managerial accounting

EIGHTH CANADIAN EDITION

Ray H. Garrison, D.B.A., CPA
Professor Emeritus
Brigham Young University

Eric W. Noreen, Ph.D., CMA
Professor Emeritus
University of Washington

Peter C. Brewer, Ph.D., CPA
Miami University—Oxford, Ohio

G. Richard Chesley, Ph.D.
Professor Emeritus
Saint Mary's University

Ray F. Carroll, Ph.D., FCGA
Dalhousie University

Alan Webb, Ph.D., CA
University of Waterloo

Toronto Montréal Boston Burr Ridge, IL Dubuque, IA Madison, WI New York San Francisco
St. Louis Bangkok Bogotá Caracas Kuala Lumpur Lisbon London Madrid
Mexico City Milan New Delhi Santiago Seoul Singapore Sydney Taipei

McGraw-Hill Ryerson

Managerial Accounting
Eighth Canadian Edition

ISBN-13: 978-0-07-098082-2
ISBN-10: 0-07-098082-9

3 4 5 6 7 8 9 10 DOW 0 9

Printed and bound in the United States of America.

Vice-President and Editor-in-Chief: Joanna Cotton
Senior Sponsoring Editor: Rhondda McNabb
Senior Marketing Manager: Joy Armitage Taylor
Senior Developmental Editor: Denise Foote
Senior Editorial Associate: Christine Lomas
Supervising Editor: Jessica Barnoski
Copy Editor: Shirley Corriveau
Senior Production Coordinator: Jennifer Hall
Cover Design: Liz Harasymczuk
Cover Image: © Frank Krahmer/Masterfile
Interior Design: Liz Harasymczuk
Page Layout: Bill Renaud
Printer: RR Donnelley/Willard

Library and Archives Canada Cataloguing in Publication

Managerial accounting / Ray H. Garrison ... [et al.]. — 8th Canadian ed.

Includes index.
ISBN 978-0-07-098082-2

1. Managerial accounting—Textbooks. I. Garrison, Ray H
HF5657.4.M38 2008 658.15'11 C2008-904100-3

Dedication

In this edition we attempt to pay tribute to our co-author and long-time colleague Ray Carroll. Up to the very days before he passed away, Ray provided valuable contributions to the eighth Canadian edition. This reflects his dedication to the book and his role as an academic. Ray will be missed by his many colleagues, students, and friends whose lives he touched and influenced.

About the Authors

Ray H. Garrison is emeritus Professor of Accounting at Brigham Young University, Provo, Utah. He received his B.S. and M.S. degrees from Brigham Young University and his D.B.A. degree from Indiana University.

As a certified public accountant, Professor Garrison has been involved in management consulting work with both national and regional accounting firms. He has published articles in *The Accounting Review, Management Accounting*, and other professional journals. Innovation in the classroom has earned Professor Garrison the Karl G. Maeser Distinguished Teaching Award from Brigham Young University.

Eric W. Noreen is Professor Emeritus of Accounting at the University of Washington and was Visiting Price Waterhouse Professor of Management Information & Control at INSEAD, an international graduate school of business located in France, and a professor at the Hong Kong University of Science and Technology.

He received his B.A. degree from the University of Washington and M.B.A. and Ph.D. degrees from Stanford University. A Certified Management Accountant, he was awarded a Certificate of Distinguished Performance by the Institute of Certified Management Accountants.

Professor Noreen has served as Associate Editor of *The Accounting Review* and the *Journal of Accounting and Economics*. He has published numerous articles in academic journals as well as won a number of awards for his teaching.

Peter C. Brewer is an Associate Professor in the Department of Accountancy at Miami University, Oxford, Ohio. He holds a B.S. degree in accounting from Penn State University, a M.S. degree in accounting from the University of Virginia, and a Ph.D. from the University of Tennessee. He has published numerous articles in a variety of journals.

Professor Brewer has received Miami University's Richard T. Farmer School of Business Teaching Excellence Award and has been recognized on two occasions by the Miami University Associated Student Government for "making a remarkable commitment to students and their educational development." He is a leader in undergraduate management accounting curriculum innovation and the use of the case method for teaching undergraduate management accounting courses. He is a frequent presenter at various professional and academic conferences and meetings.

G. Richard Chesley is Professor Emeritus of Accounting at Saint Mary's University in Halifax, Nova Scotia. He is a graduate of Mount Allison University and The Ohio State University, with B. Comm., M.A., and Ph.D. degrees. He has held appointments at Dalhousie University, the University of Pennsylvania, Hong Kong's Lingnan University, Hong Kong Baptist University, and the University of Iowa. Professor Chesley has also conducted lectures and presentations throughout Canada, the United States, and abroad, both east and west. His publications appear in *The Accounting Review*, the *Journal of Accounting Research, CA Magazine, CMA Management* magazine, and numerous books and proceedings. Research interests include Web-based reporting, non-monetary reporting, accounting regulation, and management accounting practices. In 1996, his efforts were recognized by his peers with the L. S. Rosen Outstanding Educator Award by the Canadian Academic Accounting Association. In 2005, Saint Mary's University recognized his university efforts with its inaugural Exemplary Service Award. The honourary position of Professor Emeritus was awarded by Saint Mary's University in 2007.

Ray F. Carroll was Associate Professor of Accounting at Dalhousie University in Halifax, Nova Scotia. He was a graduate of Saint Francis Xavier University, where he completed his B.B.A. and B.Ed. degrees, and Dalhousie University, from which he obtained M.B.A. and Ph.D. degrees. Professor Carroll taught at Hong Kong Baptist University and lectured in various international MBA programs throughout Hong Kong and Mainland China. His publications from recent years appeared in the *Journal of International Business, Teaching Business Ethics,* and the *Journal of Intellectual Capital*. He was a Fellow of Certified General Accountants-Canada and a member of the Institute of Management Accountants of Australia. He served as chairperson of the Canadian Certified General Accountants' National Education Committee and as a member of the American Accounting Association's Globalization Initiatives Committee. Professor Carroll passed away in February 2008 after a lengthy illness.

R. Alan Webb is an Associate Professor in the School of Accounting and Finance at the University of Waterloo. He is a graduate of Mount Allison University and the University of Alberta, with B. Comm. and Ph.D. degrees. His primary research interests are in the areas of budgeting, goal-setting, and performance measurement. Professor Webb has presented his work throughout North America and he is an Associate Editor of *Contemporary Accounting Research*. His recent publications appear in *The Accounting Review, Journal of Accounting Research, Contemporary Accounting Research, Issues in Accounting Education, CA Magazine,* and *CMA Management* magazine. He is a chartered accountant and has volunteered in numerous professional activities both in Canada and abroad.

Brief Contents

Contents

Chapter Ten
Standard Costs and Overhead Analysis 423

Chapter Eleven
Reporting for Control 494

Your guide through

For centuries, the lighthouse has stood as a beacon of guidance for mariners at sea. More than an aid to navigation, the lighthouse symbolizes safety, permanence, reliability, and the comforts of the familiar.

For this reason, we have chosen to illustrate the Canadian eighth edition of our "flagship" accounting publication, *Managerial Accounting* by Garrison, Chesley, Carroll, and Webb with an image that we feel encapsulates the greatest strengths of this market-leading text.

Garrison is your guide through the challenging waters of managerial accounting. It identifies the three functions managers must perform within their organizations—plan operations, control activities, and make decisions—and explains what accounting information is necessary for these functions, how to collect it, and how to interpret it. To achieve this, the *Managerial Accounting* eighth Canadian edition focuses, now as in the past, on three qualities:

Garrison/Chesley/Carroll/Webb:

the challenging waters of managerial accounting

Relevance. Every effort is made to help students relate the concepts in this book to the decisions made by working managers. With insightful chapter openers, scenarios and examples that reflect or discuss real-world examples, and stimulating end-of-chapter exercises. A student reading Garrison should never have to ask, "Why am I learning this?"

Balance. Garrison mixes its coverage to include a variety of business types, including not-for-profit, retail, service, and wholesale organizations, as well as manufacturing. In the Canadian eighth edition, service company examples are highlighted with icons in the margins of the text.

Clarity. Generations of students have praised Garrison for the friendliness and readability of its writing, but that's just the beginning. Technical discussions have been simplified, material has been reordered, and the entire book has been carefully retuned to make teaching—and learning—from Garrison as easy as it can be. Key term definitions and icons signifying ethics, writing, and Excel assignments continue to add clarity for both students and professors. In addition, students and professors will work with clear, well-written supplements that employ consistent terminology.

The authors' steady focus on these three core elements has led to tremendous results.

What makes Garrison such a powerful learning tool?

Managerial Accounting is full of pedagogy designed to make studying productive and hassle-free. On the following pages, you will see the kind of engaging, helpful pedagogical features that make Garrison a favourite among both teachers and students.

Service-Related Examples
Owing to the growing number of service-based companies in business today, the Canadian eighth edition uses a helpful icon to distinguish service-related examples in the text.

may give … companies a … competitive …

The most important characteristic of discretionary fixed costs is that management is not locked into its decisions regarding such costs. Discretionary costs can be adjusted from year to year or even perhaps during the course of a year if necessary.

The Trend toward Fixed Costs The trend in many companies is toward greater fixed costs relative to variable costs. Chores that used to be performed by hand have been taken over by machines. For example, grocery clerks at Loblaws and Sobeys used to key in prices by hand on cash registers. Now, most stores are equipped with bar code readers that enter price and other product information automatically. In general, competition has created pressure to give customers more value for their money—a demand that often can be satisfied only by automating business processes. For example, H&R Block used to fill out tax returns for customers mainly by hand and the advice given to a customer largely depended on the knowledge of that particular employee. Now, computer software is used to complete tax returns, and the software provides the customer with tax planning and other advice tailored to the customer's needs based on the accumulated knowledge of many experts.

As machines take over more and more of the tasks that were performed by humans, the overall demand for human workers has not diminished. The demand for "knowledge" workers—those who work primarily with their minds rather than their muscles—has grown tremendously. Knowledge workers tend to be salaried, highly trained, and difficult to replace; the costs of compensating knowledge workers are often relatively fixed and are committed rather than discretionary costs.

www.mcgrawhill.ca/olc/garrison

S

Spreadsheets
These have become an increasingly common budgeting tool for managerial accountants; therefore, to assist students in understanding how budgets look in a spreadsheet, we've included Microsoft Excel® screen captures pertaining to budgeting.

SCHEDULE 1

HAMPTON FREEZE, INC.
Sales Budget
For the Year Ended December 31, 2009

	Quarter				
	1	2	3	4	Year
Budgeted sales in units (cases of popsicles)	10,000	30,000	40,000	20,000	100,000
Selling price per unit	$20	$20	$20	$20	$20
Total sales	$200,000	$600,000	$800,000	$400,000	$2,000,000
Schedule of Expected Cash Collections					
Accounts receivable, beginning balance*	$ 90,000				$ 90,000
First-quarter sales ($200,000 × 70%, 30%)†	140,000	$ 60,000			200,000
Second-quarter sales ($600,000 × 70%, 30%)		420,000	$180,000		600,000
Third-quarter sales ($800,000 × 70%, 30%)			560,000	$240,000	800,000
Fourth-quarter sales ($400,000 × 70%)‡				280,000	280,000
Total cash collections	$230,000	$480,000	$740,000	$520,000	$1,970,000

*Cash collections from last year's fourth-quarter sales. See the December 31, 2008 balance sheet on page 388.

†Cash collections from sales are as follows: 70% collected in the quarter of sale, and the remaining 30% collected in the following quarter.

‡Uncollected fourth-quarter sales appear as accounts receivable on the company's end-of-year balance sheet (see Schedule 10 on page 389).

SCHEDULE 2

HAMPTON FREEZE, INC.
Production Budget
For the Year Ended December 31, 2009
(in cases)

	Quarter				
	1	2	3	4	Year
Budgeted sales (Schedule 1)	10,000	30,000	40,000	20,000	100,000
Add desired ending inventory of finished goods*	6,000	8,000	4,000	3,000†	3,000
Total needs	16,000	38,000	44,000	23,000	103,000
Less beginning inventory of finished goods‡	2,000	6,000	8,000	4,000	2,000
Required production	14,000	32,000	36,000	19,000	101,000

*Twenty percent of the next quarter's sales.

†Estimated.

‡The same as the prior quarter's *ending* inventory.

IN BUSINESS

Operations Drive Costs

White Grizzly Adventures is a snowcat skiing and snowboarding company in Meadow Creek, British Columbia, that is owned and operated by Brad and Carole Karafil. The company shuttles 12 guests to the top of the company's steep and tree-covered terrain in a single snowcat. Guests stay as a group at the company's lodge for a fixed number of days and are provided healthy gourmet meals.

Brad and Carole must decide each year when snowcat operations will begin in December and when they will end in early spring, and how many nonoperating days to schedule between groups of guest for maintenance and rest. This decision affects a variety of costs. Examples of costs that are fixed and variable with respect to the number of days of operation at White Grizzly include:

Costs	Cost Behaviour—Fixed or Variable with Respect to Days of Operations
Property taxes	Fixed
Summer road maintenance and tree clearing	Fixed
Lodge depreciation	Fixed
Snowcat operator and guides	Variable
Cooks and lodge help	Variable
Snowcat depreciation	Variable
Snowcat fuel	Variable
Food	Variable

Diagnosing Cost Behaviour with a Scattergram Plot

Kinh Nguyen, the chief financial office of Brentline Hospital, began his analysis of maintenance costs by collecting cost and activity data for a number of recent months. Those

Activity Level: Patient-Days	Maintenance Cost Incurred
5,600	$7,900
7,100	8,500
5,000	7,400
6,500	8,200
7,300	9,100
8,000	9,800
6,200	7,800

...st and activity data should be to plot the data on a scat... ...veals any non-linearities or other problems with the data. ...costs versus patient-days at Brentline Hospital is repro... 6–8. Two things should be noted about this scattergram: ...Y, is plotted on the vertical axis. Cost is known as the ...he amount of cost incurred during a period depends on ...period. (That is, as the level of activity increases, total

"In Business"

These helpful boxed features offer a glimpse into how real companies use the managerial accounting concepts discussed in the chapter. Every chapter contains these current examples.

PLANNING AND CONTROL

Chapters 9, 10, 11

Every organization needs to plan. **Chapter 9** describes how plans can be formalized and presented so organizations can assemble the necessary resources to carry out their plans. The details in Chapter 9 also provide a foundation for new business plans and a way of describing their strategies.

To permit managers to know if plans are achieved, a system of targets should be integrated using the same structure as the budgets presented in Chapter 9 and employing the costing approach selected from the options described in Chapters 3 to 8. Standard cos... an approach. Cos... can be developed... a system of analy... gets, termed *varia*...

Besides stan... need a means of ... a means of exter... to non-monetary... reports that show... of the business. A... the balanced sc... performance me... areas.

Section Overviews

The eighth edition is divided into five sections. One-page overviews map the chapters included and how they are related.

Opening Vignettes

These opening pieces, based on real-world scenarios, introduce the chapter and bring forward the issues, concepts, and practices to be discussed in the ensuing pages.

CHAPTER 3

LEARNING OBJECTIVES

After studying Chapter 3, you should be able to:

1. Distinguish between process costing and job-order costing and identify companies that would use each costing method.
2. Identify the documents used in a job-order costing system.
3. Compute predetermined overhead rates and explain why estimated overhead costs (rather than actual overhead costs) are used in the costing process.
4. Record the journal entries that reflect the flow of costs in a job-order costing system.
5. Apply overhead cost to Work in Process using a predetermined overhead rate.
6. Prepare schedules of cost of goods manufactured and cost of goods sold.
7. Compute under- or overapplied overhead cost and prepare the journal entry to close the balance in Manufacturing Overhead to the appropriate accounts.
8. (Appendix 3A) Explain the implications of basing the predetermined overhead rate on activity at capacity rather than on estimated activity for the period.

SYSTEMS DESIGN: JOB-ORDER COSTING

BUSINESS FOCUS

A Stringing Success

Cris Griffiths Guitar Works of Saint John's, Newfoundland, focuses on repair work and building custom guitars. Late one night while disassembling yet another guitar, Griffiths had a vision of a single bracing piece instead of the three-dozen separate internal reinforcements acoustic guitars typically have. "It was a simple idea that was easy to flesh out, but turning it from an idea into a corporation was a pretty lengthy process," he recalls. "I often say it took me six minutes to come up with the idea and six years to make it work."

Part of the problem was that using wood to make a one-piece brace was pretty much out of the question. It would take years to whittle down a wood block into a single piece, but Griffiths realized a composite material that could be punched out using injection-molding equipment could perform the same trick. Again, simple enough to conceive but it took three years before he had a solid business plan he could present to investors. Even then, Griffiths didn't have the $100,000 he needed to build a prototype, so he leveraged his existing business to the hilt, effectively putting the future of both companies on the line. Eventually, he convinced investors to pony up some seed money and he hit the road. At a Los Angeles trade show in early 2000, his guitar—lo and behold—was a hit, attracting lineups of people wanting to check out the new star.

Production started in mid-2001 and roughly $6 million was invested in the business over the next three years to keep it rolling. In 2003 the company switched to a lean manufacturing operation called the Toyota production system. That has meant a 50% cut in labour costs and manufacturing space as well as a 70% reduction in work-in-progress inventory.

Source: Andy Holloway, "Between the Rock and a Hard Place," *Canadian Business*, Dec. 27, 2004–Jan. 16, 2005, Vol. 78, Iss. 1, p. 69.

Focus on the Canadian Eighth Edition

Book Philosophy and Structure

Presenting a textbook on a topic as varied as managerial accounting is a challenge that must have a guiding philosophy.

The authors of the eighth Canadian edition believe in the framework provided by Garrison, Noreen, and Brewer in their twelfth U.S. edition. We are able to take this framework and provide a story that reflects the Canadian business and education scene. Our presentation attempts to make readers comfortable with the topic and provide the flexibility needed for the varied philosophies of Canadian users. We have tried to provide a text that can be covered in a single term yet, as our students tell us, a text that provides them with a reference book for later courses in the various programs they select.

We begin the book by describing the key players in managerial accounting, their concerns, and areas of interest followed by the developments taking place in the field. Next, we move to two areas that support managerial accounting: costing products and services, and cost behaviour. This focus is seen in Chapters 2 to 8. To permit an early view of the relevance of this foundation material, we present a simplified yet powerful analysis for decisions and the development of a cost driver, or base, creating cost behaviour.

In Chapters 9 and 10, we build the first major application of this foundation—predetermined costs described as budgets and standards—and introduce their application. Chapter 11 provides the use of predetermined costing for management control. Control requires a knowledge of costing, cost behaviour, and predetermined targets to be effective. Online Chapter 14 on financial statement analysis can be used to extend control practices to those exerted by parties external to the organization.

The second major application of costing and cost behaviour is described in chapters 12 and 13, where we first introduce costing analysis to support short-term decisions, and second, the analysis needed to support long-term decisions by management.

Not everyone can study all chapters, even though all have a place. Each of the chapters provides a selection of problems and applications focusing on manufacturing, service and not-for-profit organizations as well as international businesses so that the text reflects the variety of situations faced in today's business world. Professors will select those topics deemed appropriate for the needs of each course. What isn't covered in a course will serve as a useful reference. Online Chapter 14, for example, may be left to another course or discipline, yet managers will need to know how they are perceived by statement users external to the organization. Thus, not only is this chapter an extension of Chapter 11 on control, it also complements chapters 12 and 13 on decision analysis because external statements help to control managers and influence their decisions.

One text for a single course cannot do everything Canadian users may want, but it can provide a presentation users can understand and a foundation for later application. Clarity, balance, relevance and accuracy are necessary to the successful use of the text, our ultimate objective.

What's New in the Eighth Edition

The eighth Canadian edition has been reviewed extensively to make improvements over previous editions. The results of peer reviews and the authors' efforts are reflected in the revisions and reorganization presented in nearly every chapter. Exercises, problems, cases and research questions have been changed and new innovative topics such as the environment, XBRL and enterprise systems have been added. We believe the changes have improved an already friendly text and should facilitate an even greater understanding of key managerial accounting issues.

In the eighth edition we describe the five logical groupings of the text chapters and the connections readers should observe when studying the chapters. Section 1 groups Chapters 1 and 2 which serve as a foundation for the material in subsequent chapters. Section 2 groups Chapters 3 to 8 as a discussion of costing techniques. Costing serves as useful study for all readers and represents a primary information base for management decision making. Section 3 groups Chapters 9, 10 and 11 which cover key planning and control topics, a natural follow-up to costing techniques. Section 4 combines Chapters 12 and 13 to present the decision analysis for both short- and long-term situations. Section 5 is the logical conclusion of the discussion in the book because it covers the financial statement analysis used by the various stakeholders of the organization. The material in Chapter 14 is presented online because of the need to keep the length of the book reasonable and because some academic programs include financial statement analysis either as part of a financial accounting course or as a stand-alone course. The specific changes in each of the individual chapters of the eighth edition are presented below.

- Chapter 1 provides a discussion of how strategy, budget planning including business plans, and the environment interact with the management accountant. The section on ethics has been modified to include approaches for dealing with situations involving ethical violations. Recent developments in the business environment were rewritten to reflect changes.
- Chapter 2 retains its coverage of the nature of costs but the appendix on quality and its costs has been moved to Chapter 11 where it can be combined with the discussion of balanced scorecards.
- Chapter 3 on job costing adds a discussion on the impact of capacity definitions on costing and the information available for managers. This discussion also links to later chapters on constrained decision analysis and long-term capital budgeting.
- Chapter 4 was rewritten to provide a logical presentation of process costing and an examination of how service departments influence overhead costing. An online appendix is available for the treatment of lost units, an important issue for advancing process costing and a means of presenting a foundation for environmental cost analysis.
- Chapter 5 on activity-based costing is relocated to follow the discussion of costing techniques in Chapters 3 and 4. An extensive rewrite of this chapter highlights the importance of ABC and its limitations. A new exhibit has been developed to provide an overview of the mechanics of ABC. Also, a new appendix has been added to expand the discussion of using ABC for external reporting.
- Chapters 6 and 7 retain their popular content of cost behaviour and cost-volume-profit analysis for decision analysis material that follows. Chapter 7 also provides an online discussion of how uncertainty is incorporated in cost-volume-profit analysis.
- Chapter 8 on variable costing contains an elaboration of conversions of absorption to variable costing and vice versa. In addition, the application of variable costing to segment costing is now included because of its natural connection and the foundation it provides for budgeting, control and decision making.
- Chapter 9 now includes a more focused discussion of the master budget and incorporates the use of flexible budgets as a decision and control tool. In addition, a new comprehensive review problem has been developed. An online appendix describes inventory management practices for those seeking a more advanced discussion.
- Chapter 10 on standard costing incorporates both variable and fixed overhead analysis. The discussion of the variable overhead spending variance has been expanded to improve understanding. The material on mix and yield variances has been moved to an appendix. An online appendix on the role of learning in labour cost estimation is provided for those wishing to integrate regression analysis of cost behaviour with labour estimation in learning environments.
- Chapter 11 now presents the material on transfer pricing in the body of the chapter. The balanced scorecard section has been revised to improve focus and to incorporate quality costs. The section on international aspects of quality has been updated to include ISO 14000, which deals with environmental management systems.
- Chapter 12 on short-term decision analysis incorporates an example of variable cost pricing. A new decision aid has been added for "make or buy" decisions. The discussion of the theory of constraints has been expanded.
- Chapter 13 was rewritten to improve the logical flow of long-term budgeting and analysis. Non-tax and tax influences were incorporated in a consistent presentation of the structure of the budget and decision analysis.
- Chapter 14 is an online chapter with content similar to the seventh edition discussion of financial statement analysis. Logic and flow have been improved to suit the chapter's use by management and stakeholders.

Decision Criteria

Each chapter contains materials that provide a basis for managerial decisions. All decisions require a comparative base that enables the manager to evaluate the information. The following represents common approaches that management employs to assess the results derived from managerial accounting reports and analyses:

Chapter 1: Strategy and professional ethics
2: Financial statement rules and economic cost behaviour
3: Chart of accounts, cost comparisons, and reporting periods
4: Cost average comparisons, both historical and current
5: Activity cost comparisons
6: Cost behaviour patterns related to sales and production
7: Cost-volume-profit analyses
8: Internal management profit behaviour
9: Budgeted costs and revenues
10: Standard cost determinations for materials, labour, and overhead
11: Performance analysis and results
12: Pricing rules and differential revenues and costs
13: Long-term differential revenues and costs
14: Previous overall results and the performance of other firms

Teaching and Learning with

Managerial Accounting's technology learning solutions complement the textbook every step of the way, giving students the extra help they need while providing instructors with tools for teaching a stimulating and rewarding class.

Lyryx Assessment for Managerial Accounting

A complete online assessment system

Lyryx Assessment for Managerial Accounting is a Web-based teaching and learning tool that has captured the attention of post-secondary institutions across the country, and improved student success in managerial accounting.

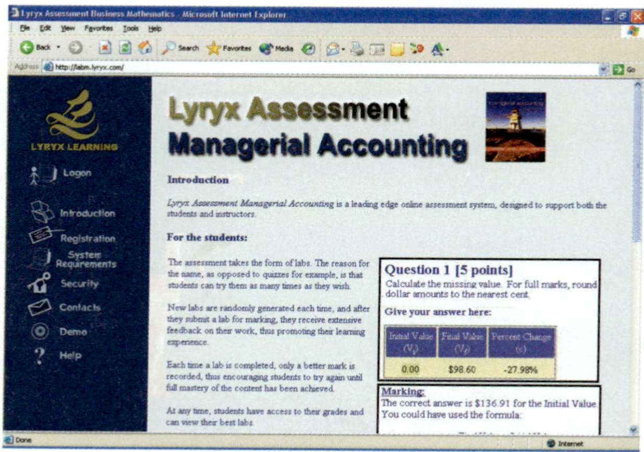

Lyryx Assessment Accounting Labs

Developed specifically for *Managerial Accounting*, Eighth Canadian Edition by Garrison, Chesley, Carroll, and Webb, **Lyryx Assessment** is a leading-edge online assessment system that delivers significant benefits to both students and instructors.

After registering their course with us, instructors can create Labs of their choice by selecting problems from our test bank and setting deadlines. Instructors have access to all the students' marks and can view their best Labs. At any time, instructors can download the class grades for their own programs to analyze individual and class performance.

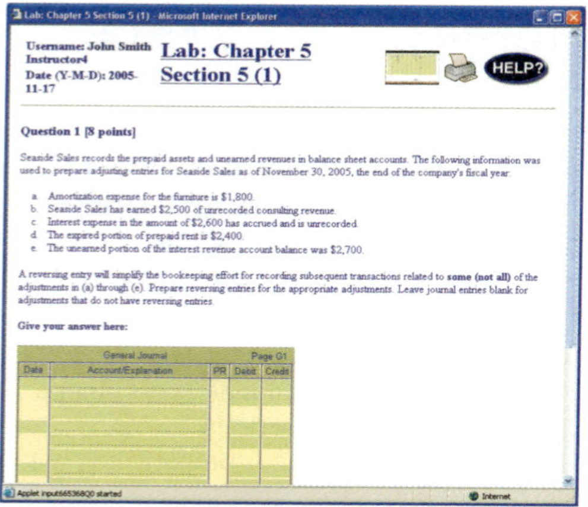

The assessment takes the form of a homework assignment called a Lab, which corresponds to the chapters in the Garrison text. The Labs are algorithmically generated and automatically graded, so students get instant scores and feedback—no need to wait until the next class to find out how well they did!

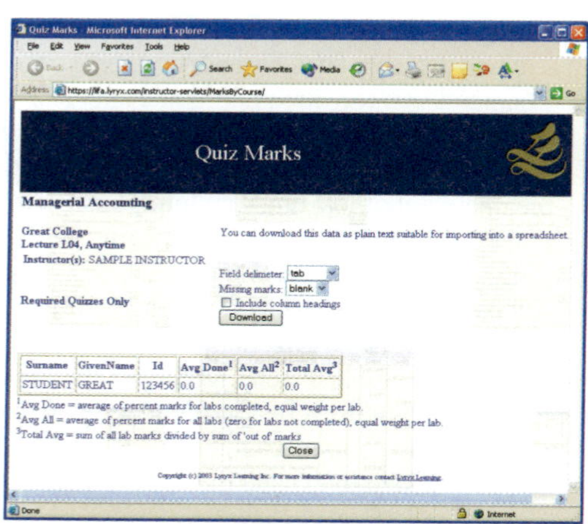

With new Labs randomly generated each time, students have unlimited opportunities to try a type of question. Student motivation is high with these Labs, because they can be tied to assessment, and because they can try as many times as they want prior to the due date, with only their best grade being recorded.

If students are doing their managerial accounting practice and homework, they will improve their performance in the course. Recent research regarding the use of Lyryx has shown when Labs are tied to assessment, even if worth only a small percentage of the total grade for the course, students *will do their homework—and more than once. The result is improved student success in managerial accounting!*

Please contact your *i*Learning Sales Specialist
for additional information on the Lyryx Assessment for Managerial Accounting.

Technology

*i*Study

In partnership with Youthography, a Canadian youth research company, and hundreds of students from across Canada, McGraw-Hill Ryerson conducted extensive student research on student study habits, behaviours, and attitudes. We asked questions and listened—and we heard some things we didn't expect. We had two goals: to help faculty be more efficient in and out of the classroom by providing a study tool that would help them improve student engagement and to help students learn their course material and get better grades. Through this research, we gained a better understanding of how students study—and how we could make vast improvements to our current online study tools. The result is a study tool that students overwhelmingly said is *better* and *there's nothing else like it out there*. *i*Study really is the first study tool built by students for students and now includes:

Study Plan
An innovative tool that helps students customize their own learning experience. Students can diagnose their knowledge pre and post test, identify the areas where they are weak, search contents of the entire learning package for content specific to the topic they're studying and add these resources to their study plan. Students told us the act of creating a study plan is how they actually study and that having the opportunity to have everything in one place, with the ability to search, customize and prioritize the class resources, was critical. No other publisher provides this type of tool and students told us without a doubt, the "Study Plan" feature is the most valuable tool they have used to help them study.

eText
Now students can search the textbook online, too! When struggling with a concept or reviewing for an exam, students can conduct key word searches to quickly find the content they need.

Homework Assessment
*i*Study assessment activities don't stop with students. There is material for instructors to leverage as well. For *Managerial Accounting*, this includes quizzes you can use in class, assign as homework, or add to exams.

Getting better grades is only a click away!
Visit www.istudyaccounting.ca.

Online Learning Centre

(**www.mcgrawhill.ca/olc/garrison**)

The Student Centre of this web site includes additional online content and an interactive student component with Excel templates (for selected problems as identified in the text by the appropriate icon), self-study multiple choice questions, and more.

Instructor Supplements

Instructor's CD-ROM

This all-in-one resource incorporates the Instructor's Manual, Solutions Manual, Computerized Test Bank, Microsoft® PowerPoint® slides, and Microsoft® Excel® templates plus solutions, each described below.

Instructor's Manual

The Instructor's Manual includes chapter overviews, assignment grids featuring levels of difficulty, and chapter-by-chapter lists of service examples.

Solutions Manual

This supplement contains completely worked-out solutions to all assignment material and a general discussion of the use of group exercises. In addition, the manual contains suggested course outlines and a listing of exercises, problems, and cases scaled according to difficulty.

Computerized Test Bank

Nearly 2,000 questions are organized by chapter and include true/false, multiple-choice, and essay questions plus computational problems. Use it to make different versions of the same test, change the answer order, edit and add questions, and conduct online testing. Technical support for this software is available. The files are also available in RTF format for printing.

Microsoft® PowerPoint® Slides

Available on the CD and on the text's web site, these slides offer a great visual complement for your lectures. A complete set of slides covers each chapter.

Microsoft® Excel® Templates

These are the solutions to the Excel templates offered to students in the Online Learning Centre.

Online Learning Centre (www.mcgrawhill.ca/olc/garrison)

Instructors can access additional problems and solutions, and downloadable supplements including the Instructor's Manual, Solutions Manual, Microsoft® PowerPoint® slides, and Microsoft® Excel® template solutions.

*i*Learning Sales Specialist

Your Integrated Learning Sales Specialist is a McGraw-Hill Ryerson representative who has the experience, product knowledge, training, and support to help you assess and integrate any of the following products, technology, and services into your course for optimum teaching and learning performance. Whether it's helping your students improve their grades, or putting your entire course online, your *i*Learning Sales Specialist is there to help you do it. Contact your local *i*Learning Sales Specialist today to learn how to maximize all of McGraw-Hill Ryerson's resources!

Primis Online

Primis Online gives you access to our resources in the best medium for your students: printed textbooks or electronic e-books. There are over 350,000 pages of content available from which you can create customized learning tools from our online database at www.mhhe.com/primis.

*i*Learning Services Program

McGraw-Hill Ryerson offers a unique *i*Learning Services package designed for Canadian faculty. Our mission is to equip providers of higher education with superior tools and resources required for excellence in teaching. For additional information visit http://www.mcgrawhill.ca/highereducation/iservices.

Reviewers

Lynn Applebaum, *Seneca College*
Dan Armishaw, *University of Ontario Institute of Technology*
Ann Bigelow, *University of Western Ontario*
Carole Bowman, *Sheridan Institute of Technology*
Donald Brown, *Brock University*
Sonja Carney, *University of Manitoba*
Lynn Carty, *Wilfrid Laurier University*
Rob Collier, *University of Ottawa*
Elliot Currie, *University of Guelph*
Annette DeWeerd, *Northern Alberta Institute of Technology*
Dennis Dober, *College of the North Atlantic*
Rob Ducharme, *University of Waterloo*
Gerry Dupont, *Carleton University*
Richard Farrar, *Conestoga College*
Michael Favere-Marchesi, *Simon Fraser University*
Ilene Gilborn, *Mount Royal College*
Sylvia Hsu, *York University*
Barbara Katz, *Kwantlen University College*
Darlene Lowe, *Grant MacEwan College*
David McConomy, *Queen's University*
Joe Nemi, *Humber College*
Cynthia Simmons, *University of Calgary*
Keith Whelan, *George Brown College*

Suggestions have been received from many of our colleagues across Canada and throughout the world who have used the prior editions of *Managerial Accounting*. This is vital feedback that we rely on in each edition. Each of those who have offered comments and suggestions has our thanks.

The efforts of many people are needed to develop and improve a text. Among these people are the reviewers and consultants who point out areas of concern, cite areas of strength, and make recommendations for change. In this regard, the professors named on this page provided feedback that was enormously helpful in preparing the Canadian eighth edition of *Managerial Accounting*.

Acknowledgements

The Canadian eighth edition of *Managerial Accounting* has benefited from the assistance of numerous individuals and groups. This assistance was invaluable in providing us with materials, review comments and suggestions, and technical assistance. Commissioned reviewers across Canada assisted with suggestions and clarifications that reflect their views of the materials they examined.

Materials were provided by the American Accounting Association, CGA-Canada, SAP Canada, and CMA-Canada. In each case, an acknowledgement is included when the material is used in the textbook. The U.S. authors acknowledge materials provided by the AICPA, the Institute of Certified Management Accountants, and the Chartered Institute of Management Accountants (United Kingdom).

Technical and secretarial assistance was provided by the editorial and technical staff of McGraw-Hill Ryerson Limited. Our book would have been impossible to produce without such help.

Despite the assistance we received, we acknowledge our responsibility for the contents of this book. We appreciate suggestions and questions from our audience.

OVERVIEW AND FOUNDATION

Chapters 1 and 2

Chapters 1 and 2 present an overview of matters that are background for subsequent chapters and that provide technical topics which appear in later chapters. Thus it is important to study these chapters carefully in order to be prepared.

Chapter 1 provides a description of what managers do and how managerial accounting can serve these needs. It also describes a few important developments in business that managerial accountants should know when working with other managers.

Chapter 2 commences with a description of how costs are classified. This description enables a proper interpretation of costs for the balance sheet and income statement. A schedule termed the Cost of Goods Manufactured Schedule presents details of manufacturing or processing costs. It provides a structure for later discussions of costing.

Cost flows are also described in Chapter 2 to permit an understanding of the interaction of costs for the study of cost behaviour.

The chapter ends with two topics important to cost control and decision analysis. Costs assigned to what is termed a "cost object" permit the development of special reports for individual areas of interest to managers. The definition of "decision focused costs," namely differential costs and sunk costs, ends the chapter. These ideas are inherent in the information needed to support decisions.

CHAPTER 1

LEARNING OBJECTIVES

After studying Chapter 1, you should be able to:

1. List the functions of managers.
2. Identify the major differences and similarities between financial and managerial accounting.
3. Describe the role of management accountants in an organization.
4. Explain the nature and importance of ethics for accountants.
5. Explain the basic concepts of lean production, six sigma, computer technology, and risk management.

MANAGERIAL ACCOUNTING AND THE BUSINESS ENVIRONMENT

BUSINESS FOCUS

Globalization: Opportunities and Threats

Advances in communications and transportation technology along with freer trade have placed Canadian companies in a global market. Globalization provides companies with the opportunity to pursue new markets leading to increased sales and income and to reduce costs due to access to alternative supply sources. For some industry sectors, such as retailing, the threat, however, is daunting. The entrance of big box stores such as Wal-Mart into Canada threatens the survival of competitors. Wal-Mart had global sales of $345 billion U.S. in 2006/07, an amount that represents 24 percent of the total Canadian economy. Wal-Mart is known for its efficiency and meticulous management of the flow of goods from its suppliers to its store shelves. To avoid being a Wal-Mart casualty Canadian companies need accounting information systems that give the latest data on revenues, costs, margins, and consumer trends. Accurate and timely accounting data on production costs and shipping, for example, is needed to help Canadian companies with decisions such as whether they should use overseas or local suppliers. Accounting data can inform managers where they can implement improvements that will lead to greater profitability. Accounting information can provide the feedback needed to control inventory and shipping costs and the data to ensure that labour costs are kept under control and conform to company policies.

Managerial accounting is concerned with providing information to managers—that is, people inside an organization who direct and control its operations. In contrast, **financial accounting** is concerned with providing information to shareholders, creditors, and others who are outside an organization. Managerial accounting provides data that help organizations run more efficiently. Financial accounting provides the scorecard by which a company's past performance is judged.

Managerial accounting
The phase of accounting concerned with providing information to managers for use in planning and controlling operations and for decision making.

Financial accounting
The phase of accounting concerned with providing information to shareholders, creditors, and others outside the organization.

Managerial accounting is concerned with determining and developing internal accounting information as a tool for helping managers make business decisions that satisfy customers while continuously monitoring costs and improving efficiencies. This requires managerial accountants to prepare a variety of reports. Some reports compare actual results to plans and to benchmarks focusing on how well managers or business units have performed. Other reports provide timely updates on key indicators such as orders received, order backlog, capacity utilization, and sales. Reports may also be prepared as needed to help investigate specific problems such as a decline in profitability of a product line or help with the decision of whether to outsource some of the business operations. Reports can also provide an analysis of a developing situation or opportunity. In contrast, financial accounting is focused on producing a limited set of specific annual and quarterly financial statements in accordance with generally accepted accounting principles (GAAP) and government regulations.

Because it is manager-oriented, any study of managerial accounting must be preceded by some understanding of what managers do, the information managers need, and the general business environment. Accordingly, the purpose of this chapter is to briefly examine these subjects.

The Work of Managers and Their Need for Managerial Accounting Information

LEARNING OBJECTIVE 1
List the functions of managers.

Every organization—large and small—has managers. Someone must be responsible for making plans, organizing resources, directing personnel, and controlling operations. This is true of the United Way, the University of Victoria, the Baptist Church, and Petro-Canada, as well as the local Max convenience store. In this chapter, we will use a particular organization—Metro Coffee, Inc.—to illustrate the work of management. What we have to say about the management of Metro Coffee, Inc., however, is very general and can be applied to virtually any organization.

Metro Coffee, Inc. operates a chain of Tim Hortons outlets that sell a full range of coffee and fast foods. The outlets are concentrated in Metro Halifax. The company has found that the best way to generate sales, and income, is to create a clean and pleasant environment. Consequently, the company puts a great deal of effort into planning the layout, decor and location of its outlets. Management knows that different types of clientele are attracted to different kinds of products and layouts. Some clients wish to sit to eat or drink while others wish to pick up meals from their vehicles.

Planning
Selecting a course of action and specifying how the action will be implemented.

Directing and motivating
Mobilizing people to carry out plans and run routine operations.

Controlling
Ensuring that the plan is actually carried out and is appropriately modified as circumstances change.

Managers at Metro Coffee, Inc., like managers everywhere, carry out three major activities—*planning, directing and motivating,* and *controlling.* **Planning** involves selecting a course of action and specifying how the action will be implemented. **Directing and motivating** involve mobilizing people to carry out plans and run routine operations. **Controlling** involves ensuring that the plan is actually carried out and is appropriately modified as circumstances change. Management accounting information plays a vital role in these basic management activities—but most particularly in the planning and control functions.

Even more than in the past, companies that now face global competition must have a viable *strategy* for succeeding in the marketplace. A **strategy** is a "game plan" that enables a company to attract customers by distinguishing itself from competitors. The focal point

Strategy
A game plan that enables a company to attract customers by distinguishing itself from competitors.

of a company's strategy should be its target customers. A company can only succeed if it creates a reason for customers to choose it over a competitor. These reasons, or what are more formally called *customer value propositions,* are the essence of strategy.

Customer value propositions tend to fall into three broad categories—*customer intimacy, operational excellence,* and *product leadership*. Companies that adopt a *customer intimacy* strategy are in essence saying to their target customers, "The reason that you should choose us is because we understand and respond to your individual needs better than our competitors." Comfort Inns, Chives Restaurant, and Tim Hortons rely primarily on a customer intimacy value proposition for their success. Companies that pursue the second customer value proposition, called *operational excellence*, are saying to their target customers, "The reason that you should choose us is because we can deliver products and services faster, more conveniently, and at a lower price than our competitors." WestJet, Wal-Mart, and Canadian National Railways are examples of companies that succeed first and foremost because of their operational excellence. Companies pursuing the third customer value proposition, called *product leadership*, are saying to their target customers, "The reason that you should choose us is because we offer higher quality products than our competitors." BMW, Rogers Communications, and RIM (the creator of the BlackBerry) are examples of companies that succeed because of their product leadership. Although one company may offer its customers a combination of these three customer value propositions, one usually outweighs the others in terms of importance.[1]

Planning

The first step in planning is to identify alternatives and then to select from among the alternatives the one that does the best job of furthering the organization's objectives. The basic objective of Metro Coffee, Inc. is to earn profits for the owners of the company by providing superior service at competitive prices in as many markets as possible. To further this objective, every year top management carefully considers a range of options, or alternatives, for expanding into new geographic markets. This year, management is considering opening new outlets in Dartmouth, Bedford, and Hubbards.

When making this and other choices, management must balance the opportunities against the demands made on the company's resources. Management knows from bitter experience that opening an outlet in a new market is a big step that cannot be taken lightly. It requires enormous amounts of time and energy from the company's most experienced, talented, and busy professionals. When the company attempted to open outlets in both Halifax and Fairview in the same year, resources were stretched too thinly. The result was that neither outlet opened on schedule, and operations in the rest of the company suffered. Therefore, entering new markets is planned very, very carefully.

Among other data, top management looks at the sales volumes, profit margins, and costs of the company's established outlets in similar markets. These data, supplied by the management accountant, are combined with projected sales volume data at the proposed new locations to estimate the profits that would be generated by the new outlets. In general, virtually all important alternatives considered by management in the planning process have some effect on revenues or costs, and management accounting data are essential in estimating those effects.

After considering all of the alternatives, Metro Coffee, Inc.'s top management decided to open an outlet in the burgeoning Hubbards market in the third quarter of the year, but to defer opening any other new outlets to another year. As soon as this decision was made, detailed plans were drawn up for all parts of the company that would be involved in the Hubbards opening. For example, the Personnel Department's travel budget was increased, since it would be providing extensive on-site training to the new personnel hired in Hubbards.

As in the Personnel Department example, the plans of management are often expressed

1. These three customer value propositions were defined by Michael Treacy and Fred Wiersema in "Customer Intimacy and Other Value Disciplines," *Harvard Business Review,* January/February 1993, pp. 84–93.

formally in **budgets**, and the term *budgeting* is applied to generally describe this part of the planning process. Budgets are usually prepared under the direction of the **controller**, who is the manager in charge of the Accounting Department. Typically, budgets are prepared annually and represent management's plans in specific, quantitative terms. In addition to a travel budget, the Personnel Department will be given goals in terms of new hires, courses taught, and detailed breakdowns of expected expenses. Similarly, the manager of each outlet will be given a target for sales volume, income, expenses, pilferage losses, and employee training. These data will be collected, analyzed, and summarized for management use in the form of budgets prepared by management accountants.

Budget
A detailed plan for the future, usually expressed in formal quantitative terms.

Controller
The manager in charge of the accounting department in an organization.

Directing and Motivating

In addition to planning for the future, managers must oversee day-to-day activities and keep the organization functioning smoothly. This requires the ability to motivate and effectively direct people. Managers assign tasks to employees, arbitrate disputes, answer questions, solve on-the-spot problems, and make many small decisions that affect customers and employees. In effect, directing is that part of the managers' work that deals with the routine and the here and now. Managerial accounting data, such as daily sales reports, are often used in this type of day-to-day decision making.

Controlling

In carrying out the **control** function, managers seek to ensure that the plan is being followed. **Feedback**, which signals whether operations are on track, is the key to effective control. In sophisticated organizations, this feedback is provided by detailed reports of various types. One of these reports, which compares budgeted to actual results, is called a **performance report**. Performance reports suggest where operations are not proceeding as planned and where some parts of the organization may require additional attention. For example, before the opening of the new Hubbards outlet in the third quarter of the year, the store's manager will be given sales volume, income, and expense targets for the fourth quarter of the year. As the fourth quarter progresses, periodic reports will be made in which the actual sales volume, income, and expenses are compared to the targets. If the actual results fall below the targets, top management is alerted that the Hubbards outlet requires more attention. Experienced personnel can be sent in to help the new manager, or top management may come to the conclusion that plans will have to be revised. As we shall see in following chapters, providing this kind of feedback to managers is one of the central purposes of managerial accounting.

Control
The process of instituting procedures and then obtaining feedback to ensure that all parts of the organization are functioning effectively and moving toward overall company goals.

Feedback
Accounting and other reports that help managers monitor performance and focus on problems and/or opportunities that might otherwise go unnoticed.

Performance report
A detailed report comparing budgeted data to actual data.

The Results of Managers' Activities

As a customer enters one of the Metro's outlets, the results of management's planning, directing and motivating, and control activities will be evident in the many details that make the difference between a pleasant and an irritating experience. The outlet will be clean, fashionably decorated, and logically laid out. Clerks will be alert, friendly, and efficient. In short, what the customer experiences doesn't simply happen; it is the result of the efforts of managers who must visualize and fit together the processes that are needed to get the job done. A role of managerial accounting is to inform and facilitate management decisions throughout these processes so that managers' efforts result in the efficient achievement of company goals.

The Planning and Control Cycle

The work of management can be summarized in a model such as the one in Exhibit 1–1. The model, which depicts the **planning and control cycle**, illustrates the smooth flow of management activities from planning through directing and motivating, controlling, and then back to planning again. All of these activities involve decision making, so it is depicted as the hub around which the other activities revolve.

Planning and control cycle
The flow of management activities through planning, directing and motivating, and controlling, and then back to planning again.

EXHIBIT 1–1 The Planning and Control Cycle

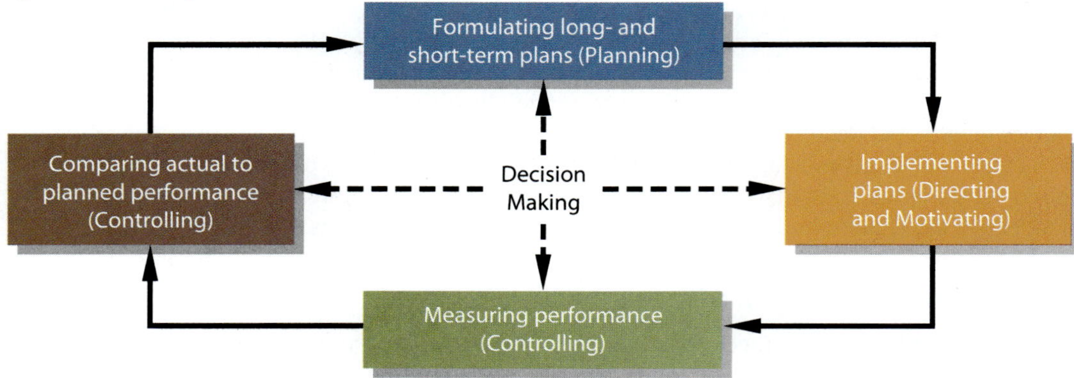

Management accounting can help serve the information needs of managers in all phases of the planning and control cycle. The management accountant can prepare detailed reports that managers need to make both day-to-day and long-term decisions. They prepare budgets to help direct resources towards the organization's goals. Later actual costs and revenues are compared with the budgeted figures and reports are prepared to inform management about any significant variances from budget. Management information needs vary from business to business but as you work your way through this book you will be introduced to many of the tools management accountants use to meet these needs. For example, managerial accountants typically provide reports that help answer questions such as the following:

How much does it cost to provide a particular good or service?
How do costs behave when the company operates at different levels of activity?
How can a company reduce costs to help improve profitability?
How many units must be sold to break even?
What will our budgets look like at different forecasted levels of activity?
Should the company add or drop a product line?
Should the company outsource some of its operations?
How should management choose when selecting among competing investment proposals?
What new projects should the company invest in and what projects should be abandoned?

The Business Plan

New businesses typically formalize their strategic planning in the form of a business plan. A business plan consists of information about the company's basic product or service and about the steps to be taken to reach its potential market. The plan includes information about production methods, the competition, the management team, details on how the business will be financed and is a key document for the organization's internal management. It is also valuable for external use in attracting resources from potential creditors and investors. The answers to many of the questions raised by providers of funds can be found in the business plan.

Exhibit 1–2[2] shows a flowchart of the steps taken in a typical business plan. The 16-week time span is for illustrative purposes only. The actual length of the business plan process varies with the nature and complexity of the venture and could span anywhere from a few weeks to several months. Note from the flow chart that it is essential for certain steps to be completed before others are begun. It makes no sense, for example, to talk about forecasting sales (step 5) until a product or service has been picked (step 3) and the market has been researched (step 4). Continuing businesses formalize part of the

2. From SIROPOLIS. *Small Business Management,* 6e. © 1997 South-Western, a part of Cengage Learning Inc. Reproduced by permission, www.cengage.com/permissions.

EXHIBIT 1–2 Flowchart of the Steps in Developing a Business Plan

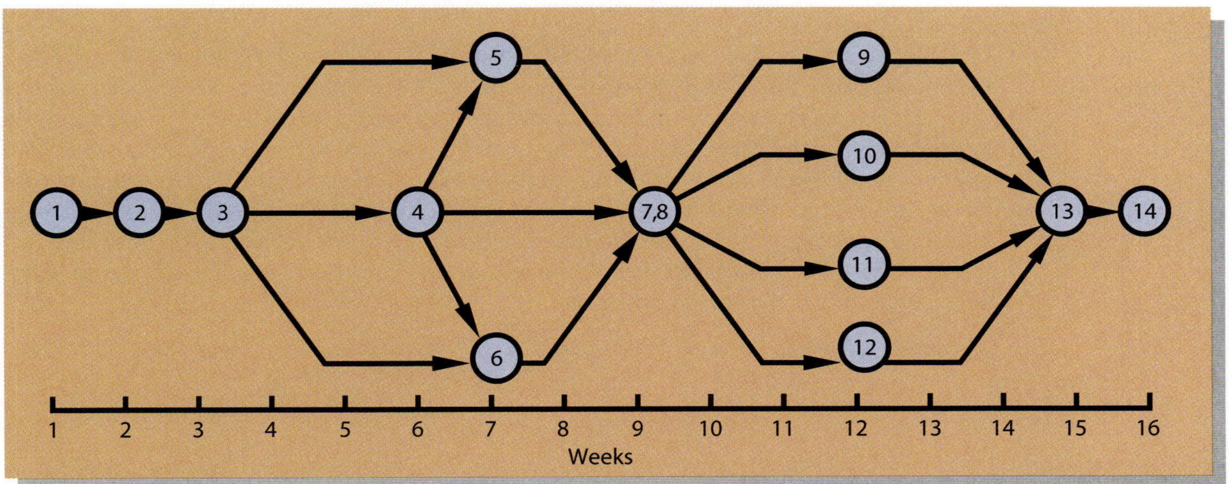

Key:
1. Decide to go into business.
2. Analyze yourself.
3. Pick product or service.
4. Research market.
5. Forecast sales revenues.
6. Pick site.
7. Develop production plan.
8. Develop marketing plan.
9. Develop personnel plan.
10. Decide whether to incorporate.
11. Explain need for records.
12. Develop insurance plan.
13. Develop financial plan.
14. Write summary overview.

Source: From SIROPOLIS. *Small Business Management*, 6e. © 1997 South-Western, a part of Cengage Learning Inc. Reproduced by permission, www.cengage.com/permissions.

financial aspects of their strategy in their annual budgets. Although some steps clearly precede others the process is not entirely linear. Development of the business plan is an interactive process. In today's volatile, fast-paced, and complex business environment, the business plan must be flexible enough to adapt in response to market changes that require new estimates and forecasts. To work well, the business plan should encourage a shared vision with clear targets and well-defined performance measures such as those discussed in later chapters of this text.

Technology can help integrate these strategic processes through the use of compatible, linked applications with automatic updates and sophisticated architecture that allows for multi-dimensional reporting, what-if analysis, and performance management. By sharing real-time transaction data, predictive models, and trend analysis across the organization, senior and departmental management can create a clear link among strategic objectives, operational plans, and personal performance goals.

A business plan requires a knowledgeable person to write the report. Since most entrepreneurs are doers rather than report writers, the preparation of the plan required to start, expand, or downsize will usually be done by someone with capabilities in both financial and business affairs, using a variety of expertise from others.

A business plan report begins with a table of contents and an executive summary. Next, the company must be described, along with its products or services and its marketing plan. Operational plans, along with management personnel and the organizational structure, will provide the substance for the financial resources needed to understand the detailed financial plans. Attachments will include competitive analysis, revenue and profit breakdowns by product and customer, and a variety of legal agreements such as contracts, patents, and confidentiality agreements for outsiders who have access to the details as a result of their study of the report.[3]

3. Eric Siegel, Brian R. Ford, and Jay Bornstein, *The Ernst & Young Business Plan Guide,* 2nd ed. (Toronto, ON: John Wiley & Sons, Inc., 1993), provides a detailed description of the contents of a business plan, along with a specific example.

IN BUSINESS

Ultra Electronics Maritime Systems is located in the Halifax Regional Municipality. It is an international leader in the design, development, and production of advanced electronic, electromechanical, and hydro-acoustic sensor systems. Strategically it operates in various countries including the United Kingdom, Japan, and France. To obtain financing for its international operations, it listed its shares on the London Stock Exchange in 1996. To provide appropriate management accounting information, it uses an enterprise information system and a broad-based scorecarding reporting of performance. Its vice-president of finance and administration is a certified management accountant who is extensively involved in strategic planning, planning, controlling, and directing operations.

Source: Robert Colman, "Navigating Strategic Change," *CMA Management*, October 2006, pp. 40–42.

Comparison of Financial and Managerial Accounting

LEARNING OBJECTIVE 2
Identify the major differences and similarities between financial and managerial accounting.

Financial accounting reports are prepared for the use of external parties such as shareholders and creditors, whereas managerial accounting reports are prepared for managers inside the organization. This contrast in basic orientation results in a number of major differences between financial and managerial accounting, even though both financial and managerial accounting rely on the same underlying financial data. These differences are summarized in Exhibit 1–3.

As shown in Exhibit 1–3, in addition to the reports being prepared for different people, financial and managerial accounting also differ in their emphasis between the past and the future, in the type of data provided to users, and in several other ways. These differences are discussed in the following paragraphs.

Emphasis on the Future

Since *planning* is such an important part of the manager's job, managerial accounting has a strong future orientation. In contrast, financial accounting primarily provides summaries of past financial transactions. These summaries may be useful in planning, but only to a point. The future is not simply a reflection of what has happened in the past. Changes are constantly taking place in economic conditions, customer needs and desires, competitive conditions, and so on. All of these changes demand that the manager's planning be based in large part on estimates of what will happen rather than on summaries of what has already happened.

Relevance of Data

Financial accounting data are expected to be objective and verifiable. However, for internal uses the manager wants information that is relevant even if it is not completely objective or verifiable. By relevant, we mean *appropriate for the problem at hand.* For example, it is difficult to verify estimated sales volumes for a proposed new outlet at Metro Coffee, Inc., but this is exactly the type of information that is most useful to managers in their decision making. The managerial accounting information system should be flexible enough to provide whatever data are relevant for a particular decision.

Less Emphasis on Precision

Making sure that dollar amounts are accurate down to the last dollar or penny takes time and effort. While that kind of accuracy is desirable for external reports, most managers

EXHIBIT 1–3 Comparison of Financial and Management Accounting

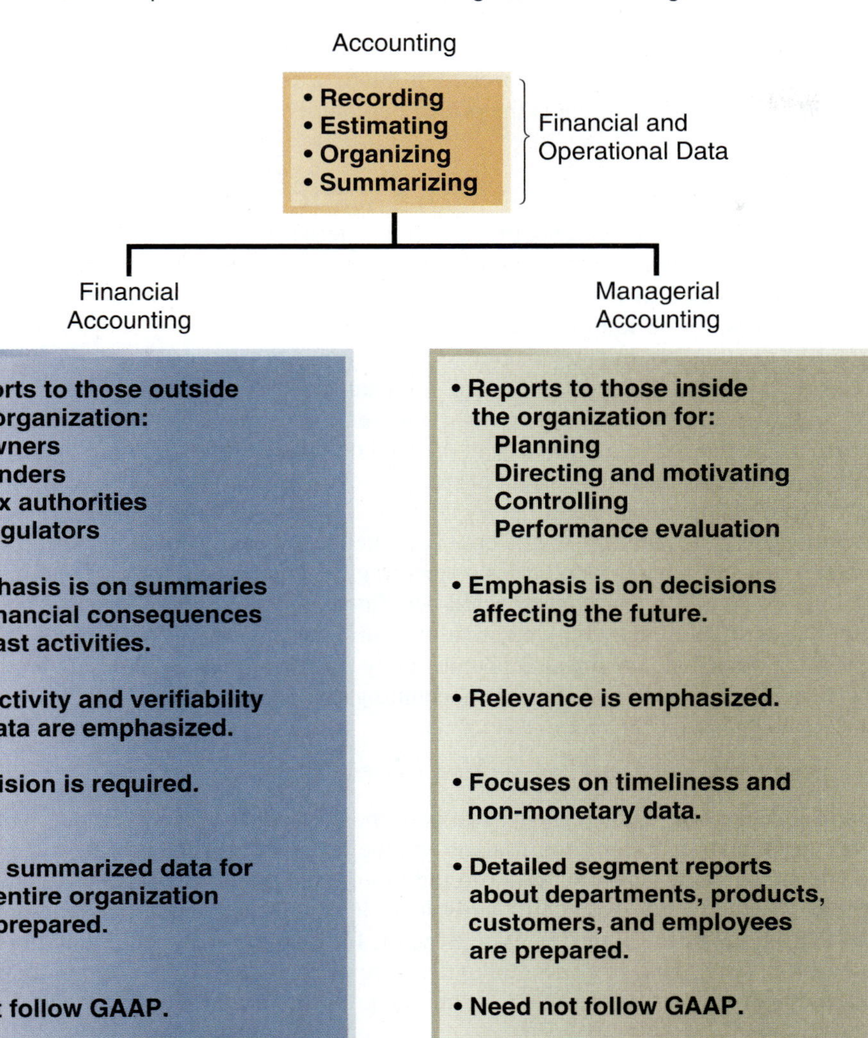

would rather have an immediate estimate than wait for a more precise answer. For this reason, managerial accountants often place less emphasis on precision than do financial accountants. In fact, one authoritative source recommends that, as a general rule, no one needs more than three significant digits in the data that are used in decision making.[4] For example, in a decision involving hundreds of millions of dollars, estimates that are rounded off to the nearest million dollars are probably good enough. In addition to placing less emphasis on precision than financial accounting, managerial accounting places more weight on non-monetary data. For example, data about customer satisfaction may be routinely used in managerial accounting reports.

Segments of an Organization

Financial accounting is primarily concerned with reporting for the company as a whole. By contrast, managerial accounting focuses much more on the parts, or **segments**, of a

Segment
Any part of an organization that can be evaluated independently of other parts and about which the manager seeks financial data.

4. *Statements on Management Accounting, Statement Number 5B, Fundamentals of Reporting Information to Managers*, Institute of Management Accountants, Montvale, NJ, p. 6.

company. These segments may be product lines, customers, sales territories, divisions, departments, or any other categorization of the company's activities that management finds useful. Financial accounting does require some breakdowns of revenues and costs by major segments in external reports, but this is a secondary emphasis. In managerial accounting, segment reporting is the primary emphasis.

Generally Accepted Accounting Principles

Financial accounting statements prepared for external users must be prepared in accordance with generally accepted accounting principles (GAAP). External users must have some assurance that the reports have been prepared in accordance with some common set of ground rules. These common ground rules enhance comparability and help reduce fraud and misrepresentation, but they do not necessarily lead to the type of reports that would be most useful in internal decision making. For example, GAAP requires that land be stated at its historical cost on financial reports. However, if management is considering moving a store to a new location and then selling the land on which the store currently sits, management would like to know the current market value of the land—a vital piece of information that is ignored under GAAP.

Managerial accounting is not bound by generally accepted accounting principles. Managers set their own ground rules concerning the content and form of internal reports. The only constraint is that the expected benefits from using the information should outweigh the costs of collecting, analyzing, and summarizing the data. Nevertheless, as we shall see in subsequent chapters, it is undeniably true that financial reporting requirements have heavily influenced management accounting practice.

Managerial Accounting—Not Mandatory

Financial accounting is mandatory; that is, it must be done. Various outside parties such as the provincial securities commissions and the tax authorities require periodic financial statements. Managerial accounting, on the other hand, is not mandatory. A company is completely free to do as much or as little as it wishes. No regulatory bodies or other outside agencies specify what is to be done or, for that matter, whether anything is to be done at all. Since managerial accounting is completely optional, the important question is always, "Is the information useful?" rather than, "Is the information required?"

Organizational Structure

LEARNING OBJECTIVE 3
Describe the role of management accountants in an organization.

Management must accomplish its objectives by working *through* people. Presidents of companies like Metro Coffee, Inc. could not possibly execute all of their companies' strategies alone; they must rely on other people. This is done by creating an organizational structure that permits effective *decentralization* of management decisions.

Decentralization

Decentralization
The delegation of decision-making authority throughout an organization by providing managers at various operating levels with the authority to make key decisions relating to their areas of responsibility.

Decentralization is the delegation of decision-making authority throughout an organization by providing managers at various operating levels with the authority to make decisions relating to their areas of responsibility. Some organizations are more decentralized than others. Because of Metro Coffee, Inc.'s geographic dispersion and the peculiarities of local markets, the company is highly decentralized.

Metro's president (also called chief executive officer or CEO) sets the broad strategy for the company and makes major strategic decisions such as opening stores in new markets, but much of the remaining decision-making authority is delegated to managers on various levels throughout the organization. These levels are as follows: The company has a number of outlets, each of which has a store manager as well as a separate manager for each section such as beverages and food. In addition, the company has support departments such as a central Purchasing Department and a Personnel Department. The organizational structure of the company is depicted in Exhibit 1–4.

The arrangement of boxes shown in Exhibit 1–4 is called an **organization chart.** The purpose of an organization chart is to show how responsibility has been divided among managers and to show formal lines of reporting and communication, or *chain of command.* Each box depicts an area of management responsibility, and the lines between the boxes show the lines of formal authority between managers. The chart tells us, for example, that the store managers are responsible to the operations vice-president. In turn, the latter is responsible to the company president, who in turn is responsible to the board of directors. Following the lines of authority and communication on the organization chart, we can see that the manager of the Hubbards outlet would ordinarily report to the operations vice-president rather than directly to the president of the company.

Organization chart
A visual diagram of a firm's organizational structure that depicts formal lines of reporting, communication, and responsibility between managers.

Informal relationships and channels of communication often develop outside the formal reporting relationships on the organization chart as a result of personal contacts between managers. The informal structure does not appear on the organization chart, but it is often vital to effective operations.

Line and Staff Relationships

An organization chart also depicts *line* and *staff* positions in an organization. A person in a **line** position is *directly* involved in achieving the basic objectives of the organization. A person in a **staff** position, by contrast, is only *indirectly* involved in achieving those basic objectives. Staff positions *support* or provide assistance to line positions or other parts of the organization, but they do not have direct authority over line positions.

Line
A position in an organization that is directly related to the achievement of the organization's basic objectives.

EXHIBIT 1–4 Organization Chart, Metro Coffee, Inc.

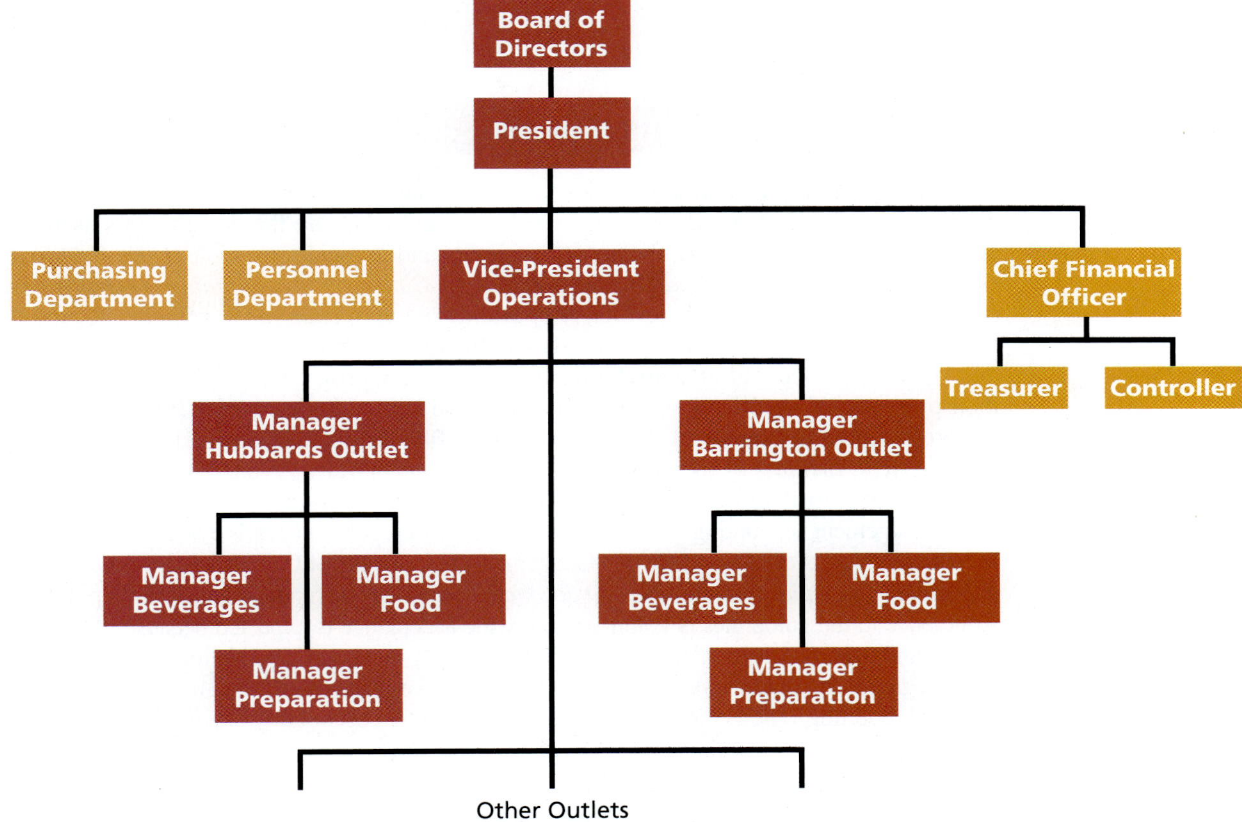

Staff
A position in an organization that is only indirectly related to the achievement of the organization's basic objectives. Such positions are supportive in nature in that they provide service or assistance to line positions or to other staff positions.

Refer again to the organization chart in Exhibit 1–4. Since the basic objective of Metro Coffee, Inc. is to sell food and beverages at a profit, those managers whose areas of responsibility are directly related to the sales effort occupy line positions. These positions, which are shown in a darker colour in the exhibit, include the managers of the various departments in each outlet, the outlet managers, the operations vice-president, and members of top management.

By contrast, the manager of the central Purchasing Department occupies a staff position, since the only function of the Purchasing Department is to support and serve the line departments by doing their purchasing for them. However, both line and staff managers have authority over the employees in their own departments.

The Controller

In Canada, the manager in charge of the Accounting Department is usually known as the *controller.* The controller, in turn, reports to the *Chief Financial Officer* (CFO). The CFO is the member of the top-management team who is given the responsibility of providing relevant and timely data to support planning and control activities and of preparing financial statements for external users. Because the controller becomes familiar with all parts of a company's operations by working with managers throughout the company, it is not unusual for the controller's office to be a stepping stone to the top position in a company.

The controller is a highly paid professional who has command over the technical details of accounting and finance, can provide leadership to other professionals in her or his department, and can analyze new and evolving situations. An effective controller is able to work well with top managers from other disciplines and can communicate technical information in a simple and clear manner.

Much of the work under the controller's responsibility involves consulting and business analysis. Many managerial accountants engaged in such activities actually identify themselves as working in finance since very few, if any, of their activities is about debits and credits or preparing journal entries. These managerial accountants see themselves as advisors who work on cross-functional teams throughout the organization.

The Professional Management Accountant

Three professional accounting organizations in Canada have members who make up the ranks of management accountants. *CGA*, *CA*, and *CMA* are the designations used by professional accountants who belong to societies and associations such as the *Certified General Accountants Association,* the *Institute of Chartered Accountants* (*L'Ordre des comptables* in Québec), and the *Society of Management Accountants.*[5] Members of these three associations work in various fields—industry, commerce, government, education, and public practice—after completing their particular programs of study and passing their professional certification examinations. In the United States, both CPAs and CMAs are professional management accountants. The CPA designation is used by members of the *American Institute of Certified Public Accountants* or various state CPA associations. CMAs are members of the *Institute of Management Accountants*.

Management accounting is not subject to the type of regulation that is evident for financial accounting. However, the Society of Management Accountants of Canada issues *management accounting guidelines and management accounting practices* on fundamental areas of practice. Adherence to the guidelines is voluntary, but wide acceptance is expected because of the relevance and expertise used in their preparation. Currently there are 65 guidelines on topics such as strategic management, risk management, performance management and measurement, and financial reporting. The Society has issued 44 management accounting practice statements on

5. Web sites for these three groups contain background information. See **http://www.cga-canada.org/**, **http://www.cica.ca/**, and **http://www.cma-canada.org/**.

topics such as risk management, performance management, and performance measurement. The difference between these two types of guides is the level of focus. Practice statements are more prescriptive in nature and contain less background discussion and research than the guidelines. New topics are continually being presented to the accounting community.

Professional Ethics

LEARNING OBJECTIVE 4
Explain the nature and importance of ethics for accountants.

A series of high profile scandals in the public and private sectors have raised deep concerns about ethics in business and government.[6] Ethics are important because they are the lubricant that keeps the economy running. As James Surowiecki writes:

> Flourishing economies require a healthy level of trust in the reliability and fairness of everyday transactions. If you assumed every potential deal was a rip-off or that the products you were buying were probably going to be lemons, then very little business would get done. More important, the cost of the transactions that did take place would be exorbitant, since you'd have to do enormous work to investigate each deal and you'd have to rely on the threat of legal action to enforce every contract. For an economy to prosper, what's needed is not a Pollyanish faith that everyone else has your best interests at heart—"caveat emptor" (buyer beware) remains an important truth—but a basic confidence in the promises and commitments that people make about their products and services.[7]

There are good reasons for companies to be concerned about their ethical reputation. A company that is not trusted by its customers, employees, and suppliers will eventually suffer. In the short run, virtue is sometimes its own reward but in the long run business ethics should be taken seriously because the very survival of the company may depend on the level of trust held by its stakeholders.

Professional accounting groups are given the right of association and certain rights of self-government by provincial governments in Canada. One inherent requirement of such rights is an expression of public service in the form of a code of ethics. Each accounting group is then permitted to operate according to the laws of the country, using its code of ethics as an operating guideline.[8]

Typically, these codes contain details of how members should conduct themselves in their dealings with the public, their association, and their fellow members. For example, accountants must maintain a level of competence appropriate to their designation. Confidentiality is essential because of the importance of the information they analyze. Integrity is maintained by avoiding conflicts of interest with their employers or clients, by communicating the limits of professional competence, and by not accepting favours that would compromise their judgement. Objectivity must be present in communications, so that recipients can receive both favourable and unfavourable information.

Professional accountants must study the full text of their code of ethics because the rules for competence, confidentiality, integrity, and objectivity are complex in real situations. In addition, procedures for resolving complex situations should be known.

Some codes of ethics give more extensive guidance than others. The Institute of Management Accountants in the United States, for example, provides quite clear guidance concerning what ethical standards to follow and also gives advice on how to resolve ethical conflict situations. This information is reproduced in Exhibit 1–5.

---

6. Examples include the Federal sponsorship scandal and others involving businesses such as Enron, WorldCom, Global Crossing, Arthur Andersen, and many others. Currently, there are also class action suits outstanding against Nortel alleging that it overstated revenues for the years 2000 and 2001.
7. James Surowiecki, "A Virtuous Cycle," *Forbes*, December 23, 2002, pp. 248–256.
8. The web sites listed in footnote 5 for Canadian accounting associations provide details about the ethical standards of their members. Also, **http://www.ifac.org/** contains ethical expectations for members of the International Federation of Accountants.

EXHIBIT 1–5 Standards of Ethical Conduct for Practitioners of Management Accounting and Financial Management

Members of the Institute of Management Accountants (IMA) shall behave ethically. A commitment to ethical professional practice includes: overarching principles that express our values, and standards that guide our conduct.

PRINCIPLES

IMA's overarching ethical principles include: Honesty, Fairness, Objectivity, and Responsibility. Members shall act in accordance with these principles and shall encourage others within their organizations to adhere to them.

STANDARDS

A member's failure to comply with the following standards may result in disciplinary action.

I. COMPETENCE

Each member has a responsibility to:

1. Maintain an appropriate level of professional expertise by continually developing knowledge and skills.
2. Perform professional duties in accordance with relevant laws, regulations, and technical standards.
3. Provide decision support information and recommendations that are accurate, clear, concise, and timely.
4. Recognize and communicate professional limitations or other constraints that would preclude responsible judgment or successful performance of an activity.

II. CONFIDENTIALITY

Each member has a responsibility to:

1. Keep information confidential except when disclosure is authorized or legally required.
2. Inform all relevant parties regarding appropriate use of confidential information. Monitor subordinates' activities to ensure compliance.
3. Refrain from using confidential information for unethical or illegal advantage.

III. INTEGRITY

Each member has a responsibility to:

1. Mitigate actual conflicts of interest. Regularly communicate with business associates to avoid apparent conflicts of interest. Advise all parties of any potential conflicts.
2. Refrain from engaging in any conduct that would prejudice carrying out duties ethically.
3. Abstain from engaging in or supporting any activity that might discredit the profession.

IV. CREDIBILITY

Each member has a responsibility to:

1. Communicate information fairly and objectively.
2. Disclose all relevant information that could reasonably be expected to influence an intended user's understanding of the reports, analyses, or recommendations.
3. Disclose delays or deficiencies in information, timeliness, processing, or internal controls in conformance with organization policy and/or applicable law.

RESOLUTION OF ETHICAL CONFLICT

In applying the Standards of Ethical Professional Practice, you may encounter problems identifying unethical behaviour or resolving an ethical conflict. When faced with ethical issues, you should follow your organization's established policies on the resolution of such conflict. If these policies do not resolve the ethical conflict, you should consider the following courses of action:

1. Discuss the issue with your immediate supervisor except when it appears that the supervisor is involved. In that case, present the issue to the next level. If you cannot achieve a satisfactory resolution, submit the issue to the next management level. If your immediate superior is the chief executive officer or equivalent, the acceptable reviewing authority may be a group such as the audit committee, executive committee, board of directors, board of trustees, or owners. Contact with levels above the immediate superior should be initiated only with your superior's knowledge, assuming he or she is not involved. Communication of such problems to authorities or individuals not employed or engaged by the organization is not considered appropriate, unless you believe there is a clear violation of the law.
2. Clarify relevant ethical issues by initiating a confidential discussion with an IMA Ethics Counselor or other impartial advisor to obtain a better understanding of possible courses of action.
3. Consult your own attorney as to legal obligations and rights concerning the ethical conflict.

Businesses are organizations of people that pursue objectives (sometimes termed *missions*). These organizations have formal relationships among their members as described by the organization chart illustrated earlier in this chapter. However, informal relationships and activities are also present that must be focused on the achievement of the objectives of a wide group of people known as *stakeholders*. Stakeholders are people within and outside the organization who have an interest in the activities of the organization. Employees, shareholders, and creditors have an obvious interest in what the organization does, but so do the public, the customers, the suppliers, and the competitors. All of these stakeholders can benefit from the organization's undertakings and they also can be harmed by these activities.

A code of ethics is prepared by an organization to reflect its value and moral system. The document specifies what is expected of its employees in their dealings with the various stakeholders. Thus, the code reflects what the organization stands for when it interacts through its employees with other stakeholders. For example, the organization may wish to pursue environmental standards in excess of those specified in local laws and regulations. The organization may wish to use the standards of conduct present in its home country rather than those of its host country in its cross-border activities. Through its code of ethics, a business can express what it stands for in its activities as well as provide its members with a guide as to how their activities should be conducted to reflect the values needed to achieve the objectives of the organization.

IN BUSINESS

Ethics Control Systems are described in The Society of Management Accountant's Management Accounting Practice number 6200. This practice guide presents the key elements needed to help ensure that a corporation's ethics are adhered to by their decision makers. The control system should contain a means of monitoring whether deviations from the stated code of ethics are made and the means of motivating compliance with the code presented to decision makers.

Source: The Society of Management Accountants of Canada, *Ethics Control Systems,* Management Accounting Practices number 6200, April 2002.

Corporate Governance

Effective *corporate governance* enhances shareholders' confidence that a company is being run in their best interests rather than in the interests of top managers. **Corporate governance** is the system by which a company is directed and controlled. If properly implemented, the corporate governance system should provide incentives for the board of directors and top management to pursue objectives that are in the interests of the company's owners and it should provide for effective monitoring of performance.[9] Many would argue that, in addition to protecting the interests of shareholders, an effective corporate governance system also should protect the interests of the company's many other *stakeholders*—its customers, creditors, employees, suppliers, and the communities within which it operates. These parties are referred to as stakeholders because their welfare is tied to the company's performance.

Corporate governance
A system by which a company is directed and controlled.

Unfortunately, history has repeatedly shown that unscrupulous top managers, if unchecked, can exploit their power to defraud stakeholders. This unpleasant reality became all too clear in 2001 when the fall of Enron kicked off a wave of corporate scandals. These scandals were characterized by financial reporting fraud and misuse of corporate funds at the very highest levels—including CEOs and CFOs. While this was disturbing in itself, it also

9. This definition of corporate governance was adapted from the 2004 report titled OECD Principles of Corporate Governance published by the Organization for Economic Co-Operation and Development.

indicated that the institutions intended to prevent such abuses weren't working, thus raising fundamental questions about the adequacy of the existing corporate governance system. In an attempt to respond to these concerns, the U.S. Congress passed the most important reform of corporate governance in many decades—*The Sarbanes-Oxley Act of 2002*.

IN BUSINESS

Spilled Milk at Parmalat

Corporate scandals have not been limited to the United States. In 2003, Parmalat, a publicly traded dairy company in Italy, went bankrupt. The CEO, Calisto Tanzi, admitted to manipulating the books for more than a decade so that he could skim off $640 million to cover losses at various of his family businesses. But the story doesn't stop there. Parmalat's balance sheet contained $13 billion in nonexistent assets, including a $5 billion Bank of America account that didn't exist. All in all, Parmalat was the biggest financial fraud in European history.

Source: Gail Edmondson, David Fairlamb, and Nanette Byrnes, "The Milk Just Keeps on Spilling," *BusinessWeek*, January 26, 2004, pp. 54–58.

Process Management

LEARNING OBJECTIVE 5
Explain the basic concepts of lean production, six sigma, computer technology, and risk management.

As discussed at the beginning of this chapter, the last two decades have been a period of tremendous turmoil and change in the business environment. Competition in many industries has become worldwide in scope, and the pace of innovation in products and services has accelerated. This has been good news for consumers, since intensified competition has generally led to lower prices, higher quality, and more choices. However, for businesses intensified global competition has presented serious challenges. More than ever companies are realizing that they must complement the functional view of their operations with a cross-functional orientation that seeks to improve the *business processes* that deliver customer value.

Business process
A series of steps that are followed in order to carry out some task in a business.

Value chain
Consists of the major business functions that add value to a company's products and services.

A **business process** is a series of steps that are followed in order to carry out some task in a business. It is quite common for the linked set of steps comprising a business process to span departmental boundaries. The term *value chain* is often used when we look at how the functional departments of an organization interact with one another to form business processes. A **value chain,** as shown in Exhibit 1–6, consists of the major business functions that add value to a company's products and services. The customer's needs are most effectively met by coordinating the business processes that span these functions.

This section discusses four different approaches to managing and improving business processes—lean production, six sigma, computer technology, and risk management. Although each is unique in certain respects, they all share the common theme of focusing on managing and improving business processes.

Lean Production

Traditionally, managers in manufacturing companies have sought to maximize production so as to spread the costs of investments in equipment and other assets over as many units

EXHIBIT 1–6 Business Functions Making Up the Value Chain

Research and Development	Product Design	Manufacturing	Marketing	Distribution	Customer Service

as possible. In addition, managers have traditionally felt that an important part of their jobs was to keep everyone busy on the theory that idleness wastes money. These traditional views, often aided and abetted by traditional management accounting practices, resulted in a number of practices that have come under criticism in recent years.

In a traditional manufacturing company, work is *pushed* through the system in order to produce as much as possible and to keep everyone busy—even if products cannot be immediately sold. This almost inevitably results in large inventories of *raw materials, work in process,* and *finished* goods. **Raw materials** are the materials that are used to make a product. **Work in process** inventories consist of units of product that are only partially complete and will require further work before they are ready for sale to a customer. **Finished goods** inventories consist of units of product that have been completed but have not yet been sold to customers.

Raw materials
Materials that are used to make a product.

Work in process
Inventories consisting of units of product that are only partially complete.

Finished goods
Inventories consisting of units of product that have been completed but have not yet been sold to customers.

The *push* process in traditional manufacturing starts by accumulating large amounts of raw material inventories from suppliers so that operations can proceed smoothly even if unanticipated disruptions occur. Next, enough materials are released to workstations to keep everyone busy. When a workstation completes its tasks, the partially completed goods (i.e., work in process) are "pushed" forward to the next workstation regardless of whether that workstation is ready to receive them. The result is that partially completed goods stack up, waiting for the next workstation to become available. They may not be completed for days, weeks, or even months. Additionally, when the units are finally completed, customers may or may not want them. If finished goods are produced faster than the market will absorb, the result is bloated finished goods inventories.

Although some may argue that maintaining large amounts of inventory has its benefits, it clearly has its costs. According to experts, in addition to tying up money, maintaining inventories encourages inefficient and sloppy work, results in too many defects, and dramatically increases the amount of time required to complete a product. For example, when partially completed goods are stored for long periods of time before being processed by the next workstation, defects introduced by the preceding workstation go unnoticed. If a machine is out of calibration or incorrect procedures are being followed, many defective units will be produced before the problem is discovered. And when the defects are finally discovered, it may be very difficult to track down the source of the problem. In addition, units may be obsolete or out of fashion by the time they are finally completed.

Large inventories of partially completed goods create many other problems that are best discussed in more advanced courses. These problems are not obvious—if they were, companies would have long ago reduced their inventories. Managers at Toyota are credited with the insight that large inventories often create many more problems than they solve. Toyota pioneered what is known today as *Lean Production*.

The Lean Thinking Model The **lean thinking model** is a five-step management approach that organizes resources such as people and machines around the flow of business processes and that pulls units through these processes in response to customer orders. The result is lower inventories, fewer defects, less wasted effort, and quicker customer response times. Exhibit 1–7 depicts the five stages of the lean thinking model.

Lean thinking model
A five-step management approach that organizes resources around the flow of business processes and pulls units through in response to customer orders.

The first step is to identify the value to customers in specific products and services. The second step is to identify the *business process* that delivers this value to customers.[10] As discussed earlier, the linked set of steps comprising a business process typically span the departmental boundaries that are specified in an organization chart. The third step is to organize work arrangements around the flow of the business process. This is often accomplished by creating what is known as a *manufacturing cell*. The cellular approach takes employees and equipment from departments that were previously separated from one another and places them side-by-side in a work space called a *cell*. The equipment within the cell is aligned in a sequential manner that follows the steps of the business process. Each employee is trained to perform all the steps within his or her own manufacturing cell.

10. The Lean Production literature uses the term *value stream* rather than *business process*.

EXHIBIT 1–7 The Lean Thinking Model

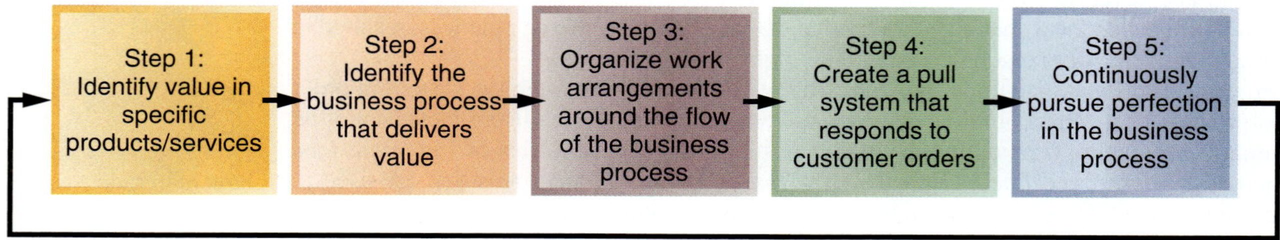

Source: This exhibit is adapted from James P. Womack and Daniel T. Jones, *Lean Thinking: Banish Waste and Create Wealth in Your Corporation*, Revised and Updated (New York, NY: Simon & Shuster, 2003).

The fourth step in the lean thinking model is to create a pull system where production is not initiated until a customer has ordered a product. Inventories are reduced to a minimum by purchasing raw materials and producing units only as needed to meet customer demand. Under ideal conditions, a company operating a pull system would purchase only enough materials each day to meet that day's needs. Moreover, the company would have no goods still in process at the end of the day, and all goods completed during the day would be shipped immediately to customers. As this sequence suggests, work takes place "just-in-time" in the sense that raw materials are received by each manufacturing cell just in time to go into production, manufactured parts are completed just in time to be assembled into products, and products are completed just in time to be shipped to customers. Not surprisingly, this facet of the lean thinking model is often called **just-in-time** production, or **JIT** for short.

Just-in-time (JIT) A pull system in the lean thinking model where production is not initiated until a customer has ordered a product.

The change from *push* to *pull* production is more profound than it may appear. Among other things, producing only in response to a customer order means that workers will be idle whenever demand falls below the company's production capacity. This can be an extremely difficult cultural change for an organization. It challenges the core beliefs of many managers and raises anxieties in workers who have become accustomed to being kept busy all of the time.

The fifth step of the lean thinking model is to continuously pursue perfection in the business process. In a traditional company, parts and materials are inspected for defects when they are received from suppliers, and assembled units are inspected as they progress along the production line. In a Lean Production system, the company's suppliers are responsible for the quality of incoming parts and materials. And instead of using quality inspectors, the company's production workers are directly responsible for spotting defective units. A worker who discovers a defect immediately stops the flow of production. Supervisors and other workers go to the cell to determine the cause of the problem and correct it before any further defective units are produced. This procedure ensures that problems are quickly identified and corrected.

The lean thinking model can also be used to improve the business processes that link companies together. The term **supply chain management** is commonly used to refer to the coordination of business processes across companies to better serve end consumers. For example Canadian Tire Corporation and Costco coordinate their business processes to ensure that tires, cleaning supplies, and garden supplies are on shelves when customers want them.

Supply chain management The coordination of business processes across companies to better serve end customers.

Six Sigma

Six Sigma is a process improvement method that relies on customer feedback and fact-based data gathering and analysis techniques to drive process improvement. Motorola and General Electric are closely identified with the emergence of the Six Sigma movement. Technically, the term Six Sigma refers to a process that generates no more than 3.4 defects per million opportunities. Because this rate of defects is so low, Six Sigma is sometimes associated with the term *zero defects*.

Six Sigma A process improvement method that relies on customer feedback and fact-based data gathering and analysis techniques to drive process improvement.

The most common framework used to guide Six Sigma process improvement efforts is known as DMAIC (pronounced: du-may-ik), which stands for Define, Measure, Analyze, Improve, and Control. As summarized in Exhibit 1–8, the Define stage of the process focuses on defining the scope and purpose of the project, the flow of the current process, and the customer's requirements. The Measure stage is used to gather baseline performance data concerning the existing process and to narrow the scope of the project to the most important problems. The Analyze stage focuses on identifying the root causes of the problems that were identified during the Measure stage. The Analyze stage often reveals that the process includes many *activities that do not add value to the product or service*. Activities that customers are not willing to pay for because they add no value are known as **non-value-added activities** and such activities should be eliminated wherever possible. During the Improve stage potential solutions are developed, evaluated, and implemented to eliminate non-value-added activities and any other problems uncovered in the Analyze stage. Finally, the objective in the Control stage is to ensure that the problems remain fixed and that the new methods are improved over time.[11]

Non-valued-added activities Activities that customers are not willing to pay for because they add no value.

Managers must be very careful when attempting to translate Six Sigma improvements into financial benefits. There are only two ways to increase profits—decrease costs or increase sales. Cutting costs may seem easy—lay off workers who are no longer needed because of improvements such as eliminating non-value-added activities. However, if this approach is taken, employees quickly get the message that process improvements lead to job losses and they will understandably resist further improvement efforts. If improvement is to continue, employees must be convinced that the end result of improvement will be more secure rather than less secure jobs. This can only happen if management uses tools such as Six Sigma to generate more business rather than to cut the workforce.

Computer Technology in Business

Computer technology is being harnessed in many ways by businesses. In this section we will discuss two of these ways—e-commerce and enterprise systems.

E-Commerce

E-commerce refers to business that is conducted using the Internet. Since the collapse of the dot.com bubble in 2001, e-commerce has slowly been rebuilding momentum. Inter-

EXHIBIT 1–8 The Six Sigma DMAIC Framework

Stage	Goals
Define	Establish the scope and purpose of the project. Diagram the flow of the current process. Establish the customer's requirements for the process.
Measure	Gather baseline performance data related to the existing process. Narrow the scope of the project to the most important problems.
Analyze	Identify the root cause(s) of the problems identified in the Measure stage.
Improve	Develop, evaluate, and implement solutions to the problems.
Control	Ensure that problems remain fixed. Seek to improve the new methods over time.

Source: Peter C. Brewer and Nancy A. Bagranoff, "Near Zero-Defect Accounting with Six Sigma," *Journal of Corporate Accounting and Finance*, January–February 2004, pp. 67–72.

11. Peter C. Brewer, "Six Sigma Helps a Company Create a Culture of Accountability," *Journal of Organizational Excellence,* Summer 2004, pp. 45–59.

net advertising is projected to exceed $12 billion per year before the end of the decade.[12] E-commerce has already had a major impact on the sale of books, music, and airline tickets. In addition to dot.com companies, established brick-and-mortar companies such as Fresh Direct, Canadian Tire, and Staples will undoubtedly continue to expand into cyberspace—both for business-to-business transactions and for retailing.

The growth in e-commerce is occurring because the Internet has important advantages over more conventional marketplaces for many kinds of transactions. For example, the Internet is an ideal technology for streamlining banking. Customers can bank and invest over the Internet rather than tying up the time of a staffperson in an office. Data and funds can be sent back and forth electronically.

Enterprise Systems[13]

Historically, most companies implemented specific software programs to support specific business functions. The accounting department would select its own software applications to meet its needs, while manufacturing would select different software programs to support its needs. The separate systems were not integrated and could not easily pass data back and forth. The end result was data duplication and data inconsistencies coupled with lengthy customer response times and high costs.

Enterprise system
A computer application designed to overcome problems in data inconsistency and duplication by integrating data across an organization into a single software system.

An **enterprise system** is designed to overcome these problems by integrating data across an organization into a single software system that enables all employees to have simultaneous access to a common set of data. There are two keys to the data integration inherent in an enterprise system. First, all data are recorded only once in the company's centralized digital data repository known as a database. When data are added to the database or are changed, the new information is simultaneously and immediately available to everyone across the organization. Second, the unique data elements contained within the database can be linked together. For example, one data element, such as a customer identification number, can be related to other data elements, such as that customer's address, billing history, shipping history, merchandise returns history, and so on. The ability to forge such relationships among data elements explains why this type of database is called a *relational database*.

Data integration helps employees communicate with one another and it also helps them communicate with their suppliers and customers. For example, consider how the *customer relationship management* process is improved when enterprise-wide information resides in one location. Whether meeting the customer's needs requires accessing information related to billing (an accounting function), delivery status (a distribution function), price quotes (a marketing function), or merchandise returns (a customer service function) the required information is readily available to the employee interacting with the customer. Though expensive and risky to install, the benefits of data integration have led many companies to invest in enterprise systems.

Enterprise Risk Management

Businesses face risks every day. Some risks are foreseeable. For example, a company could reasonably be expected to foresee the possibility of a natural disaster or a fire destroying its centralized data storage facility. Companies respond to this type of risk by maintaining off-site backup data storage facilities. Other risks are unforeseeable. For example, in 2006 Menu Foods Income Trust had to recall sales of many of its pet food products as a result of adulterated wheat gluten apparently acquired as part of the materials needed to process its

12. Stephen Baker, "Where the Real Internet Money Is Made," *BusinessWeek,* December 27, 2004, p. 99.

13 *Enterprise systems* is a broad term that encompasses many enterprise-wide computer applications such as customer relationship management and supply chain management systems. Perhaps the most frequently mentioned type of enterprise system is an Enterprise Resource Planning (ERP) system.

products. On May 2, 2007, a press release by Menu Foods suggested that this recall could cost $40 to $45 million when its 2006 sales were approximately $356 million.[14]

Every business strategy or decision involves risks. **Enterprise risk management** is a process used by a company to proactively identify and manage those risks.

Enterprise risk management A process used by a company to proactively identify and manage foreseeable risks.

Identifying and Controlling Business Risks

Companies should identify foreseeable risks before they occur rather than react to unfortunate events that have already happened. The left-hand column of Exhibit 1–9 provides 12 examples of business risks. This list is not exhaustive, rather its purpose is to illustrate the diverse nature of business risks that companies face. Whether the risks relate to the weather, computer hackers, complying with the law, employee theft, financial reporting, or strategic decision making, they all have one thing in common. If the risks are not managed effectively, they can infringe on a company's ability to meet its goals.

Once a company identifies its risks, it can respond to them in various ways such as accepting, avoiding, sharing, or reducing the risk. Perhaps the most common risk management tactic is to reduce risks by implementing specific controls. The right-hand column

EXHIBIT 1–9 Identifying and Controlling Business Risks

Examples of Business Risks	Examples of Controls to Reduce Business Risks
• Intellectual assets being stolen from computer files	• Create firewalls that prohibit computer hackers from corrupting or stealing intellectual property
• Products harming customers	• Develop a formal and rigorous new product-testing program
• Losing market share due to the unforeseen actions of competitors	• Develop an approach for legally gathering information about competitors' plans and practices
• Poor weather conditions shutting down operations	• Develop contingency plans for overcoming weather-related disruptions
• A web site malfunctioning	• Thoroughly test the web site before going "live" on the Internet
• A supplier strike halting the flow of raw materials	• Establish a relationship with two companies capable of providing needed raw materials
• A poorly designed incentive compensation system causing employees to make bad decisions	• Create a balanced set of performance measures that motivates the desired behaviour
• Financial statements unfairly reporting the value of inventory	• Count the physical inventory on hand to make sure that it agrees with the accounting records
• An employee stealing assets	• Segregate duties so that the same employee does not have physical custody of an asset and the responsibility of accounting for it
• An employee accessing unauthorized information	• Create password-protected barriers that prohibit employees from obtaining information not needed to do their jobs
• Inaccurate budget estimates causing excessive or insufficient production	• Implement a rigorous budget review process
• Failing to comply with equal employment opportunity laws	• Create a report that tracks key metrics related to compliance with the laws

14. Press release, May 9, 2007, http://www.menufoods.com/recall.

of Exhibit 1–9 provides an example of a control that could be implemented to help reduce each of the risks mentioned in the left-hand column of the exhibit.

In conclusion, a sophisticated enterprise risk management system cannot guarantee that all risks are eliminated. Nonetheless, many companies understand that managing risks is a superior alternative to reacting, perhaps too late, to unfortunate events.

Summary

Managerial accounting assists managers in carrying out their responsibilities, which include planning, directing and motivating, and controlling.

Since managerial accounting is geared to the needs of managers rather than to the needs of outsiders, it differs substantially from financial accounting. Managerial accounting is oriented more toward the future, places less emphasis on precision, emphasizes segments of an organization (rather than the organization as a whole), is not governed by generally accepted accounting principles, and is not mandatory.

Most organizations are decentralized to some degree. The organization chart depicts who works for whom in the organization and which units perform staff functions rather than line functions. Accountants perform a staff function—they support and provide assistance to others inside the organization.

Ethical standards serve a very important practical function in an advanced market economy. Without widespread adherence to ethical standards, material living standards would fall. Ethics are the lubrication that keep a market economy functioning smoothly. The Standards of Ethical Conduct for Practitioners of Management Accounting and Financial Management provide sound, practical guidelines for resolving ethical problems that might arise in an organization.

Lean Production and Six Sigma are two management approaches that focus on business processes. Lean Production organizes resources around business processes and pulls units through those processes in response to customer orders. The result is lower inventories, fewer defects, less wasted effort, and quicker customer response times. Six Sigma uses the DMAIC (Define, Measure, Analyze, Improve, and Control) framework to eliminate non-value-added activities and to improve processes.

E-commerce and enterprise systems are being used to reshape business practices. An enterprise system integrates data across the organization in a single software system that makes the same data available to all managers.

Unfortunately, trust in corporate governance systems has been undermined in recent years by numerous high-profile financial reporting scandals. The *Sarbanes-Oxley Act of 2002* was passed with the objective of improving the reliability of the financial disclosures provided by publicly traded companies.

Questions

1–1 What is the basic difference in orientation between financial and managerial accounting?
1–2 What is meant by a business strategy?
1–3 Describe the three broad categories of customer value propositions.
1–4 Describe the three major activities of a manager.
1–5 What are the four steps in the planning and control cycle?
1–6 What are the major differences between financial and managerial accounting?
1–7 Distinguish between line and staff positions in an organization.
1–8 Describe the basic responsibilities of the Chief Financial Officer.
1–9 What are the three main categories of inventories in a manufacturing company?
1–10 What are the five steps in the lean thinking model?
1–11 What are the major benefits from successful implementation of the lean thinking model?
1–12 Describe what is meant by a "pull" production system.
1–13 Briefly describe Six Sigma.
1–14 Describe the five stages in the Six Sigma DMAIC Framework.

1–15 What is an enterprise system supposed to accomplish?
1–16 Why is adherence to ethical standards important for the smooth functioning of an advanced market economy?
1–17 Describe what is meant by corporate governance.
1–18 Briefly describe what is meant by enterprise risk management.

Exercises

EXERCISE 1–1 The Roles of Managers and Management Accountants [LO1, LO3]
A number of terms that relate to organizations, the work of management, and the role of managerial accounting are listed below:

budgets	controller
decentralization	directing and motivating
feedback	financial accounting
line	managerial accounting
nonmonetary data	planning
performance report	staff
precision	Chief Financial Officer

Choose the term or terms above that most appropriately complete the following statements.

1. __________________ is concerned with providing information for the use of those who are inside the organization, whereas __________________ is concerned with providing information for the use of those who are outside the organization.
2. __________________ consists of identifying alternatives, selecting from among the alternatives the one that is best for the organization, and specifying what actions will be taken to implement the chosen alternative.
3. When __________________, managers oversee day-to-day activities and keep the organization functioning smoothly.
4. The accounting and other reports coming to management that are used in controlling the organization are called __________________.
5. The delegation of decision-making authority throughout an organization by allowing managers at various operating levels to make key decisions relating to their area of responsibility is called __________________.
6. A position on the organization chart that is directly related to achieving the basic objectives of an organization is called a __________________ position.
7. A __________________ position provides service or assistance to other parts of the organization and does not directly achieve the basic objectives of the organization.
8. The manager in charge of the accounting department is generally known as the __________________.
9. The plans of management are expressed formally in __________________.
10. A detailed report to management comparing budgeted data to actual data for a specific time period is called a __________________.
11. The __________________ is the member of the top management team who is responsible for providing timely and relevant data to support planning and control activities and for preparing financial statements for external users.
12. Managerial accounting places less emphasis on __________________ and more emphasis on __________________ than financial accounting.

EXERCISE 1–2 The Business Environment [LO5]
A number of terms are listed below:

value chain	strategy	enterprise risk management
supply chain management	Six Sigma	Internet
lean thinking model	budget	pulls
customer value proposition	business process	enterprise system
corporate governance	non-value-added activity	Just-In-Time

Required:
Choose the term or terms from the above list that most appropriately completes each of the following statements:

1. A(n) ____________ is a game plan that enables a company to attract customers by distinguishing itself from competitors.
2. ____________ is a method that relies on customer feedback and objective data gathering and analysis techniques to drive process improvement.
3. A(n) ____________ is a series of steps that are followed to carry out some task in a business.
4. The system by which a company is directed and controlled is called ____________.
5. The process used by a company to help identify the risks that it faces and to develop responses to those risks so that the company is reasonably assured of meeting its goals is known as ____________.
6. A production and inventory control system in which materials are purchased and units are produced only as needed to meet actual customer demand is known as ____________.
7. The ____________ fuels the globalization phenomenon by providing companies with greater access to geographically dispersed customers, employees, and suppliers.
8. Increasing the rate of output of a(n) ____________ as the result of an improvement effort is unlikely to have much effect on profits.
9. A(n) ____________ consists of business functions that add value to a company's products and services such as research and development, product design, manufacturing, marketing, distribution, and customer service.
10. A(n) ____________ integrates data from across an organization into a single centralized database that enables all employees to access a common set of data.
11. A management approach that coordinates business processes across companies to better serve end consumers is known as ____________.
12. The ____________ is a five-step management approach that organizes resources around the flow of business processes and that ____________ units through those processes in response to customer orders.
13. A company can only succeed if it creates a reason for customers to choose it over a competitor; in short, a ____________.
14. A(n) ____________ is a detailed plan for the future, usually expressed in formal quantitative terms.

EXERCISE 1–3 Ethics in Business [LO4]

Andy Morio was hired by a popular fast-food restaurant as an order-taker and cashier. Shortly after taking the job, he was shocked to overhear an employee bragging to a friend about shortchanging customers. He confronted the employee who then snapped back: "Mind your own business. Besides, everyone does it and the customers never miss the money." Andy didn't know how to respond to this aggressive stance.

Required:

What would be the practical consequences on the fast-food industry and on consumers if cashiers generally shortchanged customers at every opportunity?

Problems

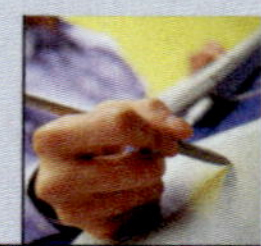

PROBLEM 1–4 Ethics in Business [LO4]

Paul Sarver is the controller of a corporation whose shares are not listed on a stock exchange. The company has just received a patent on a product that is expected to yield substantial profits in a year or two. At the moment, however, the company is experiencing financial difficulties; and because of inadequate working capital, it is on the verge of defaulting on a note held by its bank.

At the end of the most recent fiscal year, the company's president instructed Sarver not to record several invoices as accounts payable. Sarver objected since the invoices represented bona fide liabilities. However, the president insisted that the invoices not be recorded until after year-end, at which time it was expected that additional financing could be obtained. After several very strenuous objections—expressed to both the president and other members of senior management—Sarver finally complied with the president's instructions.

Required:

1. Did Sarver act in an ethical manner? Explain.
2. If the new product fails to yield substantial profits and the company becomes insolvent, can Sarver's actions be justified by the fact that he was following orders from a superior? Explain.

PROBLEM 1–5 Preparing an Organization Chart [LO1]

Winnipeg University is a large university located in Manitoba. The university is headed by a president who has five vice-presidents reporting to him. These vice-presidents are responsible for auxiliary services, admissions and records, academics, financial services (controller), and the physical plant.

In addition, the university has managers who report to these vice-presidents. These include managers for central purchasing, the university press, and the university bookstore, all of whom report to the vice-president for auxiliary services; managers for computer services and for accounting and finance, who report to the vice-president for financial services; and managers for grounds and custodial services and for plant and maintenance, who report to the vice-president for the physical plant.

The university has five faculties—business, humanities, fine arts, engineering and quantitative methods, and a law school. Each of these units has a dean who is responsible to the academic vice-president. Each faculty has several departments.

Required:

1. Prepare an organization chart for Winnipeg University.
2. Which of the positions on your chart would be line positions? Why would they be line positions? Which would be staff positions? Why?
3. Which of the positions on your chart would have a need for accounting information? Explain.

PROBLEM 1–6 Ethics in Business [LO4]

Adam Williams was recently hired as assistant controller of GroChem, Inc., which processes chemicals for use in fertilizers. Williams was selected for this position because of his past experience in chemical processing. During his first month on the job, Williams made a point of getting to know the people responsible for the plant operations and learning how things are done at GroChem.

During a conversation with the plant supervisor, Williams asked about the company procedures for handling toxic waste materials. The plant supervisor replied that he was not involved with the disposal of wastes and suggested that Williams might be wise to ignore this issue. This response strengthened Williams' determination to probe this area further to be sure that the company was not vulnerable to litigation.

Upon further investigation, Williams discovered evidence that GroChem was using a nearby residential landfill to dump toxic wastes—an illegal activity. It appeared that some members of GroChem's management team were aware of this situation and may have been involved in arranging for this dumping; however, Williams was unable to determine whether his superior, the controller, was involved.

Uncertain how he should proceed, Williams began to consider his options by outlining the following three alternative courses of action:

- Seek the advice of his superior, the controller.
- Anonymously release the information to the local newspaper.
- Discuss the situation with an outside member of the board of directors with whom he is acquainted.

Required:

1. Discuss why Adam Williams has an ethical responsibility to take some action in the matter of GroChem, Inc., and the dumping of toxic wastes. Refer to the specific standards (competence, confidentiality, integrity, and/or credibility) in the Statement of Ethical Professional Practice established by the Institute of Management Accountants to support your answer.
2. For each of the three alternative courses of action that Adam Williams has outlined, explain whether or not the action is appropriate according to the ethical practices presented in Exhibit 1–5.
3. Assume that Adam Williams sought the advice of his superior, the controller, and discovered that the controller was involved in the dumping of toxic wastes. Describe the steps that Williams should take to resolve this situation.

(CMA, adapted)

PROBLEM 1–7 Ethics in Business [LO4]

Consumers and attorney generals in more than 40 U.S. states accused a prominent nationwide chain of auto repair shops of misleading customers and selling them unnecessary parts and services, from brake jobs to front-end alignments. Lynn Sharpe Paine reported the situation as follows in "Managing for Organizational Integrity," *Harvard Business Review,* March–April, 1994:

In the face of declining revenues, shrinking market share, and an increasingly competitive market . . . management attempted to spur performance of its auto centers. . . . The automotive service advisers were given product-specific sales quotas—sell so many springs, shock absorbers, alignments, or brake jobs per shift—and paid a commission based on sales. . . . [F]ailure to meet quotas could lead to a transfer or a reduction in work hours. Some employees spoke of the "pressure, pressure, pressure" to bring in sales.

This pressure-cooker atmosphere created conditions under which employees felt that the only way to satisfy top management was by selling products and services to customers that they didn't really need.

Suppose all automotive repair businesses routinely followed the practice of attempting to sell customers unnecessary parts and services.

Required:

1. How would this behaviour affect customers? How might customers attempt to protect themselves against this behaviour?
2. How would this behaviour probably affect profits and employment in the automotive service industry?

PROBLEM 1–8 Line and Staff Positions; Organization Chart [LO1]

The Association of Medical Personnel (AMP) is a membership/educational organization that serves a wide range of individuals who work for medical institutions including hospitals, clinics, and medical practices. The membership is composed of doctors, nurses, medical assistants, and professional administrators. The purpose of the organization is to provide individuals in the medical field with a professional organization that offers educational and training opportunities through local chapters, a monthly magazine (*AMP Review*), continuing education programs, seminars, self-study courses, and research publications.

AMP is governed by a board of directors who are members elected to these positions by the membership. The chairperson of the board is the highest ranking volunteer member and presides over the board; the board establishes policy for the organization. The policies are administered and carried out by AMP's paid professional staff. The president's chief responsibility is to manage the operations of the professional staff. Like any organization, the professional staff of AMP is composed of line and staff positions. A partial organization chart of the AMP professional staff is shown in Exhibit A.

Four of the positions appearing in the organization chart are described below.

Jere Feldon, Staff Liaison to the Chairperson

Feldon is assigned to work with the chairperson of AMP by serving as an intermediary between the chairperson and the professional staff. All correspondence to the chairperson is funneled through Feldon. Feldon also works very closely with the president of AMP, especially on any matters that have to be brought to the attention of the chairperson and the board.

Lana Dickson, Director of Self-Study Programs

Dickson is responsible for developing and marketing the self-study programs offered by AMP. Self-study courses consist of DVDs and a workbook. Most of the courses are developed by outside contractors who work under her direction. Dickson relies on the director of membership marketing to assist her in marketing these courses.

Jesse Paige, Editor of Special Publications

Paige is primarily responsible for the publication and sale of any research monographs that are generated by the research department. In addition, he coordinates the publication of any special projects that may be prepared by any other AMP committees or departments. Paige also works with AMP's Publication Committee which sets policy on the types of publications that AMP should publish.

George Ackers, Manager of Personnel

Ackers works with all of the departments of AMP in hiring professional and clerical staff. The individual departments screen and interview prospective employees for professional positions, but Ackers is responsible for advertising open positions. Ackers plays a more active role in the hiring of clerical personnel by screening individuals before they are sent to the departments for interviews. In addition, Ackers coordinates the employee performance evaluation program and administers AMP's salary schedule and fringe benefit program.

Required:

1. Distinguish between line positions and staff positions in an organization by defining each. Include in your discussion the role, purpose, and importance of each.
2. Many times, conflicts will arise between line and staff managers in organizations. Discuss the characteristics of line and staff managers that may cause conflicts between the two.
3. For each of the four individuals identified by name in the text,
   a. Identify whether the individual's position is a line or staff position and explain why.
   b. Identify potential problems that could arise in each individual's position, either due to the type of position (i.e., line or staff) or to the location of the individual's position within the organization.

(CMA, adapted)

EXHIBIT A Partial Organization Chart for the Association of Medical Personnel

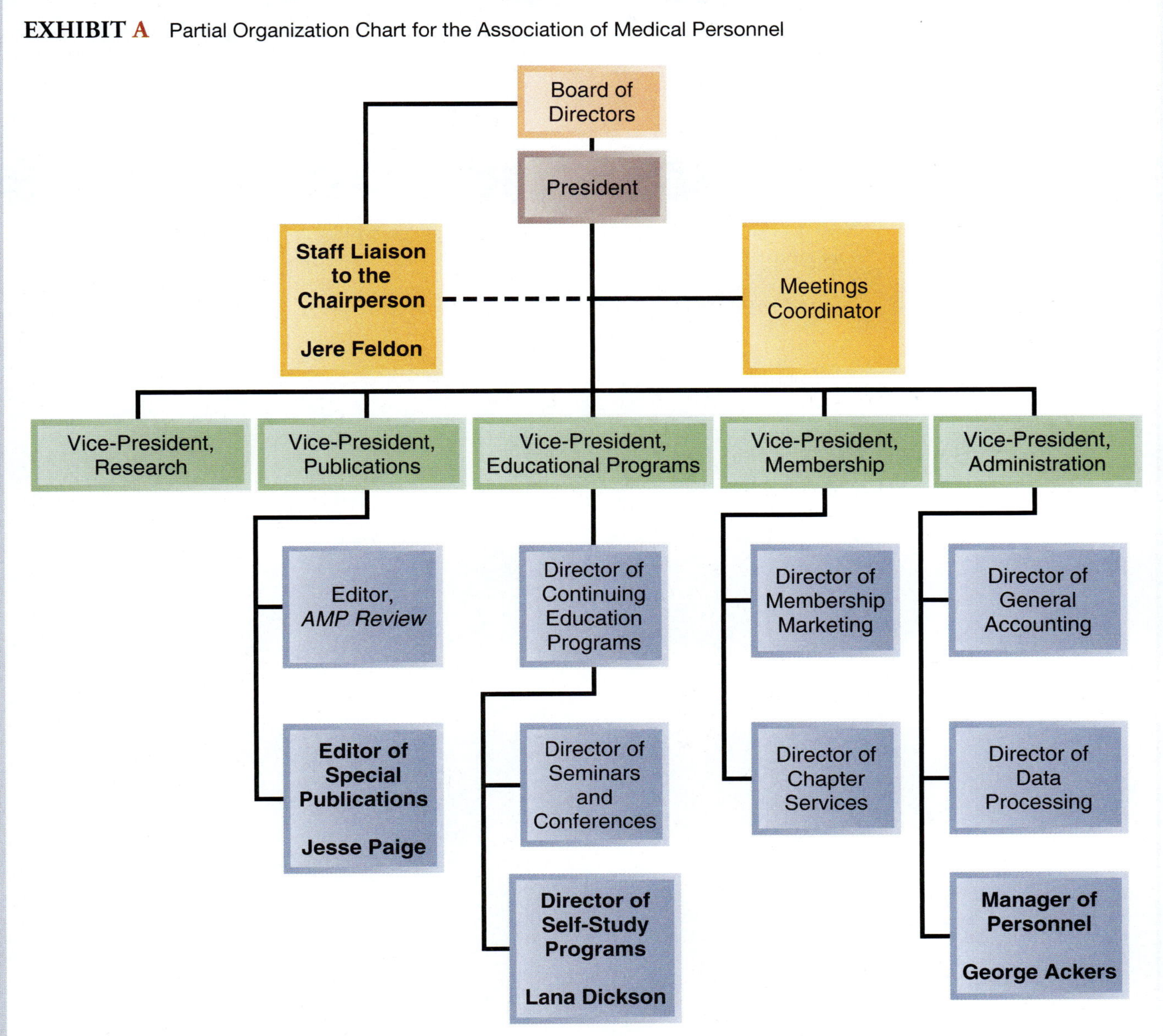

Research

R 1–9 Ethics and Governance [LO4]
Using a search of the web, investigate the governance statement presented by such organizations as Petro Canada or the Toronto Dominion Bank. Outline the practices they suggest they use, investigate if they have a code of conduct/ethics and research a blog for an indication as to whether their governance practices or code of conduct is being violated.

R 1–10 Control Practices and Technology [LO5]
RFID (Radio Frequency Identification) has been suggested as a way to revolutionize management control practices. Using a Web search, describe the nature of RFID and outline some of the problems they pose. Describe how RFID could significantly change management control practices.

R 1–11 Strategies [LO1]
Using the annual report of a major company such as Canadian Tire Corporation or Canadian National Railway, describe their strategies as presented in their Management Discussion and Analysis. Discuss whether you believe their strategy is effective against major competitors.

R 1–12 Environmental Strategies [LO5]
Using the web site for Tim Hortons, search the investor relations tab to determine the environmental policies of the company and the practices it has initiated. Discuss if such environmental policies and practices have accounting implications.

Glossary

Visit the Online Learning Centre at **http://www.mcgrawhill.ca/olc/garrison/** for a review of glossary terms and definitions.

CHAPTER 2

LEARNING OBJECTIVES

After studying Chapter 2, you should be able to:

1. Identify and give examples of each of the three basic cost elements involved in the manufacture of a product.
2. Distinguish between product costs and period costs and give examples of each.
3. Prepare an income statement including the calculation of cost of goods sold.
4. Prepare a schedule of cost of goods manufactured.
5. Explain the difference in the behaviour of variable and fixed costs.
6. Distinguish between direct and indirect costs.
7. Define and give examples of additional cost classifications used in making decisions: differential costs, opportunity costs, and sunk costs.

COST TERMS, CONCEPTS, AND CLASSIFICATIONS

BUSINESS FOCUS

Considering the Costs

Terri, the owner of a retail florist shop, has been trying to decide for some time whether she should continue to use a local courier service to deliver flowers to customers or buy a delivery truck and use one of her employees to make the deliveries. At a recent family dinner, she brought up the subject of the delivery truck with her brother-in-law, who fancies himself as an expert on all management subjects. He grabbed this opportunity to impress on Terri his understanding of costs.

In rapid-fire succession, Terri's brother-in-law told her that the fees paid to the courier to deliver flowers are a variable cost and a period cost, but the costs of the flowers are product costs rather than period costs, even though the flower costs are also variable costs. On the other hand, the depreciation of the delivery truck would be a fixed cost and a period cost. And while the fuel for the truck would be a variable cost and a differential cost, the wages of the person making the deliveries would be a fixed cost, not a differential cost, and would involve an opportunity cost. At this point, Terri excused herself—pleading that she had to help in the kitchen.

Terri felt that her brother-in-law's comments were more confusing than helpful, but she knew that she could no longer put off the decision about the delivery truck. She would have to think carefully about her costs and determine what costs should be considered in this decision.

As explained in Chapter 1, the work of management focuses on (1) planning, which includes setting objectives and outlining how to attain these objectives; (2) directing and motivating; and (3) controlling, which includes the steps to take to ensure that objectives are realized. To carry out these responsibilities, managers need *information* about the organization. From an accounting point of view, this information often relates to the costs of the organization.

In managerial accounting, the term *cost* is used in many different ways. The reason is that there are many types of costs, and these costs are classified differently according to the immediate needs of management. For example, managers may want cost data to prepare external financial reports, to prepare planning budgets, or to make decisions. Each different use of cost data requires a different classification and definition of costs. For example, the preparation of external financial reports requires the use of historical cost data, whereas decision making may require current cost data.

In this chapter, we discuss many of the possible uses of cost data and how costs are defined and classified for each use. Our first task is to explain how costs are classified for the purpose of preparing external financial reports—particularly in manufacturing or producing companies. To set the stage for this discussion, we begin the chapter by defining some terms commonly used in manufacturing and producing. This classification is general so it can serve as a framework that can be adjusted to suit the peculiarities of specific companies. For example, if a company does not have direct materials such as a public consulting firm, then they could still use direct labour and overhead.

General Cost Classifications

LEARNING OBJECTIVE 1
Identify and give examples of each of the three basic cost elements involved in the manufacture of a product.

All types of organizations incur costs—business, non-business, manufacturing, retail, and service. Generally, the kinds of costs that are incurred and the way in which these costs are classified depend on the type of organization involved. Managerial accounting is as applicable to one type of organization as to another. For this reason, we will consider in our discussion the cost characteristics of a variety of organizations—manufacturing, merchandising, and service.

Our initial focus in this chapter is on manufacturing companies, since their basic activities include most of the activities found in other types of business organizations. Manufacturing companies such as Magna, General Motors, and Sleemans acquire raw materials, produce finished goods, market, distribute, bill, and incur costs. Therefore, an understanding of costs in a manufacturing company can be very helpful in understanding costs in other types of organizations. Categories that are not applicable to a certain type of organization can be omitted. For example, Terri's Flower Shop buys flowers so it has a product cost for flower purchases but it does not grow flowers so it does not have production costs. The Flower Shop has delivery costs for its courier service which is a distribution cost. Although not discussed in the opening vignette, it would likely have marketing costs and perhaps billing costs.

Manufacturing Costs

Most manufacturing companies divide manufacturing costs into three broad categories: direct materials, direct labour, and manufacturing overhead. A discussion of each of these categories follows.

Raw materials
Any materials that go into the final product.

Direct Materials The materials that go into the final product are often termed **raw materials**. This term is somewhat misleading, since it seems to imply unprocessed natural resources like wood pulp or iron ore. Actually, *raw materials* may be used to refer to any materials that are used in the final product, and the finished product of one company can become the raw materials of another company. For example, the plastics produced by

Du Pont are a raw material used by Hewlett Packard in its personal computers. One study back in the 1990s of 37 manufacturing industries found that materials averaged about 55% of sales revenues.[1]

Direct materials are those materials that become an integral part of the finished product and that can be physically and conveniently traced to it. This would include, for example, the seats Ford purchases from subcontractors to install in its vehicles. Also included is the tiny electric motor Panasonic uses in its DVD players to make the DVD spin.

Direct materials
Those materials that become an integral part of a finished product and can be conveniently traced to it.

Sometimes it is not worth the effort to trace the costs of relatively insignificant materials to the end products. Such minor items would include the solder used to make electrical connections in a Sony TV or the glue used to assemble an Ethan Allen chair. Materials such as solder and glue are called **indirect materials** and are included as part of manufacturing overhead, which is discussed later in this section. Indirect materials can still be thought of as raw materials but they are not treated as direct materials because of their economic significance and the cost/benefit of directly tracing them to the finished products.

Indirect materials
Small items of material such as glue and nails. These items may become an integral part of a finished product but are traceable to the product only at great cost or inconvenience.

Direct Labour The term direct labour is reserved for those labour costs that can be easily (i.e., physically and conveniently) traced to individual units of product. Direct labour is sometimes called *touch labour*, since direct labour workers typically touch the product while it is being made. The labour costs of assembly-line workers, for example, would be direct labour costs, as would the labour costs of carpenters, bricklayers, and machine operators.

Direct labour
Those factory labour costs that can be traced easily to individual units of product. Also called *touch labour*.

Labour costs that cannot be physically traced to the creation of products, or that can be traced only at great cost and inconvenience, are termed **indirect labour** and treated as part of manufacturing overhead, along with indirect materials. Indirect labour includes the labour costs of janitors, supervisors, materials handlers, and night security guards. Although the efforts of these workers are essential to production, it would be either impractical or impossible to accurately trace their costs to specific units of product. Hence, such labour costs are treated as indirect labour.

Indirect labour
The labour costs of janitors, supervisors, materials handlers, and other factory workers that cannot be conveniently traced directly to particular products.

In some industries, major shifts are taking place in the structure of labour costs. Sophisticated automated equipment, operated and maintained by skilled indirect workers, is increasingly replacing direct labour. In the study of 37 manufacturing industries cited above direct labour averaged 10% of sales revenues. In a few companies, direct labour has become such a minor element of cost that it has disappeared altogether as a separate cost category. More is said in later chapters about this trend and about the impact it is having on cost systems. However, the vast majority of manufacturing and service companies throughout the world continue to recognize direct labour as a separate cost category.

Manufacturing Overhead **Manufacturing overhead**, the third element of manufacturing costs, includes all costs of manufacturing except direct materials and direct labour. Manufacturing overhead includes items such as indirect materials; indirect labour; maintenance and repairs on production equipment; and heat and light, property taxes, depreciation, and insurance on manufacturing facilities. A company also incurs costs for heat and light, property taxes, insurance, depreciation, and so forth, associated with its selling and administrative functions, but these costs are not included as part of manufacturing overhead. Only those costs associated with *operating the factory* or production facility are included in the manufacturing overhead category. Several studies have found manufacturing overhead costs to average about 16% of sales revenues.[2]

Manufacturing overhead
All costs associated with manufacturing except direct materials and direct labour.

Various names are used for manufacturing overhead, such as *indirect manufacturing cost, factory overhead,* and *factory burden.* All of these terms are synonymous with *manufacturing overhead.*

1. Germain Boer and Debra Jeter, "What's New About Modern Manufacturing? Empirical Evidence on Manufacturing Cost Changes," *Journal of Management Accounting Research*, Fall 1993, pp. 61–83.
2. J. Miller, A. DeMeyer, and J. Nakane, *Benchmarking Global Manufacturing* (Homewood, IL: Richard D. Irvin, 1992), Chapter 2. The Boer and Jeter article cited above contains a similar finding concerning the magnitude of manufacturing overhead.

Conversion cost
Direct labour cost plus manufacturing overhead cost.

Prime cost
Direct materials cost plus direct labour cost.

Manufacturing overhead combined with direct labour is called **conversion cost.** This term stems from the fact that direct labour costs and overhead costs are incurred to convert materials into finished products. Direct labour combined with direct materials is called **prime cost.**

The proportion of labour to overhead varies from company to company and even within companies within the same industry. Some automated companies have a large proportion of overhead compared to direct labour costs. Some even classify all labour as overhead. Others, such as those engaged in meat packing, have a large proportion of direct labour. Some companies buy materials partially assembled while others manufacture their subassembled parts to be used by other departments in the manufacturing process. How organizations determine their proportions of materials, labour, and overhead is a significant part of their strategic planning.

Classification of Labour Costs of Manufacturing

The classification of direct labour and indirect labour costs is relatively straightforward. Janitorial wages would usually be classified as overhead because they represent an indirect cost, as would payroll costs for supervisors, security personnel, and maintenance workers. However, the classification of idle time and overtime premiums of production workers is somewhat more difficult. For example, if three hours of a production worker's time are idle and each hour costs $12, then $36 of idle time cost usually would be charged to overhead if management felt that the cost was a general cost of all production. If, however, a specific job required idle time such as that caused by waiting for materials as a result of a specification change by the customer, then the idle time could be charged to the direct labour costs of a job. Whether the customer will pay for the charge depends on the prevailing market conditions or the contract with the customer.

Overtime premium
The extra hourly wage rate paid to workers who must work above their normal time requirements.

Overtime premiums represent the extra hourly wage rate paid to production workers who must work above their normal time requirements. For example, a worker might be paid time and a half for five overtime hours. Thus, if $12 was the base rate, the five hours would have an overtime premium of $6 × 5 hours, or $30. Classification of the overtime as direct labour or overhead depends on the cause of the overtime. A job-specific reason would dictate a direct job cost, whereas a normal overtime cost resulting from general management decisions, such as peak production needs, would dictate an overhead (indirect) charge to all jobs.

Employee benefits such as employment taxes, medical plans, and pension costs of the employer can be 30% to 40% of the base pay. Those employee benefits costs for indirect labour would obviously be classified as indirect overhead. However, the employee benefits for direct labour could justifiably be added to the base direct labour rate to specifically follow the direct labour costs on which they are based.

Non-Manufacturing Costs

Generally, non-manufacturing costs are subclassified into two categories:

1. Marketing or selling costs.
2. Administrative costs.

Marketing or selling costs
All costs necessary to secure customer orders and get the finished product or service into the hands of the customer.

Administrative costs
All executive, organizational, and clerical costs associated with the general management of an organization rather than with manufacturing, marketing, or selling.

Marketing or selling costs include all costs necessary to secure customer orders and get the finished product or service into the hands of the customer. These costs are often called *order-getting and order-filling costs.* Examples of marketing costs include order-getting costs such as those for advertising, sales travel, and sales salaries. Order-filling costs would include shipping, sales commissions, and the costs of finished goods warehouses.

Administrative costs include all executive, organizational, and clerical costs associated with the *general management* of an organization rather than with manufacturing, marketing, or selling. Examples of administrative costs include executive compensation, general accounting, secretarial, public relations, and similar costs involved in the overall, general administration of the organization *as a whole.*

Managerial accounting concepts and techniques apply just as much to non-manufacturing activities as they do to manufacturing activities. Service organizations, for example, are making increased use of cost concepts in analyzing and costing their services. Banks now use cost analysis to determine the cost of offering such services as chequing accounts, consumer loans, and credit cards, and insurance companies determine costs of servicing customers by geographic location, age, marital status, and occupation. Cost breakdowns of these types provide data for control over selling and administrative functions in the same way that manufacturing cost breakdowns provide data for controlling manufacturing functions.

Refer back to the flower shop described in the opening vignette to this chapter. Consider the wage cost of the person who prepares flower arrangements, including Terri. This person may also wait on customers, unpack purchases, prepare the payroll, and so on. How would Terri deal with such costs? She could require detailed time reports for the various activities that would permit the classification of wage costs as product costs for flower arrangements, selling costs for customer service, and administrative costs for payroll or bookkeeping. However, cost/benefit considerations would usually dictate that such a classification is unrealistic for Terri's operation. Likely Terri's wage and benefit cost would be considered administration costs, a helper's costs as selling, or Terri may not even separate selling from administrative but rather use an overall classification, operating costs. Cost/benefit analysis would dictate the answer.

IN BUSINESS

Product Costs and Period Costs: A Look Across Industries

Cost of goods sold and selling and administrative expenses expressed as a percentage of sales differ across companies and industries. For example, the U.S. data below summarize the median cost of goods sold as a percentage of sales and the median selling and administrative expense as a percentage of sales for eight different industries. Why do you think the percentages in each column differ so dramatically?

Industry	Cost of Goods Sold ÷ Sales	Selling and Administrative Expense ÷ Sales
Aerospace and Defense	79%	9%
Beverages	52%	34%
Computer Software and Services	34%	38%
Electrical Equipment and Components	64%	21%
Healthcare Services	82%	6%
Oil and Gas	90%	3%
Pharmaceuticals	31%	41%
Restaurants	78%	8%

Source: Lori Calabro, "Controlling the Flow," *CFO*, February 2005, pp. 46–50.

Product Costs versus Period Costs

LEARNING OBJECTIVE 2
Distinguish between product costs and period costs and give examples of each.

In addition to the distinction between manufacturing and non-manufacturing costs, there are other ways to look at costs. For instance, they can also be classified as either *product costs* or *period costs*. To understand the difference between product costs and period costs, we must first refresh our understanding of the matching principle from financial accounting.

Generally, costs are recognized as expenses on the income statement in the period that benefits from the cost. For example, if a company pays for liability insurance in advance for two years, the entire amount is not considered an expense of the year in which the payment is made. Instead, one-half of the cost would be recognized as an expense each year. The reason is that both years—not just the first year—benefit from the insurance payment. The unexpensed portion of the insurance payment is carried on the balance sheet as an asset called *prepaid insurance*. You should be familiar with this type of *accrual* from your financial accounting coursework.

The *matching principle* is based on the accrual concept and states that *costs incurred to generate a particular revenue should be recognized as expenses in the same period that the revenue is recognized.* This means that if a cost is incurred to acquire or make something that will eventually be sold, then the cost should be recognized as an expense only when the sale takes place—that is, when the benefit occurs. Such costs are called *product costs.*

Product Costs

Product costs
All costs that are involved in the purchase or manufacture of goods. In the case of manufactured goods, these costs consist of direct materials, direct labour, and manufacturing overhead. Also called *inventoriable costs*.

Inventoriable costs
Same as *product costs*.

For financial accounting purposes, **product costs** include all of the costs that are involved in acquiring or making a product. In the case of manufactured goods, these costs consist of direct materials, direct labour, and manufacturing overhead. Product costs are viewed as "attaching" to units of product as the goods are purchased or manufactured, and they remain attached as the goods go into inventory awaiting sale. So, initially, product costs are assigned to an inventory account on the balance sheet. When the goods are sold, the costs are released from inventory as expenses (typically called *cost of goods sold*) and matched against sales revenue. Since product costs are initially assigned to inventories, they are also known as **inventoriable costs.**

We want to emphasize that product costs are not necessarily treated as expenses in the period in which they are incurred. Rather, as explained above, they are treated as expenses in the period in which the related products *are sold.* This means that a product cost such as direct materials or direct labour might be incurred during one period but not treated as an expense until a following period when the completed product is sold. Thus product costs will be present in inventories and cost of goods sold.

IN BUSINESS

Dissecting the Costs

United Colors of Benetton, an Italian apparel company headquartered in Ponzano, is unusual in that it is involved in activities from clothing design through manufacturing, distribution, and ultimate sale to customers in Benetton retail outlets. Most companies are involved in only one or two of these activities. Looking at this company allows us to see how costs are distributed across the entire value chain. A recent income statement from the company contained the following data:

	Millions of Euros	Percent of Revenues
Revenue	€1,686	100.0%
Cost of sales	€ 929	55.1
Selling and administrative expenses:		
Payroll and related cost	€ 125	7.4
Distribution and transport	30	1.8
Sales commissions	74	4.4
Advertising and promotion	54	3.2
Depreciation and amortization	78	4.6
Other expenses	179	10.6
Total selling and administrative expenses	€ 540	32.0%

Even though this company spends large sums on advertising and runs its own shops, the cost of sales is still quite high in relation to the revenue—55.1% of revenue. And despite the company's lavish advertising campaigns, advertising and promotion costs amounted to only 3.2% of revenue. (Note: One U.S. dollar was worth about 0.7331 euros at the time of this financial report.)

Period Costs

Period costs are all of the costs that are not included in product costs. These costs are expensed on the income statement in the period in which they are incurred, using the usual rules of accrual accounting you have already learned in financial accounting. Period costs are not included as part of the cost of either purchased or manufactured goods. Sales commissions and advertising are good examples of these kinds of costs. Neither commissions nor advertising are included as part of the cost of purchased or manufactured goods. Rather, both items are treated as expenses on the income statement in the period in which they are incurred. Thus, they are said to be period costs.

Period costs
Those costs that are taken directly to the income statement as expenses in the period in which they are incurred or accrued; such costs consist of selling (marketing) and administrative expenses.

As suggested above, *all selling and administrative expenses are considered to be period costs.* Therefore, advertising, executive salaries, sales commissions, public relations, and other non-manufacturing costs discussed earlier would all be period costs. They will appear on the income statement as expenses in the period in which they are incurred. Careful analysis of the purpose of costs is necessary to separate product from period costs. For example if Terri decided to purchase a delivery truck, the depreciation of the cost of the truck would be a selling cost. If the truck was also used for picking up flowers from a supplier, then the depreciation could be separated between the product cost of flowers (freight in) and the selling costs of delivery (freight out).

Exhibit 2–1 contains a summary of the cost terms that we have introduced so far.

EXHIBIT 2–1
Summary of Cost Terms

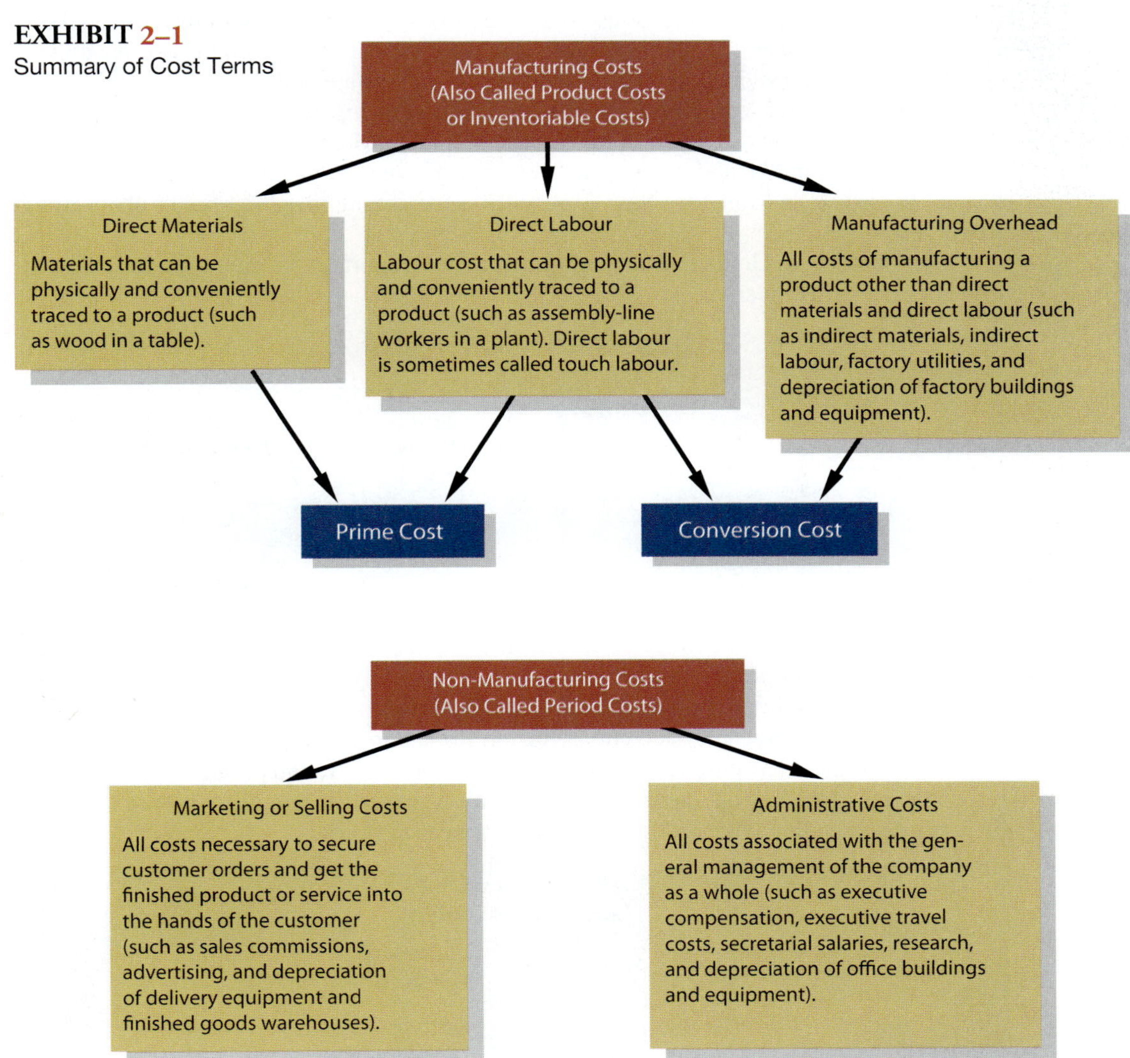

Cost Classifications on Financial Statements

In your prior accounting training, you learned that firms prepare periodic financial reports for creditors, shareholders, and others to show the financial condition of the firm and the firm's earnings performance over some specified interval. The reports you studied were probably those of merchandising companies, such as retail stores, which simply purchase goods from suppliers for resale to customers.

Financial statements prepared by a *manufacturing* company are more complex than the statements prepared by a merchandising company. Manufacturing companies are more complex organizations than merchandising companies because the manufacturing company must produce its goods as well as market them. The production process gives rise to many costs that do not exist in a merchandising company, and somehow these costs must be accounted for on the manufacturing company's financial statements. In this section, we focus our attention on how this accounting is carried out in the balance sheet and income statement.

The Balance Sheet

Raw (direct) materials The materials that are used to make a product.

Work in process Consists of units of product that are only partially complete and will require further work before they are ready for sale to a customer.

Finished goods Consist of units of product that have been completed but have not yet been sold to customers.

The balance sheet, or statement of financial position, of a manufacturing company is similar to that of a merchandising company. However, there are differences in the inventory accounts. A merchandising company has only one class of inventory—goods purchased from suppliers that are awaiting resale to customers. By contrast, manufacturing companies have three classes of inventories—**raw (direct) materials**, **work in process**, and **finished goods**. The overall inventory figure is usually broken down into these three classes of inventories and provided in a footnote to the financial statements.

We will use two companies—Graham Manufacturing and Reston Bookstore—to illustrate the concepts discussed in this section. Graham Manufacturing is located in Victoria, British Columbia, and makes precision brass fittings for yachts. Reston Bookstore is a small bookstore in Moncton, New Brunswick, specializing in selling books about Maritime Canada.

The footnotes to Graham Manufacturing's annual report reveal the following information concerning its inventories:

Graham Manufacturing Corporation
Inventory Accounts

	Beginning Balance	Ending Balance
Raw Materials	$ 60,000	$ 50,000
Work in Process	90,000	60,000
Finished Goods.	125,000	175,000
Total inventory accounts	$275,000	$285,000

Graham Manufacturing's raw materials inventory consists largely of brass rods and brass blocks. The work in process inventory consists of partially completed brass fittings. The finished goods inventory consists of brass fittings that are ready to be sold to customers.

In contrast, the inventory account at Reston Bookstore consists entirely of the costs of books the company has purchased from publishers for resale to the public. In merchandising companies like Reston, these inventories may be called *merchandise inventories.* The beginning and ending balances in this account appear as follows:

Reston Bookstore
Inventory Account

	Beginning Balance	Ending Balance
Merchandise inventory	$100,000	$150,000

EXHIBIT 2–2 Comparative Income Statements: Merchandising and Manufacturing Companies

MERCHANDISING COMPANY
Reston Bookstore

The cost of merchandise inventory purchased from outside suppliers during the period. → Add: Purchases

Sales		$1,000,000
Cost of goods sold:		
Beginning merchandise inventory	$100,000	
Add: Purchases	650,000	
Goods available for sale	750,000	
Deduct: Ending merchandise inventory	150,000	600,000
Gross margin		400,000
Less operating expenses:		
Selling expense	100,000	
Administrative expense	200,000	300,000
Operating income		$ 100,000

MANUFACTURING COMPANY
Graham Manufacturing

The manufacturing costs associated with the goods that were finished during the period. (See Exhibit 2–4 for details.) → Add: Cost of goods manufactured

Sales		$1,500,000
Cost of goods sold:		
Beginning finished goods inventory	$125,000	
Add: Cost of goods manufactured	850,000	
Goods available for sale	975,000	
Deduct: Ending finished goods inventory	175,000	800,000
Gross margin		700,000
Less operating expenses:		
Selling expense	250,000	
Administrative expense	300,000	550,000
Operating income		$ 150,000

Note: Operating income is income before interest and taxes. Interest and income taxes are ignored here.

The Income Statement

LEARNING OBJECTIVE 3
Prepare an income statement including the calculation of cost of goods sold.

Exhibit 2–2 compares the income statements of Reston Bookstore and Graham Manufacturing. For purposes of illustration, these statements contain more detail about cost of goods sold than you will generally find in published financial statements.

At first glance, the income statements of merchandising and manufacturing firms like Reston Bookstore and Graham Manufacturing are very similar. The only apparent difference is in the labels of some of the entries that go into the computation of the cost of goods sold figure. In the exhibit, the computation of cost of goods sold relies on the following basic equation for inventory accounts:

Basic Equation for Inventory Accounts

$$\text{Beginning balance} + \text{Additions to inventory} = \text{Ending balance} + \text{Withdrawals from inventory}$$

The logic underlying this equation, which applies to any inventory account, is illustrated in Exhibit 2–3. At the beginning of the period, the inventory contains a beginning balance. During the period, additions are made to the inventory through purchases or other means. The sum of the beginning balance and the additions to the account is the total amount of inventory available. During the period, withdrawals are made from inventory. Whatever is left at the end of the period after these withdrawals is the ending balance. At the end of the period, all of the inventory that was available must either be in ending inventory or must have been withdrawn from the inventory account.

EXHIBIT 2–3 Inventory Flow

Beginning balance + Additions = Total available − Withdrawals = Ending balance

These concepts are applied to determine the cost of goods sold for a merchandising company like Reston Bookstore as follows:

Cost of Goods Sold in a Merchandising Company

Beginning balance inventory + Purchases = Ending merchandising inventory + Cost of goods sold

or

Cost of goods sold = Beginning merchandise inventory + Purchases − Ending merchandise inventory

The cost of goods sold for a manufacturing company like Graham Manufacturing is determined as follows:

Cost of Goods Sold in a Manufacturing Company

Beginning finished goods inventory + Cost of goods manufactured = Ending finished goods inventory + Cost of goods sold

or

Cost of Goods Sold in a Manufacturing Company

Cost of goods sold = Beginning finished goods inventory + Cost of goods manufactured − Ending finished goods inventory

To determine the cost of goods sold in a merchandising company like Reston Bookstore, we need to know only the beginning and ending balances in the Merchandise Inventory account and the purchases. Total purchases can be determined easily in a merchandising company by simply adding together all purchases from suppliers.

Cost of goods manufactured The manufacturing costs associated with the goods that were finished during the period.

To determine the cost of goods sold in a manufacturing company like Graham Manufacturing, we need to know the *cost of goods manufactured* and the beginning and ending balances in the Finished Goods inventory account. The **cost of goods manufactured** consists of the manufacturing costs associated with goods that were *finished* during the period. The cost of goods manufactured figure for Graham Manufacturing is derived in Exhibit 2–4, which contains a *schedule of cost of goods manufactured.*

Schedule of Cost of Goods Manufactured

LEARNING OBJECTIVE 4
Prepare a schedule of cost of goods manufactured.

At first glance, the **schedule of cost of goods manufactured** in Exhibit 2–4 appears complex and perhaps even intimidating. However, it is all quite logical. The schedule of cost of goods manufactured contains the three elements of product costs that we discussed earlier—direct materials, direct labour, and manufacturing overhead. The total of these three cost elements is *not* the cost of goods manufactured, however. The reason is that some of the materials, labour, and overhead costs incurred during the period relate to goods that are not yet completed. The costs that relate to goods that are not yet completed are shown in the work in process inventory figures at the bottom of the schedule. Note that the beginning work in process inventory must be added to the manufacturing costs of the period, and the ending work in process inventory must be deducted, to arrive at the cost of goods manufactured.

The direct material cost is not simply the cost of materials purchased during the period—rather it is the cost of materials *used* during the period. The purchases of raw materials are added to the beginning balance to determine the cost of materials available for use. The ending inventory is deducted from this amount to arrive at the cost of the materials used in production. The sum of the three cost elements—materials, direct labour, and manufacturing overhead—is the **total manufacturing cost**. This is *not* the same thing, however, as the cost of goods manufactured for the period. The subtle distinction between the total manufacturing cost and the cost of goods manufactured is very easy to miss. Some of the materials, direct labour, and manufacturing overhead costs incurred during the period relate to goods that are

Schedule of costs of goods manufactured
A schedule showing the direct materials, direct labour, and manufacturing overhead costs incurred for a period and assigned to work in process and completed goods.

Total manufacturing costs
Costs that represent the direct materials used, direct labour used, and the manufacturing overhead used to perform the production work for finished or unfinished products for the period.

EXHIBIT 2–4 Schedule of Cost of Goods Manufactured

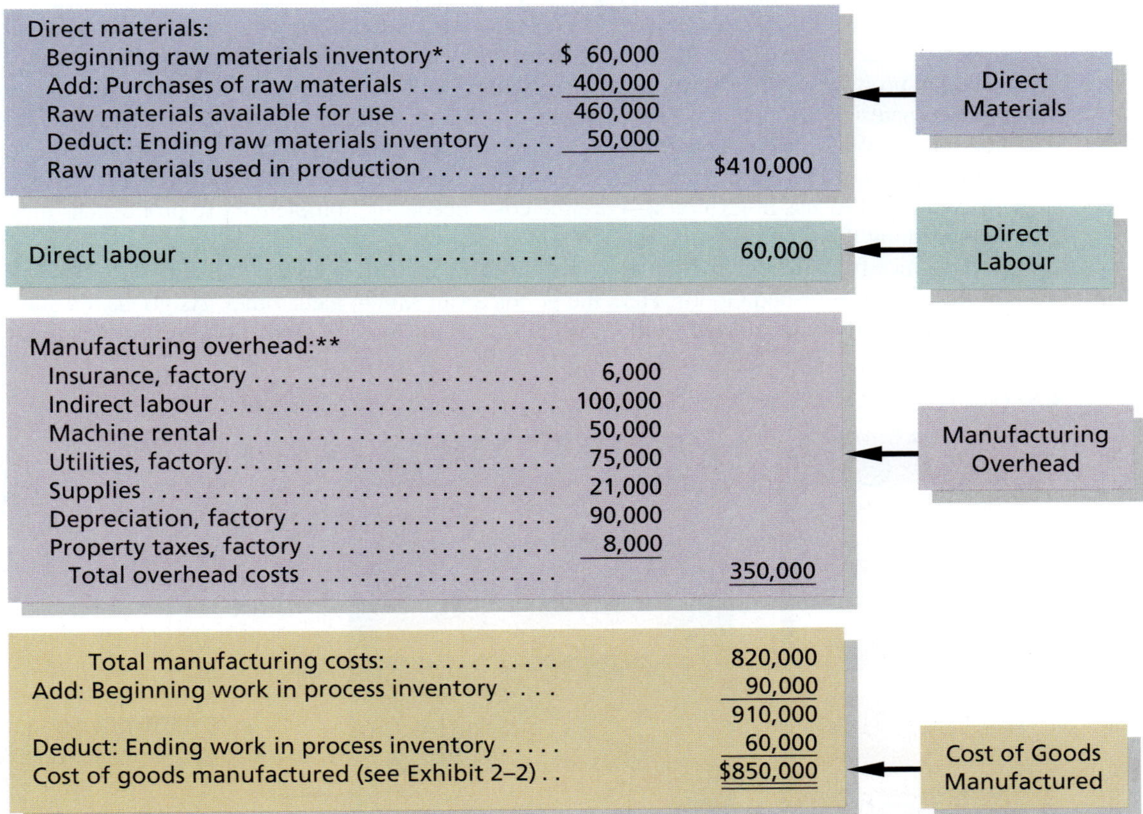

Direct materials:		
Beginning raw materials inventory*	$ 60,000	
Add: Purchases of raw materials	400,000	
Raw materials available for use	460,000	
Deduct: Ending raw materials inventory	50,000	
Raw materials used in production		$410,000
Direct labour		60,000
Manufacturing overhead:**		
Insurance, factory	6,000	
Indirect labour	100,000	
Machine rental	50,000	
Utilities, factory	75,000	
Supplies	21,000	
Depreciation, factory	90,000	
Property taxes, factory	8,000	
Total overhead costs		350,000
Total manufacturing costs:		820,000
Add: Beginning work in process inventory		90,000
		910,000
Deduct: Ending work in process inventory		60,000
Cost of goods manufactured (see Exhibit 2–2)		$850,000

*We assume in this example that the Raw Materials inventory account contains only direct materials and that indirect materials are carried in a separate Supplies account. Using a Supplies account for indirect materials is a common practice among companies. In Chapter 3, we discuss the procedure to be followed if *both* direct and indirect materials are carried in a single account.

**In Chapter 3 we will see that the manufacturing overhead section of the schedule of cost of goods manufactured can be simplified considerably by using what is called a *predetermined overhead rate.*

Cost of goods manufactured Costs that contain the direct materials used, the direct labour used, and the manufacturing overhead used for the finished production during the period.

not yet completed. As stated above, the **cost of goods manufactured** consists of the manufacturing cost associated with the goods that were *finished* during the period. Consequently, adjustments need to be made to the total manufacturing costs of the period for the partially completed goods that were in process at the beginning and at the end of the period. The costs that relate to goods that are not yet completed are shown in the work in process inventory figures at the bottom of the schedule. Note that the beginning work in process inventory must be added to the manufacturing costs of the period, and the ending work in process inventory must be deducted, to arrive at the cost of goods manufactured.

Because financial statements evident in financial accounting are for users external to the organization, accounts are often summarized so that the detail shown in Exhibits 2–2 and 2–4 would not be evident. Management accounting can, however, provide the detail shown in these exhibits. Particularly Exhibit 2–4 is not typically evident in external financial statements even though it exists internally. Privacy considerations represent part of the disclosure strategy used by managers and contained in GAAP requirements.

Product Costs—Flows

Earlier in the chapter, we defined product costs as consisting of those costs that are involved in either the purchase or the manufacture of goods. For manufactured goods, we stated that these costs consist of direct materials, direct labour, and manufacturing overhead. To understand product costs more fully, it will be helpful at this point to look briefly at the flow of costs in a manufacturing company. By doing so, we will be able to see how product costs move through the various accounts and affect the balance sheet and the income statement in the course of producing and selling products.

Exhibit 2–5 illustrates the flow of costs in a manufacturing company. Raw materials purchases are recorded in the Raw Materials inventory account. When raw materials are used in production, their costs are transferred to the Work in Process inventory account as direct materials. Notice that direct labour cost and manufacturing overhead cost are added directly to Work in Process. Work in Process can be viewed most simply as products on an assembly line. The direct materials, direct labour, and manufacturing overhead costs added to Work in Process in Exhibit 2–4 are the costs needed to complete these products as they move along this assembly line.

Notice from the exhibit that as goods are completed, their cost is transferred from Work in Process to Finished Goods. Here the goods await sale to a customer. As goods are sold, their cost is then transferred from Finished Goods to Cost of Goods Sold. It is at this point

EXHIBIT 2–5 Cost Flows and Classifications in a Manufacturing Company

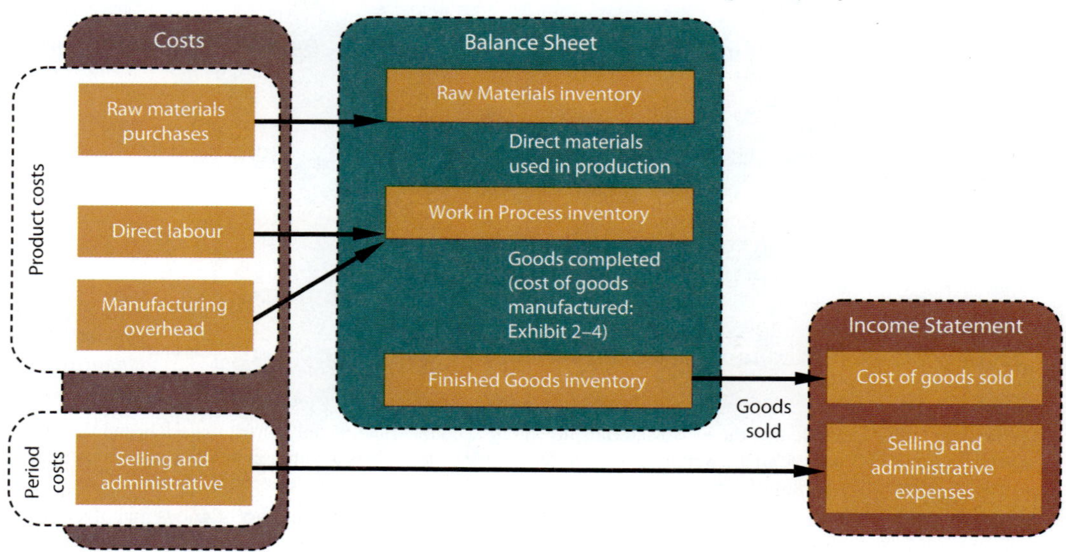

that the various materials, labour, and overhead costs that are required to make the product are finally treated as expenses.

Knowledge of cost flows is often necessary to control costs and to predict how costs interact. For example, the more the company sells, the more cost of goods sold, the more finished goods and other inventories it will usually have and the more product costs and period costs. Cost flows provide knowledge of the sequencing needed to predict the interactions of various cost categories.

Inventoriable Costs

As stated earlier, product costs are often called *inventoriable costs*. The reason is that these costs go directly into inventory accounts as they are incurred (first into Work in Process and then into Finished Goods), rather than going into expense accounts. Thus, they are termed *inventoriable costs. This is a key concept, since such costs can end up on the balance sheet as assets if goods are only partially completed or are unsold at the end of a period.* To illustrate this point, refer again to the data in Exhibit 2–5. At the end of the period, the materials, labour, and overhead costs that are associated with the units in the Work in Process and Finished Goods inventory accounts will appear on the balance sheet as part of the company's assets. As explained earlier, these costs will not become expenses until later when the goods are completed and sold.

As shown in Exhibit 2–5, selling and administrative expenses are not involved in the manufacture of a product. For this reason, they are not treated as product costs but rather as period costs that go directly into expense accounts as they are incurred.

An Example of Cost Flows

To provide an example of cost flows in a manufacturing company, assume that a company's annual insurance cost is $2,000. Three-fourths of this amount ($1,500) applies to factory operations, and one-fourth ($500) applies to selling and administrative activities. Therefore, $1,500 of the $2,000 insurance cost would be a product (inventoriable) cost and would be added to the cost of goods produced during the year. This concept is illustrated in Exhibit 2–6, where $1,500 of insurance cost is added into Work in Process. As shown

EXHIBIT 2–6 An Example of Cost Flows in a Manufacturing Company

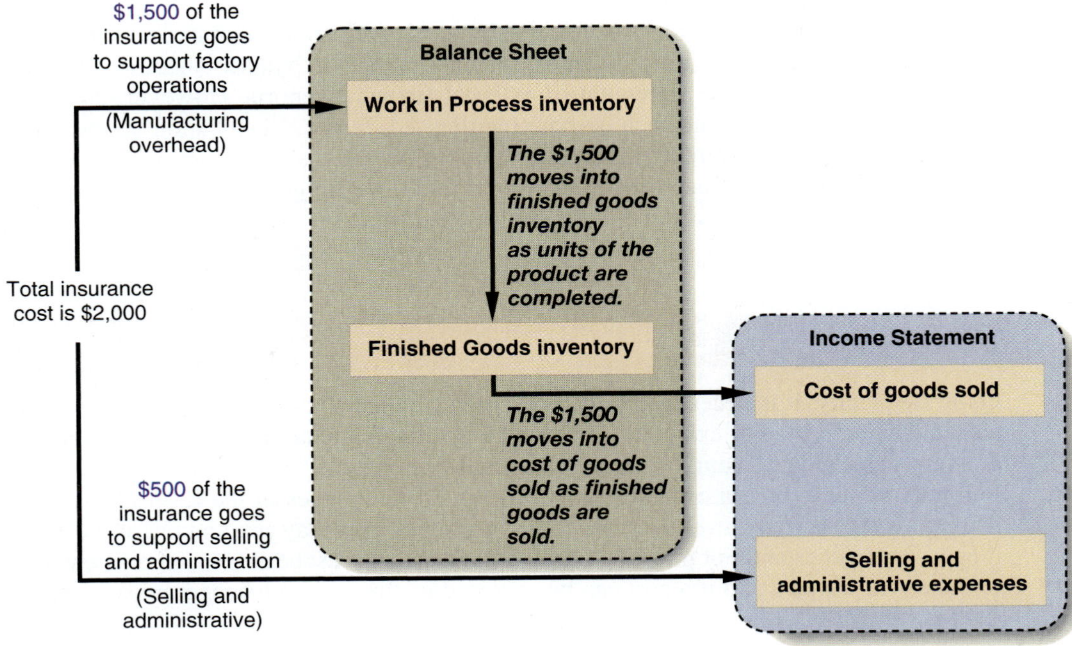

EXHIBIT 2–7 Summary of Cost Classifications

Purpose of Cost Classification	Cost Classifications
Preparing external financial statements	• Product costs (inventoriable) • Direct materials • Direct labour • Manufacturing overhead • Period costs (expensed) • Non-manufacturing costs • Marketing or selling costs • Administrative costs
Predicting cost behaviour in response to changes in activity	• Variable cost (proportional to activity) • Fixed cost (constant in total)
Assigning costs to cost objects such as departments or products	• Direct cost (can easily be traced) • Indirect cost (cannot easily be traced; must be allocated)
Making decisions	• Differential cost (differs between alternatives) • Sunk cost (past cost not affected by a decision) • Opportunity cost (forgone benefit)

in the exhibit, this portion of the year's insurance cost will not become an expense until the goods that are produced during the year are sold, and the $1,500 will remain as part of the asset, inventory (either as part of Work in Process or as part of Finished Goods), along with the other costs of producing the goods.

By contrast, the $500 of insurance costs that applies to the company's selling and administrative activities will be expensed immediately.

Thus far, we have been mainly concerned with classifications of manufacturing costs for the purpose of determining inventory valuations on the balance sheet and cost of goods sold on the income statement of external financial reports. However, costs are used for many purposes, and each purpose requires a different classification of costs. We will consider several different purposes for cost classifications in the remaining sections of this chapter. To help keep the big picture in mind, we suggest that you refer back to Exhibit 2–7 as you progress through the rest of this chapter.

Cost Classifications for Predicting Cost Behaviour

LEARNING OBJECTIVE 5
Explain the difference in the behaviour of variable and fixed costs.

Quite frequently, it is necessary to predict how a certain cost will behave in response to a change in activity. For example, Terri (in the opening vignette) needs to know how her delivery costs would change with increases and decreases in the sales of flowers. **Cost behaviour** means how a cost will react or respond to changes in the level of business activity. As the activity level rises and falls, a particular cost may rise and fall as well—or it may remain constant. For planning purposes, a manager must be able to anticipate which of these will happen, and if a cost can be expected to change, the manager must know by how much it will change. To help make such distinctions, costs are often categorized as *variable* or *fixed*.

Cost behaviour
The way in which a cost reacts or responds to changes in the level of business activity.

Variable Cost

A **variable cost** is a cost that varies, in total, in direct proportion to changes in the level of activity. The activity can be expressed in many ways, such as units produced, units sold, kilometres driven, beds occupied, lines of print, hours worked, and so forth. A good example of a variable cost is direct materials. The cost of direct materials used during a period will vary, in total, in direct proportion to the number of units that are produced. To illustrate this idea, consider the Nova Bus Corporation. Each bus requires one battery. As the output of buses increases and decreases, the number of batteries used will increase and decrease proportionately. If bus production goes up 10%, then the number of batteries used will also go up 10%. The concept of a variable cost is shown in graphic form in Exhibit 2–8.

Variable cost
A cost that varies, in total, in direct proportion to changes in the level of activity. A variable cost is constant per unit.

It is important to note that when we speak of a cost as being variable, we mean the *total* cost rises and falls as the activity level rises and falls. This idea is presented below, assuming that a battery costs $24:

Number of Buses Produced	Cost per Battery	Total Variable Cost—Batteries
1	$24	$ 24
500	24	12,000
1,000	24	24,000

One interesting aspect of variable cost behaviour is that a variable cost is constant if expressed on a *per unit* basis. Observe from the tabulation above that the per unit cost of batteries remains constant at $24 even though the total amount of cost involved increases and decreases with activity.

There are many examples of costs that are variable with respect to the products and services provided by a company. In a manufacturing company, variable costs include items such as direct materials and some elements of manufacturing overhead such as lubricants, and period costs such as shipping and sales commissions. For the present, we will also assume that direct labour is a variable cost, although as we shall see in Chapter 7, direct labour may act more like a fixed cost in many situations. In a merchandising company, variable costs include items such as cost of goods sold, commissions to salespersons, and billing costs. In a hospital, the variable costs of providing health care services to patients would include the costs of the supplies, drugs, meals, and perhaps nursing services.

When we say that a cost is variable, we ordinarily mean that it is variable with respect to the products and services the organization produces. However, cost can be variable with respect to other activities. For example, the wages paid to employees at a Rogers Video outlet will depend on the number of hours the store is open and not strictly on the number of videos rented. In this case, we would say that wage costs are variable with respect to the hours of operation. Nevertheless, when we say that a cost is variable, we ordinarily mean it is variable with respect to the volume of revenue-generating output—in other words, how many units are produced and sold, how many videos are rented, how many patients are treated, and so on.

Fixed Cost

A **fixed cost** is a cost that remains constant, in total, regardless of changes in the level of activity. Unlike variable costs, fixed costs are not affected by changes in activity. Consequently, as the activity level rises and falls, the fixed costs remain constant in

Fixed cost
A cost that remains constant, in total, regardless of changes in the level of activity within the relevant range. If a fixed cost is expressed on a per unit basis, it varies inversely with the level of activity.

EXHIBIT 2–8 Variable and Fixed Cost Behaviour

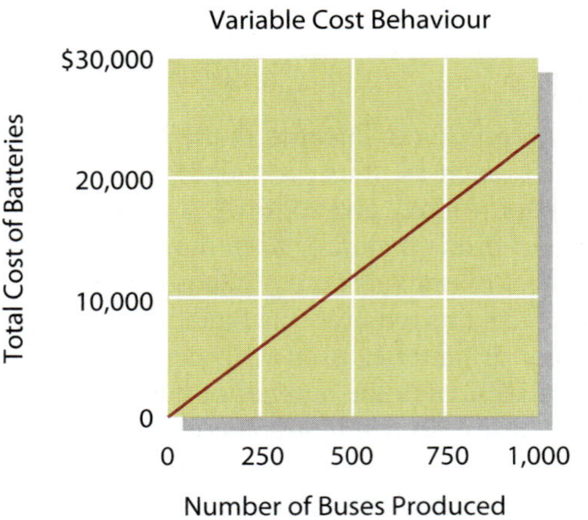

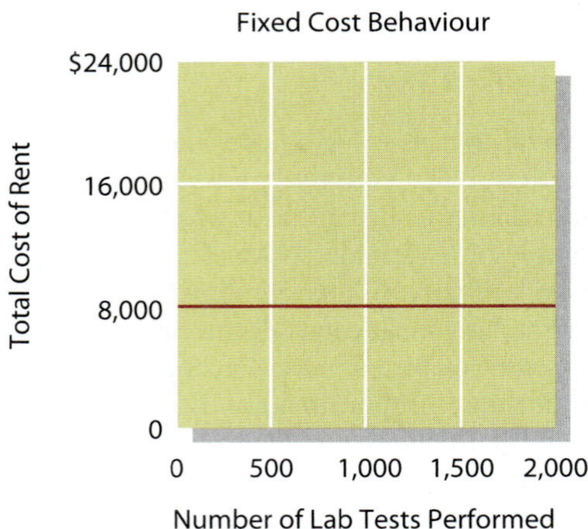

total amount unless influenced by some outside force, such as price changes. Rent is a good example of a fixed cost. Suppose the Saskatchewan Clinic rents a machine for $8,000 per month that tests blood samples for the presence of leukemia cells. The $8,000 monthly rental cost will be incurred regardless of the number of tests that may be performed during the month. The concept of a fixed cost is shown in graphic form in Exhibit 2–8.

Very few costs are completely fixed. Most will change if there is a large enough change in activity. For example, suppose that the capacity of the leukemia diagnostic machine at the Saskatchewan Clinic is 2,000 tests per month. If the clinic wishes to perform more than 2,000 tests in a month, it would be necessary to rent an additional machine, which would cause a jump in the fixed costs. When we say a cost is fixed, we mean it is fixed within some *relevant range.* The **relevant range** is the range of activity within which the assumptions about variable and fixed costs are valid. For example, the assumption that the rent for diagnostic machines is $8,000 per month is valid within the relevant range of 0 to 2,000 tests per month.

Relevant range
The range of activity within which assumptions about variable and fixed cost behaviour are valid.

Fixed costs can create difficulties if it becomes necessary to express the costs on a per unit basis. This is because if fixed costs are expressed on a per unit basis, they will react *inversely* with changes in activity. In the Saskatchewan Clinic, for example, the average cost per test will fall as the number of tests performed increases. This is because the $8,000 rental cost will be spread over more tests. Conversely, as the number of tests performed in the clinic declines, the average cost per test will rise as the $8,000 rental cost is spread over fewer tests. This concept is illustrated in the table below:

Monthly Rental Cost	Number of Tests Performed	Average Cost per Test
$8,000	10	$800
8,000	500	16
8,000	2,000	4

Note that if the Saskatchewan Clinic performs only 10 tests each month, the rental cost of the equipment will average $800 per test. But if 2,000 tests are performed each month, the average cost will drop to only $4 per test. More will be said later about the problems created for both the accountant and the manager by this variation in unit costs.

Examples of fixed costs include straight-line depreciation, insurance, property taxes, rent, supervisory salaries, administrative salaries, and advertising.

A summary of both variable and fixed cost behaviour is presented in Exhibit 2–9.

Cost	Behaviour of the Cost (within the relevant range) In Total	Per Unit
Variable cost	Total variable cost increases and decreases in proportion to changes in the activity level.	Variable costs remain constant per unit.
Fixed cost	Total fixed cost is not affected by changes in the activity level within the relevant range.	Fixed costs decrease per unit as the activity level rises and increase per unit as the activity level falls.

EXHIBIT 2–9 Summary of Variable and Fixed Cost Behaviour

Cost Classifications for Assigning Costs to Cost Objects

LEARNING OBJECTIVE 6
Distinguish between direct and indirect costs.

Costs are assigned to objects for a variety of purposes including pricing, profitability studies, and control of spending. A **cost object** is anything for which cost data are desired—including products, product lines, customers, jobs, and organizational subunits. For purposes of assigning costs to cost objects, costs are classified as either *direct* or *indirect.*

Cost object
Anything for which cost data are desired.

Direct Cost

Direct cost
A cost that can easily and conveniently be traced to the particular cost object under consideration.

A **direct cost** is a cost that can easily and conveniently be traced to the particular cost object under consideration. The concept of direct cost extends beyond just direct materials and direct labour. For example, if Reebok is assigning costs to its various regional and national sales offices, then the salary of the sales manager in its Alberta office would be a direct cost of that office.

Indirect Cost

Indirect cost
A cost that cannot easily and conveniently be traced to the particular cost object under consideration.

An **indirect cost** is a cost that cannot easily and conveniently be traced to the particular cost object under consideration. For example, a Moosehead Breweries factory may produce many varieties of beer. The factory manager's salary would be an indirect cost of a particular variety such as Dry. The reason is that the factory manager's salary is not caused by any one variety of beer but rather is incurred as a consequence of running the entire factory. *To be traced to a cost object such as a particular product, the cost must be caused by the cost object.* The factory manager's salary is called a *common cost* of producing the various products of the factory. A **common cost** is a cost that is common to a number of costing objects but cannot be traced to them individually. A common cost is a particular type of indirect cost.

Common cost
A common cost is a cost that is common to a number of costing objects but cannot be traced to them individually.

A particular cost may be direct or indirect, depending on the cost object. While the Moosehead Breweries factory manager's salary is an *indirect* cost of manufacturing Dry beer, it is a *direct* cost of the manufacturing division. In the first case, the cost object is the brand of beer. In the second case, the cost object is the entire manufacturing division.

Cost Classifications for Decision Making

LEARNING OBJECTIVE 7
Define and give examples of additional cost classifications used in making decisions: differential costs, opportunity costs, and sunk costs.

Costs are an important feature of many business decisions. In making decisions, it is essential to have a firm grasp of the concepts *differential cost, opportunity cost,* and *sunk cost.*

Differential Cost and Revenue

Decisions involve choosing among alternatives. In business decisions, each alternative will have certain costs and benefits that must be compared to the costs and benefits of the

Differential cost
A difference in cost between any two alternatives.

Differential revenue
The difference in revenue between any two alternatives.

Incremental cost
An increase in cost between two alternatives.

other available alternatives. A difference in costs between any two alternatives is known as a **differential cost.** A difference in revenues between any two alternatives is known as **differential revenue.**

A differential cost is also known as an **incremental cost,** although technically an incremental cost should refer only to an increase in cost from one alternative to another; decreases in cost should be referred to as *decremental costs.* Differential cost is a broader term, encompassing both cost increases (incremental costs) and cost decreases (decremental costs) between alternatives.

The accountant's differential cost concept can be compared to the economist's marginal cost concept. In speaking of changes in cost and revenue, the economist employs the terms *marginal cost* and *marginal revenue.* The revenue that can be obtained from selling one more unit of product is called *marginal revenue*, and the cost involved in producing one more unit of product is called *marginal cost.* The economist's marginal concept is basically the same as the accountant's differential concept applied to a single unit of output.

Differential costs can be either fixed or variable. To illustrate, assume that Nature Way Cosmetics, Inc. is thinking about changing its marketing method from distribution through retailers to distribution by door-to-door direct sale. Present costs and revenues are compared to projected costs and revenues in the following table:

	Retailer Distribution (present)	Direct Sale Distribution (proposed)	Differential Costs and Revenues
Revenues (V)	$700,000	$800,000	$100,000
Cost of goods sold (V)	350,000	400,000	50,000
Advertising (F)	80,000	45,000	(35,000)
Commissions (V)	–0–	40,000	40,000
Warehouse depreciation (F)	50,000	80,000	30,000
Other expenses (F)	60,000	60,000	–0–
Total	540,000	625,000	85,000
Operating income	$160,000	$175,000	$ 15,000

V = Variable; F = Fixed.

According to the preceding analysis, the differential revenue is $100,000 and the differential costs total $85,000, leaving a positive differential operating income of $15,000 under the proposed marketing plan.

The decision of whether Nature Way Cosmetics should stay with the present retail distribution or switch to door-to-door direct selling could be made on the basis of the operating incomes of the two alternatives. As we see in the preceding analysis, the operating income under the present distribution method is $160,000, whereas the operating income under door-to-door direct selling is estimated to be $175,000. Therefore, the door-to-door direct distribution method is preferred, since it would result in $15,000 higher operating income. Note that we would have arrived at exactly the same conclusion by simply focusing on the differential revenues, differential costs, and differential operating income, which also show a $15,000 advantage for the direct selling method.

In general, only the differences between alternatives are relevant in decisions. Those items that are the same under all alternatives and that are not affected by the decision can be ignored. For example, in the Nature Way Cosmetics example, the Other Expenses category, which is $60,000 under both alternatives, can be ignored, since it has no effect on the decision. If it was removed from the calculations, the door-to-door direct selling method would still be preferred by $15,000. This is an extremely important principle in management accounting that we will return to in later chapters. Referring back to Terri's Flower Shop, the differential costs for the delivery decision would compare the courier costs with the cost of owning and using the delivery truck. The cost of Terri's wages or the store rental would not be differential because either cost would not likely change for either alternative in the decision.

IN BUSINESS

The inquiry into the 1985 crash of Air India Flight 182 provides a lot of very sad information. However, a recent story about the testimony given at the inquiry told of an error often made in decision making. In apparent violation of Air India policy, the flight was permitted to leave Montreal because it was estimated to be too costly to keep the aircraft on the tarmac long enough to do a complete luggage check. Thus the differential cost of the flight was significant to the decision maker and was to be avoided. However, what was the differential benefit of keeping the aircraft on the ground until the check could be conducted? Maybe the decision maker did not consider this or maybe the amount was considered too small to offset the differential cost. Certainly both the differential benefit and the differential cost need to be considered before an economic decision is made.

Source: Jim Brown. "Too Costly to Keep Air India Plane on Tarmac, Inquiry Hears." The Canadian Press quoted in *The Chronicle Herald*, May 17, 2007, p. A5. Also Kim Bolan, "Cost Put Before Safety: Witness," *National Post Digital*, May 17, 2007, p. A-1.

Opportunity Cost

Opportunity cost is the potential benefit that is given up when one alternative is selected over another. To illustrate this important concept, consider the following examples:

Opportunity cost
The potential benefit that is given up when one alternative is selected over another.

Example 1

Vicki has a part-time job that pays her $100 per week while attending college. She would like to spend a week at the beach during spring break, and her employer has agreed to give her the time off, but without pay. The $100 in lost wages would be an opportunity cost of taking the week off to be at the beach.

Example 2

Suppose that The Bay is considering investing a large sum of money in land that may be a site for a future store. Rather than invest the funds in land, the company could invest the funds in high-grade securities. If the land is acquired, the opportunity cost will be the investment income that could have been realized if the securities had been purchased instead.

Example 3

Steve is employed with a company that pays him a salary of $30,000 per year. He is thinking about leaving the company and returning to school. Since returning to school would require that he give up his $30,000 salary, the forgone salary would be an opportunity cost of seeking further education.

Opportunity cost is not usually entered in the accounting records of an organization, but it is a cost that must be explicitly considered in every decision a manager makes. Virtually every alternative has some opportunity cost attached to it. In example 3 above, for instance, if Steve decides to stay at his job, there still is an opportunity cost involved: It is the higher income that could be realized in future years as a result of returning to school.

Sunk Cost

A **sunk cost** is a cost *that has already been incurred* and that cannot be changed by any decision made now or in the future. Since sunk costs cannot be changed by any decision, they are not differential costs. Therefore, they can and should be ignored when making a decision.

Sunk cost
Any cost that has already been incurred and that cannot be changed by any decision made now or in the future.

To illustrate a sunk cost, assume that a company paid $50,000 several years ago for a special-purpose machine. The machine was used to make a product that is now obsolete and is no longer being sold. Even though in hindsight the purchase of the machine may have been unwise, no amount of regret can undo that decision. And it would be folly to continue making the obsolete product in a misguided attempt to "recover" the original cost of the machine. In short, the $50,000 originally paid for the machine has already been incurred and cannot be a differential cost in any future decision. For this reason, such costs are said to be sunk and should be ignored in decisions.

Summary

In this chapter, we have looked at some of the ways in which managers classify costs. How the costs will be used—for preparing external reports, predicting cost behaviour, assigning costs to cost objects, or decision making—will dictate how the costs will be classified.

For purposes of valuing inventories and determining expenses for the balance sheet and income statement, costs are classified as either product costs or period costs. Product costs are assigned to inventories and are considered assets until the products are sold. At the point of sale, product costs become cost of goods sold on the income statement. In contrast, following the usual accrual practices, period costs are taken directly to the income statement as expenses in the period in which they are incurred.

In a merchandising company, product cost is whatever the company paid for its merchandise. For external financial reports in a manufacturing company, product costs consist of all manufacturing costs. In both kinds of companies, selling and administrative costs are considered to be period costs and are expensed as incurred.

For purposes of predicting cost behaviour—how costs will react to changes in activity—managers commonly classify costs into two categories—variable and fixed. Variable costs, in total, are strictly proportional to activity. Thus, the variable cost per unit is constant. Fixed costs, in total, remain at the same level for changes in activity that occur within the relevant range. Thus, the average fixed cost per unit decreases as the number of units increases.

For purposes of assigning costs to cost objects such as products or departments, costs are classified as direct or indirect. Direct costs can conveniently be traced to the cost objects. Indirect costs cannot conveniently be traced to cost objects.

For purposes of making decisions, the concepts of differential cost and revenue, opportunity cost, and sunk cost are of vital importance. Differential cost and revenue are the cost and revenue items that differ between alternatives. Opportunity cost is the benefit that is forgone when one alternative is selected over another. Sunk cost is a cost that occurred in the past and cannot be altered. Differential cost and opportunity cost should be carefully considered in decisions. Sunk cost is always irrelevant in decisions and should be ignored.

These various cost classifications are *different* ways of looking at costs. A particular cost, such as the cost of cheese in a taco served at Taco Bell, could be a manufacturing cost, a product cost, a variable cost, a direct cost, and a differential cost—all at the same time.

Taco Bell can be perceived as a manufacturer of fast food. The cost of the cheese in a taco would be considered a manufacturing cost and, as such, it would also be a product cost. In addition, the cost of the cheese would be considered variable with respect to the number of tacos served and would be a direct cost of serving tacos. Finally, the cost of the cheese used would be a differential cost of making and serving the tacos.

Review Problem 1: Cost Terms

Many new cost terms have been introduced in this chapter. It will take you some time to learn what each term means and how to properly classify costs in an organization. To assist in this learning process, consider the following example: Porter Company manufactures furniture, including tables. Selected costs associated with the manufacture of the tables and the general operation of the company are given below:

1. The tables are made of wood that costs $100 per table.
2. The tables are assembled by workers, at a wage cost of $40 per table.
3. Workers assembling the tables are supervised by a factory supervisor who is paid $25,000 per year.
4. Electrical costs are $2 per machine-hour. Four machine-hours are required to produce a table.

5. The depreciation cost of the machines used to make the tables totals $10,000 per year.
6. The salary of the president of Porter Company is $100,000 per year.
7. Porter Company spends $250,000 per year to advertise its products.
8. Salespersons are paid a commission of $30 for each table sold.
9. Instead of producing the tables, Porter Company could rent its factory space out at a rental income of $50,000 per year.

In the following tabulation, these costs are classified according to various cost terms used in the chapter. *Carefully study the classification of each cost.* If you don't understand why a particular cost is classified the way it is, reread the section of the chapter discussing the particular cost term. The terms *variable cost* and *fixed cost* refer to how costs behave with respect to the number of tables produced in a year.

Solution to Review Problem 1

	Variable Cost	Fixed Cost	Period (selling and administrative) Cost	Product Cost			To Units of Product		Sunk Cost	Oppor-tunity Cost
				Direct Materials	Direct Labour	Manufacturing Overhead	Direct	Indirect		
1. Wood used in a table ($100 per table)	X			X			X			
2. Labour cost to assemble a table ($40 per table)	X				X		X			
3. Salary of the factory supervisor ($25,000 per year)		X				X		X		
4. Cost of electricity to produce tables ($2 per machine-hour)	X					X		X		
5. Depreciation of machines used to produce tables ($10,000 per year)		X				X		X	X*	
6. Salary of the company president ($100,000 per year)		X	X							
7. Advertising expense ($250,000 per year)		X	X							
8. Commissions paid to salespersons ($30 per table sold)	X		X							
9. Rental income forgone on factory space										X†

*This is a sunk cost, since the outlay for the equipment was made in a previous period.

†This is an opportunity cost, since it represents the potential benefit that is lost or sacrificed as a result of using the factory space to produce tables. Opportunity cost is a special category of cost that is not ordinarily recorded in an organization's accounting books. To avoid possible confusion with other costs, we will not attempt to classify this cost in any other way except as an opportunity cost.

Review Problem 2: Schedule of Cost of Goods Manufactured and Income Statement

The following information has been taken from the accounting records of Klear-Seal Company for last year:

Selling expenses	$ 140,000
Raw materials inventory, January 1	90,000
Raw materials inventory, December 31	60,000
Utilities, factory	36,000
Direct labour cost	150,000
Depreciation, factory	162,000
Purchases of raw materials	750,000
Sales	2,500,000
Insurance, factory	40,000
Supplies, factory	15,000
Administrative expenses	270,000
Indirect labour	300,000
Maintenance, factory	87,000
Work in process inventory, January 1	180,000
Work in process inventory, December 31	100,000
Finished goods inventory, January 1	260,000
Finished goods inventory, December 31	210,000

Management wants to organize these data into a better format so that financial statements can be prepared for the year.

Required:

1. Prepare a schedule of cost of goods manufactured as in Exhibit 2–3.
2. Compute the cost of goods sold.
3. Using data as needed from (1) and (2) above, prepare an income statement.
4. Assuming production of finished and semi-finished goods amounted to 412,500 completed units for the past year, calculate the cost components of the ending finished goods inventory of 55,176 units. (Hint: The categories of costs in the ending inventory are the same as the total manufacturing costs, only the amounts are different.)

Solution to Review Problem 2

1.

KLEAR-SEAL COMPANY
Schedule of Cost of Goods Manufactured
For the Year Ended December 31

Direct materials:		
Raw materials inventory, January 1	$ 90,000	
Add: Purchases of raw materials	750,000	
Raw materials available for use	840,000	
Deduct: Raw materials inventory, December 31	60,000	
Raw materials used in production		$ 780,000
Direct labour		150,000
Manufacturing overhead:		
Utilities, factory	36,000	
Depreciation, factory	162,000	
Insurance, factory	40,000	
Supplies, factory	15,000	
Indirect labour	300,000	
Maintenance, factory	87,000	
Total overhead costs		640,000
Total manufacturing costs		1,570,000
Add: Work in process inventory, January 1		180,000
		1,750,000
Deduct: Work in process inventory, December 31		100,000
Cost of goods manufactured		$1,650,000

2. The cost of goods sold would be computed as follows:

Finished goods inventory, January 1	$ 260,000
Add: Cost of goods manufactured	1,650,000
Goods available for sale	1,910,000
Deduct: Finished goods inventory, December 31	210,000
Cost of goods sold	$1,700,000

3.

KLEAR-SEAL COMPANY
Income Statement
For the Year Ended December 31

Sales		$2,500,000
Less cost of goods sold (above)		1,700,000
Gross margin		800,000
Less selling and administrative expenses:		
Selling expenses	$140,000	
Administrative expenses	270,000	
Total expenses		410,000
Operating income		$ 390,000

4. Ending finished good inventory

Direct materials ($780,000/412,500 = $1.8909) $1.8909 × 55,176	$104,332
Direct labour ($150,000/412,500 = $0.3636) $0.3636 × 55,176	20,062*
Manufacturing overhead ($640,000/412,500 = $1.5515) $1.5515 × 55,176	85,606
Total cost	$210,000

*Rounding down is undertaken to account for unit cost rounding.

Glossary

Visit the Online Learning Centre at http://www.mcgrawhill.ca/olc/garrison/ for a review of glossary terms and definitions.

Questions

2–1 What are the three major elements of product costs in a manufacturing company?

2–2 Distinguish between the following: (a) direct materials, (b) indirect materials, (c) direct labour, (d) indirect labour, and (e) manufacturing overhead.

2–3 Explain the difference between a product cost and a period cost.

2–4 Describe how the income statement of a manufacturing company differs from the income statement of a merchandising company.

2–5 Of what value is the schedule of cost of goods manufactured? How does it tie into the income statement?

2–6 Describe how the inventory accounts of a manufacturing company differ from the inventory account of a merchandising company.

2–7 Why are product costs sometimes called inventoriable costs? Describe the flow of such costs in a manufacturing company from the point of incurrence until they finally become expenses on the income statement.

2–8 Is it possible for costs such as salaries or depreciation to end up as assets on the balance sheet? Explain.

2–9 What is meant by the term *cost behaviour*?

2–10 "A variable cost is a cost that varies per unit of product, whereas a fixed cost is constant per unit of product." Do you agree? Explain.

2–11 How do fixed costs create difficulties in costing units of product?

2–12 Why is manufacturing overhead considered an indirect cost of a unit of product?

2–13 Define the following terms: differential cost, opportunity cost, and sunk cost.

2–14 Only variable costs can be differential costs. Do you agree? Explain.

2–15 Mary Adams is employed by Acme Company. Last week she worked 34 hours assembling one of the company's products and was idle 6 hours due to material shortages. Acme's employees are engaged at their workstations for a normal 40-hour week. Ms. Adams is paid $15 per hour. Allocate her earnings between direct labour cost and manufacturing overhead cost.

2–16 John Olsen operates a stamping machine on the assembly line of Drake Manufacturing Company. Last week Mr. Olsen worked 45 hours. His basic wage rate is $14 per hour, with time and a half for overtime (time worked in excess of 40 hours per week). Allocate Mr. Olsen's wages for the week between direct labour cost and manufacturing overhead cost.

Exercises

EXERCISE 2–1 Classifying Manufacturing Costs [LO1]

Your Boat, Inc., assembles custom sailboats from components supplied by various manufacturers. The company is very small and its assembly shop and retail sales store are housed in a Gig Harbour, Ontario, boathouse. Below are listed some of the costs that are incurred at the company.

Required:

For each cost, indicate whether it would most likely be classified as direct labour, direct materials, manufacturing overhead, selling, or an administrative cost.

1. The wages of employees who build the sailboats.
2. The cost of advertising in the local newspapers.
3. The cost of an aluminum mast installed in a sailboat.
4. The wages of the assembly shop's supervisor.
5. Rent on the boathouse.
6. The wages of the company's bookkeeper.
7. Sales commissions paid to the company's salespeople.
8. Depreciation on power tools.

EXERCISE 2–2 Classification of Costs as Period or Product Costs [LO2]

Suppose that you have been given a summer job at Fairwings Avionics, a company that manufactures sophisticated radar sets for commercial aircraft. The company, which is privately owned, has approached a bank for a loan to help finance its tremendous growth. The bank requires financial statements before approving such a loan. You have been asked to help prepare the financial statements and were given the following list of costs:

1. The cost of the memory chips used in a radar set.
2. Factory heating costs.
3. Factory equipment maintenance costs.
4. Training costs for new administrative employees.
5. The cost of the solder that is used in assembling the radar sets.
6. The travel costs of the company's salespersons.
7. Wages and salaries of factory security personnel.
8. The cost of air-conditioning executive offices.
9. Wages and salaries in the department that handles billing customers.
10. Depreciation on the equipment in the fitness room used by factory workers.
11. Telephone expenses incurred by factory management.
12. The costs of shipping completed radar sets to customers.
13. The wages of the workers who assemble the radar sets.
14. The president's salary.
15. Health insurance premiums for factory personnel.

Required:

Classify the above costs as either product (inventoriable) costs or period (noninventoriable) costs for purposes of preparing the financial statements for the bank.

EXERCISE 2–3 Constructing an Income Statement [LO3]

Last month Mountain High, a mountain sporting goods retailer, had total sales of $3,200,000, selling expenses of $110,000, and administrative expenses of $470,000. The company had beginning merchandise inventory of $140,000, purchased additional merchandise inventory for $2,550,000, and had ending merchandise inventory of $180,000.

Required:
Prepare an income statement for the company for the month.

EXERCISE 2–4 Prepare a Schedule of Cost of Goods Manufactured [LO4]
Mannerman Fabrication manufactures a variety of products in its factory. Data for the most recent month's operations appear below:

Beginning raw materials inventory	$ 55,000
Purchases of raw materials	$440,000
Ending raw materials inventory	$ 65,000
Direct labour	$215,000
Manufacturing overhead	$380,000
Beginning work in process inventory	$190,000
Ending work in process inventory	$220,000

Required:
Prepare a schedule of cost of goods manufactured for the company for the month.

EXERCISE 2–5 Classification of Costs as Fixed or Variable [LO5]

Below are costs and measures of activity in a variety of organizations.

Required:
Classify each cost as variable or fixed with respect to the indicated measure of activity by placing an X in the appropriate column.

Cost	Measure of Activity	Cost Behaviour	
		Variable	Fixed
1. The cost of small glass plates used for lab tests in a medical lab	Number of lab tests performed		
2. A boutique jewellery store's cost of leasing retail space in a mall	Dollar sales		
3. Top management salaries at FedEx	Total sales		
4. Electrical costs of running production equipment at a Toyota factory	Number of vehicles produced		
5. The cost of insuring a dentist's office against fire	Patient-visits		
6. The cost of commissions paid to salespersons at a Honda dealer	Total sales		
7. The cost of heating the intensive care unit at Manitoba Hospital	Patient-days		
8. The cost of batteries installed in trucks produced at a GM factory	Number of trucks produced		
9. The salary of a university professor	Number of students taught by the professor		
10. The costs of cleaning supplies used at a fast-food restaurant to clean the kitchen and dining areas at the end of the day	Number of customers served		

EXERCISE 2–6 Identifying Direct and Indirect Costs [LO6]

The Empire Hotel is a four-star hotel located in downtown Victoria.

Required:
For each of the following costs incurred at the Empire Hotel, indicate whether it would most likely be a direct cost or an indirect cost of the specified cost object by placing an X in the appropriate column.

	Cost	Cost Object	Direct Cost	Indirect Cost
Ex.	Room service beverages	A particular hotel guest	X	
1.	The salary of the head chef	The hotel's restaurant		
2.	The salary of the head chef	A particular restaurant customer		
3.	Room cleaning supplies	A particular hotel guest		
4.	Flowers for the reception desk	A particular hotel guest		
5.	The wages of the doorman	A particular hotel guest		
6.	Room cleaning supplies	The housecleaning department		
7.	Fire insurance on the hotel building	The hotel's gym		
8.	Towels used in the gym	The hotel's gym		

EXERCISE 2–7 Differential, Opportunity, and Sunk Costs [LO7]

The Sorrento Hotel is a four-star hotel located in downtown Montreal. The hotel's operations vice-president would like to replace the hotel's antiquated computer terminals at the registration desk with attractive state-of-the-art flat-panel displays. The new displays would take less space, would consume less power than the old computer terminals, and would provide additional security since they can only be viewed from a restrictive angle. The new computer displays would not require any new wiring. The hotel's chef believes the funds would be better spent on a new bulk freezer for the kitchen.

Required:

For each of the items below, indicate by placing an X in the appropriate column whether it should be considered a differential cost, an opportunity cost, or a sunk cost in the decision to replace the old computer terminals with new flat-panel displays. If none of the categories apply for a particular item, leave all columns blank.

	Item	Differential Cost	Opportunity Cost	Sunk Cost
Ex.	Cost of electricity to run the terminals	X		
1.	Cost of the new flat-panel displays			
2.	Cost of the old computer terminals			
3.	Rent on the space occupied by the registration desk			
4.	Wages of registration desk personnel.			
5.	Benefits from a new freezer			
6.	Costs of maintaining the old computer terminals . . .			
7.	Cost of removing the old computer terminals			
8.	Cost of existing registration desk wiring			

EXERCISE 2–8 Classification of Overtime Cost [LO1]

Several weeks ago you called Jiffy Plumbing Company to have some routine repair work done on the plumbing system in your home. The plumber came about two weeks later, at four o'clock in the afternoon, and spent two hours completing your repair work. When you received your bill from the company, it contained a $75 charge for labour—$30 for the first hour and $45 for the second.

When questioned about the difference in hourly rates, the company's service manager explained that the higher rate for the second hour contained a charge for an "overtime premium," since the union required that plumbers be paid time and a half for any work in excess of eight hours per day. The service manager further explained that the company was working overtime to "catch up a little" on its backlog of work orders, but still needed to maintain a "decent" profit margin on the plumbers' time.

Required:

1. Do you agree with the company's computation of the labour charge on your job?
2. The company pays its plumbers $20 per hour for the first eight hours worked in a day and $30 per hour for any additional time worked. Show how the cost of the plumber's time for the day (nine hours) should be allocated between direct labour cost and general overhead cost on the company's books.
3. Under what circumstances might the company be justified in charging an overtime premium for repair work on your home?

EXERCISE 2–9 Product Cost Flows; Product versus Period Costs [LO2, LO3]
Ryser Company was organized on May 1. On that date the company purchased 35,000 plastic emblems, each with a peel-off adhesive backing. The front of the emblems contained the company's name, accompanied by an attractive logo. Each emblem cost Ryser Company $2.

During May, 31,000 emblems were drawn from the Raw Materials inventory account. Of these, 1,000 were taken by the sales manager to an important sales meeting with prospective customers and handed out as advertising. The remaining emblems drawn from inventory were affixed to units of the company's product that were being manufactured during May. Of the units of product having emblems affixed during May, 90% were completed and transferred from Work in Process to Finished Goods. Of the units completed during the month, 75% were sold and shipped to customers.

Required:

1. Determine the cost of emblems that would be in each of the following accounts at May 31:
   a. Raw Materials.
   b. Work in Process.
   c. Finished Goods.
   d. Cost of Goods Sold.
   e. Advertising Expense.
2. Specify whether each of the above accounts would appear on the balance sheet or on the income statement at May 31.

EXERCISE 2–10 Preparation of a Schedule of Cost of Goods Manufactured and Cost of Goods Sold [LO1, LO3, LO4]
The following cost and inventory data for the just completed year are taken from the accounting records of Eccles Company:

Costs incurred:	
Advertising expense	$100,000
Direct labour cost	$90,000
Purchases of raw materials	$132,000
Rent, factory building	$80,000
Indirect labour	$56,300
Sales commissions	$35,000
Utilities, factory	$9,000
Maintenance, factory equipment	$24,000
Supplies, factory	$700
Depreciation, office equipment	$8,000
Depreciation, factory equipment	$40,000

	Beginning of Year	End of Year
Inventories:		
Raw materials	$8,000	$10,000
Work in process	$5,000	$20,000
Finished goods	$70,000	$25,000

Required:

1. Prepare a schedule of cost of goods manufactured.
2. Prepare the cost of goods sold section of Eccles Company's income statement for the year.

EXERCISE 2–11 Classification of Costs as Variable or Fixed and as Selling and Administrative or Product [LO2, LO5]
Below are listed various costs that are found in organizations.

1. The costs of turn signal switches used at a General Motors plant. These are one of the parts installed in the steering columns assembled at the plant.
2. Interest expense on CBC's long-term debt.
3. Salespersons' commissions at Avon Products, a company that sells cosmetics door to door.
4. Insurance on one of Bombardier's factory buildings.
5. The costs of shipping brass fittings from Graham Manufacturing's plant in New Brunswick to customers in California.
6. Depreciation on the bookshelves at Reston Bookstore.

7. The costs of X-ray film at the Toronto General's radiology lab.
8. The cost of leasing an 800 telephone number at GM Canada. The monthly charge for the 800 number is independent of the number of calls taken.
9. The depreciation on the playground equipment at a McDonald's outlet.
10. The cost of mozzarella cheese used at a Pizza Hut outlet.

Required:
Classify each cost as either variable or fixed with respect to the volume of goods or services produced and sold by the organization. Also classify each cost as a selling and administrative cost or a product cost. Prepare your answer sheet as shown below. Place an X in the appropriate columns to show the proper classifications of each cost.

	Cost Behaviour			
Cost Item	Variable	Fixed	Selling and Administrative Cost	Product Cost

EXERCISE 2–12 Classification of Labour Costs [LO1]
Fred Austin is employed by White Company where he assembles a component part for one of the company's products. Fred is paid $12 per hour for regular time, and he is paid time and a half (i.e., $18 per hour) for all work in excess of 40 hours per week.

Required:
1. Assume that during a given week Fred is idle for two hours due to machine breakdowns and that he is idle for four more hours due to material shortages. No overtime is recorded for the week. Allocate Fred's wages for the week between direct labour cost and manufacturing overhead cost.
2. Assume that during a following week Fred works a total of 50 hours. He has no idle time for the week. Allocate Fred's wages for the week between direct labour cost and manufacturing overhead cost.
3. Fred's company provides an attractive package of fringe benefits for its employees. This package includes a retirement program and a health insurance program. Explain two ways that the company could handle the costs of its direct labourers' fringe benefits in its cost records.

Problems

PROBLEM 2–13 Cost Classification [LO2, LO5, LO6]
Listed below are costs found in various organizations.
1. Depreciation, executive jet.
2. Costs of shipping finished goods to customers.
3. Wood used in manufacturing furniture.
4. Sales manager's salary.
5. Electricity used in manufacturing furniture.
6. Secretary to the company president.
7. Aerosol attachment placed on a spray can produced by the company.
8. Billing costs.
9. Packing supplies for shipping products overseas.
10. Sand used in manufacturing concrete.
11. Supervisor's salary, factory.
12. Executive life insurance.
13. Sales commissions.
14. Fringe benefits, assembly-line workers.
15. Advertising costs.
16. Property taxes on finished goods warehouses.
17. Lubricants for production equipment.

Required:
Prepare an answer sheet with column headings as shown on the next page. For each cost item, indicate whether it would be variable or fixed with respect to the number of units produced and sold; and then whether it would be a selling cost, an administrative cost, or a manufacturing cost. If it is

a manufacturing cost, indicate whether it would typically be treated as a direct or indirect cost with respect to units of product. Three sample answers are provided for illustration.

Cost Item	Variable or Fixed	Selling Cost	Administrative Cost	Manufacturing (Product) Cost	
				Direct	Indirect
Direct labour	V			X	
Executive salaries...............	F		X		
Factory rent....................	F				X

PROBLEM 2–14 Classification of Labour Costs [LO1]
Lynn Bjorland is employed by Northern Laboratories and is directly involved in preparing the company's leading antibiotic drug. Lynn's basic wage rate is $24 per hour. The company pays its employees time and a half (i.e., $36 per hour) for any work in excess of 40 hours per week.

Required:
1. Suppose that in a given week Lynn works 45 hours. Compute Lynn's total wages for the week. How much of this cost would the company allocate to direct labour cost? To manufacturing overhead cost?
2. Suppose in another week that Lynn works 50 hours but is idle for 4 hours during the week due to equipment breakdowns. Compute Lynn's total wages for the week. How much of this amount would be allocated to direct labour cost? To manufacturing overhead cost?
3. Northern Laboratories has an attractive package of fringe benefits that costs the company $8 for each hour of employee time (either regular time or overtime). During a particular week, Lynn works 48 hours but is idle for 3 hours due to material shortages. Compute Lynn's total wages and fringe benefits for the week. If the company treats all fringe benefits as part of manufacturing overhead cost, how much of Lynn's wages and fringe benefits for the week would be allocated to direct labour cost? To manufacturing overhead cost?
4. Refer to the data in (3) above. If the company treats that part of fringe benefits relating to direct labour as added direct labour cost, how much of Lynn's wages and fringe benefits for the week will be allocated to direct labour cost? To manufacturing overhead cost?

PROBLEM 2–15 Cost Classification [LO1, LO2, LO5, LO7]
Several years ago Medex Company purchased a small building adjacent to its manufacturing plant in order to have room for expansion when needed. Since the company had no immediate need for the extra space, the building was rented out to another company for a rental revenue of $40,000 per year. The renter's lease will expire next month, and rather than renewing the lease, Medex Company has decided to use the building itself to manufacture a new product.

Direct materials cost for the new product will total $40 per unit. It will be necessary to hire a supervisor to oversee production. Her salary will be $2,500 per month. Workers will be hired to manufacture the new product, with direct labour cost amounting to $18 per unit. Manufacturing operations will occupy all of the building space, so it will be necessary to rent space in a warehouse nearby in order to store finished units of product. The rental cost will be $1,000 per month. In addition, the company will need to rent equipment for use in producing the new product; the rental cost will be $3,000 per month. The company will continue to depreciate the building on a straight-line basis, as in past years. Depreciation on the building is $10,000 per year.

Advertising costs for the new product will total $50,000 per year. Costs of shipping the new product to customers will be $10 per unit. Electrical costs of operating machines will be $2 per unit.

To have funds to purchase materials, meet payrolls, and so forth, the company will have to liquidate some temporary investments. These investments are presently yielding a return of $6,000 per year.

Required:
Prepare an answer sheet with the following column headings:

Name of the Cost	Variable Cost	Fixed Cost	Product Cost			Period (Selling and Administrative) Cost	Opportunity Cost	Sunk Cost
			Direct Materials	Direct Labour	Manufacturing Overhead			

List the different costs associated with the new product decision down the extreme left column (under Name of the Cost). Then place an *X* under each heading that helps to describe the type of cost involved. There may be *X*'s under several column headings for a single cost. (For example, a cost may be a fixed cost, a period cost, and a sunk cost; you would place an *X* under each of these column headings opposite the cost.)

PROBLEM 2–16 Classification of Costs as Variable or Fixed and Direct or Indirect [LO5, LO6]

Various costs associated with manufacturing operations are given below:

1. Plastic washers used to assemble autos.
2. Production superintendent's salary.
3. Wages of workers who assemble a product.
4. Electricity to run production equipment.
5. Janitorial salaries.
6. Clay used to make bricks.
7. Rent on a factory building.
8. Wood used to make skis.
9. Screws used to make furniture.
10. A supervisor's salary.
11. Cloth used to make shirts.
12. Depreciation of cafeteria equipment.
13. Glue used to make textbooks.
14. Lubricants for production equipment.
15. Paper used to make textbooks.

Required:

Classify each cost as being either variable or fixed with respect to the number of units produced and sold. Also indicate whether each cost would typically be treated as a direct cost or an indirect cost with respect to units of product. Prepare your answer sheet as shown below:

	Cost Behaviour		To Units of Product	
Cost Item	**Variable**	**Fixed**	**Direct**	**Indirect**
Example: Factory insurance		X		X

PROBLEM 2–17 Schedule of Cost of Goods Manufactured; Income Statement; Cost Behaviour [LO1, LO2, LO3, LO4, LO5]

Various cost and sales data for Medco, Inc., are given on page 59 for the just completed year:

Required:

1. Prepare a schedule of cost of goods manufactured.
2. Prepare an income statement.
3. Assume that the company produced the equivalent of 10,000 units of product during the year. What was the average cost per unit for direct materials? What was the average cost per unit for factory depreciation?
4. Assume that the company expects to produce 15,000 units of product during the coming year. What average cost per unit and what total cost would you expect the company to incur for direct materials at this level of activity? For factory depreciation? (In preparing your answer, assume that direct materials is a variable cost and that depreciation is a fixed cost; also assume that depreciation is computed on a straight-line basis.)
5. As the manager responsible for production costs, explain to the president any difference in the average costs per unit between (3) and (4) above.
6. Assuming the company produced 20,000 fully and partially finished units during the year, determine the cost components of the finished goods inventory which is composed of 4,000 finished units.

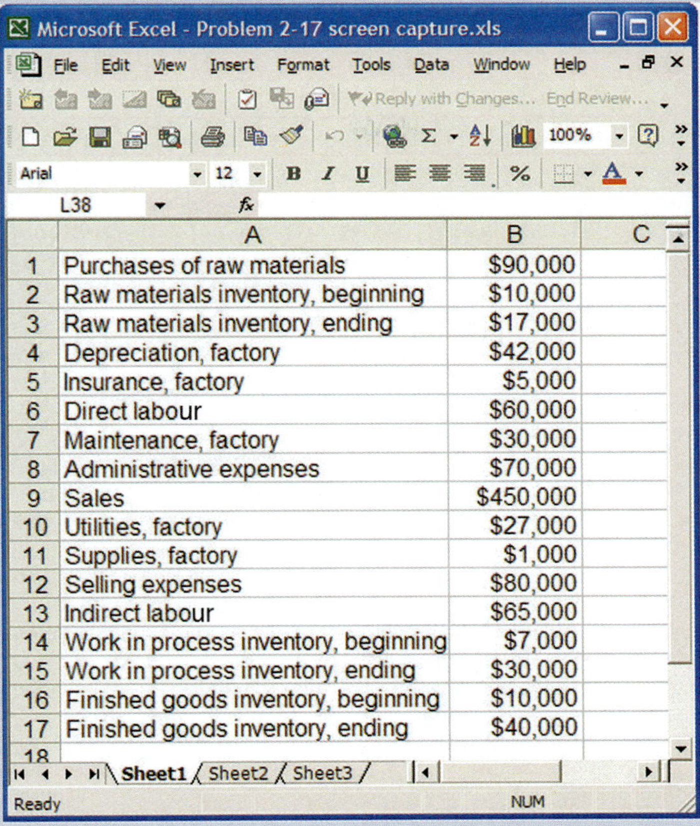

	A	B	C
1	Purchases of raw materials	$90,000	
2	Raw materials inventory, beginning	$10,000	
3	Raw materials inventory, ending	$17,000	
4	Depreciation, factory	$42,000	
5	Insurance, factory	$5,000	
6	Direct labour	$60,000	
7	Maintenance, factory	$30,000	
8	Administrative expenses	$70,000	
9	Sales	$450,000	
10	Utilities, factory	$27,000	
11	Supplies, factory	$1,000	
12	Selling expenses	$80,000	
13	Indirect labour	$65,000	
14	Work in process inventory, beginning	$7,000	
15	Work in process inventory, ending	$30,000	
16	Finished goods inventory, beginning	$10,000	
17	Finished goods inventory, ending	$40,000	
18			

PROBLEM 2–18 Classification of Salary Cost as a Period or Product Cost [LO2]
You have just been hired by EduRom Company, which was organized on January 2 of the current year. The company manufactures and sells a variety of educational DVDs for personal computers. It is your responsibility to supervise the employees who take orders from customers over the phone and to arrange for shipping orders via Federal Express, Canada Post, and other freight carriers.

The company is unsure how to classify your annual salary in its cost records. The company's cost analyst says that your salary should be classified as a manufacturing (product) cost; the controller says that it should be classified as a selling expense; and the president says that it doesn't matter which way your salary cost is classified.

Required:
1. Which viewpoint is correct? Why?
2. From the point of view of the reported operating income for the year, is the president correct in saying that it doesn't matter which way your salary cost is classified? Explain.

PROBLEM 2–19 Classification of Various Costs [LO1, LO2, LO5, LO7]

Frieda Bronkowski has invented a new type of flyswatter. After giving the matter much thought, Frieda has decided to quit her $4,000 per month job with a consulting firm and produce and sell the flyswatters full time. Frieda will rent a garage that will be used as a production plant. The rent will be $150 per month. Frieda will rent production equipment at a cost of $500 per month.

The cost of materials for each flyswatter will be $0.30. Frieda will hire workers to produce the flyswatters. They will be paid $0.50 for each completed unit. Frieda will rent a room in the house next door for use as her sales office. The rent will be $75 per month. She has arranged for the telephone company to attach a recording device to her home phone to get off-hours messages from customers. The device will increase her monthly phone bill by $20.

Frieda has some money in savings that is earning interest of $1,000 per year. These savings will be withdrawn and used for about a year to get the business going. To sell her flyswatters, Frieda will advertise heavily in the local area. Advertising costs will be $400 per month. In addition, Frieda will pay a sales commission of $0.10 for each flyswatter sold.

For the time being, Frieda does not intend to draw any salary from the new company.

Frieda has already paid the legal and filing fees to incorporate her business. These fees amounted to $600.

Required:

1. Prepare an answer sheet with the following column headings:

Name of the Cost	Variable Cost	Fixed Cost	Product Cost			Period (Selling and Administrative) Cost	Opportunity Cost	Sunk Cost
			Direct Materials	Direct Labour	Manufacturing Overhead			

   List the different costs associated with the new company down the extreme left column (under Name of Cost). Then place an *X* under each heading that helps to describe the type of cost involved. There may be *X*'s under several column headings for a single cost. (That is, a cost may be a fixed cost, a period cost, and a sunk cost; you would place an *X* under each of these column headings opposite the cost.) Under the variable cost column, list only those costs that would be variable with respect to the number of flyswatters that are produced and sold.

2. All of the costs you have listed above, except one, would be differential costs between the alternatives of Frieda producing flyswatters or staying with the consulting firm. Which cost is *not* differential? Explain.

PROBLEM 2–20 Cost Classification and Cost Behaviour [LO2, LO5, LO6]

Heritage Company manufactures a beautiful bookcase that enjoys widespread popularity. The company has a backlog of orders that is large enough to keep production going indefinitely at the plant's full capacity of 4,000 bookcases per year. Annual cost data at full capacity follow:

Direct materials used (wood and glass)	$430,000
General office salaries	$110,000
Factory supervision	$70,000
Sales commissions	$60,000
Depreciation, factory building	$105,000
Depreciation, office equipment	$2,000
Indirect materials, factory	$18,000
Factory labour (cutting and assembly)	$90,000
Advertising	$100,000
Insurance, factory	$6,000
General office supplies (billing)	$4,000
Property taxes, factory	$20,000
Utilities, factory	$45,000

Required:

1. Prepare an answer sheet with the column headings shown below. Enter each cost item on your answer sheet, placing the dollar amount under the appropriate headings. As examples, this has been done already for the first two items in the list above. Note that each cost item is classified in two ways: first, as either variable or fixed with respect to the number of units produced and sold; and second, as either a selling and administrative cost or a product cost. (If the item is a product cost, it should also be classified as either direct or indirect as shown.)

Cost Item	Cost Behaviour		Selling or Administrative Cost	Product Cost	
	Variable	Fixed		Direct	Indirect*
Materials used	$430,000			$430,000	
General office salaries		$110,000	$110,000		

*To units of product.

2. Total the dollar amounts in each of the columns in (1) above. Compute the average product cost per bookcase.
3. Due to a recession, assume that production drops to only 2,000 bookcases per year. Would you expect the average product cost per bookcase to increase, decrease, or remain unchanged? Explain. No computations are necessary.

4. Refer to the original data. The president's next-door neighbour has considered making himself a bookcase and has priced the necessary materials at a building supply store. He has asked the president whether he could purchase a bookcase from the Heritage Company "at cost," and the president has agreed to let him do so.
   a. Would you expect any disagreement between the two men over the price the neighbour should pay? Explain. What price does the president probably have in mind? The neighbour?
   b. Since the company is operating at full capacity, what cost term used in the chapter might be justification for the president to charge the full, regular price to the neighbour and still be selling "at cost"? Explain.

PROBLEM 2–21 Variable and Fixed Costs; Subtleties of Direct and Indirect Costs [LO5, LO6]

The Central Area Well-Baby Clinic provides a variety of health services to newborn babies and their parents. The clinic is organized into a number of departments, one of which is the Immunization Centre. A number of costs of the clinic and the Immunization Centre are listed below.

Example: The cost of polio immunization tablets.

a. The salary of the head nurse in the Immunization Centre.
b. Costs of incidental supplies consumed in the Immunization Centre, such as paper towels.
c. The cost of lighting and heating the Immunization Centre.
d. The cost of disposable syringes used in the Immunization Centre.
e. The salary of the Central Area Well-Baby Clinic's information systems manager.
f. The costs of mailing letters soliciting donations to the Central Area Well-Baby Clinic.
g. The wages of nurses who work in the Immunization Centre.
h. The cost of medical malpractice insurance for the Central Area Well-Baby Clinic.
i. Depreciation on the fixtures and equipment in the Immunization Centre.

Required:

For each cost listed above, indicate whether it is a direct or indirect cost of the Immunization Centre, whether it is a direct or indirect cost of immunizing particular patients, and whether it is variable or fixed with respect to the number of immunizations administered. Use the form shown below for your answer.

	Direct or Indirect Cost of the Immunization Centre		Direct or Indirect Cost of Particular Patients		Variable or Fixed with Respect to the Number of Immunizations Administered	
Item Description	**Direct**	**Indirect**	**Direct**	**Indirect**	**Variable**	**Fixed**
Example: The cost of polio immunization tablets	X		X		X	

PROBLEM 2–22 Schedule of Cost of Goods Manufactured; Income Statement [LO1, LO2, LO3, LO4]

Skyler Company was organized on November 1 of the previous year. After seven months of start-up losses, management had expected to earn a profit during June, the most recent month. Management was disappointed, however, when the income statement for June also showed a loss. June's income statement follows:

Skyler Company Income Statement For the Month Ended June 30		
Sales		$600,000
Less operating expenses:		
Selling and administrative salaries	$ 35,000	
Rent on facilities	40,000	
Purchases of raw materials	190,000	
Insurance	8,000	
Depreciation, sales equipment	10,000	
Utilities costs	50,000	
Indirect labour	108,000	
Direct labour	90,000	
Depreciation, factory equipment	12,000	
Maintenance, factory	7,000	
Advertising	80,000	630,000
Operating loss		$(30,000)

After seeing the $30,000 loss for June, Skyler's president stated, "I was sure we'd be profitable within six months, but after eight months we're still spilling red ink. Maybe it's time for us to throw in the towel and accept one of those offers we've had for the company. To make matters worse, I just heard that Linda won't be back from her surgery for at least six more weeks."

Linda is the company's controller; in her absence, the statement above was prepared by a new assistant who has had little experience in manufacturing operations. Additional information about the company follows:

a. Only 80% of the rent on facilities applies to factory operations; the remainder applies to selling and administrative activities.
b. Inventory balances at the beginning and end of the month were as follows:

	June 1	June 30
Raw materials	$17,000	$42,000
Work in process	$70,000	$85,000
Finished goods	$20,000	$60,000

c. Some 75% of the insurance and 90% of the utilities cost apply to factory operations; the remaining amounts apply to selling and administrative activities.

The president has asked you to check over the above income statement and make a recommendation as to whether the company should continue operations.

Required:

1. As one step in gathering data for a recommendation to the president, prepare a schedule of cost of goods manufactured for June.
2. As a second step, prepare a new income statement for the month.
3. Based on your statements prepared in (1) and (2) above, would you recommend that the company continue operations?

PROBLEM 2–23 Ethics and the Manager [LO2]

The top management of General Electronics, Inc., is well known for "managing by the numbers." With an eye on the company's desired growth in overall net profit, the company's CEO (chief executive officer) sets target profits at the beginning of the year for each of the company's divisions. The CEO has stated her policy as follows: "I won't interfere with operations in the divisions. I am available for advice, but the division vice-presidents are free to do anything they want so long as they hit the target profits for the year."

In November, Stan Richart, the vice-president in charge of the Cellular Telephone Technologies Division, saw that making the current year's target profit for his division was going to be very difficult. Among other actions, he directed that discretionary expenditures be delayed until the beginning of the new year. On December 30, he was angered to discover that a warehouse clerk had ordered $350,000 of cellular telephone parts earlier in December even though the parts weren't really needed by the assembly department until January or February. Contrary to common accounting practice, the General Electronics, Inc., Accounting Policy Manual states that such parts are to be recorded as an expense when delivered. To avoid recording the expense, Mr. Richart asked that the order be cancelled, but the purchasing department reported that the parts had already been delivered and the supplier would not accept returns. Since the bill had not yet been paid, Mr. Richart asked the accounting department to correct the clerk's mistake by delaying recognition of the delivery until the bill is paid in January.

Required:

1. Are Mr. Richart's actions ethical? Explain why they are or are not ethical.
2. Do the general management philosophy and accounting policies at General Electronics encourage or discourage ethical behaviour? Explain.

PROBLEM 2–24 Schedule of Cost of Goods Manufactured; Income Statement; Cost Behaviour [LO1, LO2, LO3, LO4, LO5]

The following selected account balances for the year ended December 31 are provided for Valenko Company:

Advertising expense	$215,000
Insurance, factory equipment	$8,000
Depreciation, sales equipment	$40,000
Rent, factory building	$90,000
Utilities, factory	$52,000
Sales commissions	$35,000
Cleaning supplies, factory	$6,000
Depreciation, factory equipment	$110,000
Selling and administrative salaries	$85,000
Maintenance, factory	$74,000
Direct labour	?
Purchases of raw materials	$260,000

Inventory balances at the beginning and end of the year were as follows:

	Beginning of Year	End of Year
Raw materials	$50,000	$40,000
Work in process	?	$33,000
Finished goods	$30,000	?

The total manufacturing costs for the year were $675,000; the goods available for sale totalled $720,000; and the cost of goods sold totalled $635,000.

Required:

1. Prepare a schedule of cost of goods manufactured and the cost of goods sold section of the company's income statement for the year.
2. Assume that the dollar amounts given above are for the equivalent of 30,000 units produced during the year. Compute the average cost per unit for direct materials used, and compute the average cost per unit for rent on the factory building.
3. Assume that in the following year the company expects to produce 50,000 units. What average cost per unit and total cost would you expect to be incurred for direct materials? For rent on the factory building? (Assume that direct materials is a variable cost and that rent is a fixed cost.)
4. As the manager in charge of production costs, explain to the president the reason for any difference in the average costs per unit between (2) and (3) above.

PROBLEM 2–25 Working with Incomplete Data from the Income Statement and Schedule of Cost of Goods Manufactured [LO3, LO4]

Supply the missing data in the four cases that follow. Each case is independent of the others.

	Case			
	1	2	3	4
Schedule of Cost of Goods Manufactured				
Direct materials	$ 7,000	$ 9,000	$ 6,000	$ 8,000
Direct labour	$ 2,000	$ 4,000	?	$ 3,000
Manufacturing overhead	$10,000	?	$ 7,000	$21,000
Total manufacturing costs	?	$25,000	$18,000	?
Beginning work in process inventory	?	$ 1,000	$ 2,000	?
Ending work in process inventory	$ 4,000	$ 3,500	?	$ 2,000
Cost of goods manufactured	$18,000	$?	$16,000	$31,500
Income Statement				
Sales	$25,000	$40,000	$30,000	$50,000
Beginning finished goods inventory	$ 6,000	?	$ 7,000	$ 9,000
Cost of goods manufactured	$18,000	?	$16,000	$31,500
Goods available for sale	?	?	?	?
Ending finished goods inventory	$ 9,000	$ 4,000	?	$ 7,000
Cost of goods sold	?	$26,500	$18,000	?
Gross margin	?	?	?	?
Selling and administrative expenses	$ 6,000	?	?	$10,000
Operating income	$?	$ 5,500	$ 3,000	$?

PROBLEM 2–26 Income Statement; Schedule of Cost of Goods Manufactured [LO1, LO2, LO3, LO4]

Hickey Corporation is a manufacturer that produces a single product. The following information has been taken from the company's production, sales, and cost records for the just completed year:

Production in units	30,000
Sales in units	?
Ending finished goods inventory in units	?
Sales in dollars	$650,000
Costs:	
Advertising	$50,000
Direct labour	$80,000
Indirect labour	$60,000
Raw materials purchased	$160,000
Building rent (production uses 80% of the space; administrative and sales offices use the rest)	$50,000
Utilities, factory	$35,000
Royalty paid for use of production patent, $1 per unit produced	?
Maintenance, factory	$25,000
Rent for special production equipment, $6,000 per year plus $0.10 per unit produced	?
Selling and administrative salaries	$140,000
Other factory overhead costs	$11,000
Other selling and administrative expenses	$20,000

	Beginning of Year	End of Year
Inventories:		
Raw materials	$20,000	$10,000
Work in process	$30,000	$40,000
Finished goods	$0	?

The finished goods inventory is being carried at the average unit production cost for the year. The selling price of the product is $25 per unit.

Required:

1. Prepare a schedule of cost of goods manufactured for the year.
2. Compute the following:
   a. The number of units in the finished goods inventory at the end of the year.
   b. The cost of the units in the finished goods inventory at the end of the year.
3. Prepare an income statement for the year.

Cases

CASE 2–27 Missing Data; Income Statement; Schedule of Cost of Goods Manufactured [LO1, LO2, LO3, LO4]

"I know I'm a pretty good scientist, but I guess I still have some things to learn about running a business," said Staci Morales, founder and president of Medical Technology, Inc. "Demand has been so strong for our heart monitor that I was sure we'd be profitable immediately, but just look at the gusher of red ink for the first quarter. At this rate we'll be out of business in a year." The data to which Staci was referring are shown below:

Medical Technology, Inc.
Income Statement
For the Quarter Ended June 30

Sales (16,000 monitors)		$ 975,000
Less operating expenses:		
Selling and administrative salaries	$ 90,000	
Advertising	200,000	
Cleaning supplies, factory	6,000	
Indirect labour cost	135,000	
Depreciation, office equipment	18,000	
Direct labour cost	80,000	
Raw materials purchased	310,000	
Maintenance, factory	47,000	
Rental cost, facilities	65,000	
Insurance, factory	9,000	
Utilities	40,000	
Depreciation, production equipment	75,000	
Travel, salespersons	60,000	1,135,000
Operating loss		$ (160,000)

Medical Technology was organized on April 1 of the current year to produce and market a revolutionary new heart monitor. The company's accounting system was set up by Staci's brother-in-law who had taken an accounting course about 10 years ago.

"We may not last a year if the insurance company doesn't pay the $227,000 it owes us for the 4,000 monitors lost in the truck accident last week," said Staci. "The agent says our claim is inflated, but that's a lot of baloney."

Just after the end of the quarter, a truck carrying 4,000 monitors wrecked and burned, destroying the entire load. The monitors were part of the 20,000 units completed during the quarter ended June 30. They were in a warehouse awaiting sale at quarter-end and were sold and shipped on July 3 (this sale is *not* included on the income statement above). The trucking company's insurer is liable for the cost of the goods lost. Staci's brother-in-law has determined this cost as follows:

$$\frac{\text{Total costs for the quarter}}{\text{Monitors produced during the quarter}} = \$1{,}135{,}000/20{,}000 \text{ units} = \$56.75 \text{ per unit}$$

$$4{,}000 \text{ units} \times \$56.75 \text{ per unit} = \$227{,}000$$

The following additional information is available on the company's activities during the quarter ended June 30:

a. Inventories at the beginning and end of the quarter were as follows:

	Beginning of the Quarter	End of the Quarter
Raw materials	$0	$40,000
Work in process	$0	$30,000
Finished goods	$0	?

b. Eighty percent of the rental cost for facilities and 90% of the utilities cost relate to manufacturing operations. The remaining amounts relate to selling and administrative activities.

Required:

1. What conceptual errors, if any, were made in preparing the income statement above?
2. Prepare a schedule of cost of goods manufactured for the quarter.
3. Prepare a corrected income statement for the quarter. Your statement should show in detail how the cost of goods sold is computed.
4. Do you agree that the insurance company owes Medical Technology, Inc., $227,000? Explain your answer.

CASE 2–28 Inventory Computations from Incomplete Data [LO3, LO4]

While snoozing at the controls of his Pepper Six airplane, Dunse P. Sluggard leaned heavily against the door; suddenly, the door flew open and a startled Dunse tumbled out. As he parachuted to the ground, Dunse watched helplessly as the empty plane smashed into Operex Products' plant and administrative offices.

"The insurance company will never believe this," cried Mercedes Juliet, the company's controller, as she watched the ensuing fire burn the building to the ground. "The entire company is wiped out!"

"There's no reason to even contact the insurance agent," replied Ford Romero, the company's operations manager. "We can't file a claim without records, and all we have left is this copy of last year's annual report. It shows that raw materials at the beginning of this year (January 1) totalled $30,000, work in process totalled $50,000, and finished goods totalled $90,000. But what we need is a record of these inventories as of today, and our records are up in smoke."

"All except this summary page I was working on when the plane hit the building," said Mercedes. "It shows that our sales to date this year have totalled $1,350,000 and that manufacturing overhead cost has totalled $520,000."

"Hey! This annual report is more helpful than I thought," exclaimed Ford. "I can see that our gross margin was 40% of sales. I can also see that direct labour cost is one-quarter of the manufacturing overhead cost."

"We may have a chance after all," cried Mercedes. "My summary sheet lists the sum of direct labour and direct materials at $510,000 for the year, and it says that our goods available for sale to customers this year has totalled $960,000 at cost. Now if we just knew the amount of raw materials purchased so far this year."

"I know that figure," yelled Ford. "It's $420,000! The purchasing agent gave it to me in our planning meeting yesterday."

"Fantastic," shouted Mercedes. "We'll have our claim ready before the day is over!"

To file a claim with the insurance company, Operex Products must determine the amount of cost in its inventories as of the date of the accident. You may assume that all of the materials used in production during the year were direct materials.

Required:

Determine the amount of cost in the raw materials, work in process, and finished goods inventories as of the date of the accident. (Hint: One way to proceed would be to reconstruct the various schedules and statements that would have been affected by the company's inventory accounts during the year.)

Research

R 2–29 Disclosure, Cost Classification, and External Reports [LO1, LO2, LO5]
Examine the annual report of Canadian National Railways and in particular look at the income statement. Classify as best you can the costs as variable and fixed, period and product. Contrast the cost disclosures with those presented in Chapter 2.

R 2–30 Disclosure, Cost Classification, and External Reports [LO1, LO2, LO5]
Using the most recent annual report of Barrick Gold, consider what costs are product costs and what are period costs. Also carefully consider what are the variable and what are fixed. Present your conclusions.

Comment on the extent of disclosure in the financial statements compared to that described in Chapter 2. Determine the nature of the direct materials cost, the direct labour cost, and the overhead costs. Amounts are not required.

What difficulties, if any, were encountered classifying costs?

R 2–31 Cost Classifications and Carbon Taxes [LO1, LO2, LO6]
Carbon taxes represent one means under discussions and implementation in Québec and British Columbia that are proposed as a means of reducing greenhouse gases in the environment.

Required:
1. Define the nature of a carbon tax.
2. Examine the financial statements of Tim Hortons and classify the possible impact of carbon taxes as selling, administrative, and manufacturing.
3. Discuss the possible strategic impact of a carbon tax in the operations of a sizable collection of Tim Hortons' franchises.

SECTION 2

COSTING

Chapters 3 to 8

Chapters 3 to 8 provide a comprehensive description of how costs are associated with manufacturing and other activities. In addition, these costing systems can be applied to service organizations and not-for-profit organizations. To permit costing for such specialized situations, two costing systems, job costing and process costing, can be mixed and matched.

Chapter 3 begins with the most basic and widely used costing system, *job costing*. Job costing permits costs to be assigned to specific outcomes, termed *jobs*, so that costs can be accumulated for what a company produces. In addition, manufacturing overhead, or a term often shortened to just *overhead*, is assigned by a process of averaging to determine its amount before actual overhead costs are known.

Chapter 4 introduces an averaging calculation used for costing like units, termed *process costing*. The ordering of costs learned in financial accounting, namely average and FIFO, can be applied. The idea of equivalent units is explained so partially finished work in progress can be counted in production. Chapter 4 also presents an elaboration of overhead methods so overhead can be disaggregated to cost objects, departments in this case, to permit more management control of overhead and more accurate costing.

Chapter 5 introduces another disaggregation of overhead and non-manufacturing costs according to the definition of a cost object as an activity and the use of a cost driver. By doing this, overhead costing can be improved and management can focus on managing activities rather than outcomes. Given the increasing importance of overhead to some types of organizations, methods to improve the management of overhead costs are important contributions.

Chapter 6 describes the details of cost behaviour and how costs that contain a mixture of behaviours can be analyzed.

Chapter 7 takes the idea of cost behaviour and incorporates revenues to provide commonly used tools for analysis and decision, cost-volume-profit and break-even.

Chapter 8 completes the costing segment by describing variable costing. Variable costing assigns only variable manufacturing costs to production as opposed to all manufacturing costs as was described in earlier chapters under the term *absorption costing*.

Upon the completion of Chapter 8, the costing approaches are twofold, job costing and process costing. Added to these are two definitions of costs, absorption and variable. This two by two combination can be extended using departmental and activity overhead approaches to disaggregate overhead as desired by management.

CHAPTER 3

LEARNING OBJECTIVES

After studying Chapter 3, you should be able to:

1. Distinguish between process costing and job-order costing and identify companies that would use each costing method.
2. Identify the documents used in a job-order costing system.
3. Compute predetermined overhead rates and explain why estimated overhead costs (rather than actual overhead costs) are used in the costing process.
4. Record the journal entries that reflect the flow of costs in a job-order costing system.
5. Apply overhead cost to Work in Process using a predetermined overhead rate.
6. Prepare schedules of cost of goods manufactured and cost of goods sold.
7. Compute under- or overapplied overhead cost and prepare the journal entry to close the balance in Manufacturing Overhead to the appropriate accounts.
8. (Appendix 3A) Explain the implications of basing the predetermined overhead rate on activity at capacity rather than on estimated activity for the period.

SYSTEMS DESIGN: JOB-ORDER COSTING

BUSINESS FOCUS

A Stringing Success

Cris Griffiths Guitar Works of Saint John's, Newfoundland, focuses on repair work and building custom guitars. Late one night while disassembling yet another guitar, Griffiths had a vision of a single bracing piece instead of the three-dozen separate internal reinforcements acoustic guitars typically have. "It was a simple idea that was easy to flesh out, but turning it from an idea into a corporation was a pretty lengthy process," he recalls. "I often say it took me six minutes to come up with the idea and six years to make it work."

Part of the problem was that using wood to make a one-piece brace was pretty much out of the question. It would take years to whittle down a wood block into a single piece, but Griffiths realized a composite material that could be punched out using injection-molding equipment could perform the same trick. Again, simple enough to conceive but it took three years before he had a solid business plan he could present to investors. Even then, Griffiths didn't have the $100,000 he needed to build a prototype, so he leveraged his existing business to the hilt, effectively putting the future of both companies on the line. Eventually, he convinced investors to pony up some seed money and he hit the road. At a Los Angeles trade show in early 2000, his guitar—lo and behold—was a hit, attracting lineups of people wanting to check out the new star.

Production started in mid-2001 and roughly $6 million was invested in the business over the next three years to keep it rolling. In 2003 the company switched to a lean manufacturing operation called the Toyota production system. That has meant a 50% cut in labour costs and manufacturing space as well as a 70% reduction in work-in-progress inventory.

Source: Andy Holloway, "Between the Rock and a Hard Place," *Canadian Business*, Dec. 27, 2004–Jan. 16, 2005, Vol. 78, Iss. 1, p. 69.

As discussed in Chapter 2, product costing is the process of assigning costs to the products and services provided by a company. An understanding of this costing process is vital to managers, because the way in which a product or service is costed can have a substantial impact on reported net income, as well as on key management decisions.

The essential purpose of any managerial costing system should be to provide cost data to help managers plan, control, direct, and make decisions. Nevertheless, external financial reporting and tax reporting requirements often heavily influence how costs are accumulated and summarized in managerial reports. This is true of product costing.

Absorption costing
A costing method that includes all manufacturing costs—direct materials, direct labour, and both variable and fixed overhead—as part of the cost of a finished unit of product. This term is synonymous with *full cost.*

Full cost
Same as *absorption costing.*

In this chapter and in Chapter 4, we use an *absorption costing* approach to determine product costs. This was also the method that was used in Chapter 2. In **absorption costing,** *all* manufacturing costs, fixed and variable, are assigned to units of product—units are said to *fully absorb manufacturing costs.* The absorption costing approach is also known as the **full cost** approach. Later, in Chapter 8, we look at product costing from a different point of view called *variable costing,* which is often advocated as an alternative to absorption costing. Chapter 8 also discusses the strengths and weaknesses of the two approaches.

Most companies around the world use some form of absorption costing for both external financial reporting and for tax reporting. In addition, most of these same companies also use absorption costing for managerial accounting purposes. Since absorption costing is the most common approach to product costing, we discuss it first and then deal with alternatives in subsequent chapters.

While studying product costing, we must keep in mind that the essential purpose of any costing system is to accumulate costs for managerial use. A costing system is not an end in itself. Rather, it is a managerial tool in that it exists to provide managers with the cost data needed to direct the affairs of organizations.

The design of the costing system depends on cost/benefit trade-offs as assessed by managers. The level of detail and sophistication in a cost accounting system will influence its costs of development and operation. Relevance to management and external regulatory requirements will be the benefit. Usually, more sophistication yields more benefit by providing more relevant information. But when the additional cost of providing added sophistication equals the benefits from the added relevance, the system's designer is at an optimal point in the cost/benefit trade-off and thus the added sophistication should stop.

The nature of systems design is also influenced by the nature of what is to be costed. The explanation provided in the pages that follow will focus on the nature of what is costed rather than the cost/benefit trade-offs. This will enable a description of what physically needs to be considered when the cost/benefit decision must be made. In other words, physical characteristics represent a fundamental consideration to the higher level and more subjective cost/benefit trade-off.

Absorption costing is a popular approach for determining the cost of goods sold and the cost of inventories for financial accounting and income taxes. These regulatory requirements influence how management determines costs because it may be easier and less expensive for the organization to use a single method of costing for both external and internal purposes.

Costing of products or services represents an approach that focuses on the costing of the efforts that make up the goods or services that are sold by the organization. This emphasis on costing products or services is one of the three common approaches used in managerial accounting. The discussion of costing begins with this focus because of its long tradition and its continued popularity for many types of organizations. After this approach to costing is thoroughly explored in the next few chapters, the alternatives, control and decision, will be studied so that a more complete picture will be available for your study of managerial accounting.

Process and Job-Order Costing

LEARNING OBJECTIVE 1
Distinguish between process costing and job-order costing and identify companies that would use each costing method.

In computing the cost of a product or a service, managers are faced with a difficult problem. Many costs (such as rent) do not change much from month to month, whereas production may change frequently, with production going up in one month and then down in another. In addition to variations in the level of production, several different products or services may be produced in a given period in the same facility. Under these conditions, how is it possible to accurately determine the cost of a product or service? In practice, assigning costs to products and services involves an averaging of some type across time periods and across products. The way in which this averaging is carried out will depend heavily on the type of production process involved.

Process Costing

Process costing system
A costing system used in those manufacturing situations where a single, homogeneous product (such as cement or flour) is produced for long periods of time.

A **process costing system** is used in situations where the company produces many units of a single product (such as frozen orange juice concentrate) for long periods at a time. Examples include producing paper at Bowater, refining aluminum ingots at Alcan, mixing and bottling beverages at Coca-Cola, and making wieners at J.M. Schneider Inc. All of these industries are characterized by an essentially homogeneous product that flows evenly through the production process on a continuous basis.

Process costing systems accumulate costs in a particular operation or department for an entire period (month, quarter, year) and then divide this total cost by the number of units produced during the period. The basic formula for process costing is as follows:

$$\begin{array}{c}\text{Unit product cost} \\ \text{(per litre, kilogram, bottle)}\end{array} = \frac{\text{Total manufacturing cost}}{\text{Total units produced (litres, kilograms, bottles)}}$$

Since one unit of product (litre, kilogram, bottle) is indistinguishable from any other unit of product, each unit is assigned the same average cost. This costing technique results in a broad, average unit cost figure that applies to homogeneous units flowing in a continuous stream out of the production process.

Job-Order Costing

Job-order costing system
A costing system used in situations where many different products, jobs, or services are produced each period.

A **job-order costing system** is used in situations where many *different* products are produced each period. For example, a Levi Strauss clothing factory would typically make many different types of jeans for both men and women during a month. A particular order might consist of 1,000 stonewashed men's blue denim jeans, style number A312, with a 32-inch waist and a 30-inch inseam. This order of 1,000 jeans is called a *batch* or a *job.* In a job-order costing system, costs are traced and allocated to jobs and then the costs of the job are divided by the number of units in the job to arrive at an average cost per unit.

Other examples of situations where job-order costing would be used include large-scale construction projects managed by Bechtel International, commercial aircraft produced by Bombardier, greeting cards designed and printed at Hallmark, and airline meals prepared by Cara. All of these examples are characterized by diverse outputs. Each Bechtel project is unique and different from every other—the company may be simultaneously constructing a dam in Zaire and a bridge in Indonesia. Likewise, each airline orders a different type of meal from Cara's catering service.

Job-order costing is also used extensively in service industries. Hospitals, law firms, movie studios, accounting firms, advertising agencies, and repair shops all use a variation of job-order costing to accumulate costs for accounting and billing purposes. For example, the production of the British Open golf broadcast by TSN would be suitable as a job costing project.

Although the detailed example of job-order costing provided in the following section deals with a manufacturing firm, the same basic concepts and procedures are used by many service organizations. The essential difference for service organizations is the lack of raw materials in the cost of their services. For example, a public accounting firm would have cost elements involving direct labour and overhead but not raw materials, because the firm does not make a physical item. However, to avoid duplicating the discussion that follows, the more comprehensive manufacturing environment will be presented, with the service application addressed in exercises and problems.

The record-keeping and cost assignment problems are more complex when a company sells many different products and services than when it has only a single product. Since the products are different, the costs are typically different. Consequently, cost records must be maintained for each distinct product or job. For example, a lawyer in a large criminal law practice would ordinarily keep separate records of the costs of advising and defending each of her clients. The Levi Strauss factory mentioned earlier would keep separate track of the costs of filling orders for particular styles, sizes, and colours of jeans. Thus, a job-order costing system requires more effort than a process costing system. Nevertheless, job-order costing is used by more than half the manufacturers in North America.

In this chapter, we focus on the design of a job-order costing system. In the following chapter, we focus on process costing and also look more closely at the similarities and differences between the two costing methods.

Job-Order Costing—An Overview

LEARNING OBJECTIVE 2
Identify the documents used in a job-order costing system.

To introduce job-order costing, we will follow a specific job as it progresses through the manufacturing process. This job consists of two experimental couplings that Yost Precision Machining has agreed to produce for Loops Unlimited, a manufacturer of roller coasters. Couplings connect the cars on the roller coaster and are a critical component in the performance and safety of the ride. Before we begin our discussion, recall from Chapter 2 that companies generally classify manufacturing costs into three broad categories: (1) direct materials, (2) direct labour, and (3) manufacturing overhead. As we study the operation of a job-order costing system, we will see how each of these three types of costs is recorded and accumulated.

Measuring Direct Materials Cost

Bill of materials
A document that shows the type and quantity of each major item of the materials required to make a product.

Yost Precision Machining will require four G7 connectors and two M46 housings to make the two experimental couplings for Loops Unlimited. If this were a standard product, there would be a *bill of materials* for the product. A **bill of materials** is a document that lists the type and quantity of each item of the materials needed to complete a unit of product. In this case, there is no established bill of materials, so Yost's production staff determined the materials requirements from the blueprints submitted by the customer. Each coupling requires two connectors and one housing, so to make two couplings, four connectors and two housings are required.

Materials requisition form
A detailed source document that specifies the type and quantity of materials that are to be drawn from the storeroom and identifies the job to which the costs of materials are to be charged.

A *production order* is issued when an agreement has been reached with the customer concerning the quantities, prices, and shipment date for the order. The Production Department then prepares a *materials requisition form* similar to the form in Exhibit 3–1. The **materials requisition form** is a detailed source document that (1) specifies the type and quantity of materials to be drawn from the storeroom, and (2) identifies the job to which the costs of the materials are to be charged. The form serves as a means for controlling the flow of materials into production and also for making entries in the accounting records.

The Yost Precision Machining materials requisition form in Exhibit 3–1 shows that the company's Milling Department has requisitioned two M46 housings and four G7 connectors for job 2B47. A production worker presents the completed form to the storeroom clerk who then issues the necessary raw materials. The storeroom clerk is not allowed to release materials without a completed and properly authorized requisition material requisition form.

Materials Requisition Number: 14873

Date: March 2

Job Number to Be Charged: 2B47

Department: Milling

Description	Quantity	Unit Cost	Total Cost
M46 Housing	2	$124	248
G7 Connector	4	103	412
			$660

Bill White

Authorized Signature

EXHIBIT 3–1 Materials Requisition Form

The previous paragraphs used the terms *direct materials* and *raw materials*. This distinction should be clarified. Direct materials represent materials that are directly traced to the product or service. Raw materials are ingredients that are converted into a finished product. Semi-finished materials, or supplies for a service job, could be considered direct materials if they were important enough to be directly traced to the job, but they will not be raw materials. In summary, because raw materials can be direct materials but all direct materials do not need to be raw materials, the terms often appear interchangeably in business terminology.

Job Cost Sheet

After being notified that the production order has been issued, the Accounting Department prepares a *job cost sheet* similar to the one presented in Exhibit 3–2. A **job cost sheet** is a form prepared for each separate job that records the materials, labour, and overhead costs charged to the job.

Job cost sheet A form prepared for each job that records the materials, labour, and overhead costs charged to the job.

After direct materials are issued, the Accounting Department records their costs directly on the job cost sheet. Note from Exhibit 3–2, for example, that the $660 cost for direct materials shown earlier on the materials requisition form has been charged to job 2B47 on its job cost sheet. The requisition number 14873 is also recorded on the job cost sheet to make it easier to identify the source document for the direct materials charge.

In addition to serving as a means for charging costs to jobs, the job cost sheet also serves as a key part of a firm's accounting records. Job cost sheets serve as a subsidiary ledger to the Work in Process account because the detailed records that they provide for the jobs in process add up to the balance in Work in Process.

Measuring Direct Labour Cost

Direct labour cost is handled in much the same way as direct materials cost. Direct labour consists of labour charges that are easily traced to a particular job. Labour charges that cannot be easily traced directly to any job are treated as part of manufacturing overhead. As discussed in Chapter 2, this latter category of labour costs is termed *indirect labour* and includes tasks such as maintenance, supervision, and clean-up.

Time ticket A detailed source document that is used to record an employee's hour-by-hour activities during a day.

Workers use *time tickets* to record the time they spend on each job and task. A completed **time ticket** is an hour-by-hour summary of the employee's activities throughout the day. An

IN BUSINESS

Raw Materials and Energy Costs Pressures

Energy and raw material costs are an increasing worry for global businesses according to the latest findings from the *Grant Thornton International Business Report* (IBR). The biggest worry for businesses is raw material costs with 44% of global businesses identifying these as having a major impact on cost pressures in the next 12 months, followed by 41% who were concerned about staff costs, 37% about energy costs and 34% about transport costs. Property costs (15%) are expected to have a lesser impact over the coming year.

Source: Canada News Wire, May 9, 2007.

example of an employee time ticket is shown in Exhibit 3–3. When working on a specific job, the employee enters the job number on the time ticket and notes the amount of time spent on that job. When not assigned to a particular job, the employee records the nature of the indirect labour task (such as clean-up and maintenance) and the amount of time spent on the task.

At the end of the day, the time tickets are gathered and the Accounting Department enters the direct labour-hours and costs on individual job cost sheets. (See Exhibit 3–2 for an example of how direct labour costs are entered on the job cost sheet.) The daily time tickets are source documents that are used as the basis for labour cost entries into the accounting records.

EXHIBIT 3–2 Job Cost Sheet

JOB COST SHEET

Job Number	Date Initiated
2B47	March 2
Department	**Date Completed**
Milling	
Item	**Units Completed**
For Inventory	

Direct Materials		Direct Labour			Manufacturing Overhead		
Req. No.	Amount	Ticket	Hours	Amount	Hours	Rate	Amount
14873	$660	843	5	$45			

Cost Summary		Units Shipped		
		Date	Number	Balance
Direct Materials	$			
Direct Labour	$			
Manufacturing Overhead	$			
Total Cost	$			
Unit Cost	$			

Time Ticket No.	Date
843	March 3
Employee	**Station**
Mary Holden	4

Started	Ended	Time Completed	Rate	Amount	Job Number
7:00	12:00	5.0	$9	$45	2B47
12:30	2:30	2.0	9	18	2B50
2:30	3:30	1.0	9	9	Maintenance
Totals		8.0		$72	

R.W. Pace

Supervisor

EXHIBIT 3–3 Employee Time Ticket

The system we have just described is a manual method for recording and posting labour costs. Many companies now rely on computerized systems and no longer record labour time by hand on sheets of paper. One computerized approach uses bar codes to enter the basic data into the computer. Each employee and each job has a unique bar code. When an employee begins work on a job, he or she scans three bar codes, using a handheld device much like the bar code readers at grocery store checkout stands. The first bar code indicates that a job is being started; the second is the unique bar code on the employee's identity badge; and the third is the unique bar code of the job itself. This information is fed automatically via an electronic network to a computer that notes the time and then records all of the data. When the employee completes the task, he or she scans a bar code indicating the task is complete, the bar code on the employee's identity badge, and the bar code attached to the job. This information is relayed to the computer that again notes the time, and a time ticket is automatically prepared. Since all of the source data is already in computer files, the labour costs can automatically be posted to job cost sheets (or their electronic equivalents). Computers, coupled with technology such as bar codes, can eliminate much of the drudgery involved in routine bookkeeping activities while at the same time increasing timeliness and accuracy.

IN BUSINESS

Canada's health care system gives Canadian business a striking competitive advantage with respect to labour costs. As Kirstin Downey writes:

> Employers in Canada pay only about $50 a month, or $600 a year, mostly for optional items such as eyeglasses and orthopedic shoes, said Elaine Bernard, executive director of the labour and worklife program at Harvard Law School. "Health care is significantly cheaper for corporations in Canada," she said. U.S. employers pay more than 10 times as much—an average $552 a month per employee for health insurance, according to the Kaiser Family Foundation.

Source: Kirstin Downey, "A Heftier Dose to Swallow Rising Cost of Health Care in U.S. Gives Other Developed Countries an Edge in Keeping Jobs," *Washington Post,* March 6, 2004, pp. E01.

Application of Manufacturing Overhead

LEARNING OBJECTIVE 3
Compute predetermined overhead rates and explain why estimated overhead costs (rather than actual overhead costs) are used in the costing process.

Manufacturing overhead must be included with direct materials and direct labour on the job cost sheet since manufacturing overhead is also a product cost. However, assigning manufacturing overhead to units of product can be a difficult task. There are three reasons for this.

1. Manufacturing overhead is an indirect cost. This means that it is either impossible or difficult to trace these costs to a particular product or job.
2. Manufacturing overhead consists of many different items, ranging from the grease used in machines to the annual salary of the production manager.
3. Even though output may fluctuate due to seasonal or other factors, manufacturing overhead costs tend to remain relatively constant due to the presence of fixed costs.

Allocation base
A measure of activity such as direct labour-hours or machine-hours that is used to assign costs to cost objects.

Given these problems, about the only way to assign overhead costs to products is to use an allocation process. This allocation of overhead costs is accomplished by selecting an *allocation base* that is common to all of the company's products and services. An **allocation base** is a measure such as direct labour-hours (DLH) or machine-hours (MH) that is used to assign overhead costs to products and services.

The most widely used allocation bases are direct labour-hours and direct labour cost, with machine-hours and even units of product (where a company has only a single product) also used to some extent.

Predetermined overhead rate
A rate used to charge overhead cost to jobs in production; the rate is established in advance for each period by use of estimates of total manufacturing overhead cost and of the total allocation base for the period.

Manufacturing overhead is commonly applied to products using a *predetermined overhead rate.* The **predetermined overhead rate** is computed by dividing the total estimated manufacturing overhead cost for the period by the estimated total amount of the allocation base as follows:

$$\text{Predetermined overhead rate} = \frac{\text{Estimated total manufacturing overhead cost}}{\text{Estimated total units in the allocation base}}$$

Overhead application
The process of charging manufacturing overhead cost to job cost sheets and to the Work in Process account.

Note that the predetermined overhead rate is based on *estimated* rather than actual results. This is because the *predetermined* overhead rate is computed *before* the period begins and is used to *apply* overhead cost to jobs throughout the period. The process of assigning overhead cost to jobs is called **overhead application.** The formula for determining the amount of overhead cost to apply to a particular job is:

$$\begin{array}{c}\text{Overhead applied to}\\ \text{a particular job}\end{array} = \begin{array}{c}\text{Predetermined}\\ \text{overhead rate}\end{array} \times \begin{array}{c}\text{Amount of the allocation}\\ \text{base incurred by the job}\end{array}$$

For example, if the predetermined overhead rate is \$8 per direct labour-hour, then \$8 of overhead is *applied* to a job for each direct labour-hour incurred by the job. When the allocation base is direct labour-hours, the formula becomes:

$$\begin{array}{c}\text{Overhead applied to}\\ \text{a particular job}\end{array} = \begin{array}{c}\text{Predetermined}\\ \text{overhead rate}\end{array} \times \begin{array}{c}\text{Actual direct labour hours}\\ \text{charged to the job}\end{array}$$

Using the Predetermined Overhead Rate To illustrate the steps involved in computing and using a predetermined overhead rate, let's return to Yost Precision Machining. The company has estimated its total manufacturing overhead costs will be \$320,000 for the year and its total direct labour-hours will be 40,000. Its predetermined overhead rate for the year would be \$8 per direct labour-hour, shown as follows:

$$\text{Predetermined overhead rate} = \frac{\text{Estimated total manufacturing overhead cost}}{\text{Estimated total units in the allocation base}}$$

$$\frac{\$320{,}000}{40{,}000 \text{ direct labour-hours}} = \$8 \text{ per direct labour-hour}$$

The job cost sheet in Exhibit 3–4 indicates that 27 direct labour-hours were charged to job 2B47. Therefore, a total of $216 of overhead cost would be applied to the job:

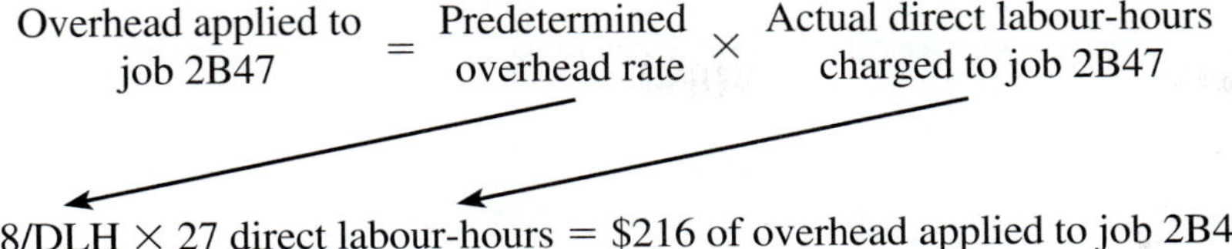

This amount of overhead has been entered on the job cost sheet in Exhibit 3–4. Note that this is *not* the actual amount of overhead caused by the job. There is no attempt to trace actual overhead costs to jobs—if that could be done, the costs would be direct costs, not overhead. The overhead assigned to the job is simply a share of the total overhead that was estimated at the beginning of the year. When a company applies overhead cost to jobs as we have done—that is, by multiplying actual activity times the predetermined overhead rate—it is called a **normal cost system.**

Normal cost system A costing system in which overhead costs are applied to jobs by multiplying a predetermined overhead rate by the actual amount of the allocation base incurred by the job.

The overhead may be applied when direct labour-hours are charged to jobs, or all of the overhead can be applied at once when the job is completed. The choice is up to the company. If a job is not completed at year-end, however, overhead should be applied to jobs so as to value the work in process inventory.

EXHIBIT 3–4 A Completed Job Cost Sheet

JOB COST SHEET

Job Number: 2B47	Date Initiated: March 2
Department: Milling	Date Completed: March 8
Item: Special order coupling	Units Completed: 2
For Inventory:	

Direct Materials		Direct Labour			Manufacturing Overhead		
Req. No.	Amount	Ticket	Hours	Amount	Hours	Rate	Amount
14873	$ 660	843	5	$ 45	27	$8/DLH	$216
14875	506	846	8	60			
14912	238	850	4	21			
	$1,404	851	10	54			
			27	$180			

Cost Summary	
Direct Materials	$1,404
Direct Labour	$ 180
Manufacturing Overhead	$ 216
Total Cost	$1,800
Unit Cost	$ 900*

Units Shipped		
Date	Number	Balance
March 8	—	2

* $1,800 ÷ 2 units = $900 per unit

The Need For a Predetermined Rate Instead of using a predetermined rate, a company could wait until the end of the accounting period to compute an actual overhead rate based on the actual total manufacturing costs and the actual total units in the allocation base for the period. However, managers cite several reasons for using predetermined overhead rates instead of actual overhead rates:

1. Managers would like to know the accounting system's valuation of completed jobs *before* the end of the accounting period. Suppose, for example, that Yost Precision Machining waits until the end of the year to compute its overhead rate. Then the cost of goods sold for job 2B47 would not be known until the close of the year, even though the job was completed and shipped to the customer in March. This problem can be reduced by computing the actual overhead more frequently, but that immediately leads to another problem, as discussed below.
2. If actual overhead rates were computed frequently, seasonal factors in overhead costs or in the allocation base could produce fluctuations in the overhead rates. For example, the costs of heating and cooling a production facility in Halifax will be highest in the winter and summer months and lowest in the spring and fall. If an overhead rate were computed each month or each quarter, the predetermined overhead rate would go up in the winter and summer and down in the spring and fall. Two identical jobs, one completed in the winter and one completed in the spring, would be assigned different costs if the overhead rate were computed on a monthly or quarterly basis. Managers generally feel that such fluctuations in overhead rates and costs serve no useful purpose and are misleading.
3. The use of a predetermined overhead rate simplifies record-keeping. To determine the overhead cost to apply to a job, the accounting staff at Yost Precision Machining simply multiplies the direct labour-hours recorded for the job by the predetermined overhead rate of $8 per direct labour-hour.

For these reasons, most companies use predetermined overhead rates rather than actual overhead rates in their cost accounting systems.

Choice of an Allocation Base for Overhead Cost

Cost driver
A factor, such as machine-hours, beds occupied, computer time, or flight-hours, that causes overhead costs.

Ideally, the allocation base used in the predetermined overhead rate should *drive* the overhead cost. A **cost driver** is a factor, such as machine-hours, beds occupied, computer time, or flight-hours, that causes overhead costs. If a base is used to compute overhead rates that does not "drive" overhead costs, then the result will be inaccurate overhead rates and distorted product costs. For example, if direct labour-hours is used to allocate overhead, but in reality overhead has little to do with direct labour-hours, then products with high direct labour-hour requirements will shoulder an unrealistic burden of overhead and will be overcosted.

Most companies use direct labour-hours or direct labour cost as the allocation base for manufacturing overhead. However, as discussed in earlier chapters, major shifts are taking place in the structure of costs in many industries. In the past, direct labour accounted for up to 60% of the cost of many products, with overhead cost making up only a portion of the remainder. This situation has been changing for two reasons. First, sophisticated automated equipment has taken over functions that used to be performed by direct labour workers. Since the costs of acquiring and maintaining such equipment are classified as overhead, this increases overhead while decreasing direct labour. Second, products are themselves becoming more sophisticated and complex and change more frequently. This increases the need for highly skilled indirect workers such as engineers. As a result of these two trends, direct labour cost is decreasing relative to overhead as a component of product costs.

In companies where direct labour and overhead costs have been moving in opposite directions, it would be difficult to argue that direct labour "drives" overhead costs. Accordingly, in recent years, managers in some companies have used *activity-based costing* principles to redesign their cost accounting systems. Activity-based costing is a costing technique that is designed to reflect more accurately the demands that products, customers, and other cost objects make on overhead resources. The activity-based approach is discussed in more detail in Chapter 5.

We hasten to add that although direct labour may not be an appropriate allocation basis in some industries, in others it continues to be a significant driver of manufacturing overhead. Indeed, most manufacturing companies in North America continue to use direct labour as the primary or secondary allocation base for manufacturing overhead. The key point is that the allocation base used by the company should really drive, or cause, overhead costs, and direct labour is not always an appropriate allocation base.

Computation of Unit Costs

With the application of Yost Precision Machining's $216 manufacturing overhead to the job cost sheet in Exhibit 3–4, the job cost sheet is almost complete. There are two final steps. First, the totals for direct materials, direct labour, and manufacturing overhead are transferred to the Cost Summary section of the job cost sheet and added together to obtain the total cost for the job. Then the total cost ($1,800) is divided by the number of units (2) to obtain the unit cost ($900). As indicated earlier, *this unit cost is an average cost and should not be interpreted as the cost that would actually be incurred if another unit were produced.* Much of the actual overhead would not change at all if another unit was produced, so the incremental cost of an additional unit is something less than the average unit cost of $900.

The completed job cost sheet will serve as the basis for valuing unsold units in ending inventory and determining cost of goods sold.

Summary of Document Flows

The sequence of events discussed above is summarized in Exhibit 3–5. A careful study of the flow of documents in this exhibit provides a good overview of the overall operation of a job-order costing system.

EXHIBIT 3–5 The Flow of Documents in a Job-Order Costing System

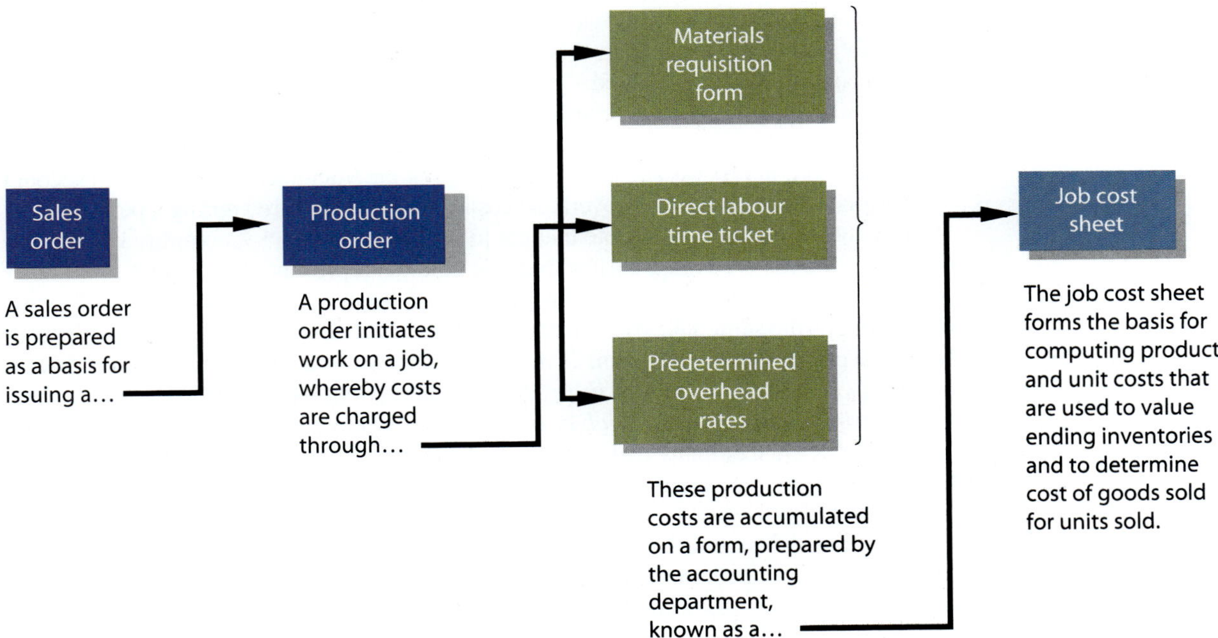

Job-Order Costing—The Flow of Costs

LEARNING OBJECTIVE 4
Record the journal entries that reflect the flow of costs in a job-order costing system.

We are now ready to take a more detailed look at the flow of costs through the company's formal accounting system. To illustrate, we shall consider a single month's activity for Rand Company, a producer of gold and silver commemorative medallions. Rand Company has two jobs in process during April, the first month of its fiscal year. Job A, a special minting of 1,000 gold medallions commemorating the world hockey championships held in Halifax, was started during March and had $30,000 in manufacturing costs already accumulated on April 1. Job B, an order for 10,000 silver medallions commemorating the same event, was started in April.

The Purchase and Issue of Materials

On April 1, Rand Company had $7,000 in raw materials on hand. During the month, the company purchased an additional $60,000 in raw materials. The purchase is recorded in journal entry (1) below:

(1)

Raw Materials	60,000	
Accounts Payable		60,000

As explained in Chapter 2, Raw Materials is an asset account. Thus, when raw materials are purchased, they are initially recorded as an asset—not as an expense.

Issue of Direct and Indirect Materials During April, $52,000 in raw materials were requisitioned from the storeroom for use in production. These raw materials include $50,000 of direct materials and $2,000 of indirect materials. Entry (2) records the issue of the materials to the production departments:

(2)

Work in Process	50,000	
Manufacturing Overhead	2,000	
Raw Materials		52,000

The materials charged to Work in Process represent direct materials for specific jobs. As these materials are entered into the Work in Process account, they are also recorded on the appropriate job cost sheets. This point is illustrated in Exhibit 3–6, where $28,000 of the $50,000 in direct materials is charged to job A's cost sheet and the remaining $22,000 is charged to job B's cost sheet. (In this example, all data are presented in summary form and the job cost sheet is abbreviated.)

The $2,000 charged to Manufacturing Overhead in entry (2) represents indirect materials used in production during April. Observe that the Manufacturing Overhead account is separate from the Work in Process account. The purpose of the Manufacturing Overhead account is to accumulate all manufacturing overhead costs as they are incurred during a period.

Before leaving Exhibit 3–6, note that the job cost sheet for job A contains a beginning balance of $30,000. We stated earlier that this balance represents the cost of work done during March that has been carried forward to April. Also note that the Work in Process account contains the same $30,000 balance. *The reason the $30,000 appears in both places is that the Work in Process account is a control account and the job cost sheets form a subsidiary ledger. Thus, the Work in Process account contains a summarized total of all costs appearing on the individual job cost sheets for all jobs in process at any given point in time.* (Since Rand Company had only job A in process at the beginning of April, job A's $30,000 balance on that date is equal to the balance in the Work in Process account.)

Issue of Direct Materials Only Sometimes the materials drawn from the Raw Materials inventory account are all direct materials. In this case, the entry to record the issue of the materials into production would be as follows:

Work in Process	XXX	
Raw Materials		XXX

EXHIBIT 3–6 Raw Materials Cost Flows

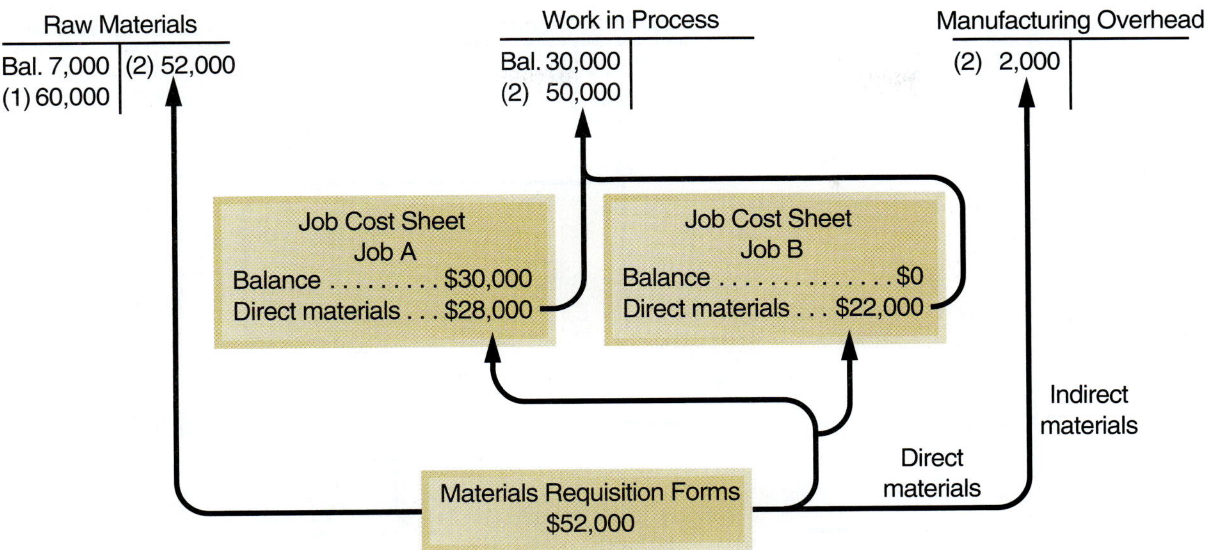

Labour Cost

As work is performed in various departments of Rand Company from day to day, employee time tickets are filled out by workers, collected, and forwarded to the Accounting Department. In the Accounting Department, the tickets are costed according to the various employee wage rates, and the resulting costs are classified as either direct or indirect labour. In April, $60,000 was recorded for direct labour and $15,000 for indirect labour resulting in the following summary entry:

(3)

Work in Process	60,000	
Manufacturing Overhead	15,000	
Salaries and Wages Payable		75,000

Only direct labour is added to the Work in Process account. For Rand Company, this amounted to $60,000 for April.

At the same time that direct labour costs are added to Work in Process, they are also added to the individual job cost sheets, as shown in Exhibit 3–7. During April, $40,000 of direct labour cost was charged to job A and the remaining $20,000 was charged to job B.

The labour costs charged to Manufacturing Overhead represent the indirect labour costs of the period, such as supervision, janitorial work, and maintenance.

Manufacturing Overhead Costs

Recall that all costs of operating the factory other than direct materials and direct labour are classified as manufacturing overhead costs. These costs are entered directly into the Manufacturing Overhead account as they are incurred. To illustrate, assume that Rand Company incurred the following general factory costs during April:

Utilities (heat, water, and power)	$21,000
Rent on factory equipment	16,000
Miscellaneous factory costs	3,000
Total	$40,000

The following entry records the incurrence of these costs:

(4)

Manufacturing Overhead	40,000	
Accounts Payable		40,000

EXHIBIT 3–7 Labour Cost Flows

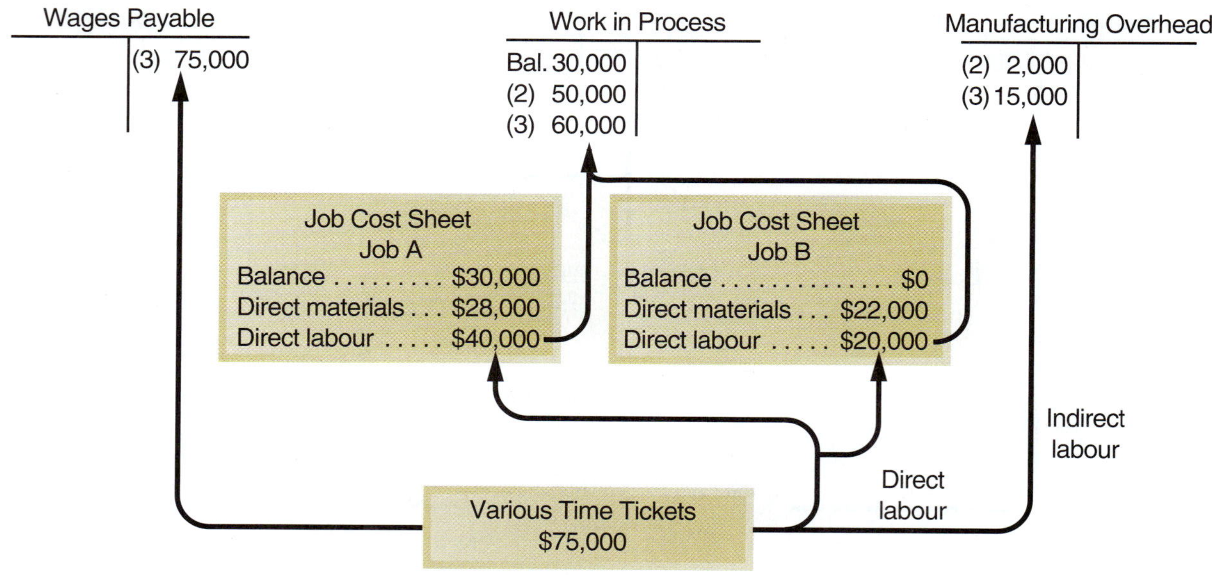

In addition, let us assume that during April, Rand Company recognized $13,000 in accrued property taxes and that $7,000 in prepaid insurance expired on factory buildings and equipment. The following entry records these items:

(5)

Manufacturing Overhead	20,000	
Property Taxes Payable		13,000
Prepaid Insurance.		7,000

Finally, assume that the company recognized $18,000 in depreciation on factory equipment during April. The following entry records the accrual of this depreciation:

(6)

Manufacturing Overhead	18,000	
Accumulated Depreciation		18,000

In short, *all* manufacturing overhead costs are recorded directly into the Manufacturing Overhead account as they are incurred day by day throughout a period. It is important to understand that Manufacturing Overhead is a control account for many—perhaps thousands—of subsidiary accounts such as Indirect Materials, Indirect Labour, Factory Utilities, and so forth. As the Manufacturing Overhead account is debited for costs during a period, the various subsidiary accounts are also debited. In the example above and also in the assignment material for this chapter, we omit the entries to the subsidiary accounts for the sake of brevity.

The Application of Manufacturing Overhead

LEARNING OBJECTIVE 5
Apply overhead cost to Work in Process using a predetermined overhead rate.

Since actual manufacturing overhead costs are charged to the Manufacturing Overhead control account rather than to Work in Process, how are manufacturing overhead costs assigned to Work in Process? The answer is, by means of the predetermined overhead rate. Recall from our discussion earlier in the chapter that a predetermined overhead rate is established at the beginning of each year. The rate is calculated by dividing the estimated total manufacturing overhead cost for the year by the estimated total units in the allocation base (measured in machine-hours, direct labour-hours, or some other base). The predetermined overhead rate is then used to apply overhead costs to jobs. For example, if direct labour-hours is the allocation base, overhead cost is applied to each job by multiplying the number of direct labour-hours charged to the job by the predetermined overhead rate.

To illustrate, assume that Rand Company has used machine-hours in computing its predetermined overhead rate and that this rate is $6 per machine-hour. Also assume that during April, 10,000 machine-hours were worked on job A and 5,000 machine-hours were worked on job B (a total of 15,000 machine-hours). Thus, $90,000 in overhead cost (15,000 machine-hours × $6 = $90,000) would be applied to Work in Process. The following entry records the application of Manufacturing Overhead to Work in Process:

(7)

Work in Process	90,000	
Manufacturing Overhead		90,000

The flow of costs through the Manufacturing Overhead account is detailed in Exhibit 3–8.

The "actual overhead costs" in the Manufacturing Overhead account shown in Exhibit 3–8 are the costs that were added to the account in entries (2)–(6). Observe that the incurrence of these actual overhead costs [entries (2)–(6)] and the application of overhead to Work in Process [entry (7)] represent two separate and entirely distinct processes.

The Concept of a Clearing Account The Manufacturing Overhead account operates as a clearing account. As we have noted, actual factory overhead costs are debited to the accounts as they are incurred day by day throughout the year. At certain intervals during the year, usually when a job is completed, overhead cost is released from the Manufacturing Overhead account and is applied to the Work in Process account by means of the predetermined overhead rate. Work in Process is debited and Manufacturing Overhead is credited. This sequence of events is illustrated as follows:

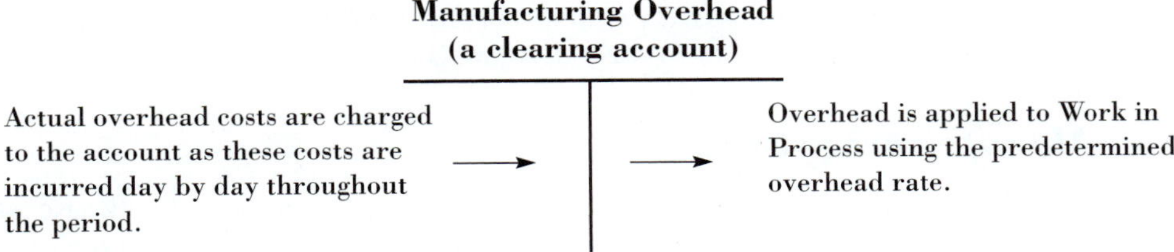

The actual overhead costs incurred and shown as debits in the manufacturing overhead account are a result of many different types of overhead costs. A brief list of some of the different types is presented in the journal entries, numbers 4, 5 and 6, or in the schedule of cost of goods manufactured, shown in Exhibit 3–11 on page 89 or previously in Exhibit 2–4 on page 39. The clearing account concept actually represents a general ledger control account for a subsidiary ledger that contains the detailed information on each type of overhead cost.

As we emphasized earlier, the predetermined overhead rate is based entirely on estimates of what overhead costs are *expected* to be, and it is established before the year begins. As a result, the overhead cost applied during a year will almost certainly turn out to be more or less than the overhead cost that is actually incurred. For example, notice from Exhibit 3–8 that Rand Company's actual overhead costs for the period are $5,000 greater than the overhead cost that has been applied to Work in Process, resulting in a $5,000 debit balance in the Manufacturing Overhead account. We will reserve discussion of what to do with this $5,000 balance until a later section in this chapter, Complications of Overhead Application.

For the moment, we can conclude by noting from Exhibit 3–8 that the cost of a completed job consists of the actual materials cost of the job, the actual labour cost of the job, and the overhead cost *applied* to the job. Pay particular attention to the following subtle but important point: *Actual overhead costs are not charged to jobs; actual overhead costs*

EXHIBIT 3–8 The Flow of Costs in Overhead Application

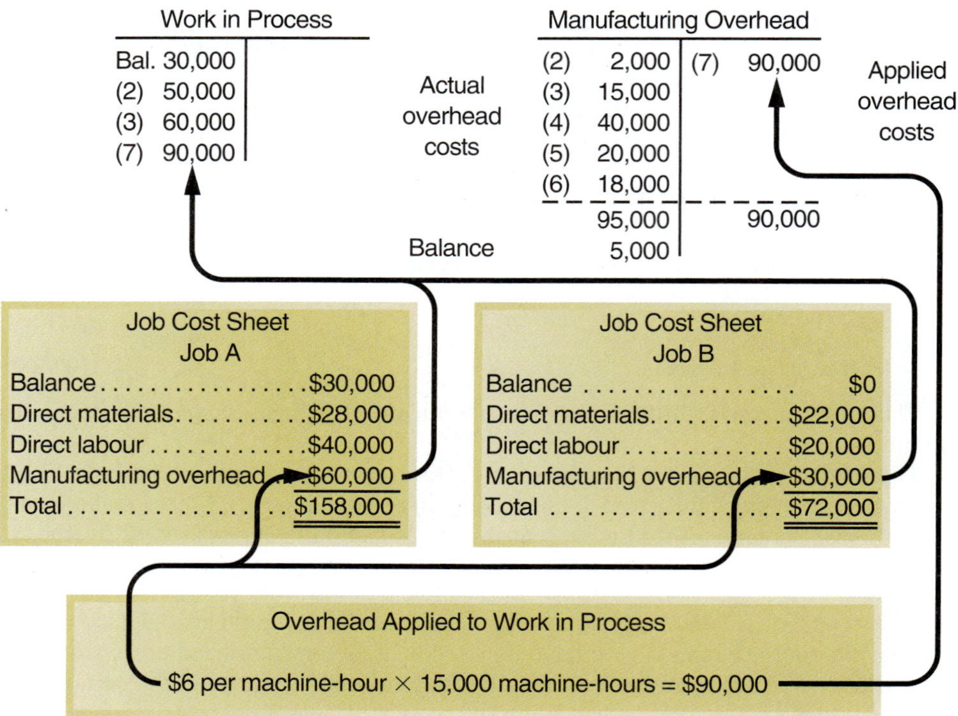

do not appear on the job cost sheet nor do they appear in the Work in Process account. Only the applied overhead cost, based on the predetermined overhead rate, appears on the job cost sheet and in the Work in Process account. Study this point carefully.

Non-Manufacturing Costs

In addition to manufacturing costs, companies also incur marketing and selling costs. As explained in Chapter 2, these costs should be treated as period expenses and charged directly to the income statement. *Non-manufacturing costs should not go into the Manufacturing Overhead account.* To illustrate the correct treatment of non-manufacturing costs, assume that Rand Company incurred $30,000 of selling and administrative costs during April. The following entry records these salaries:

(8)

Salaries Expense.	30,000	
Salaries and Wages Payable		30,000

Assume that depreciation on office equipment during April was $7,000. The entry is as follows:

(9)

Depreciation Expense.	7,000	
Accumulated Depreciation		7,000

Pay particular attention to the difference between this entry and entry (6) where we recorded depreciation on factory equipment. In journal entry (6), depreciation on factory equipment was debited to Manufacturing Overhead and is therefore a product cost. In journal entry (9) above, depreciation on office equipment was debited to Depreciation Expense. Depreciation on office equipment is considered to be a period expense rather than a product cost.

Finally, assume that advertising was $42,000 and that other selling and administrative expenses in April totalled $8,000. The following entry records these items:

(10)

Advertising Expense	42,000	
Other Selling and Administrative Expense	8,000	
Accounts Payable*		50,000

*Other accounts such as Cash may be credited.

Because the amounts in entries (8) through (10) all go directly into expense accounts, they will have no effect on product costs. The same will be true of any other selling and administrative expenses incurred during April, including sales commissions, depreciation on sales equipment, rent on office facilities, insurance on office facilities, and related costs.

The distinction between manufacturing overhead costs and non-manufacturing costs such as selling and administrative expenses is sometimes difficult because of the type of cost. For example, depreciation or salaries should be classified as product costs if related to manufacturing but are classified as period costs and expensed if related to non-manufacturing activities. In practice, the classification has to be based on what the firm does to incur the costs. If it sells or markets, then this is not production and the distinction is clear. If it involves administration then the distinction depends on what is administered and how important it is to separate production administration from overall administration. For example, if all the company does is produce the Hibernia oil platform, then administration is production (manufacturing) overhead. However, if the company is administering many jobs and marketing new jobs at the same time, it may not be able to distinguish overhead from administrative time on the part of the senior management. Thus, unless costs are needed for a cost-recovery billing, administration salaries expense may be the expeditious way to treat the salaries.

Cost of Goods Manufactured

LEARNING OBJECTIVE 6
Prepare schedules of cost of goods manufactured and cost of goods sold.

When a job has been completed, the finished output is transferred from the production departments to the finished goods warehouse. By this time, the Accounting Department will have charged the job with direct materials and direct labour cost, and manufacturing overhead will have been applied using the predetermined rate. A transfer of these costs must be made within the costing system that *parallels* the physical transfer of the goods to the finished goods warehouse. The costs of the completed job are transferred out of the Work in Process account and into the Finished Goods account. The sum of all amounts transferred between these two accounts represents the cost of goods manufactured for the period.

In the case of Rand Company, let us assume that job A was completed during April. The following entry transfers the cost of job A from Work in Process to Finished Goods:

(11)

Finished Goods	158,000	
Work in Process		158,000

The $158,000 represents the completed cost of job A, as shown on the job cost sheet in Exhibit 3–8. Since job A was the only job completed during April, the $158,000 also represents the cost of goods manufactured for the month.

Job B was not completed by month-end, so its cost will remain in the Work in Process account and carry over to the next month. If a balance sheet is prepared at the end of April, the cost accumulated thus far on job B will appear as "Work in process inventory" in the assets section.

Cost of Goods Sold

As units in finished goods are shipped to customers their cost is transferred from the Finished Goods account into the Cost of Goods Sold account. If a complete job is shipped, as in the case where a job has been done to a customer's specifications, then it is a simple matter to transfer the entire cost appearing on the job cost sheet into the Cost of Goods Sold account. In most cases, however, only a portion of the units involved in a particular job will be immediately sold. In these situations, the unit cost must be used to determine how much product cost should be removed from Finished Goods and charged to Cost of Goods Sold.

For Rand Company, we will assume that 750 of the 1,000 gold medallions in job A were shipped to customers by the end of the month for total sales revenue of $225,000. Since 1,000 units were produced and the total cost of the job from the job cost sheet was $158,000, the unit product cost was $158. The following journal entries would record the sale (all sales are on account):

(12)

Accounts Receivable	225,000	
Sales		225,000

(13)

Cost of Goods Sold	118,500	
Finished Goods		118,500
($158 per unit × 750 units = $118,500)		

With entry (13), the flow of costs through our job-order costing system is completed.

Summary of Cost Flows

To pull the entire Rand Company example together, journal entries (1) through (13) are summarized in Exhibit 3–9. The flow of costs through the accounts is presented in T-account form in Exhibit 3–10.

Exhibit 3–11 presents a schedule of cost of goods manufactured and a schedule of cost of goods sold for Rand Company. Note particularly from Exhibit 3–11 that the manufacturing overhead cost on the schedule of cost of goods manufactured is the overhead applied to jobs during the month—not the actual manufacturing overhead costs incurred. The reason for this can be traced back to journal entry (7) and the T-account for Work in Process that appears in Exhibit 3–10. Under a normal costing system as illustrated in this chapter, applied—not actual—overhead costs are applied to jobs and thus to Work in Process inventory. In contrast, in Chapter 2 actual overhead costs were assigned to Work in Process and included in the schedule of cost of goods manufactured. This is because we had not introduced the concept of normal costing in that chapter. Note also that the cost of goods manufactured for the month ($158,000) agrees with the amount transferred from Work in Process to Finished Goods for the month, as recorded earlier in entry (11). Also note that this $158,000 figure is used in computing the cost of goods sold for the month.

An income statement for April is presented in Exhibit 3–12. Observe that the cost of goods sold figure on this statement ($123,500) is carried down from Exhibit 3–11.

EXHIBIT 3–9 Summary of Rand Company Journal Entries

	Debit	Credit
(1)		
Raw Materials	60,000	
Accounts Payable		60,000
(2)		
Work in Process	50,000	
Manufacturing Overhead	2,000	
Raw Materials		52,000
(3)		
Work in Process	60,000	
Manufacturing Overhead	15,000	
Salaries and Wages Payable		75,000
(4)		
Manufacturing Overhead	40,000	
Accounts Payable		40,000
(5)		
Manufacturing Overhead	20,000	
Property Taxes Payable		13,000
Prepaid Insurance		7,000
(6)		
Manufacturing Overhead	18,000	
Accumulated Depreciation		18,000
(7)		
Work in Process	90,000	
Manufacturing Overhead		90,000
(8)		
Salaries Expense	30,000	
Salaries and Wages Payable		30,000
(9)		
Depreciation Expense	7,000	
Accumulated Depreciation		7,000
(10)		
Advertising Expense	42,000	
Other Selling and Administrative Expense	8,000	
Accounts Payable		50,000
(11)		
Finished Goods	158,000	
Work in Process		158,000
(12)		
Accounts Receivable	225,000	
Sales		225,000
(13)		
Cost of Goods Sold	118,500	
Finished Goods		118,500

EXHIBIT 3–10 Summary of Cost Flows—Rand Company

Raw Materials			
Bal.	7,000	(2)	52,000
(1)	60,000		
Bal.	15,000		

Work in Process			
Bal.	30,000	(11)	158,000
(2)	50,000		
(3)	60,000		
(7)	90,000		
Bal.	72,000		

Finished Goods			
Bal..	10,000	(13)	118,500
(11)	158,000		
Bal.	49,500		

Manufacturing Overhead			
(2)	2,000	(7)	90,000
(3)	15,000		
(4)	40,000		
(5)	20,000		
(6)	18,000		
Bal.	5,000		

Accumulated Depreciation			
			XX
		(6)	18,000
		(9)	7,000

Cost of Goods Sold			
(13)	118,500		

Accounts Payable			
			XX
		(1)	60,000
		(4)	40,000
		(10)	50,000

Salaries and Wages Payable			
			XX
		(3)	75,000
		(8)	30,000

Property Taxes Payable			
			XX
		(5)	13,000

Accounts Receivable			
	XX*		
(12)	225,000		

Prepaid Insurance			
	XX		
		(5)	7,000

Capital Stock			
			XX

Retained Earnings			
			XX

Sales			
		(12)	225,000

Salaries Expense			
(8)	30,000		

Depreciation Expense			
(9)	7,000		

Advertising Expense			
(10)	42,000		

Other Selling and Administrative Expense			
(10)	8,000		

Explanation of entries:

(1) Raw materials purchased.
(2) Direct and indirect materials issued into production.
(3) Direct and indirect factory labour cost incurred.
(4) Utilities and other factory costs incurred.
(5) Property taxes and insurance incurred on the factory.
(6) Depreciation recorded on factory assets.
(7) Overhead cost applied to Work in Process.
(8) Administrative salaries expense incurred.
(9) Depreciation recorded on office equipment.
(10) Advertising and other expense incurred.
(11) Cost of goods manufactured transferred into finished goods.
(12) Sale of job A recorded.
(13) Cost of goods sold recorded for job A.

*XX = Normal balance in the account (for example, Accounts Receivable normally carries a debit balance).

EXHIBIT 3–11 Schedules of Cost of Goods Manufactured and Cost of Goods Sold

Cost of Goods Manufactured		
Direct materials:		
Raw materials inventory, beginning	$ 7,000	
Add: Purchases of raw materials	60,000	
Total raw materials available	67,000	
Deduct: Raw materials inventory, ending	15,000	
Raw materials used in production	52,000	
Less indirect materials included in manufacturing overhead	2,000	$ 50,000
Direct labour		60,000
Manufacturing overhead applied to work in process		90,000
Total manufacturing costs		200,000
Add: Beginning work in process inventory		30,000
		230,000
Deduct: Ending work in process inventory		72,000
Cost of goods manufactured		$158,000
Cost of Goods Sold		
Finished goods inventory, beginning		$ 10,000
Add: Cost of goods manufactured		158,000
Goods available for sale		168,000
Deduct: Finished goods inventory, ending		49,500
Unadjusted cost of goods sold		118,500
Add: Underapplied overhead*		5,000
Adjusted cost of goods sold		$123,500

*Note that the underapplied overhead is added to cost of goods sold. If overhead was overapplied, it would be deducted from costs of goods sold.

EXHIBIT 3–12 Income Statement

RAND COMPANY
Income Statement
For the Month Ending April 30

Sales		$225,000
Less cost of goods sold ($118,500 + $5,000)		123,500
Gross margin		101,500
Less selling and administrative expenses:		
Salaries expense	$30,000	
Depreciation expense	7,000	
Advertising expense	42,000	
Other expense	8,000	87,000
Net income		$ 14,500

Complications of Overhead Application

We need to consider two complications relating to overhead application. These are (1) the computation of underapplied and overapplied overhead and (2) the disposition of any balance remaining in the Manufacturing Overhead account at the end of a period.

LEARNING OBJECTIVE 7
Compute under- or overapplied overhead cost and prepare the journal entry to close the balance in Manufacturing Overhead to the appropriate accounts.

Underapplied and Overapplied Overhead

Since the predetermined overhead rate is established before a period begins and is based entirely on estimated data, there generally will be a difference between the amount of overhead cost applied to Work in Process and the amount of overhead cost actually incurred

Underapplied overhead A debit balance in the Manufacturing Overhead account that arises when the amount of overhead cost actually incurred is greater than the amount of overhead cost applied to Work in Process during a period.

Overapplied overhead A credit balance in the Manufacturing Overhead account that arises when the amount of overhead cost applied to Work in Process is greater than the amount of overhead cost actually incurred during a period.

during a period. In the case of Rand Company, for example, the predetermined overhead rate of $6 per hour resulted in $90,000 of overhead cost being applied to Work in Process, whereas actual overhead costs for April proved to be $95,000 (as shown in Exhibit 3–8). The difference between the overhead cost applied to Work in Process and the actual overhead costs of a period is termed either **underapplied** or **overapplied overhead**. For Rand Company, overhead was underapplied because the applied cost ($90,000) was $5,000 less than the actual cost ($95,000). If the tables had been reversed and the company had applied $95,000 in overhead cost to Work in Process while incurring actual overhead costs of only $90,000, then the overhead would have been overapplied.

What is the cause of underapplied or overapplied overhead? The causes can be complex, and a full explanation will have to wait for Chapter 10. Nevertheless, the basic problem is that the method of applying overhead to jobs using a predetermined overhead rate assumes that actual overhead costs will be proportional to the actual amount of the allocation base incurred during the period. If, for example, the predetermined overhead rate is $6 per machine-hour, then it is assumed that actual overhead costs incurred will be $6 for every machine-hour that is actually worked. There are at least two reasons why this may not be true. First, much of the overhead often consists of fixed costs that do not change as the number of machine-hours incurred goes up or down. Second, spending on overhead items may or may not be under control. A fuller explanation of the causes of underapplied and overapplied overhead will have to wait for later chapters.

To illustrate what can happen, suppose that two companies—Turbo Crafters and Black & Howell—have prepared the following estimated data for the coming year:

	Company	
	Turbo Crafters	**Black & Howell**
Predetermined overhead rate based on	Machine-hours	Direct materials cost
Estimated manufacturing overhead (a)	$300,000 (a)	$120,000 (a)
Estimated amount of allocation base (b)	75,000	80,000
Predetermined overhead rate, (a) ÷ (b)	$4 per machine-hour	150% of direct materials cost

Note that when the allocation base is dollars—such as direct material cost in the case of Black and Howell—the predetermined overhead rate is a *percentage* of the allocation base. When dollars are divided by dollars, the result is a *percentage*.

Now assume that because of unexpected changes in overhead spending and changes in demand for the companies' products, the *actual* overhead cost and the *actual* activity recorded during the year in each company are as follows:

	Company	
	Turbo Crafters	**Black & Howell**
Actual manufacturing overhead costs	$290,000	$130,000
Actual amount of allocation base	68,000	$ 90,000

For each company, note that the actual data for both cost and the allocation base differ from the estimates used in computing the predetermined overhead rate. This results in underapplied and overapplied overhead as follows:

	Company	
	Turbo Crafters	Black & Howell
Actual manufacturing overhead cost	$290,000	$130,000
Manufactured overhead cost applied to Work in Process during the year:		
Predetermined overhead rate (a)	$4 per machine-hour	150% of direct material cost
Actual total amount of allocation base (b) . .	68,000 machine-hours	$90,000 direct material cost
Manufacturing overhead applied (a) × (b)	$272,000	$135,000
Underapplied (overapplied) manufacturing overhead	$ 18,000	$ (5,000)

For Turbo Crafters, notice that the amount of overhead cost that has been applied to Work in Process ($272,000) is less than the actual overhead cost for the year ($290,000). Therefore, overhead is underapplied. Also notice that the original estimate of overhead in Turbo Crafters ($300,000) is not directly involved in this computation. Its impact is felt only through the $4 predetermined overhead rate that is used.

For Black & Howell, the amount of overhead cost that has been applied to Work in Process ($135,000) is greater than the actual overhead cost for the year ($130,000), and so overhead is overapplied.

A summary of the concepts discussed above is presented in Exhibit 3–13.

IN BUSINESS

Overhead Costs Can Be Significant

Manufacturing overhead costs, exclusive of amortization, were $3,768,000 in the first quarter of 2007 as compared to $3,763,000 in the first quarter of 2006, representing an increase of $5,000 or 0.1%. Manufacturing overhead costs, exclusive of amortization, were 12.3% of sales in the first quarter of 2007 as compared to 9.7% in 2006. The increase in manufacturing overheads as a percentage of sales was primarily due to an underabsorption of overhead costs as a result of the lower sales volumes in the first quarter of 2007 as compared to the first quarter of 2006 and the fixed nature of certain manufacturing overhead costs.

Source: CPI Plastics Group Ltd. at www.cpiplastics.com.

EXHIBIT 3–13 Summary of Overhead Concepts

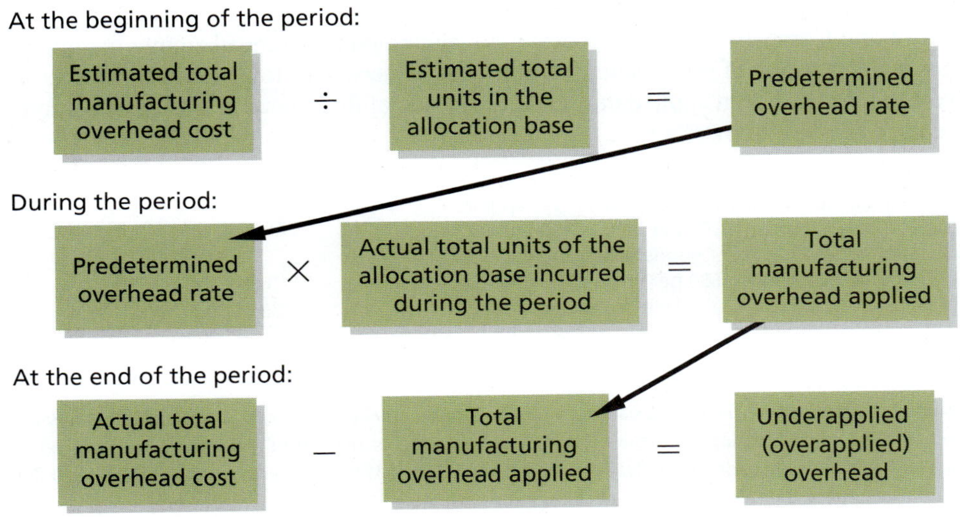

At the beginning of the period:

Estimated total manufacturing overhead cost ÷ Estimated total units in the allocation base = Predetermined overhead rate

During the period:

Predetermined overhead rate × Actual total units of the allocation base incurred during the period = Total manufacturing overhead applied

At the end of the period:

Actual total manufacturing overhead cost − Total manufacturing overhead applied = Underapplied (overapplied) overhead

Disposition of Under- or Overapplied Overhead Balances

What disposition should be made of any under- or overapplied balance remaining in the Manufacturing Overhead account at the end of a period? Generally, any balance in the account is treated in one of three ways:

1. Close out to Cost of Goods Sold.
2. Allocate between Work in Process, Finished Goods, and Cost of Goods Sold in proportion to the overhead applied during the current period in the ending balances of these accounts.[1]
3. Carry forward to the next period.

The second method, which allocates the under- or overapplied overhead among ending inventories and Cost of Goods Sold, is equivalent to using an "actual" overhead rate and is for that reason considered by many to be more accurate than the first method. Consequently, if the amount of underapplied or overapplied overhead is material, many accountants would insist that the second method be used. In problem assignments, we will always indicate which method you are to use for disposing of under- or overapplied overhead.

Close Out to Cost of Goods Sold As mentioned above, closing out the balance in Manufacturing Overhead to Cost of Goods Sold is simpler than the allocation method. Returning to the example of Rand Company, the entry to close the $5,000 of underapplied overhead to Cost of Goods Sold would be as follows:

(14)		
Cost of Goods Sold	5,000	
Manufacturing Overhead		5,000

Note that since there is a debit balance in the Manufacturing Overhead account, Manufacturing Overhead must be credited to close out the account. This has the effect of increasing Cost of Goods Sold for April to $123,500:

Unadjusted cost of goods sold [from entry (13)]	$118,500
Add underapplied overhead [entry (14) above]	5,000
Adjusted cost of goods sold	$123,500

After this adjustment has been made, Rand Company's income statement for April will appear as was shown earlier in Exhibit 3–12.

Allocate among Accounts Allocation of under- or overapplied overhead among Work in Process, Finished Goods, and Cost of Goods Sold is more accurate than closing the entire balance into Cost of Goods Sold. This allocation assigns overhead costs to where they would have gone in the first place had it not been for the errors in the estimates going into the predetermined overhead rate.

Had Rand Company chosen to allocate the underapplied overhead among the inventory accounts and cost of goods sold, it would first be necessary to determine the amount of overhead that had been applied during April in each of the accounts. The computations would have been as follows:

Overhead applied in work in process inventory, April 30	$30,000	33.33%
Overhead applied in finished goods inventory, April 30 ($60,000/1,000 units = $60 per unit) × 250 units	15,000	16.67%
Overhead applied in cost of goods sold, April ($60,000/1,000 units = $60 per unit) × 750 units	45,000	50.00%
Total overhead applied	$90,000	100.00%

1. Some firms prefer to make the allocation on the basis of the total cost of direct materials, direct labour, and applied manufacturing overhead in each of the accounts at the end of the period. This method is not as accurate as allocating the balance in the Manufacturing Overhead account on the basis of just the overhead applied in each of the accounts during the current period.

Based on the above percentages, the underapplied overhead (i.e., the debit balance in Manufacturing Overhead) would be allocated as in the following journal entry:

Work in Process (33.33% × $5,000)	1,666.50	
Finished Goods (16.67% × $5,000)	833.50	
Cost of Goods Sold (50.00% × $5,000).	2,500.00	
Manufacturing Overhead		5,000.00

Note that the first step in the allocation was to determine the amount of overhead applied in each of the accounts. For Finished Goods, for example, the total amount of overhead applied to job A, $60,000, was divided by the total number of units in job A, 1,000 units, to arrive at the average overhead applied of $60 per unit. Since 250 units from job A were still in ending finished goods inventory, the amount of overhead applied in the Finished Goods Inventory account was $60 per unit multiplied by 250 units, or $15,000 in total.

If overhead had been overapplied, the entry above would have been just the reverse, since a credit balance would have existed in the Manufacturing Overhead account.

An alternative but less accurate way to allocate under- or overapplied overhead among Work in Process, Finished Goods, and Cost of Goods Sold is to use the entire cost of manufacturing in each account.

Had we chosen to allocate the underapplied overhead in the Rand Company example, the computations and entry would have been:

Work in process inventory, April 30		$ 72,000	36.00%
Finished goods inventory, April 30		49,500	24.75
Cost of goods sold	$118,500		
Less: Work in process inventory, April 1.	30,000		
Less: Finished goods inventory, April 1	10,000	78,500	39.25
Total		$200,000	100.00%
Work in Process (36.0% × $5,000)	1,800		
Finished Goods (24.75% × $5,000)	1,237		
Cost of Goods Sold (39.25% × $5,000).	1,963		
Manufacturing Overhead		5,000	

A comparison of the percentages above with those using only overhead suggests that total manufacturing costs and overhead were not in the same proportions in each account. This difference is the inaccuracy in the problem resulting from using total manufacturing costs to conduct the allocation.

The rationale for deducting the beginning work in process and finished goods inventories from the cost of goods sold is to permit the allocation to be based on costs from the current period. By doing so, the 39.25% in the Rand Company example reflects only total manufacturing costs from April and thus corresponds to the period in which the underapplied overhead occurred. Without this adjustment, cost of goods sold would be assigned the overhead difference based on costs carried over from March and thus bear a disproportionate amount of the under- or overapplied overhead.

Carry the Balance Forward Recall the section earlier in this chapter entitled Application of Manufacturing Overhead. Notice that some firms have large seasonal variations in output while being faced with relatively constant overhead costs. Predetermined overhead was used to even out fluctuations in the cost of overhead caused by seasonal variations in output and seasonal variations in costs (e.g., heating costs). The predetermined overhead rate is computed using estimated total manufacturing costs for a year divided by estimated total units in the base. The result is an average rate. When the average predetermined rate is applied to actual production for the period, the applied overhead is determined. The under- or overapplied overhead is a result of two factors: an actual base that is different from one-twelfth of the annual estimated base and actual overhead costs that do not equal one-twelfth of the total estimated overhead costs. Therefore, for any given month, an under- or overapplied overhead amount would be expected. In some months, it would be positive; in other months, it would be negative. Over the year, these amounts may largely cancel out. If this is the situation, then significant debits and credits could be carried forward to the year-end so that a final disposition can be made either by adjusting Cost of Goods Sold or allocating (sometimes termed prorating) the amount to the inventories and Cost of Goods Sold.

The Rand Company example would be treated as follows:

Underapplied Overhead		
[a deferred debit balance on the balance sheet].	5,000	
Manufacturing Overhead.		5,000

A General Model of Product Cost Flows

The flow of costs in a product costing system is presented in the form of a T-account model in Exhibit 3–14. This model applies as much to a process costing system as it does to a job-order costing system. Examination of this model can be very helpful in gaining a perspective as to how costs enter a system, flow through it, and finally end up as Cost of Goods Sold on the income statement.

Variations from the General Model of Product Cost Flow

Costing systems can vary from what is reflected by the general model. While the general model is the most complete description, circumstances may make such a complete system too costly. For example, a system variation known as *backflush costing* can permit labour

EXHIBIT 3–14 A General Model of Cost Flows

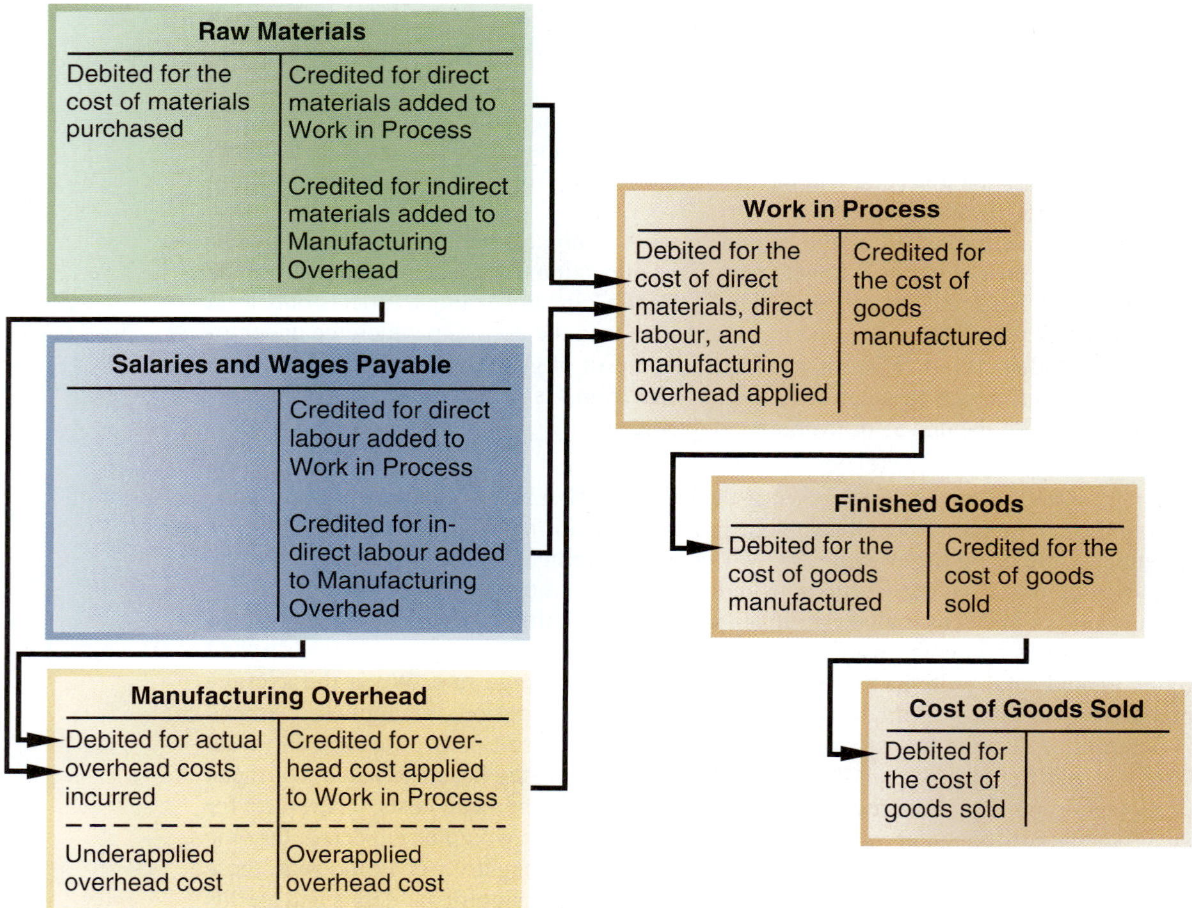

charges to be made directly to manufacturing overhead. Then, overhead is applied to the cost of completed jobs along with raw materials, so that the need to keep work in process records can be avoided. Such a minimal treatment of work in process is justified in a mechanized Lean Manufacturing (JIT) environment. Cost of completed jobs still reflects the material and overhead (including labour), but the record system reflects the simplified needs of the production environment.

Multiple Predetermined Overhead Rates

Our discussion of overhead in this chapter has assumed that there is a single predetermined overhead rate for an entire factory called a **plantwide overhead rate**. This is, in fact, a common practice—particularly in smaller companies. But in larger companies, *multiple predetermined overhead rates* are often used. In a **multiple predetermined overhead rate** system there is usually a different overhead rate for each production department. Such a system, while more complex, is considered to be more accurate, because it can reflect differences across departments in how overhead costs are incurred. For example, overhead might be allocated based on direct labour-hours in departments that are relatively labour-intensive and based on machine-hours in departments that are relatively machine-intensive. When multiple predetermined overhead rates are used, overhead is applied in each department according to its own overhead rate as a job proceeds through the department.

Plantwide overhead rate
A single predetermined overhead rate that is used throughout a plant.

Multiple predetermined overhead rates
A costing system in which there are multiple overhead cost pools with a different predetermined rate for each cost pool, rather than a single predetermined overhead rate for the entire company. Frequently, each production department is treated as a separate overhead cost pool.

To illustrate, refer to the data in the following table where Cook Company has two departments (A and B) and several jobs in process. Data is provided for two of these jobs (X and Y). If the company uses a plantwide overhead rate of \$12 (\$336,000 ÷ 28,000 DLH) then the overhead costs applied to Job X and Job Y will be \$8,400 (\$12 × 700 hours + \$12 × 0) and \$12 (\$12 × 0 hours + \$12 × 1 hour) respectively. However, if overhead is applied using department overhead rates then Job X will be assigned \$2,800 (\$4 × 700 direct labour-hours) and Job Y will be assigned \$8,400 (\$12 × 700 machine-hours).

Cook Company	Department A	Department B	Total
Overhead cost	\$84,000	\$252,000	\$336,000
Direct labour-hours	21,000	7,000	28,000 DLH
Machine-hours	7,000	21,000	28,000 MH
Overhead cost driver	21,000 DLH	21,000 MH	
Overhead rate: Plant wide			\$12 per DLH
By department	\$4/DLH	\$12/MH	
Direct labour-hours—Job X	700	0	
Direct labour-hours—Job Y	0	1	
Machine-hours—Job X	1	0	
Machine-hours—Job Y	0	700	

The decision to use a plantwide rate versus separate rates for each department comes down to cost/benefit. It is cheaper to use a plantwide rate but separate rates are more informative when the activities that drive overhead costs differ among departments. Improved decision making resulting from more accurate overhead data can justify the added costs of gathering separate departmental overhead data.

Use of Information Technology

Earlier in the chapter, we discussed how bar code technology can be used to record labour time—reducing the drudgery in that task and increasing accuracy. Bar codes have many other uses.

In a company with a well-developed bar code system, the manufacturing cycle begins with the receipt of a customer's order in electronic form. Until very recently, the order would have been received via electronic data interchange (EDI), which involves a network of computers linking organizations. An EDI network allows companies to electronically exchange business documents and other information that extend into all areas of business activity from ordering raw materials to shipping completed goods. EDI was developed in the 1980s and requires significant investments in programming and networking hardware. Recently, EDI has been challenged by a far cheaper Internet-based alternative—XML (Extensible Markup Language), an extension of HTML (Hypertext Markup Language). HTML uses codes to tell your Web browser how to display information on your screen, but the computer doesn't know what the information is—it just displays it. XML provides additional tags that identify the kind of information that is being exchanged. For example, price data might be coded as <price> 14.95 <price>. When your computer reads this data and sees the tag <price> surrounding 14.95, your computer will immediately know that this is a price. XML tags can designate many different kinds of information—customer orders, medical records, bank statements, and so on—and the tags will indicate to your computer how to display, store, and retrieve the information. Office Depot was an early adopter of XML, which it is using to facilitate e-commerce with its big customers.

Once an order has been received via EDI or over the Internet in the form of an XML file, the computer draws up a list of required raw materials and sends out electronic purchase orders to suppliers. When materials arrive at the company's plant from the suppliers, bar codes that have been applied by the suppliers are scanned to update inventory records and to trigger payment for the materials. The bar codes are scanned again when the materials are requisitioned for use in production. At that point, the computer credits the Raw Materials inventory account for the amount and type of goods requisitioned and charges the Work in Process inventory account.

A unique bar code is assigned to each job. This bar code is scanned to update Work in Process records for labour and other costs incurred in the manufacturing process. When goods are completed, another scan is performed that transfers both the cost and quantity of goods from the Work in Process inventory account to the Finished Goods inventory account, or charges Cost of Goods Sold for goods ready to be shipped.

Goods ready to be shipped are packed into containers, which are bar-coded with information that includes the customer number, the type and quantity of goods being shipped, and the order number. This bar code is then used for preparing billing information and for tracking the packed goods until placed on a carrier for shipment to the customer. Some customers require that the packed goods be bar-coded with point-of-sale labels that can be scanned at retail checkout counters. These scans allow the retailer to update inventory records, verify price, and generate a customer receipt.

In short, bar code technology is being integrated into all areas of business activity. When combined with EDI or XML, it eliminates a lot of clerical drudgery and allows companies to capture and exchange more data and to analyze and report information much more quickly and completely and with less error than with manual systems.

The integration of XML and the internal computer system for management reporting is called an *enterprise resource planning system* (ERP system). An ERP system represents a real-time computer system using a single uniform database that is coupled with modules for accounting, logistics, and human resources. Full use of these modules permits an integrated systems response for Internet-based orders in XML, supplier purchases and payables, inventory management, production, sales and receivables, treasury, and capital (fixed) assets management. Major suppliers of such ERP systems include Oracle, SAP, and Baan.[2] Other companies provide certified software that is compatible with these systems. Samples of the overall menus for SAP are shown in Exhibit 3–15.

Operationally, these systems can provide global capabilities to regulate the variety of financial accounting and tax situations and do so in the appropriate language. Combining (better known as *consolidation*) of these different reports is performed by the system, along with drill-down capabilities for investigating details.

Critical to the installation of these systems is a well-specified operating system and well-trained personnel. Configurations for these systems to suit specific industries are

2. Internet sites for these companies provide details about each of their products and services: http://www.oracle.com/, http://www.sap.com/, http://www.baan.com/, and http://www.jdedwards.com/.

EXHIBIT 3–15 Sample SAP menus[3]

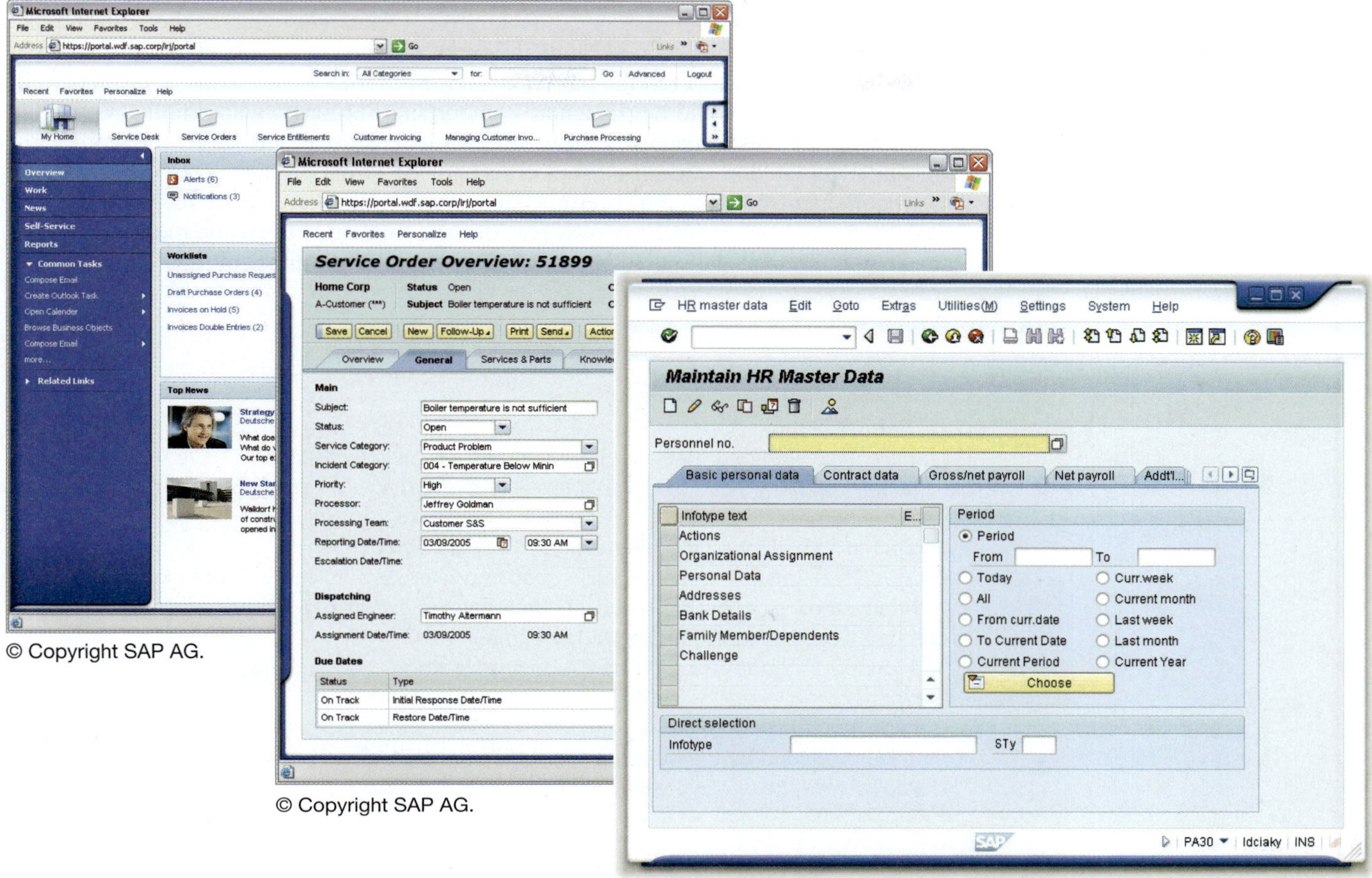

provided with the software installation. For example, SAP, the world leader in such software, provides configurations for such industries as defence, apparel, automotive, construction, chemicals, and education, to mention only a few.

ERP systems combined with Web-based software and executive decision support reporting represent the current technology used by progressive organizations in both the commercial and not-for-profit fields. The size of an organization has to be sufficient to support the larger systems mentioned here, but small business software is available to do similar activities in an appropriately simplified way.[4]

International Job Costing

Studies of the international accounting scene suggest that the general principles of product costing are universally applicable. Nevertheless, differences do exist from country to country in how specific costs are classified. For example, a study of Russian operational

3. This book contains references to the products of SAP AG, Dietmar-Hopp-Allee 16, 69190 Walldorf, Germany. The names of these products are registered and/or unregistered trademarks of SAP AG. SAP AG is neither the author nor the publisher of this book and is not responsible for its contents.

4. For background information on ERP, see Gerald Trites, *Enterprise Resource Planning* (Toronto, ON: The Canadian Institute of Chartered Accountants, 2000), and F. Robert Jacobs and D. Clay Whyback, *Why ERP? A Primer on SAP Implementation* (New York, NY: McGraw-Hill/Irwin, 2000).

accounting and statistical record-keeping, the equivalent of product costing, suggests that the required reporting structure in Russia would assign some cost elements to inventory that we might classify as selling or administrative. Other costs such as the rent on plant facilities would be classified outside of the usual overhead category. If a company was executing a contract with a foreign government, the differences in what is or is not permitted as contract costs would be particularly important. Similarly, what Public Works and Government Services Canada will allow as contract costs is described by the word "prudent" and elaborated in a specific list of costs excluded from product costs.[5] For example, these requirements would permit certain general and selling costs to be included if a prudent person would incur such costs as part of the contract. Thus, while the general principles may be similar, the specifics can vary as a result of government regulations.

IN BUSINESS

Cost Trends (2006)

Cost differentials among the returning countries (G7 plus Netherlands) have narrowed since the previous (2004) edition of *Competitive Alternatives*, with most countries moving closer to the US benchmark:

- Japan has experienced the greatest gain in cost competitiveness, assisted by the weakening of the yen relative to the US dollar, and improvements in local business costs.
- Germany, the Netherlands, France, and Italy have all experienced improvements in their cost competitiveness, relative to the US benchmark.
- The United Kingdom has retained a cost advantage over the United States, Japan, and Germany.
- Canada has retained its top ranking among G7 countries, although the size of its advantage has been reduced by the strong appreciation in value of the Canadian dollar relative to the US dollar over the last two years.

Source: *Competitive Alternatives Highlights: KPMG's Guide to International Business Costs.* www.competitivealternatives.com

Recorded Costs for Quality

Deficiencies in quality result in scrap, rework, delays in production, extra inventory, warranty claims, and poor customer relations. Such costs have been estimated at 25% to 35% of total product costs for some companies. Chapter 11 presents an elaboration of various reports used to manage quality costs.

To illustrate the accounting process for defective units, assume that 2,000 units were started for a job, but only 1,900 good units were finished. If raw material, direct labour, and overhead applied amounted to $4,800 at the end of production, then each good unit would have a unit cost of $4,800 ÷ by 1,900, or $2.53 per unit. If management wanted to charge the 100 units to all production instead of the particular 1,900-unit job, the situation could be recorded as follows:

Manufacturing Overhead	240	
Work in Process Inventory		240

Calculations:

$4,800 ÷ 2,000 units = $2.40 per unit

100 defective units would cost 100 × $2.40

The 1,900 good units would cost ($4,800 – $240) = $4,560, or $2.40 per unit.

5. Section 3, General Conditions, DSS-MAS 1031-2, "Contract Cost Principles," *Standard Acquisition Clauses and Conditions Manual*, Public Works and Government Services Canada, 1997.

Any recovery from the 100 units of scrap would be credited to manufacturing overhead or the job costs, depending on the procedure used for the initial recording. If repair or rework was undertaken on the 100 defective units, then material, direct labour, and overhead costs would be charged to the job or the overhead account to be offset by any recovery.

The logic of whether to charge scrap or rework costs to all production or to a specific job is determined by deciding if defect costs were a normal cost of all production (thus a charge to overhead) or a cost of the specific situation surrounding a particular job (thus a charge solely of that job).

Environmentally hazardous scrap or defects can require disposal costs. Such environmental costs can be presented in a manner that they would provide management with evidence of the remediation or disposal requirements for their production processes.

Summary

Job-order costing and process costing are widely used to track costs. Job-order costing is used in situations where the organization offers many different products or services, such as in furniture manufacturing, hospitals, and legal firms. Process costing is used where units of product are homogeneous, such as in flour milling or cement production.

Materials requisition forms and labour time tickets are used to assign direct materials and direct labour costs to jobs in a job-costing system. Manufacturing overhead costs are assigned to jobs through use of a predetermined overhead rate. The predetermined overhead rate is determined before the period begins by dividing the estimated total manufacturing overhead cost for the period by the estimated total allocation base for the period. The most frequently used allocation bases are direct labour-hours and machine-hours. Overhead is applied to jobs by multiplying the predetermined overhead rate by the actual amount of the allocation base used by the job.

Since the predetermined overhead rate is based on estimates, the actual overhead cost incurred during a period may be more or less than the amount of overhead cost applied to production. Such a difference is referred to as under- or overapplied overhead. The under- or overapplied overhead for a period can be (1) closed out to Cost of Goods Sold or (2) allocated among Work in Process, Finished Goods, and Cost of Goods Sold or (3) carried forward to the end of the year. When overhead is underapplied, manufacturing overhead costs have been understated and therefore inventories and/or expenses must be adjusted upward. When overhead is overapplied, manufacturing overhead costs have been overstated and therefore inventories and/or expenses must be adjusted downward.

Review Problem: Job-Order Costing

Hogle Company is a manufacturing firm that uses job-order costing. On January 1, the beginning of its fiscal year, the company's inventory balances were as follows:

Raw materials	$20,000
Work in process	15,000
Finished goods	30,000

The company applies overhead cost to jobs on the basis of machine-hours worked. For the current year, the company estimated that it would work 75,000 machine-hours and incur $450,000 in manufacturing overhead cost. The following transactions were recorded for the year:

a. Raw materials were purchased on account, $410,000.

b. Raw materials were requisitioned for use in production, $380,000 ($360,000 direct materials and $20,000 indirect materials).
c. The following costs were incurred for employee services: direct labour, $75,000; indirect labour, $110,000; sales commissions, $90,000; and administrative salaries, $200,000.
d. Sales travel costs were incurred, $17,000.
e. Utility costs were incurred in the factory, $43,000.
f. Advertising costs were incurred, $180,000.
g. Depreciation was recorded for the year, $350,000 (80% relates to factory operations, and 20% relates to selling and administrative activities).
h. Insurance expired during the year, $10,000 (70% relates to factory operations, and the remaining 30% relates to selling and administrative activities).
i. Manufacturing overhead was applied to production. Due to greater than expected demand for its products, the company worked 80,000 machine-hours during the year.
j. Goods costing $900,000 to manufacture according to their job cost sheets were completed during the year.
k. Goods were sold on account to customers during the year at a total selling price of $1,500,000. The goods cost $870,000 to manufacture according to their job cost sheets.

Required:
1. Prepare journal entries to record the preceding transactions.
2. Post the entries in (1) above to T-accounts (do not forget to enter the opening balances in the inventory accounts).
3. Is Manufacturing Overhead underapplied or overapplied for the year? Prepare a journal entry to close any balance in the Manufacturing Overhead account to Cost of Goods Sold. Do not allocate the balance between ending inventories and Cost of Goods Sold.
4. Prepare an income statement for the year and a schedule of cost of goods manufactured.

Solution to Review Problem

1.

a. Raw Materials	410,000	
Accounts Payable		410,000
b. Work in Process	360,000	
Manufacturing Overhead	20,000	
Raw Materials		380,000
c. Work in Process	75,000	
Manufacturing Overhead	110,000	
Sales Commissions Expense	90,000	
Administrative Salaries Expense	200,000	
Salaries and Wages Payable		475,000
d. Sales Travel Expense	17,000	
Accounts Payable		17,000
e. Manufacturing Overhead	43,000	
Accounts Payable		43,000
f. Advertising Expense	180,000	
Accounts Payable		180,000
g. Manufacturing Overhead	280,000	
Depreciation Expense	70,000	
Accumulated Depreciation		350,000
h. Manufacturing Overhead	7,000	
Insurance Expense	3,000	
Prepaid Insurance		10,000

i. The predetermined overhead rate for the year would be computed as follows:

$$\frac{\text{Estimated manufacturing overhead, \$450,000}}{\text{Estimated machine-hours, 75,000}} = \text{\$6 per machine-hour}$$

Based on the 80,000 machine-hours actually worked during the year, the company would have applied $480,000 in overhead cost to production: 80,000 machine-hours × $6 = $480,000. The following entry records this application of overhead cost:

Work in Process	480,000	
Manufacturing Overhead		480,000

j.	Finished Goods	900,000	
	Work in Process		900,000
k.	Accounts Receivable	1,500,000	
	Sales		1,500,000
	Cost of Goods Sold	870,000	
	Finished Goods		870,000

2.

Raw Materials

Bal.	20,000	(b)	380,000
(a)	410,000		
Bal.	50,000		

Work in Process

Bal.	15,000	(j)	900,000
(b)	360,000		
(c)	75,000		
(i)	480,000		
Bal.	30,000		

Finished Goods

Bal.	30,000	(k)	870,000
(j)	900,000		
Bal.	60,000		

Cost of Goods Sold

(k)	870,000		

Manufacturing Overhead

(b)	20,000	(i)	480,000
(c)	110,000		
(e)	43,000		
(g)	280,000		
(h)	7,000		
	460,000		480,000
		Bal.	20,000

Prepaid Insurance

		(h)	10,000

Commissions Expense

(c)	90,000		

Accumulated Depreciation

		(g)	350,000

Accounts Receivable

(k)	1,500,000		

Administrative Salary Expense

(c)	200,000		

Sales Travel Expense

(d)	17,000		

Accounts Payable

		(a)	410,000
		(d)	17,000
		(e)	43,000
		(f)	180,000

Sales

		(k)	1,500,000

Advertising Expense

(f)	180,000		

Depreciation Expense

(g)	70,000		

Salaries and Wages Payable

		(c)	475,000

Insurance Expense

(h)	3,000		

3. Manufacturing overhead is overapplied for the year. The entry to close it out to Cost of Goods Sold is as follows:

Manufacturing Overhead	20,000	
Cost of Goods Sold		20,000

4.

HOGLE COMPANY
Income Statement
For the Year Ended December 31

Sales		$1,500,000
Less cost of goods sold ($870,000 − $20,000)		850,000
Gross margin		650,000
Less selling and administrative expenses:		
Commissions expense	$ 90,000	
Administrative salaries expense	200,000	
Sales travel expense	17,000	
Advertising expense	180,000	
Depreciation expense	70,000	
Insurance expense	3,000	560,000
Operating income		$ 90,000

HOGLE COMPANY
Schedule of Cost of Goods Manufactured and
Cost of Goods Sold

Direct Materials:		
Raw materials inventory, January 1	$ 20,000	
Add: Purchases of raw materials	410,000	
Total raw materials available	430,000	
Deduct: Raw materials inventory, December 31	50,000	
Raw materials used in production	380,000	
Less: Indirect materials (below)	20,000	
Direct materials used in production		$360,000
Direct Labour		75,000
Manufacturing Overhead:		
Indirect materials	20,000	
Indirect labour	110,000	
Utilities	43,000	
Depreciation	280,000	
Insurance	7,000	
Actual overhead costs	460,000	
Add: Overapplied overhead	20,000	
Overhead applied to work in process		480,000*
Total manufacturing costs		915,000
Add: Beginning work in process inventory		15,000
		930,000
Deduct: Ending work in process inventory		30,000
Cost of goods manufactured		900,000
Add: Finished goods inventory, January 1		30,000
Goods available for sale		930,000
Deduct: Finished goods inventory, December 31		60,000
Cost of Goods Sold		870,000
Deduct: Overapplied overhead		20,000
Adjusted cost of goods sold		$850,000

*The details of manufacturing overhead may be omitted as shown in Exhibit 3–11. If these are not omitted then the overapplied overhead must be added to actual overhead costs and only the total ($480,000) is added to direct materials and direct labour. The reason is that the schedule of cost of goods manufactured represents a summary of costs flowing through the Work in Process account during a period and therefore must include only overhead applied to production. If a reverse situation had existed and overhead had been underapplied during the period, then the amount of underapplied overhead would have been deducted from actual overhead costs on the schedule. This would have brought the actual overhead costs down to the amount that had been applied to production.

Appendix 3A: The Predetermined Overhead Rate and Capacity

LEARNING OBJECTIVE 8
Explain the implications of basing the predetermined overhead rate on activity at capacity rather than on estimated activity for the period.

Companies typically base their predetermined overhead rates on the estimated, or budgeted, amount of the allocation base for the upcoming period. This is the method that is used in the chapter, but it is a practice that has recently come under severe criticism. An example will be very helpful in understanding why. Prahad Corporation manufactures music CDs for local recording studios. The company has a CD duplicating machine that is capable of producing a new CD every 10 seconds from a master CD. The company leases the CD duplicating machine for \$180,000 per year, and this is the company's only manufacturing overhead. With allowances for set-ups and maintenance, the machine is theoretically capable of producing up to 900,000 CDs per year. However, due to weak retail sales of CDs, the company's commercial customers are unlikely to order more than 600,000 CDs next year. The company uses machine time as the allocation base for applying manufacturing overhead. These data are summarized below:

PRAHAD CORPORATION DATA

Total manufacturing overhead cost	\$180,000 per year
Allocation base: machine time per CD	10 seconds per CD
Capacity	900,000 CDs per year
Budgeted output for next year	600,000 CDs

If Prahad follows common practice and computes its predetermined overhead rate using estimated, or budgeted, figures, then its predetermined overhead rate for next year would be \$0.03 per second of machine time, computed as follows:

$$\frac{\text{Estimated total manufacturing overhead cost, \$180,000}}{\text{Estimated total units in the allocation base, 600,000 CDs} \times \text{10 seconds per CD}} = \text{\$0.03 per second}$$

Since each CD requires 10 seconds of machine time, each CD will be charged for \$0.30 of overhead cost.

Critics charge that there are two problems with this procedure. First, if predetermined overhead rates are based on budgeted activity, then the unit product costs will fluctuate, depending on the budgeted level of activity for the period. For example, if the budgeted output for the year was only 300,000 CDs, the predetermined overhead rate would be \$0.06 per second of machine time or \$0.60 per CD rather than \$0.30 per CD. In general, if budgeted output falls, the overhead cost per unit will increase; it will appear that the CDs cost more to make. Managers may then be tempted to increase prices at the worst possible time—just as demand is falling.

Second, critics charge that under the traditional approach, products are charged for resources that they do not use. When the fixed costs of capacity are spread over estimated activity, the units that are produced must shoulder the costs of unused capacity. That is why the applied overhead cost per unit increases as the level of activity falls. The critics argue that products should be charged only for the capacity that they use; they should not be charged for the capacity they do not use. This can be accomplished by basing the predetermined overhead rate on capacity as follows:

$$\frac{\text{Total manufacturing overhead cost at capacity, \$180,000}}{\text{Total units in the allocation base at capacity, 900,000 CDs} \times \text{10 seconds per CD}} = \text{\$0.02 per second}$$

Since the predetermined overhead rate is \$0.02 per second, the overhead cost applied to each CD would be \$0.20. This charge is constant and would not be affected by the level of activity during a period. If output falls, the charge would still be \$0.20 per CD.

The use of capacity will almost certainly result in underapplied overhead. If actual output at Prahad Corporation is 600,000 CDs, then only \$120,000 of overhead cost would be applied to products (\$0.20 per CD × 600,000 CDs). Since the actual overhead cost is \$180,000, there would be underapplied overhead of \$60,000. In another departure from tradition, the critics suggest that the underapplied overhead that results from idle capacity should be separately disclosed on the income statement as the Cost of Unused Capacity—a period expense. Disclosing this cost as a lump sum on the income statement, rather than burying it in Cost of Goods Sold or ending inventories, makes it much more visible to managers.

Official pronouncements do not prohibit basing predetermined overhead rates on capacity for external reports. Nevertheless, basing the predetermined overhead rate on estimated, or budgeted, activity is a long-established practice in industry, and some managers and accountants may object to the large amounts of underapplied overhead that would often result from using capacity to determine predetermined overhead rates. And some may insist that the underapplied overhead be allocated among Cost of Goods Sold and ending inventories—which would defeat the purpose of basing the predetermined overhead rate on capacity.

Glossary

Visit the Online Learning Centre at **http://www.mcgrawhill.ca/olc/garrison/** for a review of glossary terms and definitions.

Questions

3–1 Why aren't actual overhead costs traced to jobs just as direct materials and direct labour costs are traced to jobs?

3–2 When would job-order costing be used instead of process costing?

3–3 What is the purpose of the job cost sheet in a job-order costing system?

3–4 What is a predetermined overhead rate, and how is it computed?

3–5 Explain how a sales order, a production order, a materials requisition form, and a labour time ticket are involved in producing and costing products.

3–6 Explain why some production costs must be assigned to products through an allocation process.

3–7 Why do companies use predetermined overhead rates rather than actual manufacturing overhead costs to apply overhead to jobs?

3–8 What factors should be considered in selecting a base to be used in computing the predetermined overhead rate?

3–9 If a company fully allocates all of its overhead costs to jobs, does this guarantee that a profit will be earned for the period?

3–10 What account is credited when overhead cost is applied to Work in Process? Would you expect the amount applied for a period to equal the actual overhead costs of the period? Why or why not?

3–11 What is underapplied overhead? Overapplied overhead? What disposition is made of these amounts at the end of the period?

3–12 Provide two reasons why overhead might be underapplied in a given year.

3–13 What adjustment is made for underapplied overhead on the schedule of cost of goods sold? What adjustment is made for overapplied overhead?

3–14 Sigma Company applies overhead cost to jobs on the basis of direct labour cost. Job A, which was started and completed during the current period, shows charges of \$5,000 for direct materials, \$8,000 for direct labour, and \$6,000 for overhead on its job cost sheet. Job B, which is still in process at year-end, shows charges of \$2,500 for direct materials and \$4,000 for direct labour. Should any overhead cost be added to Job B at year-end? Explain and show the amount.

3–15 A company assigns overhead cost to completed jobs on the basis of 125% of direct labour cost. The job cost sheet for Job 313 shows that \$10,000 in direct materials has been used on the job and that $12,000 in direct labour cost has been incurred. If 1,000 units were produced in Job 313, what is the unit product cost?

3–16 What is a plantwide overhead rate? Why are multiple overhead rates, rather than a plantwide overhead rate, used in some companies?

3–17 What happens to overhead rates based on direct labour when automated equipment replaces direct labour?

3–18 Predetermined overhead rates smooth product costs. Do you agree? Why?

3–19 Explain clearly the rationale for why under- and overapplied overhead for an interim period should be carried to the balance sheet. What conceptual factor is assumed in the argument?

3–20 Why does the calculation of the percentages for prorating the under- or overapplied overhead reduce the costs of goods sold by the opening inventories? What would happen if such a deduction were not made?

3–21 (Appendix 3A) If the plant is operated at less than capacity and the predetermined overhead rate is based on the estimated total units in the allocation base at capacity, will overhead ordinarily be overapplied or underapplied?

3–22 (Appendix 3A) Rather than netting underapplied overhead against Cost of Goods Sold or Cost of Goods Sold and ending inventories, some critics suggest an alternative way to disclose underapplied overhead. What is this alternative method?

3–23 Quality control is one way companies can become more sustainable. Explain.

Exercises

EXERCISE 3–1 Process Costing and Job-Order Costing [LO1]

Which would be more appropriate in each of the following situations—job-order costing or process costing?

a. A custom yacht builder.
b. A golf course designer.
c. A potato chip manufacturer.
d. A business consultant.
e. A plywood manufacturer.
f. A soft-drink bottler.
g. A film studio.
h. A firm that supervises bridge construction projects.
i. A manufacturer of fine custom jewellery.
j. A made-to-order clothing factory.
k. A factory making one personal computer model.
l. A fertilizer factory.

EXERCISE 3–2 Job-Order Costing Documents [LO2]

Mountain Gearing Company has incurred the following costs on Job ES34, an order for 40 gearing wheels to be delivered at the end of next month.

Direct materials:

On March 5, requisition number 870 was issued for 40 titanium blanks to be used in the special order. The blanks cost $8.00 each.

On March 8, requisition number 873 was issued for 960 hardened nibs also to be used in the special order. The nibs cost $0.60 each.

Direct labour:

On March 9, Harry Kerst worked from 9:00 A.M. until 12:15 P.M. on Job ES34. He is paid $12.00 per hour.

On March 21, Mary Rosas worked from 2:15 P.M. until 4:30 P.M. on Job ES34. She is paid $14.00 per hour.

Required:

1. On what documents would these costs be recorded?
2. How much cost should have been recorded on each of the documents for Job ES34?

EXERCISE 3–3 Compute the Predetermined Overhead Rate [LO3]

Logan Products computes its predetermined overhead rate annually on the basis of direct labour-hours. At the beginning of the year it estimated that its total manufacturing overhead would be $586,000 and the total direct labour would be 40,000 hours. Its actual total manufacturing overhead for the year was $713,400 and its actual total direct labour was 41,000 hours.

Required:

Compute the company's predetermined overhead rate for the year.

EXERCISE 3–4 Prepare Journal Entries [LO4]

Kirkaid Company recorded the following transactions for the just completed month.

a. $86,000 in raw materials were purchased on account.
b. $84,000 in raw materials were requisitioned for use in production. Of this amount, $72,000 was for direct materials and the remainder was for indirect materials.
c. Total labour wages of $108,000 were incurred. Of this amount, $105,000 was for direct labour and the remainder was for indirect labour.
d. Additional manufacturing overhead costs of $197,000 were incurred.

Required:

Record the above transactions in journal entries.

EXERCISE 3–5 Apply Overhead [LO5]

Westan Corporation uses a predetermined overhead rate of $23.10 per direct labour-hour. This predetermined rate was based on 12,000 estimated direct labour-hours and $277,200 of estimated total manufacturing overhead.

The company incurred actual total manufacturing overhead costs of $266,000 and 12,600 total direct labour-hours during the period.

Required:

Determine the amount of manufacturing overhead that would have been applied to units of product during the period.

EXERCISE 3–6 Applying Overhead; Cost of Goods Manufactured [LO5, LO6, LO7]

The following cost data relate to the manufacturing activities of Black Company during the just completed year:

Manufacturing overhead costs:	
Property taxes, factory	$ 3,000
Utilities, factory	5,000
Indirect labour	10,000
Depreciation, factory	24,000
Insurance, factory	6,000
Total actual manufacturing overhead costs	$48,000
Other costs incurred:	
Purchases of raw materials	$32,000
Direct labour cost	$40,000
Inventories:	
Raw materials, beginning	$ 8,000
Raw materials, ending	$ 7,000
Work in process, beginning	$ 6,000
Work in process, ending	$ 7,500

The company uses a predetermined overhead rate to apply overhead cost to production. The rate for the year was $5 per machine-hour; a total of 10,000 machine-hours was recorded for the year. All raw materials ultimately become direct materials—none are classified as indirect materials.

Required:

1. Compute the amount of underapplied or overapplied overhead cost for the year.
2. Prepare a schedule of cost of goods manufactured for the year.

EXERCISE 3–7 Prepare T-Accounts [LO4, LO6]

Granger Products recorded the following transactions for the just completed month. The company had no beginning inventories.

a. $75,000 in raw materials were purchased for cash.
b. $73,000 in raw materials were requisitioned for use in production. Of this amount, $67,000 was for direct materials and the remainder was for indirect materials.
c. Total labour wages of $152,000 were incurred and paid. Of this amount, $134,000 was for direct labour and the remainder was for indirect labour.
d. Additional manufacturing overhead costs of $126,000 were incurred and paid.
e. Manufacturing overhead costs of $178,000 were applied to jobs using the company's predetermined overhead rate.
f. All of the jobs in progress at the end of the month were completed and shipped to customers.
g. The underapplied or overapplied overhead for the period was closed out to Cost of Goods Sold.

Required:

1. Post the above transactions to T-accounts.
2. Determine the cost of goods sold for the period.

EXERCISE 3–8 Underapplied and Overapplied Overhead [LO7]

Cretin Enterprises uses a predetermined overhead rate of $21.40 per direct labour-hour. This predetermined rate was based on 8,000 estimated direct labour-hours and $171,200 of estimated total manufacturing overhead.

The company incurred actual total manufacturing overhead costs of $172,500 and 8,250 total direct labour-hours during the period.

Required:

1. Determine the amount of underapplied or overapplied manufacturing overhead for the period.
2. Assuming that the entire amount of the underapplied or overapplied overhead is closed out to cost of goods sold, what would be the effect of the underapplied or overapplied overhead on the company's gross margin for the period?

EXERCISE 3–9 Applying Overhead in a Service Company [LO2, LO3, LO5]

Pearson Architectural Design began operations on January 2. The following activity was recorded in the company's Work in Process account for the first month of operations:

Work in Process

Debit		Credit	
Costs of subcontracted work	90,000	To completed projects	570,000
Direct staff costs	200,000		
Studio overhead	320,000		

Pearson Architectural Design is a service firm, so the names of the accounts it uses are different from the names used in manufacturing companies. Costs of Subcontracted Work is comparable to Direct Materials; Direct Staff Costs is the same as Direct Labour; Studio Overhead is the same as Manufacturing Overhead; and Completed Projects is the same as Finished Goods. Apart from the difference in terms, the accounting methods used by the company are identical to the methods used by manufacturing companies.

Pearson Architectural Design uses a job-order costing system and applies studio overhead to Work in Process on the basis of direct staff costs. At the end of January, only one job was still in process. This job (the Krimmer Corporation Headquarters project) had been charged with $13,500 in direct staff costs.

Required:

1. Compute the predetermined overhead rate that was in use during January.
2. Complete the following job cost sheet for the partially completed Krimmer Corporation Headquarters project.

Job Cost Sheet Krimmer Corporation Headquarters Project As of January 31	
Costs of subcontracted work	$?
Direct staff costs	?
Studio overhead	?
Total cost to January 31	$?

EXERCISE 3–10 Journal Entries and T-Accounts [LO4, LO5]

Foley Company uses a job-order costing system. The following data relate to the month of October, the first month of the company's fiscal year:

a. Raw materials purchased on account, $210,000.
b. Raw materials issued to production, $190,000 (80% direct and 20% indirect).
c. Direct labour cost incurred, $49,000; and indirect labour cost incurred, $21,000.
d. Depreciation recorded on factory equipment, $105,000.
e. Other manufacturing overhead costs incurred during October, $130,000 (credit Accounts Payable).
f. The company applies manufacturing overhead cost to production on the basis of $4 per machine-hour. There were 75,000 machine-hours recorded for October.
g. Production orders costing $510,000 according to their job cost sheets were completed during October and transferred to Finished Goods.
h. Production orders that had cost $450,000 to complete according to their job cost sheets were shipped to customers during the month. These goods were sold on account at 50% above cost.

Required:

1. Prepare journal entries to record the information given above.
2. Prepare T-accounts for Manufacturing Overhead and Work in Process. Post the relevant information above to each account. Compute the ending balance in each account, assuming that Work in Process has a beginning balance of $35,000.

EXERCISE 3–11 Applying Overhead in a Service Company; Journal Entries [LO4, LO5, LO7]

Heritage Gardens uses a job-order costing system to track the costs of its landscaping projects. The company provides complete garden design and landscaping services. The following table provides data concerning the three landscaping projects that were in progress during May. There was no work in process at the beginning of May.

	Project		
	Williams	Chandler	Nguyen
Designer-hours	200	80	120
Direct materials cost	$4,800	$1,800	$3,600
Direct labour cost.	$2,400	$1,000	$1,500

Actual overhead costs were $16,000 for May. Overhead costs are applied to projects on the basis of designer-hours since most of the overhead is related to the costs of the garden design studio. The predetermined overhead rate is $45 per designer-hour. The Williams and Chandler projects were completed in May; the Nguyen project was not completed by the end of the month. No other jobs were in process during May.

Required:

1. Compute the amount of overhead cost that would have been charged to each project during May.
2. Prepare a journal entry showing the completion of the Williams and Chandler projects and the transfer of costs to the Completed Projects (i.e., Finished Goods) account.
3. What is the balance in the Work in Process account at the end of the month?
4. What is the balance in the Overhead account at the end of the month? What is this balance called?

EXERCISE 3–12 Varying Predetermined Overhead Rates [LO3, LO5]
Javadi Company makes a composting bin that is subject to wide seasonal variations in demand. Unit product costs are computed on a quarterly basis by dividing each quarter's manufacturing costs (materials, labour, and overhead) by the quarter's production in units. The company's estimated costs, by quarter, for the coming year are given below:

	Quarter			
	First	Second	Third	Fourth
Direct materials	$240,000	$120,000	$ 60,000	$180,000
Direct labour	96,000	48,000	24,000	72,000
Manufacturing overhead	228,000	204,000	192,000	216,000
Total manufacturing costs	$564,000	$372,000	$276,000	$468,000
Number of units to be produced	80,000	40,000	20,000	60,000
Estimated unit product cost	$7.05	$9.30	$13.80	$7.80

Management finds the variation in unit product costs to be confusing and difficult to work with. It has been suggested that the problem lies with manufacturing overhead, since it is the largest element of cost. Accordingly, you have been asked to find a more appropriate way of assigning manufacturing overhead cost to units of product. After some analysis, you have determined that the company's overhead costs are mostly fixed and therefore show little sensitivity to changes in the level of production.

Required:

1. The company uses a job-order costing system. How would you recommend that manufacturing overhead cost be assigned to production? Be specific, and show computations.
2. Recompute the company's unit product costs in accordance with your recommendations in (1) above.

EXERCISE 3–13 Applying Overhead; Journal Entries; Disposition of Underapplied or Overapplied Overhead [LO4, LO7]
The following information is taken from the accounts of FasGrow Company. The entries in the T-accounts are summaries of the transactions that affected those accounts during the year.

Manufacturing Overhead

(a)	380,000	(b)	410,000
		Bal.	30,000

Work in Process

Bal.	105,000	(c)	760,000
	210,000		
	115,000		
(b)	410,000		
Bal.	80,000		

Finished Goods

Bal.	160,000	(d)	820,000
(c)	760,000		
Bal.	100,000		

Cost of Goods Sold

(d)	820,000		

The overhead that had been applied to production during the year is distributed among the ending balances in the accounts as follows:

Work in Process, ending	$ 32,800
Finished Goods, ending	41,000
Cost of Goods Sold	336,200
Overhead applied	$410,000

For example, of the $80,000 ending balance in Work in Process, $32,800 was overhead that had been applied during the year.

Required:

1. Identify the reasons for entries (a) through (d).
2. Assume that the company closes any balance in the Manufacturing Overhead account directly to Cost of Goods Sold. Prepare the necessary journal entry.
3. Assume instead that the company allocates any balance in the Manufacturing Overhead account to the other accounts in proportion to the overhead applied during the year that is in the ending balance in each account. Prepare the necessary journal entry, with supporting computations.

EXERCISE 3–14 (Appendix 3A) Overhead Rates and Capacity Issues [LO3, LO5, LO7, LO8]

Estate Pension Services helps clients to set up and administer pension plans that are in compliance with tax laws and regulatory requirements. The firm uses a job-order costing system in which overhead is applied to clients' accounts on the basis of professional staff hours charged to the accounts. Data concerning two recent years appear below:

	2007	2008
Estimated professional staff hours to be charged to clients' accounts	2,400	2,250
Estimated overhead cost	$144,000	$144,000
Professional staff hours available	3,000	3,000

"Professional staff hours available" is a measure of the capacity of the firm. Any hours available that are not charged to clients' accounts represent unused capacity.

Required:

1. Jennifer Miyami is an established client whose pension plan was set up many years ago. In both 2007 and 2008, only five hours of professional staff time were charged to Ms. Miyami's account. If the company bases its predetermined overhead rate on the estimated overhead cost and the estimated professional staff hours to be charged to clients, how much overhead cost would have been applied to Ms. Miyami's account in 2007? In 2008?
2. Suppose that the company bases its predetermined overhead rate on the estimated overhead cost and the estimated professional staff hours to be charged to clients as in (1) above. Also suppose that the actual professional staff hours charged to clients' accounts and the actual overhead costs turn out to be exactly as estimated in both years. By how much would the overhead be underapplied or overapplied in 2007? In 2008?
3. Refer back to the data concerning Ms. Miyami in (1) above. If the company bases its predetermined overhead rate on the estimated overhead cost and the professional staff hours available, how much overhead cost would have been applied to Ms. Miyami's account in 2007? In 2008?
4. Suppose that the company bases its predetermined overhead rate on the estimated overhead cost and the professional staff hours available as in (3) above. Also suppose that the actual professional staff hours charged to clients' accounts and the actual overhead costs turn out to be exactly as estimated in both years. By how much would the overhead be underapplied or overapplied in 2007? In 2008?

EXERCISE 3–15 Departmental Overhead Rates [LO3, LO5]

Diewold Company has two departments, Milling and Assembly. The company uses a job-order cost system and computes a predetermined overhead rate in each department. The Milling Department bases its rate on machine-hours, and the Assembly Department bases its rate on direct labour cost. At the beginning of the year, the company made the following estimates:

	Department	
	Milling	Assembly
Direct labour-hours	8,000	75,000
Machine-hours	60,000	3,000
Manufacturing overhead cost	$510,000	$800,000
Direct labour cost	$72,000	$640,000

Required:

1. Compute the predetermined overhead rate to be used in each department.
2. Assume that the overhead rates you computed in (1) above are in effect. The job cost sheet for Job 407, which was started and completed during the year, showed the following:

	Department	
	Milling	**Assembly**
Direct labour-hours	5	20
Machine-hours	90	4
Materials requisitioned	$800	$370
Direct labour cost	$45	$160

   Compute the total overhead cost applied to Job 407.
3. Would you expect substantially different amounts of overhead cost to be charged to some jobs if the company used a plantwide overhead rate based on direct labour cost instead of using departmental rates? Explain. No computations are necessary.

EXERCISE 3–16 Applying Overhead; T-Accounts; Journal Entries [LO3, LO4, LO5, LO7]
Medusa Products uses a job-order costing system. Overhead costs are applied to jobs on the basis of machine-hours. At the beginning of the year, management estimated that the company would incur $170,000 in manufacturing overhead costs for the year and work 85,000 machine-hours.

Required:

1. Compute the company's predetermined overhead rate.
2. Assume that during the year the company actually works only 80,000 machine-hours and incurs the following costs in the Manufacturing Overhead and Work in Process accounts:

	Manufacturing Overhead			Work in Process	
(Utilities)	14,000	?	(Direct materials)	530,000	
(Insurance)	9,000		(Direct labour)	85,000	
(Maintenance)	33,000		(Overhead)	?	
(Indirect materials)	7,000				
(Indirect labour)	65,000				
(Depreciation)	40,000				

   Copy the data in the T-accounts above onto your answer sheet. Compute the amount of overhead cost that would be applied to Work in Process for the year, and make the entry in your T-accounts.
3. Compute the amount of underapplied or overapplied overhead for the year, and show the balance in your Manufacturing Overhead T-account. Prepare a journal entry to close out the balance in this account to Cost of Goods Sold.
4. Explain why the manufacturing overhead was underapplied or overapplied for the year.

EXERCISE 3–17 Applying Overhead; Journal Entries; T-Accounts [LO3, LO4, LO5]
Custom Metal Works produces castings and other metal parts to customer specifications. The company uses a job-order costing system and applies overhead costs to jobs on the basis of machine-hours. At the beginning of the year, the company estimated that it would work 576,000 machine-hours and incur $4,320,000 in manufacturing overhead cost.

The company had no work in process at the beginning of the year. The company spent the entire month of January working on one large order—Job 382, which was an order for 8,000 machined parts. Cost data for January follow:

a. Raw materials purchased on account, $315,000.
b. Raw materials requisitioned for production, $270,000 (80% direct and 20% indirect).
c. Labour cost incurred in the factory, $190,000, of which $80,000 was direct labour and $110,000 was indirect labour.
d. Depreciation recorded on factory equipment, $63,000.

e. Other manufacturing overhead costs incurred, $85,000 (credit Accounts Payable).
f. Manufacturing overhead cost was applied to production on the basis of 40,000 machine-hours actually worked during January.
g. The completed job was moved into the finished goods warehouse on January 31 to await delivery to the customer. (In computing the dollar amount for this entry, remember that the cost of a completed job consists of direct materials, direct labour, and *applied* overhead.)

Required:

1. Prepare journal entries to record items (a) through (f) above. Ignore item (g) for the moment.
2. Prepare T-accounts for Manufacturing Overhead and Work in Process. Post the relevant items from your journal entries to these T-accounts.
3. Prepare a journal entry for item (g) above.
4. Compute the unit product cost that will appear on the job cost sheet for Job 382.

Problems

PROBLEM 3–18 Comprehensive Problem [LO3, LO4, LO5, LO6, LO7]
Sovereign Millwork, Ltd., produces reproductions of antique residential moldings at a plant located in Manchester, England. Since there are hundreds of products, some of which are made only to order, the company uses a job-order costing system. On July 1, the start of the company's fiscal year, inventory account balances were as follows:

Raw Materials	£10,000
Work in Process	£4,000
Finished Goods	£8,000

The company applies overhead cost to jobs on the basis of machine-hours. For the fiscal year starting July 1, it was estimated that the plant would operate 45,000 machine-hours and incur £99,000 in manufacturing overhead cost. During the year, the following transactions were completed:

a. Raw materials purchased on account, £160,000.
b. Raw materials requisitioned for use in production, £140,000 (materials costing £120,000 were chargeable directly to jobs; the remaining materials were indirect).
c. Costs for employee services were incurred as follows:

Direct labour	£90,000
Indirect labour	£60,000
Sales commissions	£20,000
Administrative salaries	£50,000

d. Prepaid insurance expired during the year, £18,000 (£13,000 of this amount related to factory operations, and the remainder related to selling and administrative activities).
e. Utility costs incurred in the factory, £10,000.
f. Advertising costs incurred, £15,000.
g. Depreciation recorded on equipment, £25,000. (£20,000 of this amount was on equipment used in factory operations; the remaining £5,000 was on equipment used in selling and administrative activities.)
h. Manufacturing overhead cost was applied to jobs, £ ? . (The company recorded 50,000 machine-hours of operating time during the year.)
i. Goods that had cost £310,000 to manufacture according to their job cost sheets were completed.
j. Sales (all on account) to customers during the year totalled £498,000. These goods had cost £308,000 to manufacture according to their job cost sheets.

Required:

1. Prepare journal entries to record the transactions for the year.
2. Prepare T-accounts for inventories, Manufacturing Overhead, and Cost of Goods Sold. Post relevant data from your journal entries to these T-accounts (don't forget to enter the opening balances in your inventory accounts). Compute an ending balance in each account.

3. Is Manufacturing Overhead underapplied or overapplied for the year? Prepare a journal entry to close any balance in the Manufacturing Overhead account to Cost of Goods Sold.
4. Prepare an income statement for the year. (Do not prepare a schedule of cost of goods manufactured; all of the information needed for the income statement is available in the journal entries and T-accounts you have prepared.)

PROBLEM 3–19 Journal Entries; T-Accounts; Cost Flows [LO4, LO5, LO6, LO7]
Ravsten Company uses a job-order costing system. On January 1, the beginning of the current year, the company's inventory balances were as follows:

Raw materials	$16,000
Work in process...................	$10,000
Finished goods	$30,000

The company applies overhead cost to jobs on the basis of machine-hours. For the current year, the company estimated that it would work 36,000 machine-hours and incur $153,000 in manufacturing overhead cost. The following transactions were recorded for the year:

a. Raw materials purchased on account, $200,000.
b. Raw materials requisitioned for use in production, $190,000 (80% direct and 20% indirect).
c. The following costs were incurred for employee services:

Direct labour	$160,000
Indirect labour...................	$27,000
Sales commissions	$36,000
Administrative salaries	$80,000

d. Heat, power, and water costs incurred in the factory, $42,000.
e. Prepaid insurance expired during the year, $10,000 (90% relates to factory operations, and 10% relates to selling and administrative activities).
f. Advertising costs incurred, $50,000.
g. Depreciation recorded for the year, $60,000 (85% relates to factory operations, and 15% relates to selling and administrative activities).
h. Manufacturing overhead cost was applied to production. The company recorded 40,000 machine-hours for the year.
i. Goods that cost $480,000 to manufacture according to their job cost sheets were transferred to the finished goods warehouse.
j. Sales for the year totalled $700,000 and were all on account. The total cost to manufacture these goods according to their job cost sheets was $475,000.

Required:
1. Prepare journal entries to record the transactions given above.
2. Prepare T-accounts for inventories, Manufacturing Overhead, and Cost of Goods Sold. Post relevant data from your journal entries to these T-accounts (don't forget to enter the opening balances in your inventory accounts). Compute an ending balance in each account.
3. Is Manufacturing Overhead underapplied or overapplied for the year? Prepare a journal entry to close any balance in the Manufacturing Overhead account to Cost of Goods Sold.
4. Prepare an income statement for the year. (Do not prepare a schedule of cost of goods manufactured; all of the information needed for the income statement is available in the journal entries and T-accounts you have prepared.)

PROBLEM 3–20 T-Accounts; Applying Overhead [LO3, LO5, LO6, LO7]
Durham Company's trial balance as of January 1, the beginning of the current year, is is shown at the top of the next page.

Durham Company uses a job-order costing system. During the year, the following transactions took place:

a. Raw materials purchased on account, $45,000.
b. Raw materials requisitioned for use in production, $40,000 (80% direct and 20% indirect).
c. Factory utility costs incurred, $14,600.
d. Depreciation recorded on plant and equipment, $28,000. Three-fourths of the depreciation relates to factory equipment, and the remainder relates to selling and administrative equipment.

Cash	$ 8,000	
Accounts Receivable	13,000	
Raw Materials	7,000	
Work in Process	18,000	
Finished Goods	20,000	
Prepaid Insurance	4,000	
Plant and Equipment	230,000	
Accumulated Depreciation		$ 42,000
Accounts Payable		30,000
Capital Stock		150,000
Retained Earnings		78,000
Total	$300,000	$300,000

e. Costs for salaries and wages were incurred as follows:

Direct labour	$40,000
Indirect labour	$18,000
Sales commissions	$10,400
Administrative salaries	$25,000

f. Prepaid insurance expired during the year, $3,000 (80% relates to factory operations, and 20% relates to selling and administrative activities).
g. Miscellaneous selling and administrative expenses incurred, $18,000.
h. Manufacturing overhead was applied to production. The company applies overhead on the basis of 150% of direct labour cost.
i. Goods that cost $130,000 to manufacture according to their job cost sheets were transferred to the finished goods warehouse.
j. Goods that had cost $120,000 to manufacture according to their job cost sheets were sold on account for $200,000.
k. Collections from customers during the year totalled $197,000.
l. Payments to suppliers on account during the year, $100,000; and payments to employees for salaries and wages, $90,000.

Required:

1. Prepare a T-account for each account in the company's trial balance, and enter the opening balances shown above.
2. Record the transactions above directly into the T-accounts. Prepare new T-accounts as needed. Key your entries to the letters (a) through (l) above. Find the ending balance in each account.
3. Is manufacturing overhead underapplied or overapplied for the year? Make an entry in the T-accounts to close any balance in the Manufacturing Overhead account to Cost of Goods Sold.
4. Prepare an income statement for the year. (Do not prepare a schedule of cost of goods manufactured; all of the information needed for the income statement is available in the T-accounts you have prepared.)

PROBLEM 3–21 Cost Flows; T-Accounts; Income Statement [LO3, LO5, LO6, LO7]
Fantastic Props, Inc., designs and fabricates movie props such as mock-ups of star-fighters and cybernetic robots. The company's balance sheet as of January 1, the beginning of the current year, appears on the next page.

Since each prop is a unique design and may require anything from a few hours to a month or more to complete, Fantastic Props uses a job-order costing system. Overhead in the fabrication shop is charged to props on the basis of direct labour cost. The company estimated that it would incur $80,000 in manufacturing overhead and $100,000 in direct labour cost during the year. The following transactions were recorded during the year:

a. Raw materials, such as wood, paints, and metal sheeting, were purchased on account, $80,000.
b. Raw materials were issued to production, $90,000; $5,000 of this amount was for indirect materials.
c. Payroll costs incurred and paid: direct labour, $120,000; indirect labour, $30,000; and selling and administrative salaries, $75,000.

Fantastic Props, Inc.
Balance Sheet
January 1

Assets		
Current assets:		
Cash		$ 15,000
Accounts receivable		40,000
Inventories:		
Raw materials	$ 25,000	
Work in process	30,000	
Finished goods (props awaiting shipment)	45,000	100,000
Prepaid insurance		5,000
Total current assets		160,000
Buildings and equipment	500,000	
Less accumulated depreciation	210,000	290,000
Total assets		$450,000
Liabilities and Shareholders' Equity		
Accounts payable		$ 75,000
Capital stock	$250,000	
Retained earnings	125,000	375,000
Total liabilities and shareholders' equity		$450,000

d. Fabrication shop utilities costs incurred, $12,000.
e. Depreciation recorded for the year, $30,000 ($5,000 on selling and administrative assets; $25,000 on fabrication shop assets).
f. Prepaid insurance expired, $4,800 ($4,000 related to fabrication shop operations, and $800 related to selling and administrative activities).
g. Shipping expenses incurred, $40,000.
h. Other manufacturing overhead costs incurred, $17,000 (credit Accounts Payable).
i. Manufacturing overhead was applied to production. Overhead is applied on the basis of direct labour cost.
j. Movie props that cost $310,000 to produce according to their job cost sheets were completed.
k. Sales for the year totalled $450,000 and were all on account. The total cost to produce these movie props was $300,000 according to their job cost sheets.
l. Collections on account from customers, $445,000.
m. Payments on account to suppliers, $150,000.

Required:

1. Prepare a T-account for each account on the company's balance sheet, and enter the beginning balances.
2. Make entries directly into the T-accounts for the transactions given above. Create new T-accounts as needed. Determine an ending balance for each T-account.
3. Was manufacturing overhead underapplied or overapplied for the year? Assume that the company allocates any overhead balance between the Work in Process, Finished Goods, and Cost of Goods Sold accounts using the overall balances in each account. Prepare a journal entry to show the allocation. (Round allocation percentages to one decimal place.)
4. Prepare an income statement for the year. (Do not prepare a schedule of cost of goods manufactured; all of the information needed for the income statement is available in the T-accounts.)

PROBLEM 3–22 T-Accounts; Overhead Rates; Journal Entries [LO2, LO3, LO4, LO5]
Kenworth Company uses a job-order costing system. Only three jobs—Job 105, Job 106, and Job 107—were worked on during November and December. Job 105 was completed on December 10; the other two jobs were still in production on December 31, the end of the company's operating year. Data from the job cost sheets of the three jobs follows:

	Job Cost Sheet		
	Job 105	Job 106	Job 107
November costs incurred:			
Direct materials	$16,500	$9,300	$0
Direct labour	$13,000	$7,000	$0
Manufacturing overhead	$20,800	$11,200	$0
December costs incurred:			
Direct materials	$0	$8,200	$21,300
Direct labour	$4,000	$6,000	$10,000
Manufacturing overhead	?	?	?

The following additional information is available:

a. Manufacturing overhead is applied to jobs on the basis of direct labour cost.
b. Balances in the inventory accounts at November 30 were as follows:

Raw Materials	$40,000
Work in Process	?
Finished Goods	$85,000

Required:

1. Prepare T-accounts for Raw Materials, Work in Process, Finished Goods, and Manufacturing Overhead. Enter the November 30 inventory balances given above; in the case of Work in Process, compute the November 30 balance and enter it into the Work in Process T-account.
2. Prepare journal entries for *December* as follows:
   a. Prepare an entry to record the issue of materials into production and post the entry to appropriate T-accounts. (In the case of direct materials, it is not necessary to make a separate entry for each job.) Indirect materials used during December totalled $4,000.
   b. Prepare an entry to record the incurrence of labour cost and post the entry to appropriate T-accounts. (In the case of direct labour cost, it is not necessary to make a separate entry for each job.) Indirect labour cost totalled $8,000 for December.
   c. Prepare an entry to record the incurrence of $19,000 in various actual manufacturing overhead costs for December (credit Accounts Payable). Post this entry to the appropriate T-accounts.
3. What apparent predetermined overhead rate does the company use to assign overhead cost to jobs? Using this rate, prepare a journal entry to record the application of overhead cost to jobs for December (it is not necessary to make a separate entry for each job). Post this entry to the appropriate T-accounts.
4. As stated earlier, Job 105 was completed during December. Prepare a journal entry to show the transfer of this job off of the production line and into the finished goods warehouse. Post the entry to the appropriate T-accounts.
5. Determine the balance at December 31 in the Work in Process inventory account. How much of this balance consists of costs charged to Job 106? Job 107?

PROBLEM 3–23 Multiple Departments; Overhead Rates; Underapplied or Overapplied Overhead [LO3, LO5, LO7]

Winkle, Kotter, and Zale is a small law firm that contains 10 partners and 10 support persons. The firm employs a job-order costing system to accumulate costs chargeable to each client, and it is organized into two departments—the Research and Documents Department and the Litigation Department. The firm uses predetermined overhead rates to charge the costs of these departments to its clients. At the beginning of the current year, the firm's management made the following estimates for the year:

	Department	
	Research and Documents	Litigation
Research-hours	20,000	—
Direct lawyer-hours	9,000	16,000
Materials and supplies	$18,000	$5,000
Direct lawyer cost	$430,000	$800,000
Departmental overhead cost	$700,000	$320,000

The predetermined overhead rate in the Research and Documents Department is based on research-hours, and the rate in the Litigation Department is based on direct lawyer cost.

The costs charged to each client are made up of three elements: materials and supplies used, direct lawyer costs incurred, and an applied amount of overhead from each department in which work is performed on the case.

Case 618-3 was initiated on February 10 and completed on June 30. During this period, the following costs and time were recorded on the case:

	Department	
	Research and Documents	Litigation
Research-hours	18	—
Direct lawyer-hours	9	42
Materials and supplies	$50	$30
Direct lawyer cost	$410	$2,100

Required:

1. Compute the predetermined overhead rate used during the year in the Research and Documents Department. Compute the rate used in the Litigation Department.
2. Using the rates you computed in (1) above, compute the total overhead cost applied to Case 618-3.
3. What would be the total cost charged to Case 618-3? Show computations by department and in total for the case.
4. At the end of the year, the firm's records revealed the following *actual* cost and operating data for all cases handled during the year:

	Department	
	Research and Documents	Litigation
Research-hours	23,000	—
Direct lawyer-hours	8,000	15,000
Materials and supplies	$19,000	$6,000
Direct lawyer cost	$400,000	$725,000
Departmental overhead cost	$770,000	$300,000

Determine the amount of underapplied or overapplied overhead cost in each department for the year.

PROBLEM 3–24 Journal Entries; T-Accounts; Disposition of Underapplied or Overapplied Overhead; Income Statement [LO3, LO4, LO5, LO6, LO7]

Celestial Displays, Inc., puts together large-scale fireworks displays—primarily for Fourth of July celebrations sponsored by corporations and municipalities. The company assembles and orchestrates complex displays using pyrotechnic components purchased from suppliers throughout the world. The company has built a reputation for safety and for the awesome power and brilliance of its computer-controlled shows. Celestial Displays builds its own launch platforms and its own electronic controls. Because of the company's reputation, customers order shows up to a year in advance. Since each show is different in terms of duration and components used, Celestial Displays uses a job-order costing system.

Celestial Displays' trial balance as of January 1, the beginning of the current year, is given on the next page. The company charges manufacturing overhead costs to jobs on the basis of direct labour-hours. (Each customer order for a complete fireworks display is a separate job.) Management estimated that the company would incur $135,000 in manufacturing overhead costs in the fabrication and electronics shops and would work 18,000 direct labour-hours during the year. The following transactions occurred during the year:

a. Raw materials, consisting mostly of skyrockets, mortar bombs, flares, wiring, and electronic components, were purchased on account, $820,000.

b. Raw materials were issued to production, $830,000 ($13,000 of this amount was for indirect materials, and the remainder was for direct materials).

Cash	$ 9,000	
Accounts Receivable	30,000	
Raw Materials	16,000	
Work in Process	21,000	
Finished Goods	38,000	
Prepaid Insurance	7,000	
Buildings and Equipment	300,000	
Accumulated Depreciation		$128,000
Accounts Payable		60,000
Salaries and Wages Payable		3,000
Capital Stock		200,000
Retained Earnings		30,000
Total	$421,000	$421,000

c. Fabrication and electronics shop payrolls were accrued, $200,000 (70% direct labour and 30% indirect labour). A total of 20,800 direct labour-hours were worked during the year.
d. Sales and administrative salaries were accrued, $150,000.
e. The company prepaid additional insurance premiums of $38,000 during the year. Prepaid insurance expiring during the year was $40,000 (only $600 relates to selling and administrative; the other $39,400 relates to the fabrication and electronics shops because of the safety hazards involved in handling fireworks).
f. Marketing cost incurred, $100,000.
g. Depreciation charges for the year, $40,000 (70% relates to fabrication and electronics shop assets, and 30% relates to selling and administrative assets).
h. Property taxes accrued on the shop buildings, $12,600 (credit Accounts Payable).
i. Manufacturing overhead cost was applied to jobs.
j. Jobs completed during the year had a total production cost of $1,106,000 according to their job cost sheets.
k. Revenue (all on account), $1,420,000. Cost of Goods Sold (before any adjustment for underapplied or overapplied overhead), $1,120,000.
l. Cash collections on account from customers, $1,415,000.
m. Cash payments on accounts payable, $970,000. Cash payments to employees for salaries and wages, $348,000.

Required:
1. Prepare journal entries for the year's transactions.
2. Prepare a T-account for each account in the company's trial balance, and enter the opening balances given above. Post your journal entries to the T-accounts. Prepare new T-accounts as needed. Compute the ending balance in each account.
3. Is manufacturing overhead underapplied or overapplied for the year? Prepare the necessary journal entry to close the balance in the Manufacturing Overhead account to Cost of Goods Sold.
4. Prepare an income statement for the year. (Do not prepare a statement of cost of goods manufactured; all of the information needed for the income statement is available in the T-accounts.)

PROBLEM 3–25 Multiple Departments; Applying Overhead [LO3, LO5, LO7]
WoodGrain Technology makes home office furniture from fine hardwoods. The company uses a job-order costing system and predetermined overhead rates to apply manufacturing overhead cost to jobs. The predetermined overhead rate in the Preparation Department is based on machine-hours, and the rate in the Fabrication Department is based on direct materials cost. At the beginning of the year, the company's management made the following estimates for the year:

	Department	
	Preparation	**Fabrication**
Machine-hours	80,000	21,000
Direct labour-hours	35,000	65,000
Direct materials cost	$190,000	$400,000
Direct labour cost	$280,000	$530,000
Manufacturing overhead cost	$416,000	$720,000

Job 127 was started on April 1 and completed on May 12. The company's cost records show the following information concerning the job:

	Department	
	Preparation	Fabrication
Machine-hours	350	70
Direct labour-hours	80	130
Direct materials cost	$940	$1,200
Direct labour cost	$710	$980

Required:

1. Compute the predetermined overhead rate used during the year in the Preparation Department. Compute the rate used in the Fabrication Department.
2. Compute the total overhead cost applied to Job 127.
3. What would be the total cost recorded for Job 127? If the job contained 25 units, what would be the unit product cost?
4. At the end of the year, the records of WoodGrain Technology revealed the following *actual* cost and operating data for all jobs worked on during the year:

	Department	
	Preparation	Fabrication
Machine-hours	73,000	24,000
Direct labour-hours	30,000	68,000
Direct materials cost	$165,000	$420,000
Manufacturing overhead cost	$390,000	$740,000

What was the amount of underapplied or overapplied overhead in each department at the end of the year?

PROBLEM 3–26 (Appendix 3A) Predetermined Overhead Rate and Capacity [LO3, LO5, LO7, LO8]

Skid Road Recording, Inc., is a small audio recording studio located in Calgary. The company handles work for advertising agencies—primarily for radio ads—and has a few singers and bands as clients. Skid Road Recording handles all aspects of recording from editing to making a digital master from which CDs can be copied. The competition in the audio recording industry in Calgary has always been tough, but it has been getting even tougher over the last several years. The studio has been losing customers to newer studios that are equipped with more up-to-date equipment and that are able to offer very attractive prices and excellent service. Summary data concerning the last two years of operations follow:

	2007	2008
Estimated hours of studio service	1,000	750
Estimated studio overhead cost	$90,000	$90,000
Actual hours of studio service provided	900	600
Actual studio overhead cost incurred	$90,000	$90,000
Hours of studio service at capacity	1,800	1,800

The company applies studio overhead to recording jobs on the basis of the hours of studio service provided. For example, 30 hours of studio time were required to record, edit, and master the *Slug Fest* music CD for a local band. All of the studio overhead is fixed, and the actual overhead cost incurred was exactly as estimated at the beginning of the year in both 2007 and 2008.

Required:

1. Skid Road Recording computes its predetermined overhead rate at the beginning of each year based on the estimated studio overhead and the estimated hours of studio service for the year. How much overhead would have been applied to the *Slug Fest* job if it had been done in 2007? In 2008? By how much would overhead have been underapplied or overapplied in 2007? In 2008?

2. The president of Skid Road Recording has heard that some companies in the industry have changed to a system of computing the predetermined overhead rate at the beginning of each year based on the estimated studio overhead for the year and the hours of studio service that could be provided at capacity. He would like to know what effect this method would have on job costs. How much overhead would have been applied using this method to the *Slug Fest* job if it had been done in 2007? In 2008? By how much would overhead have been underapplied or overapplied in 2007 using this method? In 2008?
3. How would you interpret the underapplied or overapplied overhead that results from using studio hours at capacity to compute the predetermined overhead rate?
4. What fundamental business problem is Skid Road Recording facing? Which method of computing the predetermined overhead rate is likely to be more helpful in facing this problem? Explain.

PROBLEM 3–27 T-Account Analysis of Cost Flows [LO3, LO6, LO7]
Selected ledger accounts for Rolm Company are given below for the just completed year:

Raw Materials

Bal. 1/1	30,000	Credits	?
Debits	420,000		
Bal. 12/31	60,000		

Manufacturing Overhead

Debits	385,000	Credits	?

Work in Process

Bal. 1/1	70,000	Credits	810,000
Direct materials	320,000		
Direct labour	110,000		
Overhead	400,000		
Bal. 12/31	?		

Factory Wages Payable

Debits	179,000	Bal. 1/1	10,000
		Credits	175,000
		Bal. 12/31	6,000

Finished Goods

Bal. 1/1	40,000	Credits	?
Debits	?		
Bal. 12/31	130,000		

Cost of Goods Sold

Debits	?		

Required:
1. What was the cost of raw materials put into production during the year?
2. How much of the materials in (1) above consisted of indirect materials?
3. How much of the factory labour cost for the year consisted of indirect labour?
4. What was the cost of goods manufactured for the year?
5. What was the cost of goods sold for the year (before considering underapplied or overapplied overhead)?
6. If overhead is applied to production on the basis of direct materials cost, what rate was in effect during the year?
7. Was manufacturing overhead underapplied or overapplied? By how much?
8. Compute the ending balance in the Work in Process inventory account. Assume that this balance consists entirely of goods started during the year. If $32,000 of this balance is direct materials cost, how much of it is direct labour cost? Manufacturing overhead cost?

PROBLEM 3–28 Schedule of Cost of Goods Manufactured; Overhead Analysis [LO3, LO5, LO6, LO7]
The Pacific Manufacturing Company operates a job-order costing system and applies overhead cost to jobs on the basis of direct labour cost. In computing an overhead rate for the year, the company's estimates were: manufacturing overhead cost, $126,000; and direct labour cost, $84,000. The company has provided the following data in the form of an Excel worksheet:

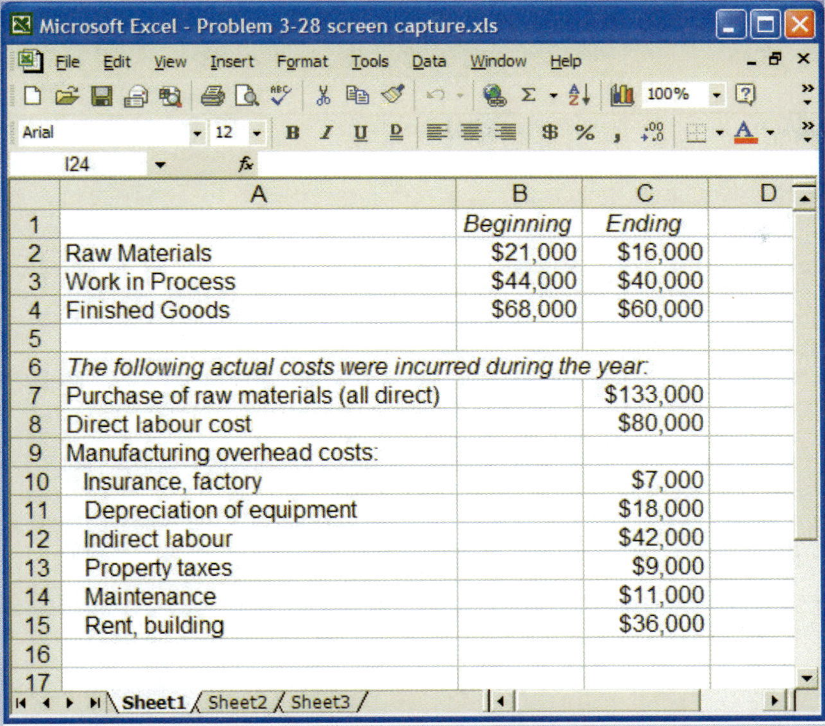

Microsoft Excel - Problem 3-28 screen capture.xls

	A	B	C
1		*Beginning*	*Ending*
2	Raw Materials	$21,000	$16,000
3	Work in Process	$44,000	$40,000
4	Finished Goods	$68,000	$60,000
5			
6	*The following actual costs were incurred during the year:*		
7	Purchase of raw materials (all direct)		$133,000
8	Direct labour cost		$80,000
9	Manufacturing overhead costs:		
10	Insurance, factory		$7,000
11	Depreciation of equipment		$18,000
12	Indirect labour		$42,000
13	Property taxes		$9,000
14	Maintenance		$11,000
15	Rent, building		$36,000
16			
17			

Required:

1. *a.* Compute the predetermined overhead rate for the year.
   b. Compute the amount of underapplied or overapplied overhead for the year.
2. Prepare a schedule of cost of goods manufactured for the year.
3. Compute the cost of goods sold for the year. (Do not include any underapplied or overapplied overhead in your cost of goods sold figure.) What options are available for disposing of underapplied or overapplied overhead?
4. Job 137 was started and completed during the year. What price would have been charged to the customer if the job required $3,200 in materials and $4,200 in direct labour cost, and the company priced its jobs at 40% above the job's cost according to the accounting system?
5. Direct labour made up $8,000 of the $40,000 ending Work in Process inventory balance. Supply the information missing below:

Direct materials	$?
Direct labour	8,000
Manufacturing overhead	?
Work in process inventory	$40,000

PROBLEM 3–29 Predetermined Overhead Rate; Disposition of Underapplied or Overapplied Overhead [LO3, LO7]

Savallas Company is highly automated and uses computers to control manufacturing operations. The company uses a job-order costing system and applies manufacturing overhead cost to products on the basis of computer-hours. The following estimates were used in preparing the predetermined overhead rate at the beginning of the year:

Computer-hours	85,000
Manufacturing overhead cost	$1,530,000

During the year, a severe economic recession resulted in cutting back production and a buildup of inventory in the company's warehouse. The company's cost records revealed the following actual cost and operating data for the year:

Computer-hours	60,000
Manufacturing overhead cost	$1,350,000
Inventories at year-end:	
Raw materials	$400,000
Work in process.	$160,000
Finished goods	$1,040,000
Cost of goods sold	$2,800,000

Required:

1. Compute the company's predetermined overhead rate for the year.
2. Compute the underapplied or overapplied overhead for the year.
3. Assume the company closes any underapplied or overapplied overhead directly to Cost of Goods Sold. Prepare the appropriate entry.
4. Assume that the company allocates any underapplied or overapplied overhead to Work in Process, Finished Goods, and Cost of Goods Sold on the basis of the amount of overhead applied during the year that remains in each account at the end of the year. These amounts are $43,200 for Work in Process, $280,800 for Finished Goods, and $756,000 for Cost of Goods Sold. Prepare the journal entry to show the allocation.
5. How much higher or lower will operating income be for the year if the underapplied or overapplied overhead is allocated rather than closed directly to Cost of Goods Sold?

PROBLEM 3–30 Comprehensive Problem: Journal Entries; T-Accounts; Financial Statements [LO3, LO4, LO5, LO6, LO7]

Southworth Company uses a job-order costing system and applies manufacturing overhead cost to jobs on the basis of the cost of direct materials used in production. At the beginning of the current year, the following estimates were made for the purpose of computing the predetermined overhead rate: manufacturing overhead cost, $248,000; and direct materials cost, $155,000. The following transactions took place during the year (all purchases and services were acquired on account):

a. Raw materials purchased, $142,000.
b. Raw materials requisitioned for use in production (all direct materials), $150,000.
c. Utility bills incurred in the factory, $21,000.
d. Costs for salaries and wages were incurred as follows:

Direct labour	$216,000
Indirect labour	$90,000
Selling and administrative salaries	$145,000

e. Maintenance costs incurred in the factory, $15,000.
f. Advertising costs incurred, $130,000.
g. Depreciation recorded for the year, $50,000 (90% relates to factory assets, and the remainder relates to selling and administrative assets).
h. Rental cost incurred on buildings, $90,000 (80% of the space is occupied by the factory, and 20% is occupied by sales and administration).
i. Miscellaneous selling and administrative costs incurred, $17,000.
j. Manufacturing overhead cost was applied to jobs, $__?__.
k. Cost of goods manufactured for the year, $590,000.
l. Sales for the year (all on account) totalled $1,000,000. These goods cost $600,000 according to their job cost sheets.

The balances in the inventory accounts at the beginning of the year were as follows:

Raw Materials	$18,000
Work in Process	$24,000
Finished Goods	$35,000

Required:

1. Prepare journal entries to record the above data.
2. Post your entries to T-accounts. (Don't forget to enter the opening inventory balances above.) Determine the ending balances in the inventory accounts and in the Manufacturing Overhead account.

3. Prepare a schedule of cost of goods manufactured.
4. Prepare a journal entry to close any balance in the Manufacturing Overhead account to Cost of Goods Sold. Prepare a schedule of cost of goods sold.
5. Prepare an income statement for the year.
6. Job 218 was one of the many jobs started and completed during the year. The job required $3,600 in direct materials and 400 hours of direct labour time at a rate of $11 per hour. If the job contained 500 units and the company billed at 75% above the unit product cost on the job cost sheet, what price per unit would have been charged to the customer?

PROBLEM 3–31 Plantwide versus Departmental Overhead Rates; Underapplied or Overapplied Overhead [LO3, LO5, LO7]

"Don't tell me we've lost another bid!" exclaimed Sandy Kovallas, president of Lenko Products, Inc. "I'm afraid so," replied Doug Martin, the operations vice-president. "One of our competitors underbid us by about $10,000 on the Hastings job." "I just can't figure it out," said Kovallas. "It seems we're either too high to get the job or too low to make any money on half the jobs we bid. What's happened?"

Lenko Products manufactures specialized goods to customers' specifications and operates a job-order costing system. Manufacturing overhead cost is applied to jobs on the basis of direct labour cost. The following estimates were made at the beginning of the year:

	Department			
	Cutting	Machining	Assembly	Total Plant
Direct labour.	$300,000	$200,000	$400,000	$900,000
Manufacturing overhead	$540,000	$800,000	$100,000	$1,440,000

Jobs require varying amounts of work in the three departments. The Hastings job, for example, would have required manufacturing costs in the three departments as follows:

	Department			
	Cutting	Machining	Assembly	Total Plant
Direct materials	$12,000	$900	$5,600	$18,500
Direct labour.	$6,500	$1,700	$13,000	$21,200
Manufacturing overhead	?	?	?	?

The company uses a plantwide overhead rate to apply manufacturing overhead cost to jobs.

Required:

1. Assuming the use of a plantwide overhead rate:
   a. Compute the rate for the current year.
   b. Determine the amount of manufacturing overhead cost that would have been applied to the Hastings job.
2. Suppose that instead of using a plantwide overhead rate, the company had used a separate predetermined overhead rate in each department. Under these conditions:
   a. Compute the rate for each department for the current year.
   b. Determine the amount of manufacturing overhead cost that would have been applied to the Hastings job.
3. Explain the difference between the manufacturing overhead that would have been applied to the Hastings job using the plantwide rate in question 1(b) above and using the departmental rates in question 2(b).
4. Assume that it is customary in the industry to bid jobs at 150% of total manufacturing cost (direct materials, direct labour, and applied overhead). What was the company's bid price on the Hastings job? What would the bid price have been if departmental overhead rates had been used to apply overhead cost?
5. At the end of the year, the company assembled the following *actual* cost data relating to all jobs worked on during the year:

	Department			
	Cutting	Machining	Assembly	Total Plant
Direct materials	$760,000	$90,000	$410,000	$1,260,000
Direct labour	$320,000	$210,000	$340,000	$870,000
Manufacturing overhead	$560,000	$830,000	$92,000	$1,482,000

Compute the underapplied or overapplied overhead for the year (*a*) assuming that a plantwide overhead rate is used, and (*b*) assuming that departmental overhead rates are used.

Cases

CASE 3–32 (Appendix 3A) Ethics; Predetermined Overhead Rate and Capacity [LO5, LO8]

Melissa Ostwerk, the new controller of TurboDrives, Inc., has just returned from a seminar on the choice of the activity level in the predetermined overhead rate. Even though the subject did not sound exciting at first, she found that there were some important ideas presented that should get a hearing at her company. After returning from the seminar, she arranged a meeting with the production manager, Jan Kingman, and the assistant production manager, Lonny Chan.

Melissa: I ran across an idea that I wanted to check out with both of you. It's about the way we compute predetermined overhead rates.

Jan: We're all ears.

Melissa: We compute the predetermined overhead rate by dividing the estimated total factory overhead for the coming year by the estimated total units produced for the coming year.

Lonny: We've been doing that as long as I've been with the company.

Jan: And it has been done that way at every other company I've worked at, except at most places they divide by direct labour-hours.

Melissa: We use units because it is simpler and we basically make one product with minor variations. But, there's another way to do it. Instead of dividing the estimated total factory overhead by the estimated total units produced for the coming year, we could divide by the total units produced at capacity.

Lonny: Oh, the Marketing Department will love that. It will drop the costs on all of our products. They'll go wild over there cutting prices.

Melissa: That is a worry, but I wanted to talk to both of you first before going over to Marketing.

Jan: Aren't you always going to have a lot of underapplied overhead?

Melissa: That's correct, but let me show you how we would handle it. Here's an example based on our budget for next year.

Budgeted (estimated) production	80,000 units
Budgeted sales	80,000 units
Capacity	100,000 units
Selling price	$70 per unit
Variable manufacturing cost	$18 per unit
Total manufacturing overhead cost (all fixed)	$2,000,000
Selling and administrative expenses (all fixed)	$1,950,000
Beginning inventories	$0

Traditional approach to computation of the predetermined overhead rate:

$$\text{Predetermined overhead rate} = \frac{\text{Estimated total manufacturing overhead cost}}{\text{Estimated total amount of the allocation base}}$$

$$= \frac{\$2{,}000{,}000}{80{,}000 \text{ units}} = \$25 \text{ per unit}$$

Budgeted Income Statement

Revenue (80,000 units × $70 per unit)		$5,600,000
Cost of goods sold:		
Variable manufacturing (80,000 units × $18 per unit)	$1,440,000	
Manufacturing overhead applied (80,000 units × $25 per unit)	2,000,000	3,440,000
Gross margin		2,160,000
Selling and administrative expenses		1,950,000
Operating income		$ 210,000

New approach to computation of the predetermined overhead rate using capacity in the denominator:

$$\text{Predetermined overhead rate} = \frac{\text{Estimated total manufacturing overhead cost at capacity}}{\text{Estimated total amount of the allocation base at capacity}}$$

$$= \frac{\$2{,}000{,}000}{100{,}000 \text{ units}} = \$20 \text{ per unit}$$

Budgeted Income Statement

Revenue (80,000 units × $70 per unit)		$5,600,000
Cost of goods sold:		
Variable manufacturing (80,000 units × $18 per unit)	$1,440,000	
Manufacturing overhead applied (80,000 units × $20 per unit)	1,600,000	3,040,000
Gross margin		2,560,000
Cost of unused capacity [(100,000 units − 80,000 units) × $20 per unit]		400,000
Selling and administrative expenses		1,950,000
Operating income		$ 210,000

Jan: Whoa!! I don't think I like the looks of that "Cost of unused capacity." If that thing shows up on the income statement, someone from headquarters is likely to come down here looking for some people to lay off.

Lonny: I'm worried about something else, too. What happens when sales are not up to expectations? Can we pull the "hat trick"?

Melissa: I'm sorry, I don't understand.

Jan: Lonny's talking about something that happens fairly regularly. When sales are down and profits look like they are going to be lower than the president told the owners they were going to be, the president comes down here and asks us to deliver some more profits.

Lonny: And we pull them out of our hat.

Jan: Yeah, we just increase production until we get the profits we want.

Melissa: I still don't understand. You mean you increase sales?

Jan: Nope, we increase production. We're the production managers, not the sales managers.

Melissa: I get it. Since you have produced more, the sales force has more units it can sell.

Jan: Nope, the marketing people don't do a thing. We just build inventories and that does the trick.

Required:

In all of the questions below, assume that the predetermined overhead rate under the traditional method is $25 per unit, and under the new method it is $20 per unit. Also assume that under the traditional method any underapplied or overapplied overhead is taken directly to the income statement as an adjustment to Cost of Goods Sold.

1. Suppose actual production is 80,000 units. Compute the operating incomes that would be realized under the traditional and new methods if actual sales are 75,000 units and everything else turns out as expected.
2. How many units would have to be produced under each of the methods in order to realize the budgeted operating income of $210,000 if actual sales are 75,000 units and everything else turns out as expected?

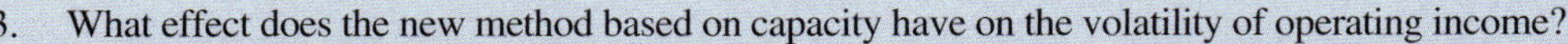

3. What effect does the new method based on capacity have on the volatility of operating income?
4. Will the "hat trick" be easier or harder to perform if the new method based on capacity is used?
5. Do you think the "hat trick" is ethical?

CASE 3–33 Critical Thinking; Interpretation of Manufacturing Overhead Rates [LO3, LO5]

Sharpton Fabricators Corporation manufactures a variety of parts for the automotive industry. The company uses a job-order costing system with a plantwide predetermined overhead rate based on direct labour-hours. On December 10, 2007, the company's controller made a preliminary estimate of the predetermined overhead rate for 2008. The new rate was based on the estimated total manufacturing overhead cost of $2,475,000 and the estimated 52,000 total direct labour-hours for 2008:

$$\text{Predetermined overhead rate} = \frac{\$2{,}475{,}000}{52{,}000 \text{ hours}}$$
$$= \$47.60 \text{ per direct labour-hour}$$

This new predetermined overhead rate was communicated to top managers in a meeting on December 11. The rate did not cause any comment because it was within a few pennies of the overhead rate that had been used during 2007. One of the subjects discussed at the meeting was a proposal by the production manager to purchase an automated milling machine centre built by Central Robotics. The president of Sharpton Fabricators, Kevin Reynolds, agreed to meet with the regional sales representative from Central Robotics to discuss the proposal.

On the day following the meeting, Mr. Reynolds met with Jay Warner, Central Robotics' sales representative. The following discussion took place:

Reynolds: Larry Winter, our production manager, asked me to meet with you since he is interested in installing an automated milling machine centre. Frankly, I am skeptical. You're going to have to show me this isn't just another expensive toy for Larry's people to play with.

Warner: That shouldn't be too difficult, Mr. Reynolds. The automated milling machine centre has three major advantages. First, it is much faster than the manual methods you are using. It can process about twice as many parts per hour as your present milling machines. Second, it is much more flexible. There are some up-front programming costs, but once those have been incurred, almost no setup is required on the machines for standard operations. You just punch in the code of the standard operation, load the machine's hopper with raw material, and the machine does the rest.

Reynolds: Yeah, but what about cost? Having twice the capacity in the milling machine area won't do us much good. That centre is idle much of the time anyway.

Warner: I was getting there. The third advantage of the automated milling machine centre is lower cost. Larry Winters and I looked over your present operations, and we estimated that the automated equipment would eliminate the need for about 6,000 direct labour-hours a year. What is your direct labour cost per hour?

Reynolds: The wage rate in the milling area averages about $21 per hour. Fringe benefits raise that figure to about $30 per hour.

Warner: Don't forget your overhead.

Reynolds: Next year the overhead rate will be about $48 per hour.

Warner: So including fringe benefits and overhead, the cost per direct labour-hour is about $78.

Reynolds: That's right.

Warner: Since you can save 6,000 direct labour-hours per year, the cost savings would amount to about $468,000 a year.

Reynolds: That's pretty impressive, but you aren't giving away this equipment are you?

Warner: Several options are available, including leasing and outright purchase. Just for comparison purposes, our 60-month lease plan would require payments of only $300,000 per year.

Reynolds: Sold! When can you install the equipment?

Shortly after this meeting, Mr. Reynolds informed the company's controller of the decision to lease the new equipment, which would be installed over the Christmas vacation period. The controller realized that this decision would require a recomputation of the predetermined overhead rate for the year 2008 since the decision would affect both the manufacturing overhead and the direct labour-hours for the year. After talking with both the production manager and the sales representative from Central Robotics, the controller discovered that in addition to the annual lease cost of $300,000, the new machine would also require a skilled technician/programmer who would have to be hired at a cost of $45,000 per year to maintain and program the equipment. Both of these costs would be included in factory overhead. There would be no other changes in total manufacturing overhead cost, which is almost entirely fixed. The controller assumed that the new machine would result in a reduction of 6,000 direct labour-hours for the year from the levels that had initially been planned.

When the revised predetermined overhead rate for the year 2008 was circulated among the company's top managers, there was considerable dismay.

Required:

1. Recompute the predetermined rate assuming that the new machine will be installed. Explain why the new predetermined overhead rate is higher (or lower) than the rate that was originally estimated for the year 2008.
2. What effect (if any) would this new rate have on the cost of jobs that do not use the new automated milling machine?
3. Why would managers be concerned about the new overhead rate?
4. After seeing the new predetermined overhead rate, the production manager admitted that he probably wouldn't be able to eliminate all of the 6,000 direct labour-hours. He had been hoping to accomplish the reduction by not replacing workers who retire or quit, but that would not be possible. As a result, the real labour savings would be only about 2,000 hours—one worker. In the light of this additional information, evaluate the original decision to acquire the automated milling machine from Central Robotics.

CASE 3–34 Ethics and the Manager [LO3, LO5, LO7]

Cristin Madsen has recently been transferred to the Appliances Division of Solequin Corporation. Shortly after taking over her new position as divisional controller, she was asked to develop the division's predetermined overhead rate for the upcoming year. The accuracy of the rate is important because it is used throughout the year and any overapplied or underapplied overhead is closed out to Cost of Goods Sold at the end of the year. Solequin Corporation uses direct labour-hours in all of its divisions as the allocation base for manufacturing overhead.

To compute the predetermined overhead rate, Cristin divided her estimate of the total manufacturing overhead for the coming year by the production manager's estimate of the total direct labour-hours for the coming year. She took her computations to the division's general manager for approval but was quite surprised when he suggested a modification in the base. Her conversation with the general manager of the Appliances Division, Lance Jusic, went like this:

Madsen: Here are my calculations for next year's predetermined overhead rate. If you approve, we can enter the rate into the computer on January 1 and be up and running in the job-order costing system right away this year.

Jusic: Thanks for coming up with the calculations so quickly, and they look just fine. There is, however, one slight modification I would like to see. Your estimate of the total direct labour-hours for the year is 110,000 hours. How about cutting that to about 105,000 hours?

Madsen: I don't know if I can do that. The production manager says she will need about 110,000 direct labour-hours to meet the sales projections for next year. Besides, there are going to be over 108,000 direct labour-hours during the current year and sales are projected to be higher next year.

Jusic: Cristin, I know all of that. I would still like to reduce the direct labour-hours in the base to something like 105,000 hours. You probably don't know that I had an agreement with your predecessor as divisional controller to shave 5% or so off the estimated direct labour-hours every year. That way, we kept a reserve that usually resulted in a big boost to operating income at the end of the fiscal year in December. We called it our Christmas bonus. Corporate headquarters always seemed as pleased as punch that we could pull off such a miracle at the end of the year. This system has worked well for many years, and I don't want to change it now.

Required:

1. Explain how shaving 5% off the estimated direct labour-hours in the base for the predetermined overhead rate usually results in a big boost in operating income at the end of the fiscal year.
2. Should Cristin Madsen go along with the general manager's request to reduce the direct labour-hours in the predetermined overhead rate computation to 105,000 direct labour-hours?

Research

R 3–35 Job Costing Systems and Risks [LO1, LO2, LO3]
The questions in this exercise are based on Bird Construction Income Fund, a general contractor that operates branches through its subsidiary, Bird Construction Company, in Toronto, Winnipeg, Calgary, Edmonton, Vancouver, and Seattle, Washington. To answer the questions, you will need to download Bird's 2006 annual report. Go to www.sedar.com and find Bird Construction by clicking "company profiles" and searching for the company under "B." You do not need to print these documents to answer the questions.

Required

1. What are the key drivers for success of Bird Construction Income Fund?
2. What business risks does Bird Construction face that may threaten the company's ability to satisfy unit-holder expectations? What are some examples of control activities that the company could use to reduce these risks?
3. Would Bird Construction be more likely to use process costing or job-order costing? Why?
4. What are some examples of Bird Construction's direct material costs? Would you expect the bill of materials for each of Bird's residential buildings to be the same or different? Why?
5. Describe the type of direct labour costs incurred by Bird Construction when constructing a residential building. Would Bird Construction use employee time tickets at their home sites under construction? Why or why not?
6. What are some examples of overhead costs that are incurred by Bird Construction to create a housing community?
7. Assume that Bird is engaged in building several planned communities. Suggest how overhead costs related to these planned communities may be assigned. From a financial reporting standpoint, why does the entity need to assign manufacturing overhead costs to cost objects? What kinds of cost related to residential construction would be included in inventory?

R 3–36 Enterprise Systems and Job Costing [LO1, LO2, LO4, LO6]
Use the web sites of Oracle or SAP to locate applications of ERP and XML to company costing operations. Form a list of five companies and determine if job costing is appropriate for them or whether any is a merchandiser.

R 3–37 Costing Systems and Overhead [LO1, LO3, LO7, LO8]
Windpower is a popular environmentally friendly electrical power-generating system. In 2006, 944 megawatts of capacity (944,000 kilowatts) were reportedly installed in Canada and much more is in the planning stages.

The Natural Resources Canada web site (www.canren.gc.ca) and the Canadian Wind Energy Association web site (www.canea.ca) provide historical, technical, and operational descriptions of activities in Canada. www.canea.ca even provides brief case studies of some Canadian projects.

Required

1. Describe how you believe the operations of wind farms would be costed. List as many cost elements as you deem appropriate.
2. Would the use of different definitions of activity amounts be useful in providing cost information?

CHAPTER 4

LEARNING OBJECTIVES

After studying Chapter 4, you should be able to:

1. Record the flow of materials, labour, and overhead through a process costing system.
2. Compute the equivalent units of production using the weighted-average method.
3. Compute the cost per equivalent unit using the weighted-average method.
4. Assign cost to units using the weighted-average method.
5. (Appendix 4A) Compute the equivalent units of production using the FIFO method.
6. (Appendix 4A) Compute the cost per equivalent unit using the FIFO method.
7. (Appendix 4A) Assign costs to units using the FIFO method.
8. (Appendix 4B) Allocate service department costs to operating department costs using the direct method.
9. (Appendix 4B) Allocate service department costs to operating department costs using the step-down method.
10. (Appendix 4B) Allocate service department costs to other departments using the reciprocal method.
11. (Online Appendix 4C) Compute the cost of lost units or shrinkage.

SYSTEMS DESIGN: PROCESS COSTING

BUSINESS FOCUS

Costing Cream Soda

Using an old family recipe, Megan started a company in Toronto that produced cream soda. At first the company struggled, but as sales increased, the company expanded rapidly. Megan soon realized that to expand any further, it would be necessary to borrow money. The investment in additional equipment was too large for her to finance out of the company's current cash flows.

Megan was disappointed to find that few banks were willing to make a loan to such a small company, but she finally found a bank that would consider her loan application. However, Megan was informed that she would have to supply up-to-date financial statements with her loan application.

Megan had never bothered with financial statements before—she felt that as long as the balance in the company's chequebook kept increasing, the company was doing fine. She wondered how she was going to determine the value of the cream soda in the work in process and finished goods inventories. The valuation of the cream soda would affect both the cost of goods sold and the inventory balances of her company. Megan thought of perhaps using job-order costing, but her company produces only one product. Raw ingredients were continually being mixed to make more cream soda, and more bottled cream soda was always coming off the end of the bottling line. Megan didn't see how she could use a job-order costing system, since the job never really ended. Perhaps there was another way to account for the costs of producing the cream soda.

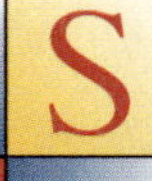

As explained in Chapter 3, there are two basic costing systems in use: job-order costing and process costing. A job-order costing system is used in situations where many different jobs or products are worked on each period. Examples of industries that would typically use job-order costing include furniture manufacturers, special-order printers, shipbuilders, and many types of service organizations, such as repair shops and professional accounting services.

Process costing
A costing method used in situations where essentially homogeneous products are produced on a continuous basis.

By contrast, **process costing** is most commonly used in industries that produce essentially homogeneous (i.e., uniform) products on a continuous basis, such as bricks, corn flakes, pop, or paper. Process costing is particularly used in companies that convert basic raw materials into homogeneous products, such as Alcan (aluminum ingots), Kimberly-Clark (toilet paper), Dover Mills (flour), Imperial Oil (gasoline and lubricating oils), and Christie's (crackers). In addition, process costing is often employed in companies that use an assembly operation, such as Panasonic (video monitors), Hewlett Packard (personal computers), General Electric (refrigerators), Toyota (automobiles), Maytag (washing machines), and Sony (DVD players). A form of process costing may also be used in utilities that produce gas, water, and electricity. As suggested by the length of this list, process costing is in very wide use.

Our purpose in this chapter is to extend the discussion of product costing to include a process costing system.

Comparison of Job-Order and Process Costing

In some ways, process costing is very similar to job-order costing, and in some ways it is very different. In this section, we focus on these similarities and differences in order to provide a foundation for the detailed discussion of process costing that follows.

Similarities between Job-Order and Process Costing

Much of what was learned in the preceding chapter about costing and cost flows applies equally well to process costing in this chapter. We are not throwing out all that we have learned about costing and starting from scratch with a whole new system. The similarities that exist between job-order and process costing can be summarized as follows:

1. Both systems have the same basic purposes—to assign materials, labour, and overhead costs to products and to provide a mechanism for computing unit costs.
2. Both systems use the same basic manufacturing accounts, including Manufacturing Overhead, Raw Materials, Work in Process, and Finished Goods.
3. The flow of costs through the manufacturing accounts is basically the same in both systems.

As can be seen from this comparison, much of the knowledge that we have already acquired about costing is applicable to a process costing system. Our task now is simply to refine and extend this knowledge to process costing.

Differences between Job-Order and Process Costing

The differences between job-order and process costing arise from two factors. The first is that the flow of units in a process costing system is more or less continuous, and the second is that these units are indistinguishable from one another. Under process costing, it makes no sense to try to identify materials, labour, and overhead costs with a particular order from a customer (as we did with job-order costing), since each order is just one of many that are filled from a continuous flow of virtually identical units from the production line. Under process costing, we accumulate costs *by department,* rather than by order, and assign these costs equally to all units that pass through the department during a period.

A further difference between the two costing systems is that the job cost sheet is not used in process costing, since the focal point of that method is departments. Instead of using job cost sheets, a document known as a **production report** is prepared for each department in which work is done on products. The production report serves several functions. It provides a summary of the number of units moving through a department during a period, and it also provides a computation of unit costs. In addition, it shows what costs were charged to the department and what disposition was made of these costs. The department production report is the key document in a process costing system.

Production report A report that summarizes all activity in a department's Work in Process account during a period and that contains three parts: a quantity schedule and a computation of equivalent units, a computation of total and unit costs, and a cost reconciliation.

The major differences between job-order and process costing are summarized in Exhibit 4–1.

EXHIBIT 4–1 Differences between Job-Order and Process Costing

Job-Order Costing	Process Costing
1. Many different jobs are worked on during each period, with each job having different production requirements.	1. A single product is produced either on a continuous basis or for long periods of time. All units of product are identical.
2. Costs are accumulated by individual job, regardless of the accounting period during which the work is done.	2. Costs are accumulated by department, during an accounting period.
3. The *job cost sheet* is the key document controlling the accumulation of costs by a job.	3. The *department production report* is the key document showing the accumulation and disposition of costs by a department.
4. Unit costs are computed *by job* on the job cost sheet.	4. Unit costs are computed *by department* on the department production report.

IN BUSINESS

Coca-Cola's Processing Departments

In 2006 Coca-Cola Company sold more than $24 billion of products in over 200 countries. Some of the key processing steps in its bottling process include washing and rinsing bottles, mixing and blending ingredients, filling and capping bottles, and labelling and packaging bottles. Raw material costs are added at various stages during this process. For example, sugar, filtered water, carbon dioxide, and syrup are added during the filling and capping step and paper labels are added during the labelling and packaging stage.

Coca-Cola's manufacturing process is well suited for process costing because it produces a continuous stream of identical bottles of soda. The material costs and conversion costs that are incurred at the various stages of the production process can be assigned to products by spreading them evenly over the total production volume.

Source: The Coca-Cola Company 2006 annual report and http://www.thecoca-colacompany.com/.

A Perspective of Process Cost Flows

Before presenting a detailed example of process costing, it will be helpful to see how manufacturing costs flow through a process costing system.

Processing Departments

Processing department Any location in an organization where work is performed on a product and where materials, labour, or overhead costs are added to the product.

A **processing department** is part of organization where work is performed on a product and where materials, labour, or overhead costs are added to the product. For example, a potato chip factory operated by Frito-Lay might have three processing departments—one for preparing potatoes, one for cooking, and one for inspecting and packaging. A brick factory might have two processing departments—one for mixing and moulding clay into brick form and one for firing the moulded brick. A company can have as many or as few processing departments as are needed to complete a product or service. Some products and services may go through several processing departments, while others may go through only one or two. Regardless of the number of departments involved, all processing departments have two essential features. First, the activity performed in the processing department must be performed uniformly on all of the units passing through it. Second, the output of the processing department must be identical.

Products in a process costing environment, such as bricks or potato chips, typically flow in a sequence from one department to another as in Exhibit 4–2.

IN BUSINESS

Cutting Conversion Costs

Cemex, SA, the world's largest cement maker, owns 54 plants. Each of these plants consumes 800 tonnes of fuel a day heating kilns to 2,700 degrees Fahrenheit. Not suprisingly, energy costs account for 40% of the company's overall conversion costs. Historically, Cemex relied exclusively on coal to heat its kilns; however, faced with soaring coal prices and shrinking profits, the company desperately needed a cheaper fuel. Cemex turned its attention to an oil industry waste product called petroleum coke that burns hotter than coal and costs half as much. The company spent about $150 million to convert its kilns to burn petroleum coke. Overall, Cemex has cut its energy bills by 17%, helping it earn higher profit margins than its biggest rivals.

Source: John Lyons, "Expensive Energy? Burn Other Stuff, One Firm Decides," *The Wall Street Journal*, September 1, 2004, pp. A1 and A8.

The Flow of Materials, Labour, and Overhead Costs

Cost accumulation is simpler in a process costing system than in a job-order costing system. In a process costing system, instead of having to trace costs to hundreds of different jobs, costs are traced to only a few processing departments. In a process costing system, production costs are not identified with specific units or batches of product. Instead, an average unit cost is computed by dividing total production costs for the period by the number of units produced during the same period. This is discussed in more detail later in this chapter.

EXHIBIT 4–2 Sequential Processing Departments

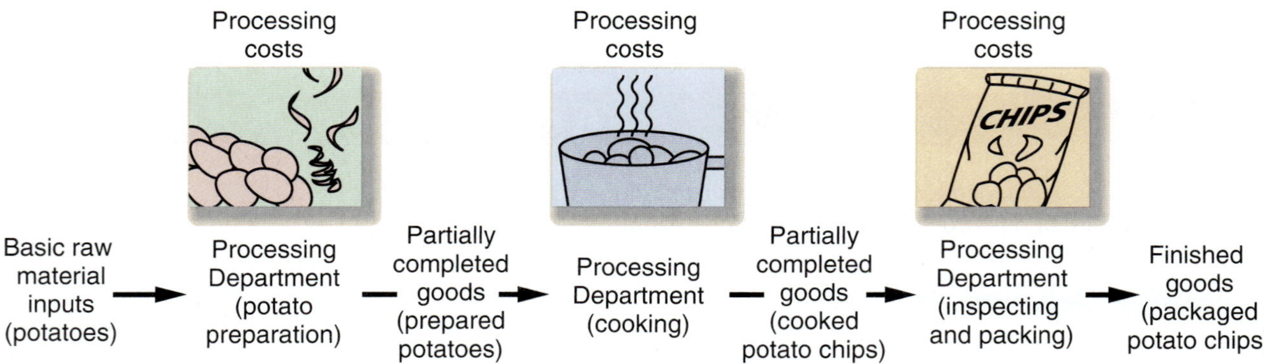

A T-account model of materials, labour, and overhead cost flows in a process costing system is given in Exhibit 4–3. Several key points should be noted from this exhibit. First, note that a separate Work in Process account is maintained for *each processing department.* In contrast, in a job-order costing system there may be only a single Work in Process account for the entire company. Second, note that the completed production of the first processing department (Department A in the exhibit) is transferred into the Work in Process account of the second processing department (Department B), where it undergoes further work. After this further work, the completed units are then transferred into Finished Goods. (In Exhibit 4–3, we show only two processing departments, but a company may have many processing departments.)

Finally, note that materials, labour, and overhead costs can be added in *any* processing department—not just the first. Costs in Department B's Work in Process account would consist of the materials, labour, and overhead costs incurred in Department B plus the costs attached to partially completed units transferred in from Department A (called **transferred-in costs**).

Transferred-in cost The cost attached to products that have been received from a prior processing department.

EXHIBIT 4–3 T-Account Model of Process Costing Flows

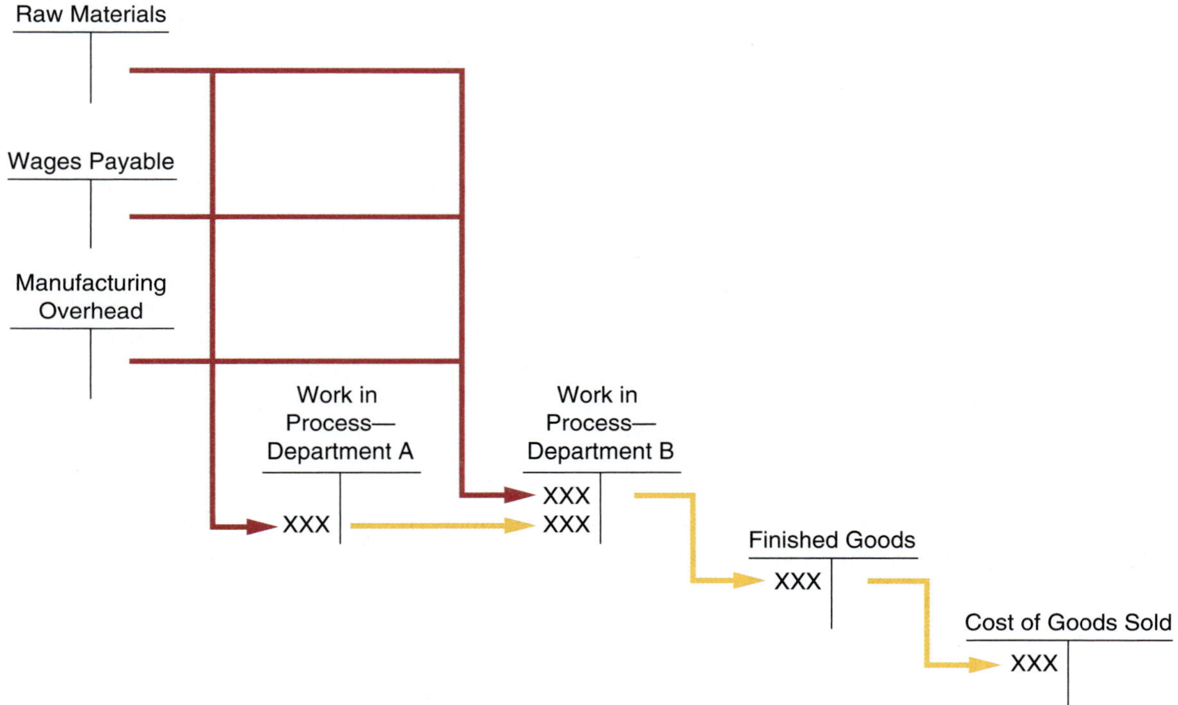

Materials, Labour, and Overhead Cost Entries

To complete our discussion of cost flows in a process costing system, in this section we show journal entries relating to materials, labour, and overhead costs at Megan's Classic Cream Soda, the company mentioned at the beginning of this chapter. Megan's company has two processing departments—Formulating and Bottling. In the Formulating Department, the various ingredients are checked for quality and then mixed and injected with carbon dioxide to create bulk cream soda. In the Bottling Department, bottles are checked for defects, filled with cream soda, capped, visually inspected again for defects, and then packed for shipping.

LEARNING OBJECTIVE 1
Record the flow of materials, labour, and overhead through a process costing system.

Materials Costs As in job-order costing, materials are drawn from the storeroom using a materials requisition form. Materials can be added in any processing department, although it is not unusual for materials to be added only in the first processing department, with subsequent departments adding only labour and overhead costs as the partially completed units move along toward completion.

At Megan's Classic Cream Soda (MCCS), some materials (water, flavourings, sugar, and carbon dioxide) are added in the Formulating Department and other materials (bottles, caps, and packing materials) are added in the Bottling Department The journal entry for placing materials into process in the first department is as follows:

Work in Process—Formulating	XXX	
Raw Materials		XXX

The journal entry to record the material used in the second processing department, the Bottling Department, is as follows:

Work in Process—Bottling	XXX	
Raw Materials		XXX

Labour Costs In process costing, labour costs are traced to departments not to individual jobs. The following entry records the labour costs in the Formulating Department at Megan's Classic Cream Soda:

Work in Process—Formulating	XXX	
Salaries and Wages Payable		XXX

Overhead Costs If production is stable from period to period and if overhead costs are incurred uniformly over the year, actual overhead costs can be charged to products. However, if production levels fluctuate or if overhead costs are not incurred uniformly, charging products with actual overhead costs will result in unit product costs that vary randomly from one period to the next. In such a situation, predetermined overhead rates should be used to charge overhead cost to products, the same as in job-order costing. When predetermined overhead rates are used, each department has its own separate rate with the rates being computed as discussed in Chapter 3. Overhead cost is then applied to units of product as the units move through the various departments. Since predetermined overhead rates are widely used in process costing, we will assume their use throughout the remainder of this chapter.

The following journal entry is used to apply overhead costs to units of product for the Formulating Departments:

Work in Process—Formulating	XXX	
Manufacturing Overhead		XXX

Completing the Cost Flows Once processing has been completed in a department, the product units are transferred to the next department for further processing, as illustrated earlier in the T-accounts in Exhibit 4–3. The following journal entry is used to transfer the costs of partially completed units from the Formulating Department to the Bottling Department:

Work in Process—Bottling	XXX	
Work in Process—Formulating		XXX

After processing has been completed in the final department, the costs of the completed units are then transferred to the Finished Goods inventory account:

Finished Goods	XXX	
Work in Process—Bottling		XXX

Finally, when a customer's order is filled and units are sold, the cost of the units is transferred to Cost of Goods Sold:

Cost of Goods Sold	XXX	
Finished Goods		XXX

To summarize, the cost flows between accounts are basically the same in a process costing system as they are in a job-order costing system. The only noticeable difference at this point is that a process costing system has a separate Work in Process account for each department.

We now turn our attention to Double Diamond Skis, a company that manufactures a high-performance deep-powder ski, and that uses process costing to determine its unit product costs. The company's production process is illustrated in Exhibit 4–4. Skis go through a sequence of five processing departments, starting with the Shaping and Milling Department and ending with the Finishing and Pairing Department. The basic idea in process costing is to add together all of the costs incurred in a department during a period and then spread those costs uniformly across the units processed in that department during that period. As we shall see, applying this simple idea involves a few complications.

Equivalent Units of Production

LEARNING OBJECTIVE 2
Compute the equivalent units of production using the weighted-average method.

After materials, labour, and overhead costs have been accumulated in a department, the department's output must be determined so that unit costs can be computed. In the simplest case average unit cost can be computed by dividing total manufacturing costs by the number of units produced during a given time period. The difficulty is that a department usually has some partially completed units in its ending inventory. It does not seem reasonable to count these partially completed units as equivalent to fully completed units when counting the department's output. Therefore, Diamond Ski will mathematically convert those

EXHIBIT 4–4 The Production Process at Double Diamond Skis*

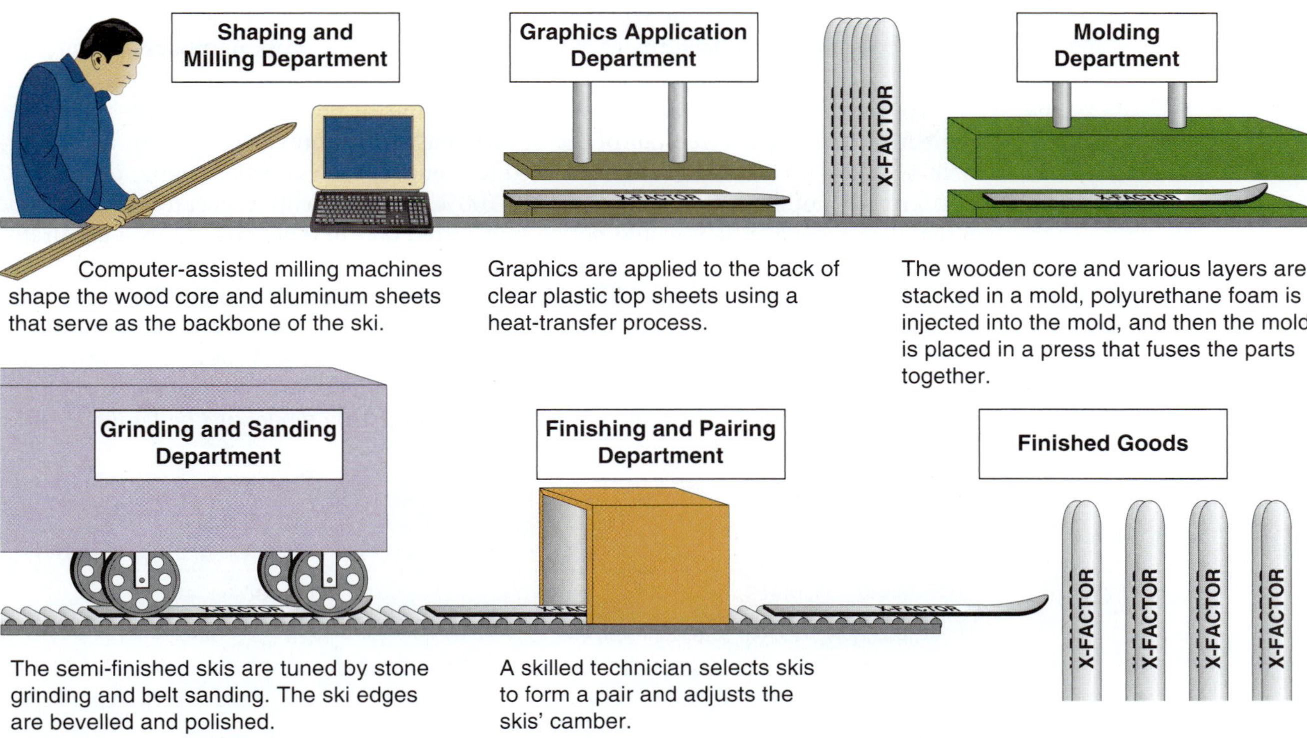

*Adapted from Bill Gout, Jesse James Duquilo, and Studio MD, "Capped Crusaders," *Skiing*, October 1993, pp. 138–144.

partially completed units into an *equivalent* number of fully completed units. In process costing, this is done using the following formula:

$$\text{Equivalent units} = \text{Number of partially completed units} \times \text{percentage completion}$$

Equivalent units
The product of the number of partially completed units and their percentage of completion with respect to a particular cost. Equivalent units are the number of complete whole units one could obtain from the materials and effort contained in partially completed units.

As the formula states, **equivalent units** is defined as the product of the number of partially completed units and the percentage completion of those units. Equivalent units are the number of complete units that could have been obtained from the materials and effort that went into the partially complete units.

For example, suppose the Moulding Department at Double Diamond has 500 units in its ending work in process inventory that are 60% complete. These 500 partially complete units are equivalent to 300 fully complete units (500 × 60% = 300). Therefore, the ending work in process inventory would be said to contain 300 equivalent units. These equivalent units would be added to any fully completed units to determine the period's output for the department—called the *equivalent units of production.*

FIFO method
A method of accounting for cost flows in a process costing system in which equivalent units and unit costs relate only to work done during the current period.

Weighted-average method
A method of process costing that blends together units and costs from both the current and prior periods.

Equivalent units of production (weighted-average method)
The units transferred to the next department (or to finished goods) during the period plus the equivalent units in the department's ending work in process inventory.

Equivalent units of production for a period can be computed in two different ways. In this chapter, we discuss the *weighted-average method.* In Appendix 4A, the *FIFO method* is discussed. The **FIFO method** of process costing is a method in which equivalent units and unit costs relate only to work done during the current period. In contrast, the **weighted-average method** blends together units and costs from the current period with units and costs from the prior period. In the weighted-average method, the **equivalent units of production** for a department are the number of units transferred to the next department (or to finished goods) plus the equivalent units in the department's ending work in process inventory.

Weighted-Average Method

Under the weighted-average method, a department's equivalent units are computed as follows:

Weighted-Average Method
(a separate calculation is made for each cost category in each processing department)

$$\text{Equivalent units of production} = \text{Units transferred to the next department or to finished goods} + \text{Equivalent units in ending work in process inventory}$$

Note that the computation of the equivalent units of production involves adding the number of units transferred out of the department to the equivalent units in the department's ending inventory. There is no need to compute the equivalent units for the units transferred out of the department—they are 100% complete with respect to the work done in that department or they would not be transferred out. In other words, each unit transferred out of the department is counted as one equivalent unit.

Consider the Shaping and Milling Department at Double Diamond. This department uses computerized milling machines to precisely shape the wooden core and metal sheets that will be used to form the backbone of the ski (see Exhibit 4–4 for an overview of the production process at Double Diamond). The following activity took place in the department in May, several months into the production of the new model of The Ultimate ski:

		Percent Completed	
	Units	Materials	Conversion
Work in process, May 1	200	55%	30%
Units started into production during May	5,000		
Units completed during May and transferred to the next department	4,800	100%*	100%*
Work in process, May 31	400	40%	25%

*It is always assumed that units transferred out of a department are 100% complete with respect to the processing done in that department.

Conversion cost Direct labour cost plus manufacturing overhead cost.

Note the use of the term *conversion* in the above table. **Conversion cost,** as defined in Chapter 2, is direct labour cost plus manufacturing overhead cost. In process costing, conversion cost is often—but not always—treated as a single element of product cost.

Note that the May 1 beginning work in process was 55% complete with respect to materials costs and 30% complete with respect to conversion costs. This means that 55% of the materials costs required to complete the units had already been incurred. Likewise, 30% of the conversion costs required to complete the units had already been incurred.

Two equivalent unit figures must be computed—one for materials and one for conversion. These computations are shown in Exhibit 4–5.

Note that the computations in Exhibit 4–5 ignore the fact that the units in the beginning work in process inventory were partially complete. For example, the 200 units in beginning inventory were already 30% complete with respect to conversion costs. The 4,800 units transferred to the next department consists of 200 units in the beginning inventory plus 4,600 units started and completed during the current period. The weighted-average method is concerned only with the 4,900 equivalent units that are in the ending inventories and in units transferred to the next department: it is not concerned with the fact that the beginning inventory was already partially complete. In other words, the 4,900 equivalent units computed using the weighted-average method include work that was accomplished in prior periods.

The weighted-average method blends together the work that was accomplished in prior periods with the work that was accomplished in the current period. In the FIFO method, the units and costs of prior periods are cleanly separated from the units and costs of the current period. Some managers believe the FIFO method is more accurate for this reason. However, the FIFO method is more complex than the weighted-average method and for that reason is covered in Appendix 4A.

Averages, in general, hide the details of the elements that make up the average. For example, the average of 2 + 4 is 3. The average of 1 + 5 is 3. If the manager is uninterested in the details of the elements, then the average provides all of the information needed. If costs from one period to the next are approximately equal (for example, 3 + 3) the average is also a reasonable representation of the results. A third explanation for the use of the average approach is the relative size of the beginning inventory of work in process compared to the current production. For example, if the beginning inventory is only one-tenth the current production, the average (weighted) of $\frac{1}{10}$ (1) + $\frac{9}{10}$ (5) = 4.60 is very accurate and very close to a FIFO result. In addition to the advantage of ease of computation, another advantage of the weighted-average method is that it generates very accurate results when costs are relatively stable from one period to the next or when the size of current production dominates the beginning inventory. All of these factors are commonly a characteristic of process cost environments!

Exhibit 4–6 provides an alternative way of looking at the computation of equivalent units of production. Study this exhibit carefully before going on.

EXHIBIT 4–5 Equivalent Units of Production: Weighted-Average Method

	Materials	Conversion
Units transferred to the next department................	4,800	4,800
Work in process, May 31:		
400 units × 40% complete with respect to materials	160	
400 units × 25% complete with respect to conversion		100
Equivalent units of production	4,960	4,900

EXHIBIT 4–6 Visual Perspective of Equivalent Units of Production

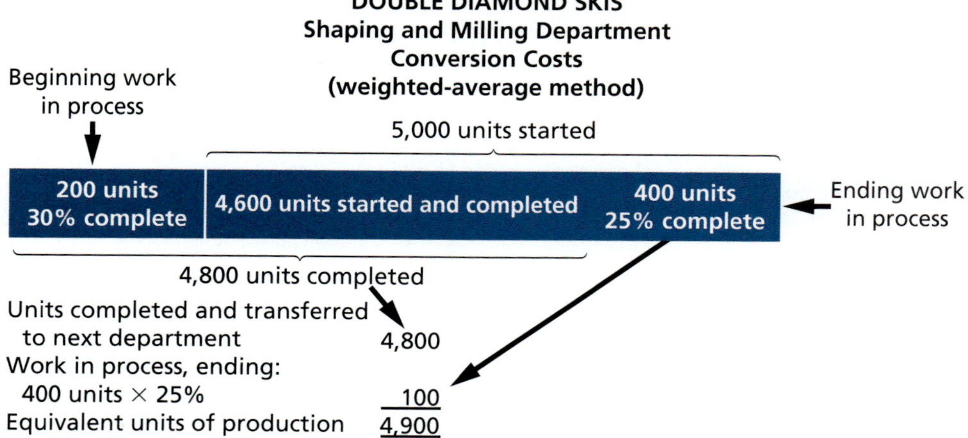

Units completed and transferred to next department	4,800
Work in process, ending: 400 units × 25%	100
Equivalent units of production	4,900

IN BUSINESS

Drug makers now use sophisticated processing systems that help catch errors as they occur rather than after the fact and cost of production reports are used to make informed decisions about expanding capacity. For example, after analyzing its production capacity, Biomedical Corporation announced that it would ship an additional 1.2 million doses of its influenza vaccine, Fluviral(R), to the Canadian market. Fluviral is produced from its two flu vaccine production facilities located in Laval and Quebec City. The Quebec City facility is undergoing expansion to increase its manufacturing capacity to about 50 million doses by 2007. The U.S. government asked Biomedical to consider sending any excess supply to the U.S. under an Investigational New Drug (IND) application. After negotiating with the FDA the company agreed to make production process changes for 2005 and beyond. With the new process in place, including a manufacturing change that is required in the U.S., it is expected that the vaccine will meet FDA approval.

Source: "ID Biomedical to Ship 1.2 Million Doses of Its Flu Vaccine to the Canadian Market," *Canada NewsWire*, Dec. 7, 2004.

Compute and Apply Costs

LEARNING OBJECTIVE 3
Compute the cost per equivalent unit using the weighted-average method.

In the last section we computed the equivalent units of production for materials and for conversion at Double Diamond Skis. In this section we will compute the cost per equivalent unit for materials and for conversion. We will then use these costs to value ending work in process and finished goods inventories. Exhibit 4–7 displays all of the data concerning May's operations in the Shaping and Milling Department that we will need to complete these tasks.

Cost per Equivalent Unit—Weighted-Average Method

In the weighted-average method, the cost per equivalent unit is computed as follows:

Weighted-Average Method
(a separate calculation is made for each cost category in each processing department)

$$\text{Cost per equivalent unit} = \frac{\text{Cost of beginning work in process inventory} + \text{Cost added during the period}}{\text{Equivalent units of production}}$$

EXHIBIT 4–7 Shaping and Milling Department Data for May Operations

Work in process, beginning:	
Units in process	200
Stage of completion with respect to materials	55%
Stage of completion with respect to conversion	30%
Costs in the beginning inventory:	
Materials cost	$ 9,600
Conversion cost	5,575
Total cost in the beginning inventory	$ 15,175
Units started into production during the period	5,000
Units completed and transferred out	4,800
Costs added to production during the period:	
Materials cost	$368,600
Conversion cost	350,900
Total cost added in the department	$719,500
Work in process, ending:	
Units in process	400
Stage of completion with respect to materials	40%
Stage of completion with respect to conversion	25%

Note that the numerator is the sum of the cost of beginning work in process inventory and of the cost added during the period. Thus, the weighted-average method blends together costs from the prior and current periods. That is why it is called the weighted-average method; it averages together units and costs from both the prior and current periods.

The costs per equivalent unit for materials and for conversion are computed below for the Shaping and Milling Department for May:

Shaping and Milling Department
Costs per Equivalent Unit

	Materials	Conversion
Cost of beginning work in process inventory	$ 9,600	$ 5,575
Costs added during the period	368,600	350,900
Total cost (a)	$378,200	$356,475
Equivalent units of production (see the computations in the previous section) (b)	4,960	4,900
Cost per equivalent unit (a) ÷ (b)	$76.25	$72.75

Applying Costs—Weighted-Average Method

LEARNING OBJECTIVE 4
Assign costs to units using the weighted-average method.

The costs per equivalent unit are used to value units in ending inventory and units that are transferred to the next department. For example, each unit transferred out of Double Diamond's Shaping and Milling Department to the Graphics Application Department, as depicted in Exhibit 4–4, will carry with it a cost of $149 ($76.25 for materials cost and $72.75 for conversion cost). Since 4,800 units were transferred out in May to the next department, the total cost assigned to those units would be $715,200 (4,800 units × $149 per unit).

A complete accounting of the costs of both ending work in process inventory and the units transferred out follows:

Shaping and Milling Department
Costs of Ending Work in Process Inventory and the Units Transferred Out

	Materials	Conversion	Total
Ending work in process inventory:			
Equivalent units of production			
400 units × 40% complete with respect to materials			
400 units × 25% complete with respect to conversion (a) . .	160	100	
Cost per equivalent unit (see above) (b)	$76.25	$72.75	
Cost of ending work in process inventory (a) × (b)	$12,200	$7,275	$19,475
Units completed and transferred out:			
Units transferred to the next department (a)	4,800	4,800	
Cost per equivalent unit (see above) (b)	$76.25	$72.75	
Cost of units transferred out (a) × (b)	$366,000	$349,200	$715,200

In each case, the equivalent units are multiplied by the cost per equivalent unit to determine the cost assigned to the units. This is done for each cost category—in this case, materials and conversion. The equivalent units for the units completed and transferred out are simply the number of units transferred to the next department because they would not have been transferred unless they were complete.

The costs assigned to ending work in process inventory and to the units transferred out reconcile with the costs we started with in Exhibit 4–7 as shown below:

Shaping and Milling Department
Cost Reconciliation

Costs to be accounted for:	
Cost of beginning work in process inventory (Exhibit 4–7)	$ 15,175
Costs added to production during the period (Exhibit 4–7).	719,500
Total cost to be accounted for.	$734,675
Costs accounted for as follows:	
Cost of ending work in process inventory (see above)	$ 19,475
Cost of units transferred out (see above).	715,200
Total cost accounted for	$734,675

The $715,200 cost of the units transferred to the next department, Graphics Application, will be accounted for in that department as "costs transferred in." It will be treated in the process costing system as just another category of costs like materials or conversion costs. The only difference is that the costs transferred in will always be 100% complete with respect to the work done in the Graphics Applications Department. Costs are passed on from one department to the next in this fashion, until they reach the last processing department, Finishing and Pairing. When the products are completed in this last department, their costs are transferred to finished goods.

Summary of Double Diamond Skis Costing

Exhibit 4–8 displays a cost of production report for the Shaping and Milling Department costs calculated on the previous pages. The production activity in units is displayed in the Quantity Schedule. This schedule summarizes the activity for the month of May and is used to begin the calculation of equivalent units of production. The schedule of costs per equivalent unit summarizes the production costs for the month of May plus the beginning work in process for May. These costs are used together with the equivalent units from the quantity schedule to compute the weighted unit costs. Finally, the production report is completed by computing the cost reconciliation. The sum of the input costs, work in process May 1 and the May production costs are tested

EXHIBIT 4–8 Production Report—Weighted-Average Method

DOUBLE DIAMOND SKIS
Shaping and Milling Department Production Report
(weighted-average method)

Quantity Schedule and Equivalent Units

	Quantity Schedule	Equivalent Units (EU) Materials	Equivalent Units (EU) Conversion
Units to be accounted for:			
Work in process, May 1 (materials 55% complete; conversion 30% complete)	200		
Started into production	5,000		
Total units	5,200		
Units accounted for as follows:			
Transferred to the next department	4,800	4,800	4,800
Work in process, May 31 (materials 40% complete; conversion 25% complete)	400	160*	100†
Total units and equivalent units of production (see Exhibit 4–5, page 137)	5,200	4,960	4,900

Costs per Equivalent Unit

	Total Cost	Materials		Conversion		Whole Unit
Cost to be accounted for:						
Work in process, May 1	$ 15,175	$ 9,600		$ 5,575		
Cost added in the Shaping and Milling Department	719,500	368,600		350,900		
Total cost (a)	$734,675	$378,200		$356,475		
Equivalent units of production (above) (b) (see above)		4,960		4,900		
Cost per EU, (a) ÷ (b) (see page 139)		$ 76.25	+	$ 72.75	=	$149.00

Cost Reconciliation

	Total Cost	Materials	Conversion
Cost accounted for as follows:			
Transferred to next department:			
4,800 units × $149.00 each (see page 140)	$715,200	4,800	4,800
Work in process, May 31:			
Materials, at $76.25 per EU (see page 140)	12,200	160	
Conversion, at $72.75 per EU	7,275		100
Total work in process, May 31	19,475		
Total cost	$734,675		

*40% × 400 units = 160 equivalent units.
†25% × 400 units = 100 equivalent units.
EU = Equivalent unit.

with the cost of units transferred to the next department and the work in process costs at May 31.

It is important to note that the costs reflected in the cost of production report for May, costs added for May, and costs transferred to the next department are the entries in the work in process account for Double Diamond Skis that will yield the May 31 ending work in process balance of $19,475 in the general ledger when these entries are added to the beginning work in process balance. The cost of production report provides the backup behind the work in process account which carries the costs.

Operation Costing

The costing systems discussed in Chapter 3 and in this chapter represent the two ends of a continuum. On one end, we have job-order costing, which is used by companies that produce many different items—generally to customers' specifications. On the other end, we have process costing, which is used by companies that produce basically homogeneous products in large quantities. Between these two extremes, there are many hybrid systems that include characteristics of both job-order and process costing. One of these hybrids is called *operation costing.*

Operation costing
A hybrid costing system used when products are manufactured in batches and when the products have some common characteristics and some individual characteristics. This system handles materials the same as in job-order costing, and labour and overhead the same as in process costing.

Operation costing is used in situations where products have some common characteristics and also some individual characteristics. Shoes, for example, have common characteristics in that all styles involve cutting and sewing that can be done on a repetitive basis, using the same equipment and following the same basic procedures. Shoes also have individual characteristics—some are made of expensive leathers and others may be made using inexpensive synthetic materials. In a situation such as this, where products have some common characteristics but also must be handled individually, operation costing may be used to determine product costs.

As mentioned above, operation costing is a hybrid system that employs aspects of both job-order and process costing. Products are typically handled in batches when operation costing is in use, with each batch charged for its own specific materials. In this sense, operation costing is similar to job-order costing. However, labour and overhead costs are accumulated by operation or by department, and these costs are assigned to units as in process costing. If shoes are being produced, for example, each shoe is charged the same per unit conversion cost, regardless of the style involved, but it is charged with its specific materials cost. Thus, the company is able to distinguish between styles in terms of materials, but it is able to employ the simplicity of a process costing system for labour and overhead costs.

Examples of other products for which operation costing may be used include electronic equipment (such as semiconductors), textiles, clothing, and jewellery (such as rings, bracelets, and medallions). Products of this type are typically produced in batches, but they can vary considerably from model to model or from style to style in terms of the cost of raw material inputs. Therefore, an operation costing system is well suited for providing cost data.

Flexible Manufacturing Systems

A plant that uses a flexible manufacturing system (FMS) is heavily automated and its activities are organized around cells, or islands, of automated equipment. The FMS concept is having a major impact on costing in several ways. One of these is through allowing companies to switch their systems from the more costly job-order approach to a less costly process or operation approach. This switching is made possible because FMS is proving to be highly efficient in reducing the set-up time required between products and jobs. With set-up time only a small fraction of previous levels, companies are able to move between products and jobs with about the same speed as if they were working in a continuous, process-type environment. The result is that these companies are able to employ process costing techniques in situations that previously required job-order costing. As the use of FMS grows (and becomes even more efficient), some managers predict that job-order costing will slowly disappear except in a few selected industries.

A further impact of FMS is through its focus on cells rather than on departments. Although production reports are still prepared in FMS settings, these reports are either much broader to include the entire production process (many cells) or much narrower to include only a single cell or workstation. If JIT is practised, then the production report becomes greatly simplified, regardless of the level at which it is prepared.

Summary

Process costing is used in situations where homogeneous products or services are produced on a continuous basis. Costs flow through the manufacturing accounts in basically the same way in a process costing system as in a job-order costing system. However, costs are accumulated by department rather than by job in process costing.

In process costing, the equivalent units of production must be determined for each cost category in each department. Under the weighted-average method, the equivalent units of production equals the number of units transferred out to the next department or to finished goods plus the equivalent units in ending work in process inventory. The equivalent units in ending inventory equals the product of the number of partially completed units in ending work in process inventory and their percentage of completion with respect to the specific cost category.

Under the weighted average method, the cost per equivalent unit for a specific cost category is computed by adding the cost of beginning work in process inventory and the cost added during the period and then dividing the result by the equivalent units of production. The cost per equivalent unit is then used to value the ending work in process inventory and the units transferred out to the next department or to finished goods.

Costs are transferred from one department to the next until the last processing department. At that point, the cost of completed units is transferred to finished goods.

Review Problem1: Process Cost Flows and Reports

Luxguard Home Paint Company produces exterior latex paint, which it sells in four-litre containers. The company has two processing departments—Base Fab and Finishing. White paint, which is used as a base for all of the company's paints, is mixed from raw ingredients in the Base Fab Department. Pigments are added to the basic white paint, the pigmented paint is squirted under pressure into four-litre containers, and the containers are labelled and packed for shipping in the Finishing Department. Information relating to the company's operations for April is as follows:

a. Raw materials were issued for use in production: Base Fab Department, $851,000, and Finishing Department, $629,000.
b. Direct labour costs were incurred: Base Fab Department, $330,000, and Finishing Department, $270,000.
c. Manufacturing overhead cost was applied: Base Fab Department, $665,000, and Finishing Department, $405,000.
d. Basic white paint was transferred from the Base Fab Department to the Finishing Department, $1,850,000.
e. Paint that had been prepared for shipping was transferred from the Finishing Department to Finished Goods, $3,200,000.

Required:

1. Prepare journal entries to record items (a) through (e) above.

2. Post the journal entries from (1) above to T-accounts. The balance in the Base Fab Department's Work in Process account on April 1 was $150,000; the balance in the Finishing Department's Work in Process account was $70,000. After posting entries to the T-accounts, find the ending balance in each department's Work in Process account.
3. Prepare a production report for the Base Fab Department for April. The following additional information is available regarding production in the Base Fab Department during April:

Production data for four-litre containers of paint:	
Units (containers) in process, April 1: 100% complete as to materials, 60% complete as to labour and overhead	30,000
Units (containers) started into production during April	420,000
Units (containers) completed and transferred to the Finishing Department	370,000
Units (containers) in process, April 30: 50% complete as to materials, 25% complete as to labour and overhead	80,000
Cost data:	
Work in process inventory, April 1:	
Materials	$ 92,000
Labour	21,000
Overhead	37,000
Total cost	$150,000
Cost added during April:	
Materials	$851,000
Labour	330,000
Overhead	665,000

Solution to Review Problem 1

1. a. Work in Process—Base Fab Department	851,000	
Work in Process—Finishing Department	629,000	
Raw Materials		1,480,000
b. Work in Process—Base Fab Department	330,000	
Work in Process—Finishing Department	270,000	
Salaries and Wages Payable		600,000
c. Work in Process—Base Fab Department	665,000	
Work in Process—Finishing Department	405,000	
Manufacturing Overhead		1,070,000
d. Work in Process—Finishing Department	1,850,000	
Work in Process—Base Fab Department		1,850,000
e. Finished Goods	3,200,000	
Work in Process—Finishing Department		3,200,000

2.

Raw Materials

Bal.	XXX	(a)	1,480,000

Salaries and Wages Payable

		(b)	600,000

Work in Process—Base Fab Department

Bal.	150,000	(d)	1,850,000
(a)	851,000		
(b)	330,000		
(c)	665,000		
Bal.	146,000		

Manufacturing Overhead

(Various actual costs)	(c)	1,070,000

Work in Process—Finishing Department

Bal.	70,000	(e)	3,200,000
(a)	629,000		
(b)	270,000		
(c)	405,000		
(d)	1,850,000		
Bal.	24,000		

Finished Goods

Bal.		XXX
(e)	3,200,000	

LUXGUARD HOME PAINT COMPANY
Production Report—Base Fab Department
For the Month Ended April 30

Quantity Schedule and Equivalent Units

	Quantity Schedule
Units (four-litre containers) to be accounted for:	
Work in process, April 1 (all materials, 60% labour and overhead added last month)	30,000
Started into production	420,000
Total units	450,000

		Equivalent Units (EU)		
		Materials	Labour	Overhead
Units (four-litre containers) accounted for as follows:				
Transferred to Finishing Department	370,000	370,000	370,000	370,000
Work in process, April 30 (materials 50% complete; labour and overhead 25% complete)	80,000	40,000*	20,000*	20,000*
Total units and equivalent units of production	450,000	410,000	390,000	390,000

Costs per Equivalent Unit

	Total Cost	Materials	Labour	Overhead	Whole Unit
Cost to be accounted for:					
Work in process, April 1	$ 150,000	$ 92,000	$ 21,000	$ 37,000	
Cost added by the Base Fab Department	1,846,000	851,000	330,000	665,000	
Total cost (a)	$1,996,000	$943,000	$351,000	$702,000	
Equivalent units of production (b) ...	—	410,000	390,000	390,000	
Cost per EU, (a) ÷ (b)	—	$2.30 +	$0.90 +	$1.80 =	$5.00

Cost Reconciliation

	Total Cost	Materials	Labour	Overhead
Cost accounted for as follows:				
Transferred to				
Finishing Department:				
370,000 units × $5.00 each . . .	$1,850,000	370,000	370,000	370,000
Work in process, April 30:				
Materials, at $2.30 per EU.	92,000	40,000		
Labour, at $0.90 per EU	18,000		20,000	
Overhead, at $1.80 per EU	36,000			20,000
Total work in process	146,000			
Total cost.	$1,996,000			

*Materials: 80,000 units × 50% = 40,000 equivalent units; labour and overhead: 80,000 units × 25% = 20,000 equivalent units.

EU = Equivalent unit.

Review Problem 2: Units and Cost Assignment

Power Company passes its product through several departments, the last of which is the finishing department. Conversion costs are added evenly throughout the process in this department. One-fourth of direct materials is added at the beginning of the process and the remaining three-fourths are added when the process is 50% complete with respect to conversion costs.

During June, 475,000 units of product were transferred to finished goods. Of these units, 100,000 units were 40% complete with respect to conversion costs at the beginning of the period and 375,000 were started and completed during the period. At the end of June, the work in process inventory comprised 225,000 units that were 30% complete with respect to conversion costs. Total costs to account for include $939,675 for conversion costs and $605,625 for direct materials.

Required:

1. Determine equivalent units of production with respect to conversion costs and with respect to direct materials for the finishing department.
2. Compute the conversion cost and the direct materials cost per equivalent unit.
3. Compute the amount of conversion cost and the amount of the direct materials cost assigned to the units completed and to the ending goods in process inventory.

Solution to Review Problem 2

1. Equivalent unit calculations:

		Equivalent Units (EU)	
		Materials	Conversion
Units accounted for as follows:			
Transferred to the next department.	475,000	475,000	475,000
Work in process, June 30:			
material, 25% complete; conversion, 30% complete)	225,000	56,250	67,500
Total units accounted for.	700,000	531,250	542,500

2. Unit cost calculations:

Conversion cost per equivalent unit = $939,675/542,500 units = $1.73

Direct materials cost per equivalent unit = $605,625/531,250 units = $1.14

3. Allocation of materials and conversion cost to products:

	Equivalent Units	Per Unit Cost	Allocated Cost
Transferred out:			
Materials	475,000	$1.14	541,500
Conversion costs	475,000	1.73	821,750
			$1,363,250 a)
Goods in Process			
Materials (225,000 × .25)	56,250	$1.14	$ 64,125
Conversion (225,000 × .3)	67,500	1.73	116,775
			180,900 b)
Total cost accounted for: a) + b)			$1,544,150

Note: Cost to account is $939,675 + $605,625 = $1,545,300. Accounted for $1,544,150. Difference of $1,150 due to rounding.

Appendix 4A: FIFO Method

LEARNING OBJECTIVE 5
Compute the equivalent units of production using the FIFO method.

The FIFO method of process costing differs from the weighted-average method in two ways: (1) the computation of equivalent units, and (2) the way in which costs of beginning inventory are treated. The FIFO method is generally considered more accurate than the weighted-average method, but it is more complex. The complexity is not a problem for computers, but the FIFO method is a little more difficult to understand and to learn than the weighted-average method.

Equivalent Units—FIFO Method

The computation of equivalent units under the FIFO method involves the following.

First, the "units transferred out" is divided into two parts. One part consists of the units from the beginning inventory that were completed and transferred out, and the other part consists of the units that were both *started* and *completed* during the current period.

Second, full consideration is given to the amount of work expended during the current period on units in the *beginning* work in process inventory as well as on units in the ending inventory. Thus, under the FIFO method, both beginning and ending inventories are converted to an equivalent units basis. For the beginning inventory, the equivalent units represent the work done to *complete* the units; for the ending inventory, the equivalent units represent the work done to bring the units to a stage of partial completion at the end of the period (the same as with the weighted-average method):

The formula for computing the equivalent units of production under the FIFO method is more complex than under the weighted-average method:

FIFO Method
(a separate calculation is made for each cost category in each processing department)

Equivalent units of production = Equivalent units to complete beginning work in process inventory*
+ Units started and completed during the period
+ Equivalent units in ending work in process inventory

$$\text{*Equivalent units to complete beginning work in process inventory} = \text{Units in beginning work in process inventory} \times \left(100\% - \text{Percentage completion of beginning work in process inventory}\right)$$

Or, the equivalent units of production can also be determined as follows:

Equivalent units of production = Units transferred out
+ Equivalent units in ending work in process inventory
− Equivalent units in beginning work in process inventory

To illustrate the FIFO method, refer again to the data for the Shaping and Milling Department at Double Diamond Skis. The department completed and transferred 4,800 units to the Graphics Application Department during May. Since 200 of these units came from the beginning inventory, the Shaping and Milling Department must have started and completed 4,600 units during May. The 200 units in the beginning inventory were 55% complete with respect to materials and only 30% complete with respect to conversion costs when the month started. Thus, to complete these units the department must have added another 45% of materials costs (100% − 55% = 45%) and another 70% of conversion costs (100% − 30% = 70%). Following this line of reasoning, the equivalent units for the department for May would be computed as shown in Exhibit 4–9.

Comparison of Equivalent Units of Production under the Weighted-Average and FIFO Methods

Stop at this point and compare the data in Exhibit 4–9 with the data in Exhibit 4–5 in the chapter, which shows the computation of equivalent units under the weighted-average method. Also refer to Exhibit 4–10, which compares the two methods.

The essential difference between the two methods is that the weighted-average method blends work and costs from the prior period with work and costs in the current period, whereas the FIFO method separates the two periods. To see this more clearly, consider the following reconciliation of the two calculations of equivalent units:

Shaping and Milling Department	Materials	Conversion
Equivalent units—weighted-average method	4,960	4,900
Less equivalent units in beginning inventory:		
200 units × 55%	110	
200 units × 30%		60
Equivalent units of production—FIFO method	4,850	4,840

From the above, it is evident that the FIFO method removes the equivalent units that were already in beginning inventory from the equivalent units as defined using the weighted-average method. Thus, the FIFO method isolates the equivalent units due to work performed during the current period. The weighted-average method blends together the equivalent units already in beginning inventory with the equivalent units due to work performed in the current period.

Cost per Equivalent Unit—FIFO Method

LEARNING OBJECTIVE 6
Compute the cost per equivalent unit using the FIFO method.

In the FIFO method, the cost per equivalent unit is computed as follows:

FIFO Method
(a separate calculation is made for each cost category in each processing department)

$$\text{Cost per equivalent unit} = \frac{\text{Cost added during the period}}{\text{Equivalent units of production}}$$

EXHIBIT 4–9 Equivalent Units of Production: FIFO Method

	Materials	Conversion
To complete beginning work in process:		
Materials: 200 units × (100% − 55%)*	90	
Conversion: 200 units × (100% − 30%)*		140
Units started and completed during the period	4,600†	4,600†
Ending work in process:		
Materials: 400 units × 40% complete	160	
Conversion: 400 units × 25% complete		100
Equivalent units of production	4,850	4,840

*This is the work needed to complete the units in beginning inventory.

†5,000 units started − 400 units in ending work in process = 4,600 units started and completed. This can also be computed as 4,800 units completed and transferred to the next department − 200 units in beginning work in process inventory. The FIFO method assumes that the units in beginning inventory are finished first.

EXHIBIT 4–10 Visual Perspective of Equivalent Units of Production—Conversion

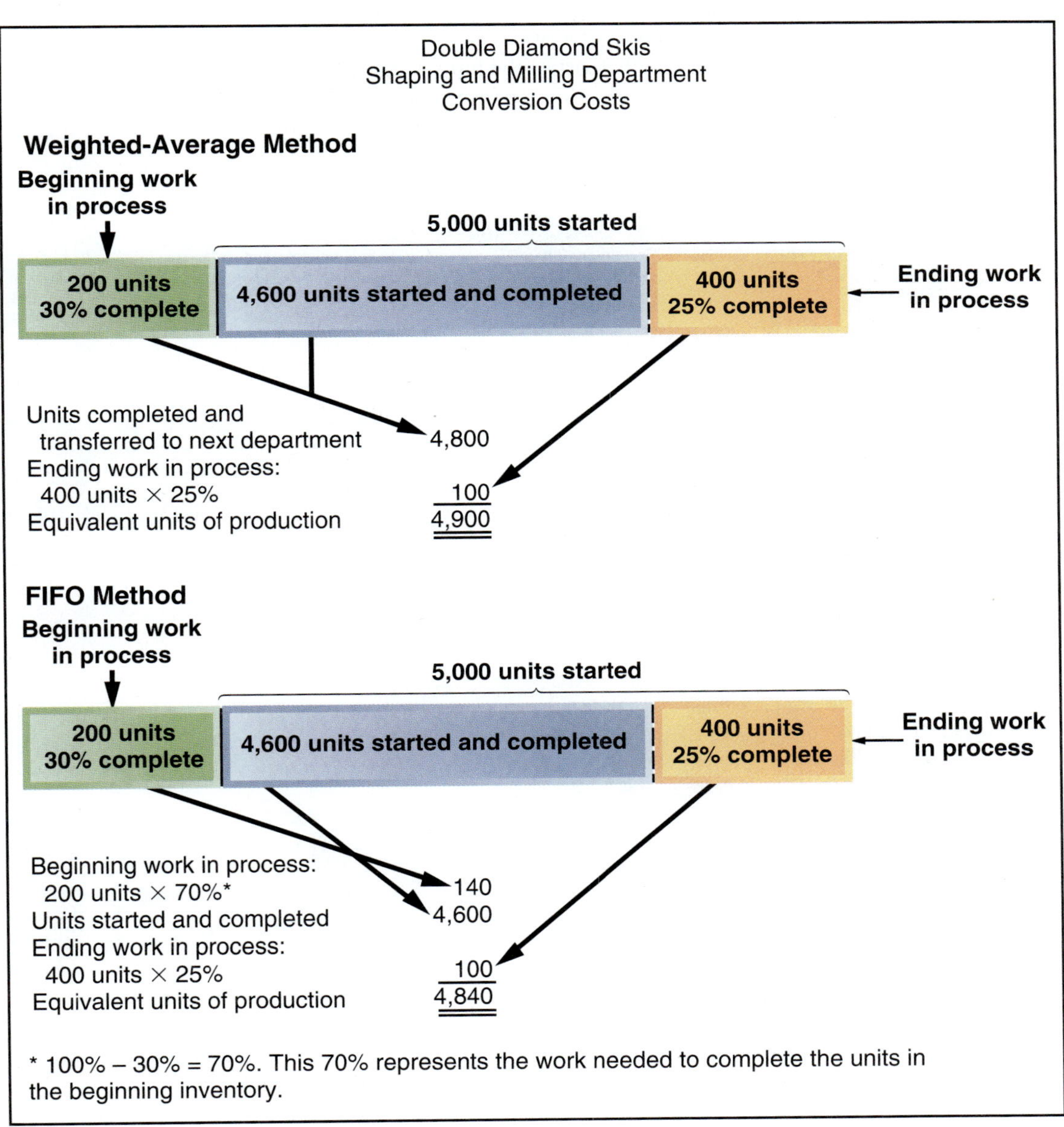

Unlike the weighted-average method, in the FIFO method the cost per equivalent unit is based only on the costs incurred in the department in the current period.

The costs per equivalent unit for materials and for conversion are computed below for the Shaping and Milling Department for May:

Applying Costs—FIFO Method

LEARNING OBJECTIVE 7
Assign costs to units using the FIFO method.

The costs per equivalent unit are used to value units in ending inventory and units that are transferred to the next department. For example, each unit transferred out of the Shaping and Milling Department to the Graphics Application Department will carry with it a cost of $148.50—$76.00 for materials cost and $72.50 for conversion cost for work done in the current period. Since 4,600 units were started and transferred out in May to the next department, the total cost assigned to those units would be $683,100 (4,600 units × $148.50 per unit).

A complete accounting of the costs of both ending work in process inventory and the units transferred out appears below. It is more complicated than the weighted average method. This is because the cost of the units transferred out consists of three separate components: (1) the cost of beginning work in process inventory; (2) the cost to complete the units in beginning work in process inventory; and (3) the cost of units started and completed during the period.

Shaping and Milling Department
Costs of Ending Work in Process Inventory and Units Transferred Out—FIFO Method

	Materials	Conversion	Total
Ending work in process inventory:			
Equivalent units of production (see Exhibit 4–9) (a)	160	100	
Cost per equivalent unit (see above) (b)	$76.00	$72.50	
Cost of ending work in process inventory (a) × (b)	$12,160	$7,250	$ 19,410
Units transferred out:			
Cost in beginning work in process inventory	$9,600	$5,575	$15,175
Cost to complete the units in beginning work in process inventory:			
Equivalent units of production required to complete the units in beginning inventory (see Exhibit 4–9) (a)	90	140	
Cost per equivalent unit (see above) (b)	$76.00	$72.50	
Cost to complete the units in beginning inventory (a) × (b)	$6,840	$10,150	$16,990
Cost of units started and completed this period:			
Units started and completed this period (see Exhibit 4–9) (a)	4,600	4,600	
Cost per equivalent unit (see above) (b)	$76.00	$72.50	
Cost of units started and completed this period (a) × (b)	$349,600	$333,500	$683,100
Total cost of units transferred out			$715,265

Again, note that the cost of the units transferred out consists of three distinct components—the cost of beginning work in process inventory, the cost to complete the units in beginning inventory, and the cost of units started and completed during the period. This is a major difference between the weighted-average and FIFO methods.

The costs assigned to ending work in process inventory and to the units transferred out reconcile with the costs we started with in Exhibit 4–7 as shown below:

Shaping and Milling Department Cost Reconciliation	
Costs to be accounted for:	
Cost of beginning work in process inventory (Exhibit 4–7)	$ 15,175
Costs added to production during the period (Exhibit 4–7)	719,500
Total cost to be accounted for	$734,675
Costs accounted for as follows:	
Cost of ending work in process inventory (see above)	$ 19,410
Cost of units transferred out (see above)	715,265
Total cost accounted for	$734,675

The $715,265 cost of the units transferred to the next department, Graphics Application, will be accounted for in that department as "costs transferred in." As in the weighted-average method, this cost will be treated in the process costing system as just another category of costs like materials or conversion costs. The only difference is that the costs transferred in will always be 100% complete with respect to the work done in the Graphics Applications Department. Costs are passed on from one department to the next in this fashion, until they reach the last processing department, Finishing and Pairing. When the products are completed in this last department, their costs are transferred to finished goods.

It is worth noting at this point the relationship of the costs reflected in the previous illustration to the schedules of cost of goods manufactured presented in Chapters 2 and 3 and the work in process general ledger account. Exhibit 3–11 will help to picture the relationships.

The cost of the beginning work in process inventory, $15,175, is the beginning general ledger balance for work in process. The total manufacturing costs of $719,500 represents the cost of raw material used, the cost of direct labour used and the manufacturing overhead applied during May. These three types of costs, $719,500, increase the work in process account for May. The cost of goods manufactured is $715,265 which represents what is transferred out of work in process for May leaving the ending work in process balance in the general ledger of $19,410. A careful tracing of the description of these costs to the schedule of costs of goods manufactured as shown in Exhibit 3–11 will assist in visualizing how the costs from the production report for process costs link to the general ledger.

A Comparison of Costing Methods

In most situations, the weighted-average and FIFO methods will produce very similar unit costs. If there never are any ending inventories, as in an ideal Lean Production (JIT) environment, the two methods will produce identical results. The reason for this is that without any ending inventories, no costs can be carried forward into the next period and the weighted-average method will base the unit costs on just the current period's costs—just as in the FIFO method. If there *are* ending inventories, either erratic input prices or erratic production levels would also be required to generate much of a difference in unit costs under the two methods. This is because the weighted-average method will blend the unit costs from the prior period with the unit costs of the current period. Unless these unit costs differ greatly, the blending will not make much difference.

Nevertheless, from the standpoint of cost control, the FIFO method is superior to the weighted-average method. Current performance should be measured in relation to costs of the current period only, and the weighted-average method mixes costs of the current period with costs of the prior period. Thus, under the weighted-average method, the manager's apparent performance in the current period is influenced by what happened in the prior period. This problem does not arise under the FIFO method because the FIFO method makes a clear distinction between costs of prior periods and costs incurred during the current period. For the same reason, the FIFO method also provides more up-to-date cost data for decision-making purposes.

On the other hand, the weighted-average method is simpler to apply than the FIFO method, but computers can handle the additional calculations with ease once they have been appropriately programmed.

Appendix 4B: Service Department Allocations

Most large organizations have both *operating departments* and *service departments.* The central purposes of the organization are carried out in the operating departments. In contrast, service departments do not directly engage in operating activities. Instead, they provide services or assistance to the operating departments. Examples of operating departments include the Surgery Department at the QEII Hospital, the Geography Department at St. Mary's, the Marketing Department at Manulife Insurance Company, and production departments at manufacturers such as Bombardier, and Michelin. In process costing, the processing departments are all operating departments. Examples of service departments include Cafeteria, Internal Auditing, Human Resources, Cost Accounting, and Purchasing.

The incurred overhead costs of operating departments commonly include allocations of costs from the service departments. To the extent that service department costs are classified as production costs, they should be included in unit product costs and thus must be allocated to operating departments in a process costing system.

The manufacturing overhead seen in the calculations of process costs shown in Chapter 4 or the job costs shown in Chapter 3 typically reflect overhead applied using a predetermined overhead rate and a base or driver that can be traced to production activity. The other side of the manufacturing overhead account shown in Exhibit 4–3 represents the actual (incurred) overhead for a given period. Actual overhead can represent a complex array of costs that are traced to both operating and service departments. To bring the service department costs to the operating costs for overhead, a method of allocation is needed.

Three approaches are used to allocate the costs of service departments to other departments: the direct method, the step-down method, and the reciprocal method. These three methods are discussed in the following sections. However, before getting into the details of these methods, a few words are in order concerning *interdepartmental services.*

Interdepartmental Services Many service departments provide services to each other, as well as to operating departments. For example, the Cafeteria Department provides meals for all employees, including those assigned to other service departments, as well as to employees of the operating departments. In turn, the Cafeteria Department may receive services from other service departments, such as from Custodial Services or from Personnel. Services provided between service departments are known as *interdepartmental* or *reciprocal services.*

IN BUSINESS

General Motors Trims Support Staff

In difficult economic times, companies frequently look to cut costs within their service departments. Because workers in service departments are not directly involved in making the products that their companies sell, they are often viewed as more expendable than their counterparts employed in operating departments. For example, General Motors (GM) responded to a slowdown in vehicle sales by telling many of its service departments to reduce their headcount by 10%. GM's operating departments were also asked to cut back, but only 3% to 7%.

Source: Dave Guilford, "GM Trims 10% in Some Areas," *Automotive News,* April 7, 2003, p.1.

Direct Method

LEARNING OBJECTIVE 8
Allocate service department costs to operating departments using the direct method.

The *direct method* is the simplest of the three cost allocation methods. It ignores the services provided by a service department to other service departments (e.g., reciprocal services) and allocates all service department costs directly to operating departments. Even if a service department (such as Personnel) provides a large amount of service to another service department (such as the cafeteria), no allocations are made between the two departments. Rather, all costs are allocated *directly* to the operating departments, bypassing the other service departments. Hence the term *direct method.*

For an example of the direct method, assume the QEII Hospital has two service departments and two operating departments as shown below. The hospital allocates its Hospital Administration costs on the basis of employee-hours and its Custodial Services costs on the basis of square metres occupied.

	Service Departments		Operating Departments		
	Hospital Administration	Custodial Services	Laboratory	Patient Care	Total
Departmental costs before allocation	$360,000	$90,000	$261,000	$689,000	$1,400,000
Employee hours.	12,000	6,000	18,000	30,000	66,000
Space occupied—square metres	1,000	20	500	4,500	6,020

The direct method of allocating the hospital's service department costs to the operating departments is shown in Exhibit 4–11. Several things should be noted in this exhibit. First, the employee-hours of the Hospital Administration Department and the Custodial Services Department are ignored when allocating the costs of Hospital Administration using the direct method. *Under the direct method, any of the allocation base attributable to the service departments themselves is ignored; only the amount of the allocation base attributable to the operating departments is used in the allocation.* Note that the same rule is used when allocating the costs of the Custodial Services Department. Even though the Hospital Administration and Custodial Services departments occupy some space, this is ignored when the Custodial Services costs are allocated. Finally, note that after all allocations have been completed, all of the service department costs are contained in the two operating departments. The operating department overhead costs would end up being assigned to production as shown in the main body of this chapter.

Although the direct method is simple, it is less accurate than the other methods because it ignores interdepartmental services.

EXHIBIT 4–11 Direct Method of Allocation

	Service Departments		Operating Departments		
	Hospital Administration	Custodial Services	Laboratory	Patient Care	Total
Departmental costs before allocation.	$360,000	$90,000	$261,000	$689,000	$1,400,000
Allocation:					
Hospital Administration costs ($^{18}/_{48}$, $^{30}/_{48}$)*	(360,000)		135,000	225,000	
Custodial Services costs ($^{5}/_{50}$, $^{45}/_{50}$)†		(90,000)	9,000	81,000	
Total cost after allocation	$ 0	$ 0	$405,000	$995,000	$1,400,000

*Based on the employee-hours in the two operating departments, which are 18,000 hours + 30,000 hours = 48,000 hours.
†Based on the space occupied by the two operating departments, which is 500 square metres + 4500 square metres = 5000 square metres.

Step-Down Method

LEARNING OBJECTIVE 9
Allocate service department costs to operating department costs using the step-down method.

Unlike the direct method, the *step-down method* provides for allocation of a service department's costs to other service departments, as well as to operating departments. The step-down method is sequential. The sequence typically begins with the department that provides the greatest amount of service to other service departments. After its costs have been allocated, the process continues, step by step, ending with the department that provides the least amount of services to other service departments. This step procedure is illustrated in graphic form in Exhibit 4–12.

Exhibit 4–13 shows the details of the step-down method. Note the following three key points about these allocations. First, under Allocation in Exhibit 4–13, you see two allocations, or steps. In the first step, the costs of Hospital Administration are allocated to another service department (Custodial Services) as well as to the operating departments. In contrast to the direct method, the allocation base for Hospital Administration costs now includes the employee-hours for Custodial Services as well as for the operating departments. However, the allocation base still excludes the employee-hours for Hospital Administration itself. *In both the direct and step-down methods, any amount of the allocation base attributable to the service department whose cost is being allocated is always ignored.* Second, looking again at Exhibit 4–12, note that in the second step under the Allocation heading, the cost of Custodial Services is allocated to the two operating departments, and none of the cost is allocated to Hospital Administration even though Hospital Administration occupies space in the building. *In the step-down method, any amount of the allocation base that is attributable to a service department whose cost has already been allocated is ignored.* After a service department's costs have been allocated, costs of other service departments are not reallocated back to it. Third, note that the cost of Custodial Services allocated to other departments in the second step ($130,000) in Exhibit 4–13 includes the costs of Hospital Administration that were allocated to Custodial Services in the first step in Exhibit 4–13.

EXHIBIT 4–12 Graphic Illustration, Step-Down Method

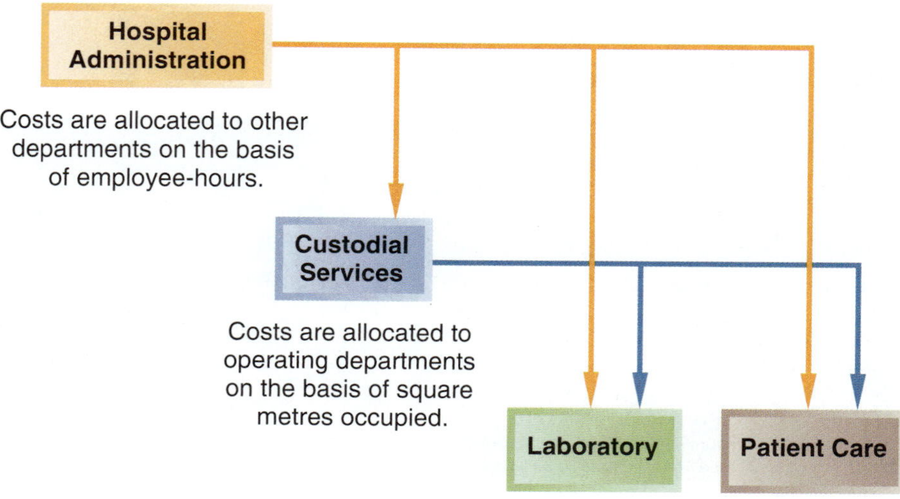

EXHIBIT 4–13 Step-Down Method of Allocation

	Service Departments		Operating Departments		
	Hospital Administration	Custodial Services	Laboratory	Patient Care	Total
Departmental costs before allocation	$360,000	$ 90,000	$261,000	$ 689,000	$1,400,000
Allocation:					
Hospital Administration costs ($^6/_{54}$, $^{18}/_{54}$, $^{30}/_{54}$)*	(360,000)	40,000	120,000	200,000	
Custodial Services costs ($^5/_{50}$, $^{45}/_{50}$)†		(130,000)	13,000	117,000	
Total cost after allocation	$ 0	$ 0	$394,000	$1,006,000	$1,400,000

*Based on the employee-hours in Custodial Services and the two operating departments, which are 6,000 hours + 18,000 hours + 30,000 hours = 54,000 hours.
†As in Exhibit 4–11, this allocation is based on the space occupied by the two operating departments.

Reciprocal Method

LEARNING OBJECTIVE 10
Allocate service department costs to other departments using the reciprocal method.

The **reciprocal method** gives full recognition to interdepartmental services. Under the step method discussed above, only partial recognition of interdepartmental services is possible, since the step method always allocates costs forward—never backward. The reciprocal method, by contrast, allocates service department costs in *both* directions. Thus, since Custodial Services in the prior example provides service for Hospital Administration, part of Custodial Services' costs will be allocated *back* to Hospital Administration if the reciprocal method is used. At the same time, part of Hospital Administration's costs will be allocated *forward* to Custodial Services. This type of reciprocal allocation requires the use of simultaneous linear equations.

Reciprocal method
A method of allocating service department costs that gives full recognition to interdepartmental services.

To illustrate reciprocal allocation, consider the following illustration in Exhibit 4–14 based on Exhibit 4–13 and the data provided about the QEII Hospital.

Note that the amount allocated by Hospital Administration had to be determined outside the schedule before the allocation was made. Similarly the Custodial Services total costs of $132,453 include what was charged from Hospital Administration. These two new amounts include the effect of the reciprocal services each department performed for the other. Once the simultaneous solutions are determined, the allocations proceed as in the step method except that allocations can go backward rather than proceed in sequence as required by the step method. Once the allocations are completed, totals for the operating departments are checked to ensure that the total overhead of $1.4 million was actually allocated. If more than two service departments exist, the solution procedure to determine the amount to be allocated commonly uses matrix inversion, which is beyond the scope of this book.

The reciprocal method has not had a long history of use in practice for two reasons. First, the computations are relatively complex. Currently, this complexity issue can be overcome by the use of computers. Second, the step method usually provides results that are a reasonable approximation of the results that the reciprocal method would provide. Thus, companies have had little motivation to use the more complex reciprocal method.

Revenue-Producing Department

To conclude our discussion of allocation methods, it is important to note that even though most service departments are cost centres and therefore generate no revenues, a few service departments such as the cafeteria may charge for the services they perform. If a service department generates revenues, these revenues should be offset against the department's costs, and only the net amount of cost remaining after this offset should be allocated to other departments within the organization. In this manner, the other departments will not be required to bear costs for which the service department has already been reimbursed.

EXHIBIT 4–14 Reciprocal Allocation

Hospital Administration (HA)

HA = 360,000 + $\frac{2}{12}$ CS

where HA denotes the costs to be allocated; that is, the direct costs plus those allocated [(1,000/(500 + 4,500 + 1,000)] = 1/6 or 2/12] from Custodial Services.

Custodial Services (CS)

CS = 90,000 + $\frac{1}{9}$ HA

where CS denotes the costs to be allocated; that is, the direct costs plus those allocated [(6,000/(18,000 + 30,000 + 6,000)] = 1/9] from Hospital Administration.

To solve (1) −360,000 = −HA + $\frac{2}{12}$ CS

(2) −90,000 = $\frac{1}{9}$ HA − CS

Multiply (2) by 9 (1) −360,000 = −HA + $\frac{2}{12}$ CS

(2) −810,000 = HA − 9 CS

Add (1) and (2) −1,170,000 = 0 − $\frac{106}{12}$ CS

CS = $132,453

Substitute in (1) − 360,000 = −HA + $\frac{2}{12}$(132,453)

HA = $360,000 + $22,076

HA = $382,076

	Service Department		Operating Department		
	Hospital Administration	Custodial Services	Laboratory	Daily Patient Care	Total
Departmental costs before allocation	$ 360,000	$ 90,000	$261,000	$ 689,000	$1,400,000
Allocation:					
Hospital Administration costs ($\frac{1}{9}$, $\frac{3}{9}$, $\frac{5}{9}$).	(382,076)	42,453	127,359	212,264	
Custodial Services costs ($\frac{2}{12}$, $\frac{1}{12}$, $\frac{9}{12}$).	22,076	(132,453)	11,038	99,339	
Totals	$ -0-	$ -0-	$399,397	$1,000,603	$1,400,000

Glossary

Visit the Online Learning Centre at http://www.mcgrawhill.ca/olc/garrison/ for a review of glossary terms and definitions.

Questions

4–1 Under what conditions would it be appropriate to use a process costing system?

4–2 In what ways are job-order and process costing similar?

4–3 Why is cost accumulation easier in a process costing system than it is in a job-order costing system?

4–4 How many Work in Process accounts are maintained in a company that uses process costing?

4–5 Assume that a company has two processing departments—Mixing and Firing. Prepare a journal entry to show a transfer of partially completed units from the Mixing Department to the Firing Department.

4–6 Assume that a company has two processing departments—Mixing followed by Firing. Explain what costs might be added to the Firing Department's Work in Process account during a period.

4–7 What is meant by the term *equivalent units of production* when the weighted-average method is used?

4–8 Watkins Trophies, Inc., produces thousands of medallions made of bronze, silver, and gold. The medallions are identical except for the materials used in their manufacture. What costing system would you advise the company to use?

4–9 How does the use of Lean Production (JIT) reduce or eliminate the difference in unit costs between FIFO and weighted-average methods of accounting for the costs of ending work in process inventory and the costs of goods transferred out?

4–10 (Appendix 4A) How does the computation of equivalent units under the FIFO method differ from the computation of equivalent units under the weighted-average method?

4–11 (Appendix 4A) From the standpoint of cost control, why is the FIFO method superior to the weighted-average method?

4–12 (Appendix 4B) What is the difference between a service department and an operating department?

4–13 (Appendix 4B) How are service department costs assigned to products?

4–14 (Appendix 4B) What are interdepartmental services?

4–15 (Appendix 4B) How are interdepartmental service costs handled under the direct method?

4–16 (Appendix 4B) How are service department costs allocated to other departments under the step-down method?

4–17 (Appendix 4B) How does the reciprocal method allocate interdepartmental services? How does the approach differ from the step method?

Exercises

EXERCISE 4–1 Process Costing Journal Entries [LO1]

Arizona Brick Corporation produces bricks in two processing departments—Molding and Firing. Information relating to the company's operations in March follows:

a. Raw materials were issued for use in production: Molding Department, $28,000; and Firing Department, $5,000.
b. Direct labour costs were incurred: Molding Department, $18,000; and Firing Department, $5,000.
c. Manufacturing overhead was applied: Molding Department, $24,000; and Firing Department, $37,000.
d. Unfired, molded bricks were transferred from the Molding Department to the Firing Department. According to the company's process costing system, the cost of the unfired, molded bricks was $67,000.
e. Finished bricks were transferred from the Firing Department to the finished goods warehouse. According to the company's process costing system, the cost of the finished bricks was $108,000.
f. Finished bricks were sold to customers. According to the company's process costing system, the cost of the finished bricks sold was $106,000.

Required:

Prepare journal entries to record items (a) through (f) above.

EXERCISE 4–2 Computation of Equivalent Units—Weighted-Average Method [LO2]

Lindex Company manufactures a product that goes through three processing departments. Information relating to activity in the first department during October is given below:

		Percent Completed	
	Units	Materials	Conversion
Work in process, October 1	50,000	90%	60%
Work in process, October 31	30,000	70%	50%

The department started 390,000 units into production during the month and transferred 410,000 completed units to the next department.

Required:
Compute the equivalent units of production for the first department for October, assuming that the company uses the weighted-average method of accounting for units and costs.

EXERCISE 4–3 Cost Per Equivalent Unit—Weighted-Average Method [LO3]
Billinstaff Industries uses the weighted-average method in its process costing system. Data for the Assembly Department for May appear below:

	Materials	Labour	Overhead
Work in process, May 1	$14,550	$23,620	$118,100
Cost added during May	$88,350	$14,330	$71,650
Equivalent units of production	1,200	1,100	1,100

Required:
Compute the cost per equivalent unit for materials, for labour, for overhead, and in total.

EXERCISE 4–4 Applying Costs to Units—Weighted-Average Method [LO4]
Data concerning a recent period's activity in the Prep Department, the first processing department in a company that uses process costing, appear below:

	Materials	Conversion
Equivalent units of production in ending work in process	300	100
Cost per equivalent unit	$31.56	$9.32

A total of 1,300 units were completed and transferred to the next processing department during the period.

Required:
Compute the cost of the units transferred to the next department during the period and the cost of ending work in process inventory.

EXERCISE 4–5 (Appendix 4A) Computation of Equivalent Units—FIFO Method [LO5]
QualCon, Inc., produces wine bottles for vintners in a process that starts in the Melt and Mold Department. Data concerning that department's operations in the most recent period appear below:

Beginning work in process:	
Units in process	400
Stage of completion with respect to materials	75%
Stage of completion with respect to conversion	25%
Units started into production during the month	42,600
Units completed and transferred out	42,500
Ending work in process:	
Units in process	500
Stage of completion with respect to materials	80%
Stage of completion with respect to conversion	30%

Required:
QualCon uses the FIFO method in its process costing system. Compute the equivalent units of production for the period for the Melt and Mold Department.

EXERCISE 4–6 (Appendix 4A) Cost per Equivalent Unit—FIFO Method [LO6]
Resprin Company uses the FIFO method in its process costing system. Data for the Assembly Department for May appear below:

	Materials	Labour	Overhead
Cost added during May	$82,560	$52,920	$132,300
Equivalent units of production	16,000	14,000	14,000

Required:
Compute the cost per equivalent unit for materials, for labour, for overhead, and in total.

EXERCISE 4–7 (Appendix 4A) Applying Costs to Units—FIFO Method [LO7]
Data concerning a recent period's activity in the Mixing Department, the first processing department in a company that uses process costing, appear below:

	Materials	Conversion
Cost of work in process inventory at the beginning of the period	$2,700	$380
Equivalent units of production in the ending work in process inventory	800	200
Equivalent units of production required to complete the beginning work in process inventory	400	700
Cost per equivalent unit for the period.	$4.40	$1.30

A total of 8,000 units were completed and transferred to the next processing department during the period. Beginning work in process inventory consisted of 1,000 units and ending work in process inventory consisted of 2,000 units.

Required:
Compute the FIFO cost of the units transferred to the next department during the period and the cost of ending work in process inventory.

EXERCISE 4–8 (Appendix 4B) Direct Method [LO8]

Ignatius College has provided the following data to be used in its service department cost allocations:

	Service Departments		Operating Departments	
	Administration	Physical Plant Services	Undergraduate Programs	Graduate Programs
Departmental costs before allocations	$2,070,000	$720,000	$23,650,000	$2,980,000
Student credit-hours			40,000	5,000
Space occupied in square metres	3,000	500	25,000	5,000

Required:
Using the direct method, allocate the costs of the service departments to the two operating departments. Allocate the costs of the Administration Department on the basis of student credit-hours and the costs of the Physical Plant Services Department on the basis of space occupied.

EXERCISE 4–9 (Appendix 4B) Step-Down Method [LO9]

University District Co-op, a foods grocery and coffee shop, has provided the following data to be used in its service department cost allocations:

	Service Departments		Operating Departments	
	Administration	Building Services	Groceries	Coffee Shop
Departmental costs before allocations.	$200,000	$60,000	$3,860,000	$340,000
Employee-hours	480	320	2,720	160
Space occupied in square metres. . .	800	1,200	9,500	500

Required:
Using the step-down method, allocate the costs of the service departments to the two operating departments. Allocate the costs of the Administration Department first on the basis of employee-hours and then the costs of the Building Services Department on the basis of space occupied.

EXERCISE 4–10 Process Costing Journal Entries [LO1]
Schneider Brot is a bread-baking company located in Aachen, Germany, near the Dutch border. The company uses a process costing system for its single product—a popular pumpernickel bread. Schneider Brot has two processing departments—Mixing and Baking. The T-accounts below show the flow of costs through the two departments in April (all amounts are in the currency euros):

Work in Process—Mixing

Balance 4/1	10,000	Transferred out	760,000
Direct materials	330,000		
Direct labour	260,000		
Overhead	190,000		

Work in Process—Baking

Balance 4/1	20,000	Transferred out	980,000
Transferred in	760,000		
Direct labour	120,000		
Overhead	90,000		

Required:
Prepare journal entries showing the flow of costs through the two processing departments during April.

EXERCISE 4–11 Equivalent Units and Cost per Equivalent Unit—Weighted-Average Method [LO2, LO3]
Kalox, Inc., manufactures an antacid product that passes through two departments. Data for May for the first department follow:

	Litres	Materials	Labour	Overhead
Work in process, May 1	80,000	$68,600	$30,000	$48,000
Litres started in process	760,000			
Litres transferred out	790,000			
Work in process, May 31	50,000			
Cost added during May		$907,200	$370,000	$592,000

The beginning work in process inventory was 80% complete with respect to materials and 75% complete with respect to labour and overhead. The ending work in process inventory was 60% complete with respect to materials and 20% complete with respect to labour and overhead.

Required:
Assume that the company uses the weighted-average method of accounting for units and costs.
1. Compute the equivalent units for May's activity for the first department.
2. Determine the costs per equivalent unit for May.

EXERCISE 4–12 (Appendix 4A) Equivalent Units and Cost per Equivalent Unit—FIFO Method [LO5, LO6]

Refer to the data for Kalox, Inc., in Exercise 4–11.

Required:
Assume that the company uses the FIFO method of accounting for units and costs.
1. Compute the equivalent units for May's activity for the first processing department.
2. Determine the costs per equivalent unit for May.

EXERCISE 4–13 (Appendix 4A) Equivalent Units; Applying Costs—FIFO Method [LO5, LO6, LO7]
Krollon Company uses the FIFO method in its process costing system. The following data are for the most recent month of operations in one of the company's processing departments:

Units in beginning inventory	400		
Units started into production	4,300		
Units in ending inventory	300		
Units transferred to the next department	4,400		
		Materials	**Conversion**
Percentage completion of beginning inventory		70%	30%
Percentage completion of ending inventory		80%	40%

The cost of beginning inventory according to the company's costing system was $7,886 of which $4,897 was for materials and the remainder was for conversion cost. The costs added during the month amounted to $181,652. The costs per equivalent unit for the month were:

	Materials	Conversion
Cost per equivalent unit	$18.20	$23.25

Required:

1. Compute the total cost per equivalent unit for the month.
2. Compute the equivalent units of material and of conversion costs in the ending inventory.
3. Compute the equivalent units of material and of conversion costs that were required to complete the beginning inventory.
4. Determine the number of units started and completed during the month.
5. Determine the costs of ending inventory and units transferred out.

EXERCISE 4–14 Equivalent Units—Weighted-Average Method [LO2]

Gulf Fisheries, Inc., processes tuna for various distributors. Two departments are involved—Cleaning and Packing. Data relating to kilograms of tuna processed in the Cleaning Department during May are given below:

	Kilograms of Tuna	Percent Completed*
Work in process, May 1	15,000	55%
Work in process, May 31	10,000	90%

*Labour and overhead only.

A total of 240,000 kilograms of tuna were started into processing during May. All materials are added at the beginning of processing in the Cleaning Department.

Required:

Compute the equivalent units for May for the Cleaning Department, assuming that the company uses the weighted-average method of accounting for units.

EXERCISE 4–15 (Appendix 4A) Equivalent Units—FIFO Method [LO5]

Refer to the data for Gulf Fisheries, Inc., in Exercise 4–14.

Required:

Compute the equivalent units for May for the Cleaning Department, assuming that the company uses the FIFO method of accounting for units.

EXERCISE 4–16 (Appendix 4B) Step-Down Method [LO9]

Arbon Company has three service departments and two operating departments. Selected data concerning the five departments are presented on the following page.

The company allocates service department costs by the step-down method in the following order: Administrative (number of employees), Janitorial (space occupied), and Equipment Maintenance (machine-hours).

Required:

Using the step-down method, allocate the service department costs to the operating departments.

	Operating Service Departments			Departments		
	Administrative	Janitorial	Equipment Maintenance	Prep	Finishing	Total
Costs	$84,000	$67,800	$36,000	$256,100	$498,600	$942,500
Number of employees	80	60	240	600	300	1,280
Square metres of space occupied	300	1,200	1,000	2,000	7,000	11,500
Machine-hours				10,000	30,000	40,000

EXERCISE 4–17 (Appendix 4B) Direct Method [LO8]
Refer to the data for Arbon Company in Exercise 4–16.

Required:
Assuming that the company uses the direct method rather than the step-down method to allocate service department costs, how much overhead cost would be assigned to each operating department?

EXERCISE 4–18 Equivalent Units and Cost per Equivalent Unit—Weighted-Average Method [LO2, LO3, LO4]
Solex Company produces a high-quality insulation material that passes through two production processes. Data for June for the first process follow:

	Units	Completion with Respect to Materials	Completion with Respect to Conversion
Work in process inventory, June 1	60,000	75%	40%
Work in process inventory, June 30	40,000	50%	25%
Materials cost in work in process inventory, June 1		$56,600	
Conversion cost in work in process inventory, June 1		$14,900	
Units started into production		280,000	
Units transferred to the next process		300,000	
Materials cost added during June		$385,000	
Conversion cost added during June		$214,500	

Required:
1. Assume that the company uses the weighted-average method of accounting for units and costs. Determine the equivalent units for June for the first process.
2. Compute the costs per equivalent unit for June for the first process.
3. Determine the total cost of ending work in process inventory and the total cost of units transferred to the next process in June.

Problems

PROBLEM 4–19 Equivalent Units, Cost per Equivalent Unit, Applying Costs—Weighted-Average Method [LO2, LO3, LO4]
Honeybutter, Inc., manufactures a product that goes through two departments prior to completion. The information shown at the top of page 163 is available about work in the first department, the Mixing Department, during June.

Required:
Assume that the company uses the weighted-average method.
1. Determine the equivalent units for June for the first process.
2. Compute the costs per equivalent unit for June for the first process.

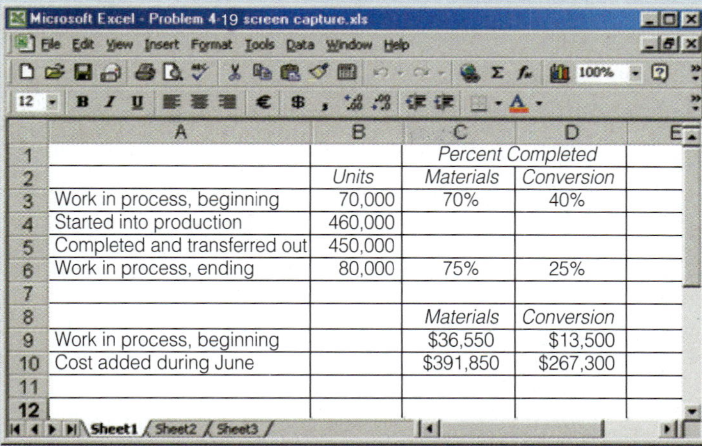

Microsoft Excel - Problem 4-19 screen capture.xls

	A	B	C	D
1			Percent Completed	
2		Units	Materials	Conversion
3	Work in process, beginning	70,000	70%	40%
4	Started into production	460,000		
5	Completed and transferred out	450,000		
6	Work in process, ending	80,000	75%	25%
7				
8			Materials	Conversion
9	Work in process, beginning		$36,550	$13,500
10	Cost added during June		$391,850	$267,300
11				
12				

3. Determine the total cost of ending work in process inventory and the total cost of units transferred to the next process in June.
4. Prepare a report that reconciles the total costs assigned to the ending work in process inventory and the units transferred out with the costs in beginning inventory and costs added during the period.

PROBLEM 4–20 (Appendix 4A) Equivalent Units, Cost per Equivalent Unit, Applying Costs—FIFO Method [LO5, LO6, LO7]

Refer to the data for the Mixing Department in Honeybutter, Inc., in Problem 4–19. Assume that the company uses the FIFO method rather than the weighted-average method in its process costing system.

Required:

1. Determine the equivalent units for June for the first process.
2. Compute the costs per equivalent unit for June for the first process.
3. Determine the total cost of ending work in process inventory and the total cost of units transferred to the next process in June.
4. Prepare a report that reconciles the total costs assigned to the ending work in process inventory and the units transferred out with the costs in beginning inventory and costs added during the period.

PROBLEM 4–21 Equivalent Units; Applying Costs—Weighted-Average Method [LO2, LO3, LO4]

The PVC Company manufactures a high-quality plastic pipe in two departments, Cooking and Molding. Materials are introduced at various points during work in the Cooking Department. After the cooking is completed, the materials are transferred into the Molding Department, in which pipe is formed.

Selected data relating to the Cooking Department during May are given below:

Production data:	
Kilograms in process, May 1: materials 100% complete, conversion 90% complete	70,000
Kilograms started into production during May	350,000
Kilograms completed and transferred to Molding	?
Kilograms in process, May 31: materials 75% complete, conversion 25% complete	40,000
Cost data:	
Work in process inventory, May 1:	
Materials cost	$86,000
Conversion cost	$36,000
Cost added during May:	
Materials cost	$447,000
Conversion cost	$198,000

The company uses the weighted-average method.

Required:

1. Compute the equivalent units of production.
2. Compute the costs per equivalent unit for May.
3. Determine the cost of ending work in process inventory and of the units transferred to the Molding Department.
4. Prepare a cost reconciliation between the costs determined in part (3) above and the cost of beginning inventory and costs added during the period.

PROBLEM 4–22 (Appendix 4A) Equivalent Units; Applying Costs—FIFO Method [LO5, LO6, LO7]

Reutter Company manufactures a single product and uses process costing. The company's product goes through two processing departments, Etching and Wiring. The following activity was recorded in the Etching Department during July:

Production data:	
Units in process, July 1: materials 60% complete, conversion 30% complete	60,000
Units started into production	510,000
Units in process, July 31: materials 80% complete, conversion 40% complete	70,000
Cost data:	
Work in process inventory, July 1:	
Materials cost	$27,000
Conversion cost	$13,000
Cost added during July:	
Materials cost	$468,000
Conversion cost	$357,000

Materials are added at several stages during the etching process. The company uses the FIFO method.

Required:

1. Compute the equivalent units of production.
2. Compute the costs per equivalent unit for July.
3. Determine the cost of ending work in process inventory and of the units transferred to the Wiring Department.
4. Prepare a cost reconciliation between the costs determined in part (3) above and the cost of beginning inventory and costs added during the period.

PROBLEM 4–23 (Appendix 4B) Step-Down Method [LO9]

Pleasant View Clinic has three service departments—Food Services, Administrative Services, and X-ray Services. The costs of these departments are allocated by the step-down method, using the allocation bases and in the order shown below:

Service Department	Costs Incurred	Base for Allocation
Food Services	Variable	Meals served
	Fixed	Peak-period needs
Administrative Services	Variable	Files processed
	Fixed	10% X-ray Services, 20% Outpatient Clinic, 30% OB Care, and 40% General Clinic
X-ray Services	Variable	X-rays taken
	Fixed	Peak-period needs

Estimated cost and operating data for all departments in the clinic for the forthcoming month are presented in the table on the top of page 165.

All billing in the clinic is done through the Outpatient Clinic, OB Care, or General Clinic. The clinic's administrator wants the costs of the three service departments allocated to these three billing centres.

Required:

Prepare the cost allocation desired by the clinic administrator. Include under each billing centre the direct costs of the centre as well as the costs allocated from the service departments.

	Food Services	Admin. Services	X-Ray Services	Outpatient Clinic	OB Care	General Clinic	Total
Variable costs	$ 73,150	$ 6,800	$38,100	$11,700	$ 14,850	$ 53,400	$198,000
Fixed costs	48,000	33,040	59,520	26,958	99,738	344,744	612,000
Total costs	$121,150	$39,840	$97,620	$38,658	$114,588	$398,144	$810,000
Meals served		1,000	500		7,000	30,000	38,500
Percent of peak-period Food Services needs		2%	1%		17%	80%	100%
Files processed			1,500	3,000	900	12,000	17,400
X-rays taken				1,200	350	8,400	9,950
Percent of peak-period X-ray Services needs				13%	3%	84%	100%

PROBLEM 4–24 Interpreting a Report—Weighted-Average Method [LO2, LO3, LO4]

Bell Computers, Ltd., located in Liverpool, England, assembles a standardized personal computer from parts it purchases from various suppliers. The production process consists of several steps, starting with assembly of the "mother" circuit board, which contains the central processing unit. This assembly takes place in the CPU Assembly Department. The company recently hired a new accountant who prepared the following report for the department for May using the weighted-average method:

Quantity Schedule	
Units to be accounted for:	
Work in process, May 1 (materials 90% complete; conversion 80% complete)	5,000
Started into production	29,000
Total units	34,000
Units accounted for as follows:	
Transferred to next department	30,000
Work in process, May 31 (materials 75% complete; conversion 50% complete)	4,000
Total units	34,000

Cost Reconciliation	
Cost to be accounted for:	
Work in process, May 1	£ 13,400
Cost added in the department	87,800
Total cost to be accounted for	£101,200
Cost accounted for as follows:	
Work in process, May 31	£ 8,200
Transferred to next department	93,000
Total cost accounted for	£101,200

The company's management would like some additional information about May's operation in the CPU Assembly Department. (The currency in England is the pound, which is denoted by the symbol £.)

Required:

1. How many units were started and completed during May?
2. What were the equivalent units for May for materials and conversion costs?
3. What were the costs per equivalent unit for May? The following additional data are available concerning the department's costs:

	Materials	Conversion	Total
Work in process, May 1	£9,000	£4,400	£13,400
Costs added during May	£57,000	£30,800	£87,800

4. Verify the accountant's ending work in process inventory figure (£8,200) given in the report.
5. The new manager of the CPU Assembly Department was asked to estimate the incremental cost of processing an additional 1,000 units through the department. He took the unit cost for an equivalent whole unit you computed in (3) above and multiplied this figure by 1,000. Will this method yield a valid estimate of incremental cost? Explain.

PROBLEM 4–25 Analysis of Work in Process T-Account—Weighted-Average Method [LO1, LO2, LO3, LO4]

Brady Products manufactures a silicone paste wax that goes through three processing departments—Cracking, Blending, and Packing. All of the raw materials are introduced at the start of work in the Cracking Department. The Work in Process T-account for the Cracking Department for May follows:

Work in Process—Cracking Department

Inventory, May 1 (35,000 kilograms, conversion 4/5 complete)	63,700	Completed and transferred to Blending (? kilograms)	?
May costs added:			
Raw materials (280,000 kilograms)	397,600		
Conversion costs	189,700		
Inventory, May 31 (45,000 kilograms, conversion 2/3 complete)	?		

The May 1 work in process inventory consists of $43,400 in materials cost and $20,300 in conversion cost. The company uses the weighted-average method.

Required:

1. Determine the equivalent units of production for May.
2. Determine the costs per equivalent unit for May.
3. Determine the cost of the units completed and transferred to Blending during May and the cost of ending work in process inventory.
4. What criticism can be made of the unit costs that you have computed if they are used to evaluate how well costs have been controlled?

PROBLEM 4–26 Equivalent Units; Costing of Inventories; Journal Entries—Weighted-Average Method [LO1, LO2, LO3, LO4]

Zap Rap, Inc., is a manufacturer of audio CDs. The company's chief financial officer is trying to verify the accuracy of the December 31 work in process and finished goods inventories prior to closing the books for the year. He strongly suspects that the year-end dollar balances are incorrect, but he believes that all the other data are accurate. The year-end balances shown on Zap Rap's books are as follows:

	Units	Costs
Work in process, Dec. 31 (materials 100% complete; conversion 50% complete)	30,000	$95,000
Finished goods, Dec. 31	50,000	$201,000

There were no finished goods inventories at the beginning of the year. The company uses the weighted-average method of process costing. There is only one processing department.

A review of the company's inventory and cost records has disclosed the following data:

		Costs	
	Units	Materials	Conversion
Work in process, Jan. 1 (materials 100% complete; conversion 80% complete)	20,000	$22,000	$48,000
Started into production	800,000		
Costs added during the year		$880,000	$2,367,000
Units completed during the year	790,000		

Required:

1. Determine the equivalent units and the costs per equivalent unit for materials and conversion for the year.
2. Determine the amount of cost that should be assigned to the ending work in process and finished goods inventories.
3. Prepare the necessary correcting journal entry to adjust the work in process and finished goods inventories to the correct balances as of December 31.
4. Determine the cost of goods sold for the year, assuming that there is no underapplied or overapplied overhead.

(CPA, adapted)

PROBLEM 4–27 Cost Flows [LO1]

Nature's Way, Inc., keeps one of its production facilities busy making a perfume called Essence de la Vache. The perfume goes through two processing departments: Blending and Bottling.

The following incomplete Work in Process account is provided for the Blending Department for March:

Work in Process—Blending

March 1 balance	32,800	Completed and transferred	
Raw materials	147,600	to Bottling (760,000 millilitres)	?
Direct labour	73,200		
Overhead	481,000		
March 31 balance	?		

The $32,800 beginning inventory in the Blending Department consisted of the following elements: raw materials, $8,000; direct labour, $4,000; and overhead applied, $20,800.

Costs incurred during March in the Bottling Department were: materials used, $45,000; direct labour, $17,000; and overhead cost applied to production, $108,000.

Required:

1. Prepare journal entries to record the costs incurred in both the Blending Department and Bottling Department during March. Key your entries to items (a) through (g) below:
   a. Raw materials were issued for use in production.
   b. Direct labour costs were incurred.
   c. Manufacturing overhead costs for the entire factory were incurred, $596,000. (Credit Accounts Payable and use a single Manufacturing Overhead control account for the entire factory.)
   d. Manufacturing overhead was applied to production using a predetermined overhead rate.
   e. Units that were complete with respect to processing in the Blending Department were transferred to the Bottling Department, $722,000.
   f. Units that were complete with respect to processing in the Bottling Department were transferred to Finished Goods, $920,000.
   g. Completed units were sold on account for $1,400,000. The cost of goods sold was $890,000.
2. Post the journal entries from (1) above to T-accounts. The following account balances existed at the beginning of March. (The beginning balance in the Blending Department's Work in Process account is given above.)

Raw Materials	$198,600
Work in Process—Bottling Department	$49,000
Finished Goods	$20,000

After posting the entries to the T-accounts, find the ending balances in the inventory accounts and the manufacturing overhead account.

4–28 (Appendix 4B) Direct and Reciprocal Methods [L08, L010]

At the beginning of this year, a group of lawyers and accountants in Calgary decided to join efforts in providing one-stop legal and accounting consulting services to industry and the government. The group established a consulting company, renting office space, and hired both professional and clerical staff.

Following several initial organizational meetings, the partners decided to divide the operation into three parts: the consulting department, the legal department, and the accounting department.

The consulting department dealt directly with the clients providing two somewhat distinct services, accounting consulting (AC) and legal consulting (LC). In its first full month of operations, this department recorded its own identifiable costs as $20,000, 30% attributed to accounting consultations and 70% to legal work. Billings to clients amounted to $30,000 and $20,500 for accounting and legal consultations, respectively. This department made use of the other two departments' services in preparing work for the external clients.

The accounting and legal departments provided professional services for each other and for the consulting department on the basis of time according to the following schedule:

	Accounting Department	Legal Department	Consulting	
			AC	LC
Accounting services (AD)	—	20%	60%	20%
Legal services (LD)	50%	—	10%	40%

The accounting department incurred $8,000 in costs in the first month and the legal department incurred $10,000. Neither department directly bills external clients.

Having completed the first month's activity, the partners are ready to evaluate the performance of the group and of the individual area. The managing partner is concerned that his organizational structure may be a major determinant of success and has asked you, as an outside consultant, to prepare some performance information for him.

Required

1. Prepare an income statement for each consulting branch separately under each of the following allocation approaches:
   a. Direct
   b. Reciprocal
2. Prepare a brief memorandum to the managing partner on the performance of the group and the individual areas. In your memorandum, comment on the usefulness of standard costing for this service organization.

(SMAC, adapted)

Cases

CASE 4–29 Ethics and the Manager; Understanding the Impact of Percentage Completion on Profit [LO2, LO3, LO4]

Thad Kostowski and Carol Lee are production managers in the Appliances Division of Mesger Corporation, which has several dozen plants scattered in locations throughout the world. Carol manages the plant located in Toronto, while Thad manages the plant in Vancouver. Production managers are paid a salary and get an additional bonus equal to 10% of their base salary if the entire division meets or exceeds its target profits for the year. The bonus is determined in March after the company's annual report has been prepared and issued to shareholders.

Late in February, Carol received a phone call from Thad that went like this:

Thad: How's it going, Carol?

Carol: Fine, Thad. How's it going with you?

Thad: Great! I just got the preliminary profit figures for the division for last year and we are within $62,500 of making the year's target profits. All we have to do is to pull a few strings, and we'll be over the top!

Carol: What do you mean?

Thad: Well, one thing that would be easy to change is your estimate of the percentage completion of your ending work in process inventories.

Carol: I don't know if I should do that, Thad. Those percentage completion numbers are supplied by Jean Jackson, my lead supervisor. I have always trusted her to provide us with good estimates. Besides, I have already sent the percentage completion figures to the corporate headquarters.

Thad: You can always tell them there was a mistake. Think about it, Carol. All of us managers are doing as much as we can to pull this bonus out of the hat. You may not want the bonus cheque, but the rest of us sure could use it.

The final processing department in Carol's production facility began the year with no work in process inventories. During the year, 270,000 units were transferred in from the prior processing department and 250,000 units were completed and sold. Costs transferred in from the prior department totalled $49,221,000. No materials are added in the final processing department. A total of $16,320,000 of conversion cost was incurred in the final processing department during the year.

Required:

1. Jean Jackson estimated that the units in ending inventory in the final processing department were 25% complete with respect to the conversion costs of the final processing department. If this estimate of the percentage completion is used, what would be the cost of goods sold for the year?
2. Does Thad Kostowski want the estimated percentage completion to be increased or decreased? Explain why.
3. What percentage completion figure would result in increasing the reported operating income by $62,500 over the operating income that would be reported if the 25% figure were used?
4. Do you think Carol Lee should go along with the request to alter estimates of the percentage completion? Why or why not?

CASE 4–30 Second Department—Weighted-Average Method [LO2, LO3, LO4]

Durall Company manufactures a plastic gasket that is used in automobile engines. The gaskets go through three processing departments: Mixing, Forming, and Stamping. The company's accountant (who is very inexperienced) has prepared a summary of production and costs for the Forming Department for October as follows:

Forming Department costs:

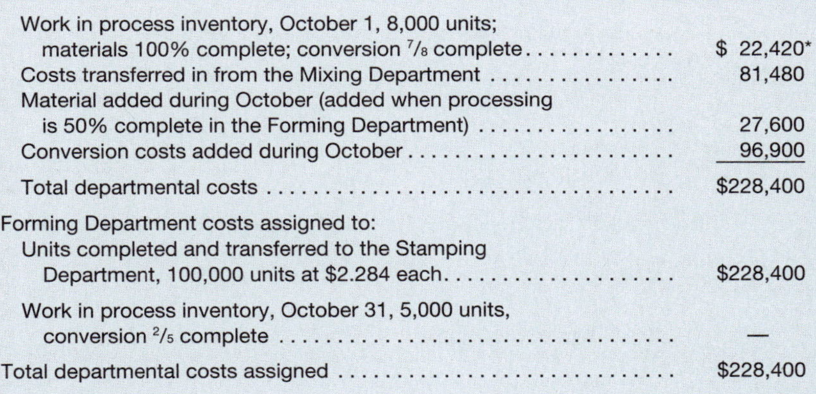

Work in process inventory, October 1, 8,000 units; materials 100% complete; conversion 7/8 complete	$ 22,420*
Costs transferred in from the Mixing Department	81,480
Material added during October (added when processing is 50% complete in the Forming Department)	27,600
Conversion costs added during October	96,900
Total departmental costs	$228,400
Forming Department costs assigned to:	
Units completed and transferred to the Stamping Department, 100,000 units at $2.284 each	$228,400
Work in process inventory, October 31, 5,000 units, conversion 2/5 complete	—
Total departmental costs assigned	$228,400

*Consists of cost transferred in, $8,820; materials cost, $3,400; and conversion costs, $10,200.

After mulling over the data above, Durall's president commented, "I can't understand what's happening here. Despite a concentrated effort at cost reduction, our unit cost actually went up in the Forming Department last month. With that kind of performance, year-end bonuses are out of the question for the people in that department."

The company uses the weighted-average method in its process costing.

Required:

1. Prepare a report for the Forming Department for October showing how much cost should have been assigned to the units completed and transferred to the Stamping Department and to the ending work in process inventory.
2. Explain to the president why the unit cost appearing on the report prepared by the accountant is so high.

CASE 4–31 (Appendix 4A) Second Department—FIFO Method [LO5, LO6, LO7]
Refer to the data for Durall Company in the preceding case. Assume that the company uses the FIFO method.

Required:

1. Prepare a report for the Forming Department for October showing how much cost should have been assigned to the units completed and transferred to the Stamping Department and to the ending work in process inventory.
2. Assume that in order to remain competitive, the company undertook a major cost-cutting program during October. Would the effects of this cost-cutting program tend to show up more under the weighted-average method or under the FIFO method? Explain your answer.

CASE 4–32 (Appendix 4B) Step-Down Method versus Direct Method [LO8, LO9]
"I can't understand what's happening here," said Mike Holt, president of Severson Products, Inc. "We always seem to bid too high on jobs that require a lot of labour time in the Finishing Department, and we always seem to get every job we bid on that requires a lot of machine time in the Milling Department. Yet we don't seem to be making much money on those Milling Department jobs. I wonder if the problem is in our overhead rates."

Severson Products manufactures high-quality wood products to customers' specifications. Some jobs take a large amount of machine work in the Milling Department, and other jobs take a large amount of hand finishing work in the Finishing Department. In addition to the Milling and Finishing departments, the company has three service departments. The costs of these service departments are allocated to other departments *in the order listed below.* (For each service department, use the most appropriate allocation base.)

	Total Labour-Hours	Square Metres of Space Occupied	Number of Employees	Machine-Hours	Direct Labour-Hours
Cafeteria	16,000	12,000	25		
Custodial Services	9,000	3,000	40		
Machinery Maintenance	15,000	10,000	60		
Milling	30,000	40,000	100	160,000	20,000
Finishing	100,000	20,000	300	40,000	70,000
	170,000	85,000	525	200,000	90,000

Budgeted overhead costs in each department for the current year are as follows:

Cafeteria	$ 320,000*
Custodial Services	65,400
Machinery Maintenance	93,600
Milling	416,000
Finishing	166,000
Total budgeted cost	$1,061,000

*This represents the amount of cost subsidized by the company.

The company has always allocated service department costs to the operating departments (Milling and Finishing) using the direct method of allocation, because of its simplicity.

Required:

1. Allocate service department costs to operating departments by the step-down method. Then compute predetermined overhead rates in the operating departments for the current year, using machine-hours as the allocation base in the Milling Department and direct labour-hours as the allocation base in the Finishing Department.
2. Repeat (1) above, this time using the direct method. Again compute predetermined overhead rates in the Milling and Finishing Departments.
3. Assume that during the current year the company bids on a job that requires machine and labour time as follows:

	Machine-Hours	Direct Labour-Hours
Milling Department	2,000	1,600
Finishing Department	800	13,000
Total hours	2,800	14,600

a. Determine the amount of overhead that would be assigned to the job if the company used the overhead rates developed in (1) above. Then determine the amount of overhead that would be assigned to the job if the company used the overhead rates developed in (2) above.

b. Explain to the president why the step-down method provides a better basis for computing predetermined overhead rates than the direct method.

Research

R 4–33 [LO1] The questions in this exercise are based on Anheuser-Busch Companies, Inc. The company had almost $15 billion in net sales in 2004. Although the company derives revenue from various sources, we are going to focus on the company's core business—beer manufacturing. To answer the questions, you will need to download and view an on-line tour of the company's beer brewing process at www.budweisertours.com/.

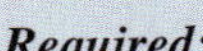

Required:

1. List each of the processing departments in Anheuser-Busch's brewing process. For each department, identify any raw materials that are added to production within that department,.
2. Would you expect Anheuser-Busch's brewing process to require fairly large amounts of manufacturing overhead costs? Why or why not?
3. Prepare a T-account model of the process costing flows for Anheuser-Busch that is similar to the one shown in Exhibit 4–3 on page 133. You need not take the diagram beyond the first two processes: Mashing and Straining.
4. Why might Anheuser-Busch use a form of operation costing as described on page 140?

CHAPTER 5

LEARNING OBJECTIVES

After studying Chapter 5, you should be able to:

1. Explain activity-based costing and how it differs from a traditional costing system.
2. Assign costs to cost pools using a first-stage allocation, and compute activity rates.
3. Assign costs to a cost object using a second-stage allocation.
4. Use activity-based costing to compute product and customer margins.
5. Compare product costs computed using traditional and activity-based costing methods.
6. (Appendix 5A) Prepare an action analysis report using activity-based costing data and interpret the report.
7. (Appendix 5B) Use activity-based costing techniques to compute unit product costs for external reports.

ACTIVITY-BASED COSTING: A TOOL TO AID DECISION MAKING

BUSINESS FOCUS

Help for an Ailing Reporting System

Toronto's Hospital for Sick Children is the largest children's hospital in Canada and has a worldwide reputation for conducting leading-edge medical research. The annual volume of activity is impressive with 15,000 inpatients and 237,000 emergency and outpatients. Prior to adopting an activity-based costing (ABC) system, financial analysis was often prepared on an ad hoc basis because the standard monthly reports were not providing managers with information useful for decision-making purposes. To address this problem, an ABC system was developed on a pilot test basis in five different operating departments, which combined had over 600 employees and an annual operating expense budget of $80 million dollars.

As is typical in ABC implementations, considerable effort was required to identify activity cost pools and activity measures in the various departments. For example, in the Health Records Department 14 different activity cost pools (e.g., emergency patient registration) and activity measures (e.g., number of patients registered) were identified. The key benefit of the new system is that operational managers now have significantly improved information with which to run their departments. In particular, the ABC system allows managers to track the actual cost per unit of an activity (e.g., cost per emergency patient registered), compare these amounts with budget, and take actions as necessary. Moreover, having accurate information on a per-activity measure basis allows managers to develop more accurate forecasts of costs given anticipated changes in overall activity levels.

Source: Brian Mackie, "Merging GPK and ABC on the Road to RCA," *Strategic Finance*, November 2006, pp. 32–39.

This chapter introduces the concept of *activity-based costing*, which has been embraced by manufacturing, service and not-for-profit organizations worldwide. **Activity-based costing (ABC)** is a costing method that is designed to provide managers with cost information for strategic and other decisions that potentially affect capacity and therefore "fixed" as well as variable costs. Activity-based costing is typically used as a supplement to, rather than as a replacement for, a company's usual costing system. Most organizations that use activity-based costing have two costing systems—the official costing system that is used for preparing external financial reports and the activity-based costing system that is used for internal decision making and for managing activities.

Activity-based costing (ABC) A costing method based on activities that is designed to provide managers with cost information for strategic and other decisions that potentially affect capacity and therefore fixed costs.

This chapter focuses primarily on ABC applications in manufacturing to provide a contrast with the material presented in earlier chapters. More specifically, Chapters 2, 3, and 4 focused on traditional absorption costing systems used by manufacturing companies to calculate unit product costs for the purpose of valuing inventories and determining cost of goods sold for external financial reports. In contrast, this chapter explains how manufacturing companies can use activity-based costing rather than traditional methods to calculate unit product costs for the purposes of managing overhead and making decisions. Because of the broad role activity-based costing can play in facilitating decisions related to product pricing, cost management, capacity utilization and customer profitability, it is important that both accountants and non-accountants understand its purpose and application.

How Costs are Treated Under Activity-Based Costing

LEARNING OBJECTIVE 1
Explain activity-based costing and how it differs from a traditional costing system.

As noted above, traditional absorption costing is designed to provide data for external financial reports. In contrast, activity-based costing is designed for use in internal decision making. As a consequence, activity-based costing differs from traditional cost accounting in several ways. In activity-based costing:

1. Non-manufacturing as well as manufacturing costs may be assigned to products, but only on a cause-and-effect basis.
2. Some manufacturing costs may be excluded from product costs.
3. Numerous **overhead cost pools** are used, each of which is allocated to products and other cost objects using its own unique measure of activity.
4. Overhead rates, or activity rates, may be based on the level of activity at capacity rather than on the budgeted level of activity.

Overhead cost pool A group of overhead cost elements.

Each of these departures from traditional costing accounting practices will be discussed in turn.[1]

Non-Manufacturing Costs and Activity-Based Costing

In traditional cost accounting, only manufacturing costs are assigned to products. Selling, general, and administrative expenses are treated as period expenses and are not assigned to products. However, many of these non-manufacturing costs are also part of the costs of producing, selling, distributing, and servicing products. For example, commissions paid to salespersons, shipping costs, and warranty repair costs can easily be traced to individual products. In this chapter, we will use the term *overhead* to refer to non-manufacturing costs as well as to indirect manufacturing costs. In activity-based costing, products are

1. T. Colwyn Jones and D. Dugdale, "The ABC Bandwagon and the Juggernaut of Modernity," *Accounting, Organizations and Society*, vol. 27, 2002, pp. 121–163, provide an interesting, if lengthy, history of various schools of thought about ABC. Many of the implicit lessons from the study are contained in the materials to follow.

assigned all of the overhead costs—non-manufacturing as well as manufacturing—that they can reasonably be supposed to have caused. In essence, we will be determining the entire cost of a product rather than just its manufacturing cost. The focus in Chapters 2, 3, and 4 was on determining just the manufacturing cost of a product.

Manufacturing Costs and Activity-Based Costing

In traditional cost accounting, *all* manufacturing costs are assigned to products—even manufacturing costs that are not caused by the products. For example, a portion of the factory security guard's wages would be allocated to each product even though the guard's wages are totally unaffected by which products are made or not made during a period. In activity-based costing, a cost is assigned to a product only if there is good reason to believe that the cost would be affected by decisions concerning the product. In activity-based costing, costs that are unaffected by product-related decisions are treated as period expenses instead of product costs. As will be seen in the example presented in this chapter, this departure from traditional costing approaches (see Chapter 3) represents one of the key benefits of activity-based costing as it results in better information for decision-making purposes.

Cost Pools, Allocation Bases, and Activity-Based Costing

Historically, cost system designs were simple and satisfactory. Typically, either one plantwide overhead cost pool or a number of departmental overhead cost pools was used to assign overhead costs to products. The plantwide and departmental approaches always had one thing in common—they relied on allocation bases such as direct labour-hours and machine-hours for allocating overhead costs to products. In the labour-intensive production processes of many years ago, direct labour was the most common choice for an overhead allocation base because it represented a large component of product costs, direct labour-hours were closely tracked, and many managers believed that direct labour-hours, the total volume of units produced, and overhead costs were highly correlated. Given that most companies at the time were producing a very limited variety of products that required similar resources to produce, allocation bases such as direct labour-hours, or even machine-hours, worked fine because in fact there was probably little difference in the overhead costs attributable to different products.

Then conditions began to change. Many tasks previously done by direct labourers were being performed by automated equipment—a component of overhead. Companies began creating new products and services at an ever-accelerating rate that differed in volume, batch size, and complexity. Managing and sustaining this product diversity required investing in many more overhead resources, such as product design engineers, that had no obvious connection to direct labour-hours or machine-hours. In this new environment, continuing to rely exclusively on a limited number of overhead cost pools and traditional allocation bases posed the risk that reported unit product costs would be distorted and, therefore, misleading when used for decision-making purposes. The activity-based approach has appeal in today's business environment because it uses more cost pools and unique measures of activity to better understand the costs of managing and sustaining product diversity.

Activity
Any event that causes the consumption of overhead resources.

Activity cost pool
A "bucket" in which costs are accumulated that relate to a single activity measure in the activity-based costing system.

Activity measure
An allocation base in an activity-based costing system; ideally a measure of the amount of activity that drives the costs in an activity cost pool; also called a cost driver.

Transaction driver
A simple count of the number of times an activity occurs.

Duration driver
A measure of the amount of time required to perform an activity.

In activity-based costing, an **activity** is any event that causes the consumption of overhead resources. An **activity cost pool** is a "bucket" in which costs are accumulated that relate to a single activity measure in the ABC system. An **activity measure** is an allocation base in an activity-based costing system. The term *cost driver* is also used to refer to an activity measure because the activity measure should "drive" the cost being allocated. The two most common types of activity measures are *transaction drivers* and *duration drivers.* **Transaction drivers** are simple counts of the number of times an activity occurs such as the number of bills sent out to customers. **Duration drivers** measure the amount of time required to perform an activity such as the time spent preparing individual bills for customers. In general, duration drivers are more accurate measures of resource consumption than transaction drivers, but they take more effort to record. For that reason, transaction drivers are often used in practice.

Many companies throughout the world continue to base overhead allocations on direct labour-hours or machine-hours. In situations where overhead costs and direct labour-hours are highly correlated or in situations where the goal of the overhead allocation process is to prepare external financial reports, this practice makes sense. However, if plantwide overhead costs do not move in tandem with plantwide direct labour-hours or machine-hours, product costs will be distorted. Activity-based costing addresses this issue by defining five levels of activity—unit-level, batch-level, product-level, customer-level, and organization-sustaining—of which only the costs and corresponding activity measures for unit-level activities relate to the volume of units produced. The remaining categories do not. These levels are described as follows:[2]

1. **Unit-level activities** are performed each time a unit is produced. The costs of unit-level activities should be proportional to the number of units produced. For example, providing power to run processing equipment would be a unit-level activity since power tends to be consumed in proportion to the number of units produced.
2. **Batch-level activities** are performed each time a batch is handled or processed, regardless of how many units are in the batch. For example, tasks such as placing purchase orders, setting up equipment, and arranging for shipments to customers are batch-level activities. They are incurred once for each batch (or customer order). Costs at the batch level depend on the number of batches processed rather than on the number of units produced, the number of units sold, or other measures of volume. For example, the cost of setting up a machine for batch processing is the same regardless of whether the batch contains 100 or 10,000 items.
3. **Product-level activities** relate to specific products and typically must be carried out regardless of how many batches are run or units of product are produced or sold. For example, activities such as designing a product, advertising a product, and maintaining a product manager and staff are all product-level activities.
4. **Customer-level activities** relate to specific customers and include activities such as sales calls, catalog mailings, and general technical support that are not tied to any specific product.
5. **Organization-sustaining activities** are carried out regardless of which customers are served, which products are produced, how many batches are run, or how many units are made. This category includes activities such as heating the factory, cleaning executive offices, providing a computer network, arranging for loans, preparing annual reports to shareholders, and so on.

Unit-level activities
Activities that arise as a result of the total volume of goods and services that are produced and that are performed each time a unit is produced.

Batch-level activities
Activities that are performed each time a batch of goods is handled or processed, regardless of how many units are in a batch. The amount of resource consumed depends on the number of batches run rather than on the number of units in the batch.

Product-level activities
Activities that relate to specific products that must be carried out regardless of how many units are produced and sold or batches run.

Customer-level activities
Activities that are carried out to support customers but that are not related to any specific product.

Organization-sustaining activities
Activities that are carried out regardless of which customers are serviced, which products are produced, how many batches are run or how many units are made.

The Costs of Idle Capacity in Activity-Based Costing

In traditional cost accounting, predetermined overhead rates are computed by dividing budgeted overhead costs by a measure of budgeted activity such as budgeted direct labour-hours. This practice results in applying the costs of unused, or idle, capacity to products, and it results in unstable unit product costs as discussed in Appendix 3A. If budgeted activity falls, the overhead rate increases because the fixed components of overhead are spread over a smaller base, resulting in increased unit product costs.

In contrast to traditional cost accounting, in activity-based costing, products are charged for the costs of capacity they use—not for the costs of capacity they don't use. In other words, the costs of idle capacity are not charged to products. This results in more stable unit costs and is consistent with the objective of assigning only those costs to products that are actually caused by the products. Instead of assigning the costs of idle capacity to products, in activity-based costing these costs are considered to be period costs that flow through to

2. Robin Cooper, "Cost Classification in Unit-Based and Activity-Based Manufacturing Cost Systems," *Journal of Cost Management,* Fall 1990, pp. 4–14.

the income statement as an expense of the current period. This treatment highlights the cost of idle capacity rather than burying it in inventory and cost of goods sold.[3]

Designing an Activity-Based Costing System

Experts agree on several essential characteristics of any successful implementation of activity-based costing. First, the initiative to implement activity-based costing must be strongly supported by top management. Second, the design and implementation of an ABC system should be the responsibility of a cross-functional team rather than of the Accounting Department. The team should include representatives from each area that will use the data provided by the ABC system. Ordinarily, this would include representatives from marketing, production, engineering, and top management, as well as technically trained accounting staff. An outside consultant who specializes in activity-based costing may serve as an advisor to the team.

Top managers must support the initiative for two reasons. First, without leadership from top management, some managers may not see any reason to change. Second, if top managers do not support the ABC system and continue to play the game by the old rules, their subordinates will quickly get the message that ABC is not important and they will abandon the ABC initiative. Time after time, when accountants have attempted to implement an ABC system on their own without top-management support and active cooperation from other managers, the results have been ignored. In addition, designing a good ABC system requires detailed knowledge of many parts of the organization's overall operations. This knowledge can come only from the people who are familiar with those operations.

To illustrate the design and use of an activity-based costing system, we use Classic Brass Inc., a company that makes two main product lines for luxury yachts—standard stanchions and custom compass housings. Based on the company's disappointing financial result for the most recent year-end (see Exhibit 5–1) senior management at Classic Brass decided that more accurate costing information was needed for making decisions

EXHIBIT 5–1 Classic Brass Income Statement

Classic Brass
Income Statement
Year Ended December 31, 2008

Sales		$3,200,000
Cost of goods sold:		
Direct materials	$ 975,000	
Direct labour	351,250	
Manufacturing overhead*	1,000,000	2,326,250
Gross margin		873,750
Selling and administrative expenses:		
Shipping expenses	65,000	
Marketing expenses	300,000	
General administrative expenses	510,000	875,000
Operating income		($ 1,250)

*The company's traditional cost system allocates manufacturing overhead to products using a plantwide overhead rate and machine-hours as the allocation base. Inventory levels did not change during the year.

3. Several *Statements on Management Accounting* issued by the Institute of Management Accountants, Montvale, New Jersey (**http://www.imanet.org/**), deal with implementing activity-based costing, including: *Statement 4T, Implementing Activity-Based Costing; Statement 4CC, Implementing Activity-Based Management;* and *Statement 4EE, Tools and Techniques for Implementing ABC/ABM*. Many of these studies are also available from the Society of Management Accountants of Canada, a joint sponsor of some of the research (**http://www.cma-canada.org/**).

such as product pricing. After studying the existing cost accounting system at Classic Brass and reviewing articles in professional and trade journals, they decided to implement an activity-based costing system. A cross-functional team was put together to design and implement the system. Like most other ABC implementations, the new ABC system would supplement, rather than replace, the existing cost accounting system, which would continue to be used for external financial reports. The new ABC system would be used to prepare special reports for management decisions such as bidding on new business.

The accounting manager drew the chart appearing in Exhibit 5–2 to explain the general structure of the ABC model. **Cost objects** such as products generate activities. For example, a customer order for a compass housing requires the activity of preparing a production order. Such an activity consumes resources. A production order uses a sheet of paper and takes time to fill out. And consumption of resources causes costs. The greater the number of sheets used to fill out production orders and the greater the amount of time devoted to filling out such orders, the greater the cost. Activity-based costing attempts to trace through these relationships to identify how products and customers affect costs.

Cost object The specific product or service to be costed.

EXHIBIT 5–2 The Activity-Based Costing Model

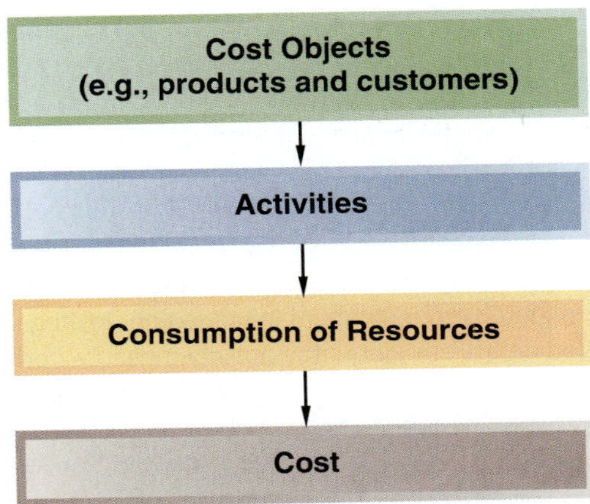

As in most companies, the ABC team at Classic Brass felt that the company's traditional cost accounting system adequately measured the direct material and direct labour costs of products since these costs are directly traced to products. Therefore, the ABC system would be concerned solely with the other costs of the company–manufacturing overhead and selling, general, and administrative costs.

The implementation process was broken down into the following five basic steps:

1. Identify and define activities, activity cost pools, and activity measures.
2. Assign overhead costs to activity cost pools.
3. Calculate activity rates.
4. Assign overhead costs to cost objects using the activity rates and activity measures.
5. Prepare management reports.

Step 1: Identify and Define Activities, Activity Cost Pools, and Activity Measures

The first major step is to identify the activities that will form the foundation for the system. This can be difficult and time-consuming, and involves a great deal of judgement. A common procedure is for the individuals on the ABC implementation team to interview people who work in overhead departments and ask them to describe their major activities. Ordinarily, this results in a very long list of activities, which can pose a problem. On one hand, the greater the number of activities tracked in the ABC system, the more accurate the costs are likely to be. On the other hand, it is costly to design, implement, maintain, and use a complex system involving large numbers of activities. Consequently, the original lengthy list of activities is usually reduced to a handful by combining similar activities. For example, several actions may be involved in handling and moving raw materials—from receiving raw materials on the loading dock to sorting them into the appropriate bins in the storeroom. All of these activities might be combined into a single activity called *materials handling*.

IN BUSINESS

Xi Agricultural Machine Company (XAMC), a state-owned manufacturer of farming equipment in China provides a good international example of the potential benefits of activity-based costing. XAMC adopted ABC because of declining profit margins, high overhead costs, and considerable production volume and complexity differences across products. Prior to adopting ABC the company used a traditional approach to allocating overhead costs to products based on direct labour-hours. Product prices are based on total costs (including overhead) plus a markup for a desired profit margin. In recent years management became increasingly concerned as demand for one of its high-volume products, a four-wheel drive tractor, began to decrease as competitors consistently underbid XAMC. Conversely, demand for one of its seeders, a low-volume, high-complexity product, was rapidly increasing as the price charged by XAMC was significantly below its competitors. Management began to suspect that its costing system was responsible for these shifts in demand.

An extensive ABC implementation process was conducted and resulted in the identification of 14 main activities. Employing the standard two-stage allocation process, the total cost of each activity was determined by management in stage one. In stage two, activity costs were assigned to products based on the amount of the activity measure consumed by each product. Activity measures were selected based on the extent to which they were correlated with the incurrence of the activity costs. The results have been dramatic. Revised product costs based on the ABC system indicated that the overhead costs of the four-wheel drive tractor had been overestimated by 46% while the overhead costs of the seeder were underestimated by 43%. Within months of implementing the ABC system, XAMC began to see the benefits of more accurate product costs as it lowered the price on its tractors and demand began to increase.

Source: Pingxin Wang, Qinglu Jin, and Thomas Lin, "How an ABC Study Helped a China State-Owned Company Stay Competitive," *Cost Management*, November–December 2005, pp. 39–47.

When combining activities in an ABC system, activities should be grouped together at the appropriate level. Batch-level activities should not be combined with unit-level activities, or product-level activities with batch-level activities, and so on. In general, it is best to combine only those activities that are highly correlated with each other within a level. For example, the number of customer orders received is likely to be highly correlated with the number of completed customer orders shipped, so these two batch-level activities (receiving and shipping orders) can usually be combined with little loss of accuracy.

At Classic Brass, the ABC team, in consultation with top managers, selected the following *activity cost pools* and *activity measures*:

Activity Cost Pools at Classic Brass

Activity Cost Pool	Activity Measure
Customer orders.	Number of customer orders
Product design	Number of product designs
Order size	Machine-hours
Customer relations	Number of active customers
Other.	Not applicable

The *Customer Orders* cost pool will be assigned all costs of resources that are consumed by taking and processing customer orders, including costs of processing paperwork and any costs involved in setting up machines for specific orders. The activity measure for this cost pool is simply the number of customer orders received. This is a *batch-level activity*, since each order generates work that occurs regardless of whether the order is for one unit or 1,000 units.

The *Product Design* cost pool will be assigned all costs of resources consumed in designing products. The activity measure for this cost pool is the number of products designed. This is a *product-level activity*, since the amount of design work on a new product does not depend on the number of units ultimately ordered or batches ultimately run.

The *Order Size* cost pool will be assigned all costs of resources consumed as a consequence of the number of units produced, including the costs of miscellaneous factory supplies, power to run machines, and some equipment depreciation. This is a *unit-level activity* since each unit requires some of these resources. The activity measure for this cost pool is machine-hours.

The *Customer Relations* cost pool will be assigned all costs associated with maintaining relations with customers, including the costs of sales calls and the costs of entertaining customers. The activity measure for this cost pool is the number of customers the company has on its active customer list. The Customer Relations cost pool represents a customer-level activity.

The *Other* cost pool will be assigned all overhead costs that are not associated with customer orders, product design, production units, or customer relations. These costs mainly consist of organization-sustaining costs and the costs of unused, idle capacity. These costs will *not* be assigned to products since they represent resources that are *not* consumed by products.

The Mechanics of Activity-Based Costing

LEARNING OBJECTIVE 2
Assign costs to cost pools using a first-stage allocation and compute activity rates.

After the ABC system had been designed, the team was ready to begin the process of actually computing the costs of products, customers, and other objects of interest. As shown in Exhibit 5–3, assigning costs to cost objects under activity-based costing is a two-stage process. In the first-stage, manufacturing and non-manufacturing overhead is allocated to the activity costs pools. In the second-stage the costs for the activities are allocated to the various cost objects. As with the traditional cost systems discussed in Chapters 3 and 4, direct costs are traced directly to cost objects. We begin our discussion of the mechanics of activity-based costing with the first-stage allocations.

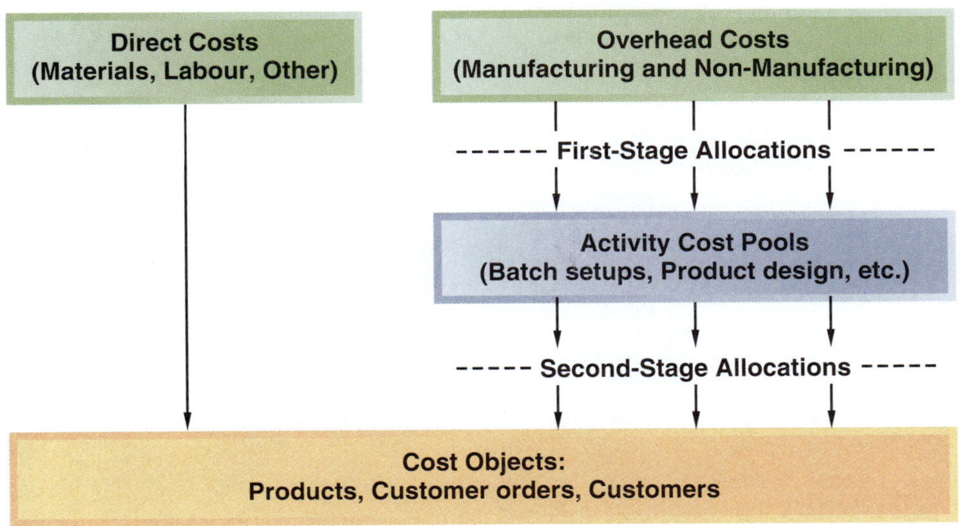

EXHIBIT 5–3 Activity-Based Costing Model

Step 2: Assign Overhead Costs to Activity Cost Pools

Exhibit 5–4 shows the annual overhead costs (both manufacturing and nonmanufacturing) that Classic Brass intends to assign to its activity cost pools. Notice the data in the exhibit are organized by department (e.g., Production, Marketing, and General Administrative). This is because the data have been extracted from the company's general ledger. General ledgers usually classify costs within the departments where the costs are incurred. For example, salaries, supplies, rent, and so forth incurred in the marketing department are charged to that department. The functional orientation of the general ledger mirrors the presentation of costs in the absorption income statement in Exhibit 5–1. In fact, you'll notice the total costs for the Production Department in Exhibit 5–4 ($1,000,000) equal the total manufacturing overhead costs from the income statement in Exhibit 5–1. Similarly, the total costs for the General Administrative and Marketing Departments in Exhibit 5–4 ($510,000 and $300,000) equal the marketing and general and administrative expenses shown in Exhibit 5–1.

Three costs included in the income statement in Exhibit 5–1—direct materials, direct labour, and shipping—are excluded from the costs shown in Exhibit 5–4. The ABC team purposely excluded these costs from Exhibit 5–4 because the existing cost system can accurately trace direct materials, direct labour, and shipping costs to products.

First-stage allocation The process by which overhead costs are assigned to activity cost pools in an activity-based costing system.

Classic Brass's activity-based costing system will divide the nine types of overhead costs in Exhibit 5–4 among its activity cost pools via an allocation process called *first-stage allocation.* The **first-stage allocation** in an ABC system is the process of assigning functionally organized overhead costs derived from a company's general ledger to the activity cost pools.

First-stage allocations are usually based on the results of interviews with employees who have first-hand knowledge of the activities. For example, Classic Brass needs to allocate $500,000 of indirect factory wages to its five activity cost pools. These allocations will be more accurate if the employees who are classified as indirect factory workers (e.g., supervisors, engineers, and quality inspectors) are asked to estimate what percentage of their time is spent dealing with customer orders, with product design, with processing units of product (i.e., order size), and with customer relations. Departmental managers are typically interviewed to determine how the nonpersonnel costs should be distributed across the activity cost pools. For example, the Classic Brass production manager would be interviewed to determine how the $300,000 of factory equipment depreciation (shown in Exhibit 5–4) should be allocated to the activity cost pools. The key question that the production manager would need to answer is "What percentage of the available machine capacity is consumed by each activity such as the number of customer orders or the number of units processed (i.e., size of orders)?"

The results of the interviews at Classic Brass are displayed in Exhibit 5–5. For example, factory equipment depreciation is distributed 20% to Customer Orders, 60% to Order

EXHIBIT 5–4 Annual Overhead Costs (both Manufacturing and Nonmanufacturing) at Classic Brass

Production Department:		
Indirect factory wages	$500,000	
Factory equipment depreciation	300,000	
Factory utilities	120,000	
Factory building lease	80,000	$1,000,000
General Administrative Department:		
Administrative wages and salaries	400,000	
Office equipment depreciation	50,000	
Administrative building lease	60,000	510,000
Marketing Department:		
Marketing wages and salaries	250,000	
Selling expenses	50,000	300,000
Total overhead cost		$1,810,000

EXHIBIT 5–5 Results of Interviews: Distribution of Resource Consumption across Activity Cost Pools

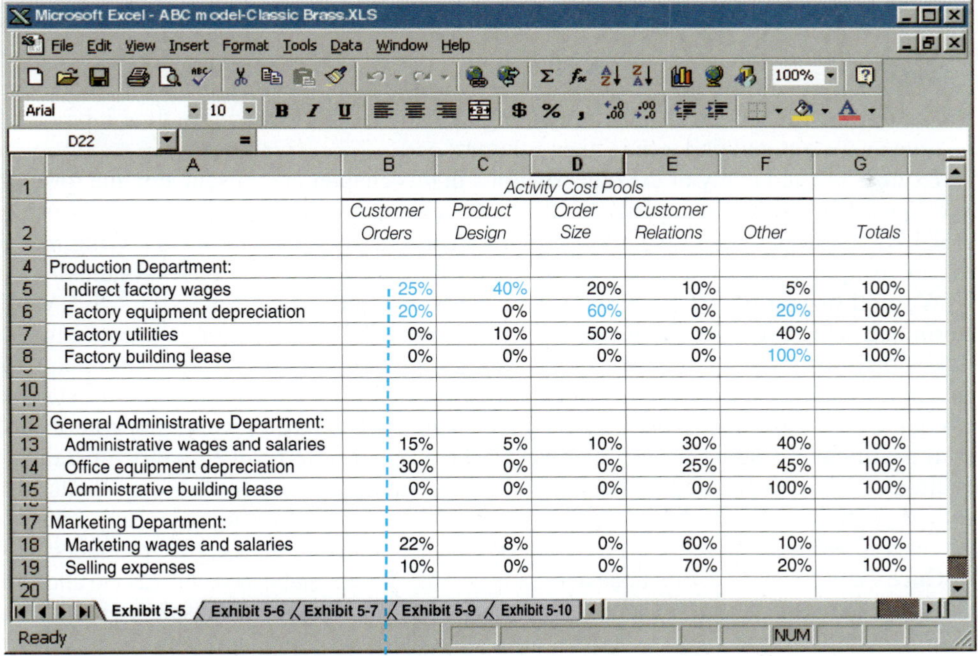

	Activity Cost Pools					
	Customer Orders	Product Design	Order Size	Customer Relations	Other	Totals
Production Department:						
Indirect factory wages	25%	40%	20%	10%	5%	100%
Factory equipment depreciation	20%	0%	60%	0%	20%	100%
Factory utilities	0%	10%	50%	0%	40%	100%
Factory building lease	0%	0%	0%	0%	100%	100%
General Administrative Department:						
Administrative wages and salaries	15%	5%	10%	30%	40%	100%
Office equipment depreciation	30%	0%	0%	25%	45%	100%
Administrative building lease	0%	0%	0%	0%	100%	100%
Marketing Department:						
Marketing wages and salaries	22%	8%	0%	60%	10%	100%
Selling expenses	10%	0%	0%	70%	20%	100%

EXHIBIT 5–6 First-Stage Allocations to Activity Cost Pools

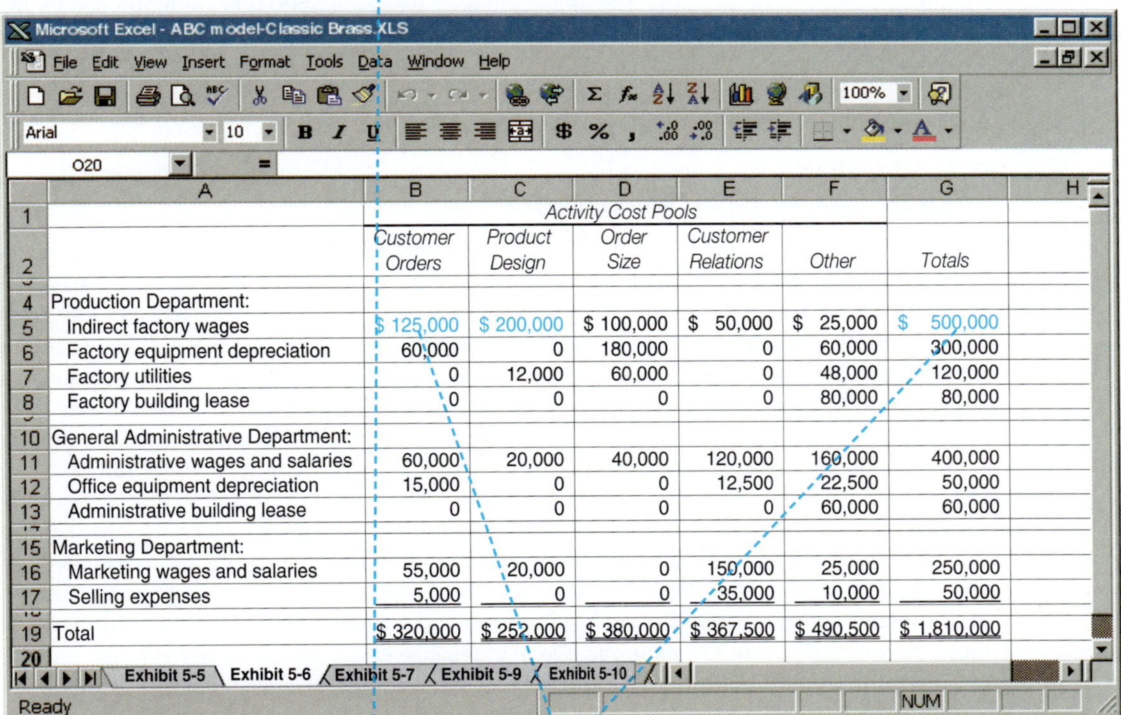

	Activity Cost Pools					
	Customer Orders	Product Design	Order Size	Customer Relations	Other	Totals
Production Department:						
Indirect factory wages	$ 125,000	$ 200,000	$ 100,000	$ 50,000	$ 25,000	$ 500,000
Factory equipment depreciation	60,000	0	180,000	0	60,000	300,000
Factory utilities	0	12,000	60,000	0	48,000	120,000
Factory building lease	0	0	0	0	80,000	80,000
General Administrative Department:						
Administrative wages and salaries	60,000	20,000	40,000	120,000	160,000	400,000
Office equipment depreciation	15,000	0	0	12,500	22,500	50,000
Administrative building lease	0	0	0	0	60,000	60,000
Marketing Department:						
Marketing wages and salaries	55,000	20,000	0	150,000	25,000	250,000
Selling expenses	5,000	0	0	35,000	10,000	50,000
Total	$ 320,000	$ 252,000	$ 380,000	$ 367,500	$ 490,500	$ 1,810,000

Exhibit 5–5 shows that Customer Orders consume 25% of the resources represented by the $500,000 of indirect factory wages.

$$25\% \times \$500{,}000 = \$125{,}000$$

Other entries in the spreadsheet are computed in a similar fashion.

Size, and 20% to the Other cost pool. The resource in this instance is machine time. According to the estimates made by the production manager, 60% of the total available machine time was used to actually process units to fill orders. This percentage is entered in the Order Size column. Each customer order requires setting up, which also requires machine time. This activity consumes 20% of the total available machine time and is entered under the Customer Orders column. The remaining 20% of available machine time represents idle time and is entered under the Other column.

Exhibit 5–5 and many of the other exhibits in this chapter are presented in the form of Excel spreadsheets. Setting up an activity-based costing system on a spreadsheet or using special ABC software can save a lot of work—particularly in situations involving many activity cost pools and in organizations that periodically update their ABC systems.

We will not go into the details of how all of the percentages in Exhibit 5–5 were determined. However, note that 100% of the factory building lease has been assigned to the Other cost pool. Classic Brass has a single production facility. It has no plans to expand or to sublease any excess space. The cost of this production facility is treated as an organization-sustaining cost because there is no way to avoid even a portion of this cost if a particular product or customer were to be dropped. (Remember that organization-sustaining costs are assigned to the Other cost pool and are not allocated to products.) In contrast, some companies have separate facilities for manufacturing specific products. The costs of these separate facilities could be directly traced to the specific products.

Once the percentage distributions in Exhibit 5–5 have been established, it is easy to allocate costs to the activity cost pools. The results of this first-stage allocation are displayed in Exhibit 5–6. Each cost is allocated across the activity cost pools by multiplying it by the percentages in Exhibit 5–5. For example, the indirect factory wages of $500,000 are multiplied by the 25% entry under Customer Orders in Exhibit 5–5 to arrive at the $125,000 entry under Customer Orders in Exhibit 5–6. Similarly, the indirect factory wages of $500,000 are multiplied by the 40% entry under Product Design in Exhibit 5–5 to arrive at the $200,000 entry under Product Design in Exhibit 5–6. All of the entries in Exhibit 5–6 are computed in this way.

Now that the first-stage allocations to the activity cost pools have been completed, the next step is to compute the activity rates.

Step 3: Calculate Activity Rates

The activity rates that will be used for assigning overhead costs to products and customers are computed in Exhibit 5–7. The ABC team determined the total activity for each cost pool that would be required to produce the company's present product mix and to serve its present customers. These numbers are listed in Exhibit 5–7. For example, the ABC team found that 400 new product designs are required each year to serve the company's present customers. The activity rates are computed by dividing the *total* cost for each activity by its *total* activity. For example, the $320,000 total annual cost for the Customer Orders cost pool is divided by the total of 1,000 customer orders per year to arrive at the activity rate of $320 per customer order. Similarly, the $252,000 *total* cost for the Product Design cost pool is divided by the *total* number of designs (i.e., 400 product designs) to determine the activity rate of $630 per design. Note that activity rates are not computed for the Other category of costs. This is because the Other cost pool consists of organization-sustaining costs and costs of idle capacity that are not allocated to products and customers. Note that the activity rates represent *average* costs. For example, the average cost of a customer order is $320.

The entries in Exhibit 5–7 indicate that on average a customer order consumes resources that cost $320; a product design consumes resources that cost $630; an order consumes resources that cost $19 per machine-hour; and maintaining relations with a customer consumes resources that cost $1,470. Note that these are *average* figures. Some members of the ABC design team at Classic Brass argued that it would be unfair to charge all new products the same $630 product design cost regardless of how much design time they actually require. After discussing the pros and cons, the team concluded that it would not be worth the effort at the present time to keep track of actual design time spent on each new product. They felt that the benefits of increased accuracy would not be great enough

EXHIBIT 5–7 Computation of Activity Rates

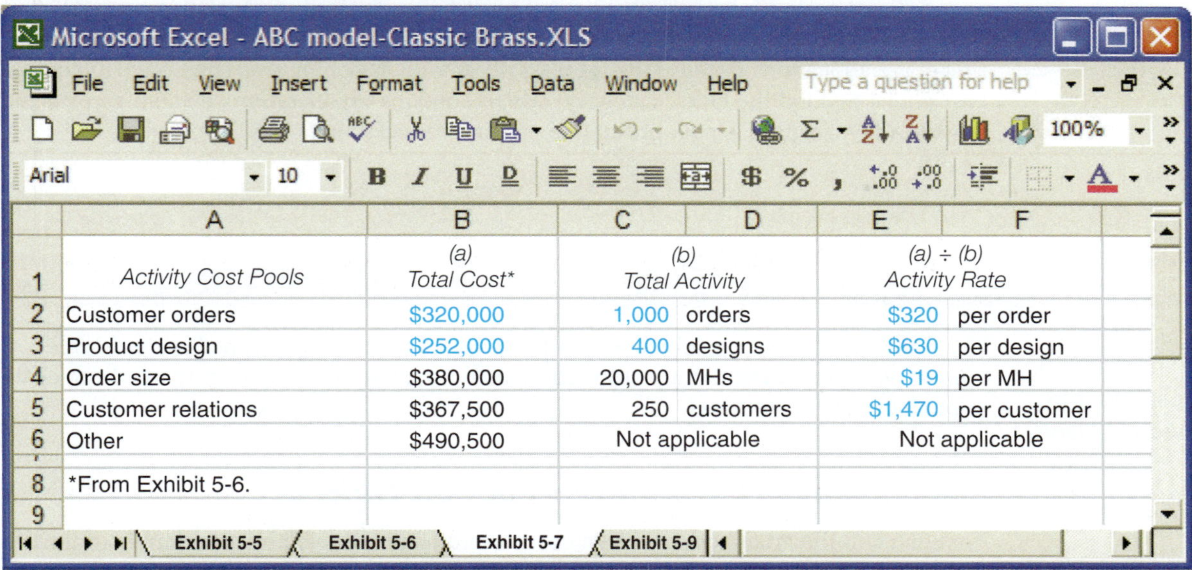

	A	B	C	D	E	F
1	*Activity Cost Pools*	*(a) Total Cost**	*(b) Total Activity*		*(a) ÷ (b) Activity Rate*	
2	Customer orders	$320,000	1,000	orders	$320	per order
3	Product design	$252,000	400	designs	$630	per design
4	Order size	$380,000	20,000	MHs	$19	per MH
5	Customer relations	$367,500	250	customers	$1,470	per customer
6	Other	$490,500	Not applicable		Not applicable	
8	*From Exhibit 5-6.					
9						

to justify the higher cost of implementing and maintaining the more detailed costing system. Similarly, some team members were uncomfortable assigning the same $1,470 cost to each customer because different customers place different demands on the resources of the company. However, while everyone agreed with this concern, the data that would be required to measure individual customers' demands on resources were not currently available. Rather than delay implementation of the ABC system, the team decided to defer such refinements to a later date.

Before proceeding, it would be helpful to review the overall process of assigning costs to products and other cost objects in an ABC system. Exhibit 5–8 builds on Exhibit 5–3 by providing a summary of the ABC system at Classic Brass. We recommend that you carefully go over this exhibit. In particular, two things about Exhibit 5–8 are important to keep

EXHIBIT 5–8 The Activity-Based Costing Model at Classic Brass

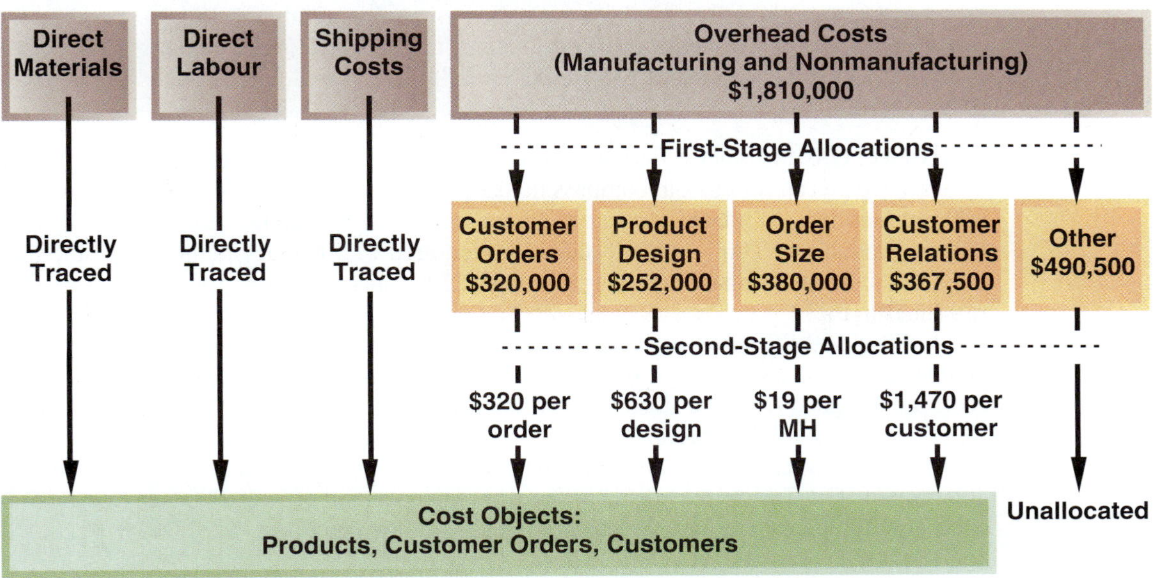

in mind. First, direct materials, direct labour and shipping costs are included because they are all direct costs of the cost objects and must be considered when analyzing total costs related to products, customer orders, and customers. These costs were not included in the first-stage allocations because that process deals with assigning overhead costs to activity cost pools. Second the Other category, which contains organization-sustaining costs and costs of idle capacity, is not allocated to products or customers.

Second-Stage Allocation of Overhead Costs

LEARNING OBJECTIVE 3
Assign costs to a cost object using a second-stage allocation.

Second-stage allocation The process by which activity rates are used to apply costs to products and customers in activity-based costing.

The fourth step in the implementation of activity-based costing is called *second-stage allocation.* In the **second-stage allocation,** activity rates are used to apply overhead costs to products and customers.

Step 4: Assign Overhead Costs to Cost Objects

First, we will illustrate how to assign costs to products followed by an example of how to assign costs to customers. The data needed by the ABC team to assign overhead costs to Classic Brass's two products—standard stanchions and custom compass housings—are as follows:

Standard Stanchions

1. This product line does not require any new design resources.
2. 30,000 units were ordered during the year, comprising 600 separate orders.
3. Each stanchion requires 35 minutes of machine time for a total of 17,500 machine-hours.

Custom Compass Housings

1. This is a custom product that requires new design resources.
2. There were 400 orders for custom compass housings. Orders for this product are placed separately from orders for standard stanchions.
3. There were 400 custom designs prepared. One custom design was prepared for each order.
4. Since some orders were for more than one unit, a total of 1,250 custom compass housings were produced during the year. A custom compass housing requires an average of 2 machine-hours for a total of 2,500 machine-hours.

Notice, 600 customer orders were placed for standard stanchions and 400 customer orders were placed for custom compass housings, for a total of 1,000 customer orders. All 400 product designs related to custom compass housings; none related to standard stanchions. Producing 30,000 standard stanchions required 17,500 machine-hours and producing 1,250 custom compass housings required 2,500 machine-hours, for a total of 20,000 machine-hours.

Exhibit 5–9 illustrates how overhead costs are assigned to the standard stanchions and custom compass housings. For example, the exhibit shows that $192,000 of overhead costs are assigned from the Customer Orders activity cost pool to the standard stanchions ($320 per order × 600 orders). Similarly, $128,000 of overhead costs are assigned from the Customer Orders activity cost pool to the custom compass housings ($320 per order × 400 orders). The Customer Orders cost pool contained a total of $320,000 (see Exhibit 5–6 or 5–7) and this total amount has been assigned to the two products ($192,000 + $128,000 = $320,000).

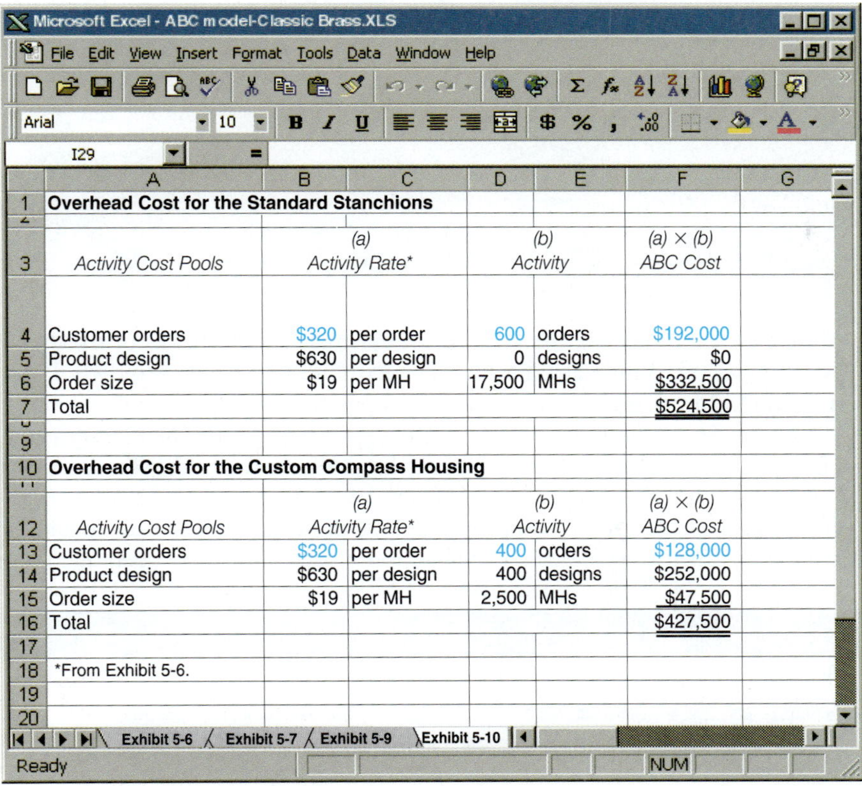

Microsoft Excel - ABC model-Classic Brass.XLS

Overhead Cost for the Standard Stanchions

Activity Cost Pools	(a) Activity Rate*		(b) Activity		(a) × (b) ABC Cost
Customer orders	$320	per order	600	orders	$192,000
Product design	$630	per design	0	designs	$0
Order size	$19	per MH	17,500	MHs	$332,500
Total					$524,500

Overhead Cost for the Custom Compass Housing

Activity Cost Pools	(a) Activity Rate*		(b) Activity		(a) × (b) ABC Cost
Customer orders	$320	per order	400	orders	$128,000
Product design	$630	per design	400	designs	$252,000
Order size	$19	per MH	2,500	MHs	$47,500
Total					$427,500

*From Exhibit 5-6.

EXHIBIT 5–9 Assigning Overhead Costs to Products

Exhibit 5–9 shows that a total of $952,000 of overhead costs is assigned to Classic Brass's two product lines—$524,500 to standard stanchions and $427,500 to custom compass housings. This amount is less than the $1,810,000 of overhead costs included in the ABC system. Why? The total amount of overhead assigned to products does not match the total amount of overhead cost in the ABC system because the ABC team purposely did not assign the $367,500 of Customer Relations and $490,500 of Other costs to products. The Customer Relations activity is a customer-level activity and the Other activity is an organization-sustaining activity—neither activity is caused by products. As shown below, when the Customer Relations and Other activity costs are added to the $952,000 of overhead costs assigned to products, the total is $1,810,000.

	Standard Stanchions	Custom Compass Housings	Total
Overhead Costs Assigned to Products			
Customer orders	$192,000	$128,000	$ 320,000
Product design	0	252,000	252,000
Order size	332,500	47,500	380,000
Subtotal	$524,500	$427,500	952,000
Overhead Costs not Assigned to Products			
Customer relations			367,500
Other			490,500
Subtotal			858,000
Total overhead cost			$1,810,000

Next, we describe another aspect of second-stage allocations—assigning activity costs to customers.

The data needed by the design team to assign overhead costs to one of its company's customers—Windward Yachts—are as follows:

Windward Yachts

1. The company placed a total of three orders.
   a. Two orders were for 150 standard stanchions per order.
   b. One order was for a single custom compass housing unit.
2. A total of 177 machine-hours were used to fulfill the three customer orders.
   a. The 300 standard stanchions required 175 machine-hours.
   b. The custom compass housing required 2 machine-hours.
3. Windward Yachts is one of 250 customers served by Classic Brass.

As shown in Exhibit 5–10, the ABC team calculated that $6,423 of overhead costs should be assigned to Windward Yachts. The exhibit shows that Windward Yachts is assigned $960 ($320 per order × 3 orders) of overhead costs from the Customer Orders activity cost pool; $630 ($630 per design × 1 design) from the Product Design cost pool; $3,363 ($19 per machine-hour × 177 machine-hours) from the Order Size cost pool; and $1,470 ($1,470 per customer × 1 customer) from the Customer Relations cost pool.

With second-stage allocations complete, the ABC design team was ready to turn its attention to creating reports that would help explain the company's first ever operating loss.

EXHIBIT 5–10 Assigning Overhead Costs to Customers

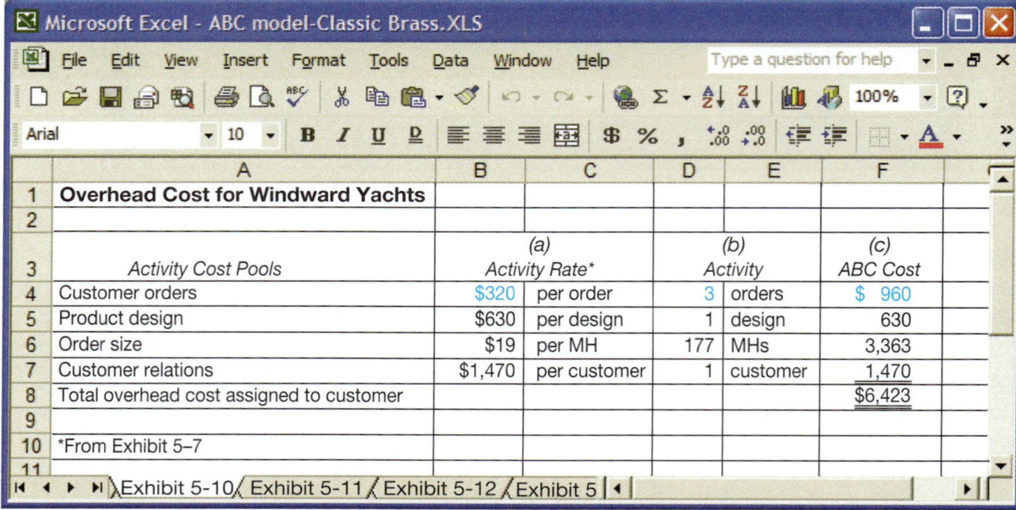

Overhead Cost for Windward Yachts

Activity Cost Pools	(a) Activity Rate*		(b) Activity		(c) ABC Cost
Customer orders	$320	per order	3	orders	$ 960
Product design	$630	per design	1	design	630
Order size	$19	per MH	177	MHs	3,363
Customer relations	$1,470	per customer	1	customer	1,470
Total overhead cost assigned to customer					$6,423

*From Exhibit 5–7

Product and Customer Margins

LEARNING OBJECTIVE 4
Use activity-based costing to compute product and customer margins.

The most common management reports prepared with ABC data are product and customer profitability reports. These reports help companies channel their resources to their most profitable growth opportunities while at the same time highlighting products and customers that drain profits. We begin by illustrating a product profitability report followed by a customer profitability report.

Step 5: Prepare Management Reports

The Classic Brass ABC team realized that the profit from a product, also called the *product margin,* is a function of the product's sales and the direct and indirect costs that the product causes. The ABC cost allocations shown in Exhibit 5–9 only summarize each product's indirect (i.e., overhead) costs. Therefore, to compute a product's profit (i.e., product margin), the design team needed to gather each product's sales and direct costs in addition to the overhead costs previously computed. The pertinent sales and direct cost data for each product are shown below. Notice the numbers in the total column agree with the income statement in Exhibit 5–1.

	Standard Stanchions	Custom Compass Housings	Total
Sales	$2,660,000	$540,000	$3,200,000
Direct costs:			
Direct materials	$905,500	$69,500	$975,000
Direct labour	$263,750	$87,500	$351,250
Shipping	$60,000	$5,000	$65,000

Having gathered the above data, the design team created the product profitability report shown in Exhibit 5–11. The report revealed that standard stanchions are profitable, with a positive product margin of $906,250, whereas the custom compass housings are unprofitable, with a negative product margin of $49,500. Keep in mind that the product profitability report purposely does not include the costs in the Customer Relations and Other activity cost pools. These costs, which total $858,000, were excluded from the report because they are not caused by the products. Customer Relations costs are caused by customers, not products. The Other costs are organization-sustaining costs that are not caused by any particular product.

EXHIBIT 5–11 Product Margins—Activity-Based Costing

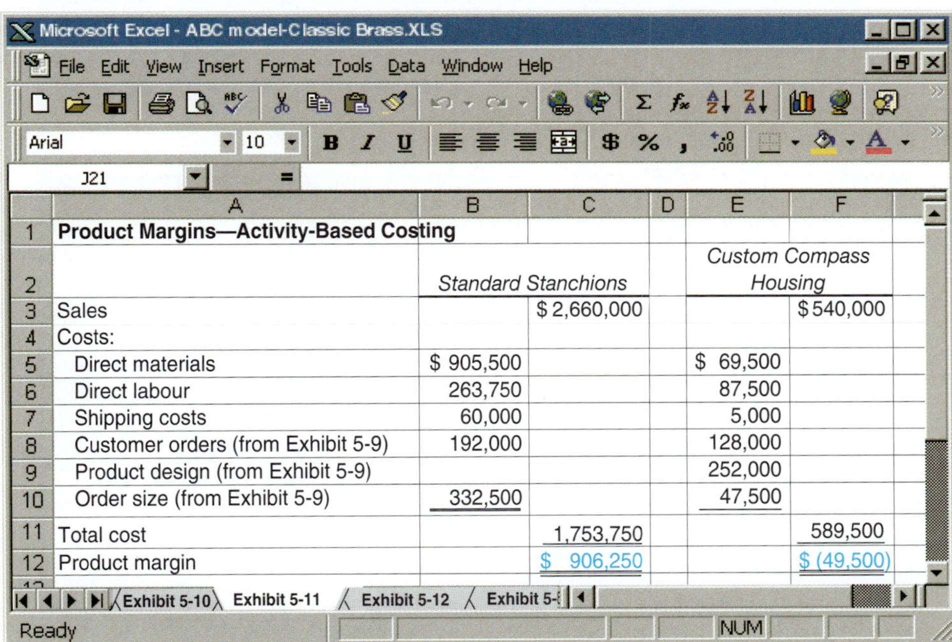

Microsoft Excel - ABC model-Classic Brass.XLS

	A	B	C	D	E	F
1	**Product Margins—Activity-Based Costing**					
2		*Standard Stanchions*			*Custom Compass Housing*	
3	Sales		$ 2,660,000			$ 540,000
4	Costs:					
5	Direct materials	$ 905,500			$ 69,500	
6	Direct labour	263,750			87,500	
7	Shipping costs	60,000			5,000	
8	Customer orders (from Exhibit 5-9)	192,000			128,000	
9	Product design (from Exhibit 5-9)				252,000	
10	Order size (from Exhibit 5-9)	332,500			47,500	
11	Total cost		1,753,750			589,500
12	Product margin		$ 906,250			$ (49,500)

Exhibit 5-10 | Exhibit 5-11 | Exhibit 5-12 | Exhibit 5-

The product margins can be reconciled with the company's operating income as follows:

	Standard Stanchions	Custom Compass Housings	Total
Sales (See Exhibit 5–11)	$2,660,000	$540,000	$3,200,000
Total costs (See Exhibit 5–11)	1,753,750	589,500	2,343,250
Product margins (See Exhibit 5–11)	$ 906,250	$ (49,500)	856,750
Overhead costs not assigned to products:			
Customer relations (See Exhibit 5–7)			367,500
Other (See Exhibit 5–7)			490,500
Total			858,000
Operating income			$ (1,250)

Next, the design team created a customer profitability report for Windward Yachts. Similar to the product profitability report, the design team needed to gather data concerning sales to Windward Yachts and the direct material, direct labour, and shipping costs associated with those sales. Those data are presented below:

	Windward Yachts
Sales	$11,350
Direct costs:	
Direct material costs	$2,123
Direct labour costs.	$1,900
Shipping costs	$205

Using these data and the data from Exhibit 5–10, the design team created the customer profitability report shown in Exhibit 5–12. The report revealed that the customer margin for Windward Yachts is $699. A similar report could be prepared for each of Classic Brass's 250 customers, thereby enabling the company to cultivate relationships with its most profitable customers, while taking steps to reduce the negative impact of unprofitable customers.

EXHIBIT 5–12 Customer Margin—Activity-Based Costing

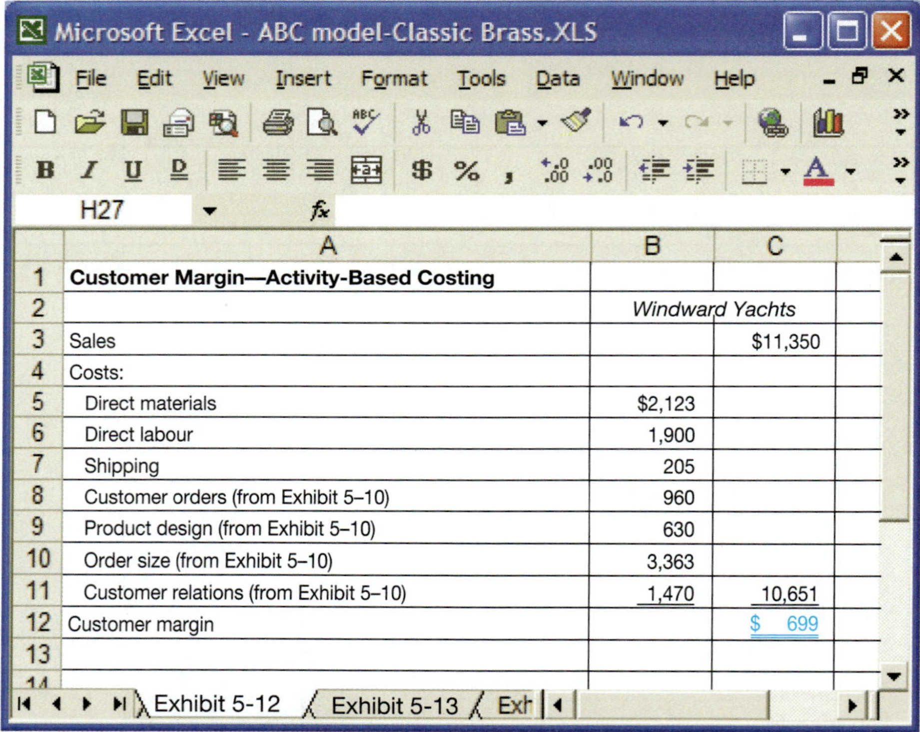

Microsoft Excel - ABC model-Classic Brass.XLS

	A	B	C
1	**Customer Margin—Activity-Based Costing**		
2		*Windward Yachts*	
3	Sales		$11,350
4	Costs:		
5	Direct materials	$2,123	
6	Direct labour	1,900	
7	Shipping	205	
8	Customer orders (from Exhibit 5–10)	960	
9	Product design (from Exhibit 5–10)	630	
10	Order size (from Exhibit 5–10)	3,363	
11	Customer relations (from Exhibit 5–10)	1,470	10,651
12	Customer margin		$ 699
13			

Comparison of Traditional and ABC Product Costs

LEARNING OBJECTIVE 5
Compare product costs computed using traditional and activity-based costing methods.

The ABC team used a two-step process to compare its traditional and ABC product costs. First, the team reviewed the product margins reported by the traditional cost system. Then, they contrasted the differences between the traditional and ABC product margins.

Product Margins Computed Using the Traditional Cost System

Classic Brass's traditional cost system assigns only manufacturing costs to products—this includes direct materials, direct labour, and manufacturing overhead. Selling and administrative costs are not assigned to products. Exhibit 5–13 shows the product margins reported by Classic Brass's traditional cost system. We will explain how these margins were calculated in three steps. First, the sales and direct materials and direct labour cost data are the same numbers used by the ABC team to prepare Exhibit 5–11. In other words, the traditional cost system and the ABC system treat these three pieces of revenue and cost data identically.

Second, the traditional cost system uses a plantwide overhead rate to assign manufacturing overhead costs to products. The numerator for the plantwide overhead rate is $1,000,000, which is the total amount of manufacturing overhead shown on the income statement in Exhibit 5–1. The footnote in Exhibit 5–1 mentions that the traditional cost system uses machine-hours to assign manufacturing overhead costs to products. The Order Size activity in Exhibit 5–7 used 20,000 machine-hours as its level of activity. These same 20,000 machine-hours would be used in the denominator of the plantwide overhead rate, which is computed as follows:

$$\text{Plantwide overhead rate} = \frac{\text{Total estimated manufacturing overhead}}{\text{Total estimated machine-hours}}$$

$$= \frac{\$1{,}000{,}000}{20{,}000 \text{ machine-hours}}$$

$$= \$50 \text{ per machine-hour}$$

Since 17,500 machine-hours were worked on standard stanchions, this product line is assigned $875,000 (17,500 machine-hours × $50 per machine-hour) of manufacturing overhead cost. Similarly, the custom compass housings required 2,500 machine-hours, so this product line is assigned $125,000 (2,500 machine-hours × $50 per machine-hour) of manufacturing overhead cost. The sales of each product minus its cost of goods sold equals the product margin of $615,750 for standard stanchions and $258,000 for custom compass housings.

Notice, the operating loss of $1,250 shown in Exhibit 5–13 agrees with the loss reported in the income statement in Exhibit 5–1 and with the loss shown in the table immediately beneath Exhibit 5–11. The company's *total* sales, *total* costs, and its resulting operating loss are the same regardless of whether you are looking at the absorption income statement in Exhibit 5–1, the ABC product profitability analysis depicted on page 187, or the traditional product profitability analysis in Exhibit 5–13. Although the "total pie" remains constant across the traditional and ABC systems, what differs is how the pie is divided between the two product lines. The traditional product margin calculations suggest that standard stanchions are generating a product margin of $615,750 and

EXHIBIT 5–13 Product Margins—Traditional Costing System

Microsoft Excel - ABC model-Classic Brass.XLS

	A	B	C	D	E	F	G	H	I
1	**Product Margins—Traditional Cost System**								
2		*Standard Stanchions*			*Custom Compass Housings*			*Total*	
3	Sales		$2,660,000			$540,000			$3,200,000
4	Cost of goods sold:								
5	Direct materials	$905,000			$ 69,500			$ 975,000	
6	Direct labour	263,750			87,500			351,250	
7	Manufacturing overhead	875,000	2,044,250		125,000	282,000		1,000,000	2,326,250
8	Product margin		$ 615,750			$258,000			873,750
9	Selling and administrative								875,000
10	Operating income								$ (1,250)
11									

Exhibit 5-12 | Exhibit 5-13 | Exhibit 5-14 | Exhibit 5-15 | Exhibit 5-

the custom compass housings a product margin of $258,000. However, these product margins differ from the ABC product margins reported in Exhibit 5–11. Indeed, the traditional cost system is sending misleading signals to Classic Brass's managers about each product's profitability. We explain why in the next section.

The Differences between ABC and Traditional Product Costs

The changes in product margins caused by switching from the traditional cost system to the activity-based costing system are shown below:

	Standard Stanchions	Custom Compass Housings
Product margins—traditional.	$615,750	$258,000
Product margins—ABC.	906,250	(49,500)
Change in reported product margins	$290,500	($307,500)

The traditional cost system overcosts the standard stanchions and consequently reports an artificially low product margin for this product. The switch to an activity-based view of product profitability increases the product margin on standard stanchions by $290,500. In contrast, the traditional cost system undercosts the custom compass housings and reports an artificially high product margin for this product. The switch to activity-based costing decreases the product margin on custom compass housings by $307,500.

The reasons for the change in reported product margins between the two costing methods are revealed in Exhibit 5–14. The top portion of the exhibit shows each product's direct and indirect cost assignments as reported by the traditional cost system in Exhibit 5–13. For example, Exhibit 5–14 includes the following costs for standard stanchions: direct materials, $905,500; direct labour, $263,750; and manufacturing overhead, $875,000. Each of these costs corresponds with those reported in Exhibit 5–13. Notice, the selling and administrative costs of $875,000 are purposely not allocated to products because these costs are considered to be period costs. Similarly, the bottom portion of Exhibit 5–14 summarizes the direct and indirect cost assignments as reported by the activity-based costing system in Exhibit 5–11. The only new information in Exhibit 5–14 is shown in the two columns of percentages. The first column of percentages shows the percentage of each cost assigned to standard stanchions. For example, the $905,500 of direct materials cost traced to standard stanchions is 92.9% of the company's total direct materials cost of $975,000. The second column of percentages does the same thing for custom compass housings.

There are three reasons why the traditional and activity-based costing systems report different product margins.

1. The traditional cost system allocates *all* manufacturing costs to products regardless of whether they consumed those costs. The ABC system does not assign manufacturing overhead costs to products for either Customer Relations activities or Other (organization-sustaining) activities because they are not caused by any particular product.
2. The traditional cost system allocates *all* manufacturing overhead costs using machine-hours, a volume-related allocation base. The ABC system uses unique activity measures (most of which are *not* volume-related) to allocate the cost of each activity cost pool selected on the basis of management's assessment of the driver of overhead costs for that activity. For example, the traditional cost system assigns 87.5% of the Product Design activity to standard stanchions even though that product caused none of these costs. Conversely, all of the Product Design activity costs should be assigned to custom compass housings, not just the 12.5% that results under the traditional system. The overall effect is that traditional cost systems overcost high-volume products (such as custom compass housings) and undercost low-volume products (such as standard stanchions) because they assign batch-level and product-level costs using volume-related allocation bases.
3. The ABC system assigns non-manufacturing overhead costs such as shipping to

EXHIBIT 5–14 A Comparison of Traditional and Activity-Based Cost Assignments

	Standard Stanchions		Custom Compass Housings		Total
	(a) Amount	(a) ÷ (c) %	(b) Amount	(b) ÷ (c) %	(c) Amount
Traditional Cost System					
Direct materials	$ 905,500	92.9%	$ 69,500	7.1%	$ 975,000
Direct labour	263,750	75.1%	87,500	24.9%	351,250
Manufacturing overhead	875,000	87.5%	125,000	12.5%	1,000,000
Total cost assigned to products	$2,044,250		$282,000		2,326,250
Selling and administrative					875,000
Total cost					$3,201,250
Activity-Based Costing System					
Direct costs:					
Direct materials	$ 905,500	92.9%	$ 69,500	7.1%	$ 975,000
Direct labour	263,750	75.1%	87,500	24.9%	351,250
Shipping	60,000	92.3%	5,000	7.7%	65,000
Indirect costs:					
Customer orders	192,000	60.0%	128,000	40.0%	320,000
Product design	0	0.0%	252,000	100.0%	252,000
Order size	332,500	87.5%	47,500	12.5%	380,000
Total cost assigned to products	$1,753,750		$589,500		2,343,250
Costs not assigned to products:					
Customer relations					367,500
Other					490,500
Total cost					$3,201,250

products on a cause-and-effect basis. The traditional cost system excludes these costs because they are classified as period costs.

Wrap-Up

Caution should be exercised before taking action based on an ABC analysis such as the one shown in Exhibits 5–11 and 5–12. The product and customer margins computed in those exhibits are a useful starting point for further analysis, but managers need to know what costs are really affected before taking any action such as dropping a product or customer or changing the prices of products or services. Appendix 5A to this chapter shows how an action analysis report can be constructed to help managers make such decisions. An **action analysis report** provides more detail about costs and how they might adjust to changes in activity than the ABC analysis presented in Exhibits 5–11 and 5–12.

Action analysis report
A report showing what costs have been assigned to a cost object, such as a product or customer, and how difficult it would be to adjust the cost if there is a change in activity.

Targeting Process Improvements

Activity-based costing can be used to identify areas that would benefit from process improvements. Indeed, managers often cite this as the major benefit of activity-based costing.[4] **Activity-based management (ABM)** is used in conjunction with activity-based costing to improve processes and reduce costs. Activity-based management is used in organizations as diverse as manufacturing companies, hospitals, and the Canadian Coast Guard.[5] When "forty percent of the cost of running a hospital involves storing, collecting

Activity-based management (ABM)
A management approach that focuses on managing activities as a way of eliminating waste and reducing delays and defects.

4. Dan Swenson, "The Benefits of Activity-Based Cost Management to the Manufacturing Industry," *Journal of Management Accounting Research* 7, Fall 1995, pp. 165–80.

5. William T. Bonner, "Stormy Waters and the Canadian Coast Guard," *CMA Magazine*, February 1998, pp. 21–26; and Michael Senyshen, "ABC/M in the Federal Government," *CGA Magazine*, December 1997, p. 19.

and moving information," there is obviously a great deal of room for eliminating waste and for improvement.[6]

The first step in any improvement program is to decide what to improve. The theory of constraints approach, which is discussed in Chapter 12 is a powerful tool for targeting the area in an organization where improvement will yield the greatest benefit. Activity-based management provides another approach. The activity rates computed in activity-based costing can provide valuable clues concerning where there is waste and scope for improvement in an organization. For example, managers at Classic Brass were surprised at the high cost of customer orders. Some customer orders are for less than $100 worth of products, and yet it costs, on average, $320 to process an order according to the activity rates calculated in Exhibit 5–7. This seemed expensive for an activity that adds no value to the product. As a consequence, the customer order processing activity was targeted for improvement.

Benchmarking provides a systematic approach to identifying the activities with the greatest room for improvement. For example, the Marketing Resources Group of a telephone company performed an ABC analysis of the activities carried out in the Accounting Department.[7] Managers computed the activity rates for the activities of the Accounting Department and then compared these rates to the costs of carrying out the same activities in other companies. Two benchmarks were used: (1) a sample of Fortune 100 companies, which are the largest 100 companies in the United States; and (2) a sample of "world-class" companies that had been identified by a consultant as having the best accounting practices in the world. These comparisons follow:

Activity	Activity Measure	Telephone Company	Fortune 100 Benchmark	World-Class Benchmark
Processing accounts receivable	Number of invoices processed	$3.80 per invoice	$15.00 per invoice	$4.60 per invoice
Processing accounts payable	Number of invoices processed	$8.90 per invoice	$7.00 per invoice	$1.80 per invoice
Processing payroll cheques	Number of cheques processed	$7.30 per cheque	$5.00 per cheque	$1.72 per cheque
Managing customer credit	Number of customer accounts	$12.00 per account	$16.00 per account	$5.60 per account

It is clear from this analysis that the telephone company does a good job of processing accounts receivable. Its average cost per invoice is $3.80, whereas the cost in other companies that are considered world class is even higher—$4.60 per invoice. On the other hand, the cost of processing payroll cheques is significantly higher at the telephone company than at benchmark companies. The cost per payroll cheque at the telephone company is $7.30 versus $5.00 at Fortune 100 companies and $1.72 at world-class companies. This suggests that it may be possible to wring some waste out of this activity using TQM, process re-engineering, or some other method.

IN BUSINESS

Tata Consultancy Services (TCS) is the largest consulting organization in India, serving both Indian and international clients. The company used activity-based management to identify problem areas in its software development business. An early finding was that "quality assurance, testing, and error-correction activities made up a significant chunk of

6. Kambiz Foroohar, "Rx: Software," *Forbes*, April 7, 1997, p. 114.

7. Steve Coburn, Hugh Grove, and Cynthia Fukami, "Benchmarking with ABCM," *Management Accounting*, January 1995, pp. 56–60.

the overall effort required to build a system, and this cost had to be kept under control to improve productivity and profitability." The company already had in place a quality management system that helped identify the types of errors that were occurring and the corrective action that would be required, but no costs were attached to these errors and actions. The activity-based management system provided this cost information, which allowed managers to set better priorities and to monitor the costs of error-detection and error-correction activities.

As another example of the usefulness of the system, 54 person-days in one software development project at TCS were charged to the activity "Waiting for client feedback"—a non-value-added activity. Investigation revealed that the client was taking a long time to review the graphical user interface (GUI) designed by TCS. The client was showing the GUI to various end users—often resulting in contradictory suggestions. The solution was to draw up guidelines for the GUI with the client, which were enforced. "As a result of this corrective action, subsequent client feedback was well within the time schedule. Most of our screens were accepted because they conformed to standards . . . ."

Source: Maha S. Mahalingam, Bala V. Balachandran, and Farooq C. Kohli, "Activity-Based Management for Systems Consulting Industry," *Journal of Cost Management*, May/June 1999, pp. 4–15.

Activity-Based Costing and External Reports

Since activity-based costing generally provides more accurate product costs than traditional costing methods, why isn't it used for external reports? Some companies *do* use activity-based costing in their external reports, but most do not. There are a number of reasons for this. First, external reports are less detailed than internal reports prepared for decision making. On the external reports, individual product costs are not reported. Cost of goods sold and inventory valuations are disclosed, but there is no breakdown of these accounts by product. If some products are undercosted and some are overcosted, the errors tend to cancel each other when the product costs are added together.

Second, an ABC system such as the one described in this chapter does not conform to generally accepted accounting principles (GAAP). As discussed in Chapter 2, product costs computed for external reports must include all of the manufacturing costs and only manufacturing costs; however, in an ABC system as described in this chapter, product costs exclude some manufacturing costs and include some non-manufacturing costs. It is possible to adjust the ABC data at the end of the period to conform to GAAP, but that requires more work. Appendix 5B presents an approach for using a modified form of ABC for external reporting purposes.

Third, auditors are likely to be uncomfortable with allocations that are based on interviews with the company's personnel. Such subjective data can easily be manipulated by management to make earnings and other key variables look more favourable.

For all of these reasons, most companies confine their ABC efforts to special studies for management, and do not attempt to integrate activity-based costing into their formal cost accounting systems.

The Limitations of Activity-Based Costing

Implementing an activity-based costing system is a major project that requires substantial resources. And once implemented, an activity-based costing system is more costly to maintain than a traditional direct labour-based costing system—data concerning numerous activity measures must be collected, checked, and entered into the system. The benefits of increased accuracy may not outweigh these costs.

IN BUSINESS

A Critical Perspective of ABC

Marconi is a Portuguese telecommunications company that encountered problems with its ABC system. The company's production managers felt that 23% of the costs included in the system were common costs that should not be allocated to products and that allocating these costs to products was not only inaccurate, but also irrelevant to their operational cost reduction efforts. Furthermore, Marconi's front-line workers resisted the ABC system because they felt it might be used to weaken their autonomy and to justify downsizing, outsourcing, and work intensification. They believed that ABC created a "turkeys queuing for Christmas syndrome" because they were expected to volunteer information to help create a cost system that could eventually lead to their demise. These two complications created a third problem—the data necessary to build the ABC cost model was provided by disgruntled and distrustful employees. Consequently, the accuracy of the data was questionable at best. In short, Marconi's experiences illustrate some of the challenges that complicate real-world ABC implementations.

Source: Maria Major and Trevor Hopper, "Managers Divided: Implementing ABC in a Portuguese Telecommunications Company," *Management Accounting Research,* June 2005, pp. 205–229.

Activity-based costing produces numbers, such as product margins, that may be at odds with the numbers produced by traditional costing systems. But managers are accustomed to using traditional costing systems to run their operations and traditional costing systems are often used in performance evaluations. Essentially, activity-based costing changes the rules of the game. It is a fact of human nature that changes in organizations, particularly those that alter the rules of the game, inevitably face resistance. This underscores the importance of top-management support and the full participation of line managers, as well as the accounting staff, in any activity-based costing initiative. If activity-based costing is viewed as an accounting initiative that does not have the full support of top management, it is doomed to failure.

In practice, most managers insist on fully allocating all costs to products, customers, and other costing objects in an activity-based costing system—including the costs of idle capacity and organization-sustaining costs. This results in overstated costs and understated margins and mistakes in pricing and other critical decisions.[8]

IN BUSINESS

In a recent survey of large manufacturing companies in Canada, nearly 66% of the respondents indicated they believed an activity-based costing system could potentially add value to their organization. However, despite acknowledging its perceived usefulness, only 39% of the responding companies had actually implemented an ABC system across all business units in the organization. Kaplan and Anderson (2007) provide some possible reasons for this relatively low adoption rate:

- High implementation and maintenance costs of ABC systems.
- Inaccuracies in activity costs due to the need for subjective estimates of the amount of time spent on various activities.
- Inability of ABC systems to completely capture the complexity of actual operations.
- Difficulties integrating ABC data from multiple business units across the organization.

8. Philip Beaulieu and Anila Lakra, "Coverage of the Criticism of Activity-Based Costing in Canadian Textbooks," *Canadian Accounting Perspectives,* vol. 4, 2005, pp. 87–109, provides relevant comments on the proper treatment of organization-sustaining activities and idle capacity based on earlier analysis in the literature.

Although ABC offers the potential for more accurate product costs, managers must carefully consider all costs of implementing, maintaining, and using the system. Further, some of the reasons cited by Kaplan and Anderson (2007) suggest that implementing a more complex costing system will not automatically result in more accurate costs. Only if estimated benefits exceed all estimated costs should the ABC implementation proceed.

Source: Alnoor Bhimani, Maurice Gosselin, Mthuli Ncube, and Hiroshi Okano, "Activity-Based Costing: How Far Have We Come Internationally?" *Cost Management*, May–June 2007, pp. 12–17; and Robert Kaplan and Steven Anderson, "The Innovation of Time-Driven Activity-Based Costing," *Cost Management*, March–April 2007, pp. 5–15.

Activity-based costing data can easily be misinterpreted and must be used with care in making decisions. Costs assigned to products, customers, and other cost objects are only *potentially* relevant. Before making any significant decisions using activity-based costing data, managers must identify which costs are really relevant for the decision at hand. See Appendix 5A to this chapter for more details.

As discussed in the previous section, reports generated by the best activity-based costing systems do not conform to generally accepted accounting principles. Consequently, an organization involved in activity-based costing should have two cost systems—one for internal use and one for preparing external reports. This is costlier than maintaining just one system and may cause confusion about which system is to be believed and relied on.

Summary

Traditional cost accounting methods suffer from several defects that can result in distorted costs for decision-making purposes. All manufacturing costs—even those that are not caused by any specific product—are allocated to products, and non-manufacturing costs that are caused by products are not assigned to products. Traditional methods also allocate the costs of idle capacity to products. In effect, products are charged for resources that they don't use. And finally, traditional methods tend to place too much reliance on unit-level allocation bases such as direct labour and machine-hours. This results in overcosting high-volume products and undercosting low-volume products and can lead to mistakes when making decisions.

Activity-based costing estimates the costs of the resources consumed by cost objects such as products and customers. The approach taken in activity-based costing assumes that cost objects generate activities that in turn consume costly resources. Activities form the link between costs and cost objects. Activity-based costing is concerned with overhead—both manufacturing overhead and selling, general, and administrative overhead. The accounting for direct labour and direct materials is usually unaffected.

To build an ABC system, companies typically choose a small set of activities that summarize much of the work performed in overhead departments. Associated with each activity is an activity cost pool. To the extent possible, overhead costs are directly traced to these activity cost pools. The remaining overhead costs are assigned to the activity cost pools in the first-stage allocation. Interviews with managers often form the basis for these allocations.

An activity rate is computed for each cost pool by dividing the costs assigned to the cost pool by the measure of activity for the cost pool. Activity rates provide useful information to managers concerning the costs of carrying out overhead activities. A particularly high cost for an activity may trigger efforts to improve the way the activity is carried out in the organization.

In the second-stage allocation, the activity rates are used to apply costs to cost objects such as products and customers. The costs computed under activity-based costing are often quite different from the costs generated by a company's traditional cost accounting system. While the ABC system is almost certainly more accurate, managers should nevertheless exercise caution before making decisions based on the ABC data. Some of the costs may not be avoidable and hence would not be relevant.

Review Problem: Activity-Based Costing

Advanced Products Corporation has supplied the following data from its activity-based costing system:

Overhead Costs	
Wages and salaries	$300,000
Other overhead costs.	100,000
Total overhead costs	$400,000

Activity Cost Pool	Activity Measure	Total Activity for the Year
Volume related.	Number of direct labour-hours	20,000 DLHs
Order related	Number of customer orders	400 orders
Customer support . . .	Number of customers	200 customers
Other	These costs are not allocated to products or customers	Not applicable

Distribution of Resource Consumption Across Activities

	Volume-Related	Order-Related	Customer Support	Other	Total
Wages and salaries	40%	30%	20%	10%	100%
Other overhead costs	30%	10%	20%	40%	100%

During the year, Advanced Products completed one order for a new customer, Shenzhen Enterprises. This customer did not order any other products during the year. Data concerning that order follow:

Data concerning the Shenzhen Enterprises Order	
Units ordered.	10 units
Direct labour-hours	2 DLHs per unit
Selling price.	$300 per unit
Direct materials	$180 per unit
Direct labour	$50 per unit

Required:

1. Prepare a report showing the first-stage allocations of overhead costs to the activity cost pools. (Use Exhibit 5–6 as a guide.)
2. Compute the activity rates for the activity cost pools. (Use Exhibit 5–7 as a guide.)
3. Prepare a report showing the overhead costs for the order from Shenzhen Enterprises. (Use Exhibit 5–10 as a guide. Do not include the customer support costs at this point in the analysis.)
4. Prepare a report showing the product margin for the order and the customer margin for Shenzhen Enterprises. (Use Exhibit 5–12 as a guide.)

Solution to Review Problem

1. The first-stage allocation is shown on the following page.

	Volume-Related	Order-Related	Customer Support	Other	Totals
Wages and salaries	$120,000	$ 90,000	$60,000	$30,000	$300,000
Other overhead costs . .	30,000	10,000	20,000	40,000	100,000
Total overhead cost. . . .	$150,000	$100,000	$80,000	$70,000	$400,000

Example: According to the distribution of resources across activities, 40% of the $300,000 wages and salaries cost is attributable to volume-related activities.

$300,000 × 40% = $120,000

Other entries in the table are determined in a similar manner.

2. Computation of activity rates:

Activity Cost Pools	(a) Total Cost	(b) Total Activity	(a) ÷ (b) Activity Rate
Volume-related	$150,000	20,000 DLHs	$7.50 per DLH
Order-related	$100,000	400 orders	$250 per order
Customer support.	$80,000	200 customers	$400 per customer

3. Computation of the overhead costs for the Shenzhen Enterprises order:

Activity Cost Pool	(a) Activity Rate	(b) Activity	(a) × (b) ABC Cost
Volume-related	$7.50 per DLH	20 DLHs*	$150
Order-related	$250 per order	1 order	250
Total			$400

*2 DLHs per unit × 10 units = 20 DLHs

4. The margins for the order and for the customer follow:

Product Profitability Analysis		
Sales (10 units × $300 per unit)		$3,000
Costs:		
Direct materials (10 units × $180 per unit)	$1,800	
Direct labour (10 units × $50 per unit)	500	
Volume overhead ($7.50 × 20 DLH).	150	
Order-related overhead	250	2,700
Product margin		$ 300

Customer Profitability Analysis	
Product margin (above)	$ 300
Less: Customer support overhead	
(1 customer @ $400 per customer)	400
Customer margin	$ (100)

Appendix 5A: ABC Action Analysis

LEARNING OBJECTIVE 6
Prepare an action analysis report using activity-based costing data and interpret the report.

A conventional ABC analysis, such as the one presented in Exhibit 5–11 in the chapter, has several important limitations. Referring back to Exhibit 5–11, recall that the custom compass housing shows a negative product margin of $49,500. Because of this apparent loss, managers were considering dropping this product. However, as the discussion among the managers revealed, it is unlikely that all of the $589,500 cost of the product would be avoided if the product was dropped. Some of these costs would continue even if the product was totally eliminated. *Before* taking action, it is vital to identify which costs would be avoided and which costs would continue. Only those costs that can be avoided are relevant in the decision. Moreover, many of the costs would require explicit management action to eliminate. If the custom compass housing product was eliminated, the direct materials cost would be avoided without any explicit management action—the materials simply wouldn't be ordered. On the other hand, if the custom compass housing product was dropped, explicit management action would be required to eliminate the salaries of overhead workers that have been assigned to the product.

Simply shifting these managed costs to other products would not solve anything. These costs would have to be eliminated or the resources shifted to a work centre that is currently a *constraint*. As will be more fully described in Chapter 12, a constraint is a resource limitation such as machine time or raw material supply, which prevents a company from fully meeting demand for its products or services. Eliminating the cost is obviously beneficial. Redeploying a resource is beneficial only if the resource is shifted to the constraint in the process. If the resource is redeployed to a work centre that is not a constraint, it would have the effect of increasing the excess capacity in that work centre—which is of no direct benefit to the company.

In addition, if some overhead costs need to be eliminated as a result of dropping a product, specific managers must be held responsible for eliminating those costs or the savings are unlikely to occur. If no one is specifically held responsible for eliminating the costs, they will almost certainly continue to be incurred. Without external pressure, managers usually avoid cutting costs in their areas of responsibility. The action analysis report developed in this appendix is intended to help top managers identify which costs are relevant in a decision and to place responsibility for the elimination of the costs on the appropriate managers.

Activity Rates—Action Analysis Report

Constructing an action analysis report begins with the results of the first-stage allocation, which is reproduced as Exhibit 5–15. In contrast to the conventional ABC analysis covered in the chapter, the calculation of the activity rates for an action analysis report is a bit more involved. In addition to computing an overall activity rate for each activity cost pool, an activity rate is computed for each cell in Exhibit 5–15. The computations of activity rates for the action analysis are carried out in Exhibit 5–16. For example, the $125,000 cost of indirect factory wages for the Customer Orders cost pool is divided by the total activity for that cost pool—1,000 orders—to arrive at the activity rate of $125 per customer order for indirect factory wages. Similarly, the $200,000 cost of indirect factory wages for the Product Design cost pool is divided by the total activity for that cost pool—400 designs—to arrive at the activity rate of $500 per design for indirect factory wages. Note that the totals at the bottom of Exhibit 5–16 agree with the overall activity rates in Exhibit 5–7 in the chapter. Exhibit 5–16, which shows the activity rates for the action analysis report, contains more detail than Exhibit 5–7, which contains the activity rates for the conventional ABC analysis.

Assignment of Overhead Costs to Products—Action Analysis Report

Similarly, computing the overhead costs to be assigned to products for an action analysis report involves more detail than for a conventional ABC analysis. The computations for Classic Brass are carried out in Exhibit 5–17. For example, the activity rate of $125 per customer order for indirect factory wages is multiplied by 600 orders for the standard stanchions to arrive at the cost of $75,000 for indirect factory wages in Exhibit 5–17. Instead of just a single cost number for each cost pool as in the conventional ABC analysis, we now have an entire cost matrix showing much more detail. Note that the column totals for the cost matrix in Exhibit 5–17 agree with the ABC costs for stanchions in Exhibit 5–9. Indeed, the conventional ABC analysis of Exhibit 5–11 can be easily constructed

EXHIBIT 5–15 First-Stage Allocations to Activity Cost Pools

	Activity Cost Pools					
	Customer Orders	*Product Design*	*Order Size*	*Customer Relations*	*Other*	*Total*
Production Department:						
Indirect factory wages	$ 125,000	$ 200,000	$ 100,000	$ 50,000	$ 25,000	$ 500,000
Factory equipment depreciation	60,000	0	180,000	0	60,000	300,000
Factory utilities	0	12,000	60,000	0	48,000	120,000
Factory building lease	0	0	0	0	80,000	80,000
General Administrative Department:						
Administrative wages and salaries	60,000	20,000	40,000	120,000	160,000	400,000
Office equipment depreciation	15,000	0	0	12,500	22,500	50,000
Administrative building lease	0	0	0	0	60,000	60,000
Marketing Department:						
Marketing wages and salaries	55,000	20,000	0	150,000	25,000	250,000
Selling expenses	5,000	0	0	35,000	10,000	50,000
Total cost	$ 320,000	$ 252,000	$ 380,000	$ 367,500	$ 490,500	$ 1,810,000

EXHIBIT 5–16 Computation of the Activity Rates for the Action Analysis Report

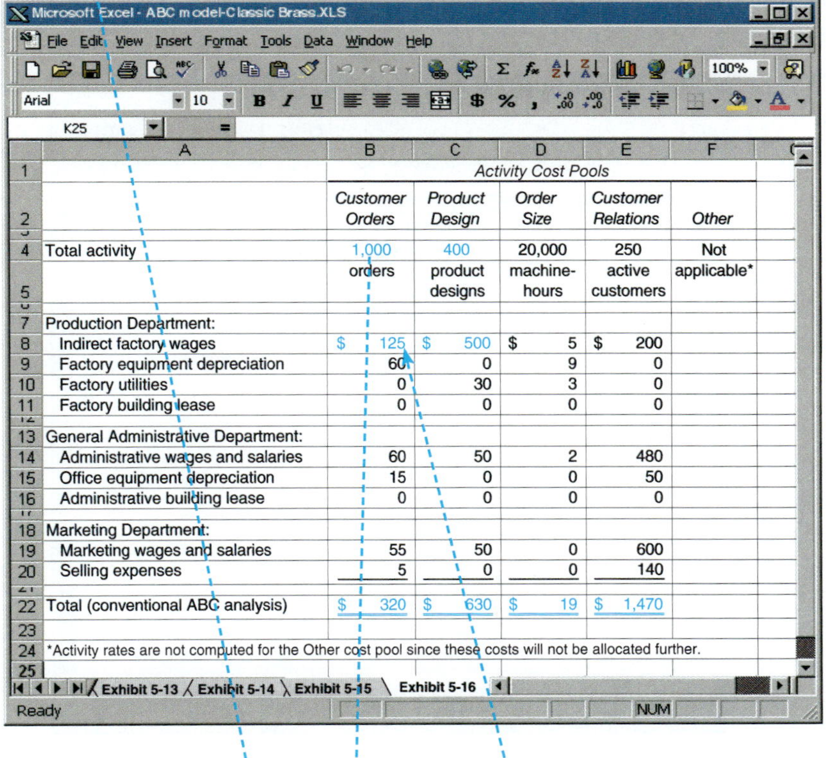

	Activity Cost Pools				
	Customer Orders	*Product Design*	*Order Size*	*Customer Relations*	*Other*
Total activity	1,000 orders	400 product designs	20,000 machine-hours	250 active customers	Not applicable*
Production Department:					
Indirect factory wages	$ 125	$ 500	$ 5	$ 200	
Factory equipment depreciation	60	0	9	0	
Factory utilities	0	30	3	0	
Factory building lease	0	0	0	0	
General Administrative Department:					
Administrative wages and salaries	60	50	2	480	
Office equipment depreciation	15	0	0	50	
Administrative building lease	0	0	0	0	
Marketing Department:					
Marketing wages and salaries	55	50	0	600	
Selling expenses	5	0	0	140	
Total (conventional ABC analysis)	$ 320	$ 630	$ 19	$ 1,470	

*Activity rates are not computed for the Other cost pool since these costs will not be allocated further.

$125,000 ÷ 1,000 orders = $125 per order.

Other entries in the spreadsheet are computed similarly.

EXHIBIT 5–17 Action Analysis Cost Matrices

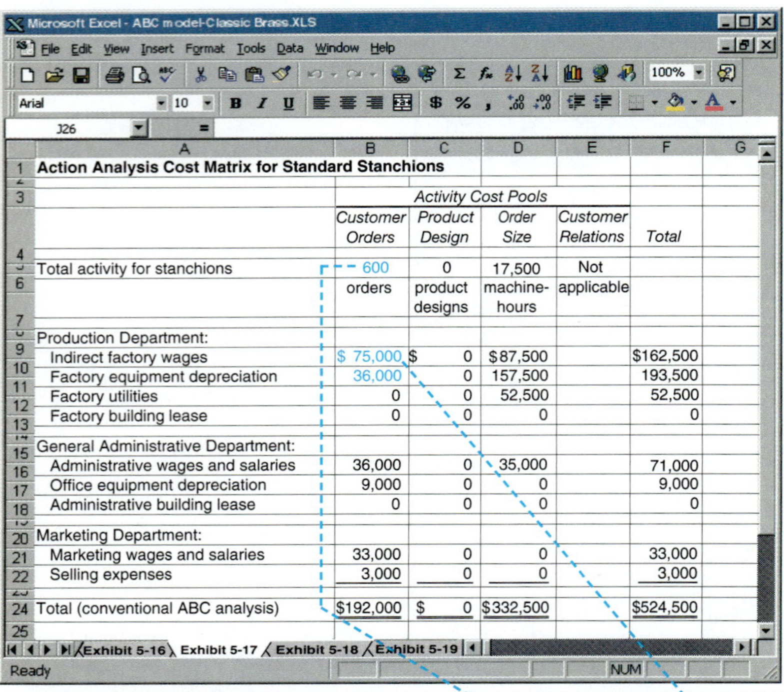

Action Analysis Cost Matrix for Standard Stanchions

	Activity Cost Pools				
	Customer Orders	*Product Design*	*Order Size*	*Customer Relations*	*Total*
Total activity for stanchions	600 orders	0 product designs	17,500 machine-hours	Not applicable	
Production Department:					
Indirect factory wages	$ 75,000	$ 0	$87,500		$162,500
Factory equipment depreciation	36,000	0	157,500		193,500
Factory utilities	0	0	52,500		52,500
Factory building lease	0	0	0		0
General Administrative Department:					
Administrative wages and salaries	36,000	0	35,000		71,000
Office equipment depreciation	9,000	0	0		9,000
Administrative building lease	0	0	0		0
Marketing Department:					
Marketing wages and salaries	33,000	0	0		33,000
Selling expenses	3,000	0	0		3,000
Total (conventional ABC analysis)	$192,000	$ 0	$332,500		$524,500

From Exhibit 5–16 the activity rate for indirect factory wages for the Customer Orders cost pool is $125 per order.

$125 per order × 600 orders = $75,000

Other entries in the table are computed in a similar way.

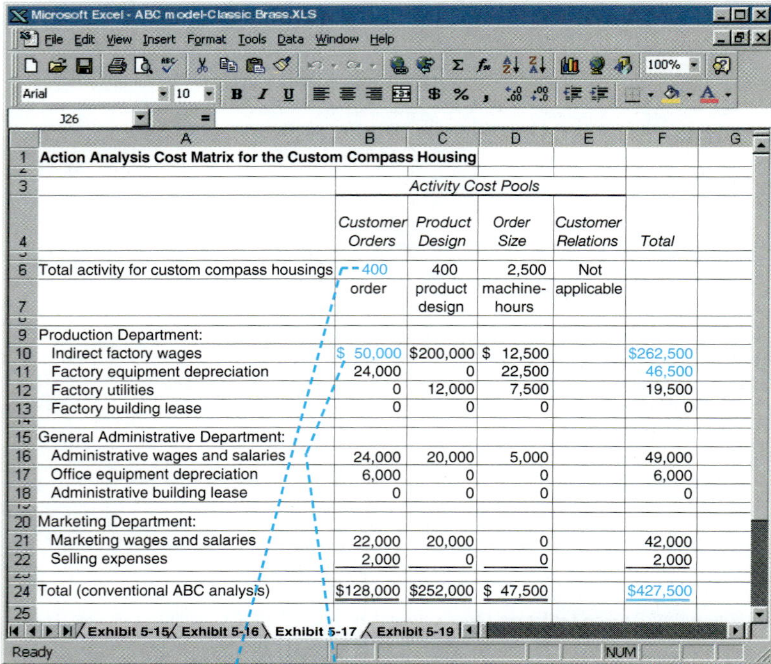

Action Analysis Cost Matrix for the Custom Compass Housing

	Activity Cost Pools				
	Customer Orders	*Product Design*	*Order Size*	*Customer Relations*	*Total*
Total activity for custom compass housings	400 order	400 product design	2,500 machine-hours	Not applicable	
Production Department:					
Indirect factory wages	$ 50,000	$200,000	$ 12,500		$262,500
Factory equipment depreciation	24,000	0	22,500		46,500
Factory utilities	0	12,000	7,500		19,500
Factory building lease	0	0	0		0
General Administrative Department:					
Administrative wages and salaries	24,000	20,000	5,000		49,000
Office equipment depreciation	6,000	0	0		6,000
Administrative building lease	0	0	0		0
Marketing Department:					
Marketing wages and salaries	22,000	20,000	0		42,000
Selling expenses	2,000	0	0		2,000
Total (conventional ABC analysis)	$128,000	$252,000	$ 47,500		$427,500

From Exhibit 5–16 the activity rate for indirect factory wages for the Customer Orders cost pool is $125 per order.

$125 per order × 400 orders = $50,000

Other entries in the table are computed in a similar way.

EXHIBIT 5–18 Ease of Adjustment Codes

Green: *Costs that adjust automatically to changes in activity without management action.*

Direct materials
Shipping costs

Yellow: *Costs that could, in principle, be adjusted to changes in activity, but management action would be required.*

Direct labour
Indirect factory wages
Factory utilities
Administrative wages and salaries
Office equipment depreciation
Marketing wages and salaries
Selling expenses

Red: *Costs that would be very difficult to adjust to changes in activity and management action would be required.*

Factory equipment depreciation
Factory building lease
Administrative building lease

using the column totals at the bottom of the cost matrices in Exhibit 5–17. In contrast, the action analysis report will be based on the row totals at the right of the cost matrices in Exhibit 5–17. In addition, the action analysis report will include a simple colour-coding scheme that will help managers identify how easily the various costs can be adjusted.

Ease of Adjustment Codes

The ABC team constructed Exhibit 5–18 to aid managers in the use of the ABC data. In this exhibit, each cost has been assigned an *ease of adjustment code*—Green, Yellow, or Red. The ease of adjustment code reflects how easily the cost could be adjusted to changes in activity.[9] Green costs are those costs that would adjust more or less automatically to changes in activity without any action by managers. For example, direct materials costs would adjust to changes in orders without any action being taken by managers. If a customer does not order stanchions, the direct materials for the stanchions would not be required and would not be ordered. Yellow costs are those costs that could be adjusted in response to changes in activity, but such adjustments require management action; the adjustment is not automatic. The ABC team believes, for example, that direct labour costs should be included in the Yellow category. Managers must make difficult decisions and take explicit action to increase or decrease, in aggregate, direct labour costs—particularly since the company has a no lay-off policy. Red costs are costs that could be adjusted to changes in activity only with a great deal of difficulty, and the adjustment would require management action. The building leases fall into this category, since it would be very difficult and expensive to break the leases.

The Action Analysis View of the ABC Data

Looking at Exhibit 5–17, the totals on the right-hand side of the table indicate that the $427,500 of overhead cost for the custom compass housing consists of $262,500 of indirect factory wages, $46,500 of factory equipment depreciation, and so on. These data are displayed in Exhibit 5–19, which shows an action analysis of the custom compass housing product. An action analysis report is a report showing what costs have been assigned to the cost object, such as a product or customer, and how difficult it would be to adjust the cost

9. The idea of using colours to code how easily costs can be adjusted was suggested to us at a seminar held by Boeing and by an article by Alfred King, "Green Dollars and Blue Dollars: The Paradox of Cost Reduction," *Journal of Cost Management*, Fall 1993, pp. 44–52.

if there is a change in activity. Note that the Red Margin at the bottom of Exhibit 5–19, ($49,500), is exactly the same as the Product Margin for the custom compass housing in Exhibit 5–11 in the chapter.

The cost data in the action analysis in Exhibit 5–19 are arranged by the colour-coded ease of adjustment. All of the Green costs—those that adjust more or less automatically to changes in activity—appear together at the top of the list of costs. These costs total $74,500 and are subtracted from the sales of $540,000 to yield a Green margin of $465,500. The same procedure is followed for the Yellow and Red costs. This action analysis indicates exactly what costs would have to be cut and how difficult it would be to cut them if the custom compass housing product was dropped. Prior to making any decision about dropping products, the managers responsible for the costs must agree to either eliminate the resources represented by those costs or to transfer the resources to an area in the organization that really needs the resources—namely, a constraint. If managers do not make such a commitment, it is likely that the costs would continue to be incurred. As a result, the company would lose the sales from the products without really saving the costs.

Wrap-Up

To be of value in the decision-making process, managers must properly interpret the results of action analysis. For example it is highly unlikely that a decision to eliminate the custom compass housings product line will allow Classic Brass to avoid an operating loss of $49,500. The reason is that the red cost (factory equipment depreciation) in Exhibit 5–19 is very difficult (if not impossible) to avoid in the short-term. Similarly, the yellow

EXHIBIT 5–19 Action Analysis of Custom Compass Housings: Activity-Based Costing System

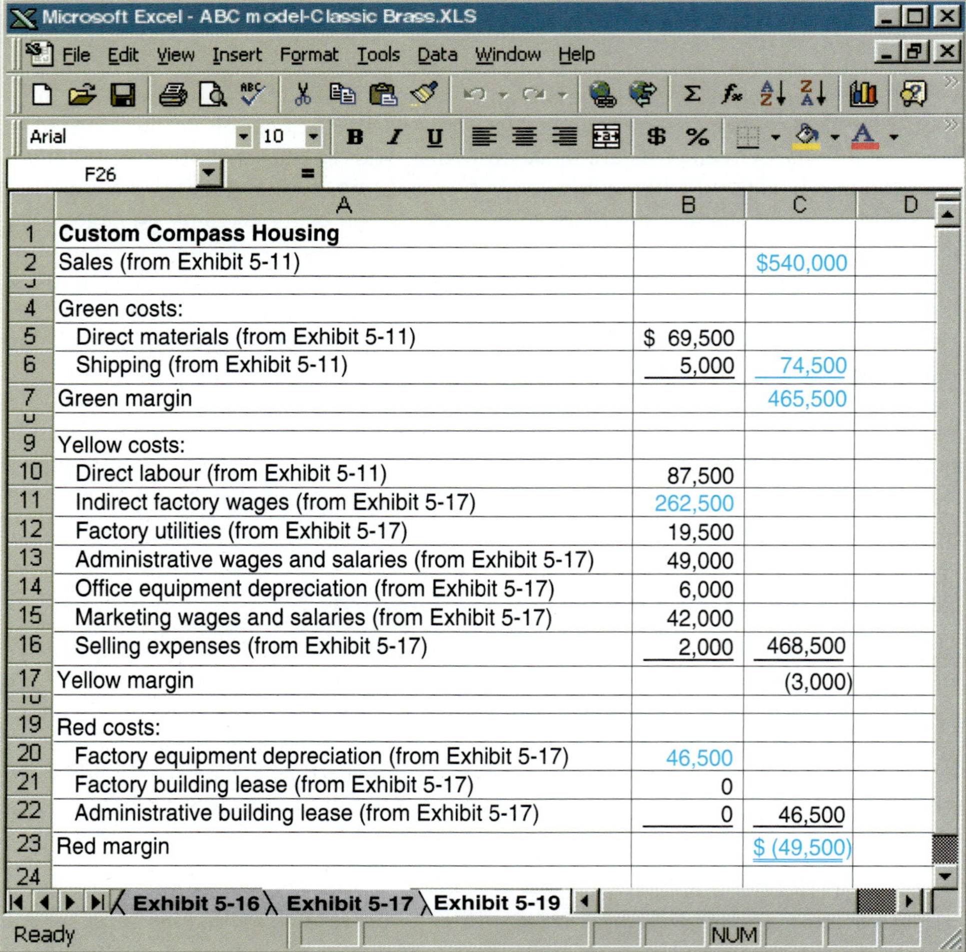

	A	B	C	D
1	**Custom Compass Housing**			
2	Sales (from Exhibit 5-11)		$540,000	
3				
4	Green costs:			
5	Direct materials (from Exhibit 5-11)	$ 69,500		
6	Shipping (from Exhibit 5-11)	5,000	74,500	
7	Green margin		465,500	
8				
9	Yellow costs:			
10	Direct labour (from Exhibit 5-11)	87,500		
11	Indirect factory wages (from Exhibit 5-17)	262,500		
12	Factory utilities (from Exhibit 5-17)	19,500		
13	Administrative wages and salaries (from Exhibit 5-17)	49,000		
14	Office equipment depreciation (from Exhibit 5-17)	6,000		
15	Marketing wages and salaries (from Exhibit 5-17)	42,000		
16	Selling expenses (from Exhibit 5-17)	2,000	468,500	
17	Yellow margin		(3,000)	
18				
19	Red costs:			
20	Factory equipment depreciation (from Exhibit 5-17)	46,500		
21	Factory building lease (from Exhibit 5-17)	0		
22	Administrative building lease (from Exhibit 5-17)	0	46,500	
23	Red margin		$ (49,500)	
24				

margin loss of $3,000 is also unlikely to represent the actual impact on profits of dropping the custom compass housings line. The largest yellow cost in Exhibit 5–19 is indirect factory wages of $262,500, which given the company's no lay-off policy, will not be avoided if the product is discontinued. Thus, while the yellow costs are adjustable if management decides to take action, eliminating the entire $468,500 is a low-probability outcome. Instead of thinking about yellow or red costs as avoidable if the product is discontinued, management is likely better served by thinking about how to reduce (not eliminate) costs such as indirect factory wages that primarily relate to the product design activity. For example, total quality management techniques could be used to identify opportunities to reduce product design costs and Classic Brass could get benchmark data from industry leaders to get a sense of efficiency gains that may be possible. By measuring the resources consumed by products (and other cost objects), a "best practice" ABC system provides a much better basis for decision making than a traditional cost accounting system that allocates overhead costs with little regard for what might be causing the overhead. A well-designed ABC system provides managers with estimates of potentially relevant costs that can be a very useful starting point for management analysis.

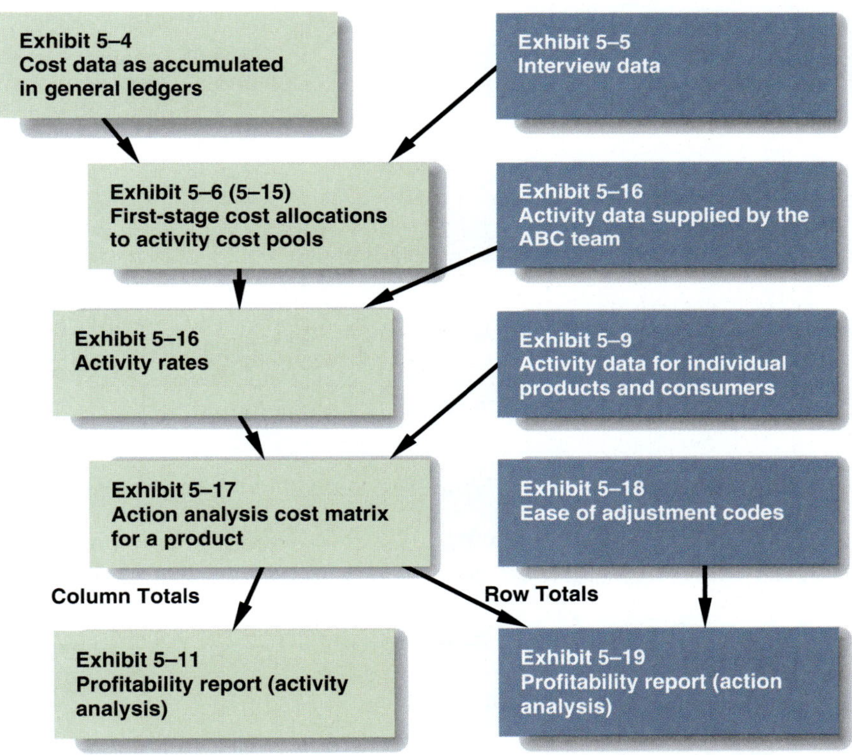

EXHIBIT 5–20 Summary of the Steps to Produce an Action Analysis Report

Appendix 5A Summary

The action analysis report illustrated in this appendix is a valuable addition to the ABC tool kit. An action analysis report provides more information for decision making than a conventional ABC analysis. The action analysis report makes it clear where costs would have to be adjusted in the organization as a result of an action. In a conventional ABC analysis, a cost such as $320 for processing an order represents costs from many parts of the organization. If an order is dropped, there will be little pressure to actually eliminate the $320 cost unless it is clear where the costs are incurred and which managers would be responsible for reducing the cost. In contrast, an action analysis report traces the costs to where they are incurred in the organization and makes it much easier to assign responsibility to managers for reducing costs. In addition, an action analysis report provides information concerning how easily a cost can be adjusted. Costs that cannot be adjusted are not relevant in a decision.

Exhibit 5–20 summarizes all of the steps required to create both an action analysis report as illustrated in this appendix and an activity analysis as shown in the chapter.

Appendix 5A Review Problem: Activity Analysis Report

Refer to the data for Advanced Products Corporation in the Review Problem at the end of the chapter on pages 196–197.

Required:

1. Compute activity rates for Advanced Products Corporation as in Exhibit 5–16.
2. Using Exhibit 5–17 as a guide, prepare a report showing the overhead costs for the Shenzhen order described in requirement 3 of the Review Problem at the end of the chapter.
3. The management of Advanced Products Corporation has assigned ease of adjustment codes to costs as follows:

Cost	Ease of Adjustment Code
Direct materials	Green
Direct labour	Yellow
Wages and salaries	Yellow
Other overhead costs	Red

Using Exhibit 5–19 as a guide, prepare an action analysis of the Shenzhen order.

Solution to Appendix 5A Review Problem

1. The activity rates are computed by dividing the costs in the cells of the first-stage allocation above by the total activity from the top of the column:

Activity Cost Pools	Volume-Related	Order-Related	Customer Support
Total activity	20,000 DLHs	400 orders	200 customers
Wages and salaries	$6.00	$225.00	$300.00
Other overhead costs	1.50	25.00	100.00
Total cost	$7.50	$250.00	$400.00

Example: $120,000 ÷ 20,000 DLHs = $6.00 per DLH

Volume-related wages and salaries from the first-stage allocation in part 1 of the end-of-chapter review problem.

2. The overhead cost for the order is computed as follows:

Activity Cost Pools	Volume-Related	Order-Related	Customer Support	Total
Total activity	20 DLHs	1 order	1 customer	
Wages and salaries	$120.00	$225.00	$300.00	$645.00
Other overhead costs	30.00	25.00	100.00	155.00
Total cost	$150.00	$250.00	$400.00	$800.00

Example: 20DLHs × $6.00 per DLH = $120.00

Activity rate for volume-related wages and salaries from part (1) above.

3. The action analysis report is constructed as follows:

Sales (10 units × $300 per unit)		$3,000
Green Costs:		
Direct materials (10 units × $180 per unit)	$1,800	1,800
Green margin		1,200
Green Costs:		
Direct labour (10 units × $50 per unit)	500	
Wages and salaries (see above)	645	1,145
Yellow margin		55
Red Costs:		
Other overhead costs (see above)	155	155
Red margin		$(100)

Appendix 5B: Using a Modified Form of Activity-Based Costing to Determine Product Costs for External Reports

LEARNING OBJECTIVE 7
Use activity-based costing techniques to compute unit product costs for external reports.

This chapter has emphasized using activity-based costing information in internal decisions. However, a modified form of activity-based costing can also be used to develop product costs for external financial reports. For this purpose, product costs include *all* manufacturing overhead costs—including organization-sustaining costs and the costs of idle capacity—and exclude all nonmanufacturing costs, even costs that are clearly caused by the products.

The simplest absorption costing systems as described in Chapter 3 assign manufacturing overhead costs to products using a single factory-wide predetermined overhead rate based on direct labour-hours or machine-hours. When activity-based costing is used to assign manufacturing overhead costs to products, a predetermined overhead rate is computed for each activity cost pool. An example will make this difference clear.

Maxtar Industries manufactures high-quality smoker/barbecue units. The company has two product lines—Premium and Standard. The company has traditionally applied manufacturing overhead costs to these products using a plantwide predetermined overhead rate based on direct labour-hours. Exhibit 5–21 details how the unit product costs of the two product lines are computed using the company's traditional costing system. The unit product cost of the Premium product line is $71.60 and the unit product cost of the Standard product line is $53.70 according to this traditional costing system.

Maxtar Industries has recently experimented with an activity-based costing approach to determining its unit product costs for external reporting purposes. The company's activity-based costing system has three activity cost pools: (1) supporting direct labour; (2) setting up machines; and (3) parts administration. The top of Exhibit 5–22 displays basic data concerning these activity cost pools. Note that the total estimated overhead cost in these three costs pools, $1,520,000, agrees with the total estimated overhead cost in the company's traditional costing system. The company's activity-based costing system simply provides an alternative way to allocate the company's manufacturing overhead across the two products.

The activity rates for the three activity cost pools are computed in the second table in Exhibit 5–22. For example, the total cost in the "setting up machines" activity cost pool, $480,000, is divided by the total activity associated with that cost pool, 800 setups, to determine the activity rate of $600 per setup.

The activity rates are used to allocate overhead costs to the two products in the third table in Exhibit 5–22. For example, the activity rate for the "setting up machines" activity cost pool, $600 per setup, is multiplied by the Premium product line's 600 setups to determine the $360,000 machine setup cost allocated to the Premium product line. The overhead cost per unit is determined at the bottom of this table by dividing the total overhead cost by the number of units produced. For example, the Premium

EXHIBIT 5–21 Maxtar Industries' Traditional Costing System

Basic Data

Total estimated manufacturing overhead cost	$1,520,000
Total estimated direct labour-hours	400,000 DLHs

	Premium	Standard
Direct materials per unit.	$40.00	$30.00
Direct labour per unit.	$24.00	$18.00
Direct labour-hours per unit.	2.0 DLHs	1.5 DLHs
Units produced	50,000 units	200,000 units

Computation of the Predetermined Overhead Rate

$$\text{Predetermined overhead rate} = \frac{\text{Total estimated manufacturing overhead}}{\text{Total estimated amount of the allocation base}}$$

$$= \frac{\$1{,}520{,}000}{400{,}000 \text{ DLHs}} = \$3.80 \text{ per DLH}$$

Traditional Unit Product Costs

	Premium	Standard
Direct materials	$40.00	$30.00
Direct labour	24.00	18.00
Manufacturing overhead (2.0 DLHs × $3.80 per DLH; 1.5 DLHs × $3.80 per DLH)	7.60	5.70
Unit product cost.	$71.60	$53.70

product line's total overhead cost of $728,000 is divided by 50,000 units to determine the $14.56 overhead cost per unit

The table at the bottom of Exhibit 5–22 displays the activity-based costing unit product costs. Note that these unit product costs differ from those computed using the company's traditional costing system in Exhibit 5–21. Because the activity-based costing system contains both a batch-level (setting up machines) and a product-level (parts administration) activity cost pool, the unit product costs under activity-based costing follow the usual pattern in which overhead costs are shifted from the high-volume to the low-volume product. The unit product cost of the Standard product line, the high-volume product, has gone down from $53.70 under the traditional costing system to $51.96 under activity-based costing. In contrast, the unit product cost of the Premium product line, the low-volume product, has increased from $71.60 under the traditional costing system to $78.56 under activity-based costing. Instead of arbitrarily assigning most of the costs of setting up machines and of parts administration to the high-volume product, the activity-based costing system more accurately assigns these costs to the two products.

EXHIBIT 5–22 Maxtar Industries' Activity-Based Costing System

Basic Data

1. Activities and Activity Measures	Estimated Overhead Cost	Expected Activity		
		Premium	Standard	Total
Supporting direct labour (DLHs)	$ 800,000	100,000	300,000	400,000
Setting up machines (setups)	480,000	600	200	800
Parts administration (part types)	240,000	140	60	200
Total manufacturing overhead cost	$1,520,000			

2. Computation of Activity Rates

Activities	(a) Estimated Overhead Cost	(b) Total Expected Activity	(a) ÷ (b) Activity Rate
Supporting direct labour	$800,000	400,000 DLHs	$2 per DLH
Setting up machines	$480,000	800 setups	$600 per setup
Parts administration	$240,000	200 part types	$1,200 per part type

3. Assigning Overhead Costs to Products:

Overhead Cost for the Premium Product

Activity Cost Pools	(a) Activity Rate	(b) Activity	(a) × (b) ABC Cost
Supporting direct labour	$2 per DLH	100,000 DLHs	$200,000
Setting up machines	$600 per setup	600 setups	360,000
Parts administration	$1,200 per part type	140 part types	168,000
Total			$728,000

Overhead Cost for the Standard Product

Activity Cost Pools	(a) Activity Rate	(b) Activity	(a) × (b) ABC Cost
Supporting direct labour	$2 per DLH	300,000 DLHs	$600,000
Setting up machines	$600 per setup	200 setups	120,000
Parts administration	$1,200 per part type	60 part types	72,000
Total			$792,000

4. Activity-Based Costing Product Costs

	Premium	Standard
Direct materials	$40.00	$30.00
Direct labour	24.00	18.00
Manufacturing overhead ($728,000 ÷ 50,000 units; $792,000 ÷ 200,000 units)	14.56	3.96
Unit product cost	$78.56	$51.96

Glossary

Visit the Online Learning Centre at http://www.mcgrawhill.ca/olc/garrison/ for a review of key terms and definitions.

Questions

5–1 In what fundamental ways does activity-based costing differ from traditional costing methods such as those described in Chapters 2 and 3?

5–2 Why is direct labour a poor base for allocating overhead in many companies?

5–3 Why are overhead rates in activity-based costing based on the level of activity at capacity rather than on the budgeted level of activity?

5–4 Which type of overhead costs are excluded from the activity-based costing approach?

5–5 What are unit-level, batch-level, product-level, customer-level, and organization-sustaining activities?

5–6 What types of costs should not be assigned to products in an activity-based costing system?

5–7 What is the difference between a transaction driver and a duration driver?

5–8 Why is the first stage of the allocation process in activity-based costing often based on interviews?

5–9 How can the activity rates (i.e., cost per activity) for the various activities be used to target process improvements?

5–10 When activity-based costing is used, why are manufacturing overhead costs often shifted from high-volume products to low-volume products?

5–11 (Appendix 5A) Why should an activity view of product margins, as in Exhibit 5–11, be supplemented with an action analysis, as in Exhibit 5–19, when making decisions about products or customers?

5–12 What is the second-stage allocation in activity-based costing?

5–13 What are the two chief limitations of activity-based costing?

5–14 Can activity-based costing be used in service organizations?

5–15 (Appendix 5B) How does the use of activity-based costing for external financial reporting differ from its use for internal decision making?

Exercises

EXERCISE 5–1 ABC Cost Hierarchy [LO1]
The following activities occur at Greenwich Corporation, a company that manufactures a variety of products.

a. Various individuals manage the parts inventories.
b. A clerk in the factory issues purchase orders for a job.
c. The personnel department trains new production workers.
d. The factory's general manager meets with other department heads such as marketing to coordinate plans.
e. Direct labour workers assemble products.
f. Engineers design new products.
g. The materials storekeeper issues raw materials to be used in jobs.
h. The maintenance department performs periodic preventive maintenance on general-use equipment.

Required:
Classify each of the activities above as either a unit-level, batch-level, product-level, or organization-sustaining activity.

EXERCISE 5–2 First-Stage Allocation [LO2]
MobileCash Corporation operates a fleet of armoured cars that make scheduled pickups and deliveries for its customers in the Toronto area. The company is implementing an activity-based costing system that has four activity cost pools: Travel, Pickup and Delivery, Customer Service, and

Other. The activity measures are kilometres for the Travel cost pool, number of pickups and deliveries for the Pickup and Delivery cost pool, and number of customers for the Customer Service cost pool. The Other cost pool has no activity measure. The following costs will be assigned using the activity-based costing system:

Driver and guard wages	$ 840,000
Vehicle operating expense	270,000
Vehicle depreciation	150,000
Customer representative salaries and expenses	180,000
Office expenses	40,000
Administrative expenses	340,000
Total cost	$1,820,000

The distribution of resource consumption across the activity cost pools is as follows:

	Travel	Pickup and Delivery	Customer Service	Other	Totals
Driver and guard wages	40%	45%	10%	5%	100%
Vehicle operating expense	75%	5%	0%	20%	100%
Vehicle depreciation	70%	10%	0%	20%	100%
Customer representative salaries and expenses	0%	0%	85%	15%	100%
Office expenses	0%	25%	35%	40%	100%
Administrative expenses	0%	5%	55%	40%	100%

Required:

Carry out the first-stage allocations of costs to activity cost pools as illustrated in Exhibit 5–6.

EXERCISE 5–3 Compute Activity Rates [LO2]

As-You-Like-It Gardening is a small gardening service that uses activity-based costing to estimate costs for pricing and other purposes. The proprietor of the company believes that costs are driven primarily by the size of customer lawns, the size of customer garden beds, the distance to travel to customers, and the number of customers. In addition, the costs of maintaining garden beds depends on whether the beds are low-maintenance beds (mainly ordinary trees and shrubs) or high-maintenance beds (mainly flowers and exotic plants). Accordingly, the company uses the five activity cost pools listed below:

Activity Cost Pool	Activity Measure
Caring for lawn	Square metres of lawn
Caring for garden beds—low maintenance	Square metres of low-maintenance beds
Caring for garden beds—high maintenance	Square metres of high-maintenance beds
Travel to jobs	Kilometres
Customer billing and service	Number of customers

The company has already carried out its first-stage allocations of costs. The company's annual costs and activities are summarized as follows:

Activity Cost Pool	Estimated Overhead Cost	Expected Activity
Caring for lawn	$77,400	180,000 square metres of lawn
Caring for garden beds—low maintenance	$30,000	24,000 square metres of low-maintenance beds
Caring for garden beds—high maintenance	$57,600	18,000 square metres of high-maintenance beds
Travel to jobs	$4,200	15,000 kilometres
Customer billing and service	$8,700	30 customers

Required:
Compute the activity rate for each of the activity cost pools.

EXERCISE 5–4 Second-Stage Allocation [LO3]
Larner Corporation is a diversified manufacturer of industrial goods. The company's activity-based costing system contains the following six activity cost pools and activity rates:

Activity Cost Pool	Activity Rates
Supporting direct labour	$7.00 per direct labour-hour
Machine processing	$3.00 per machine-hour
Machine setups	$40.00 per setup
Production orders	$160.00 per order
Shipments	$120.00 per shipment
Product sustaining.	$800 per product

Activity data have been supplied for the following products:

	Total Expected Activity	
	J78	W52
Direct labour-hours	1,000	40
Machine-hours.	3,200	30
Machine setups	5	1
Production orders	5	1
Shipments	10	1
Product sustaining	1	1

Required:
Determine the total overhead cost that would be assigned to each of the products listed above in the activity-based costing system.

EXERCISE 5–5 Product and Customer Profitability Analysis [LO3, LO4]
Updraft Systems, Inc., makes paragliders for sale through specialty sporting goods stores. The company has a standard paraglider model, but also makes custom-designed paragliders. Management has designed an activity-based costing system with the following activity cost pools and activity rates:

Activity Cost Pool	Activity Rate
Supporting manufacturing.	$18 per direct labour-hour
Order processing.	$192 per order
Custom designing	$261 per custom design
Customer service	$426 per customer

Management would like an analysis of the profitability of a particular customer, Eagle Wings, which has ordered the following products over the last 12 months:

	Standard Model	Custom Design
Number of gliders	10	2
Number of orders	1	2
Number of custom designs	0	2
Direct labour-hours per glider	28.5	32.0
Selling price per glider.	$1,650	$2,300
Direct materials cost per glider	$462	$576

The company's direct labour rate is $19 per hour.

Required:
Using the company's activity-based costing system, compute the customer margin of Eagle Wings.

EXERCISE 5–6 (Appendix 5A) Preparing an Action Analysis Report [LO6]

Pro Golf Corporation produces private label golf clubs for pro shops throughout North America. The company uses activity-based costing to evaluate the profitability of serving its customers. This analysis is based on categorizing the company's costs as follows, using the ease of adjustment colour coding scheme described in Appendix 5A:

	Ease of Adjustment Code
Direct materials	Green
Direct labour	Yellow
Indirect labour	Yellow
Factory equipment depreciation	Red
Factory administration	Red
Selling and administrative wages and salaries	Red
Selling and administrative depreciation	Red
Marketing expenses	Yellow

Management would like to evaluate the profitability of a particular customer—the Northumberland Golf Club of Pugwash, Nova Scotia. Over the past 12 months this customer submitted one order for 80 golf clubs that had to be produced in two batches due to differences in product labelling requested by the customer. Summary data concerning the order appear below:

Number of clubs	80
Number of orders	1
Number of batches	2
Direct labour-hours per club	0.3
Selling price per club	$48.00
Direct materials cost per club	$25.40
Direct labour rate per hour	$21.50

A cost analyst working in the controller's office at the company has already produced the action analysis cost matrix for the Northumberland Golf Club that follows:

Action Analysis Cost Matrix for Northumberland Golf Club

	Activity Cost Pools				
	Volume	Batch Processing	Order Processing	Customer Service	Total
Activity	24 direct labour-hours	2 batches	1 order	1 customer	
Manufacturing overhead:					
Indirect labour	$ 33.60	$51.60	$ 4.80	$ 0.00	$ 90.00
Factory equipment depreciation	105.60	0.80	0.00	0.00	106.40
Factory administration	16.80	0.60	14.00	231.00	262.40
Selling and administrative overhead:					
Wages and salaries	12.00	0.00	38.00	386.00	436.00
Depreciation	0.00	0.00	5.00	25.00	30.00
Marketing expenses	115.20	0.00	57.00	368.00	540.20
Total	$283.20	$53.00	$118.80	$1,010.00	$1,465.00

Required:

Prepare an action analysis report showing the profitability of the Northumberland Golf Club. Include direct materials and direct labour costs in the report. Use Exhibit 5–19 as a guide for organizing the report.

EXERCISE 5–7 (Appendix 5B) Activity-Based Costing Product Costs for External Reports [LO7]

Take-a-Hike Corporation makes ultra-lightweight backpacking tents. Data concerning the company's two product lines appear on the next page.

	Deluxe	Standard
Direct materials per unit.	$60.00	$45.00
Direct labour per unit.	$9.60	$7.20
Direct labour-hours per unit.	0.8 DLHs	0.6 DLHs
Estimated annual production.	10,000 units	70,000 units

The company has a traditional costing system in which manufacturing overhead is applied to units based on direct labour-hours. Data concerning manufacturing overhead and direct labour-hours for the upcoming year appear below:

Estimated total manufacturing overhead.	$290,000
Estimated total direct labour-hours	50,000 DLHS

Required:

1. Determine the unit product costs of the Deluxe and Standard products under the company's traditional costing system.
2. The company is considering replacing its traditional costing system for determining unit product costs for external reports with an activity-based costing system. The activity-based costing system would have the following three activity cost pools:

	Estimated	Expected Activity		
Activities and Activity Measures	Overhead Cost	Deluxe	Standard	Total
Supporting direct labour (direct labour-hours)	$150,000	8,000	42,000	50,000
Batch setups (setups)	60,000	200	50	250
Safety testing (tests)	80,000	80	20	100
Total manufacturing overhead cost.	$290,000			

Determine the unit product costs of the Deluxe and Standard products under the activity-based costing system.

EXERCISE 5–8 Activity Measures [LO1]

Various activities at Morales Corporation, a manufacturing company, are listed below. Each activity has been classified as unit-level, batch-level, product-level, customer-level, or organization-sustaining.

Activity	Activity Classification	Examples of Activity Measures
a. Materials are moved from the receiving dock to the assembly area by a material-handling crew	Batch-level	
b. Direct labour workers assemble various products	Unit-level	
c. Diversity training is provided to all employees in the company.	Organization-sustaining	
d. A product is designed by a cross-functional team	Product-level	
e. Equipment is set up to process a batch.	Batch-level	
f. A customer is billed for all products delivered during the month.	Customer-level	

Required:

Complete the above table by listing an example of an activity measure for each activity.

EXERCISE 5–9 Computing ABC Product Costs [LO2, LO3]

High Calibre Products Corporation makes two products, titanium Rims and Posts. Data regarding the two products follow:

	Direct Labour-Hours per Unit	Annual Production
Rims	0.40	20,000 units
Posts	0.20	80,000 units

Additional information about the company follows:

a. Rims require $17 in direct materials per unit, and Posts require $10.
b. The direct labour wage rate is $16 per hour.
c. Rims are more complex to manufacture than Posts, and they require special equipment.
d. The ABC system has the following activity cost pools:

		Estimated Overhead	Activity		
Activity Cost Pool	Activity Measure	Cost	Rims	Posts	Total
Machine setups	Number of setups	$21,600	100	80	180
Special processing...........	Machine-hours	$180,000	4,000	0	4,000
General factory	Direct labour-hours	$288,000	8,000	16,000	24,000

Required:

1. Compute the activity rate for each activity cost pool.
2. Determine the unit cost of each product according to the ABC system, including direct materials and direct labour.

EXERCISE 5–10 First-Stage Allocations [LO2]

The operations vice-president of the Regal Bank of Canada, Kristin Wu, has been interested in investigating the efficiency of the bank's operations. She has been particularly concerned about the costs of handling routine transactions at the bank and would like to compare these costs at the bank's various branches. If the branches with the most efficient operations can be identified, their methods can be studied and then replicated elsewhere. While the bank maintains meticulous records of wages and other costs, there has been no attempt thus far to show how those costs are related to the various services provided by the bank. Ms. Wu has asked your help in conducting an activity-based costing study of bank operations. In particular, she would like to know the cost of opening an account, the cost of processing deposits and withdrawals, and the cost of processing other customer transactions.

The Windsor branch of the Regal Bank of Canada has submitted the following cost data for last year:

Teller wages	$150,000
Assistant branch manager salary	70,000
Branch manager salary	85,000
Total	$305,000

Virtually all of the other costs of the branch—rent, depreciation, utilities, and so on—are organization-sustaining costs that cannot be meaningfully assigned to individual customer transactions such as depositing cheques.

In addition to the cost data above, the employees of the Windsor branch have been interviewed concerning how their time was distributed last year across the activities included in the activity-based costing study. The results of those interviews appear below:

	Distribution of Resource Consumption Across Activities				
	Opening Accounts	Processing Deposits and Withdrawals	Processing Other Customer Transactions	Other Activities	Totals
Teller wages.............	0%	75%	15%	10%	100%
Assistant branch manager salary.........	10%	15%	25%	50%	100%
Branch manager salary	0%	0%	20%	80%	100%

Required:
Prepare the first-stage allocation for Ms. Wu as illustrated in Exhibit 5–6.

EXERCISE 5–11 Computing and Interpreting Activity Rates [LO2]
(This exercise is a continuation of Exercise 5–10; it should be assigned *only* if Exercise 5–10 is also assigned.) The manager of the Windsor branch of the Regal Bank of Canada has provided the following data concerning the transactions of the branch during the past year:

Activity	Total Activity at the Windsor Branch
Opening accounts	200 accounts opened
Processing deposits and withdrawals	50,000 deposits and withdrawals
Processing other customer transactions	1,000 other customer transactions

The lowest costs reported by other branches for these activities are displayed below:

Activity	Lowest Cost Among All Regal Bank of Canada Branches
Opening accounts	$24.35 per account opened
Processing deposits and withdrawals	$2.72 per deposit or withdrawal
Processing other customer transactions	$48.90 per other customer transaction

Required:
1. Using the first-stage allocation from Exercise 5–10 and the above data, compute the activity rates for the activity-based costing system. (Use Exhibit 5–7 as a guide.) Round all computations to the nearest whole cent.
2. What do these results suggest to you concerning operations at the Windsor branch?

EXERCISE 5–12 Second-Stage Allocation to an Order [LO3]
Transvaal Mining Tools Ltd. of South Africa makes specialty tools used in the mining industry. The company uses an activity-based costing system for internal decision-making purposes. The company has four activity cost pools as listed below:

Activity Cost Pool	Activity Measure	Activity Rate
Order size	Number of direct labour-hours	R17.60 per direct labour-hour*
Customer orders	Number of customer orders	R360 per customer order
Product testing	Number of testing hours	R79 per testing hour
Selling	Number of sales calls	R1,494 per sales call

*(The currency in South Africa is the rand, denoted here by R.)

The managing director of the company would like information concerning the cost of a recently completed order for hard-rock drills. The order required 150 direct labour-hours, 18 hours of product testing, and three sales calls.

Required:
Prepare a report showing the overhead cost of the order for hard-rock drills according to the activity-based costing system. What is the total overhead cost assigned to the order?

EXERCISE 5–13 (Appendix 5A) Second-Stage Allocation to an Order Using the Action Analysis Approach [LO3, LO6]
This exercise should be assigned in conjunction with Exercise 5–12.

The results of the first-stage allocation of the activity-based costing system at Transvaal Mining Tools Ltd., in which the activity rates were computed, appear at the top of page 215.

Required:
1. Using Exhibit 5–17 as a guide, prepare a report showing the overhead cost of the order for hard-rock drills discussed in Exercise 5–12. What is the total overhead cost of the order?
2. Explain the two different perspectives this report gives to managers concerning the nature of the overhead costs involved in the order. (HINT: Look at the row and column totals of the report you have prepared.)

	Order Size	Customer Orders	Product Testing	Selling
Manufacturing overhead:				
Indirect labour	R 9.60	R 231.00	R 36.00	R 0.00
Factory depreciation	7.00	0.00	18.00	0.00
Factory utilities	0.20	0.00	1.00	0.00
Factory administration	0.00	46.00	24.00	12.00
Selling and administrative:				
Wages and salaries	0.80	72.00	0.00	965.00
Depreciation	0.00	11.00	0.00	36.00
Taxes and insurance	0.00	0.00	0.00	49.00
Selling expenses	0.00	0.00	0.00	432.00
Total overhead cost	R 17.60	R 360.00	R 79.00	R 1,494.00

EXERCISE 5–14 Cost Hierarchy [LO1]

Green Glider Corporation makes golf carts that it sells directly to golf courses throughout the world. Several basic models are available, which are modified to suit the needs of each particular golf course. A golf course located in British Columbia, for example, would typically specify that its golf carts come equipped with retractable rain-proof covers. In addition, each customer (i.e., golf course) customizes its golf carts with its own colour scheme and logo. The company typically makes all of the golf carts for a customer before starting work on the next customer's golf carts. Below are listed a number of activities and costs at Green Glider Corporation:

a. The purchasing department orders the specific colour of paint specified by the customer from the company's supplier.
b. A steering wheel is installed in a golf cart.
c. An outside lawyer draws up a new generic sales contract for the company limiting Green Glider's liability in case of accidents that involve its golf carts.
d. The company's paint shop makes a stencil for a customer's logo.
e. A sales representative visits an old customer to check on how the company's golf carts are working out and to try to make a new sale.
f. The accounts receivable department prepares the bill for a completed order.
g. Electricity is used to heat and light the factory and the administrative offices.
h. A golf cart is painted.
i. The company's engineer modifies the design of a model to eliminate a potential safety problem.
j. The marketing department has a catalogue printed and then mails copies to golf course managers.
k. Completed golf carts are individually tested on the company's test track.
l. A new model golf cart is shipped to the leading golfing trade magazine to be evaluated for the magazine's annual rating of golf carts.

Required:

Classify each of the costs or activities above as unit-level, batch-level, product-level, customer-level, or organization-sustaining. In this case, customers are golf courses, products are models of the golf cart, a batch is a specific order from a customer, and units are individual golf carts.

EXERCISE 5–15 Second-Stage Allocation and Margin Calculations [LO3, LO4]

Theatre Seating, Inc., makes high-quality adjustable seats for theatres. The company's activity-based costing system has four activity cost pools, which are listed below along with their activity measures and activity rates:

Activity Cost Pool	Activity Measure	Activity Rate
Supporting direct labour	Number of direct labour-hours	$12 per direct labour-hour
Batch processing	Number of batches	$96 per batch
Order processing	Number of orders	$284 per order
Customer service	Number of customers	$2,620 per customer

The company just completed a single order from CineMax Entertainment Corporation for 2,400 custom seats. The order was produced in four batches. Each seat required 0.8 direct labour-hours. The selling price was $137.95 per seat, the direct materials cost was $112.00 per seat, and the direct labour cost was $14.40 per seat. This was the only order from CineMax Entertainment for the year.

Required:
Using Exhibit 5–12 as a guide, prepare a report showing the customer margin on sales to CineMax Entertainment for the year.

EXERCISE 5–16 (Appendix 5A) Second-Stage Allocations and Margin Calculations Using the Action Analysis Approach [LO3, LO6]
Refer to the data for Theatre Seating, Inc., in exercise 5–15 and the following additional details concerning the activity rates:

	Activity Rates			
	Supporting Direct Labour	Batch Processing	Order Processing	Customer Service
Manufacturing overhead:				
Indirect labour	$ 1.80	$72.00	$ 18.00	$ 0.00
Factory equipment depreciation	7.35	3.25	0.00	0.00
Factory administration	2.10	7.00	28.00	268.00
Selling and administrative:				
Wages and salaries	0.50	13.00	153.00	1,864.00
Depreciation	0.00	0.75	6.00	26.00
Marketing expenses	0.25	0.00	79.00	462.00
Total activity rate	$12.00	$96.00	$284.00	$2,620.00

Management has provided their ease of adjustment codes for purposes of preparing action analyses.

	Ease of Adjustment Codes
Direct materials	Green
Direct labour	Yellow
Manufacturing overhead:	
Indirect labour	Yellow
Factory equipment depreciation	Red
Factory administration	Red
Selling and administrative:	
Wages and salaries	Red
Depreciation	Red
Marketing expenses	Yellow

Required:
Using Exhibit 5–19 as a guide, prepare an action analysis report for CineMax Entertainment similar to those prepared for products.

EXERCISE 5–17 Cost Hierarchy and Activity Measures [LO1]
Various activities at Companhia de Textils, S.A., a manufacturing company located in Brazil, are listed below. The company makes a variety of products in its plant outside Sao Paulo.

a. Preventive maintenance is performed on general-purpose production equipment.
b. Products are assembled by hand.
c. Reminder notices are sent to customers who are late in making payments.
d. Purchase orders are issued for materials to be used in production.
e. Modifications are made to product designs.
f. New employees are hired by the personnel office.
g. Machine settings are changed between batches of different products.
h. Parts inventories are maintained in the storeroom. (Each product requires its own unique parts.)
i. Insurance costs are incurred on the company's facilities.

Required:
1. Classify each of the activities as either unit-level, batch-level, product-level, customer-level, or organization-sustaining.
2. Where possible, name one or more activity measures that could be used to assign costs generated by the activity to products or customers.

EXERCISE 5–18 Comprehensive Activity-Based Costing Exercise [LO2, LO3, LO4]
Silicon Optics has supplied the following data for use in its activity-based costing system:

Overhead Costs	
Wages and salaries	$350,000
Other overhead costs	200,000
Total overhead costs	$550,000

Activity Cost Pool	Activity Measure	Total Activity
Direct labour support	Number of direct labour-hours	10,000 DLHs
Order processing	Number of orders	500 orders
Customer support	Number of customers	100 customers
Other	These costs are not allocated to products or customers	Not applicable

	Distribution of Resource Consumption Across Activity Cost Pools				
	Direct Labour Support	Order Processing	Customer Support	Other	Total
Wages and salaries	30%	35%	25%	10%	100%
Other overhead costs	25%	15%	20%	40%	100%

During the year, Silicon Optics completed an order for a special optical switch for a new customer, Indus Telecom. This customer did not order any other products during the year. Data concerning that order follow:

Data Concerning the Indus Telecom Order	
Selling price	$295 per unit
Units ordered	100 units
Direct materials	$264 per unit
Direct labour-hours	0.5 DLH per unit
Direct labour rate	$25 per DLH

Required:
1. Using Exhibit 5–6 as a guide, prepare a report showing the first-stage allocations of overhead costs to the activity cost pools.
2. Using Exhibit 5–7 as a guide, compute the activity rates for the activity cost pools.
3. Prepare a report showing the overhead costs for the order from Indus Telecom, including customer support costs.
4. Using Exhibit 5–12 as a guide, prepare a report showing the customer margin for Indus Telecom.

EXERCISE 5–19 (Appendix 5A) Comprehensive Activity-Based Costing Exercise [LO2, LO3, LO6]
Refer to the data for Silicon Optics in Exercise 5–18.

Required:
1. Using Exhibit 5–15 as a guide, prepare a report showing the first-stage allocations of overhead costs to the activity cost pools.
2. Using Exhibit 5–16 as a guide, compute the activity rates for the activity cost pools.

(Required continued on the next page)

3. Using Exhibit 5–12 as a guide, prepare a report showing the overhead costs for the order from Indus Telecom including customer support costs.
4. Using Exhibit 5–12 as a guide, prepare a report showing the customer margin for Indus Telecom.
5. Using Exhibit 5–19 as a guide, prepare an action analysis report showing the customer margin for Indus Telecom. Direct materials should be coded as a Green cost, direct labour and wages and salaries as Yellow costs, and other overhead costs as a Red cost.
6. What action, if any, do you recommend as a result of the above analyses?

EXERCISE 5–20 (Appendix 5B) Activity-Based Costing Product Costs for External Reports [LO7]

Kunkel Company makes two products and uses a traditional costing system in which a single plantwide predetermined overhead rate is computed based on direct labour-hours. Data for the two products for the upcoming year follow:

	Mercon	Wurcon
Direct materials cost per unit	$10.00	$8.00
Direct labour cost per unit	$3.00	$3.75
Direct labour-hours per unit	0.20	0.25
Number of units produced	10,000	40,000

These products are customized to some degree for specific customers.

Required:

1. The company's manufacturing overhead costs for the year are expected to be $336,000. Using the company's traditional costing system, compute the unit product costs for the two products.
2. Management is considering an activity-based costing system in which half of the overhead would continue to be allocated on the basis of direct labour-hours and half would be allocated on the basis of engineering design time. The Mercon product is expected to need 4,000 engineering design hours and the Wurcon product is also expected to need 4,000 engineering design hours. Compute the unit product costs for the two products using the proposed ABC system.
3. Explain why the unit product costs differ between the two systems.

EXERCISE 5–21 Calculating and Interpreting Activity-Based Costing Data [LO2, LO3]

Jake's Cookhouse is a popular restaurant located on Lake Huron in Sarnia. The owner of the restaurant has been trying to better understand costs at the restaurant and has hired a student intern to conduct an activity-based costing study. The intern, in consultation with the owner, identified three major activities. She then completed the first-stage allocations of costs to the activity cost pools, using data from last month's operations. The results appear below:

Activity Cost Pool	Activity Measure	Total Cost	Total Activity
Serving a party of diners	Number of parties served	$12,000	5,000 parties
Serving a diner	Number of diners served	$90,000	12,000 diners
Serving a drink	Number of drinks ordered	$26,000	10,000 drinks

The above costs include all of the costs of the restaurant except for organization-sustaining costs such as rent, property taxes, and top-management salaries. A group of diners who ask to sit at the same table are counted as a party. Some costs, such as the costs of cleaning linen, are the same whether one person is at a table or the table is full. Other costs, such as washing dishes, depend on the number of diners served.

Prior to the activity-based costing study, the owner knew very little about the costs of the restaurant. He knew that the total cost for the month (including organization-sustaining costs) was $180,000 and that 12,000 diners had been served. Therefore, the average cost per diner was $15.

Required:

1. According to the activity-based costing system, what is the total cost of serving each of the following parties of diners?
   a. A party of four diners who order three drinks in total.
   b. A party of two diners who do not order any drinks.
   c. A lone diner who orders two drinks.
2. Convert the total costs you computed in (1) above to costs per diner. In other words, what is the average cost per diner for serving each of the following parties?
   a. A party of four diners who order three drinks in total.

(Required continued on the next page)

b. A party of two diners who do not order any drinks.
c. A lone diner who orders two drinks.
3. Why do the costs per diner for the three different parties differ from each other and from the overall average cost of $15.00 per diner?

Problems

PROBLEM 5–22 Evaluating the Profitability of Services [LO2, LO3, LO4]

Happy Valley Carpet Cleaning is a small, family-owned business operating out of Penticton, British Columbia. For its services, the company has always charged a flat fee per hundred square metres of carpet cleaned. The current fee is $22.95 per hundred square metres. However, there is some question about whether the company is actually making any money on jobs for some customers—particularly those located on more remote ranches that require considerable travel time. The owner's daughter, home for the summer from college, has suggested investigating this question using activity-based costing. After some discussion, a simple system consisting of four activity cost pools seemed to be adequate. The activity cost pools and their activity measures appear below:

Activity Cost Pool	Activity Measure	Activity for the Year
Cleaning carpets	Square metres cleaned (00s)	10,000 hundred square metres
Travel to jobs	Kilometres driven	50,000 kilometres
Job support	Number of jobs	1,800 jobs
Other (costs of idle capacity and organization-sustaining costs)	None	Not applicable

The total cost of operating the company for the year is $340,000, which includes the following costs:

Wages	$140,000
Cleaning supplies	25,000
Cleaning equipment depreciation	10,000
Vehicle expenses.	30,000
Office expenses.	60,000
President's compensation.	75,000
Total cost.	$340,000

Resource consumption is distributed across the activities as follows:

	Distribution of Resource Consumption Across Activity Cost Pools				
	Cleaning Carpets	Travel to Jobs	Job Support	Other	Total
Wages	75%	15%	0%	10%	100%
Cleaning supplies	100%	0%	0%	0%	100%
Cleaning equipment depreciation	70%	0%	0%	30%	100%
Vehicle expenses	0%	80%	0%	20%	100%
Office expenses	0%	0%	60%	40%	100%
President's compensation.	0%	0%	30%	70%	100%

Job support consists of receiving calls from potential customers at the home office, scheduling jobs, billing, resolving issues, and so on.

Required:

1. Using Exhibit 5–6 as a guide, prepare the first-stage allocation of costs to the activity cost pools.
2. Using Exhibit 5–7 as a guide, compute the activity rates for the activity cost pools.

(Required continued on the next page)

3. The company recently completed a 600 square-metre carpet-cleaning job at the Grizzly Bear Ranch—a 52-kilometre round-trip journey from the company's offices in Penticton. Compute the cost of this job using the activity-based costing system.
4. The revenue from the Grizzly Bear Ranch was $137.70 (600 square-metres at $22.95 per hundred square metres). Using Exhibit 5–12 as a guide, prepare a report showing the margin from this job.
5. What do you conclude concerning the profitability of the Grizzly Bear Ranch job? Explain.
6. What advice would you give the president concerning pricing jobs in the future?

PROBLEM 5–23 (Appendix 5A) Evaluating the Profitability of Services Using an Action Analysis [LO2, LO3, LO6]

Refer to the data for Happy Valley Carpet Cleaning in Problem 5–22.

Required:

1. Using Exhibit 5–15 as a guide, prepare the first-stage allocation of costs to the activity cost pools.
2. Using Exhibit 5–16 as a guide, compute the activity rates for the activity cost pools.
3. The company recently completed a 600 square-metre carpet-cleaning job at the Grizzly Bear Ranch—a 52-kilometre round-trip journey from the company's offices in Eagle-Vail. Compute the cost of this job using the activity-based costing system.
4. The revenue from the Grizzly Bear Ranch was $137.70 (600 square-metres at $22.95 per hundred square metre). Using Exhibit 5–19 as a guide, prepare an action analysis report of the Grizzly Bear Ranch job. The president of Happy Valley Carpet Cleaning considers all of the company's costs to be Green costs except for office expenses, which are coded Yellow, and his own compensation, which is coded Red. The people who do the actual carpet cleaning are all trained part-time workers who are paid only for work actually done.
5. What do you conclude concerning the profitability of the Grizzly Bear Ranch job? Explain.
6. What advice would you give the president concerning pricing jobs in the future?

PROBLEM 5–24 (Appendix 5B) Activity-Based Costing as an Alternative to Traditional Product Costing [LO7]

Rehm Company manufactures a product that is available in both a deluxe model and a regular model. The company has manufactured the regular model for years. The deluxe model was introduced several years ago to tap a new segment of the market. Since introduction of the deluxe model, the company's profits have steadily declined, and management has become increasingly concerned about the accuracy of its costing system. Sales of the deluxe model have been increasing rapidly.

Manufacturing overhead is assigned to products on the basis of direct labour-hours. For the current year, the company has estimated that it will incur $6,000,000 in manufacturing overhead cost and produce 15,000 units of the deluxe model and 120,000 units of the regular model. The deluxe model requires 1.6 hours of direct labour time per unit, and the regular model requires 0.8 hours. Material and labour costs per unit are as follows:

	Model	
	Deluxe	Regular
Direct materials	$154	$112
Direct labour	$16	$8

Required:

1. Using direct labour-hours as the base for assigning manufacturing overhead cost to products, compute the predetermined overhead rate. Using this rate and other data from the problem, determine the unit product cost of each model.
2. Management is considering using activity-based costing to apply manufacturing overhead costs to products for external financial reports. The activity-based costing system would have the following four activity cost pools:

(Required continued on the next page)

Activity Cost Pool	Estimated Activity Measure	Overhead Costs
Purchase orders	Number of purchase orders	$ 252,000
Scrap/rework orders	Number of scrap/rework orders	648,000
Product testing	Number of tests	1,350,000
Machine related	Machine-hours	3,750,000
Total overhead cost..................		$6,000,000

Activity Measure	Expected Activity		
	Deluxe	Regular	Total
Number of purchase orders...............	400	800	1,200
Number of scrap/rework orders............	500	400	900
Number of tests........................	6,000	9,000	15,000
Machine-hours.........................	20,000	30,000	50,000

Using Exhibit 5–7 as a guide, compute the predetermined overhead rates (i.e., activity rates) for each of the four activity cost pools.

3. Using the predetermined overhead rates computed in part (2) above, do the following:
   a. Compute the total amount of manufacturing overhead cost that would be applied to each model using the activity-based costing system. After these totals have been computed, determine the amount of manufacturing overhead cost per unit for each model.
   b. Compute the unit product cost of each model (materials, labour, and manufacturing overhead).
4. From the data you have developed in (1) through (3) above, identify factors that may account for the company's declining profits.

PROBLEM 5–25 Activity-Based Costing and Bidding on Jobs [LO2, LO3]

Vance Asbestos Removal Company removes potentially toxic asbestos insulation and related products from buildings. The company's estimator has been involved in a long-simmering dispute with the on-site work supervisors. The on-site supervisors claim that the estimator does not adequately distinguish between routine work such as removal of asbestos insulation around heating pipes in older homes and nonroutine work such as removing asbestos-contaminated ceiling plaster in industrial buildings. The on-site supervisors believe that nonroutine work is far more expensive than routine work and should bear higher customer charges. The estimator sums up his position in this way: "My job is to measure the area to be cleared of asbestos. As directed by top management, I simply multiply the square metres by $4,000 per thousand square metre to determine the bid price. Since our average cost is only $3,000 per thousand square metre, that leaves enough cushion to take care of the additional costs of nonroutine work that shows up. Besides, it is difficult to know what is routine or not routine until you actually start tearing things apart."

To shed light on this controversy, the company initiated an activity-based costing study of all of its costs. Data from the activity-based costing system follow:

Activity Cost Pool	Activity Measure	Total Activity
Removing asbestos.............	Thousands of square metres	500 thousand square metres
Estimating and job setup	Number of jobs	200 jobs*
Working on nonroutine jobs	Number of nonroutine jobs	25 nonroutine jobs
Other (costs of idle capacity ...... and organization-.............. sustaining costs)	Not applicable; these costs are not allocated to jobs	

*The total number of jobs includes nonroutine jobs as well as routine jobs. Nonroutine jobs as well as routine jobs require estimating and setup work.

Wages and salaries	$ 200,000
Disposal fees	600,000
Equipment depreciation	80,000
On-site supplies	60,000
Office expenses	190,000
Licensing and insurance	370,000
Total cost	$1,500,000

	Distribution of Resource Consumption Across Activity Cost Pools				
	Removing Asbestos	Estimating and Job Setup	Working on Nonroutine Jobs	Other	Total
Wages and salaries	40%	10%	35%	15%	100%
Disposal fees	70%	0%	30%	0%	100%
Equipment depreciation	50%	0%	40%	10%	100%
On-site supplies	55%	15%	20%	10%	100%
Office expenses	10%	40%	30%	20%	100%
Licensing and insurance	50%	0%	40%	10%	100%

Required:

1. Using Exhibit 5–6 as a guide, perform the first-stage allocation of costs to the activity cost pools.
2. Using Exhibit 5–7 as a guide, compute the activity rates for the activity cost pools.
3. Using the activity rates you have computed, determine the total cost and the average cost per thousand square metre of each of the following jobs according to the activity-based costing system.
   a. A routine 2,000-square-metre asbestos removal job.
   b. A routine 4,000-square-metre asbestos removal job.
   c. A nonroutine 2,000-square-metre asbestos removal job.
4. Given the results you obtained in (3) above, do you agree with the estimator that the company's present policy for bidding on jobs is adequate?

PROBLEM 5–26 Second-Stage Allocations and Product Margins [LO3, LO4]
AnimPix, Inc., is a small company that creates computer-generated animations for films and television. Much of the company's work consists of short commercials for television, but the company also does realistic computer animations for special effects in movies.

The young founders of the company have become increasingly concerned with the economics of the business—particularly since many competitors have sprung up recently in the local area. To help understand the company's cost structure, an activity-based costing system has been designed. Three major activities are carried out in the company: animation concept, animation production, and contract administration. The animation concept activity is carried out at the contract proposal stage when the company bids on projects. This is an intensive activity that involves individuals from all parts of the company in creating storyboards and prototype stills to be shown to the prospective client. After the client has accepted a project, the animation goes into production and contract administration begins. Technical staff do almost all of the work involved in animation production, whereas the administrative staff is largely responsible for contract administration. The activity cost pools and their activity measures and rates are listed below:

Activity Cost Pool	Activity Measure	Activity Rate
Animation concept	Number of proposals	$6,000 per proposal
Animation production	Minutes of animation	$7,700 per minute of animation
Contract administration	Number of contracts	$6,600 per contract

These activity rates include all of the costs of the company, except for the costs of idle capacity and organization-sustaining costs. There are no direct labour or direct materials costs.

Preliminary analysis using these activity rates has indicated that the local commercials segment of the market may be unprofitable. This segment is highly competitive. Producers of local commercials may ask several companies like AnimPix to bid, which results in an unusually low ratio of accepted contracts to bids. Furthermore, the animation sequences tend to be much shorter for local commercials than for other work. Since animation work is billed at standard rates according to the running time of the completed animation, the revenues from these short projects tend to be below average. Data concerning activity in the local commercials market appear below:

Activity Measure	Local Commercials
Number of proposals	20
Minutes of animation	12
Number of contracts	8

The total sales for local commercials amounted to $240,000.

Required:

1. Determine the cost of the local commercials market. (Think of the local commercials market as a product.)
2. Prepare a report showing the product margin of the local commercials market. (Remember, this company has no direct materials or direct labour costs.)
3. What would you recommend to management concerning the local commercials market?

PROBLEM 5–27 (Appendix 5A) Second-Stage Allocations and Product Margins [LO3, LO6]

Refer to the data for AnimPix, Inc., in Problem 5–26. In addition, the company has provided the following details concerning its activity rates:

	Activity Rates		
	Animation Concept	Animation Production	Contract Administration
Technical staff salaries	$3,500	$5,000	$1,800
Animation equipment depreciation	600	1,500	0
Administrative wages and salaries	1,400	200	4,600
Supplies costs	300	600	100
Facility costs	200	400	100
Total	$6,000	$7,700	$6,600

Management has provided the following ease of adjustment codes for the various costs:

	Ease of Adjustment Code
Technical staff salaries	Red
Animation equipment depreciation	Red
Administrative wages and salaries	Yellow
Supplies costs	Green
Facility costs	Red

These codes created some controversy. In particular, some administrators objected to coding their own salaries Yellow, while the technical staff salaries were coded Red. However, the founders of the firm overruled these objections by pointing out that "our technical staff is our most valuable asset. Good animators are extremely difficult to find, and they would be the last to go if we had to cut back."

Required:

1. Using Exhibit 5–17 as a guide, determine the cost of the local commercials market. (Think of the local commercials market as a product.)
2. Using Exhibit 5–19 as a guide, prepare an action analysis report concerning the local commercials market. (This company has no direct materials or direct labour costs.)
3. What would you recommend to management concerning the local commercials market?

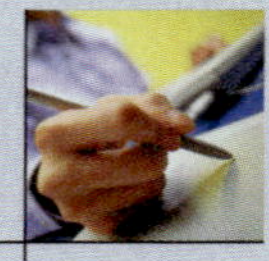

PROBLEM 5–28 (Appendix 5B) Activity-Based Costing as an Alternative to Traditional Product Costing [LO7]

For many years, Dover Company manufactured a single product called a mono-circuit. Then, three years ago, the company automated a portion of its plant and at the same time introduced a second product called a bi-circuit that has become increasingly popular. The bi-circuit product is a more complex product than the mono-circuit, requiring two hours of direct labour time per unit to manufacture, and extensive machining in the automated portion of the plant. In addition, it requires numerous inspections to ensure that high quality is maintained. The mono-circuit requires only one hour of direct labour time per unit, only a small amount of machining, and few quality control checks. Manufacturing overhead costs are assigned to the products on the basis of direct labour-hours.

Despite the growing popularity of the company's new bi-circuit, profits have declined steadily. Management is beginning to believe that the company's costing system may be faulty. Unit costs for materials and labour for the two products follow:

	Mono-Circuit	Bi-Circuit
Direct materials	$40	$80
Direct labour ($18 per hour)	$18	$36

Management estimates that the company will incur $3,000,000 in manufacturing overhead costs during the current year and that 40,000 units of the mono-circuit and 10,000 units of the bi-circuit will be produced and sold.

Required:

1. Compute the predetermined overhead rate assuming that the company continues to apply manufacturing overhead cost to products on the basis of direct labour-hours. Using this rate and other data from the problem, determine the unit product cost of each product.
2. Management is considering using activity-based costing to apply manufacturing overhead cost to products for external financial reports. Some preliminary work has been done and the data that have been collected are displayed below in the form of an Excel spreadsheet.

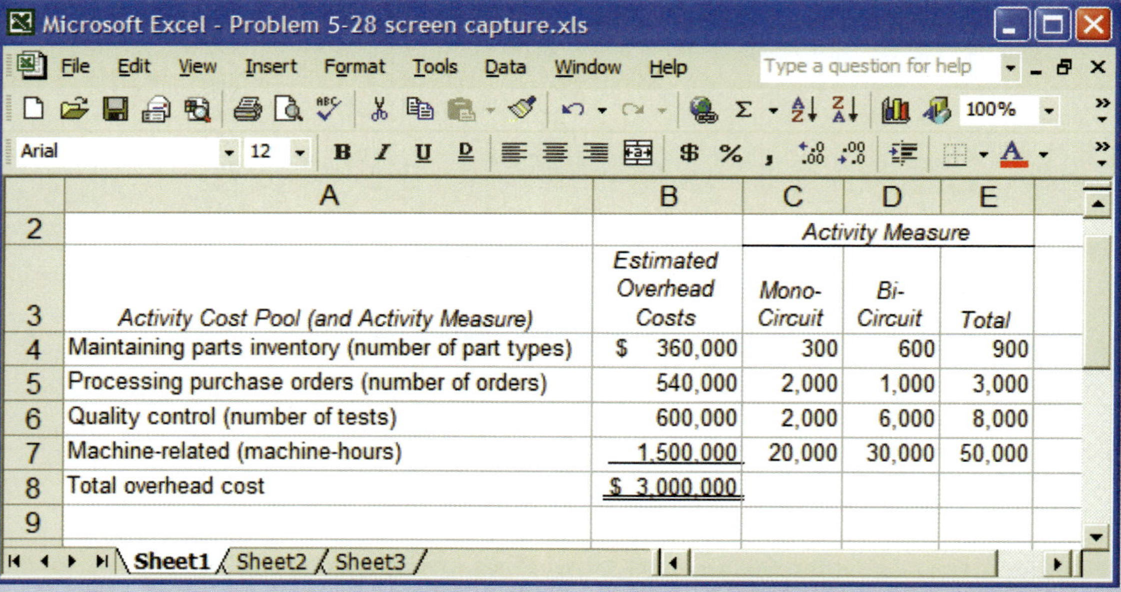

Microsoft Excel - Problem 5-28 screen capture.xls

	A	B	C	D	E
2			Activity Measure		
3	*Activity Cost Pool (and Activity Measure)*	*Estimated Overhead Costs*	*Mono-Circuit*	*Bi-Circuit*	*Total*
4	Maintaining parts inventory (number of part types)	$ 360,000	300	600	900
5	Processing purchase orders (number of orders)	540,000	2,000	1,000	3,000
6	Quality control (number of tests)	600,000	2,000	6,000	8,000
7	Machine-related (machine-hours)	1,500,000	20,000	30,000	50,000
8	Total overhead cost	$ 3,000,000			
9					

Sheet1 / Sheet2 / Sheet3

Determine the predetermined manufacturing overhead rate (i.e., activity rate) for each of the four activity cost pools.

3. Using the predetermined manufacturing overhead rates that you computed in part (2) above, do the following:
   a. Determine the total amount of manufacturing overhead cost that would be applied to each product using the activity-based costing system. After these totals have been computed, determine the amount of manufacturing overhead cost per unit of each product.
   b. Compute the unit product cost of each product.

(Required continued on the next page)

4. Look at the data you have computed in parts (1) through (3) above. In terms of manufacturing overhead cost, what factors make the bi-circuit more costly to produce than the mono-circuit? Is the bi-circuit as profitable as the company thinks it is? Explain.

PROBLEM 5–29 (Appendix 5B) Activity-Based Costing as an Alternative to Traditional Product Costing [LO7]

Erte, Inc., manufactures two models of high-pressure steam valves, the XR7 model and the ZD5 model. Data regarding the two products follow:

Product	Direct Labour-Hours	Annual Production	Total Direct Labour-Hours
XR7	0.2 DLHs per unit	20,000 units	4,000 DLHs
ZD5	0.4 DLHs per unit	40,000 units	16,000 DLHs
			20,000 DLHs

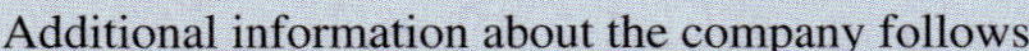

Additional information about the company follows:

a. Product XR7 requires $35 in direct materials per unit, and product ZD5 requires $25.
b. The direct labour rate is $20 per hour.
c. The company has always used direct labour-hours as the base for applying manufacturing overhead cost to products. Manufacturing overhead totals $1,480,000 per year.
d. Product XR7 is more complex to manufacture than product ZD5 and requires the use of a special milling machine.
e. Because of the special work required in (d) above, the company is considering the use of activity-based costing to apply overhead cost to products. Three activity cost pools have been identified and the first-stage allocations have been completed. Data concerning these activity cost pools appear below:

		Estimated	Estimated Total Activity		
Activity Cost Pool	Activity Measure	Total Cost	XR7	ZD5	Total
Machine setups	Number of setups	$ 180,000	150	100	250
Special milling	Machine-hours	300,000	1,000	0	1,000
General factory........	Direct labour-hours	1,000,000	4,000	16,000	20,000
		$1,480,000			

Required:

1. Assume that the company continues to use direct labour-hours as the base for applying overhead cost to products.
   a. Compute the predetermined overhead rate.
   b. Determine the unit product cost of each product.
2. Assume that the company decides to use activity-based costing to apply overhead cost to products.
   a. Compute the activity rate for each activity cost pool. Also compute the amount of overhead cost that would be applied to each product.
   b. Determine the unit product cost of each product.
3. Explain why overhead cost shifted from the high-volume product to the low-volume product under activity-based costing.

PROBLEM 5–30 (Appendix 5A) Activity Rates and Activity-Based Management [LO2, LO3, LO6]

Aegean Catering is a Greek company that provides passenger and crew meals to airlines operating out of two international airports in Athens and Corfu. The operations at the two airports are managed separately, and top management believes that there may be benefits to greater sharing of information between the two operations.

To better compare the two operations, an activity-based costing system has been designed with the active participation of the managers at both airports. The activity-based costing system is based on the activity cost pools and activity measures that appear on the next page.

Activity Cost Pool	Activity Measure
Meal preparation.	Number of meals
Flight-related activities	Number of flights
Customer service	Number of customers
Other (costs of idle capacity and organization-sustaining costs)	Not applicable

The operation at Athens International Airport (AIA) serves one million meals annually on 5,000 flights for 10 different airlines. (Each airline is considered one customer.) The annual cost of running the AIA airport operation, excluding only the costs of raw materials for meals, totals €3,675,000.

Note: The currency in Greece is the euro denoted by €.

Annual Cost of the CDG Operation	
Cooks and delivery personnel wages	€3,000,000
Kitchen supplies	37,500
Chef salaries	225,000
Equipment depreciation	75,000
Administrative wages and salaries	187,500
Building costs	150,000
Total cost.	€3,675,000

To help determine the activity rates, employees were interviewed and asked how they divided their time among the four major activities. The results of employee interviews at AIA are displayed below:

Distribution of Resource Consumption Across Activities at the AIA Operation

	Meal Preparation	Flight Related	Customer Service	Other	Total
Cooks and delivery personnel wages	75%	20%	0%	5%	100%
Kitchen supplies	100%	0%	0%	0%	100%
Chef salaries	30%	20%	40%	10%	100%
Equipment depreciation	60%	0%	0%	40%	100%
Administrative wages and salaries	0%	20%	60%	20%	100%
Building costs	0%	0%	0%	100%	100%

Required:

1. Perform the first-stage allocation of costs to the activity cost pools. (Use Exhibit 5–15 as a guide.)
2. Compute the activity rates for the activity cost pools. (Use Exhibit 5–16 as a guide.) Do not round off.
3. The Corfu operation has already concluded its activity-based costing study and has reported the following activity rates: €2.48 per meal for meal preparation; €144.50 per flight for flight-related activities; and €12,000 for customer service. Comparing the activity rates for the AIA operation you computed in part (2) above to the activity rates for Corfu, do you have any suggestions for the top management of Aegean Catering?

Cases

CASE 5–31 (Appendix 5A) Comprehensive Activity-Based Costing Case [LO2, LO3, LO5, LO6]

Victorian Windows is a small company that builds specialty wooden windows for local builders. For years the company assigned overhead costs to products based on direct labour-hours (DLHs). However, the company's president became interested in activity-based costing after reading an article about it in a trade journal. An activity-based costing design team was put together, and within a few months a simple system consisting of four activity cost pools had been designed. The activity cost pools and their activity measures appear below:

Activity Cost Pool	Activity Measure	Total Activity for the Year
Making windows	Direct labour-hours	80,000 DLHs
Processing orders	Number of orders	1,000 orders
Customer relations	Number of customers	200 customers
Other (costs of idle capacity and organization-sustaining costs)	None	Not applicable

The Processing Orders activity includes order taking, job setup, job scheduling, and so on. Direct materials and direct labour are directly assigned to jobs in both the traditional and activity-based costing systems. The total overhead cost (both nonmanufacturing and manufacturing) for the year is $1,180,000 and includes the following costs:

Manufacturing overhead costs:		
Indirect factory wages	$240,000	
Production equipment depreciation	250,000	
Other factory costs	110,000	$ 600,000
Selling and administrative expenses:		
Administrative wages and salaries	240,000	
Office expenses	60,000	
Marketing expenses	280,000	580,000
Total overhead cost		$1,180,000

Based largely on interviews with employees, the distribution of resource consumption across the activities has been estimated as follows:

	Distribution of Resource Consumption Across Activities				
	Making Windows	Processing Orders	Customer Relations	Other	Total
Indirect factory wages	25%	50%	10%	15%	100%
Production equipment depreciation	80%	0%	0%	20%	100%
Other factory costs	40%	0%	0%	60%	100%
Administrative wages and salaries	0%	25%	35%	40%	100%
Office expenses	0%	20%	30%	50%	100%
Marketing expenses	0%	0%	75%	25%	100%

Management of the company is particularly interested in measuring the profitability of two customers. One of the customers, Avon Construction, is a low-volume purchaser. The other, Lynx Builders, is a relatively high-volume purchaser. Details of these two customers' orders for the year appear below:

	Avon Construction	Lynx Builders
Number of orders during the year	2 orders	3 orders
Total direct labour-hours	250 DLHs	1,500 DLHs
Total sales	$9,995	$54,995
Total direct materials	$3,400	$17,200
Total direct labour cost	$4,500	$27,000

Required:

1. The company's traditional costing system applies manufacturing overhead to jobs strictly on the basis of direct labour-hours. Using this traditional approach, carry out the following steps:

(Required continued on the next page)

a. Compute the predetermined manufacturing overhead rate.

b. Compute the total margin for all of the windows ordered by Avon Construction according to the traditional costing system. Do the same for Lynx Builders.

2. Using activity-based costing, do the following:

a. Using Exhibit 5–15 as a guide, perform the first-stage allocation of costs to the activity cost pools.

b. Using Exhibit 5–16 as a guide, compute the activity rates for the activity cost pools.

c. Compute the overhead costs of serving each of the two customers. (You will need to construct a table like Exhibit 5–17 for each customer. However, unlike Exhibit 5–17, you should fill in the column for Customer Relations as well as the other columns. Exhibit 5–17 was constructed for a product; in this case we are interested in a customer.)

d. Management has provided the following ease of adjustment codes to use in action analysis reports:

	Ease of Adjustment Code
Direct materials	Green
Direct labour	Yellow
Indirect factory wages	Yellow
Production equipment depreciation	Yellow
Other factory costs	Yellow
Administrative wages and salaries	Red
Office expenses	Yellow
Marketing expenses	Yellow

Using Exhibit 5–19 as a guide, prepare an action analysis report showing the margin on business with Avon Construction. Repeat for Lynx Builders.

3. Does Victorian Windows appear to be losing money on either customer? Do the traditional and activity-based costing systems agree concerning the profitability of the customers? If they do not agree, which costing system do you believe? Why?

CASE 5–32 (Appendix 5B) Activity-Based Costing and Pricing [LO2, LO3, LO4, LO5, LO7] This chapter emphasizes the use of activity-based costing in internal decisions. However, a modified form of activity-based costing can also be used to develop product costs for external financial reports. For this purpose, product costs include all manufacturing overhead costs and exclude all nonmanufacturing costs. This problem illustrates such a costing system.

Java Source, Inc. (JSI), is a processor and distributor of a variety of blends of coffee. The company buys coffee beans from around the world and roasts, blends, and packages them for resale. JSI offers a large variety of different coffees that it sells to gourmet shops in one-kilogram bags. The major cost of the coffee is raw materials. However, the company's predominantly automated roasting, blending, and packing processes require a substantial amount of manufacturing overhead. The company uses relatively little direct labour.

Some of JSI's coffees are very popular and sell in large volumes, while a few of the newer blends sell in very low volumes. JSI prices its coffees at manufacturing cost plus a markup of 25%, with some adjustments made to keep the company's prices competitive.

For the coming year, JSI's budget includes estimated manufacturing overhead cost of $2,200,000. JSI assigns manufacturing overhead to products on the basis of direct labour-hours. The expected direct labour cost totals $600,000, which represents 50,000 hours of direct labour time. Based on the sales budget and expected raw materials costs, the company will purchase and use $5,000,000 of raw materials (mostly coffee beans) during the year.

The expected costs for direct materials and direct labour for one-kilogram bags of two of the company's coffee products appear below.

	Kenya Dark	Viet Select
Direct materials	$4.50	$2.90
Direct labour (0.02 hours per bag)	$0.24	$0.24

JSI's controller believes that the company's traditional costing system may be providing misleading cost information. To determine whether or not this is correct, the controller has prepared an analysis of the year's expected manufacturing overhead costs, as shown in the following table:

Activity Cost Pool	Activity Measure	Expected Activity for the Year	Expected Cost for the Year
Purchasing..........	Purchase orders	2,000 orders	$ 560,000
Material handling.....	Number of setups	1,000 setups	193,000
Quality control.......	Number of batches	500 batches	90,000
Roasting............	Roasting hours	95,000 roasting hours	1,045,000
Blending............	Blending hours	32,000 blending hours	192,000
Packaging..........	Packaging hours	24,000 packaging hours	120,000
Total manufacturing overhead cost.....			$2,200,000

Data regarding the expected production of Kenya Dark and Viet Select coffee are presented below.

	Kenya Dark	Viet Select
Expected sales....................	80,000 kilograms	4,000 kilograms
Batch size........................	5,000 kilograms	500 kilograms
Setups...........................	2 per batch	2 per batch
Purchase order size................	20,000 kilograms	500 kilograms
Roasting time per 100 kilograms.......	1.5 roasting hours	1.5 roasting hours
Blending time per 100 kilograms.......	0.5 blending hours	0.5 blending hours
Packaging time per 100 kilograms.....	0.3 packaging hours	0.3 packaging hours

Required:

1. Using direct labour-hours as the base for assigning manufacturing overhead cost to products, do the following:
   a. Determine the predetermined overhead rate that will be used during the year.
   b. Determine the unit product cost of one kilogram of the Kenya Dark coffee and one kilogram of the Viet Select coffee.
2. Using activity-based costing as the basis for assigning manufacturing overhead cost to products, do the following:
   a. Determine the total amount of manufacturing overhead cost assigned to the Kenya Dark coffee and to the Viet Select coffee for the year.
   b. Using the data developed in (2*a*) above, compute the amount of manufacturing overhead cost per kilogram of the Kenya Dark coffee and the Viet Select coffee. Round all computations to the nearest whole cent.
   c. Determine the unit product cost of one kilogram of the Kenya Dark coffee and one kilogram of the Viet Select coffee.
3. Write a brief memo to the president of JSI explaining what you have found in (1) and (2) above and discussing the implications to the company of using direct labour as the base for assigning manufacturing overhead cost to products.

(CMA, adapted)

CASE 5–33 (Appendix 5B) Contrasting Activity-Based Costing and Traditional Costing [LO2, LO3, LO4, LO7]

This chapter emphasizes the use of activity-based costing in internal decisions. However, as illustrated in Appendix 5B, a modified form of activity-based costing can also be used to develop product costs for external financial reports. For this purpose, product costs include all manufacturing overhead costs and exclude all nonmanufacturing costs. This problem illustrates such a costing system.

"Wow! Is that R-92 model ever a loser! It's time to cut back its production and shift our resources toward the new T-95 model," said Graham Thomas, executive vice-president of Thomas Products, Inc. "Just look at this income statement I've received from accounting. The T-95 is generating four times as much profit as the R-92, and it has only about one-sixth as much in sales. I'm convinced that our future depends on the T-95." The year-end statement to which Graham was referring is shown on the next page.

	Total	Model R-92	Model T-95
Sales	$11,125,000	$9,000,000	$2,125,000
Cost of goods sold	6,900,000	5,490,000	1,410,000
Gross margin	4,225,000	3,510,000	715,000
Less selling and administrative expenses	3,675,000	3,450,000	225,000
Operating income	$ 550,000	$ 60,000	$ 490,000
Number of units produced and sold		30,000	5,000

"The numbers sure look that way," replied Julie Williams, the company's sales manager. "But why isn't the competition more excited about the T-95? I know we've only been producing the model for three years, but I'm surprised that more of our competitors haven't recognized what a cash cow it is."

"I think it's our new automated plant," replied Graham. "Now it takes only two direct labour-hours to produce a unit of the R-92 and three direct labour-hours to produce a unit of the T-95. That's considerably less than it used to take us."

"I agree that automation is wonderful," replied Julie. "I suppose that's how we're able to hold down the price of the T-95. Taylor Company in England tried to bring out a T-95 but discovered they couldn't touch our price. But Taylor is killing us on the R-92 by undercutting our price with some of our best customers. I suppose they'll pick up all of our R-92 business if we move out of that market. But who cares? We don't even have to advertise the T-95; it just seems to sell itself."

"My only concern about automation is how our manufacturing overhead rate has shot up," said Graham. "Our total manufacturing overhead cost is $2,700,000. That comes out to be a hefty amount per direct labour-hour, but Dianne down in accounting has been using direct labour-hours as the base for computing overhead rates for years and doesn't want to change. I don't suppose it matters so long as costs get assigned to products."

"I've never understood that debit and credit stuff," replied Julie. "But I think you've got a problem in production. I had lunch with Janet yesterday and she complained about how complex the T-95 is to produce. Apparently they have to do a lot of setups, special soldering, and other work on the T-95 just to keep production moving. And they have to inspect every single unit."

"It'll have to wait," said Graham. "I'm writing a proposal to the board of directors to phase out the R-92. We've got to increase our bottom line or we'll all be looking for jobs."

Required:

1. Compute the predetermined overhead rate based on direct labour-hours that the company used during the year. (There was no under- or overapplied overhead for the year.)
2. Direct materials and direct labour costs per unit for the two products are as follows:

	R-92	T-95
Direct materials	$75	$120
Direct labour	$36	$ 54

   Using these data and the rate computed in part (1) above, determine the unit product cost of each product under the company's traditional costing system.
3. Assume that the company's $2,700,000 in manufacturing overhead cost can be assigned to six activity cost pools, as follows:

Activity Cost Pool (and Activity Measure)	Estimated Overhead Costs	Expected Activity Total	R-92	T-95
Machine setups (number of setups)	$ 312,000	1,600	1,000	600
Quality control (number of inspections)	540,000	9,000	4,000	5,000
Purchase orders (number of orders)	135,000	1,200	840	360
Soldering (number of solder joints)	675,000	200,000	60,000	140,000
Shipments (number of shipments)	198,000	600	400	200
Machine related (machine-hours)	840,000	70,000	30,000	40,000
	$2,700,000			

(Required continued on the next page)

Given these data, would you support a recommendation to expand sales of the T-95? Explain your position.

4. From the data you have prepared in part (3) above, why do you suppose the T-95 "just seems to sell itself"?
5. If you were president of Thomas Products, Inc., what strategy would you follow from this point forward to improve the company's overall profits?

Research

R 5–34 Activity-Based Costing Applied [LO1, LO2, LO3]

Activity-based costing can be applied in not-for-profit organizations such as colleges and universities. Arrange a meeting with an administrative officer in the business faculty of your college or university to discuss the cost allocation process currently employed and the implications of adopting an activity-based costing system.

Required:

1. Identify the key cost objects (e.g., teaching departments) currently used in the business faculty's management control system.
2. Determine how costs are currently assigned to these cost objects.
3. Determine the key activities required to support the teaching departments of the business faculty.
4. Identify an activity measure for each activity identified in part 1.
5. Qualitatively evaluate how use of an ABC system (based on the data gathered in parts 3 and 4 above) would affect the assignment of costs to the cost objects in the business faculty.

R 5–35 Benefits of Activity-Based Costing [LO1]

Implementing an activity-based costing system should only proceed if management believes the benefits of doing so will exceed the costs. The costs of an ABC system are not difficult to quantify. They would include identifying the key activities, developing an information system to record and report information, collecting data for activity measures, and maintaining the system.

Required:

1. Identify, qualitatively, some potential benefits of adopting an ABC system.
2. How could these benefits be quantified?
3. How could management deal with the uncertainty related to any potential benefits of adopting an ABC system?

R 5–36 Activity-Based Costing in Practice [LO1, LO5]

As you know, the World Wide Web is a medium that is constantly evolving. Sites come and go, and change without notice. To enable the periodic updating of site addresses, this problem has been posted to the textbook web site (www.mcgrawhill.ca/olc/garrison). After accessing the site, enter the Student Centre and select this chapter. Select and complete the Internet Exercise.

CHAPTER 6

LEARNING OBJECTIVES

After studying Chapter 6, you should be able to:

1. Describe how fixed and variable costs behave and how to use them to predict costs.
2. Explain how to analyze mixed costs.
3. Prepare an income statement using the contribution format.
4. (Appendix 6A) Elaborate on the least-squares regression method.

COST BEHAVIOUR: ANALYSIS AND USE

BUSINESS FOCUS

Costly Behaviour Required

Polytech Products of Calgary Alberta is a manufacturer and distributor of heating and cooling systems. During the 1990s, Polytech experienced rapid growth and reported in 2004 that it had 60 employees.

In 2001, management addressed a concern over its information system and implemented a new Microsoft Axapta system by August 2002. The system provides new information, reduces conflicting information in the legacy systems, lessens data entry errors and redundant entries, and improves management controls.

Costs for the new system were of two types, implementation costs for hardware, software and consulting labour of $260,000 and annual operating costs of $25,000.

The management committee needed to know how the installation costs behave so they could assess what benefits are necessary to recover their costs and the types of areas where benefits might be located.

Source: http://www.microsoft.com/resources/casestudies, April 1, 2005.

In Chapter 2, we stated costs can be classified by behaviour. *Cost behaviour* refers to how a cost will react or change as changes take place in the level of business activity. An understanding of cost behaviour is the key to many decisions in an organization. Managers who understand how costs behave are better able to predict what costs will be under various operating circumstances. Attempts at decision making without a thorough understanding of cost behaviour patterns can lead to disaster. For example, a decision to drop a particular product line might result in far less cost savings than managers had assumed—leading to a drop in profits. To avoid such problems, a manager must be able to accurately predict what costs will be at various activity levels.

This chapter briefly reviews the definitions of variable costs and fixed costs and then discusses the behaviour of these costs in greater depth than in Chapter 2. The chapter also introduces the concept of a mixed cost, which is a cost that has both variable and fixed cost elements. We conclude the chapter by introducing a new income statement format—called the *contribution format*—in which costs are organized by behaviour rather than by the traditional functions of production, sales, and administration.

Cost behaviour, as presented in this chapter, introduces the description and analytical techniques needed for all the areas of managerial accounting, that is, costing, budgeting, decision, and control. The descriptions and techniques presented here are simplified so that they are transparent but the ideas are appropriate for analysis of more complex situations that will appear in later chapters. Thus careful study of each of the discussions is important because it will be a foundation for numerous follow-up descriptions. For example, the distinction between total cost and unit cost is a major source of confusion in more complex situations.

In Chapter 2, we mentioned only variable and fixed costs. There is a third behaviour pattern, generally known as a *mixed* or *semivariable* cost. All three cost behaviour patterns—variable, fixed, and mixed—are found in most organizations. The relative proportion of each type of cost present in a firm is known as the firm's **cost structure.** For example an organization might have many fixed costs but few variable or mixed costs. Alternatively, it might have many variable costs but few fixed or mixed costs. A firm's cost structure can have a significant effect on decisions. In this chapter, we will concentrate on gaining a fuller understanding of the behaviour of each type of cost. In the next chapter, we will more fully discuss how cost structure affects decisions.

Cost structure
The relative proportion of fixed, variable, and mixed costs found within an organization.

Types of Cost Behaviour Patterns

Variable Costs

LEARNING OBJECTIVE 1
Describe how fixed and variable costs behave and how to use them to predict costs.

We explained in Chapter 2 that a variable cost is a cost whose *total dollar* amount varies in direct proportion to changes in the activity level. Direct proportion signifies that if the activity level doubles, the total dollar amount of the variable costs also doubles. If the activity level increases by only 10%, then the total dollar amount of the variable costs increases by 10% as well.

We also found in Chapter 2 that a variable cost remains constant if expressed on a *per unit* basis. To provide an example, consider Adventure Rafting, a small company that provides daylong white-water rafting excursions on rivers in the Yukon. The company provides all of the necessary equipment and experienced guides, and it serves gourmet meals to its guests. The meals are purchased from an exclusive caterer for $30 per person for a daylong excursion. If we look at the cost of the meals on a *per person* basis, the cost remains constant at $30. This $30 cost per person will not change, regardless of how many people participate in a daylong excursion. The behaviour of this variable cost, on both a per unit and a total basis, is tabulated as follows:

Number of Guests	Cost of Meals per Guest	Total Cost of Meals
250.	$30	$ 7,500
500.	30	15,000
750.	30	22,500
1,000.	30	30,000

The idea that a variable cost is constant per unit but varies in total with the activity level is crucial to an understanding of cost behaviour patterns. We will rely on this concept again and again in this chapter and in chapters ahead.

Exhibit 6–1 provides a graphic illustration of variable cost behaviour. Note that the graph of the total cost of the meals slants upward to the right. This is because the total cost of the meals is directly proportional to the number of guests. In contrast, the graph of the per unit cost of meals is flat because the cost of the meals per guest is constant at $30.

Activity base
A measure of whatever causes the incurrence of a variable cost. For example, the total cost of X-ray film in a hospital will increase as the number of X-rays taken increases. Therefore, the number of X-rays is an activity base for explaining the total cost of X-ray film.

The Activity Base For a cost to be variable, it must be variable *with respect to something*. That "something" is its *activity base.* An **activity base** is a measure of whatever causes the incurrence of variable cost. As we learned in Chapter 5 an activity base is sometimes referred to as a *cost driver.* Some of the most common activity bases are direct labour-hours, machine-hours, units produced, and units sold. Other activity bases (cost drivers) might include the number of kilometres driven by salespersons, the number of kilograms of laundry processed by a hotel, the number of letters typed by a secretary, and the number of occupied beds in a hospital.

To plan and control variable costs, a manager must be well acquainted with the various activity bases within the firm. People sometimes get the notion that if a cost doesn't vary with production or with sales, then it is not really a variable cost. This is not correct. As suggested by the range of bases or drivers listed above, costs are caused by many different activities within an organization. Whether a cost is considered to be variable depends on whether it is caused by the activity under consideration. For example, if a manager is analyzing the cost of service calls for a product warranty, the relevant activity measure will be the number of service calls made. Those costs that vary in total with the number of service calls made are the variable costs of making service calls.

EXHIBIT 6–1 Variable Cost Behaviour

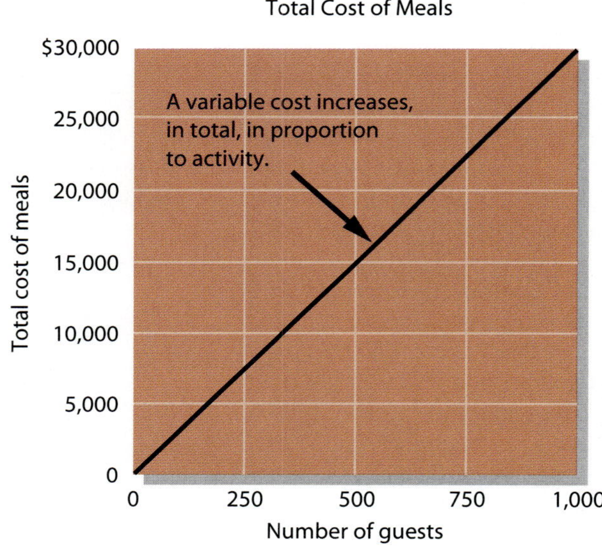

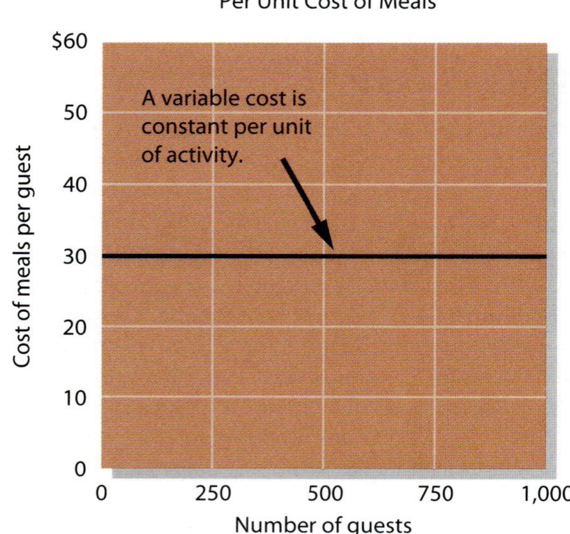

Nevertheless, unless stated otherwise, you can assume that the activity base under consideration is the total volume of goods and services produced or sold by the organization. So, for example, if we ask whether the cost of direct materials at Ford Canada is a variable cost, the answer is yes, since the cost of direct materials is variable with respect to Ford's total volume of production. We will specify the activity base only when it is something other than total production or sales.

Extent of Variable Costs The number and type of variable costs present in an organization will depend in large part on the organization's structure and purpose. A public utility like New Brunswick Power, with large investments in equipment, will tend to have few variable costs. Most of the costs are associated with its plant, and these costs tend to be insensitive to changes in levels of service provided. A company like Adventure Rafting, by contrast, will often have many variable costs; these costs will be associated with the services provided to customers.

A merchandising company like Canadian Tire or Atlantic Superstore will usually have a high proportion of variable costs in its cost structure. In most merchandising companies, the cost of merchandise purchased for resale, a variable cost, constitutes a very large component of total cost. Service companies, by contrast, have diverse cost structures. Some service companies, such as the restaurant chain Tim Hortons, have fairly large variable costs because of the costs of their raw materials. On the other hand, service companies involved in consulting, auditing, engineering, dental, medical, and architectural activities have very large fixed costs in the form of expensive facilities and highly trained salaried employees.

Some of the more frequently encountered variable costs are listed in Exhibit 6–2. This exhibit is not a complete listing of all costs that can be considered variable. Moreover, some of the costs listed in the exhibit may behave more like fixed than variable costs in some firms. We will see some examples of this later in the chapter. Nevertheless, Exhibit 6–2 provides a useful listing of many of the costs that normally would be considered variable with respect to the volume of output.

IN BUSINESS

Coping with the Fallout from September 11

Costs can change for reasons that have nothing to do with changes in volume. Filterfresh is a company that services coffee machines located in commercial offices—providing milk, sugar, cups, and coffee. The company's operations were profoundly affected by the security measures many companies initiated after the terrorist attacks on the World Trade Center and the Pentagon on September 11, 2001. Heightened security at customer locations means that Filterfresh's 250 deliverymen can no longer casually walk through a customer's lobby with a load of supplies. Now a guard typically checks the deliveryman's identification and paperwork at the loading dock and may search the van before permitting the deliveryman access to the customer's building. These delays have added an average of about an hour per day to each route, which means that Filterfresh needs 24 more delivery people to do the same work it did prior to September 11. That's a 10% increase in cost without any increase in the amount of coffee sold.

Source: Anna Bernasek, "The Friction Economy," *Fortune*, February 18, 2002, pp. 104–112

True Variable versus Step-Variable Costs

Not all variable costs have exactly the same behaviour pattern. Some variable costs behave in a *true variable* or *proportionately variable* pattern. Other variable costs behave in a *step-variable* pattern.

True Variable Costs Direct materials is a true or proportionately variable cost because the amount used during a period will vary in direct proportion to the level of

EXHIBIT 6–2 Examples of Variable Costs

Type of Organization	Costs That Are Normally Variable with Respect to Volume of Output
Merchandising company	Cost of goods (merchandise) sold
Manufacturing company	Manufacturing costs: Direct materials Direct labour* Variable portion of manufacturing overhead: Indirect materials Lubricants Supplies Power
Both merchandising and manufacturing companies	Selling, general, and administrative costs: Commissions Clerical costs, such as invoicing Shipping costs
Service organizations	Supplies, travel, clerical

*Direct labour may or may not be variable in practice. See the discussion later in this chapter.

production activity. Moreover, any amounts purchased but not used can be stored and carried forward to the next period as inventory.

Step-Variable Costs The wages of maintenance workers are often considered to be a variable cost, but this labour cost doesn't behave in quite the same way as the cost of direct materials. Unlike direct materials, the time of maintenance workers is obtainable only in large chunks. Moreover, any maintenance time not utilized cannot be stored as inventory and carried forward to the next period. If the time is not used effectively, it is gone forever. Furthermore, a maintenance crew can work at a fairly leisurely pace if pressures are light but intensify its efforts if pressures build up. For this reason, small changes in the level of production may have no effect on the number of maintenance people employed by the company.

Step-variable cost
A cost (such as the cost of a maintenance worker) that is obtainable only in large chunks and that increases and decreases only in response to fairly wide changes in the activity level.

A resource that is obtainable only in large chunks (such as maintenance workers) and whose cost increases or decreases only in response to fairly wide changes in activity is known as a **step-variable cost.** The behaviour of a step-variable cost, contrasted with the behaviour of a true variable cost, is illustrated in Exhibit 6–3.

Notice that the need for maintenance help changes only with fairly wide changes in volume and that when additional maintenance time is obtained, it comes in large, indivisible chunks. The strategy of management in dealing with step-variable costs must be to

EXHIBIT 6–3 True Variable versus Step-Variable Costs

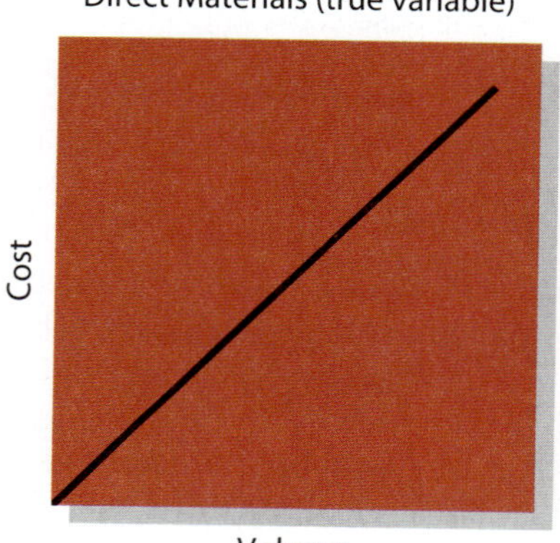

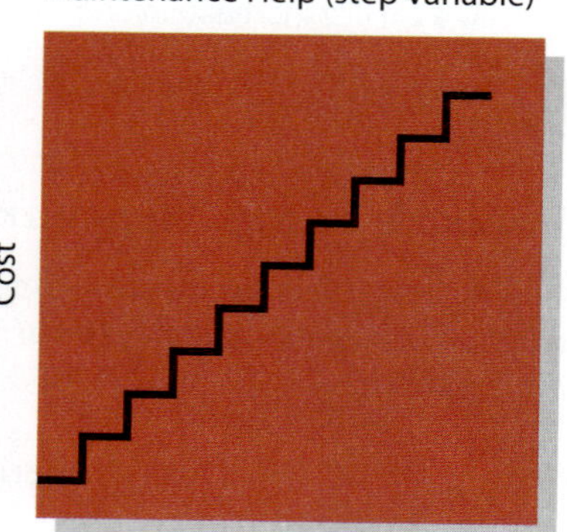

obtain the fullest use of services possible for each separate step. Great care must be taken in working with these kinds of costs to prevent "fat" from building up in an organization. There may be a tendency to employ additional help more quickly than needed, and there is a natural reluctance to lay off people when volume declines.

The Linearity Assumption and the Relevant Range

In dealing with variable costs, we have assumed a strictly linear relationship between cost and volume, except in the case of step-variable costs. Economists correctly point out that many costs that the accountant classifies as variable actually behave in a *curvilinear* fashion. The behaviour of a **curvilinear cost** is shown in Exhibit 6–4.

Curvilinear costs
A relationship between cost and activity that is a curve rather than a straight line.

Although many costs are not strictly linear when plotted as a function of volume, a curvilinear cost can be satisfactorily approximated with a straight line within a narrow band of activity known as the *relevant range.* The **relevant range** is that range of activity within which the assumptions made about cost behaviour are valid. For example, note that the dashed line in Exhibit 6–4 can be used as an approximation to the curvilinear cost with very little loss of accuracy within the shaded relevant range. However, outside of the relevant range, this particular straight line is a poor approximation to the curvilinear cost relationship. Managers should always keep in mind that a particular assumption made about cost behaviour may be invalid if activity falls outside of the relevant range.

Relevant range
The range of activity within which assumptions about variable and fixed cost behaviour are valid.

Fixed Costs

In our discussion of cost behaviour patterns in Chapter 2, we stated that total fixed costs remain constant within the relevant range of activity. To continue the Adventure Rafting example, assume the company decides to rent a building for $500 per month to store its equipment. The *total* amount of rent paid is the same regardless of the number of guests the company takes on its expeditions during any given month. This cost behaviour pattern is shown graphically in Exhibit 6–5.

Since fixed costs remain constant in total, the amount of fixed cost *per unit* basis becomes progressively smaller as the level of activity increases. If Adventure Rafting has only 250 guests in a month, the $500 fixed rental cost would amount to $2 per guest. If there are 1,000 guests, the fixed rental cost would amount to only 50 cents per guest. This aspect of the behaviour of fixed costs is also displayed in Exhibit 6–5. Note that as the number of guests increases, the average unit cost drops, but it drops at a decreasing rate. The first guests have the greatest impact on the average fixed costs per unit.

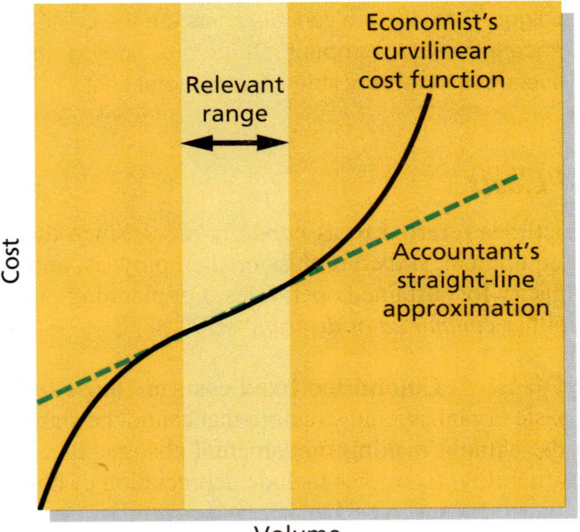

EXHIBIT 6–4 Curvilinear Costs and the Relevant Range

EXHIBIT 6–5 Fixed Cost Behaviour

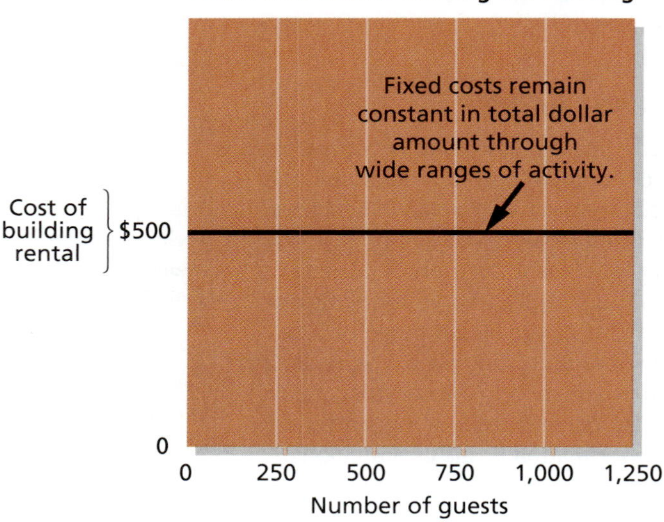

It is necessary in some contexts to express fixed costs on an average per unit basis. For example, in Chapter 2 we showed how unit product costs computed for use in external financial statements contain both variable and fixed costs. As a general rule, however, we caution against expressing fixed costs on an average per unit basis in internal reports because it creates the false impression that fixed costs are like variable costs and that total fixed costs actually change as the level of activity changes. To avoid confusion in internal reporting and decision-making situations, fixed costs should be expressed in total rather than on a per unit basis.

IN BUSINESS

Airlines have long recognized that once a flight is scheduled, the variable cost of filling a seat with a passenger is very small. The costs of the cockpit flight crew, fuel, gate rentals, maintenance, aircraft depreciation, and so on, are all basically fixed with respect to the number of passengers who actually take a particular flight. The cost of the cabin flight crew is a step-variable cost—the number of flight attendants assigned to a flight will vary with the number of passengers on the flight. The only true variable costs are the costs of meals and an almost inconsequential increase in fuel consumption. Therefore, adding one passenger to a flight brings in additional revenue but has very little effect on total cost.

Types of Fixed Costs

Fixed costs are sometimes referred to as *capacity costs*, since they result from outlays made for buildings, equipment, skilled professional employees, and other items needed to provide the basic capacity for sustained operations. For planning purposes, fixed costs can be viewed as being either *committed* or *discretionary.*

Committed fixed costs
Those fixed costs that are difficult to adjust and that relate to the investment in facilities, equipment, and the basic organizational structure of a firm.

Committed Fixed Costs **Committed fixed costs** are those investments in facilities, equipment, and the basic organizational structure that cannot be significantly reduced, even for short time periods, without making fundamental changes that would impair a firm's long-run goals or profitability. Examples include depreciation of buildings and equipment, real estate taxes, insurance expenses, and salaries of top management and operating personnel. Even if operations are interrupted or cut back, for example, a company won't usually eliminate key executive positions or sell off key facilities—the basic organizational structure and facilities ordinarily are kept intact. The costs of restoring them later are likely to be far greater than any short-run savings that might be realized.

Once a decision is made to acquire committed fixed resources, the company may be locked into that decision for many years to come. Consequently, such commitments should be made only after careful analysis of the available alternatives. Investment decisions involving committed fixed costs will be examined in Chapter 13.

Discretionary Fixed Costs **Discretionary fixed costs**, often called managed fixed costs, are those costs that arise from annual decisions by management to spend in certain fixed cost areas. Examples of discretionary fixed costs include advertising, research and development, and management training programs.

Discretionary fixed costs
Those fixed costs that arise from annual decisions by management to spend in certain fixed cost areas, such as advertising and research.

Two key differences exist between discretionary fixed costs. First, the planning horizon for a discretionary fixed cost is short term—usually a single year. By contrast, committed fixed costs have a planning horizon that encompasses many years. Second, discretionary fixed costs can be cut for short time periods with minimal damage to the long-run organizational goals. For example, spending on management development programs can be reduced because of poor economic conditions. Although some unfavourable consequences may result from the cutback, it is doubtful that these consequences would be as great as those that would result if the company decided to economize by laying off key personnel.

Caution should be taken not to confuse discretionary costs with unnecessary costs. For example, if a high-tech company such as Nortel were to cut its research and development budget, serious harm could be done to its ability to compete in the future. Similarly, cutting training costs can lead to lower employee morale and a resulting drop in productivity.

Whether a particular cost is regarded as committed or discretionary may depend on management's strategy. For example, during recessions when the level of home building is down, many construction companies lay off most of their workers and virtually disband operations. Other construction companies retain large numbers of employees on the payroll, even though the workers have little or no work to do. While these latter companies may be faced with short-term cash flow problems, it will be easier for them to respond quickly when economic conditions improve. Also the higher morale and loyalty of their employees may give these companies a significant competitive advantage.

The most important characteristic of discretionary fixed costs is that management is not locked into its decisions regarding such costs. Discretionary costs can be adjusted from year to year or even perhaps during the course of a year if necessary.

The Trend toward Fixed Costs The trend in many companies is toward greater fixed costs relative to variable costs. Chores that used to be performed by hand have been taken over by machines. For example, grocery clerks at Loblaws and Sobeys used to key in prices by hand on cash registers. Now, most stores are equipped with bar code readers that enter price and other product information automatically. In general, competition has created pressure to give customers more value for their money—a demand that often can be satisfied only by automating business processes. For example, H&R Block used to fill out tax returns for customers mainly by hand and the advice given to a customer largely depended on the knowledge of that particular employee. Now, computer software is used to complete tax returns, and the software provides the customer with tax planning and other advice tailored to the customer's needs based on the accumulated knowledge of many experts.

As machines take over more and more of the tasks that were performed by humans, the overall demand for human workers has not diminished. The demand for "knowledge" workers—those who work primarily with their minds rather than their muscles—has grown tremendously. Knowledge workers tend to be salaried, highly trained, and difficult to replace; the costs of compensating knowledge workers are often relatively fixed and are committed rather than discretionary costs.

Is Labour a Variable or a Fixed Cost? As the preceding discussion suggests, wages and salaries may be fixed or variable. The behaviour of wage and salary costs will differ from one country to another, depending on labour regulations, labour contracts, and custom. In some countries, such as France, Germany, and Japan, management has little flexibility in adjusting the labour force to changes in business activity. In countries such as Canada and the United Kingdom, management typically has much greater latitude. However, even in these less restrictive environments, managers may choose to treat employee compensation as a fixed cost for several reasons.

First, companies have become much more reluctant to decrease the workforce in response to short-term decline in sales. Most companies realize that their employees are a very valuable asset. More and more, highly skilled and trained employees are required to run a successful business, and these workers are not easy to replace. Trained workers who are laid off may never return, and layoffs undermine the morale of those workers who remain.

Second, managers do not want to be caught with a bloated payroll in an economic downturn. Therefore, there is a reluctance to add workers in response to short-term sales increases. Many companies are turning to temporary and part-time workers to take up the slack when their permanent, full-time employees are unable to handle all of the demand for the company's products and services. In such companies, labour costs are a complex mixture of fixed and variable costs.

Contract staffing enables an organization to handle increases in workloads without taking on the responsibility and expense of permanent hiring. These costs can be treated as variable costs because they will vary with changes in activity. However, regular full-time employee staffing costs are properly classified as fixed costs when they are governed by labour union agreements that stipulate fixed annual salary amounts and restrictive layoff policies.

Many major companies have undergone waves of downsizing in recent years in which large numbers of employees—particularly middle managers—have lost their jobs. It may seem that this downsizing proves that even management salaries should be regarded as variable costs, but this would not be a valid conclusion. Downsizing has been the result of attempts to re-engineer business processes and cut costs rather than a response to a decline in sales activity. This underscores an important, but subtle, point: Fixed costs can change—they just do not change in response to small changes in activity.

In summary, we cannot provide a clear-cut answer to the question "Is labour a variable or fixed cost?" It depends on how much flexibility management has to adjust the workforce and management's strategy. Nevertheless, we will assume in this text that, unless otherwise stated, direct labour is a variable cost. This assumption is more likely to be valid for companies in Canada than in countries where employment laws permit much less flexibility.

IN BUSINESS

Keeping a Lid on Fixed Costs

Summer bonuses at 247 Japanese corporations will average ¥831,009 ($7,276), up 3.05% for a fifth straight annual rise, data compiled by Nikkei Inc. shows. Automakers and steelmakers will dole out more than ¥1-million per employee on average, reflecting robust earnings. Increasingly exposed to harsh global competition, companies remain reluctant to boost base pay, which would increase fixed costs. Overall, bonuses represent an increase of 0.99 percentage points from 2.06% in 2006. Toyota Motor Corp. will top the list in yen terms. With operating profit for 2006 at a record, Toyota will pay an average of ¥1.43 million per employee. "Robust earnings will be reflected in bonuses," says Katsuaki Watanabe, Toyota's president. Japan's largest automaker kept its 2007 salary raises at the same level as a year ago. The bonuses represent variable costs, whereas salaries and wages are considered fixed in Japan.

Source: "Japanese Workers Will Have Even More to Spend This Summer, After Getting Bigger Bonuses," *National Post*, June 13, 2007.

Fixed Costs and the Relevant Range

The concept of the relevant range, which was introduced in the discussion of variable costs, is also important in understanding fixed costs—particularly discretionary fixed costs. The levels of discretionary fixed costs are typically decided at the beginning of the year and depend on the support needs of the planned programs such as advertising and training. The scope of these programs will depend, in turn, on the overall anticipated level of activity for the year. At very high levels of activity, programs are usually broadened or expanded. For example, if the company hopes to increase sales by 25%, it would probably plan for much larger advertising costs than if no sales increase was planned. So the *planned* level of activity may affect total discretionary fixed costs. However, once the total discretionary fixed costs have been budgeted, they are unaffected by the *actual* level of activity. For example, once the advertising budget has been decided on and has been spent, it will not be affected by how many units are actually sold. Therefore, the cost is fixed with respect to the *actual* number of units sold.

Discretionary fixed costs are easier to adjust than committed fixed costs. They also tend to be less "lumpy." Committed fixed costs tend to consist of costs of buildings, equipment, and the salaries of key personnel. It is difficult to buy half of a piece of equipment or to hire a quarter of a product-line manager, so the step pattern depicted in Exhibit 6–6 is typical for such costs. The relevant range of activity for a fixed cost is the range of activity over which the graph of the cost is flat, as in Exhibit 6–6. As a company expands its level of activity, it may outgrow its present facilities, or the key management team may need to be expanded. The result, of course, will be increased committed fixed costs as larger facilities are built and as new management positions are created.

One reaction to the step pattern depicted in Exhibit 6–6 is to say that discretionary and committed fixed costs are really just step-variable costs. To some extent this is true, since almost *all* costs can be adjusted in the long run. There are two major differences, however, between the step-variable costs depicted earlier in Exhibit 6–3 and the fixed costs depicted in Exhibit 6–6.

The first difference is that the step-variable costs can often be adjusted quickly as conditions change, whereas once fixed costs have been set, they often cannot be changed easily. A step-variable cost such as maintenance labour, for example, can be adjusted upward or downward by hiring and laying off maintenance workers. By contrast, once a company has signed a lease for a building, it is locked into that level of lease cost for the life of the contract.

The second difference is that the *width of the steps* depicted for step-variable costs is much narrower than the width of the steps depicted for the fixed costs in Exhibit 6–6. The width of the steps relates to volume or level of activity. For step-variable costs, the width

EXHIBIT 6–6 Fixed Costs and the Relevant Range

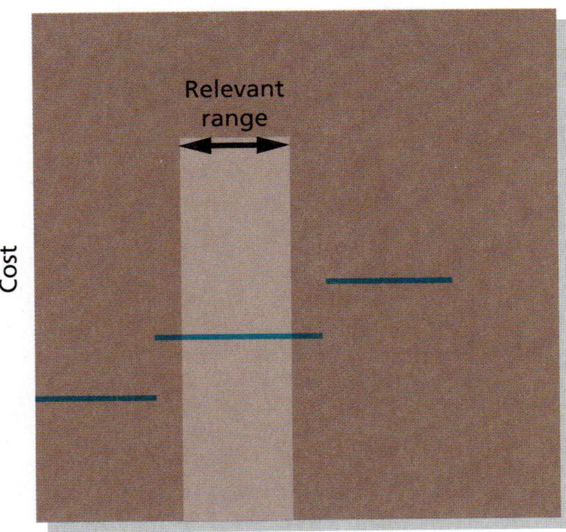

of a step may be 40 hours of activity or less if one is dealing, for example, with maintenance labour cost. For fixed costs, however, the width of a step may be *thousands* or even *tens of thousands* of hours of activity. In essence, the width of the steps for step-variable costs is generally so narrow that these costs can be treated essentially as variable costs for most purposes. The width of the steps for fixed costs, on the other hand, is so wide that these costs must generally be treated as being entirely fixed within the relevant range.

Mixed Costs

Mixed cost A cost that contains both variable and fixed cost elements.

A **mixed cost** contains both variable and fixed cost elements. Mixed costs are also known as *semivariable costs*. To continue the Adventure Rafting example, the company must pay a licence fee of $25,000 per year plus $3 per rafting party to the Yukon's Ministry of the Environment. If the company runs 1,000 rafting parties this year, then the total fees paid to the Yukon would be $28,000, made up of $25,000 in fixed cost plus $3,000 in variable cost. The behaviour of this mixed cost is shown graphically in Exhibit 6–7.

Even if Adventure fails to attract any customers and there are no rafting parties, the company will still have to pay the licence fee of $25,000. This is why the cost line in Exhibit 6–7 intersects the vertical cost axis at the $25,000 point. For each rafting party the company organizes, the total cost of the government fees will increase by $3. Therefore, the total cost line slopes upward as the variable cost element is added to the fixed cost element.

Since the mixed cost in Exhibit 6–7 is represented by a straight line, the following equation for a straight line can be used to express the relationship between mixed cost and the level of activity:

$$Y = a + bX$$

In this equation,

Y = The total mixed cost
a = The total fixed cost (the vertical intercept of the line)
b = The variable cost per unit of activity (the slope of the line)
X = The level of activity

In the case of the Yukon's fees paid by Adventure Rafting, the equation is written as follows:

$$Y = \$25,000 + \$3.00X$$

Y	$25,000	$3.00	X
Total mixed cost	Total fixed cost	Variable cost per unit of activity	Activity level

EXHIBIT 6–7 Mixed Cost Behaviour

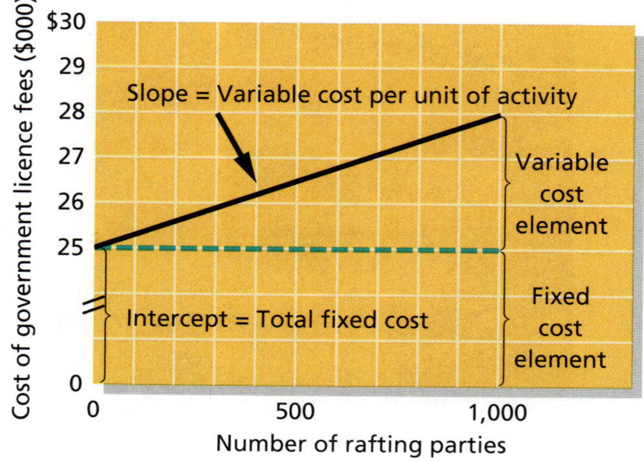

This equation makes it very easy to calculate what the total mixed cost would be for any level of activity within the relevant range. For example, suppose that the company expects to organize 800 rafting parties in the next year. Then the total government fees would be \$27,400, calculated as follows:

$$Y = \$25{,}000 + (\$3.00 \text{ per rafting party} \times 800 \text{ rafting parties})$$
$$= \$27{,}400$$

The Analysis of Mixed Costs

LEARNING OBJECTIVE 2
Explain how to analyze mixed costs.

Mixed costs are very common. For example, the cost of providing X-ray services to patients at the Queen Elizabeth II Health Sciences Centre is a mixed cost. The costs of equipment depreciation, and radiologists' and technicians' salaries are fixed, but the costs of X-ray film, power, and supplies are variable. At Air Canada, maintenance costs are a mixed cost. The company must incur fixed costs for renting maintenance facilities and for keeping skilled mechanics on the payroll, but the costs of replacement parts, lubricating oils, tires, and so forth, are variable with respect to how often and how far the company's aircraft are flown.

The fixed portion of a mixed cost represents the basic, minimum cost of just having a service *ready and available* for use. The variable portion represents the cost incurred for *actual consumption* of the service. The variable element varies in proportion to the amount of service that is consumed.

How does management go about actually estimating the fixed and variable components of a mixed cost? The most common methods used in practice are *account analysis* and the *engineering approach.*

In **account analysis,** each account under consideration is classified as either variable or fixed, based on the analyst's prior knowledge of how the cost in the account behaves. For example, direct materials would be classified as variable and a building lease cost would be classified as fixed because of the nature of those costs. The total fixed cost is the sum of the costs for the accounts that have been classified as fixed. The variable cost per unit is estimated by dividing the sum of the costs for the accounts that have been classified as variable by the total activity.

Account analysis
A method for analyzing cost behaviour in which each account under consideration is classified as either variable or fixed based on the analyst's prior knowledge of how the cost in the account behaves.

The **engineering approach** to cost analysis involves a detailed analysis of what cost behaviour should be, based on an industrial engineer's evaluation of the production methods to be used, the materials specifications, labour requirements, equipment usage, efficiency of production, power consumption, and so on. For example, Pizza Hut might use the engineering approach to estimate the cost of serving a particular take-out pizza. The cost of the pizza would be estimated by carefully costing the specific ingredients used to make the pizza, the power consumed to cook the pizza, and the cost of the container in which the pizza is delivered. The engineering approach must be used in those situations where no past experience is available concerning activity and costs. In addition, it is sometimes used together with other methods to improve the accuracy of cost analysis.

Engineering approach
A detailed analysis of cost behaviour based on an industrial engineer's evaluation of the inputs that are required to carry out a particular activity and of the prices of those inputs.

Account analysis works best when analyzing costs at a fairly aggregated level, such as the cost of caring for patients in the emergency room (ER) of the Queen Elizabeth II Health Sciences Centre. The costs of drugs, supplies, forms, wages, equipment, and so on, can be roughly classified as variable or fixed and a mixed cost formula for the overall cost of the emergency room can be estimated fairly quickly. However, this method does not recognize that some of the accounts may have elements of both fixed and variable costs. For example, the cost of electricity for the ER is a mixed cost. Most of the electricity used for heating and lighting is a fixed cost. However, the consumption of electricity increases with activity in the ER, since diagnostic equipment, operating theatre lights, defibrillators, and so on, all consume electricity. The most effective way to estimate the fixed and variable elements of such a mixed cost may be to analyze past records of cost and activity data. These records should reveal whether electrical costs vary significantly with the number of patients, and if so, by how much. The remainder of this section will be concerned with how to conduct such an analysis of past cost and activity data.

IN BUSINESS

Operations Drive Costs

White Grizzly Adventures is a snowcat skiing and snowboarding company in Meadow Creek, British Columbia, that is owned and operated by Brad and Carole Karafil. The company shuttles 12 guests to the top of the company's steep and tree-covered terrain in a single snowcat. Guests stay as a group at the company's lodge for a fixed number of days and are provided healthy gourmet meals.

Brad and Carole must decide each year when snowcat operations will begin in December and when they will end in early spring, and how many nonoperating days to schedule between groups of guest for maintenance and rest. This decision affects a variety of costs. Examples of costs that are fixed and variable with respect to the number of days of operation at White Grizzly include:

Costs	Cost Behaviour—Fixed or Variable with Respect to Days of Operations
Property taxes	Fixed
Summer road maintenance and tree clearing	Fixed
Lodge depreciation	Fixed
Snowcat operator and guides	Variable
Cooks and lodge help	Variable
Snowcat depreciation	Variable
Snowcat fuel	Variable
Food	Variable

Diagnosing Cost Behaviour with a Scattergram Plot

Kinh Nguyen, the chief financial office of Brentline Hospital, began his analysis of maintenance costs by collecting cost and activity data for a number of recent months. Those data are as follows:

Month	Activity Level: Patient-Days	Maintenance Cost Incurred
January	5,600	$7,900
February	7,100	8,500
March	5,000	7,400
April	6,500	8,200
May	7,300	9,100
June	8,000	9,800
July	6,200	7,800

Dependent variable
A variable that reacts or responds to some causal factor; total cost is the dependent variable, as represented by the letter Y, in the equation $Y = a + bX$.

Independent variable
A variable that acts as a causal factor; activity is the independent variable, as represented by the letter X, in the equation $Y = a + bX$.

The first step in analyzing the cost and activity data should be to plot the data on a scattergram. This plot immediately reveals any non-linearities or other problems with the data. The scattergram of maintenance costs versus patient-days at Brentline Hospital is reproduced in the first panel of Exhibit 6–8. Two things should be noted about this scattergram:

1. The total maintenance cost, Y, is plotted on the vertical axis. Cost is known as the **dependent variable,** since the amount of cost incurred during a period depends on the level of activity for the period. (That is, as the level of activity increases, total cost will also ordinarily increase.)
2. The activity, X (patient-days in this case), is plotted on the horizontal axis. Activity is known as the **independent variable,** since it causes variations in the cost.

From the scattergram, it is evident that maintenance costs do increase with the number of patient-days. In addition, the scattergram reveals that the relationship between maintenance costs and patient-days is approximately *linear*. In other words, the points lie more

EXHIBIT 6–8 Scattergram Method of Cost Analysis

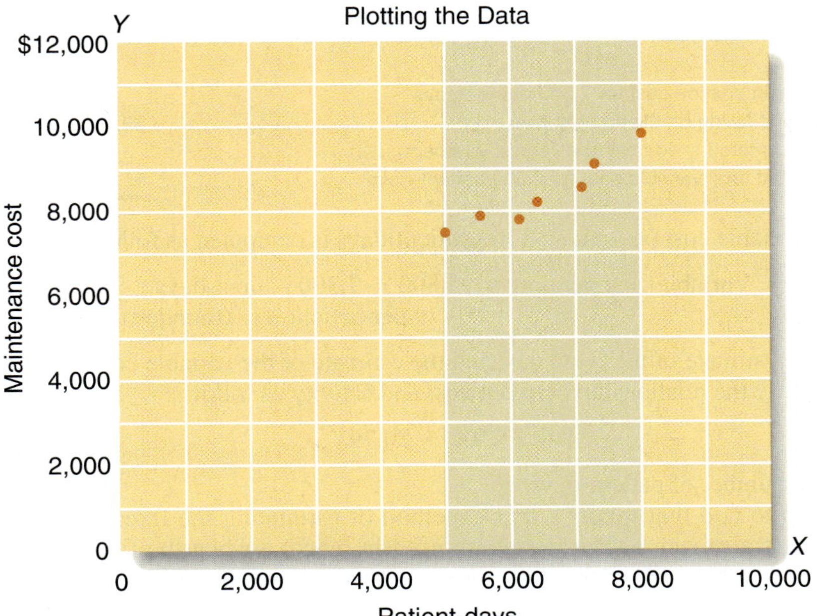

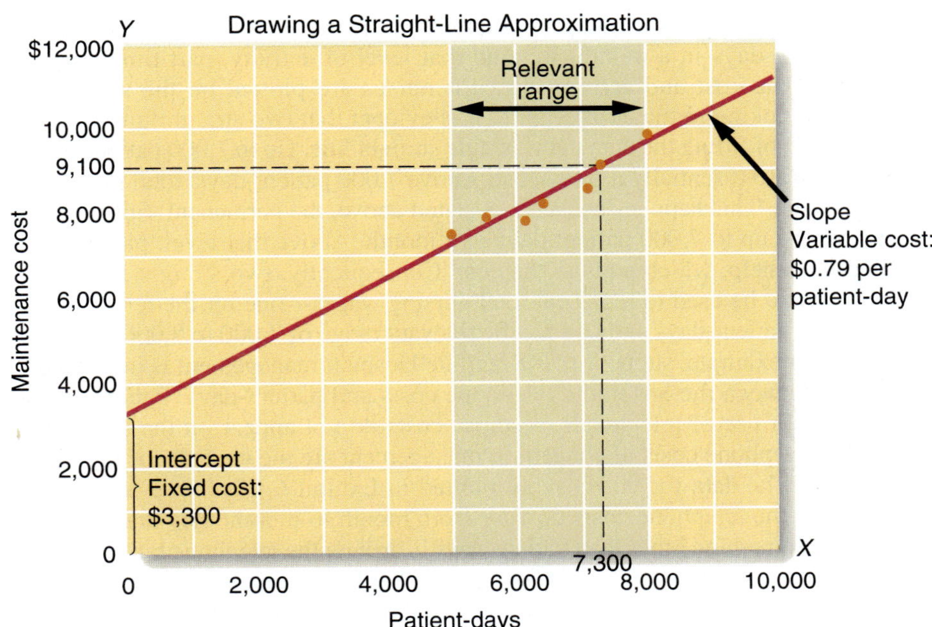

or less along a straight line. Such a straight line has been drawn using a ruler in the second panel of Exhibit 6–8. Cost behaviour is said to be **linear** whenever a straight line is a reasonable approximation for the relationship between cost and activity. Note that the data points do not fall exactly on the straight line. This will almost always happen in practice; the relationship is seldom perfectly linear.

Linear cost behaviour Cost behaviour is linear when a straight line is a reasonable approximation for the relationship between cost and activity.

Note that the straight line in Exhibit 6–8 has been drawn through the point representing 7,300 patient-days and a total maintenance cost of $9,100. Drawing the straight line through one of the data points allows the analyst to make a quick estimate of variable and fixed costs. The vertical intercept where the straight line crosses the *Y*-axis—in this case, about $3,300—is the rough estimate of the fixed cost. The variable cost can be quickly estimated by subtracting the estimated fixed cost from the total cost at the point lying on the straight line:

Total maintenance cost for 7,300 patient-days (a point falling on the straight line)	$9,100
Less estimated fixed cost (the vertical intercept)	3,300
Estimated total variable cost for 7,300 patient-days	$5,800

The average variable cost per unit at 7,300 patient-days is computed as follows:

$$\text{Variable cost per unit} = \$5{,}800 \div 7{,}300 \text{ patient-days}$$
$$= \$0.79 \text{ per patient-day (rounded)}$$

Combining the estimate of the fixed cost and the estimate of the variable cost per patient-day, we can write the relationship between cost and activity as follows:

$$Y = \$3{,}300 + \$0.79X$$

where X is the number of patient-days.

We hasten to add that this *is* a quick method of estimating the fixed and variable cost elements of a mixed cost; it is seldom used in practice when the financial implications of a decision based on the data are significant. However, setting aside the estimates of the fixed and variable cost elements, plotting the data on a scattergram is an essential diagnostic step that is too often overlooked. Suppose, for example, we had been interested in the relationship between total nursing wages and the number of patient-days at the hospital. The permanent, full-time nursing staff can handle up to 7,000 patient-days in a month. Beyond that level of activity, part-time nurses must be called in. The cost and activity data for nurses are plotted on the scattergram in Exhibit 6–9. Looking at that scattergram, it is evident that two straight lines would do a much better job of fitting the data than a single straight line. Up to 7,000 patient-days, total nursing wages are essentially a fixed cost. Above 7,000 patient-days, total nursing wages are a mixed cost. This happens because, as stated above, the permanent, full-time nursing staff can handle up to 7,000 patient-days in a month. Above that level, part-time nurses are called in to help, which adds to the cost. Consequently, two straight lines (and two equations) would be used to represent total nursing wages—one for the relevant range of 5,600 to 7,000 patient-days and one for the relevant range of 7,000 to 8,000 patient-days.

As another example, suppose that Brentline Hospital management is interested in the relationship between the hospital's telephone costs and patient-days. Patients are billed directly for their use of telephones, so those costs do not appear on the hospital's cost records. The telephone costs of concern to management are the charges for the staff's use of telephones. The data for this cost are plotted in Exhibit 6–10. It is evident from that plot that while the telephone costs do vary from month to month, they are not related to patient-days. Something other than patient-days is driving the telephone bills. Therefore, it would not make sense to analyze this cost any further by attempting to estimate a variable cost per patient-day for telephone costs. Plotting the data helps diagnose such situations.

The High-Low Method

In addition to the scattergraph method described in the preceding section, more precise methods are available for estimating fixed and variable costs. However, it must be emphasized that fixed and variable costs should be computed only if a scattergram plot confirms that the relationship is approximately linear. In the case of maintenance costs at Brentline Hospital, the relationship does appear to be linear. In the case of telephone costs, there isn't any clear relationship between telephone costs and patient-days, so there is no point in estimating how much of the cost varies with patient-days.

High-low method
A method of separating a mixed cost into its fixed and variable elements by analyzing the change in cost between the high and low levels of activity.

Assuming that the scattergram plot indicates a linear relationship between cost and activity, the fixed and variable cost elements of a mixed cost can be estimated using the *high-low method* or the *least-squares regression method.* The **high-low method** is based

EXHIBIT 6–9 More than One Relevant Range

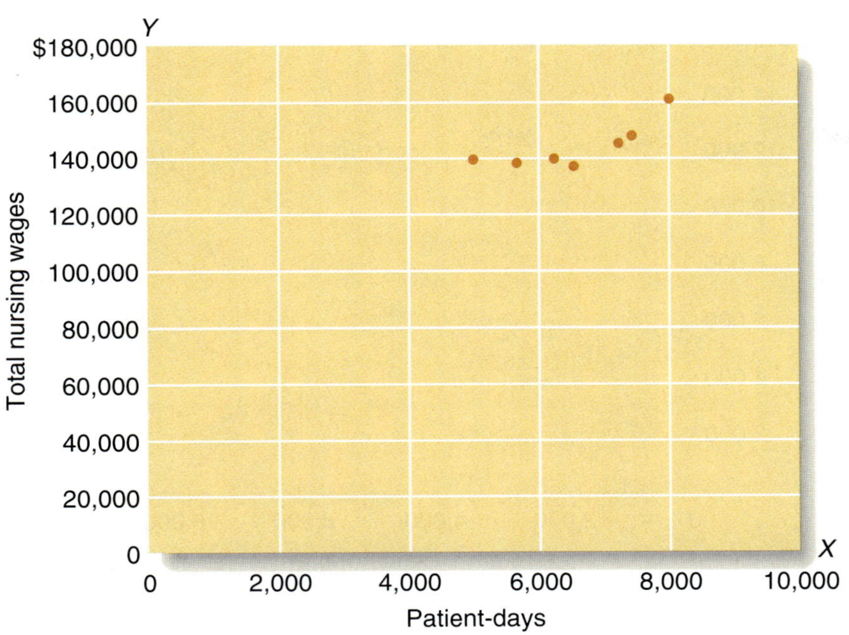

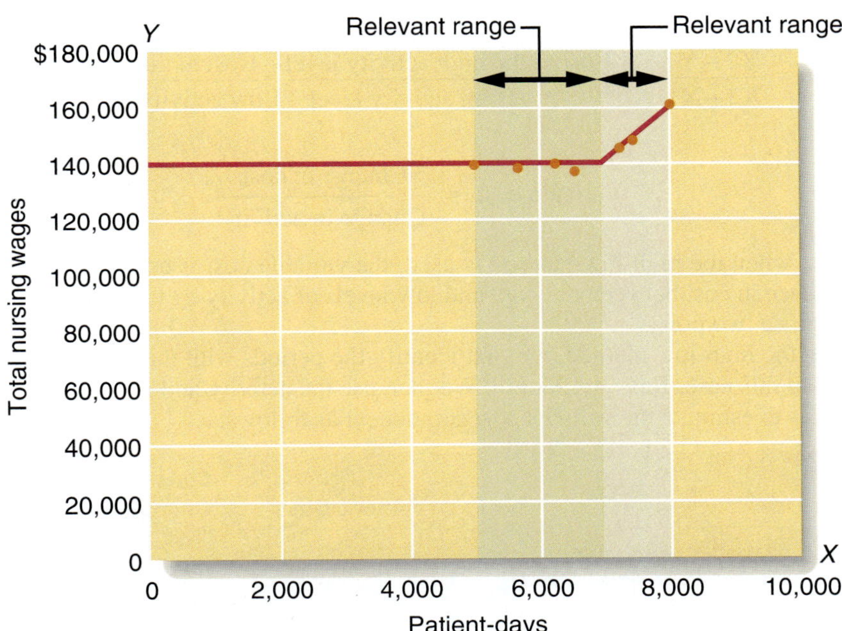

on the rise-over-run formula for the slope of a straight line. As discussed above, if the relationship between cost and activity can be represented by a straight line, then the slope of the straight line is equal to the variable cost per unit of activity. Consequently, the following formula from high school algebra can be used to estimate the variable cost:

$$\text{Variable cost} = \text{Slope of the line} = \frac{\text{Rise}}{\text{Run}} = \frac{Y_2 - Y_1}{X_2 - X_1}$$

To analyze mixed costs with the high-low method, you begin by identifying the period with the lowest level of activity and the period with the highest level of activity. The period with the lowest activity is selected as the first point in the above formula and the

EXHIBIT 6–10 A Diagnostic Scattergram Plot

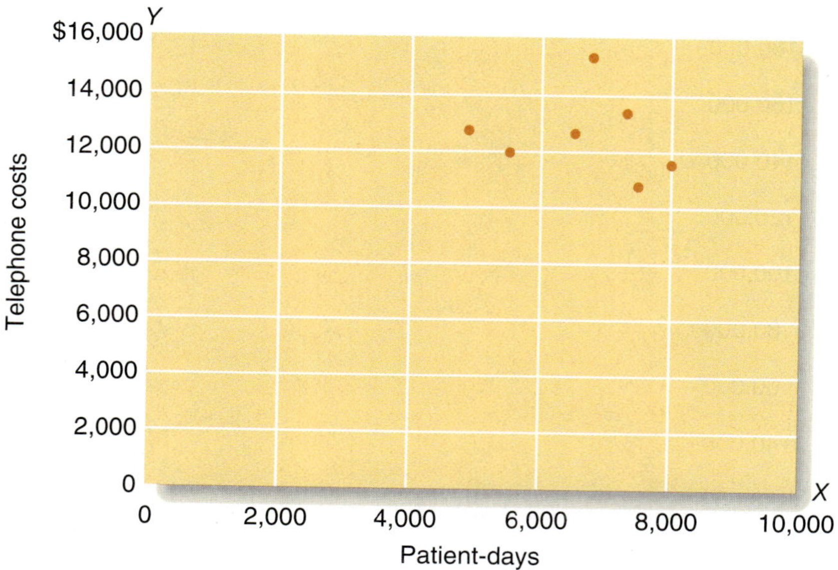

period with the highest activity is selected as the second point. Consequently, the formula becomes:

$$\text{Variable cost} = \frac{Y2 - Y1}{X2 - X1} = \frac{\text{Cost at the high activity level} - \text{Cost at the low activity level}}{\text{High activity level} - \text{Low activity level}}$$

or

$$\text{Variable cost} = \frac{\text{Change in cost}}{\text{Change in activity}}$$

Therefore, when the high-low method is used, the variable cost is estimated by dividing the difference in cost between the high and low levels of activity by the change in activity between those two points.

Using the high-low method, we first identify the periods with the highest and lowest *activity*—in this case, June and March. We then use the activity and cost data from these two periods to estimate the variable cost component as follows:

	Patient-Days	Maintenance Cost Incurred
High activity level (June)	8,000	$9,800
Low activity level (March)	5,000	7,400
Change	3,000	$2,400

$$\text{Variable cost} = \frac{\text{Change in cost}}{\text{Change in activity}} = \frac{\$2{,}400}{3{,}000 \text{ patient-days}} = \$0.80 \text{ per patient-day}$$

Having determined that the variable rate for maintenance cost is 80 cents per patient-day, we can now determine the amount of fixed cost. This is done by taking total cost at *either* the high or the low activity level and deducting the variable cost element. In the computation below, total cost at the high activity level is used in computing the fixed cost element:

$$\begin{aligned}\text{Fixed cost element} &= \text{Total cost} - \text{Variable cost element}\\ &= \$9{,}800 - (\$0.80 \text{ per patient-day} \times 8{,}000 \text{ patient-days})\\ &= \$3{,}400\end{aligned}$$

Both the variable and fixed cost elements have now been isolated. The cost of maintenance can be expressed as $3,400 per month plus 80 cents per patient-day.

The cost of maintenance can also be expressed in terms of the equation for a straight line as follows:

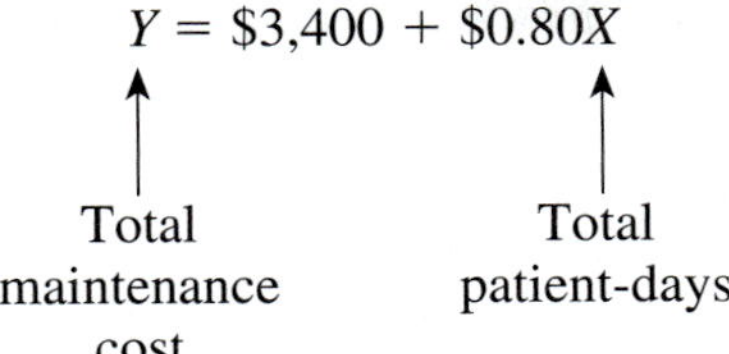

The data used in this illustration are shown graphically in Exhibit 6–11. Notice that a straight line has been drawn through the points corresponding to the low and high levels of activity. In essence, that is what the high-low method does—it draws a straight line through those two points.

Sometimes the high and low levels of activity don't coincide with the high and low amounts of cost. For example, the period that has the highest level of activity may not have the highest amount of cost. Nevertheless, the highest and lowest levels of *activity* are always used to analyze a mixed cost under the high-low method. The reason is that the analyst would like to use data that reflect the greatest possible variation in activity.

The high-low method is very simple to apply, but it suffers from a major (and sometimes critical) defect—it utilizes only two data points. Generally, two points are not enough to produce accurate results. Additionally, the periods with the highest and lowest activity tend to be unusual. A cost formula that is estimated solely using data from these unusual periods may seriously misrepresent the true cost relationship that holds during normal periods. Such a distortion is evident in Exhibit 6–11. The straight line should probably be shifted down somewhat so that it is closer to more of the data points. For these reasons, other methods of cost analysis that utilize a greater number of points will generally be more accurate than the high-low method. If a manager chooses to use the high-low method, she or he should do so with a full awareness of the method's limitations.

EXHIBIT 6–11 High-Low Method of Cost Analysis

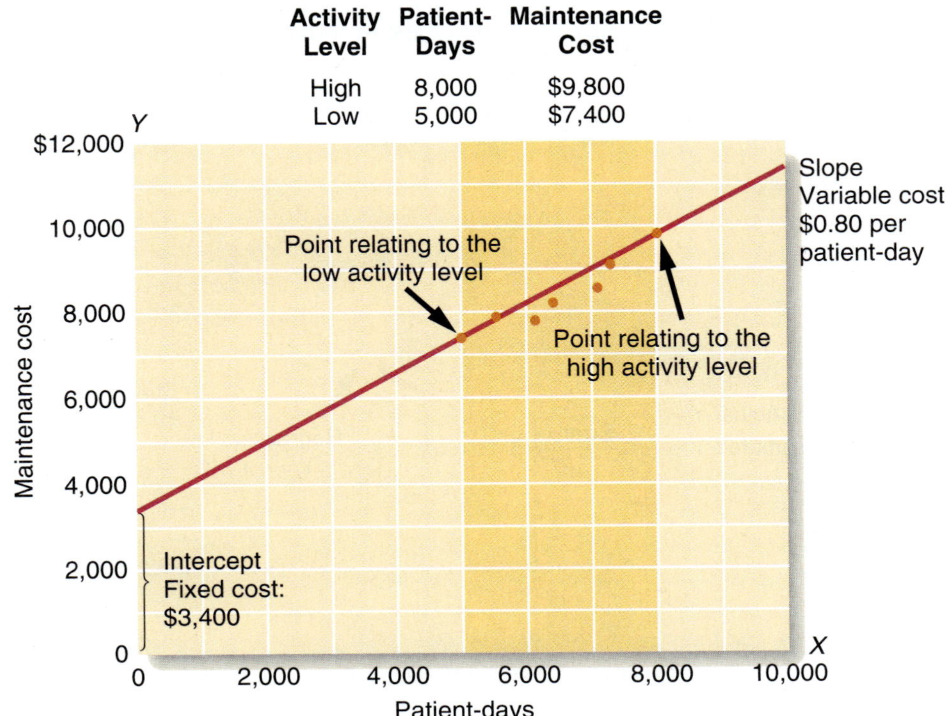

Activity Level	Patient-Days	Maintenance Cost
High	8,000	$9,800
Low	5,000	$7,400

Fortunately, modern computer software makes it very easy to use sophisticated statistical methods, such as *least-squares regression,* that use all of the data and that are capable of providing much more information than just the estimates of variable and fixed costs. The details of these statistical methods are beyond the scope of this text, but the basic approach is discussed below. Nevertheless, even if the least-squares regression approach is used, it is always a good idea to plot the data in a scattergram. By simply looking at the scattergram, you can quickly verify whether it makes sense to fit a straight line to the data using least-squares regression or some other method.

The Least-Squares Regression Method

Least-squares regression method A method of separating a mixed cost into its fixed and variable elements by fitting a regression line that minimizes the sum of the squared errors.

The **least-squares regression method**, unlike the high-low method, uses all the data to separate a mixed cost into its fixed and variable components. A *regression line* of the form $Y = a + bX$ is fitted to the data, where a represents the total fixed cost and b represents the variable cost per unit of activity. The basic idea underlying the least-squares regression method is illustrated in Exhibit 6–12 using hypothetical data points. Notice from the exhibit that the deviations from the plotted points to the regression line are measured vertically on the graph. These vertical deviations are called the *regression errors*. A regression line that perfectly explains the relationship between X and Y would have all the points on the line. There is nothing mysterious about the least-squares regression method. It computes the regression line that minimizes the sum of these squared errors. The formulas that accomplish this are fairly complex and involve numerous calculations.

Fortunately, computers are adept at carrying out the computations required by the least-squares regression formulas. The data—the observed values of X and Y—are entered into the computer, and software does the rest. In the case of the Brentline Hospital maintenance cost data, we used a statistical software package on a personal computer to calculate the following least-squares regression estimates of the total fixed cost (a) and the variable cost per unit of activity (b):

$$a = \$3{,}431$$
$$b = \$0.759$$

Therefore, using the least-squares regression method, the fixed element of the maintenance cost is \$3,431 per month and the variable portion is 75.9 cents per patient-day.

In terms of the linear equation $Y = a + bX$, the cost formula can be written as

$$Y = \$3{,}431 + \$0.759X$$

where activity (X) is expressed in patient-days.

EXHIBIT 6–12 The Concept of Least-Squares Regression

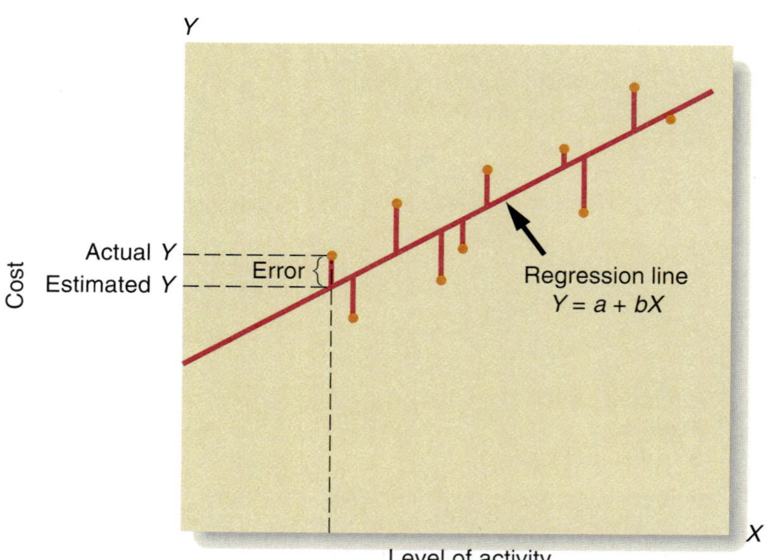

While we used statistical software to calculate the values of *a* and *b* in this example, the estimates can also be computed using a spreadsheet application such as Microsoft Excel. In Appendix 6A to this chapter, we show how this can be done.

In addition to estimates of the intercept (fixed cost) and slope (variable cost per unit), least-squares regression software ordinarily provides a number of other very useful statistics. One of these statistics is the R^2, which is a measure of "goodness of fit." The R^2 tells us the percentage of the variation in the dependent variable (cost) that is explained by variation in the independent variable (activity). The R^2 varies from 0% to 100%, and the higher the percentage, the better. A regression line that fits the data perfectly would have an R^2 of 1, but R^2 would be 0 in a situation where no fit was achieved by the regression line. In the case of the Brentline Hospital maintenance cost data, the R^2 is 0.90, which indicates that 90% of the variation in maintenance costs is explained by the variation in patient-days. This is reasonably high and is an indication of a good fit. On the other hand, a low R^2 would be an indication of a poor fit. You should always plot the data in a scattergram, but it is particularly important to check the data visually when the R^2 is low. A quick look at the scattergram can reveal that there is little real relationship between the cost and the activity or that the relationship is something other than a simple straight line. In such cases, additional analysis would be required.

Comparing Cost Estimation Methods

The three methods result in slightly different estimates of fixed and variable costs, as summarized in Exhibit 6–13. Results from the scattergram method are based on a judgmental interpretation of the visual fit of the data points. The high-low method uses only two values, corresponding to the lowest and highest patient volumes, which potentially may not be very representative of the actual data. The least-squares regression method gives the most accurate results, because it uses a statistical technique that takes all of the available data points into account.

Cost estimates resulting from any of these methods are good only if the data used for estimation are reliable. A limitation common to all three methods is that they use past data, and estimates will be inaccurate if future cost conditions change.

In summary, analysis of cost behaviour begins with a scatterplot so that the type of cost behaviour can be seen. If the trend appears to be linear, and if the amount of data permits, a linear regression will usually provide the most reasonable answer. If time or data are short, high-low will provide a reasonable approximation of the linear formula needed for subsequent applications. Complex cost behaviours will require engineering studies and/or complex statistical analysis techniques such as multiple regression. Thus, more advanced study or specialized assistance will be necessary.

Multiple Regression Analysis

In the discussion thus far, we have assumed that a single factor such as patient-days drives the variable cost component of a mixed cost. This assumption is acceptable for many mixed costs, but in some situations there may be more than one causal factor driving the variable cost element. For example, shipping costs may depend on both the number of units shipped *and* the weight of the units. In a situation such as this, *multiple regression* is necessary. **Multiple regression** is an analytical method that is used when the dependent variable (i.e., cost) is caused by more than one factor. Although adding more factors, or

Multiple regression An analytical method required in those situations where variations in a dependent variable are caused by more than one factor.

EXHIBIT 6–13 Comparison of Cost Estimation Methods

Estimation Method	Fixed Cost	Variable Cost
Scattergram	$3,300	$0.79 per patient-day
High-low	$3,400	$0.80 per patient-day
Least-squares regression	$3,431	$0.759 per patient-day

variables, makes the computations more complex, the principles involved are the same as in the simple least-squares regressions discussed above.

The Contribution Format

LEARNING OBJECTIVE 3
Prepare an income statement using the contribution format.

Contribution approach An income statement format that is geared to cost behaviour in that costs are separated into variable and fixed categories.

Separating costs into fixed and variable elements helps to predict costs and provide benchmarks. As we will see in later chapters, separating costs into fixed and variable elements is often crucial in making decisions. This crucial distinction between fixed and variable costs is at the heart of the **contribution approach** to constructing income statements. The unique thing about the contribution approach is that it provides managers with an income statement that clearly distinguishes between fixed and variable costs and therefore facilitates planning, control and decision making.

Why A New Income Statement Format?

An income statement prepared using the *traditional approach*, as illustrated in Chapter 2, is organized in a "functional" format—emphasizing the functions of production, administration, and sales. No attempt is made to distinguish between fixed or variable costs. Under the heading Administrative Expense, for example, both variable and fixed costs are lumped together.

Although an income statement prepared in the functional format may be useful for external reporting purposes, it has serious limitations when used for internal purposes. Internally, the manager needs cost data organized in a format that will facilitate planning, control, and decision making. As we will see in later chapters, these tasks are much easier when cost data are available in a fixed and variable format. The contribution approach to the income statement was developed in response to this need.

The Contribution Approach

Exhibit 6–14 illustrates the contribution approach to the income statement with a simple example based on assumed data, along with the traditional approach discussed in Chapter 2.

Contribution margin The amount remaining from sales revenues after all variable expenses have been deducted.

Notice that the contribution approach separates costs into fixed and variable categories, first deducting variable expenses from sales to obtain what is known as the *contribution margin.* The **contribution margin** is the amount remaining from sales revenues after variable expenses have been deducted. This amount *contributes* toward covering fixed expenses and then toward profits for the period.

EXHIBIT 6–14 Comparison of the Contribution Income Statement with the Traditional Income Statement

Traditional Approach (costs organized by function)		
Sales		$12,000
Less cost of goods sold		6,000*
Gross margin		6,000
Less operating expenses:		
Selling	$3,100*	
Administrative	1,900*	5,000
Operating income		$ 1,000

Contribution Approach (costs organized by behaviour)		
Sales		$12,000
Less variable expenses:		
Variable production	$2,000	
Variable selling	600	
Variable administrative	400	3,000
Contribution margin		9,000
Less fixed expenses:		
Fixed production	4,000	
Fixed selling	2,500	
Fixed administrative	1,500	8,000
Operating income		$ 1,000

*Contains both variable and fixed expenses. This is the income statement for a manufacturing company; thus, when the income statement is placed in the contribution format, the cost of goods sold figure is divided between variable production costs and fixed production costs. If this was the income statement for a *merchandising* company (which simply purchases completed goods from a supplier), then the cost of goods sold would be *all* variable.

The simplified contribution approach income statement makes a common assumption that can confuse. The variable production expenses assume production equals sales in terms of units. Thus these expenses for production like those for selling and administrative use sales volume as a driver. A more complete income statement would need to show inventory levels so that variable production costs can use production volume activity as the cost driver.

The contribution format income statement is used as an internal planning and decision-making tool. Its emphasis on cost behaviour facilitates cost-volume-profit analysis (such as we shall be doing in the next chapter), management performance appraisals, and budgeting. Moreover, the contribution approach helps managers organize data pertinent to numerous decisions such as product-line analysis, pricing, use of scarce resources, and make or buy analysis. All of these topics are covered in later chapters.

Summary

As we will see in later chapters, the ability to predict how costs will respond to changes in activity is critical for making decisions, for controlling operations, and for evaluating performance. Three major classifications of costs were discussed in this chapter—variable, fixed, and mixed. Mixed costs consist of a mixture of variable and fixed elements and a mixed cost can be expressed in equation form as $Y = a + bX$, where X is the activity, Y is the cost, a is the fixed cost element, and b is the variable cost per unit of activity. Several methods are available to estimate the fixed and variable cost components of a mixed cost using past records of cost and activity. If the relationship between cost and activity appears to be linear based on a scattergram plot, then the variable and fixed components of the mixed cost can be estimated using the quick method, the high-low method, or the least-squares regression method. The scattergraph method is based on drawing a straight line on the scatter plot and then using the slope and the intercept of the straight line to estimate the variable and fixed cost components of the mixed cost. The high-low method implicitly draws a straight line through the points of lowest activity and highest activity. In most situations, the least-squares regression method should be used in preference to both the scattergraph and the high-low methods. Computer software is widely available for using the least-squares method and a variety of useful statistics are automatically produced by most software packages, along with estimates of the intercept (fixed cost) and slope (variable cost per unit). Nevertheless, even when least-squares regression is used, the data should be plotted to confirm that the relationship is really a straight line. To complete the discussion, it should be noted that the tools of plot, account analysis, engineering and least squares can be used to analyze cost behaviour with other activity drivers. Sales and production or service levels represent only two of such drivers. Others were seen in Chapter 5.

Managers use costs organized by behaviour as a basis for many decisions. To facilitate this use, the income statement can be prepared in a contribution format. The contribution format classifies costs on the income statement by cost behaviour (i.e., variable versus fixed) rather than by the functions of production, administration, and sales.

Appendix 6A: Least Squares Regression Calculations

LEARNING OBJECTIVE 4
Elaborate on the least-squares regression method.

The least-squares regression method for estimating a linear relationship is based on the equation for a straight line:

$$Y = a + bX$$

The following formulas are used to calculate the values of the vertical intercept *(a)* and the slope *(b)* that minimize the sum of the squared errors:[1]

$$b = \frac{n(\Sigma XY) - (\Sigma X)(\Sigma Y)}{n(\Sigma X^2) - (\Sigma X)^2}$$

$$a = \frac{(\Sigma Y) - b(\Sigma X)}{n}$$

where:

X = The level of activity (independent variable)
Y = The total mixed cost (dependent variable)
a = The total fixed cost (the vertical intercept of the line)
b = The variable cost per unit of activity (the slope of the line)
n = Number of observations
Σ = Sum across all n observations

Carrying out the calculations required by the formulas is tedious at best. Fortunately, statistical software packages are widely available that perform the calculations automatically. Spreadsheet software, such as Microsoft Excel, can also be used to do least-squares regression—although it requires a little more work than specialized statistical packages do.

To illustrate how Excel can be used to calculate the intercept *a*, the slope *b*, and the R^2, we will use the Brentline Hospital data for maintenance costs on page 244. The worksheet in Exhibit 6–15 contains the data and the calculations.

As you can see, the *X* values (the independent variable) have been entered in cells B4 through B10. The *Y* values (the dependent variable) have been entered in cells C4

EXHIBIT 6–15 The Least-Squares Regression Worksheet for Brentline Hospital

Microsoft Excel = Appendix 6A.xls

File Edit View Insert Format Tools Data Window Help

G16 =

	A	B	C	D	E
1		*Patient-*	*Maintenance*		
2		*Days*	*Costs*		
3	*Month*	*X*	*Y*		
4	January	5,600	$7,900		
5	February	7,100	8,500		
6	March	5,000	7,400		
7	April	6,500	8,200		
8	May	7,300	9,100		
9	June	8,000	9,800		
10	July	6,200	7,800		
11					
12	Intercept	$3,431			
13	Slope	$0.759			
14	RSQ	0.90			
15					

Least-squares regression

Ready NUM

1. See calculus or statistics books for details concerning how these formulas are derived.

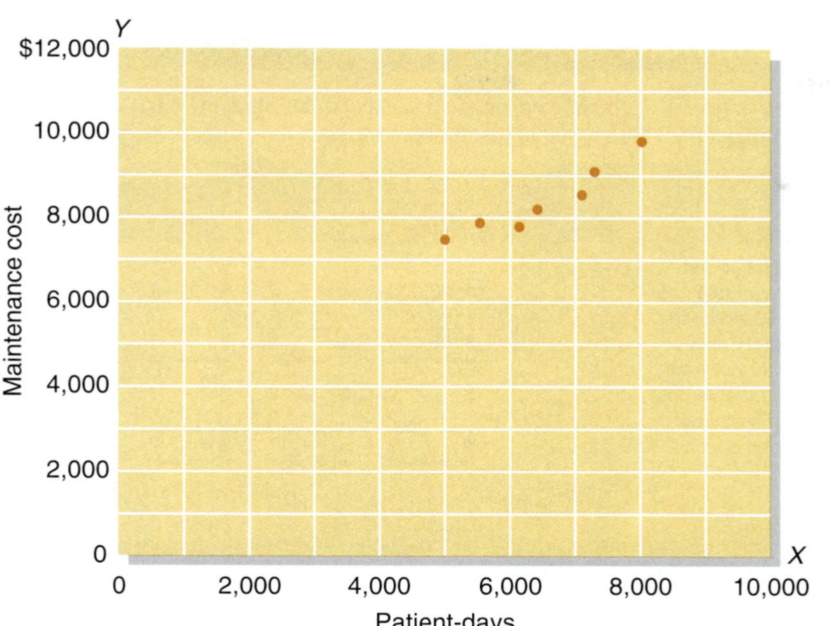

EXHIBIT 6–16 A Scattergram Plot of the Brentline Hospital Data

through C10. The slope, intercept, and R^2 are computed using the Excel functions INTERCEPT, SLOPE, and RSQ. In each case, you must specify the range of cells for the *Y* values and for the *X* values. In the Exhibit 6–15 worksheet, cell B12 contains the formula =INTERCEPT(C4:C10,B4:B10); cell B13 contains the formula =SLOPE(C4:C10,B4:B10); and cell B14 contains the formula =RSQ(C4:C10,B4:B10).

According to the calculations carried out by Excel, the fixed maintenance cost (the intercept) is $3,431 per month and the variable cost (the slope) is $0.759 per patient-day. Therefore, the cost formula for maintenance cost is:

$$Y = a + bX$$

$$Y = \$3{,}431 + \$0.759X$$

Note that the R^2 (i.e., RSQ) is 0.90, which—as previously discussed—is quite good and indicates that 90% of the variation in maintenance costs is explained by the variation in patient-days.

Plotting the data is easy in Excel. Select the range of values that you would like to plot—in this case, cells B4:C10. Then select the Chart Wizard tool on the toolbar and make the appropriate choices in the various dialogue boxes that appear. When you are finished, you should have a scattergram that looks something like the plot in Exhibit 6–16. Note that the relationship between cost and activity is approximately linear, so it is reasonable to fit a straight line to the data as we have implicitly done with the least-squares regression.

Glossary

Visit the Online Learning Centre at http:// www.mcgrawhill.ca/olc/garrison/ for a review of key terms and definitions.

Review Problem 1: Cost Behaviour

Neptune Rentals operates a boat rental service. Consider the following costs of the company over the relevant range of 5,000 to 8,000 hours of operating time for its boats:

	Hours of Operating Time			
	5,000	6,000	7,000	8,000
Total costs:				
Variable costs	$ 20,000	$?	$?	$?
Fixed costs	168,000	?	?	?
Total costs	$188,000	$?	$?	$?
Cost per hour:				
Variable cost	$?	$?	$?	$?
Fixed cost	?	?	?	?
Total cost per hour	$?	$?	$?	$?

Required:

Compute the missing amounts, assuming that cost behaviour patterns remain unchanged within the relevant range of 5,000 to 8,000 hours.

Solution to Review Problem 1

The variable cost per hour can be computed as follows:

$20,000 ÷ 5,000 hours = $4 per hour

Therefore, the missing amounts are as follows:

	Hours of Operating Time			
	5,000	6,000	7,000	8,000
Total costs:				
Variable costs				
(@ $4 per hour).	$ 20,000	$ 24,000	$ 28,000	$ 32,000
Fixed costs	168,000	168,000	168,000	168,000
Total costs	$188,000	$192,000	$196,000	$200,000
Cost per hour:				
Variable cost	$ 4.00	$ 4.00	$ 4.00	$ 4.00
Fixed cost	33.60	28.00	24.00	21.00
Total cost per hour	$ 37.60	$ 32.00	$ 28.00	$ 25.00

Observe that the total variable costs increase in proportion to the number of hours of operating time, but that these costs remain constant at $4 if expressed on a per hour basis.

In contrast, the total fixed costs do not change with changes in the level of activity. They remain constant at $168,000 within the relevant range. With increases in activity, however, the fixed cost per hour decreases, dropping from $33.60 per hour when the boats are operated 5,000 hours a period to only $21.00 per hour when the boats are operated 8,000 hours a period. *Because of this troublesome aspect of fixed costs, they are most easily (and most safely) dealt with on a total basis, rather than on a unit basis, in cost analysis work.*

Review Problem 2: High-Low Method

The administrator of Azalea Hills Hospital would like a cost formula linking the administrative costs involved in admitting patients to the number of patients admitted during a month. The admitting department's costs and the number of patients admitted during the immediately preceding eight months are given in the following table:

Month	Number of Patients Admitted	Admitting Department Costs
May	1,800	$14,700
June	1,900	$15,200
July	1,700	$13,700
August	1,600	$14,000
September	1,500	$14,300
October	1,300	$13,100
November	1,100	$12,800
December	1,500	$14,600

Required:

1. Use the high-low method to establish the fixed and variable components of admitting costs.
2. Express the fixed and variable components of admitting costs as a cost formula in the form $Y = a + bX$.

Solution to Review Problem 2

1. The first step in the high-low method is to identify the periods of the lowest and highest activity. Those periods are November (1,100 patients admitted) and June (1,900 patients admitted).

   The second step is to compute the variable cost per unit using those two data points:

Month	Number of Patients Admitted	Admitting Department Costs
High activity level (June)	1,900	$15,200
Low activity level (November)	1,100	12,800
Change	800	$ 2,400

$$\text{Variable cost} = \frac{\text{Change in cost}}{\text{Change in activity}} = \frac{\$2{,}400}{800 \text{ patients admitted}} = \$3 \text{ per patient admitted}$$

   The third step is to compute the fixed cost element by deducting the variable cost element from the total cost at either the high or low activity. In the computation below, the high point of activity is used:

$$\begin{aligned}\text{Fixed cost element} &= \text{Total cost} - \text{Variable cost element}\\ &= \$15{,}200 - (\$3 \text{ per patient admitted} \times 1{,}900 \text{ patients admitted})\\ &= \$9{,}500\end{aligned}$$

2. The cost formula is $Y = \$9{,}500 + \$3X$.

Questions

6–1 Distinguish between (*a*) a variable cost, (*b*) a fixed cost, and (*c*) a mixed cost.

6–2 What effect does an increase in volume have on—

a. Unit fixed costs?

b. Unit variable costs?

c. Total fixed costs?
d. Total variable costs?

6–3 Define the following terms: (*a*) cost behaviour and (*b*) relevant range.

6–4 What is meant by an *activity base* when dealing with variable costs? Give several examples of activity bases.

6–5 Distinguish between (*a*) a variable cost, (*b*) a mixed cost, and (*c*) a step-variable cost. Plot the three costs on a graph, with activity plotted horizontally and cost plotted vertically.

6–6 Managers often assume a strictly linear relationship between cost and volume. How can this practice be defended in light of the fact that many costs are curvilinear?

6–7 Distinguish between discretionary fixed costs and committed fixed costs.

6–8 Classify the following fixed costs as normally being either committed or discretionary:
a. Depreciation on buildings.
b. Advertising.
c. Research.
d. Long-term equipment leases.
e. Pension payments to the company's retirees.
f. Management development and training.

6–9 Does the concept of the relevant range apply to fixed costs? Explain.

6–10 What is the major disadvantage of the high-low method?

6–11 Give the general formula for a mixed cost. Which term represents the variable cost? The fixed cost?

6–12 What is meant by the term *least-squares regression?*

6–13 What is the difference between ordinary least-squares regression analysis and multiple regression analysis?

6–14 What is the difference between a contribution approach income statement and a traditional approach income statement?

6–15 What is the contribution margin?

Exercises

EXERCISE 6–1 Fixed and Variable Cost Behaviour [LO1]

Koffee Express operates a number of espresso coffee stands in busy suburban malls. The fixed weekly expense of a coffee stand is $1,100 and the variable cost per cup of coffee served is $0.26.

Required:

1. Fill in the following table with your estimates of total costs and cost per cup of coffee at the indicated levels of activity for a coffee stand. Round off the cost of a cup of coffee to the nearest tenth of a cent.

	Cups of Coffee Served in a Week		
	1,800	1,900	2,000
Fixed cost	?	?	?
Variable cost	?	?	?
Total cost	?	?	?
Cost per cup of coffee served	?	?	?

2. Does the cost per cup of coffee served increase, decrease, or remain the same as the number of cups of coffee served in a week increases? Explain.

EXERCISE 6–2 Scattergraph Analysis [LO2]

The data at the top of page 259 have been taken from the cost records of the Atlanta Processing Company. The data relate to the cost of operating one of the company's processing facilities at various levels of activity.

Month	Units Processed	Total Cost
January	8,000	$14,000
February	4,500	$10,000
March	7,000	$12,500
April	9,000	$15,500
May	3,750	$10,000
June	6,000	$12,500
July	3,000	$8,500
August	5,000	$11,500

Required:

1. Prepare a scattergraph using the above data. Plot cost on the vertical axis and activity on the horizontal axis. Fit a line to your plotted points using a ruler.
2. Using the scatttergraph method, what is the approximate monthly fixed cost? The approximate variable cost per unit processed? Show your computations.

EXERCISE 6–3 High-Low Method [LO2]

The Edelweiss Hotel has accumulated records of the total electrical costs of the hotel and the number of occupancy-days over the last year. An occupancy-day represents a room rented out for one day. The hotel's business is highly seasonal, with peaks occurring during the ski season and in the summer.

Month	Occupancy-Days	Electrical Costs
January	2,604	$6,257
February	2,856	$6,550
March	3,534	$7,986
April	1,440	$4,022
May	540	$2,289
June	1,116	$3,591
July	3,162	$7,264
August	3,608	$8,111
September	1,260	$3,707
October	186	$1,712
November	1,080	$3,321
December	2,046	$5,196

Required:

1. Using the high-low method, estimate the fixed cost of electricity per month and the variable cost of electricity per occupancy-day. Round off the fixed cost to the nearest whole dollar and the variable cost to the nearest whole cent.
2. What other factors other than occupancy-days are likely to affect the variation in electrical costs from month to month?

EXERCISE 6–4 Contribution Format Income Statement [LO3]

The Haaki Shop, Inc., is a large retailer of water sports equipment. An income statement for the company's surfboard department for a recent quarter is presented below:

The Haaki Shop, Inc. Income Statement—Surfboard Department For the Quarter Ended May 31		
Sales		$800,000
Cost of goods sold		300,000
Gross margin		500,000
Selling and administrative expenses:		
Selling expenses	$250,000	
Administrative expenses	160,000	410,000
Operating income		$ 90,000

The surfboards sell, on the average, for $400 each. The department's variable selling expenses are $50 per surfboard sold. The remaining selling expenses are fixed. The administrative expenses are 25% variable and 75% fixed. The company purchases its surfboards from a supplier at a cost of $150 per surfboard.

Required:

1. Prepare an income statement for the quarter using the contribution approach.
2. What was the contribution toward fixed expenses and profits from each surfboard sold during the quarter? (State this figure in a single dollar amount per surfboard.)

EXERCISE 6–5 (Appendix 6A) Least-Squares Regression [LO4]

EZ Rental Car offers rental cars in an off-airport location near a major tourist destination in British Columbia. Management would like to better understand the behaviour of the company's costs. One of those costs is the cost of washing cars. The company operates its own car wash facility in which each rental car that is returned is thoroughly cleaned before being released for rental to another customer. Management believes that the costs of operating the car wash should be related to the number of rental returns. Accordingly, the following data have been compiled:

Month	Rental Returns	Car Wash Costs
January	2,310	$10,113
February...........	2,453	$12,691
March.............	2,641	$10,905
April..............	2,874	$12,949
May..............	3,540	$15,334
June..............	4,861	$21,455
July..............	5,432	$21,270
August............	5,268	$19,930
September.........	4,628	$21,860
October...........	3,720	$18,383
November.........	2,106	$9,830
December.........	2,495	$11,081

Required:

Using least-squares regression, estimate the fixed cost and variable cost elements of monthly car wash costs. The fixed cost element should be estimated to the nearest dollar and the variable cost element to the nearest cent.

EXERCISE 6–6 Cost Behaviour; Contribution Format Income Statement [LO3]

Parker Company manufactures and sells a single product. A partially completed schedule of the company's total and per unit costs over a relevant range of 60,000 to 100,000 units produced and sold each year is given below:

	Units Produced and Sold		
	60,000	80,000	100,000
Total costs:			
Variable costs...........	$150,000	?	?
Fixed costs.............	360,000	?	?
Total costs..............	$510,000	?	?
Cost per unit:			
Variable cost	?	?	?
Fixed cost..............	?	?	?
Total cost per unit	?	?	?

Required:

1. Complete the schedule of the company's total and unit costs above.
2. Assume that the company produces and sells 90,000 units during the year at the selling price of $7.50 per unit. Prepare a contribution format income statement for the year.

EXERCISE 6–7 High-Low Method; Scattergraph Analysis [LO2]
Zerbel Company, a wholesaler of large, custom-built air conditioning units for commercial buildings, has noticed considerable fluctuation in its shipping expense from month to month, as shown below:

Month	Units Shipped	Total Shipping Expense
January	4	$2,200
February..........	7	$3,100
March............	5	$2,600
April	2	$1,500
May	3	$2,200
June.............	6	$3,000
July	8	$3,600

Required:
1. Using the high-low method, estimate the cost formula for shipping expense.
2. The president has no confidence in the high-low method and would like you to "check out" your results using the scattergraph method. Do the following:
   a. Prepare a scattergraph using the data given above. Plot cost on the vertical axis and activity on the horizontal axis. Use a ruler to fit a straight line to your plotted points.
   b. Using your scattergraph, estimate the approximate variable cost per unit shipped and the approximate fixed cost per month with the scattergraph method.
3. What factors, other than the number of units shipped, are likely to affect the company's shipping expense? Explain.

EXERCISE 6–8 (Appendix 6A) Least-Squares Regression [LO4]
Refer to the data for Zerbel Company in Exercise 6–7.

Required:
1. Using the least-squares regression method, estimate the cost formula for shipping expense.
2. If you also completed Exercise 6–7, prepare a simple table comparing the variable and fixed cost elements of shipping expense as computed under the scattergraph method, the high-low method, and the least-squares regression method.

EXERCISE 6–9 Cost Behaviour; High-Low Method [LO2]
Speedy Parcel Service operates a fleet of delivery trucks in a large metropolitan area. A careful study by the company's cost analyst has determined that if a truck is driven 120,000 kilometres during a year, the average operating cost is 11.6 cents per kilometre. If a truck is driven only 80,000 kilometres during a year, the average operating cost increases to 13.6 cents per kilometre.

Required:
1. Using the high-low method, estimate the variable and fixed cost elements of the annual cost of truck operation.
2. Express the variable and fixed costs in the form $Y = a + bX$.
3. If a truck were driven 100,000 kilometres during a year, what total cost would you expect to be incurred?

EXERCISE 6–10 High-Low Method; Predicting Cost [LO2]
The number of X-rays taken and X-ray costs over the last nine months in Beverly Hospital are given below:

Month	X-Rays Taken	X-Ray Costs
January	6,250	$28,000
February..........	7,000	$29,000
March............	5,000	$23,000
April	4,250	$20,000
May	4,500	$22,000
June.............	3,000	$17,000
July	3,750	$18,000
August	5,500	$24,000
September........	5,750	$26,000

Required:

1. Using the high-low method, estimate the cost formula for X-ray costs.
2. Using the cost formula you derived above, what X-ray costs would you expect to be incurred during a month in which 4,600 X-rays are taken?

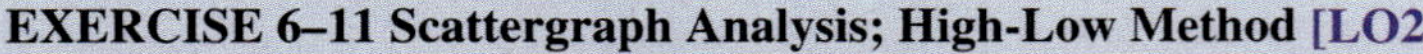

EXERCISE 6–11 Scattergraph Analysis; High-Low Method [LO2]

Refer to the data in Exercise 6–10 for Beverly Hospital.

Required:

1. Prepare a scattergraph using the data from Exercise 6–10. Plot cost on the vertical axis and activity on the horizontal axis. Using a ruler, fit a line to your plotted points.
2. Using the scattergraph method, what is the approximate monthly fixed cost for X-rays? The approximate variable cost per X-ray taken?
3. Scrutinize the points on your graph, and explain why the high-low method would or would not yield an accurate cost formula in this situation.

EXERCISE 6–12 High-Low Method; Predicting Cost [LO2]

Resort Inns, Inc., has a total of 2,000 rooms in its nationwide chain of motels. On average, 70% of the rooms are occupied each day. The company's operating costs are $21 per occupied room per day at this occupancy level, assuming a 30-day month. This $21 figure contains both variable and fixed cost elements. During October, the occupancy rate dropped to only 45%. A total of $792,000 in operating cost was incurred during October.

Required:

1. Estimate the variable cost per occupied room per day.
2. Estimate the total fixed operating costs per month.
3. Assume that the occupancy rate increases to 60% during November. What total operating costs would you expect the company to incur during November?

EXERCISE 6–13 (Appendix 6A) Least-Squares Regression [LO4]

One of Varic Company's products goes through a glazing process. The company has observed glazing costs as follows over the last six weeks:

Week	Units Produced	Total Glazing Cost
1	8	$270
2	5	$200
3	10	$310
4	4	$190
5	6	$240
6	9	$290

For planning purposes, the company's management must know the amount of variable glazing cost per unit and the total fixed glazing cost per week.

Required:

1. Using the least-squares regression method, estimate the variable and fixed elements of the glazing cost.
2. Express the cost data in (1) above in the form $Y = a + bX$.
3. If the company processes seven units next week, what would be the expected total glazing cost?

Problems

PROBLEM 6–14 (Appendix 6A) Scattergraph; Cost Behaviour; Least-Squares Regression Method [LO4]

Amanda King has just been appointed director of recreation programs for Highland Park, a rapidly growing community in Dartmouth. In the past, the city has sponsored a number of softball leagues in the summer months. From the city's cost records, Amanda has found the following total costs associated with the softball leagues over the last five years:

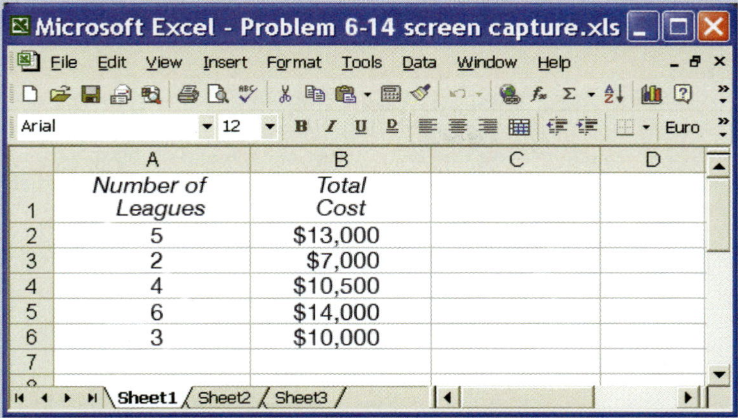
Microsoft Excel - Problem 6-14 screen capture.xls

	A	B	C	D
1	Number of Leagues	Total Cost		
2	5	$13,000		
3	2	$7,000		
4	4	$10,500		
5	6	$14,000		
6	3	$10,000		
7				

Each league requires its own paid supervisor and paid umpires as well as printed schedules and other copy work. Therefore, Amanda knows that some variable costs are associated with the leagues. She would like to know the amount of variable cost per league and the total fixed cost per year associated with the softball program. This information would help her for planning purposes.

Required:

1. Using the least-squares regression method, estimate the variable cost per league and the total fixed cost per year for the softball program.
2. Express the cost data derived in (1) above in the form $Y = a + bX$.
3. Assume that Amanda would like to expand the softball program during the coming year to involve a total of seven leagues. Compute the expected total cost for the softball program. Can you see any problem with using the cost formula from (2) above to derive this total cost figure? Explain.
4. Prepare a scattergraph, and fit a line to the plotted points using the cost formula expressed in (2) above.

PROBLEM 6–15 Contribution Format versus Traditional Income Statement [LO3]

House of Organs, Inc., purchases organs from a well-known manufacturer and sells them at the retail level. The organs sell, on the average, for $2,500 each. The average cost of an organ from the manufacturer is $1,500.

House of Organs, Inc., has always kept careful records of its costs. The costs that the company incurs in a typical month are presented below in the form of a spreadsheet:

Costs	Cost Formula
Selling:	
Advertising	$950 per month
Delivery of organs	$60 per organ sold
Sales salaries and commissions	$4,800 per month, plus 4% of sales
Utilities	$650 per month
Depreciation of sales facilities	$5,000 per month
Administrative:	
Executive salaries	$13,500 per month
Depreciation of office equipment	$900 per month
Clerical	$2,500 per month, plus $40 per organ sold
Insurance	$700 per month

During November, the company sold and delivered 60 organs.

Required:

1. Prepare an income statement for November using the traditional format with costs organized by function.
2. Redo (1) above, this time using the contribution format with costs organized by behaviour. Show costs and revenues on both a total and a per unit basis down through contribution margin.

3. Refer to the income statement you prepared in (2) above. Why might it be misleading to show the fixed costs on a per unit basis?

PROBLEM 6–16 Cost Behaviour; High-Low Method; Contribution Format Income Statement [LO2, LO3]

Frankel Ltd., a British merchandising company, is the exclusive distributor of a product that is gaining rapid market acceptance. The company's revenues and expenses (in British pounds) for the last three months are given below:

Frankel Ltd.
Comparative Income Statements
For the Three Months Ended June 30

	April	May	June
Sales in units	3,000	3,750	4,500
Sales revenue	£420,000	£525,000	£630,000
Cost of goods sold	168,000	210,000	252,000
Gross margin	252,000	315,000	378,000
Selling and administrative expenses:			
Shipping expense	44,000	50,000	56,000
Advertising expense	70,000	70,000	70,000
Salaries and commissions	107,000	125,000	143,000
Insurance expense	9,000	9,000	9,000
Depreciation expense	42,000	42,000	42,000
Total selling and administrative expenses	272,000	296,000	320,000
Operating income (loss)	£ (20,000)	£ 19,000	£ 58,000

(Note: Frankel Ltd.'s income statement has been recast in the functional format common in North America. The British currency is the pound, denoted by £.)

Required:

1. Identify each of the company's expenses (including cost of goods sold) as either variable, fixed, or mixed.
2. Using the high-low method, separate each mixed expense into variable and fixed elements. State the cost formula for each mixed expense.
3. Redo the company's income statement at the 4,500-unit level of activity using the contribution format.

PROBLEM 6–17 Identifying Cost Behaviour Patterns [LO1]

A number of graphs displaying cost behaviour patterns are shown below. The vertical axis on each graph represents total cost and the horizontal axis represents the level of activity (volume).

Required:

1. For each of the following situations, identify the graph that illustrates the cost behaviour pattern involved. Any graph may be used more than once.
   a. Electricity bill—a flat fixed charge, plus a variable cost after a certain number of kilowatt-hours are used.
   b. City water bill, which is computed as follows:

First 1,000,000 m^3 or less	$1,000 flat fee
Next 10,000 m^3	$0.003 per m^3 used
Next 10,000 m^3	$0.006 per m^3 used
Next 10,000 m^3	$0.009 per m^3 used
Etc.	Etc.

   c. Depreciation of equipment, where the amount is computed by the straight-line method. When the depreciation rate was established, it was anticipated that the obsolescence factor would be greater than the wear and tear factor.
   d. Rent on a factory building donated by the city, where the agreement calls for a fixed fee

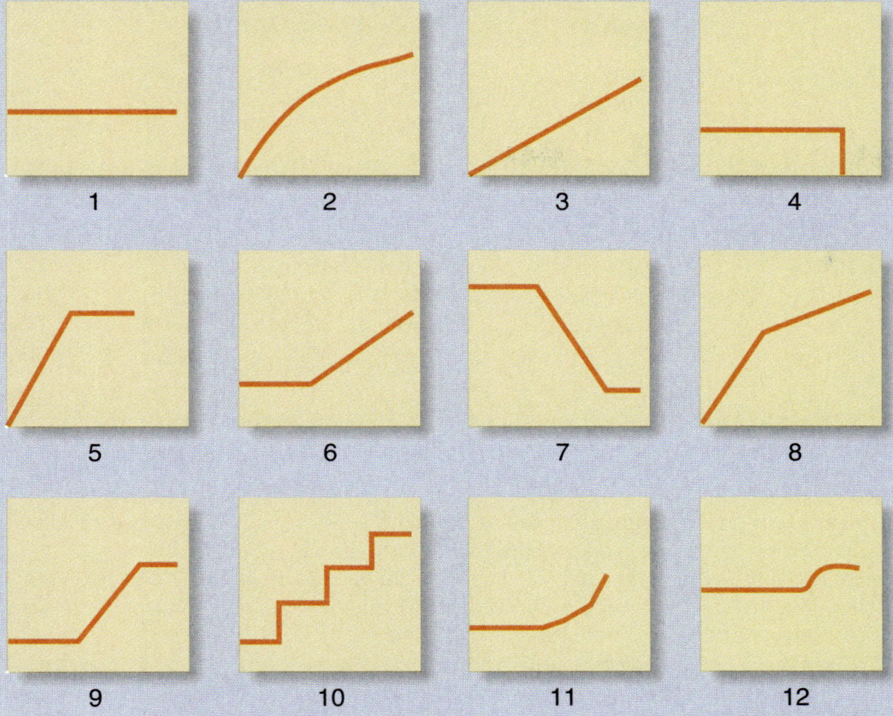

payment unless 200,000 labour-hours or more are worked, in which case no rent need be paid.

e. Cost of raw materials, where the cost starts at $7.50 per unit and then decreases by 5 cents per unit for each of the first 100 units purchased, after which it remains constant at $2.50 per unit.

f. Salaries of maintenance workers, where one maintenance worker is needed for every 1,000 hours of machine-hours or less (that is, 0 to 1,000 hours requires one maintenance worker, 1,001 to 2,000 hours requires two maintenance workers, etc.).

g. Cost of raw material used.

h. Rent on a factory building donated by the county, where the agreement calls for rent of $100,000 less $1 for each direct labour-hour worked in excess of 200,000 hours, but a minimum rental payment of $20,000 must be paid.

i. Use of a machine under a lease, where a minimum charge of $1,000 is paid for up to 400 hours of machine time. After 400 hours of machine time, an additional charge of $2 per hour is paid up to a maximum charge of $2,000 per period.

2. How would a knowledge of cost behaviour patterns such as those above be of help to a manager in analyzing the cost structure of his or her company?

(CPA, adapted)

PROBLEM 6–18 High-Low and Scattergraph Analysis [LO2]
Sebolt Wire Company heats copper ingots to very high temperatures by placing the ingots in a large heat coil. The heated ingots are then run through a shaping machine that shapes the soft ingot into wire. Due to the long heat-up time, the coil is never turned off. When an ingot is placed in the coil, the temperature is raised to an even higher level, and then the coil is allowed to drop to the "waiting" temperature between ingots. Management needs to know the variable cost of power involved in heating an ingot and the fixed cost of power during "waiting" periods. The data shown at the top of page 266 on ingots processed and power costs are available.

Required:

1. Using the high-low method, estimate a cost formula for power cost. Express the formula in the form $Y = a + bX$.
2. Prepare a scattergraph by plotting ingots processed and power cost on a graph. Fit a straight line to the plotted points using a ruler, and estimate a cost formula for power cost using the scattergraph method.

Month	Ingots	Power Cost
January	110	$5,500
February.	90	$4,500
March.	80	$4,400
April	100	$5,000
May	130	$6,000
June.	120	$5,600
July	70	$4,000
August	60	$3,200
September.	50	$3,400
October	40	$2,400

PROBLEM 6–19 (Appendix 6A) Least-Squares Regression Method [LO4]
Refer to the data for Sebolt Wire Company in Problem 6–18.

Required:
1. Using the least-squares regression method, estimate a cost formula for power cost. (Round the variable cost to the nearest cent and the fixed cost to the nearest dollar.)
2. Prepare a table showing the total fixed cost per month and the variable cost per ingot under each of the three methods used in Problems 6–18 and 6–19. Then comment on the accuracy and usefulness of the data derived by each method.

PROBLEM 6–20 (Appendix 6A) Least-Squares Regression Analysis; Contribution Format Income Statement [LO3, LO4]
Alden Company has decided to use a contribution approach income statement for internal planning purposes. The company has analyzed its expenses and has developed the following cost formulas:

Cost	Cost Formula
Cost of goods sold	$20 per unit sold
Advertising expense	$170,000 per quarter
Sales commissions	5% of sales
Administrative salaries.	$80,000 per quarter
Shipping expense	?
Depreciation expense	$50,000 per quarter

Management has concluded that shipping expense is a mixed cost, containing both variable and fixed cost elements. Units sold and the related shipping expense over the last eight quarters are given below:

Quarter	Units Sold (000)	Shipping Expense
Year 1:		
First	16	$160,000
Second	18	$175,000
Third	23	$210,000
Fourth	19	$180,000
Year 2:		
First	17	$170,000
Second	20	$190,000
Third	25	$230,000
Fourth	22	$205,000

Management would like a cost formula derived for shipping expense so that a budgeted income statement using the contribution approach can be prepared for the next quarter.

Required:
1. Using the least-squares regression method, estimate a cost formula for shipping expense. (Since the Units Sold above are in thousands of units, the variable cost you compute will also

be in thousands of units. It can be left in this form, or you can convert your variable cost to a per unit basis by dividing it by 1,000.)

2. In the first quarter of Year 3, the company plans to sell 21,000 units at a selling price of $50 per unit. Prepare a contribution format income statement for the quarter.

PROBLEM 6–21 High-Low Method; Predicting Cost [LO1, LO2]

Golden Company's total overhead cost at various levels of activity are presented below:

Month	Machine-Hours	Total Overhead Cost
March	50,000	$194,000
April	40,000	$170,200
May	60,000	$217,800
June..........	70,000	$241,600

Assume that the overhead cost above consists of utilities, supervisory salaries, and maintenance. The breakdown of these costs at the 40,000 machine-hour level of activity is as follows:

Utilities (variable)...................	$ 52,000
Supervisory salaries (fixed)	60,000
Maintenance (mixed)	58,200
Total overhead cost	$170,200

The company wants to break down the maintenance cost into its variable and fixed cost elements.

Required:

1. Estimate how much of the $241,600 of overhead cost in June was maintenance cost. (Hint: To do this, it may be helpful to first determine how much of the $241,600 consisted of utilities and supervisory salaries. Think about the behaviour of variable and fixed costs within the relevant range.)
2. Using the high-low method, estimate a cost formula for maintenance.
3. Express the company's total overhead cost in the form $Y = a + bX$.
4. What total overhead cost would you expect to be incurred at an activity level of 45,000 machine-hours?

PROBLEM 6–22 High-Low Method; Cost of Goods Manufactured [LO1, LO2]

NuWay, Inc., manufactures a single product. Selected data from the company's cost records for two recent months are given below:

	Level of Activity	
	July—Low	October—High
Number of units produced.................	9,000	12,000
Cost of goods manufactured...............	$285,000	$390,000
Work in process inventory, beginning........	$14,000	$22,000
Work in process inventory, ending	$25,000	$15,000
Direct materials cost per unit...............	$15	$15
Direct labour cost per unit..................	$6	$6
Manufacturing overhead cost, total..........	?	?

The company's manufacturing overhead cost consists of both variable and fixed cost elements. To have data available for planning, management wants to determine how much of the overhead cost is variable with units produced and how much of it is fixed per year.

Required:

1. For both July and October, estimate the amount of manufacturing overhead cost added to production. The company had no underapplied or overapplied overhead in either month. (Hint: A useful way to proceed might be to construct a schedule of cost of goods manufactured.)
2. Using the high-low method, estimate a cost formula for manufacturing overhead. Express the variable portion of the formula in terms of a variable rate per unit of product.

3. If 9,500 units are produced during a month, what would be the cost of goods manufactured? (Assume that the company's beginning work in process inventory for the month is $16,000 and that its ending work in process inventory is $19,000. Also assume that there is no underapplied or overapplied overhead cost for the month.)

PROBLEM 6–23 High-Low Method; Predicting Cost [LO1, LO2]

Echeverria SA is an Argentinian manufacturing company whose total factory overhead costs fluctuate somewhat from year to year according to the number of machine-hours worked in its production facility. These costs (in Argentinian pesos) at high and low levels of activity over recent years are given below:

	Level of Activity	
	Low	**High**
Machine-hours	60,000	80,000
Total factory overhead costs	274,000 pesos	312,000 pesos

The factory overhead costs above consist of indirect materials, rent, and maintenance. The company has analyzed these costs at the 60,000 machine-hours level of activity as follows:

Indirect materials (variable)	90,000 pesos
Rent (fixed)	130,000
Maintenance (mixed)	54,000
Total factory overhead costs	274,000 pesos

For planning purposes, the company wants to break down the maintenance cost into its variable and fixed cost elements.

Required:

1. Estimate how much of the factory overhead cost of 312,000 pesos at the high level of activity consists of maintenance cost. (Hint: To do this, it may be helpful to first determine how much of the 312,000 pesos cost consists of indirect materials and rent. Think about the behaviour of variable and fixed costs.)
2. Using the high-low method, estimate a cost formula for maintenance.
3. What *total* overhead costs would you expect the company to incur at an operating level of 65,000 machine-hours?

Cases

CASE 6–24 Scattergraph Analysis; Selection of an Activity Base [LO2]

Mapleleaf Sweepers of Toronto manufactures replacement rotary sweeper brooms for the large sweeper trucks that clear leaves and snow from city streets. The business is seasonal, with the largest demand during and just preceding the fall and winter months. Since there are so many different kinds of sweeper brooms used by its customers, Mapleleaf Sweepers makes all of its brooms to order.

The company has been analyzing its overhead accounts to determine fixed and variable components for planning purposes. At the top of page 269 are data for the company's janitorial labour costs over the last nine months.

	Number of Units Produced	Number of Janitorial Workdays	Janitorial Labour Cost
January	115	21	$3,840
February.	109	19	$3,648
March.	102	23	$4,128
April	76	20	$3,456
May	69	23	$4,320
June.	108	22	$4,032
July	77	16	$2,784
August	71	14	$2,688
September.	127	21	$3,840

The number of workdays varies from month to month due to the number of weekdays, holidays, days of vacation, and sick leave taken in the month. The number of units produced in a month varies depending on demand and the number of workdays in the month.

There are two janitors who each work an eight-hour shift each workday. They each can take up to 10 days of paid sick leave each year. Their wages on days they call in sick and their wages during paid vacations are charged to miscellaneous overhead rather than to the janitorial labour cost account.

Required:

1. Plot the janitorial labour cost and units produced on a scattergraph. (Place cost on the vertical axis and units produced on the horizontal axis.)
2. Plot the janitorial labour cost and number of workdays on a scattergraph. (Place cost on the vertical axis and the number of workdays on the horizontal axis.)
3. Which measure of activity—number of units produced or janitorial workdays—should be used as the activity base for explaining janitorial labour cost?

CASE 6–25 (Appendix 6A) Least-Squares Regression; Scattergraph; Comparison of Activity Bases [LO2, LO4]

The Hard Rock Mining Company is developing cost formulas for management planning and decision-making purposes. The company's cost analyst has concluded that utilities cost is a mixed cost, and he is attempting to find a base with which the cost might be closely correlated. The controller has suggested that tonnes mined might be a good base to use in developing a cost formula. The production superintendent disagrees; she thinks that direct labour-hours would be a better base. The cost analyst has decided to try both bases and has assembled the following information:

Quarter	Tonnes Mined (000)	Direct Labour-Hours (000)	Utilities Cost
Year 1:			
First	15	5	$50,000
Second.	11	3	$45,000
Third.	21	4	$60,000
Fourth.	12	6	$75,000
Year 2:			
First	18	10	$100,000
Second.	25	9	$105,000
Third.	30	8	$85,000
Fourth.	28	11	$120,000

Required:

1. Using tonnes mined as the independent (X) variable:
   a. Determine a cost formula for utilities cost using the least-squares regression method. (The variable cost you compute will be in thousands of tonnes. It can be left in this form, or you can convert your variable cost to a per tonne basis by dividing it by 1,000.)
   b. Prepare a scattergraph and plot the tonnes mined and utilities cost. (Place cost on the

vertical axis and tonnes mined on the horizontal axis.) Fit a straight line to the plotted points using the cost formula determined in (*a*) above.

2. Using direct labour-hours as the independent (*X*) variable, repeat the computations in (*a*) and (*b*) above.
3. Would you recommend that the company use tonnes mined or direct labour-hours as a base for planning utilities cost?

eXcel

CASE 6–26 (Appendix 6A) Analysis of Mixed Costs, Job-Order Costing, and Activity-Based Costing [LO1, LO2, LO4]

Ruedi Bärlach PLC, a company located in Gümligen, Switzerland, manufactures custom-designed high-precision industrial tools. The company has a traditional job-order costing system in which direct labour and direct materials costs are assigned directly to jobs, but factory overhead is applied to jobs using a predetermined overhead rate based on direct labour-hours. Management uses this job cost data for valuing cost of goods sold and inventories for external reports. For internal decision making, management has largely ignored this cost data since direct labour costs are basically fixed and management believes overhead costs actually have little to do with direct labour-hours. Recently, management has become interested in activity-based costing (ABC) as a way of estimating job costs and other costs for decision-making purposes.

Management assembled a cross-functional team to design a prototype ABC system. Electrical costs were among the first factory overhead costs investigated by the team. Electricity is used to provide light, to power equipment, and to heat the building in the winter. The ABC team proposed allocating electrical costs to jobs based on machine-hours since running the machines consumes significant amounts of electricity. Data assembled by the team concerning actual direct labour-hours, machine-hours, and electrical costs over a recent eight-week period have been entered into the spreadsheet that appears below. (The Swiss currency is the Swiss franc, which is denoted by SFr.)

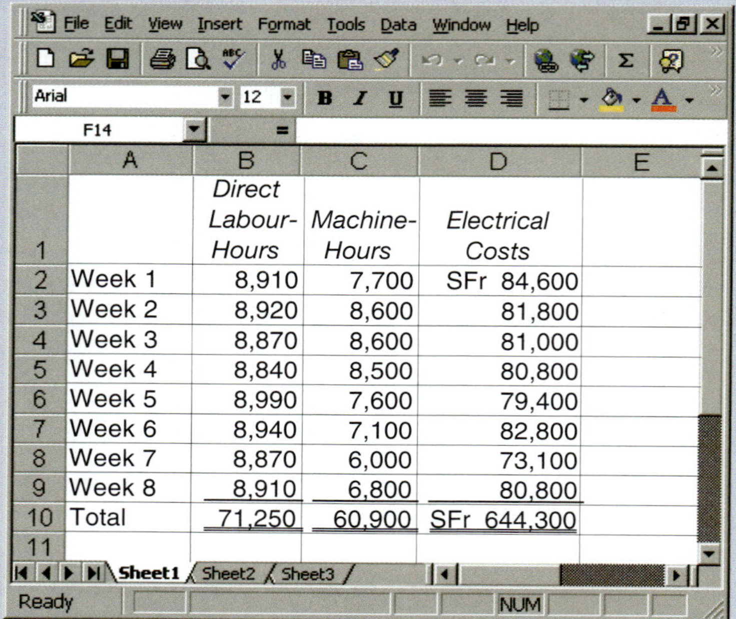

	A	B	C	D	E
1		Direct Labour-Hours	Machine-Hours	Electrical Costs	
2	Week 1	8,910	7,700	SFr 84,600	
3	Week 2	8,920	8,600	81,800	
4	Week 3	8,870	8,600	81,000	
5	Week 4	8,840	8,500	80,800	
6	Week 5	8,990	7,600	79,400	
7	Week 6	8,940	7,100	82,800	
8	Week 7	8,870	6,000	73,100	
9	Week 8	8,910	6,800	80,800	
10	Total	71,250	60,900	SFr 644,300	
11					

To help assess the effect of the proposed change to machine-hours as the allocation base, the above eight-week totals were converted to annual figures by multiplying them by six.

	Direct Labour-Hours	Machine-Hours	Electrical Costs
Estimated annual total (eight-week total above × 6)	427,500	365,400	SFr 3,865,800

Required:

1. Assume that the estimated annual totals shown above are used to compute the company's predetermined overhead rate. What would be the predetermined overhead rate for electrical costs if the allocation base is direct labour-hours? machine-hours?
2. Management intends to bid on a job for a set of custom tools for a watchmaker that would require 30 direct labour-hours and 25 machine-hours. How much electrical cost would be charged to this job using the predetermined overhead rate computed in part (1) above if the allocation base is direct labour-hours? machine-hours?
3. Prepare a scattergraph in which you plot direct labour-hours on the horizontal axis and electrical costs on the vertical axis. Prepare another scattergraph in which you plot machine-hours on the horizontal axis and electrical costs on the vertical axis. Do you agree with the ABC team that machine-hours is a better allocation base for electrical costs than direct labour-hours? Why?
4. Using machine-hours as the measure of activity and the least-squares regression method, estimate the fixed and variable components of electrical costs.
5. How much electrical cost do you think would actually be caused by the custom tool job for the toolmaker in part (2) above? Explain.
6. What factors, apart from direct labour-hours and machine-hours, are likely to affect consumption of electrical power in the company?

CASE 6–27 Analysis of Mixed Costs in a Pricing Decision [LO1, LO2, LO3]

Jasmine Lee owns a catering company that serves food and beverages at exclusive parties and business functions. Lee's business is seasonal, with a heavy schedule during the summer months and holidays and a lighter schedule at other times.

One of the major events that Lee's customers request is a cocktail party. She offers a standard cocktail party and has estimated the cost per guest for this party as follows:

Food and beverages	$17.00
Labour (0.5 hour @ $10.00 per hour)	5.00
Overhead (0.5 hour @ $18.63 per hour)	9.32
Total cost per guest	$31.32

This standard cocktail party lasts three hours and Lee hires one worker for every six guests, which is one-half hour of labour per guest. These workers are hired only as needed and are paid only for the hours they actually work.

Lee ordinarily charges $45 per guest. She is confident about her estimates of the costs of food and beverages and labour, but is not as comfortable with the estimate of overhead cost. The $18.63 overhead cost per labour-hour was determined by dividing total overhead expenses for the last 12 months by total labour-hours for the same period. Monthly data concerning overhead costs and labour-hours appear below:

Month	Labour Hours	Overhead Expenses
January	1,500	$ 44,000
February	1,680	47,200
March	1,800	48,000
April	2,520	51,200
May	2,700	53,600
June	3,300	56,800
July	3,900	59,200
August	4,500	61,600
September	4,200	60,000
October	2,700	54,400
November	1,860	49,600
December	3,900	58,400
Total	34,560	$644,000

Lee has received a request to bid on a 120-guest fund-raising cocktail party to be given next month by an important local charity. (The party would last the usual three hours.) She would like to win this contract because the guest list for this charity event includes many prominent individuals that she would like to land as future clients. Lee is confident that these potential customers would be favourably impressed by her company's services at the charity event.

Required:

1. Estimate the contribution to profit of a standard 120-guest cocktail party if Lee charges her usual price of $45 per guest. (In other words, by how much would her overall profit increase?)
2. How low could Lee bid for the charity event, in terms of a price per guest, and still not lose money on the event itself?
3. The individual who is organizing the charity's fund-raising event has indicated that he has already received a bid under $42 from another catering company. Do you think Lee should bid below her normal $45 per guest price for the charity event? Why or why not?

(CMA, adapted)

Research

R 6–28 Variable and Fixed Costs in Practice [LO1, LO2, LO3]
Form a team to investigate how an organization in your area handles variable and fixed costs. It may be in any industry and can be a business, a not-for-profit organization, or part of the government. Research the organization on the Web and in periodicals to learn what the organization does and how it has performed financially. Make an appointment to meet with the controller, chief financial officer, or with another top manager who is familiar with the financial side of the organization. After meeting with that individual, write a memo in which you discuss the following issues:

Required:

1. Does the organization distinguish between variable and fixed costs in planning and controlling operations? If not, why not?
2. If the organization does distinguish between variable and fixed costs, how are variable and fixed costs estimated? What activity bases are used? How are these activity bases selected? How often are these estimates made? Does the company prepare scattergraphs of past cost and activity data?
3. If the organization does distinguish between variable and fixed costs, how does this help managers in planning and controlling operations?

After studying Chapter 7, you should be able to:

1. Explain how changes in activity affect contribution margin and operating income.
2. Prepare and interpret a cost-volume-profit (CVP) graph.
3. Use the contribution margin ratio (CM ratio) to compute changes in contribution margin and operating income resulting from changes in sales volume.
4. Show the effects on contribution margin of changes in variable costs, fixed costs, selling price, and volume.
5. Compute the break-even point in unit sales and sales dollars.
6. Determine the level of sales needed to achieve a desired target profit.
7. Compute the margin of safety and explain its significance.
8. Explain cost structure and compute the degree of operating leverage at a particular level of sales and explain how it can be used to predict changes in operating income.
9. Compute the break-even point for a multiproduct company and explain the effects of shifts in the sales mix on contribution margin and the break-even point.
10. (Online Appendix 7A) Construct a cost-volume-profit analysis with uncertainty.

COST-VOLUME-PROFIT RELATIONSHIPS

BUSINESS FOCUS

What Happened to the Profit?

Chip Conley is CEO of Joie de Vivre Hospitality, a company that owns and operates 28 hospitality businesses. Conley summed up the company's experience after the dot.com crash and 9/11 as follows: "In the history of North American hotel markets, no hotel market has ever seen a drop in revenues as precipitous as the one in the last two years. On average, hotel revenues . . . dropped 40% to 45%. . . . We've been fortunate that our breakeven point is lower than our competition's. . . . But the problem is that the hotel business is a fixed-cost business. So in an environment where you have those precipitous drops and our costs are moderately fixed, our net incomes—well, they're not incomes anymore, they're losses."

Source: Adapted from Karen Dillon, "Shop Talk," *Inc magazine,* December 2002, pp. 111–114.

Cost-volume-profit (CVP) analysis is a powerful tool that helps managers understand the relationships among cost, volume, and profit. CVP focuses on how profits are affected by the following five elements:

1. Prices of products.
2. Volume or level of activity.
3. Per unit variable costs.
4. Total fixed costs.
5. Mix of products sold.

Because CVP analysis helps managers understand how profits are affected by these key factors, it is a vital tool in many business decisions. These decisions include what products to manufacture and services to offer, what prices to charge, what marketing stretegy to adopt, and what cost stuctures to implement. Careful study of the elements and assumptions, however, is needed to avoid mistakes and to know when to extend the ideas presented in this chapter to more complex situations. One area of potential confusion left is the use of the terms *profit* and *income* interchangeably. This confused terminology has not been corrected because the older term *profit* is often used to mean *income* by both managers and accountants.

To help understand the role of CVP analysis in business decisions, consider the case of Acoustic Concepts, Inc., a company founded by Prem Narayan. Prem, a graduate engineering student at the time, started Acoustic Concepts to market a radical new speaker that he had designed for automobile sound systems. The speaker, called the Sonic Blaster, uses an advanced microprocessor chip to boost amplification to awesome levels. Prem contracted with a Taiwanese electronics manufacturer to produce the speaker. With seed money provided by his family, Prem placed an order with the manufacturer for completed units and ran advertisements in auto magazines.

The Sonic Blaster was an almost immediate success, and sales grew to the point that Prem moved the company's headquarters out of his apartment and into rented quarters in a neighbouring industrial park. He also hired a receptionist, an accountant, a sales manager, and a small sales staff to sell the speakers to retail stores. The accountant, Bob Luchinni, had worked for several small companies where he had acted as a business advisor as well as accountant and bookkeeper.

The Basics of Cost-Volume-Profit (CVP) Analysis

LEARNING OBJECTIVE 1
Explain how changes in activity affect contribution margin and operating income.

Bob Luchinni's preparation for an upcoming meeting begins with the contribution income statement. The contribution income statement emphasizes the behaviour of costs and therefore is extremely helpful to a manager in judging the impact on profits of changes in selling price, cost, or volume. Bob will base his analysis on the following contribution income statement he prepared last month:

ACOUSTIC CONCEPTS, INC.
Contribution Income Statement
For the Month of June

	Total	Per Unit
Sales (400 speakers)	$100,000	$250
Less variable expenses	60,000	150
Contribution margin	40,000	$100
Less fixed expenses	35,000	
Operating income*	$ 5,000	

*Operating income less interest expense less income tax expense equals net income.

This contribution income statement was prepared for management's use inside the company and would not ordinarily be made available to those outside the company. Note that this statement reports sales, variable expenses, and contribution margin on both a per unit basis and a total basis. These per unit figures will be very helpful for performing the cost-volume-profit analysis that we will be studying over the next several pages. Also, note that we use operating income as our measure of profit. We ignore income taxes throughout most of this chapter so that we can more easily focus on the central issues of cost-volume-profit analysis.

Contribution Margin

As explained in Chapter 6, contribution margin is the amount remaining from sales revenue after variable expenses have been deducted. Thus, it is the amount available to cover fixed expenses and then to provide profits for the period. Notice the sequence here—contribution margin is used *first* to cover the fixed expenses, and then whatever remains goes toward profits. If the contribution margin is not sufficient to cover the fixed expenses, then a loss occurs for the period. To illustrate with an extreme example, assume that by the middle of a particular month Acoustic Concepts has been able to sell only one speaker. At that point, the company's income statement will appear as follows:

	Total	Per Unit
Sales (1 speaker)	$ 250	$250
Less variable expenses	150	150
Contribution margin	100	$100
Less fixed expenses	35,000	
Operating loss	$(34,900)	

For each additional speaker that the company is able to sell during the month, $100 more in contribution margin will become available to help cover the fixed expenses. If a second speaker is sold, for example, then the total contribution margin will increase by $100 (to a total of $200) and the company's operating loss will decrease by $100, to $34,800:

	Total	Per Unit
Sales (2 speakers)	$ 500	$250
Less variable expenses	300	150
Contribution margin	200	$100
Less fixed expenses	35,000	
Operating loss	$(34,800)	

If enough speakers can be sold to generate $35,000 in contribution margin, then all of the fixed costs will be covered and the company will have managed to at least *break even* for the month—that is, to show neither profit nor loss but just cover all of its costs. To reach the break-even point, the company will have to sell 350 speakers in a month, since each speaker sold yields $100 in contribution margin:

	Total	Per Unit
Sales (350 speakers)	$87,500	$250
Less variable expenses	52,500	150
Contribution margin	35,000	$100
Less fixed expenses	35,000	
Operating income	$ -0-	

Break-even point
The level of sales at which profit is zero. The break-even point can also be defined as the point where total sales equals total expenses or as the point where total contribution margin equals total fixed expenses. Sales – variable expenses – fixed expenses = $0.00

Computation of the break-even point is discussed in detail later in the chapter; for the moment, note that the **break-even point** is the level of sales at which profit is zero.

Once the break-even point has been reached, operating income will increase by the unit contribution margin for each additional unit sold. If 351 speakers are sold in a month, for example, then we can expect that the operating income for the month will be $100, since the company will have sold 1 speaker more than the number needed to break even:

	Total	Per Unit
Sales (351 speakers)	$87,750	$250
Less variable expenses	52,650	150
Contribution margin	35,100	$100
Less fixed expenses	35,000	
Operating income	$ 100	

If 352 speakers are sold (2 speakers above the break-even point), then we can expect that the operating income for the month will be $200, and so forth. To know what the profits will be at various levels of activity, therefore, it is not necessary for a manager to prepare a whole series of income statements. The manager can simply take the number of units to be sold in excess of the break-even point and multiply that number by the unit contribution margin. The result represents the anticipated operating profits for the period. Or, to estimate the effect of a planned increase in sales on profits, the manager can simply multiply the increase in units sold by the unit contribution margin. The result will be the expected increase in operating profits. To illustrate, if Acoustic Concepts is currently selling 400 speakers per month and plans to increase sales to 425 speakers per month, the anticipated effect on operating profits can be computed as follows:

Increased number of speakers to be sold	25
Contribution margin per speaker	×$100
Increase in operating income	$2,500

These calculations can be verified as follows:

	Sales Volume			
	400 Speakers	425 Speakers	Difference 25 Speakers	Per Unit
Sales	$100,000	$106,250	$6,250	$250
Less variable expenses	60,000	63,750	3,750	150
Contribution margin	40,000	42,500	2,500	$100
Less fixed expenses	35,000	35,000	–0–	
Operating income	$ 5,000	$ 7,500	$2,500	

To summarize, if sales are zero, the company's loss would equal its fixed expenses. Each unit that is sold reduces the loss by the amount of the unit contribution margin. Once the break-even point has been reached, each additional unit sold increases the company's operating profit by the amount of the unit contribution margin.

The simplified income statements for Acoustic Concepts illustrate the fundamentals of cost-volume-profit. Simplifications such as sales driving expenses, fixed expenses remaining fixed even for large changes in sales volumes, and the fact that no limits exist for sales levels are a few assumptions often used in even complex situations. Such simplifications permit a preliminary examination of alternatives. The contribution income statement can always be made more complex using computer spreadsheets so that "what if" analysis can be made more realistic.

IN BUSINESS

Embraer is a competitor to Bombardier Inc. Embraer, Empresa Brasileira de Aeronautica SA, has a 100-seat aircraft known as the JB001 that it expects to deliver to Jet Blue, a New York discount carrier.

An analysis of the potential benefits of the new aircraft is provided for the New York to Richmond, Virginia, route. The current fare is suggested to be $200 each way. The new aircraft provides an opportunity to cut the fare to $90 each way and to triple the customers.

Why is Jet Blue excited about the new aircraft? Does cost-volume-profit provide an answer? Should other carriers be concerned?

Source: Sean Silcoff, "Embraer Cracks New Markets," *National Post*, March 29, 2005, pp. FP1 and FP6.

CVP Relationships in Graphic Form

LEARNING OBJECTIVE 2
Prepare and interpret a cost-volume-profit (CVP) graph.

Relationships among revenue, cost, profit, and volume can be expressed graphically by preparing a **cost-volume-profit graph**. A CVP graph highlights CVP relationships over wide ranges of activity. To help explain his analysis to Prem Narayan, Bob Luchinni decided to prepare a CVP graph for Acoustic Concepts.

Cost-volume-profit (CVP) graph The relationships among revenues, costs, and level of activity in an organization presented in graphic form.

Preparing the CVP Graph

In a CVP graph (sometimes called a *break-even chart*), unit volume is commonly represented on the horizontal *x*-axis and dollars on the vertical *y*-axis. Preparing a CVP graph involves three steps as depicted in Exhibit 7–1.

1. Draw a line parallel to the volume axis to represent total fixed expenses. For Acoustic Concepts, total fixed expenses are $35,000.
2. Choose some volume of sales and plot the point representing total expenses (fixed and variable) at the activity level you have selected. In Exhibit 7–1, Bob Luchinni chose a volume of 600 speakers. Total expenses at that activity level would be as follows:

Fixed expenses	$ 35,000
Variable expenses (600 speakers × $150)	90,000
Total expenses	$125,000

   After the point has been plotted, draw a line through it back to the point where the fixed expenses line intersects the dollars axis.
3. Again choose some volume of sales and plot the point representing total sales dollars at the activity level you have selected. In Exhibit 7–1, Bob Luchinni again chose a volume of 600 speakers. Sales at that activity level total $150,000 (600 speakers × $250 per speaker). Draw a line through this point back to the origin.

The interpretation of the completed CVP graph is given in Exhibit 7–2. The anticipated profit or loss at any given level of sales is measured by the vertical distance between the total revenue line (sales) and the total expenses line (variable expenses plus fixed expenses).

The break-even point is where the total revenue and total expenses lines cross. The break-even point of 350 speakers in Exhibit 7–2 agrees with the break-even point computed earlier.

EXHIBIT 7–1 Preparing the CVP Graph

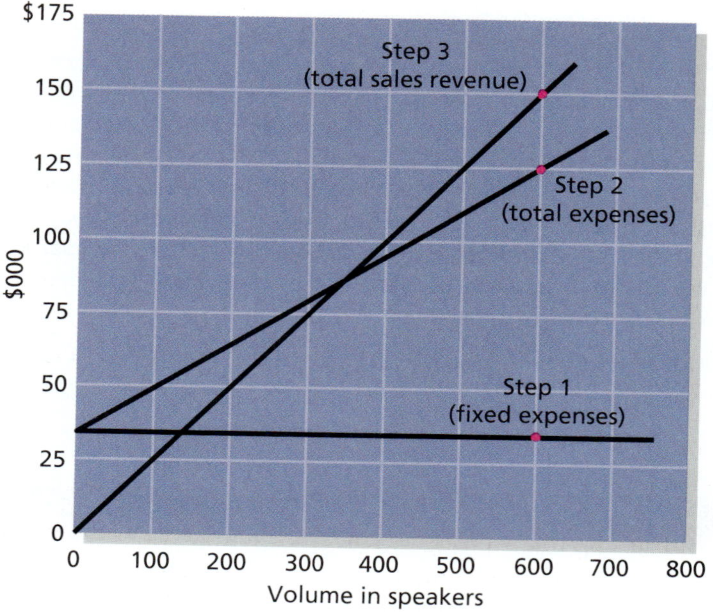

As discussed earlier, when sales are below the break-even point, in this case, 350 units, the company suffers a loss. Note that the loss (represented by the vertical distance between the total expense and total revenue lines) gets bigger as sales decline. When sales are above the break-even point, the company earns a profit and the size of the profit (represented by the vertical distance between the total revenue and total expense lines) increases as sales increase.

EXHIBIT 7–2 The Completed CVP Graph

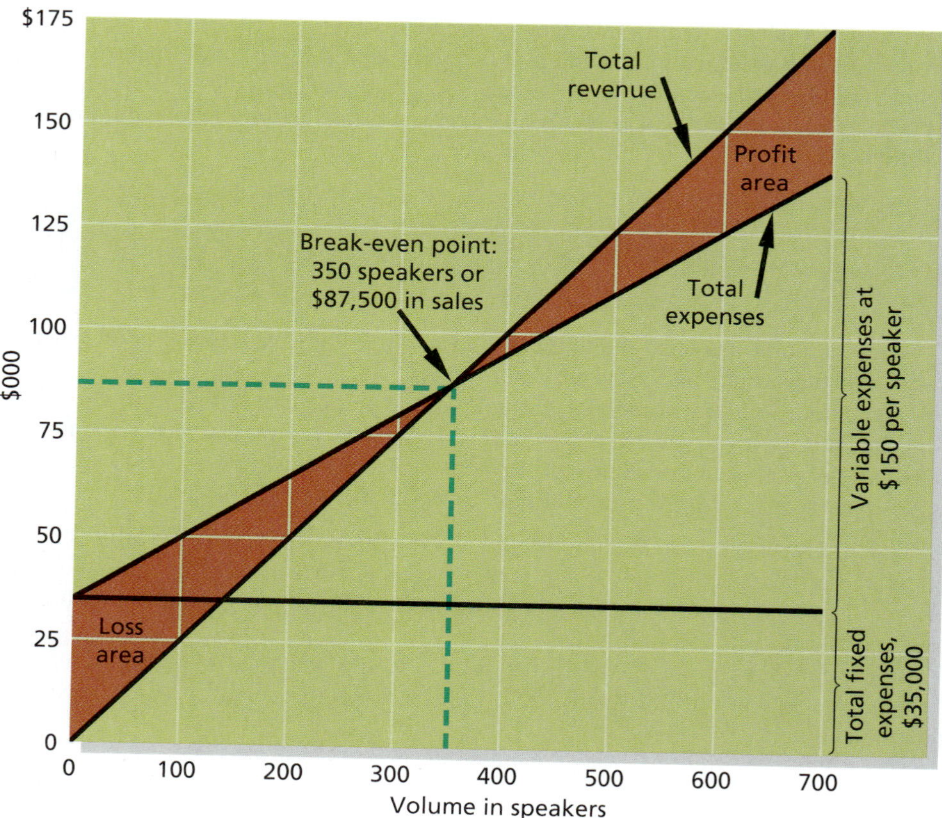

Contribution Margin (CM) Ratio

LEARNING OBJECTIVE 3
Use the contribution margin (CM) ratio to compute changes in contribution margin and operating income resulting from changes in sales volume.

In the previous section, we explored how cost-volume-profit relationships can be visualized. In this section, we show how the contribution margin can be used in cost-volume-profit calculations. As the first step, we have added a column to Acoustic Concepts' contribution income statement, in which sales revenues, variable expenses, and contribution margin are expressed as a percentage of sales:

	Total	Per Unit	Percent of Sales
Sales (400 speakers)	$100,000	$250	100%
Less variable expenses	60,000	150	60%
Contribution margin	40,000	$100	40%
Less fixed expenses.	35,000		
Operating income.	$ 5,000		

The contribution margin as a percentage of total sales is referred to as the **contribution margin (CM) ratio.** This ratio is computed as follows:

Contribution margin (CM) ratio The contribution margin as a percentage of total sales.

$$\text{CM ratio} = \frac{\text{Contribution margin}}{\text{Sales}}$$

For Acoustic Concepts, the computations are:

$$\frac{\text{Total contribution margin, \$40,000}}{\text{Total sales, \$100,000}} = 40\% \quad \text{or} \quad \frac{\text{Per unit contribution margin, \$100}}{\text{Per unit sales, \$250}} = 40\%$$

The CM ratio shows how the contribution margin will be affected by a change in total sales. Acoustic Concepts has a CM ratio of 40% meaning that for each dollar increase in sales, total contribution margin will increase by 40 cents ($1 sales × CM ratio of 40%). Operating income will also increase by 40 cents, assuming that fixed costs are not affected by the increase in sales.

As this illustration suggests, *the effect on operating income of any given dollar change in total sales can be computed in seconds by simply applying the CM ratio to the dollar change.* For example, if Acoustic Concepts plans a $30,000 increase in sales during the coming month, the contribution margin will increase by $12,000 ($30,000 increased sales × CM ratio of 40%). As we noted above, operating income will also increase by $12,000 if fixed costs do not change. This is verified by the following table:

	Sales Volume			
	Present	Expected	Increase	Percent of Sales
Sales	$100,000	$130,000	$30,000	100%
Less variable expenses.	60,000	78,000*	18,000	60%
Contribution margin	40,000	52,000	12,000	40%
Less fixed expenses	35,000	35,000	-0-	
Operating income	$ 5,000	$ 17,000	$12,000	

*$130,000 expected sales ÷ $250 per unit = 520 units. 520 units × $150 per unit = $78,000. Alternatively (1 – .40) × $130,000 = $78,000.

Some managers prefer to work with the CM ratio rather than the unit contribution margin. The CM ratio is particularly valuable in those situations where trade-offs must be made between more dollar sales of one product versus more dollar sales of another. Generally speaking, when trying to increase sales, products that yield the greatest amount of contribution margin per dollar of sales should be emphasized.

CM ratio is also helpful when working with a group of products or services where units cannot be sensibly added. For example, selling dolls and doll houses together can be added in dollars but two dolls plus one doll house does not equal three units of doll products. Because companies often work on product lines, this type of problem is often encountered.

Some Applications of CVP Concepts

LEARNING OBJECTIVE 4
Show the effects on contribution margin of changes in variable costs, fixed costs, selling price, and volume.

Bob Luchinni, the accountant at Acoustic Concepts, wanted to demonstrate to the company's president Prem Narayan how the concepts developed on the preceding pages of this text can be used in planning and decision making. Bob gathered the following basic data:

	Per Unit	Percent of Sales
Sales price	$250	100%
Less variable expenses	150	60%
Contribution margin	$100	40%

Recall that fixed expenses are $35,000 per month. Bob Luchinni will use these data to show the effects of changes in variable costs, fixed costs, sales price, and sales volume on the company's profitability.

Change in Fixed Cost and Sales Volume

Acoustic Concepts is currently selling 400 speakers per month at $250 per speaker for total monthly sales of $100,000. The sales manager feels that a $10,000 increase in the monthly advertising budget would increase monthly sales by $30,000 to a total of $130,000. Should the advertising budget be increased? The following table shows the effect of the proposed change in monthly advertising budget:

	Current Sales	Sales with Additional Advertising Budget	Difference	Percent of Sales
Sales	$100,000	$130,000	$30,000	100%
Less variable expenses	60,000	78,000*	18,000	60%
Contribution margin	40,000	52,000	12,000	40%
Less fixed expenses	35,000	45,000**	10,000	
Operating income	$ 5,000	$ 7,000	$ 2,000	

*520 units × $150 per unit = $78,000

**$35,000 plus additional $10,000 monthly advertising budget = $45,000.

Assuming no other factors to be considered, the increase in the advertising budget should be approved since it would lead to an increase in operating income of $2,000. There are two shorter ways to present this solution. The first alternative solution follows:

Alternative Solution 1

Expected total contribution margin:	
$130,000 × 40% CM ratio	$52,000
Present total contribution margin:	
$100,000 × 40% CM ratio	40,000
Incremental contribution margin	12,000
Change in fixed costs:	
Less incremental advertising expense	10,000
Increased operating income	$ 2,000

Since in this case only the fixed costs and the sales volume change, the solution can be presented in an even shorter format, as follows:

Alternative Solution 2

Incremental contribution margin:	
$30,000 × 40% CM ratio	$12,000
Less incremental advertising expense	10,000
Increased operating income	$ 2,000

Notice that this approach does not depend on a knowledge of previous sales. Also notice that it is unnecessary under either shorter approach to prepare an income statement. Both of the solutions above involve an **incremental analysis** in that they consider only those items of revenue, cost, and volume that will change if the new program is implemented. Although in each case a new income statement could have been prepared the incremental approach is simpler and more direct, and focuses attention on the specific items involved in the decision.

Incremental analysis An analytical approach that focuses only on those items of revenue, cost, and volume that will change as a result of a decision.

In economics, this incremental analysis is often termed *marginal analysis* because of the assumptions used in economics about the behaviour of revenues and costs. Accountants tend to use a more general term, *incremental*, so that less restrictive assumptions about the behaviour of revenues and costs can be made, for example step variable costs.

Change in Variable Costs and Sales Volume

Refer to the original data. Recall that Acoustic Concepts is currently selling 400 speakers per month. Management is contemplating the use of higher-quality components, which would increase variable costs (and thereby reduce the contribution margin) by $10 per speaker. However, the sales manager predicts that the higher overall quality would increase sales to 480 speakers per month. Should the higher-quality components be used? The $10 increase in variable costs will decrease the unit contribution margin by $10—from $100 to $90.

Solution

Expected total contribution margin with higher-quality components:	
480 speakers × $90 per speaker	$43,200
Present total contribution margin:	
400 speakers × $100 per speaker	40,000
Increase in total contribution margin	$ 3,200

According to this analysis, the higher-quality components should be used. Since fixed costs will not change, the $3,200 increase in contribution margin shown above should result in a $3,200 increase in operating income.

Change in Fixed Costs, Sales Price, and Sales Volume

Refer to the original data and recall again that the company is currently selling 400 speakers per month. To increase sales, the sales manager would like to cut the selling price by $20 per speaker and increase the advertising budget by $15,000 per month. The sales manager argues that if these two steps are taken, unit sales will increase by 50% to 600 speakers per month. Should the changes be made? A decrease of $20 per speaker in the selling price will cause the unit contribution margin to decrease from $100 to $80.

Solution

Expected total contribution margin with lower selling price:	
600 speakers × $80 per speaker	$48,000
Present total contribution margin:	
400 speakers × $100 per speaker	40,000
Incremental contribution margin	8,000
Change in fixed costs:	
Less incremental advertising expense	15,000
Reduction in operating income	$(7,000)

According to this analysis, the changes should not be made. The $7,000 reduction in operating income that is shown above can be verified by preparing comparative income statements as follows:

	Present 400 Speakers per Month		Expected 600 Speakers per Month		
	Total	Per Unit	Total	Per Unit	Difference
Sales	$100,000	$250	$138,000	$230	$38,000
Less variable expenses	60,000	150	90,000	150	30,000
Contribution margin	40,000	$100	48,000	$ 80	8,000
Less fixed expenses	35,000		50,000*		15,000
Operating income (loss)	$ 5,000		$ (2,000)		$(7,000)

*35,000 + Additional monthly advertising budget of $15,000 = $50,000.

Change in Variable Cost, Fixed Cost, and Sales Volume

Refer to the original data. As before, the company is currently selling 400 speakers per month. The sales manager would like to pay sales persons a commission of $15 per speaker sold, rather than the flat salaries that now total $6,000 per month. The sales manager is confident that the change will increase monthly sales by 15% to 460 speakers per month. Should the change be made?

Solution

Changing the sales staff from a salaried basis to a commission basis will affect both fixed and variable costs. Fixed costs will decrease by $6,000, from $35,000 to $29,000. Variable costs will increase by $15, from $150 to $165, and the unit contribution margin will decrease from $100 to $85.

Expected total contribution margin with sales staff on commission:	
460 speakers × $85 per speaker	$39,100
Present total contribution margin:	
400 speakers × $100 per speaker	40,000
Decrease in total contribution margin	(900)
Change in fixed costs:	
Add salaries avoided if a commission is paid	6,000
Increase in operating income	$ 5,100

According to this analysis, the change should be made. Again, the same answer can be obtained by preparing comparative income statements:

	Present 400 Speakers per Month		Expected 460 Speakers per Month		Difference: Increase or (Decrease) in Net Income
	Total	Per Unit	Total	Per Unit	
Sales	$100,000	$250	$115,000	$250	$15,000
Less variable expenses	60,000	150	75,900	165	(15,900)
Contribution margin	40,000	$100	39,100	$ 85	(900)
Less fixed expenses	35,000		29,000		6,000
Operating income	$ 5,000		$ 10,100		$ 5,100

Change in Regular Sales Price

Refer to the original data where Acoustic Concepts is currently selling 400 speakers per month. The company has an opportunity to make a bulk sale of 150 speakers to a wholesaler if an acceptable price can be worked out. This sale would not disturb the company's regular sales and would not affect the company's total fixed expenses. What price per speaker should be quoted to the wholesaler if Acoustic Concepts wants to increase its monthly profits by $3,000?

Variable cost per speaker	$150
Desired profit per speaker:	
$3,000 ÷ 150 speakers	20
Quoted price per speaker	$170

Notice that no fixed expenses are included in the computation. This is because fixed expenses are not affected by the bulk sale, so all of the additional revenue that is in excess of variable costs goes to increasing the profits of the company.

If Acoustic Concepts had been operating at a loss rather than at a profit, many managers would look at the situation somewhat differently. Instead of a modest profit of $3,000, many managers would attempt to reverse all or part of the company's overall loss by quoting a higher price. To illustrate this point, assume that Acoustic Concepts presently has a loss of $6,000 this month and that the company would like to make enough money on the bulk sale of speakers to turn this loss into a profit of $3,000. Under these circumstances, the quoted price on the 150 new speakers would be computed as shown below:

Variable cost per speaker	$150
Present net loss:	
$6,000 ÷ 150 speakers	40
Desired profit:	
$3,000 ÷ 150 speakers	20
Quoted price per speaker	$210

The $210 price we have computed represents a substantial discount from the $250 regular selling price per speaker. Thus, both the wholesaler and the company would benefit from the bulk order at this price. This will not always happen, however. By attempting to cover all of the company's losses on one special order, a manager may quote such a high price that the order is lost. Any price greater than $150 will help to reduce the company's loss. A manager must always keep such market considerations in mind when deciding on prices.

As noted above, this example assumes that the bulk order will not affect sales to regular customers. There may be serious strategic implications to accepting this bulk order if this assumption does not hold. Will negative consequences result from accepting this bulk order? For example, existing customers may find out about this order and demand the same low price, or they may simply buy from competitors. Will this bulk sale lead to more orders from the new customer? In summary, managers should consider both the short-term and long-range strategic effects before deciding to accept or reject the bulk order.

Importance of the Contribution Margin

As stated in the introduction to this chapter, CVP analysis seeks the most profitable combination of variable costs, fixed costs, selling price, and sales volume. The above examples show that the effect on the contribution margin is a major consideration in deciding on the most profitable combination of these factors. We have seen that profits can sometimes be improved by reducing the contribution margin if fixed costs can be reduced by a greater amount. More commonly, however, we have seen that the way to improve profits is to increase the total contribution margin figure. Sometimes this can be done by reducing the selling price and thereby increasing volume; sometimes it can be done by increasing the fixed costs (such as advertising) and thereby increasing volume; and sometimes it can be done by trading off variable and fixed costs with appropriate changes in volume. Many other combinations of factors are possible.

The size of the unit contribution margin figure (and the size of the CM ratio) will have a significant influence on what steps a company is willing to take to improve profits. For example, the greater the unit contribution margin, the greater is the amount that a company will be willing to spend in order to increase unit sales. This explains in part why companies with high unit contribution margins (such as auto manufacturers) advertise so heavily, while companies with low unit contribution margins (such as dishware manufacturers) tend to spend much less for advertising.

In short, the effect on the contribution margin is the key to many decisions.

Break-Even Analysis

LEARNING OBJECTIVE 5
Compute the break-even point in unit sales and sales dollars.

Break-even analysis is an aspect of CVP analysis that is designed to answer questions such as how far sales could drop before the company begins to lose money.

Break-Even Computations

Earlier in the chapter, we defined the break-even point to be the level of sales at which the company's profit (operating income) is zero. The break-even point can be computed using either the *equation method* or the *contribution margin method*—the two methods are equivalent.

Equation method
A method of computing break-even sales using the contribution format income statement.

The Equation Method The **equation method** translates the contribution format income statement illustrated earlier in the chapter into an equation form as follows:

$$\text{Profits} = (\text{Sales} - \text{Variable expenses}) - \text{Fixed expenses}$$

Rearranging this equation slightly yields the following equation, which is widely used in CVP analysis:

$$\text{Sales} = \text{Variable expenses} + \text{Fixed expenses} + \text{Profits}$$

At the break-even point, profits are zero. Therefore, the break-even point can be computed by finding that point where sales just equal the total of the variable expenses plus the fixed expenses. For Acoustic Concepts, the break-even point in unit sales, Q, can be computed as follows:

$$\text{Sales} = \text{Variable expenses} + \text{Fixed expenses} + \text{Profits}$$

$$\begin{aligned} \$250Q &= \$150Q + \$35{,}000 + \$0 \\ \$100Q &= \$35{,}000 \\ Q &= \$35{,}000 \div 100 \\ Q &= 350 \text{ speakers} \end{aligned}$$

where:

$$\begin{aligned} Q &= \text{Number (quantity) of speakers sold} \\ \$250 &= \text{Unit sales price} \\ \$150 &= \text{Unit variable expenses} \\ \$35{,}000 &= \text{Total fixed expenses} \end{aligned}$$

The break-even point in sales dollars can be computed by multiplying the break-even level of unit sales by the selling price per unit:

$$350 \text{ speakers} \times \$250 = \$87{,}500$$

The break-even in total sales dollars, X, can also be directly computed as follows:

$$\text{Sales} = \text{Variable expenses} + \text{Fixed expenses} + \text{Profits}$$

$$\begin{aligned} X &= 0.60X + \$35{,}000 + \$0 \\ 0.40X &= \$35{,}000 \\ X &= \$35{,}000 \div 0.40 \\ X &= \$87{,}500 \end{aligned}$$

where:

$$\begin{aligned} X &= \text{Total sales dollars} \\ 0.60 &= \text{Variable expenses as a percentage of sales} \\ \$35{,}000 &= \text{Total fixed expenses} \end{aligned}$$

Note that in the above analysis the *variable expense ratio* is used. The **variable expense ratio** is the ratio of variable expenses to sales dollars. It can be computed by dividing the total variable expenses by the total sales dollars, or in a single product analysis, it can be computed by dividing the variable cost per unit by the unit selling price.

Variable expense ratio The ratio of variable expenses to sales dollars.

Also note that the use of the ratios in the above analysis yields a break-even point expressed in sales dollars rather than in units sold. If desired, the break-even point in units sold can be computed as follows:

$$\$87{,}500 \div \$250 = 350 \text{ speakers}$$

The Contribution Margin Method The **contribution margin method** is a short-cut version of the equation method already described. The approach centres on the idea discussed earlier that each unit sold provides a certain amount of contribution margin that goes toward covering fixed costs. To find how many units must be sold to break even, divide the total fixed costs by the unit contribution margin:

Contribution margin method A method of computing the break-even point in which the fixed expenses are divided by the contribution margin per unit.

$$\text{Break-even point in units sold} = \frac{\text{Fixed expenses}}{\text{Unit contribution margin}}$$

Each speaker generates a contribution margin of \$100 (\$250 selling price, less \$150 variable expenses). Since the total fixed expenses are \$35,000, the break-even point is as follows:

$$\frac{\text{Fixed expenses}}{\text{Unit contribution margin}} = \frac{\$35{,}000}{\$100 \text{ per speaker}} = 350 \text{ speakers}$$

A variation of this method uses the CM ratio instead of the unit contribution margin. The result is the break-even in total sales dollars rather than in total units sold.

$$\text{Break-even point in total sales dollars} = \frac{\text{Fixed expenses}}{\text{CM ratio}}$$

In the Acoustic Concepts example, the calculations are as follows:

$$\frac{\text{Fixed expenses}}{\text{CM ratio}} = \frac{\$35{,}000}{40\%} = \$87{,}500$$

This approach, based on the CM ratio, is particularly useful when a company has multiple product lines and wishes to compute a single break-even point for the company as a whole. More is said on this point in a later section entitled The Concept of Sales Mix.

Target Operating Profit Analysis

LEARNING OBJECTIVE 6
Determine the level of sales needed to achieve a desired target profit.

CVP formulas can be used to determine the sales volume needed to achieve a target operating profit. Suppose that Prem Narayan of Acoustic Concepts would like to earn a target operating profit of $40,000 per month. How many speakers would have to be sold?

The CVP Equation

One approach is to use the equation method. Instead of solving for the unit sales where operating profits are zero, you instead solve for the unit sales where operating profits are $40,000:

$$\text{Sales} = \text{Variable expenses} + \text{Fixed expenses} + \text{Profits}$$

$$\begin{aligned} \$250Q &= \$150Q + \$35{,}000 + \$40{,}000 \\ \$100Q &= \$75{,}000 \\ Q &= \$75{,}000 \div \$100 \\ Q &= 750 \text{ speakers} \end{aligned}$$

where:

$$\begin{aligned} Q &= \text{Number of speakers sold} \\ \$250 &= \text{Unit sales price} \\ \$150 &= \text{Unit variable expenses} \\ \$35{,}000 &= \text{Total fixed expenses} \\ \$40{,}000 &= \text{Target operating profit} \end{aligned}$$

Thus, the target operating profit can be achieved by selling 750 speakers per month, which represents $187,500 in total sales ($250 × 750 speakers).

The Contribution Margin Approach

A second approach involves expanding the contribution margin formula to include the target operating profit:

$$\text{Units sold to attain the target profit} = \frac{\text{Fixed expenses} + \text{Target operating profit}}{\text{Unit contribution margin}}$$

$$\frac{\$35{,}000 \text{ fixed expenses} + \$40{,}000 \text{ target operating profit}}{\$100 \text{ contribution margin per speaker}} = 750 \text{ speakers}$$

This approach gives the same answer as the equation method since it is simply a short-cut version of the equation method. Similarly, the dollar sales needed to attain the target operating profit can be computed as follows:

$$\text{Dollar sales to attain target profit} = \frac{\text{Fixed expenses} + \text{Target operating profit}}{\text{CM ratio}}$$

$$= \frac{\$35{,}000 + \$40{,}000}{0.40}$$

$$= \$187{,}500$$

The problem of computing a desired dollar sales level is very similar to the problem of finding a break-even point. In the case of finding a break-even point the target operating profit is zero. For any targeted amount of sales above zero we simply add the desired profit to fixed expenses because the target profit is another fixed amount that must be covered.

After-Tax Analysis

Operating profit in the preceding analysis has ignored income taxes and is actually income before taxes. In general, operating income after tax can be computed as a fixed percentage of income before taxes. To calculate the income taxes, we simply multiply the tax rate (t) by the operating income before taxes (B). After-tax profit is equal to profit before taxes times 1 minus the tax rate and is derived as follows:

$$\begin{aligned} \text{Income after taxes} &= \text{Before-tax profit} - \text{Taxes} \\ &= B - t(B) \\ &= B(1 - t) \end{aligned}$$

Dividing both sides by $(1 - t)$, income before taxes is equal to income after taxes divided by 1 minus the tax rate $(1 - t)$:

$$B = \frac{\text{Income after taxes}}{(1 - t)}$$

Using the previous example, assume that the tax rate is 30% and the target operating profit is $48,000 after taxes. The target profit can be achieved by selling 1,036 speakers. The appropriate formula to use would be:

$$\frac{\text{Fixed expenses} + [(\text{Target after-tax profit})/(1 - \text{tax rate})]}{\text{Contribution margin per unit}}$$

$$\frac{\$35{,}000 + [\$48{,}000/(1 - 0.3)]}{\$100} = 1{,}036 \text{ speakers (rounded)}$$

The Margin of Safety

LEARNING OBJECTIVE 7
Compute the margin of safety and explain its significance.

The **margin of safety** is the excess of budgeted (or actual) sales over the break-even volume of sales. It states the amount by which sales can drop before losses begin to be incurred. The higher the margin of safety, the lower the risk of not breaking even. The formula for its calculation is as follows:

$$\text{Margin of safety} = \text{Total budgeted (or actual) sales} - \text{Break-even sales}$$

Margin of safety
The excess of budgeted (or actual) sales over the break-even volume of sales.

The margin of safety can also be expressed in percentage form. This percentage is obtained by dividing the margin of safety in dollar terms by total sales:

$$\text{Margin of safety percentage} = \frac{\text{Margin of safety in dollars}}{\text{Total budgeted (or actual) sales}}$$

The calculations for the margin of safety for Acoustic Concepts are as follows:

Sales (at the current volume of 400 speakers) (a)	$100,000
Break-even sales (at 350 speakers)	87,500
Margin of safety (in dollars) (b)	$ 12,500
Margin of safety as a percentage of sales, (b) ÷ (a)	12.5%

This margin of safety means that at the current level of sales and with the company's current prices and costs, a reduction in sales of $12,500, or 12.5%, would result in just breaking even.

In a single-product firm like Acoustic Concepts, the margin of safety can also be expressed in terms of the number of units sold by dividing the margin of safety in dollars by the selling price per unit. In this case, the margin of safety is 50 speakers ($12,500 ÷ $250 per speaker = 50 speakers).

IN BUSINESS

The company eToys, which sells toys on the Internet, lost $190 million in 1999 on sales of $151 million. One major cost was advertising: eToys spent about $37 on advertising for each $100 of sales. Other e-tailers were spending even more—in some cases, up to $460 on advertising for each $100 in sales!

eToys does have some advantages over brick-and-mortar stores such as Toys "R" Us. For example, eToys has much lower inventory costs, since it needs to keep on hand only one or two of a slow-moving item, whereas a traditional store has to fully stock its shelves. Also, brick-and-mortar retail spaces in malls and elsewhere cost money—on average, about 7% of sales. However, e-tailers such as eToys have their own disadvantages. Customers can "pick and pack" their own items at a brick-and-mortar outlet, but e-tailers have to pay employees to carry out this task, which costs approximately $33 for every $100 of sales. Also the technology to sell on the Net is not free: eToys paid some $29 on its Web site and related technology for every $100 in sales. However, many of these costs of selling on the Net are fixed. Toby Lenk, the CEO of eToys, estimates that the company will pass the break-even point somewhere between $750 million and $950 million in sales—representing less than 1% of the market for toys.

Source: Erin Kelly, "The Last e-Store on the Block," *Fortune*, September 18, 2000, pp. 214–20.

CVP Considerations in Choosing a Cost Structure

LEARNING OBJECTIVE 8
Explain cost structure and compute the degree of operating leverage at a particular level of sales and explain how it can be used to predict changes in operating income.

Cost structure refers to the relative proportion of fixed and variable costs in an organization. An organization often has some latitude in trading off between fixed and variable costs. For example, fixed investments in automated equipment can reduce variable labour costs. In this section, we discuss the choice of a cost structure, focusing on the effect of cost structure on profit stability, in which *operating leverage* plays a key role.

Cost Structure and Profit Stability

Cost structure The relative proportion of fixed and variable costs in an organization.

Which cost structure is better—high variable costs and low fixed costs, or the opposite? To show what is needed to answer this question, refer to the income statements given below for two blueberry farms. Bogside Farm depends on migrant workers to pick its berries by hand, whereas Sterling Farm has invested in expensive berry-picking machines. Consequently, Bogside Farm has higher variable costs, but Sterling Farm has higher fixed costs:

	Bogside Farm		Sterling Farm	
	Amount	**Percent**	**Amount**	**Percent**
Sales	$100,000	100%	$100,000	100%
Less variable expenses	60,000	60%	30,000	30%
Contribution margin	40,000	40%	70,000	70%
Less fixed expenses	30,000		60,000	
Operating income	$ 10,000		$ 10,000	

Which farm has the better cost structure? The answer depends on many factors, including the long-run trend in sales, year-to-year fluctuations in the level of sales, and the attitude of the owners toward risk. If sales are expected to be above $100,000 in the future, then Sterling Farm probably has the better cost structure. The reason is that its CM ratio is higher, and its profits will therefore increase more rapidly as sales increase. To illustrate, assume that each farm experiences a 10% increase in sales without any increase in fixed costs. The new income statements would be as follows:

	Bogside Farm		Sterling Farm	
	Amount	**Percent**	**Amount**	**Percent**
Sales	$110,000	100%	$110,000	100%
Less variable expenses	66,000	60%	33,000	30%
Contribution margin	44,000	40%	77,000	70%
Less fixed expenses	30,000		60,000	
Operating income	$ 14,000		$ 17,000	

Sterling Farm has experienced a greater increase in operating income due to its higher CM ratio even though the increase in sales was the same for both farms.

What if sales drop below $100,000? What are the break-even points of the two farms? What are their margins of safety? The computations needed to answer these questions are carried out as follows, using the contribution margin method:

	Bogside Farm	Sterling Farm
Fixed expenses	$ 30,000	$ 60,000
Contribution margin ratio	÷40%	÷70%
Break-even in total sales dollars	$ 75,000	$ 85,714
Total current sales (a)	$100,000	$100,000
Break-even sales	75,000	85,714
Margin of safety in sales dollars (b)	$ 25,000	$ 14,286
Margin of safety as a percentage of sales, (b) ÷ (a)	25.0%	14.3%

This analysis makes it clear that Bogside Farm is less vulnerable to downturns than Sterling Farm. We can identify two reasons for this. First, due to its lower fixed expenses, Bogside Farm has a lower break-even point and a higher margin of safety, as shown by the computations above. Therefore, it will not incur losses as quickly as Sterling Farm in periods of sharply declining sales. Second, due to its lower CM ratio, Bogside Farm will not lose contribution margin as rapidly as Sterling Farm when sales fall off. Thus, Bogside Farm's income will be less volatile. We saw earlier that this is a drawback when sales increase, but it provides more protection when sales drop.

To summarize, without knowing the future, it is not obvious which cost structure is better. Both have advantages and disadvantages. Sterling Farm, with its higher fixed costs and lower variable costs, will experience wider swings in operating income as changes take place in sales, with greater profits in good years and greater losses in bad years. Bogside Farm, with its lower fixed costs and higher variable costs, will enjoy greater stability in operating income and will be more protected from losses during bad years, but at the cost of lower operating income in good years.

IN BUSINESS

Both JetBlue and United Airlines use an Airbus 235 to fly from Dulles International Airport near Washington, DC, to Oakland, California. Both planes have a pilot, copilot, and four flight attendants. That is where the similarity ends. Based on 2002 data, the pilot on the United flight earned $16,350 to $18,000 a month compared to $6,800 per month for the JetBlue pilot. United's senior flight attendants on the plane earned more than $41,000 per year; whereas the JetBlue attendants were paid $16,800 to $27,000 per year. Largely because of the higher labour costs at United, its costs of operating the flight were more than 60% higher than JetBlue's costs. Due to intense fare competition from JetBlue and other low-cost carriers, United was unable to cover its higher operating costs on this and many other flights. Consequently, United went into bankruptcy at the end of 2002.

Source: Susan Carey, "Costly Race in the Sky," *The Wall Street Journal*, September 9, 2002, pp. B1 and B3.

Operating Leverage

Operating leverage
A measure of how sensitive operating income is to a given percentage change in sales. It is computed by dividing the contribution margin by operating income.

A lever is a tool for multiplying force. Using a lever, a massive object can be moved with only a modest amount of force. In business, *operating leverage* serves a similar purpose. **Operating leverage** is a measure of how sensitive operating income is to percentage changes in sales. Operating leverage acts as a multiplier. If operating leverage is high, a small percentage increase in sales can produce a much larger percentage increase in operating income.

Operating leverage can be illustrated by returning to the data given above for the two blueberry farms. We previously showed that a 10% increase in sales (from $100,000 to $110,000 for each farm) results in a 70% increase in the operating income of Sterling Farm (from $10,000 to $17,000) and only a 40% increase in the operating income of Bogside Farm (from $10,000 to $14,000). Thus, for a 10% increase in sales, Sterling Farm experiences a much greater percentage increase in profits than does Bogside Farm. Therefore, Sterling Farm has greater operating leverage than Bogside Farm.

Degree of operating leverage
A measure, at a given level of sales, of how a percentage change in sales volume will affect profits. The degree of operating leverage is computed by dividing contribution margin by operating income.

The **degree of operating leverage** at a given level of sales is computed by the following formula:

$$\text{Degree of operating leverage} = \frac{\text{Contribution margin}}{\text{Operating income}}$$

The degree of operating leverage is a measure, at a given level of sales, of how a percentage change in sales volume will affect profits. To illustrate, the degree of operating leverage for the two farms at a $100,000 sales level would be as follows:

$$\text{Bogside Farm: } \frac{\$40{,}000}{\$10{,}000} = 4$$

$$\text{Sterling Farm: } \frac{\$70{,}000}{\$10{,}000} = 7$$

Since the degree of operating leverage for Bogside Farm is 4, the farm's operating income grows four times as fast as its sales. Similarly, Sterling Farm's operating income grows seven times as fast as its sales. Thus, if sales increase by 10%, then we can expect the operating income of Bogside Farm to increase by four times this amount, or by 40%, and the operating income of Sterling Farm to increase by seven times this amount, or by 70%.

	(1) Percent Increase in Sales	(2) Degree of Operating Leverage	(3) Percent Increase in Operating Income (1) × (2)
Bogside Farm	10%	4	40%
Sterling Farm	10%	7	70%

What is responsible for the higher operating leverage at Sterling Farm? The only difference between the two farms is their cost structure. If two companies have the same total revenue and same total expense but different cost structures, then the company with the higher proportion of fixed costs in its cost structure will have higher operating leverage. Referring back to the original example on page 289, when both farms have sales of $100,000 and total expenses of $90,000, one-third of Bogside Farm's costs are fixed but two-thirds of Sterling Farm's costs are fixed. As a consequence, Sterling's degree of operating leverage is higher than Bogside's.[1]

The degree of operating leverage is greatest at sales levels near the break-even point and decreases as sales and profits rise. This can be seen from the tabulation below, which shows the degree of operating leverage for Bogside Farm at various sales levels. (Data used earlier for Bogside Farm are shown in colour.)

Sales	$75,000	$80,000	$100,000	$150,000	$225,000
Less variable expenses.	45,000	48,000	60,000	90,000	135,000
Contribution margin (a)	30,000	32,000	40,000	60,000	90,000
Less fixed expenses	30,000	30,000	30,000	30,000	30,000
Operating income (b)	$ -0-	$ 2,000	$ 10,000	$ 30,000	$ 60,000
Degree of operating leverage, (a) ÷ (b)	∞	16	4	2	1.5

Thus, a 10% increase in sales would increase operating profits by only 15% (10% × 1.5) if the company was operating at a $225,000 sales level, as compared to the 40% increase we computed earlier at the $100,000 sales level. The degree of operating leverage will continue to decrease the further the company moves from its break-even point. At the break-even point, the degree of operating leverage will be infinitely large ($30,000 contribution margin ÷ $0 operating income = ∞).

A manager can use the degree of operating leverage to quickly estimate what effect various percentage changes in sales will have on profits, without the necessity of preparing detailed income statements. As shown by our examples, the effects of operating leverage can be dramatic. If a company is near its break-even point, then even small percentage increases in sales can yield large percentage increases in profits. *This explains*

1. See Richard A. Lord, "Interpreting and Measuring Operating Leverage," *Issues in Accounting Education,* Fall 1995, pp. 317–29, for an extensive discussion of the impact of cost structure on the degree of operating leverage.

why management will often work very hard for only a small increase in sales volume. If the degree of operating leverage is 5, then a 6% increase in sales would translate into a 30% increase in profits.

In summary, we can predict the percentage change in operating income before taxes (OIBT) resulting from a given percentage change in sales. The following equation does this by multiplying the percentage change in sales by the degree of operating leverage:

$$\%\Delta \text{ OIBT} = \%\Delta \text{ Sales} \times \text{Degree of operating leverage}$$

Automation: Risks and Rewards from a CVP Perspective

We have noted in preceding chapters that several factors, including the move toward flexible manufacturing systems and other uses of automation, have resulted in a shift toward greater fixed costs and less variable costs in organizations. In turn, this shift in cost structure has had an impact on the CM ratio, the break-even point, and the degree of operating leverage.

Many benefits can accrue from automation, but certain risks are introduced when a company moves toward greater amounts of fixed costs. These risks suggest that management must be careful as it automates to ensure that investment decisions are made in accordance with a carefully devised long-run strategy. This point is discussed further in Chapter 13 where we deal with investment decisions in an automated environment.

Indifference Analysis

We have seen that cost-volume-profit analysis is a decision tool that can be used as input for decisions about the profitability of individual products. CVP analysis is also useful for aiding decisions about the comparative profitability of alternative products or methods of production. The analysis focuses on cost behaviour in relation to changes in activity level. Relative profitability depends on activity level. A product with a high level of fixed costs will require a higher sales activity level to generate a profit than will a product with low fixed costs and comparatively high variable costs. Cost-volume-profit analyses facilitate the comparison of alternatives with different fixed and variable cost structures.

To illustrate, assume that Goodwin Company has decided to introduce a new product that can be manufactured by either a labour-intensive production (LIP) system or a capital-intensive production (CIP) system. The manufacturing method will not affect the quality of the product. The estimated manufacturing costs of a labour-intensive production system and a capital-intensive production system are as follows:

	Labour-Intensive Production System		Capital-Intensive Production System	
Selling price per unit sold		$30.00		$30.00
Direct material		6.00		5.00
Direct labour-hours (DLH)	0.8 DLH @ $9	7.20	0.5 DLH@ $12	6.00
Variable overhead	0.8 DLH @ $6	4.80	0.5 DLH @ $6	3.00
Variable selling expense		2.00		2.00
Total variable costs		20.00		16.00
Contribution margin		$10.00		$14.00
Fixed overhead*		$1,200,000.00		$2,550,000.00
Fixed selling expenses		$ 600,000.00		$ 600,000.00
Break-even sales		$5,400,000.00		$6,750,000.00
Break-even units		180,000		225,000

*These costs are directly traceable to the new product line. They would not be incurred if the new product was not produced.

We can calculate the point at which Goodwin will be indifferent about using a labour-intensive production system or a capital-intensive production system as follows:

1. Determine the unit CM times the number of units (Q) minus total fixed costs of each alternative.

2. Set up an equation with each alternative on opposite sides of the equal sign.
3. Solve for Q, the indifference point.

$$\$10Q - \$1{,}800{,}000 = \$14Q - \$3{,}150{,}000$$
$$\$4Q = \$1{,}350{,}000$$
$$Q = 337{,}500 \text{ units}$$

Note from line 2 of the equation that the $4 change in contribution margin is on the left-hand side of the equation, and the $1,350,000 on the right-hand side of the equation is the change in fixed costs. The indifference point can therefore be found quickly by dividing the change in fixed cost by the change in contribution margin for each alternative:

$$\frac{\text{Fixed cost of CIP} - \text{Fixed cost of LIP}}{\text{CM of CIP} - \text{CM of LIP}} = \frac{\$3{,}150{,}000 - \$1{,}8000{,}000}{\$14 - \$10} = \frac{\$1{,}350{,}000}{\$4} = 337{,}500 \text{ units}$$

At sales below the indifference point of 337,500 units, profitability will be higher for LIP. Sales above the indifference point will generate higher profitability for CIP, because CIP generates a higher contribution margin per unit than LIP does.

The Concept of Sales Mix

Before concluding our discussion of CVP concepts, we will consider the effect of changes in sales mix on a firm's profits.

LEARNING OBJECTIVE 9
Compute the break-even point for a multiproduct company and explain the effects of shifts in the sales mix on contribution margin and the break-even point.

The Definition of Sales Mix

The term **sales mix** refers to the relative proportions in which a company's products are sold. Managers try to achieve the combination, or mix, that will yield the greatest amount of profits. Most companies have several products, and often these products are not equally profitable; therefore, profits will depend to some extent on the company's sales mix. Profits will be greater if high-margin rather than low-margin items make up a relatively large proportion of total sales.

Changes in the sales mix can cause perplexing variations in a company's profits. A shift in the sales mix from high-margin items to low-margin items can cause total profits to decrease even though total sales may increase. Conversely, a shift in the sales mix from low-margin items to high-margin items can cause the reverse effect—total profits may increase even though total sales decrease. It is one thing to achieve a particular sales volume, but it is quite another to sell the most profitable mix of products.

Sales mix
The relative proportions in which a company's products are sold. Sales mix is computed by expressing the sales of each product as a percentage of total sales.

IN BUSINESS

Kodak dominates the film industry in the U.S., selling two out of every three rolls of film. It also processes 40% of all film dropped off for developing. Unfortunately for Kodak, this revenue stream is threatened by digital cameras, which do not use film at all. To counter this threat, Kodak has moved into the digital market with its own line of digital cameras and various services, but sales of digital products undeniably cut into the company's film business. "Chief Financial Officer Robert Brust has 'stress-tested' profit models based on how quickly digital cameras may spread. If half of homes go digital, . . . Kodak's sales would rise 10% a year—but profits would go up only 8% a year. Cost cuts couldn't come fast enough to offset a slide in film sales and the margin pressure from selling cheap digital cameras." The sales mix is moving in the wrong direction, given the company's current cost structure and competitive prices.

Source: Bruce Upbin, "Kodak's Digital Moment," *Forbes*, August 21, 2000, pp. 106–112.

Sales Mix and Break-Even Analysis

If a company sells more than one product, break-even analysis is somewhat more complex than discussed to this point. The reason is that different products will have different selling prices, different costs, and different contribution margins. Consequently, the break-even point will depend on the mix in which the various products are sold. To illustrate, consider Sound Unlimited, a small company that imports DVDs from France for use in personal computers. At present, the company distributes the following to retail computer stores: the Le Louvre DVD, a multimedia free-form tour of the famous art museum in Paris; and the Le Vin DVD, which features the wines and wine-growing regions of France. Both multimedia products have sound, photos, video clips, and sophisticated software. The company's September sales, expenses, and break-even point are shown in Exhibit 7–3.

As shown in the exhibit, the break-even point is $60,000 in sales, which was computed by dividing the fixed costs by the company's *overall* CM ratio of 45%. But $60,000 in sales represents the break-even point for the company only as long as the sales mix does not change. *If the sales mix changes, then the break-even point will also change.* This is illustrated by the results for October in which the sales mix shifted away from the more profitable Le Vin DVD (which has a 50% CM ratio) toward the less profitable Le Louvre DVD (which has only a 25% CM ratio). These results appear in Exhibit 7–4.

EXHIBIT 7–3 Multiple-Product Break-Even Analysis

SOUND UNLIMITED
Contribution Income Statement
For the Month of September

	Le Louvre DVD		Le Vin DVD		Total	
	Amount	**Percent**	**Amount**	**Percent**	**Amount**	**Percent**
Sales	$20,000	100%	$80,000	100%	$100,000	100%
Variable expenses	15,000	75%	40,000	50%	55,000	55%
Contribution margin	$ 5,000	25%	$40,000	50%	45,000	45%
Fixed expenses					27,000	
Operating income					$ 18,000	

Computation of the break-even point:

$$\frac{\text{Fixed expenses}}{\text{Overall CM ratio}} = \frac{\$27{,}000}{0.45} = \$60{,}000$$

Verification of the break-even point:

	Le Louvre DVD	Le Vin DVD	Total
Current dollar sales	$20,000	$80,000	$100,000
Percentage of total dollar sales	20%	80%	100%
Sales at the break-even point	$12,000	$48,000	$60,000

	Le Louvre DVD		Le Vin DVD		Total	
	Amount	**Percent**	**Amount**	**Percent**	**Amount**	**Percent**
Sales	$12,000	100%	$48,000	100%	$ 60,000	100%
Variable expenses	9,000	75%	24,000	50%	33,000	55%
Contribution margin	$ 3,000	25%	$24,000	50%	27,000	45%
Fixed expenses					27,000	
Operating income					$ 0	

EXHIBIT 7–4 Multiple-Product Break-Even Analysis: A Shift in Sales Mix (see Exhibit 7–3)

SOUND UNLIMITED
Contribution Income Statement
For the Month of October

	Le Louvre DVD		Le Vin DVD		Total	
	Amount	**Percent**	**Amount**	**Percent**	**Amount**	**Percent**
Sales	$80,000	100%	$20,000	100%	$100,000	100%
Less variable expenses	60,000	75%	10,000	50%	70,000	70%
Contribution margin	$20,000	25%	$10,000	50%	30,000	30%
Less Fixed expenses					27,000	
Operating income					$ 3,000	

Computation of the break-even point:

$$\frac{\text{Fixed expenses}}{\text{Overall CM ratio}} = \frac{\$27{,}000}{0.30} = \$90{,}000$$

Although sales have remained unchanged at $100,000, the sales mix is exactly the reverse of what it was in Exhibit 7–3, with the bulk of the sales now coming from the less profitable Le Louvre DVD. Notice that this shift in the sales mix has caused both the overall CM ratio and total profits to drop sharply from the prior month—the overall CM ratio has dropped from 45% in September to only 30% in October, and operating income has dropped from $18,000 to only $3,000. In addition, with the drop in the overall CM ratio, the company's break-even point is no longer $60,000 in sales. Since the company is now realizing less average contribution margin per dollar of sales, it takes more sales to cover the same amount of fixed costs. Thus, the break-even point has increased from $60,000 to $90,000 in sales per year.

In preparing a break-even analysis, some assumptions must be made concerning the sales mix. Usually the assumption is that it will not change. However, if the manager knows that shifts in various factors (consumer tastes, market share, and so forth) are causing shifts in the sales mix, then these factors must be explicitly considered in any CVP computations. Otherwise, the manager may make decisions on the basis of outmoded or faulty data.

Assumptions of CVP Analysis

A number of assumptions typically underlie CVP analysis:

1. Selling price is constant throughout the entire relevant range. The price of a product or service will not change as volume changes.
2. Costs are linear throughout the entire relevant range, and they can accurately be divided into variable and fixed elements. The variable element is constant per unit, and the fixed element is constant in total over the entire relevant range.
3. In multiproduct companies, the sales mix is constant.
4. In manufacturing companies, inventories do not change. The number of units produced equals the number of units sold (this assumption is considered further in the next chapter).

While some of these assumptions may be violated in practice, the results of CVP analysis are often "good enough" to be quite useful. For example, in most multiproduct companies, the sales mix is constant enough that the results of CVP analysis are reasonably valid.

Perhaps the greatest danger lies in relying on simple CVP analysis when a manager is contemplating a large change in volume that lies outside of the relevant range. For example, a manager might contemplate increasing the level of sales far beyond what the company has ever experienced. However, even in these situations, a manager can adjust the model as we have done in this chapter to take into account anticipated changes in selling prices, fixed costs, and the sales mix that would otherwise violate the assumptions. For example, in a decision that would affect fixed costs, the change in fixed costs can explicitly be taken into account as illustrated earlier in the chapter in the Acoustic Concepts example on page 280.

Summary

CVP analysis is based on a simple model of how profits respond to prices, costs, and volume. This model can be used to answer a variety of critical questions such as what the company's break-even volume is, what its margin of safety is, and what is likely to happen if specific changes are made in prices, costs, and volume.

A CVP graph depicts the relationships between sales volume in units, on the one hand, and fixed expenses, variable expenses, total expenses, total sales, and profits on the other hand. The CVP graph is useful for developing intuition about how costs and profits respond to changes in sales volume.

The contribution margin ratio is the ratio of the total contribution margin to total sales. This ratio can be used to quickly estimate what effect a change in total sales would have on operating income. The ratio is also useful in break-even analysis.

The break-even point is the level of sales (in units or in dollars) at which the company just breaks even. The break-even point can be computed using several different techniques that are all based on the simple CVP model. With slight modification, the same technique can be used to compute the level of sales required to attain a target profit.

The margin of safety is the amount by which the company's current sales exceed break-even sales.

The degree of operating leverage allows quick estimation of what effect a given percentage in sales would have on the company's operating income. The higher the degree of operating leverage, the greater is the effect on the company's profits. The degree of operating leverage is not constant—it depends on the company's current level of sales.

The profits of a multiproduct company are affected by its sales mix. Changes in the sales mix can affect the break-even point, margin of safety, and other critical measures.

Review Problem: CVP Relationships

Voltar Company manufactures and sells a telephone answering machine. The company's contribution format income statement for the most recent year is given below:

	Total	Per Unit	Percent of Sales
Sales (20,000 units)	$1,200,000	$60	100%
Less variable expenses	900,000	45	? %
Contribution margin	300,000	$15	? %
Less fixed expenses	240,000		
Operating income	$ 60,000		

Management is anxious to improve the company's profit performance and has asked for several items of information.

Required:

1. Compute the company's CM ratio and variable expense ratio.
2. Compute the company's break-even point in both units and sales dollars. Use the equation method.
3. Assume that sales increase by $400,000 next year. If cost behaviour patterns remain unchanged, by how much will the company's operating income increase? Use the CM ratio to determine your answer.
4. Refer to original data. Assume that next year management wants the company to earn a minimum profit of $90,000. How many units will have to be sold to meet this target profit figure?
5. Refer to the original data. Compute the company's margin of safety in both dollar and percentage form.
6. *a.* Compute the company's degree of operating leverage at the present level of sales.
   b. Assume that, through a more intense effort by the sales staff, the company's sales increase by 8% next year. By what percentage would you expect operating income to increase? Use the operating leverage concept to obtain your answer.
   c. Verify your answer to (*b*) by preparing a new income statement showing an 8% increase in sales.
7. In an effort to increase sales and profits, management is considering the use of a higher-quality speaker. The higher-quality speaker would increase variable costs by $3 per unit, but management could eliminate one quality inspector who is paid a salary of $30,000 per year. The sales manager estimates that the higher-quality speaker would increase annual sales by at least 20%.
   a. Assuming that changes are made as described above, prepare a projected income statement for next year. Show data on a total, per unit, and percentage basis.
   b. Compute the company's new break-even point in both units and dollars of sales. Use the contribution margin method.
   c. Would you recommend that the changes be made?

Solution to Review Problem

1. CM ratio:

$$\frac{\text{Contribution margin, \$15}}{\text{Selling price, \$60}} = 25\%$$

Variable expense ratio:

$$\frac{\text{Variable expense, \$45}}{\text{Selling price, \$60}} = 75\%$$

2.

$$\text{Sales} = \text{Variable expenses} + \text{Fixed expenses} + \text{Profits}$$

$$\$60Q = \$45Q + \$240{,}000 + \$0$$

$$\$15Q = \$240{,}000$$

$$Q = \$240{,}000 \div \$15$$

$$Q = 16{,}000 \text{ units; or at \$60 per unit, \$960,000}$$

Alternative solution:

$$X = 0.75X + \$240{,}000 + \$0$$

$$0.25X = \$240{,}000$$

$$X = \$240{,}000 \div 0.25$$

$$X = \$960{,}000\text{; or at \$60 per unit, 16,000 units}$$

3.

Increase in sales	$400,000
Multiply by the CM ratio.	× 25%
Expected increase in contribution margin.	$100,000

Since the fixed expenses are not expected to change, operating income will increase by the entire $100,000 increase in contribution margin computed above.

4. Equation method:

$$\text{Sales} = \text{Variable expenses} + \text{Fixed expenses} + \text{Profits}$$

$$\$60Q = \$45Q + \$240{,}000 + \$90{,}000$$

$$\$15Q = \$330{,}000$$

$$Q = \$330{,}000 \div \$15$$

$$Q = 22{,}000 \text{ units}$$

Contribution margin method:

$$\frac{\text{Fixed expenses} + \text{Target profit}}{\text{Contribution margin per unit}} = \frac{\$240{,}000 + \$90{,}000}{\$15} = 22{,}000 \text{ units}$$

5. Total sales − Break-even sales = Margin of safety in dollars
$1,200,000 − $960,000 = $240,000

$$\frac{\text{Margin of safety in dollars, } \$240{,}000}{\text{Total sales, } \$1{,}200{,}000} = 20\%$$

6. *a.* $\frac{\text{Contribution margin, } \$300{,}000}{\text{Operating income, } \$60{,}000} = 5$ (degree of operating leverage)

b.

Expected increase in sales	8%
Degree of operating leverage	× 5%
Expected increase in operating income	40%

c. If sales increase by 8%, then 21,600 units (20,000 × 1.08 = 21,600) will be sold next year. The new income statement will be as follows:

	Total	Per Unit	Percent of Sales
Sales (21,600 units)	$1,296,000	$60	100%
Less variable expenses	972,000	45	75%
Contribution margin	324,000	$15	25%
Less fixed expenses.......	240,000		
Operating income.........	$ 84,000		

Thus, the $84,000 expected operating income for next year represents a 40% increase over the $60,000 operating income earned during the current year:

$$\frac{\$84{,}000 - \$60{,}000 = \$24{,}000}{\$60{,}000} = 40\% \text{ increase}$$

Note from the income statement above that the increase in sales from 20,000 to 21,600 units has resulted in increases in *both* total sales and total variable expenses. It is a common error to overlook the increase in variable expenses when preparing a projected income statement.

7. *a.* A 20% increase in sales would result in 24,000 units being sold next year: 20,000 units × 1.20 = 24,000 units.

	Total	Per Unit	Percent of Sales
Sales (24,000 units)	$1,440,000	$60	100%
Less variable expenses	1,152,000	48*	80%
Contribution margin	288,000	$12	20%
Less fixed expenses.......	210,000†		
Operating income.........	$ 78,000		

*$45 + $3 = $48; $48 ÷ $60 = 80%.
†$240,000 − $30,000 = $210,000.

Note that the change in per unit variable expenses results in a change in both the per unit contribution margin and the CM ratio.

b.

$$\text{Break-even in unit sales} = \frac{\text{Fixed expenses}}{\text{Contribution margin per unit}}$$

$$= \frac{\$210{,}000}{\$12 \text{ per unit}} = 17{,}500$$

$$\text{Break-even in sales dollars} = \frac{\text{Fixed expenses}}{\text{Contribution margin ratio}}$$

$$= \frac{\$210{,}000}{0.20} = \$1{,}050{,}000$$

c. Yes, based on these data the changes should be made. The changes will increase the company's operating income from the present $60,000 to $78,000 per year. Although the changes will also result in a higher break-even point (17,500 units as compared to the present 16,000 units), the company's margin of safety will actually be wider than before:

Margin of safety in dollars = Total sales − Break-even sales
$1,440,000 − $1,050,000 = $390,000

As shown in (5) above, the company's present margin of safety is only $240,000. Thus, several benefits will result from the proposed changes.

Glossary

Visit the Online Learning Centre at **http://www.mcgrawhill.ca/olc/garrison/** for a review of key terms and definitions.

Questions

7–1 What is meant by a product's contribution margin ratio? How is this ratio useful in planning business operations?

7–2 Often the most direct route to a business decision is an incremental analysis. What is meant by an *incremental analysis?*

7–3 Company A's costs are mostly variable, whereas Company B's costs are mostly fixed. When sales increase, which company will tend to realize the greatest increase in profits? Explain.

7–4 What is meant by the term *operating leverage?*

7–5 What is meant by the term *break-even point?*

7–6 A 10% decrease in the selling price of a product will have the same effect on net income before tax as a 10% increase in variable expenses. Do you agree? Why or why not?

7–7 Name three approaches to break-even analysis. Briefly explain how each approach works.

7–8 In response to a request from your immediate supervisor, you have prepared a CVP graph portraying the cost and revenue characteristics of your company's product and operations. Explain how the lines on the graph and the break-even point would change if (*a*) the selling price per unit decreased, (*b*) fixed cost increased throughout the entire range of activity portrayed on the graph, and (*c*) variable cost per unit increased.

7–9 What effect would a 30% income tax rate have on the CVP formula?

7–10 What is meant by the margin of safety?

7–11 Companies X and Y are in the same industry. Company X is highly automated, whereas Company Y relies primarily on labour to make its products. If sales and total expenses in the two companies are about the same, which company would you expect to have the lower margin of safety? Why?

7–12 What is meant by the term *sales mix?* What assumption is usually made concerning sales mix in CVP analysis?

7–13 Explain how a shift in the sales mix could result in both a higher break-even point and a lower operating income.

Exercises

EXERCISE 7–1 Preparing a Contribution Format Income Statement [LO1]
Wheeler Corporation's most recent income statement follows on the next page.

Required:
Prepare a new contribution format income statement under each of the following conditions (consider each case independently):

1. The sales volume increases by 50 units.

	Total	Per Unit
Sales (8,000 units)	$208,000	$26.00
Variable expenses.	144,000	18.00
Contribution margin	64,000	$ 8.00
Fixed expenses.	56,000	
Operating income	$ 8,000	

2. The sales volume declines by 50 units.
3. The sales volume is 7,000 units.

EXERCISE 7–2 Prepare a Cost-Volume-Profit (CVP) Graph [LO2]
Katara Enterprises distributes a single product whose selling price is $36 and whose variable cost is $24 per unit. The company's monthly fixed expense is $12,000.

Required:
1. Prepare a cost-volume-profit graph for the company up to a sales level of 2,000 units.
2. Estimate the company's break-even point in unit sales using your cost-volume-profit graph.

EXERCISE 7–3 Computing and Using the CM Ratio [LO3]
Last month when Harrison Creations, Inc., sold 40,000 units, total sales were $300,000, total variable expenses were $240,000, and total fixed expenses were $45,000.

Required:
1. What is the company's contribution margin (CM) ratio?
2. Estimate the change in the company's operating income if it were to increase its total sales by $1,500.

EXERCISE 7–4 Changes in Variable Costs, Fixed Costs, Selling Price, and Volume [LO4]
Data for Herron Corporation are shown below:

	Per Unit	Percent of Sales
Selling price	$75	100%
Variable expenses	45	60%
Contribution margin	$30	40%

Fixed expenses are $75,000 per month and the company is selling 3,000 units per month.

Required:
1. The marketing manager argues that an $8,000 increase in the monthly advertising budget would increase monthly sales by $15,000. Should the advertising budget be increased?
2. Refer to the original data. Management is considering using higher-quality components that would increase the variable cost by $3 per unit. The marketing manager believes the higher-quality product would increase sales by 15% per month. Should the higher-quality components be used?

EXERCISE 7–5 Compute the Break-Even Point [LO5]
Maxson Products distributes a single product, a woven basket whose selling price is $8 and whose variable cost is $6 per unit. The company's monthly fixed expense is $5,500.

Required:
1. Solve for the company's break-even point in unit sales using the equation method.
2. Solve for the company's break-even point in sales dollars using the equation method and the CM ratio.
3. Solve for the company's break-even point in unit sales using the contribution margin method.
4. Solve for the company's break-even point in sales dollars using the contribution margin method and the CM ratio.

EXERCISE 7–6 Compute the Level of Sales Required to Attain a Target Profit [LO6]
Liman Corporation has a single product whose selling price is $140 and whose variable cost is $60 per unit. The company's monthly fixed expense is $40,000.

Required:
1. Using the equation method, solve for the unit sales that are required to earn a target profit before tax of $6,000.
2. Using the contribution margin approach, solve for the dollar sales that are required to earn a target profit before tax of $8,000.
3. Calculate the number of units that needs to be sold to earn an after tax income of $7,700 assigning a tax rate of 30%.

EXERCISE 7–7 Compute the Margin of Safety [LO7]
Mohan Corporation is a distributor of a sun umbrella used at resort hotels. Data concerning the next month's budget appear below:

Selling price	$25 per unit
Variable expense	$15 per unit
Fixed expense	$8,500 per month
Unit sales	1,000 units per month

Required:
1. Compute the company's margin of safety.
2. Compute the company's margin of safety as a percentage of its sales.

EXERCISE 7–8 Compute and Use the Degree of Operating Leverage [LO8]
Eneliko Company installs home theatre systems. The company's most recent monthly contribution format income statement appears below:

	Amount	Percent of Sales
Sales.	$120,000	100%
Variable expenses.	84,000	70%
Contribution margin	36,000	30%
Fixed expenses	24,000	
Operating income	$ 12,000	

Required:
1. Compute the company's degree of operating leverage.
2. Using the degree of operating leverage, estimate the impact on operating income of a 10% increase in sales.
3. Verify your estimate from part (2) above by constructing a new contribution format income statement for the company assuming a 10% increase in sales.

EXERCISE 7–9 Compute the Break-Even Point for a Multiproduct Company [LO9]
Lucky Products markets two computer games: Predator and Runway. A contribution format income statement for a recent month for the two games appears below:

	Predator	Runway	Total
Sales.	$100,000	$50,000	$150,000
Variable expenses.	25,000	5,000	30,000
Contribution margin	$ 75,000	$45,000	120,000
Fixed expenses			90,000
Operating income			$ 30,000

Required:
1. Compute the overall contribution margin (CM) ratio for the company.

2. Compute the overall break-even point for the company in sales dollars.
3. Verify the overall break-even point for the company by constructing a contribution format income statement showing the appropriate levels of sales for the two products.

EXERCISE 7–10 Break-Even Analysis; Target Profit; Margin of Safety; CM Ratio [LO1, LO3, LO5, LO6, LO7]

Pringle Company distributes a single product. The company's sales and expenses for a recent month follow:

	Total	Per Unit
Sales	$600,000	$40
Variable expenses	420,000	28
Contribution margin	180,000	$12
Fixed expenses	150,000	
Operating income	$ 30,000	

Required:

1. What is the monthly break-even point in units sold and in sales dollars?
2. Without performing computations, what is the total contribution margin at the break-even point?
3. How many units would have to be sold each month to earn a target profit of $18,000? Use the contribution margin method. Verify your answer by preparing a contribution format income statement at the target level of sales.
4. Refer to the original data. Compute the company's margin of safety in both dollar and percentage terms.
5. What is the company's CM ratio? If monthly sales increase by $80,000 and there is no change in fixed expenses, by how much would you expect monthly operating income to increase?

EXERCISE 7–11 Break-Even Analysis and CVP Graphing [LO2, LO4, LO5]

Chi Omega Sorority is planning its annual Riverboat Extravaganza. The Extravaganza committee has assembled the following expected costs for the event:

Dinner (per person)	$7
Favours and program (per person)	$3
Band	$1,500
Tickets and advertising	$700
Riverboat rental	$4,800
Floorshow and strolling entertainers	$1,000

The committee members would like to charge $30 per person for the evening's activities.

Required:

1. Compute the break-even point for the Extravaganza (in terms of the number of persons that must attend).
2. Assume only 250 persons attended the Extravaganza last year. If the same number attend this year, what price per ticket must be charged to break even?
3. Refer to the original data ($30 ticket price per person). Prepare a CVP graph for the Extravaganza from zero tickets up to 600 tickets sold.

EXERCISE 7–12 Using a Contribution Format Income Statement [LO1, LO4]

Porter Company's most recent contribution format income statement is shown below:

	Total	Per Unit
Sales (30,000 units)	$150,000	$5
Variable expenses	90,000	3
Contribution margin	60,000	$2
Fixed expenses	50,000	
Operating income	$ 10,000	

Required:

Prepare a new contribution format income statement under each of the following conditions (consider each case independently):

1. The number of units sold increases by 15%.
2. The selling price decreases by 50 cents per unit, and the number of units sold increases by 20%.
3. The selling price increases by 50 cents per unit, fixed expenses increase by $10,000, and the number of units sold decreases by 5%.
4. Variable expenses increase by 20 cents per unit, the selling price increases by 12%, and the number of units sold decreases by 10%.

EXERCISE 7–13 Missing Data; Basic CVP Concepts [LO1]

Fill in the missing amounts in each of the eight case situations below. Each case is independent of the others. (Hint: One way to find the missing amounts would be to prepare a contribution format income statement for each case, enter the known data, and then compute the missing items.)

a. Assume that only one product is being sold in each of the four following case situations:

Case	Units Sold	Sales	Variable Expenses	Contribution Margin per Unit	Fixed Expenses	Operating Income (Loss)
1	9,000	$270,000	$162,000	$?	$90,000	$?
2	?	$350,000	?	$15	$170,000	$40,000
3	20,000	?	$280,000	$6	?	$35,000
4	5,000	$160,000	?	?	$82,000	($12,000)

b. Assume that more than one product is being sold in each of the four following case situations:

Case	Sales	Variable Expenses	Average Contribution Margin (Percent)	Fixed Expenses	Operating Income (Loss)
1	$450,000	$?	40%	$?	$65,000
2	$200,000	$130,000	?	$60,000	?
3	?	?	80%	$470,000	$90,000
4	$300,000	$90,000	?	?	($15,000)

EXERCISE 7–14 Break-Even and Target Profit Analysis [LO3, LO4, LO5, LO6]

Super Sales Company is the exclusive distributor for a revolutionary bookbag. The product sells for $60 per unit and has a CM ratio of 40%. The company's fixed expenses are $360,000 per year.

Required:

1. What are the variable expenses per unit?
2. Using the equation method:
   a. What is the break-even point in units and in sales dollars?
   b. What sales level in units and in sales dollars is required to earn an operating income of $90,000?
   c. Assume that through negotiation with the manufacturer the Super Sales Company is able to reduce its variable expenses by $3 per unit. What is the company's new break-even point in units and in sales dollars?
3. Repeat (2) above using the contribution margin method.
4. Referring to the original data, what sales level in dollars is required to earn an annual profit of $90,000 after taxes if the company's tax rate is 30%?

EXERCISE 7–15 Operating Leverage [LO4, LO8]

Superior Door Company sells prehung doors to home builders. The doors are sold for $60 each. Variable costs are $42 per door, and fixed costs total $450,000 per year. The company is currently selling 30,000 doors per year.

Required:

1. Prepare a contribution format income statement for the company at the present level of sales and compute the degree of operating leverage.
2. Management is confident that the company can sell 37,500 doors next year (an increase of 7,500 doors, or 25%, over current sales). Compute the following:
   a. The expected percentage increase in operating income for next year.
   b. The expected operating income for next year. (Do not prepare an income statement; use the degree of operating leverage to compute your answer.)

EXERCISE 7–16 Break-Even and Target Profit Analysis [LO4, LO5, LO6]
Reveen Products sells camping equipment. One of the company's products, a camp lantern, sells for $90 per unit. Variable expenses are $63 per lantern, and fixed expenses associated with the lantern total $135,000 per month.

Required:

1. Compute the company's break-even point in number of lanterns and in total sales dollars.
2. If the variable expenses per lantern increase as a percentage of the selling price, will it result in a higher or a lower break-even point? Why? (Assume that the fixed expenses remain unchanged.)
3. At present, the company is selling 8,000 lanterns per month. The sales manager is convinced that a 10% reduction in the selling price will result in a 25% increase in the number of lanterns sold each month. Prepare two contribution income statements, one under present operating conditions, and one as operations would appear after the proposed changes. Show both total and per unit data on your statements.
4. Refer to the data in (3) above. How many lanterns would have to be sold at the new selling price to yield a minimum operating income of $72,000 per month?

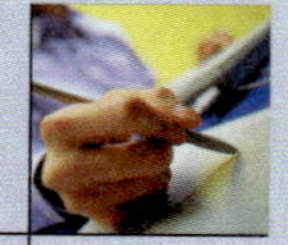

EXERCISE 7–17 Multiproduct Break-Even Analysis [LO9]
Okabee Enterprises is the distributor for two products, Model A100 and Model B900. Monthly sales and the contribution margin ratios for the two products follow:

	Product		
	Model A100	Model B900	Total
Sales	$700,000	$300,000	$1,000,000
Contribution margin ratio	60%	70%	?

The company's fixed expenses total $598,500 per month.

Required:

1. Prepare a contribution format income statement for the company as a whole.
2. Compute the break-even point for the company based on the current sales mix.
3. If sales increase by $50,000 per month, by how much would you expect operating income to increase? What are your assumptions?

Problems

PROBLEM 7–18 Basic CVP Analysis [LO1, LO3, LO4, LO5, LO8]
Stratford Company distributes a lightweight lawn chair that sells for $15 per unit. Variable costs are $6 per unit, and fixed costs total $180,000 annually.

Required:

Answer the following independent questions:

1. What is the product's CM ratio?
2. Use the CM ratio to determine the break-even point in sales dollars.
3. The company estimates that sales will increase by $45,000 during the coming year due to increased demand. By how much should operating income increase?
4. Assume that the operating results for last year were as follows:

Sales	$360,000
Variable expenses	144,000
Contribution margin	216,000
Fixed expenses	180,000
Operating income	$ 36,000

a. Compute the degree of operating leverage at the current level of sales.
b. The president expects sales to increase by 15% next year. By how much should operating income increase?

5. Refer to the original data. Assume that the company sold 28,000 units last year. The sales manager is convinced that a 10% reduction in the selling price, combined with a $70,000 increase in advertising expenditures, would cause annual sales in units to increase by 50%. Prepare two contribution format income statements, one showing the results of last year's operations and one showing what the results of operations would be if these changes were made. Would you recommend that the company do as the sales manager suggests?
6. Refer to the original data. Assume again that the company sold 28,000 units last year. The president feels that it would be unwise to change the selling price. Instead, he wants to increase the sales commission by $2 per unit. He thinks that this move, combined with some increase in advertising, would cause annual sales to double. By how much could advertising be increased with profits remaining unchanged? Do not prepare an income statement; use the incremental analysis approach.

PROBLEM 7–19 Basics of CVP Analysis; Cost Structure [LO1, LO3, LO4, LO5, LO6]

Memofax, Inc., produces memory enhancement kits for fax machines. Sales have been very erratic, with some months showing a profit and some months showing a loss. The company's contribution format income statement for the most recent month is given below:

Sales (13,500 units at $20 per unit)	$270,000
Variable expenses	189,000
Contribution margin	81,000
Fixed expenses	90,000
Operating loss	$ (9,000)

Required:

1. Compute the company's CM ratio and its break-even point in both units and dollars.
2. The sales manager feels that an $8,000 increase in the monthly advertising budget, combined with an intensified effort by the sales staff, will result in a $70,000 increase in monthly sales. If the sales manager is right, what will be the effect on the company's monthly operating income or loss? (Use the incremental approach in preparing your answer.)
3. Refer to the original data. The president is convinced that a 10% reduction in the selling price, combined with an increase of $35,000 in the monthly advertising budget, will cause unit sales to double. What will the new contribution format income statement look like if these changes are adopted?
4. Refer to the original data. The company's advertising agency thinks that a new package would help sales. The new package being proposed would increase packaging costs by $0.60 per unit. Assuming no other changes, how many units would have to be sold each month to earn a profit of $4,500?
5. Refer to the original data. By automating certain operations, the company could slash its variable expenses in half. However, fixed costs would increase by $118,000 per month.
   a. Compute the new CM ratio and the new break-even point in both units and dollars.
   b. Assume that the company expects to sell 20,000 units next month. Prepare two contribution format income statements, one assuming that operations are not automated and one assuming that they are.
   c. Would you recommend that the company automate its operations? Explain.

PROBLEM 7–20 Sales Mix; Multiproduct Break-Even Analysis [LO9]
Marlin Company, a wholesale distributor, has been operating for only a few months. The company sells three products—sinks, mirrors, and vanities. Budgeted sales by product and in total for the coming month are shown below:

	Product						Total	
	Sinks		Mirrors		Vanities			
Percentage of total sales	48%		20%		32%		100%	
Sales	$240,000	100%	$100,000	100%	$160,000	100%	$500,000	100%
Variable expenses	72,000	30%	80,000	80%	88,000	55%	240,000	48%
Contribution margin	$168,000	70%	$ 20,000	20%	$ 72,000	45%	260,000	52%
Fixed expenses							223,600	
Operating income							$ 36,400	

$$\text{Break-even point in sales dollars} = \frac{\text{Fixed expenses}}{\text{CM ratio}} = \frac{\$223{,}600}{0.52} = \$430{,}000$$

As shown by these data, operating income is budgeted at $36,400 for the month, and break-even sales at $430,000.

Assume that actual sales for the month total $500,000 as planned. Actual sales by product are: sinks, $160,000; mirrors, $200,000; and vanities, $140,000.

Required:

1. Prepare a contribution format income statement for the month based on actual sales data. Present the income statement in the format shown above.
2. Compute the break-even point in sales dollars for the month, based on your actual data.
3. Considering the fact that the company met its $500,000 sales budget for the month, the president is shocked at the results shown on your income statement in (1) above. Prepare a brief memo for the president explaining why both the operating results and the break-even point in sales dollars are different from what was budgeted.

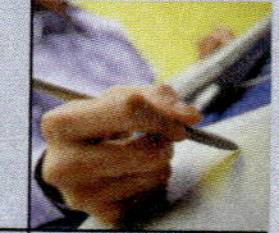

PROBLEM 7–21 Basic CVP Analysis; Graphing [LO1, LO2, LO4, LO5]
Shirts Unlimited operates a chain of shirt stores around the country. The stores carry many styles of shirts that are all sold at the same price. To encourage sales personnel to be aggressive in their sales efforts, the company pays a substantial sales commission on each shirt sold. Sales personnel also receive a small basic salary.

The following worksheet contains cost and revenue data for Store 36. These data are typical of the company's many outlets:

Microsoft Excel - Problem 7-21 screen capture.xls

	A	B	C
1		*Per Shirt*	
2	Selling price	$ 40.00	
3			
4	Variable expenses:		
5	Invoice cost	$ 18.00	
6	Sales commission	7.00	
7	Total variable expenses	$ 25.00	
8			
9		*Annual*	
10	Fixed expenses:		
11	Advertising	$ 80,000	
12	Rent	150,000	
13	Salaries	70,000	
14	Total fixed expenses	$300,000	
15			

Sheet1 / Sheet2 / Sheet3

Shirts Unlimited is a fairly new organization. The company has asked you, as a member of its planning group, to assist in some basic analysis of its stores and company policies.

Required:

1. Calculate the annual break-even point in dollar sales and in unit sales for Store 36.
2. Prepare a CVP graph showing cost and revenue data for Store 36 from zero shirts up to 30,000 shirts sold each year. Clearly indicate the break-even point on the graph.
3. If 19,000 shirts are sold in a year, what would be Store 36's operating income or loss?
4. The company is considering paying the store manager of Store 36 an incentive commission of $3 per shirt (in addition to the salesperson's commissions). If this change is made, what will be the new break-even point in dollar sales and in unit sales?
5. Refer to the original data. As an alternative to (4) above, the company is considering paying the store manager a $3 commission on each shirt sold in excess of the break-even point. If this change is made, what will be the store's operating income or loss if 23,500 shirts are sold in a year?
6. Refer to the original data. The company is considering eliminating sales commissions entirely in its stores and increasing fixed salaries by $107,000 annually.
   a. If this change is made, what will be the new break-even point in dollar sales and in unit sales in Store 36?
   b. Would you recommend that the change be made? Explain.

PROBLEM 7–22 Break-Even Analysis; Pricing [LO1, LO4, LO5]

Detmer Holdings AG of Zurich, Switzerland, has just introduced a new fashion watch for which the company is trying to find an optimal selling price. Marketing studies suggest that the company can increase sales by 5,000 units for each SFr2 per unit reduction in the selling price. (SFr2 denotes 2 Swiss francs.) The company's present selling price is SFr90 per unit, and variable expenses are SFr60 per unit. Fixed expenses are SFr840,000 per year. The present annual sales volume (at the SFr90 selling price) is 25,000 units.

Required:

1. What is the present yearly operating income or loss?
2. What is the present break-even point in units and in Swiss franc sales?
3. Assuming that the marketing studies are correct, what is the *maximum* profit that the company can earn yearly? At how many units and at what selling price per unit would the company generate this profit?
4. What would be the break-even point in units and in Swiss franc sales using the selling price you determined in (3) above (i.e., the selling price at the level of maximum profits)? Why is this break-even point different from the break-even point you computed in (2) above?

PROBLEM 7–23 Graphing; Incremental Analysis; Operating Leverage [LO2, LO4, LO5, LO6, LO8]

Teri Hall has recently opened Sheer Elegance, Inc., a store specializing in fashionable stockings. Ms. Hall has just completed a course in managerial accounting, and she believes that she can apply certain aspects of the course to her business. She is particularly interested in adopting the cost-volume-profit (CVP) approach to decision making. Thus, she has prepared the following analysis:

Sales price per pair of stockings	$2.00
Variable expense per pair of stockings.	0.80
Contribution margin per pair of stockings	$1.20
Fixed expense per year:	
Building rental	$12,000
Equipment depreciation	3,000
Selling	30,000
Administrative	15,000
Total fixed expense.	$60,000

Required:

1. How many pairs of stockings must be sold to break even? What does this represent in total dollar sales?

2. Prepare a CVP graph for the store from zero pairs up to 70,000 pairs of stockings sold each year. Indicate the break-even point on the graph.
3. How many pairs of stockings must be sold to earn a $9,000 target profit for the first year?
4. Ms. Hall now has one full-time and one part-time salesperson working in the store. It will cost her an additional $8,000 per year to convert the part-time position to a full-time position. Ms. Hall believes that the change would bring in an additional $20,000 in sales each year. Should she convert the position? Use the incremental approach. (Do not prepare an income statement.)
5. Refer to the original data. Actual operating results for the first year are as follows:

Sales.	$125,000
Variable expenses.	50,000
Contribution margin	75,000
Fixed expenses	60,000
Operating income	$ 15,000

a. What is the store's degree of operating leverage?
b. Ms. Hall is confident that with some effort she can increase sales by 20% next year. What would be the expected percentage increase in operating income? Use the degree of operating leverage concept to compute your answer.

PROBLEM 7–24 Break-Even and Target Profit Analysis [LO5, LO6]
The Marbury Stein Shop sells steins from all parts of the world. The owner of the shop, Clint Marbury, is thinking of expanding his operations by hiring local college students, on a commission basis, to sell steins at the local college. The steins will bear the school emblem.

These steins must be ordered from the manufacturer three months in advance, and because of the unique emblem of each college, they cannot be returned. The steins would cost Mr. Marbury $15 each with a minimum order of 200 steins. Any additional steins would have to be ordered in increments of 50.

Since Mr. Marbury's plan would not require any additional facilities, the only costs associated with the project would be the cost of the steins and the cost of sales commissions. The selling price of the steins would be $30 each. Mr. Marbury would pay the students a commission of $6 for each stein sold.

Required:
1. To make the project worthwhile in terms of his own time, Mr. Marbury would require a $7,200 operating income for the first six months of the venture. What level of sales in units and dollars would be required to attain this target operating income? Show all computations.
2. Assume that the venture is undertaken and an order is placed for 200 steins. What would be Mr. Marbury's break-even point in units and in sales dollars? Show computations, and explain the reasoning behind your answer.

PROBLEM 7–25 Sales Mix; Break-Even Analysis; Margin of Safety [LO7, LO9]
Puleva Milenario SA, a company located in Toledo, Spain, manufactures and sells two models of luxuriously finished cutlery—Alvaro and Bazan. Present revenue, cost, and unit sales data for the two products appear below. All currency amounts are stated in terms of euros, which are indicated by the symbol €.

	Alvaro	Bazan
Selling price per unit.	€4.00	€6.00
Variable expenses per unit	€2.40	€1.20
Number of units sold monthly.	200 units	80 units

Fixed expenses are €660 per month.

Required:
1. Assuming the sales mix above, do the following:
   a. Prepare a contribution format income statement showing both euro and percent columns for each product and for the company as a whole.

   b. Compute the break-even point in euros for the company as a whole and the margin of safety in both euros and percent of sales.
2. The company has developed another product, Cano, that the company plans to sell for €8 each. At this price, the company expects to sell 40 units per month of the product. The variable expense would be €6 per unit. The company's fixed expenses would not change.
   a. Prepare another contribution format income statement, including sales of Cano (sales of the other two products would not change).
   b. Compute the company's new break-even point in euros for the company as a whole and the new margin of safety in both euros and percent of sales.
3. The president of the company was puzzled by your analysis. He did not understand why the break-even point has gone up even though there has been no increase in fixed expenses and the addition of the new product has increased the total contribution margin. Explain to the president what has happened.

PROBLEM 7–26 Sales Mix; Multiproduct Break-Even Analysis [LO9]

Topper Sports, Inc., produces high-quality sports equipment. The company's Racket Division manufactures three tennis rackets—the Standard, the Deluxe, and the Pro—that are widely used in amateur play. Selected information on the rackets is given below:

	Standard	Deluxe	Pro
Selling price per racket	$40.00	$60.00	$90.00
Variable expenses per racket:			
Production	$22.00	$27.00	$31.50
Selling (5% of selling price)	$2.00	$3.00	$4.50

All sales are made through the company's own retail outlets. The Racket Division has the following fixed costs:

	Per Month
Fixed production costs	$120,000
Advertising expense	100,000
Administrative salaries.	50,000
Total.	$270,000

Sales, in units, over the past two months have been as follows:

	Standard	Deluxe	Pro	Total
April	2,000	1,000	5,000	8,000
May	8,000	1,000	3,000	12,000

Required:

1. Using the contribution approach, prepare an income statement for April and an income statement for May, with the following headings:

	Standard		Deluxe		Pro		Total	
	Amount	Percent	Amount	Percent	Amount	Percent	Amount	Percent
Sales . . .								
Etc.								

   Place the fixed expenses only in the Total column. Do not show percentages for the fixed expenses.
2. Upon seeing the income statements in (1) above, the president stated, "I can't believe this! We sold 50% more rackets in May than in April, yet profits went down. It's obvious that costs are out of control in that division." What other explanation can you give for the drop in operating income?
3. Compute the Racket Division's break-even point in dollar sales for April.

4. Has May's break-even point in dollar sales gone up or down from April's break-even point? Explain without computing a break-even point for May.
5. Assume that sales of the Standard racket increase by $20,000. What would be the effect on operating income? What would be the effect if Pro racket sales increased by $20,000? Do not prepare income statements; use the incremental analysis approach in determining your answer.

PROBLEM 7–27 Various CVP Questions: Break-Even Point; Cost Structure; Target Sales [LO1, LO3, LO4, LO5, LO6, LO8]

Tyrene Products manufactures recreational equipment. One of the company's products, a skateboard, sells for $37.50. The skateboards are manufactured in an antiquated plant that relies heavily on direct labour workers. Thus, variable costs are high, totalling $22.50 per skateboard.

Over the past year the company sold 40,000 skateboards, with the following operating results:

Sales (40,000 skateboards)	$1,500,000
Variable expenses	900,000
Contribution margin	600,000
Fixed expenses	480,000
Operating income	$ 120,000

Management is anxious to maintain and perhaps even improve its present level of income from the skateboards.

Required:

1. Compute (*a*) the CM ratio and the break-even point in skateboards, and (*b*) the degree of operating leverage at last year's level of sales.
2. Due to an increase in labour rates, the company estimates that variable costs will increase by $3 per skateboard next year. If this change takes place and the selling price per skateboard remains constant at $37.50, what will be the new CM ratio and the new break-even point in skateboards?
3. Refer to the data in (2) above. If the expected change in variable costs takes place, how many skateboards will have to be sold next year to earn the same operating income ($120,000) as last year?
4. Refer again to the data in (2) above. The president has decided that the company may have to raise the selling price of its skateboards. If Tyrene Products wants to maintain *the same CM ratio as last year,* what selling price per skateboard must it charge next year to cover the increased labour costs?
5. Refer to the original data. The company is considering the construction of a new, automated plant. The new plant would slash variable costs by 40%, but it would cause fixed costs to increase by 90%. If the new plant is built, what would be the company's new CM ratio and new break-even point in skateboards?
6. Refer to the data in (5) above.
   a. If the new plant is built, how many skateboards will have to be sold next year to earn the same operating income, $120,000, as last year?
   b. Assume that the new plant is constructed and that next year the company manufactures and sells 40,000 skateboards (the same number as sold last year). Prepare a contribution format income statement, and compute the degree of operating leverage.
   c. If you were a member of top management, would you have been in favour of constructing the new plant? Explain.
7. Refer to the data in part (a) of item 6 above. If the new plant is built, how many skateboards will have to be sold next year to earn an after-tax net income of $120,000 assuming that the company tax rate is 30%?

PROBLEM 7–28 Interpretive Questions on the CVP Graph [LO2, LO5]

A CVP graph, as illustrated on the next page, is a useful technique for showing relationships between an organization's costs, volume, and profits.

Required:

1. Identify the numbered components in the CVP graph.

2. State the effect of each of the following actions on line 3, line 9, and the break-even point. For line 3 and line 9, state whether the action will cause the line to:
   Remain unchanged.
   Shift upward.
   Shift downward.
   Have a steeper slope (i.e., rotate upward).
   Have a flatter slope (i.e., rotate downward).
   Shift upward *and* have a steeper slope.
   Shift upward *and* have a flatter slope.
   Shift downward *and* have a steeper slope.
   Shift downward *and* have a flatter slope.

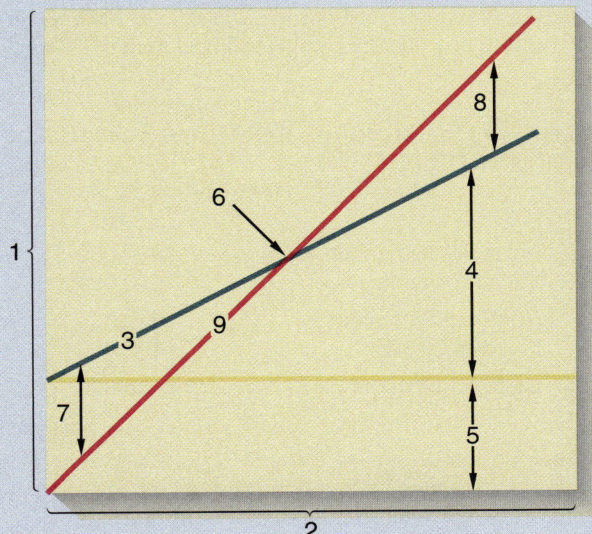

In the case of the break-even point, state whether the action will cause the break-even point to:
   Remain unchanged.
   Increase.
   Decrease.
   Probably change, but the direction is uncertain.

Treat each case independently.

x. *Example*. Fixed costs are increased by $20,000 each period.
   Answer (see choices above): Line 3: Shift upward.
   Line 9: Remain unchanged.
   Break-even point: Increase.

a. The unit selling price is decreased from $30 to $27.

b. The per unit variable costs are increased from $12 to $15.

c. The total fixed costs are reduced by $40,000.

d. Five thousand fewer units are sold during the period than were budgeted.

e. Due to purchasing a robot to perform a task that was previously done by workers, fixed costs are increased by $25,000 per period, and variable costs are reduced by $8 per unit.

f. As a result of a decrease in the cost of materials, both unit variable costs and the selling price are decreased by $3.

g. Advertising costs are increased by $50,000 per period, resulting in a 10% increase in the number of units sold.

h. Due to paying salespeople a commission rather than a flat salary, fixed costs are reduced by $21,000 per period, and unit variable costs are increased by $6.

PROBLEM 7–29 Changes in Fixed and Variable Costs; Break-Even and Target Profit Analysis [LO4, LO5, LO6]

Novelties, Inc., produces and sells highly faddish products directed toward the preteen market. A new product has come onto the market that the company is anxious to produce and sell. Enough capacity exists in the company's plant to produce 30,000 units each month. Variable costs to manufacture and sell one unit would be $1.60, and fixed costs would total $40,000 per month.

The Marketing Department predicts that demand for the product will exceed the 30,000 units that the company is able to produce. Additional production capacity can be rented from another company at a fixed cost of $2,000 per month. Variable costs in the rented facility would total $1.75 per unit, due to somewhat less efficient operations than in the main plant. The product would sell for $2.50 per unit.

Required:

1. Compute the monthly break-even point for the new product in units and in total dollar sales. Show all computations in good form.
2. How many units must be sold each month to make a monthly operating income of $9,000?
3. If the sales manager receives a bonus of 15 cents for each unit sold in excess of the break-even point, how many units must be sold each month to earn a return of 25% on the monthly investment in fixed costs?

PROBLEM 7–30 Changes in Cost Structure; Break-Even Analysis; Operating Leverage; Margin of Safety [LO4, LO5, LO7, LO8]

Frieden Company's contribution format income statement for the most recent month is given below:

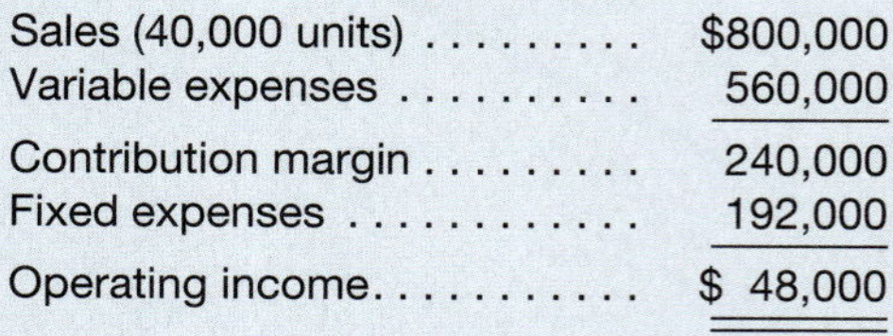

Sales (40,000 units)	$800,000
Variable expenses	560,000
Contribution margin	240,000
Fixed expenses	192,000
Operating income.	$ 48,000

The industry in which Frieden Company operates is quite sensitive to cyclical movements in the economy. Thus, profits vary considerably from year to year according to general economic conditions. The company has a large amount of unused capacity and is studying ways of improving profits.

Required:

1. New equipment has come on the market that would allow Frieden Company to automate a portion of its operations. Variable costs would be reduced by $6 per unit. However, fixed costs would increase to a total of $432,000 each month. Prepare two contribution format income statements, one showing present operations and one showing how operations would appear if the new equipment is purchased. Show an Amount column, a Per Unit column, and a Percent column on each statement. Do not show percentages for the fixed costs.
2. Refer to the income statements in (1) above. For both present operations and the proposed new operations, compute (*a*) the degree of operating leverage, (*b*) the break-even point in dollars, and (*c*) the margin of safety in both dollar and percentage terms.
3. Refer again to the data in (1) above. As a manager, what factor would be paramount in your mind in deciding whether to purchase the new equipment? (You may assume that ample funds are available to make the purchase.)
4. Refer to the original data. Rather than purchase new equipment, the marketing manager argues that the company's marketing strategy should be changed. Instead of paying sales commissions, which are included in variable expenses, the marketing manager suggests that salespersons be paid fixed salaries and that the company invest heavily in advertising. The marketing manager claims that this new approach would increase unit sales by 50% without any change in selling price; the company's new monthly fixed expenses would be $240,000; and its operating income would increase by 25%. Compute the break-even point in dollar sales for the company under the new marketing strategy. Do you agree with the marketing manager's proposal?

Problem 7–31 Changes in Cost Structure, Break-Even Analysis: Indifference [LO4, LO5, LO6]

Szeto Manufacturing Co. is presently manufacturing a new product for the following costs:

Direct materials per unit	$6
Direct labour per unit	0.8 DLH @$15/DLH
Variable overhead per unit	2/3 of direct labour costs

Fixed manufacturing costs	$1,200,000
Fixed selling and administration costs	$2,000,000
Selling price per unit	$40
Variable selling costs per unit	$2

The production manager feels that savings could be achieved by automating the plant. If the plant were automated, the costs would shift as follows:

Direct materials cost per unit	$5.50
Direct labour per unit	0.5 DLH @$20/DLH
Variable overhead per unit	½ of direct labour costs
Fixed manufacturing costs	$1,600,000

There would be no change to any other costs or to the selling price.

Required

1. Calculate the break-even point in annual units of sales if the new product if Szeto Manufacturing uses the:
   a. present method of production.
   b. automated method of production.
2. Calculate the annual number of units of sales up to which Szeto Manufacturing would be indifferent about which manufacturing method is used. If demand exceeds this amount, which method of production should be used?
3. Identify four factors that Szeto Manufacturing might consider before selecting either the present method of production or the automated method of production.

(CGA-Canada adapted)

PROBLEM 7–32 Changes in Cost Structure, Break-Even Analysis, Target Profit [LO5, LO6, LO8]

Warton Ltd. is considering replacing an existing machine with a new and faster machine that will produce a more reliable product (that is, better tolerances). The switch to a new machine resulting in a superior product is expected to allow Warton to increase its sales price for the product. The switch will increase fixed costs, but not the variable costs. Cost and revenue estimates are as follows.

Cost Item	Old Machine	New Machine
Monthly fixed costs	$120,000	$250,000
Variable cost per unit	14	14
Sales price per unit	18	20

Required

1. Determine the break-even point in units for the two machines.
2. Determine the sales level in units at which the new machine will achieve a 10% target profit-to-sales ratio (ignore taxes).
3. Determine the sales level at which profits will be the same for either the old or new machine.
4. Which machine represents a lower risk if demand is uncertain? Explain.

(CGA-Canada adapted)

Cases

CASE 7–33 Break-Evens for Individual Products in a Multiproduct Company [LO5, LO9]

Jasmine Park encountered her boss, Rick Gompers, at the pop machine in the lobby. Rick is the vice-president of marketing at Down South Lures Corporation. Jasmine was puzzled by some calculations she had been doing, so she asked him:

Jasmine: "Rick, I'm not sure how to go about answering the questions that came up at the meeting with the president yesterday."

Rick: "What's the problem?"

Jasmine: "The president wanted to know the break even for each of the company's products, but I am having trouble figuring them out."

Rick: "I'm sure you can handle it, Jasmine. And, by the way, I need your analysis on my desk tomorrow morning at 8:00 sharp so I can look at it before the follow-up meeting at 9:00."

Down South Lures makes three fishing lures in its manufacturing facility in Toronto. Data concerning these products appear below.

	Frog	Minnow	Worm
Normal annual sales volume	100,000	200,000	300,000
Unit selling price	$2.00	$1.40	$0.80
Variable cost per unit	$1.20	$0.80	$0.50

Total fixed expenses for the entire company are $282,000 per year.

All three products are sold in highly competitive markets, so the company is unable to raise its prices without losing unacceptable numbers of customers.

The company has no work in process or finished goods inventories due to an extremely effective just-in-time manufacturing system.

Required:

1. What is the company's overall break-even point in total sales dollars?
2. Of the total fixed costs of $282,000, $18,000 could be avoided if the Frog lure product were dropped, $96,000 if the Minnow lure product were dropped, and $60,000 if the Worm lure product were dropped. The remaining fixed costs of $108,000 consist of common fixed costs such as administrative salaries and rent on the factory building that could be avoided only by going out of business entirely.
   a. What is the break-even point in units for each product?
   b. If the company sells exactly the break-even quantity of each product, what will be the overall profit of the company? Explain this result.

CASE 7–34 Cost Structure; Break-Even Point; Target Profits [LO4, LO5, LO6]

Marston Corporation manufactures disposable thermometers that are sold to hospitals through a network of independent sales agents located in the United States and Canada. These sales agents sell a variety of products to hospitals in addition to Marston's disposable thermometer. The sales agents are currently paid an 18% commission on sales, and this commission rate was used when Marston's management prepared the following budgeted income statement for the upcoming year.

MARSTON CORPORATION Budgeted Income Statement		
Sales		$30,000,000
Cost of goods sold:		
Variable	$17,400,000	
Fixed	2,800,000	20,200,000
Gross margin		9,800,000
Selling and administrative expenses:		
Commissions	5,400,000	
Fixed advertising expense	800,000	
Fixed administrative expense	3,200,000	9,400,000
Operating income		$ 400,000

Since the completion of the above statement, Marston's management has learned that the independent sales agents are demanding an increase in the commission rate to 20% of sales for the upcoming year. This would be the third increase in commissions demanded by the independent sales agents in five years. As a result, Marston's management has decided to investigate the possibility of hiring its own sales staff to replace the independent sales agents.

Marston's controller estimates that the company will have to hire eight salespeople to cover the current market area, and the total annual payroll cost of these employees will be about $700,000, including fringe benefits. The salespeople will also be paid commissions of 10% of sales. Travel and entertainment expenses are expected to total about $400,000 for the year. The company will also have to hire a sales manager and support staff whose salaries and fringe benefits will come to $200,000 per year. To make up for the promotions that the independent sales agents had been running on behalf of Marston, management believes that the company's budget for fixed advertising expenses should be increased by $500,000.

Required:

1. Assuming sales of $30,000,000, construct a budgeted contribution format income statement for the upcoming year for each of the following alternatives:
   a. The independent sales agents' commission rate remains unchanged at 18%.
   b. The independent sales agents' commission rate increases to 20%.
   c. The company employs its own sales force.
2. Calculate Marston Corporation's break-even point in sales dollars for the upcoming year assuming the following:
   a. The independent sales agents' commission rate remains unchanged at 18%.
   b. The independent sales agents' commission rate increases to 20%.
   c. The company employs its own sales force.
3. Refer to your answer to (1)(b) above. If the company employs its own sales force, what volume of sales would be necessary to generate the operating income the company would realize if sales are $30,000,000 and the company continues to sell through agents (at a 20% commission rate)?
4. Determine the volume of sales at which operating income would be equal regardless of whether Marston Corporation sells through agents (at a 20% commission rate) or employs its own sales force.
5. Prepare a graph on which you plot the profits for both of the following alternatives.
   a. The independent sales agents' commission rate increases to 20%.
   b. The company employs its own sales force.
   On the graph, use total sales revenue as the measure of activity.
6. Write a memo to the president of Marston Corporation in which you make a recommendation as to whether the company should continue to use independent sales agents (at a 20% commission rate) or employ its own sales force. Fully explain the reasons for your recommendation in the memo.

(CMA, adapted)

CASE 7–35 Break-Even Analysis with Step Fixed Costs [LO5, LO6]

The Cardiac Care Department at St. Andrew's General Clinics has a capacity of 70 beds and operates 24 hours a day year-around. The measure of activity in the department is patient-days, where one patient-day represents one patient occupying a bed for one day. The average revenue per patient-day is $480 and the average variable cost per patient-day is $180. The fixed cost of the department (not including personnel costs) is $2,740,000.

The only personnel directly employed by the Cardiac Care Department are aides, nurses, and supervising nurses. The clinic has minimum staffing requirements for the department based on total annual patient-days in Cardiac Care. Clinic requirements, beginning at the minimum expected level of activity, follow:

Annual Patient-Days	Aides	Nurses	Supervising Nurses
10,000–12,000	7	15	3
12,001–13,750	8	15	3
13,751–16,500	9	16	4
16,501–18,250	10	16	4
18,251–20,750	10	17	5
20,751–23,000	11	18	5

These staffing levels represent full-time equivalents, and it should be assumed that the Cardiac Care Department always employs only the minimum number of required full-time equivalent personnel.

Average annual salaries for each class of employee are: aides, $36,000; nurses, $58,000; and supervising nurses, $76,000.

Required:

1. Compute the total fixed costs (including the salaries of aides, nurses, and supervising nurses) in the Cardiac Care Department for each level of activity shown above (i.e., total fixed costs at

the 10,000–12,000 patient-day level of activity, total fixed costs at the 12,001–13,750 patient-day level of activity, etc.).

2. Compute the minimum number of patient-days required for the Cardiac Care Department to break even.
3. Determine the minimum number of patient-days required for the Cardiac Care Department to earn an annual "profit" of $720,000.

(CPA, adapted)

Research

R 7–36 Cost-Volume-Profit Disclosures [LO3, LO4, LO5, LO6, LO7, LO8, LO9]
The questions in this exercise are based on the Benetton Group, a company headquartered in Italy and known in North America primarily for one of its brands of fashion apparel—United Colors of Benetton. To answer the questions, you will need to download the Benetton Group's 2004 Annual Report at www.benetton.com/investors. You do not need to print this document to answer the questions.

Required:

1. How do the formats of the income statements shown on pages 33 and 50 of Benetton's annual report differ from one another (disregard everything beneath the line titled "income from operations")? Which expenses shown on page 50 appear to have been reclassified as variable selling costs on page 33?
2. Why do you think cost of sales is included in the computation of contribution margin on page 33?
3. Perform two separate computations of Benetton's break-even point in euros. For the first computation, use data from 2003. For the second computation, use data from 2004. Why do the numbers that you computed differ from one another?
4. What sales volume would have been necessary in 2004 for Benetton to attain a target income from operations of €300 million?
5. Compute Benetton's margin of safety using data from 2003 and 2004. Why do your answers for the two years differ from one another?
6. What is Benetton's degree of operating leverage in 2004? If Benetton's sales in 2004 had been 6% higher than what is shown in the annual report, what income from operations would the company have earned? What percentage increase in income from operations does this represent?
7. What income from operations would Benetton have earned in 2004 if it had invested an additional €10 million in advertising and promotions and realized a 3% increase in sales? As an alternative, what income from operations would Benetton have earned if it not only invested an additional €10 million in advertising and promotions but also raised its sales commission rate to 6% of sales, thereby generating a 5% increase in sales? Which of these two scenarios would have been preferable for Benetton?
8. Assume that total sales in 2004 remained unchanged at €1,686 million (as shown on pages 33 and 50); however, the Casual sector sales were €1,554 million, the Sportswear and Equipment sector sales were €45million, and the Manufacturing and Other sector sales were €87 million. What income from operations would Benetton have earned with this sales mix? (Hint: look at pages 36 and 37 of the annual report.) Why is the income from operations under this scenario different from what is shown in the annual report?

CHAPTER 8

LEARNING OBJECTIVES

After studying Chapter 8, you should be able to:

1. Explain how variable costing differs from absorption costing and compute unit product costs under each method.

2. Prepare income statements using both variable and absorption costing.

3. Reconcile variable costing and absorption costing operating incomes and explain why the two amounts differ.

4. Explain the advantages and disadvantages of both variable and absorption costing.

5. Explain how the use of lean production reduces the difference between reported operating income under the variable and absorption costing methods.

6. Prepare a segmented income statement using the contribution format and explain the difference between traceable fixed costs and common fixed costs.

VARIABLE COSTING: A TOOL FOR MANAGEMENT

BUSINESS FOCUS

Manipulating Profits

Tina Xu is employed as an investment analyst in Toronto. She has just received the current annual report of Andersen Transformers Limited and is puzzled by several items in the report.

Andersen Transformers' ending inventory was 40% higher than the previous year's amount and operating income had risen, even though sales had remained relatively stable.

How can building inventories increase profits without any increases in sales? As we will see in this chapter, absorption costing—the most widely used method of determining product costs—can be used to artificially increase profits by increasing the quantity of units produced.

Two general approaches are used in manufacturing companies for costing products for the purposes of valuing inventories and cost of goods sold. One approach, called *absorption costing,* was discussed in Chapters 2 and 3. Absorption costing is generally used for external financial reports. The other approach, called *variable costing,* is preferred by some managers for internal decision making and must be used when an income statement is prepared in the contribution format. Ordinarily, absorption costing and variable costing produce different figures for operating income, and the difference can be quite large. In addition to showing how these two methods differ, we will consider the arguments for and against each costing method and we will show how management decisions can be affected by the costing method chosen.

In Chapters 6 and 7, the presentations generally assumed inventories were insignificant or that production equals sales. This assumption is reasonable in some situations as shall be presented later in this chapter. However, inventories can be important to income results in other situations. The explanations to follow will show what is involved when production does not equal sales and thus production is a cost driver rather than sales. Also the analysis will include the elements of production costs rather than using only the total production costs.

Overview of Absorption and Variable Cost

LEARNING OBJECTIVE 1
Explain how variable costing differs from absorption costing and compute unit product costs under each method.

In the last two chapters, we learned that the contribution format income statement and cost-volume-profit (CVP) analysis are valuable management tools. Both of these tools emphasize cost behaviour and require that managers carefully distinguish between variable and fixed costs. Absorption costing, which was discussed in Chapters 2 and 3, assigns both variable and fixed costs to products—mingling them in a way that makes it difficult for managers to distinguish between them. In contrast, variable costing focuses on *cost behaviour*, clearly separating fixed from variable costs. One of the strengths of variable costing is that it harmonizes with both the contribution approach and the CVP concepts discussed in the preceding chapters.

Absorption Costing

Absorption costing
A costing method that includes all manufacturing costs—direct materials, direct labour, and both variable and fixed manufacturing overhead—in the cost of a unit of product. Absorption costing is also referred to as the *full cost method.*

Full cost method
Same as *absorption costing.*

In Chapter 3, we learned that **absorption costing** treats *all* manufacturing costs as product costs, regardless of whether they are variable or fixed. The cost of a unit of product under the absorption costing method therefore consists of direct materials, direct labour, and *both* variable and fixed overhead. Thus, absorption costing allocates a portion of fixed manufacturing overhead cost to each unit of product, along with the variable manufacturing costs. Because absorption costing includes all manufacuring costs as product costs, it is frequently referred to as the **full cost method**.

Variable Costing

Variable costing
A costing method that includes only variable manufacturing costs—direct materials, direct labour, and variable manufacturing overhead—in the cost of a unit of product.

Under **variable costing**, only those manufacturing costs that vary with output are treated as product costs. This would generally include direct materials, direct labour, and the variable portion of manufacturing overhead. Fixed manufacturing overhead is not treated as a product cost under this method. Rather, fixed manufacturing overhead is treated as a period cost and, like selling and administrative expenses, it is charged off in its entirety against revenue each period. Consequently, the cost of a unit of product in inventory or in cost of goods sold under the variable costing method does not contain any of fixed overhead cost.

Variable costing is sometimes referred to as **direct costing** or **marginal costing.** The term *direct costing* was popular for many years, but it is slowly disappearing from day-to-day use. The term *variable costing* is more descriptive of the way in which product costs are computed when a contribution income statement is prepared.

Selling and Administrative Expense

To complete this summary comparison of absorption and variable costing, we need to consider briefly the handling of selling and administrative expenses. These expenses are rarely treated as product costs, regardless of the costing method in use. Thus, under either absorption or variable costing, selling and administrative expenses are always treated as period costs (expenses) and deducted from revenues as incurred.

Exhibit 8–1 summarizes the classification of costs under both absorption and variable costing.

Direct costing
Same as *variable costing.*

Marginal costing
Same as *variable costing.*

EXHIBIT 8–1 Cost Classifications—Absorption versus Variable Costing

Absorption Costing		Variable Costing
Product costs	Direct materials	Product costs
Product costs	Direct labour	Product costs
Product costs	Variable manufacturing overhead	Product costs
Product costs	Fixed manufacturing overhead	Period costs
Period costs	Variable selling and administrative expenses	Period costs
Period costs	Fixed selling and administrative expenses	Period costs

Unit Cost Computations

To illustrate the computation of unit product costs under both absorption and variable costing, consider Boley Company, a small company that produces a single product and has the following cost structure:

Number of units produced each year	6,000
Variable costs per unit:	
Direct materials	$ 2
Direct labour	4
Variable manufacturing overhead	1
Variable selling and administrative expenses	3
Fixed costs per year:	
Fixed manufacturing overhead	30,000
Fixed selling and administrative expenses	10,000

Under the absorption costing method, *all* manufacturing costs, variable and fixed, are included when determining the unit product cost. Thus, if the company sells a unit of product and absorption costing is being used, then $12 (consisting of $7 variable cost and $5 fixed cost) will be deducted on the income statement as cost of goods sold. Similarly, any unsold units will be carried as inventory on the balance sheet at $12 each.

Absorption Costing	
Direct materials	$ 2
Direct labour	4
Variable manufacturing overhead	1
Total variable production cost	7
Fixed manufacturing overhead ($30,000 ÷ 6,000 units of product)	5
Unit product cost	$12

Under the variable costing method, only the variable manufacturing costs are included in product costs. Therefore, if the company sells a unit of product, only $7 will be deducted as cost of goods sold, and unsold units will be carried in the balance sheet inventory account at only $7 each.

Variable Costing

Direct materials	$ 2
Direct labour	4
Variable manufacturing overhead	1
Unit product cost	$ 7

(The $30,000 fixed manufacturing overhead in variable costing will be charged off in total against income as a period expense along with the selling and administrative expenses.)

Income Comparison of Absorption and Variable Costing

LEARNING OBJECTIVE 2
Prepare income statements using both variable and absorption costing.

Income statements prepared under the absorption and variable costing approaches are shown in Exhibit 8–2. In preparing these statements, we use the data for Boley Company presented earlier, along with other information about the company as given below:

Units in beginning inventory	–0–
Units produced	6,000
Units sold	5,000
Units in ending inventory	1,000
Selling price per unit	$ 20
Selling and administrative expenses:	
Variable per unit	$ 3
Fixed per year	$10,000

	Absorption Costing	Variable Costing
Unit product cost:		
Direct materials	$ 2	$ 2
Direct labour	4	4
Variable manufacturing overhead	1	1
Fixed manufacturing overhead ($30,000 ÷ 6,000 units)	5	—
Unit product cost	$12	$ 7

Several points can be made about the financial statements in Exhibit 8–2:

Fixed manufacturing overhead cost deferred in inventory
The portion of the fixed manufacturing overhead cost of a period that goes into inventory under the absorption costing method as a result of production exceeding sales.

1. Under the absorption costing method, if there is an ending inventory the fixed manufacturing costs associated with the inventory will be carried forward as a balance sheet account, inventory, rather than being treated as a period cost. Such a deferral of costs is known as **fixed manufacturing overhead cost deferred in inventory.** The process involved can be explained by referring to the data for Boley Company. During the current period, Boley Company produced 6,000 units but sold only 5,000 units, thus leaving 1,000 unsold units in the ending inventory. Under the absorption costing method, each unit produced was assigned $5 in fixed overhead cost (see the unit cost computations above). Therefore, each of the 1,000 units going into inventory at the end of the period has $5 in fixed manufacturing overhead cost attached to it, or a total of $5,000 for the 1,000 units. *This fixed manufacturing overhead cost of the*

EXHIBIT 8–2 Comparison of Absorption and Variable Costing—Boley Company

Absorption Costing		
Sales (5,000 units × $20 per unit)		$100,000
Less cost of goods sold:		
Beginning inventory	$ -0-	
Add cost of goods manufactured (6,000 units × $12 per unit)	72,000	
Goods available for sale	72,000	
Less ending inventory (1,000 units × $12 per unit)	12,000	
Cost of goods sold		60,000
Gross margin		40,000
Less selling and administrative expenses (5,000 units × $3 variable per unit + $10,000 fixed)		25,000
Operating income		$ 15,000
Variable Costing		
Sales (5,000 units × $20 per unit)		$100,000
Less variable expenses:		
Variable cost of goods sold:		
Beginning inventory	$ -0-	
Add variable manufacturing costs (6,000 units × $7 per unit)	42,000	
Goods available for sale	42,000	
Less ending inventory (1,000 units × $7 per unit)	7,000	
Variable cost of goods sold	35,000	
Variable selling and administrative expenses (5,000 units × $3 per unit)	15,000	50,000
Contribution margin		50,000
Less fixed expenses:		
Fixed manufacturing overhead	30,000	
Fixed selling and administrative expenses	10,000	40,000
Operating income		$ 10,000

Note the difference in ending inventories. Fixed manufacturing overhead cost at $5 per unit is included under the absorption approach. This explains the difference in ending inventory and in operating income (1,000 units × $5 per unit = $5,000).

current period is deferred in inventory to the next period, when, hopefully, these units will be taken out of inventory and sold. The deferral of $5,000 of fixed manufacturing overhead costs can be seen clearly by analyzing the ending inventory under the absorption costing method:

Variable manufacturing costs: 1,000 units × $7.	$ 7,000
Fixed manufacturing overhead costs: 1,000 units × $5.	5,000
Total inventory value	$12,000

In summary, under absorption costing, of the $30,000 in fixed manufacturing overhead costs incurred during the period, only $25,000 (5,000 units sold × $5) has been included in cost of goods sold. The remaining $5,000 (1,000 units *not* sold × $5) has been deferred in inventory to the next period.

2. Under the variable costing method, the entire $30,000 in fixed manufacturing overhead costs has been treated as an expense of the current period (see the bottom portion of the variable costing income statement).
3. The ending inventory figure under the variable costing method is $5,000 lower than it is under the absorption costing method. The reason is that under variable costing,

only the variable manufacturing costs are assigned to units of product and therefore included in inventory:

Variable manufacturing costs: 1,000 units × $7	$7,000

The $5,000 difference in ending inventories explains the difference in operating income reported between the two costing methods. Operating income is $5,000 *higher* under absorption costing since, as already explained, $5,000 of fixed manufacturing overhead cost has been deferred in inventory to the next period under that costing method.

4. The absorption costing income statement makes no distinction between fixed and variable costs; therefore, it is not well suited for CVP computations, which are important for good planning and control. To generate data for CVP analysis, it would be necessary to spend time reworking and reclassifying costs on the absorption statement.
5. The variable costing approach to costing units of product blends very well with the contribution approach to the income statement, since both concepts are based on the idea of classifying costs by behaviour. The variable costing data in Exhibit 8–2 could be used immediately in CVP computations.

Careful reading of the previous two sections, unit cost calculations and income comparisons of absorption and variable costing, may have created confusion when the fixed overhead unit cost was calculated. Chapter 3, Exhibit 3–13 and Appendix 3A, suggest the use of a predetermined overhead rate. Such a rate would be applicable to the unit cost of fixed overhead and the unit cost of variable overhead used here. However, in the examples in this chapter we used actual overhead rates rather than predetermined ones in order to reduce unneeded discussion. What is illustrated about the effects of inventory on the difference in operating income will hold regardless of the use of actual or predetermined overhead rates. Later chapters will show full treatment of predetermined overhead rates to prove this assertion.

Essentially, the difference between the absorption costing method and the variable costing method centres on timing. Advocates of variable costing say that fixed manufacturing costs should be expensed immediately in total, whereas advocates of absorption costing say that fixed manufacturing costs should be charged against revenues bit by bit as units of product are sold. Any units of product not sold under absorption costing result in fixed costs being inventoried and carried forward as *assets* to the next period. We will defer discussing the arguments presented by each side in this dispute until after we have a better understanding of the two methods. Nevertheless, as we will see in the discussion of Emerald Isle Knitters, the use of absorption costing can sometimes produce strange effects on income statements.

Extended Comparison of Income Data

LEARNING OBJECTIVE 3
Reconcile variable costing and absorption costing operating incomes and explain why the two amounts differ.

Emerald Isle Knitters Ltd. of Galway, Republic of Ireland, is a small company that manufactures traditional wool, fisherman sweaters.

The basic data appear in the first part of Exhibit 8–3, on page 323, and the absorption costing income statements as reported to the bank for the last three years appear in the first part on page 324. Sean MacLafferty, the company accountant, decided to try using the variable costing approach to see what effect that might have on operating income. The variable costing income statements for the last three years appear in the lower part on page 324.

Note that Emerald Isle Knitters maintained a steady rate of production per year of 25,000 sweaters. However, sales varied from year to year. In year 1, production and sales were equal. In year 2, production exceeded sales due to a cancelled order. In year 3, sales recovered and exceeded production. As a consequence, inventories did not change during year 1, inventories increased during year 2, and inventories decreased during year 3. *The change in inventories during the year is the key to understanding how absorption costing differs from variable costing.* Note that when inventories increase in year 2, absorption costing operating income exceeds variable costing operating income. When inventories decrease in year 3, the opposite occurs—variable costing operating income exceeds absorption costing operating income. And when there is no change in inventories, as in year 1, there is no difference in operating income between the two methods. Why is this? The reasons are discussed below and are briefly summarized in Exhibit 8–4.

1. When production and sales are equal, as in year 1 for Emerald Isle Knitters, operating income will generally be the same regardless of whether absorption or variable costing is used. The reason is as follows: The *only* difference that can exist between absorption and variable costing operating incomes is the amount of fixed manufacturing overhead recognized as expense on the income statement. When everything that is produced in the year is sold, all of the fixed manufacturing overhead assigned to units of product under absorption costing become part of the current year's cost of goods sold. Under variable costing, the total fixed manufacturing overhead flows directly to the income statement as an expense. So under either method, when production equals sales (and hence there is no change in inventories), all of the fixed manufacturing overhead incurred during the year flows through to the income statement as expense. Therefore, the operating income under the two methods is the same.
2. When production exceeds sales (see year 2 in Exhibit 8–3), the operating income reported under absorption costing will generally be greater than the operating income

EXHIBIT 8–3 Absorption and Variable Costing Data—Emerald Isle Knitters, Ltd.

Basic Data

Selling price per unit sold	€ 20
Variable manufacturing cost per unit produced	7
Fixed manufacturing overhead costs per year	150,000
Variable selling and administrative expenses per unit sold	1
Fixed selling and administrative expenses per year	90,000

	Year 1	Year 2	Year 3	Three Years Together
Units in beginning inventory	–0–	–0–	5,000	–0–
Units produced	25,000	25,000	25,000	75,000
Units sold	25,000	20,000	30,000	75,000
Units in ending inventory	–0–	5,000	–0–	–0–

Unit Product Costs

	Year 1	Year 2	Year 3
Under variable costing (variable manufacturing costs only)	€ 7	€ 7	€ 7
Under absorption costing:			
Variable manufacturing costs	€ 7	€ 7	€ 7
Fixed manufacturing overhead costs (€150,000 spread over the number of units produced in each year)	6	6	6
Total absorption cost per unit	€13	€13	€13

continued

EXHIBIT 8–3 *concluded*

	Year 1		Year 2		Year 3		Three Years Together	
Absorption Costing								
Sales		€500,000		€400,000		€600,000		€1,500,000
Less cost of goods sold:								
Beginning inventory	€ -0-		€ -0-		€ 65,000		€ -0-	
Add cost of goods manufactured (25,000 units × €13 per unit)	325,000		325,000		325,000		975,000	
Goods available for sale	325,000		325,000		390,000		975,000	
Less ending inventory (5,000 units × €13 per unit)	-0-		65,000		-0-		-0-	
Cost of goods sold		325,000		260,000		390,000		975,000
Gross margin		175,000		140,000		210,000		525,000
Less selling and administrative expenses		115,000*		110,000*		120,000*		345,000
Operating income		€ 60,000		€ 30,000		€ 90,000		€ 180,000

*The selling and administrative expenses are computed as follows:
Year 1: 25,000 units × €1 per unit variable + €90,000 fixed = €115,000.
Year 2: 20,000 units × €1 per unit variable + €90,000 fixed = €110,000.
Year 3: 30,000 units × €1 per unit variable + €90,000 fixed = €120,000.

	Year 1		Year 2		Year 3		Three Years Together	
Variable Costing								
Sales		€500,000		€400,000		€600,000		€1,500,000
Less variable expenses:								
Variable cost of goods sold:								
Beginning inventory	€ -0-		€ -0-		€ 35,000		€ -0-	
Add variable manufacturing costs (25,000 units × €7 per unit)	175,000		175,000		175,000		525,000	
Goods available for sale	175,000		175,000		210,000		525,000	
Less ending inventory (5,000 units × €7 per unit)	-0-		35,000		-0-		-0-	
Variable cost of goods sold	175,000*		140,000*		210,000*		525,000	
Variable selling and administrative expenses (€1 per unit sold)	25,000	200,000	20,000	160,000	30,000	240,000	75,000	600,000
Contribution margin		300,000		240,000		360,000		900,000
Less fixed expenses:								
Fixed manufacturing overhead	150,000		150,000		150,000		450,000	
Fixed selling and administrative expenses	90,000	240,000	90,000	240,000	90,000	240,000	270,000	720,000
Operating income		€ 60,000		€ -0-		€120,000		€ 180,000

*The variable cost of goods sold could have been computed more simply as follows:
Year 1: 25,000 units sold × €7 per unit = €175,000.
Year 2: 20,000 units sold × €7 per unit = €140,000.
Year 3: 30,000 units sold × €7 per unit = €210,000.

EXHIBIT 8–4 Comparative Income Effects—Absorption and Variable Costing

Relationship between Production and Sales for the Period	Effect on Inventories	Relationship between Absorption and Variable Costing Operating Incomes
Production = Sales	No change in inventories	Absorption costing operating income = Variable costing operating income
Production > Sales	Inventories increase	Absorption costing operating income > Variable costing operating income*
Production < Sales	Inventories decrease	Absorption costing operating income < Variable costing operating income†

*Operating income is higher under absorption costing, since fixed manufacturing overhead cost is *deferred* in inventory under absorption costing as inventories increase.

†Operating income is lower under absorption costing, since fixed manufacturing overhead cost is *released* from inventory under absorption costing as inventories decrease.

reported under variable costing. This occurs because under absorption costing, part of the fixed manufacturing overhead costs of the current period is deferred in inventory. In year 2, for example, €30,000 of fixed manufacturing overhead costs (5,000 units × €6 per unit) has been applied to units in ending inventory. These costs are excluded from cost of goods sold.

Under variable costing, however, *all* of the fixed manufacturing overhead costs of year 2 has been immediately expensed. As a result, the operating income for year 2 under variable costing is €30,000 *lower* than it is under absorption costing. Exhibit 8–5 contains a reconciliation of the variable costing and absorption costing operating income figures.

3. When production is less than sales (see year 3 in Exhibit 8–3), the operating income reported under the absorption costing approach will generally be less than the operating income reported under the variable costing approach. This happens because as inventories are drawn down, the fixed manufacturing overhead costs that were previously deferred in inventory under absorption costing are released and charged against income (known as **fixed manufacturing overhead cost released from inventory**). In year 3, for example, the €30,000 in fixed manufacturing overhead costs deferred in inventory under the absorption approach from year 2 to year 3 is released

Fixed manufacturing overhead cost released from inventory The portion of the fixed manufacturing overhead cost of a prior period that becomes an expense of the current period under the absorption costing method as a result of sales exceeding production.

EXHIBIT 8–5 Reconciliation of Variable Costing and Absorption Costing—Operating Income Data from Exhibit 8–3

	Year 1	Year 2	Year 3
Variable costing operating income.	€60,000	€ -0-	€120,000
Add fixed manufacturing overhead costs deferred in inventory under absorption costing (5,000 units ×€6 per unit)	-0-	30,000	-0-
Deduct fixed manufacturing overhead costs released from inventory under absorption costing (5,000 units × €6 per unit).	-0-	-0-	(30,000)
Absorption costing operating income	€60,000	€30,000	€ 90,000

from inventory because these units were sold. As a result, the cost of goods sold for year 3 contains not only all of the fixed manufacturing overhead costs for year 3 (since all that was produced in year 3 was sold in year 3) but €30,000 of fixed manufacturing overhead costs from year 2 as well.

By contrast, under variable costing only the fixed manufacturing overhead costs of year 3 have been charged against year 3. The result is that operating income under variable costing is €30,000 *higher* than it is under absorption costing. Exhibit 8–5 contains a reconciliation of the variable costing and absorption costing operating income figures for year 3.

Careful reading of Exhibit 8–3 will raise the question as to why operating income is not influenced by changes in inventories when variable costing is used. The reason is that variable costing releases variable costs from inventory to cost of goods sold in amounts that are based on the volume of sales. Thus production does not influence the cost of goods sold because fixed manufacturing overhead is fixed and not released as cost of goods sold as it was with absorption costing.

4. Over an *extended* period of time, the cumulative operating income figures reported under absorption costing and variable costing will tend to be the same. The reason is that over the long run, sales cannot exceed production, nor can production much exceed sales. The shorter the time period, the more the operating income figures will tend to differ.

Effect of Changes in Production on Operating Income

In the Emerald Isle Knitters example in the preceding section, production was constant and sales fluctuated over the three-year period. Since sales fluctuated, the income statements Sean MacLafferty presented in Exhibit 8–3 allowed us to see the effect of changes in sales on operating income under both variable and absorption costing.

To further investigate the differences between variable and absorption costing, Sean next put together the hypothetical example in Exhibit 8–6. In this hypothetical example, sales are constant and production fluctuates (the opposite of Exhibit 8–3). The purpose of Exhibit 8–6 is to illustrate the effect of changes in *production* on operating income under both variable and absorption costing.

Variable Costing

Operating income is *not* affected by changes in production under variable costing. Notice from Exhibit 8–6 that operating income is the same for all three years under the variable costing approach, although production exceeds sales in one year and is less than sales in another year. In short, a change in production has no effect on operating income when variable costing is used.

Absorption Costing

Operating income *is* affected by changes in production under absorption costing. As shown in Exhibit 8–6, operating income under the absorption approach goes up in year 2, in response to the increase in production for that year, and then goes down in year 3, in response to the drop in production for that year. Note particularly that operating income goes up and down between these two years *even though the same number of units is sold in each year.* The reason for this effect can be traced to the shifting of fixed manufacturing overhead costs between periods under the absorption costing method as a result of changes in inventory.

As shown in Exhibit 8–6, production exceeds sales in year 2, resulting in an increase of 10,000 units in inventory. Each unit produced during year 2 has €6 in fixed manufacturing overhead costs attached to it (see the unit cost computations at the top of Exhibit 8–6). Therefore, €60,000 (10,000 units × €6) of the fixed manufacturing overhead costs of year 2 are not charged against that year but rather are added to the inventory account (along with the variable manufacturing costs). The operating income of year 2 rises sharply, because these costs are deferred in inventories, even though the same number of units is sold in year 2 as in the other years.

The reverse effect occurs in year 3. Since sales exceed production in year 3, that year is forced to cover all of its own fixed manufacturing overhead costs as well as the fixed manufacturing overhead costs carried forward in inventory from year 2. A substantial drop in operating income during year 3 results from the release of fixed manufacturing overhead costs from inventories, despite the fact that the same number of units is sold in that year as in the other years.

The variable costing and absorption costing operating incomes are reconciled in Exhibit 8–7. This exhibit shows that the differences in operating income can be traced to the effects of changes in inventories on absorption costing operating income. Under absorption costing, fixed manufacturing overhead costs are deferred in inventory when inventories increase and are released from inventory when inventory decreases.

EXHIBIT 8–6 Sensitivity of Costing Methods to Changes in Production—Hypothetical Data

Basic Data			
Selling price per unit sold			€ 25
Variable manufacturing cost per unit produced			10
Fixed manufacturing overhead costs per year			300,000
Variable selling and administrative expenses per unit sold			1
Fixed selling and administrative expenses per year			200,000
	Year 1	**Year 2**	**Year 3**
Units in beginning inventory	–0–	–0–	10,000
Units produced	40,000	50,000	30,000
Units sold	40,000	40,000	40,000
Units in ending inventory	–0–	10,000	–0–
Unit Product Costs			
Under variable costing (variable manufacturing costs only)	€10.00	€10.00	€10.00
Under absorption costing			
Variable manufacturing costs	€10.00	€10.00	€10.00
Fixed manufacturing overhead costs (€300,000 total spread over the number of units produced in each year)	7.50	6.00	10.00
Total absorption cost per unit	€17.50	€16.00	€20.00

continued

EXHIBIT 8–6 *concluded*

	Year 1		Year 2		Year 3	
Absorption Costing						
Sales (40,000 units)		€1,000,000		€1,000,000		€1,000,000
Less cost of goods sold:						
Beginning inventory	€ -0-		€ -0-		€160,000	
Add cost of goods manufactured	700,000*		800,000*		600,000*	
Goods available for sale	700,000		800,000		760,000	
Less ending inventory	-0-		160,000†		-0-	
Cost of goods sold		700,000		640,000		760,000
Gross margin		300,000		360,000		240,000
Less selling and administrative expenses (40,000 units × €1 per unit + €200,000)		240,000		240,000		240,000
Operating income		€ 60,000		€ 120,000		€ -0-

*Cost of goods manufactured:
Year 1: 40,000 units × €17.50 per unit = €700,000.
Year 2: 50,000 units × €16.00 per unit = €800,000.
Year 3: 30,000 units × €20.00 per unit = €600,000.
†Ending inventory, year 2: 10,000 units × €16 per unit = €160,000.

	Year 1		Year 2		Year 3	
Variable Costing						
Sales (40,000 units)		€1,000,000		€1,000,000		€1,000,000
Less variable expenses:						
Variable cost of goods sold:						
Beginning inventory	€ -0-		€ -0-		€100,000	
Add variable manufacturing costs at €10 per unit produced	400,000		500,000		300,000	
Goods available for sale	400,000		500,000		400,000	
Less ending inventory	-0-		100,000†		-0-	
Variable cost of goods sold	400,000		400,000		400,000	
Variable selling and administrative expenses	40,000	440,000	40,000	440,000	40,000	440,000
Contribution margin		560,000		560,000		560,000
Less fixed expenses:						
Fixed manufacturing overhead	300,000		300,000		300,000	
Fixed selling and administrative expenses	200,000	500,000	200,000	500,000	200,000	500,000
Operating income		€ 60,000		€ 60,000		€ 60,000

†Ending inventory, year 2: 10,000 units × €10 per unit = €100,000.

	Year 1	Year 2	Year 3
Variable costing operating income.	€60,000	€ 60,000	€60,000
Add fixed manufacturing overhead costs deferred in inventory under absorption costing (10,000 units × €6 per unit)	-0-	60,000	-0-
Deduct fixed manufacturing overhead costs released from inventory under absorption costing (10,000 units × €6 per unit)	-0-	-0-	(60,000)
Absorption costing operating income	€60,000	€120,000	€ 0

EXHIBIT 8–7 Reconciliation of Variable Costing and Absorption Costing—Operating Income Data from Exhibit 8–6

Choosing a Costing Method

The Impact on the Manager

LEARNING OBJECTIVE 4
Explain the advantages and disadvantages of both variable and absorption costing.

Opponents of absorption costing argue that shifting fixed manufacturing overhead cost between periods can be confusing and can lead to misinterpretations and even to faulty decisions. Look again at the data in Exhibit 8–6; a manager might wonder why operating income went up substantially in year 2 under absorption costing when sales remained the same as in the prior year. Was it a result of lower selling costs, or more efficient operations, or was some other factor involved? A manager cannot say by simply looking at the absorption costing income statement. Then in year 3, operating income drops sharply, even though again the same number of units is sold as in the other two years. Why would income rise in one year and then drop in the next? The figures seem erratic and contradictory and can lead to confusion and a loss of confidence in the integrity of the statement data.

By contrast, the variable costing income statements in Exhibit 8–6 are clear and easy to understand. Sales remain constant over the three-year period covered in the exhibit, so both contribution margin and operating income also remain constant. The statements are consistent with what managers would expect to happen under the circumstances, so they tend to generate confidence rather than confusion.

Under variable costing, essentially revenue drives operating income. Under absorption costing both revenue and production drive operating income. The two drivers create confusion for the user of operating income because it is difficult to perceive income without selling the production, something absorption costing does.

To avoid mistakes when absorption costing is used, readers of financial statements should be alert to changes in inventory levels. Under absorption costing, if there is an increase in inventories, fixed manufacturing overhead costs are deferred in inventories and operating income is increased. If there is a decrease in inventories, fixed manufacturing overhead costs are released from inventories and operating income decreases. Thus, fluctuations in operating income can be due to changes in inventories rather than to changes in sales.

IN BUSINESS

While managers can artificially increase operating income under absorption costing by producing more than is really necessary and building up inventories, a few unscrupulous managers have stepped over the line into the area of outright fraud. By claiming inventories that don't exist, an unethical manager can produce instant profits and dress up the balance sheet. Since the value of ending inventories is subtracted from the cost of goods available for sale in order to arrive at the cost of goods sold, phantom inventories directly reduce cost of goods sold. Phantom inventories also beef up the balance sheet by increasing assets.

Auditors attempt to uncover such fraud by physically verifying the existence of inventory reported on the balance sheet. This is done by counting random samples of perhaps 5% to 10% of reported inventory items. However, this audit approach is not always effective.

Jed Connelly, the top American executive at Nissan North America, admits: "We had a lot of excess production that we had to force on the market." Nissan liked to run its factories at capacity, regardless of how well the cars were selling, because under its bookkeeping rules (presumably absorption costing), the factories would then generate a profit. As a consequence, Nissan dealers had to slash prices and offer big rebates to sell their cars. According to *Fortune* magazine, "Years of discounting and distress sales seriously undercut the value of the Nissan brand. While Toyota stood for quality, customers came to Nissan to get a better deal."

In 1999 after Renault of France purchased a 44% interest in Nissan, a major turn around was accomplished under the direction of the new CEO from Renault, Carlos Ghosn. Employee layoffs, factory closures, elimination of product models and new designs have made Nissan number two in Japan and a company with the highest operating margin of large volume carmakers.

Despite the success since 1999, the new Nissan factory in the United States has reported production quality problems for the North American segment that need to be addressed, a task directed by the CEO Carlos Ghosn.

Thus cost and quality are important issues for firms that extend beyond the accounting incentives of absorption costing.

Source: Alex Taylor III, "The Man Who Wants to Change Japan Inc.," *Fortune*, December 20, 1999, pp. 189–198; "The $10 Billion Man: Face Value," *The Economist*, London, February 26, 2005, vol. 374, p. 76.

CVP Analysis and Absorption Costing

Absorption costing is widely used for both internal and external reports. Many firms use the absorption approach exclusively because of its focus on *full* costing of units of product. A weakness of the method, however, is its inability to dovetail well with CVP analysis.

To illustrate, refer again to Exhibit 8–3. Let us compute the break-even point for Emerald Isle Knitters. To obtain the break-even point, we divide total fixed costs by the contribution margin per unit:

Selling price per unit	€ 20
Variable costs per unit	8
Contribution margin per unit	€ 12
Fixed manufacturing overhead costs	€150,000
Fixed selling and administrative costs	90,000
Total fixed costs	€240,000

$$\frac{\text{Total fixed costs}}{\text{Contribution margin per unit}} = \frac{€240{,}000}{€12} = 20{,}000 \text{ units}$$

The break-even point is 20,000 units. Notice from Exhibit 8–3 that in year 2, the firm sold exactly 20,000 units, the break-even volume. Under the contribution approach, using variable costing, the firm does break even in year 2, showing zero operating income. *Under absorption costing, however, the firm shows a positive operating income of €30,000 for year 2.* How can this be? How can absorption costing produce a positive operating income when the firm sold exactly the break-even volume of units?

The answer lies in the fact that €30,000 in fixed manufacturing overhead costs were deferred in inventory during year 2 under absorption costing and therefore did not appear as expenses. By deferring these fixed manufacturing overhead costs in inventory, the income statement shows a profit even though the company sold exactly the break-even volume of units. Absorption costing runs into similar kinds of difficulty in other areas of CVP analysis, which assumes that variable costing is being used.

Absorption break-even analysis would require the analysis of two drivers, sales and production. By determining various levels for each driver, a zero operating income could be determined. But like the truism from mathematics, a single equation does not provide a unique solution when there are two unknowns. Various possible sales and production levels that can create a break-even operating income would be what break-even means here. For example see year three of Exhibit 8–6 where 40,000 units were sold and 30,000 units were produced. Operating income is zero, or break-even.

Decision Making

A basic problem with absorption costing is that fixed manufacturing overhead costs appear to be variable with respect to the number of units sold, but they are not. For example, in Exhibit 8–3, the absorption unit product cost is €13, but the variable portion of this cost is only €7. Since the product costs are stated on a per unit basis, managers may mistakenly believe that if another unit is produced, it will cost the company €13.

The misperception that absorption unit product costs are variable can lead to many managerial problems, including inappropriate pricing decisions and decisions to drop products that are in fact profitable. These problems with absorption costing product costs will be discussed more fully in later chapters.

External Reporting and Income Taxes

Practically speaking, absorption costing is required for external reports in the United States and is the predominant method used in Canada. In Canada, accounting standards for external reporting require a company to assign to work in process and finished goods the laid-down cost of materials plus the cost of direct labour and the applicable share of overhead expenses.[1] This implies that both variable and absorption costing is required in Canada after January 1, 2008. For income tax purposes in Canada, *Interpretation Bulletin 473* permits both variable and absorption costing for the purposes of determining taxable income.[2]

Even if a company uses absorption costing for its external reports, a manager can use variable costing statements for internal reports. No particular accounting problems are created by using *both* costing methods—the variable costing method for internal reports and the absorption costing method for external reports. As we demonstrated earlier in Exhibits 8–5 and 8–7, the adjustment from variable costing operating income to absorption costing operating income is a simple one that can be made easily at year-end. Computer systems such as those described in Chapter 3 can make the conversion as long as the information is contained in the supporting data base.

Top executives of publicly held corporations are typically evaluated based on the earnings reported in the external financial reports presented to shareholders. This creates a problem for top executives who might otherwise favour using variable costing for internal reports. They may feel that since they are evaluated based on absorption costing reports, decisions should also be based on absorption costing data.

Advantages of Variable Costing and the Contribution Approach

As stated earlier, even if the absorption approach is used for external reporting purposes, variable costing, together with the contribution margin format income statement, is an appealing alternative for internal reports. The advantages of variable costing can be summarized as follows:

1. Data required for CVP analysis can be taken directly from a contribution margin format income statement. These data are not available on a conventional absorption costing statement.

1. *Canadian Institute of Chartered Accountants' Handbook*, section 3031, "Inventories," paragraph 13. Note, the requirement of absorption costing in Canada is a change from previous practices to make Canada comparable to international accounting standards.
2. Inventory valuation, paragraph 12, IT-473R, December 21, 1998, www.cra-arc.gc.ca.

2. Under variable costing, the profit for a period is not affected by changes in inventories. Other things remaining equal (i.e., selling prices, costs, sales mix, etc.), profits move in the same direction as sales when variable costing is used.
3. Managers often assume that unit product costs are variable costs. This is a problem under absorption costing because unit product costs are a combination of both fixed and variable costs. Under variable costing, unit product costs do not contain fixed costs.
4. The impact of fixed costs on profits is emphasized under the variable costing and contribution approach. The total amount of fixed costs appears explicitly on the income statement, highlighting that the whole amount of fixed costs must be covered for the company to be truly profitable. Under absorption costing, the fixed costs are mingled together with the variable costs and are buried in cost of goods sold and in ending inventories.
5. Variable costing data make it easier to estimate the profitability of products, customers, and other segments of the business. With absorption costing, profitability is obscured by arbitrary allocations of fixed costs. These issues will be discussed in later chapters.
6. Variable costing ties in with cost control methods such as standard costs and flexible budgets, which will be covered in later chapters.
7. Variable costing operating income is closer to net cash flow than absorption costing operating income. This is particularly important for companies with potential cash flow problems.

With all of these advantages, one might wonder why absorption costing continues to be used almost exclusively for external reporting and why it is the predominant choice for internal reports as well. This is partly due to tradition, but absorption costing is also attractive to many accountants and managers because they believe it better matches costs with revenues. Advocates of absorption costing argue that *all* manufacturing costs must be assigned to products in order to properly match the costs of producing units of product with the revenues from the units when they are sold. The fixed costs of depreciation, taxes, insurance, supervisory salaries, and so on, are just as essential to manufacturing products as are the variable costs.

Advocates of variable costing argue that fixed manufacturing costs are not really the costs of any particular unit of product. These costs are incurred in order to have the *capacity* to make products during a particular period and will be incurred even if nothing is made during the period. Moreover, whether a unit is made or not, the fixed manufacturing costs will be exactly the same. Therefore, variable costing advocates argue that fixed manufacturing costs are not part of the costs of producing a particular unit of product and thus the matching principle dictates that fixed manufacturing costs should be charged to the current period.

Another downside of absorption or full costing is that it can be used by an unethical manager to deliberately mislead others. This is possible because reported profits are affected by inventory build-ups or drawdowns if fixed costs are included in inventory. During periods of inventory build-up, less than a year's fixed costs will be expensed and during years in which inventory is reduced, more than a year's fixed costs will be expensed. An unethical manager whose bonus is based on operating income, for example, could make profits appear higher by simply building up inventory levels, since there is a direct relationship between ending inventory and operating income. Those responsible for performance evaluation should look beyond the bottom line to identify such abuses.

One restriction on the unethical use of absorption costing to increase operating income by building ending inventories is the application of the generally accepted accounting principle of lower of cost or market. The ending inventory has to be examined for its saleability by determining its market value. If market is below cost then a loss is recorded in the income statement of the current period. Thus if the excess inventory could not be sold, a write-down is expected which would reduce but not necessarily eliminate the operating income resulting from the inventory buildup. Whether the result would make absorption operating income equal to variable operating income is a question of the specifics and thus unlikely to be exactly equal.

At any rate, absorption costing is a generally accepted method for preparing mandatory external financial reports. Probably because of the cost and possible confusion of maintaining two separate costing systems—one for external reporting and one for internal reporting—most companies use absorption costing for both external and internal reports.

There may also be important strategic reasons for using absorption costing. Senior management, for example, may fear that variable costing will result in an overemphasis on contribution margin and lead to insufficient attention to the management of fixed costs. Decision makers may focus too much on short-run profitability and bring long-run harm to the company. For example, long-term profitability will suffer if managers, lured by the attractiveness of high contribution margins, set product prices too low because of blindness to the existence of fixed costs. This is a particular risk in those industries in which the trend has been for cost structures to shift away from variable costs. Judging from the dominant use of absorption costing, it appears that managers have generally concluded that the incremental benefits of variable costing information are outweighed by these strategic factors and the additional costs of maintaining parallel systems.

IN BUSINESS

Albert J. Dunlap, who relishes the nickname "Chainsaw Al," left Sunbeam Corporation under a cloud after three years as CEO. Dunlap was hired to turn around Sunbeam with his well-known cost-cutting and disregard for the sensibilities of existing employees.

Three years later, Dunlap had been fired by the board of directors amid well-publicized concerns about his aggressive accounting practices. In addition to questionable accounting practices, Dunlap left a legacy of excess inventories. Dunlap's successors complain that eliminating those excess inventories has required the company to keep production levels well under capacity. Since Sunbeam, like almost all other companies, uses absorption costing to prepare its external financial reports, liquidating these excess inventories depresses the company's profits.

The aggressive accounting practices at Sunbeam have been characterized as a disaster such as those seen at Enron and WorldCom. The aftermath included the bankruptcy and reorganization of Sunbeam, the permanent banning of Mr. Dunlap as an executive of a public company, a fine of $500,000 by the SEC, and a $15 million personal settlement of a shareholder lawsuit.

Sunbeam was reorganized to become American Household Inc. which was recently sold for $746 million.

Sources: Michael Schroeder, "Dunlap Settles Fraud Charges with the SEC," *Wall Street Journal*, September 5, 2002, p. C1. Dennis K. Berman and Henny Sender, "Jarden Is Set to Acquire American Household; Consumer-Products Firm is to pay $746 million for Successor to Sunbeam," *The Wall Street Journal*, September 20, 2004, p. A6.

Impact of Lean Production

LEARNING OBJECTIVE 5
Explain how the use of lean production reduces the difference between reported operating income under the variable and absorption costing methods.

As discussed in this chapter, variable and absorption costing will produce different operating income figures whenever the number of units produced is different from the number of units sold—in other words, whenever there is a change in the number of units in inventory. We have also learned that the absorption costing operating income figure can be erratic, sometimes moving in a direction that is opposite from the movement in sales.

When companies use lean production methods, these problems are reduced. The erratic movement of operating income under absorption costing and the difference in operating income between absorption and variable costing occur because of changes in the number of units in inventory. Under lean production, goods are produced to customers' orders and the goal is to eliminate finished goods inventories entirely and reduce work in process inventory to almost nothing. If there is very little inventory, then changes in inventories will be very small and both variable and absorption costing will show basically the same operating income figure. In that case, absorption costing operating income will move in the same direction as movements in sales.

Of course, the cost of a unit of product will still be different between variable and absorption costing, as explained earlier in the chapter. But when lean production is used, the differences in operating income will largely disappear.

Segment Reporting

LEARNING OBJECTIVE 6
Prepare a segmented income statement using the contribution format and explain the difference between traceable fixed costs and common fixed costs.

To operate effectively, managers and decision makers must have a great deal more information available to them than the information provided by a single company-wide income statement. Whether prepared on a variable costing or absorption basis such statements usually provide only a summary of overall operations; as such, they typically do not contain enough detail to allow the manager or investor to detect problems that may exist in the organization. For example, some product lines may be profitable while others are unprofitable; some sales territories may have a poor sales mix or may be overlooking sales opportunities. Managers may wish to analyze the results at a more detailed level to see if some salespeople are more effective than others, or to see if some producing divisions are effectively or ineffectively using their capacity and/or resources. To uncover such problems the manager may need not one but several income statements that focus on the segments of a company. The preparation of income statements of this type is known as *segmented reporting*.

Segment
Any part or activity of an organization about which a manager seeks cost, revenue, or profit data.

A **segment** is any part or activity of an organization about which a manager seeks cost, revenue, or profit data. Examples of segments would include sales territories, individual stores or other retail outlets, service centres, manufacturing divisions or plants, marketing departments, individual customers, and product lines.

An operating segment for financial accounting purposes is a component of an enterprise that:[3]

- Engages in business activities from which it may earn revenues and incur expenses
- Whose operating results are regularly reviewed by the enterprise's chief operating decision maker to make decisions about resources to be allocated to the segment and access its performance, and
- For which discrete financial information is available.

Differing Levels of Segmented Statements

Segmented statements can be prepared for different levels of activity in an organization and in differing formats, Exhibit 8–8 illustrates three levels of segmented statements for SoftSolutions Inc., presented in a widely used format. The contribution format income statement for the entire company appears at the very top of the exhibit under the column labelled Total Company. Immediately to the right of this column are two columns—one for each of the two divisions. We can see that the Business Products Division's segment margin is $60,000 and the Consumer Products Division's is $40,000. These segment margins show the company's divisional managers how much each of their divisions is contributing to the company's profits.

Segmented income statements can be prepared for activities at many levels in a company. The divisions are segmented according to their major product lines. In the case of the Consumer Products Division, the product lines are animation and computer games. Going even further, each of the product lines is segmented according to how they are sold—in retail stores or by online sales. Notice that as we go from one segmented statement to another, we are looking at smaller and smaller pieces of the company. While not shown in Exhibit 8–8, segmented income statements could have also been prepared for the major product lines in the Business Products Division.

The benefits accruing to the manager from a series of statements such as those contained in Exhibit 8–8 are substantial. By carefully examining trends and results in each segment, the manager can gain considerable insight into the company as a whole, and

3. CICA Handbook, Section 1701, paragraph 10.

perhaps discover opportunities and courses of action that would otherwise have remained hidden from view. Advanced computer-based information systems make it easier to construct such statements and to keep them continuously current.

One obvious question becomes evident from a careful review of Exhibit 8–8: Why break down results by divisions first, product lines next, and then sales territories? The order of break-

EXHIBIT 8–8 SoftSolutions, Inc.—Segmented Income Statements in the Contribution Format

Segments Defined as Divisions

	Total Company	Divisions: Business Products Division	Divisions: Consumer Products Division
Sales	$500,000	$300,000	$200,000
Variable expenses:			
Variable cost of goods sold	180,000	120,000	60,000
Other variable expenses	50,000	30,000	20,000
Total variable expenses	230,000	150,000	80,000
Contribution margin	270,000	150,000	120,000
Traceable fixed expenses	170,000	90,000	80,000*
Divisional segment margin	100,000	$ 60,000	$ 40,000
Common fixed expenses not traceable to individual divisions	85,000		
Operating income	$ 15,000		

Segments Defined as Product Lines of the Consumer Products Division

	Consumer Products Division	Product Line: Computer Animation	Product Line: Computer Games
Sales	$200,000	$ 75,000	$125,000
Variable expenses:			
Variable cost of goods sold	60,000	20,000	40,000
Other variable expenses	20,000	5,000	15,000
Total variable expenses	80,000	25,000	55,000
Contribution margin	120,000	50,000	70,000
Traceable fixed expenses	70,000	30,000	40,000
Product-line segment margin	50,000	$ 20,000	$ 30,000
Common fixed expenses not traceable to individual product lines	10,000		
Divisional segment margin	$ 40,000		

Segments Defined as Sales Territories for One Product Line, Computer Games, of the Consumer Products Division

	Computer Games	Sales Territories: Online Sales	Sales Territories: Retail Stores
Sales	$125,000	$100,000	$ 25,000
Variable expenses:			
Variable cost of goods sold	40,000	32,000	8,000
Other variable expenses	15,000	5,000	10,000
Total variable expenses	55,000	37,000	18,000
Contribution margin	70,000	63,000	7,000
Traceable fixed expenses	25,000	15,000	10,000
Sales-channel segment margin	45,000	$ 48,000	$ (3,000)
Common fixed expenses not traceable to individual sales channels	15,000		
Product-line segment margin	$ 30,000		

*Notice that this $80,000 in traceable fixed expenses is divided into two parts when the Consumer Products Division is broken down into product lines—$70,000 traceable and $10,000 common. The reasons for this are discussed later in the section "Traceable Costs Can Become Common."

down depends on what information is desired. Certainly it might be advantageous to begin with each sales territories. Then it would be possible to examine product lines for each sales territory, and then divisions for each product line. This alternative would permit a product line comparison between divisions. What management wants to learn and the types of comparisons desired are factors used for deciding the order of breakdown. The order of the breakdown should not affect the numbers, but it can alter what appears on a given report and the ease of review.

Assigning Costs to Segments

Segmented statements for internal use are typically prepared in the contribution format. The same costing guidelines are used in preparing these statements as are used in preparing a contribution statement generally, with one exception. This lies in the handling of fixed costs. Notice from Exhibit 8–8 that the fixed costs are divided into two parts on a segmented statement—one part labelled *traceable* and the other part labelled *common*. Only those fixed costs labelled traceable are charged to the various segments. If a fixed cost is not traceable directly to some segment, then it is treated as a common cost and kept separate from the segments themselves. Thus, under the contribution approach, a cost is never arbitrarily assigned to a segment of an organization.

In summary, two guidelines are followed in assigning costs to the various segments of a company under the contribution approach:

1. First, according to cost behaviour patterns (i.e. variable and fixed).
2. Second, according to whether the costs are directly traceable to the segments involved.

We now consider various aspects of Exhibit 8–8 in more depth.

Sales and Contribution Margin

To prepare segmented statements for management purposes, it is necessary to keep records of sales by individual segment, as well as in total for the organization. After deducting related variable expenses, a contribution margin figure can be computed for each segment, as illustrated in Exhibit 8–8.

Recall from our discussion of variable costing that the contribution margin is an extremely useful piece of data to the manager—particularly for determining the effect on net income of increases or decreases in sales volume. If sales volume goes up or down, the effect on operating income can be easily computed by simply multiplying the unit contribution margin by the change in units sold or by multiplying the change in sales dollars by the C/M ratio. One assumption implicit here is that selling prices and variable costs do not change with changes in volume. Segmented statements give the manager the ability to make such computations on a product-by-product, division-by-division, or territory-by-territory basis, thereby providing the information needed to show up areas of weakness or to capitalize on areas of strength.

The contribution margin is basically a short-run planning tool. As such, it is especially valuable in decisions relating to temporary uses of capacity, to special orders, or to short-run product line promotion. Decisions relative to the short run usually involve only variable costs and revenues, which of course are the very elements involved in contribution margin. By carefully monitoring segment contribution margin and segment contribution margin ratios, the manager is in a position to make those short-run decisions that maximize each segment's contribution to the overall profitability of the organization. Such decisions will be discussed in detail in Chapter 12.

The Importance of Fixed Costs

The emphasis we place on the usefulness of the contribution margin should not be taken as a suggestion that fixed costs are not important. Fixed costs are very important in any organization. What the contribution approach does imply is that *different costs are needed for different purposes*. For one purpose, variable costs and revenues alone may be adequate for a manager's needs; for another purpose, his or her needs may encompass the fixed costs as well.

The breaking apart of fixed and variable costs also emphasizes to management that the costs are controlled differently and that these differences must be kept clearly in mind for both short-run and long-run planning. Moreover, the grouping of fixed costs under the contribution approach highlights the fact that, after the fixed costs have been covered, operating income increases to the extent of the contribution margin generated on each additional unit sold. All of these concepts are useful to the manager *internally* for planning purposes.

Traceable and Common Fixed Costs

Traceable fixed costs can be defined as those fixed costs that can be identified with a particular segment and that arise because of the existence of the segment—if the segment had never existed, the fixed cost would not have been incurred, and/or if the segment were eliminated, the fixed cost would disappear. Only the traceable fixed costs are charged to particular segments. If a cost is not traceable to a segment, then it is not assigned to the segment. Examples of traceable fixed costs include the following:

Traceable fixed costs
Fixed costs that can be identified with a particular segment and that arise because of the existence of the segment.

- The salary of the Fritos product manager at PepsiCo is a *traceable* fixed cost of the Fritos business segment of PepsiCo.
- The maintenance cost for the building in which a Challenger jet is assembled is a *traceable* fixed cost of the Challenger business segment of Bombardier Ltd.

A **common fixed cost** is a fixed cost that supports the operations of more than one segment but is not traceable in whole or in part to any one segment. Even if the segment were entirely eliminated, there would be no change in a true common fixed cost. Note the following:

Common fixed costs
A fixed cost that supports the operations of more than one segment but is not traceable in whole or in part to any one segment.

- The salary of the CEO of General Motors Canada is a *common* fixed cost of the various divisions of General Motors Canada.
- The cost of the automatic bar-coding machine at SoftSolutions is a *common* fixed cost of the Consumer Products Division and of the Business Products Division.
- The cost of the receptionist's salary at an office shared by a number of doctors is a *common* fixed cost of the doctors. The cost is traceable to the office, but not to any one of the doctors individually.

Common fixed costs are not allocated to segments but simply deducted in total amount to arrive at the income for the company as a whole (see Exhibit 8–8). The managerial accountant may contend that nothing is added to the overall usefulness of a segmented statement by allocating the common costs among segments. Rather, the accountant would argue that such allocations tend to reduce the usefulness of segmented statements. The reason is that arbitrary allocations draw attention away from those costs that are traceable to a segment and that should form a basis for appraising performance.

Moreover, it is argued that any attempt to allocate common fixed costs among segments may result in misleading data or may obscure important relationships between segment revenues and segment earnings. Arbitrary allocation of common fixed costs often results in a segment appearing to be unprofitable, whereas it may be contributing substantially above its own traceable costs toward the overall profitability of a firm. In such cases, the allocated costs may lead to the unwise elimination of a segment and to a decrease in profits for the company as a whole because common costs do not disappear if the segment is closed down.

A word of caution is necessary here. Management reaction to common costs may help control the growth of such costs. Managers may use common cost allocation as a form of cost price or as a signal about the benefits received from headquarters and thus modify their actions for the common good of the organization. Empirical investigations suggest firms often allocate common costs to segments for a number of reasons. Rigorous analysis of the treatment of uncontrollable costs and allocated common costs suggests there may be benefit to charging managers with uncontrollable costs or allocating common costs to segments. Managerial behaviour is complex and investigation of it often finds results that were previously thought to be fallacious but may not be so. Some of these issues will be elaborated in Chapter 11.

Identifying Traceable Fixed Costs

The distinction between traceable and common fixed costs is crucial in segmented reporting, because traceable fixed costs are charged to the segments, but common fixed costs are not. In an actual situation it is sometimes hard to determine whether a cost should be classified as traceable or common.

The general guideline is to treat as traceable costs *only those costs that would disappear over time if the segment itself disappeared*. For example, if the Consumer Products Division in Exhibit 8–8 were sold or discontinued, it would no longer be necessary to pay the division manager's salary. Therefore the division manager's salary should be classified as a traceable fixed cost of the Consumer Products Division. On the other hand, the president of the company undoubtedly would continue to be paid even if the Consumer Products Division were dropped. In fact, he or she might even be paid more if dropping the division was a good idea. Therefore, the president's salary is common to both divisions and should not be charged to either division.

There will always be some costs that fall between the traceable and common categories, and considerable care and good judgement will be required for their proper classification. The important point is to resist the temptation to allocate costs (such as depreciation of corporate facilities) that are clearly common and that will continue regardless of whether the segment exists or not. *Any allocation of common costs to segments reduces the value of the segment margin as a guide to long-run segment profitability and segment performance.*

Breakdown of Traceable Fixed Costs

In preparing segmented income statements, some manager's like to separate the traceable fixed costs into two classes—discretionary and committed. As discussed in Chapter 6, discretionary fixed costs are under the immediate control of the manager, whereas committed fixed costs are not. Therefore, a breakdown of the traceable fixed costs into these two classes allows a company to make a distinction between the performance of the segment manager and the performance of the segment as a long-term investment.

In some situations, this distinction in performance can be very important. A top-flight manager, for example, may be assigned to a division that has an antiquated plant or that is saddled with other committed fixed costs that are beyond the segment manager's control. Under these conditions, it would be unfair to judge the segment manager's performance simply on the basis of overall margin generated by the segment. Rather, in these circumstances, the discretionary fixed costs should be separated from the committed fixed costs and deducted as a separate group from the segment's contribution margin. The amount remaining after deducting the discretionary fixed costs, sometimes called a *segment performance margin*, should then be used as a basis for evaluating the segment manager's performance. This would be a valid measure of performance, as the amount involved would represent the margin generated by the segment after deducting all costs controllable by the segment manager. The committed fixed costs of a segment can be broken down in still other ways. However, the preceding discussion is adequate for our purposes.

Activity-Based Costing Some costs are easy to identify as traceable costs. For example, the costs of advertising Crest toothpaste on television are clearly traceable to Crest. A more difficult situation arises when a building, machine, or other resource is shared by two or more segments. For example, assume that a multiproduct company leases warehouse space that is used for storing the full range of its products. Would the lease cost of the warehouse be a traceable or a common cost of the products? Managers familiar with activity-based costing might argue that the lease is traceable and should be assigned to the products according to how much space the products use in the warehouse. In like manner, these managers would argue that order processing costs, sales support costs, and other selling, general, and administrative (SG&A) expenses should also be charged to segments according to the segments' consumption of SG&A resources.

To illustrate, consider Holt Corporation, a company that manufactures concrete pipe for industrial uses. The company has three products—9-inch pipe, 12-inch pipe, and 18-inch pipe. Space is leased in a large warehouse on a yearly basis as needed. The lease cost of this space is $10 per square metre per year. The 9-inch pipe occupies 400 square metres of space, 12-inch pipe occupies 1,600 square metres, and 18-inch pipe occupies 2,000 square metres. The company also has an order-processing department that incurred $150,000 in order-processing costs last year. Management believes that order-processing costs are driven by the number of orders placed by customers in a year. Last year, 2,500 orders were placed, of which 1,200 were for 9-inch pipe, 800 were for 12-inch pipe, and 500 were for 18-inch pipe. Given these data, the following costs would be assigned to each product using the activity-based costing approach:

Warehouse space cost:	
9-inch pipe: $10 × 400 square metres	$ 4,000
12-inch pipe: $10 × 1,600 square metres	16,000
18-inch pipe: $10 × 2,000 square metres.....	20,000
Total cost assigned	$40,000
Order processing costs:	
$150,000 ÷ 2,500 orders = $60 per order	
9-inch pipe: $60 × 1,200 orders	$ 72,000
12-inch pipe: $60 × 800 orders	48,000
18-inch pipe: $60 × 500 orders	30,000
Total cost assigned	$150,000

This method of assigning costs combines the strength of activity-based costing with the power of the contribution approach and greatly enhances the manager's ability to measure the profitability and performance of segments. However, managers must still ask themselves if the costs would in fact disappear over time if the segment itself disappeared. In the case of Holt Corporation, it is clear that the $20,000 in warehousing costs for the 18-inch pipe would be eliminated if the 18-inch pipe were no longer being produced. The company would simply rent less warehouse space the following year. However, suppose the company owns the warehouse. Then it is not so clear that the $20,000 of the cost of the warehouse would really disappear if the 18-inch pipes were discontinued as a product. The company warehouse might simply be empty while the costs of the warehouse continue to be incurred.

Traceable Costs Can Become Common

Fixed costs that are traceable to one segment may be common costs of another segment. This is because there are limits to how finely a cost can be separated without resorting to arbitrary allocation. The more finely segments are defined, the more costs there are that are common.

This concept can be seen in Exhibit 8–9. Notice that when segments are defined as divisions, the Consumer Products Division has $80,000 in traceable fixed expenses. Only $70,000 of this amount remains traceable, however, when we narrow our definition to that of the product lines. Notice that the other $10,000 then becomes a common cost of these product lines of the Consumer Products Division.

Why would $10,000 of traceable fixed cost become a common cost when the division is divided into product lines? The $10,000 is the monthly salary of the manager of the Consumer Products Division. This salary is a traceable cost of the division as a whole, but is a common cost of the division's product lines. The manager's salary is a necessary cost of having the two product lines, but even it one of the product lines were discontinued entirely, the manager's salary would probably not be cut. Therefore, none of the manger's salary can really be traced to the individual products.

The $70,000 traceable fixed cost of the product lines consists of the cost of product-specific advertising. A total of $30,000 was spent on advertising animation software and

EXHIBIT 8–9 Reclassification of Traceable Fixed Expenses from Exhibit 8–8

	Total Company	Segment: Business Products Division	Segment: Consumer Products Division
Contribution margin	$270,000	$150,000	$120,000
Traceable fixed expenses	170,000	90,000	80,000

	Consumer Products Division	Segment: Computer Animation	Segment: Computer Games
Contribution margin	$120,000	$50,000	$70,000
Traceable fixed expenses	70,000	30,000	40,000
Product-line segment margin	50,000	$20,000	0$30,000
Common fixed expenses	10,000		
Divisional segment margin	$ 40,000		

$40,000 was spent on advertising computer games. These costs can clearly be traced to the individual product lines.

Segment Margin

Segment margin A segment margin is obtained by deducting a segment's traceable fixed costs from the segment's contribution margin.

Observe from Exhibit 8–8 that the **segment margin** is obtained by deducting a segment's traceable fixed costs from the segment's contribution margin. It represents the margin available after a segment has covered all of its own costs. The segment margin is the best gage of the long-run profitability of a segment, because it includes only those costs that are caused by the segment. The term long-run is applied here because fixed costs could be altered if the segment were eliminated. If a segment cannot cover its own costs, that segment probably should be dropped (unless it is essential to sales of other segments). Notice from Exhibit 8–8, for example, that the Retail Stores sales channel has a negative segment margin. This means that the segment is not generating enough revenue to cover its own costs. In fact, it is detracting from profits in that its $3,000 loss must be covered by other segments. Retention or elimination of product lines and other segments is covered in more depth in Chapter 12.

From a decision-making point of view, the segment margin is most useful in major decisions that affect capacity such as dropping a segment. By contrast, as noted earlier, the contribution margin is most useful in decisions relating to short-run changes, such as pricing of special orders that involve temporary use of existing capacity.

Segment Reporting for Financial Accounting

Conflicting reports between segment profits for internal management and those required for external statement users are now minimized as a result of the changes to Section 1701 of the *CICA Handbook*. Segmented reports prepared for external users must use the same methods and definitions that the companies use in internal segmented reports that are prepared to aid in making operating decisions. This is a very unusual requirement. Companies are not ordinarily required to report the same data to external users that are reported internally for decision-making purposes. This requirement has some serious drawbacks. First, segmented data are often highly sensitive and companies are reluctant to release such data to the public for the simple reason that their competitors will then have access to the data. Second, segmented statements prepared in accordance with GAAP do not distinguish between fixed and variable costs and between traceable and common costs. Indeed, the segmented income statements illustrated earlier in this chapter do not conform to GAAP for that reason. To avoid the complications of reconciling non-GAAP segment earnings with GAAP consolidated earnings, it is likely that at least some managers will choose to construct their segmented financial statements in a manner that conforms with GAAP. This will result in more occurrences of the problems discussed in the following section.

Hindrances to Proper Cost Assignment

Costs must be properly assigned to segments. All of the costs attributable to a segment—and only those costs—should be assigned to the segment. Unfortunately, companies often make mistakes when assigning costs to segments. They omit some costs, inappropriately assign traceable fixed costs, and arbitrarily allocate common fixed costs.

Omission of Costs

The costs assigned to a segment should include all costs attributable to that segment from the company's entire value chain as discussed in Chapter 1. All of these functions, from research and development, through product design, manufacturing, marketing, distribution, and customer service, are required to bring a product or service to the customer and generate revenues.

However, as discussed in Chapters 2, 3 and earlier in this chapter, only manufacturing costs are included in product costs under absorption costing, which is widely regarded as required for financial reporting. To avoid having to maintain two costing systems and to provide consistency between internal and external reports, many companies also use absorption costing for their internal reports such as segmented income statements. As a result, such companies omit from their profitability analysis part or all of the "upstream" costs in the value chain, which consist of research and development and product design, and the "downstream" costs, which consist of marketing, distribution, and customer service. Yet these nonmanufacturing costs are just as essential as manufacturing costs in determining product profitability. These upstream and downstream costs, which are usually included in selling and administrative expenses on the income statement can represent half or more of the total costs of an organization. If either the upstream or downstream costs are omitted in profitability analysis, then the product is undercosted and management may unwittingly develop and maintain products that result in losses in the long run.

Inappropriate Methods for Assigning Traceable Costs among Segments

In addition to omitting costs, many companies do not correctly handle traceable fixed expenses on segmented income statements. First, they may not trace fixed expenses to segments even when it is feasible to do so. Second, they may use inappropriate allocation bases to allocate traceable fixed expenses to segments.

Failure to Trace Costs Directly Costs that can be traced directly to a specific company segment should be charged directly to that segment and should not be allocated to other segments. For example, the rent for a branch office of an insurance company should be charged directly against the branch to which it relates rather than included in a companywide overhead pool and then spread throughout the company.

Inappropriate Allocation Base Some companies allocate costs to segments using arbitrary bases such as sales dollars or cost of goods sold. For example, under the sales dollars approach, costs are allocated to the various segments according to the percentage of company sales generated by each segment. Thus, if a segment generates 20% of the company's sales, it is allocated 20% of the company's Selling General and Administrative (SG&A) expenses as its "fair share." This same basic procedure is followed if costs of goods sold or some other measure is used as the allocation base.

Costs should be allocated to segments for internal decision-making purposes only when the allocation base actually drives the cost being allocated (or is very highly correlated with the real cost driver). For example, sales should be used to allocate selling and administrative expenses only if a 10% increase in sales will result in a 10% increase in selling and administrative expenses. To the extent that selling and administrative expenses are not driven by sales volume, these expenses will be improperly allocated—with a disproportionately high percentage of the selling and administrative expenses assigned to the segments with the largest sales.

Arbitrarily Dividing Common Costs among Segments The third business practice that leads to distorted segment costs is the practice of assigning non-traceable costs to segments. For example, some companies allocate the costs of the corporate headquarters building to products on segment reports. However, in a multiproduct company, no single product is likely to be responsible for any significant amount of this cost. Even if a product were eliminated entirely, there would usually be no significant effect on any of the costs of the corporate headquarters building. In short, there is no cause-and-effect relation between the cost of the corporate headquarters building and the existence of any one product. As a consequence, any allocation of the costs of the corporate headquarters building to the products must be arbitrary.

Common costs like the costs of the corporate headquarters building are necessary, of course, to have a functioning organization. The common practice of arbitrarily allocating these costs to segments is often justified on the grounds that "someone" has to "cover the common cost." While it is undeniably true that the common costs must be covered, arbitrarily allocating common costs to segments does not ensure that this will happen. In fact, adding a share of common costs to the real costs of a segment may make an otherwise profitable segment appear to be unprofitable. If a manager eliminates the apparently unprofitable segment, the real traceable costs of the segment will be saved, but its revenues will be lost. What happens to the common fixed costs that were allocated to the segment? They don't disappear; they are reallocated to the remaining segments of the company. That makes all of the remaining segments appear to be less profitable—possibly resulting in dropping other segments. The net effect will be to reduce the profits of the company as a whole and make it even more difficult to "cover the common costs."

Additionally, common fixed costs are not manageable by the manager to whom they are arbitrarily allocated; they are the responsibility of higher-level managers. Allocating common fixed costs to responsibility centres is counterproductive in a responsibility accounting system. When common fixed costs are allocated to managers, they are held responsible for those costs even though they cannot control them.

In summary, the way many companies handle segment reporting results in cost distortion. This distortion results from three practices—the failure to trace costs directly to a specific segment when it is feasible to do so, the use of inappropriate bases for allocating costs, and the allocation of common costs to segments. These practices are widespread. One study found that 60% of the companies surveyed made no attempt to assign selling and administrative costs to segments on a cause-and-effect basis.[4]

The examples of segment reporting provided in Exhibits 8–8 and 8–9 avoid many of the problems encountered by companies who do not use variable costing. Variable costing permits a clearer allocation of costs to segments because it avoids the distortions created by the allocation of fixed manufacturing overhead that would be present with the use of absorption costing. Thus our suggestion is to use variable costing for segment reports and allocate fixed manufacturing overhead as a period expense based on the criterion of traceability, that is, *fixed costs that will disappear over time if the segment itself disappears.*

4. James R. Emore and Joseph A. Ness, "The Slow Pace of Meaningful Change in Cost Systems," *Journal of Cost Management* 4, p. 39.

Summary

Variable and absorption costing are alternative methods of determining unit product costs. Under variable costing, only those production costs that vary with output are treated as product costs. This includes direct materials, variable overhead, and ordinarily, direct labour. Fixed manufacturing overhead is treated as a period cost and charged off against revenue as it is incurred, the same as selling and administrative expenses. By contrast, absorption costing treats fixed manufacturing overhead as a product cost, along with direct materials, direct labour, and variable overhead.

Since absorption costing treats fixed manufacturing overhead as a product cost, a portion of fixed manufacturing overhead is assigned to each unit as it is produced. If units of product are unsold at the end of a period, then the fixed manufacturing overhead cost attached to the units is carried with them into the inventory account and deferred to the next period. When these units are later sold, the fixed manufacturing overhead cost attached to them is released from the inventory account and charged against revenues as a part of cost of goods sold. Thus, under absorption costing, it is possible to defer a portion of the fixed manufacturing overhead cost of one period to the next period through the inventory account.

Unfortunately, this shifting of fixed manufacturing overhead cost between periods can cause operating income to fluctuate erratically and can result in confusion and unwise decisions on the part of management. To guard against mistakes when they interpret income statement data, managers should be alert to any changes that may have taken place in inventory levels or in unit product costs during the period.

Practically speaking, variable costing cannot be used externally for financial reporting purposes in certain jurisdictions. However, it may be used internally for planning purposes. The variable costing approach dovetails well with CVP concepts that are often indispensable in profit planning and decision making.

Segment income statements provide information for evaluating the profitability and performance of divisions, product lines, sales territories, and other company segments. Under the contribution approach variable costs and fixed costs are clearly distinguished from each other and only those costs that are traceable to a segment are assigned to the segment. A cost is considered traceable to a segment only if the cost is caused by the segment and could be avoided by eliminating the segment. Fixed common costs are not allocated to segments. The segment margin consists of revenues, less variable expenses, less traceable fixed expenses of the segment.

Review Problem 1: Contrasting Variable and Absorption Costing

Dexter Company produces and sells a single product, a wooden hand loom for weaving small items such as scarves. Selected cost and operating data relating to the product for two years are given below:

Selling price per unit	$ 50	
Manufacturing costs:		
Variable per unit produced:		
Direct materials	11	
Direct labour	6	
Variable overhead	3	
Fixed per year	120,000	
Selling and administrative costs:		
Variable per unit sold	5	
Fixed per year	70,000	
	Year 1	**Year 2**
Units in beginning inventory	–0–	2,000
Units produced during the year	10,000	6,000
Units sold during the year	8,000	8,000
Units in ending inventory	2,000	–0–

Required:

1. Assume that the company uses absorption costing.
   a. Compute the unit product cost in each year.
   b. Prepare an income statement for each year.
2. Assume that the company uses variable costing.
   a. Compute the unit product cost in each year.
   b. Prepare an income statement for each year.
3. Reconcile the variable costing and absorption costing operating incomes.

Solution to Review Problem 1

1. *a.* Under absorption costing, all manufacturing costs, variable and fixed, are included in unit product costs:

	Year 1	Year 2
Direct materials	$11	$11
Direct labour	6	6
Variable manufacturing overhead	3	3
Fixed manufacturing overhead		
($120,000 ÷ 10,000 units)	12	
($120,000 ÷ 6,000 units)		20
Unit product cost	$32	$40

b. The absorption costing income statements follow:

	Year 1		Year 2	
Sales (8,000 units × $50 per unit)		$400,000		$400,000
Less cost of goods sold:				
Beginning inventory	$ –0–		$ 64,000	
Add cost of goods manufactured				
(10,000 units × $32 per unit)	320,000			
(6,000 units × $40 per unit)			240,000	
Goods available for sale	320,000		304,000	
Less ending inventory (2,000 units × $32 per unit; 0 units)	64,000	256,000	–0–	304,000
Gross margin		144,000		96,000
Less selling and administrative expenses		110,000*		110,000*
Operating income		$ 34,000		$(14,000)

*Selling and administrative expenses:

Variable (8,000 units × $5 per unit)	$ 40,000
Fixed per year	70,000
Total	$110,000

2. *a.* Under variable costing, only the variable manufacturing costs are included in unit product costs:

	Year 1	Year 2
Direct materials	$11	$11
Direct labour	6	6
Variable manufacturing overhead	3	3
Unit product cost	$20	$20

b. The variable costing income statements follow. Notice that the variable cost of goods sold is computed in a simpler, more direct manner than in the examples provided earlier. On a variable costing income statement, either approach to computing the cost of goods sold followed in this chapter is acceptable.

	Year 1		Year 2	
Sales (8,000 units × $50 per unit)		$400,000		$400,000
Less variable expenses:				
Variable cost of goods sold (8,000 units × $20 per unit)	$160,000		$160,000	
Variable selling and administrative expenses (8,000 units × $5 per unit)	40,000		40,000	
Contribution margin		200,000		200,000
Less fixed expenses:				
Fixed manufacturing overhead	120,000		120,000	
Fixed selling and administrative expenses	70,000	190,000	70,000	190,000
Operating income		$ 10,000		$ 10,000

3. The reconciliation of the variable and absorption costing operating incomes follows:

	Year 1	Year 2
Variable costing operating income	$10,000	$10,000
Add fixed manufacturing overhead costs deferred in inventory under absorption costing (2,000 units × $12 per unit)	24,000	
Deduct fixed manufacturing overhead costs released from inventory under absorption costing (2,000 units × $12 per unit)		24,000
Absorption costing operating income	$34,000	$(14,000)

Review Problem 2: Segmented Statements

The business staff of the law firm Frampton, Davis & Smythe has constructed the following report which breaks down the firm's overall results for last month into two main business segments—family law and commercial law:

However, this report is not quite correct. The common fixed expenses such as the managing partner's salary, general administrative expenses, and general firm advertising have been allocated to the two segments based on revenues from clients.

	Total	Family Law	Commercial Law
Revenues from clients	$1,000,000	$400,000	$600,000
Variable expenses	220,000	100,000	120,000
Contribution margin	780,000	300,000	480,000
Traceable fixed expenses	670,000	280,000	390,000
Segment margin	110,000	20,000	90,000
Common fixed expenses	60,000	24,000	36,000
Operating income	$ 50,000	$ (4,000)	$ 54,000

Required:

1. Redo the segment report, eliminating the allocation of common fixed expenses. Would the firm be better off financially if the family law segment were dropped? (Note: Many of the firm's commercial law clients also use the firm for their family law requirements such as drawing up wills.)
2. The firm's advertising agency has proposed an ad campaign targeted at boosting the revenues of the family law segment. The ad campaign would cost $20,000, and the advertising agency claims that it would increase family law revenues by $100,000. The managing partner of Frampton, Davis & Smythe believes this increase in business could be accommodated without

any increase in fixed expenses. What effect would this ad campaign have on the family law segment margin and on the firm's overall operating income?

Solution to Review Problem 2

1. The corrected segmented income statement appears below:

	Total	Family Law	Commercial Law
Revenues from clients	$1,000,000	$400,000	$600,000
Variable expenses	220,000	100,000	120,000
Contribution margin	780,000	300,000	480,000
Traceable fixed expenses	670,000	280,000	390,000
Segment margin	110,000	$ 20,000	$ 90,000
Common fixed expenses	60,000		
Operating income	$ 50,000		

No, the firm would not be financially better off if the family law practice were dropped. The family law segment is covering all of its own costs and is contributing $20,000 per month to covering the common fixed expenses of the firm. While the segment margin for family law is much lower than for commercial law, it is still profitable. Moreover, family law may be a service that the firm must provide to its commercial clients in order to remain competitive.

2. The ad campaign would increase the family law segment margin by $55,000 as follows:

Increased revenues from clients	$100,000
Family law contribution margin ratio ($300,000 ÷ $400,000)	× 75%
Incremental contribution margin	$ 75,000
Less cost of the ad campaign	20,000
Increased segment margin	$ 55,000

Since there would be no increase in fixed expenses (including common fixed expenses), the increase in overall operating income is also $55,000.

Glossary

Visit the Online Learning Centre at http://www.mcgrawhill.ca/olc/garrison/ for a review of key terms and definitions.

Questions

8–1 What is the basic difference between absorption costing and variable costing?

8–2 Are selling and administrative expenses treated as product costs or as period costs under variable costing?

8–3 Explain how fixed manufacturing overhead costs are shifted from one period to another under absorption costing.

8–4 What arguments can be advanced in favour of treating fixed manufacturing overhead costs as product costs?

8–5 What arguments can be advanced in favour of treating fixed manufacturing overhead costs as period costs?

8–6 If production and sales are equal, which method would you expect to show the higher operating income, variable costing or absorption costing? Why?

8–7 If production exceeds sales, which method would you expect to show the higher operating income, variable costing or absorption costing? Why?

8–8 If fixed manufacturing overhead costs are released from inventory under absorption costing, what does this tell you about the level of production in relation to the level of sales?

8–9 Parker Company had $5,000,000 in sales and reported a $300,000 loss in its annual report to shareholders. According to a CVP analysis prepared for management's use, $5,000,000 in sales is the break-even point for the company. Did the company's inventory level increase, decrease, or remain unchanged? Explain.

8–10 Under absorption costing, how is it possible to increase operating income without increasing sales?

8–11 How is the use of variable costing limited?

8–12 How does Lean Production reduce or eliminate the difference in reported operating income between absorption and variable costing?

8–13 What is a segment of an organization? Give several examples of segments.

8–14 What costs are assigned to a segment under the contribution approach?

8–15 Distinguish between a traceable cost and a common cost. Give several examples of each.

8–16 Explain how the segment margin differs from the contribution margin.

8–17 Why aren't common costs allocated to segments under the contribution approach?

8–18 How is it possible for a cost that is traceable to a segment to become a common cost if the segment is divided into further segments?

Exercises

EXERCISE 8–1 Variable and Absorption Costing Unit Product Costs [LO1]

Shastri Bicycle of Bombay, India, produces an inexpensive, yet rugged, bicycle for use on the city's crowded streets that it sells for 500 rupees. (Indian currency is denominated in rupees, denoted by R.) Selected data for the company's operations last year follow:

Units in beginning inventory	0
Units produced	10,000
Units sold	8,000
Units in ending inventory	2,000
Variable costs per unit:	
Direct materials	R120
Direct labour	R140
Variable manufacturing overhead	R50
Variable selling and administrative	R20
Fixed costs:	
Fixed manufacturing overhead	R600,000
Fixed selling and administrative	R400,000

Required:

1. Assume that the company uses absorption costing. Compute the unit product cost for one bicycle.
2. Assume that the company uses variable costing. Compute the unit product cost for one bicycle.

EXERCISE 8–2 Variable Costing Income Statement; Explanation of Difference in Operating Income [LO2]

Refer to the data in Exercise 8–1 for Shastri Bicycle. An absorption costing income statement prepared by the company's accountant appears on the next page.

Required:

1. Determine how much of the ending inventory of R740,000 above consists of fixed manufacturing overhead cost deferred in inventory to the next period.
2. Prepare an income statement for the year using the variable costing method. Explain the difference in operating income between the two costing methods.

EXERCISE 8–3 Reconciliation of Absorption and Variable Costing Operating Incomes [LO3]

High Tension Transformers, Inc., manufactures heavy-duty transformers for electrical switching stations. The company uses variable costing for internal management reports and absorption costing for external reports to shareholders, creditors, and the government. The company has provided the data for Years 1, 2, and 3 shown on the next page.

Absorption Costing Income Statement for Exercise 8–2:

Sales (8,000 units × R500 per unit)		R4,000,000
Cost of goods sold:		
Beginning inventory	R 0	
Add cost of goods manufactured (10,000 units × R __?__ per unit)	3,700,000	
Goods available for sale	3,700,000	
Less ending inventory (2,000 units × R __?__ per unit)	740,000	2,960,000
Gross margin		1,040,000
Selling and administrative expenses:		
Variable selling and administrative	160,000	
Fixed selling and administrative	400,000	560,000
Operating income		R 480,000

Exercise 8–3 continued:

The company's fixed manufacturing overhead per unit was constant at $450 for all three years.

	Year 1	Year 2	Year 3
Inventories:			
Beginning (units)	180	150	160
Ending (units)	150	160	200
Variable costing operating income	$292,400	$269,200	$251,800

Required:

1. Determine each year's absorption costing operating income. Present your answer in the form of a reconciliation report such as the one shown in Exhibit 8–7.
2. In Year 4, the company's variable costing operating income was $240,200 and its absorption costing operating income was $267,200. Did inventories increase or decrease during Year 4? How much fixed manufacturing overhead cost was deferred or released from inventory during Year 4?

EXERCISE 8–4 Evaluating Absorption and Variable Costing as Alternative Costing Methods [LO4]

The questions below pertain to two different scenarios involving a manufacturing company. In each scenario, the cost structure of the company is constant from year to year. Selling prices, unit variable costs, and total fixed costs are the same in every year. However, unit sales and/or unit production levels may vary from year to year.

Required:

1. Consider the following data for scenario A:

	Year 1	Year 2	Year 3
Variable costing operating income	$16,847	$16,847	$16,847
Absorption costing operating income	$16,847	$29,378	$6,018

   a. Were unit sales constant from year to year? Explain.
   b. What was the relation between unit sales and unit production levels in each year? For each year, indicate whether inventories grew or shrank.

2. Consider the following data for scenario B:

	Year 1	Year 2	Year 3
Variable costing operating income (loss)	$16,847	($18,153)	($53,153)
Absorption costing operating income	$16,847	$17,583	$18,318

a. Were unit sales constant from year to year? Explain.
b. What was the relation between unit sales and unit production levels in each year? For each year, indicate whether inventories grew or shrank.

3. Given the patterns of operating income in scenarios A and B above, which costing method, variable costing or absorption costing, do you believe provides a better reflection of economic reality? Explain.

EXERCISE 8–5 Variable Costing Unit Product Cost and Income Statement; Break-Even [LO1, LO2]

CompuDesk, Inc., makes an oak desk specially designed for personal computers. The desk sells for $200. Data for last year's operations follow:

Units in beginning inventory	0
Units produced	10,000
Units sold	9,000
Units in ending inventory	1,000
Variable costs per unit:	
Direct materials	$ 60
Direct labour	30
Variable manufacturing overhead	10
Variable selling and administrative	20
Total variable cost per unit	$ 120
Fixed costs:	
Fixed manufacturing overhead	$300,000
Fixed selling and administrative	450,000
Total fixed costs	$750,000

Required:

1. Assume that the company uses variable costing. Compute the unit product cost for one computer desk.
2. Assume that the company uses variable costing. Prepare a contribution format income statement for the year.
3. What is the company's break-even point in terms of units sold?

EXERCISE 8–6 Absorption Costing Unit Product Cost and Income Statement [LO1, LO2]

Refer to the data in Exercise 8–5 for CompuDesk. Assume in this exercise that the company uses absorption costing.

Required:

1. Compute the unit product cost for one computer desk.
2. Prepare an income statement for the year.

EXERCISE 8–7 Variable and Absorption Costing Unit Product Costs and Income Statements [LO1, LO2]

Maxwell Company manufactures and sells a single product. The following costs were incurred during the company's first year of operations:

Variable costs per unit:	
Manufacturing:	
Direct materials	$18
Direct labour	$7
Variable manufacturing overhead	$2
Variable selling and administrative	$5
Fixed costs per year:	
Fixed manufacturing overhead	$160,000
Fixed selling and administrative expenses	$110,000

During the year, the company produced 20,000 units and sold 16,000 units. The selling price of the company's product is $50 per unit.

Required:

1. Assume that the company uses absorption costing:
   a. Compute the unit product cost.
   b. Prepare an income statement for the year.
2. Assume that the company uses variable costing:
   a. Compute the unit product cost.
   b. Prepare an income statement for the year.

EXERCISE 8–8 Inferring Costing Method; Unit Product Cost [LO1, LO4]
Amcor, Inc., incurs the following costs to produce and sell a single product.

Variable costs per unit:	
Direct materials	$10
Direct labour	$5
Variable manufacturing overhead	$2
Variable selling and administrative expenses	$4
Fixed costs per year:	
Fixed manufacturing overhead	$90,000
Fixed selling and administrative expenses	$300,000

During the last year, 30,000 units were produced and 25,000 units were sold. The Finished Goods inventory account at the end of the year shows a balance of $85,000 for the 5,000 unsold units.

Required:

1. Is the company using absorption costing or variable costing to cost units in the Finished Goods inventory account? Show computations to support your answer.
2. Assume that the company wishes to prepare financial statements for the year to issue to its shareholders.
   a. Is the $85,000 figure for Finished Goods inventory the correct amount to use on these statements for external reporting purposes? Explain.
   b. At what dollar amount *should* the 5,000 units be carried in inventory for external reporting purposes?

EXERCISE 8–9 Variable Costing Income Statement; Reconciliation [LO2, LO3]
Morey Company has just completed its first year of operations. The company's absorption costing income statement for the year appears below:

MOREY COMPANY INCOME STATEMENT		
Sales (40,000 units at $33.75 per unit)		$1,350,000
Cost of goods sold:		
Beginning inventory	$ 0	
Add cost of goods manufactured (50,000 units at $21 per unit)	1,050,000	
Goods available for sale	1,050,000	
Less ending inventory (10,000 units at $21 per unit)	210,000	840,000
Gross margin		510,000
Selling and administrative expenses		420,000
Operating income		$ 90,000

The company's selling and administrative expenses consist of $300,000 per year in fixed expenses and $3 per unit sold in variable expenses. The company's $21 per unit product cost given above is computed as follows:

Direct materials	$10
Direct labour	4
Variable manufacturing overhead	2
Fixed manufacturing overhead ($250,000 ÷ 50,000 units)	5
Unit product cost	$21

Required:

1. Redo the company's income statement in the contribution format using variable costing.
2. Reconcile any difference between the operating income on your variable costing income statement and the operating income on the absorption costing income statement above.

EXERCISE 8–10 Basic Segmented Income Statement [LO6]

Caltec, Inc., produces and sells recordable CD and DVD packs. Revenue and cost information relating to the products follow:

	Product	
	CD	DVD
Selling price per pack	$8.00	$25.00
Variable expenses per pack	$3.20	$17.50
Traceable fixed expenses per year	$138,000	$45,000

Common fixed expenses in the company total $105,000 annually. Last year the company produced and sold 37,500 CD packs and 18,000 DVD packs.

Required:

Prepare a contribution format income statement for the year segmented by product lines.

EXERCISE 8–11 Segmented Income Statement [LO6]

Bovine Company, a wholesale distributor of DVDs, has been experiencing losses for some time, as shown by its most recent monthly contribution format income statement below:

Sales.	$1,500,000
Variable expenses	588,000
Contribution margin	912,000
Fixed expenses	945,000
Operating loss	$ (33,000)

Required:

1. Prepare a contribution format income statement segmented by geographic market, as desired by the president.
2. The company's sales manager believes that sales in the Central geographic market could be increased by 15% if monthly advertising were increased by $25,000. Would you recommend the increased advertising? Show computations to support your answer.

In an effort to isolate the problem, the president has asked for an income statement segmented by geographic market. Accordingly, the Accounting Department has developed the following:

	Geographic Market		
	South	Central	North
Sales	$400,000	$600,000	$500,000
Variable expenses as a percentage of sales	52%	30%	40%
Traceable fixed expenses	$240,000	$330,000	$200,000

EXERCISE 8–12 Working with a Segmented Income Statement [LO6]

Marple Associates is a consulting firm that specializes in information systems for construction and landscaping companies. The firm has two offices—one in Toronto and one in Vancouver. The firm classifies the direct costs of consulting jobs as variable costs. A segmented contribution format income statement for the company's most recent year is given on the next page.

Required:

1. By how much would the company's operating income increase if Vancouver increased its sales by $75,000 per year? Assume no change in cost behaviour patterns.
2. Refer to the original data. Assume that sales in Toronto increase by $50,000 next year and that sales in Vancouver remain unchanged. Assume no change in fixed costs.

	Total Company		Office: Toronto		Office: Vancouver	
Sales	$750,000	100.0%	$150,000	100%	$600,000	100%
Variable expenses	405,000	54.0	45,000	30	360,000	60
Contribution margin	345,000	46.0	105,000	70	240,000	40
Traceable fixed expenses	168,000	22.4	78,000	52	90,000	15
Office segment margin	177,000	23.6	$ 27,000	18%	$150,000	25%
Common fixed expenses not traceable to offices	120,000	16.0				
Operating income	$ 57,000	7.6%				

a. Prepare a new segmented income statement for the company using the above format. Show both amounts and percentages.

b. Observe from the income statement you have prepared that the CM ratio for Toronto has remained unchanged at 70% (the same as in the above data) but that the segment margin ratio has changed. How do you explain the change in the segment margin ratio?

EXERCISE 8–13 Working with a Segmented Income Statement [LO6]
Refer to the data in Exercise 8–12. Assume that Vancouver's sales by major market are as follows:

	Vancouver		Market: Construction Clients		Market: Landscaping Clients	
Sales	$600,000	100%	$400,000	100%	$200,000	100%
Variable expenses	360,000	60	260,000	65	100,000	50
Contribution margin	240,000	40	140,000	35	100,000	50
Traceable fixed expenses	72,000	12	20,000	5	52,000	26
Market segment margin	168,000	28	$120,000	30%	$ 48,000	24%
Common fixed expenses not traceable to markets	18,000	3				
Office segment margin	$150,000	25%				

The company would like to initiate an intensive advertising campaign in one of the two markets during the next month. The campaign would cost $8,000. Marketing studies indicate that such a campaign would increase sales in the construction market by $70,000 or increase sales in the landscaping market by $60,000.

Required:
1. In which of the markets would you recommend that the company focus its advertising campaign? Show computations to support your answer.
2. In Exercise 8–12, Vancouver shows $90,000 in traceable fixed expenses. What happened to the $90,000 in this exercise?

Problems

PROBLEM 8–14 Variable Costing Income Statement; Reconciliation [LO2, LO3]
During Denton Company's first two years of operations, the company reported absorption costing operating income as shown on the next page.

Production and cost data for the two years are given below:

	Year 1	Year 2
Units produced	25,000	25,000
Units sold	20,000	30,000

	Year 1	Year 2
Sales (at $50 per unit)	$1,000,000	$1,500,000
Cost of goods sold:		
Beginning inventory	0	170,000
Add cost of goods manufactured (at $34 per unit)	850,000	850,000
Goods available for sale	850,000	1,020,000
Less ending inventory (at $34 per unit)	170,000	0
Cost of goods sold	680,000	1,020,000
Gross margin	320,000	480,000
Selling and administrative expenses*	310,000	340,000
Operating income	$ 10,000	$ 140,000

*$3 per unit variable; $250,000 fixed each year.

The company's $34 unit product cost is computed as follows:

Direct materials	$ 8
Direct labour	10
Variable manufacturing overhead	2
Fixed manufacturing overhead ($350,000 ÷ 25,000 units)	14
Unit product cost	$34

Required:

1. Prepare a variable costing income statement for each year in the contribution format.
2. Reconcile the absorption costing and variable costing operating income figures for each year.

PROBLEM 8–15 Variable and Absorption Costing Unit Product Costs and Income Statements; Explanation of Difference in Operating Income [LO1, LO2, LO3]

Wiengot Antennas, Inc., produces and sells a unique type of TV antenna. The company has just opened a new plant to manufacture the antenna, and the following cost and revenue data have been provided for the first month of plant's operation in the form of a worksheet.

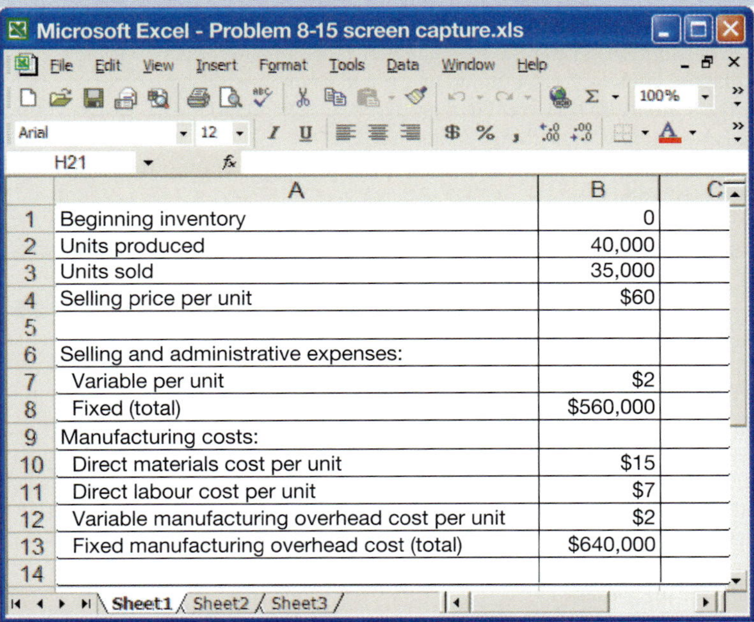

Microsoft Excel - Problem 8-15 screen capture.xls

	A	B
1	Beginning inventory	0
2	Units produced	40,000
3	Units sold	35,000
4	Selling price per unit	$60
5		
6	Selling and administrative expenses:	
7	Variable per unit	$2
8	Fixed (total)	$560,000
9	Manufacturing costs:	
10	Direct materials cost per unit	$15
11	Direct labour cost per unit	$7
12	Variable manufacturing overhead cost per unit	$2
13	Fixed manufacturing overhead cost (total)	$640,000
14		

Since the new antenna is unique in design, management is anxious to see how profitable it will be and has asked that an income statement be prepared for the month.

Required:

1. Assume that the company uses absorption costing.
   a. Determine the unit product cost.
   b. Prepare an income statement for the month.
2. Assume that the company uses variable costing.
   a. Determine the unit product cost.
   b. Prepare a contribution format income statement for the month.
3. Explain the reason for any difference in the ending inventory balances under the two costing methods and the impact of this difference on reported operating income.

PROBLEM 8–16 Comprehensive Problem with Labour Fixed [LO1, LO2, LO3, LO4]

Advance Products, Inc., has just organized a new division to manufacture and sell specially designed tables built for personal computers using select hardwoods. The division's monthly costs are shown in the schedule below:

Manufacturing costs:	
Variable costs per unit:	
Direct materials	$86
Variable manufacturing overhead	$4
Fixed manufacturing overhead costs (total)	$240,000
Selling and administrative costs:	
Variable	15% of sales
Fixed (total)	$160,000

Advance Products regards all of its workers as full-time employees and the company has a long-standing no-layoff policy. Furthermore, production is highly automated. Accordingly, the company includes its labour costs in its fixed manufacturing overhead. The tables sell for $250 each.

During the first month of operations, the following activity was recorded:

Units produced	4,000
Units sold	3,200

Required:

1. Compute the unit product cost under:
   a. Absorption costing.
   b. Variable costing.
2. Prepare an income statement for the month using absorption costing.
3. Prepare a contribution format income statement for the month using variable costing.
4. Assume that the company must obtain additional financing. As a member of top management, which of the statements that you have prepared in (2) and (3) above would you prefer to take with you as you negotiate with the bank? Why?
5. Reconcile the absorption costing and variable costing operating income figures in (2) and (3) above.

PROBLEM 8–17 Absorption and Variable Costing; Production Constant, Sales Fluctuate [LO1, LO2, LO3, LO4]

Sandi Scott obtained a patent on a small electronic device and organized Scott Products, Inc., to produce and sell the device. During the first month of operations, the device was very well received on the market, so Ms. Scott looked forward to a healthy profit. For this reason, she was surprised to see a loss for the month on her income statement. This statement was prepared by her accounting service, which takes great pride in providing its clients with timely financial data. The statement is shown on the next page.

Ms. Scott is discouraged over the loss shown for the month, particularly since she had planned to use the statement to encourage investors to purchase stock in the new company. A friend, who is an accountant, insists that the company should be using absorption costing rather than variable costing. He argues that if absorption costing had been used, the company would probably have reported a profit for the month.

Selected cost data relating to the product and to the first month of operations follow:

Units produced	50,000
Units sold	40,000
Variable costs per unit:	
Direct materials	$1.00
Direct labour	$0.80
Variable manufacturing overhead	$0.20
Variable selling and administrative expenses	$0.75

SCOTT PRODUCTS, INC. INCOME STATEMENT		
Sales (40,000 units)		$200,000
Variable expenses:		
Variable cost of goods sold*	$80,000	
Variable selling and administrative expenses	30,000	110,000
Contribution margin		90,000
Fixed expenses:		
Fixed manufacturing overhead	75,000	
Fixed selling and administrative expenses	20,000	95,000
Operating loss		$ (5,000)

*Consists of direct materials, direct labour, and variable manufacturing overhead.

Required:

1. Complete the following:
   a. Compute the unit product cost under absorption costing.
   b. Redo the company's income statement for the month using absorption costing.
   c. Reconcile the variable and absorption costing operating income (loss) figures.
2. Was the accountant correct in suggesting that the company really earned a "profit" for the month? Explain.
3. During the second month of operations, the company again produced 50,000 units but sold 60,000 units. (Assume no change in total fixed costs.)
   a. Prepare a contribution format income statement for the month using variable costing.
   b. Prepare an income statement for the month using absorption costing.
   c. Reconcile the variable costing and absorption costing operating income figures.

PROBLEM 8–18 Prepare and Reconcile Variable Costing Statements [LO1, LO2, LO3, LO4]

Linden Company manufactures and sells a single product. Cost data for the product follow:

Variable costs per unit:	
Direct materials	$ 6
Direct labour	12
Variable factory overhead	4
Variable selling and administrative	3
Total variable costs per unit	$25
Fixed costs per month:	
Fixed manufacturing overhead	$240,000
Fixed selling and administrative	180,000
Total fixed cost per month	$420,000

The product sells for $40 per unit. Production and sales data for May and June, the first two months of operations, are as follows:

	Units Produced	Units Sold
May.	30,000	26,000
June	30,000	34,000

Income statements prepared by the Accounting Department, using absorption costing, are presented below:

	May	June
Sales	$1,040,000	$1,360,000
Cost of goods sold:		
Beginning inventory	0	120,000
Add cost of goods manufactured.	900,000	900,000
Goods available for sale.	900,000	1,020,000
Less ending inventory.	120,000	0
Cost of goods sold.	780,000	1,020,000
Gross margin	260,000	340,000
Selling and administrative expenses	258,000	282,000
Operating income.	$ 2,000	$ 58,000

Required:

1. Determine the unit product cost under:
   a. Absorption costing.
   b. Variable costing.
2. Prepare variable costing income statements for May and June using the contribution approach.
3. Reconcile the variable costing and absorption costing operating income figures.
4. The company's Accounting Department has determined the break-even point to be 28,000 units per month, computed as follows:

$$\frac{\text{Fixed cost per month}}{\text{Unit contribution margin}} = \frac{\$420{,}000}{\$15 \text{ per unit}} = 28{,}000 \text{ units}$$

Upon receiving this figure, the president commented, "There's something peculiar here. The controller says that the break-even point is 28,000 units per month. Yet we sold only 26,000 units in May, and the income statement we received showed a $2,000 profit. Which figure do we believe?" Prepare a brief explanation of what happened on the May income statement.

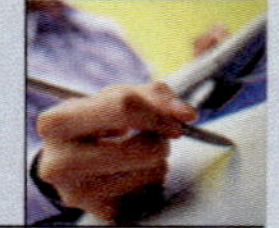

PROBLEM 8–19 Incentives Created by Absorption Costing; Ethics and the Manager [LO2, LO4]

Aristotle Constantinos, the manager of DuraProducts' Australian Division, is trying to set the production schedule for the last quarter of the year. The Australian Division had planned to sell 100,000 units during the year, but current projections indicate sales will be only 78,000 units in total. By September 30 the following activity had been reported:

	Units
Inventory, January 1.	0
Production	72,000
Sales	60,000
Inventory, September 30	12,000

Demand has been soft, and the sales forecast for the last quarter is only 18,000 units.

The division can rent warehouse space to store up to 30,000 units. The division should maintain a minimum inventory level of at least 1,500 units. Mr. Constantinos is aware that production must be at least 6,000 units per quarter in order to retain a nucleus of key employees. Maximum production capacity is 45,000 units per quarter.

Due to the nature of the division's operations, fixed manufacturing overhead is a major element of product cost.

Required:

1. Assume that the division is using variable costing. How many units should be scheduled for production during the last quarter of the year? (The basic formula for computing the required production for a period in a company is: Expected sales + Desired ending inventory − Beginning inventory = Required production.) Show computations and explain your answer. Will the number of units scheduled for production affect the division's reported profit for the year? Explain.
2. Assume that the division is using absorption costing and that the divisional manager is given an annual bonus based on the division's operating income. If Mr. Constantinos wants to maximize his division's operating income for the year, how many units should be scheduled for production during the last quarter? [See the formula in (1) above.] Explain.
3. Identify the ethical issues involved in the decision Mr. Constantinos must make about the level of production for the last quarter of the year.

PROBLEM 8–20 Comparison of Costing Methods [LO1, LO2, LO3, LO4]

Alta Products Ltd. has just created a new division to manufacture and sell DVD players. The facility is highly automated and thus has high monthly fixed costs, as shown in the following schedule of budgeted monthly costs. This schedule was prepared based on an expectation of a monthly production volume of 1,500 units.

During August 2008, the following activity was recorded:

Units produced	1,500
Units sold	1,200
Selling price per unit	$150

Manufacturing costs:	
Variable cost per unit:	
Direct material	$25
Direct Labour	30
Variable overhead	5
Total fixed overhead	$60,000
Selling and administrative costs:	
Variable	6% of sales
Fixed	$45,000

Required:

1. Prepare an income statement for the month ended August 31, 2008, under absorption costing.
2. Prepare an income statement for the month ended August 31, 2008 under variable costing.
3. Beginning with absorption costing reconcile the absorption costing and variable costing income figures for the month.
4. What are some of the arguments in favour of using variable costing? What are some of the arguments in favour of using absorption costing?

(CGA-Canada adapted)

PROBLEM 8–21 Comparison of Costing Methods [LO1, LO2, LO3, LO4]

The following information relates to Mucktar Ltd. during the first quarter of 2008:

	January	February	March
Unit sales	12,000	14,000	18,000
Sales price per unit	$12	$12	$12
Variable manufacturing cost per unit	5	5	5
Variable selling expense	2	2	2
Unit production	15,000	18,000	13,000

Additional data:

a. On January 1, there were 2,000 units on hand.

b. Fixed overhead cost is $3,00 per unit and is applied to units of product on the basis of a production volume of 14,000 units per month. Costs of goods sold is adjusted for any over- or underapplied fixed manufacturing overhead.

c. Mucktar Ltd. uses FIFO inventory flow. Work in process inventories are not material and are to be ignored.

d. Fixed selling and administrative expenses total $22,000 per month.

Required:

1. Prepare quarterly income statements using:
   a. absorption costing
   b. variable costing
2. Explain why, under absorption costing, monthly profits have moved erratically over the quarter and have not moved in correlation with changes in sales volume. Include a reconciliation of absorption and variable costing in your answer.
3. Identify the advantages and disadvantages of using variable costing for internal reporting purposes.

(CGA-Canada adapted)

PROBLEM 8–22 Variable Costing Income Statements; Sales Constant; Production Varies; Lean Production [LO1, LO2, LO3, LO4, LO5]

"Can someone explain to me what's wrong with these statements?" asked Cheri Reynolds, president of Milex Corporation. "They just don't make sense. We sold the same number of units this year as we did last year, yet our profits have tripled! Who messed up the calculations?"

The absorption costing income statements to which Ms. Reynolds was referring are shown below:

	Year 1	Year 2
Sales (40,000 units each year)	$1,250,000	$1,250,000
Cost of goods sold	840,000	720,000
Gross margin	410,000	530,000
Selling and administrative expenses	350,000	350,000
Operating income	$ 60,000	$ 180,000

In the first year, the company produced and sold 40,000 units; in the second year, the company again sold 40,000 units, but it increased production to 50,000 units, as shown below:

	Year 1	Year 2
Production in units	40,000	50,000
Sales in units	40,000	40,000
Variable manufacturing cost per unit produced	$6	$6
Variable selling and administrative expense per unit sold	$2	$2
Fixed manufacturing overhead costs (total)	$600,000	$600,000

Milex Corporation applies fixed manufacturing overhead costs to its only product on the basis of each year's production. (Thus, a new fixed manufacturing overhead rate is computed each year, as in Exhibit 8–6.)

Required:

1. Compute the unit product cost for each year under:
   a. Absorption costing.
   b. Variable costing.
2. Prepare a contribution format income statement for each year using variable costing.
3. Reconcile the variable costing and absorption costing operating income figures for each year.
4. Explain to the president why the operating income for Year 2 was higher than for Year 1 under absorption costing, although the same number of units was sold in each year.
5. *a.* Explain how operations would have differed in Year 2 if the company had been using Lean Production and inventories had been eliminated.
   b. If Lean Production had been in use during Year 2 and ending inventories were zero, what would the company's operating income have been under absorption costing? Explain the reason for any difference between this income figure and the figure reported by the company in the statements above.

PROBLEM 8–23 Prepare and Interpret Statements; Changes in Both Sales and Production; Lean Production [LO1, LO2, LO3, LO4, LO5]

Memotec, Inc., manufactures and sells a unique electronic part. Operating results for the first three years of activity were as follows (absorption costing basis):

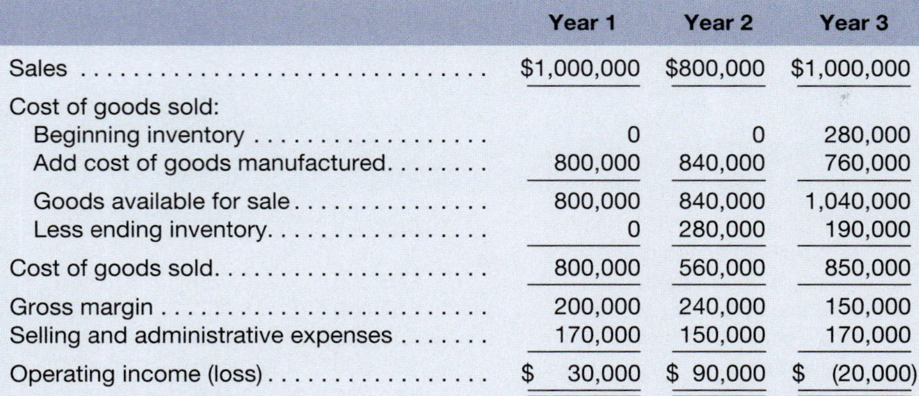

	Year 1	Year 2	Year 3
Sales	$1,000,000	$800,000	$1,000,000
Cost of goods sold:			
Beginning inventory	0	0	280,000
Add cost of goods manufactured.	800,000	840,000	760,000
Goods available for sale.	800,000	840,000	1,040,000
Less ending inventory.	0	280,000	190,000
Cost of goods sold.	800,000	560,000	850,000
Gross margin	200,000	240,000	150,000
Selling and administrative expenses	170,000	150,000	170,000
Operating income (loss)	$ 30,000	$ 90,000	$ (20,000)

Sales dropped by 20% during Year 2 due to the entry of several foreign competitors into the market. Memotec had expected sales to remain constant at 50,000 units for the year; production was set at 60,000 units in order to build a buffer of protection against unexpected spurts in demand. By the start of Year 3, management could see that spurts in demand were unlikely and that the inventory was excessive. To work off the excessive inventories, Memotec cut back production during Year 3, as shown below:

	Year 1	Year 2	Year 3
Production in units	50,000	60,000	40,000
Sales in units	50,000	40,000	50,000

Additional information about the company follows:

a. The company's plant is highly automated. Variable manufacturing costs (direct materials, direct labour, and variable manufacturing overhead) total only $4 per unit, and fixed manufacturing overhead costs total $600,000 per year.

b. Fixed manufacturing overhead costs are applied to units of product on the basis of each year's production. (That is, a new fixed overhead rate is computed each year, as in Exhibit 8–6).

c. Variable selling and administrative expenses are $2 per unit sold. Fixed selling and administrative expenses total $70,000 per year.

d. The company uses a FIFO inventory flow assumption.

Memotec's management can't understand why profits tripled during Year 2 when sales dropped by 20%, and why a loss was incurred during Year 3 when sales recovered to previous levels.

Required:

1. Prepare a contribution format income statement for each year using variable costing.
2. Refer to the absorption costing income statements above.
   a. Compute the unit product cost in each year under absorption costing. (Show how much of this cost is variable and how much is fixed.)
   b. Reconcile the variable costing and absorption costing operating income figures for each year.
3. Refer again to the absorption costing income statements. Explain why operating income was higher in Year 2 than it was in Year 1 under the absorption approach, in light of the fact that fewer units were sold in Year 2 than in Year 1.
4. Refer again to the absorption costing income statements. Explain why the company suffered a loss in Year 3 but reported a profit in Year 1, although the same number of units was sold in each year.
5. *a.* Explain how operations would have differed in Year 2 and Year 3 if the company had been using Lean Production with the result that ending inventory was zero.
   b. If Lean Production had been in use during Year 2 and Year 3, what would the company's operating income (or loss) have been in each year under absorption costing? Explain the reason for any differences between these income figures and the figures reported by the company in the statements above.

PROBLEM 8–24 Restructuring a Segmented Income Statement [LO6]
Brabant NV of the Netherlands is a wholesale distributor of Dutch cheeses that it sells throughout the European Community. Unfortunately, the company's profits have been declining, which has caused considerable concern. To help understand the condition of the company, the managing director of the company has requested that the monthly income statement be segmented by sales territory. Accordingly, the company's accounting department has prepared the following statement for March, the more recent month. (The Dutch currency is the euro which is designated by €.)

	Sales Territory		
	Southern Europe	Middle Europe	Northern Europe
Sales	€300,000	€800,000	€700,000
Territorial expenses (traceable):			
Cost of goods sold.	93,000	240,000	315,000
Salaries.	54,000	56,000	112,000
Insurance	9,000	16,000	14,000
Advertising	105,000	240,000	245,000
Depreciation.	21,000	32,000	28,000
Shipping	15,000	32,000	42,000
Total territorial expenses	297,000	616,000	756,000
Territorial income (loss) before corporate expenses	3,000	184,000	(56,000)
Corporate expenses:			
Advertising (general).	15,000	40,000	35,000
General administrative	20,000	20,000	20,000
Total corporate expenses	35,000	60,000	55,000
Operating income (loss).	€(32,000)	€124,000	€(111,000)

Cost of goods sold and shipping expenses are both variable; other costs are all fixed. Brabant NV purchases cheeses at auction and from farmers' cooperatives, and it distributes them in the three territories listed above. Each of the three sales territories has its own manager and sales staff. The cheeses vary widely in profitability; some have a high margin and some have a low margin. (Certain cheeses, after having been aged for long periods, are the most expensive and carry the highest margins.)

Required:

1. List any disadvantages or weaknesses that you see to the statement format illustrated above.
2. Explain the basis that is apparently being used to allocate the corporate expenses to the territories. Do you agree with these allocations? Explain.
3. Prepare a new segmented contribution format income statement for May. Show a Total column as well as data for each territory. Include percentages on your statement for all columns. Carry percentages to one decimal place.
4. Analyze the statement that you prepared in (3) above. What points that might help to improve the company's performance would you bring to management's attention?

PROBLEM 8–25 Segment Reporting and Decision Making [LO6]
The most recent monthly contribution format income statement for Reston Company is given below:

RESTON COMPANY INCOME STATEMENT FOR THE MONTH ENDED MAY 31		
Sales	$900,000	100.0%
Variable expenses	408,000	45.3
Contribution margin.	492,000	54.7
Fixed expenses	465,000	51.7
Operating income	$ 27,000	3.0%

Management is disappointed with the company's performance and is wondering what can be done to improve profits. By examining sales and cost records, you have determined the following:

a. The company is divided into two sales territories—Central and Eastern. The Central Territory recorded $400,000 in sales and $208,000 in variable expenses during May. The remaining sales and variable expenses were recorded in the Eastern Territory. Fixed expenses of $160,000 and $130,000 are traceable to the Central and Eastern Territories, respectively. The rest of the fixed expenses are common to the two territories.
b. The company is the exclusive distributor for two products—Awls and Pows. Sales of Awls and Pows totalled $100,000 and $300,000, respectively, in the Central Territory during May. Variable expenses are 25% of the selling price for Awls and 61% for Pows. Cost records show that $60,000 of the Central Territory's fixed expenses are traceable to Awls and $54,000 to Pows, with the remainder common to the two products.

Required:

1. Prepare contribution format segmented income statements, first showing the total company broken down between sales territories and then showing the Central Territory broken down by product line. Show both Amount and Percent columns for the company in total and for each segment. Round percentage computations to one decimal place.
2. Look at the statement you have prepared showing the total company segmented by sales territory. What points revealed by this statement should be brought to management's attention?
3. Look at the statement you have prepared showing the Central Territory segmented by product lines. What points revealed by this statement should be brought to management's attention?

PROBLEM 8–26 Basic Segmented Statement; Activity-Based Cost Assignment [LO6]

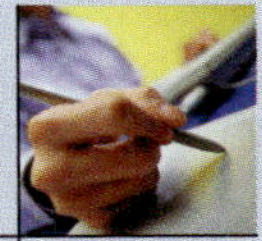

Vega Foods, Inc., has recently purchased a small mill that it intends to operate as one of its subsidiaries. The newly acquired mill has three products that it offers for sale—wheat cereal, pancake mix, and flour. Each product sells for $10 per package. Materials, labour, and other variable production costs are $3.00 per bag of wheat cereal, $4.20 per bag of pancake mix, and $1.80 per bag of flour. Sales commissions are 10% of sales for any product. All other costs are fixed.

The mill's income statement for the most recent month is given below:

		Product Line		
	Total Company	Wheat Cereal	Pancake Mix	Flour
Sales	$600,000	$200,000	$300,000	$100,000
Expenses:				
Materials, labour, and other	204,000	60,000	126,000	18,000
Sales commissions	60,000	20,000	30,000	10,000
Advertising	123,000	48,000	60,000	15,000
Salaries	66,000	34,000	21,000	11,000
Equipment depreciation	30,000	10,000	15,000	5,000
Warehouse rent	12,000	4,000	6,000	2,000
General administration	90,000	30,000	30,000	30,000
Total expenses	585,000	206,000	288,000	91,000
Operating income (loss)	$ 15,000	$ (6,000)	$ 12,000	$ 9,000

The following additional information is available about the company:

a. The same equipment is used to mill and package all three products. In the above income statement, equipment depreciation has been allocated on the basis of sales dollars. An analysis of equipment usage indicates that it is used 40% of the time to make wheat cereal, 50% of the time to make pancake mix, and 10% of the time to make flour.
b. All three products are stored in the same warehouse. In the above income statement, the warehouse rent has been allocated on the basis of sales dollars. The warehouse contains 24,000 square metres of space, of which 8,000 square metres are used for wheat cereal, 14,000 square metres are used for pancake mix, and 2,000 square metres are used for flour. The warehouse space costs the company $0.50 per square metre to rent.
c. The general administration costs relate to the administration of the company as a whole. In the above income statement, these costs have been divided equally among the three product lines.
d. All other costs are traceable to the product lines.

Vega Foods' management is anxious to improve the mill's 2.5% margin on sales.

Required:

1. Prepare a new contribution format segmented income statement for the month. Adjust the allocations as required.
2. After seeing the income statement in the main body of the problem, management has decided to eliminate the wheat cereal, because it is not returning a profit, and to focus all available resources on promoting the pancake mix.
   a. Based on the statement you have prepared, do you agree with the decision to eliminate the wheat cereal? Explain.
   b. Based on the statement you have prepared, do you agree with the decision to focus all available resources on promoting the pancake mix? Assume that an ample market is available for all three products. (Hint: compute the contribution margin ratio for each product.)

PROBLEM 8–27 Finely Segmented Income Statements [LO6]

Severo S.A. of Sao Paulo, Brazil, is organized into two divisions. The company's contribution format segmented income statement (in terms of the Brazilian currency Real) for last month is given below:

		Divisions	
	Total Company	Cloth	Leather
Sales	R3,500,000	R2,000,000	R1,500,000
Variable expenses	1,721,000	960,000	761,000
Contribution margin	1,779,000	1,040,000	739,000
Traceable fixed expenses:			
Advertising	612,000	300,000	312,000
Administration	427,000	210,000	217,000
Depreciation	229,000	115,000	114,000
Total traceable fixed expenses	1,268,000	625,000	643,000
Divisional segment margin	511,000	R 415,000	R 96,000
Common fixed expenses	390,000		
Operating income	R 121,000		

Top management can't understand why the Leather Division has such a low segment margin when its sales are only 25% less than sales in the Cloth Division. As one step in isolating the problem, management has directed that the Leather Division be further segmented into product lines. The following information is available on the product lines in the Leather Division:

	Leather Division Product Lines		
	Garments	Shoes	Handbags
Sales	R500,000	R700,000	R300,000
Traceable fixed expenses:			
Advertising	R80,000	R112,000	R120,000
Administration	R30,000	R35,000	R42,000
Depreciation	R25,000	R56,000	R33,000
Variable expenses as a percentage of sales	65%	40%	52%

Analysis shows that R110,000 of the Leather Division's administration expenses are common to the product lines.

Required:

1. Prepare a contribution format segmented income statement for the Leather Division with segments defined as product lines.
2. Management is surprised by the handbag product line's poor showing and would like to have the product line segmented by market. The following information is available about the markets in which the handbag line is sold:

	Handbag Markets	
	Domestic	Foreign
Sales	R200,000	R100,000
Traceable fixed expenses:		
Advertising	R40,000	R80,000
Variable expenses as a percentage of sales	43%	70%

All of the handbag product line's administration expenses and depreciation are common to the markets in which the product is sold. Prepare a contribution format segmented income statement for the handbag product line with segments defined as markets.

3. Refer to the statement prepared in (1) above. The sales manager wants to run a special promotional campaign on one of the product lines over the next month. A marketing study indicates that such a campaign would increase sales of the garment product line by R200,000 or sales of the shoes product line by R145,000. The campaign would cost R30,000. Show computations to determine which product line should be chosen.

Cases

CASE 8–28 Ethics and the Manager; Absorption Costing Income Statements [LO2, LO4]

Michael Lee was hired as chief executive officer (CEO) in late November by the board of directors of Hunter Electronics, a company that produces a state-of-the-art DVD drive for personal computers. The previous CEO had been fired by the board due to a series of questionable business practices including prematurely recording revenues on products that had not yet been shipped to customers.

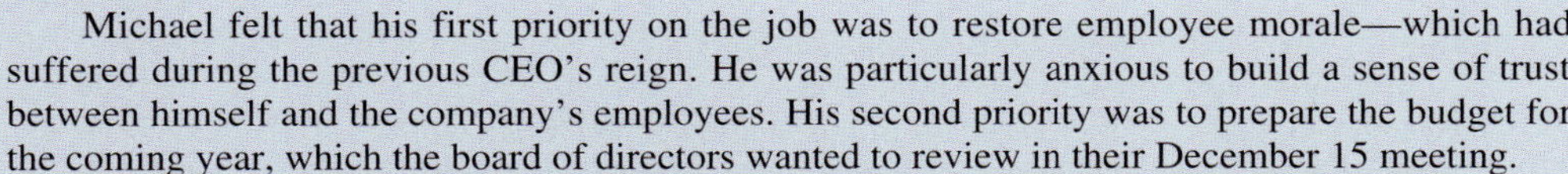

Michael felt that his first priority on the job was to restore employee morale—which had suffered during the previous CEO's reign. He was particularly anxious to build a sense of trust between himself and the company's employees. His second priority was to prepare the budget for the coming year, which the board of directors wanted to review in their December 15 meeting.

After hammering out the details in meetings with key managers, Michael was able to put together a budget that he felt the company could realistically meet during the coming year. That budget appears below:

BASIC BUDGET DATA	
Units in beginning inventory	0
Units produced	200,000
Units sold	200,000
Units in ending inventory	0
Variable costs per unit:	
Direct materials	$ 50
Direct labour	40
Variable manufacturing overhead	20
Variable selling and administrative	10
Total variable cost per unit	$120
Fixed costs:	
Fixed manufacturing overhead	$ 8,400,000
Fixed selling and administrative	3,600,000
Total fixed costs	$12,000,000

HUNTER ELECTRONICS BUDGETED INCOME STATEMENT (ABSORPTION METHOD)		
Sales (200,000 units)		$40,000,000
Cost of goods sold:		
Beginning inventory	$ 0	
Add cost of goods manufactured (200,000 × $152 per unit)	30,400,000	
Goods available for sale	30,400,000	
Less ending inventory	0	30,400,000
Gross margin		9,600,000
Selling and administrative expenses:		
Variable selling and administrative	2,000,000	
Fixed selling and administrative	3,600,000	5,600,000
Operating income		$ 4,000,000

While the board of directors did not oppose the budget, they made it clear that the budget was not as ambitious as they had hoped. The most influential member of the board stated that "managers should have to really stretch to meet profit goals." After some discussion, the board decided to set a profit goal of $4,800,000 for the coming year. To provide strong incentives and a win-win situation, the board agreed to pay out bonuses to top managers of $200,000 if this profit goal was eventually met. Michael's share of the bonus pool would be $50,000. The bonus would be all-or-nothing. If actual operating income turned out to be $4,800,000 or more, the bonus would be paid. Otherwise, no bonus would be allowed.

Required:

1. Assuming that the company does not build up its inventory (i.e., production equals sales) and its selling price and cost structure remain the same, how many units of the DVD drive would have to be sold to meet the target operating income of $4,800,000?
2. Verify your answer to (1) above by constructing a revised budget and budgeted absorption costing income statement that yields a operating income of $4,800,000.
3. Unfortunately, by October of the next year it had become clear that the company would not be able to make the $4,800,000 target profit. In fact, it looked like the company would wind-up the year as originally planned, with sales of 200,000 units, no ending inventories, and a profit of $4,000,000.

   Several managers who were reluctant to lose their year-end bonuses approached Michael and suggested that the company could still show a profit of $4,800,000. The managers argued that at the present rate of sales, there was enough capacity to produce tens of thousands of additional DVD drives for the warehouse. Overtime costs might have to be incurred, but all of this additional cost would be assigned to the DVD drives in ending inventory.

   If sales are 200,000 units for the year and the selling price and cost structure remain the same, how many units would have to be produced to show a profit of at least $4,800,000 under absorption costing? (Round your answer up to the nearest whole unit.)
4. Verify your answer to (3) above by constructing an absorption costing income statement.
5. Do you think Michael Lee should approve the plan to build ending inventories in order to attain the target profit?
6. What advice would you give to the board of directors concerning how they determine bonuses in the future?

CASE 8–29 The Case of the Perplexed President; Lean Production [LO2, LO3, LO4, LO5]
John Ovard, president of Mylar, Inc., was looking forward to receiving the company's second quarter income statement. He knew that the sales budget of 20,000 units sold had been met during the second quarter and that this represented a 25% increase in sales over the first quarter. He was especially happy about the increase in sales, since Mylar was about to approach its bank for additional loan money for expansion purposes. He anticipated that the strong second-quarter results would be a real plus in persuading the bank to extend the additional credit.

For this reason, Mr. Ovard was shocked when he received the second-quarter income statement below, which showed a substantial drop in absorption costing operating income from the first quarter.

MYLAR, INC. INCOME STATEMENTS FOR THE FIRST TWO QUARTERS	First Quarter		Second Quarter	
Sales		$1,600,000		$2,000,000
Cost of goods sold:				
Beginning inventory	$ 210,000		$ 490,000	
Add cost of goods manufactured	1,400,000		980,000	
Goods available for sale	1,610,000		1,470,000	
Less ending inventory	490,000		70,000	
Cost of goods sold	1,120,000		1,400,000	
Add underapplied overhead	0	1,120,000	240,000	1,640,000
Gross margin		480,000		360,000
Selling and administrative expenses		310,000		330,000
Operating income		$ 170,000		$ 30,000

Mr. Ovard was certain there had to be an error somewhere and immediately called the controller into his office to find the problem. The controller stated, "That operating income is correct, John. Sales went up during the second quarter, but the problem is in production. You see, we budgeted to produce 20,000 units each quarter, but a strike in one of our supplier's plants forced us to cut production back to only 14,000 units in the second quarter. That's what caused the drop in operating income."

Mr. Ovard was angered by the controller's explanation. "I call you in here to find out why income dropped when sales went up, and you talk about production! So what if production was off? What does that have to do with the sales that we made? If sales go up, then income ought to go up. If your statements can't show a simple thing like that, then we're due for some changes in your area!"

Budgeted production and sales for the year, along with actual production and sales for the first two quarters, are given below:

	Quarter			
	First	Second	Third	Fourth
Budgeted sales (units)	16,000	20,000	20,000	24,000
Actual sales (units)	16,000	20,000	—	—
Budgeted production (units)	20,000	20,000	20,000	20,000
Actual production (units)	20,000	14,000	—	—

The company's plant is heavily automated, so fixed manufacturing overhead costs total $800,000 per quarter. Variable manufacturing costs are $30 per unit. The fixed manufacturing overhead cost is applied to units of product at the rate of $40 per unit (based on the budgeted production shown above). Any underapplied or overapplied overhead is closed directly to cost of goods sold for the quarter.

The company had 3,000 units in inventory to start the first quarter and uses the FIFO inventory flow assumption. Variable selling and administrative expenses are $5 per unit sold.

Required:

1. What characteristic of absorption costing caused the drop in operating income for the second quarter and what could the controller have said to explain the problem?
2. Prepare a contribution format income statement for each quarter using variable costing.
3. Reconcile the absorption costing and the variable costing operating income figures for each quarter.
4. Identify and discuss the advantages and disadvantages of using the variable costing method for internal reporting purposes.
5. Assume that the company had introduced Lean Production methods at the beginning of the second quarter, resulting in zero ending inventory. (Sales and production during the first quarter were as shown above.)

a. How many units would have been produced during the second quarter under Lean Production?

b. Starting with the third quarter, would you expect any difference between the operating income reported under absorption costing and under variable costing? Explain why there would or would not be any difference.

CASE 8–30 Service Organization; Segment Reporting [LO6]

The American Association of Acupuncturists is a professional association for acupuncturists that has 10,000 members. The association operates from a central headquarters but has local chapters throughout North America. The association's monthly journal, *American Acupuncture,* features recent developments in the field. The association also publishes special reports and books, and it sponsors courses that qualify members for the continuing professional education credit required by certification boards. The association's statement of revenues and expenses for the current year is presented below:

AMERICAN ASSOCIATION OF ACUPUNCTURISTS STATEMENT OF REVENUES AND EXPENSES FOR THE YEAR ENDED DECEMBER 31	
Revenues	$970,000
Expenses:	
Salaries	440,000
Occupancy costs	120,000
Distributions to local chapters	210,000
Printing	82,000
Mailing	24,000
Continuing education instructors' fees	60,000
General and administrative	27,000
Total expenses	963,000
Excess of revenues over expenses	$ 7,000

The board of directors of the association has requested that you construct a segmented income statement that shows the financial contribution of each of the association's four major programs—membership service, journal, books and reports, and continuing education. The following data have been gathered to aid you:

a. Membership dues are $60 per year, of which $15 covers a one-year subscription to the association's journal. The other $45 pays for general membership services.

b. One-year subscriptions to *American Acupuncture* are sold to nonmembers and libraries at $20 per subscription. A total of 1,000 of these subscriptions were sold last year. In addition to subscriptions, the journal generated $50,000 in advertising revenues. The costs per journal subscription, for members as well as nonmembers, were $4 for printing and $1 for mailing.

c. A variety of technical reports and professional books were sold for a total of $70,000 during the year. Printing costs for these materials totalled $25,000, and mailing costs totalled $8,000.

d. The association offers a number of continuing education courses. The courses generated revenues of $230,000 last year.

e. Salary costs and space occupied by each program and the central staff follow:

	Salaries	Space Occupied (square feet)
Membership services	$170,000	3,000
Journal	60,000	1,000
Books and reports	40,000	1,000
Continuing education	50,000	2,000
Central staff	120,000	3,000
Total	$440,000	10,000

f. The $120,000 in occupancy costs incurred last year includes $20,000 in rental cost for a portion of the warehouse used by the Membership Services program for storage purposes. The association has a flexible rental agreement that allows it to pay rent only on the warehouse space it uses.

g. Printing costs other than for journal subscriptions and for books and reports related to Continuing Education.
h. Distributions to local chapters are for general membership services.
i. General and administrative expenses include costs relating to overall administration of the association as a whole. The association's central staff does some mailing of materials for general administrative purposes.
j. The expenses that can be traced or assigned to the central staff, as well as any other expenses that are not traceable to the programs, will be treated as common costs. It is not necessary to distinguish between variable and fixed costs.

Required:
1. Prepare a contribution format segmented income statement for the American Association of Acupuncturists for last year. This statement should show the segment margin for each program as well as results for the association as a whole.
2. Give arguments for and against allocating all costs of the association to the four programs.

(CMA, adapted)

Research

R 8–31 Group Exercise: College Segment Reports [LO2, LO3, LO4]

Obtain a copy of your college or university's most recent financial report prepared for internal use.

Required:
1. Does the financial report break down the results into major segments such as schools, academic departments, intercollegiate sports, and so on? Can you determine the financial contribution (i.e., revenues less expenses) of each segment from the report?
2. If the report attempts to show the financial contribution of each major segment, does the report follow the principles for segment reporting provided in the chapter? If not, what principles are violated and what harm, if any, can occur as a result of violating those principles?

R 8–32 Group Exercise: Who Needs Customers? I Can Make Money Without Them [LO1, LO3, LO4]

Tough times can bring out the worst in people. When companies are desperate to stay in business or to report more favourable earnings to the market, some managers just can't seem to resist the temptation to manipulate reported profits. Unfortunately, inventory is sometimes a tempting target of such manipulation. It is important to know how such earnings distortion can occur, whether they result from intentional actions or innocent miscalculations.

Required:
1. What product cost concept is the basis for inventory valuation and cost of goods sold determination for external financial reporting purposes?
2. Explain the concept of "phantom" or "illusory" profits. Could a firm with sales below the break-even point report profits? Explain.
3. Find an article from the business press that reports on a company that has boosted reported profits by manipulation inventory.

R 8–33 Recognition and Segment Reporting [LO1, LO4, LO6]

Suncor Energy Inc. (www.suncor.com) is a major player in the tar sands of western Canada. A lot of environmental issues are associated with oil and gas operations. Suncor has used extensive environmental reporting for more than 10 years.

The environmental report for Suncor is a large document but a summary report is provided that outlines the elements of their vision for "responsible energy development." They summarize their challenges in five key areas: community, sustainability, climate change, water management, and labour shortages.

Required:
1. Read the summary report of Suncor's sustainability activities and outline what they state as accomplishments for the most recent year.
2. Examine the comparable annual financial statements. Do not attempt to download the whole report because it is a very large document. Assess how these sustainable actions would appear in the financial statements or why they would not appear.
3. For any items located in part 2, determine whether or not segment reporting or variable costing would assist with the disclosure of sustainable reporting in the financial statements.

PLANNING AND CONTROL

Chapters 9, 10, 11

Every organization needs to plan. **Chapter 9** describes how plans can be formalized and presented so organizations can assemble the necessary resources to carry out their plans. The details in Chapter 9 also provide a foundation for new business plans and a way of describing their strategies.

To permit managers to know if plans are achieved, a system of targets should be integrated using the same structure as the budgets presented in Chapter 9 and employing the costing approach selected from the options described in Chapters 3 to 8. Standard costing in **Chapter 10** provides such an approach. Cost targets, termed *standard costs*, can be developed in many situations and if they are, a system of analysis of deviations from these targets, termed *variances*, is possible.

Besides standard cost variances, businesses need a means of analyzing their performance and a means of extending performance assessments to non-monetary areas. **Chapter 11** describes reports that show the results of various aspects of the business. Also presented is a description of the balanced scorecard which is used to extend performance measures beyond non-monetary areas.

CHAPTER 9

LEARNING OBJECTIVES

After studying Chapter 9, you should be able to:

1. Explain why organizations budget and the processes they use to create budgets.
2. Prepare the supporting components of a master budget and the budgeted financial statements.
3. Prepare a flexible budget and explain the need for the flexible budget approach.
4. Prepare a performance report using the flexible budget approach.
5. Describe variations in the master budget process when applying it to not-for-profit and activity-based situations.
6. (Online Appendix 9A) Compute the optimum inventory level and order size.

BUDGETING

BUSINESS FOCUS

Big League Budgeting

In 2005 the National Hockey League (NHL) and its players signed a new collective bargaining agreement (CBA). One of the key features of the new CBA is that it effectively establishes a budget (salary cap) for each team's spending on player salaries. For the 2007–2008 season each team in the league must spend a minimum of $34 million on player salaries but cannot spend more than $50.3 million. The objective of having each team assigned the same budget range for player salaries is to create greater parity in the league by allowing teams in smaller markets, such as Ottawa, to compete with teams in larger markets such as New York.

Having a set budget range has forced teams to plan very carefully in deciding which players to sign and for how long. Deciding how to allocate the salary budget is very important as it can have a dramatic impact on a team's on-ice success. Moreover, unlike most organizations, decisions made by NHL teams in allocating their salary budget are subjected to intense scrutiny by the press, other teams, hockey analysts, and of course, the fans. For example, many experts questioned the New York Rangers decision to sign two high-priced unrestricted free agents in the summer of 2007. The two signings used $14 million of their $50 million salary budget. Whether the decision to use 30% of the salaries budget on just two players will lead to a successful season for the Rangers will only be determined once the games begin.

As you will see in this chapter, many organizations use budgets as a tool for making resource allocation decisions. While these decisions are not as public as those made by NHL teams, the objective is similar: to allocate budgeted resources in a way that gives the organization its best chance for success.

Source: Wayne Scanlan, "Players Get What Market Will Bear; NHL Salary Cap can Hurt or Reward, Depending on Need," *National Post*, July 6, 2007, pp. B9.

Budgets are an important tool used by management to communicate financial objectives for the coming year (or years), allocate resources and coordinate activities across the different functional areas within the organization. Budgets can also be an important tool used by managers to periodically compare actual performance on revenues, expenses and profits to the plan. When actual results are significantly better than budget, management will seek explanations as to the causes and attempt to identify whether or not the favourable trend will continue. If actual results are significantly worse than budget, management will also seek to understand the causes and take corrective action when necessary. In this chapter we focus on both the steps involved in preparing budgets as well as some of the issues that influence how managers use and respond to budgets.

The Basic Framework of Budgeting

Definition of Budgeting

LEARNING OBJECTIVE 1
Explain why organizations budget and the processes they use to create budgets.

A **budget** is a detailed plan for the acquisition and use of financial and other resources over a specified time period. It represents a plan for the future expressed in formal quantitative terms. The act of preparing a budget is called *budgeting.* The use of budgets to control a firm's activities is known as *budgetary control.*

The **master budget** is a summary of a company's plans that sets specific targets for sales, production, distribution, and financing activities. It generally culminates in a cash budget, a budgeted income statement, and a budgeted balance sheet. In short, it represents a comprehensive financial expression of management's plans for the future and how these plans are to be accomplished.

Budget
A detailed plan for the acquisition and use of financial and other resources over a specified time period.

Master budget
A summary of a company's plans in which specific targets are set for sales, production, distribution, and financing activities; generally culminates in a cash budget, budgeted income statement, and budgeted balance sheet.

Planning
Developing objectives and preparing budgets to achieve these objectives.

Control
Those steps taken by management that attempt to increase the likelihood that the objectives developed at the planning stage are attained and to ensure that all parts of the organization function in a manner consistent with organizational policies.

Budgets Dual Role: Planning and Control

It is widely accepted that budgets serve as both a planning and control tool in organizations. However, the terms **planning** and **control** are often confused, and occasionally these terms are used in such a way as to suggest that they mean the same thing. Actually, planning and control are two quite distinct concepts. Planning involves developing objectives and preparing various budgets to achieve these objectives. Control involves the steps taken by management to increase the likelihood that the objectives developed at the planning stage are attained, and to ensure that all parts of the organization function in a manner consistent with organizational policies. To be completely effective, a good budgeting system must provide for *both* planning and control. Good planning without effective control is time wasted. On the other hand, unless plans are laid down in advance, there are no objectives toward which control can be directed.

Advantages of Budgeting

Some managers claim that budgeting is a waste of time. These managers argue that while budgeting may work well in *some* situations, it would never work well in their companies because operations are too complex or because there are too many uncertainties. Actually these complexities and uncertainties provide one of the important justifications for budgeting: to analyze the situation on paper before consuming the resources necessary to try it in reality. Managers usually will have informal plans even before they become involved in developing their budgets. The budget process provides a mechanism for quantifying the financial consequences of these plans.

Companies realize many benefits from a budgeting program including:

1. Budgets provide a means of *communicating* management's plans throughout the organization.

2. Budgets force managers to *think about* and plan for the future. In the absence of the necessity to prepare a budget, many managers might spend considerable time dealing with daily emergencies.
3. The budgeting process provides a means of *allocating resources* to those parts of the organization where they can be used most effectively.
4. The budgeting process can uncover potential **bottlenecks** before they occur.
5. Budgets *coordinate* the activities of the entire organization by *integrating* the plans of the various parts. Budgeting helps to ensure that everyone in the organization is pulling in the same direction.
6. Budgets define goals and objectives that can serve as *benchmarks* for evaluating subsequent performance.

Bottlenecks
A machine, activity or process that limits total output because it is operating at capacity.

Responsibility Accounting

Most of what we say in this chapter and in the next two chapters is concerned with *responsibility accounting*. The basic idea behind **responsibility accounting** is that a manager should be held responsible for those items—and *only* those items—that the manager can actually influence to a significant extent. Each line item (i.e., revenue or cost) in the budget is made the responsibility of a manager, and that manager is held responsible for subsequent deviations between budgeted goals and actual results. This concept is central to any effective profit planning and control system. Someone must be held responsible for each cost or else no one will be responsible, and the cost will inevitably grow out of control.

Responsibility accounting
A system of accountability in which managers are held responsible for those items of revenue and cost—and *only* those items—over which the manager can exert significant influence. The managers are held responsible for differences between budgeted and actual results.

Being held responsible for costs does not mean that the manager is penalized if the actual results do not measure up to the budgeted goals. However, the manager should take the initiative to correct any unfavourable discrepancies, should understand the source of significant favourable or unfavourable discrepancies, and should be prepared to explain the reasons for discrepancies to higher management. The point of an effective responsibility system is to make sure that nothing "falls through the cracks," that the organization reacts quickly and appropriately to deviations from its plans, and that the organization learns from the feedback it gets by comparing budgeted goals to actual results.

Choosing a Budget Period

Operating budgets are ordinarily set to cover a one-year period. The one-year period should correspond to the company's fiscal year so that the budget figures can be compared with the actual results. Many companies divide their budget year into four quarters. The first quarter is then subdivided into months, and monthly budget figures are established. The last three quarters are carried in the budget at quarterly totals only. As the year progresses, the figures for the second quarter are broken down into monthly amounts, then the third-quarter figures are broken down, and so forth. This approach has the advantage of requiring periodic review and reappraisal of budget data throughout the year.

Continuous or *perpetual budgets* are used by a significant number of organizations. A **continuous** or **perpetual budget** is a 12-month budget that rolls forward one month (or quarter) as the current month (or quarter) is completed. In other words, one month (or quarter) is added to the end of the budget as each month (or quarter) comes to a close. This approach keeps managers focused at least one year ahead so that they do not become too narrowly focused on short-term results.

Continuous or perpetual budget
A 12-month budget that rolls forward one month as the current month is completed.

In this chapter, we will focus on one-year operating budgets. However, using basically the same techniques, operating budgets can be prepared for periods that extend over many years. It may be difficult to accurately forecast sales and required data much beyond a year, but even rough estimates can be invaluable in uncovering potential problems and opportunities that would otherwise be overlooked.

The Participative Budget

The success of a budget program will be determined in large part by the way in which the budget is developed. The most successful budget programs involve managers with cost control responsibilities in preparing their own budget estimates—rather than having a budget imposed from above. This approach to preparing budget data is particularly important if the budget is to be used to control and evaluate a manager's activities. If a budget is imposed on a manager from above, it may generate resentment and ill will rather than cooperation and increased productivity.

Participative budget A method of preparing budgets in which managers prepare their own budgets. These budgets are then reviewed by the manager's supervisor, and any issues are resolved by mutual agreement.

Self-imposed budget Same as *participative budget*.

A **participative budget** or **self-imposed budget** is a budget that is prepared with the full cooperation and participation of managers at all levels. Exhibit 9–1 illustrates this approach to budget preparation.

A number of advantages are commonly cited for such self-imposed budgets:

1. Individuals at all levels of the organization are recognized as members of the team whose views and judgements are valued by top management.
2. Budget estimates prepared by front-line managers are often more accurate and reliable than estimates prepared by top managers who have less detailed knowledge of market factors and day-to-day operations.
3. Motivation is generally higher when individuals participate in setting their own goals than when the goals are imposed from above. Self-imposed budgets create commitment to attaining the goal.
4. A manager who is not able to meet a budget that has been imposed from above can always say that the budget was unrealistic and impossible to meet. With a self-imposed budget, this excuse is not available.

Budget estimates prepared by lower-level managers cannot necessarily be accepted without question by higher levels of management. If no system of checks and balances is present, self-imposed budgets may be too loose and allow too much "budgetary slack." The result will be inefficiency and waste. Therefore, before

EXHIBIT 9–1 The Initial Flow of Budget Data in a Participative Budgeting System

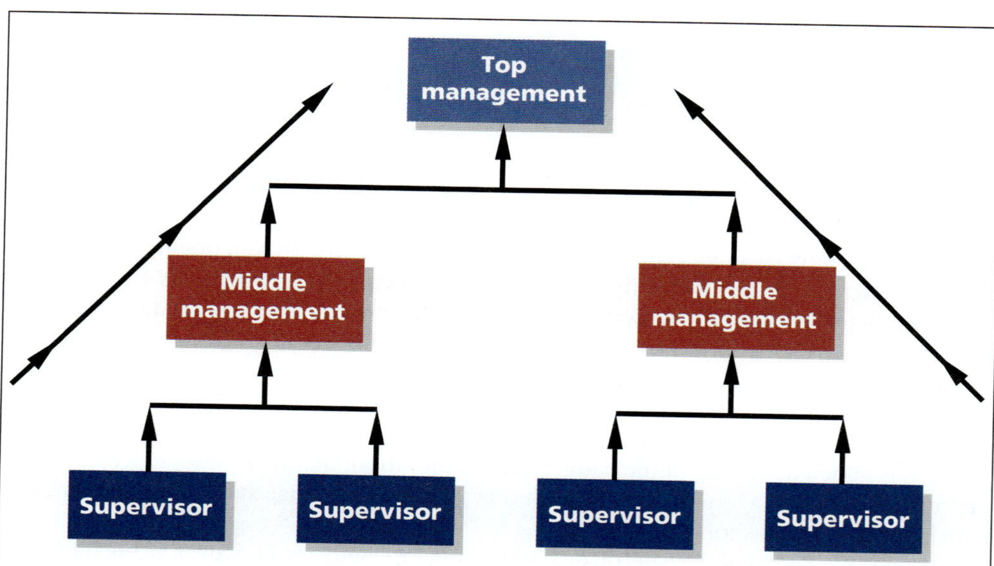

The initial flow of budget data in a participative system is from lower levels of responsibility to higher levels of responsibility. Each person with responsibility for cost control will prepare his or her own budget estimates and submit them to the next higher level of management. These estimates are reviewed and consolidated as they move upward in the organization.

budgets are accepted, they must be carefully reviewed by immediate superiors. If changes from the original budget seem desirable, the items in question are discussed and modified as necessary by mutual consent.

All levels of an organization should work together to produce the budget. Since top management is generally unfamiliar with detailed, day-to-day operations, it should rely on subordinates to provide detailed budget information. On the other hand, top management has a perspective on the company as a whole that is vital in making broad policy decisions in budget preparation. Each level of responsibility in an organization should contribute in the way that it best can in a *cooperative* effort to develop an integrated budget document.

In an effort to ensure an efficient and effective budgeting process, many companies use a **budget committee.** This committee is typically responsible for overall policy matters related to the budget program and for coordinating the preparation of the budget itself. Committee membership usually consists of the president, heads of functional areas (e.g., sales, production, purchasing), and the controller. The budget committee handles any disagreements or problems that arise during the budgeting process, such as those between lower-level managers and their supervisors when budget reviews are being conducted. Importantly, the budget committee also approves the final budget and receives periodic progress reports regarding the company's success in meeting its targets.

Budget committee
A group of key management personnel responsible for: overall policy matters related to the budget program, coordinating the preparation of the budget, handling disputes related to the budget, and approving the final budget.

To be successful, a participative approach to setting budgets requires that all managers understand and agree with the organization's strategy. Otherwise, the budgets proposed by the lower-level managers will lack coherent direction. Chapter 12 discusses in greater detail how a company can formulate its strategy and communicate it throughout the organization.

Most companies do not follow the budgeting process we have described. Typically, top managers initiate the budget process by issuing broad guidelines in terms of overall target profits or sales. Lower-level managers are directed to prepare budgets that meet those targets. The difficulty is that the targets set by top managers may be unrealistically high or may allow too much slack. If the targets are too high and employees know they are unrealistic, motivation will suffer. If the targets allow too much slack, waste will occur. Unfortunately, top managers are often not in a position to know whether the targets they have set are appropriate. Admittedly, however, in a pure participative budgeting system, lower-level managers may be tempted to build into their budgets a great deal of budgetary slack limiting their usefulness as a planning or contract tool.[1] Nevertheless, because of the motivational advantages of self-imposed budgets, top managers should be cautious about setting inflexible targets or otherwise imposing limits on the budgeting process.

The Matter of Human Relations

Whether or not a budget program is accepted by lower management personnel will be reflective of (1) the degree to which top management accepts the budget program as a vital part of the company's activities, and (2) the way in which top management uses budgeted data. If a budget program is to be successful, it must have the complete acceptance and support of the persons who occupy key management positions. If lower or middle management personnel sense that top management simply tolerates budgeting as a necessary evil, then their own attitudes will reflect a similar lack of enthusiasm. If top management is not enthusiastic about and committed to the budget program, then it is unlikely that anyone else in the organization will be either.

In administering the budget program, top management should not use the budget as a means of pressuring employees or as a way to find someone to blame for a

1. Stan Davis, Todd De Zoort and Lori Kopp, "The Effect of Obedience Pressure and Perceived Responsibility on Management Accountants' Creation of Budgetary Slack," *Behavioural Research in Accounting 18*, 2006, 19–36.

particular problem. This can cause resentment, tension, and mistrust rather than greater cooperation and productivity. Unfortunately, research suggests that the budget is often used as a pressure device and that great emphasis is placed on "meeting the budget" under all circumstances.

It is easy to become preoccupied with the technical aspects of the budget to the exclusion of the human aspects. Management should remember that the purposes of the budget are to motivate employees and to coordinate their efforts. Preoccupation with cost reductions in the budget, or being rigid and inflexible is usually counterproductive and can lead to poor morale because people feel undervalued. An over-emphasis on cost reduction rather than value creation can lead to budget games by which managers skillfully time revenues, expenditures and investments in the short-term, sometimes to the detriment of long-term performance. An important objective is that the budget be designed as a positive aid in achieving both individual and company goals.

An important issue in developing a budget is the difficulty of the targets. If the targets are too difficult, employees will know they are unrealistic and motivation will suffer. If the targets are too easy then waste will occur. Some experts argue that budget targets should be very challenging and should require managers to stretch to meet them. Even the most capable managers may have to scramble to meet such a "stretch budget" and they may not always succeed. In practice, most companies set their budget targets at a "highly achievable" level.[2] A highly achievable budget may be challenging, but it can usually be met by competent managers exerting reasonable effort.

Bonuses based on meeting and exceeding budgets are often an element of management compensation. Typically, no bonus is paid unless the budget is met. The bonus often increases when the budget target is exceeded, but the bonus is usually capped at some level. Managers who have such a bonus plan or whose performance is evaluated based on meeting budget targets usually prefer to be evaluated based on highly achievable budgets than on stretch budgets. Highly achievable budgets can generate greater commitment to the budget and may result in less undesirable behaviour by managers intent on earning their bonuses.

IN BUSINESS

A manager's compensation is often tied to the budget. Typically, no bonus is paid unless a minimum performance hurdle such as 80% of the budget target is attained. Once that hurdle is passed, the manager's bonus increases until a cap is reached. That cap is often set at 120% of the budget target.

This common method of tying a manager's compensation to the budget has some serious negative side effects. For example, a marketing manager for a big beverage company intentionally grossly understated demand for the company's products for an upcoming major holiday so that the budget target for revenues would be low and easy to beat. Unfortunately, the company tied its production to this biased forecast and ran out of products to sell during the height of the holiday selling season.

As another example, near the end of the year another group of managers announced a price increase of 10% effective January 2 of the following year. Why would they do this? By announcing this price increase, managers hoped that customers would order before year end, helping managers meet their sales targets for the current year. Sales in the following year would, of course, drop. What trick would managers pull to meet their sales targets next year in the face of this drop in demand?

Sources: Michael C. Jensen, "Corporate Budgeting is Broken—Let's Fix it," *Harvard Business Review*, November, 2001; and Michael C. Jensen, "Why Pay People to Lie?" *The Wall Street Journal*, January 8, 2001, p. A32.

2. Joseph Fisher, Sean Peffer, and Geoff Sprinkle, "Budget-based Contracts, Budget-levels, and Group Performance," *Journal of Management Accounting Research* 15, 2003, 51–74.

Zero-Based Budgeting

In the traditional approach to budgeting, the manager starts with last year's budget and adds to it (or subtracts from it) according to anticipated needs. This is an incremental approach to budgeting in which the previous year's budget is taken for granted as a baseline.

Zero-base budgeting is an alternative approach that is sometimes used—particularly in the governmental and not-for-profit sectors of the economy. Under a **zero-base budget,** managers are required to justify *all* budgeted expenditures, not just changes in the budget from the previous year. The baseline is zero rather than last year's budget.

Zero-base budget
A method of budgeting in which managers are required to justify all costs as if the programs involved were being proposed for the first time.

A zero-base budget requires considerable documentation. The manager must prepare a series of "decision packages" in which all of the activities of the department are ranked according to their relative importance and the cost of each activity is identified. Higher-level managers then review the decision packages and cut back in those areas that appear to be less critical or whose costs do not appear to be justified.

A key issue for companies that use this approach is the frequency of the zero-base review. Critics argue that properly executed zero-base budgeting is too time-consuming and costly to justify on an annual basis. In addition, critics argue that annual reviews can become mechanical, limiting the benefits of zero-based budgeting. Whether or not a company should use an annual review is a matter of judgement. However, most managers would at least agree that on occasion zero-base reviews can be very helpful.

The Master Budget: An Overview

LEARNING OBJECTIVE 2
Prepare the supporting components of a master budget and the budgeted financial statements.

The master budget consists of a number of separate but interdependent budgets. Exhibit 9–2 provides an overview of the various parts of the master budget and how they are related.

The Sales Budget A **sales budget** is a detailed schedule showing the expected sales for the budget period; typically, it is expressed in both dollars and units of product. An accurate sales budget is the key to the entire budgeting process. All of the other parts of the master budget are dependent on the sales budget in some way, as illustrated in Exhibit 9–2. Thus, if the sales budget is poorly done, then the rest of the budgeting process is of limited value.

Sales budget
A detailed schedule showing the expected sales for coming periods; these sales are typically expressed in both dollars and units.

The sales budget will help determine how many units will have to be produced. Thus, the production budget is prepared after the sales budget. The production budget in turn is used to determine the budgets for manufacturing costs including the direct materials budget, the direct labour budget, and the manufacturing overhead budget. These budgets are then combined with data from the sales budget and the selling and administrative expense budget to determine the cash budget. In essence, the sales budget triggers a chain reaction that leads to the development of the other budgets.

As shown in Exhibit 9–2, the selling and administrative expense budget is both dependent on and a determinant of the sales budget. This reciprocal relationship arises because sales will in part be determined by the funds committed for advertising and sales promotion.

The Cash Budget Once the operating budgets (sales, production, and so on) have been established, the cash budget and other financial budgets can be prepared. A **cash budget** is a detailed plan showing how cash resources will be acquired and used over some specified time period. Observe from Exhibit 9–2 that all of the operating budgets have an impact on the cash budget. In the case of the sales budget, the impact comes from the planned cash receipts to be received from sales. In the case of the other budgets, the impact comes from the planned cash expenditures within the budgets themselves.

Cash budget
A detailed plan showing how cash resources will be acquired and used over some specific time period.

Sales Forecasting—A Critical Step

The sales budget is usually based on the company's *sales forecast.* Sales from prior years are commonly used as a starting point in preparing the sales forecast. In addition, the manager may examine the company's unfilled back orders, the company's pricing policy and marketing

EXHIBIT 9–2 The Master Budget Interrelationships

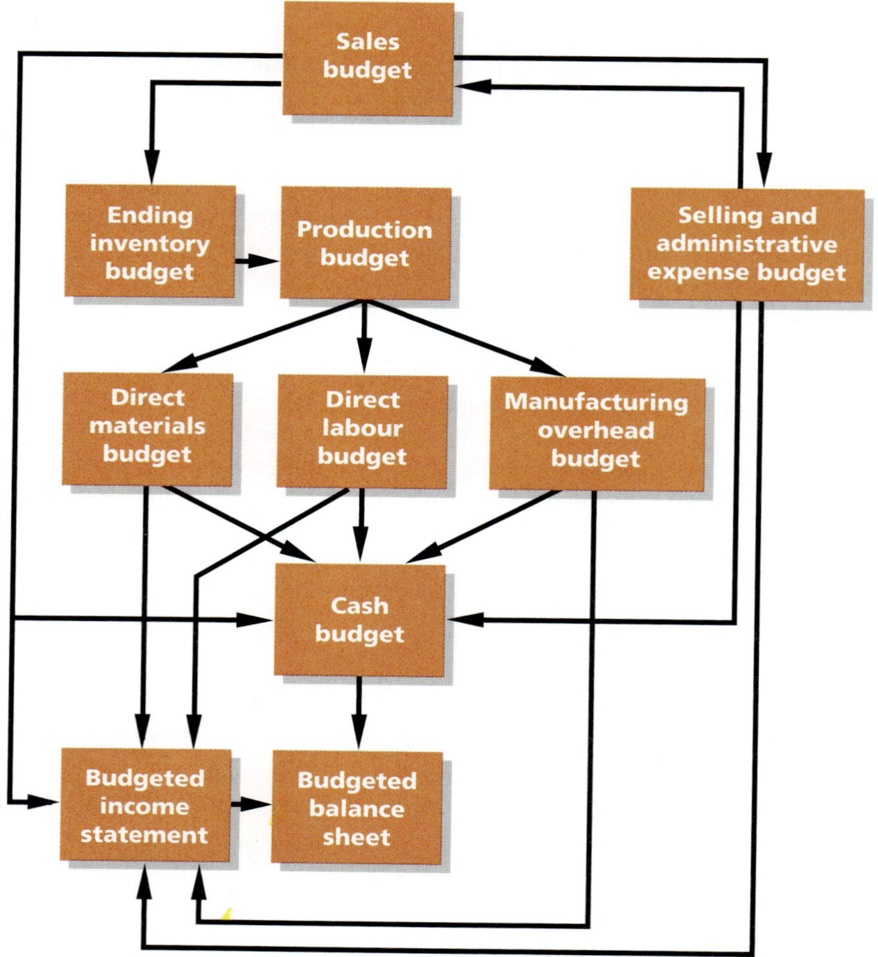

Note: For merchandising companies the production budget is replaced by a merchandise purchases budget and there would not be a manufacturing overhead budget.

Source: Nicholas C. Siropolis, *Small Business Management: A Guide to Entrepreneurship*, Second Edition, Copyright © 1982 by Houghton Mifflin Company. Reprinted with permission.

plans, trends in the industry, and general economic conditions. Sophisticated statistical tools may be used to analyze the data and to build models that are helpful in predicting key factors influencing the company's sales. The In Business feature on the next page suggests how some companies are using rolling sales forecasts to enhance planning and reduce gaming behaviour. However, we will not go into the details of how sales forecasts are made.

Preparing the Master Budget

Tom Wills is the majority shareholder and chief executive officer of Hampton Freeze, Inc., a company he started in 2007. The company makes premium popsicles using only natural ingredients and featuring exotic flavours such as tangy tangerine and minty mango. The company's business is highly seasonal, with most of the sales occurring in spring and summer.

In 2008, the company's second year of operations, there was a major cash crunch in the first and second quarters that almost forced the company into bankruptcy. In spite of this, 2008 turned out to be overall a very successful year in terms of both cash flow and net income. Toward the end of 2008, Tom decided to hire a professional financial manager. Tom interviewed several promising candidates for the job and settled on Larry Giano, who had considerable experience in the packaged foods industry.

IN BUSINESS

Borealis is a company headquartered in Copenhagen, Denmark, that produces polymers for the plastics industry. Thomas Boesen, the company's financial controller, felt that the traditional budgeting process has outlived its usefulness—markets were changing so fast that the budget was out of date within weeks of its publication. Moreover, since budgets were used to control and evaluate the performance of managers, they were subject to considerable gaming behaviour that reduced their accuracy and usefulness. So over a five-year period the company phased out its traditional budgets and replaced them with rolling forecasts and several other management tools. Instead of holding managers to a budget, targets based on competitors' performance were set for variable costs, fixed costs, and operating margins. Managers were given the freedom to spend money as needed to meet these competitive benchmarks. Since the rolling forecasts of financial results were not used to control spending or to evaluate managers' performance, managers had little incentive to "game the system," and hence the forecasts were more accurate than those obtained through the traditional budgeting process.

Source: Professor Bjorn Jorgensen, *Borealis*, Harvard Business School Case 9–102-048, Rev: May 9, 2002.

Larry convinced Tom that to help avoid the problems experienced in 2008, a master budget should be prepared for 2009. In his planning for the budgeting process, Larry drew up the following list of documents that would be a part of the master budget:

1. A sales budget, including a schedule of expected cash collections.
2. A production budget (or merchandise purchases budget for a merchandising company).
3. A direct materials budget, including a schedule of expected cash disbursements for raw materials.
4. A direct labour budget.
5. A manufacturing overhead budget.
6. An ending finished goods inventory budget.
7. A selling and administrative expense budget.
8. A cash budget.
9. A budgeted income statement.
10. A budgeted balance sheet.

Larry felt it was important to get everyone's cooperation in the budgeting process, so he asked Tom to call a companywide meeting in which the budgeting process would be explained. At the meeting, there was initially some grumbling, but Tom was able to convince nearly everyone of the necessity for planning and getting better control over spending. It helped that the cash crisis earlier in the year was still fresh in everyone's minds.

In the months that followed, Larry worked closely with all of the managers involved in the master budget, gathering data from them and making sure that they understood and fully supported the parts of the master budget that would affect them. In subsequent years, Larry hoped to turn the whole budgeting process over to the managers and to take a more advisory role.

The interdependent documents that Larry Giano prepared for Hampton Freeze are Schedules 1 through 10 of his company's master budget. In the following sections, we will study these schedules.

The Sales Budget

The sales budget is the starting point in preparing the master budget. As shown earlier in Exhibit 9–2, all other items in the master budget, including production, purchases, inventories, and expenses, depend on it in some way.

The sales budget is constructed by multiplying the budgeted sales in units by the selling price. Schedule 1 on the next page contains the sales budget for Hampton Freeze for the year 2009, by quarters. Notice from the schedule that the company plans to sell 100,000 cases of popsicles during the year, with sales peaking in the third quarter.

A schedule of expected cash collections, such as the one that appears in Schedule 1 for Hampton Freeze, is prepared after the sales budget. This schedule will be needed later to prepare the cash budget. Cash collections consist of collections on sales made to customers in prior periods plus collections on sales made in the current budget period. At Hampton Freeze, experience has shown that 70% of sales is collected in the quarter in which the sale is made and the remaining 30% is collected in the following quarter. So, for example, 70% of the first quarter sales of $200,000 (or $140,000) is collected during the first quarter and 30% (or $60,000) is collected during the second quarter.

The Production Budget

Production budget A detailed plan showing the number of units that must be produced during a period in order to meet both sales and inventory needs.

The **production budget** is prepared after the sales budget. The production budget lists the number of units that must be produced during each budget period to meet sales needs and to provide for the desired ending inventory. Production needs can be determined as follows:

Budgeted sales in units	XXXX
Add desired ending inventory	XXXX
Total needs	XXXX
Less beginning inventory	XXXX
Required production	XXXX

Schedule 2, which appears on the next page, contains the production budget for Hampton Freeze.

Note that production requirements for a quarter are influenced by the desired level of the ending inventory. Inventories should be carefully planned. Excessive inventories tie up funds and create storage problems. Insufficient inventories can lead to lost sales or crash production efforts in the following period. At Hampton Freeze, management believes that an ending inventory equal to 20% of the next quarter's sales strikes the appropriate balance.

Inventory Purchases—Merchandising Firm

Hampton Freeze prepares a production budget, since it is a *manufacturing* firm. If it was a *merchandising* firm, then instead of a production budget, it would prepare a merchandise purchases budget showing the amount of goods to be purchased from its suppliers during the period. The merchandise purchases budget is in the same basic format as the production budget, except that it shows goods to be purchased rather than goods to be produced, as shown below:

Budgeted sales	XXXXX
Add desired ending merchandise inventory	XXXXX
Total needs	XXXXX
Less beginning merchandise inventory	XXXXX
Required purchases	XXXXX

The merchandising firm would prepare a merchandise purchases budget such as the one above for each item carried in inventory. The merchandise purchases budget can be expressed in terms of either units or the purchase cost of those units. So, for example,

SCHEDULE 1

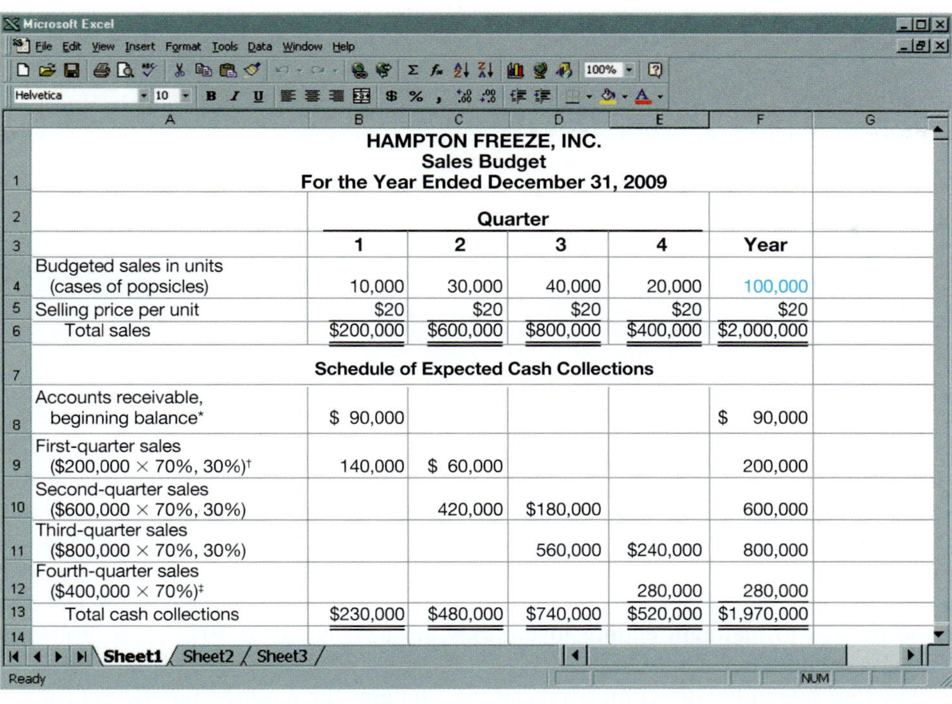

HAMPTON FREEZE, INC. Sales Budget For the Year Ended December 31, 2009					
	Quarter				
	1	2	3	4	Year
Budgeted sales in units (cases of popsicles)	10,000	30,000	40,000	20,000	100,000
Selling price per unit	$20	$20	$20	$20	$20
Total sales	$200,000	$600,000	$800,000	$400,000	$2,000,000
Schedule of Expected Cash Collections					
Accounts receivable, beginning balance*	$ 90,000				$ 90,000
First-quarter sales ($200,000 × 70%, 30%)†	140,000	$ 60,000			200,000
Second-quarter sales ($600,000 × 70%, 30%)		420,000	$180,000		600,000
Third-quarter sales ($800,000 × 70%, 30%)			560,000	$240,000	800,000
Fourth-quarter sales ($400,000 × 70%)‡				280,000	280,000
Total cash collections	$230,000	$480,000	$740,000	$520,000	$1,970,000

*Cash collections from last year's fourth-quarter sales. See the December 31, 2008 balance sheet on page 388.

†Cash collections from sales are as follows: 70% collected in the quarter of sale, and the remaining 30% collected in the following quarter.

‡Uncollected fourth-quarter sales appear as accounts receivable on the company's end-of-year balance sheet (see Schedule 10 on page 389).

SCHEDULE 2

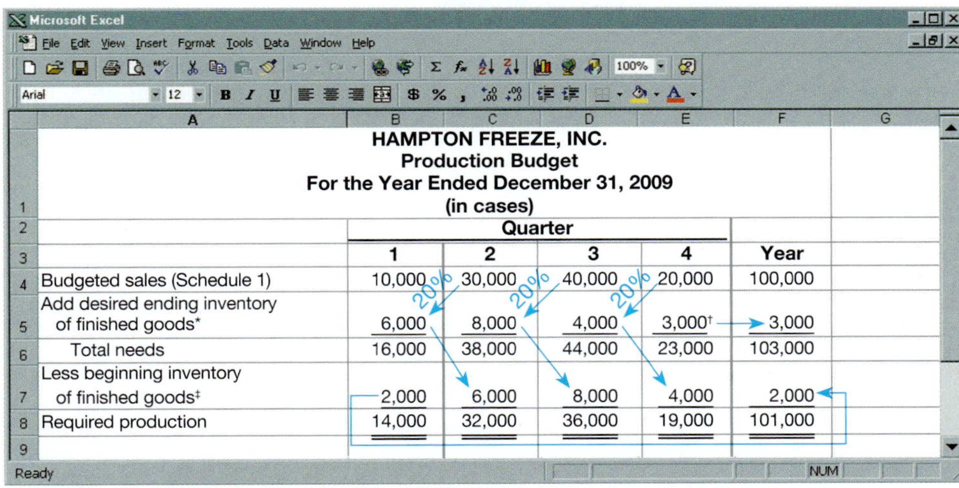

HAMPTON FREEZE, INC. Production Budget For the Year Ended December 31, 2009 (in cases)					
	Quarter				
	1	2	3	4	Year
Budgeted sales (Schedule 1)	10,000	30,000	40,000	20,000	100,000
Add desired ending inventory of finished goods*	6,000	8,000	4,000	3,000†	3,000
Total needs	16,000	38,000	44,000	23,000	103,000
Less beginning inventory of finished goods‡	2,000	6,000	8,000	4,000	2,000
Required production	14,000	32,000	36,000	19,000	101,000

*Twenty percent of the next quarter's sales.

†Estimated.

‡The same as the prior quarter's *ending* inventory.

the budgeted sales shown in the table on the previous page can be expressed in terms of either the number of units sold or the purchase cost of the units sold. Some large retail organizations make such computations on a frequent basis (particularly at peak seasons) to ensure that adequate quantities are on hand to meet customer needs.

The Direct Materials Budget

Direct materials budget A detailed plan showing the amount of raw materials that must be purchased during a period to meet both production and inventory needs.

After the production requirements have been computed, a **direct materials budget** can be prepared. The direct materials budget details the raw materials that must be purchased to fulfil the production budget and to provide for adequate inventories. The required purchases of raw materials are computed as follows:

Raw materials needed to meet the production schedule	XXXXX
Add desired ending inventory of raw materials	XXXXX
Total raw materials needs	XXXXX
Less beginning inventory of raw materials..................	XXXXX
Raw materials to be purchased	XXXXX

Schedule 3 contains the direct materials budget for Hampton Freeze. The only raw material included in that budget is high fructose sugar, which is the major ingredient in popsicles other than water. The remaining raw materials are relatively insignificant and are included in variable manufacturing overhead. Notice that materials requirements are first determined in units (kilograms, litres, and so on) and then translated into dollars by multiplying by the appropriate unit cost. Also note that the management of Hampton Freeze desires to maintain ending inventories of sugar equal to 10% of the following quarter's production needs.

The first line in the direct materials budget contains the required production for each quarter, which is taken directly from the production budget (Schedule 2). Looking at the

SCHEDULE 3

HAMPTON FREEZE, INC.
Direct Materials Budget
For the Year Ended December 31, 2009

	Quarter 1	2	3	4	Year
Units to be produced (Schedule 2)	14,000	32,000	36,000	19,000	101,000
Raw materials needed per unit (kilograms)	5	5	5	5	5
Production needs (kilograms)	70,000	160,000	180,000	95,000	505,000
Add desired ending inventory of raw materials (kilograms)*	16,000	18,000	9,500	7,500	7,500
Total needs (kilograms)	86,000	178,000	189,500	102,500	512,500
Less beginning inventory of raw materials (kilograms)	7,000	16,000	18,000	9,500	7,000
Raw materials to be purchased (kilograms)	79,000	162,000	171,500	93,000	505,500
Cost of raw materials to be purchased at $0.60 per kilogram	$ 47,400	$ 97,200	$ 102,900	$ 55,800	$ 303,300

*10% of the next quarter's production needs. For example, the second-quarter production needs are 160,000 kilograms. Therefore, the desired ending inventory for the first quarter would be 10%×160,000 kilograms = 16,000 kilograms. The ending inventory of 7,500 kilograms for the fourth quarter is estimated.

Schedule of Expected Cash Disbursements for Materials

	1	2	3	4	Year
Accounts payable 12/31/08	$ 25,800				$ 25,800
First-quarter purchases ($47,400 x 50%, 50%)	23,700	$ 23,700			47,400
Second-quarter purchases ($97,200 x 50%, 50%)		48,600	$ 48,600		97,200
Third-quarter purchases ($102,900 x 50%, 50%)			51,450	$ 51,450	102,900
Fourth-quarter purchases ($55,800 x 50%)				27,900	27,900
Total cash disbursements	$ 49,500	$ 72,300	$ 100,050	$ 79,350	$ 301,200

first quarter, since the production schedule calls for production of 14,000 cases of popsicles and each case requires 5 kilograms of sugar, the total production needs are 70,000 kilograms of sugar (14,000 cases × 5 kilograms per case). In addition, management wants to have ending inventories of 16,000 kilograms of sugar, which is 10% of the following quarter's needs of 160,000 kilograms. Consequently, the total needs are for 86,000 kilograms (70,000 kilograms for the current quarter's production plus 16,000 kilograms for the desired ending inventory). However, since the company already has 7,000 kilograms in beginning inventory, only 79,000 kilograms of sugar (86,000 kilograms – 7,000 kilograms) will need to be purchased. Finally, the cost of the raw materials purchased is determined by multiplying the amount of raw material to be purchased by the cost per unit of the raw material. In this case, since 79,000 kilograms of sugar will have to be purchased during the first quarter and sugar costs $0.60 per kilogram, the total cost will be $47,400 (79,000 kilograms × $0.60 per kilogram).

As with the production budget, the amounts listed under the Year column are not always the sum of the quarterly amounts. The desired ending inventory of raw materials for the year is the same as the desired ending inventory of raw materials for the fourth quarter. Likewise, the beginning inventory of raw materials for the year is the same as the beginning inventory of raw materials for the first quarter

The direct materials budget is usually accompanied by a schedule of expected cash disbursements for raw materials. This schedule is needed to prepare the overall cash budget. Disbursements for raw materials consist of payments for purchases on account in prior periods plus any payments for purchases in the current budget period. Schedule 3 contains such a schedule of cash disbursements.

Ordinarily, companies do not immediately pay their suppliers. At Hampton Freeze, the policy is to pay for 50% of purchases in the quarter in which the purchase is made and 50% in the following quarter, so while the company intends to purchase $47,400 worth of sugar in the first quarter, the company will only pay for half, $23,700, in the first quarter and the other half will be paid in the second quarter. The company will also pay $25,800 in the first quarter for sugar that was purchased on account in the previous quarter, but not yet paid for. This is the beginning balance in the accounts payable. Therefore, the total cash disbursements for sugar in the first quarter are $49,500 – the $25,800 payment for sugar acquired in the previous quarter plus the $23,700 payment for sugar acquired during the first quarter.

The Direct Labour Budget

The **direct labour budget** is also developed from the production budget. By knowing in advance just what will be needed in the way of labour time throughout the budget year, the company can develop plans to adjust the labour force as the situation may require. Firms that neglect to budget run the risk of facing labour shortages or having to hire and lay off at awkward times. Erratic labour policies can lead to insecurity and inefficiency on the part of employees.

Direct labour budget
A detailed plan showing labour requirements over some specific time period.

To compute direct labour requirements, the number of units of finished product to be produced each period (month, quarter, and so on) is multiplied by the number of direct labour-hours required to produce a single unit. For example, 14,000 cases are to be produced in the first quarter and each case requires 0.40 direct labour-hours, so a total of 5,600 direct labour-hours (14,000 cases × 0.40 direct labour-hours per case) will be required in the first quarter. The direct labour requirements can then be translated into expected direct labour costs. How this is done will depend on the labour policy of the firm. In Schedule 4 on page 382, the management of Hampton Freeze has assumed that the direct labour force will be adjusted as the work requirements change from quarter to quarter. In that case, the total direct labour cost is computed by simply multiplying the direct labour-hour requirements by the direct labour rate per hour. The direct labour-hour requirement can then be translated into budgeted direct labour costs by multiplying the direct labour-hour requirement by the direct labour rate per hour. For example, the direct labour cost in the first quarter is $84,000 (5,600 direct labour-hours × $15 per direct labour-hour).

However, many companies have employment policies or contracts that prevent them from laying off and rehiring workers as needed. Suppose, for example, that Hampton Freeze has 25 workers who are classified as direct labour and each of them is guaranteed

SCHEDULE 4

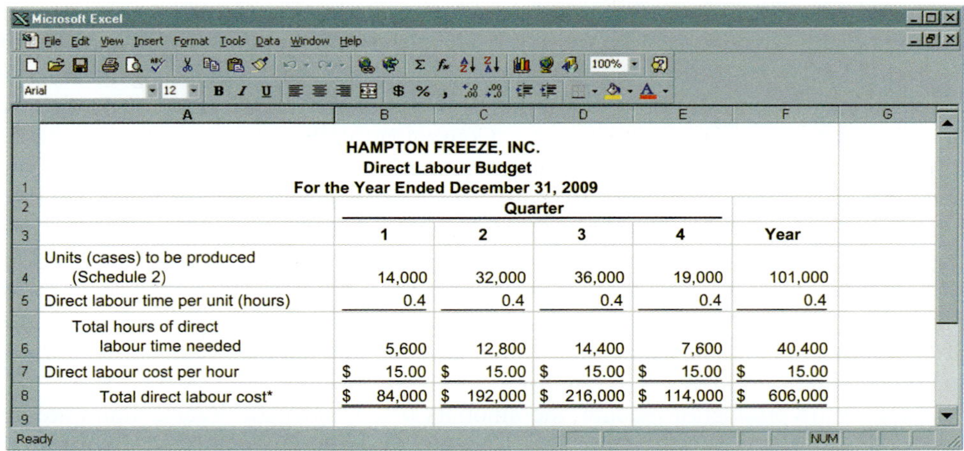

	HAMPTON FREEZE, INC. Direct Labour Budget For the Year Ended December 31, 2009				
	Quarter				
	1	2	3	4	Year
Units (cases) to be produced (Schedule 2)	14,000	32,000	36,000	19,000	101,000
Direct labour time per unit (hours)	0.4	0.4	0.4	0.4	0.4
Total hours of direct labour time needed	5,600	12,800	14,400	7,600	40,400
Direct labour cost per hour	$ 15.00	$ 15.00	$ 15.00	$ 15.00	$ 15.00
Total direct labour cost*	$ 84,000	$ 192,000	$ 216,000	$ 114,000	$ 606,000

*This schedule assumes that the direct labour workforce will be fully adjusted to the workload (i.e., "Total hours of direct labour time needed") each quarter.

at least 480 hours of pay each quarter at a rate of $15 per hour. In that case, the minimum direct labour cost for a quarter would be as follows:

$$25 \text{ workers} \times 480 \text{ hours} \times \$15 = \$180{,}000$$

Note that in this case, the direct labour costs for the first and fourth quarters would have to be increased to $180,000.

The Manufacturing Overhead Budget

Manufacturing overhead budget A detailed plan showing the indirect production costs that will be incurred over a specified time period.

The **manufacturing overhead budget** provides a schedule of all costs of production other than direct materials and direct labour. Schedule 5 shows the manufacturing overhead budget for Hampton Freeze. Note how the production costs are separated into variable and fixed components. The variable component is $4 per direct labour-hour. The fixed component is $60,600 per quarter. Because the variable component of the manufacturing overhead depends on direct labour, the first line in the manufacturing overhead budget consists of the budgeted direct labour-hours from the direct labour budget (Schedule 4). The budgeted direct labour-hours in each quarter are multiplied by the variable overhead rate to determine the variable component of manufacturing overhead. For example, the variable manufacturing overhead for the first quarter is $22,400 (5,600 direct labour-hours × $4.00 per direct labour-hour). This is added to the fixed manufacturing overhead for the quarter to determine the total manufacturing overhead for the quarter. For example, the total manufacturing overhead for the first quarter is $83,000 ($22,400 + $60,600).

In most cases, fixed costs are the costs of supplying capacity to do things like make products, process purchase orders, handle customer calls, and so on. The amount of capacity that will be utilized depends on the expected level of activity for the period. If the expected level of activity is greater than the company's current capacity, then fixed costs may have to be increased. Or, if the expected level is appreciably below the company's current capacity, then it may be desirable to decrease fixed costs if that is possible. However, once the level of fixed costs has been determined in the budget, the costs really are fixed. Therefore, the time to adjust fixed costs is during the budgeting process. To determine the appropriate level of fixed costs at budget time, an activity-based costing system, as described in Chapter 5, can be very helpful. It can help answer questions like, "How many clerks will we need to hire to process the anticipated number of purchase orders next year?" For simplicity, we assume in all of the budgeting examples in this book that the appropriate levels of fixed costs have already been determined for the budget with the aid of activity-based costing or some other method.

The last line of Schedule 5 for Hampton Freeze shows its budgeted cash disbursements for manufacturing overhead. Since some of the overhead costs are not cash outflows, the total

SCHEDULE 5

HAMPTON FREEZE, INC.					
Manufacturing Overhead Budget					
For the Year Ended December 31, 2009					
	Quarter				
	1	*2*	*3*	*4*	*Year*
Budgeted direct labour-hours (Schedule 4)	5,600	12,800	14,400	7,600	40,400
Variable overhead rate	$ 4.00	$ 4.00	$ 4.00	$ 4.00	$ 4.00
Variable manufacturing overhead	$ 22,400	$ 51,200	$ 57,600	$ 30,400	$ 161,600
Fixed manufacturing overhead	60,600	60,600	60,600	60,600	242,400
Total manufacturing overhead	83,000	111,800	118,200	91,000	404,000
Less depreciation	(15,000)	(15,000)	(15,000)	(15,000)	(60,000)
Cash disbursements for manufacturing overhead	$ 68,000	$ 96,800	$ 103,200	$ 76,000	$ 344,000
Total manufacturing overhead (a)					$ 404,000
Budgeted direct labour-hours (b)					40,400
Predetermined overhead rate for the year (a)÷(b)					$ 10.00

budgeted manufacturing overhead costs must be adjusted to determine the cash disbursements for manufacturing overhead. At Hampton Freeze, the only significant non-cash manufacturing overhead cost is depreciation, which is $15,000 per quarter. These non-cash depreciation charges are deducted from the total budgeted manufacturing overhead to determine the expected cash disbursements. Hampton Freeze pays all overhead costs involving cash disbursements in the quarter incurred. Note that the company's predetermined overhead rate for the year will be $10 per direct labour-hour, which is determined by dividing the total budgeted manufacturing overhead for the year by the total budgeted direct labour-hours for the year.

The Ending Finished Goods Inventory Budget

After completing Schedules 1 to 5, Larry Giano had all of the data he needed to compute unit product costs. This computation was needed for two reasons: first, to determine cost of goods sold on the budgeted income statement and second, to identify the amount to put on the balance sheet inventory account for unsold units. The carrying cost of the unsold units is computed on the **ending finished goods inventory budget.**

Ending finished goods inventory budget
A budget showing the dollar amount of cost expected to appear on the balance sheet for unsold units at the end of a period.

Larry Giano considered using variable costing in preparing Hampton Freeze's budget statements, but he decided to use absorption costing instead since the bank would very likely require that absorption costing be used. He also knew that it would be easy to convert the absorption costing financial statements to a variable costing basis later. At this point, the primary concern was to determine what financing, if any, would be required in the year 2009 and then to arrange for that financing from the bank.

The unit product cost computations are shown in Schedule 6. For Hampton Freeze, the absorption costing unit product cost is $13 per case of popsicles—consisting of $3 of direct materials, $6 of direct labour, and $4 of manufacturing overhead. For convenience, the manufacturing overhead is applied to units of product on the basis of direct labour-hours. The budgeted carrying cost of the expected ending inventory is $39,000.

The Selling and Administrative Expense Budget

The **selling and administrative expense budget** lists the budgeted expenses for areas other than manufacturing. In large organizations, this budget would be a compilation of many smaller, individual budgets submitted by department heads and other persons responsible for selling and administrative expenses. For example, the marketing manager in a large organization would submit a budget detailing the advertising expenses for each budget period.

Selling and administrative expense budget
A detailed schedule of planned expenses that will be incurred in areas other than manufacturing during a budget period.

Schedule 7 contains the selling and administrative expense budget for Hampton Freeze.

SCHEDULE 6

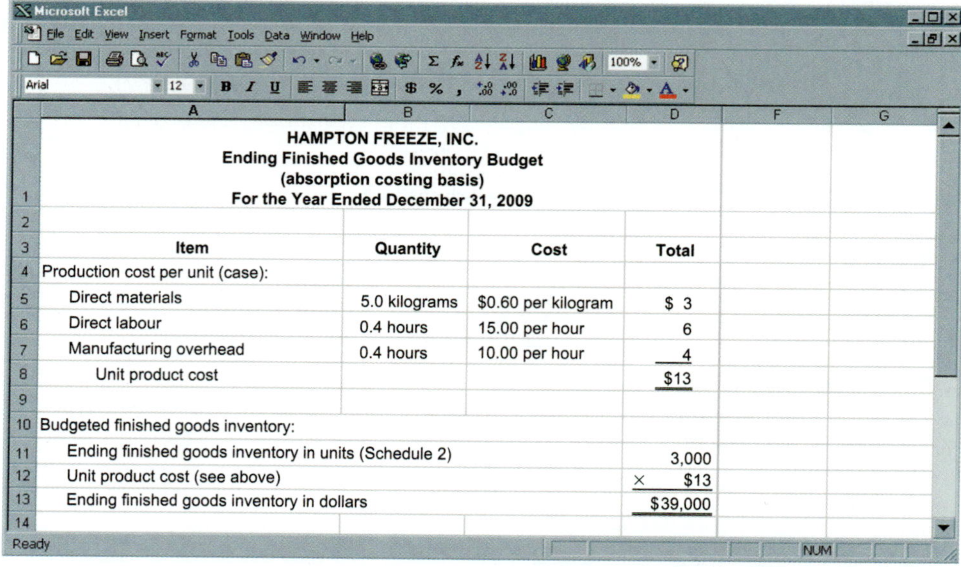

HAMPTON FREEZE, INC.
Ending Finished Goods Inventory Budget
(absorption costing basis)
For the Year Ended December 31, 2009

Item	Quantity	Cost	Total
Production cost per unit (case):			
Direct materials	5.0 kilograms	$0.60 per kilogram	$ 3
Direct labour	0.4 hours	15.00 per hour	6
Manufacturing overhead	0.4 hours	10.00 per hour	4
Unit product cost			$13
Budgeted finished goods inventory:			
Ending finished goods inventory in units (Schedule 2)			3,000
Unit product cost (see above)			× $13
Ending finished goods inventory in dollars			$39,000

Like the manufacturing overhead budget, the selling and administrative expense budget is divided into variable and fixed cost components. For Hampton Freeze, the variable selling and administrative expense is $1.80 per case. Consequently, budgeted sales in cases for each quarter are entered at the top of the schedule. These data are taken from the sales budget (Schedule 1). The budgeted variable selling and administrative expenses are determined by multiplying the budgeted cases sold by the variable selling and administrative expense per case. For example, the budgeted variable selling and administrative expense for the first quarter is $18,000 (10,000 cases × $1.80 per case). The fixed selling and administrative expenses (all given data) are then added to the variable selling and administrative expenses to arrive at the total budgeted selling and administrative expenses.

Finally, to determine the cash disbursements for selling and administrative expenses the total budgeted expenses are adjusted by subtracting any non-cash items included in the budget, and adding any cash expenditures not reflected in the budgeted amounts. As shown in Schedule 7, there are three items that must be subtracted: depreciation of $2,000 per quarter because this is a non-cash expense; insurance of $9,912 per quarter because although this is an expense under accrual accounting, it does not represent an actual outflow of cash each quarter; and property taxes of $4,538 because this too is an expense under accrual accounting, but not a cash outflow each quarter. Two cash disbursements are added: the insurance premium payments of $1,900 and $37,750 in the second and third quarters respectively; and the property tax payment of $18,150 made in the fourth quarter. Each of these additions is necessary to reflect the actual timing of the cash outflows for insurance and property taxes.

The Cash Budget

As illustrated in Exhibit 9–2 on page 376, the cash budget pulls together much of the data developed in the preceding steps. It is a good idea to restudy Exhibit 9–2 to get the big picture firmly in mind before moving on.

The cash budget is composed of four major sections:

1. Receipts section.
2. Disbursements section.
3. Cash excess or deficiency section.
4. Financing section.

The receipts section consists of a listing of all of the cash inflows, except for financing, expected during the budget period. Generally, the major source of receipts will be from sales.

The disbursements section consists of all cash payments that are planned for the budget

SCHEDULE 7

HAMPTON FREEZE, INC. **Selling and Administrative Expense Budget** **For the Year Ended December 31, 2009**					
	Quarter				
	1	**2**	**3**	**4**	**Year**
Budgeted sales in cases (Schedule 1)	10,000	30,000	40,000	20,000	100,000
Variable selling and administrative expenses per case*	$1.80	$1.80	$1.80	$1.80	$1.80
Budgeted variable expense	$18,000	$ 54,000	$ 72,000	$ 36,000	$180,000
Budgeted fixed selling and administrative expenses					
Advertising	40,000	40,000	40,000	40,000	160,000
Executive salaries	35,000	35,000	35,000	35,000	140,000
Insurance	9,912	9,912	9,912	9,912	39,648
Property taxes	4,538	4,538	4,538	4,538	18,152
Depreciation	2,000	2,000	2,000	2,000	8,000
Total budgeted fixed selling and administrative expenses	91,450	91,450	91,450	91,450	365,800
Total budgeted selling and administrative expenses	109,450	145,450	163,450	127,450	545,800
Less depreciation expense	(2,000)	(2,000)	(2,000)	(2,000)	(8,000)
Less insurance expense	(9,912)	(9,912)	(9,912)	(9,912)	(39,648)
Add insurance premium payment		1,900	37,750		39,650
Less property tax expense	(4,538)	(4,538)	(4,538)	(4,538)	(18,152)
Add property tax paid				18,150	18,150
Cash disbursements for selling and administrative expenses	$93,000	$130,900	$184,750	$129,150	$537,800

*Commissions, clerical, and shipping.

period. These payments will include raw materials purchases, direct labour payments, manufacturing overhead costs, and so on, as contained in their respective budgets. In addition, other cash disbursements, such as equipment purchases, dividends, and other cash withdrawals by owners, are listed.

The cash excess or deficiency section is computed as follows:

Cash balance, beginning	XXXX
Add receipts	XXXX
Total cash available before financing	XXXX
Less disbursements	XXXX
Excess (deficiency) of cash available over disbursements	XXXX

If there is a cash deficiency during any budget period, the company will need to borrow funds. If there is a cash excess during any budget period, funds borrowed in previous periods can be repaid or the idle funds can be placed in short-term or other investments.

The financing section provides a detailed account of the borrowings and repayments projected to take place during the budget period. It also includes detail of interest payments that will be due on money borrowed. Banks are becoming increasingly insistent that firms in need of borrowed money give long advance notice of the amounts and times that funds will be needed. This permits the banks to plan and helps to assure that funds will be ready when needed. Moreover, careful planning of cash needs via the budgeting process avoids unpleasant surprises for companies as well. Few things are more disruptive to an organization than to run into unexpected difficulties in the Cash account. A well-coordinated budgeting program eliminates uncertainty as to what the cash situation will be in two months, six months, or a year from now.

Generally speaking, the cash budget should be broken down into time periods that are as short as feasible. There can be considerable fluctuations in cash balances that would be hidden by looking at a longer time period. While a monthly cash budget is most common, many firms budget cash on a weekly or even daily basis. Larry Giano has prepared a quarterly cash budget for Hampton Freeze that can be further refined as necessary. This budget appears in Schedule 8. The cash budget builds on the earlier schedules and on additional data that are provided as follows:

- The beginning cash balance is $42,500.
- Management plans to spend $50,000 during the year on equipment purchases: $30,000 in the first quarter and $20,000 in the second quarter.
- The board of directors has approved cash dividends of $17,500 per quarter.
- Management would like to have a cash balance of at least $40,000 at the beginning of each quarter for contingencies.
- Hampton Freeze has an open line of credit with a bank that enables the company to borrow at a 10% interest rate per year. To simplify the calculations in the example: (1) all borrowing and repayments are in round $1,000 amounts and (2) all borrowing would occur at the beginning of quarters and all repayments would be made at the end of quarters. To simplify our example we assume that interest would be due when repayments are made and only on the amount of principal that is repaid. However, in

SCHEDULE 8

HAMPTON FREEZE, INC.
Cash Budget
For the Year Ended December 31, 2009

	Schedule	Quarter 1	Quarter 2	Quarter 3	Quarter 4	Year
Cash balance, beginning		$42,500	$40,000	$40,000	$40,500	$42,500
Add receipts:						
Collections from customers	1	230,000	480,000	740,000	520,000	1,970,000
Total cash available before current financing		272,500	520,000	780,000	560,500	2,012,500
Less disbursements:						
Direct materials	3	49,500	72,300	100,050	79,350	301,200
Direct labour	4	84,000	192,000	216,000	114,000	606,000
Manufacturing overhead	5	68,000	96,800	103,200	76,000	344,000
Selling and administrative	7	93,000	130,900	184,750	129,150	537,800
Income taxes	9	10,500	10,500	10,500	10,500	42,000
Equipment purchases		30,000	20,000	—	—	50,000
Dividends		17,500	17,500	17,500	17,500	70,000
Total disbursements		352,500	540,000	632,000	426,500	1,951,000
Excess (deficiency) of cash available over disbursements		(80,000)	(20,000)	148,000	134,000	61,500
Financing:						
Borrowings (at beginning)		120,000	60,000	—	—	180,000
Repayments (at end)		—	—	(100,000)	(80,000)	(180,000)
Interest (at 10% per annum)†		—	—	(7,500)†	(6,500)†	(14,000)
Total financing		120,000	60,000	(107,500)	(86,500)	(14,000)
Cash balance, ending		$40,000	$40,000	$40,500	$47,500	$47,500

† The interest payments relate only to the principal being repaid at the time it is repaid. For example, the interest in quarter 3 relates only to the interest due on the $100,000 principal being repaid from quarter 1 borrowing, as follows: $100,000 × 10% × 3/4 = $7,500. The interest paid in quarter 4 is computed as follows:

$20,000 × 10% × 1 year.	$2,000
$60,000 × 10% × ¾	4,500
Total interest paid	$6,500

practice, banks and other creditors typically require interest payments each month based on the average loan balance outstanding for that period.

The cash budget is prepared one quarter at a time, starting with the first quarter. Larry began the cash budget by entering the beginning cash balance of $42,500 for the first quarter. Receipts—in this case, just the $230,000 in cash collections from customers—are added to the beginning balance to arrive at the total cash available of $272,500. Since the total disbursements are $352,500 and the total cash available is only $272,500, there is a shortfall of $80,000. Since management would like to have a beginning cash balance of at least $40,000 for the second quarter, the company will need to borrow $120,000.

Required Borrowings at the End of the First Quarter	
Desired ending cash balance	$ 40,000
Plus deficiency of cash available over disbursements	80,000
Required borrowings.	$120,000

The second quarter of the cash budget is handled similarly. Note that the ending cash balance for the first quarter is brought forward as the beginning cash balance for the second quarter. Also note that additional borrowing is required in the second quarter because of the continued cash shortfall.

Required Borrowings at the End of the Second Quarter	
Desired ending cash balance	$40,000
Plus deficiency of cash available over disbursements	20,000
Required borrowings.	$60,000

In the third quarter, the cash flow situation improves dramatically and the excess of cash available over disbursements is $148,000. This makes it possible for the company to repay part of its loan from the bank, which now totals $180,000. How much can be repaid? The total amount of the principal and interest that can be repaid is determined as follows:

Total Maximum Feasible Loan Payments at the End of the Third Quarter	
Excess of cash available over disbursements	$148,000
Less desired ending cash balance	40,000
Maximum feasible principal and interest payment	$108,000

The next step—figuring out the exact amount of the loan payment—is tricky since interest must be paid on the principal amount that is repaid. In this case, the principal amount that is repaid must be less than $108,000, so we know that we would be paying off part of the loan that was taken out at the beginning of the first quarter. Since the repayment would be made at the end of the third quarter, interest would have accrued for three quarters. So the interest owed would be ¾ of 10%, or 7.5%. Either a trial-and-error or an algebraic approach will lead to the conclusion that the maximum principal repayment that can be made is $100,000. The interest payment would be 7.5% of this amount, or $7,500—making the total payment $107,500.

In the case of Hampton Freeze, all loans have been repaid by year-end. If all loans are not repaid and a budgeted income statement or balance sheet is being prepared, then interest must be accrued on the unpaid loans. This interest will *not* appear on the cash budget (since it has not yet been paid), but it will appear as part of interest expense on the budgeted income statement and as a liability on the budgeted balance sheet.

As with the production and raw materials budgets, the amounts under the Year column in the cash budget are not always the sum of the amounts for the four quarters. In particular, the beginning cash balance for the year is the same as the beginning cash balance for the first quarter and the ending cash balance is the same as the ending cash balance for the fourth quarter. Also, note that the beginning cash balance for any quarter is the same as the ending cash balance for the previous quarter.

The Budgeted Income Statement

A budgeted income statement can be prepared from the data developed in Schedules 1–8. *The budgeted income statement is one of the key schedules in the budget process.* It shows the company's planned profit for the upcoming budget period, and it stands as a benchmark against which subsequent company performance can be measured. Schedule 9 contains the budgeted income statement for Hampton Freeze.

The Budgeted Balance Sheet

The budgeted balance sheet is developed by beginning with the balance sheet for the fiscal period just ended, and adjusting it for the data contained in the other budgets. Hampton Freeze's budgeted balance sheet is presented in Schedule 10.

Some of the data on the budgeted balance sheet have been taken from the company's end-of-year balance sheet for 2008, which appears below:

HAMPTON FREEZE, INC.
Balance Sheet
December 31, 2008

Assets		
Current assets:		
Cash	$ 42,500	
Accounts receivable	90,000	
Raw materials inventory (7,000 kilograms)	4,200	
Finished goods inventory (2,000 cases)	26,000	
Total current assets		$162,700
Plant and equipment:		
Land	80,000	
Buildings and equipment	700,000	
Accumulated depreciation	(292,000)	
Plant and equipment, net		488,000
Total assets		$650,700
Liabilities and Shareholders' Equity		
Current liabilities:		
Accounts payable (raw materials)		$ 25,800
Shareholders' equity:		
Common shares, no par	$175,000	
Retained earnings	449,900	
Total shareholders' equity		624,900
Total liabilities and shareholders' equity		$650,700

Careful observation of the income statement (Schedule 9), the balance sheet (Schedule 10), and the cash budget (Schedule 8) would reveal that a significant item represented by income taxes has been simplified. Income taxes, while pertinent to budgets, have been simplified to avoid overdoing the complexity of the presentation. Given that income taxes can represent a significant percent of net income, this matter is serious.

In organizations, income taxes may not be administered at the level of the responsibility centre being budgeted. The specialized nature of the area means that taxes may require management by specialists at the headquarters level. In addition, income taxation is a companywide charge that may be difficult to break down by responsibility centre.

SCHEDULE 9

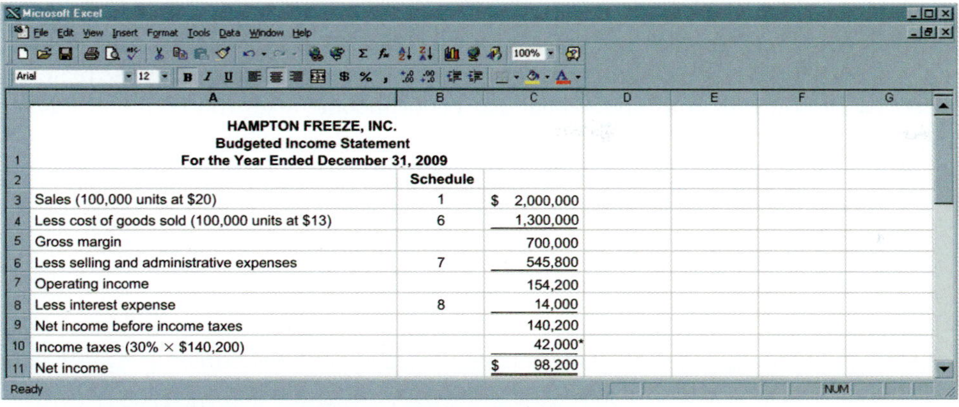

HAMPTON FREEZE, INC. Budgeted Income Statement For the Year Ended December 31, 2009	Schedule	
Sales (100,000 units at $20)	1	$ 2,000,000
Less cost of goods sold (100,000 units at $13)	6	1,300,000
Gross margin		700,000
Less selling and administrative expenses	7	545,800
Operating income		154,200
Less interest expense	8	14,000
Net income before income taxes		140,200
Income taxes (30% × $140,200)		42,000*
Net income		$ 98,200

*Difference of $60 due to rounding (.3 × $140,200 = $42,060)

SCHEDULE 10

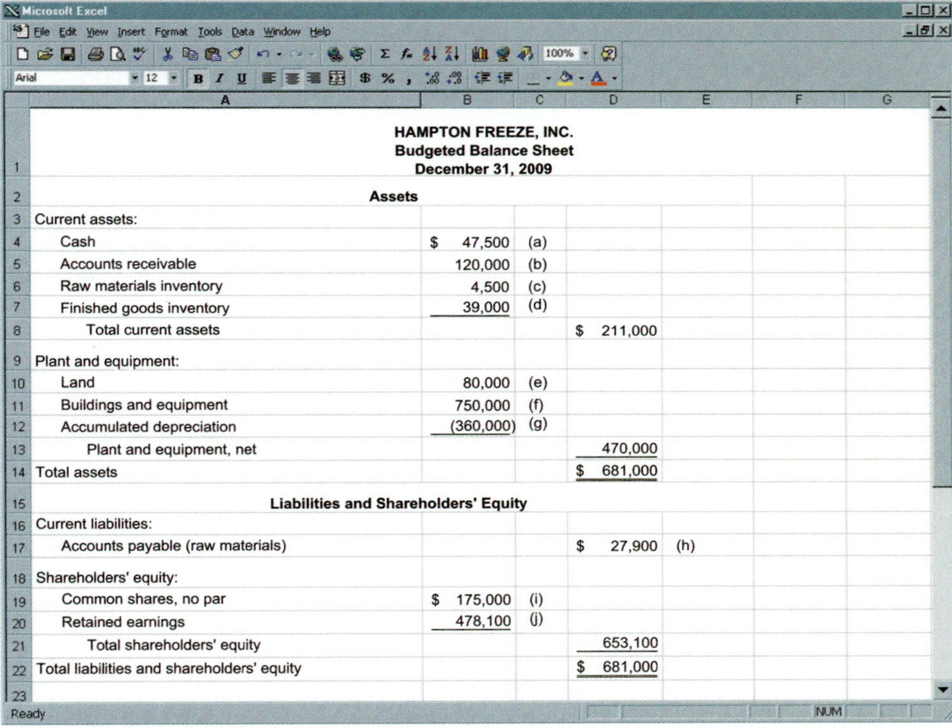

HAMPTON FREEZE, INC. Budgeted Balance Sheet December 31, 2009				
Assets				
Current assets:				
Cash	$ 47,500	(a)		
Accounts receivable	120,000	(b)		
Raw materials inventory	4,500	(c)		
Finished goods inventory	39,000	(d)		
Total current assets			$ 211,000	
Plant and equipment:				
Land	80,000	(e)		
Buildings and equipment	750,000	(f)		
Accumulated depreciation	(360,000)	(g)		
Plant and equipment, net			470,000	
Total assets			$ 681,000	
Liabilities and Shareholders' Equity				
Current liabilities:				
Accounts payable (raw materials)			$ 27,900	(h)
Shareholders' equity:				
Common shares, no par	$ 175,000	(i)		
Retained earnings	478,100	(j)		
Total shareholders' equity			653,100	
Total liabilities and shareholders' equity			$ 681,000	

Explanation of December 31, 2009, balance sheet figures:

a. The ending cash balance, as projected by the cash budget in Schedule 8.
b. Thirty percent of fourth-quarter sales, from Schedule 1 ($400,000 × 30% = $120,000).
c. From Schedule 3, the ending raw materials inventory will be 7,500 kilograms. This material costs $0.60 per kilogram. Therefore, the ending inventory in dollars will be 7,500 kilograms × $0.60 = $4,500.
d. From Schedule 6.
e. From the December 31, 2008, balance sheet (no change).
f. The December 31, 2008, balance sheet indicated a balance of $700,000. During 2009, $50,000 additional equipment will be purchased (see Schedule 8), bringing the December 31, 2009, balance to $750,000.
g. The December 31, 2008, balance sheet indicated a balance of $292,000. During 2009, $68,000 of depreciation will be taken ($60,000 on Schedule 5 and $8,000 on Schedule 7), bringing the December 31, 2009, balance to $360,000.
h. One-half of the fourth-quarter raw materials purchases, from Schedule 3.
i. From the December 31, 2008, balance sheet (no change).
j.

December 31, 2008, balance	$449,900
Add net income, from Schedule 9	98,200
	548,100
Deduct dividends paid, from Schedule 8.	70,000
December 31, 2009, balance	$478,100

Some of the detail about income taxes is partially described in Chapter 13 when capital budgeting (long term) is presented. Here the complexity of capital cost allowance, capital gains and losses, recaptures, and terminal losses are an integral part of the required budgets. To introduce the full operational aspects of income taxes to the master budget requires the consideration of future tax liabilities and assets, instalments, and loss carry-overs. Advanced discussions of budgeting can present these issues within the analysis after the necessary background study is made of the tax rules.

IN BUSINESS

The example presented in this chapter on preparing a master budget illustrates how much time and effort goes into the process. Imagine how much more effort would be required to prepare a master budget for a company with multiple divisions operating in different countries. Given the increasing complexity of organizations over the past few decades, many have questioned whether the benefits of preparing detailed operating budgets exceed the costs. A recent survey of 212 managers directly involved in the budgeting process at U.S. companies gathered evidence on their perceptions of both the benefits and limitations of budgets.

Over 70% of the respondents agreed that budgets are indispensable as a management tool. When asked to give the budgeting process an overall score with respect to the value added to the organization, the average grade assigned was 70 out of 100. Further, over 33% of the managers gave the budgeting process a grade of 80 or above. Importantly, managers were asked to assign this grade after taking into account the cost of preparing budgets (time and effort) and the dysfunctional consequences (e.g., budget slack) that might occur when budgets are used as a control tool.

Many of the key criticisms of the budgeting process identified by managers relate to how quickly it can become out of date if significant changes occur in the organization's operating environment. Nearly 50% of the respondents indicated that to combat this problem, they either prepare rolling budgets or use a form of flexible budgets (discussed later in this chapter) in an effort to retain the control benefits of the budget process. Overall, while the budgeting process is not without its problems, this study shows that many managers continue to believe the benefits exceed the costs.

Source: Theresa Libby and Murray Lindsay, "Beyond Budgeting or Better Budgeting," *Strategic Finance*, August 2007, pp. 47–51.

Flexible Budget

LEARNING OBJECTIVE 3
Prepare a flexible budget and explain the need for the flexible budget approach.

Static budget
A budget designed for only the planned level of activity.

Flexible budget
A budget that provides estimates of what revenues and costs should be for any level of activity within a specified range.

The budgets presented in Schedules 1–10 are static budgets. A **static budget** is prepared only for the planned or budgeted level of activity. In our example, that level of activity was the forecast sales volume of 100,000 units. While this approach is suitable for planning purposes, it can be inadequate for control purposes if the actual level of activity during a period differs significantly from the budgeted level. Specifically, the problem that arises when a significant difference exists between actual and budgeted levels of activity is that it becomes very difficult to evaluate how well the manager did in generating revenues and controlling costs. For example, if actual activity levels are higher than expected, actual revenues and variable costs will be higher than static budget amounts. Should we conclude that the manager did a good job in generating revenues, but not so well in controlling costs? Clearly this would not be a fair evaluation since the reason that costs are above budget is that the volume of actual activity exceeded the static budget amount. Thus another approach is needed in order to restore the usefulness of budgets as a control tool.

Flexible budgets take into account changes in revenues and costs that should occur as a consequence of changes in activity. A **flexible budget** provides estimates of what revenues and costs should be for any level of activity within a specified range. When a flexible budget is used in performance evaluation, actual revenues and costs are compared to what the *revenues and costs should have been for the actual level of activity during the period* rather than to the planned budgeted revenues and costs from the static budget. This is a very important distinction—particularly for variable costs. If adjustments for the level of activity are not made it is very difficult to interpret differences between actual and budgeted revenues and costs.

How a Flexible Budget Works

The basic idea of the flexible budget approach is that the budget is adjusted to show what revenues and costs *should be* for a specific level of activity. To illustrate how a flexible budget works, we use the data from the Hampton Freeze Inc. example to develop income statements for different levels of activity within a range of annual sales of 90,000 units to 110,000 units. To simplify the example, we have omitted interest expense and income tax expense although both could easily be included using the steps presented in preparing the static budget. Note that although Exhibit 9–3 presents an annual flexible budget, the same approach can be used in developing flexible budgets for shorter reporting periods such as quarters or months. Also note that the flexible budget income statements in Exhibit 9–3 have been prepared using the variable costing approach covered in Chapter 7. As a result, the operating income shown in Exhibit 9–3 for sales of 100,000 units is $151,800 while the operating income shown on Schedule 9 on page 389 is $154,200. This difference of $2,400 arises because operating income in Schedule 9 was calculated using absorption costing and an additional 1,000 units of finished goods inventory were added in 2009 (Schedule 2). The additional manufacturing overhead deferred in finished goods inventory using absorption costing is $2,400: 1,000 units × $2.40 per unit of fixed overhead ($6 per hour × 0.4 hours per unit). The rate of $6 per hour for fixed overhead is based on the total

EXHIBIT 9–3 Flexible Budget Income Statement

HAMPTON FREEZE, INC.
Flexible Budget
For the Year Ended December 31, 2009

	Budgeted Amount Per Unit	Sales in Units		
		90,000	100,000	110,000
Sales	$20.00	$1,800,000	$2,000,000	$2,200,000
Less variable expenses				
Direct materials*	3.00	270,000	300,000	330,000
Direct labour*	6.00	540,000	600,000	660,000
Variable manufacturing overhead#	1.60	144,000	160,000	176,000
Selling and administrative+	1.80	162,000	180,000	198,000
Total variable expenses	2.40	1,116,000	1,240,000	1,364,000
Contribution margin	$ 7.60	684,000	760,000	836,000
Less fixed expenses				
Manufacturing overhead**		242,400	242,400	242,400
Selling and administrative##		365,800	365,800	365,800
Total fixed expenses		608,200	608,200	608,200
Operating income		$ 75,800	$ 151,800	$ 227,800

*Per unit amount as per Schedule 6
#Variable overhead cost per hour (Schedule 5) multiplied by hours per unit (Schedule 6): $4 × 0.4 = $1.60
+Per unit amount as per Schedule 7
**Total budgeted fixed overhead expense as per Schedule 5
##Total budgeted fixed selling and administrative expenses as per Schedule 7

rate of $10 per hour (Schedule 6) less $4 per hour for variable overhead (Schedule 5). We use variable costing to emphasize the revenue and cost behaviour patterns expected over this relevant range of activity. Specifically, the selling price and variable costs per unit are expected to remain constant while total fixed costs are not expected to change over the relevant range.

The calculation of the revenues and expenses in Exhibit 9–3 is straightforward. The amounts *per unit* for sales and variable expenses are multiplied by the activity level (units) to arrive at the totals for the year. For example, for an activity level of 90,000 units, total sales are calculated as: $20.00 × 90,000 = $1,800,000. Each of the variable expense line items is calculated in a similar fashion. Fixed costs are not expected to change over the relevant range of activity so they stay the same for each activity level shown in Exhibit 9–3. The flexible budget provides a useful tool in estimating operating income at different levels of activity. As illustrated in Exhibit 9–3, a 10,000 unit change in sales volume, above or below the budgeted level of 100,000 units causes a $76,000 change in operating income, which can be calculated as: 10,000 units × $7.60 per unit contribution margin. Importantly, a flexible budget can be developed for any level of activity within the relevant range of activity. Thus if actual sales volume for the year is 95,000 units, a flexible budget can be prepared showing what revenues and costs should have been for that level of activity.

Using the Flexible Budgeting Concept in Performance Evaluation

LEARNING OBJECTIVE 4
Prepare a performance report using the flexible budget approach.

Flexible budget variance
The difference between actual and flexible budget amounts for revenues and expenses.

Static budget variance
The difference between actual and static budget amounts for revenues and expenses.

To demonstrate the benefits of using the flexible budgeting approach to evaluate performance, we continue with our example of Hampton Freeze Inc. The flexible budget performance report shown in Exhibit 9–4 has three main components. First, it presents actual revenues and expenses for the year given actual sales of 110,000 units. Second, it contains a flexible budget based on actual sales of 110,000 units using the revenues and expenses from Exhibit 9–3. Third, it shows the **flexible budget variance**, the difference between actual results and the flexible budget with unfavourable and favourable variances labelled "u" and "f" respectively. As shown in Exhibit 9–4 actual operating income for 2009 was $161,500 while the flexible budget indicates that at an actual volume of 110,000 unit sales, $227,800 should have been earned. The flexible budget variances for the individual line items tell the story as to why the unfavourable operating income variance of $66,300 occurred. The largest contributing factor was the unfavourable sales variance of $55,000 so management will want to determine why the actual selling price of $19.50 per unit ($2,145,000 ÷ 110,000) differed from the budget of $20 per unit. Cost control also appears to have been a problem for many of the variable expenses at Hampton Freeze Inc., which in total were $11,000 above budget. As will be further explored in Chapter 10, the flexible budget variances for manufacturing costs (direct materials, direct labour, variable overhead) could have been caused by actual unit prices for production inputs differing from budget, or the actual quantities used in producing the 110,000 units differing from budget. Management will want to know how each of these two factors contributed to the variances shown in Exhibit 9–4.

The value of the flexible budget performance report can be further illustrated by examining Exhibit 9–5, which presents a static budget performance report. The **static budget variances** in Exhibit 9–5 represent the differences between actual results (activity level of 110,000 units) and the static budget amounts (activity level of 100,000 units). The operating income variance is $9,700 favourable suggesting that overall, Hampton Freeze Inc. had a good year. However this is very misleading as it is largely attributable to the favourable sales variance of $145,000, which relates to selling 10,000 more units than planned in the static budget. While selling more units than planned is a good thing from a revenue perspective, the static budget variances for the variable expense items are not useful in evaluating how well managers did in controlling costs at actual levels of activity.

EXHIBIT 9–4 Flexible Budget Performance Report

HAMPTON FREEZE, INC.
Flexible Budget Performance Report
For the Year Ended December 31, 2009

	Budgeted Amount Per Unit	Actual (110,000 units)	Flexible Budget (110,000 units)	Flexible Budget Variance++
Sales	$20.00	$2,145,000	$2,200,000	$55,000 u
Less variable expenses				
Direct materials*	3.00	335,500	330,000	5,500 u
Direct labour*	6.00	671,000	660,000	11,000 u
Variable manufacturing overhead#	1.60	165,000	176,000	11,000 f
Selling and administrative+	1.80	203,500	198,000	5,500 u
Total variable expenses	2.40	1,375,000	1,364,000	11,000 u
Contribution margin	$7.60	770,000	836,000	66,000 u
Less fixed expenses				
Manufacturing overhead**		241,000	242,400	1,400 f
Selling and administrative##		367,500	365,800	1,700 u
Total fixed expenses		608,500	608,200	300 u
Operating income		$ 161,500	$ 227,800	$66,300 u

*Per unit amount as per Schedule 6
#Variable overhead cost per hour (Schedule 5) multiplied by hours per unit (Schedule 6): $4 × 0.4 = $1.60
+Per unit amount as per Schedule 7
**Total budgeted fixed overhead expense as per Schedule 5
##Total budgeted fixed selling and administrative expenses as per Schedule 7
++u = unfavourable variance; f = favourable variance

As shown in Exhibit 9–5, total actual variable expenses were $135,000 above the static budget but much of this increase relates to the 10,000 unit difference in the volume of activity. Hence, the key benefit of the flexible budget performance report shown in Exhibit 9–4 is that it removes the effects of any volume differences between actual results and the static budget. This allows for a much more meaningful analysis of how well managers did in generating revenue and controlling costs.

Finally, some companies integrate the information contained in Exhibits 9–4 and 9–5 in preparing a comprehensive performance report that includes actual results along with both flexible and static budget amounts. An example of this type of report is shown in Exhibit 9–6. Note that the total favourable static budget variance of $9,700 is the same as calculated in Exhibit 9–5, but Exhibit 9–6 shows that it consists of two components: (1) an unfavourable flexible budget variance of $66,300 from Exhibit 9–4; and (2) a favourable $76,000 **sales volume variance**. The *sales volume variance* represents the difference between the flexible and static budget amounts for revenues and expenses. Because both the flexible and static budgets are prepared using budgeted amounts per unit, the only difference that can arise between them relates to the actual level of activity differing from the static budget level. For example, the favourable sales volume variance of $200,000 for sales is calculated as follows: (110,000 units – 100,000 units) × $20 per unit. The sales volume variances for variable expenses are calculated in a similar fashion. Because total budgeted fixed expenses are constant within the relevant range of activity, no differences between the flexible and static budgets arise for these items. The advantage of preparing a comprehensive report such as that shown in Exhibit 9–6 is that it helps managers isolate the part of the static-budget variance caused solely by volume differences, from that caused by other factors such as actual unit prices differing from budget. We further explore the factors that can cause sales volume variances in Chapter 11.

Sales volume variance
The difference between flexible and static budget amounts for revenues and expenses.

EXHIBIT 9–5 Static Budget Performance Report

HAMPTON FREEZE, INC.
Static Budget Performance Report
For the Year Ended December 31, 2009

	Budgeted Amount Per Unit	Actual (110,000 units)	Static Budget (100,000 units)	Static Budget Variance++
Sales	$20.00	$2,145,000	$2,000,000	$145,000 f
Less variable expenses				
Direct materials*	3.00	335,500	300,000	35,500 u
Direct labour*	6.00	671,000	600,000	71,000 u
Variable manufacturing overhead#	1.60	165,000	160,000	5,000 u
Selling and administrative+	1.80	203,500	180,000	23,500 u
Total variable expenses	12.40	1,375,000	1,240,000	135,000 u
Contribution margin	$ 7.60	770,000	760,000	10,000 f
Less fixed expenses				
Manufacturing overhead**		241,000	242,400	1,400 f
Selling and administrative##		367,500	365,800	1,700 u
Total fixed expenses		608,500	608,200	300 u
Operating income		$ 161,500	$ 151,800	$ 9,700 f

*Per unit amount as per Schedule 6
#Variable overhead cost per hour (Schedule 5) multiplied by hours per unit (Schedule 6): $4 × 0.4 = $1.60
+Per unit amount as per Schedule 7
**Total budgeted fixed overhead expense as per Schedule 5
##Total budgeted fixed selling and administrative expenses as per Schedule 7
++u = unfavourable variance; f = favourable variance

EXHIBIT 9–6 Comprehensive Performance Report

HAMPTON FREEZE, INC.
Comprehensive Performance Report+
For the Year Ended December 31, 2009

	Actual (110,000 units)	Flexible Budget Variance*	Flexible Budget (110,000 units)	Sales Volume Variance*	Static Budget (100,000 units)
Sales	$2,145,000	$55,000 u	$2,200,000	$200,000 f	$2,000,000
Less variable expenses					
Direct materials	335,500	5,500 u	330,000	30,000 u	300,000
Direct labour	671,000	11,000 u	660,000	60,000 u	600,000
Variable manufacturing overhead	165,000	11,000 f	176,000	16,000 u	160,000
Selling and administrative+	203,500	5,500 u	198,000	18,000 u	180,000
Total variable expenses	1,375,000	11,000 u	1,364,000	124,000 u	1,240,000
Contribution margin	770,000	66,000 u	836,000	76,000 f	760,000
Less fixed expenses					
Manufacturing overhead	241,000	1,400 f	242,400	0 –	242,400
Selling and administrative	367,500	1,700 u	365,800	0 –	365,800
Total fixed expenses	608,500	300 u	608,200	0 –	608,200
Operating income	$ 161,500	$66,300 u	$ 227,800	$ 76,000 f	$ 151,800

$9,700 f
Total static-budget variance

+All actual and flexible budget amounts as per Exhibit 9–4; all static budget amounts as per Exhibit 9–5.
*u = unfavourable variance; f = favourable variance

IN BUSINESS

The use of flexible budgets is one way of addressing the problem of actual activity levels differing significantly from those included in the static budget. However, proponents of the beyond budgeting (BB) approach claim flexible budgets do not go far enough in addressing the deficiencies of the static budget approach. The BB approach still involves the use of budgets for planning purposes but does not use them for control purposes. Under the BB approach, performance targets can be based either on the results of other divisions in the same organization or on those of leading competitors. This approach to setting targets can avoid some of the potential problems associated with participative budgeting where managers may be able to negotiate relatively easy performance targets.

Another key feature of the BB approach is the use of hindsight to subjectively adjust the budget at the end of a reporting period. These subjective adjustments go beyond the simple volume adjustment used in the flexible budgeting approach and can incorporate other major events that occurred during the year affecting selling prices or the costs associated with the products or services offered by the organization. Importantly, the BB approach also requires an evaluation of whether the actual volume of activity achieved (e.g., unit sales) was the desired level. For example, if actual unit sales were 100,000 while the static budget was based on 120,000 units, the flexible budget approach would restate all budget figures using 100,000 units as the new basis. Conversely, the BB approach would assess whether 100,000 units was the best the company could have done given the circumstances. This assessment could result in a restatement of the budget using a level of activity greater than 100,000 units.

The appeal of the BB approach is that it provides much greater flexibility in evaluating the performance of a manager by incorporating subjectivity in the process. However, this greater use of subjectivity can also lead to concerns about the consistency and fairness of the evaluation process. Even if the process is well intentioned, if managers do not believe they are being evaluated fairly, motivation and performance may suffer.

Source: Stephen Hansen, David Otley, and Wim Van der Stede, "Practice Developments in Budgeting: An Overview and Research Perspective," *Journal of Management Accounting Research*, 2003, pp. 95–115

Budgeting for Not-for-Profit Entities

LEARNING OBJECTIVE 5
Describe variations in the master budget process when applying it to not-for-profit and activity-based situations.

Up to this point, we have discussed budgeting in the context of profit-seeking enterprises. The sales estimate is the critical factor on which the rest of the master budget depends. Inaccurate sales estimates create additional inaccuracies in all other budgets. With profit-oriented bodies, there is an intricate relationship between expenses and revenues. With not-for-profit (NFP) entities, there is often no relationship between revenues expected to be received and expenditures expected to be incurred. Examples of NFP entities include municipal, provincial, and federal governmental units as well as hospitals, universities, voluntary associations, professional associations, and many others. The profit motive is replaced with a service orientation in NFP organizations. Budget information is gathered to assist in decisions regarding what programs and expenditures the entity will undertake. Subsequently the NFP entity estimates what revenues are needed to support these programs and anticipated expenditures. Revenue sources may be in the form of grants, donations, or special tax or membership levies. The very survival of NFP organizations such as art galleries depends on their ability to attract donors.

Accountability is of critical importance to most NFP entities. To ensure continued support from contributors, it is advantageous to have a budgeting process in place to assist in planning how resources are effectively and efficiently used. Budgets of NFP entities should be formally approved by the entity's governing body. A formally approved budget sends a signal to employees and volunteers alike that the governing body is committed to meeting revenue and expenditure goals.

A budget can be prepared either on an expenditure basis or on a program basis. An expenditure-based budget simply lists the total expected costs of such items as rent, insurance, salaries, and depreciation but does not detail how much of these various expenses relate to particular programs. For many NFP organizations there is a need to report information on the basis of programs rather than line-item expenses. Preparation of the budget on the basis of programs facilitates performance evaluation and allows for the comparison of budgeted with actual revenues and expenses of each program. This should aid decision making about resource allocation among various programs. Budgeting by program also facilitates a stewardship objective by providing information in a format permitting determination of whether designated funds are being spent as intended.

IN BUSINESS

Given the importance of government budgets, the CICA's Public Sector Accounting Board (PSAB) commissioned a research report to survey current practice. The survey looks at the basis of accounting and accounting policies used by Canadian federal, provincial and territorial governments in their budgets and estimates (appropriations) as compared with those adopted in their summary financial statements. Planning, budgeting, and reporting are elements of a government's performance management and accountability framework. The report discusses each of these elements. Traditionally, the approach begins with priority setting and planning, followed by the budgeting process and ending with reporting and auditing. The survey findings indicate a clear trend for senior governments in Canada: (1) to move to accrual-based accounting, (2) to prepare a summary budget, and (3) to change certain significant accounting policies to be in line with the recommendations set out in the Public Sector Accounting Handbook.

Source: Excerpted from J. Paul-Emile, "Accounting Bases Used in Canadian Government Budgeting," *CA Magazine*, Toronto, January/February 2005, vol. 138, iss. 1, p. 18. Reproduced by permission from *CA Magazine* produced by the Canadian Institute of Chartered Accountants, Toronto, Canada.

Activity-Based Budgeting

Activity-based budgeting A type of budgeting in which emphasis is placed on budgeting the costs of the activities needed to produce and market the firm's goods and services.

In Chapter 5, we saw that activity-based costing has been developed to help provide the manager with more accurate product or service costs. More accurate costs should translate into better decision making and tighter control over costs. Activity-based costing principles can also be applied to budgeting. With **activity-based budgeting**, the emphasis is on budgeting the costs of the activities needed to produce and market the firm's goods and services.

Activity-based budgeting involves several stages. First, the budgeted cost of accomplishing each unit of activity is determined. Recall that an activity is a cost driver, such as machine set-up, a purchase order, a quality inspection, or a maintenance request. Next, sales and production targets are used to estimate the demand for these activities. The unit cost of each activity is then multiplied by the expected demand to determine the total cost of each activity. The result is a budget based on activities that drive costs rather than the traditional budget based on business functions and expense classifications.

For activity budgeting, costs within the responsibility centre are classified by activity, and activity drivers other than simple quantities produced or sold are identified. Activities such as quality inspections, materials handling, assembly, shipping, purchasing, and so on are identified, measured, and costed. These costs are then compiled to present the overall costs of the product or services if overall results are desired. The activity costing presented in Chapter 5 illustrates how activity budgets could be presented.

The detail of applying activity-based costing techniques to budgeting technically requires reversal of the ABC approach. Instead of going from costs of resources, to activities, and then to the costs of outputs, activity-based budgeting goes from outputs to their costs, to the costs of the required activities, and then to the costs of procuring the required resources needed to produce the outputs. Such a reversal can result in inaccuracies in the budgets for the resources when the resources do not have a simple linear relationship to the outputs. Careful adjustments may be needed to compensate for the difficulties that this reversal of the costing process may cause.[3]

International Aspects of Budgeting

A multinational company (MNC) faces special problems when preparing a budget. These problems arise because of fluctuations in foreign currency exchange rates, the high inflation rates found in some countries, and local economic conditions and governmental policies that affect everything from labour costs to marketing practices.

Fluctuations in foreign currency exchange rates create unique budgeting problems. Exporters may be able to predict with some accuracy their sales in the local foreign currency such as dollars or euros. However, the amounts they eventually receive in their own currency will depend on the currency exchange rates that prevail at the time. If, for example, the currency exchange rates are less favourable than expected, the company will ultimately receive in its own currency less than it had anticipated.

Companies that are heavily involved in export operations often hedge their exposure to exchange rate fluctuations by buying and selling sophisticated financial contracts. These hedges ensure that if the company loses money in its exporting operations because of exchange rate fluctuations, it will make up that loss with gains on its financial contracts. The details of such hedging operations are covered in finance textbooks. When an MNC uses hedging operations, the costs of those activities should be budgeted along with other expenses.

Some MNCs have operations in countries with very high inflation rates—sometimes exceeding 100% a year. Such high inflation rates—called *hyperinflation*—can render a budget obsolete very quickly. A common budgeting tactic in such countries is to reduce the lead time for preparing the budget and to revise the budget frequently throughout the year in the light of the actual inflation experienced to date.

In addition to problems with exchange rates and inflation, MNCs must be sensitive to government policies in the countries in which they operate that might affect labour costs, equipment purchases, cash management, or other budget items.

Summary

Our purpose has been to present an overview of the budgeting process and to show how the various operating budgets relate to each other. We have seen how the sales budget forms the foundation for profit planning. Once the sales budget has been set, the production budget and the selling and administrative budget can be prepared since they depend on how many units are to be sold. The production budget determines how many units are to be produced, so after it is prepared, the various manufacturing cost budgets can be prepared. All of these various budgets feed into the cash budget and the budgeted income statement and balance sheet. There are many connections between these various parts of the master budget. For example, the schedule of expected cash collections, which is completed in connection with the sales budget, provides data for both the cash budget and the budgeted balance sheet.

3. Robin Cooper and Regine Slagmulder, "Activity-Based Budgeting—Parts 1 and 2," *Strategic Finance*, September 2000, pp. 85–86, and October 2000, pp. 26–28.

We have also presented an approach that some companies use to address the limitations that arise with static budgets when actual activity levels differ from budgeted levels. The use of flexible budgets involves restating the budget at the end of a reporting period using actual activity levels. This revised budget then provides a better tool for evaluating managers' performance in generating revenue and controlling costs, given the actual volume of activity.

The material in this chapter is just an introduction to budgeting and profit planning. In later chapters, we will see how budgets are used to control day-to-day operations and how they are used in performance evaluation.

Review Problem: Completing a Master Budget

The following data relate to the operations of Soper Company, a wholesale distributor of consumer goods:

Current assets as of March 31:	
Cash	$8,000
Accounts receivable	$20,000
Inventory	$36,000
Building and equipment, net	$120,000
Accounts payable	$21,750
Common shares	$150,000
Retained earnings	$12,250

a. The gross margin is 25% of sales.
b. Actual and budgeted sales data:

March (actual)	$50,000
April	$60,000
May	$72,000
June	$90,000
July	$48,000

c. Sales are 60% for cash and 40% on credit. Credit sales are collected in the month following sale. The accounts receivable at March 31 are a result of March credit sales.
d. Each month's ending inventory should equal 80% of the following month's budgeted cost of goods sold.
e. One-half of a month's inventory purchases is paid for in the month of purchase; the other half is paid for in the following month. The accounts payable at March 31 are the result of March purchases of inventory.
f. Monthly expenses are as follows: commissions, 12% of sales; rent, $2,500 per month; other expenses (excluding depreciation), 6% of sales. Assume that these expenses are paid monthly. Depreciation is $900 per month (includes depreciation on new assets).
g. Equipment costing $1,500 will be purchased for cash in April.
h. The company must maintain a minimum cash balance of $4,000. An open line of credit is available at a local bank. All borrowing is done at the beginning of a month, and all repayments are made at the end of a month; borrowing must be in multiples of $1,000. The annual interest rate is 12%. Interest is paid only at the time of repayment of principal; calculate interest on whole months ($\frac{1}{12}$, $\frac{2}{12}$, and so forth).

Required:
Using the preceding data:

1. Complete the following:

Schedule of Expected Cash Collections	April	May	June	Quarter
Cash sales	$36,000			
Credit sales	20,000			
Total collections	$56,000			

2. Complete the following:

Merchandise Purchases Budget	April	May	June	Quarter
Budgeted cost of goods sold	$45,000*	$54,000		
Add desired ending inventory	43,200†			
Total needs	88,200			
Less beginning inventory	36,000			
Required purchases	$52,200			

*For April sales: $60,000 sales × 75% cost ratio = $45,000.
†$54,000 × 80% = $43,200

Schedule of Expected Cash Disbursements—Merchandise Purchases	April	May	June	Quarter
March purchases	$21,750			$21,750
April purchases	26,100	$26,100		52,200
May purchases				
June purchases				
Total disbursements	$47,850			

3. Complete the following:

Schedule of Expected Cash Disbursements—Operating Expenses	April	May	June	Quarter
Commissions	$ 7,200			
Rent	2,500			
Other expenses	3,600			
Total disbursements	$13,300			

4. Complete the following cash budget:

Cash Budget	April	May	June	Quarter
Cash balance, beginning	$ 8,000			
Add cash collections	56,000			
Total cash available	$64,000			

continued

	April	May	June	Quarter
Less cash disbursements:				
For inventory	$47,850			
For expenses	13,300			
For equipment	1,500			
Total cash disbursements	62,650			
Excess (deficiency) of cash	$ 1,350			
Financing:				
Etc.				

5. Prepare an absorption costing income statement, similar to the one shown in Schedule 9 in the text, for the quarter ended June 30.
6. Prepare a balance sheet as of June 30.

Solution to Review Problem

1. Schedule of expected cash collections:

	April	May	June	Quarter
Cash sales	$36,000*	$43,200	$54,000	$133,200
Credit sales[1]	20,000*	24,000	28,800	72,800
Total collections	$56,000*	$67,200	$82,800	$206,000

[1]40% of the preceding month's sales.
*Given.

2. Inventory purchases budget:

	April	May	June	Quarter
Budgeted cost of goods sold[1]	$45,000*	$54,000*	$67,500	$166,500
Add desired ending inventory[2]	43,200*	54,000	28,800	28,800
Total needs	88,200*	108,000	96,300	195,300
Less beginning inventory	36,000*	43,200	54,000	36,000
Required purchases	$52,200*	$64,800	$42,300	$159,300

[1]For April sales: $60,000 sales × 75% cost ratio = $45,000.
[2]At April 30: $54,000 × 80% = $43,200.
At June 30: July sales $48,000 × 75% cost ratio × 80% = $28,800.
*Given.

Schedule of Expected Cash Disbursements—Purchases

	April	May	June	Quarter
March purchases	$21,750*			$21,750*
April purchases	26,100*	$26,100*		52,200*
May purchases		32,400	$32,400	64,800
June purchases			21,150	21,150
Total disbursements	$47,850*	$58,500	$53,550	$159,900

*Given.

3. Schedule of Expected Cash Disbursements—Operating Expenses

	April	May	June	Quarter
Commissions	$ 7,200*	$ 8,640	$10,800	$26,640
Rent	2,500*	2,500	2,500	7,500
Other expenses	3,600*	4,320	5,400	13,320
Total disbursements	$13,300*	$15,460	$18,700	$47,460

*Given.

4. Cash budget:

	April	May	June	Quarter
Cash balance, beginning	$ 8,000*	$ 4,350	$ 4,590	$ 8,000
Add cash collections	56,000*	67,200	82,800	206,000
Total cash available	64,000*	71,550	87,390	214,000
Less disbursements:				
For inventory	47,850*	58,500	53,550	159,900
For expenses	13,300*	15,460	18,700	47,460
For equipment	1,500*	—	—	1,500
Total disbursements	62,650*	73,960	72,250	208,860
Excess (deficiency) of cash	1,350*	(2,410)	15,140	5,140
Financing:				
Borrowings	3,000	7,000	—	10,000
Repayments	—	—	(10,000)	(10,000)
Interest	—	—	(230)[1]	(230)
Total financing	3,000	7,000	(10,230)	(230)
Cash balance, ending	$ 4,350	$ 4,590	$ 4,910	$ 4,910

[1]$3,000 × 12% × 3/12 =	$ 90
7,000 × 12% × 2/12 =	140
Total interest	$230

*Given.

5.

SOPER COMPANY
Income Statement
For the Quarter Ended June 30

Sales ($60,000 + $72,000 + $90,000)		$222,000
Less cost of goods sold:		
Beginning inventory (Given)	$ 36,000	
Add purchases (Part 2)	159,300	
Goods available for sale	195,300	
Ending inventory (Part 2)	28,800	166,500*
Gross margin		55,500
Less operating expenses:		
Commissions (Part 3)	26,640	
Rent (Part 3)	7,500	
Depreciation ($900 x 3)	2,700	
Other expenses (Part 3)	13,320	50,160
Operating income		5,340
Less interest expense (Part 4)		230
Net income		$ 5,110

*A simpler computation would be: $222,000 × 75% = $166,500.

6.

SOPER COMPANY Balance Sheet June 30		
Assets		
Current assets:		
Cash (Part 4)		$ 4,910
Accounts receivable ($90,000 × 40%)		36,000
Inventory (Part 2)		28,800
Total current assets		69,710
Building and equipment—net ($120,000 + $1,500 − $2,700)		118,800
Total assets		$188,510
Liabilities and Shareholders' Equity		
Accounts payable (Part 2: $42,300 × 50%)		$ 21,150
Shareholders' equity:		
Common shares (Given)	$150,000	
Retained earnings*	17,360	167,360
Total liabilities and shareholders' equity		$188,510
*Retained earnings, beginning	$ 12,250	
Add net income	5,110	
Retained earnings, ending	$ 17,360	

Glossary

Visit the Online Learning Centre at http://www.mcgrawhill.ca/olc/garrison/ for a review of key terms and definitions.

Questions

9–1 What is a budget? What is budgetary control?

9–2 Discuss some of the major benefits to be gained from budgeting.

9–3 What is meant by the term *responsibility accounting?*

9–4 What is a master budget? Briefly describe its contents.

9–5 Why is the sales forecast the starting point in budgeting?

9–6 "As a practical matter, planning and control mean exactly the same thing." Do you agree? Explain.

9–7 What is a perpetual budget?

9–8 What is a participative budget? What are the major advantages of participative budgets? What caution must be exercised in their use?

9–9 How can budgeting assist a firm in its employment policies?

9–10 How does zero-based budgeting differ from traditional budgeting?

9–11 "The principal purpose of the cash budget is to see how much cash the company will have in the bank at the end of the year." Do you agree? Explain.

9–12 Which budget schedule replaces the production budget for merchandising companies?

9–13 Which is a better basis for evaluating actual results, budgeted performance or past performance? Why?

9–14 What is the role of the budget committee?

9–15 "To a large extent, the success of a budget program hinges on education and good salesmanship." Do you agree? Explain.

9–16 "With profit, not-for-profit, and government entities, there is generally a direct relationship between revenues and expenditures." Do you agree with this statement? Why or why not?

9–17 Describe the difference between a static budget and a flexible budget.

Exercises

EXERCISE 9–1 Schedule of Expected Cash Collections [LO2]
Peak sales for Eastern Products, a wholesale distributor of leaf rakes, occur in August. The company's sales budget for the third quarter showing these peak sales is given below:

	July	August	September	Total
Budgeted sales (all on account)	$600,000	$900,000	$500,000	$2,000,000

From past experience, the company has learned that 20% of a month's sales are collected in the month of sale, another 70% are collected in the month following sale, and the remaining 10% are collected in the second month following sale. Bad debts are negligible and can be ignored. May sales totalled $430,000, and June sales totalled $540,000.

Required:
1. Prepare a schedule of expected cash collections from sales, by month and in total, for the third quarter.
2. Assume that the company will prepare a budgeted balance sheet as of September 30. Compute the accounts receivable as of that date.

EXERCISE 9–2 Production Budget [LO2]
Sounds Good has budgeted the sales of its innovative MP3 player over the next four months as follows:

	Sales in Units
July.	30,000
August	45,000
September	60,000
October	50,000

The company is now in the process of preparing a production budget for the third quarter. Past experience has shown that end-of-month inventories of finished goods must equal 10% of the next month's sales. The inventory at the end of June was 3,000 units.

Required:
Prepare a production budget for the third quarter showing the number of units to be produced each month and for the quarter in total.

EXERCISE 9–3 Direct Materials Budget [LO2]
Office Wizards, Inc., has developed a very powerful electronic calculator. Each calculator requires three small "chips" that cost $2 each and are purchased from an overseas supplier. Office Wizards has prepared a production budget for the calculator by quarters for Year 2 and for the first quarter of Year 3, as shown below:

	Year 2				Year 3
	First	Second	Third	Fourth	First
Budgeted production, in calculators	120,000	190,000	300,000	200,000	160,000

The chip used in production of the calculator is sometimes hard to get, so it is necessary to carry large inventories as a precaution against stockouts. For this reason, the inventory of chips at the end of a quarter must be equal to 20% of the following quarter's production needs. Some 72,000 chips will be on hand to start the first quarter of Year 2.

Required:
Prepare a direct materials budget for chips, by quarter and in total, for Year 2. At the bottom of your budget, show the dollar amount of purchases for each quarter and for the year in total.

EXERCISE 9–4 Direct Labour Budget [LO2]
The Production Department of the Oceanview Plant of Roth Corporation has submitted the following forecast of units to be produced at the plant for each quarter of the upcoming fiscal year. The plant produces high-end outdoor barbecue grills.

	1st Quarter	2nd Quarter	3rd Quarter	4th Quarter
Units to be produced	5,000	4,400	4,500	4,900

Each unit requires 0.40 direct labour-hours and direct labour-hour workers are paid $11 per hour.

Required:

1. Construct the company's direct labour budget for the upcoming fiscal year, assuming that the direct labour workforce is adjusted each quarter to match the number of hours required to produce the forecasted number of units produced.
2. Construct the company's direct labour budget for the upcoming fiscal year, assuming that the direct labour workforce is *not* adjusted each quarter. Instead, assume that the company's direct labour workforce consists of permanent employees who are guaranteed to be paid for at least 1,800 hours of work each quarter. If the number of required direct labour-hours is less than this number, the workers are paid for 1,800 hours anyway. Any hours worked in excess of 1,800 hours in a quarter are paid at the rate of 1.5 times the normal hourly rate for direct labour.

EXERCISE 9–5 Manufacturing Overhead Budget [LO2]
The direct labour budget of Small Corporation for the upcoming fiscal year contains the following details concerning budgeted direct labour-hours.

	1st Quarter	2nd Quarter	3rd Quarter	4th Quarter
Budgeted direct labour-hours	5,000	4,800	5,200	5,400

The company's variable manufacturing overhead rate is $1.75 per direct labour-hour and the company's fixed manufacturing overhead is $35,000 per quarter. The only noncash item included in the fixed manufacturing overhead is depreciation, which is $15,000 per quarter.

Required:

1. Construct the company's manufacturing overhead budget for the upcoming fiscal year.
2. Compute the company's manufacturing overhead rate (including both variable and fixed manufacturing overhead) for the upcoming fiscal year. Round off to the nearest whole cent.

EXERCISE 9–6 Selling and Administrative Expense Budget [LO2]
The budgeted unit sales of Hirst Company for the upcoming fiscal year are provided below:

	1st Quarter	2nd Quarter	3rd Quarter	4th Quarter
Budgeted unit sales............	12,000	14,000	11,000	10,000

The company's variable selling and administrative expenses per unit are $2.75. Fixed selling and administrative expenses include advertising expenses of $12,000 per quarter, executive salaries of $40,000 per quarter, and depreciation of $16,000 per quarter. In addition, the company will make insurance payments of $6,000 in the 2nd Quarter and $6,000 in the 4th Quarter. Finally, property taxes of $6,000 will be paid in the 3rd Quarter.

Required:
Prepare the company's selling and administrative expense budget for the upcoming fiscal year.

EXERCISE 9–7 Cash Budget Analysis [LO2]
A cash budget, by quarters, is given below for a retail company (000 omitted). The company requires a minimum cash balance of $5,000 to start each quarter.

Required:
Fill in the missing amounts in the table that follows.

	Quarter				
	1	2	3	4	Year
Cash balance, beginning	$ 9	$?	$?	$?	$?
Add collections from customers	?	?	125	?	391
Total cash available	85	?	?	?	?
Less disbursements:					
Purchases of inventory	40	58	?	32	?
Operating expenses	?	42	54	?	180
Equipment purchases	10	8	8	?	36
Dividends	2	2	2	2	?
Total disbursements	?	110	?	?	?
Excess (deficiency) of cash available over disbursements	(3)	?	30	?	?
Financing:					
Borrowings	?	20	—	—	?
Repayments (including interest)*	—	—	(?)	(7)	(?)
Total financing	?	?	?	?	?
Cash balance, ending	$?	$?	$?	$?	$?

*Interest will total $4,000 for the year.

EXERCISE 9–8 Preparing a Flexible Budget [LO3]
An incomplete monthly flexible budget is given below for Auto Bath Inc., a company that owns and operates a large automatic carwash facility near Thunder Bay, Ontario.

AUTO BATH INC.
Flexible Budget

		Monthly Activity (cars)		
	Per Car	7,000	8,000	9,000
Sales	?	?	$80,000	?
Variable expenses:				
Cleaning supplies	?	?	6,000	?
Utilities	?	?	4,800	?
Maintenance	?	?	1,200	?
Total variable expenses	?	?	?	?
Contribution margin	?	?	?	?
Fixed expenses:				
Operator wages		?	10,000	?
Depreciation		?	20,000	?
Rent		?	8,000	?
Insurance		?	1,000	?
Selling and administrative		?	4,000	?
Total fixed expenses		?	43,000	?
Operating income		?	?	?

Required:
Fill in the missing data in the flexible budget.

EXERCISE 9–9 Flexible Budget Performance Report [LO3, LO4]
Refer to the data in Exercise 9–8. Auto Bath Inc.'s actual level of activity was 8,300 cars. The actual revenues and expenses for August are given below:

	Actuals for 8,300 cars
Sales	$83,000
Variable expenses:	
Cleaning supplies	6,350
Utilities	4,865
Maintenance	1,600
Fixed expenses:	
Operator wages	10,050
Depreciation	20,200
Rent	8,000
Insurance	1,100
Selling and administrative	3,800

Required:

1. Prepare a flexible budget performance report for August using Exhibit 9–4 as your guide.
2. Prepare a comprehensive performance report for August using Exhibit 9–6 as your guide. Assume that the static budget for August was based on an activity level of 8,000 cars.

Problems

PROBLEM 9–10 Behavioural Aspects of Budgeting [LO1]

Five years ago, Phil Davis left his position at a large company to start Integrated Solutions Co. (ISC), a software design company. ISC's first product was a unique software package that seamlessly integrates networked PCs. Robust sales of this initial product permitted the company to begin development of other software products and to hire additional personnel. The staff at ISC quickly grew from three people working out of Davis's basement to over 70 individuals working in leased spaces at an industrial park. Continued growth led Davis to hire seasoned marketing, distribution, and production managers and an experienced accountant, Jan Smith.

Recently, Davis decided that the company had become too large to run on an informal basis and that a formalized planning and control program centred around a budget was necessary. Davis asked the accountant, Jan Smith, to work with him in developing the initial budget for ISC.

Davis forecasted sales revenues based on his projections for both the market growth for the initial software and successful completion of new products. Smith used this data to construct the master budget for the company, which he then broke down into departmental budgets. Davis and Smith met a number of times over a three-week period to hammer out the details of the budgets.

When Davis and Smith were satisfied with their work, the various departmental budgets were distributed to the department managers with a cover letter explaining ISC's new budgeting system. The letter requested everyone's assistance in working together to achieve the budget objectives.

Several of the department managers were displeased with how the budgeting process was undertaken. In discussing the situation among themselves, they felt that some of the budget projections were overly optimistic and not realistically attainable.

Required:

1. How does the budgeting process Davis and Smith used at ISC differ from recommended practice?
2. What are the behavioural implications of the way Davis and Smith went about preparing the master budget? (CMA, adapted)

PROBLEM 9–11 Schedules of Expected Cash Collections and Disbursements [LO2]

Calgon Products, a distributor of organic beverages, needs a cash budget for September. The following information is available:

a. The cash balance at the beginning of September is $9,000.
b. Actual sales for July and August and expected sales for September are as shown on the next page. Sales on account are collected over a three-month period as follows: 10% collected in the month of sale, 70% collected in the month following sale, and 18% collected in the second month following sale. The remaining 2% is uncollectible.
c. Purchases of inventory will total $25,000 for September. Twenty percent of a month's inventory purchases are paid for during the month of purchase. The accounts payable remaining

	July	August	September
Cash sales	$ 6,500	$ 5,250	$ 7,400
Sales on account	20,000	30,000	40,000
Total sales	$26,500	$35,250	$47,400

from August's inventory purchases total $16,000, all of which will be paid in September.

d. Selling and administrative expenses are budgeted at $13,000 for September. Of this amount, $4,000 is for depreciation.

e. Equipment costing $18,000 will be purchased for cash during September, and dividends totalling $3,000 will be paid during the month.

f. The company maintains a minimum cash balance of $5,000. An open line of credit is available from the company's bank to bolster the cash position as needed.

Required:

1. Prepare a schedule of expected cash collections for September.
2. Prepare a schedule of expected cash disbursements during September for inventory purchases.
3. Prepare a cash budget for September. Indicate in the financing section any borrowing that will be needed during September.

PROBLEM 9–12 Behavioural Aspects of Budgeting; Ethics and the Manager [LO1]

Granger Stokes, managing partner of the venture capital firm of Halston and Stokes, was dissatisfied with the top management of PrimeDrive, a manufacturer of computer disk drives. Halston and Stokes had invested $20 million in PrimeDrive, and the return on their investment had been unsatisfactory for several years. In a tense meeting of the board of directors of PrimeDrive, Stokes exercised his firm's rights as the major equity investor in PrimeDrive and fired PrimeDrive's chief executive officer (CEO). He then quickly moved to have the board of directors of PrimeDrive appoint himself as the new CEO.

Stokes prided himself on his hard-driving management style. At the first management meeting, he asked two of the managers to stand and fired them on the spot, just to show everyone who was in control of the company. At the budget review meeting that followed, he ripped up the departmental budgets that had been submitted for his review and yelled at the managers for their "wimpy, do nothing targets." He then ordered everyone to submit new budgets calling for at least a 40% increase in sales volume and announced that he would not accept excuses for results that fell below budget.

Keri Kalani, an accountant working for the production manager at PrimeDrive, discovered toward the end of the year that her boss had not been scrapping defective disk drives that had been returned by customers. Instead, he had been shipping them in new cartons to other customers to avoid booking losses. Quality control had deteriorated during the year as a result of the push for increased volume, and returns of defective TRX drives were running as high as 15% of the new drives shipped. When she confronted her boss with her discovery, he told her to mind her own business. And then, to justify his actions, he said, "All of us managers are finding ways to hit Stokes's targets."

Required:

1. Is Granger Stokes using budgets as a planning and control tool?
2. What are the behavioural consequences of the way budgets are being used at PrimeDrive?
3. What, if anything, do you think Keri Kalani should do?

PROBLEM 9–13 Production and Direct Materials Budgets [LO2]

Fedy Toys manufactures and distributes a number of products to retailers. One of these products, Playclay, requires three kilograms of material A135 in the manufacture of each unit. The company is now planning raw materials needs for the third quarter—July, August, and September. Peak sales of Playclay occur in the third quarter of each year. To keep production and shipments moving smoothly, the company has the following inventory requirements:

a. The finished goods inventory on hand at the end of each month must be equal to 5,000 units plus 30% of the next month's sales. The finished goods inventory on June 30 is budgeted to be 17,000 units.

b. The raw materials inventory on hand at the end of each month must be equal to one-half of the following month's production needs for raw materials. The raw materials inventory on June 30 for material A135 is budgeted to be 64,500 kilograms.

c. The company maintains no work in process inventories.

A sales budget for Playclay for the last six months of the year follows.

	Budgeted Sales in Units
July	40,000
August	50,000
September	70,000
October	35,000
November	20,000
December	10,000

Required:

1. Prepare a production budget for Playclay for the months July, August, September, and October.
2. Examine the production budget that you prepared. Why will the company produce more units than it sells in July and August and less units than it sells in September and October?
3. Prepare a direct materials budget showing the quantity of material A135 to be purchased for July, August, and September and for the quarter in total.

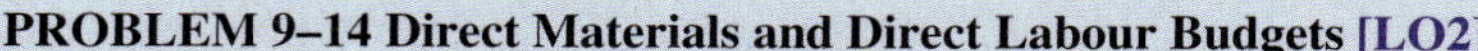

PROBLEM 9–14 Direct Materials and Direct Labour Budgets [LO2]

The production department of Taylor Company has submitted the following forecast of units to be produced by quarter for the upcoming fiscal year.

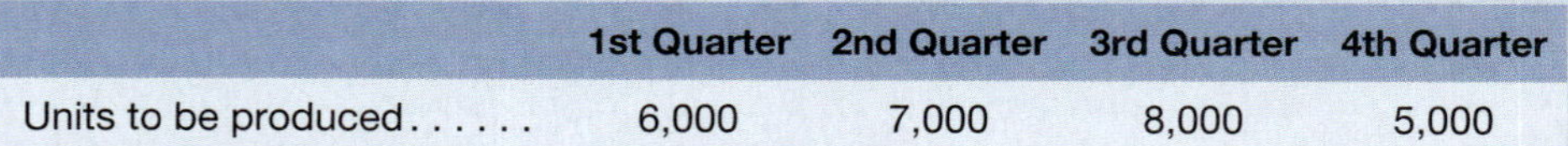

	1st Quarter	2nd Quarter	3rd Quarter	4th Quarter
Units to be produced	6,000	7,000	8,000	5,000

In addition, the beginning raw materials inventory for the 1st Quarter is budgeted to be 3,600 kilograms and the beginning accounts payable for the 1st Quarter is budgeted to be $11,775.

Each unit requires three kilograms of raw material that costs $2.50 per kilogram. Management desires to end each quarter with a raw materials inventory equal to 20% of the following quarter's production needs. The desired ending inventory for the 4th Quarter is 3,700 kilograms. Management plans to pay for 70% of raw material purchases in the quarter acquired and 30% in the following quarter. Each unit requires 0.50 direct labour-hours and direct labour-hour workers are paid $12 per hour.

Required:

1. Prepare the company's direct materials budget and schedule of expected cash disbursements for materials for the upcoming fiscal year.
2. Prepare the company's direct labour budget for the upcoming fiscal year, assuming that the direct labour workforce is adjusted each quarter to match the number of hours required to produce the forecasted number of units produced.

PROBLEM 9–15 Direct Labour and Manufacturing Overhead Budgets [LO2]

The Production Department of Milverton Corporation has submitted the following forecast of units to be produced by quarter for the upcoming fiscal year.

	1st Quarter	2nd Quarter	3rd Quarter	4th Quarter
Units to be produced	16,000	15,000	14,000	15,000

Each unit requires 0.80 direct labour-hours and direct labour-hour workers are paid $11.50 per hour.

In addition, the variable manufacturing overhead rate is $2.50 per direct labour-hour. The fixed manufacturing overhead is $90,000 per quarter. The only noncash element of manufacturing overhead is depreciation, which is $34,000 per quarter.

Required:

1. Prepare the company's direct labour budget for the upcoming fiscal year, assuming that the direct labour workforce is adjusted each quarter to match the number of hours required to produce the forecasted number of units produced.
2. Prepare the company's manufacturing overhead budget.

PROBLEM 9–16 Schedule of Expected Cash Collections; Cash Budget [LO2]

Jodi Horton, president of the retailer Crestline Products, has just approached the company's bank with a request for a $30,000, 90-day loan. The purpose of the loan is to assist the company in acquiring inventories in support of peak April sales. Since the company has had some difficulty in paying off its loans in the past, the loan officer has asked for a cash budget to help determine whether the loan should be made. The following data are available for the months April–June, during which the loan will be used:

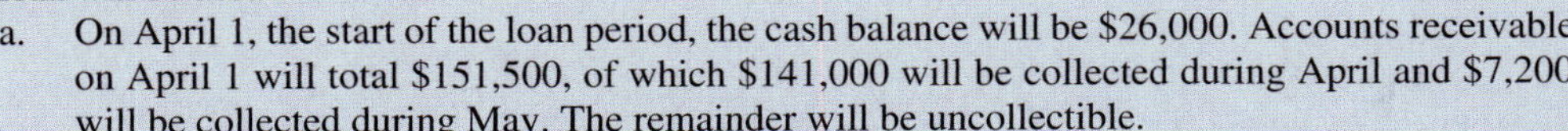

a. On April 1, the start of the loan period, the cash balance will be $26,000. Accounts receivable on April 1 will total $151,500, of which $141,000 will be collected during April and $7,200 will be collected during May. The remainder will be uncollectible.

b. Past experience shows that 20% of a month's sales are collected in the month of sale, 75% in the month following sale, and 4% in the second month following sale. The other 1% represents bad debts that are never collected. Budgeted sales and expenses for the three-month period follow:

	April	May	June
Sales (all on account)	$200,000	$300,000	$250,000
Merchandise purchases	$120,000	$180,000	$150,000
Payroll	$9,000	$9,000	$8,000
Lease payments	$15,000	$15,000	$15,000
Advertising	$70,000	$80,000	$60,000
Equipment purchases	$8,000	—	—
Depreciation	$10,000	$10,000	$10,000

c. Merchandise purchases are paid in full during the month following purchase. Accounts payable for merchandise purchases on March 31, which will be paid during April, total $108,000.

d. In preparing the cash budget, assume that the $30,000 loan will be made in April and repaid in June. Interest on the loan will total $1,200.

Required:

1. Prepare a schedule of expected cash collections for April, May, and June and for the three months in total.
2. Prepare a cash budget, by month and in total, for the three-month period.
3. If the company needs a minimum cash balance of $20,000 to start each month, can the loan be repaid as planned? Explain.

PROBLEM 9–17 Cash Budget; Income Statement; Balance Sheet [LO2]

The balance sheet of Pixelize, Inc., a distributor of photographic supplies, as of May 31 is given below:

PIXELIZE, INC. Balance Sheet May 31	
Assets	
Cash	$ 8,000
Accounts receivable	72,000
Inventory	30,000
Buildings and equipment, net of depreciation	500,000
Total assets	$610,000
Liabilities and Shareholders' Equity	
Accounts payable	$ 90,000
Note payable	15,000
Common shares	420,000
Retained earnings	85,000
Total liabilities and shareholders' equity	$610,000

Pixelize, Inc., has not budgeted previously, and for this reason it is limiting its master budget planning horizon to just one month ahead—namely, June. The company has assembled the following budgeted data relating to June:

a. Sales are budgeted at $250,000. Of these sales, $60,000 will be for cash; the remainder will be credit sales. One-half of a month's credit sales are collected in the month the sales are made, and the remainder is collected the following month. All of the May 31 accounts receivable will be collected in June.
b. Purchases of inventory are expected to total $200,000 during June. These purchases will all be on account. Forty percent of all inventory purchases are paid for in the month of purchase; the remainder are paid in the following month. All of the May 31 accounts payable to suppliers will be paid during June.
c. The June 30 inventory balance is budgeted at $40,000.
d. Selling and administrative expenses for June are budgeted at $51,000, exclusive of depreciation. These expenses will be paid in cash. Depreciation is budgeted at $2,000 for the month.
e. The note payable on the May 31 balance sheet will be paid during June. The company's interest expense for June (on all borrowing) will be $500, which will be paid in cash.
f. New warehouse equipment costing $9,000 will be purchased for cash during June.
g. During June, the company will borrow $18,000 from its bank by giving a new note payable to the bank for that amount. The new note will be due in one year.

Required:
1. Prepare a cash budget for June. Support your budget with a schedule of expected cash collections from sales and a schedule of expected cash disbursements for inventory purchases.
2. Prepare a budgeted income statement for June. Use the absorption costing income statement format as shown in Schedule 9.
3. Prepare a budgeted balance sheet as of June 30.

PROBLEM 9–18 Integration of Sales, Production, and Direct Materials Budgets [LO2]
Dolphin, Inc., manufactures an advanced swim fin for scuba divers. Management is now preparing detailed budgets for the third quarter, July through September, and has assembled the following information to assist in preparing the budget:
a. The Marketing Department has estimated sales as follows for the remainder of the year (in pairs of swim fins):

July	6,000	October	4,000
August	7,000	November	3,000
September	5,000	December	3,000

The selling price of the swim fins is $50 per pair.
b. All sales are on account. Based on past experience, sales are expected to be collected in the following pattern:

40% in the month of sale
50% in the month following sale
10% uncollectible

The beginning accounts receivable balance (excluding uncollectible amounts) on July 1 will be $130,000.
c. The company maintains finished goods inventories equal to 10% of the following month's sales. The inventory of finished goods on July 1 will be 600 pairs.
d. Each pair of swim fins requires 2 kilograms of geico compound. To prevent shortages, the company would like the inventory of geico compound on hand at the end of each month to be equal to 20% of the following month's production needs. The inventory of geico compound on hand on July 1 will be 2,440 kilograms.
e. Geico compound costs $2.50 per kilogram. Dolphin pays for 60% of its purchases in the month of purchase; the remainder is paid for in the following month. The accounts payable balance for geico compound purchases will be $11,400 on July 1.

Required:
1. Prepare a sales budget, by month and in total, for the third quarter. (Show your budget in both pairs of swim fins and dollars.) Also prepare a schedule of expected cash collections, by month and in total, for the third quarter.
2. Prepare a production budget for each of the months July through October.
3. Prepare a direct materials budget for geico compound, by month and in total, for the third quarter. Also prepare a schedule of expected cash disbursements for geico compound, by month and in total, for the third quarter.

(Required continued on the next page)

PROBLEM 9–19 Completing a Master Budget [LO2]
Nordic Company, a merchandising company, prepares its master budget on a quarterly basis. The following data have been assembled to assist in preparation of the master budget for the second quarter.

a. As of March 31 (the end of the prior quarter), the company's balance sheet showed the following account balances:

Cash	$ 9,000	
Accounts receivable	48,000	
Inventory	12,600	
Buildings and equipment (net)	214,100	
Accounts payable		$ 18,300
Common shares		190,000
Retained earnings		75,400
	$283,700	$283,700

b. Actual sales for March and budgeted sales for April–July are as follows:

March (actual)	$60,000
April	$70,000
May	$85,000
June	$90,000
July	$50,000

c. Sales are 20% for cash and 80% on credit. All payments on credit sales are collected in the month following the sale. The accounts receivable at March 31 are a result of March credit sales.

d. The company's gross margin percentage is 40% of sales. (In other words, cost of goods sold is 60% of sales.)

e. Monthly expenses are budgeted as follows: salaries and wages, $7,500 per month; shipping, 6% of sales; advertising, $6,000 per month; other expenses, 4% of sales. Depreciation, including depreciation on new assets acquired during the quarter, will be $6,000 for the quarter.

f. Each month's ending inventory should equal 30% of the following month's cost of goods sold.

g. Half of a month's inventory purchases are paid for in the month of purchase and half in the following month.

h. Equipment purchases during the quarter will be as follows: April, $11,500; and May, $3,000.

i. Dividends totalling $3,500 will be declared and paid in June.

j. Management wants to maintain a minimum cash balance of $8,000. The company has an agreement with a local bank that allows the company to borrow in increments of $1,000 at the beginning of each month, up to a total loan balance of $20,000. The interest rate on these loans is 1% per month, and for simplicity, we will assume that interest is not compounded. The company would, as far as it is able, repay the loan plus accumulated interest at the end of the quarter.

Required:
Using the data above, complete the following statements and schedules for the second quarter:

1. Schedule of expected cash collections:

	April	May	June	Total
Cash sales	$14,000			
Credit sales	48,000			
Total collections	$62,000			

2. *a.* Merchandise purchases budget:

	April	May	June	Total
Budgeted cost of goods sold	$42,000*	$51,000		
Add desired ending inventory	15,300†			
Total needs	57,300			
Less beginning inventory	12,600			
Required purchases	$44,700			

*$70,000 sales × 60% = $42,000.
†$51,000 × 30% = $15,300.

b. Schedule of expected cash disbursements for merchandise purchases:

	April	May	June	Total
For March purchases	$18,300			$18,300
For April purchases	22,350	$22,350		44,700
For May purchases				
For June purchases				
Total cash disbursements for purchases	$40,650			

3. Schedule of expected cash disbursements for selling and administrative expenses:

	April	May	June	Total
Salaries and wages	$ 7,500			
Shipping	4,200			
Advertising	6,000			
Other expenses	2,800			
Total cash disbursements for operating expenses	$20,500			

4. Cash budget:

	April	May	June	Total
Cash balance, beginning	$ 9,000			
Add cash collections	62,000			
Total cash available	71,000			
Less cash disbursements:				
For inventory purchases	40,650			
For selling and administrative expenses	20,500			
For equipment purchases	11,500			
For dividends	—			
Total cash disbursements	72,650			
Excess (deficiency) of cash	$ (1,650)			
Financing				
Etc.				

5. Prepare an absorption costing income statement for the quarter ending June 30 as shown in Schedule 9 in the chapter.
6. Prepare a balance sheet as of June 30.

PROBLEM 9–20 Cash Budget with Supporting Schedules [LO2]

The president of Cleantech, Inc., has just approached the company's bank seeking short-term financing for the coming year, Year 2. Cleantech is a distributor of commercial vacuum cleaners. The bank has stated that the loan request must be accompanied by a detailed cash budget that shows the quarters in which financing will be needed, as well as the amounts that will be needed and the quarters in which repayments can be made.

To provide this information for the bank, the president has directed that the following data be gathered from which a cash budget can be prepared:

a. Budgeted sales and merchandise purchases for Year 2, as well as actual sales and purchases for the last quarter of Year 1, are as follows:

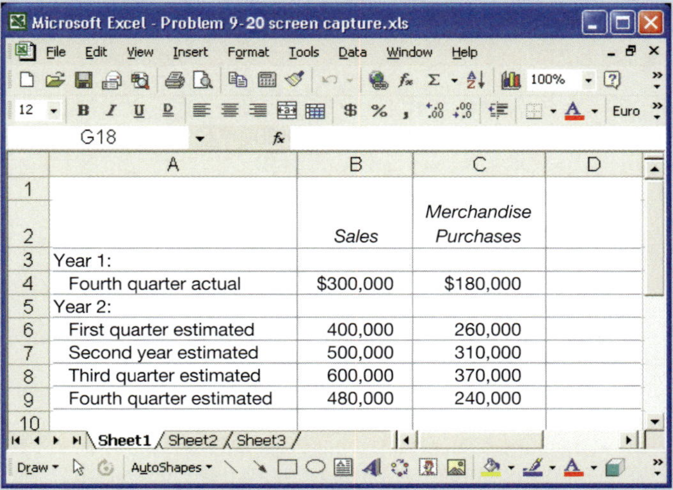

	Sales	Merchandise Purchases
Year 1:		
Fourth quarter actual	$300,000	$180,000
Year 2:		
First quarter estimated	400,000	260,000
Second year estimated	500,000	310,000
Third quarter estimated	600,000	370,000
Fourth quarter estimated	480,000	240,000

b. The company typically collects 33% of a quarter's sales before the quarter ends and another 65% in the following quarter. The remainder is uncollectible. This pattern of collections is now being experienced in the actual data for the Year 1 fourth quarter.

c. Some 20% of a quarter's merchandise purchases are paid for within the quarter. The remainder is paid in the following quarter.

d. Operating expenses for Year 2 are budgeted at $90,000 per quarter plus 12% of sales. Of the fixed amount, $20,000 each quarter is depreciation.

e. The company will pay $10,000 in cash dividends each quarter.

f. Land purchases will be made as follows during the year: $80,000 in the second quarter and $48,500 in the third quarter.

g. The Cash account contained $20,000 at the end of Year 1. The company must maintain a minimum cash balance of at least $18,000.

h. The company has an agreement with a local bank that allows the company to borrow in increments of $10,000 at the beginning of each quarter, up to a total loan balance of $100,000. The interest rate on these loans is 1% per month, and for simplicity, we will assume that interest is not compounded. The company would, as far as it is able, repay the loan plus accumulated interest at the end of the year.

i. At present, the company has no loans outstanding.

Required:

1. Prepare the following, by quarter and in total, for Year 2:
   a. A schedule of expected cash collections on sales.
   b. A schedule of expected cash disbursements for merchandise purchases.
2. Compute the expected cash disbursements for operating expenses, by quarter and in total, for Year 2.
3. Prepare a cash budget by quarter and in total for Year 2.

PROBLEM 9–21 Cash Budget with Supporting Schedules [LO2]

Scott Products, Inc., is a merchandising company that sells binders, paper, and other school supplies. The company is planning its cash needs for the third quarter. In the past, Scott Products has had to borrow money during the third quarter to support peak sales of back-to-school materials, which occur during August. The following information has been assembled to assist in preparing a cash budget for the quarter:

a. Budgeted monthly absorption costing income statements for July–October are as follows:

	July	August	September	October
Sales	$40,000	$70,000	$50,000	$45,000
Cost of goods sold	24,000	42,000	30,000	27,000
Gross margin	16,000	28,000	20,000	18,000
Selling and administrative expenses:				
Selling expense	7,200	11,700	8,500	7,300
Administrative expense*	5,600	7,200	6,100	5,900
Total expenses	12,800	18,900	14,600	13,200
Operating income	$ 3,200	$ 9,100	$ 5,400	$ 4,800

*Includes $2,000 depreciation each month.

b. Sales are 20% for cash and 80% on credit.

c. Credit sales are collected over a three-month period with 10% collected in the month of sale, 70% in the month following sale, and 20% in the second month following sale. May sales totalled $30,000, and June sales totalled $36,000.

d. Inventory purchases are paid for within 15 days. Therefore, 50% of a month's inventory purchases are paid for in the month of purchase. The remaining 50% is paid in the following month. Accounts payable for inventory purchases at June 30 total $11,700.

e. The company maintains its ending inventory levels at 75% of the cost of the merchandise to be sold in the following month. The merchandise inventory at June 30 is $18,000.

f. Land costing $4,500 will be purchased in July.

g. Dividends of $1,000 will be declared and paid in September.

h. The cash balance on June 30 is $8,000; the company must maintain a cash balance of at least this amount at the end of each month.

i. The company has an agreement with a local bank that allows the company to borrow in increments of $1,000 at the beginning of each month, up to a total loan balance of $40,000. The interest rate on these loans is 1% per month, and for simplicity, we will assume that interest is not compounded. The company would, as far as it is able, repay the loan plus accumulated interest at the end of the quarter.

Required:

1. Prepare a schedule of expected cash collections for July, August, and September and for the quarter in total.
2. Prepare the following for merchandise inventory:
   a. A merchandise purchases budget for July, August, and September.
   b. A schedule of expected cash disbursements for merchandise purchases for July, August, and September and for the quarter in total.
3. Prepare a cash budget for July, August, and September and for the quarter in total.

PROBLEM 9–22 Integrated Operating Budgets [LO2]

The East Division of Kensic Company manufactures a vital component that is used in one of Kensic's major product lines. The East Division has been experiencing some difficulty in coordinating activities between its various departments, which has resulted in some shortages of the component at critical times. To overcome the shortages, the manager of East Division has decided to initiate a monthly budgeting system that is integrated between departments.

The first budget is to be for the second quarter of the current year. To assist in creating the budget, the divisional controller has accumulated the following information:

Sales. Sales through the first three months of the current year were 32,000 units. Actual sales in units for January, February, and March, and planned sales in units over the next five months, are given below:

January (actual)	6,000
February (actual)	10,000
March (actual)	16,000
April (planned)	20,000
May (planned)	35,000
June (planned)	50,000
July (planned).	45,000
August (planned)	30,000

In total, the East Division expects to produce and sell 250,000 units during the current year.

Direct Material. Two different materials are used in the production of the component. Data regarding these materials are given below:

Direct Material	Units of Direct Materials per Finished Component	Cost per Unit	Inventory at March 31
No. 208	4 kilograms	$5.00	46,000 kilograms
No. 311	9 metres	$2.00	69,000 metres

Material No. 208 is sometimes in short supply. Therefore, the East Division requires that enough of the material be on hand at the end of each month to provide for 50% of the following month's production needs. Material No. 311 is easier to get, so only one-third of the following month's production needs must be on hand at the end of each month.

Direct Labour. The East Division has three departments through which the components must pass before they are completed. Information relating to direct labour in these departments is given below:

Department	Direct Labour-Hours per Finished Component	Cost per Direct Labour-Hour
Shaping	0.25	$18.00
Assembly	0.70	$16.00
Finishing	0.10	$20.00

Direct labour is adjusted to the workload each month.

Manufacturing Overhead. East Division manufactured 32,000 components during the first three months of the current year. The actual variable overhead costs incurred during this three-month period are shown below. East Division's controller believes that the variable overhead costs incurred during the last nine months of the year will be at the same rate per component as experienced during the first three months.

Utilities	$ 57,000
Indirect labour	31,000
Supplies	16,000
Other.	8,000
Total variable overhead	$112,000

The actual fixed manufacturing overhead costs incurred during the first three months was $1,170,000. The East Division has budgeted fixed manufacturing overhead costs for the entire year as follows:

Supervision	$ 872,000
Property taxes	143,000
Depreciation.	2,910,000
Insurance	631,000
Other	72,000
Total fixed manufacturing overhead	$4,628,000

Finished Goods Inventory. The desired monthly ending finished goods inventory is 20% of the next month's estimated sales. The East Division has 4,000 units in finished goods inventory on March 31.

Required:

1. Prepare a production budget for the East Division for the second quarter ending June 30. Show computations by month and in total for the quarter.
2. Prepare a direct materials budget for each type of material for the second quarter ending June 30. Again show computations by month and in total for the quarter.
3. Prepare a direct labour budget for the second quarter ending June 30. This time it is *not* necessary to show monthly figures; show quarterly totals only. Assume that the workforce is adjusted as work requirements change.
4. Assume that the company plans to produce a total of 250,000 units for the year. Prepare a manufacturing overhead budget for the nine-month period ending December 31. (Do not compute a predetermined overhead rate.) Again, it is *not* necessary to show monthly figures.

(CMA, adapted)

PROBLEM 9–23 Completing a Master Budget [LO2]

The following data relate to the operations of Lim Corporation, a wholesale distributor of consumer goods:

Current assets as of December 31:	
Cash	$6,000
Accounts receivable	$36,000
Inventory	$9,800
Buildings and equipment, net	$110,885
Accounts payable	$32,550
Common shares	$100,000
Retained earnings	$30,135

a. The gross margin is 30% of sales. (In other words, cost of goods sold is 70% of sales.)

b. Actual and budgeted sales data are as follows:

December (actual)	$60,000
January	$70,000
February	$80,000
March	$85,000
April	$55,000

c. Sales are 40% for cash and 60% on credit. Credit sales are collected in the month following sale. The accounts receivable at December 31 are the result of December credit sales.

d. Each month's ending inventory should equal 20% of the following month's budgeted cost of goods sold.

e. One-quarter of a month's inventory purchases is paid for in the month of purchase; the other three-quarters is paid for in the following month. The accounts payable at December 31 are the result of December purchases of inventory.

f. Monthly expenses are as follows: commissions, $12,000; rent, $1,800; other expenses (excluding depreciation), 8% of sales. Assume that these expenses are paid monthly. Depreciation is $2,400 for the quarter and includes depreciation on new assets acquired during the quarter.

g. Equipment will be acquired for cash: $3,000 in January and $8,000 in February.

h. Management would like to maintain a minimum cash balance of $5,000 at the end of each month. The company has an agreement with a local bank that allows the company to borrow in increments of $1,000 at the beginning of each month, up to a total loan balance of $50,000. The interest rate on these loans is 1% per month, and for simplicity, we will assume that interest is not compounded. The company would, as far as it is able, repay the loan plus accumulated interest at the end of the quarter.

Required:

Using the data above:

1. Complete the following schedule:

Schedule of Expected Cash Collections	January	February	March	Quarter
Cash sales	$28,000			
Credit sales	36,000			
Total collections	$64,000			

2. Complete the following:

Merchandise Purchases Budget	January	February	March	Quarter
Budgeted cost of goods sold	$49,000*			
Add desired ending inventory	11,200†			
Total needs	60,200			
Less beginning inventory	9,800			
Required purchases	$50,400			

*$70,000 sales × 70% = $49,000.
†$80,000 × 70% × 20% = $11,200.

Schedule of Expected Cash Disbursements—Merchandise Purchases	January	February	March	Quarter
December purchases	$32,550*			$32,550
January purchases	12,600	$37,800		50,400
February purchases				
March purchases				
Total disbursements	$45,150			

*Beginning balance of the accounts payable.

3. Complete the following schedule:

Schedule of Expected Cash Disbursements—Selling and Administrative Expenses	January	February	March	Quarter
Commissions	$12,000			
Rent	1,800			
Other expenses	5,600			
Total disbursements	$19,400			

4. Complete the following cash budget:

	January	February	March	Quarter
Cash balance, beginning	$ 6,000			
Add cash collections	64,000			
Total cash available	70,000			
Less cash disbursements:				
For inventory	45,150			
For operating expenses	19,400			
For equipment	3,000			
Total cash disbursements	67,550			
Excess (deficiency) of cash	$ 2,450			
Financing				
Etc.				

(Required continued on the next page)

5. Prepare an absorption costing income statement, similar to the one shown in Schedule 9 on page 389, for the quarter ended March 31.
6. Prepare a balance sheet as of March 31.

PROBLEM 9–24 Applying the Flexible Budget Approach [LO3, LO4]
The KGV Blood Bank, a private charity partly supported by government grants, is located on the Caribbean island of St. Lucia. The blood bank has just finished its operations for September, which was a particularly busy month due to a powerful hurricane that hit neighbouring islands, causing many injuries. The hurricane largely bypassed St. Lucia, but residents of St. Lucia willingly donated their blood to help people on other islands. As a consequence, the blood bank collected and processed over 25% more blood than had been originally planned for the month.

A report prepared by a government official comparing actual costs to costs included in the static budget for the blood bank appears below. (The currency on St. Lucia is the East Caribbean dollar.) Continued support from the government depends on the blood bank's ability to demonstrate control over its costs.

KGV BLOOD BANK
Cost Control Report
For the Month Ended September 30

	Actual	Static Budget	Static Budget Variance
Litres of blood collected	780	600	180
Variable costs:			
Medical supplies	$ 9,252	$ 7,110	$2,142 U
Lab tests	10,782	8,610	2,172 U
Refreshments for donors	1,186	960	226 U
Administrative supplies	189	150	39 U
Total variable cost	21,409	16,830	4,579 U
Fixed costs:			
Staff salaries	13,200	13,200	0
Equipment depreciation	2,100	1,900	200 U
Rent	1,500	1,500	0
Utilities	324	300	24 U
Total fixed cost	17,124	16,900	224 U
Total cost	$38,533	$33,730	$4,803 U

The managing director of the blood bank was very unhappy with this report, claiming that his costs were higher than expected due to the emergency on the neighbouring islands. He also pointed out that the additional costs had been fully covered by payments from grateful recipients on the other islands. The government official who prepared the report countered that all of the figures had been submitted by the blood bank to the government; he was just pointing out that actual costs were a lot higher than promised in the budget.

Required:
1. Prepare a new performance report for September using the flexible budget approach. (Note: Even though there are no revenues in this setting, the flexible budget approach can still be used to prepare a flexible budget performance report. Use Exhibit 9–4 as your guide)
2. Do you think any of the variances in the report you prepared should be investigated? Why?

Cases

CASE 9–25 Evaluating a Company's Budget Procedures [LO1]

Tom Emory and Jim Morris strolled back to their plant from the administrative offices of Ferguson & Son Manufacturing Company. Tom is manager of the machine shop in the company's factory; Jim is manager of the equipment maintenance department.

The men had just attended the monthly performance evaluation meeting for plant department heads. These meetings had been held on the third Tuesday of each month since Robert Ferguson, Jr., the president's son, had become plant manager a year earlier.

As they were walking, Tom Emory spoke: "Boy, I hate those meetings! I never know whether my department's accounting reports will show good or bad performance. I'm beginning to expect the worst. If the accountants say I saved the company a dollar, I'm called 'Sir,' but if I spend even a little too much—boy, do I get in trouble. I don't know if I can hold on until I retire."

Tom had just been given the worst evaluation he had ever received in his long career with Ferguson & Son. He was the most respected of the experienced machinists in the company. He had been with Ferguson & Son for many years and was promoted to supervisor of the machine shop when the company expanded and moved to its present location. The president (Robert Ferguson, Sr.) had often stated that the company's success was due to the high-quality work of machinists like Tom. As supervisor, Tom stressed the importance of craftsmanship and told his workers that he wanted no sloppy work coming from his department.

When Robert Ferguson, Jr., became the plant manager, he directed that monthly performance comparisons be made between actual and budgeted costs for each department. The departmental budgets were intended to encourage the supervisors to reduce inefficiencies and to seek cost reduction opportunities. The company controller was instructed to have his staff "tighten" the budget slightly whenever a department attained its budget in a given month; this was done to reinforce the plant manager's desire to reduce costs. The young plant manager often stressed the importance of continued progress toward attaining the budget; he also made it known that he kept a file of these performance reports for future reference when he succeeded his father.

Tom Emory's conversation with Jim Morris continued as follows:

Emory: I really don't understand. We've worked so hard to meet the budget, and the minute we do so they tighten it on us. We can't work any faster and still maintain quality. I think my men are ready to quit trying. Besides, those reports don't tell the whole story. We always seem to be interrupting the big jobs for all those small rush orders. All that setup and machine adjustment time is killing us. And quite frankly, Jim, you were no help. When our hydraulic press broke down last month, your people were nowhere to be found. We had to take it apart ourselves and got stuck with all that idle time.

Morris: I'm sorry about that, Tom, but you know my department has had trouble making budget, too. We were running well behind at the time of that problem, and if we'd spent a day on that old machine, we would never have made it up. Instead we made the scheduled inspections of the forklift trucks because we knew we could do those in less than the budgeted time.

Emory: Well, Jim, at least you have some options. I'm locked into what the scheduling department assigns to me and you know they're being harassed by sales for those special orders. Incidentally, why didn't your report show all the supplies you guys wasted last month when you were working in Bill's department?

Morris: We're not out of the woods on that deal yet. We charged the maximum we could to other work and haven't even reported some of it yet.

Emory: Well, I'm glad you have a way of getting out of the pressure. The accountants seem to know everything that's happening in my department, sometimes even before I do. I thought all that budget and accounting stuff was supposed to help, but it just gets me into trouble. It's all a big pain. I'm trying to put out quality work; they're trying to save pennies.

Required:

1. Identify the problems that appear to exist in Ferguson & Son Manufacturing Company's budgetary control system and explain how the problems are likely to reduce the effectiveness of the system.
2. Explain how Ferguson & Son Manufacturing Company's budgetary control system could be revised to improve its effectiveness.

(CMA, adapted)

CASE 9–26 Master Budget with Supporting Schedules [LO2]

You have just been hired as a management trainee by Formalwear Sales Company, a nationwide distributor of a designer's silk ties. The company has an exclusive franchise on the distribution of the ties, and sales have grown so rapidly over the last few years that it has become necessary to add new members to the management team. You have been given responsibility for all planning and budgeting. Your first assignment is to prepare a master budget for the next three months, starting April 1. You are anxious to make a favourable impression on the president and have assembled the information below.

The company desires a minimum ending cash balance each month of $10,000. The ties are sold to retailers for $8 each. Recent and forecasted sales in units are as follows:

January (actual)	20,000	June	60,000
February (actual)	24,000	July	40,000
March (actual)	28,000	August	36,000
April	35,000	September	32,000
May	45,000		

The large buildup in sales before and during June is due to Father's Day. Ending inventories are supposed to equal 90% of the next month's sales in units. The ties cost the company $5 each.

Purchases are paid for as follows: 50% in the month of purchase and the remaining 50% in the following month. All sales are on credit, with no discount, and payable within 15 days. The company has found, however, that only 25% of a month's sales are collected by month-end. An additional 50% is collected in the following month, and the remaining 25% is collected in the second month following sale. Bad debts have been negligible.

The company's monthly operating expenses are given below:

Variable:	
Sales commissions	$1 per tie
Fixed:	
Wages and salaries	$22,000
Utilities	$14,000
Insurance	$1,200
Depreciation	$1,500
Miscellaneous	$3,000

All operating expenses are paid during the month, in cash, with the exception of depreciation and insurance expired. Land will be purchased during May for $25,000 cash. The company declares dividends of $12,000 each quarter, payable in the first month of the following quarter. The company's balance sheet at March 31 is given below:

Assets	
Cash	$ 14,000
Accounts receivable ($48,000 February sales; $168,000 March sales)	216,000
Inventory (31,500 units)	157,500
Prepaid insurance	14,400
Fixed assets, net of depreciation	172,700
Total assets	$574,600
Liabilities and Shareholders' Equity	
Accounts payable	$ 85,750
Dividends payable	12,000
Common shares	300,000
Retained earnings	176,850
Total liabilities and shareholders' equity	$574,600

The company has an agreement with a bank that allows the company to borrow in increments of $1,000 at the beginning of each month, up to a total loan balance of $40,000. The interest rate on these loans is 1% per month, and for simplicity, we will assume that interest is not compounded. At the end of the quarter, the company would pay the bank all of the accumulated interest on the loan and as much of the loan as possible (in increments of $1,000), while still retaining at least $10,000 in cash.

Required:

Prepare a master budget for the three-month period ending June 30. Include the following detailed budgets:

1. *a.* A sales budget by month and in total.
   b. A schedule of expected cash collections from sales, by month and in total.
   c. A merchandise purchases budget in units and in dollars. Show the budget by month and in total.
   d. A schedule of expected cash disbursements for merchandise purchases, by month and in total.
2. A cash budget. Show the budget by month and in total.
3. A budgeted income statement for the three-month period ending June 30. Use the contribution approach.
4. A budgeted balance sheet as of June 30.

CASE 9–27 Selling Expense Flexible Budget [LO3, LO4]

Mark Fletcher, president of SoftGro Inc., was looking forward to seeing the performance reports for November because he knew the company's sales for the month had exceeded budget by a considerable margin. SoftGro, a distributor of educational software packages, had been growing steadily for approximately two years. Fletcher's biggest challenge at this point was to ensure that the company did not lose control of expenses during this growth period. When Fletcher received the November reports, he was dismayed to see the large unfavourable variance in the company's monthly selling expense report that is presented below:

SOFTGRO INC.
Monthly Selling Expense Report
November

		November		
	Annual Budget	Static Budget	Actual	Static Budget Variance
Unit sales	2,000,000	280,000	310,000	30,000 F
Dollar sales	$80,000,000	$11,200,000	$12,400,000	$1,200,000 F
Orders processed	54,000	6,500	5,800	700 U
Salespersons per month	90	90	96	6 U
Expenses:				
Advertising	$19,800,000	$ 1,650,000	$ 1,660,000	$ 10,000 U
Staff salaries	1,500,000	125,000	125,000	0
Sales salaries	1,296,000	108,000	115,400	7,400 U
Commissions	3,200,000	448,000	496,000	48,000 U
Per diem expense	1,782,000	148,500	162,600	14,100 U
Office expense	4,080,000	340,000	358,400	18,400 U
Shipping expense	6,750,000	902,500	976,500	74,000 U
Total expense	$38,408,000	$ 3,722,000	$ 3,893,900	$ 171,900 U

Fletcher called in the company's new controller, Susan Porter, to discuss the implications of the variances reported for November and to plan a strategy for improving performance. Porter suggested that the reporting format the company had been using might not be giving Fletcher a true picture of the company's operations and proposed that SoftGro implement flexible budgeting for reporting purposes. Porter offered to redo the monthly selling expense report for November using flexible budgeting so that Fletcher could compare the two reports and see the advantages of flexible budgeting.

After some analysis, Porter derived the following data about the company's selling expenses:

a. The total compensation paid to the sales force consists of both a monthly base salary and a commission. The commission varies with sales dollars.

b. Sales office expense is a mixed cost with the variable portion related to the number of orders processed. The fixed portion of office expense is $3,000,000 annually and is incurred uniformly throughout the year.
c. Subsequent to the adoption of the annual budget for the current year, SoftGro decided to open a new sales territory. As a consequence, approval was given to hire six additional salespersons effective November 1. Porter decided that these additional six people should be recognized in her revised report.
d. Per diem reimbursement to the sales force, while a fixed amount per day, is variable with the number of salespersons and the number of days spent travelling. SoftGro's original budget was based on an average sales force of 90 persons throughout the year with each salesperson travelling 15 days per month.
e. The company's shipping expense is a mixed cost with the variable portion, $3 per unit, dependent on the number of units sold. The fixed portion is incurred uniformly throughout the year.

Using the data above, Porter believed she would be able to redo the November report and present it to Fletcher for his review.

Required:

1. Describe the benefits of flexible budgeting, and explain why Susan Porter would propose that SoftGro use flexible budgeting in this situation.
2. Prepare a revised comprehensive performance report for November that would permit Mark Fletcher to more clearly evaluate SoftGro's control over selling expenses. Use Exhibit 9–6 as your guide.
3. Of the total unfavourable static budget variance of $171,900, how much relates to actual activity levels differing from the static budget.

(CMA, adapted)

Research

R 9–28 Budgeting at Not-for-Profit Organizations [LO5]
Form a team to examine how a large not-for-profit organization in your area develops and uses its operating budgets. Make an appointment to meet with the individual responsible for the budgeting process and discuss the following issues.

Required:

1. How are budgets set each year? Is a zero-based budgeting approach used or are budgets based on prior year amounts adjusted for anticipated changes in the coming year?
2. How challenging are the budget targets?
3. How long does the budget process take and who is involved?
4. Is the budget prepared on an expenditure basis or a program basis?
5. How often are actual results compared to the budget?
6. Is any follow-up done if actual amounts differ significantly from the budget?
7. Are flexible budgets used?
8. What are the major strengths and weaknesses of the budgeting process used by the organization?

R 9–29 Challenges with Budgeting [LO1]
As you know, the World Wide Web is a medium that is constantly evolving. Sites come and go, and change without notice. To enable the periodic updating of site addresses, this problem has been posted to the textbook web site (**www.mcgrawhill.ca/olc/garrison**). After accessing the site, enter the Student Centre and select this chapter. Select and complete the Internet Exercise.

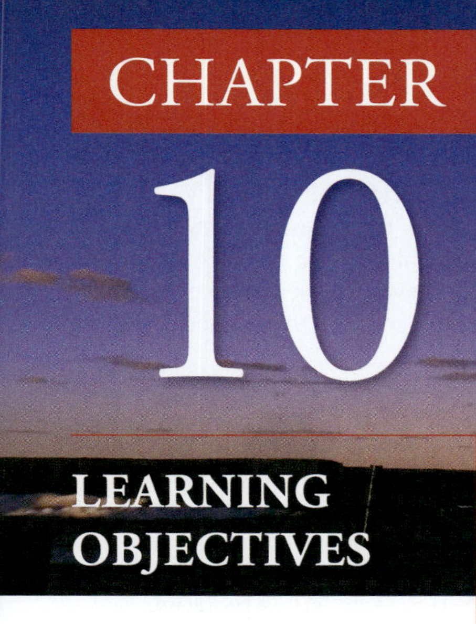

CHAPTER 10

LEARNING OBJECTIVES

After studying Chapter 10, you should be able to:

1. Explain how direct materials standards and direct labour standards are set.
2. Compute the direct materials price and quantity variances and explain their significance.
3. Compute the direct labour rate and efficiency variances and explain their significance.
4. Compute the variable manufacturing overhead spending and efficiency variances.
5. Explain the significance of the denominator activity figure in determining the standard cost of a unit of product.
6. Compute and interpret the fixed overhead budget and volume variances.
7. Prepare a performance report for manufacturing overhead and perform analysis of capacity utilization.
8. (Appendix 10A) Compute the mix and yield variances for materials and explain their significance.
9. (Appendix 10B) Prepare journal entries to record standard costs and variances.
10. (Online Appendix 10C) Compute labour time when learning is present.

STANDARD COSTS AND OVERHEAD ANALYSIS

BUSINESS FOCUS

Managing Distribution Costs

Rising fuel costs in recent years have created pressure for many organizations to find ways to improve the management of the distribution function. For many manufacturing companies, the cost of shipping products to wholesalers, retailers and the final customer represents a significant portion of their overall cost structure. To address these issues, Catalyst Paper Corporation, a pulp and paper manufacturer based in British Columbia, has developed a comprehensive approach for managing its distribution costs.

At Catalyst Paper, shipping products to customers involves a complex network of manufacturing plants, warehouses, transportation modes (e.g., rail versus truck), and carriers within modes of transportation. To improve control over shipping expenses, analysts at Catalyst Paper have developed a model that they use to budget the cost of each shipment made to a customer throughout the year. The model is very elaborate and requires estimates of: the mode of transportation to be used for each shipment (e.g., rail, truck, container ship); the specific carrier that will be used within a transportation mode (e.g., ABC Trucking); the rates charged by that carrier; and the warehouse(s) that will be used to fill the order. Combining all of these estimates allows Catalyst to calculate the budgeted or "standard cost" for each shipment made to a customer. At the end of each month, company analysts compare the actual shipping costs to the standard amounts estimated by their model. Variances between the actual and standard costs can be caused by several factors including using different transportation modes (rail instead of truck), different carriers (DEF Trucking instead of ABC Trucking) or using different warehouses to source the order, compared to the plan. The model developed by Catalyst allows analysts to determine the portion of the total variance between actual and standard shipping expenses attributable to each of these factors. Once the causes of the variance have been identified, managers can identify follow-up action aimed at eliminating or reducing unfavourable variances in future periods (e.g., switch to a less expensive transportation mode).

Prior to developing their analytical model, managers at Catalyst could not pinpoint the cause of unfavourable variances in any given month. Thanks to the new approach, management believes they have a better understanding of the drivers of distribution costs. They also believe it has improved their ability to both plan and control distribution costs.

Source: Kevin Gaffney, Valeri Gladkikh, and Alan Webb, "A Case Study of a Variance Analysis Framework for Managing Distribution Costs," *Accounting Perspectives*, Volume 6, 2007, pp. 167–190.

Chapter 10 continues our three-chapter study of planning, control, and performance measurement. Quite often, these terms carry with them negative connotations. Indeed, performance measurements can be used counterproductively to create fear, to cast blame, and to punish. However, if used properly, as explained in the following quotation, performance measurement serves a vital function in both daily life and in organizations:

> Imagine you want to improve your basketball shooting skill. You know that practice will help, so you go to the basketball court. There you start shooting toward the hoop, but as soon as the ball gets close to the rim your vision goes blurry for a second, so that you cannot observe where the ball ended up in relation to the target (left, right, in front, too far back, inside the hoop?). It would be pretty difficult to improve under those conditions. . . .
>
> Or imagine someone engaging in a weight loss program. A normal step in such programs is to purchase a scale to be able to track one's progress: Is this program working? Am I losing weight? A positive answer would be encouraging and would motivate me to keep up the effort, while a negative answer might lead me to reflect on the process: Am I working on the right diet and exercise program? Am I doing everything I am supposed to? Suppose you don't want to set up a sophisticated measurement system and decide to forgo the scale. You would still have some idea of how well you are doing from simple methods such as clothes feeling looser, a belt that fastens at a different hole, or simply via observation in a mirror! Now, imagine trying to sustain a weight loss program without any feedback on how well you are doing.
>
> In these examples, availability of quantitative measures of performance can yield two types of benefits: First, performance feedback can help improve the "production process" through a better understanding of what works and what doesn't; e.g., shooting this way works better than shooting that way. Second, feedback on performance can sustain motivation and effort, because it is encouraging and/or because it suggests that more effort is required for the goal to be met.[1]

In the same way, performance measurement can be helpful in an organization. It can provide feedback concerning what works and what does not work, and it can help motivate people to sustain their efforts.

Our study of performance measurement begins with the production function. In this chapter we see how various measures are used to control operations and to evaluate performance in this key operating area. Even though we are starting with an operational area, keep in mind that performance measures should be derived from the organization's overall strategy. For example, a company like Cervélo that bases its strategy on designing and producing world-class racing bicycles should use different performance measures than a company like Purolator Courier where on-time delivery, customer convenience, and low cost are key competitive advantages. Cervélo may want to keep close track of the percentage of revenues from new models introduced within the last year; whereas Purolator may want to closely monitor the percentage of packages delivered on time. In Chapter 11, we will have more to say concerning the role of strategy in the selection of performance measures when we discuss the balanced scorecard. But first we will see how *standard costs* are used by managers to help control costs.

Companies in highly competitive industries like Purolator, WestJet, MDG, and Cervélo must be able to provide high-quality goods and services at low cost. If they do not, their customers will buy from more efficient competitors. Stated in the starkest terms, managers must obtain inputs such as raw materials and electricity at the lowest possible prices and must use them as effectively as possible—while maintaining or increasing the quality of what they sell. If inputs are purchased at prices that are too high or more input is used than is really necessary, higher costs will result.

1. Soumitra Dutta and Jean-François Manzoni, *Process Reengineering, Organizational Change and Performance Improvement* (New York: McGraw-Hill), Chapter IV.

How do managers control the prices that are paid for inputs and the quantities that are used? They could examine every transaction in detail, but this obviously would be an inefficient use of management time. For many companies, the answer to this control problem lies at least partially in *standard costs.*

Budgeting, as described in Chapter 9, focuses on planning but is employed for control purposes where desired by management. Standards represent specific elements of budgets such as material requirements or labour requirements as well as overhead projections. Standards thus serve both a planning function and a control function. Whether or not organizations employ standard costs to formally cost jobs (Chapter 3) or processes (Chapter 4) is one of the decisions managers must make when implementing financial systems. If they decide to use actual costs for jobs or processes, they still can employ standard cost practices for budgeting and operational planning.

Controlling overhead costs is also a major concern for managers in business, government and not-for-profit organizations. Indeed overhead is a major cost, if not the major cost in many large organizations. Control of overhead costs poses special problems in part because they are more difficult to understand than direct materials and direct labour. Overhead is made up of numerous individual items, some of which are small in dollar amounts. Further, some overhead costs are variable and others are fixed. In this chapter we extend the concept of flexible budgets introduced in Chapter 9 to their use in controlling overhead costs. We also address the analysis and reporting of overhead costs within a standard cost system.

IN BUSINESS

The Brass Products Division at Parker Hannifin Corporation, known as Parker Brass, is a world-class manufacturer of tube and brass fittings, valves, hose and hose fittings. Management at the company uses variances from its standard costing system to target problem areas for improvement. If a production variance exceeds 5% of sales, the responsible manager is required to explain the variance and to propose a plan of action to correct the detected problems. In the past, variances were reported at the end of the month—often several weeks after a particular job had been completed. Now, a variance report is generated the day after a job is completed and summary variance reports are prepared weekly. These more frequent reports help managers take more timely corrective action.

Source: David Johnsen and Parvez Sopariwala, "Standard Costing Is Alive and Well at Parker Brass," *Management Accounting Quarterly*, Winter 2000, pp. 12–20.

Standard Costs—Management by Exception

A *standard* is a benchmark or "norm" for measuring performance. Standards are found everywhere. Your doctor evaluates your weight using standards that have been set for individuals of your age, height, and gender. The food we eat in restaurants must be prepared under specified standards of cleanliness. The buildings we live in must conform to standards set in building codes. Standards are also widely used in managerial accounting, where they relate to the *quantity* and *cost* of inputs used in manufacturing goods or providing services.

Quantity and cost standards are set for each major input such as raw materials and labour time. *Quantity standards* specify how much of an input should be used to make a unit of product or provide a unit of service. *Cost (price) standards* specify how much should be paid for each unit of the input. Actual quantities and actual costs of inputs are compared to these standards. If either the quantity or the cost of inputs departs significantly from the standards, managers investigate the discrepancy to find the cause of the problem and eliminate it. This process is called **management by exception.**

Management by exception
A system of management in which standards are set for various operating activities which are then periodically compared to actual results. Any differences that are deemed significant are brought to the attention of management as "exceptions."

In our daily lives, we operate in a management by exception mode most of the time. Consider what happens when you sit down in the driver's seat of your car. You put the key in the ignition, you turn the key, and your car starts. Your expectation (standard) that the car will start is met; you do not have to open the car hood and check the battery, the connecting cables, the fuel lines, and so on. If you turn the key and the car does not start, then you have a discrepancy (variance). Your expectations are not met, and you need to investigate why. Note that even if the car starts after a second try, it would be wise to investigate anyway. The fact that the expectation was not met should be viewed as an opportunity to uncover the cause of the problem rather than as simply an annoyance. If the underlying cause is not discovered and corrected, the problem may recur and become much worse.

This basic approach to identifying and solving problems is used in the *variance analysis cycle*, which is illustrated in Exhibit 10–1. The cycle begins with the preparation of standard cost performance reports in the Accounting Department. These reports highlight the variances, which are the differences between actual results and what should have occurred according to the standards. The variances raise questions. Why did the variance occur? Why is this variance larger than it was last period? The significant variances are investigated to discover their root causes. Corrective actions are taken, and then next period's operations are carried out. The cycle then begins again with the preparation of a new standard cost performance for the most recent period. The emphasis should be highlighting problems, finding their root causes, and taking corrective action. The goal is to improve operations—not to assign blame.

Who Uses Standard Costs?

Manufacturing, service, food, and not-for-profit organizations all make use of standards to some extent. Auto service centres like Canadian Tire, for example, often set specific labour time standards for the completion of certain work tasks, such as installing a water pump or doing a valve job, and then measure actual performance against these standards. Fast-food outlets such as Harvey's have exacting standards as to the quantity of meat put into a sandwich, as well as standards for the cost of the meat. Hospitals have standard costs (for food, laundry, and other items) for each occupied bed per day, as well as standard time allowances for certain routine activities, such as laboratory tests. In short, you are likely to run into standard costs in virtually any line of business that you enter.

Standard cost card
A detailed listing of the standard amounts of materials, labour, and overhead that should go into a unit of product, multiplied by the standard price or rate that has been set for each cost element.

Manufacturing companies often have highly developed standard costing systems in which standards relating to materials, labour, and overhead are developed in detail for each separate product. A **standard cost card** shows the standard quantities and costs of the inputs required to produce a unit of a specific product. In the following section, we provide a detailed example of the setting of standard costs and the preparation of a standard cost card.

EXHIBIT 10–1 The Variance Analysis Cycle

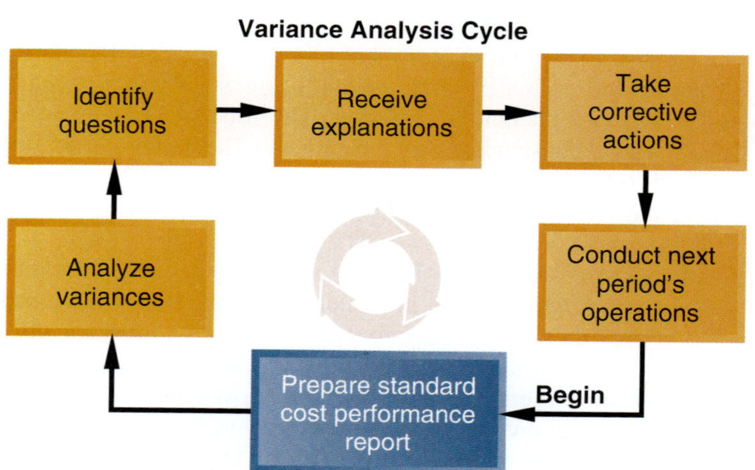

Setting Standard Costs

Setting price and quantity standards ideally combines the expertise of everyone who has responsibility for purchasing and using inputs. In a manufacturing setting, this might include accountants, purchasing managers, engineers, production supervisors, line managers, and production workers. Past records of purchase prices and of input usage can be helpful in setting standards. However, the standards should be designed to encourage efficient *future* operations, not a repetition of *past* operations, that may or may not have been efficient.

LEARNING OBJECTIVE 1
Explain how direct materials standards and direct labour standards are set.

Ideal versus Practical Standards

Should standards be attainable all of the time, part of the time, or almost none of the time? Opinions vary, but standards tend to fall into one of two categories—either ideal or practical.

Ideal standards are those that can be attained only under the best circumstances. They allow for no machine breakdowns or other work interruptions, and they call for a level of effort that can be attained only by the most skilled and efficient employees working at peak effort 100% of the time. Some managers feel that such standards have a motivational value. These managers argue that even though employees know they will rarely meet the standard, it is a constant reminder of the need for ever-increasing efficiency and effort. Few firms use ideal standards. Most managers feel that ideal standards tend to discourage even the most diligent workers. Moreover, when ideal standards are used, variances from the standards have little meaning. Large variances from the ideal are normal and it is difficult to "manage by exception."

Ideal standards
Standards that allow for no machine breakdowns or other work interruptions and that require peak efficiency at all times.

Practical standards are defined as standards that are "tight but attainable." They allow for normal machine downtime and employee rest periods, and they can be attained through reasonable, although highly efficient, efforts by the average employee. Variances from practical standards typically signal a need for management attention because they represent deviations that fall outside of normal operating conditions. In addition to signalling abnormal conditions, they can also be used in forecasting cash flows and in planning inventory. By contrast, ideal standards cannot be used in forecasting and planning; they do not allow for normal inefficiencies, and therefore they result in unrealistic planning and forecasting figures.

Practical standards
Standards that allow for normal machine downtime and other work interruptions and that can be attained through reasonable, although highly efficient, efforts by the average employee.

Throughout the remainder of this chapter, we will assume the use of practical rather than ideal standards.

Setting Direct Materials Standards

We will use the Colonial Pewter Company to illustrate the development and application of a standard cost system. The company was organized a year ago and its only product at present is a reproduction of an eighteenth-century pewter bookend. The bookend is made largely by hand, using traditional metal-working tools. Consequently, the manufacturing process is very labour-intensive and requires a high level of skill.

Colonial Pewter has recently expanded its workforce to take advantage of unexpected demand for the bookends as gifts. The company started with a small group of experienced pewter workers but has had to hire less experienced workers as a result of the expansion. Terry Sherman is the controller of the company. He has been asked by Colonial Pewter's president to develop a system that would allow the company to periodically evaluate the productivity of its employees, the efficiency of raw material usage and the prices paid for labour and materials.

Terry Sherman's first task was to prepare price and quantity standards for the company's only significant raw material, pewter ingots. The **standard price per unit** for direct materials should reflect the final, delivered cost of the materials, net of any discounts taken. After consulting with the purchasing manager, Terry prepared the following documentation for the standard price of a kilogram of pewter in ingot form:

Standard price per unit
The price that should be paid for a single unit of materials, including allowances for quality, quantity purchased, shipping, receiving, and other such costs, net of any discounts allowed.

Purchase price, top-grade pewter ingots	$ 3.60
Freight, by truck, from the supplier's warehouse	0.44
Receiving and handling	0.05
Less purchase discount.	(0.09)
Standard price per kilogram	$ 4.00

Notice that the standard price reflects a particular grade of material (top quality) delivered by a particular type of carrier (truck). Allowances have also been made for handling and discounts. If everything proceeds according to these expectations, the net standard price of a kilogram of pewter should therefore be $4.

Standard quantity per unit The amount of materials that should be required to complete a single unit of product, including allowances for normal waste, spoilage, rejects, and similar inefficiencies.

The **standard quantity per unit** for direct materials should reflect the amount of material going into each unit of finished product, as well as an allowance for unavoidable waste, spoilage, and other normal inefficiencies. After consulting with the production manager, Terry Sherman prepared the following documentation for the standard quantity of pewter going into a pair of bookends:

Material requirements as specified in the bill of materials for a pair of bookends, in kilograms	2.7
Allowance for waste and spoilage, in kilograms.	0.2
Allowance for rejects, in kilograms	0.1
Standard quantity per pair of bookends, in kilograms	3.0

Bill of materials A listing of the quantity of each type of material required to manufacture a unit of product.

A **bill of materials** details the type and quantity of each item of material that should be used in a product. As shown above, it should be adjusted for waste and other factors when determining the standard quantity per unit of product. "Waste and spoilage" refers to materials that are wasted as a normal part of the production process or that spoil before they are used. "Rejects" refers to the direct material contained in units that are defective and must be scrapped.

Although it is common to recognize allowances for waste, spoilage, and rejects when setting standard costs, this practice is now coming into question. Those involved in total quality management (TQM) and similar management approaches argue that no amount of waste or defects should be tolerated. If allowances for waste, spoilage, and rejects are built into the standard cost, the levels of those allowances should be periodically reviewed and reduced over time to reflect improved processes, better training, and better equipment.

Once the price and quantity standards have been set, the standard cost of material per unit of finished product can be computed as follows:

$$3.0 \text{ kilograms per unit} \times \$4 \text{ per kilogram} = \$12 \text{ per unit}$$

This $12 cost figure will appear as one item on the standard cost card of the product.

Setting Direct Labour Standards

Standard rate per hour The labour rate that should be incurred per hour of labour time, including employement taxes, employee benefits, and other such labour costs.

Direct labour price and quantity standards are usually expressed in terms of a labour rate and labour-hours. The **standard rate per hour** for direct labour would include not only wages earned but also employee benefits (e.g., employment insurance, extended medical insurance, etc.) and other labour costs. Using wage records and in consultation with the production manager, Terry determined the standard rate per hour at the Colonial Pewter Company as follows:

Basic average wage rate per hour.	$10
Employment taxes at 10% of the basic rate . . .	1
Employee benefits at 30% of the basic rate . . .	3
Standard rate per direct labour-hour.	$14

Many companies prepare a single standard rate for all employees in a department. This standard rate reflects the expected "mix" of workers, even though the actual wage rates may vary somewhat from individual to individual due to differing skills or seniority. According to the standard computed above, the direct labour rate for Colonial Pewter should average $14 per hour.

The standard direct labour time required to complete a unit of product (generally called the **standard hours per unit**) is perhaps the single most difficult standard to determine. One approach is to break down each task into elemental body movements (such as reaching, pushing, and turning over). Published tables of standard times for such movements are available. These times can be applied to the movements and then added together to determine the total standard time allowed per operation. Another approach is for an industrial engineer to do a time and motion study, which involves recording the time required for certain tasks. As stated earlier, the standard time should include allowances for breaks, personal needs of employees, clean-up, and machine downtime. After consulting with the production manager, Terry prepared the following documentation for the standard hours per unit:

Standard hours per unit The amount of labour time that should be required to complete a single unit of product, including allowances for breaks, machine downtime, clean-up, rejects, and other normal inefficiencies.

Basic labour time per unit, in hours	1.9
Allowance for breaks and personal needs	0.1
Allowance for clean-up and machine downtime	0.3
Allowance for rejects	0.2
Standard labour-hours per unit of product	2.5

Once the rate and time standards have been set, the standard labour cost per unit of product can be computed as follows:

$$2.5 \text{ hours per unit} \times \$14 \text{ per hour} = \$35 \text{ per unit}$$

This $35 cost figure appears along with direct materials as one item on the standard cost card of the product.

Standard labour-hours have declined in relative importance for some organizations. This is particularly true in highly automated manufacturing firms. However, for many service organizations and numerous other construction and processing organizations, labour remains an important input to the production and service activities. For these organizations standard labour-hours inform workers and managers what is expected and how labour should be used. More specifically, standards and the resulting comparisons to actual labour-hours may serve to motivate workers and managers. Labour standards can influence individuals in setting their own goals.

Setting Variable Manufacturing Overhead Standards

As with direct labour, the price and quantity standards for variable manufacturing overhead are generally expressed in terms of rate and hours. The rate represents *the variable portion of the predetermined overhead rate* discussed in Chapter 3. Developing the rate requires an estimate of both the unit cost of the variable overhead items used in production (indirect supplies, indirect labour, etc.) as well as the quantity required for the planned level of production. The unit costs are relatively straight-forward to estimate and can be based on prior year amounts or existing contractual agreements with suppliers that lock in prices. The estimated quantities for variable overhead items can be estimated using actual results from prior periods. The hours represent whatever hours base is used to apply overhead to units of product (usually machine-hours or direct labour-hours, as we learned in Chapter 3). As noted above, the number of hours required per unit can be based on published tables of standard times or on time and motion studies. At Colonial Pewter, the variable portion of the predetermined overhead rate is $3 per direct labour-hour. Therefore, the standard variable manufacturing overhead cost per unit is computed as follows:

$$2.5 \text{ hours per unit} \times \$3 \text{ per hour} = \$7.50 \text{ per unit}$$

This $7.50 cost figure appears along with direct materials and direct labour as one item on the standard cost card from variable production costs in Exhibit 10–2. Observe that the **standard cost per unit** is computed by multiplying the standard quantity or hours by the standard price or rate. We expand our discussion of standard costs to include fixed manufacturing overhead later in this chapter.

EXHIBIT 10–2 Standard Cost Card—Variable Production Cost

Inputs	(1) Standard Quantity or Hours	(2) Standard Price or Rate	(3) Standard Cost (1) × (2)
Direct materials	3.0 kilograms	$ 4.00	$12.00
Direct labour	2.5 hours	14.00	35.00
Variable manufacturing overhead	2.5 hours	3.00	7.50
Total standard variable cost per unit			$54.50

Standard cost per unit The standard cost of a unit of product as shown on the standard cost card; it is computed by multiplying the standard quantity or hours by the standard price or rate for each cost element.

Are Standards the Same as Budgets?

Standards and budgets are very similar. The major distinction between the two terms is that a standard is a *unit* amount, whereas a budget is a *total* amount. The standard cost for materials at Colonial Pewter is $12 per pair of bookends. If 1,000 pairs of bookends are to be manufactured during a budgeting period, then the budgeted cost of materials would be $12,000. In effect, *a standard can be viewed as the budgeted cost for one unit of product.*

A General Model for Variance Analysis

An important reason for separating standards into two categories—price and quantity—is that different managers are usually responsible for buying and for using inputs and these two activities occur at different points in time. In the case of raw materials, for example, the purchasing manager is responsible for the price, and this responsibility is exercised at the time of purchase. In contrast, the production manager is responsible for the amount of the raw material used, and this responsibility is exercised when the materials are used in production, which may be many weeks or months after the purchase date. It is important, therefore, that we separate discrepancies due to deviations from price standards from those due to deviations from quantity standards. Differences between *standard* prices and *actual* prices and *standard* quantities and *actual* quantities are called **variances**. The act of computing and interpreting variances is called *variance analysis.*

Variance The difference between standard prices and quantities and actual prices and quantities.

A general model for computing standard cost variances for variable costs is presented in Exhibit 10–3. This model isolates price variances from quantity variances and shows how each of these variances is computed. We will use this model to compute variances for direct materials, direct labour, and variable manufacturing overhead. We will discuss the model for calculating and interpreting fixed overhead variances later in this chapter.

Four things should be noted from Exhibit 10–3. First, note that a price variance and a quantity variance can be computed for all three variable cost elements—direct materials, direct labour, and variable manufacturing overhead—even though the variance is not called by the same name in all cases. For example, a price variance is called a *materials price variance* in the case of direct materials but a *labour rate variance* in the case of direct labour and an *overhead spending variance* in the case of variable manufacturing overhead.

Second, note that even though a price variance may be called by different names, it is computed in exactly the same way, regardless of whether one is dealing with direct materials, direct labour, or variable manufacturing overhead. The same is true with the quantity variance.

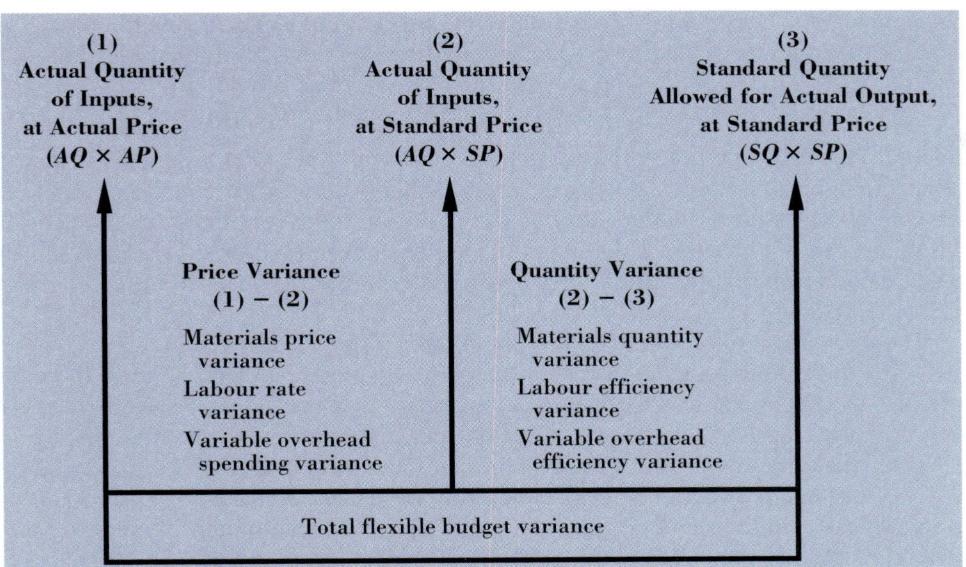

EXHIBIT 10–3 A General Model for Variance Analysis—Variable Production Costs

Third, note that variance analysis is actually a type of input-output analysis. The inputs represent the actual quantity of direct materials, direct labour, and variable manufacturing overhead used; the output represents the good production of the period, expressed in terms of the *standard quantity (or the standard hours) allowed for the actual output* (see column 3 in Exhibit 10–3). By **standard quantity allowed** or **standard hours allowed,** we mean the amount of direct materials, direct labour, or variable manufacturing overhead *that should have been used* to produce the actual output of the period. This could be more or could be less materials, labour, or overhead than was *actually* used, depending on the efficiency or inefficiency of operations. The standard quantity allowed is computed by multiplying the actual output in units by the standard input allowed per unit.

Standard quantity allowed The amount of materials that should have been used to complete the period's output, as computed by multiplying the actual number of units produced by the standard quantity per unit.

Standard hours allowed The time that should have been taken to complete the period's output, as computed by multiplying the actual number of units produced by the standard hours per unit.

Fourth, note that the amount in column 3 (SQ × SP) of Exhibit 10–3 represents the flexible budget for the period. In Chapter 9 we prepared a simplified version of a flexible budget based on the *actual* quantity of units produced for the period multiplied by the *budgeted* cost per unit. When a standard cost system is being used, the flexible budget is based on the *standard quantity allowed* for the *actual* output achieved multiplied by the *standard price* per unit. As will be illustrated in the sections that follow, this revised approach to calculating the flexible budget permits the flexible budget variance for a period to be broken down into its price (rate or spending) and quantity (efficiency) components.

For the analysis of variances, it is key to note the difference between unit cost standards and total cost standards. For example, material has a standard unit cost of $4.00 per kilogram (Exhibit 10–2) but because 3 kilograms are used per pair of bookends, the production unit, the standard cost per pair is $12. However, when we look at the variances we need to consider the standard quantity for the period's production, 2,000 pairs. Thus we need to carefully determine what standard we are considering, unit of material, unit of production, or standard quantity for the actual amount of production for the period.

With this general model as a foundation, we will now examine the price and quantity variances in more detail.

Using Standard Costs—Direct Materials Variances

LEARNING OBJECTIVE 2
Compute the direct materials price and quantity variances and explain their significance.

After determining Colonial Pewter Company's standard costs for direct materials, direct labour, and variable manufacturing overhead, Terry Sherman's next step was to compute the company's variances for June, the most recent month. As discussed in the preceding section, variances are computed by comparing standard costs to actual costs. To facilitate this comparison, Terry referred to the standard cost data contained in Exhibit 10–2. This exhibit shows that the standard cost of direct materials per unit of product is as follows:

$$3.0 \text{ kilograms per unit} \times \$4 \text{ per kilogram} = \$12 \text{ per unit}$$

Colonial Pewter's purchasing records for June showed that 6,500 kilograms of pewter were purchased at a cost of $3.80 per kilogram. This cost figure included freight and handling and was net of the quantity discount. All of the material purchased was used during June to manufacture 2,000 pairs of pewter bookends. Using these data and the standard costs from Exhibit 10–2, Terry computed the price and quantity variances shown in Exhibit 10–4.

The three arrows in Exhibit 10–4 point to three different total cost figures. The first, $24,700, refers to the actual total cost of the pewter that was purchased during June. The second, $26,000, refers to what the actual quantity of pewter would have cost if it had been purchased at the standard price of $4.00 per kilogram rather than the actual price of $3.80 per kilogram. The difference between these two figures, $1,300 ($26,000 − $24,700), is the price variance. It exists because the actual purchase price was $0.20 per kilogram less than the standard purchase price. Since 6,500 kilograms were purchased, the total amount of the variance is $1,300 ($0.20 per kilogram × 6,500 kilograms). This variance is labelled *favourable* (denoted by F), since the actual purchase price was less than the standard purchase price. A price variance is labelled *unfavourable* (denoted by U) if the actual price exceeds the standard price.

The third arrow in Exhibit 10–4 points to $24,000—the cost (i.e., the flexible budget amount) that the pewter would have been had it been purchased at the standard price and only the amount allowed by the standard quantity had been used. The standards call for 3 kilograms of pewter per unit. Since 2,000 pairs of bookends were produced, 6,000 kilograms of pewter should have been used. This is referred to as the *standard quantity allowed for the actual output*. If this 6,000 kilograms of pewter had been purchased at the standard price of $4.00 per kilogram, the company would have spent $24,000. The difference between this figure, $24,000, and the figure at the end of the middle arrow in Exhibit 10–4, $26,000, is the quantity variance of $2,000.

To understand this quantity variance, note that the actual amount of pewter used in production was 6,500 kilograms. However, the standard amount of pewter allowed for the actual output is only 6,000 kilograms. Therefore, in total, 500 kilograms too much pewter was used to produce the actual output. To express this in dollar terms, the 500 kilograms is multiplied by the standard price of $4.00 per kilogram to yield the quantity variance of $2,000. Why is the standard price, rather than the actual price, of the pewter used in this calculation? The production manager is ordinarily responsible for the quantity variance.

EXHIBIT 10–4 Variance Analysis—Direct Materials

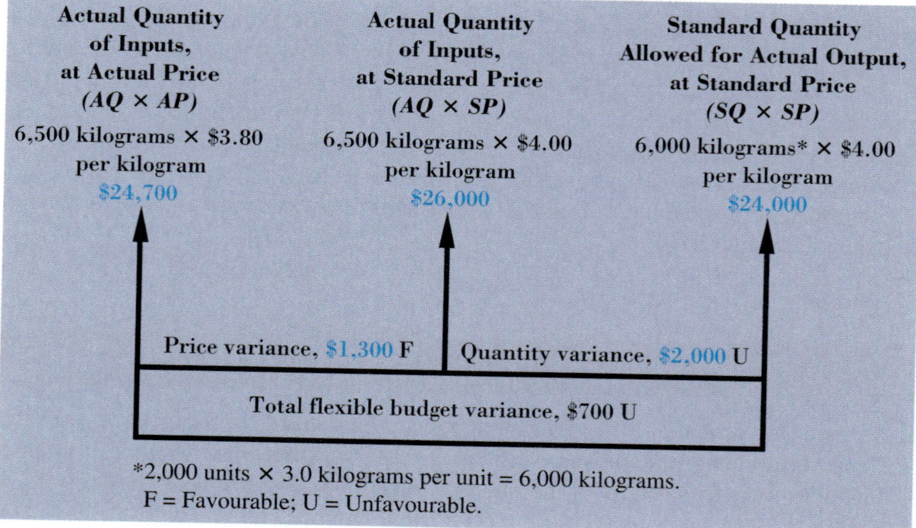

*2,000 units × 3.0 kilograms per unit = 6,000 kilograms.
F = Favourable; U = Unfavourable.

If the actual price was used in the calculation of the quantity variance, the production manager would be held responsible for the efficiency or inefficiency of the purchasing manager. Apart from being unfair, time-consuming debates between the production manager and purchasing manager could occur every time the actual price of an input is above its standard price. To avoid these debates that can be an unproductive distraction to managers, the standard price is used when computing the quantity variance.

The quantity variance in Exhibit 10–4 is labelled *unfavourable* (denoted by U). This is because more pewter was used to produce the actual output than is called for by the standard. A quantity variance is labelled *unfavourable* if the actual quantity exceeds the standard quantity and is labelled *favourable* if the actual quantity is less than the standard quantity.

The computations in Exhibit 10–4 reflect the fact that all of the material purchased during June was also used during June. How are the variances computed if a different amount of material is purchased than is used? To illustrate, assume that during June the company purchased 6,500 kilograms of materials, as before, but used only 5,000 kilograms of material during the month and produced only 1,600 units. In this case, the price variance and quantity variance would be as shown in Exhibit 10–5.

For two reasons, companies compute the materials price variance when materials are purchased rather than when they are used in production. First, delaying the computation of the price variance until the materials are used would result in less-timely variance reports. Second, by computing the price variance when the materials are purchased, the materials can be carried in the inventory accounts at their standard costs. This greatly simplifies bookkeeping. Note, however, that the problem of determining the purchase price variance at a different time than the materials usage variance would not occur in a strict JIT environment. See Appendix 10B at the end of the chapter for an explanation of how the simplified bookkeeping works in a standard costing system where inventory of direct materials exists.

Note from Exhibit 10–5 that the price variance is computed on the entire amount of material purchased (6,500 kilograms), as before, whereas the quantity variance is computed only on the portion of this material used in production during the month (5,000 kilograms). A quantity variance on the 1,500 kilograms of material that were purchased during the month but *not* used in production (6,500 kilograms purchased − 5,000 kilograms used = 1,500 kilograms unused) will be computed in a future period when these materials are drawn out of inventory and used in production. The situation illustrated

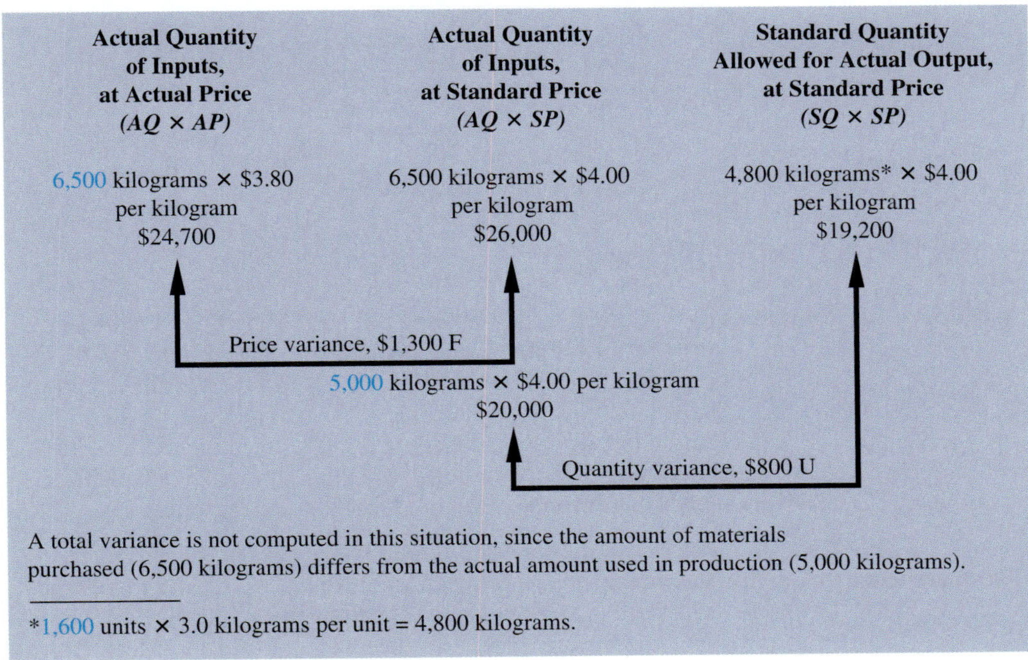

EXHIBIT 10–5 Variance Analysis—Direct Materials, When the Amount Purchased Differs from the Amount Used

in Exhibit 10–5 is common for companies that purchase materials well in advance of use and store the materials in warehouses while awaiting the production process.

Materials Price Variance—A Closer Look

Materials price variance
A measure of the difference between the actual unit price paid for an item and the standard price, multiplied by the quantity purchased.

A **materials price variance** measures the difference between what is paid for a given quantity of materials and what should have been paid according to the standard that has been set. From Exhibits 10–4 and 10–5, this difference can be expressed by the following formula:

$$\text{Materials price variance} = (AQ \times AP) - (AQ \times SP)$$

Actual Quantity Purchased; Actual Price; Standard Price

The formula can be factored into simpler form as follows:

$$\text{Materials price variance} = AQ(AP - SP)$$

Some managers prefer this simpler formula, since it permits variance computations to be made very quickly. Using the data from Exhibits 10–4 and 10–5 in this formula, we have the following:

$$6{,}500 \text{ kilograms } (\$3.80 \text{ per kilogram} - \$4.00 \text{ per kilogram}) = \$1{,}300 \text{ F}$$

Notice that the answer is the same as that yielded in Exhibit 10–4. Also note that a negative variance because of the order of the calculation is always labelled as *favourable* (F) and a positive variance is always labelled as *unfavourable* (U) when the formula approach is used. This will be true of all variance formulas in this and later chapters.

Variance reports are often issued in a tabular format that shows the details and explanation of particular variances. Following is an example of such a report that has been provided by the purchasing manager:

COLONIAL PEWTER COMPANY
Performance Report—Purchasing Department

Item Purchased	(1) Quantity Purchased	(2) Actual Price	(3) Standard Price	(4) Difference in Price (2) − (3)	(5) Total Price Variance (1) × (4)	Explanation
Pewter	6,500 kilograms	$3.80	$4.00	$0.20	$1,300 F	Bargained for an especially favourable price.

F = Favourable; U = Unfavourable.

Isolation of Variances Variances should be isolated and brought to the attention of management as quickly as possible so that problems can be promptly identified and corrected. The most significant variances should be viewed as "red flags"; an exception has occurred that requires explanation by the responsible manager and perhaps follow-up effort. The performance report itself may contain explanations for the variances, as illustrated above. In the case of Colonial Pewter Company, the purchasing manager said that the favourable price variance resulted from bargaining for an especially good price.

Responsibility for the Variance Who is responsible for the materials price variance? Generally speaking, the purchasing manager has control over the price paid for goods and is therefore responsible for any price variances. Many factors influence the prices paid for goods, including how many units are ordered in a lot, how the order is delivered, whether the order is a rush order, and the quality of materials purchased. A deviation in any of these factors from what was assumed when the standards were set can result in a price variance. For example, purchase of second-grade materials rather than top-grade materials may result in a favourable price variance, since the lower-grade materials would generally be less costly (but perhaps less suitable for production).

However, someone other than the purchasing manager could be responsible for a materials price variance. Production may be scheduled in such a way, for example, that the purchasing manager must request delivery by airfreight, rather than by truck. In these cases, the production manager would bear responsibility for the resulting price variances.

A word of caution is in order. Variance analysis should not be used as an excuse to assign blame. The emphasis must be on the control function in the sense of *supporting* the line managers and *assisting* them in meeting the goals that they have participated in setting for the company. In short, the emphasis should be positive rather than negative. Excessive dwelling on what has already happened, particularly in terms of trying to find someone to blame, can be destructive to the functioning of an organization.

Materials Quantity Variance—A Closer Look

The **materials quantity variance** measures the difference between the quantity of materials used in production and the quantity that should have been used, according to the standard that has been set. Although the variance is concerned with the physical usage of materials, it is generally stated in dollar terms, as shown in Exhibit 10–4. The formula for the materials quantity variance is as follows:

Materials quantity variance
A measure of the difference between the actual quantity of materials used in production and the standard quantity allowed, multiplied by the standard price per unit of materials.

$$\text{Materials quantity variance} = (AQ \times SP) - (SQ \times SP)$$

AQ = Actual Quantity Used; SP = Standard Price; SQ = Standard Quantity Allowed for Actual Output

Again, the formula can be factored into simpler terms:

$$\text{Materials quantity variance} = SP(AQ - SQ)$$

Using the data from Exhibit 10–4 in the formula, we have the following:

$4.00 per kilogram (6,500 kilograms − 6,000 kilograms*) = $2,000 U

*2,000 units × 3.0 kilograms per unit = 6,000 kilograms.

The answer, of course, is the same as that yielded in Exhibit 10–4. The data might appear as follows if a formal performance report was prepared:

COLONIAL PEWTER COMPANY
Performance Report—Production Department

Type of Materials	(1) Standard Price	(2) Actual Quantity	(3) Standard Quantity Allowed	(4) Difference in Quantity (2) − (3)	(5) Total Quantity Variance (1) × (4)	Explanation
Pewter	$4.00	6,500 kg	6,000 kg	500 kg	$2,000 U	Low-grade materials unsuitable for production

U = Unfavourable.

The materials quantity variance is best isolated at the time that materials are placed into production. Materials are drawn for the number of units to be produced, according to the standard bill of materials for each unit. Any additional materials are usually drawn with an excess materials requisition, which is different from the normal requisition. This procedure calls attention to the excessive usage of materials *while production is still in process* and provides an opportunity for early control of any developing problem.

Excessive usage of materials can result from many factors, including faulty machines, inferior quality of materials, untrained workers, and poor supervision. Generally speaking, it is the responsibility of the production department to see that material usage is kept in line with standards. There may be times, however, when the *purchasing* department may be responsible for an unfavourable materials quantity variance. If the purchasing department obtains inferior-quality materials in an effort to economize on price, the materials may be unsuitable for use and may result in excessive waste. Thus, purchasing rather than production would be responsible for the quantity variance. At Colonial Pewter, the production manager said that low-grade materials were the cause of the unfavourable materials quantity variance for June.

IN BUSINESS

Management at an unnamed breakfast cereal company became concerned about the apparent waste of raisins in one of its products. A box of the product was supposed to contain 300 grams of cereal and 50 grams of raisins. However, the production process had been using an average of 60 grams of raisins per box. To correct the problem, a bonus was offered to employees if the consumption of raisins dropped to 52.5 grams per box or less—which would allow for about 5% waste. Within a month, the target was hit and bonuses were distributed. However, another problem began to appear. Market studies indicated that customers had become dissatisfied with the amount of raisins in the product. Workers had hit the 52.5 grams per box target by drastically reducing the amount of raisins in rush orders. Boxes of the completed product are ordinarily weighed and if the weight is less than 350 grams, the box is rejected. However, rush orders aren't weighed since that would slow down the production process. Consequently, workers were reducing the raisins in rush orders so as to hit the overall target of 52.5 grams of raisins per box. This resulted in substandard boxes of cereal in rush orders and customer complaints. Clearly, managers need to be very careful when they set targets and standards. They may not get what they bargained for. Subsequent investigation by an internal auditor revealed that, due to statistical fluctuations, an average of about 60 grams of raisins must be used to ensure that every box contains at least 50 grams of raisins.

Source: Harper A. Roehm and Joseph R. Castellano, "The Danger of Relying on Accounting Numbers Alone," *Management Accounting Quarterly*, Fall 1999, pp. 4–9.

Using Standard Costs—Direct Labour Variances

LEARNING OBJECTIVE 3
Compute the direct labour rate and efficiency variances and explain their significance.

Terry's next step in determining Colonial Pewter's variances for June was to compute the direct labour variances for the month. Recall from Exhibit 10–2 that the standard direct labour cost per unit of product is $35, computed as follows:

2.5 hours per unit × $14 per hour = $35 per unit

During June, the company paid its direct labour workers $74,250, including employment taxes and benefits, for 5,400 hours of work. This was an average of $13.75 per hour. Using these data and the standard costs from Exhibit 10–2, Terry computed the direct labour rate and efficiency variances that appear in Exhibit 10–6.

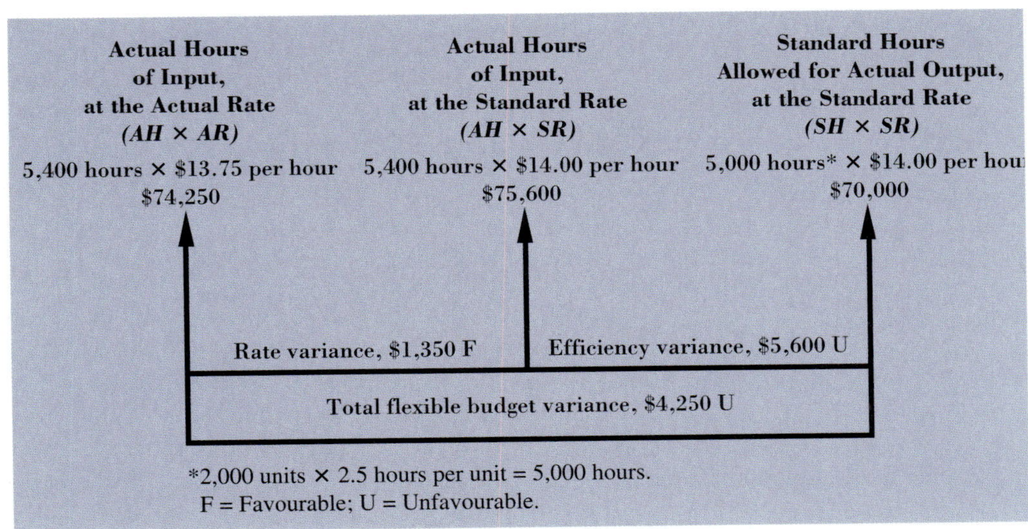

EXHIBIT 10–6 Variance Analysis—Direct Labour

Notice that the column headings in Exhibit 10–6 are the same as those used in the prior two exhibits, except that in Exhibit 10–6 the terms *hours* and *rate* are used in place of the terms *quantity* and *price.*

Labour Rate Variance—A Closer Look

As explained earlier, the price variance for direct labour is commonly termed a **labour rate variance**. This variance measures any deviation from standard in the average hourly rate paid to direct labour workers. The formula for the labour rate variance is expressed as follows:

Labour rate variance A measure of the difference between the actual hourly labour rate and the standard rate, multiplied by the number of hours worked during the period.

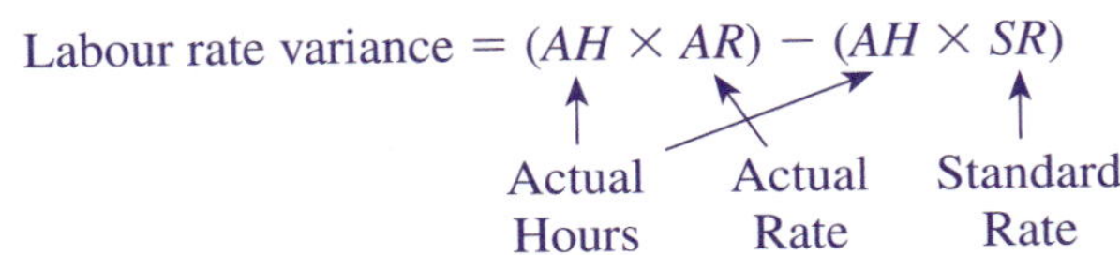

The formula can be factored into simpler form as follows:

$$\text{Labour rate variance} = AH(AR - SR)$$

Using the data from Exhibit 10–6 in the formula, we have the following:

$$5{,}400 \text{ hours } (\$13.75 \text{ per hour} - \$14.00 \text{ per hour}) = \$1{,}350 \text{ F}$$

In most companies, the rates paid to workers are quite predictable. Nevertheless, rate variances can arise through the way labour is used. Skilled workers with high hourly rates of pay may be given duties that require little skill and call for low hourly rates of pay. This will result in unfavourable labour rate variances, since the actual hourly rate of pay will exceed the standard rate specified for the particular task being performed. A reverse situation exists when unskilled or untrained workers are assigned to jobs that require higher levels of skill or training. The lower pay scale for these workers will result in favourable rate variances, although the workers may be inefficient. Finally, unfavourable rate variances can arise from overtime work at premium rates if any portion of the overtime premium is added to the direct labour account.

Who is responsible for controlling the labour rate variance? Since rate variances generally arise as a result of how labour is used, production supervisors bear responsibility for seeing that labour rate variances are kept under control.

Labour Efficiency Variance—A Closer Look

Labour efficiency variance A measure of the difference between the actual hours taken to complete a task and the standard hours allowed, multiplied by the standard hourly labour rate.

The quantity variance for direct labour, more commonly called the **labour efficiency variance**, measures the productivity of labour time. No variance is more closely watched by management, since it is widely believed that increasing the productivity of direct labour time is vital to reducing costs. The formula for the labour efficiency variance is expressed as follows:

$$\text{Labour efficiency variance} = (AH \times SR) - (SH \times SR)$$

where AH = Actual Hours, SR = Standard Rate, SH = Standard Hours Allowed for Actual Output

Factored into simpler terms, the formula is as follows:

$$\text{Labour efficiency variance} = SR(AH - SH)$$

Using the data from Exhibit 10–6 in the formula, we have the following:

$$\$14.00 \text{ per hour } (5{,}400 \text{ hours} - 5{,}000 \text{ hours*}) = \$5{,}600 \text{ U}$$

*2,000 units × 2.5 hours per unit = 5,000 hours.

Possible causes of an unfavourable labour efficiency variance include poorly trained or motivated workers; poor-quality materials, requiring more labour time in processing; faulty equipment, causing breakdowns and work interruptions; poor supervision of workers; and inaccurate standards. The managers in charge of production would generally be responsible for control of the labour efficiency variance. However, the variance might be chargeable to purchasing if the acquisition of poor materials resulted in excessive labour processing time.

Insufficient demand for the company's products may be another important cause of an unfavourable labour efficiency variance. Managers in some companies argue that it is difficult, and perhaps unwise, to constantly adjust the workforce in response to changes in the amount of work that needs to be done. In such companies, the direct labour workforce is

IN BUSINESS

Does Direct Labour Variance Reporting Increase Productivity?

Professors Rajiv Banker, Sarv Devaraj, Roger Schroeder, and Kingshuk Sinha studied the direct labour variance reporting practices at 18 plants of a Fortune 500 manufacturing company. Seven of the plants eliminated direct labour variance reporting and the other 11 plants did not. The group of seven plants that eliminated direct labour variance reporting experienced an 11% decline in labour productivity, which was significantly greater than the decline experienced by the other 11 plants. The authors estimated that the annual loss due to the decline in labour productivity across the seven plants of $1,996,000 was only partially offset by the $200,000 saved by eliminating the need to track direct labour variances.

While these findings suggest that direct labour variance reporting is a useful tool for monitoring direct labour workers, advocates of Lean Production would argue otherwise. They would claim that direct labour variance reporting is a non-value-added activity that encourages excessive production and demoralizes direct labour workers. The two points of view provide an interesting opportunity to debate the appropriate role of management accounting within organizations.

Source: Rajiv Banker, Sarv Devaraj, Roger Schroeder, and Kingshuk Sinha, "Performance Impact of the Elimination of Direct Labour Variance Reporting: A Field Study," *Journal of Accounting Research*, September 2002, pp. 1013–1036.

essentially fixed in the short run. If demand is insufficient to keep everyone busy, workers are not laid off. In this case, if demand falls below the level needed to keep everyone busy, an unfavourable labour efficiency variance will often be recorded.

If customer orders are insufficient to keep the workers busy, the work centre manager has two options—either accept an unfavourable labour efficiency variance or build-up inventory.[2] A central lesson of Lean Production is that building inventory with no immediate prospect of sale is a bad idea. Excessive inventory—particularly work in process inventory—leads to high defect rates, obsolete goods, and generally inefficient operations. As a consequence, when the workforce is basically fixed in the short term, managers must be cautious about how labour efficiency variances are used. Some advocate dispensing with labour efficiency variances entirely in such situations—at least for the purposes of motivating and controlling workers on the shop floor.

Using Standard Costs—Variable Manufacturing Overhead Variances

LEARNING OBJECTIVE 4
Compute the variable manufacturing overhead spending and efficiency variances.

The next step in Terry's analysis of Colonial Pewter's variances for June was to compute the variable manufacturing overhead variances. The variable portion of manufacturing overhead can be analyzed using the same basic formulas that are used to analyze direct materials and direct labour. Recall from Exhibit 10–2 that the standard variable manufacturing overhead is $7.50 per unit of product, computed as follows:

$$2.5 \text{ hours per unit} \times \$3.00 \text{ per hour} = \$7.50 \text{ per unit}$$

Colonial Pewter's cost records showed that the total actual variable manufacturing overhead cost for June was $15,390. Recall from the earlier discussion of the direct labour variances that 5,400 hours of direct labour time were recorded during the month and that the company produced 2,000 pairs of bookends. Terry's analysis of this overhead data appears in Exhibit 10–7.

Notice the similarities between Exhibits 10–6 and 10–7. These similarities arise from the fact that direct labour-hours are being used as a base for allocating overhead cost to units of product; thus, the same hourly figures appear in Exhibit 10–7 for variable manufacturing overhead as in Exhibit 10–6 for direct labour. The main difference between the two exhibits is in the standard hourly rate being used, which in this company is much lower for variable manufacturing overhead. However, the format of the variance analysis

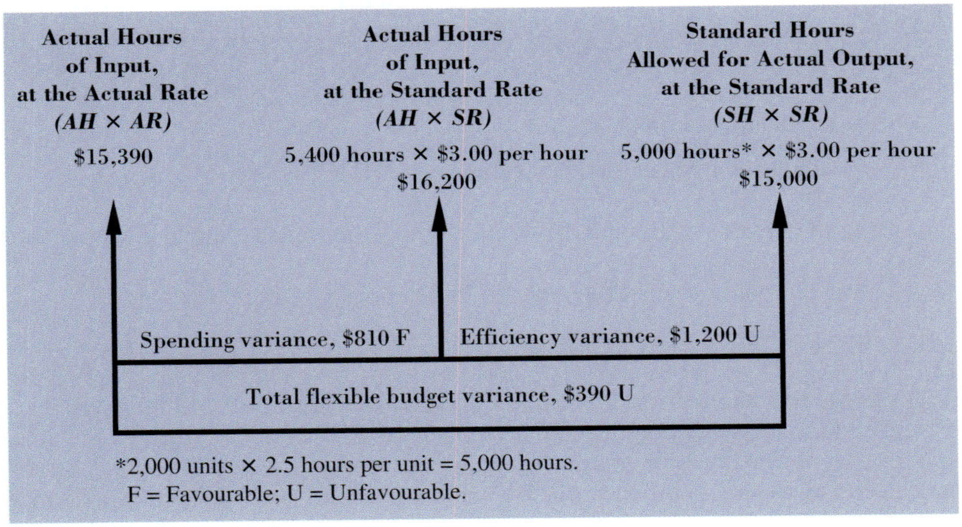

EXHIBIT 10–7 Variance Analysis—Variable Manufacturing Overhead

Actual Hours of Input, at the Actual Rate *(AH × AR)*	Actual Hours of Input, at the Standard Rate *(AH × SR)*	Standard Hours Allowed for Actual Output, at the Standard Rate *(SH × SR)*
$15,390	5,400 hours × $3.00 per hour $16,200	5,000 hours* × $3.00 per hour $15,000

Spending variance, $810 F | Efficiency variance, $1,200 U

Total flexible budget variance, $390 U

*2,000 units × 2.5 hours per unit = 5,000 hours.
F = Favourable; U = Unfavourable.

2. For further discussion, see Eliyahu M. Goldratt and Jeff Cox, *The Goal,* 2nd rev. ed. (Croton-on-Hudson, NY: North River Press, 1992).

for variable manufacturing overhead is the same if machine hours or material quantities or some other base were used.

Variable Manufacturing Overhead Variances—A Closer Look

Variable overhead spending variance
The difference between the actual variable overhead cost incurred during a period and the standard cost that should have been incurred based on the actual activity of the period.

The formula for **variable overhead spending variance** is expressed as follows:

$$\text{Variable overhead spending variance} = (AH \times AR) - (AH \times SR)$$

Actual Hours (AH); Actual Rate (AR); Standard Rate (SR)

Using the data from Exhibit 10–7, we have the following:

$$(5{,}400 \times \$2.85) - (5{,}400 \times \$3.00) = \$810\text{F}$$

Or, factored into simpler terms:

$$\text{Variable overhead spending variance} = AH(AR - SR)$$

Using the data from Exhibit 10–7 in the formula, we have the following:

5,400 hours ($2.85 per hour* − $3.00 per hour) = $810 F

*$15,390 ÷ 5,400 hours = $2.85 per hour.

As will be explained below, the actual rate of $2.85 per hour incorporates both the price and quantity of all actual variable overhead items used during the period. As such it represents a mixture of many individual actual rates (cost per kilogram of indirect materials, rate per hour of indirect labour, etc.) and cannot be interpreted the same way as the actual price for direct materials or the actual rate for direct labour.

Variable overhead efficiency variance
The difference between the actual activity (direct labour-hours, machine-hours, or some other base) of a period and the standard activity allowed, multiplied by the variable part of the predetermined overhead rate.

The formula for the **variable overhead efficiency variance** is expressed as follows:

$$\text{Variable overhead efficiency variance} = (AH \times SR) - (SH \times SR)$$

Actual Hours (AH); Standard Rate (SR); Standard Hours Allowed for Actual Output (SH)

Or, factored into simpler terms:

$$\text{Variable overhead efficiency variance} = SR(AH - SH)$$

Again using the data from Exhibit 10–7, the computation of the variance would be as follows:

$3 per hour (5,400 hours − 5,000 hours*) = $1,200 U

*2,000 units × 2.5 hours per unit = 5,000 hours.

Interpreting the Spending Variance The variable overhead spending variance is most useful to managers when the cost driver for variable overhead really is the actual number of labour or machine hours worked. In other words, when the actual variable overhead costs vary in proportion with the actual number of hours worked in a period then the variable overhead spending variance can be informative. An overhead spending variance can occur, if either (*a*) the actual purchase price of the variable overhead items differs from the standards or (*b*) the actual quantity of variable overhead items used differs from the standards.

To illustrate the two distinct components of the spending variance, we will further consider the Colonial Pewter Company example. Assume that the variable manufacturing overhead rate of $3 per hour shown in Exhibit 10–2 is calculated as follows:

$$\text{Predetermined variable overhead rate} = \frac{\text{Estimated June total variable overhead cost}}{\text{Estimated June total direct labour hours}}$$

$$\$3 = \$15{,}000 \div 5{,}000 \text{ (2,000 units} \times \text{2.5 hours per unit} = \text{5,000 hours)}$$

Further assume that the $15,000 of total variable manufacturing overhead costs consists of the following three items:

Indirect labour	$7,500
Indirect materials	5,000
Utilities	2,500
Total variable overhead	$15,000

The rate of $3 per hour incorporates estimates of both the *price* per unit that will be paid for each item included in variable overhead (e.g., indirect materials) and the *quantity* of those items that will be used for each direct labour hour worked on the product.[3] For example, assume that Terry's estimate of $5,000 for indirect materials is based on expected usage of 200 kilograms of finishing materials at a cost of $25 per kilogram. This implies that 0.04 kilograms of indirect materials will be used for *each hour* worked on a pair of bookends (200 kilograms ÷ 5,000 hours). Given these characteristics of the predetermined overhead rate, two factors can cause the budgeted rate of $3 per hour to differ from the actual rate of $2.85 ($15,390 ÷ 5,400 hours) per hour implied by Exhibit 10–7. First, given the favourable spending variance for June, it may be that the actual cost of indirect materials was less than $25 per kilogram. Second, less than 0.04 kilograms of indirect materials may have been used per hour in producing 2,000 pairs of bookends in June. Of course, various combinations of these factors can also lead to the favourable spending variance such as lower prices *and* more efficient use of indirect materials. Alternatively, higher prices could be more than offset by more efficient use of indirect materials.

In principle the price and quantity components of the spending variance could be separately reported. However this is seldom done as typically the price element will be small so the variance will mainly be influenced by how efficiently the quantities of variable overhead resources are used, such as indirect materials. Even though the price and quantity components are rarely broken out, the spending variance is useful to managers. For example, an unfavourable spending variance tells managers they must find ways to acquire overhead items at cheaper prices, use lower quantities of them, or both.

Interpreting the Efficiency Variance Like the variable overhead spending variance, the variable overhead efficiency variance is useful only if the cost driver for variable overhead really is the actual hours worked. Then any increase or decrease in hours actually worked should result in an increase or decrease in variable overhead costs actually incurred. The variable overhead efficiency variance is an estimate of the effect on variable overhead costs of efficiencies or inefficiencies in the use of the base (i.e., hours). In a sense, the term *variable overhead efficiency variance* is a misnomer. It seems to suggest that it measures the efficiency with which variable overhead resources were used. It does not. It is an estimate of the indirect effect on variable overhead costs of efficiency or inefficiency in the use of the activity base.

This point can be illustrated by looking again at Exhibit 10–7. Four hundred more labour-hours were used during June than should have been used to produce the period's output. Each of these hours presumably required the incurrence of $3.00 of variable

3. Recall from Chapter 3 that using predetermined overhead application rates negates the need to track the actual quantity of variable overhead items used when assigning costs to products or services.

overhead cost, resulting in an unfavourable variance of $1,200 (400 hours × $3.00 = $1,200). Although this $1,200 variance is called an *overhead efficiency variance*, it could better be called a *labour-hours efficiency variance*, since it results from using too many labour-hours rather than from inefficient use of overhead resources. However, the term *overhead efficiency variance* is so firmly ingrained in day-to-day use that a change is unlikely. Even so, be careful to interpret the variance with a clear understanding of what it really measures. It is worth noting that the efficiency variance for variable overhead can only be calculated if a standard exists for hours *allowed* for the actual quantity of output achieved for a period. In the absence of a quantity standard for any input, only the spending variance can be calculated as will be illustrated later in this chapter.

Control of the Efficiency Variance Who is responsible for control of the overhead efficiency variance? Since the variance really reflects efficiency in the utilization of the base underlying the flexible budget, whoever is responsible for control of this base is responsible for control of the variance. If the base is direct labour-hours, then the supervisor responsible for the use of labour time will be responsible for any overhead efficiency variance.

Before proceeding further, we suggest that you pause at this point and go back and review the data contained in Exhibits 10–2 through 10–7. These exhibits and the accompanying text discussion provide a comprehensive, integrated illustration of standard setting and variance analysis.

Overhead Rates and Fixed Overhead Analysis

LEARNING OBJECTIVE 5
Explain the significance of the denominator activity figure in determining the standard cost of a unit of product.

The detailed analysis of fixed overhead differs considerably from the analysis of variable overhead discussed in the previous section, simply because of the difference in the nature of the costs involved. To provide a background for our discussion, we will first review briefly the need for, and computation of, predetermined overhead rates. This review will be helpful, since the predetermined overhead rate plays a major role in fixed overhead analysis. We will then show how fixed overhead variances are computed and make some observations as to their usefulness to managers.

Flexible Budgets and Overhead Rates

Fixed costs come in large, indivisible pieces that by definition do not change with changes in the level of activity within the relevant range. As we learned in Chapter 3, this creates a problem in product costing, since a given level of fixed overhead cost spread over a small number of units will result in a higher cost per unit than if the same amount of cost is spread over a large number of units. Consider the data in the following table:

Month	(1) Fixed Overhead Cost	(2) Number of Units Produced	(3) Unit Cost (1) ÷ (2)
January	$6,000	1,000	$6.00
February	6,000	1,500	4.00
March	6,000	800	7.50

Notice that the large number of units produced in February results in a low unit cost ($4.00), whereas the small number of units produced in March results in a high unit cost ($7.50). This problem arises only in connection with the fixed portion of overhead, since by definition the variable portion of overhead remains constant on a per unit basis, rising and falling in total proportionately with changes in the activity level. Most managers feel that the fixed portion of unit cost should be stabilized so that a single unit cost figure can be used throughout the year. As we learned in Chapter 3, this stability can be accomplished through use of the predetermined overhead rate.

We will be analyzing the fixed overhead costs of Colonial Pewter Company using the flexible budget of the company—including fixed costs—as displayed in Exhibit 10–8. Note that the budgeted total fixed overhead costs amount to $300,000 within the relevant range of activity.

Denominator Activity The formula that we used in Chapter 3 to compute the predetermined overhead rate is as follows (MH: machine-hours; DLH: direct labour-hours):

$$\text{Predetermined overhead rate} = \frac{\text{Estimated total manufacturing overhead cost}}{\text{Estimated total units in the base (MH, DLH, etc.)}}$$

The estimated total units in the base in the formula for the predetermined overhead rate is called the **denominator activity.** Recall from our discussion in Chapter 3 that once an estimated activity level (denominator activity) has been chosen, it remains unchanged throughout the year, even if the actual activity turns out to be different from what was estimated. The reason for not changing the denominator is to maintain stability in the amount of overhead applied to each unit of product, regardless of when it is produced during the year.

Denominator activity The activity figure used to compute the predetermined overhead rate.

Computing the Overhead Rate When we discussed predetermined overhead rates in Chapter 3, we didn't explain how the estimated total manufacturing cost was determined. This figure can be derived from the flexible budget. Once the denominator level of activity has been chosen, the flexible budget can be used to determine the total amount of overhead cost that should be incurred at that level of activity. The predetermined overhead rate can then be computed using the following variation on the basic formula for the predetermined overhead rate:

$$\text{Predetermined overhead rate} = \frac{\text{Overhead from the flexible budget at the denominator level of activity}}{\text{Denominator level of activity}}$$

To illustrate, refer to Colonial Pewter Company's flexible budget for manufacturing overhead shown in Exhibit 10–8. Suppose that the budgeted activity level for the year is 50,000 direct labour-hours (DLH) and that this will be used as the denominator activity

EXHIBIT 10–8 Flexible Budget Schedule

COLONIAL PEWTER COMPANY
Flexible Budgets at Various Levels of Activity

Overhead Costs	Cost Formula (per direct labour-hour)	Annual Activity (in direct labour-hours) 40,000	50,000	60,000
Variable overhead costs				
Indirect labour	$1.50	$ 60,000	$ 75,000	$ 90,000
Lubricants	1.00	40,000	50,000	60,000
Power	0.50	20,000	25,000	30,000
Total variable overhead cost	$3.00	120,000	150,000	180,000
Fixed overhead costs:				
Depreciation		120,000	120,000	120,000
Supervisory salaries		144,000	144,000	144,000
Insurance		36,000	36,000	36,000
Total fixed overhead cost		300,000	300,000	300,000
Total overhead cost		$420,000	$450,000	$480,000

in the formula for the predetermined overhead rate. The numerator in the formula is the estimated total overhead cost of $450,000 when the activity is 50,000 DLH. This figure is taken from the flexible budget in Exhibit 10–8. Therefore, the predetermined overhead rate for Colonial Pewter Company will be computed as follows:

$$\frac{\$450{,}000}{50{,}000 \text{ DLH}} = \$9.00 \text{ per direct labour-hour}$$

The company can also break its predetermined overhead rate down into variable and fixed elements rather than using a single combined figure:

$$\text{Variable element: } \frac{\$150{,}000}{50{,}000 \text{ DLH}} = \$3.00 \text{ per direct labour-hour}$$

$$\text{Fixed element: } \frac{\$300{,}000}{50{,}000 \text{ DLH}} = \$6.00 \text{ per direct labour-hour}$$

For every direct labour-hour of operation, work in process will be charged with $9.00 of overhead, of which $3.00 will be variable overhead and $6.00 will be fixed overhead. If a pair of bookends takes two and one-half direct labour-hours to complete, then its cost will include $7.50 variable overhead and $15 fixed overhead, as per the revised standard cost card shown in Exhibit 10–9 that now includes fixed manufacturing overhead.

In summary, the flexible budget provides the estimated overhead cost needed to compute the predetermined overhead rate. Thus, the flexible budget plays a key role in determining the amount of fixed and variable overhead cost that will be charged to units of product.

EXHIBIT 10–9 Standard Cost Card—Absorption Cost

	(1) Standard Quantity or Hours	(2) Standard Price or Rate	(3) Standard Cost (1) × (2)
Inputs			
Direct materials (from Exhibit 10–2)	3.0 kilograms	$4.00	$12.00
Direct labour (from Exhibit 10–2)	2.5 hours	14.00	35.00
Variable manufacturing overhead (from Exhibit 10–2)	2.5 hours	3.00	7.50
Fixed manufacturing overhead	2.5 hours	6.00	15.00
Total standard cost per unit			$69.50

Overhead Application and Fixed Overhead Variances

LEARNING OBJECTIVE 6
Compute and interpret the fixed overhead budget and volume variances.

To understand the fixed overhead variances, it is necessary first to understand how overhead is applied to work in process in a standard cost system. Therefore, we examine the details of the application process next.

Overhead Application in a Standard Cost System

In Chapter 3, recall that we applied overhead to work in process on the basis of actual hours of activity (multiplied by the predetermined overhead rate). This procedure was correct, since at the time we were dealing with a normal cost system.[4] However, we are now dealing with a

4. Normal cost systems are defined in Chapter 3.

standard cost system. In such a system, overhead is applied to work in process on the basis of the *standard hours allowed for the actual output of the period* rather than on the basis of the actual number of hours worked. This point is illustrated in Exhibit 10–10. In a standard cost system, every unit of product moving along the production line bears the same amount of overhead cost, regardless of any variations in efficiency that may have been involved in its production.

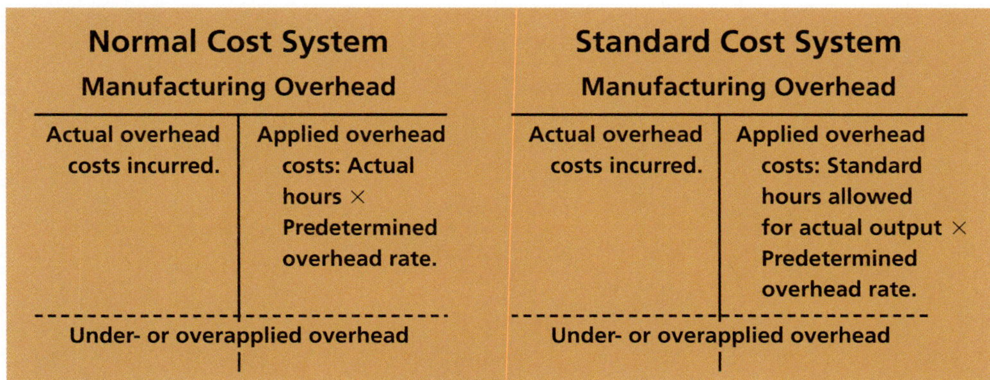

EXHIBIT 10–10 Applied Overhead Costs: Normal Cost System versus Standard Cost System

The Fixed Overhead Variances

To illustrate the computation of fixed overhead variances, we will refer again to the data for Colonial Pewter Company:

Denominator activity in direct labour-hours . . .	50,000
Budgeted annual fixed overhead costs.	$300,000
Fixed portion of the predetermined overhead rate (computed earlier).	$6

Let us assume that the following actual operating results were recorded for the month of June:

Actual direct labour-hours	5,400
Standard direct labour-hours allowed*	5,000
Actual fixed overhead costs:	
Depreciation	$10,000
Supervisory salaries	14,000
Insurance.	3,500
Total actual cost	$27,500

*For the actual production in June.

From these data, two variances can be computed for fixed overhead—a *budget variance* and a *volume variance.* The variances for the month of June are shown in Exhibit 10–11.

Notice from the exhibit that overhead has been applied to work in process on the basis of 5,000 standard hours allowed for the output of June rather than on the basis of 5,400 actual hours worked. As stated earlier, this keeps unit costs from being affected by any variations in efficiency.

The Budget Variance—A Closer Look

The **budget variance** is the difference between the actual fixed overhead costs incurred during the period and the budgeted fixed overhead costs as contained in the flexible budget. It can be computed as shown in Exhibit 10–11 or by using the following formula:

$$\text{Budget variance} = \text{Actual fixed overhead cost} - \text{Flexible budget fixed overhead cost}$$

Budget variance A measure of the difference between the actual fixed overhead costs incurred during the period and budgeted fixed overhead costs as contained in the flexible budget.

EXHIBIT 10–11 Computation of the June Fixed Overhead Variances

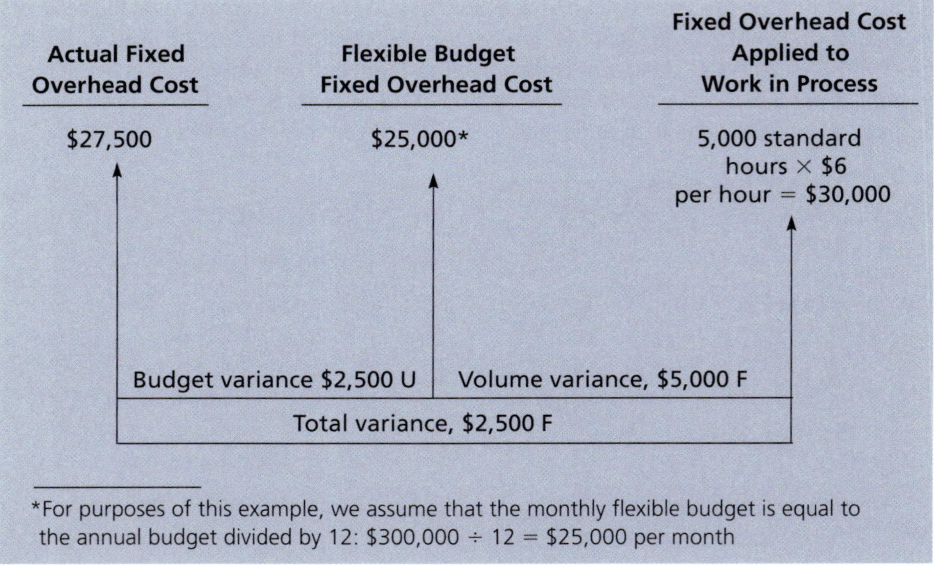

Applying this formula to Colonial Pewter Company, the budget variance would be as follows:

$$\$27{,}500 - \$25{,}000 = \$2{,}500\text{ U}$$

Budget variances for fixed overhead can be very useful, since they represent the difference between how much should have been spent (according to the flexible budget) and how much was actually spent. For the month of June, Colonial Pewter's actual fixed costs were $2,500 higher than budget and management may want to identify which specific fixed overhead items have caused this variance. We will present a detailed performance report for overhead costs later in this chapter.

The Volume Variance—A Closer Look

The volume variance is a measure of utilization of plant facilities. The variance arises whenever the standard hours allowed for the actual output of a period are different from the denominator activity level that was planned when the period began. It can be computed as shown in Exhibit 10–11 or by means of the following formula:

$$\text{Volume variance} = \begin{matrix}\text{Fixed portion of} \\ \text{the predetermined} \\ \text{overhead rate}\end{matrix} \times \left(\begin{matrix}\text{Denominator} \\ \text{hours}\end{matrix} - \begin{matrix}\text{Standard hours} \\ \text{allowed}\end{matrix}\right)$$

Applying this formula to Colonial Pewter Company, the volume variance would be computed as follows:

$$\$6\text{ per DLH }(4{,}167 - 5{,}000) = \$4{,}998\text{ F}$$

As discussed in Chapter 3, predetermined overhead rates are often prepared on an annual basis to avoid distortions in product costs caused by seasonal fluctuations in overhead items (e.g., heating costs). Colonial Pewter's rate of $6 per hour for fixed overhead is based on estimated annual fixed costs of $300,000 and an annual denominator activity level of 50,000 labour hours. However, to facilitate the calculation of a volume variance for the *month* of June, Terry assigned the annual denominator activity of 50,000 direct labour hours evenly to each month. Therefore, denominator activity for June is: 50,000 ÷ 12 = 4,167.[5] Except for a $2 rounding difference, the $4,998 volume variance above

5. If a company does employ monthly denominator activity levels and overhead application rates, then these would be used in the monthly fixed manufacturing overhead variance calculations.

agrees with the amount shown in Exhibit 10–11. Importantly, when calculating the volume variance for the year, Terry will use the total annual denominator activity level of 50,000 hours and the standard hours allowed for the total production output for the year.

As stated earlier, the volume variance is a measure of utilization of available plant facilities. A favourable variance, as above, means that the company operated at an activity level *above* that planned for the period. An unfavourable variance would mean that the company operated at an activity level *below* than that planned for the period.

It is important to note that the volume variance does not measure over- or underspending. A company normally would incur the same dollar amount of fixed overhead cost regardless of whether the period's activity was above or below the planned (denominator) level. Also note that fixed overhead does not have an efficiency variance because the fixed overhead budget for the actual direct labour-hours, 5,400, is the same as the fixed overhead budget for 5,000 standard direct labour-hours, namely $25,000. The volume variance only occurs as a result of the standard and denominator direct labour-hours difference, 400 direct labour-hours. In short, the volume variance is an activity-related variance. It is explainable only by activity and is controllable only through activity.

To summarize:

1. If the denominator activity and the standard hours allowed for the output of the period are the same, then there is no volume variance.
2. If the denominator activity is greater than the standard hours allowed for the output of the period, then the volume variance is unfavourable, signifying an underutilization of available facilities.
3. If the denominator activity is less than the standard hours allowed for the output of the period, then the volume variance is favourable, signifying a higher utilization of available facilities than was planned.

Graphic Analysis of Fixed Overhead Variances

Some insights into the budget and volume variances can be gained through graphic analysis. A graph containing these variances is presented in Exhibit 10–12.

As shown in the graph, fixed overhead cost is applied to work in process at the predetermined rate of $6 for each standard hour of activity. (The applied-cost line is the upward-sloping line on the graph.) Since a denominator level of 4,167 direct labour-

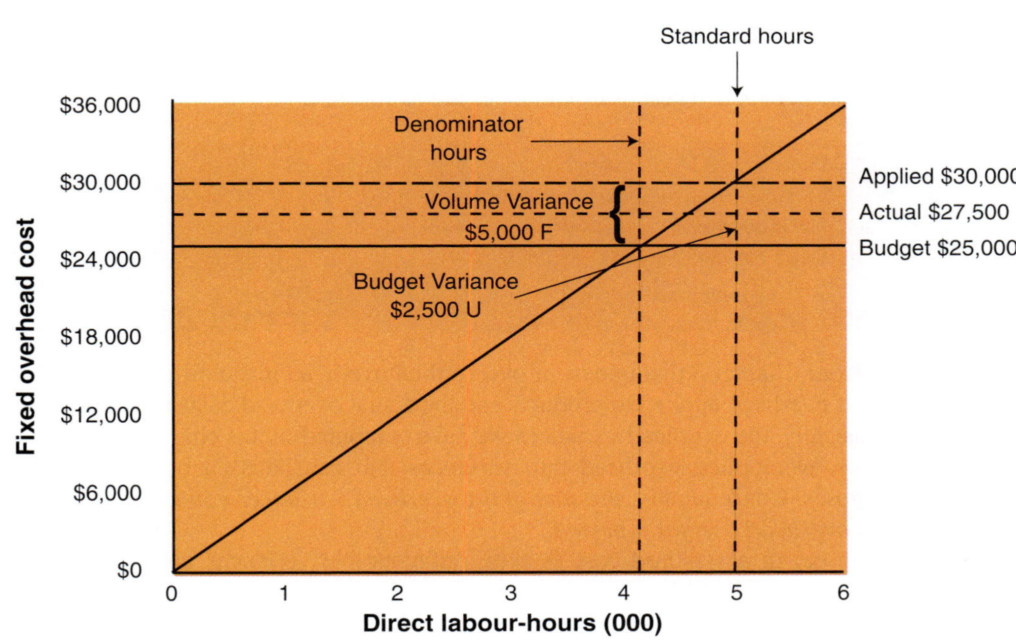

EXHIBIT 10–12 Graphic Analysis of Fixed Overhead Variances

hours was used for June, the applied-cost line crosses the budget-cost line at exactly the 4,167 direct labour-hour point. Thus, if the denominator hours and the standard hours allowed for the output are the same, there can be no volume variance, since the applied-cost line and the budget-cost line will exactly meet on the graph. It is only when the standard hours differ from the denominator hours that a volume variance can arise.

In this case, the standard hours allowed for the actual output (5,000 hours) are more than the denominator hours (4,167 hours) for June; the result is a favourable volume variance, since more cost was applied to production than was originally budgeted. If the situation had been reversed and the standard hours allowed for the actual output had been less than the denominator hours, then the volume variance on the graph would have been unfavourable.

Cautions in Fixed Overhead Analysis

The reason we get a volume variance for fixed overhead is that the total fixed cost does not depend on activity; yet when applying the costs to work in process, we act *as if* the fixed costs were variable and depended on activity. This point can be seen from the graph in Exhibit 10–12. Notice from the graph that the fixed overhead costs are applied to work in process at a rate of $6 per hour *as if* they were variable. Treating these costs as if they were variable is necessary for product costing purposes, but there are some real dangers here. The manager can easily become misled and start thinking of the fixed costs as if they were *in fact* variable.

The manager must keep clearly in mind that fixed overhead costs come in large, indivisible pieces. Expressing fixed costs on a unit or per hour basis, although necessary for product costing for external reports, is artificial. Increases or decreases in activity in fact have no effect on total fixed costs within the relevant range of activity. Even though fixed costs are expressed on a unit or per hour basis, they are *not* proportional to activity. In a sense, the volume variance is the error that occurs as a result of treating fixed costs as variable costs in the costing system.

Because of the confusion that can arise concerning the interpretation of the volume variance, some companies present the volume variance in physical units (hours) rather than in dollars. These companies feel that stating the variance in physical units gives management a clearer signal concerning the cause of the variance.

Overhead Variances and Under- or Overapplied Overhead Cost

Four variances relating to overhead cost have been computed for Colonial Pewter Company in this chapter. These four variances are as follows:

Variable overhead spending variance (p. 439). . . .	$ 810 F
Variable overhead efficiency variance (p. 439) . . .	1,200 U
Fixed overhead budget variance (p. 446).	2,500 U
Fixed overhead volume variance (p. 446)	5,000 F
Total overhead variance.	$2,110 F

Recall from Chapter 3 that under- or overapplied overhead is the difference between the amount of overhead applied to products and the actual overhead costs incurred during a period. Basically, the overhead variances we have computed in this chapter break down the under- or overapplied overhead into variances that can be used by managers for control purposes. Consequently, *the sum of the overhead variances equals the under- or overapplied overhead cost for a period.*

Furthermore, in a standard cost system, unfavourable variances are equivalent to underapplied overhead and favourable variances are equivalent to overapplied overhead.

Unfavourable variances occur because more was spent on overhead than the standards allow. Underapplied overhead occurs when more was spent on overhead than was applied to products during the period. But in a standard costing system, the standard amount of overhead allowed is exactly the same amount of overhead applied to products. Therefore, in a standard costing system, unfavourable variances and underapplied overhead are the same thing, as are favourable variances and overapplied overhead.

For Colonial Pewter Company, the total overhead variance was $2,110 favourable. Therefore, its overhead cost was overapplied by $2,110 for the year. To reinforce this concept, carefully study the review problem at the end of the chapter.

Overhead Performance Reporting and Capacity Analysis

LEARNING OBJECTIVE 7
Prepare a performance report for manufacturing overhead and perform analysis of capacity utilization.

Terry completes his analysis of overhead spending at Colonial Pewter Company in June by preparing the performance report shown in Exhibit 10–13. The report builds on the analysis of variable and fixed overhead presented, respectively, in Exhibits 10–7 and 10–11 by providing details on the individual items included in each category. This additional level of detail allows managers to determine the amount that each overhead item contributes to the spending (budget) and efficiency variances.

Two things should be noted about Exhibit 10–13. First, because Terry has developed a standard cost system and wants to report both the spending and efficiency variances for variable overhead costs, he has included budgeted costs for both the actual direct labour-hours used (5,400), and the standard direct labour-hours allowed (5,000) for the 2,000 units produced in June. As a result, the sum of the individual spending ($810 F) and efficiency ($1,200 U) variances reported in Exhibit 10–13 corresponds to the overall calculations shown in Exhibit 10–7. The second issue to note in Exhibit 10–13 is that for fixed overhead costs, there are no efficiency variances included; only budget variances are calculated. This is consistent with Exhibit 10–11, which illustrates that for fixed overhead, it is not possible to calculate an efficiency variance. As discussed earlier, this is because within the relevant range of activity, fixed costs do not change as the activity level changes. Therefore, the budget for each fixed overhead item is the same in columns (2) and (3) of Exhibit 10–13 even though the activity level differs by 400 hours (5,400 – 5,000) across these two columns. For control purposes, the budget variance for fixed overhead is the key tool. By comparing what was actually spent on each fixed overhead item to the budget, Terry can determine how well the managers responsible for these line items did in controlling costs.

Preparing an overhead performance report that contains both spending and efficiency variances is only possible if a standard cost system is in place. In the absence of a standard cost system, column (3) in Exhibit 10–13 would not exist since it represents the standard direct labour hours allowed for the actual output achieved. However, even if a standard cost system is not being used, an overhead performance report can still be prepared but it will include *only* the spending and budget variances. An example of this type of report is presented in Exhibit 10–14. Note that the spending and budget variances shown in Exhibit 10–14, are the same as those reported in Exhibit 10–13. The only difference between the two performance reports is that Exhibit 10–13, based on the standard cost system developed at Colonial Pewter, also includes efficiency variances.

After preparing the performance report, managers still have to decide whether the variances that have been calculated require further action. For example, the $2,000 unfavourable fixed overhead budget variance for supervisory salaries is the largest single variance for the month of June. Should it be investigated? Should answers be sought as to the cause of the variance? Identifying which variances to target for investigation is an important part of the variance analysis cycle presented in Exhibit 10–1. In the next section we examine how managers make these decisions.

EXHIBIT 10–13 An Overhead Performance Report

COLONIAL PEWTER CORPORATION
Overhead Performance Report
For the Month Ended June 30

Actual production (units)	2,000
Actual direct labour-hours	5,400
Standard direct labour-hours allowed	5,000

Budget allowances are based on the direct labour-hours that should have been used (5,000) to produce 2,000 units and the hours actually worked (5,400).

This approach yields both a spending and an efficiency variance for variable manufacturing overhead.

Overhead Costs	Cost Formula (per Direct Labour-Hour)	(1) Actual Costs 5,400 Direct Labour-Hours	(2) Budget Based on 5,400 Direct Labour-Hours	(3) Budget Based on 5,000 Direct Labour-Hours	Total Variance (1) – (3)	Breakdown of the Total Variance: Spending (Budget) Variance (1) – (2)	Breakdown of the Total Variance: Efficiency Variance (2) – (3)
Variable overhead costs							
Indirect labour	$1.50	$ 7,830	$ 8,100	$ 7,500	$330 U	$270 F	$ 600 U
Lubricants	1.00	5,022	5,400	5,000	22 U	378 F	400 U
Power	0.50	2,538	2,700	2,500	38 U	162 F	200 U
Total variable overhead cost	$3.00	15,390	16,200	15,000	390 U	810 F	1,200 U
Fixed overhead costs							
Depreciation		10,000	10,000	10,000	0	0	–
Supervisory salaries		14,000	12,000	12,000	2,000 U	2,000 U	–
Insurance		3,500	3,000	3,000	500 U	500 U	–
Total fixed overhead cost		27,500	25,000	25,000	2,500 U	2,500 U	–
Total overhead cost		$42,890	$41,200	$40,000	$2,890 U	$1,690 U	$1,200 U

EXHIBIT 10–14 An Overhead Performance Report with Only Spending or Budget Variances

COLONIAL PEWTER CORPORATION
Overhead Performance Report
For the Month Ended June 30

Actual production (units)	2,000			
Actual direct labour-hours	5,400			

Overhead Costs	**Cost Formula (per Direct Labour-Hour)**	**(1) Actual Costs 5,400 Direct Labour-Hours**	**(2) Budget Based on 5,400 Direct Labour-Hours**	**Spending (Budget) Variance (1) – (2)**
Variable overhead costs				
Indirect labour	$1.50	$ 7,830	$ 8,100	$ 270 F
Lubricants	1.00	5,022	5,400	378 F
Power	0.50	2,538	2,700	162 F
Total variable overhead cost	$3.00	15,390	16,200	810 F
Fixed overhead costs				
Depreciation		10,000	10,000	0
Supervisory salaries		14,000	12,000	2,000 U
Insurance		3,500	3,000	500 U
Total fixed overhead cost		27,500	25,000	2,500 U
Total overhead cost		$42,890	$41,200	$1,690 U

IN BUSINESS

Overhead Accounts: Fertile Ground for Fraud

Particularly in small companies, the controller may be the only person who understands concepts such as overhead variances and overapplied and underapplied overhead. Furthermore, a small company controller may be able to both authorize cash disbursements and account for them. Since small, closely held companies often do not hire external auditors, these circumstances create an ideal environment for fraud.

Such was the case in a small manufacturing company with 100 employees and $30 million in annual sales. The controller embezzled nearly $1 million from the company over three years by writing cheques to himself. The consultant who uncovered the fraud was tipped off by the unusually high overhead variances that resulted from the controller recording fictitious expenses in the overhead accounts to offset his fraudulent cash withdrawals. After the fraud was exposed, the company implemented various controls to reduce the risk of future problems. These controls included hiring an internal auditor and requiring periodic review of overhead variances to identify and explain significant discrepancies.

Source: John B. MacArthur, Bobby E. Waldrup, and Gary R. Fane, "Caution: Fraud Overhead," *Strategic Finance*, October 2004, pp. 28–32.

Capacity Analysis for Management

Colonial Pewter Company has a budgeted production level of 20,000 pairs of bookends. This activity level was used earlier in this chapter to determine a standard cost per pair of bookends of $69.50 based on 20,000 units or 50,000 direct labour-hours (see Exhibit 10–9). Assume now that the year has ended and 16,000 pairs of bookends have been sold.

Theoretical capacity The volume of activity resulting from operations conducted 24 hours per day, 7 days per week, 365 days per year, with no downtime.

Practical capacity The productive capacity of operations at a theoretical level less unavoidable downtime.

If all available production time was used and no waste occurred, Colonial Pewter could reach a level of capacity known as **theoretical capacity**. This level of capacity would require operations to be conducted around the clock, 365 days per year, with no downtime, similar to the definition of an ideal standard presented earlier in this chapter. If the denominator level of 20,000 units or 50,000 direct labour-hours represented 50% of the theoretical capacity, then Colonial Pewter could produce 40,000 units (20,000 ÷ 0.50) in 100,000 hours.

Practical capacity represents what could be produced if unavoidable downtime was subtracted from theoretical capacity. Maintenance, breakdowns, and set-up times for new operations are considered to be unavoidable downtime. If the denominator level was 80% of practical capacity, then 25,000 units (20,000 ÷ 0.80) could be produced using 62,500 direct labour-hours.

Capacity analysis would proceed by first examining the overhead cost (variable + fixed) at each level of capacity.

	Total Overhead Costs
Theoretical	(100,000 DLH × $3.00) + $300,000 = $600,000
Practical	(62,500 DLH × $3.00) + $300,000 = $487,500
Denominator.........	(50,000 DLH × $3.00) + $300,000 = $450,000
Actual	(40,000 DLH × $3.00) + $300,000 = $420,000

If Colonial Pewter can sell all that it can produce at $80 per unit, then an indication of the opportunity cost incurred of not operating at the various levels of capacity can be computed as follows:

	Contribution Margin	Total Overhead	Operating Income
Theoretical	40,000 units × ($80.00 − $47.00) −	$600,000 =	$720,000
Practical	25,000 units × ($80.00 − $47.00) −	$487,500 =	$337,500
Denominator.........	20,000 units × ($80.00 − $47.00) −	$450,000 =	$210,000
Actual	16,000 units × ($80.00 − $47.00) −	$420,000 =	$108,000

Note that $47 is composed of the standard materials cost of $12 per unit and the standard direct labour cost of $35 per unit shown in Exhibit 10–9. The remaining variable production cost of $3 for overhead is included in the overhead charges calculated above.

To calculate the opportunity cost of operating at 16,000 units (a profit of $108,000) we begin by looking at what additional profit would have been possible at the theoretical capacity: $720,000 – $108,000, or $612,000 in lost profits. By examining marketing strategies to sell an additional 24,000 units (40,000 – 16,000), management might be able to significantly improve its profit picture. Analysis would also have to be conducted to evaluate the potential impact of any additional unit sales on set-up costs, maintenance, wastage, etc.

When budgeting, both short term as presented in Chapter 9 or long term as will be presented in Chapter 13, capacity analysis is an important strategic planning tool. Capacity costs and changes in capacity require time, so capacity utilization, bottlenecks, and marketing opportunies are important areas for investigation.

Variance Investigation Decisions and Management by Exception

Variance analysis and performance reports are important elements of *management by exception*, which is an approach that emphasizes focusing on those areas of responsibility where goals and expectations are not being met.

The budgets and standards discussed in this chapter and in the preceding chapter reflect management's plans. If all goes according to plan, there will be little difference between actual results and the budgets and standards. However, if actual results do not conform to the budget and to standards, the performance reporting system sends a signal to the manager that an "exception" has occurred. This signal is in the form of a variance from the budget or standards.

However, are all variances worth investigating? The answer is no. Differences between actual results and what was expected will almost always occur. If every variance was investigated, management would spend a great deal of time tracking down immaterial differences. Variances may occur for any of a variety of reasons—only some of which warrant management attention. For example, hotter-than-normal weather in the summer may result in higher-than-expected electrical bills for air conditioning. Because of unpredictable random factors, every cost category will produce a variance of some kind.

How should managers decide which variances are worth investigating? One indicator is the size of the variance. A variance of $5 is probably not big enough to warrant attention, whereas a variance of $5,000 might well be worth tracking down. Another indicator is the size of the variance relative to the amount of spending involved. A variance that is only 0.1% of spending on an item is very likely due to random factors. On the other hand, a variance of 10% of spending is much more likely to be a signal that something is wrong and should be investigated.

A more reliable approach is to plot variance data on a statistical control chart, as illustrated in Exhibit 10–15. The basic idea underlying a statistical control chart is that some random fluctuations in variances from period to period are normal and to be expected even when costs are well under control. A variance should be investigated only when it is unusual relative to that normal level of random fluctuation. Typically, the standard deviation of the variances is used as the measure of the normal level of fluctuations. Often a simple decision rule is adopted such as "investigate all variances that are more than *X* standard deviations from zero." In the control chart in Exhibit 10–15, *X* is 1.0. That is, the decision rule in this company is to investigate all variances that are more than one standard deviation in either direction (favourable or unfavourable) from zero. This means that the variances in weeks 7, 11, and 17 would have been investigated, but none of the others.

What value of *X* should be chosen? The greater the value of *X*, the wider the band of acceptable variances that would not be investigated. Thus, the greater the value of *X*, the less time will be spent tracking down variances, but the more likely it is that a real out-of-control situation would be overlooked. Ordinarily, if *X* is selected to be 1.0, roughly 30% of all variances will trigger an investigation even when there is no real problem. If *X* is set at 1.5, the figure drops to about 13%. If *X* is set at 2.0, the figure drops all the way to about 5%.

In addition to watching for unusually large variances, the pattern of the variances should be monitored. For example, a series of steadily increasing variances should trigger an investigation even if none of the variances is large enough by itself to warrant investigation.

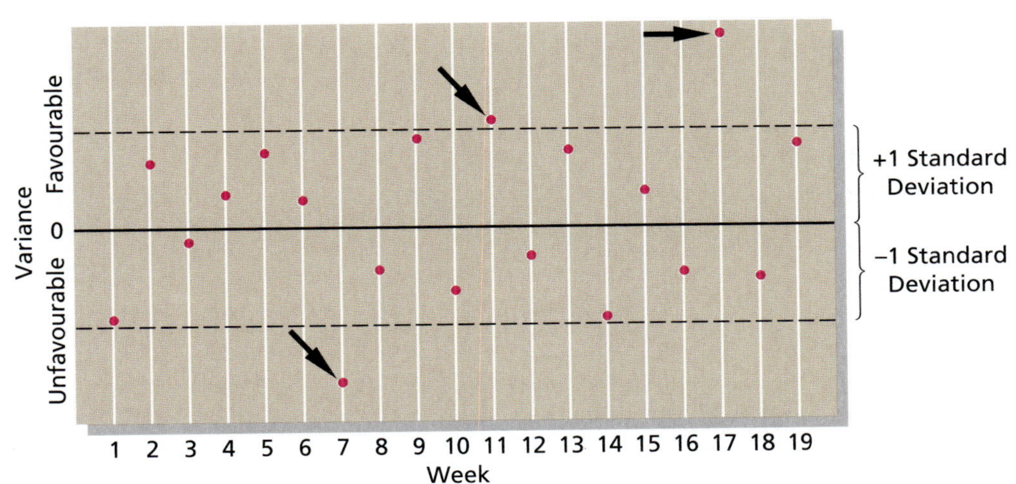

EXHIBIT 10–15 A Statistical Control Chart

IN BUSINESS

Standard costs have a 100-year history in modern business practice. Modern computer systems have integrated standard cost practices on systems designed for a wide variety of organizations. Material requirements planning (MRP), supply chain management, and human resource management are a few of the terms used by modern computer systems that incorporate standard costs for planning, bidding, customer relationship management, inventory management, and production planning.

One example of a modern application of standards is described by Nova Chemicals Corporation for the standardization of its maintenance practices for its 23 plants operating in Canada, United States and Europe. Nova claims the modern computer and management system they implemented provides standardization company wide, performance indicators, and accurate data for the management of maintenance. Estimates by Nova suggest the new systems saved approximately 15% on their maintenance costs alone.

Source: Nova Chemicals, www.sap.com/industries.

International Uses of Standard Costs

Standard costs are used by companies worldwide. A comparative study of cost accounting practices found that three-fourths of the companies surveyed in the United Kingdom, two-thirds of the companies surveyed in Canada, and 40% of the companies surveyed in Japan used standard cost systems.[6]

Standard costs were first introduced in Japan after World War II. Nippon Electronics Company (NEC) was one of the first Japanese companies to adopt standard costs for all of its products. Many other Japanese companies followed NEC's lead after the war and developed standard cost systems. The ways in which these standard costs are used in Japan—and also in the other countries cited above—are shown in Exhibit 10–16.

Over time, the pattern of use shown in Exhibit 10–16 may change, but at present managers can expect to encounter standard costs in most industrialized nations. Moreover, the most important uses are for cost management and budgetary planning purposes.

EXHIBIT 10–16 Uses of Standard Costs in Four Countries

	Canada	United States	United Kingdom	Japan
Cost management	2	1*	2	1
Budgetary planning and control†	1	2	3	3
Pricing decisions	3	3	1	2
Financial statement preparation	4	4	4	4

*The numbers 1 through 4 denote importance of use, from greatest to least.
†Includes management planning.

Source: Compiled from data in a study by Shin'ichi Inoue, "Comparative Studies of Recent Development of Cost Management Problems in U.S.A., U.K., Canada, and Japan," *Research Paper No. 29*, Kagawa University, March 1988, p. 20.

6. Shin'ichi Inoue, "Comparative Studies of Recent Development of Cost Management Problems in U.S.A., U.K., Canada, and Japan," Research Paper No. 29, Kagawa University, March 1988, p. 17. The study included 95 United States companies, 52 United Kingdom companies, 82 Canadian companies, and 646 Japanese companies.

Evaluation of Controls Based on Standard Costs

Advantages of Standard Costs

Standard cost systems have a number of advantages:

1. As stated earlier, the use of standard costs is a key element in a management by exception approach. If costs remain within the standards, managers can focus on other issues. When costs fall significantly outside the standards, managers are alerted that there may be problems requiring attention. This approach helps managers focus on important issues.
2. Standards that are viewed as reasonable by employees can promote economy and efficiency. They provide benchmarks that individuals can use to judge their own performance.
3. Standard costs can greatly simplify bookkeeping. Instead of recording actual costs for each job, the standard costs for materials, labour, and overhead can be charged to jobs.
4. Standard costs fit naturally in an integrated system of "responsibility accounting." The standards establish what costs should be, who should be responsible for them, and whether actual costs are under control.

Potential Problems with the Use of Standard Costs

The use of standard costs can present a number of potential problems. Most of these problems result from improper use of standard costs and the management by exception principle or from using standard costs in situations in which they are not appropriate.

1. Standard cost variance reports are usually prepared on a monthly basis and often are released days or even weeks after the end of the month. As a consequence, the information in the reports may be very outdated. Timely, frequent reports that are approximately correct are better than infrequent reports that are very precise but out of date by the time they are released. As mentioned earlier, some companies are now reporting other key operating data daily or even more frequently.
2. If managers are insensitive and use variance reports to lay blame, morale may suffer. If variances are used to lay blame, subordinates may be tempted to cover up unfavourable variances or take actions that are not in the best interests of the company to make sure the variances are favourable. For example, workers may exert high effort to increase output at the end of the month to avoid an unfavourable labour efficiency variance. In the rush to increase output, quality may suffer.
3. Labour quantity standards and efficiency variances make two important assumptions. First, they assume that the production process is labour-paced; if labour works faster, output will go up. However, output in many companies is no longer determined by how fast labour works; rather, it is determined by the processing speed of machines. Second, the computations assume that labour is a variable cost. However, as discussed in earlier chapters, in many companies, direct labour may essentially be fixed. If labour is fixed, then an undue emphasis on labour efficiency variances creates pressure to build excess work in process and finished goods inventories.
4. In some cases, a "favourable" variance can be as bad or worse than an "unfavourable" variance. For example, Harvey's has a standard for the amount of hamburger meat that should be in a burger. If there is a "favourable" variance, it means that less meat was used than the standard specifies. The result is a substandard burger and possibly a dissatisfied customer.
5. There may be a tendency with standard cost reporting systems to emphasize meeting the standards to the exclusion of other important objectives, such as maintaining and improving quality, on-time delivery, and customer satisfaction. This tendency can be reduced by using supplemental performance measures that focus on these other objectives.

6. Just meeting standards may not be sufficient; continual improvement may be necessary to survive in the current competitive environment. For this reason, some companies focus on the trends in the standard cost variances—aiming for continual improvement rather than just meeting the standards. In other companies, engineered standards are being replaced either by a rolling average of actual costs, which is expected to decline, or by very challenging target costs.

In summary, managers should exercise considerable care in their use of a standard cost system. It is particularly important that managers go out of their way to focus on the positive, rather than just on the negative, and to be aware of possible unintended consequences.

Nevertheless, standard costs are still found in the vast majority of manufacturing companies and in many service companies, although their use is changing. For evaluating performance, standard cost variances may be supplanted in the future by a particularly interesting development known as the *balanced scorecard,* which is discussed in Chapter 11.

IN BUSINESS

Significant increases in healthcare costs over the past several decades in Canada, the United States and other countries worldwide has prompted calls for new measures directed at improving cost control. In a recent article, Thibadoux, Scheidt, and Luckey (2007) explored the possible development and use of the standard costing methodology in the U.S. healthcare system. Developing standard costs would involve the use of evidence-based best practices (EBBP), which are clinical guidelines for diagnosis and treatment, derived from scientific research. EBBP prescribe a standard approach to be followed by physicians in treating patients involving the use of published checklists for every major diagnostic related group (DRG). An example of a DRG would be cardiac disease by-pass surgery. By determining the cost of each "step" included in the EBBP checklist for a particular DRG, a standard cost could be developed for diagnosing and treating each patient. Actual costs could then be compared to the standard cost and variances investigated.

Interviews with several practising physicians about the possible use of standard costs in the healthcare system suggest the disadvantages may outweigh the benefits. While some interviewees indicated that a standard costing approach could be useful in identifying possible causes of cost increases, most had serious concerns about the concept. For example, many noted that being held responsible for adhering to standard costs could lead to decisions aimed more at controlling costs than ensuring the well-being of their patients. Similarly, others indicated that interpreting variances from standard costs could also be problematic in that a favourable cost variance could mean poor care had been given to the patient. Finally, some respondents stated that unlike manufacturing companies where relatively precise standards can be developed for production, the approach used to treat a serious illness can vary considerably from one patient to the next. Therefore they questioned whether meaningful standards could even be developed.

Whether or not healthcare administrators adopt the standard costing methodology remains to be seen. However, it is interesting to note the similarities between the problems identified by physicians with standard costs and those noted earlier in this chapter.

Source: Greg Thibadoux, Marsha Scheidt, and Elizabeth Luckey, "Accounting and Medicine: An Exploratory Investigation into Physicians' Attitudes Toward the Use of Standard Cost-Accounting Methods in Medicine," *Journal of Business Ethics* 75, 2007 pp. 137–149.

Summary

A standard is a benchmark or "norm" for measuring performance. In business organizations, standards are set for both the cost and the quantity of inputs needed to manufacture goods or to provide services. Quantity standards indicate how much of a cost element, such as labour time or raw materials, should be used in manufacturing a unit of product or in providing a unit of service. Cost standards indicate what the cost of the time or the materials should be.

Standards are normally practical in nature, meaning that they can be attained by reasonable, although highly efficient, efforts. Such standards are generally felt to have a favourable motivational impact on employees.

When standards are compared to actual performance, the difference is referred to as a *variance.* Variances are computed and reported to management on a regular basis for both the price and the quantity elements of materials, labour, and variable overhead. Price, rate and spending variances for inputs are computed by taking the difference between the actual and standard prices of the inputs and multiplying the result by the amount of input purchased. Quantity and efficiency variances are computed by taking the difference between the actual amount of the input used and the amount of input that is allowed for the actual output, and then multiplying the result by the standard price of the input.

Two variances also exist for fixed overhead. The budget variance is simply the difference between the actual and budgeted amounts for total fixed overhead costs. The volume variance is the difference between the amount of fixed overhead cost applied to inventory and the total amount of fixed overhead that was originally budgeted for the period. The budget variance is a measure of the extent to which fixed overhead spending was under control. The volume variance is the consequence of treating fixed costs as if they are variable and is more difficult to meaningfully interpret. However, at a general level, the volume variance represents the difference between planned and actual use of production facilities. The sum of the four variances for variable and fixed overhead equals the over or underapplied amount for the reporting period. Unfavaourable variances are equivalent to underapplied overhead while favourable variances are equivalent to overapplied overhead.

Not all variances require management time or attention. Only unusual or particularly significant variances should be investigated—otherwise a great deal of time would be spent investigating unimportant matters. Additionally, it should be emphasized that the point of the investigation should not be to find someone to blame. The point of the investigation is to pinpoint the problem so that it can be fixed and operations improved.

Traditional standard cost variance reports should often be supplemented with other performance measures. Overemphasis on standard cost variances may lead to problems in other critical areas such as product quality, inventory levels, and on-time delivery.

Review Problem: Standard Costs

Dawson Toys, Ltd. produces a toy called the Maze. Overhead is applied to products on the basis of direct labour-hours. The company has recently implemented a standard cost system to help control costs and has established the following standards for the Maze toys:

Direct materials: 6 microns per toy at $0.50 per micron
Direct labour: 1.3 hours per toy at $8 per hour
Variable manufacturing overhead: 1.3 hours per toy at $4 per hour
Fixed manufacturing overhead: 1.3 hours per toy at $6 per hour

During July, the company produced 3,000 Maze toys. The fixed overhead expense budget for July was $24,180 with 4,030 direct labour-hours as the denominator level of activity. Production data for the month on the toys follow:

Direct materials: 25,000 microns were purchased at a cost of $0.48 per micron. 5,000 of these microns were still in inventory at the end of the month.
Direct labour: 4,000 direct labour-hours were worked at a cost of $36,000.
Variable overhead: Actual cost in July was $17,000.
Fixed overhead: Actual cost in July was $25,000.

Required:

1. Compute the materials, labour, variable manufacturing overhead and fixed manufacturing overhead variances.
2. Calculate total over- or underapplied overhead for July.

Solution to Review Problem

1. **Materials Variances**

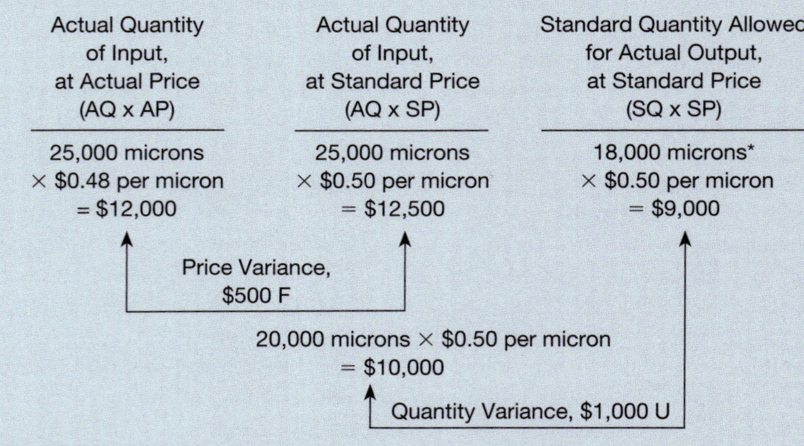

*3,000 toys × 6 microns per toy = 18,000 microns

A total variance is not computed in this situation because the amount of materials purchased (25,000 microns) differs from the amount of materials used in production (20,000 microns).

Using the formulas in the chapter, the same variances would be computed as:

Materials price variance = AQ (AP – SP)
25,000 microns ($0.48 per micron – $0.50 per micron) = $500 F

Materials quantity variance = SP (AQ – SQ)
$0.50 per micron (20,000 microns – 18,000 microns) = $1,000 U

Direct Labour Variances

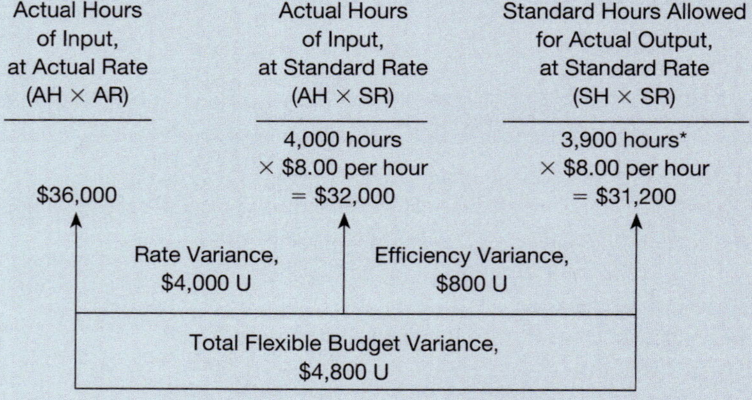

*3,000 toys × 1.3 hours per toy = 3,900 hours

Using the formulas in the chapter, the same variances would be computed as:

Labour rate variance = AH (AR – SR)
4,000 hours ($9.00 per hour* – $8.00 per hour) = $4,000 U

*$36,000 ÷ 4,000 hours = $9.00 per hour

Labour efficiency variance = SR (AH – SH)
$8.00 per hour (4,000 hours – 3,900 hours) = $800 U

Variable Manufacturing Overhead Variances

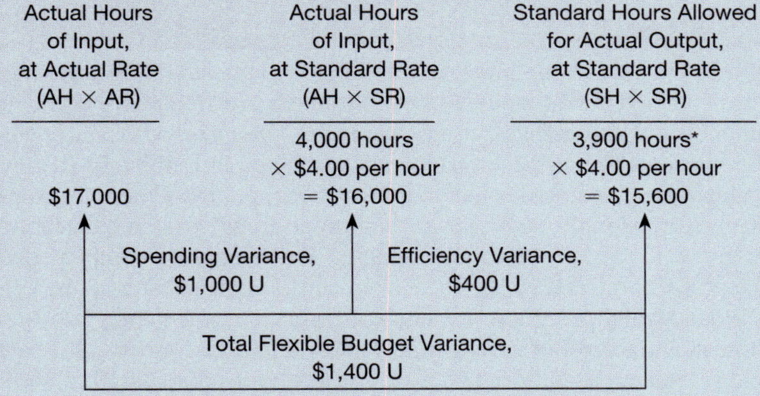

Using the formulas in the chapter, the same variances would be computed as:

Variable overhead spending variance = AH (AR – SR)
4,000 hours ($4.25 per hour* – $4.00 per hour) = $1,000 U

*$17,000 ÷ 4,000 hours = $4.25 per hour

Variable overhead efficiency variance = SR (AH – SH)
$4.00 per hour (4,000 hours – 3,900 hours) = $400 U

Fixed Manufacturing Overhead Variances

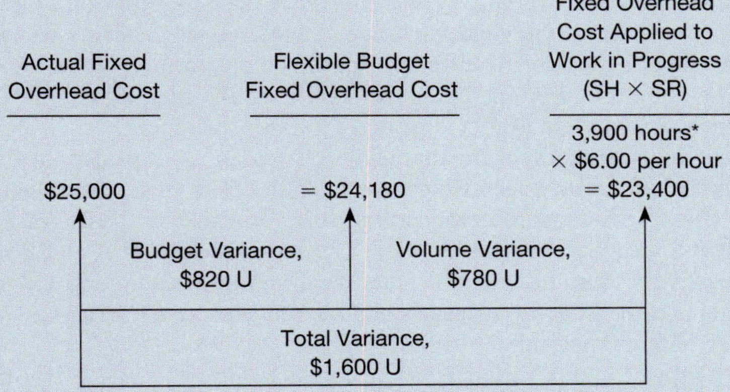

Using the formula in the chapter, the volume variance would be computed as:
$6 (4,030 – 3900) = $780 U

2. Actual overhead costs incurred:

Variable	$17,000
Fixed	25,000
Total	$42,000

Overhead costs applied:

Variable	$15,600
Fixed	23,400
Total	$39,000

Therefore, overhead is underapplied by $3,000 ($42,000 – $39,000)

Appendix 10A: Further Analysis of Materials Variances

LEARNING OBJECTIVE 8
Compute the mix and yield variances for materials and explain their significance.

A survey of the cost accounting practices of the 1,000 largest U.S. industrial companies[7] found that two other types of standard cost variances are frequently computed.[8] These are subcomponents of the material usage variance: a *materials mix* and *materials yield variance.* A representation of these variances is presented in Exhibit 10–17.

The production of most goods generally requires input from more than one material. Chemical firms, for example, may use varying proportions of interchangeable materials. The same is true with food processing companies. For example, a company that produces flour with a mixture of red and white wheat may, on occasion, substitute one kind of wheat for another. When legally permitted, a manufacturer of canned fruit may substitute peaches for pears and a manufacturer of sausages may substitute pork for beef. The calculation of mix and yield variances is appropriate only if different types of material can be substituted for one another. A **mix variance** results if the actual mix of materials differs from the budgeted mix of materials. The budgeted mix reflects a proportional mix of materials that is expected to be used to produce a given product. A mix variance is calculated to determine the effects of a change in the materials mix on the total materials cost. The mix variance is favourable if the actual mix is cheaper than the standard mix. This means that a greater proportion of less-expensive materials was used in the blend. The mix variance is unfavourable if the actual mix is more expensive than the standard mix because a greater proportion of more-expensive materials was used. Where a manager has control over the composition of the mix, the mix variance can be a useful measure of the manager's performance.

Mix variance
The dollar effect of a difference between the actual mix of materials and the budgeted mix of materials on total materials cost.

The amount of quantity variance remaining after deducting the mix variance from the total quantity variance is the **yield variance.** A yield variance occurs when the actual combination of inputs generates a different rate of output from what would have been produced by the input mix used in setting the standards. In other words, the actual yield differs from the standard yield expected from a given mix of inputs.

Yield variance
The portion of the efficiency variance that is not the mix variance. It occurs when the actual yield differs from the standard yield expected from a given mix of inputs.

To illustrate the calculation of the mix and yield variances, assume that Cape Breton Chemical Company combines secret ingredients A and B to make a product known as super-cleaner Bjax. The standard composition calls for a mix of 2 kilograms of A and 3 kilograms of B to produce one unit of Bjax. The standard mix for A and B is therefore ⅖ and ⅗, respectively. Assume that 150 units were produced using 350 kilograms of A and 450 kilograms of B. Material A has a standard unit price of $1.50 and material B has a standard price of $2.50 per unit.

For a given input, the mix variance can be calculated in two steps. First, multiply the budgeted mix percentage by the actual *total* input and subtract the actual quantity. This is the mix variance expressed in physical terms. Second, multiply your answer from step one by the standard cost of the input:

$$\text{Mix variance} = \left[\text{Actual quantity} - \left(\text{Budgeted \%} \times \text{Total input}\right)\right] \times \text{Standard price}$$

7. Max Laudeman and F. W. Schaeberle, "The Cost Accounting Practices of Firms Using Standard Costs," *Cost and Management,* July–August 1985, pp. 21–25.
8. Ibid.

EXHIBIT 10–17 Extended Model for Variance Analysis—Materials

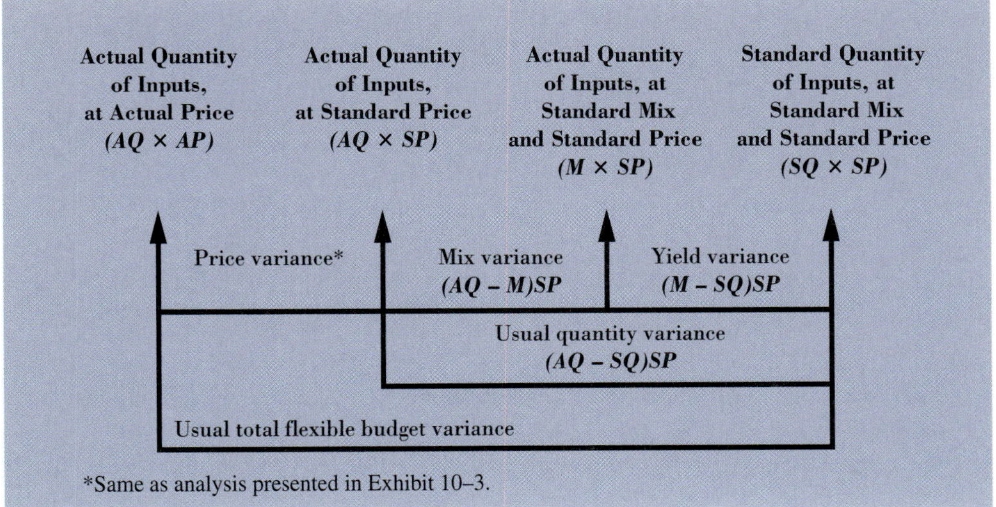

For material A, this would be:

$$[350 - \tfrac{2}{5}(350 + 450)] \times \$1.50 = \$45\text{ U}$$

Similarly, for material B, the mix variance is:

$$[450 - \tfrac{3}{5}(350 + 450)] \times \$2.50 = \$75\text{ F}$$

The budgeted percent times the total input of material A is 320 [⅖(350 + 450)] kilograms. This is the amount of material A that would have been used if the budget had been adhered to. Since the amount of material used, 350 kilograms, exceeds the budgeted amount, the mix variance is unfavourable. If the budget had been adhered to in the case of material B, 480 [⅗(350 + 450)] kilograms would have been used. Since the actual usage of material B was only 450 kilograms, the material mix variance of material B is favourable.

Yield variance = [(Budgeted % × Total Input) – Standard Quantity] × Standard Price

Note the mix variance is always calculated before the yield variance so that the mix effect is isolated from the quantity or yield amount.

The variances can also be calculated using the following notation. For material A:

$$\text{Mix variance} = (AQ_A - M_A)SP_A$$
$$= [350 - \tfrac{2}{5}(350 + 450)]\$1.50 = \$45\text{ U}$$

$$\text{Yield variance} = (M_A - SQ_A)SP_A$$
$$= [\tfrac{2}{5}(350 + 450) - 150(2)]\$1.50 = \$30\text{ U}$$

$$\text{Total material quantity variance} = (AQ_A - SQ_A)SP_A$$
$$= (350 - 150(2))\$1.50 = \$75\text{ U}$$

or mix variance + yield variance

$45 U + $30 U = $75 U

where

AQ_A is the actual quantity used of material A.
M_A is the standard mix of material A actually used.
SQ_A is the standard quantity of material A.

For material B:

$$\text{Mix variance} = [450 - \tfrac{3}{5}(350 + 450)]\$2.50 = \$75\text{ F}$$
$$\text{Yield variance} = [\tfrac{3}{5}(350 + 450) - 3(150)]\$2.50 = \$75\text{ U}$$
$$\text{Total material quantity variance} = [450 - 3(150)]\$2.50 = \$0$$

or

$$\$75\text{ F} - \$75\text{ U} = \$0$$

Labour efficiency variances, described earlier in the chapter, can be analyzed in a similar manner if the composition of a work group is provided in the standard. For example, if all junior staff members are assigned to other jobs, a public accounting firm might assign a senior staff member to a job that would normally be done by more junior personnel. The standard mix of employees can be applied to the total hours worked in the group to determine the standard mix for each employee group.

The calculation of mix and yield variances provides a means of separating the quantity variance into a set of constituents. This breakdown can be meaningful where managers are able to change the mix in production, thereby affecting the quantities of each type of material used. If the standard mix is the ideal, then departures from this mix should be made evident to statement users.

Managers, however, should carefully examine the effect of mix and yield variances to see how other costs, such as labour and overhead, are affected by the change in mix and its effect on yield. Often there are interrelationships among the mix, yield, and materials price variances. For example, a production manager may respond to changes in relative prices of inputs by changing the mix. The new mix may, in turn, affect the yield. If examined in isolation, the appropriateness of the decision to change the mix could not be properly assessed. This raises performance evaluation issues. The budgeted mix is no longer optimal and, therefore, cannot be used as a valid benchmark for evaluating the manager's performance.

One problem of mix and yield variances stems from its use of standard prices. When prices differ from standard, it is the change in actual relative prices within the composition of materials that may make changes in the mix and yield worthwhile. The fact that these price changes are held constant when calculating the mix and usage variances makes it difficult to interpret the effectiveness of managerial decisions to make changes in the mix of inputs. Conceptually, these variances can be left in physical units. Multiplying by standard prices is to facilitate aggregation by providing a common denominator.

Appendix 10B: General Ledger Entries to Record Variances

LEARNING OBJECTIVE 9
Prepare journal entries to record standard costs and variances.

Although standard costs and variances can be computed and used by management without being formally entered into the accounting records, most organizations prefer to make formal entries. Formal entry tends to give variances a greater emphasis than informal, off-the-record computations. This emphasis gives a clear signal of management's desire to keep costs within the limits that have been set. In addition, formal use of standard costs considerably simplifies the bookkeeping process. Inventories and cost of goods sold can be valued at their standard costs—eliminating the need to keep track of the actual cost of each unit.

Direct Materials Variances

To illustrate the general ledger entries needed to record standard cost variances, we will return to the data contained in the review problem at the end of the chapter. The entry to record the purchase of direct materials would be as follows:

Raw Materials (25,000 microns at $0.50 per micron).	12,500	
Materials Price Variance (25,000 microns at $0.02 per micron F)		500
Accounts Payable (25,000 microns at $0.48 per micron)		12,000

Notice that the price variance is recognized when purchases are made, rather than when materials are actually used in production. This permits the price variance to be isolated early, and it also permits the materials to be carried in the inventory account at standard cost. As direct materials are later drawn from inventory and used in production, the quantity variance is isolated as follows:

Work in Process (18,000 microns at $0.50 per micron)	9,000	
Materials Quantity Variance (2,000 microns U at $0.50 per micron) . .	1,000	
Raw Materials (20,000 microns at $0.50 per micron)		10,000

Thus, direct materials enter into the Work in Process account at standard cost, in terms of both price and quantity. Notice that the favourable price variance is a credit and the unfavourable quantity variance is a debit.

The term direct materials is not the same as raw materials even though they are often used interchangeably. Technically, raw materials refer to materials that are basic to the production process and usually no processing has been done that changes their nature. Direct materials refer to materials identified in the product as opposed to indirect supplies or materials that are not identified in the product. For example, oil is a direct material for the production of electricity and it is considered a raw material by most. Steel is a direct material in the production of automobiles. However, a car seat is a direct material, not a raw material. Because of the confusion we will consider the two terms interchangeable unless an obvious distinction is necessary.

Direct Labour Variances

Referring again to the cost data in the review problem at the end of the chapter, the general ledger entry to record the incurrence of direct labour cost would be:

Work in Process (3,900 hours at $8.00 per hour).	31,200	
Labour Efficiency Variance (100 hours U at $8.00 per hour)	800	
Labour Rate Variance (4,000 hours at $1.00 per hour U).	4,000	
Wages Payable (4,000 hours at $9.00 per hour).		36,000

Thus, as with direct materials, direct labour costs enter into the Work in Process account at standard, both in terms of the rate and in terms of the hours allowed for the actual production of the period.

Variable and Fixed Manufacturing Overhead Variances

Referring to the cost data in the review problem at the end of the chapter, the entries to record actual overhead, the application of overhead, the overhead variances, and the disposition of underapplied overhead for July are shown below.

To record actual variable and fixed overhead for July:

Overhead costs ($17,000 + $25,000).	42,000	
Various credits such as accounts payable		42,000

To record the application of variable overhead (3,900 × $4) and fixed overhead (3,900 × $6) in July:

Work in Progress ($15,600 + $23,400)	39,000	
Overhead costs		39,000

To record the overhead variances and the disposition of underapplied overhead for July:

Variable overhead spending variance	1,000	
Variable overhead efficiency variance	400	
Fixed overhead budget variance	820	
Fixed overhead volume variance	780	
Overhead costs		3,000

Cost Flows in a Standard Cost System

The flows of costs through the company's accounts are illustrated for direct materials and direct labour in Exhibit 10–18. Note that entries into the various inventory accounts are made at standard cost—not actual cost. The differences between actual and standard costs are entered into special accounts that accumulate the various standard cost variances. Ordinarily, these standard cost variance accounts are closed out to Cost of Goods Sold at the end of the period. Unfavourable variances increase Cost of Goods Sold, and favourable variances decrease Cost of Goods Sold.

EXHIBIT 10–18
Cash Flows in a Standard Cost System

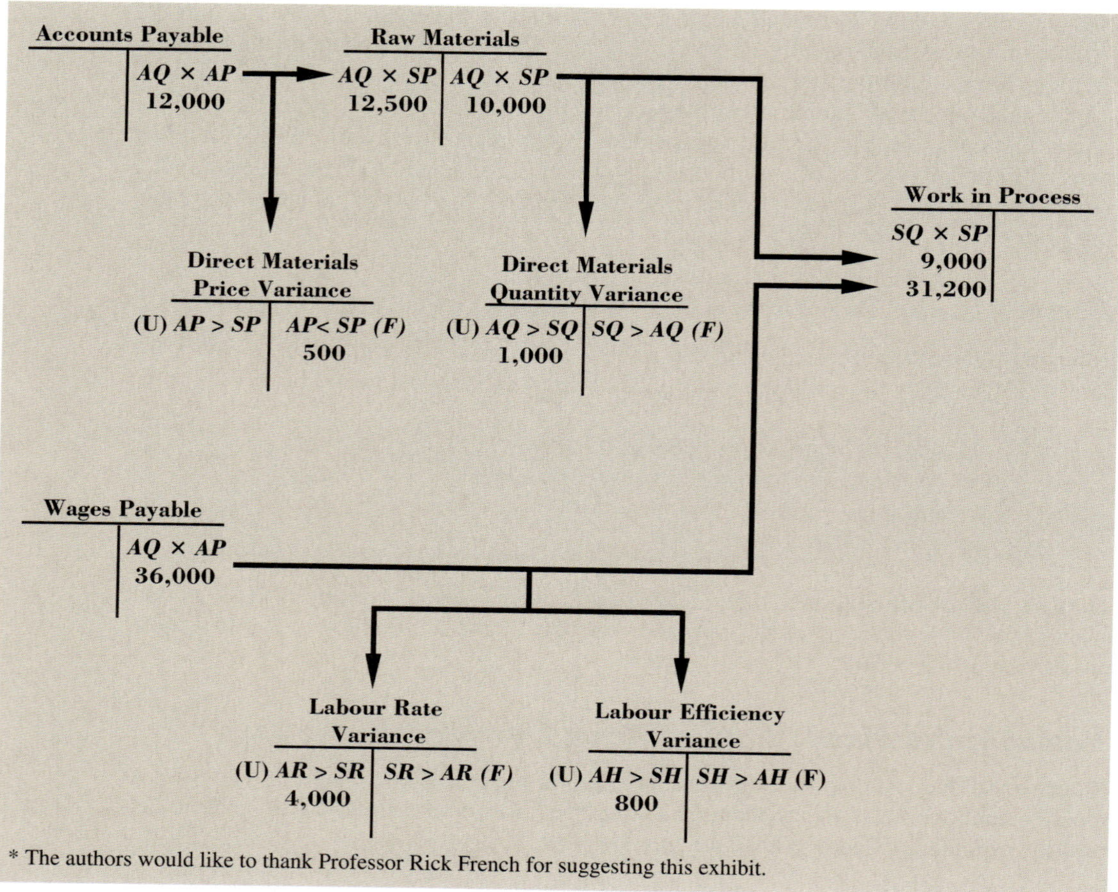

* The authors would like to thank Professor Rick French for suggesting this exhibit.

Glossary

Visit the Online Learning Centre at **http://www.mcgrawhill.ca/olc/garrison/** for a review of key terms and definitions.

Questions

10–1 What is a quantity standard? What is a price standard?

10–2 Distinguish between ideal and practical standards.

10–3 If employees are constantly unable to meet a standard, what effect would you expect this to have on their productivity?

10–4 What is the difference between a standard and a budget?

10–5 What is meant by the term, *management by exception*?

10–6 Why are variances generally segregated in terms of a price variance and a quantity variance?

10–7 Who is generally responsible for the materials price variance? The materials quantity variance? The labour efficiency variance?

10–8 The materials price variance can be computed at what two different points in time? Which point is better and why?

10–9 What effect, if any, would you expect purchasing poor-quality materials to have on direct labour variances?

10–10 If variable manufacturing overhead is applied to production on the basis of direct labour hours and the direct labour efficiency variance is unfavourable, will the variable overhead efficiency variance be favourable or unfavourable, or could it be either? Explain.

10–11 What is meant by the term *denominator level of activity*?

10–12 Why do we apply overhead to work in process on the basis of standard hours allowed in Chapter 10 when we applied it on the basis of actual hours in Chapter 3? What is the difference in costing systems between the two chapters?

10–13 In a standard cost system, what two variances are computed for fixed manufacturing overhead?

10–14 What does the fixed overhead budget variance measure?

10–15 Under what circumstances would you expect the volume variance to be favourable? Unfavourable? Does the volume variance measure deviations in spending for fixed overhead items? Explain.

10–16 How might the volume variance be measured other than in dollars?

10–17 In Chapter 3, you became acquainted with the concept of under- or overapplied overhead. The under- or overapplied overhead can be broken down into what four variances?

10–18 If factory overhead is overapplied for August, would you expect the total of the overhead variances to be favourable or unfavourable?

10–19 What is a statistical control chart, and how is it used?

10–20 Why can undue emphasis on labour efficiency variances lead to excess work in process inventories?

10–21 Capacity analysis extends beyond typical variance analysis of overhead. How are different definitions of capacity used as a starting point for capacity analysis?

10–22 (Appendix 10A) What is a mix variance? What is a yield variance?

10–23 (Appendix 10B) What are the advantages of making formal journal entries in the accounting records for variances?

Exercises

EXERCISE 10–1 Setting Standards; Preparing a Standard Cost Card [LO1]

Svenska Pharmicia, a Swedish pharmaceutical company, makes an anticoagulant drug. The main ingredient in the drug is a raw material called Alpha SR40. Information concerning the purchase and use of Alpha SR40 follows:

Purchase of Alpha SR40: The raw material Alpha SR40 is purchased in 2-kilogram containers at a cost of 3,000 Kr per kilogram. (The Swedish currency is the krona, which is abbreviated as Kr.) A discount of 2% is offered by the supplier for payment within 10 days and

Svenska Pharmicia takes all discounts. Shipping costs, which Svenska Pharmicia must pay, amount to 1,000 Kr for an average shipment of ten 2-kilogram containers.

Use of Alpha SR40: The bill of materials calls for 6 grams of Alpha SR40 per capsule of the anticoagulant drug. (A kilogram equals 1,000 grams.) About 4% of all Alpha SR40 purchased is rejected as unsuitable before being used to make the anticoagulant drug. In addition, after the addition of Alpha SR40, about 1 out of every 26 capsules is rejected at final inspection, due to defects of one sort or another in the capsule.

Required:

1. Compute the standard purchase price for one gram of Alpha SR40.
2. Compute the standard quantity of Alpha SR40 (in grams) per capsule that passes final inspection. (Carry computations to two decimal places.)
3. Using the data from (1) and (2) above, prepare a standard cost card showing the standard cost of Alpha SR40 per capsule of the anticoagulant drug.

EXERCISE 10–2 Material Variances [LO2]

Harmon Household Products, Inc., manufactures a number of consumer items for general household use. One of these products, a chopping board, requires an expensive hardwood. During a recent month, the company manufactured 12,000 chopping boards using 11,000 metres of hardwood. The hardwood cost the company $56,100.

The company's standards for one chopping board are .8 metres of hardwood, at a cost of $5.40 per metre.

Required:

1. What cost for wood should have been incurred to make 12,000 chopping boards? How much greater or less is this than the cost that was incurred?
2. Break down the difference computed in (1) above into a materials price variance and a materials quantity variance.

EXERCISE 10–3 Direct Labour Variances [LO3]

AirMeals, Inc., prepares in-flight meals for a number of major airlines. One of the company's products is stuffed cannelloni with roasted pepper sauce, fresh baby corn, and spring salad. During the most recent week, the company prepared 6,000 of these meals using 1,150 direct labour-hours. The company paid these direct labour workers a total of $11,500 for this work, or $10 per hour.

According to the standard cost card for this meal, it should require 0.20 direct labour-hours at a cost of $9.50 per hour.

Required:

1. What direct labour cost should have been incurred to prepare 6,000 meals? How much does this differ from the actual direct labour cost?
2. Break down the difference computed in (1) above into a labour rate variance and a labour efficiency variance.

EXERCISE 10–4 Variable Overhead Variances [LO4]

Order Up, Inc., provides order fulfillment services for dot.com merchants. The company maintains warehouses that stock items carried by its dot.com clients. When a client receives an order from a customer, the order is forwarded to Order Up, which pulls the item from storage, packs it, and ships it to the customer. The company uses a predetermined variable overhead rate based on direct labour-hours.

In the most recent month, 140,000 items were shipped to customers using 5,800 direct labour-hours. The company incurred a total of $15,950 in variable overhead costs.

According to the company's standards, 0.04 direct labour-hours are required to fulfill an order for one item and the variable overhead rate is $2.80 per direct labour-hour.

Required:

1. What variable overhead cost should have been incurred to fill the orders for the 140,000 items? How much does this differ from the actual variable overhead cost?
2. Break down the difference computed in (1) above into a variable overhead spending variance and a variable overhead efficiency variance.

EXERCISE 10–5 Fixed Overhead Variances [LO5, LO6]

Lusive Corporation has a standard cost system in which it applies overhead to products based on the standard direct labour-hours allowed for the actual output of the period. Data concerning the most recent year appear below:

Total budgeted fixed overhead cost for the year	$400,000
Actual fixed overhead cost for the year	$394,000
Budgeted standard direct labour-hours (denominator level of activity)	50,000
Actual direct labour-hours	51,000
Standard direct labour-hours allowed for the actual output	48,000

Required:

1. Compute the fixed portion of the predetermined overhead rate for the year.
2. Compute the fixed overhead budget and volume variances.

EXERCISE 10–6 Variable Overhead Performance Report [LO7]

Jessel Corporation bases its variable overhead performance report on the actual direct labour-hours of the period. Data concerning the most recent year that ended on December 31 are as follows:

Budgeted direct labour-hours	42,000
Actual direct labour-hours	44,000
Standard direct labour-hours allowed	45,000
Cost formula (per direct labour-hour):	
Indirect labour	$0.90
Supplies	$0.15
Electricity	$0.05
Actual costs incurred:	
Indirect labour	$42,000
Supplies	$6,900
Electricity	$1,800

Required:

Prepare a variable overhead performance report using the format in Exhibit 10–13. Compute both variable overhead spending and efficiency variances.

EXERCISE 10–7 (Appendix 10A) Mix and Yield Variances [LO8]

The Caledon Company uses standard costs to account for its production of widgets. The standard cost of a widget is given as follows for materials and direct labour:

Material A	15 kilograms at 80 cents	$12.00
Material B	4 kilograms at $2.25	9.00
Direct Labour	5 hours at $12.00	60.00

Both material A and material B are added at the start of the process. Production data for June 2008 are as follows:

a. Beginning work process, 10,000 units, 30% complete.
b. Started during June, 40,000 units.
c. Ending work in process, 12,000 units, 60% complete.
d. No units were spoiled.
e. 620,000 kilograms of material A were issued to production.
f. 150,000 kilograms of material B were used during June.
g. Direct labour worked 212,000 hours at a cost of $2,597,000 for the month.

Required:

Determine all of the material and labour variances possible from the preceding data for the month of June.

EXERCISE 10–8 (Appendix 10B) Recording Variances in the General Ledger [LO9]

Kinkel Corporation makes a product with the following standard costs for direct material and direct labour:

Direct material: 1.50 metres at $5.40 per metre . .	$8.10
Direct labour: 0.25 hours at $14.00 per hour	$3.50

During the most recent month, 8,000 units were produced. The costs associated with the month's production of this product were as follows:

Material purchased: 15,000 metres at $5.60 per metre	$84,000
Material used in production: 11,900 metres	—
Direct labour: 1,950 hours at $14.20 per hour	$27,690

The standard cost variances for direct material and direct labour are:

Materials price variance: 15,000 metres at $0.20 per metre U . . .	$3,000 U
Materials quantity variance: 100 metres at $5.40 per metre F. . . .	$540 F
Labour rate variance: 1,950 hours at $0.20 per hour U	$390 U
Labour efficiency variance: 50 hours at $14.00 per hour F	$700 F

Required:

1. Prepare the journal entry to record the purchase of materials on account for the month.
2. Prepare the journal entry to record the use of materials for the month.
3. Prepare the journal entry to record the incurrence of direct labour cost for the month.

EXERCISE 10–9 Setting Standards [LO1]

Czar Nicholas Chocolatier, Ltd., makes premium handcrafted chocolate confections in London. The owner of the company is setting up a standard cost system and has collected the following data for one of the company's products, the Imperial Truffle. This product is made with the finest white chocolate and various fillings. The data below pertain only to the white chocolate used in the product. (The currency in the United Kingdom is the British pound sterling, which is denoted by £.):

Material requirements, kilograms of white chocolate per dozen truffles . .	0.80 kilograms
Allowance for waste, kilograms of white chocolate per dozen truffles. . . .	0.02 kilograms
Allowance for rejects, kilograms of white chocolate per dozen truffles . . .	0.03 kilograms
Purchase price, finest grade white chocolate	£9.00 per kilogram
Purchase discount.	5% of purchase price
Shipping cost from the supplier in Belgium	£0.20 per kilogram
Receiving and handling cost	£0.05 per kilogram

Required:

1. Determine the standard price of a kilogram of white chocolate.
2. Determine the standard quantity of white chocolate for a dozen truffles.
3. Determine the standard cost of the white chocolate in a dozen truffles.

EXERCISE 10–10 Material and Labour Variances [LO2, LO3]

Topper Toys has developed a new toy called the Brainbuster. The company has a standard cost system to help control costs and has established the following standards for the Brainbuster toy:

Direct materials: 8 diodes per toy at $0.30 per diode
Direct labour: 1.2 hours per toy at $7 per hour

During August, the company produced 5,000 Brainbuster toys. Production data on the toy for August follow:

Direct materials: 70,000 diodes were purchased at a cost of $0.28 per diode. 20,000 of these diodes were still in inventory at the end of the month. (There was no opening inventory.)
Direct labour: 6,400 direct labour-hours were worked at a cost of $48,000.

Required:

1. Compute the following variances for August:
   a. Direct materials price and quantity variances.
   b. Direct labour rate and efficiency variances.
2. Prepare a brief explanation of the possible causes of each variance.

EXERCISE 10–11 Material and Labour Variances [LO2, LO3]
Sonne Company produces a perfume called Whim. The direct materials and direct labour standards for one bottle of Whim are given below:

	Standard Quantity or Hours	Standard Price or Rate	Standard Cost
Direct materials......	7.2 grams	$2.50 per gram	$18.00
Direct labour	0.4 hours	$10.00 per hour	$4.00

During the most recent month, the following activity was recorded:

a. Twenty thousand grams of material were purchased at a cost of $2.40 per gram.
b. All of the material was used to produce 2,500 bottles of Whim.
c. Nine hundred hours of direct labour time were recorded at a total labour cost of $10,800.

Required:

1. Compute the direct materials price and quantity variances for the month.
2. Compute the direct labour rate and efficiency variances for the month.

EXERCISE 10–12 Material Variances [LO2]
Refer to the data in Exercise 10–11. Assume that instead of producing 2,500 bottles of Whim during the month, the company produced only 2,000 bottles using 16,000 grams of material. (The rest of the material purchased remained in raw materials inventory.)

Required:
Compute the direct materials price and quantity variances for the month.

EXERCISE 10–13 Labour and Variable Manufacturing Overhead Variances [LO3, LO4]
Hollowell Audio, Inc., manufactures military-specification compact discs. The company uses standards to control its costs. The labour standards that have been set for one disc are as follows:

Standard Hours	Standard Rate per Hour	Standard Cost
24 minutes	$12.00	$4.80

During July, 8,500 hours of direct labour time were recorded to make 20,000 discs. The direct labour cost totalled $98,600 for the month.

Required:

1. What direct labour cost should have been incurred to make the 20,000 discs? By how much does this differ from the cost that was incurred?
2. Break down the difference in cost from (1) above into a labour rate variance and a labour efficiency variance.
3. The budgeted variable manufacturing overhead rate is $8 per direct labour-hour. During July, the company incurred $78,200 in variable manufacturing overhead cost. Compute the variable overhead spending and efficiency variances for the month.

EXERCISE 10–14 Working Backwards from Labour Variances [LO3]
Worldwide Credit Card, Inc., uses standards to control the labour time involved in opening mail from card holders and recording the enclosed remittances. Incoming mail is gathered into batches, and a standard time is set for opening and recording each batch. The labour standards relating to one batch are as follows:

	Standard Hours	Standard Rate	Standard Cost
Per batch	2.5	$12.00	$30.00

The record showing the time spent last week in opening batches of mail has been misplaced. However, the batch supervisor recalls that 168 batches were received and opened during the week, and the controller recalls the following variance data relating to these batches:

Total labour variance	$660 U
Labour rate variance	$300 F

Required:

1. Determine the number of actual labour-hours spent opening batches during the week.
2. Determine the actual hourly rate paid to employees for opening batches last week.

(Hint: A useful way to proceed would be to work from known to unknown data either by using the variance formulas or by using the columnar format shown in Exhibit 10–6.)

EXERCISE 10–15 Predetermined Overhead Rate; Overhead Variances [LO4, LO5, LO6]
Weller Company's flexible budget for manufacturing overhead (in condensed form) follows:

Overhead Costs	Cost Formula (per machine-hour)	Machine-Hours		
		8,000	9,000	10,000
Variable cost	$1.05	$ 8,400	$ 9,450	$10,500
Fixed cost.............		24,800	24,800	24,800
Total overhead cost		$33,200	$34,250	$35,300

The following information is available for a recent period:

a. The denominator activity of 8,000 machine-hours was chosen to compute the predetermined overhead rate.
b. At the 8,000 standard machine-hours level of activity, the company should produce 3,200 units of product.
c. The company's actual operating results were as follows:

Number of units produced.........	3,500
Actual machine-hours	8,500
Actual variable overhead costs	$9,860
Actual fixed overhead costs........	$25,100

Required:

1. Compute the predetermined overhead rate and break it down into variable and fixed cost elements.
2. What were the standard hours allowed for the year's actual output?
3. Compute the variable overhead spending and efficiency variances and the fixed overhead budget and volume variances.

EXERCISE 10–16 Using Fixed Overhead Variances [LO5, LO6]
The standard cost card for the single product manufactured by Prince Company is given below:

Standard Cost Card—Per Unit	
Direct materials, 3.5 metres at $4 per metre	$14.00
Direct labour, 0.8 direct labour-hours at $18 per direct labour-hour.......	14.40
Variable overhead, 0.8 direct labour-hours at $2.50 per direct labour-hour	2.00
Fixed overhead, 0.8 direct labour-hours at $6 per direct labour-hour	4.80
Total standard cost per unit	$35.20

Last year, the company produced 10,000 units of product and worked 8,200 actual direct labour-hours. Manufacturing overhead cost is applied to production on the basis of direct labour-hours. Selected data relating to the company's fixed manufacturing overhead cost for the year are shown at the top of the next page.

Required:

1. What were the standard hours allowed for the year's production?
2. What was the amount of budgeted fixed overhead cost for the year?
3. What was the budget variance for the year?
4. What denominator activity level did the company use in setting the predetermined overhead rate for the year?

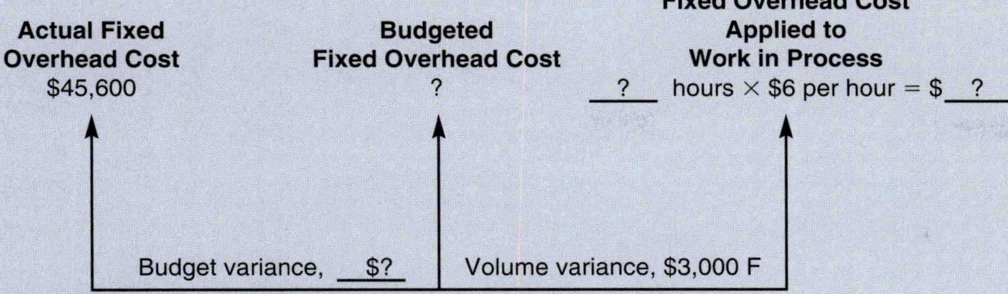

EXERCISE 10–17 Fixed Overhead Variances [LO5, LO6]
Selected operating information on three different companies for a recent period is given below:

	Company		
	X	Y	Z
Full-capacity direct labour-hours	20,000	9,000	10,000
Budgeted direct labour-hours*.	19,000	8,500	8,000
Actual direct labour-hours	19,500	8,000	9,000
Standard direct labour-hours allowed for actual output	18,500	8,250	9,500

*Denominator activity for computing the predetermined overhead rate.

Required:
For each company, state whether the volume variance would be favourable or unfavourable; also, explain in each case *why* the volume variance would be favourable or unfavourable.

EXERCISE 10–18 Overhead Performance Report with Both Spending and Efficiency Variances [LO4, LO7]
The cheque-clearing office of San Juan Bank is responsible for processing all cheques that come to the bank for payment. Managers at the bank believe that variable overhead costs are essentially proportional to the number of labour-hours worked in the office, so labour-hours are used as the activity base when preparing variable overhead budgets and performance reports. Data for October, the most recent month, appear below:

Budgeted labour-hours	865
Actual labour-hours	860
Standard labour-hours allowed for the actual number of cheques processed . . .	880

	Cost Formula (per labour-hour)	Actual Costs Incurred in October
Variable overhead costs:		
Office supplies	$0.15	$ 146
Staff coffee lounge	0.05	124
Indirect labour	3.25	2,790
Total variable overhead cost	$3.45	$3,060

Fixed overhead at San Juan Bank consists entirely of supervisory salaries and is applied at the rate of $5 per direct labour-hour. Actual fixed overhead costs totalled $4,200 in October while the flexible budget was $4,000 for the month.

Required:
Prepare an overhead performance report for October for the cheque-clearing office that includes both spending and efficiency variances for variable overhead and the budget

variance for fixed overhead. Use Exhibit 10–13 as a guide in preparing the performance report.

EXERCISE 10–19 (Appendix 10A) Mix and Yield Variances, [LO8]
Davis Division uses three secret materials. A, B, and C, to produce its product Corzon. The materials are mixed in the following standard proportions to yield 100 litres of Corzon:

Secret Material	Quantity (Litres)	Cost per Litre
A	80	$ 4.00
B	40	$ 8.00
C	30	$20.00

It requires 50 hours of direct labour at $20.00 per hour to produce 100 litres of Corzon.

On average, the division can produce and sell 200,000 litres of Corzon per month. In a recent month, the division used the following amounts of materials and labour to produce 175,000 litres of Corzon:

Secret Material	Quantity (Litres)	Total Actual Cost
A	159,000	$ 647,130
B	72,000	580,204
C	44,000	870,000
	275,000	$2,097,334
Direct labour	91,000 hours	$1,380,000

Required:

1. Calculate the following materials variances for Corzon:
   a. Price.
   b. Quantity.
   c. Mix.
   d. Yield.
2. The supervisor on the Corzon product line argued that the workers were operating at standard, if not better, despite a large unfavourable labour efficiency variance of $52,500. Is the supervisor correct? Why or why not?

(SMAC, Adapted)

EXERCISE 10–20 (Appendix 10B) Material and Labour Variances; Journal Entries [LO2, LO3, LO9]
Marmot Products, Inc., began production of a new product on April 1. The company uses a standard cost system and has established the following standards for one unit of the new product: During April, the following activity was recorded regarding the new product:

	Standard Quantity or Hours	Standard Price or Rate	Standard Cost
Direct materials. . . .	3.5 metres	$6 per metre	$21
Direct labour.	0.4 hours	$10 per hour	$4

a. Purchased 7,000 metres of material at a cost of $5.75 per metre.
b. Used 6,000 metres of material to produce 1,500 units of the new product.
c. Worked 725 direct labour-hours on the new product at a cost of $8,120.

Required:

1. For direct materials:
   a. Compute the direct materials price and quantity variances.
   b. Prepare journal entries to record the purchase of materials and the use of materials in production.
2. For direct labour:
   a. Compute the direct labour rate and efficiency variances.

b. Prepare journal entries to record the incurrence of direct labour cost for the month.

3. Post the entries you have prepared to the T-accounts below:

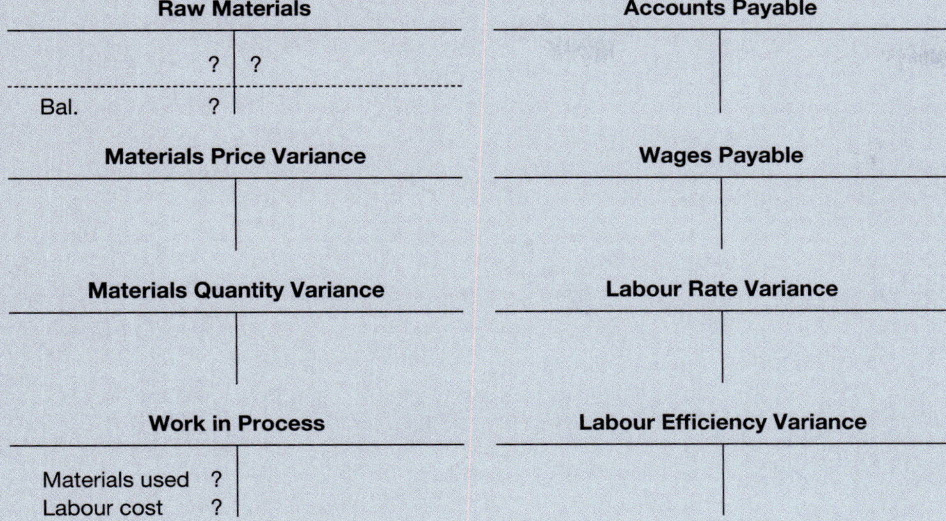

EXERCISE 10–21 Capacity Analysis [LO7]

Johnson Company produces leather seats for racing bikes. The standard cost per seat is as follows:

Direct materials	$28
Direct labour	12
Variable overhead (2 machine-hours at $3.00)*	6
Fixed overhead (2 machine-hours at $12.00)*	24
Total standard cost per seat	$70

*Overhead rates are based on a denominator activity level of 50,000 machine-hours.

During 2008, Johnson Company produced and sold 22,000 seats. Management believes that the denominator level of activity represents 75% of theoretical capacity and 80% of practical capacity.

Required:

1. Calculate the total overhead costs at the following levels of activity: theoretical, practical, denominator, and actual (2008).
2. Assuming Johnson Company can sell all of the seats it can produce for $75 per unit, calculate the opportunity loss of producing 22,000 seats in 2008 compared to the following capacity utilization alternatives: theoretical, practical, and denominator.

Problems

PROBLEM 10–22 Comprehensive Variance Analysis [LO2, LO3, LO4]

Hamilton Company's Stoney Creek Plant produces precast ingots for industrial use. Carlos Santiago, who was recently appointed general manager of the Stoney Creek Plant, has just been handed the plant's income statement for October. The statement is shown on the next page.

Mr. Santiago was shocked to see the loss for the month, particularly since sales were exactly as budgeted. He stated, "I sure hope the plant has a standard cost system in operation. If it doesn't, I won't have the slightest idea of where to start looking for the problem."

The plant does use a standard cost system, with the standard variable cost per ingot details shown on the next page.

Mr. Santiago has determined that during October the plant produced 5,000 ingots and incurred the following costs:

a. Purchased 25,000 kilograms of materials at a cost of $2.95 per kilogram. There were no raw materials in inventory at the beginning of the month.

b. Used 19,800 kilograms of materials in production. (Finished goods and work in process inventories are insignificant and can be ignored.)

c. Worked 3,600 direct labour-hours at a cost of $8.70 per hour.
d. Incurred a total variable manufacturing overhead cost of $4,320 for the month. A total of 1,800 machine-hours was recorded.
It is the company's policy to close all variances to cost of goods sold on a monthly basis.

	Budgeted	Actual
Sales (5,000 ingots)	$250,000	$250,000
Variable expenses:		
Variable cost of goods sold*	80,000	96,390
Variable selling expenses	20,000	20,000
Total variable expenses	100,000	116,390
Contribution margin	150,000	133,610
Fixed expenses:		
Manufacturing overhead.	60,000	59,000
Selling and administrative.	75,000	75,000
Total fixed expenses.	135,000	134,000
Operating income (loss)	$ 15,000	$ (390)

*Contains direct materials, direct labour, and variable manufacturing overhead.

	Standard Quantity or Hours	Standard Price or Rate	Standard Cost
Direct materials	4.0 kilograms	$2.50 per kilogram	$10.00
Direct labour	0.6 hours	$9.00 per hour	5.40
Variable manufacturing overhead	0.3 hours*	$2.00 per hour	0.60
Total standard variable cost			$16.00

*Based on machine-hours.

Required:

1. Compute the following variances for October:
   a. Direct materials price and quantity variances.
   b. Direct labour rate and efficiency variances.
   c. Variable manufacturing overhead spending and efficiency variances.
2. Summarize the variances that you computed in (1) above by showing the net overall favourable or unfavourable variance for October. What impact did this figure have on the company's income statement?
3. Pick out the two most significant variances that you computed in (1) above. Explain to Mr. Santiago possible causes of these variances.

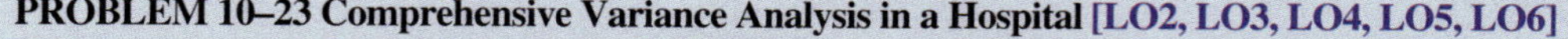

PROBLEM 10–23 Comprehensive Variance Analysis in a Hospital [LO2, LO3, LO4, LO5, LO6]
"What's going on in that lab?" asked Derek Warren, chief administrator for Cottonwood Hospital, as he studied the prior month's reports. "Every month the lab teeters between a profit and a loss. Are we going to have to increase our lab fees again?"

"We can't," replied Lois Ankers, the controller. "We're getting *lots* of complaints about the last increase, particularly from the insurance companies and governmental health units. They're now paying only about 80% of what we bill. I'm beginning to think the problem is on the cost side."

To determine if lab costs are in line with other hospitals, Mr. Warren has asked you to evaluate the costs for the past month. Ms. Ankers has provided you with the following information:

a. Two basic types of tests are performed in the lab—smears and blood tests. During the past month, 2,700 smears and 900 blood tests were performed in the lab.
b. Small glass plates are used in both types of tests. During the past month, the hospital purchased 16,000 plates at a cost of $38,400. This cost is net of a 4% purchase discount. A total of 2,000 of

these plates were unused at the end of the month; no plates were on hand at the beginning of the month.

c. During the past month, 1,800 hours of labour time were used in performing smears and blood tests. The cost of this labour time was $18,450.

d. The lab's variable overhead cost last month totalled $11,700.

e. Fixed overhead cost last month totalled $10,400.

Cottonwood Hospital has never used standard costs. By searching industry literature, however, you have determined the following nationwide averages for hospital labs:

Plates: Three plates are required per lab test. These plates cost $2.50 each and are disposed of after the test is completed.

Labour: Each smear should require 0.3 hours to complete, and each blood test should require 0.6 hours to complete. The average cost of this lab time is $12 per hour.

Overhead: Overhead cost is based on direct labour-hours. The average rate of variable overhead is $6 per hour. The average rate of fixed overhead is $8 per hour. These rates are based on a denominator activity level of 1,250 hours per month.

Required:

1. Compute the materials price variance for the plates purchased last month, and compute a materials quantity variance for the plates used last month.
2. For labour cost in the lab:
   a. Compute a labour rate variance and a labour efficiency variance.
   b. In most hospitals, three-fourths of the workers in the lab are certified technicians and one-fourth are assistants. In an effort to reduce costs, Cottonwood Hospital employs only one-half certified technicians and one-half assistants. Would you recommend that this policy be continued? Explain.
3. Compute the variable overhead spending and efficiency variances. Is there any relation between the variable overhead efficiency variance and the labour efficiency variance? Explain.
4. Compute the fixed overhead budget and volume variances.

PROBLEM 10–24 Comprehensive Standard Cost Variances [LO2, LO3, LO4, LO5, LO6]
"It certainly is nice to see that small variance on the income statement after all the trouble we've had lately in controlling manufacturing costs," said Linda White, vice-president of Molina Company. "The $12,250 overall manufacturing variance reported last period is well below the 3% limit we have set for variances. We need to congratulate everybody on a job well done."

The company produces and sells a single product. The standard cost card for the product follows:

Standard Cost Card—Per Unit	
Direct materials, 4 metres at $3.50 per metre	$14
Direct labour, 1.5 direct labour-hours at $12 per direct labour-hour	18
Variable overhead, 1.5 direct labour-hours at $2 per direct labour-hour	3
Fixed overhead, 1.5 direct-labour hours at $6 per direct labour-hour	9
Standard cost per unit	$44

The following additional information is available for the year just completed:

a. The company manufactured 20,000 units of product during the year.

b. A total of 78,000 metres of material was purchased during the year at a cost of $3.75 per metre. All of this material was used to manufacture the 20,000 units. There were no beginning or ending inventories for the year.

c. The company worked 32,500 direct labour-hours during the year at a cost of $11.80 per hour.

d. Overhead cost is applied to products on the basis of standard direct labour-hours. Data relating to manufacturing overhead costs follow:

Denominator activity level (direct labour-hours)	25,000
Budgeted fixed overhead costs (from the flexible budget)	$150,000
Actual fixed overhead costs	$148,000
Actual variable overhead costs	$68,250

Required:

1. Compute the direct materials price and quantity variances for the year.
2. Compute the direct labour rate and efficiency variances for the year.
3. For manufacturing overhead, compute the following:
   a. The variable overhead spending and efficiency variances for the year.
   b. The fixed overhead budget and volume variances for the year.
4. Total the variances you have computed, and compare the net amount with the $12,250 mentioned by the vice-president. Do you agree that everyone should be congratulated for a job well done? Explain.

PROBLEM 10–25 Applying Overhead; Overhead Variances [LO4, LO5, LO6]
Highland Shortbread, Ltd., of Aberdeen, Scotland, produces a single product and uses a standard cost system to help control costs. Manufacturing overhead is applied to production on the basis of standard machine-hours. According to the company's flexible budget, the following overhead costs should be incurred at an activity level of 18,000 machine-hours (the denominator activity level chosen for the year):

Variable manufacturing overhead cost	£ 31,500
Fixed manufacturing overhead cost	72,000
Total manufacturing overhead cost.......	£103,500

During the year, the following operating results were recorded:

Actual machine-hours worked	15,000
Standard machine-hours allowed	16,000
Actual variable manufacturing overhead cost incurred	£26,500
Actual fixed manufacturing overhead cost incurred.......	£70,000

At the end of the year, the company's Manufacturing Overhead account contained the following data:

Manufacturing Overhead			
Actual costs	96,500	Applied costs	92,000
	4,500		

Management would like to determine the cause of the £4,500 underapplied overhead.

Required:

1. Compute the predetermined overhead rate for the year. Break it down into variable and fixed cost elements.
2. Show how the £92,000 "Applied costs" figure in the Manufacturing Overhead account was computed.
3. Analyze the £4,500 underapplied overhead figure in terms of the variable overhead spending and efficiency variances and the fixed overhead budget and volume variances.
4. Explain the meaning of each variance that you computed in (3) above.

PROBLEM 10–26 (Appendix 10B) Comprehensive Variance Analysis; Journal Entries [LO2, LO3, LO4, LO5, LO6, LO9]
Haliburton Mills, Inc., is a large producer of men's and women's clothing. The company uses standard costs for all of its products. The standard costs and actual costs for a recent period are given on the top of page 477 for one of the company's product lines (per unit of product):

During this period, the company produced 4,800 units of product. A comparison of standard and actual costs for the period on a total cost basis is also given on page 477.

There was no inventory of materials on hand to start the period. During the period, 21,120 metres of materials were purchased and used in production. The denominator level of activity for the period was 6,860 hours.

	Standard Cost	Actual Cost
Direct materials:		
Standard: 4.0 metres at $3.60 per metre	$14.40	
Actual: 4.4 metres at $3.35 per metre.		$14.74
Direct labour:		
Standard: 1.6 hours at $4.50 per hour	7.20	
Actual: 1.4 hours at $4.85 per hour.		6.79
Variable manufacturing overhead:		
Standard: 1.6 hours at $1.80 per hour	2.88	
Actual: 1.4 hours at $2.15 per hour.		3.01
Fixed manufacturing overhead:		
Standard: 1.6 hours at $3.00 per hour	4.80	
Actual: 1.4 hours at $3.05 per hour.		4.27
Total cost per unit	$29.28	$28.81

Actual costs: 4,800 units at $28.81.	$138,288
Standard costs: 4,800 units at $29.28	140,544
Difference in cost—favourable	$ 2,256

Required:

1. For direct materials:
   a. Compute the price and quantity variances for the period.
   b. Prepare journal entries to record all activity relating to direct materials for the period.
2. For direct labour:
   a. Compute the rate and efficiency variances.
   b. Prepare a journal entry to record the incurrence of direct labour cost for the period.
3. Compute the variable manufacturing overhead spending and efficiency variances.
4. Compute the fixed overhead budget and volume variances.
5. On seeing the $2,256 total cost variance, the company's president stated. It's obvious that our costs are well under control." Do you agree? Explain.
6. State possible causes of each variance that you have computed.

PROBLEM 10–27 Basic Variance Analysis [LO2, LO3, LO4]

Barberry, Inc., manufactures a product called Fruta. The company uses a variable costing in conjunction with standard cost system and has established the following standards for one unit of Fruta:

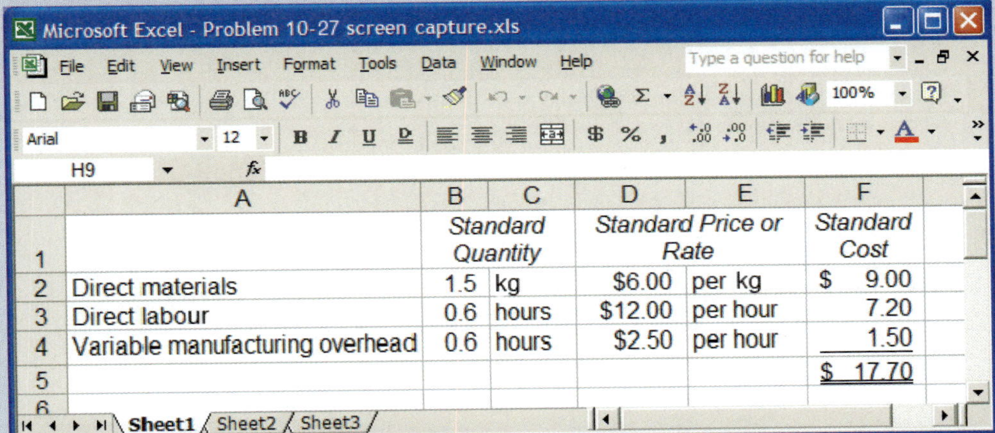

	A	B	C	D	E	F
1		Standard Quantity		Standard Price or Rate		Standard Cost
2	Direct materials	1.5	kg	$6.00	per kg	$ 9.00
3	Direct labour	0.6	hours	$12.00	per hour	7.20
4	Variable manufacturing overhead	0.6	hours	$2.50	per hour	1.50
5						$ 17.70

During June, the company recorded this activity relative to production of Fruta:

a. The company produced 3,000 units during June.
b. A total of 8,000 kilograms of material were purchased at a cost of $46,000.
c. There was no beginning inventory of materials; however, at the end of the month, 2,000 kilograms of material remained in ending inventory.

d. The company employs 10 persons to work on the production of Fruta. During June, each worked an average of 160 hours at an average rate of $12.50 per hour.
e. Variable manufacturing overhead is assigned to Fruta on the basis of direct labour-hours. Variable manufacturing overhead costs during June totalled $3,600.

The company's management is anxious to determine the efficiency of the Fruta production activities.

Required:

1. For direct materials used in the production of Fruta:
   a. Compute the price and quantity variances.
   b. The materials were purchased from a new supplier who is anxious to enter into a long-term purchase contract. Would you recommend that the company sign the contract? Explain.
2. For labour employed in the production of Fruta:
   a. Compute the rate and efficiency variances.
   b. In the past, the 10 persons employed in the production of Fruta consisted of 4 senior workers and 6 assistants. During June, the company experimented with 5 senior workers and 5 assistants. Would you recommend that the new labour mix be continued? Explain.
3. Compute the variable overhead spending and efficiency variances. What relation can you see between this efficiency variance and the labour efficiency variance?

PROBLEM 10–28 Overhead Performance Report [LO7]

Elgin Company has recently introduced budgeting as an integral part of its corporate planning process. An inexperienced member of the accounting staff was given the assignment of constructing a flexible budget for manufacturing overhead costs and prepared it in the format that follows:

Percentage of Capacity	80%	100%
Machine-hours	40,000	50,000
Utilities	$ 41,000	$ 49,000
Supplies	4,000	5,000
Indirect labour	8,000	10,000
Maintenance	37,000	41,000
Supervision	10,000	10,000
Total manufacturing overhead cost	$100,000	$115,000

The company assigns manufacturing overhead costs to production on the basis of standard machine-hours. The cost formulas used to prepare the budgeted figures above are relevant over a range of 80% to 100% of capacity in a month. The managers who will be working under these budgets have control over both fixed and variable manufacturing overhead costs.

Required:

1. Use the high-low method to separate fixed and variable costs.
2. Come up with a single cost formula for all overhead costs based on your analysis in part 1. (Hint: Your cost formula should be of the form: $y = a + bx$.)
3. During May, the company operated at 86% of machine-hour capacity. Actual manufacturing overhead costs incurred during the month were as follows:

Utilities	$ 42,540
Supplies	6,450
Indirect labour	9,890
Maintenance	35,190
Supervision	10,000
Total actual manufacturing overhead cost	$104,070

   Fixed costs had no budget variances. Prepare an overhead performance report for May. Include both fixed and variable costs in your report (in separate sections). Structure your report so that it shows only a spending variance for variable overhead. The company originally budgeted to work 40,000 machine-hours during the month; standard hours allowed for the month's production totalled 41,000 machine-hours. (Use Exhibit 10–14 as a guide.)
4. Explain possible causes of the spending variance for supplies.

PROBLEM 10–29 Setting Standards [LO1]

L'Essence is a small cosmetics company located in the perfume centre of Grasse in southern France. The company plans to introduce a new body oil, called Energique, for which it needs to develop a standard product cost. The following information is available on the production of Energique:

a. The Energique base is made by mixing select lanolin and alcohol. Some loss in volume occurs for both the lanolin and the alcohol during the mixing process. As a result, each 100-litre batch of Energique base requires 100 litres of lanolin and 8 litres of alcohol.

b. After the base has been prepared, a highly concentrated lilac powder is added to impart a pleasing scent. Only 200 grams of the powder are added to each 100-litre batch. The addition of the lilac powder does not affect the total liquid volume.

c. Both the lanolin and the lilac powder are subject to some contamination from naturally occurring materials. For example, the lilac powder often contains some traces of insects that are not detected and removed when the lilac petals are processed. Occasionally such contaminants interact in ways that result in an unacceptable product with an unpleasant odour. About one 100-litre batch in twenty is rejected as unsuitable for sale for this reason and is thrown away.

d. It takes a worker two hours to process one 100-litre batch of Energique. Employees work an eight-hour day, including two hours per day for lunch, rest breaks, and cleanup.

Required:

1. Determine the standard quantity for each of the raw materials needed to produce an acceptable 100-litre batch of Energique.
2. Determine the standard labour time allowed to produce an acceptable 100-litre batch of Energique.
3. The standard prices for direct materials and direct labour in euros (€) appear below:

Lanolin	€16 per litre
Alcohol	€2 per litre
Lilac powder	€1 per gram
Direct labour cost	€12 per hour

Prepare a standard cost card for materials and labour for one acceptable 100-litre batch of Energique.

(CMA, adapted)

PROBLEM 10–30 Applying Overhead; Overhead Variances [LO4, LO5, LO6]

Wymont Company produces a single product that requires a large amount of labour time. Overhead cost is applied on the basis of standard direct labour-hours. The company's condensed flexible budget for manufacturing overhead is given below:

Overhead Costs	Cost Formula (per DLH)	Direct Labour-Hours		
		24,000	30,000	36,000
Variable manufacturing overhead cost	$2	$ 48,000	$ 60,000	$ 72,000
Fixed manufacturing overhead cost		180,000	180,000	180,000
Total manufacturing overhead cost		$228,000	$240,000	$252,000

The company's product requires 4 metres of direct material that has a standard cost of $3 per metre. The product requires 1.5 hours of direct labour time. The standard labour rate is $12 per hour.

During the year, the company had planned to operate at a denominator activity level of 30,000 direct labour-hours and to produce 20,000 units of product. Actual activity and costs for the year were as follows:

Number of units produced	22,000
Actual direct labour-hours worked	35,000
Actual variable manufacturing overhead cost incurred	$63,000
Actual fixed manufacturing overhead cost incurred	$181,000

Required:

1. Compute the predetermined overhead rate for the year. Break the rate down into variable and fixed components.
2. Prepare a standard cost card for the company's product; show the details for all manufacturing costs on your standard cost card.
3. *a.* Compute the standard direct labour-hours allowed for the year's production.
   b. Complete the following Manufacturing Overhead T-account for the year:

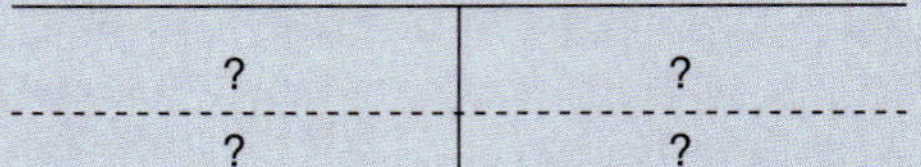

4. Determine the reason for the underapplied or overapplied overhead from (3) above by computing the variable overhead spending and efficiency variances and the fixed overhead budget and volume variances.
5. Suppose the company had chosen 36,000 direct labour-hours as the denominator activity rather than 30,000 hours. State which, if any, of the variances computed in (4) above would have changed, and explain how the variance(s) would have changed. No computations are necessary.

PROBLEM 10–31 Flexible Budget and Overhead Performance Report [LO4, LO5, LO6, LO7]

Durrant Company has had great difficulty in controlling manufacturing overhead costs. At a recent convention, the president heard about a control device for overhead costs known as a flexible budget, and he has hired you to implement this budgeting program in Durrant Company. After some effort, you have developed the following cost formulas for the company's Machining Department. These costs are based on a normal operating range of 10,000 to 20,000 machine-hours per month:

Overhead Cost	Cost Formula
Utilities	$0.70 per machine-hour
Lubricants.	$1.00 per machine-hour plus $8,000 per month
Machine setup	$0.20 per machine-hour
Indirect labour	$0.60 per machine-hour plus $120,000 per month
Depreciation	$32,000 per month

During March, the first month after your preparation of the above data, the Machining Department worked 18,000 machine-hours and produced 9,000 units of product. The actual manufacturing overhead costs for March were as follows:

Utilities	$ 12,000
Lubricants	24,500
Machine setup	4,800
Indirect labour	132,500
Depreciation.	32,000
Total manufacturing overhead cost	$205,800

Fixed costs had no budget variances. The department had originally been budgeted to work 20,000 machine-hours during March.

Required:

1. Prepare an overhead performance report for the Machining Department for the month of March. Include both variable and fixed costs in the report (in separate sections). Show only a spending variance on the report. (Use Exhibit 10–14 as your guide.)
2. What additional information would you need to compute an overhead efficiency variance for the department?

PROBLEM 10–32 Evaluating an Overhead Performance Report [LO5, LO6, LO7]

Ronald Davis, superintendent of Mason Company's Milling Department, is very happy with his performance report for the past month. The report follows:

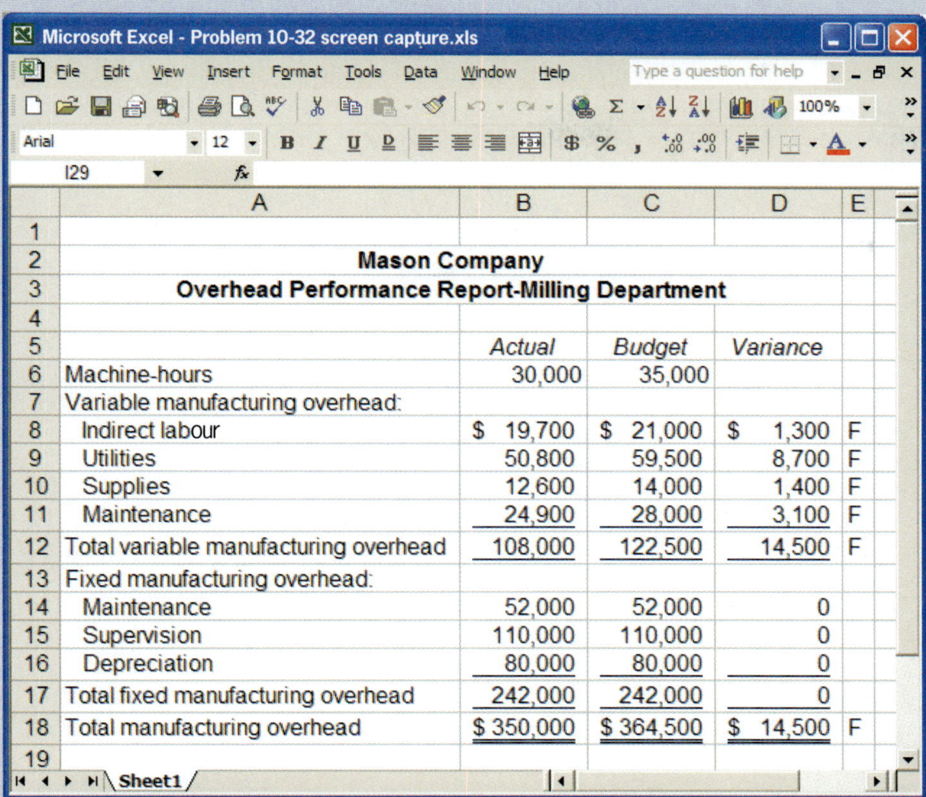

Microsoft Excel - Problem 10-32 screen capture.xls

Mason Company
Overhead Performance Report-Milling Department

	Actual	Budget	Variance	
Machine-hours	30,000	35,000		
Variable manufacturing overhead:				
Indirect labour	$ 19,700	$ 21,000	$ 1,300	F
Utilities	50,800	59,500	8,700	F
Supplies	12,600	14,000	1,400	F
Maintenance	24,900	28,000	3,100	F
Total variable manufacturing overhead	108,000	122,500	14,500	F
Fixed manufacturing overhead:				
Maintenance	52,000	52,000	0	
Supervision	110,000	110,000	0	
Depreciation	80,000	80,000	0	
Total fixed manufacturing overhead	242,000	242,000	0	
Total manufacturing overhead	$ 350,000	$ 364,500	$ 14,500	F

Upon receiving a copy of this report, John Arnold, the production manager, commented, "I've been getting these reports for months now, and I still can't see how they help me assess efficiency and cost control in that department. I agree that the budget for the month was 35,000 machine-hours, but that represents 17,500 units of product, since it should take two hours to produce one unit. The department produced only 14,000 units during the month, and took 30,000 machine-hours to do it. Why do all the variances turn up favourable?"

Required:

1. In answer to Mr. Arnold's question, why are all the variances favourable? Evaluate the performance report.
2. Prepare a new overhead performance report that will help Mr. Arnold assess efficiency and cost control in the Milling Department. (Hint: Exhibit 10–13 may be helpful in structuring your report.)

PROBLEM 10–33 Selection of a Denominator; Overhead Analysis; Standard Cost Card [LO1, LO4, LO5, LO6]

The condensed flexible budget for manufacturing overhead of the Scott Company is as follows:

Overhead Costs	Cost Formula (per DLH)	Direct Labour-Hours		
		30,000	40,000	50,000
Variable manufacturing overhead cost	$2.50	$ 75,000	$100,000	$125,000
Fixed manufacturing overhead cost		320,000	320,000	320,000
Total manufacturing overhead cost.......		$395,000	$420,000	$445,000

The company produces a single product that requires 2.5 direct labour-hours to complete. The direct labour wage rate is $20 per hour. Three metres of raw material are required for each unit of product, at a cost of $5 per metre.

Demand for the company's product differs widely from year to year. Expected activity for this year is 50,000 direct labour-hours; normal activity is 40,000 direct labour-hours per year.

Required:

1. Assume that the company chooses 40,000 direct labour-hours as the denominator level of activity. Compute the predetermined overhead rate, breaking it down into fixed and variable cost components.
2. Assume that the company chooses 50,000 direct labour-hours as the denominator level of activity. Repeat the computations in (1) above.
3. Complete two standard cost cards as outlined below.

Denominator Activity: 40,000 DLHs	
Direct materials, 3 metres at $5 per metre . .	$15.00
Direct labour, ?	?
Variable manufacturing overhead, ?	?
Fixed manufacturing overhead, ?	?
Total standard cost per unit.	$?

Denominator Activity: 50,000 DLHs	
Direct materials, 3 metres at $5 per metre . .	$15.00
Direct labour, ?	?
Variable manufacturing overhead, ?	?
Fixed manufacturing overhead, ?	?
Total standard cost per unit.	$?

4. Assume that 48,000 actual hours are worked during the year, and that 18,500 units are produced. Actual manufacturing overhead costs for the year are as follows:

Variable manufacturing overhead cost	$124,800
Fixed manufacturing overhead cost	321,700
Total manufacturing overhead cost.	$446,500

a. Compute the standard hours allowed for the year's actual output.

b. Compute the missing items from the Manufacturing Overhead account below. Assume that the company uses 40,000 direct labour-hours (normal activity) as the denominator activity figure in computing overhead rates, as you have used in (1) above.

Manufacturing Overhead		
Actual costs	446,500	?
	?	?

c. Analyze your underapplied or overapplied overhead balance in terms of variable overhead spending and efficiency variances and fixed overhead budget and volume variances.

5. Looking at the variances that you have computed, what appears to be the major disadvantage of using normal activity rather than expected actual activity as a denominator in computing the predetermined overhead rate? What advantages can you see to offset this disadvantage?

PROBLEM 10–34 Developing Standard Costs [LO1]

Le Forestier, S.A., is a small company that processes wild mushrooms found in the forests of central France. For many years, Le Forestier's products have had strong sales in France. However, companies from other countries in the European common market such as Italy and Spain have begun marketing similar products in France, and price competition has become increasingly intense. Jean Leveque, the company's controller, is planning to implement a standard cost system for Le Forestier and has gathered considerable information from the purchasing and production managers concerning production and material requirements for Le Forestier's products. Leveque believes that the use of standard costing will allow Le Forestier to improve cost control and thereby better compete with the new entrants into the French market.

Le Forestier's most popular product is dried chanterelle mushrooms, which are sold in small vacuum-packed jars. Each jar contains 15 grams of dried mushrooms. Fresh mushrooms are purchased for €60 per kilogram in bulk from individuals who gather them from local forests. (€ stands for euro, the currency used in France, and a kilogram is 1,000 grams.) Because of imperfections in the mushrooms and normal spoilage, one-quarter of the fresh mushrooms are discarded. Fifteen minutes is the direct labour time required for inspecting and sorting per kilogram of fresh mushrooms. After sorting and inspecting, the acceptable mushrooms are flash-dried, which requires 10 minutes of direct labour time per kilogram of acceptable, sorted, and inspected fresh mushrooms. The flash-drying removes most of the moisture content of the mushrooms and therefore drastically reduces their weight. Flash-drying reduces the weight of the acceptable mushrooms by 80%. As a consequence, a kilogram of *acceptable* fresh mushrooms yields only about 200 grams of dried mushrooms. After drying, the mushrooms are vacuum-packed in small jars and labels are applied.

Direct labour is paid at the rate of €12 per hour. The cost of the glass jars, lids, and labels is €10 per 100 jars. The labour time required to pack 100 jars is 10 minutes.

Required:

1. Develop the standard cost for the direct labour and materials cost components of a single jar of dried chanterelle mushrooms, including the costs of the mushrooms, inspecting and sorting, drying, and packing.
2. Jean Leveque wonders who should be held responsible—the purchasing manager or the production manager—for the materials variances for the chanterelle mushrooms.
   a. Who should be held responsible for the materials price variances for the chanterelle mushrooms? Explain.
   b. Who should be held responsible for the materials quantity variances for the chanterelle mushrooms? Explain.

PROBLEM 10–35 Materials and Labour Variances; Computations from Incomplete Data [LO1, LO2, LO3]

Topaz Company produces a single product. The company has set standards as follows for materials and labour:

	Direct Materials	Direct Labour
Standard quantity or hours per unit . . .	? kilograms	2.5 hours
Standard price or rate	? per kilogram	$9 per hour
Standard cost per unit	?	$22.50

During the past month, the company purchased 6,000 kilograms of direct materials at a cost of $16,500. All of this material was used in the production of 1,400 units of product. Direct labour cost totalled $28,500 for the month. The following variances have been computed:

Materials quantity variance . . .	$1,200 U
Total materials variance	$300 F
Labour efficiency variance . . .	$4,500 F

Required:

1. For direct materials:
   a. Compute the standard price per kilogram for materials.
   b. Compute the standard quantity allowed for materials for the month's production.
   c. Compute the standard quantity of materials allowed per unit of product.
2. For direct labour:
   a. Compute the actual direct labour cost per hour for the month.
   b. Compute the labour rate variance.

(Hint: In completing the problem, it may be helpful to move from known to unknown data either by using the variance formulas or by using the columnar format shown in Exhibits 10–4 and 10–6.)

PROBLEM 10–36 (Appendix 10B) Comprehensive Variance Analysis with Incomplete Data; Journal Entries [LO2, LO3, LO4, LO5, LO6, LO9]

Topline Surf Boards manufactures a single product. The standard cost of one unit of this product is as follows:

Direct materials: 2 metres at $3 per metre	$ 6.00
Direct labour: 1 hour at $4.50 per hour	4.50
Variable manufacturing overhead: 1 hour at $3 per hour	3.00
Fixed manufacturing overhead: 1 hour at $5 per hour	5.00
Total standard variable cost per unit	$18.50

During October, 6,000 units were produced. Selected data relating to the month's production follow:

Material purchased: 20,000 metres at $2.85 per metre	$57,000
Material used in production: 12,650 metres	—
Direct labour: __?__ hours at $ __?__ per hour.	$27,950
Variable manufacturing overhead cost incurred	$20,475
Variable manufacturing overhead efficiency variance . .	$1,500 U
Denominator level of activity for October	6,200 hours
Fixed manufacturing overhead budget variance.	1,000 U

There was no beginning inventory of raw materials. The variable and fixed manufacturing overhead rates are based on direct labour-hours.

Required:

1. For direct materials:
   a. Compute the price and quantity variances for October.
   b. Prepare journal entries to record activity for October.
2. For direct labour:
   a. Compute the rate and efficiency variances for October.
   b. Prepare a journal entry to record labour activity for October.
3. For variable manufacturing overhead:
   a. Compute the spending variance for October, and verify the efficiency variance given above.
   b. If manufacturing overhead is applied to production on the basis of direct labour-hours, is it possible to have a favourable direct labour efficiency variance and an unfavourable variable overhead efficiency variance? Explain.
4. For fixed manufacturing overhead:
   a. Compute the volume variance for October.
   b. Compute actual costs for October.
5. State possible causes of each variance that you have computed.

PROBLEM 10–37 Comprehensive Variance Analysis [LO2, LO3, LO4, LO5, LO6]
Helix Company produces several products in its factory, including a karate robe. The company uses a standard cost system to assist in the control of costs. According to the standards that have been set for the robes, the factory has a denominator activity level of 780 direct labour-hours each month which should result in the production of 1,950 robes. The standard costs associated with this level of production are as follows:

	Total	Per Unit of Product
Direct materials	$35,490	$18.20
Direct labour	$7,020	3.60
Variable manufacturing overhead*	$2,340	1.20
Fixed manufacturing overhead*	$4,680	2.40
		$25.40

*Based on direct labour-hours

During April, the factory worked only 760 direct labour-hours and produced 2,000 robes. The following actual costs were recorded during the month:

	Total	Per Unit of Product
Direct materials (6,000 metres)	$36,000	$18.00
Direct labour	$7,600	3.80
Variable manufacturing overhead	$3,800	1.90
Fixed manufacturing overhead	$4,600	2.30
		$26.00

At standard, each robe should require 2.8 metres of material. All of the materials purchased during the month were used in production.

Required:

Compute the following variances for April:

1. The materials price and quantity variances.
2. The labour rate and efficiency variances.
3. The variable manufacturing overhead spending and efficiency variances.
4. The fixed manufacturing overhead budget and volume variances.

PROBLEM 10–38 Overhead Performance Report [LO7]

Ronson Products, Ltd., an Australian company, has the following cost formulas (expressed in Australian dollars) for variable overhead costs in one of its machine shops:

Variable Overhead Cost	Cost Formula (per machine-hour)
Supplies.........	$0.70
Power	1.20
Lubrication.......	0.50
Wearing tools	3.10
Total	$5.50

The flexible budget amounts for fixed overhead costs in July are as follows:

Fixed Overhead Cost	Flexible Budget
Depreciation	$10,000
Supervisory salaries	14,000
Maintenance...........	3,000
Total	$27,000

During July, the machine shop was scheduled to work 3,200 machine-hours and to produce 16,000 units of product. The standard machine time per unit of product is 0.2 hours. A severe storm during the month forced the company to close for several days, which reduced the level of output for the month. Actual results for July were as follows:

Actual machine-hours worked	2,700
Actual number of units produced	14,000

Actual costs for July were:

Overhead Costs	Total Actual Cost	Per Machine-Hour
Variable overhead costs:		
Supplies	$1,836	$0.68
Power	3,348	1.24
Lubrication	1,485	0.55
Wearing tools	8,154	3.02
Total variable overhead	14,823	$5.49
Fixed overhead costs:		
Depreciation	10,000	–
Supervisory salaries	14,600	–
Maintenance	2,500	–
Total fixed overhead	27,100	–
Total overhead	$41,923	

Required:

Prepare an overhead performance report including both variable and fixed overhead for the machine shop for July. Use column headings in your report as shown below:

Overhead Item	Cost Formula (per MH)	Actual Costs Incurred, 2,700 MHs	Flexible Budget Based on 2,700 MHs	Flexible Budget Based on 2,800 MHs	Total Variance	Breakdown of the Total Variance	
						Spending Variance	Efficiency Variance

PROBLEM 10–39 (Appendix 10A) Mix and Yield Variances [LO8]

Dundas Company manufactures and sells two special purpose cleaning solvents, Brill and Daz. The two products emerge from the same production process, which requires three materials: C12, D24, and E48. The division developed standard costs for these two solvents as shown below.

Normal monthly volume is 22,000 kilograms of input materials processed or 20,000 kilograms of good output. Some variations of input quantities are permissible without affecting the quality of the finished products.

Joint Processing Costs		
Materials—C12	12 kilograms at $4.80 per kilogram	$ 57.60
—D24	8 kilograms at 8.40 per kilogram	67.20
—E48	2 kilograms at 10.30 per kilogram	20.60
Total materials input	22 kilograms	145.40
Labour (applied at $11.20 per kilogram × 22 kilograms)		246.40
Overhead—Variable (applied at $5.60 per kilogram × 22 kilograms)		123.20
—Fixed (applied at $10.00 per kilogram × 22 kilograms)		220.00
Joint costs to produce 20 kilograms of good output		$735.00

Costs Assigned to the Two Joint Products Using Market Value

Product	Good Output	Per Kilogram	Total	Joint* Costs	Standard Cost Per Kilogram
Brill	14 kilograms	$40	$560	$420.00	$30.00
Daz	6 kilograms	70	420	315.00	52.50
	20 kilograms		$980	$735.00	

*Joint costs are allocated to the products on the basis of market value.

Materials are purchased from another division and are readily available; therefore, very little raw material inventory is kept by Dundas Company. Material prices are negotiated annually between the divisions. All production is finished daily; therefore, there are no work in process inventories.

Actual production of good output in July amounted to 22,800 kilograms. The production costs were calculated as follows:

Materials input—C12.	15,000 kilograms at $4.80 per kilogram	$ 72,000
—D24.	8,100 kilograms at 8.40 per kilogram	68,040
—E48.	2,200 kilograms at 10.30 per kilogram	22,660
Total Input	25,300 kilograms	$162,700
Labour for 25,300 kilograms processed		$283,360
Good output: Brill 15,800 kilograms		
Daz 7,000 kilograms		

Required:

Calculate the material and labour cost variances in as much detail as the data permit for the Dundas Company for the month of July. Comment on the performance of the production function of the Dundas Company during July by explaining the significance of the variances you calculated.

(SMAC, Adapted)

PROBLEM 10–40 Capacity Analysis [LO7]

The Yardman Company produces electric weed trimmers, among other products. The following standard costs per unit are associated with the trimmers:

Item	Quantity	Cost per unit
Direct materials	4 pieces at $5.00	$20.00
Direct labour.	2 hours at $12.00	24.00
Variable overhead . . .	2 hours at $3.00	6.00
Fixed overhead	2 hours at $5.00	10.00
Total		$60.00

Normal activity of 60,000 hours was used as the denominator level. Other possible capacity levels were:

Expected annual	55,000 hours
Practical annual	75,000 hours
Theoretical annual	100,000 hours

An analysis of the difference between practical and theoretical capacity for the past year showed the following: 10,000 hours were not used because management decided not to employ two crews of workers. A further 5,000 hours of capacity had to be assigned to set-up when machines were switched from one product to another. Another 5,000 hours was not used because scheduled maintenance of production equipment was required. Finally, the remaining 5,000 hours of theoretical capacity was not used because existing markets could not use all of the theoretical capacity without a substantial reduction in selling price. Management approached the Marketing department to determine what pricing policy would be needed to move from the denominator level of activity (30,000 units) to practical capacity (37,500 units). Marketing suggested that a price reduction of 10% below the existing selling price of $80 would increase demand from 30,000 units to 37,500 units.

Marketing also indicated that to move from practical capacity (37,500 units) to theoretical capacity (50,000 units) two crews would need to be hired, set-ups eliminated, and maintenance deferred. A further 10% price reduction below the existing $80 would also be needed to increase demand by another 12,500 units.

Required:

Analyze the profit implications of the potential capacity selections available to management at Yardman.

Cases

CASE 10–41 Ethics and the Manager; Rigging Standards [LO1]

Stacy Cummins, the newly hired controller at Merced Home Products, Inc., was disturbed by what she had discovered about the standard costs at the Home Security Division. In looking over the past several years of quarterly earnings reports at the Home Security Division, she noticed that the first-quarter earnings were always poor, the second-quarter earnings were slightly better, the third-quarter earnings were again slightly better, and the fourth quarter always ended with a spectacular performance in which the Home Security Division managed to meet or exceed its target profit for the year. She also was concerned to find letters from the company's external auditors to top management warning about an unusual use of standard costs at the Home Security Division.

When Ms. Cummins ran across these letters, she asked the assistant controller, Gary Farber, if he knew what was going on at the Home Security Division. Gary said that it was common knowledge in the company that the vice-president in charge of the Home Security Division, Preston Lansing, had rigged the standards at his division in order to produce the same quarterly earnings pattern every year. According to company policy, variances are taken directly to the income statement as an adjustment to cost of goods sold.

Favourable variances have the effect of increasing operating income, and unfavourable variances have the effect of decreasing operating income. Lansing had rigged the standards so that there were always large favourable variances. Company policy was a little vague about when these variances have to be reported on the divisional income statements. While the intent was clearly to recognize variances on the income statement in the period in which they arise, nothing in the company's accounting manuals actually explicitly required this. So for many years Lansing had followed a practice of saving up the favourable variances and using them to create a nice smooth pattern of earnings growth in the first three quarters, followed by a big "Christmas present" of an extremely good fourth quarter. (Financial reporting regulations forbid carrying variances forward from one year to the next on the annual audited financial statements, so all of the variances must appear on the divisional income statement by the end of the year.)

Ms. Cummins was concerned about these revelations and attempted to bring up the subject with the president of Merced Home Products but was told that "we all know what Lansing's doing, but as long as he continues to turn in such good reports, don't bother him." When Ms. Cummins asked if the board of directors was aware of the situation, the president somewhat testily replied, "Of course they are aware."

Required:

1. How did Preston Lansing probably "rig" the standard costs—are the standards set too high or too low? Explain.
2. Should Preston Lansing be permitted to continue his practice of managing reported earnings?
3. What should Stacy Cummins do in this situation?

CASE 10–42 Behavioural Impact of Standard Costs and Variances [LO1]

Terry Travers is the manufacturing supervisor of Aurora Manufacturing Company, which produces a variety of plastic products. Some of these products are standard items that are listed in the company's catalogue, while others are made to customer specifications. Each month, Travers receives a performance report showing the budget for the month, the actual activity, and the variance between budget and actual. Part of Travers' annual performance evaluation is based on his department's performance against budget. Aurora's purchasing manager, Sally Christensen, also receives monthly performance reports and she, too, is evaluated in part on the basis of these reports.

The monthly reports for June had just been distributed when Travers met Christensen in the hallway outside their offices. Scowling, Travers began the conversation, "I see we have another set of monthly performance reports hand-delivered by that not very nice junior employee in the budget office. He seemed pleased to tell me that I'm in trouble with my performance again."

Christensen: I got the same treatment. All I ever hear about are the things I've done wrong. Now I'll have to spend a lot of time reviewing the report and preparing explanations. The worst part is that it's now the 21st of July so the information is almost a month old, and we have to spend all this time on history.

Travers: My biggest gripe is that our production activity varies a lot from month to month, but we're given an annual budget that's written in stone. Last month we were shut down for three days when a strike delayed delivery of the basic ingredient used in our plastic formulation, and we had already exhausted our inventory. You know about that problem, though, because we asked you to call all over the country to find an alternate source of supply. When we got what we needed on a rush basis, we had to pay more than we normally do.

Christensen: I expect problems like that to pop up from time to time—that's part of my job—but now we'll both have to take a careful look at our reports to see where the charges are reflected for that rush order. Every month I spend more time making sure I should be charged for each item reported than I do making plans for my department's daily work. It's really frustrating to see charges for things I have no control over.

Travers: The way we get information doesn't help, either. I don't get copies of the reports you get, yet a lot of what I do is affected by your department, and by most of our other departments. Why do the budget and accounting people assume that I should only be told about my operations even though the president regularly gives us pep talks about how we all need to work together as a team?

Christensen: I seem to get more reports than I need, and I am never asked to comment on them until top management calls me on the carpet about my department's shortcomings. Do you ever hear comments when your department shines?

Travers: I guess they don't have time to review the good news. One of my problems is that all the reports are in dollars and cents. I work with people, machines, and materials. I need information to help me solve *this* month's problems—not another report of the dollars expended *last* month or the month before.

Required:

1. Based on the conversation between Terry Travers and Sally Christensen, describe the likely motivation and behaviour of these two employees resulting from Aurora Manufacturing Company's standard cost and variance reporting system.
2. When properly implemented, both employees and companies should benefit from a system involving standard costs and variances.
   a. Describe the benefits that can be realized from a standard cost system.
   b. Based on the situation presented above, recommend ways for Aurora Manufacturing Company to improve its standard cost and variance reporting system so as to increase employee motivation.

(CMA, adapted)

CASE 10–43 Ethics and the Manager [LO7]

Lance Prating is the controller of the Red Deer manufacturing facility of Tech Systems, Incorporated. Among the many reports that must be filed with corporate headquarters is the annual overhead performance report. The report covers the year which ends on December 31 and is due at corporate headquarters shortly after the beginning of the new year. Prating does not like putting work off to the last minute, so just before Christmas he put together a preliminary draft of the overhead performance report. Some adjustments would later be required for the few transactions that occur between Christmas and New Year's Day. A copy of the preliminary draft report, which Prating completed on December 21, is shown on the next page.

Tab Kapp, the general manager at the Red Deer facility, asked to see a copy of the preliminary draft report at 4:45 P.M. on December 23. Prating carried a copy of the report to Kapp's office where the following discussion took place:

Kapp: Wow! Almost all of the variances on the report are unfavourable. The only thing that looks good at all are the favourable variances for supervisory salaries and for industrial engineering. How did we have an unfavourable variance for depreciation?

Prating: Do you remember that milling machine that broke down because the wrong lubricant was used by the machine operator?

Kapp: Only vaguely.

Prating: It turned out we couldn't fix it. We had to scrap the machine and buy a new one.

Kapp: This report doesn't look good. I was raked over the coals last year when we had just a few unfavourable variances.

Prating: I'm afraid the final report is going to look even worse.

Kapp: Oh?

Prating: The line item for industrial engineering on the report is for work we hired Klein Engineering to do for us on a contract basis. The original contract was for $160,000, but we asked them to do some additional work that was not in the contract. Under the terms of the contract, we have to reimburse Klein Engineering for the costs of the additional work. The $154,000 in actual costs that appear on the preliminary draft report reflects only their billings through December 21. The last bill they had sent us was on November 28, and they completed the project just last week. Yesterday I got a call from Maria over at Klein and she said they would be sending us a final bill for the project before the end of the year. The total bill, including the reimbursements for the additional work, is going to be . . .

Kapp: I am not sure I want to hear this.

Prating: $176,000.

Kapp: Ouch!

Prating: The additional work we asked them to do added $16,000 to the cost of the project.

Kapp: No way can I turn in a performance report with an overall unfavourable variance. They'll kill me at corporate headquarters. Call up Maria at Klein and ask her not to send the bill until after the first of the year. We have to have that $6,000 favourable variance for industrial engineering on the performance report.

Red Deer Manufacturing Facility
Overhead Performance Report
December 21 Preliminary Draft

Budgeted machine-hours	100,000
Actual machine-hours	90,000

Overhead Costs	Cost Formula (per machine-hour)	Actual Costs for 90,000 Machine-Hours	Flexible Budget Based on 90,000 Machine-Hours	Spending or Budget Variance
Variable overhead costs:				
Power	$0.03	$ 2,840	$ 2,700	$ 140 U
Supplies	0.86	79,060	77,400	1,660 U
Abrasives	0.34	32,580	30,600	1,980 U
Total variable overhead cost	$1.23	114,480	110,700	3,780 U
Fixed overhead costs:				
Depreciation		228,300	226,500	1,800 U
Supervisory salaries		187,300	189,000	1,700 F
Insurance		23,000	23,000	0
Industrial engineering		154,000	160,000	6,000 F
Factory building lease		46,000	46,000	0
Total fixed overhead cost.		638,600	644,500	5,900 F
Total overhead cost		$753,080	$755,200	$2,120 F

Required:

What should Lance Prating do? Explain.

CASE 10–44 Working Backwards from Variance Data [LO2, LO3, LO4, LO6]

You have recently graduated from university and have accepted a position with Vibiz, Inc., the manufacturer of a popular consumer product. During your first week on the job, the vice-president has been favourably impressed with your work. She has been so impressed, in fact, that yesterday she called you into her office and asked you to attend the executive committee meeting this morning for the purpose of leading a discussion on the variances reported for last period. Anxious to favourably impress the executive committee, you took the variances and supporting data home last night on a memory stick to study.

Unfortunately, when you tried to open the files this morning some of them had become corrupted. All you could retrieve is shown at the top of the next page.

You recall that manufacturing overhead cost is applied to production on the basis of direct labour-hours and that all of the materials purchased during the period were used in production. Since the company uses JIT to control work flows, work in process inventories are insignificant and can be ignored.

Standard Cost Card

Direct materials, 6 kilograms at $6 per kilogram	$36.00
Direct labour, 0.8 direct labour-hours at $30 per direct labour-hour	24.00
Variable manufacturing overhead, 0.8 direct labour-hours at $6 per direct labour-hour	4.80
Fixed manufacturing overhead, 0.8 direct labour-hours at $14 per direct labour-hour	11.20
Standard cost per unit	$76.00

	Total Standard Cost*	Variances Reported			
		Price or Rate	Spending or Budget	Quantity or Efficiency	Volume
Direct materials	$810,000	$13,800 F		$18,000 U	
Direct labour	$540,000	$29,100 U		$42,000 U	
Variable manufacturing overhead	$108,000		$2,600 F	$?† U	
Fixed manufacturing overhead	$252,000		$1,000 F		$28,000 U

*Applied to Work in Process during the period.
†Data corrupted.

It is now 8:30 A.M. The executive committee meeting starts in just one hour; you realize that to avoid looking like a bungling fool you must somehow generate the necessary "backup" data for the variances before the meeting begins. Without backup data it will be impossible to lead the discussion or answer any questions.

Required:

1. How many units were produced last period? (Think hard about this one!)
2. How many kilograms of direct material were purchased and used in production?
3. What was the actual cost per kilogram of material?
4. How many actual direct labour-hours were worked during the period?
5. What was the actual rate paid per direct labour-hour?
6. How much actual variable manufacturing overhead cost was incurred during the period?
7. What is the total fixed manufacturing overhead cost in the company's flexible budget?
8. What were the denominator direct labour-hours for last period?

CASE 10–45 Full Variance Analysis: Direct Costing [LO3, LO4, LO5, LO6]

Abbotsford Tech Limited manufactures and distributes intergrated circuits for electronics firms. In December 2007, Abbotsford required a bank loan and the bank manager insisted that Christy Dasilva, Abbotsford's president, prepare a budget for 2008. In January 2009 Abbotsford needed an additional loan and Dasilva asked her accountant to prepare a budget for 2009 to show the bank manager. Dasilva was concerned because Abbotsford's profit for 2008 was considerably less than the 2008 budget figure given the bank and she knew that the bank manager would want to know why. As a first step in analyzing the differences, Dasilva copied the 2008 actual figures onto a 2008 bank budget form shown at the top of the next page.

Required:

1. Redraft the budget to show the 2008 static budget, flexible budget, actual, and variances from the flexible budget, with contribution margins separately identified.
2. Present quantitive analysis to demonstrate to management the main causes for the variance from the flexible budget, as a basis both for taking corrective action and for explaining the variance from the static budget to the bank manager.
3. If anticipated 2009 operating results are similar to 2008, explain to the bank manager how much of the loan you would be able to repay from 2009 earnings. (Assume no changes in accounts receivable and accounts payable.)
4. If competition became intense in 2009, and Abbotsford was operating well below capacity at 85,000 units, explain with calculation the minimum bid you would make on an order for 10,000 units.
5. What changes to the management accounting and reporting system for Abbotsford Tech would you propose?

(CGAC, Adapted)

Abbotsford Tech Limted
2008 Budget Prepared for Bank Loan

	Dollars in (000s)		
	Static Budget	**Actual**	**Variance**
Sales—units	110,000	105,000	5,000 U
Sales—dollars	$5,500	$5,040	$ 460 U
Cost of sales:			
Materials	880	842	38 F
Labour	1,760	1,690	70 F
Overhead.	440	410	30 F
Fixed factory overhead	600	606	6 U
	3,680	3,548	132 F
Gross profit	1,820	1,492	328 U
Selling expenses:			
Variable	440	418	22 F
Fixed	200	204	4 U
Administration—fixed	400	394	6 F
	1,040	1,016	24 F
Profit before income tax	780	476	304 U
Income tax	312	190	122 F
Net earnings	$ 468	$ 286	$ 182 U

Standard Costs on Which Budget Is Based

		Standard per Unit
Sales price		$50
Direct Material		$ 8
Labour 1/2 hour at $32 per hour		16
Overhead 1/2 hour at $8 per hour		4
Fixed factory overhead:		
Depreciation	$400,000	
Other	200,000	
	600,000	
Standard output 100,000 units at 1/2 hour = 50,000 direct labour hours		
($600,000 ÷ 50,000) × 1/2 hour		6
Selling expenses:		
Variable		4
Fixed $200,000 ÷ 100,000 units		2
Administration Fixed:		
$400,000 ÷ 100,000 units		4
		$44

Standard costs were used for preparing bids whereas the cost accounting system recorded actual costs.

Research

R 10–46 Standard Costing in Practice [LO1]
Identify a company in your local area that is likely to use standards and conduct variance analysis, such as a manufacturer, a chain restaurant, a service department at an auto dealership or a commercial bakery. Once you have determined that the company uses standards, set up a meeting with a manager in the financial reporting department.

Required:
At the meeting, get answers to the following questions:

1. Which types of variances are calculated (price, efficiency, etc.)?
2. How often are they calculated?
3. How do managers decide which variances to investigate?
4. Are favourable and unfavourable variances investigated?
5. What is the mechanism for reviewing the explanations provided for variances?
6. What are some examples of corrective actions taken as the result of a variance investigation?
7. How often are standards updated or revised?

R 10–47 Overhead Reporting and Control [LO7]
Identify a company in your local area that is likely to have significant manufacturing overhead costs. An example would be a manufacturing company that has automated at least some of its production activities.

Once you have determined that the company uses standards, set up a meeting with a manager in the financial reporting department.

Required:
At the meeting, get answers to the following questions:
1. How are overhead costs controlled in the organization?
2. What types of performance reports are prepared for overhead?
3. How often are performance reports prepared for overhead?
4. Does the company distinguish between variable and fixed overhead in its reporting and control system?
5. How are overhead costs allocated to products or services?
6. What is the biggest challenge in managing overhead costs?

R 10–48 Issues with Standard Costs [LO1]
As you know, the World Wide Web is a medium that is constantly evolving. Sites come and go, and change without notice. To enable the periodic updating of site addresses, this problem has been posted to the textbook web site (**www.mcgrawhill.ca/olc/garrison**). After accessing the site, enter the Student Centre and select this chapter. Select and complete the Internet Exercise.

CHAPTER 11

LEARNING OBJECTIVES

After studying Chapter 11, you should be able to:

1. Differentiate among responsibility centres such as cost centres, profit centres, and investment centres, and explain how performance is measured in each.
2. Determine the range, if any, within which a negotiated transfer price should fall and explain other approaches to setting the transfer price.
3. Analyze the return on investment (ROI).
4. Compute residual income and describe the strengths and weaknesses of this method of measuring performance.
5. Explain the use of balanced scorecards to assess performance.
6. Identify the four types of quality costs, explain their interaction and prepare a quality cost report.
7. (Appendix 11A) Analyze variances from sales budgets.
8. (Appendix 11B) Analyze marketing expenses using cost drivers.

REPORTING FOR CONTROL

BUSINESS FOCUS

Managing Performance: How Well Are We Doing?

A recent survey of nearly 2,100 financial professionals at Canadian companies was conducted to find out how well Canadian companies are doing at managing their financial and operational performance. In light of the amount of attention given in the business press over the past 10 years to the development and use of more sophisticated performance measurement systems, some of the findings are surprising. For example, when asked to rate the overall performance of their organization (e.g., revenues, profits) almost one-third of respondents indicated that it is *below* target. Of those companies attempting to use more comprehensive performance measurement systems that incorporate both financial and non-financial metrics (e.g., number of customer complaints), almost half claimed they did not believe it had helped their financial performance. Perhaps even more surprising is the finding that a large majority of the respondents indicated that they were in the very early stages of developing better performance measurement systems. Of these respondents, many claimed they still use traditional reporting and control systems focused on financial performance measures and are just beginning to implement non-financial metrics.

These results suggest that despite the growing popularity of comprehensive performance measurement approaches such as the balanced scorecard (discussed in this chapter), many companies are struggling to put the pieces together. The survey responses provide some clues as to the nature of the obstacles. First, many companies are not doing a good job of linking their performance measures to the strategic objectives of the firm. The survey respondents who are having success in managing performance indicated that identifying the key drivers of strategic performance and measuring them is critically important. Second, the cost and difficulty of acquiring data for some performance measures (e.g., customer satisfaction) can be prohibitive. Many companies know what they want to measure, but gathering and analyzing the data is expensive. Finally, many companies fail to set specific targets for the metrics used at the departmental or individual level. While having organizational level targets for revenue growth or return on investment is important, it is essential to cascade these goals to the lower levels of the organization to ensure all employees understand their performance expectations.

Source: Robert Angel and Daryl-Lynn Carlson, "Why Don't They Just Do It," *CA Magazine*, August 2007, pp. 28–33.

Managers of organizations determine the direction they wish the organization to take. *Strategic planning* is the term applied to this planning process. Budgeting is the financial expression of the plans. The short-term version of budgeting was presented in Chapter 9, while Chapter 13 describes long-term capital budgets. Planning, however, is only part of the management process. Through a combination of feedback of actual results, comparisons to budgets, comparisons to results of previous periods, and even comparisons to other organizations, managers attempt to ensure that the organization moves in the planned direction, termed performance assessment or control.

Managers control the organization using a variety of approaches. Accounting reports of financial results represent one important approach to controlling operations because such reports provide a means of obtaining comparisons to budgets, to previous results, and to the results of other organizations, as well as providing a knowledge of actual financial results. Such financial comparisons also serve as a base for reward schemes or contracts used to motivate managers to work toward the achievement of planned goals and objectives.

These financial performance reports can be constructed in various ways so that they better serve the specific control functions that management desires. As this chapter illustrates, responsibility centre reporting, investment performance, and profitability analysis are three commonly used reporting structures that provide somewhat different types of information. Each presents information in a manner that permits a different view of the organization and a different aspect of organizational control. Understanding how the aspects change and why managers would want these changes will permit you to integrate the concepts of control with reports about standard cost variances, cost of production, and flexible budget analyses described in earlier chapters.

The modern manufacturing environment has promoted the need for flexibility in management to accompany flexibility in production. Flexibility in management requires timely and accurate decisions by members of the organization ranging from top management to the production worker. Timely and accurate decisions require timely and accurate control information appropriate to this wide range of organizational personnel. Providing information to operating or production workers so they can monitor and conrol their operations has posed an interesting challenge for accountants. Traditional reports have been considered too aggregated for operating workers. Accounting formats often represent approaches that are not well understood by production workers. Monthly reports, the common management accounting reporting period, are not timely enough to provide a review of operations that may change daily. Some accounting conventions, such as expensing items that are viewed as assets, can distort realities or misdirect attention so that incorrect control decisions can occur.

Study is ongoing to rectify some of the deficiencies. Increasingly, companies are using non-financial indicators of performance such as scrap levels, rework efforts, market share, employee morale, pollutant discharges, and customer satisfaction. The process of collecting and presenting these data on a real-time basis is assisted by computer systems. Properly configured enterprise resource planning (ERP) systems enable the operational and financial data to be maintained consistently by using a common interactive database. A sufficiently large computer system with well-specified operational practices can provide the timely data needed for operational purposes. The term *balanced scorecard* is a best practice approach accepted by ERP system suppliers and others as a means of organizing and presenting this array of data.

This chapter provides an explanation of common financial performance indicators as well as the balanced scorecard, a performance measurement framework that incorporates non-financial indicators. More than ever, organizations are using a combination of financial and non-financial measures in their reporting and control systems. Integrating material on performance from previous chapters with discussions in this and later chapters will provide you with a foundation for understanding developments in performance reporting.

Decentralization in Organizations

Decentralized organization An organization in which decision making is spread throughout the organization rather than being confined to a few top executives.

In a **decentralized organization** decision making is spread throughout the organization, rather than being confined to a few top executives. All large organizations are decentralized to some extent out of necessity. At one extreme, a strongly decentralized organization is one in which there are few, if any, constraints on the freedom of even the lowest-level managers and employees to make decisions. At the other extreme, in a strongly centralized organization, lower-level managers have little freedom to make decisions. Most organizations fall somewhere between these two extremes.

Decentralization and Segment Reporting

Effective decentralization requires *segment reporting* to permit an analysis and evaluation of the decisions made by the segment managers. In addition to the companywide income statement, reports are needed for individual segments of the organization. In Chapter 8, a segment was defined as a part or activity of an organization about which managers would like cost, revenue, or profit data. As we saw in Chapter 8, a company's operations can be segmented in many ways. For example, a grocery store chain like Loblaws or Sobeys can segment its business by geographic region, by individual store, by the nature of the merchandise (i.e., fresh foods, canned goods, paper goods), by brand name, and so on. In this chapter, we consider segment reporting again as part of our discussion of responsibility centres, which are defined in the next section. As we will see, it is possible to classify segments according to managers' ability to control revenues, costs and profits. Importantly, the tools used to evaluate segment managers' performance depend directly on what they have control over. You may find it useful at this point to review the details of preparing segment reports presented in Chapter 8, including the distinction between traceable and common costs.

Cost, Profit, and Investment Centres

LEARNING OBJECTIVE 1
Differentiate among responsibility centres such as cost centres, profit centres, and investment centres, and explain how performance is measured in each.

Responsibility centre Any business segment whose manager has control over cost or profit or the use of investment funds.

Cost centre A business segment whose manager has control over cost but has no control over revenue or the use of investment funds.

Profit centre A business segment whose manager has control over cost and revenue but has no control over the use of investment funds.

A **responsibility centre** is broadly defined as any part of an organization whose manager has control over and is accountable for cost, profit, or investments. The three primary types of responsibility centres are cost centres, profit centres, and investment centres.[1] As discussed below, organizations categorize responsibility centres into one of these three types based on the manager's authority to control cost, revenue, and investment funds.

Cost Centre A **cost centre** is a business segment whose manager has control over costs but not over revenue or investment funds. Service departments, such as accounting, finance, general administration, legal, personnel, and so on, are usually considered to be cost centres. In addition, manufacturing facilities are often considered to be cost centres. The managers of cost centres are expected to minimize cost while providing the level of services or the amount of products demanded by the other parts of the organization. For example, the manager of a production facility would be evaluated at least in part by comparing actual costs to how much the costs should have been for the actual number of units produced during the period. Standard cost variances and flexible budget variances discussed in Chapter 10 are often used to evaluate cost centre performance. However, as pointed out in Chapter 8, managers should not be held accountable for controlling common costs, arbitrarily allocated to their segment.

Profit Centre In contrast to a cost centre, a **profit centre** is any business segment whose manager has control over both cost and revenue. Like a cost centre, however, a

1. Some companies classify business segments that are responsible mainly for generating revenue, such as an insurance sales office, as *revenue centres.* Other companies would consider this to be just another type of profit centre, since costs of some kind (salaries, rent, utilities) are usually deducted from the revenues in the segment's income statement.

profit centre manager generally does not have control over investment funds. For example, the manager in charge of one of six resorts would be responsible for both the revenues and costs, and hence the profits, of the resort but may not have control over major investments in the resort. Profit centre managers are often evaluated by comparing actual profit to targeted or budgeted profit.

Investment Centre An **investment centre** is any segment of an organization whose manager has control over cost, revenue, and investments in operating assets. For example, the president of General Motors Canada would have a great deal of discretion over investments in the division. The president of the division would be responsible for initiating investment proposals, such as funding research into more fuel-efficient engines for sport-utility vehicles. Once the proposal has been approved by the top level of managers at General Motors Canada and the board of directors, the president of the division would then be responsible for making sure that the investment pays off. Investment centre managers are usually evaluated using return on investment or residual income measures, as discussed later in the chapter.

Investment centre A business segment whose manager has control over cost and revenue and also has control over the use of investment funds.

A partial organization chart for Universal Foods Corporation, a company in the snack food and beverage industry, appears in Exhibit 11–1. This partial organization chart indicates how the various business segments of the company are classified in terms of responsibility. Note that the cost centres are the departments and work centres that do not generate significant revenues by themselves. These are staff departments such as finance, legal, and personnel, and operating units such as the bottling plant, warehouse, and beverage distribution centre. The profit centres are business segments that generate revenues and include the beverage, salty snacks, and confections product segments. The vice-president of operations oversees allocation of investment funds across the product segments and is responsible for revenues and costs, and so is treated as an investment centre. And finally, corporate headquarters is an investment centre, since it is responsible for all revenues, costs, and investments.

EXHIBIT 11–1 Business Segments Classified as Cost, Profit, and Investment Centres

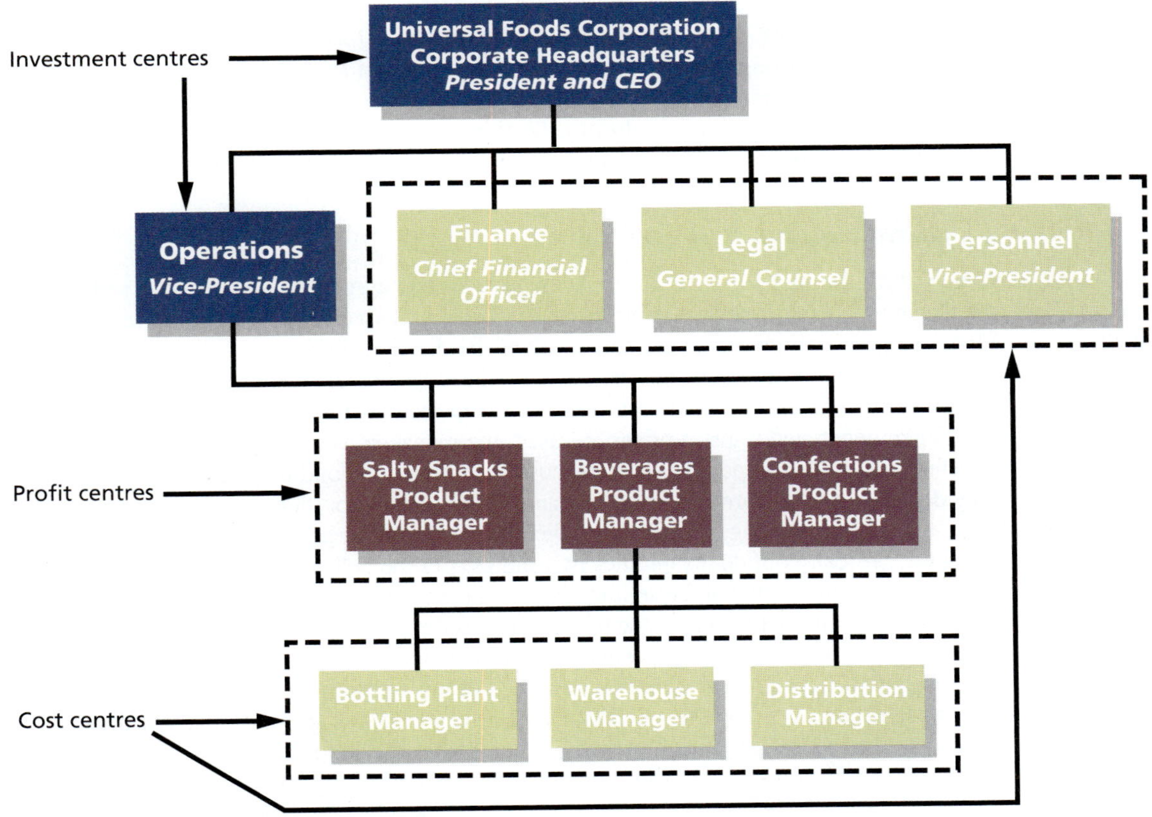

Transfer Pricing

LEARNING OBJECTIVE 2
Determine the range, if any, within which a negotiated transfer price should fall and explain other approaches to setting the transfer price.

Transfer price
The price charged when one division or segment provides goods or services to another division or segment of an organization.

In the previous section we discussed various issues related to responsibility centre reporting and profitability analysis. In this section we discuss another key issue that arises when segments of the same company (often referred to as divisions) supply goods and services to each other. The issue is determining the transfer price of the goods or services being sold between segments. A **transfer price** is the price charged when one segment sells goods or services to another segment of the same company. Because the dollar amount of these transfers can be very large, the transfer price at which they occur can have a significant impact on the profits of both the buying and selling segment. As a result, managers are intensely interested in how transfer prices are set.

As an example of a transfer pricing scenario, most companies in the oil industry, such as Imperial, Shell, and Petro-Canada, have petroleum refining and retail sales divisions that are evaluated on the basis of ROI or residual income, two performance measures discussed in detail, later in this chapter. The petroleum refining division processes crude oil into gasoline, kerosene, lubricants, and other end products. The retail sales division takes gasoline and other products from the refining division and sells them through the company's chain of service stations. Each product has a price for transfers within the company. Suppose the transfer price for gasoline is $1.00 per litre. Then the refining division gets credit for $1.00 per litre of revenue on its segment report and the retailing division must deduct $1.00 per litre as an expense on its segment report. Clearly, the refining division would like the transfer price to be as high as possible, whereas the retailing division would like the transfer price to be as low as possible. However, the transaction has no direct effect on the entire company's reported profit because the revenue recorded for the transfer by the selling division is exactly offset by the cost recorded by the buying divisions.

Three common approaches are used to set transfer prices:

1. Allow the managers involved in the transfer to negotiate their own transfer prices.
2. Set transfer prices at cost using either variable cost or full absorption cost.
3. Set transfer prices at the market price.

We consider each of these transfer pricing methods in turn, beginning with negotiated transfer prices. Throughout the discussion, keep in mind that *the fundamental objective in setting transfer prices is to motivate the managers to act in the best interests of the overall company.* In contrast, **suboptimization** occurs when managers do not act in the best interests of the overall company or even in the best interests of their own segment.

Suboptimization
An overall level of profitability that is less than a segment or a company is capable of earning.

Negotiated Transfer Prices

Negotiated transfer price
A transfer price agreed on between buying and selling divisions.

A **negotiated transfer price** is a transfer price that is agreed on between the selling and purchasing segments or divisions. Negotiated transfer prices have several important advantages. First, this approach preserves the autonomy of the divisions and is consistent with the spirit of decentralization. Second, the managers of the divisions are likely to have much better information about the potential costs and benefits of the transfer than others in the company.

When negotiated transfer prices are used, the managers who are involved in a proposed transfer within the company meet to discuss the terms and conditions of the transfer. They may decide not to go through with the transfer, but if they do, they must agree to a transfer price. Generally speaking, we cannot predict the exact transfer price to which they will agree. However, we can confidently predict two things: (1) the selling division will agree to the transfer only if the profits of the selling division increase as a result of the transfer, and (2) the purchasing division will agree to the transfer only if the profits of the purchasing division also increase as a result of the transfer. This may seem obvious, but it is an important point.

Clearly, if the transfer price is below the selling division's cost, a loss will occur on the transaction and the selling division will refuse to agree to the transfer. Likewise, if the transfer price is set too high, it will be impossible for the purchasing division to make any profit on the transferred item. For any given proposed transfer, the transfer price has both a lower limit (determined by the situation of the selling division) and an upper limit (determined by the situation of the purchasing division). The actual transfer price agreed to by the two division managers can fall anywhere between those two limits. These limits determine the **range of acceptable transfer prices**—the range of transfer prices within which the profits of both divisions participating in a transfer would increase.

Range of acceptable transfer prices
The range of transfer prices within which the profits of both the selling division and the purchasing division would increase as a result of a transfer.

An example will help illustrate negotiated transfer prices. Harrison Ltd. owns fast-food restaurants and snack food and beverage manufacturers in Atlantic Canada. One of the restaurants, Pizza Place, serves a variety of beverages along with pizzas. One of the beverages is ginger beer, which is served on tap. Harrison has just purchased a new division, Cumberland Beverages, that produces ginger beer. The managing director of Cumberland Beverages has approached the managing director of Pizza Place about purchasing Cumberland Beverages ginger beer for sale at Pizza Place restaurants rather than its usual brand of ginger beer. Managers at Pizza Place agree that the quality of Cumberland Beverages' ginger beer is comparable to the quality of their regular brand. It is just a question of price. The basic facts follow:

Cumberland Beverages:	
Ginger beer production capacity per month	10,000 barrels
Variable cost per barrel of ginger beer	$8 per barrel
Fixed costs per month	$70,000
Selling price of Cumberland Beverages ginger beer on the outside market	$20 per barrel
Pizza Place:	
Purchase price of regular brand of ginger beer	$18 per barrel
Monthly consumption of ginger beer	2,000 barrels

The Selling Division's Lowest Acceptable Transfer Price The selling division, Cumberland Beverages, will be interested in a proposed transfer only if its profit increases. Clearly, the transfer price must not fall below the variable cost per barrel of $8. In addition, if Cumberland Beverages has insufficient capacity to fill the Pizza Place order, then it would have to give up some of its regular sales. Cumberland Beverages would expect to be compensated for the contribution margin on these lost sales. In summary, if the transfer has no effect on fixed costs, then from the selling division's standpoint, the transfer price must cover both the variable costs of producing the transferred units and any opportunity costs from lost sales.

Seller's perspective:

$$\text{Transfer price} \geq \begin{matrix}\text{Variable cost} \\ \text{per unit}\end{matrix} + \frac{\text{Total contribution margin on lost sales}}{\text{Number of units transferred}}$$

The Purchasing Division's Highest Acceptable Transfer Price The purchasing division, Pizza Place, will be interested in the proposal only if its profit increases. In cases like this where a purchasing division has an outside supplier, the purchasing division's decision is simple. Buy from the inside supplier if the price is less than the price offered by the outside supplier.

Purchaser's perspective:

$$\text{Transfer price} \leq \text{Cost of buying from outside supplier}$$

We will consider several different hypothetical situations and see what the range of acceptable transfer prices would be in each situation.

Selling Division with Idle Capacity Suppose that Cumberland Beverages has sufficient idle capacity to satisfy the demand for ginger beer from Pizza Place without cutting into sales of ginger beer to its regular customers. To be specific, let's suppose that Cumberland Beverages is selling only 7,000 barrels of ginger beer per month on the outside market. That leaves unused capacity of 3,000 barrels per month—more than enough to satisfy Pizza

Place's requirement of 2,000 barrels per month. What range of transfer prices, if any, would make both divisions better off with the transfer of 2,000 barrels per month?

1. The selling division, Cumberland Beverages, will be interested in the proposal only if:

$$\text{Transfer price} \geq \frac{\text{Variable cost}}{\text{per unit}} + \frac{\text{Total contribution margin on lost sales}}{\text{Number of units transferred}}$$

Since Cumberland Beverages has ample idle capacity, there are no lost outside sales. And since the variable cost per unit is $8, the lowest acceptable transfer price as far as the selling division is concerned is also $8:

$$\text{Transfer price} \geq \$8 + \frac{\$0}{2{,}000} = \$8$$

2. The purchasing division, Pizza Place, can buy similar ginger beer from an outside vendor for $18 per barrel. Therefore, Pizza Place would be unwilling to pay more than $18 per barrel for Cumberland Beverages' ginger beer:

$$\text{Transfer price} \leq \text{Cost of buying from outside supplier} = \$18$$

3. Combining the requirements of both the selling division and the purchasing division, the acceptable range of transfer prices in this situation is:

$$\$8 \leq \text{Transfer price} \leq \$18$$

Assuming that the managers understand their own businesses and that they are cooperative, they should be able to agree on a transfer price within this range.

Selling Division with No Idle Capacity Suppose that Cumberland Beverages has *no* idle capacity; it is selling 10,000 barrels of ginger beer a month on the outside market at $20 per barrel. To fill the order from Pizza Place, Cumberland Beverages would have to divert 2,000 barrels from its regular customers. What range of transfer prices, if any, would make both divisions better off transferring the 2,000 barrels within the company?

1. The selling division, Cumberland Beverages, will be interested in the proposal only if:

$$\text{Transfer price} \geq \frac{\text{Variable cost}}{\text{per unit}} + \frac{\text{Total contribution margin on lost sales}}{\text{Number of units transferred}}$$

Since Cumberland Beverages has no idle capacity, there *are* lost outside sales. The contribution margin per barrel on these outside sales is $12 ($20 − $8):

$$\text{Transfer price} \geq \$8 + \frac{(\$20 - \$8) \times 2{,}000}{2{,}000} = \$8 + (\$20 - \$8) = \$20$$

Thus, as far as the selling division is concerned, the transfer price must at least cover the revenue on the lost sales, which is $20 per barrel. This makes sense since the cost of producing the 2,000 barrels is the same whether they are sold on the inside market or on the outside. The only difference is that the selling division loses the revenue of $20 per barrel if it transfers the barrels to Pizza Place.

2. As before, the purchasing division, Pizza Place, would be unwilling to pay more than the $18 per barrel it is already paying for similar ginger beer from its regular supplier:

$$\text{Transfer price} \leq \text{Cost of buying from outside supplier} = \$18$$

3. Therefore, the selling division would insist on a transfer price of at least $20, but the purchasing division would refuse any transfer price above $18. It is impossible to satisfy both division managers simultaneously; there can be no agreement on a transfer price and no transfer will take place. Is this good? The answer is yes. From the standpoint of the entire company, the transfer does not make sense. Why give up sales of $20 to save $18?

Basically, the transfer price is a mechanism for dividing between the two divisions any profit the entire company earns as a result of the transfer. If the company loses money on the transfer, there will be no profit to divide up, and it will be impossible for the two divisions to come to an agreement. On the other hand, if the company makes money on the transfer, there will be a potential profit to share, and it will always be possible for the two divisions to find a mutually agreeable transfer price that increases the profits of both divisions. If the pie is bigger, it is always possible to divide it up in such a way that everyone has a bigger piece.

Selling Division with Some Idle Capacity Suppose now that Cumberland Beverages is selling 9,000 barrels of ginger beer per month on the outside market. Pizza Place can sell only one kind of ginger beer on tap. It cannot buy 1,000 barrels from Cumberland Beverages and 1,000 barrels from its regular supplier; it must buy all of its ginger beer from one source.

To fill the entire 2,000-barrel per month order from Pizza Place, Cumberland Beverages would have to divert 1,000 barrels from its regular customers who are paying $20 per barrel. The other 1,000 barrels can be made using idle capacity. What range of transfer prices, if any, would make both divisions better off transferring the 2,000 barrels within the company?

1. As before, the selling division, Cumberland Beverages, will insist on a transfer price that at least covers its variable cost and opportunity cost:

$$\text{Transfer price} \geq \frac{\text{Variable cost}}{\text{per unit}} + \frac{\text{Total contribution margin on lost sales}}{\text{Number of units transferred}}$$

Since Cumberland Beverages does not have enough idle capacity to fill the entire order for 2,000 barrels, there *are* lost outside sales. The contribution margin per barrel on the 1,000 barrels of lost outside sales is $12 ($20 − $8):

$$\text{Transfer price} \geq \$8 + \frac{(\$20 - \$8) \times 1{,}000}{2{,}000} = \$8 + \$6 = \$14$$

Thus, as far as the selling division is concerned, the transfer price must cover the variable cost of $8 plus the average opportunity cost of lost sales of $6.

2. As before, the purchasing division, Pizza Place, would be unwilling to pay more than the $18 per barrel it pays its regular supplier:

$$\text{Transfer price} \leq \text{Cost of buying from outside suppliers} = \$18$$

3. Combining the requirements for both the selling and purchasing divisions, the range of acceptable transfer prices is:

$$\$14 \leq \text{Transfer price} \leq \$18$$

Again, assuming that the managers understand their own businesses and that they are cooperative, they should be able to agree on a transfer price within this range.

No Outside Supplier If Pizza Place has no outside supplier for the ginger beer, the highest price the purchasing division would be willing to pay depends on how much the purchasing division expects to make on the transferred units—excluding the transfer price. If, for example, Pizza Place expects to earn $30 per barrel of ginger beer after paying its own expenses, then it should be willing to pay up to $30 per barrel to Cumberland Beverages. Remember, however, that this assumes Pizza Place cannot buy ginger beer from other sources.

Evaluation of Negotiated Transfer Prices As discussed earlier, if a transfer within the company would result in higher overall profits for the company, there is always a range of transfer prices within which both the selling and purchasing division would also have higher profits if they agree to the transfer. Therefore, if the managers understand their own businesses and are cooperative, then they should always be able to agree on a transfer price if it is in the best interests of the company that they do so.

Unfortunately not all managers understand their own businesses and not all managers are cooperative. As a result, negotiations often break down even when it would be in the managers' own best interests to come to an agreement. Sometimes that is the fault of the way managers are evaluated. If managers are pitted against each other rather than against their own past performance or reasonable benchmarks, a non-cooperative atmosphere is almost guaranteed. Nevertheless, it must be admitted that even with the best performance evaluation system, some people by nature are not cooperative.

Given the potential problems of the negotiation process, most companies rely on some other means of setting transfer prices. Unfortunately, as we will see below the alternatives to negotiated transfer prices have their own serious drawbacks.

Transfers to the Selling Division at Cost

Many companies set transfer prices at either the variable cost or full absorption cost incurred by the selling division. Although the cost approach to setting transfer prices is relatively simple to apply, it has some major defects.

First, the use of cost—particularly full cost—as a transfer price can lead to bad decisions and thus suboptimization. Return to the example involving the ginger beer. The full cost of ginger beer can never be less than $15 per barrel ($8 per barrel variable cost + $7 per barrel fixed cost at capacity). What if the cost of buying the ginger beer from an outside supplier is less than $15—for example, $14 per barrel? If the transfer price was bureaucratically set at full cost, then Pizza Place would never want to buy ginger beer from Cumberland Beverages, since it could buy its ginger beer from the outside supplier at less cost. However, from the standpoint of the company as a whole, ginger beer should be transferred from Cumberland Beverages to Pizza Place whenever Cumberland Beverages has more than 1,000 units of idle capacity. Why? Because when Cumberland Beverages has more than 1,000 units of idle capacity, the total transfer price (including the opportunity cost) will be less than the $14 per barrel to buy from outside suppliers.[2]

Second, if cost is used as the transfer price, the selling division will never show a profit on any internal transfer. The only division that shows a profit is the division that makes the final sale to an outside party.

A third problem with cost-based prices is that they do not provide incentives to control costs. If the costs of one division are simply passed on to the next, then there is little incentive for anyone to work to reduce costs. This problem can be overcome to some extent by using standard costs rather than actual costs for transfer prices.

Despite these shortcomings, cost-based transfer prices are commonly used in practice. Advocates argue that they are easily understood and convenient to use.

Transfers at Market Price

Market price
The price being charged for an item on the open (intermediate) market.

Intermediate market
A market in which a transferred product or service is sold in its present form to outside customers.

Some form of competitive **market price** (i.e., the price charged for an item on the open market) is often regarded as the best approach to the transfer pricing problem—particularly if transfer price negotiations routinely become bogged down.

The market price approach is designed for situations in which there is an *intermediate market* for the transferred product or service. By **intermediate market,** we mean a market in which the product or service is sold in its present form to outside customers. If the selling division has no idle capacity, the market price in the intermediate market is the

2. Recall from the example on page 501 that when Cumberland Beverages has 1,000 units of idle capacity, the minimum transfer price was calculated to be $14 ($8 + [($20 − $8) × 1,000/2,000]). Therefore if idle capacity is greater than 1,000 units, then the transfer price will always be less than the outside purchase price of $14 and the transfer should occur. For example if idle capacity is 1,200 units, then the transfer price would be $12.80 calculated as: ($8 + [($20 − $8) × 800/2,000]).

perfect choice for the transfer price. The reason for this is that if the selling division can sell a transferred item on the outside market instead, then the real cost of the transfer as far as the company is concerned is the opportunity cost of the lost revenue on the outside sale. Whether the item is transferred internally or sold on the outside intermediate market, the production costs are exactly the same. If the market price is used as the transfer price, the selling division manager will not lose anything by making the transfer, and the purchasing division manager will get the correct signal about how much it really costs the company for the transfer to take place.

While the market price works well when there is no idle capacity, difficulties occur when the selling division has idle capacity. Recalling once again the ginger beer example, the outside market price for the ginger beer produced by Cumberland Beverages is $20 per barrel. However, Pizza Place can purchase all of the ginger beer it wants from outside suppliers for $18 per barrel. Why would Pizza Place ever buy from Cumberland Beverages if Pizza Place is forced to pay Cumberland Beverages' market price? In some market price-based transfer pricing schemes, the transfer price would be lowered to $18, the outside vendor's market price, and Pizza Place would be directed to buy from Cumberland Beverages, as long as Cumberland Beverages is willing to sell. This scheme can work reasonably well, but a drawback is that managers at Pizza Place will regard the cost of ginger beer as $18 rather than the $8, which is the real cost to the company when the selling division has sufficient idle capacity to fill the entire order. Consequently, the managers of Pizza Place will make pricing and other decisions based on an incorrect cost.

Unfortunately, none of the possible solutions to the transfer pricing problem are perfect—not even market-based transfer prices.

IN BUSINESS

Although using the market price as the basis for setting transfer prices seems simple in theory, in practice it appears that managers of selling divisions may take other considerations into account. In a study examining how experienced managers set transfer prices when an external market exists for their product, researchers find that fairness concerns come into play. Specifically, managers of selling divisions were less likely to use the market price as the transfer price if doing so resulted in disproportionately larger profits for their division compared to the buying division. Selling division managers indicated that they believed accepting a lower transfer price than they could have received based on market prices was fairer as it allowed both the buying and selling managers to more equally share the financial benefits arising from the transaction. Moreover, the selling division managers claimed that being seen as fair negotiators was important when they expected future interactions with the buying division manager.

Source: Joan Luft and Robert Libby, "Profit Comparisons, Market Prices and Managers' Judgments about Negotiated Transfer Prices," *The Accounting Review*, April 1997, pp. 217–229.

Divisional Autonomy and Suboptimization

The principles of decentralization suggest that companies should grant managers autonomy to set transfer prices and to decide whether to sell internally or externally. It may be very difficult for top managers to accept this principle when their subordinate managers are about to make a suboptimal decision. However, if top management intervenes, the purposes of decentralization are defeated. Furthermore, to impose the correct transfer price, top managers would have to know details about the buying and selling divisions' outside market, variable costs, and capacity utilization. The whole premise of decentralization is that local managers have access to better information for operational decisions than top managers at corporate headquarters.

Of course, if a division manager consistently makes suboptimal decisions, the performance of the division will suffer. The offending manager's compensation will be adversely affected and promotion will become less likely. However, if top managers wish to create a culture of autonomy and independent profit responsibility, they must allow their subordinate managers to control their own destiny—even to the extent of granting their managers the right to make mistakes.

International Aspects of Transfer Pricing

Transfer pricing is used worldwide to control the flow of goods and services between segments of an organization. However, the objectives of transfer pricing change when a multinational corporation (MNC) is involved and the goods and services being transferred must cross international borders. The objectives of international transfer pricing, as compared to domestic transfer pricing, are summarized below.

Transfer Pricing Objectives[3]

Domestic	International
Greater divisional autonomy	Less taxes, duties and tariffs
Greater motivation for managers	Less foreign exchange risks
Better performance evaluation	Better competitive position
Better goal congruence	Better governmental relations

As shown, the objectives of international transfer pricing focus on minimizing taxes, duties, and foreign exchange risks, along with enhancing a company's competitive position and improving its relations with foreign governments. Although domestic objectives such as managerial motivation and divisional autonomy are always desirable in an organization, they usually become secondary when international transfers are involved. Companies will focus instead on charging a transfer price that will reduce its total tax bill or that will strengthen a foreign subsidiary.

For example, charging a low transfer price for parts shipped to a foreign subsidiary may reduce Customs duty payments as the parts cross international borders, or it may help the subsidiary to compete in foreign markets by keeping the subsidiary's costs low. On the other hand, charging a high transfer price may help an MNC draw profits out of a country that has stringent controls on foreign remittances, or it may allow an MNC to shift income from a country that has high income tax rates to a country that has low rates.

Transfer prices have a significant influence on a firm's duties and income taxes. Given that transfer prices are set by parties who are not independent of each other (non-arm's length), the opportunity exists to minimize taxes by shifting profit to low-tax jurisdictions or by minimizing duties paid. The Canada Revenue Agency (CRA) seeks Canada's fair share of tax revenue by adopting policies and practices based on the principle of arm's length pricing. In simple cases, management simply needs to show CRA that the transfer price is comparable to an appropriately arm's length market price. In other cases, complex cost/profit allocation processes have to be documented by the company, together with the reasons for adopting such processes for determining the transfer price. Severe penalties exist for violations of the arm's length market price rule of the Income Tax Act, section 247, in foreign dealings with non-arm's length parties of an organization.[4]

In summary, managers need to be sensitive to legal rules in establishing transfer prices. In particular, the strict practices demonstrated with foreign transfer prices by the CRA rules illustrate the potential issues associated with provincial sales taxes, foreign trade practices under NAFTA and GATT, and the income tax provisions dealing with artificial tax-based transactions used to manipulate income taxes.

3. Based on Wagdy M. Abdallah, "Guidelines for CEOs in Transfer Pricing Policies," *Management Accounting* 70, no. 3, September 1988, p. 61.

4. Stephanie de Breyne, "Transfer Pricing: Get It In Writing, " *CMA Magazine,* February 1998, p. 36, and Hendrick Swaneveld and Martin Przysuski, "Transfer Pricing Now a Canadian Priority," *CMA Management,* April 2002, pp. 42–44.

Evaluating Investment Centre Performance—Return on Investment

Thus far in the chapter we have focused on how to properly assign costs to responsibility centres and how to set transfer prices on goods an services being transferred between segments within the same organization. These are important issues when evaluating cost and profit centres. However, evaluating an investment centre's performance requires more than accurate cost and segment margin reporting. In addition, an investment centre is responsible for earning an adequate return on investment. The next two sections of this chapter present two methods for evaluating this aspect of an investment centre's performance. The first method is called *return on investment (ROI)*. The second method is called *residual income*.

LEARNING OBJECTIVE 3
Analyze the return on investment (ROI).

The Return on Investment (ROI) Formula

The **return on investment (ROI)** is defined as operating income divided by average operating assets:

Return on investment (ROI) Operating income divided by average operating assets. ROI also equals margin multiplied by turnover.

$$\text{ROI} = \frac{\text{Operating income}}{\text{Average operating assets}}$$

The higher the return on investment (ROI) of a business segment, the greater the profit generated per dollar invested in the segment's operating assets.

Operating Income and Operating Assets Defined

Note that *operating income,* rather than net income, is used in the ROI formula. **Operating income** is income before interest and taxes and is sometimes referred to as EBIT (earnings before interest and taxes). The reason for using operating income in the formula is that the income figure used should be consistent with the base to which it is applied. Notice that the base (i.e., denominator) consists of *operating assets.* Thus, to be consistent we use operating income in the numerator because no debt is included in the denominator, and interest expense is paid for by the profits from the operating assets and thus is a distribution of those profits rather than an expense.

Operating income Income before interest and income taxes have been deducted.

Operating assets include cash, accounts receivable, inventory, plant and equipment, and all other assets held for productive use in the organization. Examples of assets that would not be included in the operating assets category (i.e., examples of non-operating assets) would include land held for future use, an investment in another company, or a factory building rented to someone else. The operating assets base used in the formula is typically computed as the average of the operating assets between the beginning and the end of the year.

Operating assets Cash, accounts receivable, inventory, plant and equipment, and all other assets held for productive use in an organization.

Plant and Equipment: Net Book Value or Gross Cost?

A major issue in ROI computations is the dollar amount of plant and equipment that should be included in the operating assets base. To illustrate the problem involved, assume that a company reports the following amounts for plant and equipment on its balance sheet:

Plant and equipment	$3,000,000
Less accumulated depreciation	900,000
Net book value	$2,100,000

What dollar amount of plant and equipment should the company include with its operating assets in computing ROI? One widely used approach is to include only the plant and equipment's *net book value*—that is, the plant's original cost less accumulated depreciation

($2,100,000 in the example above). A second approach is to ignore depreciation and include the plant's entire *gross cost* in the operating assets base ($3,000,000 in the example above). Both of these approaches are used in actual practice, even though they will obviously yield very different operating asset and ROI figures.

The following arguments can be raised for using net book value to measure operating assets and for using gross cost to measure operating assets in ROI computation:

Arguments for Using Net Book Value to Measure Operating Assets in ROI Computations:

1. The net book value method is consistent with how plant and equipment are reported on the balance sheet (i.e., cost less accumulated depreciation to date).
2. The net book value method is consistent with the computation of operating income, which includes depreciation as an operating expense.

Arguments for Using Gross Cost to Measure Operating Assets in ROI Computations:

1. The gross cost method eliminates both the age of equipment and the method of depreciation as factors in ROI computations. (Under the net book value method, ROI will tend to increase over time as net book value declines due to depreciation.)
2. The gross cost method does not discourage replacement of old, worn-out equipment. (Under the net book value method, replacing fully depreciated equipment with new equipment can have a dramatic, adverse effect on ROI.)

Managers generally view consistency as the most important of the considerations above. As a result, a majority of companies use the net book value approach in ROI computations. In this text, we will also use the net book value approach unless a specific exercise or problem directs otherwise.

Understanding ROI

The equation for ROI, operating income divided by average operating assets, does not provide much help to managers interested in taking actions to improve their ROI. It only offers two levers for improving performance—operating income and average operating assets. Fortunately, ROI can also be expressed as follows:

$$\text{ROI} = \text{Margin} \times \text{Turnover}$$

where

$$\text{Margin} = \frac{\text{Operating income}}{\text{Sales}}$$

and

$$\text{Turnover} = \frac{\text{Sales}}{\text{Average operating assets}}$$

Margin
Operating income divided by sales.

Turnover
The amount of sales generated in an investment centre for each dollar invested in operating assets. Sales divided by average operating assets.

The **margin** is a measure of management's ability to control operating expenses in relation to sales. The lower operating expenses are per dollar of sales, the higher the margin earned. **Turnover** is a measure of the sales that are generated for each dollar invested in operating assets. Note that the sales terms in the margin and turnover formulas cancel out when they are multiplied together, yielding the original formula for ROI stated in terms of operating income and average operating assets. So either formula for ROI will give the same answer. However, the margin and turnover formulation provides some additional insights.

From a manager's perspective, margin and turnover are very important concepts. Margin is ordinarily improved by increasing sales or reducing operating expenses, including cost of goods sold and selling and administrative expenses. Some managers tend to focus too much on margin and ignore turnover. However, turnover incorporates a crucial area of a manager's responsibility—the investment in operating assets. Excessive funds tied up in operating assets (e.g., cash, accounts receivable, inventories, plant and equipment, and other assets) depress turnover and lower ROI. In fact, inefficient use of operating assets can be just as much of a drag on profitability as excessive operating expenses, which depress margin.

E.I. du Pont de Nemours and Company (better known as DuPont) pioneered the use of ROI and recognized the importance of looking at both margin and turnover in assessing a manager's performance. ROI is now widely used as the key measure of investment centre performance. ROI reflects in a single figure many aspects of the manager's responsibilities. It can be compared to the returns of other investment centres in the organization, the returns of other companies in the industry, and to the past returns of the investment centre itself.

DuPont also developed the diagram that appears in Exhibit 11–2. This exhibit helps managers understand how they can improve ROI. Any increase in ROI must involve at least one of the following:

1. Increased sales
2. Reduced operating expenses
3. Reduced operating assets

Many actions involve combinations of changes in sales, expenses, and operating assets. For example, a manager may make an investment in (i.e., increase) operating assets to reduce operating expenses or increase sales. Whether the net effect is favourable or not is judged in terms of its overall impact on ROI.

To illustrate how ROI is impacted by various actions, we will use the Monthaven outlet of the Burger Grill chain as an example. Burger Grill is a small chain of upscale casual restaurants that has been rapidly adding outlets via franchising. The Monthaven franchise is owned by a group of local surgeons who have little time to devote to management and little expertise in business matters. Therefore, they delegate operating decisions—including decisions concerning investments in operating assets such

EXHIBIT 11–2 Elements of Return on Investment (ROI)

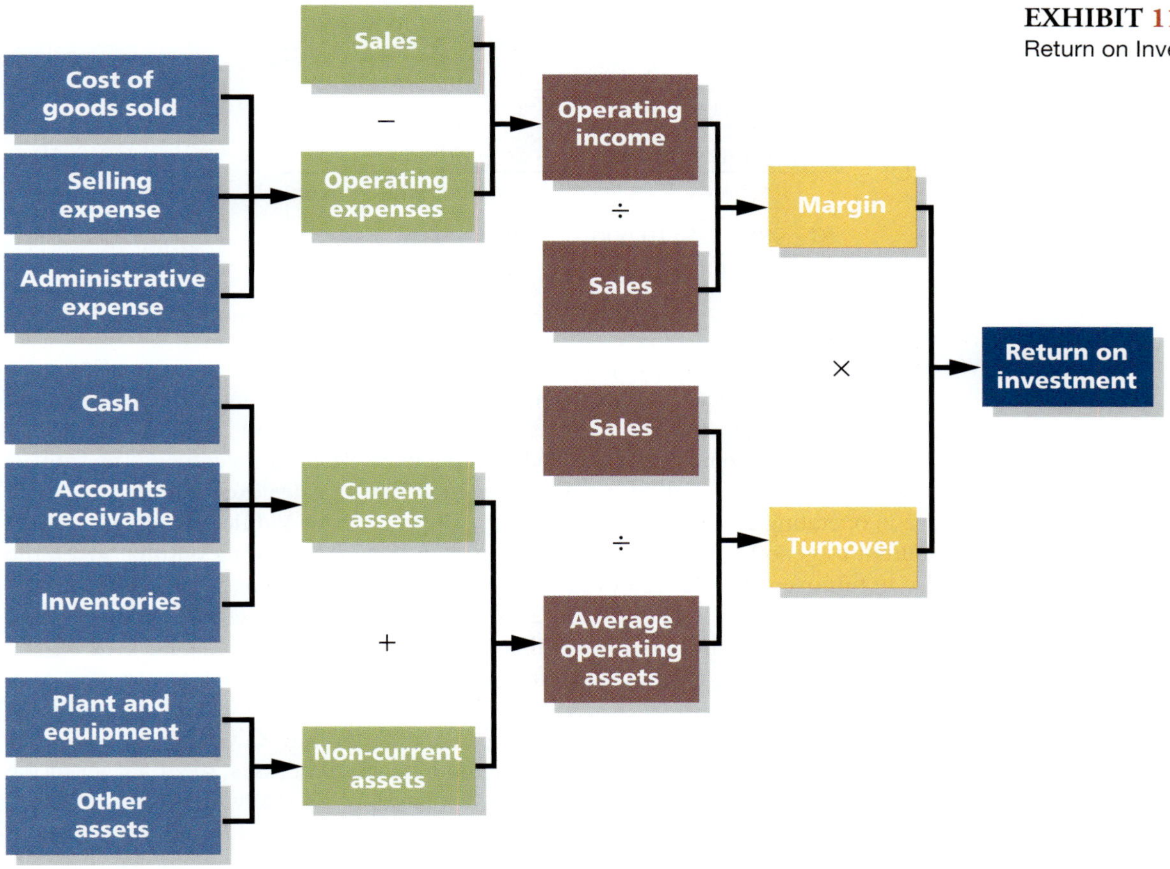

Cost of goods sold
Selling expense
Administrative expense
Sales
–
Operating expenses
Operating income
÷
Sales
Margin
×
Return on investment
Cash
Accounts receivable
Inventories
Current assets
+
Plant and equipment
Other assets
Non-current assets
Sales
÷
Average operating assets
Turnover

as inventories—to a professional manager they have hired. The manager is evaluated largely based on the ROI the franchise generates.

The following data represent the results of operations for the most recent month:

Sales	$100,000
Operating expenses	$90,000
Operating income	$10,000
Average operating assets	$50,000

The return on investment (ROI) for the month is computed as follows:

$$\text{ROI} = \frac{\text{Operating income}}{\text{Sales}} \times \frac{\text{Sales}}{\text{Average operating assets}}$$

$$= \frac{\$10,000}{\$100,000} \times \frac{\$100,000}{\$50,000}$$

$$= 10\% \times 2 = 20\%$$

Example 1: Increased Sales without Any Increase in Operating Assets Assume that the manager of the Monthaven Burger Grill can increase sales by 10% without any increase in operating assets. The increase in sales will require additional operating expenses. However, operating expenses include some fixed expenses, which would probably not be affected by a 10% increase in sales. Therefore, the increase in operating expenses would probably be less than 10%; let's assume the increase is 7.8%. Under those assumptions, the new operating income would be $12,980, an increase of 29.8%, determined as follows:

Sales (1.10 × $100,000)	$110,000
Operating expenses (1.078 × $90,000)	97,020
Operating income	$ 12,980

In this case, the new ROI would be:

$$\text{ROI} = \frac{\text{Operating income}}{\text{Sales}} \times \frac{\text{Sales}}{\text{Average operating assets}}$$

$$= \frac{\$12,980}{\$110,000} \times \frac{\$110,000}{\$50,000}$$

$$= 11.8\% \times 2.2 = 25.96\% \text{ (as compared to 20\% originally)}$$

When sales are increased *without* an increase in operating assets, both the margin and turnover are likely to be affected. In the example above, because sales increased by 10% and operating expenses increased by only 7.8%, the margin increased to 11.8% (up from 10%). This improvement in the margin combined with the increase in turnover to 2.2 (up from 2) led to the gain in ROI. Clearly if the percentage increase in sales exceeds the percentage increase in operating expenses, ROI will always improve, if no additional operating assets are required to generate the new sales. However, it is worth pointing out that given the increase in turnover, the old ROI of 20% could have been maintained as long as the new margin did not fall below 9.09% (20% ÷ 2.2). If the new margin exceeds 9.09%, as it does in the example, ROI will increase. Using this type of analysis can help managers assess the extent to which operating expenses can increase before ROI begins to decrease.

Example 2: Decreased Operating Expenses with No Change in Sales or Operating Assets Assume that by improving business processes, the manager of the Monthaven Burger Grill can reduce operating expenses by $1,000 without any effect on sales or operating assets. This reduction in operating expenses would result in increasing operating income by $1,000, from $10,000 to $11,000. The new ROI would be:

$$\text{ROI} = \frac{\text{Operating income}}{\text{Sales}} \times \frac{\text{Sales}}{\text{Average operating assets}}$$

$$= \frac{\$11{,}000}{\$100{,}000} \times \frac{\$100{,}000}{\$50{,}000}$$

$$= 11\% \times 2 = 22\% \text{ (as compared to 20\% originally)}$$

When margins or profits are being squeezed, the first line of attack is often to cut costs. Discretionary fixed costs are particularly vulnerable to cuts. However, managers must be careful not to cut too much or in the wrong place. Inappropriate cost cutting can lead to decreased sales, increased costs elsewhere, and a drop in morale.

Example 3: Decreased Operating Assets with No Change in Sales or Operating Expenses Assume that the manager of the Monthaven Burger Grill uses Lean Production techniques to reduce inventories by $10,000. This might actually have a positive effect on sales (through fresher ingredients) and on operating expenses (through reduced inventory spoilage), but for the sake of illustration, suppose the reduction in inventories has no effect on sales or operating expenses. The reduction in inventories will reduce average operating assets by $10,000, from $50,000 down to $40,000. The new ROI would be:

$$\text{ROI} = \frac{\text{Operating income}}{\text{Sales}} \times \frac{\text{Sales}}{\text{Average operating assets}}$$

$$= \frac{\$10{,}000}{\$100{,}000} \times \frac{\$100{,}000}{\$40{,}000}$$

$$= 10\% \times 2.5 = 25\% \text{ (as compared to 20\% originally)}$$

In this example, Lean Production was used to reduce operating assets. Another common tactic for reducing operating assets is to speed up the collection of accounts receivable. For example, many companies encourage customers to pay electronically rather than by mail.

IN BUSINESS

JIT and ROI Improvement

A study of companies that adopted just-in-time (JIT) in comparison to a control group that did not adopt JIT, found that the JIT adopters improved their ROIs more. The JIT adopters' success resulted from improvements in both profit margins and asset turnover. The elimination of inventories in JIT reduces total assets, but more important, it leads to process improvements as production problems are exposed. When production problems and non-value-added activities are eliminated, costs go down.

Source: Michael R. Kinney and William F. Wempe, "Further Evidence on the Extent and Origins of JIT's Profitability Effects," *The Accounting Review*, January 2002, pp. 203–225.

Example 4: Invest in Operating Assets to Increase Sales Assume that the manager of the Monthaven Burger Grill invests $2,000 in a state-of-the-art soft-serve ice cream machine that can dispense a number of different flavours. This new machine will boost sales by $4,000, but will require additional operating expenses of $1,000. Thus, operating income will increase by $3,000, to $13,000. The new ROI will be:

$$\text{ROI} = \frac{\text{Operating income}}{\text{Sales}} \times \frac{\text{Sales}}{\text{Average operating assets}}$$

$$= \frac{\$13{,}000}{\$104{,}000} \times \frac{\$104{,}000}{\$52{,}000}$$

$$= 12.5\% \times 2 = 25\% \text{ (as compared to 20\% originally)}$$

In this particular example, the investment had no effect on turnover, which remained at 2, so there had to be an increase in margin in order to improve the ROI.

IN BUSINESS

As part of a proposal to persuade Ford Motor Company Limited to construct a $750 million assembly plant in St. Thomas, Ontario, the Canadian Auto Workers (CAW) union estimated that the return on investment (ROI) would be 18.3% per year over a seven-year period. The proposal calculated that a similar assembly plant built in the United States or Mexico would yield annual ROI of 4.9% and 9.2% respectively. The superior ROI from the Canadian plant would stem, in part, from the CAW's suggestion to limit spending on operating assets by combining the new plant with an existing assembly plant in St. Thomas. Further, the proposal indicates that the operating margin would be strengthened by the CAW agreeing to initially set employees' wages at 75% of the levels earned at other assembly plant sites. The CAW proposal provides a good example of how both components of ROI, margin and turnover, can be managed to maximize potential profits in an organization.

Source: Tony Van Alphen, "CAW Makes Unusual Pitch to Ford: Wage Concessions Part of Proposed Assembly Plant for St. Thomas," *Toronto Star*, Augst 30, 2006, p. F1.

Criticisms of ROI

Although ROI is widely used in evaluating performance, it is not a perfect tool. The method is subject to the following criticisms:

1. Just telling managers to increase ROI may not be enough. Managers may not know how to increase ROI; they may increase ROI in a way that is inconsistent with the company's strategy; or they may take actions that increase ROI in the short run but harm the company in the long run (such as cutting back on research and development).
2. A manager who takes over a business segment typically inherits many committed costs over which the manager has no control. These committed costs may be relevant in assessing the performance of the business segment as an investment but make it difficult to fairly assess the performance of the manager relative to other managers.
3. As discussed in the next section, a manager who is evaluated based on ROI may reject profitable investment opportunities.

Residual Income

LEARNING OBJECTIVE 4
Compute residual income and describe the strengths and weaknesses of this method of measuring performance.

Residual income
The operating income that an investment centre earns above the required return on its operating assets.

Economic value added (EVA®)
A concept similar to residual income.

Another approach to measuring an investment centre's performance focuses on a concept known as *residual income.* **Residual income** is the operating income that an investment centre earns above the minimum required return on its operating assets. Thus we use operating income as defined with ROI but reduce it by a special charge computed as a percentage of average operating assets. In equation form, residual income is calculated as follows:

$$\text{Residual Income} = \text{Operating Income} - \left(\text{Average operating assets} \times \text{Minimum required rate of return}\right)$$

Economic value added (EVA®) is a similar concept that differs in some details from residual income.[5] For example, under the economic value added concept, funds used for

5. The basic idea underlying residual income and economic value added has been around for more than a hundred years. In recent years, economic value added has been popularized and trademarked by the consulting firm Stern, Stewart & Co.

research and development are treated as investments rather than as expenses. However, for our purposes, we will not draw any distinction between residual income and economic value added. We will illustrate residual income because the adjustments for EVA® are complex and would create more confusion than is appropriate for this introduction.

When residual income or EVA® is used to measure performance, the purpose is to maximize the total amount of residual income or EVA®, not to maximize overall ROI. Organizations as diverse as Loblaws, Quaker Oats, and Domtar have embraced some version of residual income in recent years.

For purposes of illustration, consider the following data for an investment centre—the Whitehorse Division of Yukon Marine Services Corporation.

YUKON MARINE SERVICES CORPORATION
Whitehorse Division
Basic Data for Performance Evaluation

Average operating assets.	$100,000
Operating income.	$ 20,000
Minimum required rate of return	15%

Yukon Marine Services Corporation has long had a policy of evaluating investment centre managers based on ROI, but it is considering a switch to residual income. The controller of the company, who is in favour of the change to residual income, has provided the following table that shows how the performance of the division would be evaluated under each of the two methods:

YUKON MARINE SERVICES CORPORATION
Whitehorse Division
Alternative Performance Measures

	ROI	Residual Income
Average operating assets	$100,000 (a)	$100,000
Operating income	$ 20,000 (b)	$ 20,000
ROI, (b) 4 (a).	20%	
Minimum required return (15% 3 $100,000)		15,000
Residual income		$ 5,000

The reasoning underlying the residual income calculation is straightforward. The company is able to earn a rate of return of at least 15% on its investments. Since the company has invested $100,000 in the Whitehorse Division in the form of operating assets, the company should be able to earn at least $15,000 (15% × $100,000) on this investment. Since the Whitehorse Division's operating income is $20,000, the residual income exceeds the minimum required return by $5,000. If residual income is adopted as the performance measure to replace ROI, the manager of the Whitehorse Division would be evaluated based on the growth from year to year in residual income.

Motivation and Residual Income

One of the primary reasons why the controller of Yukon Marine Services Corporation would like to switch from ROI to residual income has to do with how managers view new investments under the two performance measurement schemes. The residual income approach encourages managers to make investments that are profitable for the entire company but that would be rejected by managers who are evaluated by the ROI formula.

To illustrate this problem, suppose that the manager of the Whitehorse Division is considering purchasing a computerized diagnostic machine to aid in servicing marine diesel engines. The machine would cost $25,000 and is expected to generate additional operating income of $4,500 a year. From the standpoint of the company, this would be a good investment since it promises a rate of return of 18% ($4,500 ÷ $25,000), which is in excess of the company's minimum required rate of return of 15%.

If the manager of the Whitehorse Division is evaluated based on residual income, she would be in favour of the investment in the diagnostic machine evaluated below:

YUKON MARINE SERVICES CORPORATION
Whitehorse Division
Performance Evaluated Using Residual Income

	Present	New Project	Overall
Average operating assets	$100,000	$25,000	$125,000
Operating income	$ 20,000	$ 4,500	$ 24,500
Minimum required return	15,000	3,750*	18,750
Residual income	$ 5,000	$ 750	$ 5,750

*$25,000 × 15% = $3,750.

Since the project would increase the residual income of the Whitehorse Division, the manager would want to invest in the new diagnostic machine.

Now suppose that the manager of the Whitehorse Division is evaluated based on ROI. The effect of the diagnostic machine on the division's ROI is computed below:

YUKON MARINE SERVICES CORPORATION
Whitehorse Division
Performance Evaluated Using ROI

	Present	New Project	Overall
Average operating assets (a)	$100,000	$25,000	$125,000
Operating income (b)	$ 20,000	$ 4,500*	$ 24,500
ROI, (b) ÷ (a)	20%	18%	19.6%

*$25,000 × 18% = $4,500.

The new project reduces the division's ROI from 20% to 19.6%. This happens because the 18% rate of return on the new diagnostic machine, while above the company's 15% minimum rate of return, is below the division's present ROI of 20%. Therefore, the new diagnostic machine would reduce the division's ROI, even though it would be a good investment from the standpoint of the company as a whole. If the manager of the division is evaluated based on ROI, she will be reluctant to even propose such an investment.

Generally, a manager who is evaluated based on ROI will want to reject any project whose rate of return is below the division's current ROI even if the rate of return on the project is above the minimum required rate of return for the entire company. In contrast, any project whose rate of return is above the minimum required rate of return for the company will result in an increase in residual income and thus add value for the shareholders. Since it is in the best interests of the company as a whole to accept any project whose rate of return is above the minimum required rate of return, managers who are evaluated based on residual income will tend to make better decisions concerning investment projects than managers who are evaluated based on ROI.

IN BUSINESS

Aligning the incentives of managers with those of shareholders is a major challenge at many companies. Some are turning to measures such as residual income or EVA® to motivate managers to take actions that are in the best interests of the organization as a whole. A common approach is to set targets for a measure such as EVA® and pay managers a bonus if they meet or exceed the target. However, if they fall short of the target, there may be no bonus paid or it may be significantly smaller than if they had reached the target. For example, Loblaws Companies Limited reported that both of their two senior executives, the chairman and the president, did not receive a bonus in 2005 because the company failed to achieve the specified targets for EVA.

Source: Bloomberg Business News, "Loblaw Executives Forego 2005 Bonuses," *The Globe and Mail*, March 18, 2006, p. B3.

Divisional Comparison and Residual Income

The residual income approach has one major disadvantage. It cannot be used to compare the performance of divisions of different sizes. You would expect larger divisions to have more residual income than smaller divisions, not necessarily because they are better managed but simply because they are bigger.

As an example, consider the following residual income computations for Division X and Division Y:

	Division	
	X	Y
Average operating assets (a)	$1,000,000	$250,000
Operating income	$ 120,000	$ 40,000
Minimum required return: 10% × (a)	100,000	25,000
Residual income	$ 20,000	$ 15,000

Observe that Division X has slightly more residual income than Division Y, but that Division X has $1,000,000 in operating assets as compared to only $250,000 in operating assets for Division Y. Thus, Division X's greater residual income is probably more a result of its size than the quality of its management. In fact, it appears that the smaller division is better managed, since it has been able to generate nearly as much residual income with only one-fourth as much in operating assets with which to work. This problem can be reduced to some degree by focusing on the percentage change in residual income from year to year rather than on the absolute amount of the residual income.

Criticisms of Residual Income

As shown above, compared to ROI, the use of residual income can lead managers to make decisions more consistent with shareholders' objectives. Further, some claim that residual income is more closely related to shareholder returns than other metrics such as sales growth, net income or ROI. However the following criticisms of residual income, are worth noting:

1. Residual income is based on historical accounting data, which means that in particular, the accounting values used for capital assets can suffer from being out of date when costs are rising. This can lead to inflated amounts for residual income.

2. The residual income approach does not indicate what earnings *should* be for a particular business unit. A means of comparison is needed, which could involve using external benchmarks based on key competitors or evaluating trends in residual income over time (e.g., tracking the percentage change over several periods).
3. Calculating residual income requires numerous adjustments to financial information recorded using generally accepted accounting principles that can increase the cost of preparing the information.
4. Residual income is a financial metric that does not incorporate important leading non-financial indicators of success such as employee motivation or customer satisfaction.

Balanced Scorecard

LEARNING OBJECTIVE 5
Explain the use of balanced scorecards to assess performance.

Balanced scorecard
An integrated set of performance measures that is derived from and supports the organization's strategy.

A **balanced scorecard** consists of an integrated set of performance measures that is derived from the company's strategy and that supports the company's strategy throughout the organization.[6,7] A strategy is essentially a theory about how to achieve the organization's goals and deals with issues such as how to attract customers, what products or services to sell, what markets to enter, and how to compete with rivals. According to some experts, there are three potentially successful generic strategic approaches to outperforming competitors:[8]

1. **Cost leadership:** By maintaining low cost through efficiency relative to competitors, a company will be able to make superior profits at current industry prices. Alternatively, the company can become a price leader because other firms are unable to undercut its prices. Low costs may also serve as a barrier against potential new market entrants and thereby protect long-term profitability. However, technological change or imitation of low-cost techniques by rivals can threaten the success of this strategy.
2. **Differentiation:** For products or services that are perceived as unique, customers sometimes will pay premium prices, giving the company higher profit margins. This cushion of higher profits reduces the effect of supplier or buyer power. Brand loyalty, however, may fail if the cost differential between the firm and the cost leader in the industry becomes too wide.
3. **Focus or niche:** By serving a narrow, strategic target market more effectively than rivals who are competing more broadly, a firm may be able to achieve superior profitability. The risk of being overtaken by broad-target firms who have economies of scale is a constant threat to the success of this strategy.

Under the balanced scorecard approach, top management translates its strategy into performance measures that employees can understand and can do something about. For example, the length of time passengers have to wait in line to have their baggage checked might be a performance measure for the supervisor in charge of the Air Canada check-in

---

6. The balanced scorecard concept was promoted by Robert Kaplan and David Norton. For further details, see their articles "The Balanced Scorecard—Measures That Drive Performance," *Harvard Business Review*, January/February 1992, pp. 71–79; "Using the Balanced Scorecard as a Strategic Management System," *Harvard Business Review*, January/February 1996, pp. 75–85; "Why Does a Business Need a Balanced Scorecard?" *Journal of Cost Management*, May/June 1997, pp. 5–10; and their book *Translating Strategy into Action: The Balanced Scorecard* (Boston, MA: Harvard Business School Press, 1996).
7. In the 1960s, the French developed a concept similar to the balanced scorecard called *Tableau de Bord* or "dashboard." For details, see Michel Lebas, "Managerial Accounting in France: Overview of Past Tradition and Current Practice," *The European Accounting Review* 3, no. 3, 1994, pp. 471–87; and Marc Epstein and Jean-François Manzoni, "The Balanced Scorecard and the Tableau de Bord: Translating Strategy into Action," *Management Accounting*, August 1997, pp. 28–36.
8. Michael E. Porter, *Competitive Strategy: Creating and Sustaining Superior Performance* (New York, NY: Free Press, 1985).

counter at the Vancouver airport. This performance measure is easily understood by the supervisor, and can be improved by the supervisor's actions.

Common Characteristics of Balanced Scorecards

Performance measures used in the balanced scorecard approach tend to fall into the four groups illustrated in Exhibit 11–3: financial, customer, internal business processes, and learning and growth. Internal business processes are what the company does in an attempt to satisfy customers. For example, in a manufacturing company, assembling a product is an internal business process. For an airline, handling baggage is an internal business process. The basic idea is that learning is necessary to improve internal business processes; improving business processes is necessary to improve customer satisfaction; and improving customer satisfaction is necessary to improve financial results.

Note that the emphasis in Exhibit 11–3 is on *improvement*—not on just attaining some specific objective such as profits of $10 million. In the balanced scorecard approach, continual improvement is encouraged. In many industries, this is a matter of survival. If an organization does not continually improve, it will eventually lose out to competitors that do.

Financial performance measures appear at the top of Exhibit 11–3. Ultimately, most companies exist to provide financial rewards to owners. There are exceptions. Some companies—for example, The Body Shop—may have loftier goals, such as providing environmentally friendly products to consumers. However, even non-profit organizations must generate enough financial resources to stay in operation.

However, for several reasons, financial performance measures (even ROI or EVA®) are not sufficient in themselves—they should be integrated with nonfinancial measures in a well-designed balanced scorecard. First, financial measures are lag indicators that report on the results of past actions. In contrast, nonfinancial measures of key success drivers such as customer satisfaction are leading indicators of future financial performance. Second, top managers are ordinarily responsible for the financial performance measures—not

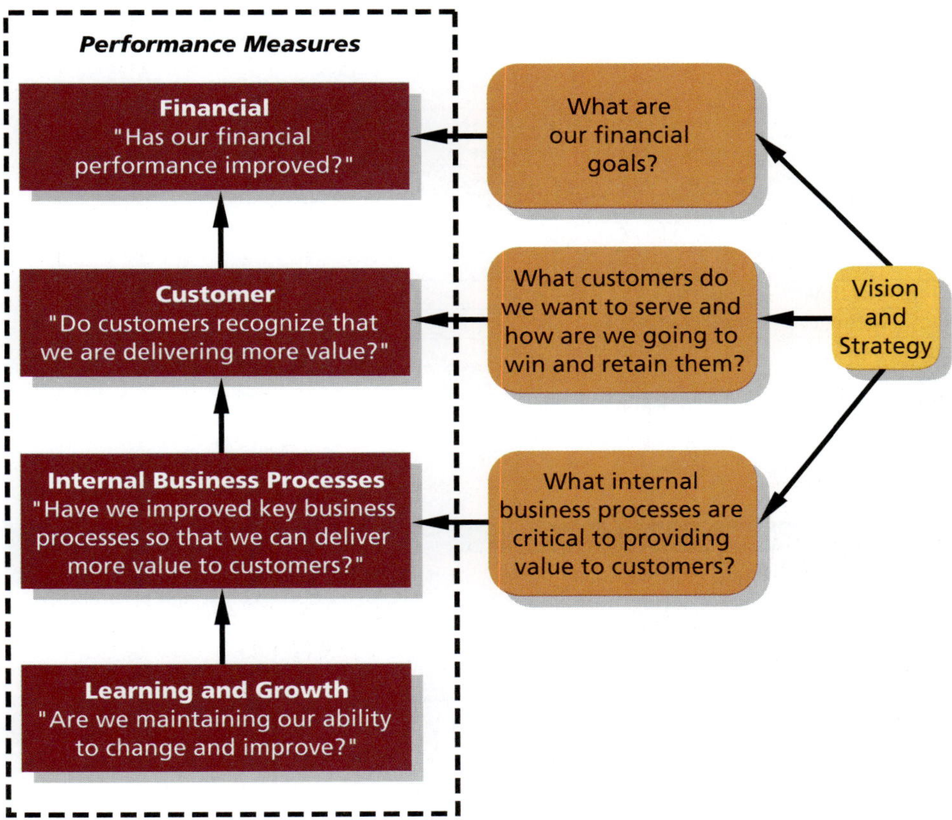

EXHIBIT 11–3 From Strategy to Perfomance Measures: The Balanced Scorecard

lower-level managers. The supervisor in charge of checking in passengers can be held responsible for how long passengers have to wait in line. However, this supervisor cannot reasonably be held responsible for the entire company's profit. That is the responsibility of the airline's top managers.

Exhibit 11–4 lists some examples of performance measures that can be found in the customer, internal business process and learning and growth categories of the balanced scorecards at many companies. However, few companies, if any, would use all of these performance measures, and almost all companies would add other performance measures. Managers should carefully select the performance measures for their company's balanced scorecard, keeping the following points in mind. First, the performance measures should be consistent with, and follow from, the company's strategy. If the performance measures are not consistent with the company's strategy, people will find themselves working at cross-purposes. Second, the scorecard should not have too many performance measures. This can lead to a lack of focus and confusion.

While the entire organization will have an overall balanced scorecard, each responsible individual may have his or her own personal scorecard as well. This scorecard should

EXHIBIT 11–4 Examples of Performance Measures for Balanced Scorecards

Customer Perspective

Performance Measure	Desired Change
Customer satisfaction as measured by survey results	+
Number of customer complaints	−
Market share	+
Product returns as a percentage of sales	−
Percentage of customers retained from last period	+
Number of new customers	+

Internal Business Processes Perspective

Performance Measure	Desired Change
Percentage of sales from new products	+
Time to introduce new products to market	−
Percentage of customer calls answered within 20 seconds	+
On-time deliveries as a percentage of all deliveries	+
Work in process inventory as a percentage of sales	−
Unfavourable standard cost variances	−
Defect-free units as a percentage of completed units	+
Delivery cycle time*	−
Throughput time*	−
Manufacturing cycle efficiency*	+
Quality costs*	−
Set-up time	−
Time from call by customer to repair of product	−
Percent of customer complaints settled on first contact	+
Time to settle a customer claim	−

Learning and Growth Perspective

Performance Measure	Desired Change
Suggestions per employee	+
Value-added employee†	+
Employee turnover	−
Hours of in-house training per employee	+

*Explained later in this chapter.

†Value-added is revenue less externally purchased materials, supplies, and services.

consist of items the individual can personally influence that relate directly to the performance measures on the overall balanced scorecard (e.g. hours spent in training courses). The performance measures on this personal scorecard should not be overly influenced by actions taken by others in the company or by events that are outside of the individual's control. Also, the personal scorecard measures should not lead an individual to take actions that are inconsistent with the organization's objectives

With those broad principles in mind, we will now take a look at how a company's strategy affects its balanced scorecard.

A Company's Strategy and the Balanced Scorecard

Returning to the performance measures in Exhibit 11–3, each company must decide which customers to target and what internal business processes are crucial to attracting and retaining those customers. Different companies, having different strategies, will target different customers with different kinds of products and services. Take the automobile industry as an example. BMW stresses engineering and handling; Volvo, safety; Jaguar, luxury detailing; Corvette, racy styling; and Toyota, reliability. Because of these differences in emphases, a one-size-fits-all approach to performance measurement will not work even within this one industry. Performance measures must be tailored to the specific strategy of each company.

Suppose, for example, that Jaguar's strategy is to offer distinctive, richly finished luxury automobiles to wealthy individuals who prize handcrafted, individualized products. Part of Jaguar's strategy might be to create such a large number of options for details, such as leather seats, interior and exterior colour combinations, and wooden looking dashboards, that each car becomes virtually one of a kind. For example, instead of just offering tan or blue leather seats in standard cowhide, the company may offer customers the choice of an almost infinite palette of colours in any of a number of different exotic leathers. For such a system to work effectively, Jaguar would have to be able to deliver a completely customized car within a reasonable amount of time—and without incurring more cost for this customization than the customer is willing to pay. Exhibit 11–5 suggests how Jaguar might reflect this strategy in its balanced scorecard.

If the balanced scorecard is correctly constructed, the performance measures should be linked together on a cause-and-effect basis. Each link can then be read as an hypothesis in the form "If we improve this performance measure, then this other performance measure should also improve." Starting from the bottom of Exhibit 11–5, we can read the links between performance measures as follows. If employees acquire the skills to install new options more effectively, then the company can offer more options and the options can be installed in less time. If more options are available and they are installed in less time, then customer surveys should show greater satisfaction with the range of options available. If customer satisfaction improves, then the number of cars sold should increase. In addition, if customer satisfaction improves, the company should be able to maintain or increase its selling prices, and if the time to install options decreases, the costs of installing the options should decrease. Together, this should result in an increase in the contribution margin per car. If the contribution margin per car increases and more cars are sold, the result should be an increase in profits.

In essence, the balanced scorecard illustrates a theory of how the company can attain its desired outcomes (financial, in this case) by taking concrete actions. While the strategy laid out in Exhibit 11–5 seems plausible, it should be regarded as only a theory that should be discarded if it proves to be invalid. For example, if the company succeeds in increasing the number of options available and in decreasing the time required to install options and yet there is no increase in customer satisfaction, the number of cars sold, the contribution margin per car, or profits, the strategy would have to be reconsidered. One of the advantages of the balanced scorecard is that it can be used to continually test the theories underlying management's strategy. If a strategy is not working, it should become evident when some of the predicted effects (i.e., more car sales) do not occur. Without this feedback, management may drift on indefinitely with an ineffective strategy based on faulty assumptions.

EXHIBIT 11–5 A Possible Strategy at Jaguar and the Balanced Scorecard

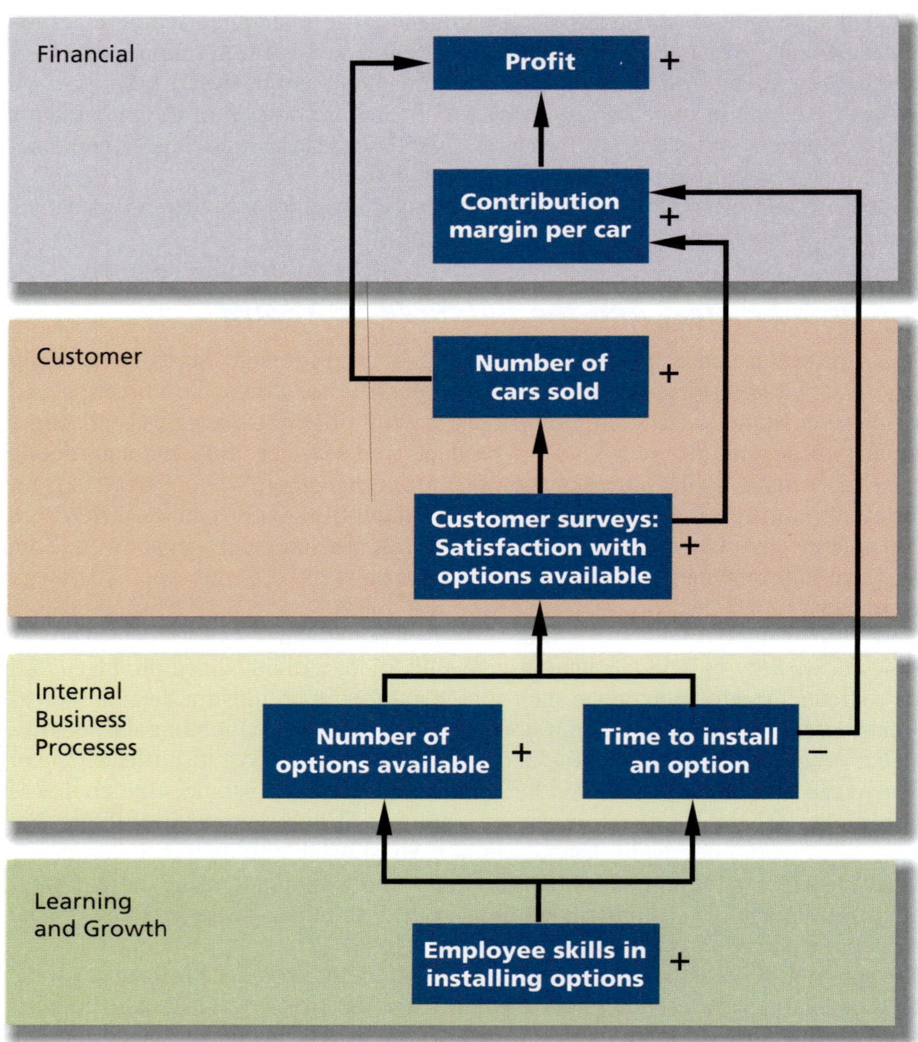

IN BUSINESS

Cause-and-Effect Is the Key

Professors Christopher D. Ittner and David F. Larcker surveyed 157 companies and found that only 23% consistently verified the hypothesized cause-and-effect linkages embedded in their balanced scorecards. These companies earned a 5.14% higher return on common shareholders' equity than the 77% of companies that did not verify their cause-and-effect linkages.

The authors found that most companies do not verify cause-and-effect linkages because they erroneously believe that they are self-evident. For example, one fast-food chain chose employee turnover as a performance measure believing that its positive effects on profits were obvious. However, the professors' research revealed that the fast-food chain's profitability was only influenced by turnover among its supervisors, not lower-level employees. A broad measure of employee turnover did not help explain differences in profitability across restaurants.

Source: Christopher D. Ittner and David F. Larcker, "Coming Up Short on Nonfinancial Performance Measurement," *Harvard Business Review,* November 2003, pp. 88–95.

Tying Compensation to the Balanced Scorecard

Incentive compensation for employees, such as bonuses, can, and probably should, be tied to balanced scorecard performance measures. However, this should be done only after the organization has been successfully managed with the scorecard for some time—perhaps a year or more. Managers must be confident that the performance measures are reliable, sensible, understood by those who are being evaluated, and not easily manipulated. As Robert Kaplan and David Norton, the promotors of the balanced scorecard concept point out, "compensation is such a powerful lever that you have to be pretty confident that you have the right measures and have good data for the measures before making the link."[9]

Advantages of Timely Feedback

Whatever performance measures are used, they should be reported on a frequent and timely basis. For example, data about defects should be reported to the responsible managers at least once a day so that action can be quickly taken if an unusual number of defects occurs. In the most advanced companies, any defect is reported *immediately,* and its cause is tracked down before any more defects occur. Another common characteristic of the performance measures under the balanced scorecard approach is that managers focus on *trends* in the performance measures over time. The emphasis is on progress and *improvement* rather than on meeting any specific standard.

IN BUSINESS

A Picture is Worth a Thousand Numbers

Graphics are routinely integrated in Balanced Scorecard reports, with data often displayed on a "dashboard" with representations of gauges and digital readouts. At Beverage Can Americas Co. in Chicago, a division of London-based Rexam Plc., executive dashboards and scorecards are being rolled out to thousands of employees. "Each worker sees a handful of metrics that pertain to his or her job, which are represented as green, yellow, or red icons depending on whether they are satisfactory, borderline, or subpar."

Source: Scott Leibs, "Now You See It," *CFO,* July 2002, pp. 61–66.

Some Measures of Internal Business Process Performance

Internal business process performance measures included on a balanced scorecard provide feedback needed for improving these processes. This information is essential for making cost and quality improvements that lead to greater profitability and customer satisfaction.

Most of the performance measures listed in Exhibit 11–4 are self-explanatory. However, three are not—*delivery cycle time*, *throughput time*, and *manufacturing cycle efficiency (MCE)*. Because of their importance to organizations and their common use in balanced scorecards, they are discussed next.

Delivery Cycle Time The amount of time from when an order is received from a customer to when the completed order is shipped is called **delivery cycle time.** This time is clearly a key concern to many customers, who would like the delivery cycle time to be as short as possible. Cutting the delivery cycle time may give a company a key competitive advantage—and may be necessary for survival—and therefore many companies would include this performance measure on their balanced scorecard.

Delivery cycle time
The amount of time required from receipt of an order from a customer to shipment of the completed goods.

9. Lori Calabro, "On Balance: A CFO Interview," *CFO,* February 2001, pp. 73–78.

Throughput time The amount of time required to turn raw materials into completed products.

Throughput (Manufacturing Cycle) Time

The amount of time required to turn raw materials into completed products is called **throughput time,** or *manufacturing cycle time*. The relationship between the delivery cycle time and the throughput (manufacturing cycle) time is illustrated in Exhibit 11–6.

Note that, as shown in Exhibit 11–6, the throughput time, or manufacturing cycle time, is made up of process time, inspection time, move time, and queue time. *Process time* is the amount of time in which work is actually done on the product. *Inspection time* is the amount of time spent ensuring that the product is not defective. *Move time* is the time required to move materials or partially completed products from workstation to workstation. *Queue time* is the amount of time a product spends waiting to be worked on, to be moved, to be inspected, or in storage waiting to be shipped.

As shown at the bottom of Exhibit 11–6, the only one of these four activities that adds value to the product is process time. The other three activities—inspecting, moving, and queueing—add no value and should be eliminated as much as possible.

Manufacturing cycle efficiency (MCE) Process (value-added) time as a percentage of throughput time.

Manufacturing Cycle Efficiency (MCE)

Through concerted efforts to eliminate the *non-value-added* activities of inspecting, moving, and queueing, some companies have reduced their throughput time to only a fraction of previous levels. In turn, this has helped to reduce the delivery cycle time from months to only weeks or hours. The throughput time, which is considered to be a key measure in delivery performance, can be put into better perspective by computing the **manufacturing cycle efficiency (MCE).** The MCE is computed by relating the value-added time to the throughput time. The formula is as follows:

$$\text{MCE} = \frac{\text{Value-added time}}{\text{Throughput (manufacturing cycle) time}}$$

If the MCE is less than 1, then non-value-added time is present in the production process. An MCE of 0.5, for example, would mean that half of the total production time consisted of inspection, moving, and similar non-value-added activities. In many manufacturing companies, the MCE is less than 0.1 (10%), which means that 90% of the time a unit is in process is spent on activities that do not add value to the product.[10] By monitoring the MCE, companies are able to reduce non-value-added activities and thus get products into the hands of customers more quickly and at a lower cost.

EXHIBIT 11–6 Delivery Cycle Time and Throughput (Manufacturing Cycle) Time

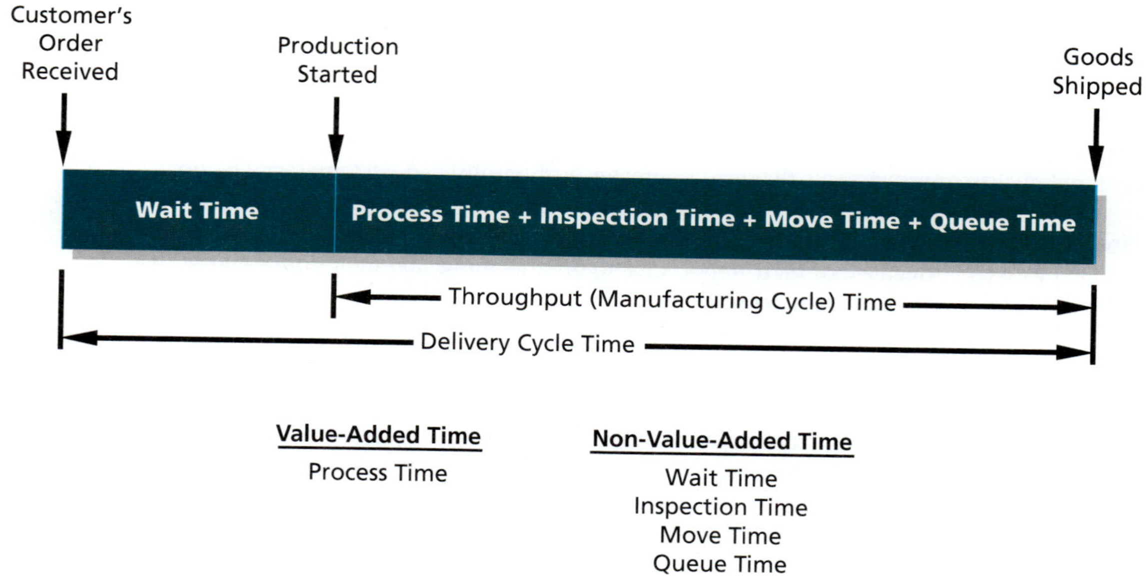

10. Callie Berlinger and James A. Brimson, eds., *Cost Management for Today's Advanced Manufacturing* (Boston, MA: Harvard Business School Press, 1988), p. 4.

To provide a numeric example of these measures, assume the following data for Novex Company:

Novex Company keeps careful track of the time relating to orders and their production. During the most recent quarter, the following average times were recorded for each unit or order:

	Days
Wait time	17.0
Inspection time	0.4
Process time	2.0
Move time	0.6
Queue time	5.0

Goods are shipped as soon as production is completed.

Based on this data, we can calculate the following:

1. Throughput time, or velocity of production.
2. Manufacturing cycle efficiency (MCE).
3. Percentage of the production time spent in non-value-added activities.
4. Delivery cycle time.

The calculations are as follows:

1. Throughput time = Process time + Inspection time + Move time + Queue time
   = 2.0 days + 0.4 days + 0.6 days + 5.0 days
   = 8.0 days
2. Only process time represents value-added time; therefore, the computation of the MCE would be as follows:

$$\text{MCE} = \frac{\text{Value-added time, 2.0 days}}{\text{Throughput time, 8.0 days}}$$
$$= 0.25$$

   Thus, once put into production, a typical unit is actually being worked on only 25% of the time.
3. Since the MCE is 25%, the complement of this figure, or 75% of the total production time, is spent in non-value-added activities.
4. Delivery cycle time = Wait time + Throughput time
   = 17.0 days + 8.0 days
   = 25.0 days

IN BUSINESS

Banks ordinarily require three to four weeks to approve an application for a mortgage loan on a house. The application form includes the individual's employment history, income, and financial assets and liabilities. Personnel at the bank check credit references and review the entire application before granting the loan. A manager at one bank wondered why this process takes so long and asked employees to keep track of how much time they actually worked on processing an application. He discovered that processing an application took on average 26 days, but only about 15 minutes of this time was actual work. All of the rest of the time the application was waiting in someone's in-basket. The manufacturing cycle efficiency (MCE) was therefore only 0.0004 (15 minutes/[26 days × 24 hours per day × 60 minutes per hour]). By redesigning and automating the process, the cycle time was cut down to 15 minutes and the MCE rose to 1.0. Loan applicants can now have a cup of coffee while waiting for approval.

Source: Robert Kaplan and David Norton, *Translating Strategy into Action: The Balanced Scoreboard* (Boston, MA: Harvard Business School Press, 1996), pp. 118–19.

Some Final Observations Concerning the Balanced Scorecard We would like to emphasize a few points concerning the balanced scorecard. First, the balanced scorecard should be tailored to the company's strategy; each company's balanced scorecard should be unique. The examples given in this chapter are just that—examples. They should not be interpreted as general templates to be fitted to each company. Second, the balanced scorecard reflects a particular strategy, or theory, about how a company can further its objectives by taking specific actions. The theory should be viewed as tentative and subject to change if the actions do not in fact lead to attaining the company's financial and other goals. If the theory (i.e., strategy) changes, then the performance measures on the balanced scorecard should also change. The balanced scorecard should be viewed as a dynamic system that evolves as the company's strategy evolves. Third, while the balanced scorecard is an important component of an organization's reporting and control system, it is not the only piece. Numerous supporting schedules and supplementary information will also be regularly prepared and used by managers to monitor and control the day-to-day activities under their responsibility. An example of the need for additional reporting beyond the summary information contained in a balanced scorecard is presented in the next section where quality costs are discussed Thus a balanced scorecard does not replace the need for the regular preparation and use of detailed reports on key operating activities.

Cost of Quality

LEARNING OBJECTIVE 6
Identify the four types of quality costs, explain their interaction, and prepare a quality cost report.

One of the internal business process measures shown in Exhibit 11–4 that many companies include on their balanced scorecard is quality costs. This is usually a summary metric made up of different types or categories of quality costs. Increasingly, managers at both manufacturing and service companies are emphasizing the importance of understanding the various kinds of quality costs and how they can be managed. In this section we discuss the types of quality costs and their interaction as well as illustrate how some companies extend the reporting of these costs beyond the summary metrics included in the scorecard.

A company may have a product with a high-quality design that uses high-quality components, but if the product is poorly assembled or has other defects, the company will have high warranty repair costs and dissatisfied customers. People who are dissatisfied with a product are unlikely to buy the product again and may tell others about their bad experiences. This is the worst possible sort of advertising. To prevent such problems, companies have been expending a great deal of effort to reduce defects. The objective is to have high *quality of conformance*.

IN BUSINESS

Who Is Laughing Now?

There was time when Hyundai's product quality was the laughing stock of the automobile industry. However, in 2004 Hyundai's vehicles tied Toyota and Honda for the top spot in J.D. Power and Associates' study of initial vehicle quality. In that same year, Consumer Reports rated Hyundai's Sonata the most reliable car on the road. Why the dramatic turnabout? The company expanded its quality department to 1,000 employees—a tenfold increase—and required the department to report directly to the company's chairman, Mong-Koo Chung. Now, employees are paid bonuses for sharing and implementing ideas for improvement. "At Hyundai's Asian factory outside Seoul, workers have dropped 25,000 ideas into the suggestion box, of which 30% have been adopted." When test drives revealed a flaw in the Sonata's front door, it took engineers two months to create a solution that cost 40 cents per car. Had the same problem occurred a few years ago, one manager at Hyundai commented "we'd probably leave it."

Source: Joann Muller and Robyn Meredith, "Last Laugh," *Forbes*, April, 18, 2005, pp. 98–104.

Quality of Conformance

A product that meets or exceeds its design specifications and is free of defects that mar its appearance or degrade its performance is said to have high **quality of conformance**. Note that if an economy car is free of defects, it can have a quality of conformance that is just as high as a defect-free luxury car. The purchasers of economy cars cannot expect their cars to be as opulently equipped as luxury cars, but they can and do expect them to be free of defects.

Quality of conformance
The degree to which a product or service meets or exceeds its design specifications and is free of defects or other problems that mar its appearance or degrade its performance.

Preventing, detecting, and dealing with defects cause costs that are called *quality costs* or the *cost of quality*. The use of the term *quality cost* is confusing to some people. It does not refer to costs such as using a higher-grade leather to make a wallet or using 14K gold instead of gold-plating in jewellery. Instead, the term **quality cost** refers to all of the costs that are incurred to prevent defects or that are incurred as a result of defects occurring.

Quality cost
Costs that are incurred to prevent defective products from falling into the hands of customers or that are incurred as a result of defective units.

Quality costs can be broken down into four broad groups. Two of these groups—known as *prevention costs* and *appraisal costs*—are incurred in an effort to keep defective products from falling into the hands of customers. The other two groups—known as *internal failure costs* and *external failure costs*—are incurred because defects are produced despite efforts to prevent them. Examples of specific costs involved in each of these four groups are given in Exhibit 11–7.

Several things should be noted about the quality costs shown in the exhibit. First, quality costs do not relate to just manufacturing; rather, they relate to all of the activities in a company from initial research and development (R&D) through customer service. Second, the number of costs associated with quality is very large; therefore, total quality cost can be quite high unless management gives this area special attention. Finally, the costs in the four groupings are quite different. We will now look at each of these groupings more closely.

Prevention Costs

Generally the most effective way to minimize quality costs while maintaining high-quality output is to avoid having quality problems arise in the first place. This is the purpose of **prevention costs**; such costs relate to any activity that reduces the number of defects in products or services. Companies have learned that it is much less costly to prevent a problem from ever happening than it is to find and correct the problem after it has occurred.

Prevention costs
Costs that are incurred to keep defects from occurring.

Note from Exhibit 11–7 that prevention costs include activities relating to quality circles and statistical process control. **Quality circles** consist of small groups of employees that meet on a regular basis to discuss ways to improve the quality of output. Both management and workers are included in these circles. Quality circles are widely used

Quality circles
Small groups of employees that meet on a regular basis to discuss ways of improving quality.

EXHIBIT 11–7 Typical Quality Costs

Prevention Costs
Systems development
Quality engineering
Quality training
Quality circles
Statistical process control activities
Supervision of prevention activities
Quality data gathering, analysis, and reporting
Quality improvement projects
Technical support provided to suppliers
Audits of the effectiveness of the quality system

Appraisal Costs
Test and inspection of incoming materials
Test and inspection of in-process goods
Final product testing and inspection
Supplies used in testing and inspection
Supervision of testing and inspection activities
Depreciation of test equipment
Maintenance of test equipment
Plant utilities in the inspection area
Field testing and appraisal at customer site

Internal Failure Costs
Net cost of scrap
Net cost of spoilage
Rework labour and overhead
Reinspection of reworked products
Retesting of reworked products
Downtime caused by quality problems
Disposal of defective products
Analysis of the cause of defects in production
Re-entering data because of keying errors
Debugging software errors

External Failure Costs
Cost of field servicing and handling complaints
Warranty repairs and replacements
Repairs and replacements beyond the warranty period
Product recalls
Liability arising from defective products
Returns and allowances arising from quality problems
Lost sales arising from a reputation for poor quality

in manufacturing companies, utilities, health care organizations, banks, and many other organizations.

Statistical process control A charting technique used to monitor the quality of work being done at a workstation for the purpose of immediately correcting any problems.

Statistical process control is a technique used to detect whether a process is in or out of control. An out-of-control process results in defective units and may be caused by a miscalibrated machine or some other factor. In statistical process control, workers use charts to monitor the quality of units that pass through their workstations. Using these charts, workers can quickly spot processes that are out of control and that are creating defects. Problems can be immediately corrected and further defects prevented rather than waiting for an inspector to catch the defects later.

Note also from the list of prevention costs in Exhibit 11–7 that some companies provide technical support to their suppliers as a way of preventing defects. Particularly in just-in-time (JIT) systems, such support to suppliers is vital. In a JIT system, parts are delivered from suppliers just in time and in just the correct quantity to fill customer orders. If a defective part is received from a supplier, the part cannot be used and the order for the ultimate customer cannot be filled on time. Hence, every part received from a supplier must be free of defects. Consequently, companies that use JIT often require that their suppliers use sophisticated quality control programs such as statistical process control and that their suppliers certify that they will deliver parts and materials that are free of defects.

Appraisal Costs

Appraisal costs Costs that are incurred to identify defective products before the products are shipped to customers.

Any defective parts and products should be caught as early as possible. **Appraisal costs**, which are sometimes called *inspection costs*, are incurred to identify defective products *before* the products are shipped to customers. Unfortunately, performing appraisal activities doesn't keep defects from happening again, and most managers now realize that maintaining an army of inspectors is a costly (and ineffective) approach to quality control.

The late professor John K. Shank of Dartmouth College once stated, "The old-style approach was to say, 'We've got great quality. We have 40 quality control inspectors in the factory.' Then somebody realized that if you need 40 inspectors, it must be a lousy factory. So now the trick is to run a factory without any quality control inspectors; each employee is his or her own quality control person."[11]

Employees are increasingly being asked to be responsible for their own quality control. This approach, along with designing products to be easy to manufacture properly, allows quality to be built into products rather than relying on inspection to get the defects out.

Internal Failure Costs

Internal failure costs Costs that are incurred as a result of identifying defective products before they are shipped to customers.

Failure costs are incurred when a product fails to conform to its design specifications. Failure costs can be either internal or external. **Internal failure costs** result from identification of defects during the appraisal process. Such costs include scrap, rejected products, reworking of defective units, and downtime caused by quality problems. It is crucial that defects be discovered before a product is shipped to customers. Of course, the more effective a company's appraisal activities, the greater the chance of catching defects internally and the greater the level of internal failure costs (as compared to external failure costs). Unfortunately, appraisal activities focus on symptoms rather than on causes and they do nothing to reduce the number of defective items. However, appraisal activities do bring defects to the attention of management, which may lead to efforts to increase prevention activities so that the defects do not happen.

External Failure Costs

External failure costs Costs that are incurred when a product or service that is defective is delivered to a customer.

External failure costs result when a defective product is delivered to a customer. As shown in Exhibit 11–7, external failure costs include warranty repairs and replacements, product recalls, liability arising from legal action against a company, and lost sales arising from a reputation for poor quality. Such costs can significantly reduce profits.

11. Robert W. Casey, "The Changing World of the CEO," *PPM World* 24, no. 2, 1990, p. 31.

In the past, some managers have taken the attitude, "Let's go ahead and ship everything to customers, and we'll take care of any problems under the warranty." This attitude generally results in high external failure costs, customer ill will, and declining market share and profits.

Distribution of Quality Costs

Studies show that quality costs for some U.S. companies range between 10% and 20% of total sales, whereas experts say that these costs should be more in the 2% to 4% range. How does a company reduce its total quality cost? The answer lies in how the quality costs are distributed. Refer to the graph in Exhibit 11–8, which shows total quality costs as a function of the quality of conformance.

The graph shows that when the quality of conformance is low, total quality cost is high and that most of this cost consists of internal and external failure costs. A low quality of conformance means that a high percentage of units are defective and hence the company must incur high failure costs. However, as a company spends more and more on prevention and appraisal, the percentage of defective units drops. This results in lower costs of internal and external failure. Ordinarily, total quality cost drops rapidly as the quality of conformance increases. Thus, a company can reduce its total quality cost by focusing its efforts on prevention and appraisal. The cost savings from reduced defects usually exceed the costs of the additional prevention and appraisal efforts.

The graph in Exhibit 11–8 has been drawn so that the total quality cost is minimized when the quality of conformance is less than 100%. However, some experts contend that the total quality cost is not minimized until the quality of conformance is 100% and there are no defects. Indeed, many companies have found that the total quality costs seem to keep dropping even when the quality of conformance approaches 100% and defect rates are as low as one in a million units. Others argue that eventually total quality cost increases as the quality of conformance increases. However, in most companies, this does not seem to happen until the quality of conformance is very close to 100% and defect rates are very close to zero.

As a company's quality program becomes more refined and as its failure costs begin to fall, prevention activities usually become more effective than appraisal activities. Appraisal can only find defects, whereas prevention can eliminate them. The best way to prevent defects from happening is to design processes that reduce the likelihood of defects and to continually monitor processes using statistical process control methods.

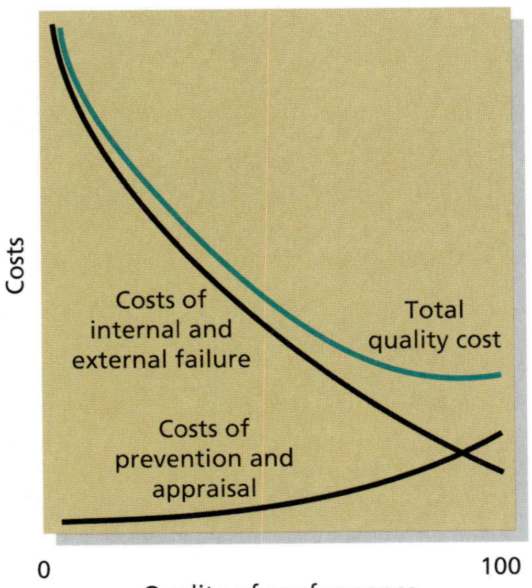

EXHIBIT 11–8 Effect of Quality Costs on Quality of Conformance

Quality Cost Reports

Quality cost report
A report that details prevention costs, appraisal costs, and the costs of internal and external failures.

As an initial step in quality improvement programs, companies often construct a *quality cost report* that provides an estimate of the financial consequences of the company's current level of defects. A **quality cost report** details the prevention costs, appraisal costs, and costs of internal and external failures that arise from the company's current level of defective products and services. A typical quality cost report is shown in Exhibit 11–9. For companies that use a balanced scorecard, this type of quality cost report would serve as a supplement to the summary information contained in the scorecard. For example, companies might choose to report only the total cost of quality in the balanced scorecard, or the total for each of the four quality cost categories. The quality cost report would then provide important details about the composition of the summary amounts.

Several things should be noted from the data in the exhibit. First, Ventura Company's quality costs are poorly distributed in both years, with most of the costs being traceable to either internal failure or external failure. The external failure costs are particularly high in year 1 in comparison to other costs.

Second, the company increased its spending on prevention and appraisal activities in year 2. As a result, internal failure costs go up in that year (from $2 million in year 1 to $3 million in year 2), but external failure costs drop sharply (from $5.15 million in year 1 to only $2 million in year 2). Because of the increase in appraisal activity in year 2, more defects are being caught inside the company before goods are shipped to customers. This results in more cost for scrap, rework, and so forth, but saves huge amounts in warranty repairs, warranty replacements, and other external failure costs.

EXHIBIT 11–9 Quality Cost Report

Ventura Company
Quality Cost Report
For Years 1 and 2

	Year 1		Year 2	
	Amount	Percent*	Amount	Percent*
Prevention costs:				
Systems development	$ 270,000	0.54%	$ 400,000	0.80%
Quality training	130,000	0.26%	210,000	0.42%
Supervision of prevention activities	40,000	0.08%	70,000	0.14%
Quality improvement projects	210,000	0.42%	320,000	0.64%
Total prevention cost	650,000	1.30%	1,000,000	2.00%
Appraisal costs:				
Inspection	560,000	1.12%	600,000	1.20%
Reliability testing	420,000	0.84%	580,000	1.16%
Supervision of testing and inspection	80,000	0.16%	120,000	0.24%
Depreciation of test equipment	140,000	0.28%	200,000	0.40%
Total appraisal cost	1,200,000	2.40%	1,500,000	3.00%
Internal failure costs:				
Net cost of scrap	750,000	1.50%	900,000	1.80%
Rework labour and overhead	810,000	1.62%	1,430,000	2.86%
Downtime due to defects in quality	100,000	0.20%	170,000	0.34%
Disposal of defective products	340,000	0.68%	500,000	1.00%
Total internal failure cost	2,000,000	4.00%	3,000,000	6.00%
External failure costs:				
Warranty repairs	900,000	1.80%	400,000	0.80%
Warranty replacements	2,300,000	4.60%	870,000	1.74%
Allowances	630,000	1.26%	130,000	0.26%
Cost of field servicing	1,320,000	2.64%	600,000	1.20%
Total external failure cost	5,150,000	10.30%	2,000,000	4.00%
Total quality cost	$9,000,000	18.00%	$7,500,000	15.00%

*As a percentage of total sales. In each year sales totalled $50,000,000.

Third, as a result of greater emphasis on prevention and appraisal, *total* quality cost has decreased in year 2. As continued emphasis is placed on prevention and appraisal in future years, total quality cost should continue to decrease. Moreover, appraisal costs should also decrease as more effort is put into prevention.

Quality Cost Reports in Graphic Form

As a supplement to the quality cost report shown in Exhibit 11–9, companies frequently prepare quality cost information in graphic form. Graphic presentations include pie charts, bar graphs, trend lines, etc. The data for Ventura Company from Exhibit 11–9 are presented in bar graph form in Exhibit 11–10.

The first bar graph in Exhibit 11–10 is scaled in terms of dollars of quality cost, and the second is scaled in terms of quality cost as a percentage of sales. In both graphs, appraisal costs are stacked on top of prevention costs, internal failure costs are stacked on top of the sum of prevention costs plus appraisal costs, and so forth. The percentage figures in the second graph show that total quality cost equals 18% of sales in year 1 and 15% of sales in year 2, the same as reported earlier in Exhibit 11–9.

Data in graphic form help managers to see trends more clearly and to see the magnitude of the various costs in relation to each other. Such graphs are easily prepared using computer graphics packages.

Uses of Quality Cost Information

The information provided by a quality cost report is used by managers in several ways. First, quality cost information helps managers see the financial significance of defects. Managers usually are not aware of the magnitude of their quality costs because they cut across departmental lines and are not normally tracked and accumulated by the cost system.

Second, quality cost information helps managers identify the relative importance of the quality problems faced by the firm. For example, the quality cost report may show that scrap is a major quality problem or that the company is incurring significant warranty costs. With this information, managers have a better idea of where to focus efforts.

Third, quality cost information helps managers see whether their quality costs are poorly distributed. In general, quality costs should be distributed more toward prevention and appraisal activities and less toward failures.

Counterbalancing these uses, three limitations of quality cost information should be

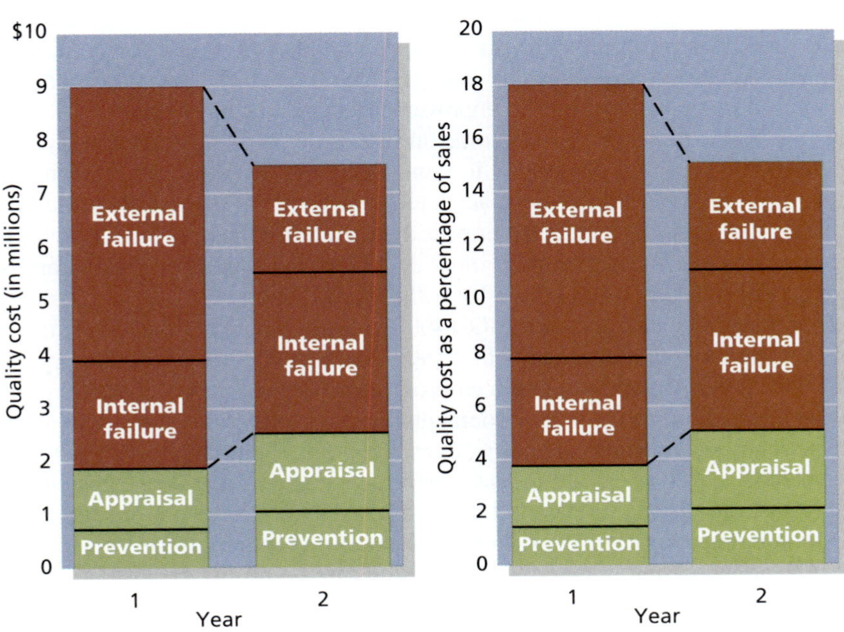

EXHIBIT 11–10 Quality Costs in Graphic Form

recognized. First, simply measuring and reporting quality costs does not solve quality problems. Problems can be solved only by taking action. Second, results usually lag behind quality improvement programs. Initially, total quality cost may even increase as quality control systems are designed and installed. Decreases in these costs may not begin to occur until the quality program has been in effect for a year or more. And third, the most important quality cost, lost sales arising from customer ill will, is usually omitted from the quality cost report because it is difficult to estimate.

Typically, during the initial years of a quality improvement program, the benefits of compiling a quality cost report outweigh the costs and limitations of the reports. As managers gain experience in balancing prevention and appraisal activities, the need for quality cost reports often diminishes.

International Aspects of Quality

Many of the tools used in quality management today were developed in Japan after World War II. In statistical process control, Japanese companies borrowed heavily from the work of W. Edwards Deming. However, Japanese companies are largely responsible for quality circles, JIT, the idea that quality is everyone's responsibility, and the emphasis on prevention rather than on inspection.

In the 1980s, quality re-emerged as a pivotal factor in the market. Many companies now find that it is impossible to effectively compete without a very strong quality program in place. This is particularly true of companies that wish to compete in the European market.

ISO 9000 standards
Quality control requirements issued by the International Standards Organization.

The International Organization for Standardization (ISO), based in Geneva, Switzerland, has established quality control guidelines known as the **ISO 9000 standards**. Many companies and organizations in Europe will buy only from ISO 9000 standard-certified suppliers. This means that the suppliers must demonstrate to a certifying agency that:

1. A quality control system is in use, and the system clearly defines an expected level of quality.
2. The system is fully operational and is backed up with detailed documentation of quality control procedures.
3. The intended level of quality is being achieved on a sustained, consistent basis.

The key to receiving certification under the ISO 9000 standards is documentation. It is one thing for a company to say that it has a quality control system in operation, but it is quite different to be able to document the steps in that system. Under ISO 9000, this documentation must be so detailed and precise that if all of the employees in a company were suddenly replaced, the new employees could use the documentation to make the product exactly as it was made by the former employees. Even companies with good quality control systems find that it takes up to two years of painstaking work to develop this detailed documentation. But companies often find that compiling this documentation results in improvements in their quality systems.

The ISO 9000 standards have become an international measure of quality. Although the standards were widely developed to control the quality of goods sold in European countries, they have become widely accepted elsewhere as well. Companies in North America that export to Europe often expect their own suppliers to comply with the ISO 9000 standards, since these exporters must document the quality of the materials going into their products as part of their own ISO 9000 certification.

In 1996 the ISO came out with ISO 14000, a set of standards that detail the requirements for an environmental management system (EMS). ISO 14000 provides organizations with a tool to: identify and control the environmental impact of its activities, products or services; continually improve its environmental performance; and develop an approach to setting environmental performance objectives and goals.[12] Although ISO 14000 does not identify specific levels of environmental performance (e.g., greenhouse gas emissions) it has established a common framework that can be used by organizations and their stakeholders when communicating about environmental issues. Although not yet as widely adopted as ISO 9000, an increasing number of organizations are becoming ISO 14000 certified.

12. See the ISO web site at www.iso.org/iso/home.htm.

Summary

A responsibility centre is any segment of an organization whose manager has control over and is accountable for cost, profit, or investments. Responsibility centre managers are evaluated based on what they can control. A cost centre is a business segment whose manager has control over costs only. A profit centre is a segment whose manager controls revenues and costs but not investments in operating assets. An investment centre manager controls profits and investments in operating assets. Responsibility centre reporting and evaluation is an important part of decentralization as it permits an assessment of the effectiveness of managers' decision making.

When products or services are transferred from one segment to another, a transfer price must be determined. Transfer pricing has no impact on overall company profits since the revenues recorded by the selling segment are exactly offset by the costs of the buying segment. However, because the profits of the individual segments *are* affected by the transfer price, managers are very concerned about the price that is set. The key objective in setting the transfer price is to motivate managers to take actions that are in the best interest of the overall company. Three approaches to setting transfer prices are possible: let managers negotiate their own price; base the price on the cost (variable or full absorption) of the products or services being transferred; or use the market price for the goods or services. When negotiating a transfer price, the minimum acceptable price for the selling division should be variable costs plus any opportunity costs incurred on the transaction. The buying division should not be willing to pay the selling division more than the price being charged by an external supplier.

For purposes of evaluating the performance of managers, there are at least three kinds of business segments—cost centres, profit centres, and investment centres. Return on investment (ROI) is widely used to evaluate investment centre performance. However, there is a trend toward using residual income or economic value added instead of ROI. The residual income and economic value added approaches encourage profitable investments in many situations where the ROI approach would discourage investment.

The balanced scorecard is a promising approach to managing organizations. A balanced scorecard consists of an integrated system of performance measures that are derived from and support the company's strategy. Different companies will have different balanced scorecards because they have different strategies. A well-constructed balanced scorecard provides a means for guiding the company and also provides feedback concerning the effectiveness of the company's strategy.

Internal business process measures are an integral part of a balanced scorecard. Examples of these measures that are tracked by many companies include delivery cycle time, manufacturing cycle time, manufacturing cycle efficiency, and quality costs. Quality costs are incurred to prevent defects and also arise when defects do occur. They can be classified into four broad groups: prevention costs, appraisal costs, internal failure costs, and external failure costs.

Review Problem 1: Transfer Pricing

Situation A

Collyer Products, Inc. has a Valve Division that manufactures and sells a standard valve as follows:

Capacity in units	100,000
Selling price to outside customers on the intermediate market	$15
Variable costs per unit	8
Fixed costs per unit (based on capacity)	5

The company has a Pump Division that could use this valve in the manufacture of one of its pumps. The Pump Division is currently purchasing 10,000 valves per year from an overseas supplier at a cost of $14 per valve.

Required:

1. Assume that the Valve Division has ample idle capacity to handle all of the Pump Division's needs. What is the acceptable range, if any, for the transfer price between the two divisions?
2. Assume that the Valve Division is selling all that it can produce to outside customers on the intermediate market. What is the acceptable range, if any, for the transfer price between the two divisions?
3. Assume again that the Valve Division is selling all that it can produce to outside customers on the intermediate market. Also assume that $2 in variable expenses can be avoided on transfers within the company, due to reduced selling costs. What is the acceptable range, if any, for the transfer price between the two divisions?

Solution to Situation A

1. Since the Valve Division has idle capacity, it does not have to give up any outside sales to take on the Pump Division's business. Applying the formula for the lowest acceptable transfer price from the viewpoint of the selling division, we get:

$$\text{Transfer price} \geq \begin{matrix}\text{Variable cost}\\ \text{per unit}\end{matrix} + \frac{\text{Total contribution margin on lost sales}}{\text{Number of units transferred}}$$

$$\text{Transfer price} \geq \$8 + \frac{\$0}{10{,}000} = \$8$$

The Pump Division would be unwilling to pay more than $14, the price it is currently paying an outside supplier for its valves. Therefore, the transfer price must fall within the range:

$$\$8 \leq \text{Transfer price} \leq \$14$$

2. Since the Valve Division is selling all that it can produce on the intermediate market, it would have to give up some of these outside sales to take on the Pump Division's business. Thus, the Valve Division has an opportunity cost that is the total contribution margin on lost sales:

$$\text{Transfer price} \geq \begin{matrix}\text{Variable cost}\\ \text{per unit}\end{matrix} + \frac{\text{Total contribution margin on lost sales}}{\text{Number of units transferred}}$$

$$\text{Transfer price} \geq \$8 + \frac{(\$15 - \$8) \times 10{,}000}{10{,}000} = \$8 + \$7 = \$15$$

Since the Pump Division can purchase valves from an outside supplier at only $14 per unit, no transfers will be made between the two divisions.

3. Applying the formula for the lowest acceptable price from the viewpoint of the selling division, we get:

$$\text{Transfer price} \geq \begin{matrix}\text{Variable cost}\\ \text{per unit}\end{matrix} + \frac{\text{Total contribution margin on lost sales}}{\text{Number of units transferred}}$$

$$\text{Transfer price} \geq (\$8 - \$2) + \frac{(\$15 - \$8) \times 10{,}000}{10{,}000} = \$6 + \$7 = \$13$$

In this case, the transfer price must fall within the range:

$$\$13 \leq \text{Transfer price} \leq \$14$$

Situation B

Referring to the original data in situation A above, assume the Pump Division needs 20,000 special high-pressure valves per year. The Valve Division's variable costs to manufacture and ship the special valve would be $10 per unit. To produce these special valves, the Valve Division would have to reduce its production and sales of regular valves from 100,000 units per year to 70,000 units per year.

Required:
As far as the Valve Division is concerned, what is the lowest acceptable transfer price?

Solution to Situation B

To produce the 20,000 special valves, the Valve Division will have to give up sales to outside customers of 30,000 regular valves. Applying the formula for the lowest acceptable price from the viewpoint of the selling division, we get:

$$\text{Transfer price} \geq \begin{matrix}\text{Variable cost}\\ \text{per unit}\end{matrix} + \frac{\text{Total contribution margin on lost sales}}{\text{Number of units transferred}}$$

$$\text{Transfer price} \geq \$10 + \frac{(\$15 - \$8) \times 30{,}000}{20{,}000} = \$10 + \$10.50 = \$20.50$$

Review Problem 2: Return on Investment (ROI) and Residual Income

Selected operating data for two divisions of Outback Brewing, Ltd., of Australia are given below:

	Division	
	Queensland	**New South Wales**
Sales	$4,000,000	$7,000,000
Average total operating assets	$2,000,000	$2,000,000
Operating income	$360,000	$420,000
Property, plant, and equipment (net)	$950,000	$800,000

Required:
1. Compute the rate of return for each division using the return on investment (ROI) formula stated in terms of margin and turnover.
2. Compute residual income for each division assuming the required rate of return is 15%.

Solution to Review Problem 2

1. ROI computations:

$$\text{ROI} = \text{Margin} \times \text{Turnover}$$
$$= \frac{\text{Operating income}}{\text{Sales}} \times \frac{\text{Sales}}{\text{Average operating assets}}$$

Queensland Division:

$$\text{ROI} = \frac{\$360{,}000}{\$4{,}000{,}000} \times \frac{\$4{,}000{,}000}{\$2{,}000{,}000}$$
$$= 9\% \times 2 = 18\%$$

New South Wales Division:

$$\text{ROI} = \frac{\$420{,}000}{\$7{,}000{,}000} \times \frac{\$7{,}000{,}000}{\$2{,}000{,}000}$$
$$= 6\% \times 3.5 = 21\%$$

2. Residual income for each division is calculated as follows:

   Queensland Division:
   \$360,000 − (\$2,000,000 × 15%) = \$60,000

   New South Wales Division:
   \$420,000 − (\$2,000,000 × 15%) = \$120,000

Appendix 11A: Profitability Analysis

A frequently overlooked way to analyze profitability is by customer. Although managers generally assume that a dollar of sales to one customer is just as profitable as a dollar of sales to any other customer, this assumption may not be correct. The reason is that customers have varying demands for resource-consuming activities, just as products, markets, or other segments of a company have varying demands. For example, some customers order in smaller lots and more frequently than other customers, requiring more paperwork and materials handling. Some customers order non-standard parts that require special engineering work, special machinery set-ups, and perhaps special packaging and handling. Other customers always seem to be in a hurry and want special expediting and delivery services. Customers who demand high levels of these resource-consuming activities should not be cross-subsidized by customers who demand little in the way of customized services, special packaging, and so forth. However, unless the activities that are provided for customer support are traced to the company's various customers, cross-subsidization almost certainly will occur.

After the various customer-support activities in a company have been identified, the costs of providing these activities should be charged to the customers who require them. Thus, a customer who requires special accounts receivable terms, many small orders and deliveries, the packing of goods in shop-ready containers, and specialized field service should be quoted a price that reflects these costly activities. This is why we stated in earlier chapters that suppliers who make deliveries to customers in a JIT environment frequently quote prices that are somewhat higher than prices charged by other suppliers. The higher prices are needed to compensate these suppliers for the special activities required on their part to support JIT customers.

Businesses that have analyzed customer profitability have been surprised to find that a fairly small number of customers are apparently responsible for most of their profits. It is also common to find that a small number of customers consume far more resources than are warranted by the revenue generated.

Sales Variance Analysis

LEARNING OBJECTIVE 7
Analyze variances from sales budgets.

Segment reporting, first discussed in Chapter 8 and continued in this chapter as part of our discussion of responsibility centres, represents an important tool for evaluating managers' performance. As pointed out, the metrics used to evaluate managers depend on what they have control over. Cost centre managers will be evaluated on the basis of how well they did in controlling costs while investment centre managers can be evaluated using more comprehensive measures such as ROI or residual income. However, segmented profitability analysis can also be combined with the variance analysis discussed in Chapter 10 to generate a series of performance reports so that prices and volumes (quantities) can be compared to targets set by the budgeting process. The interaction of price and quantity represents important information for businesses to analyze to determine why the strategic goals and specific budgeted targets were not achieved. Managers want to know the effects of market volume changes, market penetration or share changes, sales mix changes, and price changes. Each of these elements can be isolated but the true test of management is to reconstitute the combination needed for a new marketing strategy. Variances from previous results can provide a valuable start for this process.

The ability to have segment revenue data for analysis depends on the coding attached to the revenue information. Geographic market, product line, customer, and sales personnel are common classifications. Managers, with the assistance of the accountant, must decide what they wish to know and what classifications can be realistically structured, given the degree of substitutes and complements that exist, the number of products that exist, and the nature of meaningful groupings.

To illustrate the nature of variance reporting in the revenue area, consider the following example for Ace Video Company.

Budget sales in units:	
Deluxe video game.	10,000
Standard video game. . . .	5,000
Budget price:	
Deluxe	$60
Standard.	$30
Market volume expected:	
Deluxe	70,000
Standard.	90,000
Budget variable expense:	
Deluxe	$24
Standard.	$15

The sales price for the deluxe video game was reduced to $54 from the anticipated $60. This resulted in a $48,000 increase in revenue. The standard video game price was increased by $3 per unit, resulting in a revenue decrease of $18,000. The reasoning behind the price and revenue changes is something marketing management should explain so that a new pricing strategy can be considered.

Actual results for the period were:

Unit sales:	
Deluxe	12,000
Standard.	4,000
Sales prices:	
Deluxe	$54
Standard.	$33
Market volume:	
Deluxe	75,000
Standard.	85,000

Exhibit 11–11 presents a summary of the relationships among budgeted and actual results.

Analysis of revenue variances can proceed as follows:

$$\textbf{Sales price variance} = \left(\text{Actual sales price} - \text{Budgeted sales price}\right) \times \text{Actual sales volume}$$

Sales price variance Actual sales price minus budgeted sales price, multiplied by actual sales quantity.

Deluxe	($54 − $60) × 12,000 units =	$72,000 U
Standard	($33 − $30) × 4,000 units =	12,000 F
	Total sales price variance =	$60,000 U

Note in Exhibit 11–11 that the total $60,000 unfavourable sales price variance in contribution margin resulting from the change in sales price is calculated using actual sales volume in units times the difference in sales price (actual versus budget) because actual and budgeted variable costs per unit are the same.

Firms often wish to know how well they are performing compared to the market for their product. If the total market demand changes, they want to evaluate the impact on

EXHIBIT 11–11 Actual and Budgeted Results: Ace Video Company

	Actual Results		Flexible Budget		Master Budget	
Revenue:						
Deluxe	(12,000 × $54)	$648,000	(12,000 × $60)	$720,000	(10,000 × $60)	$600,000
Standard	(4,000 × $33)	132,000	(4,000 × $30)	120,000	(5,000 × $30)	150,000
		780,000		840,000		750,000
Variable expenses:						
Deluxe	(12,000 × $24)	288,000	(12,000 × $24)	288,000	(10,000 × $24)	240,000
Standard	(4,000 × $15)	60,000	(4,000 × $15)	60,000	(5,000 × $15)	75,000
		348,000		348,000		315,000
Contribution margin		$432,000		$492,000		$435,000
		Sales Price Variance			Sales Volume Variance	
Total variances		$60,000 U			$57,000 F	

profits. Importantly, to avoid the problems associated with the arbitrary allocation of common costs first discussed in Chapter 8, the variances that follow focus on the effects of volume, quantity, and mix changes on contribution margin. If these changes also impacted the segment's traceable fixed costs, managers would also want to analyze these effects but this is beyond the scope of our discussion. *Market volume variances* and *market share variances* can provide a method of seeing the contribution margin effects of market volume changes or changes in the portion of the market, termed *market share* or *market penetration*, captured by the firm.

We begin with the market volume variance, holding market share constant.

Market volume variance
Actual market volume minus budget market volume times anticipated market share, multiplied by budgeted contribution margin.

$$\text{Market volume variance} = \begin{pmatrix}\text{Actual market volume} - \text{Budget market volume}\end{pmatrix} \times \text{Anticipated market share percentage} \times \text{Budgeted contribution margin per unit}$$

Deluxe	(75,000 − 70,000) × (10,000/70,000) × ($60 − $24) =	$25,714 F
Standard	(85,000 − 90,000) × (5,000/90,000) × ($30 − $15) =	$ 4,167 U
Total		$21,547 F

The market volume variance represents the effect on contribution margin of the total market size (demand) differing from what was anticipated. Using Ace Video's budgeted market share percentages for each product, the analysis above indicates that the net effect of higher than anticipated total market demand for Deluxe video games and lower than anticipated total market demand for Standard video games is an increase in contribution margin of $21,547. This variance, although favourable, is not the result of any actions taken by Ace Video managers; instead it simply reflects the impact on contribution margin of the total market demand for video games differing from the estimates prepared by the company.

To calculate the impact on contribution margin of Ace Video's market share differing from budget, holding the effects of total market demand constant, we use the following approach:

Market share variance
Actual sales volume minus the anticipated portion of the actual market volume, multiplied by budgeted contribution margin per unit.

$$\text{Market share variance} = \text{Actual sales quantity} - \left[\text{Actual market volume} \times \text{Anticipated market share percentage}\right] \times \text{Budgeted contribution margin per unit}$$

Deluxe	{12,000 − [75,000 × (10,000/70,000)]} × ($60 − $24) =	$46,286 F
Standard	{4,000 − [85,000 × (5,000/90,000)]} × ($30 − $15) =	10,833 U
Total		$35,453 F

The favourable market share variance of $35,453 reflects the net effect of Ace Video enjoying a higher than budgeted market share for Deluxe video games (16% actual versus 14.3% budgeted) but a lower than budgeted market share for Standard video games (4.7% versus 5.6%).[13] The market share variance can be influenced by actions taken by managers. For example the favourable market share variance for Deluxe video games is likely in part attributable to the $6 per unit price decrease. Another controllable factor that could influence the market share variance is a change to the company's marketing campaign.

Two aspects of the market volume variance and market share variance are worth emphasizing. First, each variance was calculated at the contribution margin level rather than individually analyzing revenues and variable expenses. This permits a direct evaluation of the profit effect of actual sales volumes differing from the master budget. Second, the use of the budgeted contribution margin per unit isolates the effects of volume variances from those of price (or cost) variances. The impact of actual selling prices differing from budget is captured by the sales price variance while the impact of actual variable costs per unit differing from budget was analyzed in Chapter 10.

The market volume variance and the market share variance help managers understand why actual sales quantities were 12,000 units for Deluxe and 4,000 units for Standard compared to budgeted unit sales of 10,000 and 5,000 respectively. In total these volume differences resulted in the following contribution margin variances:

Deluxe	(12,000 − 10,000) × ($60 − $24) =	$72,000 F
Standard	(4,000 − 5,000) × ($30 − $15) =	15,000 U
Total		$57,000 F
Composition: Market volume	=	$21,547 F
Market share	=	35,453 F
		$57,000 F

An alternative view of sales volume variances can be generated by examining sales mix and sales quantity variances in terms of their relationship to the budgeted contribution margin. For this approach to be meaningful, management must be in a position to control the mix of products it sells in the market. While alternative formulations are possible using gross margins, sales prices, or weighted average contribution margins, the straightforward use of contributions will be employed in the illustration that follows so the principle can be understood.

$$\textbf{Sales mix variance} = \left(\text{Actual sales quantity} - \text{Actual sales quantity at anticipated sales mix}\right) \times \text{Budgeted contribution margin per unit}$$

Deluxe	{[12,000 − 16,000* × (10/15)]} × ($60 − $24) =	$48,000 F
Standard	{[4,000 − 16,000 × (5/15)]} × ($30 − $15) =	20,000 U
Total sales mix variance	=	$28,000 F

*Note: 16,000 units = (12,000 + 4,000) and 10/15 is the anticipated proportion of Deluxe sales while 5/15 is the anticipated Standard mix proportion.

$$\textbf{Sales quantity variance} = \left\{\left[\text{Actual sales quantity at anticipated sales mix}\right] - \text{Anticipated sales quantity}\right\} \times \text{Budgeted contribution margin per unit}$$

13. Actual market shares for Deluxe and Standard video games are calculated as follows: Deluxe 16% = 12,000/75,000; Standard 4.7% = 4,000/85,000. Budgeted market shares for Deluxe and Standard video games are calculated as follows: Deluxe 14.3% = 10,000/70,000; Standard 5.6% = 5,000/90,000.

Deluxe	{[16,000 × (10/15)] − 10,000} × ($60 − $24) =	$24,000 F
Standard	{[16,000 × (5/15)] − 5,000} × ($30 − $15) =	5,000 F
Total sales quantity variance		$29,000 F

The total sales volume variance is $57,000 favourable, composed of the following:

Sales mix	$28,000 F
Sales quantity.....	29,000 F
Total	$57,000 F

The sales mix variance quantifies the effects on contribution margin of selling the two products in a mix that differs from the original budget. As shown in the analysis above, Ace Video had a budgeted mix of 66.7% Deluxe games (10,000/15,000) and 33.3% Standard games (5,000/15,000). However, the actual mix turned out to be 75% Deluxe games (12,000/16,000) and 25% Standard games (4,000/16,000). Selling a higher proportion of Deluxe games generates a favourable total sales mix variance because Deluxe has a contribution margin of $36 per unit compared to $15 per unit for Standard. The sales quantity variance isolates the effects on contribution margin of unit sales differing from the budget, holding constant the sales mix at the budgeted proportions. Because total sales quantity was 16,000 units compared to the budget of 15,000 units, the total quantity variance is favourable.[14]

Appendix 11B: Marketing Expense

LEARNING OBJECTIVE 8
Analyze marketing expenses using cost drivers.

Knowledge of the nature and behaviour of marketing expenses provides managers with information about the costs of their marketing endeavours. Such information represents a significant aspect of marketing efforts, one that is needed to complement the pricing strategy previously discussed. Transport, warehousing, selling, advertising, and credit are some of the key factors managers need to consider in their marketing strategy. Accurate cost behaviour and allocation by the accounting function can assist marketing decision makers.

Accountants typically decompose marketing expense into two general categories, order-getting and order-filling. Order-getting costs are the pure marketing costs such as advertising, selling commissions, and travel. Order-filling includes the costs of warehousing, transportation, packing, and credit. Order-getting costs tend to be somewhat more discretionary than order-filling because order-filling occurs after the sale rather than to obtain the sale. Nevertheless, marketing managers need to understand the cost behaviour associated with both sets of costs so that analysis can be conducted to decide what should be done and how. Consider the following data:

Driver Analysis	Total for Period
Transport (kilometres to customer)................................	390 km
Jones Ltd.—30 km per shipment	
Smith Ltd.—60 km per shipment	
Selling (hours spent on customers per period)........................	150 hours
Jones Ltd.—50 hours	
Smith Ltd.—100 hours	

continued

14. Because the sales quantity variance holds sales mix constant at the budgeted proportions, it can also be calculated using a weighted average contribution margin approach. The weighted average contribution margin, using the budgeted sales mix is $29 per unit: (10/15 × $36) + (5/15 × $15). The total sales quantity variance = (Actual total sales quantity − Budgeted total sales quantity) × Budgeted average contribution margin per unit. Using the data from our example: (16,000 − 15,000) × $29 = $29,000 F.

continued

Advertising (cost of medium per period)	$4,000
Jones Ltd.—3 weight for mostly television (75% of total)	
Smith Ltd.—1 weight for mostly Internet (25% of total)	
Warehousing (space occupied)	5,880 m³
Product A—50 cubic metres per unit	
Product B—80 cubic metres per unit	
Credit/Collection (invoices per shipment—Jones requires more time to pay and line-item invoicing):	
Jones Ltd.—1 invoice per shipment, 10 units per invoice (4 of A, 6 of B)	5 shipments
Smith Ltd.—1 invoice per shipment, 10 units per invoice (6 of A, 4 of B)	4 shipments

	Total Costs and Per Unit Amounts for Period		
	Total	Driver Level	Unit
Transport	$ 1,950	390 km	$5 per km
Selling	7,500	150 hrs	$50 per hr
Advertising	4,000	—	—
Warehousing	6,500	5,880 m³*	$1.105 per m³
Credit/Collection	750	9 invoices**	$83.33 per invoice
Total	$20,700		

*[(4 × 5) + (6 × 4) × 50m³] + [(6 × 5) + (4 × 4) × 80m³]
**(1 × 5) + (1 × 4)

When costs for a period are associated with their drivers and drivers can be associated with customers, marketing costs can be allocated to particular customers.

	Costs to Customer		
	Jones Ltd.	Smith Ltd.	Total
Transport:			
$5/km × 5 shipments × 30 km	$750		
$5/km × 4 shipments × 60 km		$1,200	$1,950
Selling:			
$50/hr × 50 hours	2,500		
$50/hr × 100 hours		5,000	7,500
Advertising: 3/4 × $4,000	3,000		
1/4 × $4,000		1,000	4,000
Warehousing:			
$1.105 m³ × 5 × [(4 × 50) + (6 × 80)]	3,760*		
$1.105 m³ × 4 × [(6 × 50) + (4 × 80)]		2,740	6,500
Credit/Collection:			
$83.33/invoice × 1 × 5	417		
$83.33/invoice × 1 × 4		333	750
	$10,427	$10,273	$20,700

*Rounded up. 5 shipments × m³ per shipment.

	Costs to Products		
	Product A	Product B	Total
Transport—common	—	—	$1,950
Selling—common	—	—	7,500
Advertising—common	—	—	4,000
Warehousing:			
$1.105 m³ × [(4 × 5) + (6 × 4)] × 50 m³	$2,431		
$1.105 m³ × [(6 × 5) + (4 × 4)] × 80 m³		$4,069*	$6,500
Credit/Collection—common	—	—	750
	$2,431	$4,069	$20,700

*Rounded up. Cost per m³ × units of product × space occupied per unit of A or B.

If the data are allocated to the two products, A and B, then the marketing expense can be broken down for the warehousing. However, the other costs cannot be broken down because transport, selling, and advertising are independent of the type of product, and are treated as common costs for the product breakdown above. Similarly, credit/collection are treated as common costs since invoicing and collection costs are not driven by product type. Only warehousing is a function of the product type and thus can be broken down by product type as well as by customer.

Marketing expense analysis uses the concepts of drivers to provide alternative views of the relationship of marketing costs to sales. The complexity of the analysis depends on the ability to define appropriate cost drivers for the marketing costs in a manner similar to the approach used with overhead costs as explained in Chapter 5. To avoid arbitrary allocations, expenses that do not have suitable drivers should be treated as common costs that are not incremental for the particular categories of the analysis being conducted. Management may decide that further analysis of these common costs can result in refined driver definitions, which in turn will permit cause/effect allocations of common marketing costs.

Summary

Analysis of customer profitability by including drivers for marketing and administration can provide opportunities for important strategic decisions. Knowledge of the profitability of customers or customer classes can facilitate selling decisions, surcharges for extra services, cross-selling opportunities, and changes in marketing approaches. Enterprise resource planning or similar computer systems can make the detailed analysis feasible and provide personnel with ratings of customer types so that the appropriate approach can be instituted for individual customers. With a wide variety of products and services, such analysis can be important, because all customers are not necessarily homogeneous and thus not equally profitable. Also, increases in sales value do not necessarily equate to increases in profitability because of the cost of providing the product services that customers demand.

Review Problem 3: Customer Profitability Analysis

The Leo company produces and sells two product lines with budgeted revenues and expenses as follows.

	Spars	Masts
Expected total industry sales.	48,000 units	85,000 units
Expected Leo Company sales.	4,200 units	17,000 units
Expected selling price	$200 per unit	$300 per unit
Expected cost of manufacturing (40% fixed)	110 per unit	180 per unit
Expected selling and administration costs (70% fixed). .	60 per unit	70 per unit
Expected product profit margin.	$30 per unit	$ 50 per unit
Actual results for 2008 included:		
Actual total industry sales	60,000 units	100,000 units
Actual Leo Company sales	6,000 units	18,000 units
Actual selling price.	$180 per unit	$300 per unit

All costs behaved exactly as expected.

W. Gallant, vice-president of marketing and sales, has requested that the employees of his department be paid a bonus for the year based on the fact that they have been able to increase sales by 2,800 units over budget level for the year, an increase of over 13%.

Required:

1. Calculate the changes in overall company profits caused by the following factors:
   a. Sales price
   b. Sales mix
   c. Sales quanitity

d. Market share
e. Market volume

Solution to Review Problem 3

1. **Budgeted Contribution Margin:**

	Spars	Masts
Selling price	$200	$300
Variable costs:		
Manufacturing	66	108
Selling & administration	18	21
Total variable costs	84	129
Budgeted contribution margin per unit	$116	$171

a. **Sales Price Variance:**

Spars ($180 – $200) x 6,000 =	$120,000	U
Masts ($300 – $300) x 18,000 =	–0–	
Total	$120,000	U

b. **Sales Mix Variance:**

Spars [6,000 – (4,200/21,200 x 24,000)] x $116 =	$144,453	F
Masts [18,000 – (17,000/21,200 x 24,000)] x $171 =	212,943	U
	$ 68,490	U

c. **Sales Quantity Variance:**

Spars [(4,200/21,200 x 24,000) – 4,200] x $116 =	$ 64,347	F
Masts [(17,000/21,200 x 24,000) – 17,000] x $171 =	383,943	F
	$448,290	F

d. **Market Share Variance:**

Spars [6,000 – (4,200/48,000 x 60,000)] x $116 =	$ 87,000	F
Masts [18,000 – (17,000/85,000 x 100,000)] x $171 =	342,000	U
	$255,000	U

e. **Market Volume Variance:**

Spars [(60,000 – 48,000) x (4,200/48,000)] x $116 =	$121,800	F
Masts [(100,000 – 85,000) x (17,000/85,000)] x $171=	513,000	F
	$634,800	F

Glossary

Visit the Online Learning Centre at http://www.mcgrawhill.ca/olc/garrison/ for a review of key terms and definitions.

Questions

11–1 What is meant by the term *decentralization*?
11–2 Distinguish between a cost centre, a profit centre, and an investment centre.
11–3 From the standpoint of a selling division that has idle capacity, what is the minimum acceptable transfer price for an item?
11–4 From the standpoint of a selling division that has *no* idle capacity, what is the minimum acceptable transfer price for an item?
11-5 What are the advantages and disadvantages of cost-based transfer prices?
11–6 If a market price for a product can be determined, why is it not always the best transfer price?
11–7 What is meant by the terms *margin* and *turnover*?
11–8 What are the three approaches to improving return on investment (ROI)?
11–9 What is meant by the term *residual income*?
11–10 In what way can the use of ROI for investment centres lead to bad decisions? How does the residual income approach overcome this problem?
11–11 Should residual income be used to compare divisions of different sizes? Why or why not?

11–12 What are the four groups of performance measures typically included in a balanced scorecard?

11–13 Why do the measures used in a balanced scorecard differ from company to company?

11–14 Why does the balanced scorecard include financial performance measures as well as measures of how well internal business processes are doing?

11–15 What is the difference between delivery cycle time and throughput time? What four elements make up throughput time? Into what two classes can these four elements be placed?

11–16 Costs associated with the quality of conformance can be broken down into four broad groups. What are these four groups and how do they differ?

11–17 In their efforts to reduce the total cost of quality, should companies generally focus on decreasing prevention and appraisal costs?

11–18 What is likely the most effective way to reduce a company's total quality costs?

11–19 What are the main uses of quality cost reports?

11–20 (Appendix 11A) What is the advantage of examining a customer's profits over other segment analysis?

11–21 (Appendix 11A) What is the *market share variance* and is it controllable by managers?

11–22 (Appendix 11A) What is the *sales mix variance* and is it controllable by managers?

11–23 (Appendix 11B) What are the two categories of marketing expenses?

Exercises

EXERCISE 11–1 Transfer Pricing Situations [LO2]

In each of the cases below, assume that Division X has a product that can be sold either to outside customers or to Division Y of the same company for use in its production process. The managers of the divisions are evaluated based on their divisional profits.

	Case	
	A	B
Division X:		
Capacity in units	100,000	100,000
Number of units being sold to outside customers	100,000	80,000
Selling price per unit to outside customers	$50	$35
Variable costs per unit	$30	$20
Fixed costs per unit (based on capacity)	$8	$6
Division Y:		
Number of units needed for production	20,000	20,000
Purchase price per unit now being paid to an outside supplier	$47	$34

Required:

1. Refer to the data in case A above. Assume that $2 per unit in variable selling costs can be avoided on intracompany sales. If the managers are free to negotiate and make decisions on their own, will a transfer take place? If so, within what range will the transfer price fall? Explain.
2. Refer to the data in case B above. In this case there will be no reduction in variable selling costs on intracompany sales. If the managers are free to negotiate and make decisions on their own, will a transfer take place? If so, within what range will the transfer price fall? Explain.

EXERCISE 11–2 Compute the Return on Investment (ROI) [LO3]

Tundra Services Company, a division of a major oil company, provides various services to the operators of the North Slope oil field in Northern Alberta. Data concerning the most recent year appear on the next page.

Sales	$18,000,000
Operating income	$5,400,000
Average operating assets	$36,000,000

Required:
1. Compute the margin for Tundra Services Company.
2. Compute the turnover for Tundra Services Company.
3. Compute the return on investment (ROI) for Tundra Services Company.

EXERCISE 11–3 Residual Income [LO4]

Midlands Design Ltd. of Manchester, England, is a company specializing in providing design services to residential developers. Last year the company had operating income of £400,000 on sales of £2,000,000. The company's average operating assets for the year were £2,200,000 and its minimum required rate of return was 16%.

Required:
Compute the company's residual income for the year.

EXERCISE 11–4 Classification of Quality Costs [LO6]

Below are listed a number of activities that are part of a company's quality control system:

a. Repairs of goods still under warranty.
b. Customer returns due to defects.
c. Statistical process control.
d. Disposal of spoiled goods.
e. Maintaining testing equipment.
f. Inspecting finished goods.
g. Downtime caused by quality problems.
h. Debugging errors in software.
i. Recalls of defective products.
j. Training quality engineers.
k. Re-entering data due to typing errors.
l. Inspecting materials received from suppliers.
m. Audits of the quality system.
n. Supervision of testing personnel.
o. Rework labour.

Required:
1. Classify the costs associated with each of these activities into one of the following categories: prevention cost, appraisal cost, internal failure cost, or external failure cost.
2. Which of the four types of costs listed in (1) above are incurred to keep poor quality of conformance from occurring? Which of the four types of costs are incurred because poor quality of conformance has occurred?

EXERCISE 11–5 Transfer Pricing from Viewpoint of the Entire Company [LO2]

Division A manufactures components for plasma TVs. The components can be sold either to Division B of the same company or to outside customers. Last year, the following activity was recorded in Division A:

Selling price per component	$525
Variable cost per component	$390
Number of components:	
Produced during the year	20,000
Sold to outside customers	16,000
Sold to Division B	4,000

Sales to Division B were at the same price as sales to outside customers. The components purchased by Division B were used in a TV set manufactured by that division. Division B incurred $900 in additional variable cost per TV and then sold the TVs for $1,800 each.

Required:
1. Prepare income statements for last year for Division A, Division B, and the company as a whole.
2. Assume that Division A's manufacturing capacity is 20,000 components per year. Next year, Division B wants to purchase 5,000 components from Division A, rather than only 4,000 components as in last year. (Components of this type are not available from outside sources.) From the standpoint of the company as a whole, should Division A sell the 1,000 additional components to Division B, or should it continue to sell them to outside customers? Explain.

EXERCISE 11–6 Computing and Interpreting Return on Investment (ROI) [LO3]
Selected operating data on the two divisions of York Company are given below:

	Division	
	Eastern	Western
Sales	$1,000,000	$1,750,000
Average operating assets	$500,000	$500,000
Operating income	$90,000	$105,000
Property, plant, and equipment	$250,000	$200,000

Required:

1. Compute the rate of return for each division using the return on investment (ROI) formula stated in terms of margin and turnover.
2. Which divisional manager seems to be doing the better job? Why?

EXERCISE 11–7 Evaluating New Investments Using Return on Investment (ROI) and Residual Income [LO3, LO4]
Selected sales and operating data for three divisions of three different companies are given below:

	Division A	Division B	Division C
Sales	$6,000,000	$10,000,000	$8,000,000
Average operating assets	$1,500,000	$5,000,000	$2,000,000
Operating income	$300,000	$900,000	$180,000
Minimum required rate of return	15%	18%	12%

Required:

1. Compute the return on investment (ROI) for each division, using the formula stated in terms of margin and turnover.
2. Compute the residual income for each division.
3. Assume that each division is presented with an investment opportunity that would yield a rate of return of 17%.
   a. If performance is being measured by ROI, which division or divisions will probably accept the opportunity? Reject? Why?
   b. If performance is being measured by residual income, which division or divisions will probably accept the opportunity? Reject? Why?

EXERCISE 11–8 Creating a Balanced Scorecard [LO5]
Mason Paper Company (MPC) manufactures commodity grade papers for use in computer printers and photocopiers. MPC has reported operating losses for the last two years due to intense price pressure from much larger competitors. The MPC management team—including Kristen Townsend (CEO), Mike Martinez (vice-president of Manufacturing), Tom Andrews (vice-president of Marketing), and Wendy Chen (CFO)—is contemplating a change in strategy to save the company from impending bankruptcy. Excerpts from a recent management team meeting are shown below:

Townsend: As we all know, the commodity paper manufacturing business is all about economies of scale. The largest competitors with the lowest cost per unit win. The limited capacity of our older machines prohibits us from competing in the high-volume commodity paper grades. Furthermore, expanding our capacity by acquiring a new paper-making machine is out of the question given the extraordinarily high price tag. Therefore, I propose that we abandon cost reduction as a strategic goal and instead pursue manufacturing flexibility as the key to our future success.

Chen: Manufacturing flexibility? What does that mean?

Martinez: It means we have to abandon our "crank out as many tonnes of paper as possible" mentality. Instead, we need to pursue the low-volume business opportunities that exist in the nonstandard, specialized paper grades. To succeed in this regard, we'll need to improve our flexibility in three ways. First, we must improve our ability to switch between paper grades. Right now, we require an average of four hours to change over to another paper grade. Timely customer deliveries are a function of changeover performance. Second, we need to expand the range of paper grades that we can manufacture. Currently, we can only manufacture three paper grades. Our customers must perceive that we are a "one-stop shop" that can meet all of their paper grade needs. Third, we will need to improve our yields (e.g., tonnes of acceptable output relative to total tonnes processed) in the nonstandard paper grades. Our percentage of waste within these grades will be unacceptably high unless we do something to improve our processes. Our variable costs will go through the roof if we cannot increase our yields!

Chen: Wait just a minute! These changes are going to destroy our equipment utilization numbers!

Andrews: You're right Wendy; however, equipment utilization is not the name of the game when it comes to competing in terms of flexibility. Our customers don't care about our equipment utilization. Instead, as Mike just alluded to, they want just-in-time delivery of smaller quantities of a full range of paper grades. If we can shrink the elapsed time from order placement to order delivery and expand our product offerings, it will increase sales from current customers and bring in new customers. Furthermore, we will be able to charge a premium price because of the limited competition within this niche from our cost-focused larger competitors. Our contribution margin per tonne should drastically improve!

Martinez: Of course, executing the change in strategy will not be easy. We'll need to make a substantial investment in training because ultimately it is our people who create our flexible manufacturing capabilities.

Chen: If we adopt this new strategy, it is definitely going to impact how we measure performance. We'll need to create measures that motivate our employees to make decisions that support our flexibility goals.

Townsend: Wendy, you hit the nail right on the head. For our next meeting, could you pull together some potential measures that support our new strategy?

Required:

1. Contrast MPC's previous manufacturing strategy with its new manufacturing strategy.
2. Generally speaking, why would a company that changes its strategic goals need to change its performance measurement system as well? What are some examples of measures that would have been appropriate for MPC prior to its change in strategy? Why would those measures fail to support MPC's new strategy?
3. Using Exhibit 11–3 as a guide, construct a balanced scorecard that would support MPC's new manufacturing strategy. Use arrows to show the causal links between the performance measures and show whether the performance measure should increase or decrease over time. Feel free to create measures that may not be specifically mentioned in the chapter, but nonetheless make sense given the strategic goals of the company.
4. What hypotheses are built into MPC's balanced scorecard? Which of these hypotheses do you believe are most questionable and why?

EXERCISE 11–9 Measures of Internal Business Process Performance [LO5]

Lipex, Ltd., of Birmingham, England, is interested in cutting the amount of time between when a customer places an order and when the order is completed. For the first quarter of the year, the following data were reported:

Inspection time	0.5 days
Process time	2.8 days
Wait time	16.0 days
Queue time..........	4.0 days
Move time	0.7 days

Required:

1. Compute the throughput time.
2. Compute the manufacturing cycle efficiency (MCE) for the quarter.
3. What percentage of the throughput time was spent on non-value-added activities?
4. Compute the delivery cycle time.
5. If by using Lean Production all queue time can be eliminated in production, what will be the new MCE?

EXERCISE 11–10 Quality Cost Report [LO6]

Yedder Enterprises was a pioneer in designing and producing precision surgical lasers. Yedder's product was brilliantly designed, but the manufacturing process was neglected by management with a consequence that quality problems have been chronic. When customers complained about defective units, Yedder would simply send out a repair person or replace the defective unit with a new one. Recently, several competitors came out with similar products without Yedder's quality problems, and as a consequence Yedder's sales have declined.

To rescue the situation, Yedder embarked on an intensive campaign to strengthen its quality control at the beginning of the current year. These efforts met with some success—the downward slide in sales was reversed, and sales grew from $95 million last year to $100 million this year. To help monitor the company's progress, costs relating to quality and quality control were compiled for last year and for the first full year of the quality campaign this year. The costs, which do not include the lost sales due to a reputation for poor quality, appear below:

	Costs (in thousands)	
	Last Year	This Year
Product recalls	$3,500	$600
Systems development	$120	$680
Inspection	$1,700	$2,770
Net cost of scrap	$800	$1,300
Supplies used in testing	$30	$40
Warranty repairs	$3,300	$2,800
Rework labour	$1,400	$1,600
Statistical process control	$0	$270
Customer returns of defective goods	$3,200	$200
Cost of testing equipment	$270	$390
Quality engineering	$1,080	$1,650
Downtime due to quality problems	$600	$1,100

Required:

1. Prepare a quality cost report for both this year and last year. Carry percentage computations to two decimal places.
2. Prepare a bar graph showing the distribution of the various quality costs by category.
3. Prepare a written evaluation to accompany the reports you have prepared in (1) and (2) above. This evaluation should discuss the distribution of quality costs in the company, changes in the distribution over the last year, and any other information you believe would be useful to management.

EXERCISE 11–11 (Appendix 11A) Variance Analysis [LO7]

Johnston Company (JC) sells two types of bicycles with details as follows for 2008:

	Mountain	Road
Plan		
Expected total industry unit sales	96,000	170,000
Budgeted JC unit sales	8,400	34,000
Budgeted selling price per unit	$1,200	$1,600
Budgeted variable costs per unit	$ 968	$1,258
Actuals		
Actual total industry unit sales	120,000	200,000
Actual JC unit sales	12,000	36,000
Actual selling price per unit	$1,240	$1,575
Actual contribution margin per unit	$1,000	$1,275

Required:

1 Calculate the budgeted contribution margin for each model.

2. Calculate the following variances:
   a. Sales price
   b. Market volume
   c. Market share
   d. Sales mix
   e. Sales quantity

EXERCISE 11–12 Transfer Pricing Basics [LO2]
Gerbig Company's Electrical Division produces a high-quality transformer. Sales and cost data on the transformer follow:

Selling price per unit on the outside market	$40
Variable costs per unit	$21
Fixed costs per unit (based on capacity).......	$9
Capacity in units	60,000

Gerbig Company has a Motor Division that would like to begin purchasing this transformer from the Electrical Division. The Motor Division is currently purchasing 10,000 transformers each year from another company at a cost of $38 per transformer. Gerbig Company evaluates its division managers on the basis of divisional profits.

Required:

1. Assume that the Electrical Division is now selling only 50,000 transformers each year to outside customers.
   a. From the standpoint of the Electrical Division, what is the lowest acceptable transfer price for transformers sold to the Motor Division?
   b. From the standpoint of the Motor Division, what is the highest acceptable transfer price for transformers acquired from the Electrical Division?
   c. If left free to negotiate without interference, would you expect the division managers to voluntarily agree to the transfer of 10,000 transformers from the Electrical Division to the Motor Division? Why or why not?
   d. From the standpoint of the entire company, should a transfer take place? Why or why not?
2. Assume that the Electrical Division is now selling all of the transformers it can produce to outside customers.
   a. From the standpoint of the Electrical Division, what is the lowest acceptable transfer price for transformers sold to the Motor Division?
   b. From the standpoint of the Motor Division, what is the highest acceptable transfer price for transformers acquired from the Electrical Division?
   c. If left free to negotiate without interference, would you expect the division managers to voluntarily agree to the transfer of 10,000 transformers from the Electrical Division to the Motor Division? Why or why not?
   d. From the standpoint of the entire company, should a transfer take place? Why or why not?

EXERCISE 11–13 Contrasting Return on Investment (ROI) and Residual Income [LO3, LO4]
Rains Nickless Ltd. of Australia has two divisions that operate in Perth and Darwin. Selected data on the two divisions follow:

	Division	
	Perth	Darwin
Sales	$9,000,000	$20,000,000
Operating income............	$630,000	$1,800,000
Average operating assets	$3,000,000	$10,000,000

Required:

1. Compute the return on investment (ROI) for each division.
2. Assume that the company evaluates performance using residual income and that the minimum required rate of return for any division is 16%. Compute the residual income for each division.
3. Is the Darwin Division's greater residual income an indication that it is better managed? Explain.

EXERCISE 11–14 Return on Investment (ROI) and Residual Income Relations [LO3, LO4]
A family friend has asked your help in analyzing the operations of three anonymous companies operating in the same service sector industry. Supply the missing data in the table at the top of the next page.

	Company		
	A	B	C
Sales	$400,000	$750,000	$600,000
Operating income	$?	$45,000	$?
Average operating assets	$160,000	?	$150,000
Return on investment (ROI)	20%	18%	?
Minimum required rate of return:			
Percentage	15%	?	12%
Dollar amount	$?	$50,000	$?
Residual income	$?	$?	$6,000

EXERCISE 11–15 Return on Investment (ROI) Relations [LO3]
Provide the missing data in the following table:

	Division		
	Fab	Consulting	IT
Sales	$800,000	$?	$?
Operating income	$72,000	$?	$40,000
Average operating assets	$?	$130,000	$?
Margin	?	4%	8%
Turnover	?	5	?
Return on investment (ROI)	18%	?	20%

EXERCISE 11–16 Effects of Changes in Profits and Assets on Return on Investment (ROI) [LO3]
The Abs Shoppe is a regional chain of health clubs. The managers of the clubs, who have authority to make investments as needed, are evaluated based largely on return on investment (ROI). The Abs Shoppe reported the following results for the past year:

Sales	$800,000
Operating income	$16,000
Average operating assets	$100,000

Required:
The following questions are to be considered independently. Carry out all computations to two decimal places.

1. Compute the club's return on investment (ROI).
2. Assume that the manager of the club is able to increase sales by $80,000 and that as a result operating income increases by $6,000. Further assume that this is possible without any increase in operating assets. What would be the club's return on investment (ROI)?
3. Assume that the manager of the club is able to reduce expenses by $3,200 without any change in sales or operating assets. What would be the club's return on investment (ROI)?
4. Assume that the manager of the club is able to reduce operating assets by $20,000 without any change in sales or operating income. What would be the club's return on investment (ROI)?

EXERCISE 11–17 Measures of Internal Business Process Performance [LO5]
MacIntyre Fabrications, Ltd., of Aberdeen, Scotland, has recently begun a continuous improvement campaign in conjunction with a move toward Lean Production. Management has developed new performance measures as part of this campaign. The following operating data have been gathered over the last four months:

	Month			
	1	2	3	4
Throughput time	?	?	?	?
Manufacturing cycle efficiency	?	?	?	?
Delivery cycle time	?	?	?	?
Percentage of on-time deliveries	72%	73%	78%	85%
Total sales (units)	10,540	10,570	10,550	10,490

Management would like to know the company's throughput time, manufacturing cycle efficiency, and delivery cycle time. The data to compute these measures have been gathered and appear below:

	Month			
	1	2	3	4
Move time per unit, in days	0.5	0.5	0.4	0.5
Process time per unit, in days	0.6	0.5	0.5	0.4
Wait time per order before start of production, in days.	9.6	8.7	5.3	4.7
Queue time per unit, in days	3.6	3.6	2.6	1.7
Inspection time per unit, in days	0.7	0.7	0.4	0.3

Required:

1. For each month, compute the following:
   a. The throughput time.
   b. The manufacturing cycle efficiency (MCE).
   c. The delivery cycle time.
2. Using the performance measures given in the problem and those you computed in (1) above, identify whether the trend over the four months is generally favourable, generally unfavourable, or mixed. What areas apparently require improvement and how might they be improved?
3. Refer to the move time, process time, and so forth, given above for month 4.
   a. Assume that in month 5 the move time, process time, and so forth, are the same as for month 4, except that through the implementation of Lean Production, the company is able to completely eliminate the queue time during production. Compute the new throughput time and MCE.
   b. Assume that in month 6 the move time, process time, and so forth, are the same as for month 4, except that the company is able to completely eliminate both the queue time during production and the inspection time. Compute the new throughput time and MCE.

Problems

PROBLEM 11–18 Basic Transfer Pricing [LO2]

In cases 1–3 below, assume that Division A has a product that can be sold either to Division B of the same company or to outside customers. The managers of both divisions are evaluated based on their own division's return on investment (ROI). The managers are free to decide if they will participate in any internal transfers. All transfer prices are negotiated. Treat each case independently.

	Case			
	1	2	3	4
Division A:				
Capacity in units	50,000	300,000	100,000	200,000
Number of units now being sold to outside customers.	50,000	300,000	75,000	200,000
Selling price per unit to outside customers	$100	$40	$60	$45
Variable costs per unit	$63	$19	$35	$30
Fixed costs per unit (based on capacity)	$25	$8	$17	$6
Division B:				
Number of units needed annually	10,000	70,000	20,000	60,000
Purchase price now being paid to an outside supplier.	$92	$39	$60*	—

*Before any purchase discount.

Required:

1. Refer to case 1 on the previous page. A study has indicated that Division A can avoid $5 per unit in variable costs on any sales to Division B. Will the managers agree to a transfer and if so, within what range will the transfer price be? Explain.
2. Refer to case 2 on the previous page. Assume that Division A can avoid $4 per unit in variable costs on any sales to Division B.
   a. Would you expect any disagreement between the two divisional managers over what the transfer price should be? Explain.
   b. Assume that Division A offers to sell 70,000 units to Division B for $38 per unit and that Division B refuses this price. What will be the loss in potential profits for the company as a whole?
3. Refer to case 3 on the previous page. Assume that Division B is now receiving a 5% price discount from the outside supplier.
   a. Will the managers agree to a transfer? If so, within what range will the transfer price be?
   b. Assume that Division B offers to purchase 20,000 units from Division A at $52 per unit. If Division A accepts this price, would you expect its ROI to increase, decrease, or remain unchanged? Why?
4. Refer to case 4 on the previous page. Assume that Division B wants Division A to provide it with 60,000 units of a *different* product from the one that Division A is now producing. The new product would require $25 per unit in variable costs and would require that Division A cut back production of its present product by 30,000 units annually. What is the lowest acceptable transfer price from Division A's perspective?

PROBLEM 11–19 Comparison of Performance Using Return on Investment (ROI) [LO3]
Comparative data on three companies in the same service industry are given below:

	Company		
	A	B	C
Sales	$4,000,000	$1,500,000	$?
Operating income	$560,000	$210,000	$?
Average operating assets	$2,000,000	?	$3,000,000
Margin	?	?	3.5%
Turnover	?	?	2
Return on investment (ROI)	?	7%	?

Required:

1. What advantages are there to breaking down the ROI computation into two separate elements, margin and turnover?
2. Fill in the missing information above, and comment on the relative performance of the three companies in as much detail as the data permit. Make *specific recommendations* about how to improve the ROI.

(Adapted from National Association of Accountants, *Research Report No. 35,* p. 34)

PROBLEM 11–20 Return on Investment (ROI) and Residual Income [LO3, LO4]
"I know headquarters wants us to add that new product line," said Fred Halloway, manager of Kirsi Products' East Division. "But I want to see the numbers before I make a move. Our division's return on investment (ROI) has led the company for three years, and I don't want any letdown."

Kirsi Products is a decentralized wholesaler with four autonomous divisions. The divisions are evaluated on the basis of ROI, with year-end bonuses given to divisional managers who have the highest ROI. Operating results for the company's East Division for last year are given below:

Sales	$21,000,000
Variable expenses	13,400,000
Contribution margin	7,600,000
Fixed expenses	5,920,000
Operating income	$ 1,680,000
Divisional operating assets	$ 5,250,000

The company had an overall ROI of 18% last year (considering all divisions). The company's East Division has an opportunity to add a new product line that would require an investment of $3,000,000. The cost and revenue characteristics of the new product line per year would be as follows:

Sales................	$9,000,000
Variable expenses......	65% of sales
Fixed expenses........	$2,520,000

Required:

1. Compute the East Division's ROI for last year; also compute the ROI as it would appear if the new product line is added.
2. If you were in Fred Halloway's position, would you accept or reject the new product line? Explain.
3. Why do you suppose headquarters is anxious for the East Division to add the new product line?
4. Suppose that the company's minimum required rate of return on operating assets is 15% and that performance is evaluated using residual income.
   a. Compute the East Division's residual income for last year; also compute the residual income as it would appear if the new product line is added.
   b. Under these circumstances, if you were in Fred Halloway's position would you accept or reject the new product line? Explain.

PROBLEM 11–21 Creating Balanced Scorecards that Support Different Strategies [LO5]

The Performance Consulting Group (PCG) helps companies build balanced scorecards. As part of its marketing efforts, PCG conducts an annual balanced scorecard workshop for prospective clients. As PCG's newest employee, your boss has asked you to participate in this year's workshop by explaining to attendees how a company's strategy determines the measures that are appropriate for its balanced scorecard. Your boss has provided you with the excerpts below from the annual reports of two current PCG clients. She has asked you to use these excerpts in your portion of the workshop.

Excerpt from Applied Pharmaceuticals' annual report:

> The keys to our business are consistent and timely new product introductions and manufacturing process integrity. The new product introduction side of the equation is a function of research and development (R&D) yield (e.g., the number of marketable drug compounds created relative to the total number of potential compounds pursued). We seek to optimize our R&D yield and first-to-market capability by investing in state-of-the-art technology, hiring the highest possible percentage of the "best and the brightest" engineers that we pursue, and providing world-class training to those engineers. Manufacturing process integrity is all about establishing world-class quality specifications and then relentlessly engaging in prevention and appraisal activities to minimize defect rates. Our customers must have an awareness of and respect for our brand image of being "first to market and first in quality." If we deliver on this pledge to our customers, then our financial goal of increasing our return on shareholders' equity should take care of itself.

Excerpt from Destination Resorts International's annual report:

> Our business succeeds or fails based on the quality of the service that our front-line employees provide to customers. Therefore, it is imperative that we strive to maintain high employee morale and minimize employee turnover. In addition, it is critical that we train our employees to use technology to create one seamless worldwide experience for our repeat customers. Once an employee enters a customer preference (e.g., provide two extra pillows in the room, deliver fresh brewed coffee to the room at 8:00 A.M., etc.) into our database, our worldwide workforce strives to ensure that a customer will never need to repeat it at any of our destination resorts. If we properly train and retain a motivated workforce, we should see continuous improvement in our percentage of error-free repeat customer check-ins, the time taken to resolve customer complaints, and our independently assessed room cleanliness. This in turn should drive improvement in our customer retention, which is the key to meeting our revenue growth goals.

Required:

1. Based on the excerpts above, compare and contrast the strategies of Applied Pharmaceuticals and Destination Resorts International.
2. Select balanced scorecard measures for each company and link the scorecard measures using the framework from Exhibit 11–3. Use arrows to show the causal links between

the performance measures and show whether the performance measure should increase or decrease over time. Feel free to create measures that may not be specifically mentioned in the chapter, but nonetheless make sense given the strategic goals of each company.

3. What hypotheses are built into each balanced scorecard? Why do the hypotheses differ between the two companies?

PROBLEM 11–22 Analyzing a Quality Cost Report [LO6]

Bergen, Inc., produces telephone equipment at its Quebec plant. In recent years, the company's market share has been eroded by stiff competition from Asian and European competitors. Price and product quality are the two key areas in which companies compete in this market.

Two years ago, Jean Houle, Bergen's president, decided to devote more resources to improving product quality after learning that his company's products had been ranked fourth in quality in a survey of telephone equipment users. He believed that Bergen could no longer afford to ignore the importance of product quality. Houle set up a task force that he headed to implement a formal quality improvement program. Included on this task force were representatives from engineering, sales, customer service, production, and accounting. This broad representation was needed because Houle believed that this was a companywide program, and that all employees should share the responsibility for its success.

After the first meeting of the task force, Pascale Richard, manager of sales, asked Guy Laflamme, production manager, what he thought of the proposed program. Laflamme replied, "I have reservations. Quality is too abstract to be attaching costs to it and then to be holding you and me responsible for cost improvements. I like to work with goals that I can see and count! I'm nervous about having my annual bonus based on a decrease in quality costs; there are too many variables that we have no control over."

Bergen's quality improvement program has now been in operation for two years. The company's most recent quality cost report is shown below.

Bergen, Inc.
Quality Cost Report
(in thousands)

	Year 1	Year 2
Prevention costs:		
Machine maintenance	$ 215	$ 160
Training suppliers	5	15
Design reviews	20	95
Total prevention cost	240	270
Appraisal costs:		
Incoming inspection	45	22
Final testing	160	94
Total appraisal cost	205	116
Internal failure costs:		
Rework	120	62
Scrap	68	40
Total internal failure cost	188	102
External failure costs:		
Warranty repairs	69	23
Customer returns	262	80
Total external failure cost	331	103
Total quality cost	$ 964	$ 591
Total production cost	$4,120	$4,510

As they were reviewing the report, Richard asked Laflamme what he now thought of the quality improvement program. "The work is really moving through the production department," Laflamme replied. "We used to spend time helping the customer service department solve their problems, but they are leaving us alone these days. I have no complaints so far, and I'm relieved to see that the new quality improvement hasn't adversely affected our bonuses. I'm anxious to see if it increases our bonuses in the future."

Required:

1. By analyzing the company's quality cost report, determine if Bergen, Inc.'s quality improvement program has been successful. *List specific evidence to support your answer.* Show percentage figures in two ways: first, as a percentage of total production cost; and second, as a percentage of total quality cost. Carry all computations to one decimal place.
2. Discuss why Laflamme's current reaction to the quality improvement program is more favourable than his initial reaction.
3. Jean Houle believed that the quality improvement program was essential and that Bergen, Inc., could no longer afford to ignore the importance of product quality. Discuss how Bergen, Inc., could measure the opportunity cost of not implementing the quality improvement program.

(CMA, adapted)

PROBLEM 11–23 (Appendix 11A) Variance Analysis [LO7]

Rest Easy produces two types of mattresses: Regular and Heavenly. Budgeted and actual data for 2008 were as follows:

	Master Budget		Actual	
	Regular	**Heavenly**	**Regular**	**Heavenly**
Price per unit	$300	$800	$325	$700
Variable costs per unit	$220	$590	$238	$583
Unit Sales.	4,500	5,500	7,200	4,800

Market Data for 2008:
Expected total market unit sales of mattresses: Regular 300,000; Heavenly 200,000
Actual total market sales of beds: Regular 444,444; Heavenly 222,223

Required:

1. Calculate the following variances
   a. Sales price
   b. Market volume
   c. Market share
   d. Sales mix
   e. Sales quantity
2. During 2008, Big Sleep, one of Rest Easy's key competitors introduced an aggressive new marketing campaign that includes online advertising. Big Sleep also reduced prices on their mattress that competes directly with Rest Easy's Heavenly model. Management at Rest Easy decided to follow suit by reducing the price on the Heavenly model but decided against changing their marketing approach. Using any of the variances that you believe are relevant from part 1 above, evaluate the decisions made by Rest Easy's managers regarding the Heavenly model.

PROBLEM 11–24 Transfer Pricing with an Outside Market [LO2]

Galati Products, Inc., has just purchased a small company that specializes in the manufacture of electronic tuners that are used as a component part of TV sets. Galati Products, Inc., is a decentralized company, and it will treat the newly acquired company as an autonomous division with full profit responsibility. The new division, called the Tuner Division, has the following revenue and costs associated with each tuner that it manufactures and sells:

Selling price		$20
Expenses:		
Variable	$11	
Fixed (based on a capacity of 100,000 tuners per year)	6	17
Operating income		$3

Galati Products also has an Assembly Division that assembles TV sets. This division is currently purchasing 30,000 tuners per year from an overseas supplier at a cost of $20 per tuner, less a 10% purchase discount. The president of Galati Products is anxious to have the Assembly Division begin purchasing its tuners from the newly acquired Tuner Division in order to "keep the profits within the corporate family."

Required:

For (1) and (2) below, assume that the Tuner Division can sell all of its output to outside TV manufacturers at the normal $20 price.

1. Are the managers of the Tuner and Assembly Divisions likely to voluntarily agree to a transfer price for 30,000 tuners each year? Why or why not?
2. If the Tuner Division meets the price that the Assembly Division is currently paying to its overseas supplier and sells 30,000 tuners to the Assembly Division each year, what will be the effect on the profits of the Tuner Division, the Assembly Division, and the company as a whole?

For (3) through (6) below, assume that the Tuner Division is currently selling only 60,000 tuners each year to outside TV manufacturers at the stated $20 price.

3. Are the managers of the Tuner and Assembly Divisions likely to voluntarily agree to a transfer price for 30,000 tuners each year? Why or why not?
4. Suppose that the Assembly Division's overseas supplier drops its price (net of the purchase discount) to only $16 per tuner. Should the Tuner Division meet this price? Explain. If the Tuner Division does *not* meet this price, what will be the effect on the profits of the company as a whole?
5. Refer to (4) above. If the Tuner Division refuses to meet the $16 price, should the Assembly Division be required to purchase from the Tuner Division at a higher price for the good of the company as a whole? Explain.
6. Refer to (4) above. Assume that due to inflexible management policies, the Assembly Division is required to purchase 30,000 tuners each year from the Tuner Division at $20 per tuner. What will be the effect on the profits of the company as a whole?

PROBLEM 11–25 Return on Investment (ROI) and Residual Income [LO3, LO4]

Financial data for Bridger, Inc., for last year are as follows:

Bridger, Inc. Balance Sheet	Ending Balance	Beginning Balance
Assets		
Cash	$ 130,000	$ 125,000
Accounts receivable	480,000	340,000
Inventory	490,000	570,000
Plant and equipment, net	820,000	845,000
Investment in Brier Company	430,000	400,000
Land (undeveloped)	250,000	250,000
Total assets	$2,600,000	$2,530,000
Liabilities and Shareholders' Equity		
Accounts payable	$ 340,000	$ 380,000
Long-term debt	1,000,000	1,000,000
Shareholders' equity	1,260,000	1,150,000
Total liabilities and shareholders' equity	$2,600,000	$2,530,000

Bridger, Inc. Income Statement		
Sales		$4,180,000
Operating expenses		3,553,000
Operating income		627,000
Interest and taxes:		
Interest expense	$120,000	
Tax expense	200,000	320,000
Net income		$ 307,000

The company paid dividends of $197,000 last year. The "Investment in Brier Company" on the balance sheet represents an investment in the common shares of another company.

Required:

1. Compute the company's margin, turnover, and return on investment (ROI) for last year.
2. The board of directors of Bridger, Inc., has set a minimum required return of 20%. What was the company's residual income last year?

PROBLEM 11–26 Internal Business Process Performance Measures [LO5]

Exeter Corporation has recently begun a continuous improvement campaign. As a consequence, there have been many changes in operating procedures. Progress has been slow, particularly in trying to develop new performance measures for the factory.

Management has been gathering the following data over the past four months:

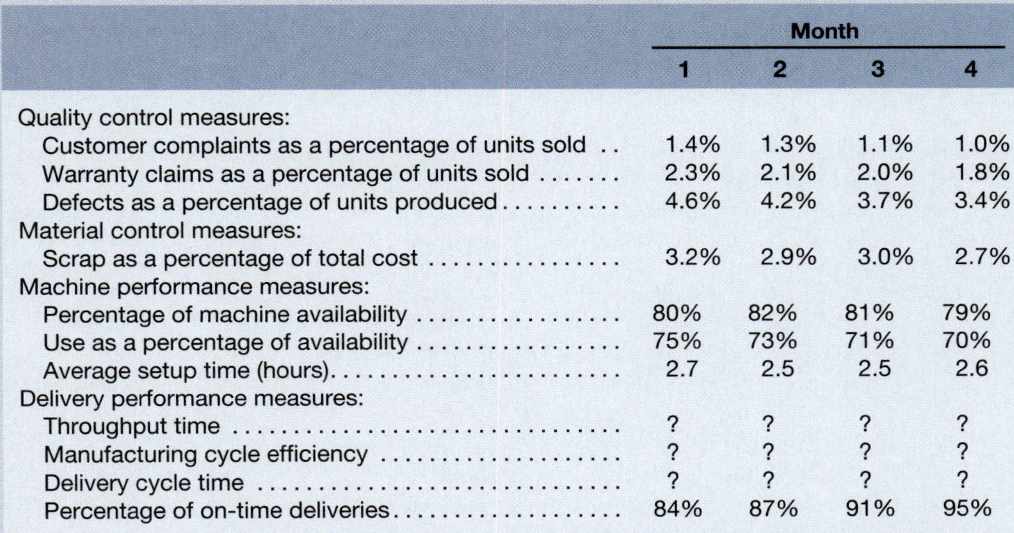

	Month			
	1	2	3	4
Quality control measures:				
Customer complaints as a percentage of units sold	1.4%	1.3%	1.1%	1.0%
Warranty claims as a percentage of units sold	2.3%	2.1%	2.0%	1.8%
Defects as a percentage of units produced	4.6%	4.2%	3.7%	3.4%
Material control measures:				
Scrap as a percentage of total cost	3.2%	2.9%	3.0%	2.7%
Machine performance measures:				
Percentage of machine availability	80%	82%	81%	79%
Use as a percentage of availability	75%	73%	71%	70%
Average setup time (hours)	2.7	2.5	2.5	2.6
Delivery performance measures:				
Throughput time	?	?	?	?
Manufacturing cycle efficiency	?	?	?	?
Delivery cycle time	?	?	?	?
Percentage of on-time deliveries	84%	87%	91%	95%

The president has attended conferences at which the importance of throughput time, manufacturing cycle efficiency, and delivery cycle time were stressed, but no one at the company is sure how they are computed. The data to compute these measures have been gathered and appear below:

	Month			
	1	2	3	4
Wait time per order before start of production, in days	16.7	15.2	12.3	9.6
Inspection time per unit, in days	0.1	0.3	0.6	0.8
Process time per unit, in days	0.6	0.6	0.6	0.6
Queue time per unit, in days	5.6	5.7	5.6	5.7
Move time per unit, in days	1.4	1.3	1.3	1.4

Required:

1. For each month, compute the following operating performance measures:
   a. Throughput time.
   b. Manufacturing cycle efficiency (MCE).
   c. Delivery cycle time.
2. Using the performance measures given in the problem and those you computed in (1) above, do the following:
   a. Identify areas where the company seems to be improving.
   b. Identify areas where the company seems to be deteriorating or stagnating.
   c. Explain why you think some specific areas are improving while others are not.
3. Refer to the move time, process time, and so forth, given above for month 4.
   a. Assume that in month 5 the move time, process time, and so forth, are the same as for month 4, except that through the implementation of Lean Production, the company is able to completely eliminate the queue time during production. Compute the new throughput time and MCE.

b. Assume that in month 6 the move time, process time, and so forth, are the same as for month 4, except that the company is able to completely eliminate both the queue time during production and the inspection time. Compute the new throughput time and MCE.

PROBLEM 11–27 Building a Balanced Scorecard [LO5]

Deer Creek ski resort was for many years a small, family-owned resort serving day skiers from nearby towns. Deer Creek was recently acquired by Mountain Associates, a major ski resort operator with several destination resorts in western Canada. The new owners have plans to upgrade the resort into a destination resort for vacationers staying for a week or more. As part of this plan, the new owners would like to make major improvements in the Lynx Lair Lodge, the resort's on-the-hill fast-food restaurant. The menu at the Lodge is very limited—hamburgers, hot dogs, chili, tuna fish sandwiches, french fries, and packaged snacks. The previous owners of the resort had felt no urgency to upgrade the food service at the Lodge since there is little competition. If skiers want lunch on the mountain, the only alternatives are the Lynx Lair Lodge or a brown bag lunch brought from home.

As part of the deal when acquiring Deer Creek, Mountain Associates agreed to retain all of the current employees of the resort. The manager of the Lodge, while hardworking and enthusiastic, has very little experience in the restaurant business. The manager is responsible for selecting the menu, finding and training employees, and overseeing daily operations. The kitchen staff prepares food and washes dishes. The dining room staff takes orders, serves as cashiers, and cleans the dining room area.

Shortly after taking over Deer Creek, management of Mountain Associates held a day-long meeting with all of the employees of the Lynx Lair Lodge to discuss the future of the ski resort and management's plans for the Lodge. At the end of this meeting, top management and Lodge employees created a balanced scorecard for the Lodge that would help guide operations for the coming ski season. Almost everyone who participated in the meeting seemed to be enthusiastic about the scorecard and management's plans for the Lodge.

The following performance measures were included on the balanced scorecard for the Lynx Lair Lodge:

- Customer satisfaction with service, as measured by customer surveys.
- Total Lynx Lair Lodge profit.
- Dining area cleanliness, as rated by a representative from Mountain Associates management.
- Average time to prepare an order.
- Customer satisfaction with menu choices, as measured by surveys.
- Average time to take an order.
- Percentage of kitchen staff completing institutional cooking course at the local community college.
- Sales.
- Percentage of dining room staff completing hospitality course at the local community college.
- Number of menu items.

Mountain Associates will pay for the costs of staff attending courses at the local community college.

Required:

1. Using the above performance measures, construct a balanced scorecard for the Lynx Lair Lodge. Use Exhibit 11–3 as a guide. Use arrows to show causal links and indicate with a + or − whether the performance measure should increase or decrease.
2. What hypotheses are built into the balanced scorecard for the Lynx Lair Lodge? Which of these hypotheses do you believe are most questionable? Why?
3. How will management know if one of the hypotheses underlying the balanced scorecard is false?

PROBLEM 11–28 Cost-Volume-Profit Analysis; Return on Investment (ROI); Transfer Pricing [LO2, LO3]

The Switch division of Tornax, Inc., produces a small switch that is used by various companies as a component part in their products. Tornax, Inc., operates its divisions as autonomous units, giving its divisional managers great discretion in pricing and other decisions. Each division is expected to generate a minimum required rate of return of at least 14% on its operating assets. The Switch Division has average operating assets of $700,000. The switches are sold for $5 each. Variable costs are $3 per switch, and fixed costs total $462,000 per year. The division has a capacity of 300,000 switches each year.

Required:

1. How many switches must the Switch Division sell each year to generate the desired rate of return on its assets?
   a. What is the margin earned at this level of sales?
   b. What is the turnover at this level of sales?
2. Assume that the Switch Division's current ROI equals the minimum required rate of 14%. In order to increase the division's ROI, the divisional manager wants to increase the selling price per switch by 4%. Market studies indicate that an increase in the selling price would cause sales to drop by 20,000 units each year. However, operating assets could be reduced by $50,000 due to decreased needs for accounts receivable and inventory. Compute the margin, turnover, and ROI if these changes are made.
3. Refer to the original data. Assume again that the Switch Division's current ROI equals the minimum required rate of 14%. Rather than increase the selling price, the sales manager wants to reduce the selling price per switch by 4%. Market studies indicate that this would fill the plant to capacity. In order to carry the greater level of sales, however, operating assets would increase by $50,000. Compute the margin, turnover, and ROI if these changes are made.
4. Refer to the original data. Assume that the normal volume of sales is 280,000 switches each year at a price of $5 per switch. Another division of the company is currently purchasing 20,000 switches each year from an overseas supplier, at a price of $4.25 per switch. The manager of the Switch Division has refused to meet this price, pointing out that it would result in a loss for his division:

Selling price per switch		$4.25
Cost per switch:		
Variable	$3.00	
Fixed ($462,000 ÷ 300,000 switches) . . .	1.54	4.54
Operating loss per switch.		$(0.29)

The manager of the Switch Division also points out that the normal $5 selling price barely allows his division to earn the required 14% rate of return. "If we take on some business at only $4.25 per unit, then our ROI is obviously going to suffer," he reasons, "and maintaining that ROI figure is the key to my future. Besides, taking on these extra units would require us to increase our operating assets by at least $50,000 due to the larger inventories and accounts receivable we would be carrying." Would you recommend that the Switch Division sell to the other division at $4.25? Show ROI computations to support your answer.

PROBLEM 11–29 Return on Investment (ROI) Analysis [LO3]
The contribution format income statement for Westex, Inc., for its most recent period is given below:

Microsoft Excel - Problem 11-29 screen capture.xls

	A	B	C	D
1			*Total*	*Unit*
2	Sales		$1,000,000	$50.00
3	Less variable expenses		600,000	30.00
4	Contribution margin		400,000	20.00
5	Less fixed expenses		320,000	16.00
6	Operating income		80,000	4.00
7	Less income taxes @	40%	32,000	1.60
8	Operating income		$ 48,000	$ 2.40
9				

The company had average operating assets of $500,000 during the period.

Required:

1. Compute the company's return on investment (ROI) for the period using the ROI formula stated in terms of margin and turnover.

For each of the following questions, indicate whether the margin and turnover will increase, decrease, or remain unchanged as a result of the events described, and then compute the new ROI figure. Consider each question separately, starting in each case from the original ROI computed in (1) above.

2. The company achieves cost savings of $10,000 per period by using less costly materials.
3. Using Lean Production, the company is able to reduce the average level of inventory by $100,000. (The released funds are used to pay off bank loans.)
4. Sales are increased by $100,000; operating assets remain unchanged.
5. The company issues bonds and uses the proceeds to purchase $125,000 in machinery and equipment at the beginning of the period. Interest on the bonds is $15,000 per period. Sales remain unchanged. The new, more efficient equipment reduces production costs by $5,000 per period.
6. The company invests $180,000 of cash (received on accounts receivable) in a plot of land that is to be held for possible future use as a plant site.
7. Obsolete inventory carried on the books at a cost of $20,000 is scrapped and written off as a loss.

PROBLEM 11–30 Market-Based Transfer Price [LO2]

Damico Company's Board Division manufactures an electronic control board that is widely used in high-definition (HD) DVD players. The cost per control board is as follows:

Variable cost per board	$120
Fixed cost per board	30*
Total cost per board	$150

*Based on a capacity of 800,000 boards per year.

Part of the Board Division's output is sold to outside manufacturers of HD-DVD players, and part is sold to Damico Company's Consumer Products Division, which produces a DVD player under the Damico name. The Board Division charges a selling price of $190 per control board for all sales, both internal and external.

The costs, revenues, and operating income associated with the Consumer Products Division's HD-DVD player are given below:

Selling price per player		$580
Variable costs per player:		
Cost of the control board	$190	
Variable cost of other parts	230	
Total variable costs		420
Contribution margin		160
Fixed costs per player		85*
Operating income per player		$ 75

*Based on a capacity of 200,000 HD-DVD players per year.

The Consumer Products Division has an order from an overseas distributor for 5,000 HD-DVD players. The distributor wants to pay only $400 per DVD player.

Required:

1. Assume that the Consumer Products Division has enough idle capacity to fill the 5,000-unit order. Is the division likely to accept the $400 price, or to reject it? Explain.
2. Assume that both the Board Division and the Consumer Products Division have idle capacity. Under these conditions, would rejecting the $400 price be advantageous for the company as a whole, or would it result in the loss of potential profits? Show computations to support your answer.

(Required continued on the next page)

3. Assume that the Board Division is operating at capacity and could sell all of its control boards to outside manufacturers of HD-DVD players. Assume, however, that the Consumer Products Division has enough idle capacity to fill the 5,000-unit order. Under these conditions, compute the profit impact to the Consumer Products Division of accepting the order at the $400 price.
4. What conclusions do you draw concerning the use of market price as a transfer price in intra-company transactions?

PROBLEM 11–31 (Appendix 11B) Costing for Customers [LO8]
Clearview Manufacturing and Distributing Ltd. distributes its preformed windows throughout eastern Canada to two classes of customers, wholesalers and contractors. In an effort to analyze its marketing expenses by distribution channel, the following statistics were obtained:

	Wholesalers	Contractors
Units sold	6,000	7,500
Kilometres travelled	90,000	126,000
Orders	3,600	4,500
Customers	114	480
Costs:		
Warehousing per unit	$10.00	$13.00
Transport	$1.80 per kilometre	
Credit and collection	$0.60 per order plus $150 per customer	
Selling	$2.00 per order	
Advertising	$100.00 per customer	

Required:
1. Analyze the marketing costs by customer class.
2. Clearview is considering purchasing its own truck and hiring a driver for $48,000 per year. Determine how much it could afford to spend on a truck in year one (capital plus operating costs) to equal its current costs.

Cases

CASE 11–32 Transfer Pricing; Divisional Performance [LO2]
Stanco, Inc., is a decentralized organization with five divisions. The company's Electronics Division produces a variety of electronics items, including an XL5 circuit board. The division (which is operating at capacity) sells the XL5 circuit board to regular customers for $12.50 each. The circuit boards have a variable production cost of $8.25 each.

The company's Clock Division has asked the Electronics Division to supply it with a large quantity of XL5 circuit boards for only $9 each. The Clock Division, which is operating at only 60% of capacity, will put the circuit boards into a timing device that it will produce and sell to a large oven manufacturer. The cost of the timing device being manufactured by the Clock Division follows:

XL5 circuit board (desired cost)	$ 9.00
Other purchased parts (from outside vendors)	30.00
Other variable costs	20.75
Fixed overhead and administrative costs	10.00
Total cost per timing device	$69.75

The manager of the Clock Division feels that she can't quote a price greater than $70 per timing device to the oven manufacturer if her division is to get the job. As shown above, in order to keep the price at $70 or less, she can't pay more than $9 per unit to the Electronics Division for the XL5 circuit boards. Although the $9 price for the XL5 circuit boards represents a substantial discount from the normal $12.50 price, she feels that the price concession is necessary for her division to get the oven manufacturer contract and thereby keep its core of highly trained people.

The company uses return on investment (ROI) to measure divisional performance.

Required:

1. Assume that you are the manager of the Electronics Division. Would you recommend that your division supply the XL5 circuit boards to the Clock Division for $9 each as requested? Why or why not? Show all computations.
2. Would it be profitable for the company as a whole for the Electronics Division to supply the Clock Division with the circuit boards for $9 each? Explain your answer.
3. In principle, should it be possible for the two managers to agree to a transfer price in this particular situation? If so, within what range would that transfer price lie?
4. Discuss the organizational and manager behaviour problems, if any, inherent in this situation. What would you advise the company's president to do in this situation?

(CMA, adapted)

CASE 11–33 Balanced Scorecard [LO5]

Weierman Department Store is located in the downtown area of a medium-sized city in Western Canada. While the store had been profitable for many years, it is facing increasing competition from large national chains that have set up stores in the city's suburbs. Recently the downtown area has been undergoing revitalization, and the owners of Weierman Department Store are somewhat optimistic that profitability can be restored.

In an attempt to accelerate the return to profitability, the management of Weierman Department Store is in the process of designing a balanced scorecard for the company. Management believes the company should focus on two key problems. First, customers are taking longer and longer to pay the bills they incur on the department store's charge card, and they have far more bad debts than are normal for the industry. If this problem were solved, the company would have more cash to make much needed renovations. Investigation has revealed that much of the problem with late payments and unpaid bills is apparently due to disputed bills that are the result of incorrect charges on the customer bills. These incorrect charges usually occur because salesclerks enter data incorrectly on the charge account slip. Second, the company has been incurring large losses on unsold seasonal apparel. Such items are ordinarily resold at a loss to discount stores that specialize in such distress items.

The meeting in which the balanced scorecard approach was discussed was disorganized and ineffectively led—possibly because no one other than one of the vice-presidents had read anything about how to put a balanced scorecard together. Nevertheless, a number of potential performance measures were suggested by various managers as follows.

Performance measures suggested by various managers:

- Total sales revenue.
- Percentage of salesclerks trained to correctly enter data on charge account slips.
- Customer satisfaction with accuracy of charge account bills from monthly customer survey.
- Sales per employee.
- Travel expenses for buyers for trips to fashion shows.
- Average age of accounts receivables.
- Courtesy shown by junior staff members to senior staff members based on surveys of senior staff.
- Unsold inventory at the end of the season as a percentage of total cost of sales.
- Sales per square metre of floor space.
- Percentage of suppliers making just-in-time deliveries.
- Quality of food in the staff cafeteria based on staff surveys.
- Written-off accounts receivables (bad debts) as a percentage of sales.
- Percentage of charge account bills containing errors.
- Percentage of employees who have attended the city's cultural diversity workshop.
- Total profit.
- Profit per employee.

Required:

1. As someone with more knowledge of the balanced scorecard than almost anyone else in the company, you have been asked to build an integrated balanced scorecard. In your scorecard, use only performance measures suggested by the managers above. You do not have to use all of the performance measures suggested by the managers, but you should build a balanced scorecard that reveals a strategy for dealing with the problems with accounts receivable and with unsold merchandise. Construct the balanced scorecard following the format used in Exhibit 11–3. Do not be particularly concerned with whether a specific performance measure falls within the learning and growth, internal business process, customer, or financial perspective. However, clearly show the causal links between

the performance measures with arrows and whether the performance measures should show increases or decreases.

2. Assume that the company adopts your balanced scorecard. After operating for a year, there are improvements in some performance measures but not in others. What should management do next?
3. *a.* Suppose that customers express greater satisfaction with the accuracy of their charge account bills but the performance measures for the average age of accounts receivable and for bad debts do not improve. Explain why this might happen.
   b. Suppose that the performance measures for the average age of accounts receivable, bad debts, and unsold inventory improve, but total profits do not. Explain why this might happen. Assume in your answer that the explanation lies within the company.

CASE 11–34 Return on Investment (ROI) and Residual Income; Decentralization [LO3, LO4]

Kaiser Industries produces tool and die machinery for manufacturers. The company expanded vertically several years ago by acquiring Superior Steel Company, one of its suppliers of alloy steel plates. Kaiser decided to maintain Superior's separate identity and therefore established the Superior Steel Division as one of its investment centres.

Kaiser evaluates its divisions on the basis of ROI. Management bonuses are also based on ROI. All investments in operating assets are expected to earn a minimum required rate of return of 11%.

Superior' ROI has ranged from 14% to 17% since it was acquired by Kaiser. During the past year, Superior had an investment opportunity that would yield an estimated rate of return of 13%. Superior' management decided against the investment because it believed the investment would decrease the division's overall ROI.

Last year's absorption costing income statement for Superior Steel Division follows. The division's operating assets employed were $6,480,000 at the end of the year, which represents an 8% increase over the previous year-end balance.

SUPERIOR STEEL DIVISION
Divisional Income Statement
For the Year Ended December 31

Sales		$15,600,000
Cost of goods sold		8,250,000
Gross margin..................		7,350,000
Less operating expenses:		
Selling expenses	$2,810,000	
Administrative expenses	3,604,000	6,414,000
Operating income		$ 936,000

Required:

1. Compute the following performance measures for the Superior Steel Division:
   a. ROI. (Remember, ROI is based on the *average* operating assets, computed from the beginning-of-year and end-of-year balances.) State ROI in terms of margin and turnover.
   b. Residual income.
2. Would the management of Superior Steel Division have been more likely to accept the investment opportunity it had last year if residual income were used as a performance measure instead of ROI? Explain.
3. The Superior Steel Division is a separate investment centre within Kaiser Industries. Identify the items Superior must be free to control if it is to be evaluated fairly by either the ROI or residual income performance measures.

(CMA, adapted)

Research

R 11–35 ROI and Residual Income Management [LO3, LO4]

The key elements included in the calculation of ROI are summarized in Exhibit 11–2. Take a moment and review the exhibit.

Required:

1. If managers are rewarded for attaining ROI targets (e.g., 20%), what actions might they take that allow them to achieve the target in the short run, but that might be harmful to the organization in the long run?
2. Would the use of residual income to evaluate a manager's performance overcome the problems you identified in part 1?
3. How can organizations reduce the likelihood that managers will take the actions identified in part 1?

R 11–36 Performance Measurement [LO5]

Contact a financial manager (e.g., CFO, controller, assistant controller) at a medium or large manufacturing or service company located nearby your college or university.

Required:

Make an appointment to meet the manager to discuss the following:

1. What is the company's strategy?
2. Does the company use a balanced scorecard? If yes, what measures are included on the scorecard? How were these measures selected? To what extent are the performance measures based on the company's strategic objectives?
3. If the company uses a balanced scorecard, at what levels of the organization is it used? For example scorecards can be prepared for the overall organization, business divisions, departments, work teams and individual employees.
4. If the company does not use a balanced scorecard, are any non-financial measures regularly reported (e.g., customer satisfaction, defect rates, etc.)? Why were these measures chosen?
5. If the company uses a balanced scorecard or at least reports some non-financial measures, are they linked to employees' incentives? If yes, how?
6. If non-financial measures are not used by the company, why?
7. What key financial measures are used by the company? Does the company track ROI or residual income?

R 11–37 Control Issues in Practice [LO2, LO3, LO4, LO5]

As you know, the World Wide Web is a medium that is constantly evolving. Sites come and go, and change without notice. To enable the periodic updating of site addresses, this problem has been posted to the textbook web site (www.mcgrawhill.ca/olc/garrison). After accessing the site, enter the Student Centre and select this chapter. Select and complete the Internet Exercise.

SECTION 4

SHORT-TERM AND LONG-TERM DECISIONS

Chapters 12 and 13

Two environments are commonly used to characterize decision analysis. **Chapter 12** presents approaches to short-term decision analysis where decisions need to examine differential revenues and differential costs without the need to consider the cost of interest. Various commonly encountered short-term situations are described in this chapter.

Long-term decision analysis is typically distinguished by the introduction of interest into the differential analysis. The approach is commonly termed capital budgeting. **Chapter 13** introduces income taxes into the differential analysis because of their importance and their unique effect. These tax effects are termed tax shields. Completion of the decision analysis in this chapter demonstrates a sound operational and strategic decision approach where interest and income taxes can influence the results.

After studying Chapter 12, you should be able to:

1. Distinguish between relevant and irrelevant costs in decision making.
2. Prepare analyses for various decision situations.
3. Determine the most profitable use of a constrained resource and the value of obtaining more of the constrained resource.
4. (Appendix 12A) Compute selling prices based on costs.
5. (Appendix 12A) Compute target costs based on selling prices.

RELEVANT COSTS FOR DECISION MAKING

BUSINESS FOCUS

Expanding Operations at WestJet

As one of the two major Canadian airlines, WestJet faces an ongoing challenge of deciding which destinations to serve both within Canada and internationally. In making decisions about which flights to add or drop, one of the items considered by airlines such as WestJet is the "load factor" which is the percentage of seats sold on any given flight. Because many of the costs per flight are fixed (e.g., flight preparation, insurance, flight assistants wages) the load factor is important to monitor and manage since a minimum number of seats must be sold in order for each flight to break even. Moreover, a flight will only improve the company's profitability if the total contribution margin (flight capacity × load factor × contribution margin per passenger) *exceeds* the total relevant fixed costs of that flight. Accordingly, WestJet's shareholders would likely be encouraged by news that the company's average load factor for all flights during the first quarter of 2007 was 81.1%, up from 79.4% in 2006.

Recent announcements by WestJet to increase the number of weekly flights from Vancouver to Hawaii as well as adding new flights to destinations in Eastern Canada would have been based, in part, on the type of analysis described above. Importantly, the analysis of whether to add or drop flights to any destination should ignore costs that are not affected by the decision. For example, if WestJet does not need to increase the number of administrative staff it employs to add new flights to Hawaii, then the wages paid to these employees are irrelevant to the decision. These costs will be incurred, whether or not the new flights are added. Conversely, any additional costs that will be incurred as a result of adding flights, such as increased advertising, insurance, and airport fees, are relevant to the decision and should be considered.

Properly analyzing the expected effects of expanding or reducing capacity through the addition or discontinuation of flights is critical to airlines such as WestJet. Increasing capacity is only warranted if it will eventually lead to increases in profits.

Source: Excerpted from "WestJet Announces Record April Load Factor" (May 3, 2007) and "WestJet Airlines Adds to Daily Winter Flights to Hawaii" (May 1, 2007), www.westjet.com.

Decision making is a critical aspect of managing an organization. Managers are constantly faced with problems of deciding which products or services to offer, the production methods to use, whether to make or buy component parts, what prices to charge, whether to accept special orders at special prices, how to allocate limited resources, and so on. In each case, the decision should lead to outcomes that contribute to achieving the performance goals identified as part of the organization's strategic objectives (e.g., grow revenues, reduce costs, improve return on investment, etc.). However, decision making is a complex process. Numerous alternatives may exist for each decision situation and large amounts of data must be analyzed, only some of which are relevant.

How can managers cope with these complexities in an effort to consistently make good decisions? The key is to identify and compare *only* the relevant costs and benefits for each alternative. **Relevant costs** are those that differ among the alternatives under consideration. A key challenge for managers, and fundamental to good decision making, is differentiating between relevant and irrelevant costs. This is critical because consideration of irrelevant costs wastes managers' time and effort, and can lead to the wrong decisions. Further complicating matters is the fact that the relevance of specific costs and benefits depends on the decision situation. For example, a product supervisor's salary is typically irrelevant in deciding whether or not to accept a special order from a customer but can be relevant when deciding whether to keep or drop that product line. The purpose of this chapter is to provide a framework for distinguishing between relevant and irrelevant costs by illustrating their use in a wide range of decision-making situations.

Relevant cost
A cost that differs between alternatives in a particular decision. In managerial accounting, this term is synonymous with avoidable cost and differential cost.

We begin the chapter by developing a general framework for identifying relevant costs and benefits. We then apply this framework to a variety of non-recurring situations to illustrate how the relevance of a cost or benefit depends on the type of decision being made. Next we turn our attention to analyzing situations where managers must decide how to allocate a limited resource such as labour hours. Finally, the relation between relevant costs and pricing issues is further examined in the appendix.

Two aspects of the decision situations and the related analysis presented in this chapter are important to emphasize. First, none of the situations involve capital expenditures (e.g., replacing production equipment) where the time value of money can be an important factor in the analysis. This type of analysis, termed *capital budgeting*, is covered in Chapter 13. Second, the key criterion used in the various decision situations presented in the chapter is the maximization of operating income. However, in practice managers may also consider qualitative factors when making decisions. For example, when deciding whether to keep or drop a product or segment, the effect on employee morale and the impact on the company's reputation with its customers may be important, but very difficult or costly to quantify. The extent to which qualitative factors influence a decision will vary from situation to situation but they are often taken into account.

Cost Concepts for Decision Making

LEARNING OBJECTIVE 1
Distinguish between relevant and irrelevant costs in decision making.

Four cost terms discussed in Chapter 2 are particularly applicable to this chapter. These terms are *differential costs, incremental costs, opportunity costs,* and *sunk costs.* You may find it helpful to turn back to Chapter 2 and review the concepts before reading on.

Identifying Relevant Costs and Benefits

Because it is fundamental to the proper analysis of the various decision situations covered in this chapter, we begin by identifying the nature of relevant costs and benefits. Only those costs and benefits that differ in total between alternatives are relevant in a decision. If a cost will be the same regardless of the alternative selected, then the decision has no effect on the cost and it can be ignored. For example, if you are trying to decide whether to go to a movie or to rent a DVD for the evening, the lease payments on your car are irrelevant. Whether you go to a movie or rent a DVD, the lease payments will be exactly the same and are therefore irrelevant in the decision. On the other hand, the cost of the movie ticket and the cost of renting the DVD would be relevant in the decision because they are *avoidable costs.*

Avoidable cost
Any cost that can be eliminated (in whole or in part) by choosing one alternative over another in a decision-making situation. In managerial accounting, this term is synonymous with *relevant cost* and *differential cost.*

An **avoidable cost** is a cost that can be eliminated in whole or in part by choosing one alternative over another. By choosing the alternative of going to the movie, the cost of renting the DVD can be avoided. By choosing the alternative of renting the DVD, the cost of the movie ticket can be avoided. Therefore, the cost of the movie ticket and the cost of renting the DVD are both avoidable costs. On the other hand, the lease payments on the car are not an avoidable cost of either alternative. You would continue to lease your car under either alternative. Avoidable costs are relevant costs. Unavoidable costs are irrelevant costs.

Two broad categories of costs are never relevant in decisions. These irrelevant costs are:

1. Sunk costs (e.g., previously owned DVD player).
2. Future costs that do not differ between the alternatives (e.g., lease payments for movie decision).

Sunk cost
Any cost that has already been incurred and that cannot be changed by any decision made now or in the future.

As we learned in Chapter 2, a **sunk cost** is a cost that has already been incurred and that cannot be avoided, regardless of what a manager decides to do. Sunk costs are always the same, no matter what alternatives are being considered, and they are therefore always irrelevant and should be ignored. On the other hand, future costs that do differ between alternatives *are* relevant. For example, when deciding whether to go to a movie or rent a DVD, the cost of buying a movie ticket and the cost of renting a DVD have not yet been incurred. These are future costs that differ between alternatives when the decision is being made and therefore are relevant.

Differential cost
Any cost that differs between alternatives in a decision-making situation. In managerial accounting, this term is synonymous with avoidable cost and relevant cost.

Along with sunk cost, the term **differential cost** was introduced in Chapter 2. In managerial accounting, the terms *avoidable cost, differential cost, incremental cost,* and *relevant cost* are often used interchangeably. To identify the costs and benefits that are relevant in a particular decision situation, these steps can be followed:

1. Eliminate costs and benefits that do not differ between alternatives. These irrelevant costs consist of (a) sunk costs and (b) future costs that do not differ between alternatives.
2. Use the remaining costs and benefits that do differ between alternatives in making the decision. The costs that remain are the differential, or avoidable, costs.

Different Costs for Different Purposes

We need to recognize from the outset of our discussion that costs that are relevant in one decision situation are not necessarily relevant in another. Simply put, this means that *the manager needs different costs for different purposes.* For one purpose, a particular group of costs may be relevant; for another purpose, an entirely different group of costs may be relevant. Thus, in *each* decision situation the manager must examine the data at hand and isolate the relevant costs. Otherwise, the manager runs the risk of being misled by irrelevant data.

The concept of "different costs for different purposes" is basic to managerial accounting; we will see its application frequently in the pages that follow.

An Example of Identifying Relevant Costs and Benefits

Cynthia is currently a student in an MBA program in Halifax and would like to visit a friend in Moncton over the weekend. She is trying to decide whether to drive or take the train. Because she is on a tight budget, she wants to carefully consider the costs of the two alternatives. If one alternative is far less expensive than the other, that may be decisive in her choice. By car, the distance between her apartment in Halifax and her friend's apartment in Moncton is 265 kilometres. Cynthia has compiled the list of items (shown in the table on the next page) to consider.

Which costs and benefits are relevant in this decision? Remember, only those costs and benefits that differ between alternatives are relevant. Everything else is irrelevant and can be ignored.

Start at the top of the list with item (a): the original cost of the car is a sunk cost. This cost has already been incurred and therefore can never differ between alternatives. Consequently, it is irrelevant and can be ignored. The same is true of the accounting depreciation of $2,800 per year, which simply spreads the sunk cost across a number of years.

Automobile Costs

	Item	Annual Cost of Fixed Items	Cost per km (based on 16,000 km per year)
(a)	Annual straight-line depreciation on car [($24,000 original cost − $10,000 estimated resale value in 5 years)/5 years]	$2,800	$0.175
(b)	Cost of gasoline ($1.30 per litre ÷ 10 kilometres per litre)		0.130
(c)	Annual cost of auto insurance and licence	2,000	0.125
(d)	Maintenance and repairs		0.041
(e)	Parking fees at university ($45 per month × 8 months)	360	0.023
(f)	Tires ($900 to replace all 4 tires every 50,000 kilometres)		$0.018
(g)	Total average cost per kilometre		$0.512

Additional Data

	Item	
(h)	Cost of round-trip VIA ticket	$125
(i)	Benefit of relaxing and being able to study during the train ride rather than having to drive	?
(j)	Cost of putting the cat in a kennel while gone	$40
(k)	Benefit of having a car available in Moncton	?
(l)	Hassle of parking the car in Moncton	?
(m)	Cost of parking the car in Moncton	$25 per day

Move down the list to item (b): the cost of gasoline consumed by driving to Moncton would clearly be a relevant cost in this decision. If Cynthia takes the train, this cost would not be incurred. Hence, the cost differs between alternatives and is therefore relevant.

Item (c), the annual cost of auto insurance and licence, is not relevant. Whether Cynthia takes the train or drives on this particular trip, her annual auto insurance premium and her auto licence fee will remain the same.[1]

Item (d), the cost of maintenance and repairs, is relevant. While maintenance and repair costs have a large random component, over the long run they should be more or less proportional to the amount the car is driven. Thus, the average cost of $0.041 per kilometre is a reasonable estimate to use.

Item (e), the monthly fee that Cynthia pays to park at her university during the academic year, would not be relevant in the decision of how to get to Moncton. Regardless of which alternative she selects—driving or taking the train—she will still need to pay for parking at school.

Item (f), the cost of replacing all four tires ($900) every 50,000 kilometres is relevant. The more often Cynthia uses her car the sooner she will have to replace the tires.

1. If Cynthia has an accident while driving to Moncton or back, this might affect her insurance premium when the policy is renewed. If the expected cost of the increase in the insurance premium could be estimated, it would be a relevant cost of this particular trip, but the normal amount of the insurance premium is not relevant in any case.

Therefore, the $0.018 per kilometre for tires is appropriate to use in deciding whether to drive or take the train.

Item (g) is the total average cost of $0.512 per kilometre. As discussed above, some elements of this total are relevant, but some are not relevant. Since it contains some irrelevant costs, it would be incorrect to estimate the cost of driving to Moncton and back by simply multiplying the $0.512 by 530 kilometres (265 kilometres each way × 2). This erroneous approach would yield a cost of driving of $271.36. Unfortunately, such mistakes are often made in both personal life and in business. Since the total cost is stated on a per-kilometre basis, people are easily misled. Often people think that if the cost is stated as $0.512 per kilometre, the cost of driving 100 kilometres is $51.20. But it is not. Many of the costs included in the $0.512 cost per kilometre are sunk and/or fixed and will not increase if the car is driven another 100 kilometres. The $0.512 is an average cost, not an incremental cost. Study such unitized costs carefully (i.e., costs stated in terms of a dollar amount per unit, per kilometre, per direct labour-hour, per machine-hour, and so on)—they are often misleading.

Item (h), the $125 cost of a round-trip ticket on VIA, is clearly relevant in this decision. If Cynthia drives, she would not have to buy the ticket.

Item (i) is relevant to the decision, even if it is difficult to put a dollar value on relaxing and being able to study while on the train. It is relevant because it is a benefit that is available under one alternative but not under the other.

Item (j), the cost of putting Cynthia's cat in the kennel while she is gone, is clearly irrelevant in this decision. Whether she takes the train or drives to Moncton, she will still need to put her cat in a kennel.

Like item (i), items (k) and (l) are relevant to the decision even if it is difficult to measure their dollar impacts.

Item (m), the cost of parking in Moncton, is relevant to the decision.

Bringing together all of the relevant data, Cynthia would estimate the relative costs of driving and taking the train as follows:

Relevant financial cost of driving to Moncton:	
Gasoline (530 kilometres at $0.13 per kilometre)	$ 68.90
Maintenance and repairs (530 kilometres @ $0.041 per km)	21.73
Tires (530 kilometres @ $0.018 per km)	9.54
Cost of parking the car in Moncton (2 days @ $25 per day)	50.00
Total	$150.17
Relevant financial cost of taking the train to Moncton:	
Cost of round-trip VIA ticket from Halifax to Moncton	$125.00

What should Cynthia do? From a purely financial standpoint, it would be cheaper by $25.17 ($150.17 – $125.00) to take the train. Cynthia has to decide whether the benefit of having the car available in Moncton justifies the higher cost of driving.

In this example, we focused on identifying the relevant costs and benefits—everything else was ignored. In the next example, we will begin the analysis by including all of the costs and benefits—relevant or not. We will see that if we are very careful, we will still get the correct answer because the irrelevant costs and benefits will cancel out when we compare the alternatives.

Reconciling the Total and Differential Approaches

Oak Harbour Woodworks is considering a new labour-saving machine that rents for $3,000 per year. The machine will be used on the company's coat rack production line. Data concerning the company's annual sales and costs of coat racks with and without the new machine are shown in the table on the next page.

Given the annual sales and the price and cost data in this table, the operating income for the product under the two alternatives can be computed as shown in Exhibit 12–1.

Note that the operating income is higher by $12,000 with the new machine, so that is the better alternative. Note also that the $12,000 advantage for the new machine can be obtained

EXHIBIT 12–1 Total and Differential Costs

	Current Situation	Situation with New Machine	Differential Costs and Benefits
Sales (5,000 units @ $40 per unit)	$200,000	$200,000	$ –0–
Less variable expenses:			
Direct materials (5,000 units @ $14 per unit)	70,000	70,000	–0–
Direct labour (5,000 units @ $8 and $5 per unit)	40,000	25,000	15,000
Variable overhead (5,000 units @ $2 per unit)	10,000	10,000	–0–
Total variable expenses	120,000	105,000	
Contribution margin	80,000	95,000	
Less fixed expenses:			
Other	62,000	62,000	–0–
Rent of new machine	–0–	3,000	(3,000)
Total fixed expenses	62,000	65,000	
Operating income	$ 18,000	$ 30,000	$12,000

in two different ways. It is the difference between the $30,000 operating income with the new machine and the $18,000 operating income for the current situation. It is also the sum of the differential costs and benefits as shown in the last column of Exhibit 12–1. A positive number in the Differential Costs and Benefits column indicates that the difference between the alternatives favours the new machine; a negative number indicates that the difference favours the current situation. A zero in that column simply means that the total amount for the item is exactly the same for both alternatives. Thus, since the difference in the operating incomes equals the sum of the differences for the individual items, any cost or benefit that is the same for both alternatives will have no impact on which alternative is preferred. This is the reason that costs and benefits that do not differ between alternatives are irrelevant and can be ignored. If we properly account for them, they will cancel out when we compare the alternatives.

	Current Situation	Situation with the New Machine
Units produced and sold..........	5,000	5,000
Selling price per unit..........	$ 40	$ 40
Direct materials cost per unit	14	14
Direct labour cost per unit..........	8	5
Variable overhead cost per unit	2	2
Fixed costs, other..........	62,000	62,000
Fixed costs, new machine	—	3,000

We could have arrived at the same solution more quickly by ignoring the irrelevant costs and benefits:

- The selling price per unit and the number of units sold do not differ between the alternatives. Therefore, the total sales revenues are exactly the same for the two alternatives as shown in Exhibit 12–1. Since the sales revenues are exactly the same, they have no effect on the difference in operating income between the two alternatives. That is shown in the last column in Exhibit 12–1, which indicates a $0 differential benefit.
- The direct materials cost per unit, the variable overhead cost per unit, and the number of units produced and sold do not differ between the alternatives. Consequently, the direct materials cost and the variable overhead cost will be the same for the two alternatives and can be ignored.

- The "other" fixed expenses do not differ between the alternatives, so they can be ignored as well.

Indeed, the only costs that do differ between the alternatives are direct labour costs and the fixed rental cost of the new machine. Hence, these are the only relevant costs. The two alternatives can be compared based on just these relevant costs:

Net advantage to renting the new machine:	
Decrease in direct labour costs (5,000 units at a cost savings of $3 per unit)	$15,000
Increase in fixed expenses (rent)	(3,000)
Net annual cost savings from renting the new machine	$12,000

Thus, if we focus on just the relevant costs and benefits, we get exactly the same answer that we got when we listed all of the costs and benefits—including those that do not differ between the alternatives and hence are irrelevant. We get the same answer because the only costs and benefits that matter in the final comparison of the operating incomes are those that differ between the two alternatives and hence are not zero in the last column of Exhibit 12–1. Those two relevant costs are both listed in the above analysis showing the net advantage to renting the new machine.

Why Isolate Relevant Costs?

In the preceding example, we used two different approaches to analyze the alternatives. First, we considered only the relevant costs; and second, we considered all costs, both those that were relevant and those that were not. We obtained the same answer under both approaches. It would be natural to ask, "Why bother to isolate relevant costs when total costs will do the job just as well?" Isolating relevant costs is desirable for at least two reasons.

First, only rarely will enough information be available to prepare a detailed income statement for both alternatives as we have done in the preceding examples. Assume, for example, that you are called on to make a decision relating to a *single operation* of a multidepartmental, multiproduct firm. Under these circumstances, it would be virtually impossible to prepare an income statement of any type. You would have to rely on your ability to recognize which costs are relevant and which are not in order to assemble the data necessary to make a decision.

Second, combining irrelevant costs with relevant costs may cause confusion and distract attention from the matters that are really critical. Furthermore, the danger always exists that an irrelevant piece of data may be used improperly, resulting in an incorrect decision. Indeed, research shows that managers will often attempt to use *all* information provided, relevant and irrelevant, when making a decision.[2] The best approach is to discard irrelevant data and base the decision entirely on the relevant data.

Relevant cost analysis, combined with the contribution approach to the income statement, provides a powerful tool for making decisions. We will investigate various uses of this tool in the remaining sections of this chapter.

Analysis of Various Decision Situations

LEARNING OBJECTIVE 2
Prepare analyses for various decision situations.

Periodically, managers are faced with making non-routine or special decisions. Should a product line or segment be kept or dropped? Should a product component be made internally or purchased from an external supplier (outsourced)? Should special orders

2. K. Siegel-Jacobs and F. Yates, "Effects of Procedural and Outcome Accountability on Judgment Quality," *Organizational Behaviour and Human Decision Processes,* 1996, 65(1), pp. 7–17.

be accepted or rejected? Should a product be sold as is, or processed further? While on the surface these may appear to be very different decision situations, the approach to the analysis is similar in each case. For each situation, the relevant costs and benefits must be quantified, and the alternative with the most favourable impact on operating income selected. In some situations the analysis will consist only of a comparison of relevant costs (make versus buy) while in others both relevant benefits and relevant costs will be involved (keep or drop a product). As will be illustrated in the examples of each decision situation that follows, the challenge for managers is identifying and quantifying the relevant costs and benefits.

Adding and Dropping Product Lines and Other Segments

Decisions relating to whether existing product lines or other segments of a company should be dropped and new ones added are among the most difficult that a manager has to make. In such decisions, many qualitative and quantitative factors must be considered. Ultimately, however, any final decision to drop an old segment or to add a new one is going to hinge primarily on the impact the decision will have on operating income. To assess this impact, it is necessary to make a careful analysis of the costs involved.

Consider the three major product lines of AFM Electronics—televisions, stereos, and cameras. Sales and cost information for the preceding month for each separate product line and for the company in total are given in Exhibit 12–2.

What can be done to improve the company's overall performance? One product line—cameras—shows an operating loss for the month. Perhaps dropping this line would cause profits in the company as a whole to improve. In deciding whether the line should be dropped, management should employ the reasoning that follows.

If the cameras line is dropped, then the company will lose $16,000 per month in contribution margin. By dropping the line, however, it may be possible to avoid some fixed costs by, for example, discharging certain employees or reducing advertising costs. If by dropping the cameras line the company is able to avoid more in fixed costs than it loses in contribution margin, then it will be better off if the line is eliminated, because overall operating income should improve. On the other hand, if the company is not able to avoid as much in fixed costs as it loses in contribution margin, then the cameras line should be retained. In short, the manager should ask, "What costs can I avoid if I drop this product line?"

As we have seen from our earlier discussion, not all costs are avoidable. For example, some of the costs associated with a product line may be sunk costs. Other costs may be

EXHIBIT 12–2 AFM Electronics Product Lines

		Product Line		
	Total	Televisions	Stereos	Cameras
Sales	$340,000	$187,500	$112,500	$40,000
Less variable expenses	136,500	75,000	37,500	24,000
Contribution margin	203,500	112,500	75,000	16,000
Less fixed expenses:				
Salaries	69,400	44,250	18,750	6,400
Advertising	17,950	1,500	11,250	5,200
Utilities	2,300	750	750	800
Depreciation—fixtures	6,100	1,500	3,000	1,600
Rent	27,200	15,000	9,000	3,200
Insurance	4,150	3,000	750	400
General administrative	40,800	22,500	13,500	4,800
Total fixed expenses	167,900	88,500	57,000	22,400
Operating income (loss)	$ 35,600	$24,000	$18,000	$ (6,400)

allocated common costs that will not differ in total regardless of whether the product line is dropped or retained. As discussed in Chapter 5, an activity-based costing analysis may be used to help identify the relevant costs.

To show how the manager should proceed in a product-line analysis, suppose that the management of AFM Electronics has analyzed the costs being charged to the three product lines and has determined the following:

1. The salaries expense represents salaries paid to employees working directly in each product-line area. All of the employees working in cameras would be discharged if the line is dropped.
2. The advertising expense represents direct advertising of each product line and is avoidable if the line is dropped.
3. The utilities expense represents utilities costs for the entire company. The amount charged to each product line is an allocation based on space occupied and is not avoidable if the product line is dropped.
4. The depreciation expense represents depreciation on fixtures used for display of the various product lines. Although the fixtures are nearly new, they are custom-built and will have little resale value if the cameras line is dropped.
5. The rent expense represents rent on the entire building housing the company; it is allocated to the product lines on the basis of sales dollars. The monthly rent of $27,200 is fixed under a long-term lease agreement.
6. The insurance expense represents insurance carried on inventories within each of the three product-line areas.
7. The general administrative expense represents the costs of accounting, purchasing, and general management, which are allocated to the product lines on the basis of sales dollars. Total administrative costs will not change if the cameras line is dropped.

With this information, management can identify costs that can and cannot be avoided if the product line is dropped (see the following).

	Total Cost	Not Avoidable*	Avoidable
Salaries	$ 6,400		$ 6,400
Advertising	5,200		5,200
Utilities	800	$ 800	
Depreciation—fixtures	1,600	1,600	
Rent	3,200	3,200	
Insurance	400		400
General administrative	4,800	4,800	
Total fixed expenses	$22,400	$10,400	$12,000

*These costs represent either (1) sunk costs or (2) future costs that will not change if the cameras line is retained or discontinued.

To determine how dropping the line will affect the overall profits of the company, we can compare the contribution margin that will be lost to the costs that can be avoided if the line is dropped:

Contribution margin lost if the cameras line is discontinued (see Exhibit 12–2)	$(16,000)
Less fixed costs that can be avoided if the cameras line is discontinued (see above)	12,000
Decrease in overall company operating income	$ (4,000)

In this case, the fixed costs that can be avoided by dropping the product line are less than the contribution margin that will be lost. Therefore, based on the data given, the cameras line should not be discontinued unless a more profitable use can be found for the floor and counter space that it is occupying.

A Comparative Format

Some managers prefer to approach decisions of this type by preparing comparative income statements showing the effects on the company as a whole of either keeping or dropping the product line in question. A comparative analysis of this type for AFM Electronics is shown in Exhibit 12–3.

As shown by column 3 in the Exhibit, overall company operating income will decrease by $4,000 each period if the cameras line is dropped. This is the same answer, of course, as we obtained in our earlier analysis.

Beware of Allocated Fixed Costs

Our conclusion that the cameras line should not be dropped seems to conflict with the data shown earlier in Exhibit 12–2. Recall from the exhibit that the cameras line is showing a loss rather than a profit. Why keep a line that is showing a loss? The explanation for this apparent inconsistency lies at least in part with the common fixed costs that are being allocated to the product lines. As we observed in Chapter 8, one of the great dangers in allocating common fixed costs is that such allocations can make a product line (or other segment of a business) *look* less profitable than it really is. By allocating the common fixed costs among all product lines, the cameras line has been made to *look* as if it was unprofitable, whereas, in fact, dropping the line would result in a decrease in overall company operating income. This point can be seen clearly if we recast the data in Exhibit 12–2 and eliminate the allocation of the common fixed costs. This recasting of data—using the segmented approach from Chapter 8—is shown in Exhibit 12–4.

Exhibit 12–4 gives us a much different perspective of the cameras line than does Exhibit 12–2. As shown in Exhibit 12–4, the cameras line is covering all of its own traceable fixed costs and is generating a $2,400 segment margin toward covering the common fixed costs of the company. Unless another product line can be found that will generate a greater segment margin than this, the company would be better off keeping the

EXHIBIT 12–3 A Comparative Format for Product-Line Analysis

	Keep Cameras	Drop Cameras	Difference: Operating Income Increase or (Decrease)
Sales	$40,000	$ –0–	$(40,000)
Less variable expenses	24,000	–0–	24,000
Contribution margin	16,000	–0–	(16,000)
Less fixed expenses:			
Salaries	6,400	–0–	6,400
Advertising	5,200	–0–	5,200
Utilities	800	800	–0–
Depreciation—fixtures	1,600	1,600	–0–
Rent	3,200	3,200	–0–
Insurance	400	–0–	400
General administrative	4,800	4,800	–0–
Total fixed expenses	22,400	10,400	12,000
Operating income (loss)	$ (6,400)	$(10,400)	$ (4,000)

EXHIBIT 12–4 AFM Electronics Produce Lines—Recast in Contribution Format (from Exhibit 12–2)

		Product Line		
	Total	Televisions	Stereos	Cameras
Sales	$340,000	$187,500	$112,500	$40,000
Less variable expenses	136,500	75,000	37,500	24,000
Contribution margin	203,500	112,500	75,000	16,000
Less traceable fixed expenses:				
Salaries	69,400	44,250	18,750	6,400
Advertising	17,950	1,500	11,250	5,200
Depreciation—fixtures	6,100	1,500	3,000	1,600
Insurance	4,150	3,000	750	400
Total fixed expenses	97,600	50,250	33,750	13,600
Product-line segment margin	105,900	$ 62,250	$41,250	$ 2,400*
Less common fixed expenses:				
Utilities	2,300			
Rent	27,200			
General administrative	40,800			
Total	70,300			
Operating income	$ 35,600			

*If the cameras line is dropped, this $2,400 in segment margin will be lost to the company. In addition, we have seen that the $1,600 depreciation on the fixtures is a sunk cost that cannot be avoided. The sum of these two figures ($2,400 + $1,600 = $4,000) would be the decrease in the company's overall profits if the cameras line was discontinued.

cameras line. By keeping the line, the company's overall operating income will be higher than if the product line was dropped.[3]

Additionally, we should note that managers may choose to retain an unprofitable product line if the line is necessary to the sale of other products or if it serves as a "magnet" to attract customers. Bread, for example, is not an especially profitable line in food stores, but customers expect it to be available, and many would undoubtedly shift their buying elsewhere if a particular store decided to stop carrying it. Accordingly, to the extent that dropping a product line or segment results in decreases (or increases) to sales of other products or segments, the related impact on contribution margin should be included in the keep versus drop analysis.

The Make or Buy Decision

Many steps may be involved in getting a finished product into the hands of a consumer. First, raw materials may have to be obtained through mining, drilling, growing crops, raising animals, and so forth. Second, these raw materials may have to be processed to remove impurities and to extract the desirable and usable materials. Third, the usable materials may have to undergo some preliminary fabrication so as to be usable in final products. For example, cotton must be made into thread and textiles before being made into clothing. Fourth, the actual manufacturing of the finished product must take place. And finally, the finished product must be distributed to the ultimate consumer. Each of these steps is part of the value chain discussed in Chapter 1.

3. An alternative way of formulating the analysis is to start with the cameras net loss of $(6,400) from Exhibit 12–2 and add back the non-avoidable (irrelevant) expenses of $10,400 to arrive at the relevant benefit (segment margin) of $4,000 that would be forgone if the product line were to be discontinued.

Decision *Aid*

KEEP OR DROP A PRODUCT/SEGMENT

Relevant Costs and Benefits

- Contribution margin (CM) lost if dropped
- Fixed costs avoided if dropped
- CM lost/gained on *other* products/segments

Irrelevant Costs

- Allocated common costs
- Sunk costs

Decision Rule:

Keep if: CM lost (*all* products/segments) > fixed costs avoided + CM gained (*other* products/segments)

Drop if: CM lost (*all* products/segments) < fixed costs avoided + CM gained (*other* products/segments)

Separate companies may carry out each of the steps in the value chain or a single company may carry out several of the steps. When a company is involved in more than one of these steps in the entire value chain, it is following a policy of **vertical integration.** Vertical integration is very common. Some firms control *all* of the activities in the value chain from producing basic raw materials right up to the final distribution of finished goods. Other firms are content to integrate on a smaller scale by purchasing many of the parts and materials that go into their finished products.

A decision to produce a fabricated part internally, rather than to buy the part externally from a supplier, is called a **make or buy decision.** Indeed, any decision relating to vertical integration is a make or buy decision, since the company is deciding whether to meet its own needs internally or to buy externally.

Vertical integration
The involvement by a company in more than one of the steps from production of basic raw materials to the manufacture and distribution of a finished product.

Make or buy decision
A decision as to whether an item should be produced internally or purchased from an outside supplier.

Strategic Aspects of the Make or Buy Decision

Integration provides certain advantages. An integrated firm is less dependent on its suppliers and may be able to ensure a smoother flow of parts and materials for production than a non-integrated firm. For example, a strike against a major parts supplier can interrupt the operations of a non-integrated firm for many months, whereas an integrated firm that is producing its own parts might be able to continue operations. Also, many firms feel that they can control quality better by producing their own parts and materials, rather than by relying on the quality control standards of outside suppliers.

The advantages of integration are counterbalanced by some advantages of using external suppliers. By pooling demand from a number of firms, a supplier may be able to enjoy economies of scale in research and development and in manufacturing. These economies of scale can result in higher quality and lower costs than would be possible if the firm was to attempt to make the parts on its own. A company must be careful, however, to retain control over activities that are essential to maintaining its competitive position. For example, Hewlett-Packard controls the software for a laser printer it makes in cooperation with Canon Inc. of Japan to prevent Canon from coming out with a competing product. The present trend appears to be toward less vertical integration, with some companies like Nokia Corp., the world's largest cellphone maker, focused on hardware while teaming up with companies such as Microsoft to acquire the email software used in its phones.[4] These factors suggest that the make or buy decision should be made very carefully.

4. David Pringle, "Nokia, Microsoft Bury Hatchet," *The Globe and Mail,* February 2005, p. B14.

An Example of Make or Buy

To provide an illustration of a make or buy decision, consider Mountain Goat Cycles. The company is now producing the heavy-duty gear shifters used in its most popular line of mountain bikes. The company's Accounting Department reports the following costs of producing the shifter internally:

	Per Unit	8,000 Units
Direct materials	$ 6	$ 48,000
Direct labour	4	32,000
Variable overhead	1	8,000
Supervisor's salary	3	24,000
Depreciation of special equipment	2	16,000
Allocated general overhead	5	40,000
Total cost	$21	$168,000

An outside supplier has offered to sell Mountain Goat Cycles 8,000 shifters per year at a price of only $19 each. Should the company stop producing the shifters internally and start purchasing them from the outside supplier? To approach the decision from a financial point of view, the manager should again focus on the differential costs. As we have seen, the differential costs can be obtained by eliminating those costs that are not avoidable—that is, by eliminating (1) the sunk costs and (2) the future costs that will continue regardless of whether the shifters are produced internally or purchased outside. The costs that remain after making these eliminations are the costs that are avoidable to the company by purchasing outside. If these avoidable costs are less than the outside purchase price, then the company should continue to manufacture its own shifters and reject the outside supplier's offer. That is, the company should purchase outside only if the outside purchase price is less than the costs that can be avoided internally as a result of stopping production of the shifters.

Looking at the data above, note first that depreciation of special equipment is listed as one of the costs of producing the shifters internally. Since the equipment has already been purchased, this depreciation is a sunk cost and is therefore irrelevant. If the equipment could be sold, its salvage value would be relevant. Or if the machine could be used to make other products, this could be relevant as well. However, we will assume that the equipment has no salvage value and that it has no other use except making the heavy-duty gear shifters.

Also note that the company is allocating a portion of its general overhead costs to the shifters. Any portion of this general overhead cost that would actually be eliminated if the gear shifters were purchased rather than made would be relevant in the analysis. However, it is likely that the general overhead costs allocated to the gear shifters are in fact common to all items produced in the factory and would continue unchanged even if the shifters are purchased from the outside. Such allocated common costs are not differential costs (because they do not differ between the make or buy alternatives) and should be eliminated from the analysis along with the sunk costs.

The variable costs of producing the shifters (materials, labour, and variable overhead) are differential costs, because they can be avoided by buying the shifters from the outside supplier. If the supervisor can be discharged and her salary avoided by buying the shifters, then it too will be a differential cost and relevant to the decision. Assuming that both the variable costs and the supervisor's salary can be avoided by buying from the outside supplier, then the analysis takes the form shown in Exhibit 12–5.

Since it costs $5 less per unit to continue to make the shifters, Mountain Goat Cycles should reject the outside supplier's offer. However, there is one additional factor that the company may wish to consider before coming to a final decision. This factor is the opportunity cost of the space now being used to produce the shifters.

EXHIBIT 12–5 Mountain Goat Cycles Make or Buy Analysis

	Production "Cost" per Unit	Per Unit Differential Costs		Total Differential Costs—8,000 Units	
		Make	Buy	Make	Buy
Direct materials	$ 6	$ 6		$ 48,000	
Direct labour	4	4		32,000	
Variable overhead	1	1		8,000	
Supervisor's salary	3	3		24,000	
Depreciation of special equipment	2	—		—	
Allocated general overhead	5	—		—	
Outside purchase price			$19		$152,000
Total cost	$21	$14	$19	$112,000	$152,000
Difference in favour of continuing to make		$5		$40,000	

Opportunity Cost

If the space now being used to produce the shifters *would otherwise be idle,* then Mountain Goat Cycles should continue to produce its own shifters and the supplier's offer should be rejected, as stated above. Idle space that has no alternative use has an opportunity cost of zero.

But what if the space now being used to produce shifters could be used for some other purpose? In that case, the space would have an opportunity cost that would have to be considered in assessing the desirability of the supplier's offer. What would this opportunity cost be? It would be the segment margin that could be derived from the best alternative use of the space.

To illustrate, assume that the space now being used to produce shifters could be used to produce disc brakes that would generate a segment margin of $60,000 per year. Under these conditions, Mountain Goat Cycles would be better off to accept the supplier's offer and to use the available space to produce the new product line:

	Make	Buy
Differential cost per unit (see Exhibit 12–5)	$ 14	$ 19
Number of units needed annually	× 8,000	× 8,000
Total annual cost	112,000	152,000
Opportunity cost—segment margin forgone on a potential new product line	60,000	—
Total cost	$172,000	$152,000
Difference in favour of purchasing from the outside supplier	$ 20,000[5]	

5. An alternative approach to the analysis is to add the incremental unit cost of continuing to make the shifters of $14 (see Exhibit 12–5) to the opportunity cost per unit of $7.50 ($60,000 opportunity cost ÷ 8,000 units), giving a total of $21.50. Since $21.50 is greater than the purchase price of $19 per unit, Mountain Goat Cycle should buy the shifter.

Opportunity costs are not recorded in accounts of an organization because they do not represent actual dollar outlays. Rather, they represent economic benefits that are *forgone* as a result of pursuing some course of action. Because of this, opportunity costs are often erroneously ignored by managers when making decisions.[6] The opportunity costs of Mountain Goat Cycles are sufficiently large in this case to make continued production of the shifters very costly from an economic point of view.

Decision *Aid*

MAKE OR BUY

Relevant Costs

- Incremental costs of making the product (variable and fixed)
- Opportunity cost of utilizing space to make the product
- Outside purchase price

Irrelevant Costs

- Allocated common costs
- Sunk costs

Total relevant costs of making = incremental costs + opportunity costs

Decision Rule:

Make if: total relevant costs of making < outside purchase price
Buy if: total relevant costs of making > outside purchase price

IN BUSINESS

Companies regularly review the outsourcing arrangements they have in place to meet their production needs in the short and long-term. For financial or strategic reasons, production that had been previously outsourced may be "in-sourced," which means the use of an external supplier is discontinued and production is done internally. For example, if the cost of outsourcing becomes too high or it becomes more economically feasible to increase production capacity, companies may decide to increase the extent of vertical integration. Thus, "make or buy" decision are not seen as irreversible, but instead are monitored and managed on an ongoing basis to ensure that the company's objectives are being met.

A good example of the management of outsourcing arrangements is provided by BMW's recent announcement that they would no longer be using the services of Magna International Incorporated (a Canadian-based company) to produce the X3, one of their sport utility vehicles. Magna produced 113,000 X3s in 2006 at their plant in Austria. Citing the high cost of outsourcing, BMW announced that they would be moving the production to their own plant in South Carolina. BMW officials also noted that moving production of the X3 to the United States, the biggest market for the vehicle, also protects the company against the possibility of further declines in the value of the U.S. dollar.

Source: Greg Keenan, "BMW Decision Costly for Magna's Austrian Operation," *The Globe and Mail*, May 16, 2007, B4.

6. S. Vera-Munoz. "The Effects of Accounting Knowledge and Context on the Omission of Opportunity Costs in Resource Allocation Decisions," *The Accounting Review*, 1998, 73 (1), pp. 47–72.

Special Orders

Managers often must evaluate whether a *special order* should be accepted, and if the order is accepted, the price that should be charged. A **special order** is a one-time order that is not considered part of the company's normal ongoing business. The objective in setting a price for special orders is to achieve positive incremental operating income. To illustrate, Mountain Goat Cycles has just received a request from the Edmonton Police Department to produce 100 specially modified mountain bikes at a price of $279 each. The bikes would be used to patrol some of the more densely populated residential sections of the city. Mountain Goat Cycles can easily modify its City Cruiser model to fit the specifications of the Edmonton Police. The normal selling price of the City Cruiser bike is $349, and its unit product cost is $282 as shown below:

Special order
A one-time order that is not considered part of the company's normal ongoing business.

Direct materials	$186
Direct labour	45
Manufacturing overhead	51
Unit product cost	$282

The variable portion of the above manufacturing overhead is $6 per unit. The order would have no effect on the company's total fixed manufacturing overhead costs.

The modifications to the bikes consist of welded brackets to hold radios, nightsticks, and other gear. These modifications would require $17 in incremental variable costs. In addition, the company would have to pay a graphics design studio $1,200 to design and cut stencils that would be used for spray painting the Edmonton Police Department's logo and other identifying marks on the bikes.

This order should have no effect on the company's other sales. The production manager says that she can handle the special order without disrupting any of the regular scheduled production.

What effect would accepting this order have on the company's operating income?

Only the incremental costs and benefits are relevant. Since the existing fixed manufacturing overhead costs would not be affected by the order, they are not incremental costs and therefore are not relevant. The incremental operating income can be computed as follows:

	Per Unit	Total 100 Bikes
Incremental revenue	$279	$27,900
Incremental costs:		
Variable costs:		
Direct materials	186	18,600
Direct labour	45	4,500
Variable manufacturing overhead	6	600
Special modifications	17	1,700
Total variable cost	$254	25,400
Fixed cost:		
Purchase of stencils		1,200
Total incremental cost		26,600
Incremental operating income		$ 1,300

Therefore, even though the price on the special order ($279) is below the normal unit product cost ($282) and the order would require incurring additional costs, the order would result in an increase in operating income. In general, a special order is profitable as long as the incremental revenue from the special order exceeds the incremental costs of the order.

However, in performing the analysis it is important to make sure that there is indeed idle capacity and that the special order does not cut into normal sales. For example, what if Mountain Goat Cycle is already operating at 100% of capacity and normally sells all the bikes it can produce for $349 each? What is the opportunity cost of accepting the order? Should they accept the $279 price? If not, what is the minimum price they should accept? To answer these questions, the analysis can be conducted as follows:

	Per Unit
(a) Opportunity Costs:	
Normal selling price	$349
Less variable costs:	
Direct materials	186
Direct labour	45
Variable overhead	6
Total variable costs	$237
Contribution margin forgone	$112*
(b) Total relevant costs:	
Incremental costs:	
Variable ($237 + $17)	$254
Fixed ($1,200/100)	12
	$266
Opportunity costs	112
Total	$378

* If Mountain Goat Cycle is operating at 100% capacity, every bike they sell to the Edmonton Police Department means forgoing the contribution margin of $112 they would have earned on a sale to a regular customer. This is the per unit opportunity cost of accepting the special order.

Since the total relevant costs of $378 exceed the offer price of $279, Mountain Goat Cycle should decline the offer. Indeed, to be no worse off from a financial perspective, the minimum price that should be charged on the special order is $378 per bike. At this price, management should be indifferent between filling the special order and continuing to sell all it can produce to regular customers.

Decision *Aid*

ACCEPT OR REJECT A SPECIAL ORDER

Relevant Costs and Benefits

- Incremental costs of filling the order (variable and fixed)
- Opportunity cost of filling the order
- Incremental revenues from the order

Irrelevant Costs

- Allocated common costs
- Sunk costs

Total Relevant Costs = incremental costs + opportunity costs

Decision Rule:

Accept if: incremental revenues > total relevant costs
Reject if: incremental revenues < total relevant costs

Joint Product Costs and The Sell or Process Further Decision

In some industries, a number of end products are produced from a single raw material input. For example, in the petroleum refining industry a large number of products are extracted from crude oil, including gasoline, jet fuel, home heating oil, lubricants, asphalt, and various organic chemicals. Another example is provided by the St. Thomas Wool Cooperative of British Columbia. The company buys raw wool from local sheepherders, separates the wool into three grades—coarse, fine, and superfine—and then dyes the wool using traditional methods that rely on pigments from local materials. Exhibit 12–6 contains a diagram of the production process.

At St. Thomas Wool Cooperative, coarse wool, fine wool, and superfine wool are produced from one input—raw wool. Two or more products that are produced from a common input are known as **joint products.** The term **joint product costs** is used to describe those manufacturing costs that are incurred in producing joint products up to the split-off point. The **split-off point** is the point in the manufacturing process at which the joint products can be recognized as separate products. This does not occur at St. Thomas

Joint products Two or more items that are produced from a common input.

Joint product costs Costs that are incurred up to the split-off point in producing joint products.

Split-off point That point in the manufacturing process where some or all of the joint products can be recognized as individual products.

EXHIBIT 12–6 Joint Products

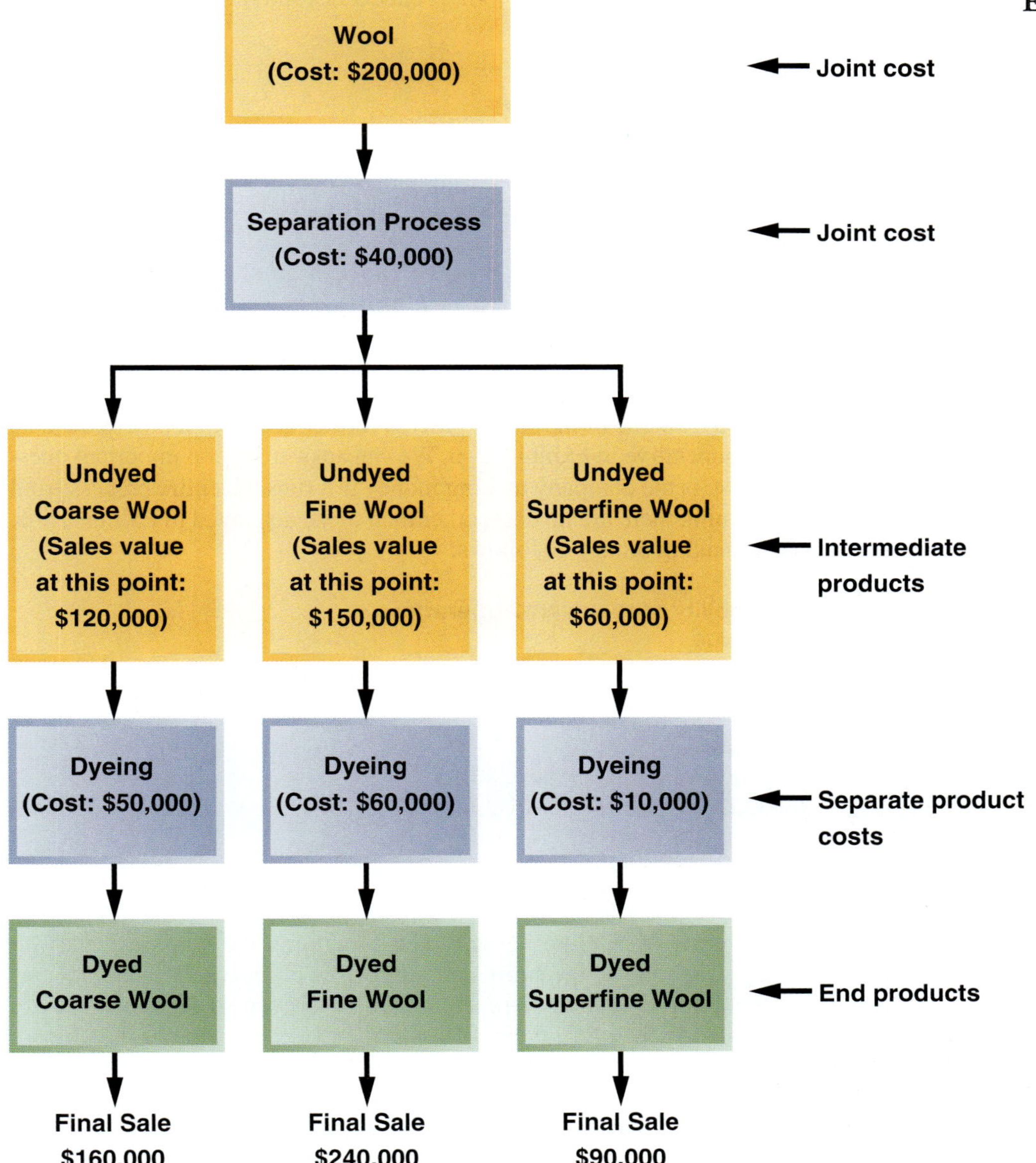

Cooperative until the raw wool has gone through the separating process. At St. Thomas Wool Cooperative, the joint costs are the $200,000 cost of the raw wool and the $40,000 cost of separating the wool. The undyed wool is called an *intermediate product* because it is not finished at this point. Nevertheless, a market does exist for undyed wool—although at a significantly lower price than finished, dyed wool.

The Pitfalls of Allocation

Joint product costs are really common costs incurred to simultaneously produce a variety of end products. Traditional cost accounting books contain various approaches to allocating these common costs among the different products at the split-off point. A typical approach is to allocate the joint product costs according to the relative sales value of the end products.

Although allocation of joint product costs is needed for some purposes, such as balance sheet inventory valuation, allocations of this kind should be viewed with great caution *internally* in the decision making process. As will be discussed in the next section, because allocated joint product costs are sunk costs, they should never be used when making decisions about what to do with the joint products beyond the split-off point (i.e., sell immediately or process further).

Sell or Process Further Decisions

Sell or process further decision
A decision as to whether a joint product should be sold at the split-off point or processed further and sold at a later time in a different form.

Deciding what to do with a product from the split-off point forward is known as a **sell or process further decision**. Joint costs are irrelevant in these decisions because by the time one arrives at the split-off point, the joint product costs have already been incurred and therefore are sunk costs.

It will always be profitable to continue processing a joint product after the split-off point *as long as the incremental revenue from such processing exceeds the incremental processing cost incurred after the split-off point.* Joint product costs that already have been incurred up to the split-off point are sunk costs, which are always irrelevant in decisions concerning what to do from the split-off point forward.

To provide a detailed example of the sell or process further decision, return to the data for St. Thomas Wool Cooperative in Exhibit 12–6. We can answer several important questions using this data. First, is the company making money if it runs the entire process from beginning to end? Assuming there are no costs other than those displayed in Exhibit 12–6, the company is indeed making money as follows:

Analysis of the profitability of the overall operation:		
Combined final sales value		
($160,000 + $240,000 + $90,000)		$490,000
Less costs of producing the end products:		
Cost of wool	$200,000	
Cost of separating wool	40,000	
Combined costs of dyeing		
($50,000 + $60,000 + $10,000)	120,000	360,000
Profit		$130,000

Note that the joint costs of buying the wool and separating the wool *are* relevant when considering the profitability of the entire operation. This is because these joint costs *could* be avoided if the entire operation were shut down. However, these joint costs are *not* relevant when considering the profitability of any one product. As long as the process is being run to make the other products, no additional joint costs are incurred to make the specific product in question.

Even though the company is making money overall, it may be losing money on one or more of the products. If the company buys wool and runs the separation process, it will get all three intermediate products. Nothing can be done about that. However, each of these products can be sold *as is* without further processing. It may be that the company would be better off selling one or more of the products prior to dyeing to avoid the dyeing costs. The appropriate way to make this choice is to compare the incremental revenues to the incremental costs from further processing as follows in Exhibit 12–7.

EXHIBIT 12–7 Sell or Process Further Decision

	Coarse Wool	Fine Wool	Superfine Wool
Final sales value after further processing	$160,000	$240,000	$90,000
Less sales value at the split-off point	120,000	150,000	60,000
Incremental revenue from further processing	40,000	90,000	30,000
Less cost of further processing (dyeing)	50,000	60,000	10,000
Profit (loss) from further processing.	$ (10,000)	$ 30,000	$20,000

As this analysis shows, the company would be better off selling the undyed coarse wool as is rather than processing it further. The other two products should be processed further and dyed before selling them.

Note that the joint costs of the wool ($200,000) and of the wool separation process ($40,000) play no role in the decision to sell or further process the intermediate products. These joint costs are relevant in a decision of whether to buy wool and to run the wool separation process, but they are not relevant in decisions about what to do with the intermediate products once they have been separated.

Decision *Aid*

SELL OR PROCESS FURTHER

Relevant Costs and Benefits

- Incremental costs of further processing
- Incremental revenues from further processing

Irrelevant Costs

- Allocated joint product costs

Decision Rule:

Process further if: incremental revenues > incremental costs of further processing
Sell at split-off if: incremental revenues < incremental costs of further processing

Utilization of a Constrained Resource

LEARNING OBJECTIVE 3
Determine the most profitable use of a constrained resource and the value of obtaining more of the constrained resource.

Another decision situation managers often face is the problem of how to utilize a constrained resource. When a limited resource of some type restricts a company's ability to fully satisfy demand for its products or services, the company is said to have a **constraint**. A convenience store has limited shelf space so it must decide which products to sell. Manufacturing firms may have constraints on machine-hours, labour-hours or the amount of raw materials available for production. The **theory of constraints (TOC)** maintains that effectively managing a constraint is important to the financial success of an organization. The challenge for managers is deciding how best to utilize the constrained resource in order to maximize the company's profits. As will be illustrated below, fixed

Constraint
A limitation under which a company must operate, such as limited machine time available or limited raw materials available, that restricts the company's ability to satisfy demand.

Theory of constraints (TOC)
A management approach that emphasizes the importance of managing constraints.

costs are usually unaffected by the allocation of the constrained resource in the short-run, so the focus will be on analyzing and maximizing contribution margin.

Contribution Margin in Relation to a Constrained Resource

To maximize total contribution margin, a firm should not necessarily promote those products that have the highest *unit* contribution margins. Rather, total contribution margin will be maximized by promoting those products or accepting those orders that provide the highest unit contribution margin *in relation to the constrained resource.* To illustrate, Mountain Goat Cycles makes a line of panniers—a saddlebag for bicycles. There are two models of panniers—a touring model and a mountain model. Cost and revenue data for the two models of panniers are given below:

	Model	
	Mountain Pannier	Touring Pannier
Selling price per unit.	$40	$50
Variable cost per unit	30	42
Contribution margin per unit	$10	$ 8
Contribution margin (CM) ratio.	25%	16%

The mountain pannier appears to be much more profitable than the touring pannier. It has a $10 per unit contribution margin as compared to only $8 per unit for the touring model, and it has a 25% CM ratio as compared to only 16% for the touring model.

But now let us add one more piece of information—the plant that makes the panniers is operating at capacity. Ordinarily this does not mean that every machine and every person in the plant is working at the maximum possible rate. Because machines have different capacities, some machines will be operating at less than 100% of capacity. However, if the plant as a whole cannot produce any more units, some machine or process must be operating at capacity. The machine or process that is limiting overall output is called the **bottleneck**—it is the constraint.

Bottleneck
A machine or process that limits total output because it is operating at capacity.

At Mountain Goat Cycles, the bottleneck is a particular stitching machine. The mountain pannier requires four minutes of stitching time, and each unit of the touring pannier requires two minutes of stitching time. Since this stitching machine already has more work than it can handle, something will have to be cut back. In this situation, which product is more profitable? To answer this question, the manager should look at the *contribution margin per unit of the constrained resource,* also known as the **profitability index**. This figure is computed by dividing the contribution margin by the amount of the constrained resource a unit of product requires. These calculations are carried out below for the mountain and touring panniers.

Profitability Index =

$$\frac{\text{Contribution margin per unit}}{\text{Quantity of constrained resource required per unit}}$$

	Model	
	Mountain Pannier	Touring Pannier
Contribution margin per unit (a)	$10.00	$8.00
Time on the stitching machine required to produce one unit (b)	4 min.	2 min.
Contribution margin per unit of the constrained resource, (a) ÷ (b)	$2.50/min.	$4.00/min.

Using the profitability index, it is easy to decide which product is less profitable and should be de-emphasized. Each minute of processing time on the stitching machine that is devoted to the touring pannier results in an increase of $4 in contribution margin and profits. The comparable figure for the mountain pannier is only $2.50 per minute. Therefore, the touring model should be emphasized. Even though the mountain model has the larger per unit contribution margin and the larger CM ratio, the touring model provides the larger contribution margin in relation to the constrained resource.

To verify that the touring model is indeed the more profitable product, suppose an hour of additional stitching time is available and that there are unfilled orders for both products. The additional hour on the stitching machine could be used to make either 15 mountain panniers (60 minutes ÷ 4 minutes) or 30 touring panniers (60 minutes ÷ 2 minutes), with the following consequences:

	Model	
	Mountain Pannier	Touring Pannier
Contribution margin per unit (a)	$ 10	$ 8
Additional units that can be processed in one hour	× 15	× 30
Additional contribution margin	$150	$240

The analysis illustrated in this example generalizes well to situations where demand exceeds capacity and managers must allocate a constrained resource to three or more products. Demand should be fully satisfied for the product with the highest profitability index. Any capacity that remains should then be allocated to the product with the second highest profitability index, and so on until all available capacity has been utilized. Simply looking at unit contribution margins alone is not enough when constraints exist; contribution margin per unit of the scarce resource must guide decision making.

IN BUSINESS

Indalex Aluminum Solutions Group is the largest producer of soft alloy extrusions in North America. The company has installed a new generation of business intelligence software created by pVelocity, Inc., of Toronto, Canada. The software "provides decision makers across our entire manufacturing enterprise with time-based financial metrics using TOC concepts to identify bottlenecks." And, it "shifts the focus of a manufacturing company from traditional cost accounting measurements to measuring the generation of dollars per unit of time." For example, instead of emphasizing products with the largest gross margins or contribution margins, the software helps managers to identify and emphasize the products that maximize the contribution margin per unit of the constrained resource.

Source: Mike Alger, "Managing a Business as a Portfolio of Customers," *Strategic Finance*, June 2003, pp. 54–57.

Managing Constraints

Profits can be increased by effectively managing the organization's constraints. One aspect of managing constraints is to decide how to best utilize them. As discussed above, if the constraint is a bottleneck in the production process, the manager should select the product mix that maximizes the total contribution margin. In addition, the manager should take an active role in managing the constraint itself. Management should focus efforts on increasing the efficiency of the bottleneck operation (constraint) and on increasing its capacity. Such efforts directly increase the output of finished goods and will often pay off in an almost immediate increase in profits.

It is often possible for a manager to effectively increase the capacity of the bottleneck,

Relaxing (or elevating) the constraint
An action that increases the capacity of a bottleneck.

which is called **relaxing (or elevating) the constraint.** For example, the stitching machine operator could be asked to work overtime. This would result in more available stitching time and hence more finished goods that can be sold. The benefits from relaxing the constraint in such a manner are often enormous and can easily be quantified. The manager should first ask, "What would I do with additional capacity at the bottleneck if it was available?" In the previous example, for touring (mountain) panniers, the additional capacity was worth $4 ($2.50) per minute or $240 ($150) per hour because adding an hour of capacity would generate an additional $240 ($150) of contribution margin if it were used solely to process more touring (mountain) panniers. Based on the profitability indices, additional capacity should first be allocated to production of touring panniers, followed by mountain panniers if any capacity remains. Since overtime pay for the operator is likely to be much less than $240 (or $150 for that matter!), running the stitching machine on overtime would be an excellent way to increase the company's profits while satisfying its customers at the same time.

The implications are clear: Managers should focus much of their attention on managing bottlenecks. As we have discussed, managers should emphasize products that most profitably utilize the constrained resource. They should also make sure that products are processed smoothly through the bottlenecks, with minimal lost time due to breakdowns and set-ups. And they should try to find ways to increase the capacity at the bottlenecks, which can be accomplished in a number of ways, including:

- Working overtime on the bottleneck.
- Subcontracting some of the processing that would be done at the bottleneck.
- Shifting workers from processes that are not bottlenecks to the process that *is* a bottleneck.
- Focusing business process improvement efforts such as TQM and business process re-engineering on the bottleneck.
- Reducing defective units. Each defective unit that is processed through the bottleneck and subsequently scrapped takes the place of a good unit that could be sold.

The last three methods of increasing the capacity of the bottleneck are particularly attractive, because they are low-cost interventions and may even yield additional cost savings.

Bottlenecks, as the name implies, represent restrictions to the productive capacity of an organization. As the discussions about capacity in Chapter 10 suggested, numerous types of restrictions can exist, thus preventing the organization from producing at practical capacity. Chapter 10 provided a discussion of how management may try to analyze the implications of various forms of capacity restrictions. The implications of administrative decisions about work shift numbers or maintenance practices, as well as available back-up capacity for breakdowns and other stoppages, can be analyzed to see what needs to be addressed by management to improve the economic performance of the organization.

The Problem of Multiple Constraints

What does a firm do if it has more than one potential constraint? For example, a firm may have limited raw materials, limited direct labour-hours available, limited floor space, and limited advertising dollars to spend on product promotion. How would it proceed to find the right combination of products to produce? The proper combination or "mix" of products can be found by use of a quantitative method known as *linear programming,* which is covered in quantitative methods and operations management courses.

Activity-Based Costing and Relevant Costs

As discussed in Chapter 5, activity-based costing improves the traceability of costs by focusing on the activities caused by a product or other segment. However, managers should exercise caution against assuming that if a cost is traceable to a segment, then the cost is automatically an avoidable cost. That is not true. Costs provided by a well-designed activity-based costing system are only relevant if they are actually avoidable. Costs that are not avoidable should be ignored.

To illustrate, refer again to the data relating to the cameras line in Exhibit 12–4. The $1,600 depreciation on fixtures is a traceable cost of the camera lines because it relates to activities in that department. We found, however, that the $1,600 is not avoidable if the cameras line is dropped. The key lesson here is that a sunk cost such as depreciation of existing equipment is still a sunk cost regardless of whether it is traced directly to a particular segment on an activity basis, allocated to all segments on the basis of labour-hours, or treated in some other way in the costing process. Regardless of the cost assignment method managers must apply the principles discussed in this chapter to determine the costs that are avoidable in each situation.[7]

Summary

The analysis presented for the various decision situations examined in this chapter illustrate one pervasive concept: When making decisions, managers should only consider those costs and benefits that will be incurred or realized in the future and that differ among the alternatives. Application of this concept ensures that only relevant costs, including opportunity costs, are considered and that irrelevant items such as sunk or common costs are ignored. Because technological advances have increased the availability of data for decision making, it is more important than ever that managers be able to consistently differentiate between relevant and irrelevant information. The examples in the chapter show that the relevance of particular costs and benefits depends on the type of decision situation and decision aids were provided in each case to summarize the appropriate approach to the analysis.

A simple approach was also illustrated for allocating a constrained resource when demand exceeds production capacity in the short-run. Use of the profitability index permits identification of the product that is most profitable per unit of the constrained resource and guides the resource allocation process.

Chapter 13 continues our examination of relevant costs in the context of long-run investment decisions.

Review Problem: Relevant Costs

The St. Albert Cycle Company manufactures three types of bicycles—a dirt bike, a mountain bike, and a racing bike. Data on sales and expenses for the past quarter follow:

	Total	Dirt Bikes	Mountain Bikes	Racing Bikes
Sales	$300,000	$90,000	$150,000	$60,000
Less variable manufacturing and selling expenses	120,000	27,000	60,000	33,000
Contribution margin	180,000	63,000	90,000	27,000

continued

7. For further discussion, see Douglas Sharp and Linda P. Christensen, "A New View of Activity-Based Costing," *Management Accounting* 73, no. 7, September 1991, pp. 32–34; and Maurice L. Hirsch, Jr. and Michael C. Nibbelin, "Incremental, Separable, Sunk, and Common Costs in Activity-Based Costing," *Journal of Cost Management* 6, no. 1, Spring 1992, pp. 39–47.

	Total	Dirt Bikes	Mountain Bikes	Racing Bikes
Less fixed expenses:				
Advertising, traceable.	30,000	10,000	14,000	6,000
Depreciation of special equipment	23,000	6,000	9,000	8,000
Salaries of product-line managers	35,000	12,000	13,000	10,000
Allocated common fixed expenses*.	60,000	18,000	30,000	12,000
Total fixed expenses	148,000	46,000	66,000	36,000
Operating income (loss).	$ 32,000	$17,000	$ 24,000	$(9,000)

*Allocated on the basis of sales dollars.

Management is concerned about the continued losses shown by the racing bikes and wants a recommendation as to whether or not the line should be discontinued. The special equipment used to produce racing bikes has no resale value and does not wear out.

Required:

1. Should production and sale of the racing bikes be discontinued? Explain. Show computations to support your answer.
2. Recast the above data in a format that would be more usable to management in assessing the long-run profitability of the various product lines.

Solution to Review Problem

1. No, production and sale of the racing bikes should not be discontinued. If the racing bikes were discontinued, then the operating income for the company as a whole would decrease by $11,000 each quarter:

Lost contribution margin		$(27,000)
Fixed costs that can be avoided:		
Advertising, traceable	$ 6,000	
Salary of the product line manager	10,000	16,000
Decrease in operating income for the company as a whole		$(11,000)

The depreciation of the special equipment is a sunk cost and is not relevant to the decision. The common costs are allocated and will continue regardless of whether or not the racing bikes are discontinued; thus, they are not relevant to the decision.

Alternative Solution:

	Current Total	Total if Racing Bikes Are Dropped	Difference: Operating Income Increase or (Decrease) if Dropped
Sales.	$300,000	$240,000	$(60,000)
Less variable expenses	120,000	87,000	33,000
Contribution margin	180,000	153,000	(27,000)
Less fixed expenses:			
Advertising, traceable.	30,000	24,000	6,000
Depreciation on special equipment* . . .	23,000	23,000	0
Salaries of product managers	35,000	25,000	10,000
Common allocated costs	60,000	60,000	0
Total fixed expenses	148,000	132,000	16,000
Operating income	$ 32,000	$ 21,000	$ (11,000)

*Includes pro-rated loss on the special equipment if it is disposed of.

2. The segmented report can be improved by eliminating the allocation of the common fixed expenses. Following the format introduced in Chapter 8 for a segmented income statement, a better report would be:

	Total	Dirt Bikes	Mountain Bikes	Racing Bikes
Sales	$300,000	$90,000	$150,000	$60,000
Less variable manufacturing and selling expenses	120,000	27,000	60,000	33,000
Contribution margin	180,000	63,000	90,000	27,000
Less traceable fixed expenses:				
Advertising	30,000	10,000	14,000	6,000
Depreciation of special equipment	23,000	6,000	9,000	8,000
Salaries of the product line managers	35,000	12,000	13,000	10,000
Total traceable fixed expenses	88,000	28,000	36,000	24,000
Product line segment margin	92,000	$35,000	$ 54,000	$ 3,000
Less common fixed expenses	60,000			
Operating income	$ 32,000			

Appendix 12A: Pricing Products and Services

LEARNING OBJECTIVE 4
Compute selling prices based on costs.

Our consideration of special orders in Chapter 12 focused on non-routine situations where companies receive an offer for a product or service at a specific price. By comparing the relevant costs that would be incurred if the offer was accepted to the offer price, managers can determine the incremental effect on operating income. In this appendix we expand our discussion of the relation between relevant costs and pricing issues to include two distinct pricing situations requiring on-going analysis by managers. First, we examine situations where companies are faced with the problem of setting their own prices for products or services. In this setting we present two approaches to setting prices based on costs. Second, we examine a setting where the company offers a product or service that competes with other similar products or services for which a market price already exists. In this setting, we introduce the concept of target costing. Importantly, in both settings managers must identify and use relevant cost information to make decisions that are in the best interests of the company. Setting prices is a critical decision for managers. If the price is set too high, customers will avoid purchasing the company's products. If the price is set too low, the company's costs may not be covered.

Cost-Plus Pricing

The usual approach in pricing is to *mark up* cost.[8] A product's **markup** is the difference between its selling price and its cost. The markup is usually expressed as a percentage of cost. This approach is called **cost-plus pricing** because the predetermined markup percentage is applied to the cost base to determine a target selling price.

Markup
The difference between the selling price of a product or service and its cost. The markup is usually expressed as a percentage of cost.

Cost-plus pricing
A pricing method in which a predetermined markup is applied to a cost base to determine the target selling price.

$$\text{Selling price} = \text{Cost} + (\text{Markup percentage} \times \text{Cost})$$

8. There are some legal restrictions on prices. Competition laws prohibit "predatory" prices, which are generally interpreted by the courts to mean a price below average variable cost. "Price discrimination"—charging different prices to customers in the same market for the same product or service—is also prohibited by the law.

For example, if a company uses a markup of 50%, it adds 50% to the costs of its products to determine the selling price. If a product costs $10, then the company would charge $15 for the product.

There are two key issues when the cost-plus approach to pricing is used. First, what costs are relevant to the pricing decision? Second, how should the markup be determined? Several alternative approaches are considered in this appendix.

As discussed in Chapters 2 through 8 and Chapter 10, various definitions of cost exist, each of which could be used as the base for setting a selling price. To provide a coherent illustration of cost-plus pricing, absorption costing as described in Chapters 2, 3, 4, and 8 will be presented first. We will then present an example of cost-plus pricing using the total variable costing approach.

Setting a Target Selling Price Using the Absorption Costing Approach

To illustrate, let us assume that the management of Roper Company wants to set the selling price on a product that has just undergone some design modifications. The Accounting Department has provided cost estimates for the redesigned product as shown below:

	Per Unit	Total
Direct materials	$12	
Direct labour	8	
Variable manufacturing overhead	6	
Fixed manufacturing overhead	—	$140,000
Variable selling, general, and administrative expenses	4	
Fixed selling, general, and administrative expenses	—	120,000

The first step in the absorption costing approach to cost-plus pricing is to compute the unit product cost. For Roper Company, this amounts to $40 per unit at a volume of 10,000 units, as shown in the first part of Exhibit 12–8.

Roper Company has a general policy of marking up unit product costs by 50%. A price quotation sheet for the company prepared using the absorption approach is also presented in Exhibit 12–8. Note that selling, general, and administrative (SG&A) costs are not included in the cost base. Instead, the markup is supposed to cover these expenses. Next we examine how some companies compute these markup percentages.

Determining the Markup Percentage

How did Roper Company arrive at its markup percentage of 50%? This figure could be based on industry norms or just a company tradition that seems to work. The markup percentage may also be the result of an explicit computation. As we have discussed, the markup over cost ideally should be largely determined by market conditions. However, a popular approach is to at least start with a markup based on cost and desired profit. The reasoning goes like this: The markup must be large enough to cover SG&A expenses

EXHIBIT 12–8 Price Quotation Sheet—Absorption Basis (10,000 Units)

Direct materials	$12
Direct labour	8
Variable manufacturing overhead	6
Fixed manufacturing overhead (based on 10,000 units)	14
Unit product cost	40
Markup to cover selling, general, and administrative expenses and desired profit—50% of unit manufacturing cost	20
Target selling price	$60

and provide an adequate return on investment (ROI). Given the forecasted unit sales, the markup can be computed as follows:

$$\text{Markup percentage on absorption cost} = \frac{\begin{pmatrix}\text{Required ROI} \\ \times \text{ Investment}\end{pmatrix} + \text{SG\&A expenses}}{\text{Unit sales} \times \text{Unit product cost}}$$

To show how the formula above is applied, assume Roper Company must invest \$200,000 to produce and market 10,000 units of the product each year. The \$200,000 investment covers purchase of equipment and funds needed to carry inventories and accounts receivable. If Roper Company requires a 20% ROI, then the markup for the product would be determined as follows:

$$\text{Markup percentage on absorption cost} = \frac{\begin{pmatrix}20\% \\ \times \$200{,}000\end{pmatrix} + \left((\$4 \times 10{,}000) + \$120{,}000\right)}{10{,}000 \times \$40}$$

$$\text{Markup percentage on absorption cost} = \frac{\$40{,}000 + \$160{,}000}{\$400{,}000} = 50\%$$

As shown earlier, this markup of 50% leads to a target selling price of \$60 for the Roper Company product. As shown in Exhibit 12–9, *if the company actually sells 10,000 units* of the product at this price, and actual costs are as expected, the company's ROI on this product will indeed be 20%. If it turns out that more than 10,000 units are sold at this price, the ROI will be greater than 20%. If fewer than 10,000 units are sold, the ROI will be less than 20%. *The required ROI will be attained only if the forecasted unit sales volume is attained,* and actual costs equal expected costs for that level of sales activity.

Problems with the Absorption Costing Approach

Using the absorption costing approach, the pricing problem looks deceptively simple. All you have to do is compute your unit product cost, decide how much profit you want, and

EXHIBIT 12–9 Income Statement and ROI Analysis—Roper Company
Actual Unit Sales = 10,000 Units; Selling Price = \$60

Direct materials	\$12
Direct labour	8
Variable manufacturing overhead	6
Fixed manufacturing overhead (\$140,000 ÷ 10,000 units)	14
Unit product cost	\$40

ROPER COMPANY
Absorption Costing Income Statement

Sales (\$60 × 10,000 units)	\$600,000
Less cost of goods sold (\$40 × 10,000 units)	400,000
Gross margin	200,000
Less selling, general, and administration expenses (\$4 × 10,000 units + \$120,000)	160,000
Operating income	\$ 40,000

ROI

$$\text{ROI} = \frac{\text{Operating income}}{\text{Average operating assets}}$$

$$= \frac{\$40{,}000}{\$200{,}000}$$

$$= 20\%$$

then set your price. It appears that you can ignore demand and arrive at a price that will safely yield whatever profit you want. However, as noted above, the absorption costing approach relies on a forecast of unit sales. Neither the markup nor the unit product cost can be computed without such a forecast.

The absorption costing approach essentially assumes that customers *need* the forecasted unit sales and will pay whatever price the company decides to charge. However, customers have a choice. If the price is too high, they can buy from a competitor or they may choose not to buy at all. Suppose, for example, that when Roper Company sets its price at $60, it sells only 7,000 units rather than the 10,000 units forecasted. As shown in Exhibit 12–10, the company would then have a loss of $50,000 on the product instead of a profit of $40,000. Some managers believe that the absorption costing approach to pricing is safe. This is an illusion. The absorption costing approach is safe only as long as customers choose to buy at least as many units as managers forecasted they would buy and costs behave exactly as predicted.

Setting a Target Selling Price Using the Variable Costing Approach

Some companies use a variable costing approach to determine the target selling price based either on variable manufacturing costs or total variable costs. The key advantages of the variable costing approach are: (1) it is consistent with the cost-volume-profit analysis presented in Chapter 6, which allows managers to determine the profit effects of changes in price and volume; and (2) it avoids the need to arbitrarily allocate common fixed costs to specific products.

To illustrate the use of the variable costing approach using total variable costs we return to the Roper Company example.[9] The revised formula for calculating the markup is as follows:

$$\text{Markup percentage on total variable cost} = \frac{(\text{Required ROI} \times \text{Investment}) + \text{Total fixed expenses}}{\text{Unit sales} \times \text{Unit total variable costs}}$$

EXHIBIT 12–10 Income Statement and ROI Analysis—Roper Company Actual Unit Sales = 7,000 Units; Selling Price = $60

Direct materials	$ 12
Direct labour	8
Variable manufacturing overhead	6
Fixed manufacturing overhead ($140,000 ÷ 7,000 units)	20
Unit product cost	$46

ROPER COMPANY
Absorption Costing Income Statement

Sales ($60 × 7,000 units)	$420,000
Less cost of goods sold ($46 × 7,000 units)	322,000
Gross margin	98,000
Less selling, general, and administration expenses ($4 × 7,000 units + $120,000)	148,000
Operating income	$ (50,000)

ROI

$$\text{ROI} = \frac{\text{Operating income}}{\text{Average operating assets}}$$

$$= \frac{(\$50{,}000)}{\$200{,}000}$$

$$= -25\%$$

9. The variable manufacturing cost approach would exclude variable SG&A expenses from the cost base and instead include them in the numerator. Otherwise it is the same as the total variable costing approach.

The numerator now includes fixed manufacturing overhead costs and the denominator includes both manufacturing and SG&A variable expenses. The reasoning under this approach is that the markup must result in a contribution margin that covers all fixed expenses *and* leads to the required level of profit.

The calculations for the Roper Company data are as follows:

$$\text{Markup percentage on total variable cost} = \frac{(20\% \times \$200{,}000) + \$140{,}000 + \$120{,}000}{10{,}000 \times \$30\ (\$12 + \$8 + \$6 + \$4)}$$

$$\text{Markup percentage on total variable cost} = \frac{\$40{,}000 + \$260{,}000}{\$300{,}000} = 100\%$$

A markup of 100% under the total variable costing approach results in the same $60 per unit selling price as the absorption costing approach: $30 + (100% x $30) = $60. By comparison, the markup required under the absorption costing approach is only 50% because the cost base ($40) is higher by virtue of including *all* manufacturing costs (variable and fixed). This highlights the need for managers using the total variable costing approach to remember that the markup must cover all costs, variable *and* fixed. While the ROI method of determining the markup explicitly incorporates all fixed costs in the calculations, other approaches such as industry norms or company tradition may not. Importantly, regardless of the method used to calculate the cost base or the markup percentage, managers must be diligent in ensuring that all costs are covered.

Setting a Target Selling Price for Service Companies Using Time and Materials Pricing

A variation of cost-plus pricing used by some companies, particularly in service industries, is called **time and materials pricing**. Under this approach, two pricing rates are established, one based on direct labour time and the other based on the cost of direct material used.

Time and materials pricing A pricing method, often used in service firms, in which two pricing rates are established—one based on direct labour time and the other based on direct materials used.

This pricing method is widely used in repair shops and printing shops, and by many professionals such as engineers and lawyers. The time and materials rates are usually market-determined. In other words, the rates are determined by the interplay of supply and demand and by competitive conditions in the industry. However, some companies set the rates using a process similar to the process followed in the absorption costing approach to cost-plus pricing. In this case, the rates include allowances for selling, general, and administrative expenses; for other direct and indirect costs; and for a desired profit. This section will show how the rates might be set using the cost-plus approach.

Time Component

The time component is typically expressed as a rate per hour of labour. The rate is computed by adding together three elements: (1) the direct costs of the employee, including salary and benefits; (2) a pro rata allowance for selling, general, and administrative expenses of the organization; and (3) an allowance for a desired profit per hour of employee time. In some organizations (such as a repair shop), the same hourly rate will be charged regardless of which employee actually works on the job; in other organizations, the rate may vary by employee. For example, in a public accounting firm, the rate charged for a new assistant accountant's time will generally be less than the rate charged for an experienced senior accountant or for a partner.

Materials Component

Materials loading charge A markup applied to the cost of materials that is designed to cover the costs of ordering, handling, and carrying materials in inventory and to provide for some profit.

The materials component is determined by adding a **materials loading charge** to the invoice price of any materials used on the job. The materials loading charge is designed to cover the costs of ordering, handling, and carrying materials in inventory, plus a profit margin on the materials themselves.

An Example of Time and Materials Pricing

To provide an example of time and materials pricing, we use data from The Quality Auto Shop. The following costs for repairs and parts have been budgeted for the coming year:

	Repairs	Parts
Mechanics' wages	$300,000	$ —
Service manager—salary	40,000	—
Parts manager—salary	—	36,000
Clerical assistant—salary	18,000	15,000
Retirement and insurance—16% of salaries and wages	57,280	8,160
Supplies	720	540
Utilities	36,000	20,800
Property taxes	8,400	1,900
Depreciation	91,600	37,600
Invoice cost of parts used	—	400,000
Total budgeted cost	$552,000	$520,000

The company expects to bill customers for 24,000 hours of repair time. A profit of $7 per hour of repair time is considered to be feasible, given the competitive conditions in the market. For parts, the competitive markup on the invoice cost of parts used is 15%.

Exhibit 12–11 shows the computation of the billing rate and the materials loading charge to be used for the next year. Note that the billing rate, or time component, is $30 per hour of repair time and the materials loading charge is 45% of the invoice cost of parts used. Using these rates, a repair job that requires 4.5 hours of mechanics' time and $200 in parts would be billed as follows:

Labour time: 4.5 hours × $30		$135
Parts used:		
Invoice cost	$200	
Materials loading charge: 45% × $200	90	290
Total price of the job		$425

Rather than using labour-hours as the basis for computing the time rate, a machine shop, a printing shop, or a similar organization might use machine-hours.

This method of setting prices is a variation of the absorption costing approach. As such, it is not surprising that it suffers from the same problem: Customers may not be willing to pay the rates that have been computed. If actual business is less than the forecasted 24,000 hours and $400,000 worth of parts, or actual costs exceed estimates, the profit objectives will not be met and the company may not even break even.

Target Costing

LEARNING OBJECTIVE 5
Compute target costs based on selling prices.

Our discussion so far has presumed that a product has already been developed, has been costed, and is ready to be marketed as soon as a price is set. In many cases, the sequence of events is just the reverse. That is, the company will already *know* what price should be charged, and the problem will be to *develop a product* that can be marketed profitably at the desired price. Even in this situation, where the normal sequence of events is reversed, cost is still a crucial factor. The company's approach will be to employ *target costing*. **Target costing** is the process of determining the maximum allowable cost for a new product and then developing a prototype that can be profitably made for that maximum target cost figure. Many companies use

EXHIBIT 12–11 Time and Materials Pricing

	Time Component: Repairs		Parts: Material Loading Charge	
	Total	**Per Hour***	**Total**	**Percent†**
Cost of mechanics time:				
Mechanics wages	$300,000			
Retirement and insurance (16% of wages)	48,000			
Total cost	348,000	$14.50		
For repairs—other cost of repair service. For parts—costs of ordering, handling, and storing parts:				
Repairs service manager—salary	40,000		$ —	
Parts manager—salary	—		36,000	
Clerical assistant—salary	18,000		15,000	
Retirement and insurance (16% of salaries)	9,280		8,160	
Supplies	720		540	
Utilities	36,000		20,800	
Property taxes	8,400		1,900	
Depreciation	91,600		37,600	
Total cost	204,000	8.50	120,000	30%
Desired profit:				
24,000 hours × $7	168,000	7.00	—	
15% × $400,000	—		60,000	15%
Total amount to be billed	$720,000	$30.00	$180,000	45%

*Based on 24,000 hours.

†Based on $400,000 invoice cost of parts. The charge for ordering, handling, and storing parts, for example, is computed as follows: $120,000 cost ÷ $400,000 invoice cost = 30%.

target costing, including Chrysler, Ford, ITT Automotive, NEC, Nissan, Sharp, Texas Instruments, and Toyota.

The target cost for a product is computed by starting with the product's anticipated selling price and then deducting the desired profit, as follows:

Target cost = Anticipated selling price − Desired profit

The product development team is given the responsibility of designing the product so that it can be made for no more than the target cost.

Target costing The process of determining the maximum allowable cost for a new product and then developing a prototype that can be profitably manufactured and distributed for that maximum target cost figure.

Reasons for Using Target Costing

The target costing approach was developed in recognition of two important characteristics of markets and costs. The first is that many companies have less control over price than they would like. The market (i.e., supply and demand) really determines prices, and a company that attempts to ignore this does so at its peril. Therefore, the anticipated market price is taken as a given in target costing. The second observation is that most of the cost of a product is determined in the design stage. Once a product has been designed and has gone into production, not much can be done to significantly reduce its cost. Most of the opportunities to reduce cost come from designing the product so that it is simple to make, uses inexpensive parts, and is robust and reliable. If the company has little control over market price and little control over cost once the product has gone into production, then it follows that the major opportunities for affecting profit come in the design stage, where valuable features for which customers are willing to pay can be added and where most of the costs are really determined. So that is where the effort is concentrated—in designing and developing the product. The difference between target costing and other approaches to product development is profound. Instead of designing the product and then finding out how much it costs, the target cost is set first and then the product is designed so that the target cost is attained.

Effective target costing requires a detailed understanding of the customer; what is valued; the full costs of production, including long-term investments; and a detailed breakdown of the target cost. A management philosophy of customer focus and cost reduction (Kaizen costing) is part of the organizational package that will help a company to realize the full benefits of target costing.[10]

An Example of Target Costing

For a simple numerical example of target costing, assume the following situation: AFM Electronics feels that there is a market niche for stereo headphones with certain new features. Surveying the features and prices of headphones already on the market, the Marketing Department believes that a price of $60 would be about right for the new headphones. At that price, Marketing estimates that 80,000 of the new headphones could be sold annually. To design, develop, and produce these new headphones, an investment of $4,000,000 would be required. The company desires a 30% ROI. Given these data, the target cost to manufacture, sell, distribute, and service one pair of headphones is $45, as shown below:

Projected sales (80,000 headphones × $60)	$4,800,000
Less desired profit (30% × $4,000,000)............	1,200,000
Target cost for 80,000 headphones	$3,600,000
Target cost per pair of headphone ($3,600,000 ÷ 80,000 headphones).............	$45.00

This $45 target cost would be broken down into target costs for the various functions: manufacturing, marketing, distribution, after-sales service, and so on. Each functional area would be responsible for keeping its actual costs within the target.

Pricing and "The Law"

The federal Competition Act[11] restricts certain pricing practices to encourage competition and to protect consumers. For example, different prices cannot be charged for goods of like quality and quantity sold at the same time. In addition, a manufacturer can only suggest a list price; it cannot mandate this price to its retailers. Court proceedings represent only one of a variety of means used by the Industry Canada's Competition Bureau to enforce the Act.

International restrictions on pricing appear in antidumping and subsidy laws. Prohibitions exist on the sale of products below cost (that is, full absorption cost) in international markets or the use of government subsidies to achieve the same end. GATT and NAFTA disputes provide obvious examples of the need for cost information to substantiate pricing.

10. A more detailed discussion of the use of target costing as a philosophy for strategic planning and control can be found in "Implementing Target Costing," *Management Accounting Guidelines*, The Society of Management Accountants of Canada, 1999.

11. Department of Justice Canada web site: **http://laws.justice.gc.ca/en**.

IN BUSINESS

Conventional target costing wisdom suggests that the approach is most beneficial when applied early in a product's life cycle. This is based on claims that approximately 80% of a product's costs are fixed (i.e., difficult to reduce) once the design phase has been completed. While many companies such as Toyota and Mitsubishi do employ target costing at the design stage of the product, others have found the approach can be successfully applied at the manufacturing stage. The Montclair Papers Division of Mohawk Forest Products is a good example.

After losing a bid to a key competitor on one of its paper products, management at Montclair began to question the validity of its standard costing system. Montclair's standard cost for the product on which they lost the bid was $2,900 per tonne, which was over $1,400 per tonne more than the *price* bid by its competitor! Spurred on by this vast difference in costs, management at Montclair adopted an aggressive target costing exercise in order to re-engineer the manufacturing process for product. Using the price bid by their competitor as the starting point, Montclair then deducted the desired profit for the product to arrive at a target cost of $1,162. To achieve this target cost, management identified costing saving opportunities in each of the major activities involved in manufacturing and distributing the product. Eighteen months after adopting target costing, Montclair had reduced manufacturing costs to the target level, and through use of the Kaizen approach of continuous cost reductions, planned further reductions of $330 per tonne. Montclair's successful application of target costing provides evidence that the approach can yield benefits at the post-design phase of a product's life cycle.

Source: John K. Shank and Joseph Fisher, "Case Study: Target Costing as a Strategic Tool," *Sloan Management Review*, Fall 1999, 41(1), pp. 73–82.

Appendix 12A Summary

This appendix extended our discussion of the relation between relevant costs and pricing issues. Companies offering products and services where a market price is not readily available often use cost-plus pricing. One approach to cost-plus pricing uses absorption unit product costs as the cost base with the markup calculated to cover both non-manufacturing costs and to provide an adequate ROI. Another approach uses total variable costs as the base with the markup covering all fixed costs and providing an adequate ROI. Companies in the service industry often use a variation of the cost-plus approach called time and materials pricing. Two pricing rates are established, one for direct labour time and the other for direct material costs. The degree to which either cost-plus pricing or time and materials pricing will lead to the desired profits critically depends on the accuracy of both the sales forecasts and the cost estimates.

Some companies develop and sell products or services for which an established market and price already exist. Target costing can be used in such situations. Desired profit is deducted from the estimated market price to determine the product's target cost. The product design and development team then has the responsibility of ensuring that the actual cost of the new product does not exceed the target cost.

Glossary

Visit the Online Learning Centre at **http://www.mcgrawhill.ca/olc/garrison/** for a review of key terms and definitions.

Questions

12–1 What is a *relevant cost?*

12–2 Define the following terms: *incremental cost, opportunity cost,* and *sunk cost.*

12–3 Are variable costs always relevant costs? Explain.

12–4 Depreciation (as shown on the income statement) is an expense to a company, but this same expense is irrelevant in decision making. Explain why this is so.

12–5 "Sunk costs are easy to spot—they're simply the fixed costs associated with a decision." Do you agree? Explain.

12–6 "Variable costs and differential costs mean the same thing." Do you agree? Explain.

12–7 "All future costs are relevant in decision making." Do you agree? Why?

12–8 Davis Company is considering dropping one of its product lines. What costs of the product line would be relevant to this decision? Irrelevant?

12–9 "If a product line is generating a loss, then that's pretty good evidence that the product line should be discontinued." Do you agree? Explain.

12–10 What is the danger in allocating common fixed costs among product lines or other segments of an organization?

12–11 How does opportunity cost enter into the make or buy decision?

12–12 A successful owner of a small business stated: "We have the best technology, the best products and the best people in the world. We have no constraints." Do you agree?

12–13 List four ways to increase capacity at bottlenecks.

12–14 How should the relative profitability of products be determined when trying to decide how to allocate a constrained resource such as machine hours?

12–15 Define the following terms: *joint products, joint product costs,* and *split-off point.*

12–16 From a decision-making point of view, what pitfalls are there in allocating common costs among joint products?

12–17 What guideline can be used in determining whether a joint product should be sold at the split-off point or processed further?

12–18 Airlines sometimes offer reduced rates during certain times of the week to members of a businessperson's family if they accompany him or her on trips. How does the concept of relevant costs enter into the decision to offer reduced rates of this type?

12–19 (Appendix 12A) What is meant by cost-plus pricing?

12–20 (Appendix 12A) When the absorption costing approach to cost-plus pricing is used, how is the desired profit determined?

12–21 (Appendix 12A) What is target costing? How do target costs enter into the pricing decision?

12–22 (Appendix 12A) What type of companies would you expect to be using time and materials pricing?

Exercises

EXERCISE 12–1 Identifying Relevant Costs [LO1]

A number of costs are listed on the next page that may be relevant in decisions faced by the management of Poulsen & Sonner A/S, a Danish furniture manufacturer:

Required:

Copy the information from the next page onto your answer sheet and place an X in the appropriate column to indicate whether each item is relevant or not relevant in the following situations. Requirement 1 relates to Case 1 and requirement 2 relates to Case 2. Consider the two cases independently.

1. The company chronically runs at capacity and the old Model A3000 machine is the company's constraint. Management is considering the purchase of a new Model B3800 machine to use in addition to the company's present Model A3000 machine. The old Model A3000 machine will continue to be used to capacity as before, with the new Model B3800 being used to expand production. The increase in volume will be large enough to require increases in fixed selling expenses and in general administrative overhead, but not in the general fixed manufacturing overhead.
2. The old Model A3000 machine is not the company's constraint, but management is considering replacing it with a new Model B3800 machine because of the potential savings in direct

Item	Case 1		Case 2	
	Relevant	Not Relevant	Relevant	Not Relevant
a. Sales revenue				
b. Direct materials				
c. Direct labour				
d. Variable manufacturing overhead				
e. Book value—Model A3000 machine				
f. Disposal value—Model A3000 machine				
g. Depreciation—Model A3000 machine				
h. Market value—Model B3800 machine (cost)				
i. Fixed manufacturing overhead (general)				
j. Variable selling expense				
k. Fixed selling expense				
l. General administrative overhead				

materials cost with the new machine. The Model A3000 machine would be sold. This change will have no effect on production or sales, other than some savings in direct materials costs due to less waste.

EXERCISE 12–2 Dropping or Retaining a Segment [LO2]

Cumberland County Senior Services is a nonprofit organization devoted to providing essential services to seniors who live in their own homes within the Cumberland County area. Three services are provided for seniors—home nursing, meals on wheels, and housekeeping. In the home nursing program, nurses visit seniors on a regular basis to check on their general health and to perform tests ordered by their physicians. The meals on wheels program delivers a hot meal once a day to each senior enrolled in the program. The housekeeping service provides weekly housecleaning and maintenance services. Data on revenue and expenses for the past year follow:

	Total	Home Nursing	Meals on Wheels	Housekeeping
Revenues	$900,000	$260,000	$400,000	$240,000
Variable expenses	490,000	120,000	210,000	160,000
Contribution margin	410,000	140,000	190,000	80,000
Fixed expenses:				
Depreciation	68,000	8,000	40,000	20,000
Liability insurance	42,000	20,000	7,000	15,000
Program administrators' salaries	115,000	40,000	38,000	37,000
General administrative overhead*	180,000	52,000	80,000	48,000
Total fixed expenses	405,000	120,000	165,000	120,000
Operating income (loss)	$ 5,000	$ 20,000	$ 25,000	$ (40,000)

*Allocated on the basis of program revenues.

The head administrator of Cumberland County Senior Services, Judith Miyama, is concerned about the organization's finances and considers the operating income of $5,000 last year to be razor-thin. (Last year's results were very similar to the results for previous years and are representative of what would be expected in the future.) She feels that the organization should be building its financial reserves at a more rapid rate in order to prepare for the next inevitable recession. After seeing the above report, Ms. Miyama asked for more information about the financial advisability of perhaps discontinuing the housekeeping program.

The depreciation in housekeeping is for a small van that is used to carry the housekeepers and their equipment from job to job. If the program were discontinued, the van would be donated to a charitable organization. Depreciation charges assume zero salvage value. None of the general administrative overhead would be avoided if the housekeeping program were dropped, but the liability insurance and the salary of the program administrator would be avoided.

Required:

1. Should the housekeeping program be discontinued? Explain. Show computations to support your answer.
2. Recast the above data in a format that would be more useful to management in assessing the long-run financial viability of the various services.

EXERCISE 12–3 Make or Buy a Component [LO2]

Climate-Control, Inc., manufactures a variety of heating and air-conditioning units. The company is currently manufacturing all of its own component parts. An outside supplier has offered to sell a thermostat to Climate-Control for $20 per unit. To evaluate this offer, Climate-Control, Inc., has gathered the following information relating to its own cost of producing the thermostat internally:

	Per Unit	15,000 Units per Year
Direct materials	$ 6	$ 90,000
Direct labour	8	120,000
Variable manufacturing overhead	1	15,000
Fixed manufacturing overhead, traceable	5*	75,000
Fixed manufacturing overhead, common, but allocated	10	150,000
Total cost	$30	$450,000

*40% supervisory salaries; 60% depreciation of special equipment (no resale value).

Required:

1. Assuming that the company has no alternative use for the facilities now being used to produce the thermostat, should the outside supplier's offer be accepted? Show all computations.
2. Suppose that if the thermostats were purchased, Climate-Control, Inc., could use the freed capacity to launch a new product. The segment margin of the new product would be $65,000 per year. Should Climate-Control, Inc., accept the offer to buy the thermostats from the outside supplier for $20 each? Show computations.

EXERCISE 12–4 Evaluating a Special Order [LO2]

Miyamoto Jewelers is considering a special order for 10 handcrafted gold bracelets to be given as gifts to members of a wedding party. The normal selling price of a gold bracelet is $389.95 and its unit product cost is $264.00 as shown below:

Direct materials	$143.00
Direct labour	86.00
Manufacturing overhead	35.00
Unit product cost	$264.00

Most of the manufacturing overhead is fixed and unaffected by variations in how much jewelry is produced in any given period. However, $7 of the overhead is variable with respect to the number of bracelets produced. The customer who is interested in the special bracelet order would like special filigree applied to the bracelets. This filigree would require additional materials costing $6 per bracelet and would also require acquisition of a special tool costing $465 that would have no other use once the special order is completed. This order would have no effect on the company's regular sales and the order could be fulfilled using the company's existing capacity without affecting any other order.

Required:

What effect would accepting this order have on the company's operating income if a special price of $349.95 is offered per bracelet for this order? Should the special order be accepted at this price?

EXERCISE 12–5 Utilization of a Constrained Resource [LO3]

Banner Company produces three products: A, B, and C. The selling price, variable costs, and contribution margin for one unit of each product follow:

	Product		
	A	B	C
Selling price	$60	$90	$80
Variable costs:			
Direct materials	27	14	40
Direct labour	12	32	16
Variable manufacturing overhead	3	8	4
Total variable cost	42	54	60
Contribution margin	$18	$36	$20
Contribution margin ratio	30%	40%	25%

Due to a strike in the plant of one of its competitors, demand for the company's products far exceeds its capacity to produce. Management is trying to determine which product(s) to concentrate on next week in filling its backlog of orders. The direct labour rate is $8 per hour, and only 3,000 hours of labour time are available each week.

Required:

1. Compute the amount of contribution margin that will be obtained per hour of labour time spent on each product.
2. Which orders would you recommend that the company work on next week—the orders for product A, product B, or product C? Show computations.
3. By paying overtime wages, more than 3,000 hours of direct labour time can be made available next week. Up to how much should the company be willing to pay per hour in overtime wages as long as there is unfilled demand for the three products? Explain.

EXERCISE 12–6 Sell or Process Further [LO2]

Solex Company manufactures three products from a common input in a joint processing operation. Joint processing costs up to the split-off point total $100,000 per year. The company allocates these costs to the joint products on the basis of their total sales value at the split-off point. These sales values are as follows: product X, $50,000; product Y, $90,000; and product Z, $60,000.

Each product may be sold at the split-off point or processed further. Additional processing requires no special facilities. The additional processing costs and the sales value after further processing for each product (on an annual basis) are shown below:

Product	Additional Processing Costs	Sales Value
X	$35,000	$80,000
Y	$40,000	$150,000
Z	$12,000	$75,000

Required:

Which product or products should be sold at the split-off point, and which product or products should be processed further? Show computations.

EXERCISE 12–7 Identification of Relevant Costs [LO1]

Hart Company sells and delivers office furniture in the Maritime provinces.

The costs associated with the acquisition and annual operation of a delivery truck are given below:

Insurance	$1,750
Licenses	$250
Taxes (vehicle)	$150
Garage rent for parking (per truck)	$1,350
Depreciation ($30,000 ÷ 5 years)	$6,000*
Gasoline, oil, tires, and repairs	$0.16 per kilometre

*Based on obsolescence rather than on wear and tear.

Required:

1. Assume that Hart Company has purchased one truck that has been driven 50,000 kilometres during the first year. Compute the average cost per kilometre of owning and operating the truck.
2. At the beginning of the second year, Hart Company is unsure whether to use the truck or leave it parked in the garage and have all hauling done commercially. (The government requires the payment of vehicle taxes even if the vehicle isn't used.) What costs from the previous list are relevant to this decision? Explain.
3. Assume that the company decides to use the truck during the second year. Near year-end an order is received from a customer over 1,000 kilometres away. What costs from the previous list are relevant in a decision between using the truck to make the delivery and having the delivery done commercially? Explain.
4. Occasionally, the company could use two trucks at the same time. For this reason, some thought is being given to purchasing a second truck. The total kilometres driven would be the same as if only one truck were owned. What costs from the previous list are relevant to a decision over whether to purchase the second truck? Explain.

EXERCISE 12–8 Dropping or Retaining a Segment [LO2]

Boyle's Home Centre, a retailing company, has two departments, Bath and Kitchen. The company's most recent monthly contribution format income statement follows:

		Department	
	Total	Bath	Kitchen
Sales	$5,000,000	$1,000,000	$4,000,000
Variable expenses	1,900,000	300,000	1,600,000
Contribution margin	3,100,000	700,000	2,400,000
Fixed expenses	2,700,000	900,000	1,800,000
Operating income (loss)	$ 400,000	$ (200,000)	$ 600,000

A study indicates that $370,000 of the fixed expenses being charged to the Bath Department are sunk costs or allocated costs that will continue even if the Bath Department is dropped. In addition, the elimination of the Bath Department would result in a 10% decrease in the sales of the Kitchen Department.

Required:

If the Bath Department is dropped, what will be the effect on the operating income of the company as a whole?

EXERCISE 12–9 Make or Buy a Component [LO2]

For many years, Diehl Company has produced a small electrical part that it uses in the production of its standard line of diesel tractors. The company's unit product cost for the part, based on a production level of 60,000 parts per year, is as follows:

	Per Part	Total
Direct materials	$ 4.00	
Direct labour	2.75	
Variable manufacturing overhead	0.50	
Fixed manufacturing overhead, traceable	3.00	$180,000
Fixed manufacturing overhead, common (allocated on the basis of labour-hours)	2.25	$135,000
Unit product cost	$12.50	

An outside supplier has offered to supply the electrical parts to the Diehl Company for only $10.00 per part. One-third of the traceable fixed manufacturing cost is supervisory salaries and other costs that can be eliminated if the parts are purchased. The other two-thirds of the traceable fixed manufacturing costs consist of depreciation of special equipment that has no resale value. Economic depreciation on this equipment is due to obsolescence rather than wear and tear. The decision to buy the parts from the outside supplier would have no effect on the common fixed costs of the company, and the space being used to produce the parts would otherwise be idle.

Required:
Prepare computations showing how much profits would increase or decrease as a result of purchasing the parts from the outside supplier rather than making them inside the company.

EXERCISE 12–10 Special Order [LO2]

Glade Company produces a single product. The costs of producing and selling a single unit of this product at the company's current activity level of 8,000 units per month are:

Direct materials	$2.50
Direct labour	$3.00
Variable manufacturing overhead	$0.50
Fixed manufacturing overhead	$4.25
Variable selling and administrative expenses	$1.50
Fixed selling and administrative expenses	$2.00

The normal selling price is $15 per unit. The company's capacity is 10,000 units per month. An order has been received from a potential customer overseas for 2,000 units at a price of $12.00 per unit. This order would not affect regular sales.

Required:
1. If the order is accepted, by how much will monthly profits increase or decrease? (The order would not change the company's total fixed costs.)
2. Assume the company has 500 units of this product left over from last year that are inferior to the current model. The units must be sold through regular channels at reduced prices. What unit cost is relevant for establishing a minimum selling price for these units? Explain.

EXERCISE 12–11 Utilization of a Constrained Resource [LO3]
Shelby Company produces three products: product X, product Y, and product Z. Data concerning the three products follow (per unit):

	Product X	Product Y	Product Z
Selling price	$80	$56	$70
Less variable expenses:			
Direct materials	24	15	9
Labour and overhead	24	27	40
Total variable expenses	48	42	49
Contribution margin	$32	$14	$21
Contribution margin ratio	40%	25%	30%

Demand for the company's products is very strong, with far more orders each month than the company can produce with the available raw materials. The same material is used in each product. The material costs $3 per kilogram, with a maximum of 5,000 kilograms available each month.

Required:
Which orders would you advise the company to accept first, those for product X, for product Y, or for product Z? Which orders second? Third?

EXERCISE 12–12 Sell or Process Further [LO2]
Morrell Company produces several products from processing krypton, a rare mineral. Material and processing costs total $30,000 per tonne, one-third of which are allocated to the product merifulon. The merifulon produced from a tonne of krypton can either be sold at the split-off point, or processed further at a cost of $13,000 and then sold for $60,000. The sales value of merifulon at the split-off point is $40,000.

Required:
Should merifulon be processed further or sold at the split-off point?

EXERCISE 12–13 Volume Trade-Off Decision [LO3]
Car Art makes miniature reproductions of classic sports cars. The bottleneck in the production process is applying several coats of paint on each car. This process requires the attention of the shop's most experienced craftsman. A total of 7,200 hours is available per year in this bottleneck operation. Data concerning the company's four products appear below:

	Corvette	Porsche	Ferrari	Jaguar
Unit contribution margin	$100	$64	$70	$144
Annual demand (units)	160	240	200	280
Hours required in the bottleneck operation per unit	10	8	14	16

No fixed costs could be avoided by modifying how many units are produced of any product or even by dropping any one of the products.

Required:
1. Is there sufficient capacity in the bottleneck operation to satisfy demand for all products?
2. What is the optimal production plan for the year?
3. What would be the total contribution margin for the optimal production plan you have proposed?

EXERCISE 12–14 Identification of Relevant Costs [LO1]
Bill has just returned from a duck hunting trip in Northern Ontario. He has brought home eight ducks. Bill's friend, John, disapproves of duck hunting, and to discourage Bill from further hunting, John has presented him with the following cost estimates:

Camper and equipment:	
Cost, $16,000; usable for eight seasons; 10 hunting trips per season	$200
Travel expense (pickup truck):	
100 kilometres at $0.35 per kilometre (gas, oil, and tires—$0.25 per kilometre; depreciation and insurance—$0.10 per kilometre)	35
Shotgun shells (two boxes)	20
Boat:	
Cost, $4,000, usable for eight seasons; 10 hunting trips per season	50
Hunting license:	
Cost, $30 for the season; 10 hunting trips per season	3
Money lost playing poker:	
Loss, $40 (Bill plays poker every weekend)	40
Coffee beans:	
Cost, $20	20
Total cost of the trip	$368
Cost per duck ($368 ÷ 8 ducks)	$ 46

Required:
1. Assuming that the duck hunting trip Bill has just completed is typical, what costs are relevant to a decision as to whether Bill should go duck hunting again this season?
2. Suppose that Bill gets lucky on his next hunting trip and shoots 10 ducks in the amount of time it took him to shoot 8 ducks on his last trip. How much would it have cost him to shoot the last two ducks? Explain.
3. Which costs are relevant in a decision of whether Bill should give up hunting? Explain.

EXERCISE 12–15 Dropping or Retaining a Segment [LO2]
Dexter Products, Inc., manufactures and sells a number of items, including an overnight case. The company has been experiencing losses on the overnight case for some time, as shown on the contribution format income statement on the next page.

Discontinuing the overnight cases would not affect sales of other product lines and would have no noticeable effect on the company's total general factory overhead or total purchasing department expenses.

Dexter Products, Inc. Income Statement—Overnight Cases For the Quarter Ended June 30		
Sales		$450,000
Variable expenses:		
Variable manufacturing expenses	$130,000	
Sales commissions	48,000	
Shipping	12,000	
Total variable expenses		190,000
Contribution margin		260,000
Fixed expenses:		
Salary of product-line manager	21,000	
General factory overhead	104,000*	
Depreciation of equipment (no resale value)	36,000	
Advertising—traceable	110,000	
Insurance on inventories	9,000	
Purchasing department	50,000†	
Total fixed expenses		330,000
Operating loss		$ (70,000)

*Allocated on the basis of machine-hours.
†Allocated on the basis of sales dollars.

Required:
Would you recommend that the company discontinue the manufacture and sale of overnight cases? Support your answer with appropriate computations.

EXERCISE 12–16 Make or Buy a Component [LO2]
Royal Company manufactures 20,000 units of part R-3 each year for use on its production line. At this level of activity, the cost per unit for part R-3 follows:

Direct materials	$ 4.80
Direct labour	7.00
Variable manufacturing overhead	3.20
Fixed manufacturing overhead	10.00
Total cost per part	$25.00

An outside supplier has offered to sell 20,000 units of part R-3 each year to Royal Company for $23.50 per part. If Royal Company accepts this offer, the facilities now being used to manufacture part R-3 could be rented to another company at an annual rental of $150,000. However, Royal Company has determined that $6 of the fixed manufacturing overhead being applied to part R-3 would continue even if part R-3 were purchased from the outside supplier.

Required:
Prepare computations showing how much profits will increase or decrease if the outside supplier's offer is accepted.

EXERCISE 12–17 (Appendix 12A) Absorption Costing and Total Variable Costing Approaches to Setting a Selling Price [LO4]
Nash Limited is considering the introduction of a new product. Management has gathered the following information:

Number of units to be produced and sold each year	20,000
Unit product cost	$32
Projected annual selling and administrative expenses	$80,000
Estimated investment required by the company	$800,000
Desired return on investment (ROI)	16%

Required:

1. Using the absorption costing approach to cost-plus pricing, compute the markup the company will have to use to achieve the desired ROI.
2. Assume that the $32 unit product cost includes $6 per unit for fixed manufacturing overhead based on producing and selling 20,000 units each year. Also assume that $52,000 of the total selling and administrative expenses of $80,000 is fixed. The remainder is variable. Use the total variable costing approach to calculate the markup the company will have to use to achieve the desired ROI.
3. Compute the target selling price per unit under each pricing approach from parts 1 and 2 above.

EXERCISE 12–18 (Appendix 12A) Target Costing [LO5]
Little River Cycles (LRC) produces and distributes carbon fibre road bikes. Management is eager to take advantage of the growing market for these bikes. To be competitive, LRC's sales manager estimates that the bike can't be priced at more than $2,000. At this price management thinks they can sell 1,000 bikes per year. Producing the bikes will require an initial investment of $2,000,000 and the company's target ROI is 25%.

Required:
Calculate the target cost of one carbon fibre road bike.

EXERCISE 12–19 (Appendix 12A) Time and Materials Pricing [LO4]
Ronnie's Repair Company provides repair services for small engines and uses time and materials pricing. The company has budgeted the following costs for next year:

Mechanic's wages and benefits	$900,000
Other repair costs, except for parts-related costs . .	$450,000
Costs of ordering, handling, and storing parts	40% of invoice cost

In total, the company expects to log 50,000 hours of billable repair time next year. According to competitive conditions, the company believes it should aim for a profit of $8 per hour of each mechanic's time. The competitive markup on parts is 40% of invoice cost.

Required:

1. Compute the time rate and the material loading charge that would be used to bill jobs.
2. One of the company's mechanics has just completed a repair job that required 12 hours of time and $100 in parts (invoice cost). Compute the amount that would be billed for the job.

Problems

PROBLEM 12–20 Dropping or Retaining a Tour [LO2]
Maple Leaf Tours, Inc., operates tours throughout Canada. A study has indicated that some of the tours are not profitable, and consideration is being given to dropping these tours to improve the company's overall operating performance.

One such tour is a three-day Heritage Farms bus tour conducted in the Maritimes. An income statement from a typical Heritage Farms tour is given on the next page.

The following additional information is available about the tour:

a. Bus drivers are paid fixed annual salaries; tour guides are paid for each tour conducted.
b. The "Bus maintenance and preparation" cost above is an allocation of the salaries of mechanics and other service personnel who are responsible for keeping the company's fleet of buses in good operating condition.
c. Depreciation of buses is due to obsolescence. Depreciation due to wear and tear is negligible.
d. Liability insurance premiums are based on the number of buses in the company's fleet.
e. Dropping the Heritage Farms bus tour would not allow Maple Leaf Tours to reduce the number of buses in its fleet, the number of bus drivers on the payroll, or the size of the maintenance and preparation staff.

Ticket revenue (100 seat capacity × 40% occupancy × $75 ticket price per person)	$3,000	100%
Variable expenses ($22.50 per person)	900	30
Contribution margin	2,100	70%
Tour expenses:		
Tour promotion	600	
Salary of bus driver	350	
Fee, tour guide	700	
Fuel for bus	125	
Depreciation of bus	450	
Liability insurance, bus	200	
Overnight parking fees, bus	50	
Room and meals, bus driver and tour guide	175	
Bus maintenance and preparation	300	
Total tour expenses	2,950	
Operating loss	$ (850)	

Required:

1. Prepare an analysis showing what the impact will be on the company's profits if this tour is discontinued.
2. The company's tour director has been criticized because only about 50% of the seats on Maple Leaf's tours are being filled as compared to an industry average of 60%. The tour director has explained that Maple Leaf's average seat occupancy could be improved considerably by eliminating about 10% of its tours, but that doing so would reduce profits. Explain how this could happen.

PROBLEM 12–21 Sell or Process Further [LO2]

Valley Meat Processing Corporation is a major processor of beef and other meat products. The company has a large amount of T-bone steak on hand, and it is trying to decide whether to sell the T-bone steaks as is or to process them further into filet mignon and New York-cut steaks.

Management believes that a kilogram of T-bone steak would yield the following profit:

Wholesale selling price ($16.00 per kilogram)	$16.00
Less joint costs incurred up to the split-off point where T-bone steak can be identified as a separate product	12.00
Profit per kilogram	$ 4.00

As mentioned above, instead of being sold as is, the T-bone steaks could be further processed into filet mignon and New York-cut steaks. Cutting one side of a T-bone steak provides the filet mignon, and cutting the other side provides the New York cut. One 480-gram T-bone steak cut in this way will yield one 181-gram filet mignon and one 241-gram New York cut; the remaining grams are waste. The cost of processing the T-bone steaks into these cuts is $1.40 per kilogram. The filet mignon can be sold retail for $26 per kilogram, and the New York-cut can be sold wholesale for $22 per kilogram.

Required:

1. Determine the profit for each 480-gram T-bone steak processed further into filet mignon and New York-cut steaks.
2. Would you recommend that the T-bone steaks be sold as is or processed further? Why?

(Prepared from a situation suggested by Professor John W. Hardy.)

PROBLEM 12–22 Close or Retain a Store [LO2]

Thrifty Markets, Inc., operates three stores in a large metropolitan area. The company's segmented absorption costing income statement for the last quarter is given on the next page.

Management is very concerned about the Downtown Store's inability to show a profit, and consideration is being given to closing the store. The company has asked you to make a recommendation as to what course of action should be taken. Additional information available on the store is shown on the next page.

Thrifty Markets, Inc.
Income Statement
For the Quarter Ended March 31

	Total	Uptown Store	Downtown Store	Westpark Store
Sales	$2,500,000	$900,000	$600,000	$1,000,000
Cost of goods sold	1,450,000	513,000	372,000	565,000
Gross margin	1,050,000	387,000	228,000	435,000
Selling and administrative expenses:				
Selling expenses:				
Direct advertising	118,500	40,000	36,000	42,500
General advertising*	20,000	7,200	4,800	8,000
Sales salaries	157,000	52,000	45,000	60,000
Delivery salaries	30,000	10,000	10,000	10,000
Store rent	215,000	70,000	65,000	80,000
Depreciation of store fixtures	46,950	18,300	8,800	19,850
Depreciation of delivery equipment	27,000	9,000	9,000	9,000
Total selling expenses	614,450	206,500	178,600	229,350
Administrative expenses:				
Store management salaries	63,000	20,000	18,000	25,000
General office salaries*	50,000	18,000	12,000	20,000
Utilities	89,800	31,000	27,200	31,600
Insurance on fixtures and inventory	25,500	8,000	9,000	8,500
Employment taxes	36,000	12,000	10,200	13,800
General office expenses—other*	25,000	9,000	6,000	10,000
Total administrative expenses	289,300	98,000	82,400	108,900
Total operating expenses	903,750	304,500	261,000	338,250
Operating income (loss)	$ 146,250	$ 82,500	$ (33,000)	$ 96,750

*Allocated on the basis of sales dollars.

a. The manager of the store has been with the company for many years; he would be retained and transferred to another position in the company if the store were closed. His salary is $6,000 per month, or $18,000 per quarter. If the store were not closed, a new employee would be hired to fill the other position at a salary of $5,000 per month.
b. The lease on the building housing the Downtown Store can be broken with no penalty.
c. The fixtures being used in the Downtown Store would be transferred to the other two stores if the Downtown Store were closed.
d. The company's employment taxes are 12% of salaries.
e. A single delivery crew serves all three stores. One delivery person could be discharged if the Downtown Store were closed; this person's salary amounts to $7,000 per quarter. The delivery equipment would be distributed to the other stores. The equipment does not wear out through use, but it does eventually become obsolete.
f. One-third of the Downtown Store's insurance relates to its fixtures.
g. The general office salaries and other expenses relate to the general management of Thrifty Markets, Inc. The employee in the general office who is responsible for the Downtown Store would be discharged if the store were closed. This employee's compensation amounts to $8,000 per quarter.

Required:

1. Prepare a schedule showing the change in revenues and expenses and the impact on the overall company operating income that would result if the Downtown Store were closed.
2. Based on your computations in (1) above, what recommendation would you make to the management of Thrifty Markets, Inc.?

(Required continued on the next page)

3. Assume that if the Downtown Store were closed, sales in the Uptown Store would increase by $200,000 per quarter due to loyal customers shifting their buying to the Uptown Store. The Uptown Store has ample capacity to handle the increased sales, and its gross margin is 43% of sales. What effect would these factors have on your recommendation concerning the Downtown Store? Show computations.

PROBLEM 12–23 Make or Buy Decision [LO2]

Berger Company manufactures a variety of ballpoint pens. The company has just received an offer from an outside supplier to provide the ink cartridge for the company's Zippo pen line, at a price of $0.48 per dozen cartridges. The company is interested in this offer, since its own production of cartridges is at capacity.

Berger Company estimates that if the supplier's offer were accepted, the direct labour and variable manufacturing overhead costs of the Zippo pen line would be reduced by 10% and the direct materials cost would be reduced by 20%.

Under present operations, Berger Company manufactures all of its own pens from start to finish. The Zippo pens are sold through wholesalers at $4 per box. Each box contains one dozen pens. Fixed manufacturing overhead costs charged to the Zippo pen line total $50,000 each year. (The same equipment and facilities are used to produce several pen lines.) The present cost of producing one dozen Zippo pens (one box) is given below:

Direct materials	$1.50
Direct labour	1.00
Manufacturing overhead	0.80*
Total cost	$3.30

*Includes both variable and fixed manufacturing overhead, based on production of 100,000 boxes of pens each year.

Required:

1. Should Berger Company accept the outside supplier's offer? Show computations.
2. What is the maximum price that Berger Company should be willing to pay the outside supplier per dozen cartridges? Explain.
3. Due to the bankruptcy of a competitor, Berger Company expects to sell 150,000 boxes of Zippo pens next year. As stated above, the company presently has enough capacity to produce the cartridges for only 100,000 boxes of Zippo pens annually. By incurring $30,000 in added fixed cost each year, the company could expand its production of cartridges to satisfy the anticipated demand for Zippo pens. The variable cost per unit to produce the additional cartridges would be the same as at present. Under these circumstances, how many boxes of cartridges should be purchased from the outside supplier and how many should be made by Berger? Show computations to support your answer.
4. What qualitative factors should Berger Company consider in determining whether it should make or buy the ink cartridges?

(CMA, adapted)

PROBLEM 12–24 Relevant Cost Analysis in a Variety of Situations [LO2]

Ovation Company has a single product called a Bit. The company normally produces and sells 60,000 Bits each year at a selling price of $32 per unit. The company's unit costs at this level of activity are given below:

Direct materials	$10.00	
Direct labour	4.50	
Variable manufacturing overhead	2.30	
Fixed manufacturing overhead	5.00	($300,000 total)
Variable selling expenses	1.20	
Fixed selling expenses	3.50	($210,000 total)
Total cost per unit	$26.50	

A number of questions relating to the production and sale of Bits follow. Each question is independent.

Required:

1. Assume that Ovation Company has sufficient capacity to produce 90,000 Bits each year without any increase in fixed manufacturing overhead costs. The company could increase its sales by 25% above the present 60,000 units each year if it were willing to increase the fixed selling expenses by $80,000. Would the increased fixed selling expenses be justified?
2. Assume again that Ovation Company has sufficient capacity to produce 90,000 Bits each year. A customer in a foreign market wants to purchase 20,000 Bits. Import duties on the Bits would be $1.70 per unit, and costs for permits and licenses would be $9,000. The only selling costs that would be associated with the order would be $3.20 per unit shipping cost. Compute the per unit break-even price on this order.
3. The company has 1,000 Bits on hand that have some irregularities and are therefore considered to be "seconds." Due to the irregularities, it will be impossible to sell these units at the normal price through regular distribution channels. What unit cost figure is relevant for setting a minimum selling price? Explain.
4. Due to a strike in its supplier's plant, Ovation Company is unable to purchase more material for the production of Bits. The strike is expected to last for two months. Ovation Company has enough material on hand to operate at 30% of normal levels for the two-month period. As an alternative, Ovation could close its plant down entirely for the two months. If the plant were closed, fixed manufacturing overhead costs would continue at 60% of their normal level during the two-month period and the fixed selling expenses would be reduced by 20%. What would be the impact on profits of closing the plant for the two-month period?
5. An outside manufacturer has offered to produce Bits and ship them directly to Ovation's customers. If Ovation Company accepts this offer, the facilities that it uses to produce Bits would be idle; however, fixed manufacturing overhead costs would be reduced by 75%. Since the outside manufacturer would pay for all shipping costs, the variable selling expenses would be only two-thirds of their present amount. Compute the unit cost that is relevant for comparison to the price quoted by the outside manufacturer.

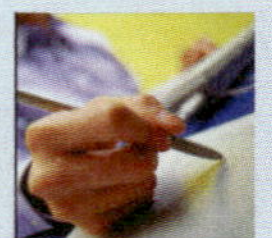

PROBLEM 12–25 Shutting Down or Continuing to Operate a Plant [LO2]

(Note: This type of decision is similar to dropping a product line.)

Hallas Company manufactures a fast-bonding glue in its Ontario plant. The company normally produces and sells 40,000 litres of the glue each month. This glue, which is known as MJ-7, is used in the wood industry to manufacture plywood. The selling price of MJ-7 is $35 per litre, variable costs are $21 per litre, fixed manufacturing overhead costs in the plant total $230,000 per month, and the fixed selling costs total $310,000 per month.

Strikes in the mills that purchase the bulk of the MJ-7 glue have caused Hallas Company's sales to temporarily drop to only 11,000 litres per month. Hallas Company's management estimates that the strikes will last for two months, after which sales of MJ-7 should return to normal. Due to the current low level of sales, Hallas Company's management is thinking about closing down the Ontario plant during the strike.

If Hallas Company does close down the Ontario plant, fixed manufacturing overhead costs can be reduced by $60,000 per month and fixed selling costs can be reduced by 10%. Start-up costs at the end of the shutdown period would total $14,000. Since Hallas Company uses Lean Production methods, no inventories are on hand.

Required:

1. Assuming that the strikes continue for two months, would you recommend that Hallas Company close the Ontario plant? Explain. Show computations to support your answer.
2. At what level of sales (in litres) for the two-month period should Hallas Company be indifferent between closing the plant or keeping it open? Show computations. (Hint: This is a type of break-even analysis, except that the fixed cost portion of your break-even computation should include only those fixed costs that are relevant [i.e., avoidable] over the two-month period.)

PROBLEM 12–26 Make or Buy Analysis [LO2]

"That old equipment for producing subassemblies is worn out," said Paul Taylor, president of Timkin Company. "We need to make a decision quickly." The company is trying to decide whether it should rent new equipment and continue to make its subassemblies internally or whether it should discontinue production of its subassemblies and purchase them from an outside supplier. The alternatives follow:

Alternative 1: Rent new equipment for producing the subassemblies for $60,000 per year.
Alternative 2: Purchase subassemblies from an outside supplier for $8 each.

Timkin Company's present costs per unit of producing the subassemblies internally (with the old equipment) are given below. These costs are based on a current activity level of 40,000 subassemblies per year:

Direct materials	$ 2.75
Direct labour	4.00
Variable overhead	0.60
Fixed overhead ($0.75 supervision, $0.90 depreciation, and $2 general company overhead)	3.65
Total cost per unit	$11.00

The new equipment would be more efficient and, according to the manufacturer, would reduce direct labour costs and variable overhead costs by 25%. Supervision cost ($30,000 per year) and direct materials cost per unit would not be affected by the new equipment. The new equipment's capacity would be 60,000 subassemblies per year.

The total general company overhead would be unaffected by this decision.

Required:

1. The president is unsure what the company should do and would like an analysis showing the unit costs and total costs for each of the two alternatives given above. Assume that 40,000 subassemblies are needed each year. Which course of action would you recommend to the president?
2. Would your recommendation in (1) above be the same if the company's needs were (*a*) 50,000 subassemblies per year, or (*b*) 60,000 subassemblies per year? Show computations in good form.
3. What other factors would you recommend that the company consider before making a decision?

PROBLEM 12–27 Accept or Reject a Special Order [LO2]

Moore Company manufactures and sells a single product called a Lop. Operating at capacity, the company can produce and sell 30,000 Lops per year. Costs associated with this level of production and sales are given below:

	Unit	Total
Direct materials	$15	$ 450,000
Direct labour	8	240,000
Variable manufacturing overhead	3	90,000
Fixed manufacturing overhead	9	270,000
Variable selling expense	4	120,000
Fixed selling expense	6	180,000
Total cost	$45	$1,350,000

The Lops normally sell for $50 each. Fixed manufacturing overhead is constant at $270,000 per year within the range of 25,000 through 30,000 Lops per year.

Required:

1. Assume that due to a recession, Moore Company expects to sell only 25,000 Lops through regular channels next year. A large retail chain has offered to purchase 5,000 Lops if Moore is willing to accept a 16% discount off the regular price. There would be no sales commissions on this order; thus, variable selling expenses would be slashed by 75%. However, Moore Company would have to purchase a special machine to engrave the retail chain's name on the 5,000 units. This machine would cost $10,000. Moore Company has no assurance that the retail chain will purchase additional units in the future. Determine the impact on profits next year if this special order is accepted.
2. Refer to the original data. Assume again that Moore Company expects to sell only 25,000 Lops through regular channels next year. The Quebec government would like to make a one-time-only purchase of 5,000 Lops. The government would pay a fixed fee of $1.80 per Lop,

and it would reimburse Moore Company for all costs of production (variable and fixed) associated with the units. Since the government would pick up the Lops with its own trucks, there would be no variable selling expenses associated with this order. If Moore Company accepts the order, by how much will profits increase or decrease for the year?

3. Assume the same situation as that described in (2) above, except that the company expects to sell 30,000 Lops through regular channels next year. Thus, accepting the Quebec government's order would require giving up regular sales of 5,000 Lops. If the government's order is accepted, by how much will profits increase or decrease from what they would be if the 5,000 Lops were sold through regular channels?

PROBLEM 12–28 Utilization of a Constrained Resource [LO3]

The Brandilyn Toy Company manufactures a line of dolls and a doll dress sewing kit. Demand for the dolls is increasing, and management requests assistance from you in determining the best sales and production mix for the coming year. The company has provided the following data:

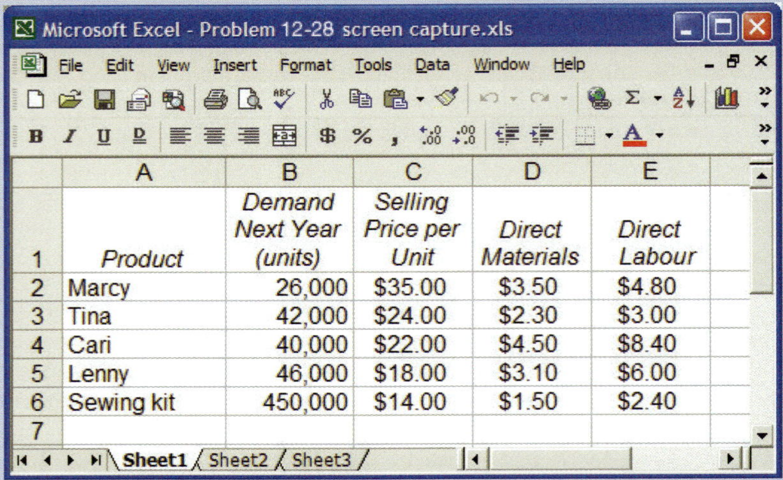

	A	B	C	D	E
1	Product	Demand Next Year (units)	Selling Price per Unit	Direct Materials	Direct Labour
2	Marcy	26,000	$35.00	$3.50	$4.80
3	Tina	42,000	$24.00	$2.30	$3.00
4	Cari	40,000	$22.00	$4.50	$8.40
5	Lenny	46,000	$18.00	$3.10	$6.00
6	Sewing kit	450,000	$14.00	$1.50	$2.40
7					

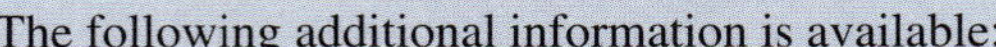

The following additional information is available:

a. The company's plant has a capacity of 150,000 direct labour-hours per year on a single-shift basis. The company's present employees and equipment can produce all five products.

b. The direct labour rate of $12.00 per hour is expected to remain unchanged during the coming year.

c. Fixed costs total $356,000 per year. Variable overhead costs are $4.00 per direct labour-hour.

d. All of the company's nonmanufacturing costs are fixed.

e. The company's finished goods inventory is negligible and can be ignored.

Required:

1. Determine the contribution margin per direct labour-hour expended on each product.
2. Prepare a schedule showing the total direct labour-hours that will be required to produce the units estimated to be sold during the coming year.
3. Examine the data you have computed in (1) and (2) above. How would you allocate the 150,000 direct labour-hours of capacity to Brandilyn Toy Company's various products?
4. What is the highest price, in terms of a rate per hour, that Brandilyn Toy Company should be willing to pay for additional capacity (that is, for added direct labour time)?
5. Identify ways in which the company might be able to obtain additional output so that it would not have to leave some demand for its products unsatisfied.

(CMA, adapted)

PROBLEM 12–29 Sell or Process Further [LO2]

Tidy Corporation produces a variety of cleaning compounds and solutions for both industrial and household use. While most of its products are processed independently, a few are related, such as the company's Grit 337 and its Sparkle silver polish.

Grit 337 is a coarse cleaning powder with many industrial uses. It costs $1.60 a kilogram to make, and it has a selling price of $2.00 a kilogram. A small portion of the annual production of Grit 337 is retained in the factory for further processing. It is combined with several other ingredients to form a paste that is marketed as Sparkle silver polish. The silver polish sells for $4.00 per jar.

This further processing requires one-fourth kilogram of Grit 337 per jar of silver polish. The additional direct costs involved in the processing of a jar of silver polish are:

Other ingredients	$0.65
Direct labour...........	1.48
Total direct cost	$2.13

Overhead costs associated with the processing of the silver polish are:

Variable manufacturing overhead cost.............	25% of direct labour cost
Fixed manufacturing overhead cost (per month):	
Production supervisor.........................	$3,000
Depreciation of mixing equipment	$1,400

The production supervisor has no duties other than to oversee production of the silver polish. The mixing equipment, purchased two years ago, is special-purpose equipment acquired specifically to produce the silver polish. Its resale value is negligible and it does not wear out through use.

Direct labour is a variable cost at Tidy Corporation.

Advertising costs for the silver polish total $4,000 per month. Variable selling costs associated with the silver polish are 7.5% of sales.

Due to a recent decline in the demand for silver polish, the company is wondering whether its continued production is advisable. The sales manager feels that it would be more profitable to sell all of the Grit 337 as a cleaning powder.

Required:

1. What is the incremental contribution margin per jar from further processing of Grit 337 into silver polish?
2. What is the minimum number of jars of silver polish that must be sold each month to justify the continued processing of Grit 337 into silver polish? Explain. Show all computations in good form.

PROBLEM 12–30 (Appendix 12A) Standard Costs; Absorption Costing and Total Variable Costing Approach to Setting Prices [LO4]

Corporate Clothing, Inc. has designed a business suit that is about to be introduced on the market. A standard cost card has been prepared for the new suit, as follows:

	Standard Quantity or Hours	Standard Price or Rate	Standard Cost
Direct materials	5.0 metres	$ 5.00 per metre	$25.00
Direct labour	2.0 hours	14.00 per hour	28.00
Manufacturing overhead ($^1/_6$ variable)	2.0 hours	12.00 per hour	24.00
Total standard cost per suit......			$77.00

The following additional information relating to the new suit is available:

a. The only variable selling, general, or administrative costs will be $8 per suit for shipping. Fixed selling, general, and administrative costs will be (per year):

Salaries	$ 90,000
Advertising and other..........	400,000
Total.......................	$490,000

b. Since the company manufactures many products, it is felt that no more than 20,000 hours of labour time per year can be devoted to production of the new suits.

c. An investment of $1,000,000 will be necessary to carry inventories and accounts receivable and to purchase some new equipment. The company desires a 20% return on investment (ROI) in new product lines.

d. Manufacturing overhead costs are allocated to products on the basis of direct labour-hours.

Required:

1. Assume that the company uses the absorption approach to cost-plus pricing.
   a. Compute the markup that the company needs on the suits to achieve a 20% ROI if it sells all of the suits it can produce using 20,000 hours of labour time.
   b. Using the markup you have computed, prepare a price quote sheet for a single suit.
   c. Assume that the company is able to sell all of the suits that it can produce. Prepare an income statement for the first year of activity, and compute the company's ROI for the year on the suits, using the ROI formula from Chapter 11.
2. Repeat requirements 1*a* and 1*b* above assuming that the company uses the total variable costing approach to cost-plus pricing.
3. After marketing the suits for several years, the company is experiencing a fall-off in demand due to an economic recession. A large retail outlet will make a bulk purchase of suits if its label is sewn in and if an acceptable price can be worked out. What is the minimum acceptable price for this order?

PROBLEM 12–31 (Appendix 12A) Target Costing [LO5]

Free Riders, Inc. sells motorcycles throughout most of Canada. Management is considering adding a scooter to its line-up. Management will negotiate the price of the scooters with its Alberta-based manufacturer.

Management of Free Riders believes the scooters can be sold to its customers for $4,000 each. At that price, annual sales of the scooters should be 200 units. If the scooters are added to Free Riders's product lines, the company will have to invest $200,000 in inventories and special warehouse fixtures. The variable cost of selling the scooters would be $1,000 per unit.

Required:

1. If Free Riders requires a 20% return on investment (ROI), what is the maximum amount the company would be willing to pay the manufacturer for the scooters?
2. After many hours of negotiations, management has concluded that the manufacturer is unwilling to sell the scooters at a low enough price for Free Riders to earn its 20% required ROI. Apart from simply giving up on the idea of adding the scooters to Free Riders' product lines, what could management do?

PROBLEM 12–32 (Appendix 12A) Time and Material Pricing [LO4]

Computer Repair, Inc. uses time and materials pricing, and each year it reviews its rates in light of the actual costs incurred in the prior year. Actual costs incurred last year in connection with repair work and in connection with the company's parts inventory are shown below.

Customers were billed for 20,000 hours of repair work last year.

The company has a target profit of $10 per hour of repair service time and a target profit of 40% of the invoice cost of parts used. During the past year, the company billed repair service time at $50 per hour and added a material loading charge of 40% to parts. Management feels these rates may now be inadequate, since costs have risen somewhat over the last year.

	Repairs	Parts
Repair technicians—wages	$480,000	
Repair service manager—salary	56,000	
Parts manager—salary		$60,000
Repairs and parts assistant—salary	28,800	7,500
Retirement benefits (20% of salaries and wages)	112,960	13,500
Health insurance (5% of salaries and wages)	28,240	3,375
Utilities	120,000	24,000
Truck operating costs	19,200	
Property taxes	9,280	5,400
Liability and fire insurance	6,720	3,000
Supplies	1,200	225
Rent—Building	38,400	33,000
Depreciation—trucks and equipment	59,200	
Invoice cost of parts used		600,000
Total costs for the year	$960,000	$750,000

Required:

1. Using the data on the previous page, compute the following:
   a. The rate that would be charged per hour of repair service time using time and materials pricing.
   b. The materials loading charge that would be used in billing jobs. The materials loading charge should be expressed as a percentage of the invoice cost.
2. Assume that the company adopts the rates that you have computed in (1) above. What should be the total price charged on a repair job that requires 6 hours of service time and parts with an invoice cost of $500?
3. If the company adopts the rates that you have computed in (1) above, would you expect the company's profits to improve?

Cases

CASE 12–33 Integrative Case: Relevant Costs; Pricing [LO1, LO4]

Jenco Incorporated's only product is a combination fertilizer-weed killer called Fertikil. Fertikil is sold nationwide through normal marketing channels to retail nurseries and garden stores.

Taylor Nursery plans to sell a similar fertilizer weed killer compound through its regional nursery chain under its own private label. Taylor does not have manufacturing facilities of its own, so it has asked Jenco (and several other companies) to submit a bid for manufacturing and delivering a 25,000 kilogram order of the private brand compound to Taylor. While the chemical composition of the Taylor compound differs from that of Fertikil, the manufacturing processes are very similar.

The Taylor compound would be produced in 1,000 kilogram lots. Each lot would require 30 direct labour-hours and the following chemicals:

Chemicals	Quantity in Kilograms
CW–3	400
JX–6	300
MZ–8	200
BE–7.	100

The first three chemicals (CW–3, JX–6, and MZ–8) are all used in the production of Fertikil. BE–7 was used in another compound that Jenco discontinued several months ago. The supply of BE–7 that Jenco had on hand when the other compound was discontinued was not discarded. Jenco could sell its supply of BE–7 at the prevailing market price less $0.10 per kilogram selling and handling expenses.

Jenco also has on hand a chemical called CN–5, which was manufactured for use in another product that is no longer produced. CN–5, which cannot be used in Fertikil, can be substituted for CW–3 on a one-for-one basis without affecting the quality of the Taylor compound. The CN–5 in inventory has a salvage value of $500.

Inventory and cost data for the chemicals that can be used to produce the Taylor compound are as shown below:

Raw Material	Kilograms in Inventory	Actual Price per Kilogram When Purchased	Current Market Price per Kilogram
CW–3	22,000	$0.80	$0.90
JX–6	5,000	0.55	0.60
MZ–8.	8,000	1.40	1.60
BE–7	4,000	0.60	0.65
CN–5.	5,500	0.75	(Salvage)

The current direct labour rate is $14 per hour. The predetermined overhead rate is based on direct labour-hours (DLH). The predetermined overhead rate for the current year, based on a two-shift capacity of 400,000 total DLH with no overtime, is as follows:

Variable manufacturing overhead	$ 4.50 per DLH
Fixed manufacturing overhead	7.50 per DLH
Combined rate	$12.00 per DLH

Jenco's production manager reports that the present equipment and facilities are adequate to manufacture the Taylor compound. Therefore, the order would have no effect on total fixed manufacturing overhead costs. However, Jenco is within 400 hours of its two-shift capacity this month. Any additional hours beyond 400 hours must be done in overtime. If need be, the Taylor compound could be produced on regular time by shifting a portion of Fertikil production to overtime. Jenco's rate for overtime hours is 1½ times the regular pay rate, or $21 per hour. There is no allowance for any overtime premium in the predetermined overhead rate.

Required:

1. Jenco, has decided to submit a bid for a 25,000 kilogram order of Taylor Nursery's new compound. The order must be delivered by the end of the current month. Taylor Nursery has indicated that this is a one-time order that will not be repeated. Calculate the lowest price that Jenco could bid for the order without reducing its operating income.
2. Refer to the original data. Assume that Taylor Nursery plans to place regular orders for 25,000 kilogram lots of the new compound during the coming year. Jenco expects the demand for Fertikil to remain strong. Therefore, the recurring orders from Taylor Nursery would put Jenco over its two-shift capacity. However, production could be scheduled so that 60% of each Taylor Nursery order could be completed during regular hours. As another option, some Fertikil production could be shifted temporarily to overtime so that the Taylor Nursery orders could be produced on regular time. Current market prices are the best available estimates of future market prices.

   Jenco's standard markup policy for new products is 40% of the full manufacturing cost, including fixed manufacturing overhead. Calculate the price that Jenco would quote Taylor Nursery for each 25,000 kilogram lot of the new compound, assuming that it is to be treated as a new product and this pricing policy is followed.

CASE 12–34 Decentralization and Relevant Costs [LO2]

Hub Corporation consists of three decentralized divisions—East Division, West Division, and Central Division. The president of Hub has given the managers of the three divisions the authority to decide whether they will sell to outside customers on the intermediate market or sell to other divisions within the company. The divisions are autonomous in that each divisional manager has power to set selling prices to outside customers and to set transfer prices to other divisions. (A transfer price is a price one division charges another division of the same company for a product or service it supplies to that division.) Divisional managers are evaluated and compensated on the basis of their divisions' profits.

The manager of the West Division is considering two alternative orders. Data on the orders are provided below:

a. The Central Division needs 2,000 motors that can be supplied by the West Division at a transfer price of $1,600 per motor. To manufacture these motors, West would purchase component parts from the East Division at a transfer price of $400 per part. (Each motor would require one part.) East would incur variable costs for these parts of $200 each. In addition, each part would require 2.5 hours of machine time at the East Division's general fixed overhead rate of $38 per hour. West Division would then further process these parts, incurring variable costs of $450 per motor. The motors would require 5 hours of machine time each in West's plant at its general fixed overhead rate of $23 per hour.

   If the Central Division can't obtain the motors from the West Division, it will purchase the motors from Bedford Corporation, which has offered to supply the same motors to Central Division at a price of $1,500 per motor. To manufacture these motors, Bedford Corporation would also have to purchase a component part from East Division. This would be a different component part than that needed by the West Division. It would cost East $175 in variable cost to produce, and East would sell it to Bedford Corporation for $350 per part on an order of 2,000 parts. Because of its intricate design, this part would also require 2.5 hours of machine time.

b. Spruce Corporation wants to place an order with the West Division for 2,500 units of a motor that is similar to the motor needed by the Central Division. Spruce has offered to pay $1,200 per motor. To manufacture these motors, West Division would again have to purchase a component part from the East Division. This part would cost East Division $100 per part in variable cost to produce, and East would sell it to West Division at a transfer price of $200 per part. This part would require 2 hours of machine time in East's plant. West Division would further process these parts, incurring variable costs of $500 per motor. This work would require 4 hours of machine time in West Division.

The West Division's plant capacity is limited, and the division can accept only the order from the Central Division or the order from Spruce, but not both. The president of Hub and the manager of the West Division both agree that it would not be beneficial to increase capacity at this time. The company's total general fixed overhead would not be affected by this decision.

Required:

1. If the manager of the West Division wants to maximize the division's profits, which order should be accepted—the order from the Central Division or the order from Spruce Corporation? Support your answer with appropriate computations.
2. For the sake of discussion, assume that the West Division decides to accept the order from Spruce Corporation. Determine if this decision is in the best interests of Hub *as a whole.* Explain your answer. Support your answer with appropriate computations.

(CMA, adapted)

CASE 12–35 Sell or Process Further Decision [LO2]

Manitoba Mills has a plant that can mill wheat grain into a cracked wheat cereal and then further mill the cracked wheat into flour. The company can sell all the cracked wheat cereal that it can produce at a selling price of $615 per tonne. In the past, the company has sold only part of its cracked wheat as cereal and has retained the rest for further milling into flour. The flour has been selling for $875 per tonne, but recently the price has become unstable and has dropped to $780 per tonne. The costs and revenues associated with a tonne of flour follow:

		Per Tonne of Flour
Selling price		$780
Cost to manufacture:		
Raw materials:		
Enrichment materials	$100	
Cracked wheat	590	690
Direct labour		25
Manufacturing overhead		75
Manufacturing profit (loss)		$ (10)

Because of the weak price for flour, the sales manager believes that the company should discontinue milling flour and use its entire milling capacity to produce cracked wheat to sell as cereal.

The same milling equipment is used for both products. Milling one tonne of cracked wheat into one tonne of flour requires the same capacity as milling one tonne of wheat grain into one tonne of cracked wheat. Hence, the choice is between one tonne of flour and two tonnes of cracked wheat. Current cost and revenue data on the cracked wheat cereal follow:

		Per Tonne of Cracked Wheat
Selling price		$615
Cost to manufacture:		
Wheat grain	$490	
Direct labour	25	
Manufacturing overhead	75	590
Manufacturing profit		$ 25

The sales manager argues that since the present $780 per tonne price for the flour results in a $10 per tonne loss, the milling of flour should not be resumed until the price per tonne rises above $790.

The company assigns manufacturing overhead cost to the two products on the basis of milling hours. The same amount of time is required to mill either a tonne of cracked wheat or a tonne of flour. Virtually all manufacturing overhead costs are fixed. Materials and labour costs are variable.

The company can sell all of the cracked wheat and flour it can produce at the current market prices.

Required:

1. Do you agree with the sales manager that the company should discontinue milling flour and use the entire milling capacity to mill cracked wheat if the price of flour remains at $780 per tonne? Support your answer with computations and explanations.
2. What is the lowest price that the company should accept for a tonne of flour? Again support your answer with computations and explanations.

CASE 12–36 Plant Closing Decision [LO1, LO2]

Automotive Interiors (AI) manufactures seats for automobiles, vans, trucks, and boats. The company has a number of plants, including the Woodstock Cover Plant, which makes seat covers.

Bill Rice is the plant manager at the Woodstock Plant but also serves as the regional production manager for the company. His budget as the regional manager is charged to the Woodstock Cover Plant.

Rice has just heard that AI has received a bid from an outside vendor to supply the equivalent of the entire annual output of the Woodstock Plant for $42 million. Rice was astonished at the low outside bid because the budget for the Woodstock Plant's operating costs for the coming year was set at $48.6 million. If this bid is accepted, the Woodstock Plant will be closed down.

The budget for the Woodstock Cover Plant's operating costs for the coming year is presented on the next page. Additional facts regarding the plant's operations are as follows:

a. Due to the plant's commitment to use high-quality fabrics in all of its products, the Purchasing Department was instructed to place blanket purchase orders with major suppliers to ensure the receipt of sufficient materials for the coming year. If these orders are canceled as a consequence of the plant closing, termination charges would amount to 25% of the cost of direct materials.

b. Approximately 350 employees will lose their jobs if the plant is closed. This includes all of the direct labourers and supervisors, management and staff, and the plumbers, electricians, and other skilled workers classified as indirect plant workers. Some of these workers would have difficulty finding new jobs. Nearly all the production workers would have difficulty matching the plant's base pay of $12.50 per hour, which is the highest in the area. A clause in the plant's contract with the union may help some employees; the company must provide employment assistance and job training to its former employees for 12 months after a plant closing. The estimated cost to administer this service would be $1.6 million.

c. Some employees would probably choose early retirement because AI has an excellent pension plan. In fact, $1.4 million of the annual pension expenditures would continue whether the plant is open or not.

d. Rice and his regional staff would not be affected by the closing of the Woodstock plant. They would still be responsible for running three other area plants.

e. If the plant were closed, the company would realize about $4 million salvage value for the equipment in the plant. If the plant remains open, there are no plans to make any significant investments in new equipment or buildings. The old equipment is adequate for the job and should last indefinitely.

Required:

1. Without regard to costs, identify the advantages to AI of continuing to obtain covers from its own Woodstock Cover Plant.
2. AI plans to prepare a financial analysis that will be used in deciding whether or not to close the Woodstock Cover Plant. Management has asked you to identify:
   a. The annual budgeted costs that are relevant to the decision regarding closing the plant (show the dollar amounts).
   b. The annual budgeted costs that are not relevant to the decision regarding closing the plant and explain why they are not relevant (again show the dollar amounts).
   c. Any nonrecurring costs that would arise due to the closing of the plant and explain how they would affect the decision (again show any dollar amounts).

(Required continued on the next page)

Woodstock Cover Plant Annual Budget for Operating Costs		
Materials		$16,000,000
Labour:		
Direct	$13,400,000	
Supervision	800,000	
Indirect plant	3,800,000	18,000,000
Overhead:		
Depreciation—equipment	2,600,000	
Depreciation—building	4,200,000	
Pension expense	3,200,000	
Plant manager and staff*	1,200,000	
Corporate expenses**	3,400,000	14,600,000
Total budgeted costs		$48,600,000

*Expense for Rice and his regional staff.
**Fixed corporate expenses allocated to plants and other operating units based on total budgeted wage and salary costs.

3. Looking at the data you have prepared in (2) above, should the plant be closed? Show computations and explain your answer.
4. Identify any revenues or costs not specifically mentioned in the problem that AI should consider before making a decision.

(CMA, adapted)

CASE 12–37 Make or Buy; Utilization of a Constrained Resource [LO1, LO2, LO3]

Store-It, Inc., sells a wide range of drums, bins, boxes, and other containers that are used in the chemical industry. One of the company's products is a heavy-duty corrosion-resistant metal drum, called the AUD drum, used to store toxic wastes. Production is constrained by the capacity of an automated welding machine that is used to make precision welds. A total of 2,000 hours of welding time is available annually on the machine. Since each drum requires 0.4 hours of welding time, annual production is limited to 5,000 drums. At present, the welding machine is used exclusively to make the AUD drums. The accounting department has provided the following financial data concerning the AUD drums:

AUD Drums		
Selling price per drum		$149.00
Cost per drum:		
Direct materials	$52.10	
Direct labour ($18 per hour)	3.60	
Manufacturing overhead	4.50	
Selling and administrative expense	29.80	90.00
Margin per drum		$ 59.00

Management believes 6,000 AUD drums could be sold each year if the company had sufficient manufacturing capacity. As an alternative to adding another welding machine, management has considered buying additional drums from an outside supplier. Bentley Industries, Inc., a supplier of quality products, would be able to provide up to 4,000 AUD-type drums per year at a price of $138 per drum, which Store-It would resell to its customers at its normal selling price after appropriate relabelling.

Sharon Doane, Store-It's production manager, has suggested that the company could make better use of the welding machine by manufacturing bike frames, which would require 0.5 hours of welding time per frame and yet sell for far more than the drums. Sharon believes that Store-It could sell up to 1,600 bike frames per year to bike manufacturers at a price of $239 each. The accounting department has provided the following data concerning the proposed new product:

Bike Frames		
Selling price per frame		$239.00
Cost per frame:		
Direct materials	$99.40	
Direct labour ($18 per hour)	28.80	
Manufacturing overhead	36.00	
Selling and administrative expense	47.80	212.00
Margin per frame		$ 27.00

The bike frames could be produced with existing equipment and personnel. Manufacturing overhead is allocated to products on the basis of direct labour-hours. Most of the manufacturing overhead consists of fixed common costs such as rent on the factory building, but some of it is variable. The variable manufacturing overhead has been estimated at $1.35 per AUD drum and $1.90 per bike frame. The variable manufacturing overhead cost would not be incurred on drums acquired from the outside supplier.

Selling and administrative expenses are allocated to products on the basis of revenues. Almost all of the selling and administrative expenses are fixed common costs, but it has been estimated that variable selling and administrative expenses amount to $0.75 per AUD drum whether made or purchased and would be $1.30 per bike frame.

All of the company's employees—direct and indirect—are paid for full 40-hour workweeks and the company has a policy of laying off workers only in major recessions.

Required:

1. Should the financial analysis prepared by the company be used in deciding which product to sell? Why?
2. Compute the contribution margin per unit for:
   a. Purchased AUD drums.
   b. Manufactured AUD drums.
   c. Manufactured bike frames.
3. Determine the number of AUD drums (if any) that should be purchased and the number of AUD drums and/or bike frames (if any) that should be manufactured. What is the increase in operating income that would result from this plan over current operations?

   As soon as your analysis was shown to the top management team at Store-It, several managers got into an argument concerning how direct labour costs should be treated when making this decision. One manager argued that direct labour is always treated as a variable cost in textbooks and in practice and has always been considered a variable cost at Store-It. After all, "direct" means you can directly trace the cost to products. "If direct labour is not a variable cost, what is?" Another manager argued just as strenuously that direct labour should be considered a fixed cost at Store-It. No one had been laid off in over a decade, and for all practical purposes, everyone at the plant is on a monthly salary. Everyone classified as direct labour works a regular 40-hour workweek and overtime has not been necessary since the company adopted just-in-time techniques. Whether the welding machine is used to make drums or frames, the total payroll would be exactly the same. There is enough slack, in the form of idle time, to accommodate any increase in total direct labour time that the bike frames would require.
4. Redo requirements (2) and (3) above, making the opposite assumption about direct labour from the one you originally made. In other words, if you treated direct labour as a variable cost, redo the analysis treating it as a fixed cost. If you treated direct labour as a fixed cost, redo the analysis treating it as a variable cost.
5. What do you think is the correct way to treat direct labour cost in this situation—as variable or as fixed?

Research

R 12–38 Managing Constraints in a Manufacturing Firm [LO3]
Identify a manufacturing company in your local area and make an appointment to meet with a production manager.

Required:
At the meeting with the production manager, seek answers to the following questions:
1. What constraints (bottlenecks) exist in the production process?
2. What approaches has the company used in reducing the constraints?
3. What was the estimated cost of reducing the constraints?
4. What long-term solution was implemented, if any, to eliminate the constraint?

R 12–39 Dropping a Product or Service: Beyond the Numbers [LO2]
One of the decisions facing managers illustrated in Chapter 12 is whether to keep or drop an existing product, service, or operating segment. The analysis presented indicates that if the costs avoided by dropping the product or segment exceed the contribution margin lost, then "drop" is the correct decision from a financial perspective. However, when companies decide to drop a major product, service or operating segment, there may be non-financial consequences involving suppliers, creditors, employees, and customers.

Required:
Identify, using any examples you can find from the business press, some non-financial consequences that may occur when an organization decides to drop a major product, service, or operating segment.

R 12–40 Decision Making in Practice [LO1, LO2]
As you know, the World Wide Web is a medium that is constantly evolving. Sites come and go, and change without notice. To enable the periodic updating of site addresses, this problem has been posted to the textbook web site (www.mcgrawhill.ca/olc/garrison). After accessing the site, enter the Student Centre and select this chapter. Select and complete the Internet Exercise.

CHAPTER 13

LEARNING OBJECTIVES

After studying Chapter 13, you should be able to:

1. Determine the payback period for an investment.
2. Compute the simple rate of return for an investment.
3. Evaluate the acceptability of an investment project using the net present value method.
4. Evaluate the acceptability of an investment project using the internal rate of return method.
5. Evaluate an investment project that has uncertain cash flows.
6. Rank investment projects in order of preference.
7. Include income taxes in a capital budgeting analysis.
8. (Appendix 13A) Explain present value concepts and the use of present value tables.

CAPITAL BUDGETING DECISIONS

BUSINESS FOCUS

Planned Capital Spending

Capital programs are a major concern for natural resource companies. Petro-Canada, for example, incurred capital and exploration expenditures of $3,485 million in 2006, down 5% compared to 2005 due to lower investment in Oil Sands assets. According to the company's 2006 annual report, capital expenditures were expected to increase in 2007. More than 60% of planned capital expenditures support delivering profitable new growth, and funding exploration and new ventures. This estimate is up from nearly 53% in these categories in 2006. The remaining 40% of the 2007 planned capital expenditures are directed toward replacing reserves in core areas, enhancing existing assets, improving base business profitability and complying with regulations. The regulatory compliance portion of the program was greater in 2006, primarily reflecting expenditures to produce cleaner burning fuels at downstream refineries. The following table summarizes Petro-Canada's expected capital expenditures for 2007 according to the company's 2006 annual report:

Capital program by investment priority:	(millions of dollars)
Complying with regulations	$ 100
Enhancing existing assets	240
Improving base business profitability	160
Replacing reserves in core areas	1,025
Advancing new growth projects	2,020
Investing in exploration and new ventures	515
Total	$4,060

Budgeting for such programs, termed capital budgeting, is of critical importance for companies such as Petro-Canada.

Source: Petro-Canada, 2006 Annual Report.

The term **capital budgeting** is used to describe how managers plan significant outlays on projects that have long-term implications, such as the purchase of new equipment and the introduction of new products. In a recent fiscal year, BCE Inc. had capital expenditures reaching $3.1 billion. Most companies have many more potential projects than can actually be funded. Hence, managers must carefully select those projects that promise the greatest future return. How well managers make these capital budgeting decisions is a critical factor in the long-run profitability of the company.

Capital budgeting The process of planning significant outlays on projects that have long-term implications, such as the purchase of new equipment or the introduction of a new product.

Capital budgeting involves *investment*—a company must commit funds now in order to receive a return in the future. Investments are not limited to stocks and bonds. Purchase of inventory or equipment is also an investment. For example, Tim Hortons makes an investment when it opens a new restaurant. McCain Foods makes an investment when it installs a new computer to handle customer billing. Chrysler Canada Inc. makes an investment when it redesigns a product such as the Jeep Eagle and must retool its production lines. With a combination of public and private funding, universities such as UBC, U of T, McGill, Dalhousie, and Memorial make substantial expenditures in medical research. All of these investments are characterized by a commitment of funds today in the expectation of receiving a return in the future in the form of additional cash inflows or reduced cash outflows.

Capital Budgeting—Planning Investments

Typical Capital Budgeting Decisions

Any decision that involves an outlay now in order to obtain some return (increase in revenue or reduction in costs) in the future is a capital budgeting decision. Typical capital budgeting decisions include:

1. ***Cost-reduction decisions.*** Should new equipment be purchased to reduce costs?
2. ***Expansion decisions.*** Should a new plant, warehouse, or other facility be acquired to increase capacity and production?
3. ***Equipment selection decisions.*** Which of several available machines should be purchased?
4. ***Lease or buy decisions.*** Should new equipment be leased or purchased?
5. ***Equipment replacement decisions.*** Should old equipment be replaced now or later?

Capital budgeting decisions tend to fall into two broad categories—*screening decisions* and *preference decisions*. **Screening decisions** are those relating to whether a proposed project is accepted. For example, a firm may have a policy of accepting projects only if they promise a return of 20% on the investment. The required rate of return is the minimum rate of return a project must yield to be acceptable.

Screening decision A decision as to whether a proposed investment meets some preset standard of acceptance.

Preference decisions, by contrast, relate to selecting from among several acceptable alternates. To illustrate, a firm may be considering five different machines to replace an existing machine on the assembly line. The choice of which machine to purchase is a *preference* decision.

Preference decision A decision as to which of several competing acceptable investment proposals is best.

In this chapter, we initially discuss screening decisions.

Approaches to Capital Budgeting Decisions

LEARNING OBJECTIVE 1
Determine the payback period for an investment.

Payback period
The length of time that it takes for a project to recover its initial cost out of the cash receipts that it generates.

In this section, we discuss two methods, known as *payback* and *simple rate of return.*

The Payback Method

The payback method focuses on the *payback period.* The **payback period** is the length of time that it takes for a project to recoup its initial cost out of the cash receipts that it generates. This period is sometimes referred to as "the time that it takes for an investment to pay for itself." The basic premise of the payback method is that the more quickly the cost of an investment can be recovered, the more desirable is the investment.

The payback period is expressed in years. *When the net annual cash inflow is the same every year,* the following formula can be used to compute the payback period:

$$\text{Payback period} = \frac{\text{Investment required}}{\text{Net annual cash inflow*}} \qquad (1)$$

*If new equipment is replacing old equipment, this becomes incremental net annual cash inflow.

To illustrate the payback method, assume the following data:

Example A

York Company needs a new milling machine. The company is considering two machines: machine A and machine B. Machine A costs $15,000 and will reduce operating costs by $5,000 per year. Machine B costs only $12,000 but will also reduce operating costs by $5,000 per year.

Which machine should be purchased according to the payback method?

$$\text{Machine A payback period} = \frac{\$15{,}000}{\$5{,}000} = 3.0 \text{ years}$$

$$\text{Machine B payback period} = \frac{\$12{,}000}{\$5{,}000} = 2.4 \text{ years}$$

According to the payback calculations, York Company should purchase machine B, since it has a shorter payback period than machine A.

Evaluation of the Payback Method

The payback method is not a true measure of the profitability of an investment. Rather, it simply tells the manager how many years will be required to recover the original investment. Unfortunately, a shorter payback period does not always mean that one investment is more desirable than another.

To illustrate refer back to the example above. Since machine B has a shorter payback period than machine A, it *appears* that machine B is more desirable than machine A. But if we add one more piece of data, this illusion quickly disappears. Machine A has a projected 10-year life, and machine B has a projected 5-year life. It would take two purchases of machine B to provide the same length of service as would be provided by a single purchase of machine A. Under these circumstances, machine A would be a much better investment than machine B, even though machine B has a shorter payback period. Unfortunately, the payback method has no inherent mechanism for highlighting differences in useful life between investments. Such differences can be very important, and relying on payback alone may result in incorrect decisions.

A further criticism of the payback method is that it does not adequately consider the time value of money. A cash inflow to be received several years in the future is weighed equally with a cash inflow to be received right now. To illustrate, assume that for an investment of $8,000 you can purchase either of the two following streams of cash inflows:

Year	0	1	2	3	4	5	6	7	8
Stream 1		–0–	–0–	–0–	$8,000	$2,000	$2,000	$2,000	$2,000
Stream 2		$2,000	$2,000	$2,000	$2,000	$8,000	–0–	–0–	–0–

Which stream of cash inflows would you prefer to receive in return for your $8,000 investment? Each stream has a payback period of 4.0 years. Therefore, if payback alone was relied on in making the decision, you would be forced to say that the streams are equally desirable. However, from the point of view of the time value of money, stream 2 is much more desirable than stream 1 because the return occurs sooner.

On the other hand, under certain conditions the payback method can be very useful. For one thing, it can help identify which investment proposals are in the "ballpark." That is, it can be used as a screening tool to help answer the question, "Should I consider this proposal further?" If a proposal doesn't provide a payback within some specified period, then there may be no need to consider it further. In addition, the payback period is often of great importance to firms that are "cash poor." When a firm is cash poor, a project with a short payback period but a low rate of return might be preferred over another project because the company may simply need a faster recovery of its cash investment. Finally, the payback method is sometimes used in industries where products become obsolete very rapidly—such as consumer electronics. Since products may last only a year or two, the payback period on investments must be very short.

IN BUSINESS

Investing in an energy solution can benefit hotels in many ways ranging from conservation to guest satisfaction (GSI) according to research conducted by Direct Energy Business Services. Hotels that have recently invested in total energy management solutions have also reduced their operating costs by as much as 24% per annum. With larger hotels, this equates to approximately $1.5 million per year, or an average of $644 per room per year.

The research, conducted with hotel properties across Canada whose energy management projects varied widely, shows that paying close attention to this back-of-house strategy that encompasses how a property buys, converts, uses and disposes of its energy, usually has a payback of three to five years and attractive ROI of up to 33%. For one hotel, whose solution had a price tag of more than $3.7 million and resulted in savings of more than $650,000 per annum, when combined with incentives the simple payback was 5.6 years. In particular projects like lighting upgrades or automation can return investments in less than four years.

Source: Excerpted from "New Research Shows Managing Energy Benefits, ROI, Conservation and Guest Satisfaction," *Direct Energy Business Services*, Feb. 15, 2005.

An Extended Example of Payback

As shown by formula (1) given earlier, the payback period is computed by dividing the investment in a project by the net annual cash inflows that the project will generate. If new equipment is replacing old equipment, then any salvage value to be received on disposal of the old equipment should be deducted from the cost of the new equipment, and only the *incremental* investment should be used in the payback computation. In addition, any depreciation deducted in arriving at the project's operating income must be added back to obtain the project's expected net annual cash inflow. To illustrate, consider the following data:

Example B

Goodtime Fun Centres, Inc. operates amusement parks. Some of the vending machines in one of its parks provide very little revenue, so the company is considering removing the machines and installing equipment to dispense soft ice cream. The equipment would cost $80,000 and have an eight-year useful life with no salvage value. Incremental annual revenues and costs associated with the sale of ice cream would be as follows:

Sales	$150,000
Less cost of ingredients	90,000
Contribution margin	60,000
Less fixed expenses:	
Salaries	27,000
Maintenance	3,000
Depreciation	10,000
Total fixed expenses	40,000
Operating income	$ 20,000

The vending machines can be sold for a $5,000 scrap value. The company will not purchase equipment unless it has a payback period of three years or less. Does the ice cream dispenser pass this criterion?

Exhibit 13–1 shows the computation of the payback period for the ice cream dispenser. Several things should be noted. First, depreciation is added back to operating income to obtain the net annual cash inflow from the new equipment. Depreciation is not a cash outlay; thus, it must be added back to adjust operating income to a cash basis. Second, the payback computation deducts the salvage value of the old machines from the cost of the new equipment so that only the incremental investment is used in computing the payback period.

Since the proposed equipment has a payback period of less than three years, the company's payback requirement has been met.

EXHIBIT 13–1 Computation of the Payback Period

Step 1: *Compute the net annual cash inflow.* Since the net annual cash inflow is not given, it must be computed before the payback period can be determined:

Operating income (given above)	$20,000
Add: Noncash deduction for depreciation	10,000
Net annual cash inflow	$30,000

Step 2: *Compute the payback period.* Using the net annual cash inflow figure from above, the payback period can be determined as follows:

Cost of the new equipment	$80,000
Less salvage value of old equipment	5,000
Investment required	$75,000

$$\text{Payback period} = \frac{\text{Investment required}}{\text{Net annual cash inflow}}$$

$$= \frac{\$75{,}000}{\$30{,}000} = 2.5 \text{ years}$$

Payback and Uneven Cash Flows

When the cash flows associated with an investment project change from year to year, the simple payback formula that we outlined earlier cannot be used. Consider the following data:

Year	Investment	Cash Inflow
1	$4,000	$1,000
2		-0-
3		2,000
4	2,000	1,000
5		500
6		3,000
7		2,000
8		2,000

What is the payback period on this investment? The answer is 5.5 years, but to obtain this figure it is necessary to track the unrecovered investment year by year. The steps involved in this process are shown in Exhibit 13–2. By the middle of the sixth year, sufficient cash inflows will have been realized to recover the entire investment of $6,000 ($4,000 + $2,000).

The Simple Rate of Return Method

LEARNING OBJECTIVE 2
Compute the simple rate of return for an investment.

The **simple rate of return** method is another capital budgeting technique that does not involve discounted cash flows. The method is also known as the *accounting rate of return,* or *the unadjusted rate of return.*

Unlike the other capital budgeting methods that we have discussed, the simple rate of return method does not focus on cash flows. Rather, it focuses on accounting operating income. The approach is to estimate the revenues that will be generated by a proposed investment and then deduct from these revenues all of the projected operating expenses associated with the project. This operating income figure is then related to the initial investment in the project, as shown in the following formula:

$$\text{Simple rate of return} = \frac{\text{Incremental revenues} - \text{Incremental expenses, including depreciation} = \text{Incremental operating income}}{\text{Initial investment*}} \quad (2)$$

*The investment should be reduced by any salvage from the sale of old equipment.

Simple rate of return The rate of return computed by dividing a project's annual accounting operating income by the initial investment required.

Or, if a cost reduction project is involved, the formula becomes:

$$\text{Simple rate of return} = \frac{\text{Cost savings} - \text{Depreciation on new equipment}}{\text{Initial investment*}} \quad (3)$$

*Any salvage from the sale of old equipment should be deducted from the initial investment.

The logic of deducting depreciation on the investment in new equipment is subject to potential confusion given how the initial investment is handled in later discussions. Deducting depreciation expense in formula 2 or 3 permits the simple rate of return to parallel accounting results used in the return on investment (ROI) described in Chapter 11. Also the investment is changed to the return over the life of the investment by the periodic depreciation, a process that is permitted if timing of costs and revenues is considered to be unimportant to the assessment of the investment.

EXHIBIT 13–2 Payback Calculation and Uneven Cash Flows

Year	Investment (a)	Cash Inflow (b)	Unrecovered Investment* (c)
1	$4,000	$1,000	$3,000
2		-0-	$3,000
3		$2,000	$1,000
4	$2,000	$1,000	$2,000
5		$ 500	$1,500
6		$3,000	-0-
7		$2,000	-0-

*Year X unrecovered investment, column (c) = Year X − 1 unrecovered investment, column (c) + Year X investment, column (a) − Year X cash inflow, column (b)

Example C

Brigham Tea, Inc. is a processor of a low-acid tea. The company is contemplating purchasing equipment for an additional processing line. The additional processing line would increase revenues by $90,000 per year. Incremental cash operating expenses would be $40,000 per year. The equipment would cost $180,000 and have a nine-year life. No salvage value is projected.

The simple rate of return for this example is calculated as follows:

$$\text{Simple rate of return} = \frac{\left[\begin{array}{c}\$90{,}000\\ \text{Incremental}\\ \text{revenues}\end{array}\right] - \left[\begin{array}{c}\$40{,}000 \text{ Cash operating expenses}\\ + \$20{,}000 \text{ Depreciation}\end{array}\right]}{\$180{,}000 \text{ Initial investment}}$$

$$= \frac{\$30{,}000}{\$180{,}000}$$

$$= 16.7\%$$

Example D

Midwest Farms, Inc. hires people on a part-time basis to sort eggs. The cost of this hand-sorting process is $30,000 per year. The company is investigating the purchase of an egg-sorting machine that would cost $90,000 and have a 15-year useful life. The machine would have negligible salvage value, and it would cost $10,000 per year to operate and maintain. The egg-sorting equipment currently being used could be sold now for a scrap value of $2,500.

A cost reduction project is involved in this situation. By applying the formula for the simple rate of return found in equation (3), we can compute the simple rate of return as follows:

$$\text{Simple rate of return} = \frac{\$20{,}000^{*} \text{ Cost savings} - \$6{,}000^{\dagger} \text{ Depreciation on new equipment}}{\$90{,}000 - \$2{,}500}$$

$$= 16.0\%$$

*$30,000 − $10,000 = $20,000 cost savings.
†$90,000 ÷ 15 years = $6,000 depreciation.

Criticisms of the Simple Rate of Return

The most damaging criticism of the simple rate of return method is that it does not adequately consider the time value of money. The simple rate of return method considers a dollar received 10 years from now just as valuable as a dollar received today. Thus, the simple rate of return can be misleading if the alternatives being considered have different cash flow patterns. For example, assume that project A has a high simple rate of return but yields the bulk of its cash flows many years from now. Another project, B, has a somewhat lower simple rate of return but yields the bulk of its cash flows over the next few years. Project A has a higher simple rate of return than project B; however, project B might in fact be a much better investment if the time value of money was considered. In contrast, the net present value method which we introduce next, provides a single number that summarizes all of the cash flows over the entire useful life of the project.

Given the criticisms mentioned, simple rate of return does provide information consistent with the return on investment described in Chapter 11. Thus the simple rate of return provides information to management about what the potential impact of the investment might be on the performance assessment of managers.

The Time Value of Money

As stated earlier, capital investments commonly promise returns that extend over fairly long periods of time. Therefore, in approaching capital budgeting decisions, it is necessary to employ techniques that recognize the *time value of money.* A dollar today is worth more than a dollar a year from now. The same concept applies in choosing between investment projects. Projects that promise returns earlier in time are preferable to those that promise later returns.

The capital budgeting techniques that recognize the time value of money involve *discounted cash flows.* We will spend the rest of this chapter illustrating the use of discounted cash flow methods in making capital budgeting decisions. If you are not already familiar with discounting and the use of present value tables, you should read Appendix 13A, The Concept of Present Value, at the end of this chapter before proceeding any further.

IN BUSINESS

Choosing a Cat

Sometimes a long-term decision does not have to involve present value calculations or any other sophisticated analytical technique. White Grizzly Adventures of Meadow Creek, British Columbia, needs two snowcats for its powder skiing operations—one for shuttling guests to the top of the mountain and one to be held in reserve in case of mechanical problems with the first. Bombardier of Canada sells new snowcats for $250,000 and used, reconditioned snowcats for $150,000. In either case, the snowcats are good for about 5,000 hours of operation before they need to be reconditioned. From White Grizzly's perspective, the choice is clear. Since both new and reconditioned snowcats last about 5,000 hours, but the reconditioned snowcats cost $100,000 less, the reconditioned snowcats are the obvious choice. They may not have all of the latest bells and whistles, but they get the job done at a price a small operation can afford.

Bombardier snowcats do not have passenger cabs as standard equipment. To save money, White Grizzly builds its own custom-designed passenger cab for about $15,000, using recycled Ford Escort seats and industrial-strength aluminum for the frame and siding. If purchased retail, a passenger cab would cost about twice as much and would not be as well suited for snowcat skiing.

Source: Brad and Carole Karafil, owners and operators of White Grizzly Adventures, www.whitegrizzly.com.

Discounted Cash Flows—the Net Present Value Method

LEARNING OBJECTIVE 3
Evaluate the acceptability of an investment project using the net present value method.

Two approaches to making capital budgeting decisions use discounted cash flows. One is the *net present value method,* and the other is the *internal rate of return method* (sometimes called the *time-adjusted rate of return method*). The net present value method is discussed in this section; the internal rate of return method is discussed in the following section.

The Net Present Value Method Illustrated

Under the net present value method, the present value of a project's cash inflows is compared to the present value of the project's cash outflows. The difference between the

Net present value The difference between the present value of the cash inflows and the present value of the cash outflows associated with an investment project.

present value of these cash flows, called the **net present value**, determines whether or not the project is an acceptable investment. To illustrate, let us assume the following data:

Example E

Harper Company is contemplating the purchase of a machine capable of performing certain operations that are now performed manually. The machine will cost $50,000, and it will last for five years. At the end of the five-year period, the machine will have a zero scrap value. Use of the machine will reduce labour costs by $18,000 per year. Harper Company requires a minimum return of 20% before taxes on all investment projects.

Should the machine be purchased? Harper Company must determine whether a cash investment now of $50,000 can be justified if it will result in an $18,000 reduction in cost each year over the next five years. It may appear that the answer is obvious since the total cost savings are $90,000 ($18,000 per year × 5 years). However, the company can earn a 20% return by investing its money elsewhere. It is not enough that the cost reductions cover just the original cost of the machine; they must also yield at least a 20% return or the company would be better off investing the money elsewhere.

To determine whether the investment is desirable, the stream of annual $18,000 cost savings is discounted to its present value, which is then compared to the cost of the new machine. Since Harper Company requires a minimum return of 20% on all investment projects, this rate is used in the discounting process and is called the *discount rate*. Exhibit 13–3 shows how this analysis is done.

According to the analysis, Harper Company should purchase the new machine. The present value of the cost savings is $53,838, as compared to a present value of only $50,000 for the investment required (cost of the machine). Deducting the present value of the investment required from the present value of the cost savings gives a *net present value* of $3,838. Whenever the net present value is zero or greater, as in our example, an investment project is acceptable. Whenever the net present value is negative (the present value of the cash outflows exceeds the present value of the cash inflows), an investment project is not acceptable. In summary:

If the Net Present Value Is . . .	Then the Project Is . . .
Positive	Acceptable, since it promises a return greater than the required rate of return.
Zero	Acceptable, since it promises a return equal to the required rate of return.
Negative	Not acceptable, since it promises a return less than the required rate of return.

EXHIBIT 13–3 Net Present Value Analysis of a Proposed Project

Initial cost	$50,000
Life of the project (years)	5
Annual cost savings	$18,000
Salvage value	–0–
Required rate of return	20%

Item	Year(s)	Amount of Cash Flow	20% Factor	Present Value of Cash Flows
Annual cost savings	1–5	$ 18,000	2.991*	$ 53,838
Initial investment	Now	(50,000)	1.000	(50,000)
Net present value				$ 3,838

*From Exhibit 13–23 in Appendix 13A at the end of this chapter.

A full interpretation of the solution would be as follows: The new machine promises more than the required 20% rate of return. This is evident from the positive net present value of $3,838. Harper Company could spend up to $53,838 for the new machine and still obtain the minimum required 20% rate of return. The net present value of $3,838, therefore, shows the amount of "cushion" or "margin of error." One way to look at this is that the company could underestimate the cost of the new machine by up to $3,838, or overestimate the net present value of the future cash savings by up to $3,838, and the project would still be financially attractive. If the present value of the cost savings was only $50,000 instead of $53,838, the project would still generate the required 20% return.

Emphasis on Cash Flows

In capital budgeting decisions, the focus is on cash flows and not on accounting income. Accounting income is based on accruals that ignore the timing of cash flows into and out of an organization. From a capital budgeting standpoint, the timing of cash flows is critical, since a dollar received today is more valuable than a dollar received in the future. Therefore, even though the accounting income figure is useful for many things, it is not used in discounted cash flow analysis. Instead of determining accounting income, the manager must concentrate on identifying the specific cash flows associated with an investment project.

Although the specific cash flows will vary from project to project, certain types of cash flows tend to recur, as explained in the following paragraphs.

Typical Cash Outflows Most projects will have an immediate cash outflow in the form of an initial investment in equipment or other assets. Any salvage value realized from the sale of old equipment can be recognized as a cash inflow or as a reduction in the required investment. In addition, some projects require that a company expand its working capital. **Working capital** is current assets (cash, accounts receivable, and inventory) less current liabilities. When a company takes on a new project, the balances in the current asset accounts will often increase. For example, opening a new Bay department store would require additional cash in sales registers, increased accounts receivable for new customers, and more inventory to stock the shelves. These additional working capital needs should be treated as part of the initial investment in a project. Also, many projects require periodic outlays for repairs and maintenance and for additional operating costs. These should all be treated as cash outflows for capital budgeting purposes.

Working capital
The excess of current assets over current liabilities.

Typical Cash Inflows On the cash inflow side, a project will normally either increase revenues or reduce costs. Either way, the amount involved should be treated as a cash inflow for capital budgeting purposes. Notice that from a cash flows standpoint, a *reduction in costs is equivalent to an increase in revenues.* Cash inflows are also frequently realized from selling equipment for its salvage value when a project is terminated, although the company may actually have to pay for the cost of disposing of some low-value or hazardous items. In addition, any working capital that was tied up in the project can be released for use elsewhere at the end of the project and should be treated as a cash inflow. Working capital is released, for example, when a company sells off its inventory or collects its receivables. (If the released working capital is not shown as a cash inflow at the termination of a project, then the project appears to be charged for the use of the funds forever!)

In summary, the following types of cash flows are common in business investment projects:

Cash outflows:

Initial investment (including installation costs).

Increased working capital needs.

Repairs and maintenance.

Incremental operating costs.

Cash inflows:

Incremental revenues.

Reduction in costs.

Salvage value.

Release of working capital.

Recovery of the Original Investment

When computing the present value of a project, depreciation is not deducted for two reasons. First, depreciation is not a current cash outflow.[1] As discussed previously, discounted cash flow methods of making capital budgeting decisions focus on *cash flows.* Although depreciation is used in computing net income for financial statements, it is not relevant in an analytical framework that focuses on cash flows.

A second reason for not deducting depreciation is that discounted cash flow methods *automatically* provide for return of the original investment, thereby making a deduction for depreciation unnecessary. To demonstrate this point, let us assume the following data:

Example F

Carver Dental Clinic is considering the purchase of an attachment for its X-ray machine that will cost $3,170. The attachment will be usable for four years, after which time it will have no salvage value. It will increase net cash inflows by $1,000 per year in the X-ray department. The clinic's board of directors has instructed that no investments are to be made unless they have an annual return of at least 10%.

A present value analysis of the desirability of purchasing the X-ray attachment is presented in Exhibit 13–4. Notice that the attachment promises exactly a 10% return on the original investment, since the net present value is zero at a 10% discount rate.

Each annual $1,000 cash inflow arising from use of the attachment is made up of two parts. One part represents a recovery of a portion of the original $3,170 paid for the attachment, and the other part represents a return on this investment. The breakdown of each year's $1,000 cash inflow between recovery *of* investment and return *on* investment is shown in Exhibit 13–5.

The first year's $1,000 cash inflow consists of a $317 interest return (10%) *on* the $3,170 original investment, plus a $683 return *of* that investment. Since the amount of the unrecovered investment decreases over the four years, the dollar amount of the interest return also decreases. By the end of the fourth year, all $3,170 of the original investment has been recovered.

EXHIBIT 13–4 Carver Dental Clinic—Net Present Value Analysis of X-Ray Attachment

Initial cost	$3,170
Life of the project (years)	4
Annual net cash inflow	$1,000
Salvage value	–0–
Required rate of return	10%

Item	Year(s)	Amount of Cash Flow	10% Factor	Present Value of Cash Flows
Annual net cash inflow	1–4	$ 1,000	3.170*	$ 3,170
Initial investment	Now	(3,170)	1.000	(3,170)
Net present value				$ –0–

*From Exhibit 13–23 in Appendix 13A.

1. Although depreciation itself is not a cash flow, it does have an effect on cash outflows for income taxes. We will look at this effect when we discuss the impact of income taxes on capital budgeting later in the chapter.

EXHIBIT 13–5 Carver Dental Clinic—Breakdown of Annual Cash Inflows

Year	(1) Investment Outstanding during the Year	(2) Cash Inflow	(3) Return on Investment (1) × 10%	(4) Recovery of Investment during the Year (2) — (3)	(5) Unrecovered Investment at the End of the Year (1) — (4)
1	$3,170	$1,000	$317	$ 683	$2,487
2	2,487	1,000	249	751	1,736
3	1,736	1,000	173	827	909
4	909	1,000	91	909	–0–
Total investment recovered				$3,170	

Simplifying Assumptions

Two simplifying assumptions are usually made in net present value analyis.

The first assumption is that all cash flows other than the initial investment occur at the end of periods. This is somewhat unrealistic in that cash flows typically occur *throughout* a period—not only at year end. The purpose of this assumption is just to simplify computations and it does not affect the accuracy in a significant manner in most cases.

The second assumption is that all cash flows generated by an investment project are immediately reinvested at a rate of return equal to the discount rate. Unless these conditions are met, the return computed for the project will not be accurate. We used a discount rate of 10% for the Carver Dental Clinic in Exhibit 13–4. Unless the funds released each period are immediately reinvested at a 10% return, the net present value computed for the X-ray attachment will be misstated.

Choosing a Discount Rate

A positive net present value means that the project's return exceeds the discount rate. A negative net present value indicates that the project's return is less than the discount rate. Therefore, if the company's minimum required rate of return is used as the discount rate, a project with a positive net present value has a return that exceeds the minimum required rate of return and is acceptable. Contrarily, a project with a negative net present value has a return than is less than the minimum required rate of return and is unacceptable.

The firm's *cost of capital* is usually regarded as the most appropriate choice for the discount rate. The **cost of capital** is the average rate of return the company must pay to its long-term creditors and shareholders for the use of their funds. The cost of capital is the minimum required rate of return, because if a project's rate of return is less than the cost of capital, company earnings will not be enough to compensate its creditors and shareholders. Therefore, any rate of return less than the cost of capital should not be accepted.

Cost of capital The overall cost to an organization of obtaining investment funds, including the cost of both debt sources and equity sources. (Same as *hurdle rate, cut-off rate,* and *required rate of return.*)

The mechanics involved in cost of capital computations are covered in finance texts and will not be considered here. The cost of capital is known by various names. It is sometimes called the *hurdle rate*, the *cut-off rate*, or the *required rate of return*.

Most finance specialists would agree that a before-tax cost of capital of 16–20% would be typical for an average industrial corporation. The appropriate after-tax figure would depend on the corporation's tax circumstances, but it would probably average around 10–12%. Among the top Canadian wealth producers, this cost of capital is comparatively high. For example, Barrick Gold Corp.'s 16.6% cost of capital, and Placer Dome Inc.'s 17.2% well outpace the 11% average cost of 300 ranked Canadian companies.[2]

2. "*Financial Post* MVA List," *Financial Post,* June 22/24, 1996, pp. 43–47.

An Extended Example of the Net Present Value Method

To conclude our discussion of the net present value method, we present an extended example of how it is used in analyzing an investment proposal, which will help to tie together (and to reinforce) many of the ideas developed so far.

Example G

Under a special licensing arrangement, Swinyard Company has an opportunity to market a new product in western Canada for a five-year period. The product would be purchased from the manufacturer, with Swinyard Company responsible for all costs of promotion and distribution. The licensing arrangement could be renewed at the end of the five-year period at the option of the manufacturer. After careful study, Swinyard Company has estimated that the following costs and revenues would be associated with the new product:

Cost of equipment needed	$ 60,000
Working capital needed	100,000
Overhaul of the equipment in four years	5,000
Salvage value of the equipment in five years	10,000
Annual revenues and costs:	
Sales revenues	200,000
Cost of goods sold	125,000
Out-of-pocket operating costs (for salaries, advertising, and other direct costs)	35,000

At the end of the five-year period, the working capital would be released for investment elsewhere if the manufacturer decided not to renew the licensing arrangement. Swinyard Company's discount rate and cost of capital is 14%. Would you recommend that the new product be introduced?

This example involves a variety of cash inflows and cash outflows. The solution is given in Exhibit 13–6.

Notice particularly how the working capital is handled in this exhibit. It is counted as a cash outflow at the beginning of the project and as a cash inflow when it is released at the end of the project. Also notice how the sales revenues, cost of goods sold, and out-of-pocket costs are handled. **Out-of-pocket costs** are actual cash outlays for salaries, advertising, and other operating expenses. Depreciation would not be an out-of-pocket cost, since it involves no current cash outlay.

Out of pocket costs
Actual cash outlays for operating costs.

Since the overall net present value is positive, the new product should be added, assuming the company has no better use for the investment funds.

EXHIBIT 13–6 The Net Present Value Method—An Extended Example

Sales revenues	$200,000
Less cost of goods sold	125,000
Less out-of-pocket costs for salaries, advertising, etc.	35,000
Annual net cash inflows	$ 40,000

Item	Year(s)	Amount of Cash Flows	14% Factor	Present Value of Cash Flows
Purchase of equipment	Now	$ (60,000)	1.000	$ (60,000)
Working capital needed	Now	(100,000)	1.000	(100,000)
Overhaul of equipment	4	(5,000)	0.592*	(2,960)
Annual net cash inflows from sales of the product line	1–5	40,000	3.433†	137,320
Salvage value of the equipment	5	10,000	0.519*	5,190
Working capital released	5	100,000	0.519*	51,900
Net present value				$ 31,450

*From Exhibit 13–22 in Appendix 13A.

†From Exhibit 13–23 in Appendix 13A.

Discounted Cash Flows—The Internal Rate of Return Method

The **internal rate of return** (or **time-adjusted rate of return**) can be defined as the interest yield promised by an investment project over its useful life. It is sometimes referred to simply as the **yield** on a project. The internal rate of return is computed by finding the discount rate that equates the present value of a project's cash outflows with the present value of its cash inflows. In other words, the internal rate of return is that discount rate that results in a net present value of zero.

LEARNING OBJECTIVE 4
Evaluate the acceptability of an investment project using the internal rate of return method.

Internal rate of return
The discount rate at which the net present value of an investment project is zero; thus, the internal rate of return represents the interest yield promised by a project over its useful life. This term is synonymous with *time-adjusted rate of return.*

Time-adjusted rate of return
Same as *internal rate of return.*

Yield
A term synonymous with *internal rate of return* and *time-adjusted rate of return.*

The Internal Rate of Return Method Illustrated

To illustrate the internal rate of return method, let us assume the following data:

Example H

Glendale School District is considering the purchase of a large tractor-pulled lawnmower. At present, the lawn is mowed using a small hand-pushed gas mower. The large, tractor-pulled mower will cost $16,950 and will have a useful life of 10 years. It will have only a negligible scrap value, which can be ignored. The tractor-pulled mower would do the job much more quickly than the old mower and would result in a labour savings of $3,000 per year.

To compute the internal rate of return promised by the new mower, we must find the discount rate that will cause the net present value of the project to be zero. How do we do this? The simplest and most direct approach *when the net cash inflow is the same every year* is to divide the investment in the project by the expected net annual cash inflow. This computation will yield a factor from which the internal rate of return can be determined. The formula is as follows:

$$\text{Factor of the internal rate of return} = \frac{\text{Investment required}}{\text{Net annual cash inflow}} \qquad (4)$$

The factor derived from this formula is then located in the present value tables to see what rate of return it represents. Using this formula and the data for Glendale School District's proposed project, we get:

$$\frac{\text{Investment required}}{\text{Net annual cash inflow}} = \frac{\$16{,}950}{\$3{,}000} = 5.650$$

Thus, the discount factor that will equate a series of $3,000 cash inflows with a present investment of $16,950 is 5.650. Now we need to find this factor in Exhibit 13–23 in Appendix 13A to see what rate of return it represents. We should use the 10-period line in Exhibit 13–23 since the cash flows for the project continue for 10 years. If we scan along the 10-period line, we find that a factor of 5.650 represents a 12% rate of return. Therefore, the internal rate of return promised by the mower project is 12%. We can verify this by computing the project's net present value using a 12% discount rate. This computation is shown in Exhibit 13–7.

Notice from Exhibit 13–7 that using a 12% discount rate equates the present value of the annual cash inflows with the present value of the investment required in the project, leaving a zero net present value. The 12% rate therefore represents the internal rate of return promised by the project.

Salvage Value and Other Cash Flows

The technique just demonstrated works very well if a project's cash flows are identical every year. But what if they are not? For example, what if a project will have some salvage value at the end of its life in addition to the annual cash inflows? Under these circumstances, a trial-and-error process is necessary to find the rate of return that will equate the cash inflows with the cash outflows. The trial-and-error

EXHIBIT 13–7 Evaluation of the Mower Purchase Using a 12% Discount Rate

Initial cost	$16,950
Life of the project (years)	10
Annual cost savings	$ 3,000
Salvage value	–0–

Item	Year(s)	Amount of Cash Flow	12% Factor	Present Value of Cash Flows
Annual cost savings	1–10	$ 3,000	5.650*	$ 16,950
Initial investment	Now	(16,950)	1.000	(16,950)
Net present value				$ –0–

*From Exhibit 13–23 in Appendix 13A.

process can be carried out by hand, or it can be carried out in seconds by means of computer software programs such as spreadsheets that perform the necessary computations. In short, erratic or uneven cash flows should not prevent a manager from determining a project's internal rate of return.

Using the Internal Rate of Return

Required rate of return The minimum rate of return that an investment project must yield to be acceptable.

Once the internal rate of return has been computed, what does the manager do with the information? The internal rate of return is compared to the company's *required rate of return.* The **required rate of return** is the minimum rate of return that an investment project must yield to be acceptable. If the internal rate of return is *equal* to or *greater* than the required rate of return, then the project is acceptable. If it is *less* than the required rate of return, then the project is rejected. Quite often, the company's cost of capital is used as the required rate of return. The reasoning is that if a project cannot provide a rate of return at least as great as the cost of the funds invested in it, then it is not profitable.

In the case of the Glendale School District example used earlier, let us assume that the district has set a minimum required rate of return of 15% on all projects. Since the large mower's internal rate of return is only 12%, it does not meet the criterion and would therefore be rejected as a project.

The Cost of Capital as a Screening Tool

As we have seen in preceding examples, the cost of capital often operates as a *screening* device, helping the manager screen out undesirable investment projects. This screening is accomplished in different ways, depending on whether the company is using the internal rate of return method or the net present value method in its capital budgeting analysis.

When the internal rate of return method is used, the cost of capital is used as the *hurdle rate* that a project must clear for acceptance. If the internal rate of return of a project is not great enough to clear the cost of capital hurdle, then the project is ordinarily rejected. We saw the application of this idea in the Glendale School District example, where the hurdle rate was set at 15%.

When the net present value method is used, the cost of capital is the *discount rate* used to compute the net present value of a proposed project. Any project yielding a negative net present value is rejected unless other factors are significant enough to require its acceptance.

The use of the cost of capital as a screening tool is summarized in Exhibit 13–8.

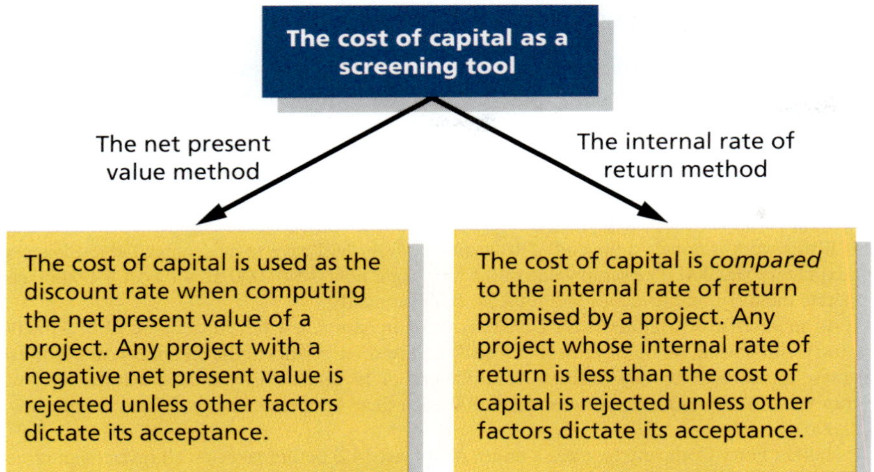

EXHIBIT 13–8 Capital Budgeting Screening Decisions

Comparison of the Net Present Value and the Internal Rate of Return Methods

The net present value method has several important advantages over the internal rate of return method.

First, the net present value method is often simpler to use. As mentioned earlier, the internal rate of return method may require using a trial-and-error process to find the discount rate that results in a net present value of zero. However, this very laborious process can be automated using a computer spreadsheet.

Second, the internal rate of return method makes a questionable assumption. Both methods assume that cash flows generated by a project during its useful life are immediately reinvested elsewhere. However, the two methods make different assumptions concerning the rate of return that is earned on those cash flows. The net present value method assumes that the rate of return is the discount rate, whereas the internal rate of return method assumes that the rate of return is the internal rate of return on the project. Specifically, if the internal rate of return of the project is high, this assumption may not be realistic. It is generally more realistic to assume that cash inflows can be reinvested at a rate of return equal to the discount rate—particularly if the discount rate is the company's cost of capital or an opportunity rate of return. For example, if the discount rate is the company's cost of capital, this rate of return can actually be realized by paying off the company's creditors and buying back the company's shares with cash flows from the project. In short, when the net present value method and the internal rate of return method do not agree concerning the attractiveness of a project, it is best to go with the net present value method. Of the two methods, it makes the more realistic assumption about the rate of return that can be earned on cash flows from the project.

Expanding the Net Present Value Method

So far all of our examples have involved only a single investment alternative. We will now expand the net present value method to include two alternatives. In addition, we will integrate the concept of relevant costs into the discounted cash flow analysis.

The net present value method can be used to compare competing investment projects in two ways. One is the *total-cost approach,* and the other is the *incremental-cost approach.* Each approach is illustrated in the following sections.

The Total-Cost Approach

The total-cost approach is the most flexible method for comparing competing projects. To illustrate the mechanics of the approach, let us assume the following data:

Example I

Halifax Ferry Company provides a ferry service across the Halifax Harbour. One of its ferryboats is in poor condition. This ferry can be renovated at an immediate cost of $200,000. Further repairs and an overhaul of the motor will be needed five years from now at a cost of $80,000. In all, the ferry will be usable for 10 years if this work is done. At the end of 10 years, the ferry will have to be scrapped at a salvage value of approximately $60,000. The scrap value of the ferry right now is $70,000. It will cost $300,000 each year to operate the ferry, and revenues will total $400,000 annually.

As an alternative, Halifax Ferry Company can purchase a new ferryboat at a cost of $360,000. The new ferry will have a life of 10 years, but it will require some repairs at the end of 5 years. It is estimated that these repairs will amount to $30,000. At the end of 10 years, it is estimated that the ferry will have a scrap value of $60,000. It will cost $210,000 each year to operate the ferry, and revenues will total $400,000 annually.

Halifax Ferry Company requires a return of at least 14% before taxes on all investment projects.

Should the company purchase the new ferry or renovate the old ferry? Using the total-cost approach, Exhibit 13–9 gives the solution.

Two points should be noted from the exhibit. First, *all* cash inflows and *all* cash outflows are included in the solution under each alternative. No effort has been made to isolate those cash flows that are relevant to the decision and those that are not relevant. The inclusion of all cash flows associated with each alternative gives the approach its name—the *total-cost* approach.

Second, notice that a net present value figure is computed for each of the two alternatives. This is a distinct advantage of the total-cost approach in that an unlimited number of alternatives can be compared side by side to determine the best action. For example, another alternative for Halifax Ferry Company would be to get out of the ferry business entirely. If management desired, the net present value of this alternative could be computed to compare with the alternatives shown in Exhibit 13–9. Still other alternatives might be open to the company. Once management has determined the net present value of each alternative that it wishes to consider, it can select the course of action that promises to be the most profitable. In this case, given only the two alternatives, the data indicate that the most profitable course is to purchase the new ferry.[3]

The Incremental-Cost Approach

When only two alternatives are being considered, the incremental-cost approach offers a simpler and more direct route to a decision. Unlike the total-cost approach, it focuses only on differential costs.[4] The procedure is to include in the discounted cash flow analysis only those costs and revenues that *differ* between the two alternatives being considered. To illustrate, refer again to the data in example I relating to Halifax Ferry Company. The solution using only differential costs is presented in Exhibit 13–10.

Two things should be noted from the data in this exhibit. First, notice that the net present value of $405,390 in favour of buying shown in Exhibit 13–10 agrees with the net present value shown under the total-cost approach in Exhibit 13–9. This agreement should be expected, since the two approaches are just different roads to the same destination.

Second, notice that the costs used in Exhibit 13–10 are just the differences between the costs shown for the two alternatives in the prior exhibit. For example, the $160,000 incremental investment required to purchase the new ferry in Exhibit 13–10 is the

3. The alternative with the highest net present value is not always the best choice, although it is the best choice in this case. For further discussion, see the section Preference Decisions—The Ranking of Investment Projects, later in this chapter.

4. Technically, the incremental-cost approach is misnamed, since it focuses on differential costs (that is, on both cost increases and decreases) rather than just on incremental costs. As used here, the term *incremental costs* should be interpreted broadly to include both cost increases and cost decreases.

EXHIBIT 13–9 The Total-Cost Approach to Project Selection

	New Ferry	Old Ferry
Annual revenues	$400,000	$400,000
Annual cash operating costs	210,000	300,000
Net annual cash inflows	$190,000	$100,000

Item	Year(s)	Amount of Cash Flows	14% Factor*	Present Value of Cash Flows
Buy the new ferry:				
Initial investment	Now	$(360,000)	1.000	$(360,000)
Repairs in five years	5	(30,000)	0.519	(15,570)
Net annual cash inflows	1–10	190,000	5.216	991,040
Salvage of the old ferry	Now	70,000	1.000	70,000
Salvage of the new ferry	10	60,000	0.270	16,200
Net present value				701,670
Keep the old ferry:				
Initial repairs	Now	$(200,000)	1.000	(200,000)
Repairs in five years	5	(80,000)	0.519	(41,520)
Net annual cash inflows	1–10	100,000	5.216	521,600
Salvage of the old ferry	10	60,000	0.270	16,200
Net present value				296,280
Net present value in favour of buying the new ferry				$405,390

*All factors are from Exhibits 13–22 and 13–23 in Appendix 13A.

difference between the $360,000 cost of the new ferry and the $200,000 cost required to renovate the old ferry from Exhibit 13–9. The other figures in Exhibit 13–10 have been computed in the same way.

Least-Cost Decisions

Some decisions do not involve revenues. For example, a company may be trying to decide whether to lease or to buy an executive jet. In situations such as this, where no revenues are involved, the most desirable alternative will be the one that promises the *least total*

EXHIBIT 13–10 The Incremental-Cost Approach to Project Selection

Item	Year(s)	Amount of Cash Flows	14% Factor*	Present Value of Cash Flows
Incremental investment required to purchase the new ferry	Now	$(160,000)	1.000	$(160,000)
Repairs in five years avoided	5	50,000	0.519	25,950
Increased net annual cash inflows	1–10	90,000	5.216	469,440
Salvage of the old ferry	Now	70,000	1.000	70,000
Difference in salvage value in 10 years	10	–0–	0.270	–0–
Net present value in favour of buying the new ferry				$405,390

*All factors are from Exhibits 13–22 and 13–23 in Appendix 13A.

cost from the present value perspective. Hence, these are known as least-cost decisions. To illustrate a least-cost decision, assume the following data:

Example J

Val-Tek Company is considering the replacement of an old threading machine. A new threading machine is available that could substantially reduce annual operating costs. Selected data relating to the old and the new machines are presented below:

	Old Machine	New Machine
Purchase cost when new	$200,000	$250,000
Salvage value now	30,000	—
Annual cash operating costs	150,000	90,000
Overhaul needed immediately	40,000	—
Salvage value in six years	-0-	50,000
Remaining life	6 years	6 years

Val-Tek Company's cost of capital is 10%.

Exhibit 13–11 presents the alternatives using the total-cost approach. As shown in the exhibit, the new machine has the lowest total cost when the present value of the net cash outflows is considered. An analysis of the two alternatives using the incremental-cost approach is presented in Exhibit 13–12. As before, the data in this exhibit represent the differences between the alternatives after all irrelevant cash flows have been eliminated, namely those that do not change with a change in alternatives.

EXHIBIT 13–11 The Total-Cost Approach (Least-Cost Decision)

Item	Year(s)	Amount of Cash Flows	10% Factor*	Present Value of Cash Flows
Buy the new machine:				
Initial investment	Now	$(250,000)	1.000	$(250,000)†
Salvage of the old machine	Now	30,000	1.000	30,000†
Annual cash operating costs	1–6	(90,000)	4.355	(391,950)
Salvage of the new machine	6	50,000	0.564	28,200
Present value of net cash outflows				(583,750)
Keep the old machine:				
Overhaul needed now	Now	$ (40,000)	1.000	$ (40,000)
Annual cash operating costs	1–6	(150,000)	4.355	(653,250)
Present value of net cash outflows				(693,250)
Net present value in favour of buying the new machine				$ 109,500

*All factors are from Exhibits 13–22 and 13–23 in Appendix 13A.

†These two items could be netted into a single $220,000 incremental-cost figure ($250,000 − $30,000 = $220,000).

EXHIBIT 13–12 The Incremental-Cost Approach (Least-Cost Decision)

Item	Year(s)	Amount of Cash Flows	10% Factor*	Present Value of Cash Flows
Incremental investment required to purchase the new machine	Now	$(210,000)	1.000	$(210,000)†
Salvage of the old machine	Now	30,000	1.000	30,000†
Savings in annual cash operating costs	1–6	60,000	4.355	261,300
Difference in salvage value in six years	6	50,000	0.564	28,200
Net present value in favour of buying the new machine				$109,500

*All factors are from Exhibits 13–22 and 13–23 in Appendix 13A.

†These two items could be netted into a single $180,000 incremental-cost figure ($210,000 − $30,000 = $180,000).

Capital Budgeting and Non-Profit Organizations

Capital budgeting concepts can be applied in all types of organizations. Note, for example, the different types of organizations used in the examples in this chapter. These organizations include a dental clinic, a company working under a licensing agreement, a school district, a company operating a ferryboat service, and a manufacturing company. The diversity of these examples shows the range and power of discounted cash flow methods.

One problem faced by *non-profit* organizations in capital budgeting is determining the proper discount rate. Some non-profit organizations use, as their discount rate, the rate of interest that could be earned by placing money in an endowment fund rather than spending it on capital improvements, and others use discount rates that are set somewhat arbitrarily by governing boards.

The greatest danger lies in using a discount rate that is too low. Most government agencies, for example, at one time used the interest rate on government bonds as their discount rate. It is now recognized that this rate is too low and has resulted in the acceptance of many projects that should not have been undertaken.[5] The problem has not been resolved in Canada but in the United States, the Office of Management and Budget has specified that federal government units must use a discount rate of at least 10% on all projects.[6] For non-profit units such as schools and hospitals, it is generally recommended that the discount rate should "approximate the average rate of return on private sector investments."[7]

Uncertain Cash Flows

LEARNING OBJECTIVE 5
Evaluate an investment project that has uncertain cash flows.

The analysis to this point in the chapter has assumed that all of the future cash flows are known with certainty. However, future cash flows are often uncertain or difficult to estimate. A number of techniques are available for handling this complication. Some of these techniques are quite technical—involving computer simulations or advanced mathematical skills—and some are beyond the scope of this book. However, we can provide some very useful information to managers without getting too technical.

5. See *Federal Capital Budgeting: A Collection of Haphazard Practices*, GAO, P.O. Box 6015, Gaithersburg, MD, PAD-81-19, February 26, 1981.
6. *Office of Management and Budget Circular No. A-94*, March 1972. The U.S. Postal Service is exempted from the 10% rate as are all water resource projects and all lease or buy decisions.
7. Robert N. Anthony and David W. Young, *Management Control in Nonprofit Organizations*, 5th ed. (Homewood, IL: Richard D. Irwin, Inc., 1994), p. 445.

An Example of Uncertain Cash Flows

As an example of difficult-to-estimate future cash flows, consider the case of investments in automated equipment. The up-front costs of automated equipment and the tangible benefits, such as reductions in operating costs and waste, tend to be relatively easy to estimate. However, the intangible benefits, such as greater reliability, greater speed, and higher quality, are more difficult to quantify in terms of future cash flows. These intangible benefits certainly affect future cash flows—particularly in terms of increased sales and perhaps higher selling prices—but the cash flow effects are difficult to estimate. What can be done?

A fairly simple procedure can be followed when the intangible benefits are likely to be significant. Suppose, for example, that a company with a 12% cost of capital is considering purchasing automated equipment that would have a 10-year useful life. Also suppose that a discounted cash flow analysis of just the tangible costs and benefits shows a negative net present value of $226,000. Clearly, if the intangible benefits are large enough, they could turn this negative net present value into a positive net present value. In this case, the amount of additional cash flow per year from the intangible benefits that would be needed to make the project financially attractive can be computed as follows:

Net present value excluding the intangible benefits (negative)	$(226,000)
Present value factor for an annuity at 12% for 10 periods (from Exhibit 13–23 in Appendix 13A)	5.650

$$\frac{\text{Net present value, \$(226,000)}}{\text{Present value factor, 5.650}} = \$40,000$$

Thus, if intangible benefits such as greater flexibility, higher quality of output, and avoidance of capital decay are worth at least $40,000 per year to the company, then the automated equipment should be purchased. If, in the judgement of management, these intangible benefits are *not* worth $40,000 per year, then the automated equipment should not be purchased.

This technique can be used in other situations in which the future benefits of a current investment are uncertain or intangible. For example, this technique can be used when the salvage value is difficult to estimate. To illustrate, suppose that all of the cash flows from an investment in a supertanker have been estimated, other than its salvage value in 20 years. Using a discount rate of 12%, management has determined that the net present value of all these cash flows is a negative $1.04 million. This negative net present value would be offset by the salvage value of the supertanker. How large would the salvage value have to be to make this investment attractive?

Net present value excluding salvage value (negative)	$(1,040,000)
Present value factor at 12% for 20 periods (from Exhibit 13–22 in Appendix 13A)	0.104

$$\frac{\text{Net present value to be offset, \$1,040,000}}{\text{Present value factor, 0.104}} = \$10,000,000$$

Thus, if the salvage value of the tanker in 20 years is at least $10 million, its net present value would be positive and the investment would be made. However, if management believes the salvage value is unlikely to be as large as $10 million, the investment should not be made.

Real Options

The analysis in this chapter has assumed that an investment cannot be postponed and that, once started, nothing can be done to alter the course of the project. In reality, investments can often be postponed. Postponement is a particularly attractive option when the net present value of the project is modest using current estimates of future cash flows, but the future cash flows involve a great deal of uncertainty that may be resolved over time.

Similarly, once an investment is made, management can often exploit changes in the business environment and take actions that enhance future cash flows. For example, buying a supertanker provides management with a number of options, some of which may become more attractive as time passes. Instead of operating the supertanker itself, the company may decide to lease it to another operator if the rental rates become high enough. Or, if a supertanker shortage develops, management may decide to sell the supertanker and take a gain. In the case of an investment in automated equipment, management may initially buy only the basic model without costly add-ons, but keep the option open to add more capacity and capability later.

The ability to delay the start of a project, to expand it if conditions are favourable, to cut losses if they are unfavourable, and to otherwise modify plans as business conditions change adds value to many investments. These advantages can be quantified using what is called *real option analysis*, but the techniques are beyond the scope of this book.

Preference Decisions–The Ranking of Investment Projects

LEARNING OBJECTIVE 6
Rank investment projects in order of preference.

When considering investment opportunities, managers must make two types of decisions—screening decisions and preference decisions. Screening decisions, which come first, pertain to whether or not some proposed investment is acceptable. Preference decisions come *after* screening decisions and attempt to answer the following question: "How do the remaining investment proposals, all of which have been screened and provide an acceptable rate of return, rank in terms of preference? That is, which one(s) would be *best* for the firm to accept?"

Preference decisions are more difficult to make than screening decisions because investment funds are usually limited. This often requires that some (perhaps many) otherwise very profitable investment opportunities must be passed up.

Sometimes preference decisions are called *ranking decisions*, or *rationing decisions*, because they ration limited investment funds among many competing alternatives. Hence, the more reliable alternatives must be ranked. Either the internal rate of return method or the net present value method can be used in making preference decisions. However, as discussed earlier, if the two methods are in conflict, it is best to use the more reliable net present value method.

IN BUSINESS

With an eye on environmental concerns, the board of directors of Royal Dutch/Shell, the Anglo-Dutch energy company, has decided that all large projects must explicitly take into account the likely future costs of abating carbon emissions. Calculations must assume a cost of $5 per tonne of carbon dioxide emission in 2005 through 2009, rising to $20 per tonne from 2010 onward. A Shell manager explains: "We know that $5 and $20 are surely the wrong prices, but everyone else who assumes a carbon price of zero in the future will be more wrong. This is not altruism. We see it as giving us a competitive edge."

Source: "Big Business Bows to Global Warming," *The Economist*, December 2, 2000, p. 1.

Internal Rate of Return Method

When using the internal rate of return method to rank competing investment projects, the preference rule is: *The higher the internal rate of return, the more desirable the project.* An investment project with an internal rate of return of 18% is preferable to another project that promises a return of only 15%. Internal rate of return is widely used to rank projects.

Net Present Value Method

Unfortunately, the net present value of one project cannot be compared directly to the net present value of another project unless the investments in the projects are of equal size. For example, assume that a company is considering two competing investments, as shown below:

	Investment	
	A	B
Investment required	$(80,000)	$(5,000)
Present value of cash inflows.	81,000	6,000
Net present value	$ 1,000	$ 1,000

Although each project has a net present value of $1,000, the projects are not equally desirable if funds available for investment are limited. The project requiring an investment of only $5,000 is much more desirable when funds are limited than the project requiring an investment of $80,000. To compare the two projects on a valid basis, the present value of the cash inflows should be divided by the investment required. The result is called the **profitability index**. The formula for the profitability index follows:

Profitability index
The ratio of the present value of a project's cash inflows to the investment required.

$$\text{Profitability index} = \frac{\text{Present value of cash inflows}}{\text{Investment required}} \tag{5}$$

The profitability indexes for the two investments above would be computed as follows:

	Investment	
	A	B
Present value of cash inflows (a)	$81,000	$6,000
Investment required (b).	$80,000	$5,000
Profitability index, (a) ÷ (b)	1.01	1.20

When using the profitability index to rank competing investment projects, the preference rule is: *The higher the profitability index, the more desirable the project.* Applying this rule to the two investments above, investment B should be chosen over investment A.

The profitability index is an application of the techniques for utilizing scarce resources discussed in Chapter 12. In this case, the scarce resource is the limited funds available for investment, and the profitability index is similar to the contribution margin per unit of the scarce resource.

A few details should be clarified with respect to the computation of the profitability index. The "Investment required" refers to any cash outflows that occur at the beginning of the project, reduced by any salvage value recovered from the sale of old equipment. "Investment required" also includes any investment in working capital that the project may need.

Comparing the Preference Rules

The profitability index is conceptually superior to the internal rate of return as a method of making preference decisions. This is because the profitability index will always give the correct signal as to the relative desirability of alternatives, even if the alternatives have different lives and different patterns of earnings. By contrast, if lives are unequal, the internal rate of return method can lead the manager to make incorrect decisions. Assume the following situation:

Example K

Parker Company is considering two investment proposals, only one of which can be accepted. Project A requires an investment of $5,000 and will provide a single cash inflow of $6,000 in one year. Therefore, it promises an internal rate of return of 20%. Project B also requires an investment of $5,000. It will provide cash inflows of $1,360 each year for six years. Its internal rate of return is 16%. Which project should be accepted?

Although project A promises an internal rate of return of 20%, as compared to only 16% for project B, project A is not necessarily preferable over project B. It is preferable *only* if the funds released at the end of the year under project A can be reinvested at a high rate of return in some *other* project for the five remaining years. Otherwise, project B, which promises a return of 16% over the *entire* six years, is more desirable.

Let us assume that the company in this example has an after-tax cost of capital of 12%. The net present value method, with the profitability index, would rank the two proposals as follows:

	Project	
	A	B
Present value of cash inflows:		
$6,000 received at the end of one year at 12% factor (factor of 0.893)	$5,358 (a)	
$1,360 received at the end of each year for six years at 12% (factor of 4.111)		$5,591 (a)
Investment required	$5,000 (b)	$5,000 (b)
Profitability index, (a) ÷ (b)	1.07	1.12

The profitability index indicates that project B is more desirable than project A. This is in fact the case if the funds released from project A at the end of one year can be reinvested at only 12% (the cost of capital). Although the computations will not be shown here, in order for project A to be more desirable than project B, the funds released from project A would have to be reinvested at a rate of return *greater* than 14% for the remaining five years.

In short, the internal rate of return method of ranking tends to favour short-term, high-yield projects, whereas the net present value method of ranking (using the profitability index) tends to favour longer-term projects.

The internal rate of return method is problematic. It assumes that funds can be reinvested at a particular project's yield. The problem becomes apparent in the context of MacInnis Company of Kitchener, Ontario. If MacInnis has projects in Cambridge, Guelph, and Waterloo that have internal rates of return of 20%, 15%, and 10%, respectively, it is nonsense to differentiate among the cash flows and assume that a dollar returned from the Waterloo project will earn less than a dollar returned from the Cambridge project. Obviously, a dollar is a dollar regardless of the project from which it comes. The net present value method does not suffer from this flaw but assumes that funds can be reinvested at the firm's cost of capital. Because the net present value is conceptually superior, it should be used in ranking projects that are mutually exclusive. However, in choosing among projects that have the same net present values, the internal rates of return should be used to rank them. Projects should then be chosen based on the highest internal rates of return.

Although the net present value method is conceptually superior to the internal rate of return method, there are practical reasons for decision makers to choose the latter. Managers typically make project investment decisions within a four- or five-year planning horizon. Faced with this time constraint, projects will be ranked according to their terminal values at the end of the planning horizon. Estimated cash flows after the planning period may be perceived by managers to be too uncertain to be reliable. Projects with larger internal rate of return values will have cash flow patterns with higher short-term terminal values. In summary, although there are problems with the internal rate of return method over the entire life of a project, it will accurately evaluate projects within the planning horizon.

Post-Appraisal of Investment Projects

Post-appraisal
Following up on a project that has been approved to see if expected results are realized.

A *post-appraisal* should be conducted after an investment project has been approved and implemented. A **post-appraisal** involves checking whether or not expected results are actually realized. This is a key part of the capital budgeting process that helps keep managers committed to their investment proposals. Any tendency to inflate the benefits or downplay the costs in a proposal should become evident after the post-appraisal. The post-appraisal also provides an opportunity to reinforce and possibly expand successful projects and to cut losses on floundering projects.

The same capital budgeting method should be used in the post-appraisal that was used in the original approval process. That is, if a project was approved on the basis of a net present value analysis, then the same procedure should be used in performing the post-appraisal. However, the data used in the post-appraisal analysis should be *actual observed data* rather than estimated data. This gives management an opportunity to make a side-by-side comparison to see how well the project has succeeded. It also helps assure that estimated data received on future proposals will be carefully prepared, since the persons submitting the data will know that their estimates will be compared to the actual results in the post-appraisal process.

Monitoring of capital budgeting projects may also help improve the quality of similar investment proposals. Care should be exercised, however, when trying to use past experience as a guide to future decisions because assumptions about the business environment may no longer be valid.

To avoid a liquidity crunch, the firm must respond quickly to significant overruns that require unplanned cash outflows. It may be necessary to arrange additional financing or to amend plans.

The post-appraisal should answer a variety of questions: Was the capital budgeting decision consistent with overall corporate strategy? Did the project meet the specifications that were set out in the appropriation request? Were the original specifications realistically and honestly determined? Were any additional expenditures properly authorized? A proper review may be tedious and time-consuming, and special care should be taken in making assertions about cause and effect. It is often difficult to relate particular costs and revenues to a specific project. This is especially true if there are several projects on-line simultaneously and is absolutely true if there is synergy among the projects.[8] A cost/benefit trade-off is necessary when deciding how many company sources are to be devoted to the post-appraisal.

To ensure objectivity, the post-appraisal should be performed by an individual or team that has not been directly involved in the actual project. The post-appraisal should not be aimed at placing blame, but should be an accountability process aimed at improving control and a learning process that will improve estimates of future projects.

---

8. Synergy occurs when the projects working together generate greater revenue than the sum of the revenues of all projects acting independently.

IN BUSINESS

The post-appraisal process can be applied in the context of *economic value creation* (EVA®). Economic value is a financial performance measure based on a firm's residual wealth calculated by deducting cost of capital from its net operating profit[1] after taxes as expressed by the following formula:

$$\text{EVA} = \text{NOPAT} - \text{Capital charge}$$

For example, assume that a firm employing $2,500,000 of capital with a 15% cost of capital reports a net operating profit after taxes of $1,000,000. EVA would equal $625,000.

$$\text{EVA}^{®} = \$1{,}000{,}000 - (15\% \times \$2{,}500{,}000) = \$625{,}000$$

When considering strategic or major operating decisions, 15 (73%) of the respondents in a recent Canadian study indicated that they ''always'' or ''often'' explicitly use EVA to evaluate their decisions.

Supporters of EVA claim that it allows managers to measure actual value creation performance and that EVA tracks shareholder wealth better than traditional accounting measures such as net income or earnings per share. The Canadian study found inconclusive evidence on whether the effect of EVA actually brings about greater shareholder value. Of the companies surveyed 50% were underperforming their TSX sectoral indices. Of the other 50%, 36% are outperforming their TSX sectoral indices, and the remaining companies were at a similar level with comparable companies that did not use EVA.

Source: Howard Armitage, Ellen Wong, and Alan Douglas, "The Pursuit of Value," *CMA Management Accounting Magazine*, November 2003.

1. It is common to adjust NOPAT for so called "accounting distortions" affecting inventory, deferred taxes and intangibles. Adjustments, for example, include capitalizing operating leases and adding back Research and Development cost and other intangible costs.

Income Taxes in Capital Budgeting Decisions

LEARNING OBJECTIVE 7
Include income taxes in a capital budgeting analysis.

In our discussion of capital budgeting, we ignored income taxes until now for two reasons. First, some organizations do not pay income taxes. Not-for-profit organizations, such as hospitals and charitable foundations, and governmental agencies are exempt from income taxes. Second, capital budgeting is complex and is best absorbed in small doses. Now that we have a solid groundwork in the concepts of present value and discounting, we can explore the effects of income taxes on capital budgeting decisions.

The Canadian income tax regulations are enormously complex. We only scratch the surface in this text. To keep the subject within reasonable bounds, we have made many simplifying assumptions about the tax regulations throughout this section. Among the most important of these assumptions are: (1) taxable income equals net income as computed for financial reports; and (2) the tax rate is a flat percentage of taxable income. The actual tax regulations are far more complex than this; however, the simplifications that we make throughout this section allow us to cover the most important implications of income taxes for capital budgeting without getting bogged down in details.

The Concept of After-Tax Cost

Businesses, like individuals, must pay income taxes. In the case of businesses, the amount of income tax that must be paid is determined by the company's net taxable income.

Tax-deductible expenses (tax deductions) decrease the company's net taxable income and hence reduce the taxes the company must pay. For this reason, expenses are often stated on an *after-tax* basis. For example, if a company pays rent of $10 million per year but this expense results in a reduction in income taxes of $3 million, the after-tax cost of the rent is $7 million. An expenditure net of its tax effect is known as **after-tax cost**.

After-tax cost
The amount of net cash outflow resulting from a tax-deductible cash expense after income tax effects have been considered. The amount is determined by multiplying the tax-deductible cash expense by (1 – Tax rate).

To illustrate, assume that a company with a tax rate of 30% is contemplating a training program that costs $60,000. What impact will this have on the company's taxes? To keep matters simple, let's suppose the training program has no immediate effect on sales. How much does the company actually pay for the training program after taking into account the impact of this expense on taxes? The answer is $42,000 as shown in Exhibit 13–13. While the training program costs $60,000 before taxes, it would reduce the company's taxes by $18,000, so its *after-tax* cost would be only $42,000. This $18,000 reduction in taxes can also be calculated directly by simply multiplying $60,000 by the 30% tax rate.

The after-tax cost of any tax-deductible cash expense can be determined using the following formula:[9]

$$\begin{array}{c}\text{After-tax cost}\\ \text{(net cash outflow)}\end{array} = (1 - \text{Tax rate}) \times \text{Tax-deductible cash expense} \qquad (6)$$

We can verify the accuracy of this formula by applying it to the $60,000 training program expenditure:

$$(1 - 0.30) \times \$60{,}000 = \$42{,}000 \text{ after-tax cost of the training program}$$

After-tax benefit
The amount of net cash inflow realized from a taxable cash receipt after income tax effects have been considered. The amount is determined by multiplying the taxable cash receipt by (1 – Tax rate).

This formula is very useful since it provides the actual amount of cash a company must pay after taking into consideration tax effects. It is this actual, after-tax, cash outflow that should be used in capital budgeting decisions.

Similar reasoning applies to revenues and other *taxable* cash inflows. Since these cash receipts are taxable, the company must pay out a portion of them in taxes. The **after-tax benefit,** or net cash inflow, realized from a particular cash receipt can be obtained by applying a simple variation of the cash expenditure formula used above:

EXHIBIT 13–13 The Computation of After-Tax Cost

	Without Training Program	With Training Program
Sales	$850,000	$850,000
Less tax-deductible expenses:		
Salaries, insurance, and other	700,000	700,000
New training program		60,000
Total expenses	700,000	760,000
Taxable income	$150,000	$ 90,000
Income taxes (30%)	$ 45,000	$ 27,000

Cost of new training program	$60,000
Less: Reduction in income taxes ($45,000 – $27,000)	18,000
After-tax cost of the new training program	$42,000

9. This formula assumes that a company is operating at a profit; if it is operating at a loss, the tax situation can be very complex. For simplicity, we assume in all examples, exercises, and problems that the company is operating at a profit.

$$\text{After-tax benefit (net cash inflow)} = (1 - \text{Tax rate}) \times \text{Taxable cash receipt} \qquad (7)$$

We emphasize the term *taxable cash receipt* because not all cash inflows are taxable. For example, the release of working capital at the termination of an investment project would not be a taxable cash inflow. It is not counted as income for either financial accounting or income tax reporting purposes since it is simply a recovery of the initial investment.

Capital Cost Allowance (CCA) Tax Shield

Because capital cost allowance (CCA) is not a cash flow, it was ignored in this chapter in all discounted cash flow computations. However, CCA does affect the taxes that must be paid and therefore has an indirect effect on the company's cash flows.

To illustrate the effect of CCA deductions on tax payments, consider a company with annual cash sales of $500,000 and cash operating expenses of $310,000. In addition, the company has a depreciable asset on which the CCA deduction is $90,000 per year. The tax rate is 30%. As shown in Exhibit 13–14, the CCA deduction reduces the company's taxes by $27,000. In effect, the CCA deduction of $90,000 *shields* $90,000 in revenues from taxation and thereby *reduces* the amount of taxes that the company must pay. Because CCA deductions shield revenues from taxation, they are generally referred to as a **capital cost allowance tax shield.**[10] The reduction in tax payments made possible by the CCA tax shield is equal to the amount of the CCA deduction, multiplied by the tax rate as follows:

$$\text{Tax savings from the CCA tax shield} = \text{Tax rate} \times \text{CCA deduction} \qquad (8)$$

We can verify this formula by applying it to the $90,000 CCA deduction in our example:

$$0.30 \times \$90{,}000 = \$27{,}000 \text{ reduction in tax payments}$$

In this section, when we estimate after-tax cash flows for capital budgeting decisions, we will include the tax savings provided by the CCA tax shield.

Rules for CCA are complex and most companies take advantage of accelerated methods allowed under the tax regulations. These accelerated methods usually result in a reduction in current taxes and an offsetting increase in future taxes. This shifting of part of the tax burden from the current year to future years is advantageous from a present value point of view, since a dollar today is worth more than a dollar in the future. A summary of the concepts we have introduced so far is given in Exhibit 13–15.

Capital Cost Allowance Instead of Depreciation

Capital cost allowance is the Canada Revenue Agency's counterpart to depreciation. Depreciation is the allocation of the cost of an asset over its useful life. The amount deducted each period for financial statement reporting purposes is based on generally accepted accounting principles (GAAP). For income tax purposes, however, depreciation is not an allowable expense. Instead, a capital cost allowance is permitted by regulations that accompany the Canadian Income Tax Act. A CCA deduction is allowed for business-

10. The term *capital cost allowance tax shield* may convey the impression that there is something underhanded about capital cost allowance deductions—that companies are getting some sort of a special tax break. However, to use the CCA deduction, a company must have already acquired a depreciable asset—which typically requires a cash outflow. Essentially, the tax regulations require companies to delay recognizing the cash outflow as an expense until CCA charges are recorded.

EXHIBIT 13–14 The Effect of CCA Deductions on Tax Payments

	Without CCA Deduction	With CCA Deduction
Sales	$500,000	$500,000
Cash operating expenses	310,000	310,000
Cash flow from operations	190,000	190,000
Capital cost allowance	—	90,000
Taxable income	$190,000	$100,000
Income taxes (30%)	$ 57,000	$ 30,000

$27,000 lower taxes with the CCA deduction

Cash flow comparison:		
Cash flow from operations (above)	$190,000	$190,000
Income taxes (above)	57,000	30,000
Net cash flow	$133,000	$160,000

$27,000 greater cash flow with the CCA deduction

related capital property such as equipment and automobiles. See Exhibit 13–15 for a summary of required adjustments when income taxes are considered.

The income tax regulations group assets into classes and each class is then assigned a maximum capital cost allowance rate for tax reporting purposes. Maximum capital cost allowance rates are prescribed by the regulations in the Income Tax Act for approximately 44 classes or pools of assets. A company has the option of deducting capital cost allowance for each asset class for any amount ranging from zero to the maximum amount prescribed by the Act. The CCA rate applicable to each class is usually intended to reflect the economic life of the assets of that class. Where the CCA rate is clearly in excess of that required to reflect the economic useful life, it can be considered to be an accelerated CCA.

These prescribed rates are subject to governmental change. Examples of these assets pools and maximum prescribed rates follow:

Asset	Class	Maximum Rate
Non-residential buildings	1	6%
Automobiles	10	30%
Computer equipment	45	55%
Computer software	12	100%
Assets not included in other classes	8	20%

EXHIBIT 13–15 Tax Adjustments Required in a Capital Budgeting Analysis

Item	Treatment
Tax-deductible cash expense*	Multiply by (1 − Tax rate) to get after-tax cost.
Taxable cash receipt*	Multiply by (1 − Tax rate) to get after-tax cash inflow.
CCA deduction	Multiply by the tax rate to get the tax savings from the CCA tax shield.

*Cash expenses can be deducted from the cash receipts and the difference multiplied by (1 – Tax rate). See the example at the top of Exhibit 13–16 on page 651.

Capital cost allowance is calculated essentially by applying the prescribed rate to a declining balance called the **undepreciated capital cost (UCC)**. For net additions to each asset class during the year, however, only one-half of the prescribed rate is permitted. Under this half-year rule, only half of the normal CCA for most assets is allowed as a tax-deductible expense in the year during which the asset is acquired. The management accountant may occasionally have to seek the advice of a tax expert to assist in capital budgeting analysis.

Undepreciated capital cost (UCC)
The remaining book value of an asset class or pool of assets that is available for tax-deductible depreciation (capital cost allowance). The maximum amount of capital cost allowance that can be deducted in a taxation year of a particular CCA class is the UCC multiplied by the CCA rate for that asset class.

Example L

Toronto Ltd. has obtained a $30,000 loan to acquire a truck. Assuming that the company will have a taxable income indefinitely into the future, calculate the present value of the capital cost allowance tax shield for the first three years if the cost of capital is 10% and the tax rate is 40%.

(1) Year	(2) Undepreciated Capital Cost	(3) CCA (2) × 30%	(4) Tax Savings (3) × 40%	(5) PV Factor at 10 %	(6) PV of Tax Savings (4) × (5)
1	$30,000	$4,500*	$1,800	0.909	$1,636
2	25,500	7,650	3,060	0.826	2,528
3	17,850	5,355	2,142	0.751	1,609

*$30,000 × .30 × (1/2) = $4,500

Because the capital cost allowance is calculated on a declining balance of a pool of assets rather than on a single asset, a business is able to obtain tax savings from a project even after its disposition. As long as there are other assets in the pool and the proceeds from disposal are less than the UCC for the class, tax savings can be realized in perpetuity.

It can be shown mathematically that the present value of this infinite stream of tax savings from a declining balance capital cost allowance is calculated by what is referred to as the *CCA tax shield formula*:

$$PV = \frac{Cdt}{d + k} \times \frac{1 + 0.5k}{1 + k} \qquad (9)$$

where

C = The capital cost of the asset added to the asset pool.
d = CCA rate.
t = The firm's marginal income tax rate.
k = The cost of capital.

$\frac{1 + 0.5k}{1 + k}$ = The correction factor to account for the provision that only one-half of the capital cost of an asset is included in UCC during the year of acquisition.

For the previous example, the present value of the CCA tax shield is:

$$\frac{\$30{,}000 \times 0.3 \times 0.4}{0.3 + 0.10} \times \frac{1 + 0.5 \times 0.10}{1 + 0.10} = \$9{,}000 \times 0.95455 = \$8{,}591$$

Example M

Using the data in the previous example, calculate the present value of the CCA tax shield, assuming that other assets remain in the pool and the asset is disposed of for $6,000 after five years' use.

The sale of the asset results in a cash inflow at the end of year 5. This disposal results in the asset pool balance (UCC) being reduced by the $6,000 proceeds. The present value of the CCA tax shield is also reduced, because from the end of year 5 onward, CCA will be applied to a smaller UCC balance than it otherwise would have been without the asset disposal. If S represents salvage value, the CCA tax shield formula must be adjusted by deducting:

$$\frac{Sdt}{d + k} \times (1 + k)^{-n} \tag{10}$$

where

$$\frac{Sdt}{d + k}$$

calculates the present value of the lost tax shield at the end of year 5 ($n = 5$). This lost tax shield is then discounted to time period zero by multiplying it by $(1 + k)^{-n}$ or by using Exhibit 13–22. The present value of the tax shield is calculated to be $7,473.

IN BUSINESS

Managers should be alert to income tax changes that could have an effect on the company's bottom line. For example, in the 2004 Federal Budget capital cost allowance changes were made that allowed companies to depreciate computers and computer infrastructure 50% more aggressively. The previous CCA rate of 30% was increased to 45% of the undepreciated value (UCC). The CCA rate for broadband, Internet and other data-network infrastructure equipment was increased from 20% to 30%. In the 2007 Federal Budget the CCA on computer equipment was increased to 55%. Keeping up to date with tax changes can be quite challenging.

Example of Income Taxes and Capital Budgeting

Armed with an understanding of after-tax cost, after-tax revenue, and the CCA tax shield, we are now prepared to examine a comprehensive example of income taxes and capital budgeting.

Holland Company owns the mineral rights to land that has a deposit of ore. The company is uncertain whether it should purchase equipment and open a mine on the property. After careful study, the following data have been assembled by the company:

Cost of equipment needed	$300,000
Working capital needed	75,000
Estimated annual cash receipts from sales of ore	250,000
Estimated annual cash expenses for salaries, insurance, utilities, and other cash expenses of mining the ore	170,000
Cost of road repairs needed in 6 years	40,000
Salvage value of the equipment in 10 years	100,000

The ore in the mine would be exhausted after 10 years of mining activity, at which time the mine would be closed. The equipment would then be sold for its salvage value. Holland Company uses a 20% rate, assuming no salvage value, to compute CCA deductions for tax purposes. The company's after-tax cost of capital is 12% and its tax rate is 30%.

Should Holland Company purchase the equipment and open a mine on the property? The solution to the problem is given in Exhibit 13–16. We suggest that you go through this solution item by item and note the following points:

Cost of new equipment. The initial investment of $300,000 in the new equipment is included in full, with no reductions for taxes. This represents an *investment,* not an expense, so no tax adjustment is made. (Only revenues and expenses are adjusted for the effects of taxes.) However, this investment does affect taxes through the CCA deductions that are considered below.

Working capital. Observe that the working capital needed for the project is included in full, with no reductions for taxes. Like the cost of new equipment, working capital is an investment and not an expense so no tax adjustment is made. Also observe that no tax adjustment is made when the working capital is released at the end of the project's life. The release of working capital is not a taxable cash flow, since it merely represents a return of investment funds back to the company.

Net annual cash receipts. The net annual cash receipts from sales of ore are adjusted for the effects of income taxes, as discussed earlier in the chapter. Note at the top of Exhibit 13–16 that the annual cash expenses are deducted from the annual cash receipts to obtain the net cash receipts. This just simplifies computations.

Road repairs. Since the road repairs occur just once (in the sixth year), they are treated separately from other expenses. Road repairs would be a tax-deductible cash expense, and therefore they are adjusted for the effects of income taxes, as discussed earlier in the chapter.

Capital cost allowance deductions. The tax savings provided by CCA deductions are essentially an annuity that is included in the present value computations using the CCA tax shield formula.

Salvage value of equipment. The salvage value of $100,000 results in the present value inflow of $32,200. However, later in the analysis, note that the present value of the tax shield is reduced. The value of $6,900 is the present value at the end of year 10 of the

EXHIBIT 13–16 Example of Income Taxes and Capital Budgeting

	Per Year
Cash receipts from sales of ore	$250,000
Less payments for salaries, insurance, utilities, and other cash expenses	170,000
Net cash receipts	$ 80,000

Items and Computations	Year(s)	(1) Amount	(2) Tax Effect*	After-Tax Cash Flows (1) × (2)	12% Factor	Present Value of Cash Flows
Cost of new equipment	Now	$(300,000)	—	$(300,000)	1.000	$(300,000)
Working capital needed	Now	(75,000)	—	(75,000)	1.000	(75,000)
Net annual cash receipts	1–10	80,000	1–0.30	56,000	5.650	316,400
Road repairs	6	(40,000)	1–0.30	(28,000)	.507	(14,196)
Salvage value of equipment	10	100,000	—	100,000	.322	32,200
Release of working capital	10	75,000	—	75,000	.322	24,150
Subtotal						$ (16,446)

Present value of CCA tax shield:

$$PV = \frac{Cdt}{d+k} \times \frac{(1+.5k)}{1+k} - \frac{S \times d \times t}{d+k} \times (1+k)^{-n}$$

$$PV = \frac{\$300{,}000 \times .3 \times .3}{.3+.12} \times \frac{1.06}{1.12} - \frac{\$100{,}000 \times .3 \times .3}{.3+.12} \times (1+.12)^{-10}$$

$$PV = \$64{,}285.71 \times .9464 - \$21{,}428.57 \times .322$$

$PV = \$60{,}840.00 - \$6{,}900.00$ 53,940

Net present value .... $ 37,494

*Taxable cash receipts and tax-deductible cash expenses are multiplied by (1 − Tax rate) to determine the after-tax cash flow. CCA deductions are multiplied by the tax rate itself to determine the after-tax cash flow (i.e., tax savings from the CCA tax shield).

lost tax shield from the salvage. This amount therefore must be discounted to *now* by multiplying it by the present value factor of $1 at the end of 10 periods $(1 + 0.12)^{-10}$.

Since the net present value of the proposed mining project is positive, the equipment should be purchased and the mine opened. Study Exhibit 13–16 thoroughly—*it is a key exhibit!*

Behavioural Considerations

The chapter thus far has emphasized the technical aspects of capital budgeting. The management accountant should also be cognizant of important behavioural considerations. An understanding of the functional and dysfunctional consequences of human input provides deeper insight into the whole capital budgeting process.

Capital budgeting projects require creativity, judgement, and the ability to see ideas through to implementation. The entire capital budgeting process from idea generation to implementation can provide valuable training for managers. There may be non-financial reasons for accepting certain projects. Some marginal projects may be accepted because they provide good experience and training benefits.

Estimates of cash flows, discount rates, and salvage values may be affected by the attitudes of individual managers toward risk. Risk-averse managers tend to use more conservative figures in their estimates than those managers who tend to seek risk and take on more venturesome projects.

The micropolitics of organizations may also affect the capital budgeting process. Key managers may favour their own pet projects. Self-identification with projects may obscure management judgement of when to abandon a particular project. Obtaining truthful estimates may become problematic. Internal politics may also influence how projects are awarded. With only limited company funds available for capital investments, a division with several good investment proposals may be denied acceptance of some proposals for less profitable projects of other divisions. Such sharing of projects may be seen as necessary to maintain harmony and to give the appearance of fairness.

The capital budgeting process itself may create additional pressure on top management. Projects often have to go through several layers of approval before reaching top management. It may be difficult to reject projects already approved by managers at lower levels. On the other hand, some projects that are rejected at lower levels, and thus never reach the purview of top management, may actually be acceptable to top management because they help diversify the firm's overall risk.

Projects involving employee safety, or environmental or consumer safety, or which impact heavily on the firm's social environment may have to be evaluated by non-financial criteria. Other projects that cannot be justified on financial grounds may have to be undertaken in order to conform to municipal, provincial, or federal laws.

In summary, the capital budgeting process involves more factors than first meet the eye. A purely quantitative approach to capital budgeting is not sufficient. Any model developed to solve capital budgeting problems is not broad enough to encompass all decision variables. Important qualitative factors imposed on the process by the political and social environment within the firm may strongly influence capital budgeting decisions. All levels of management should take a broad view, and reward systems within the firm should be flexible enough to encourage the acceptance of projects that lead to optimal capital investment decisions.

Summary

Some companies prefer to use either payback or the simple rate of return to evaluate investment proposals. The payback period is the number of periods required to recover the initial investment in the project. The simple rate of return is determined by dividing a project's accounting income by the initial investment in the project.

Investment decisions should take into account the time value of money, since a dollar today is more valuable than a dollar received in the future. The net present value and internal rate of return methods both reflect this fact. In the net present value method, value of the cash outflows is called the project's net present value. If the net present value of the project is negative, the project is rejected. The discount rate in the net present value method is usually a minimum required rate of return, such as the company's cost of capital.

The internal rate of return is the rate of return that equates the present value of the cash inflows and the present value of cash outflows, resulting in a zero net present value. If the internal rate of return is less than the company's minimum required rate of return, the project is rejected.

After rejecting projects whose net present values are negative or whose internal rates of return are less than the minimum required rate of return, the company may still have more projects than can be supported with available funds. The remaining projects can be ranked using either the profitability index or their internal rates of return. The profitability index is computed by dividing the present value of the project's future net cash inflows by the required initial investment.

After a project has been approved, a post-appraisal should be performed to see whether expected results are actually being realized. This is a key part of the capital budgeting process, since it tends to strengthen the quality of the estimates going into investment proposals and affords management with an early opportunity to recognize any developing problems or opportunities.

Unless a company is a tax-exempt organization, such as a not-for-profit school or governmental unit, income taxes should be considered in making capital budgeting decisions. Tax deductible cash expenditures and taxable cash receipts are placed on an after-tax basis by multiplying them by (1 – Tax rate). Only the after-tax amount should be used in determining the desirability of an investment proposal.

Although CCA is not a cash outflow, it is a valid deduction for tax purposes and therefore affects income tax payments. The CCA tax shield—computed by multiplying the CCA deduction by tax rate itself—also results in income tax savings. Finally, behavioural considerations may play a strong role in the capital budgeting process. Important qualitative factors may reverse a decision made solely on a quantitative basis.

Review Problem 1: Basic Present Value Computations

Each of the following situations is independent. Work out your own solution to each situation, and then check it against the solution provided.

1. John plans to retire in 12 years. Upon retiring, he would like to take an extended vacation, which he expects will cost at least $40,000. What lump-sum amount must he invest now to have $40,000 at the end of 12 years if the rate of return is:
   a. Eight percent?
   b. Twelve percent?
2. The Morgans would like to send their daughter to a music camp at the end of each of the next five years. The camp costs $1,000 a year. What lump-sum amount would have to be invested now to have $1,000 at the end of each year if the rate of return is:
   a. Eight percent?
   b. Twelve percent?
3. You have just received an inheritance from a relative. You can either receive a $200,000 lump-sum amount at the end of 10 years or receive $14,000 at the end of each year for the next 10 years. If your discount rate is 12%, which alternative would you prefer?

Solution to Review Problem 1

1. *a.* The amount that must be invested now would be the present value of the $40,000, using a discount rate of 8%. From Exhibit 13–22 in Appendix 13A, the factor for a discount rate

of 8% for 12 periods is 0.397. Multiplying this discount factor by the $40,000 needed in 12 years will give the amount of the present investment required: $40,000 × 0.397 = $15,880.

b. We will proceed as we did in (*a*) above, but this time we will use a discount rate of 12%. From Exhibit 13–22 in Appendix 13A, the factor for a discount rate of 12% for 12 periods is 0.257. Multiplying this discount factor by the $40,000 needed in 12 years will give the amount of the present investment required: $40,000 × 0.257 = $10,280.

Notice that as the discount rate (desired rate of return) increases, the present value decreases.

2. This part differs from (1) above in that we are now dealing with an annuity rather than with a single future sum. The amount that must be invested now is the present value of the $1,000 needed at the end of each year for five years. Since we are dealing with an annuity, or a series of annual cash flows, we must refer to Exhibit 13–23 in Appendix 13A for the appropriate discount factor.

   a. From Exhibit 13–23 in Appendix 13A, the discount factor for 8% for five periods is 3.993. Therefore, the amount that must be invested now to have $1,000 available at the end of each year for five years is $1,000 × 3.993 = $3,993.

   b. From Exhibit 13–23 in Appendix 13A, the discount factor for 12% for five periods is 3.605. Therefore, the amount that must be invested now to have $1,000 available at the end of each year for five years is $1,000 × 3.605 = $3,605.

   Again, notice that as the discount rate increases, the present value decreases. When the rate of return increases, less must be invested today to yield a given amount in the future.

3. For this part we will need to refer to both Exhibits 13–22 and 13–23 in Appendix 13A. From Exhibit 13–22, we will need to find the discount factor for 12% for 10 periods, then apply it to the $200,000 lump sum to be received in 10 years. From Exhibit 13–23, we will need to find the discount factor for 12% for 10 periods, then apply it to the series of $14,000 payments to be received over the 10-year period. Whichever alternative has the higher present value is the one that should be selected.

   $200,000 × 0.322 = $64,400

   $14,000 × 5.650 = $79,100

   Thus, you should prefer to receive the $14,000 per year for 10 years rather than the $200,000 lump sum. This means that you could invest the $14,000 received at the end of each year at 12% and have *more* than $200,000 at the end of 10 years.

Review Problem 2: Comparison of Capital Budgeting Methods

Lamar Company is considering a project that would have an eight-year life and require a $2,400,000 investment in equipment. At the end of eight years, the project would terminate and the equipment would have no salvage value. The project would provide operating income each year as follows:

Sales		$3,000,000
Variable expenses		1,800,000
Contribution margin		1,200,000
Fixed expenses:		
Advertising, salaries, and other fixed out-of-pocket costs	$700,000	
Depreciation	300,000	
Total fixed expenses		1,000,000
Operating income		$ 200,000

The company's discount rate is 12%.

Required:

1. Compute the net annual cash inflow from the project.
2. Compute the project's net present value. Is the project acceptable?

3. Find the project's internal rate of return to the nearest whole percent.
4. Compute the project's payback period.
5. Compute the project's simple rate of return.

Solution to Review Problem 2

1. The net annual cash inflow can be computed by deducting the cash expenses from sales:

Sales	$3,000,000
Variable expenses	1,800,000
Contribution margin	1,200,000
Advertising, salaries, and other fixed out-of-pocket costs	700,000
Net annual cash inflow	$ 500,000

Or the net annual cash inflow can be computed by adding depreciation back to operating income:

Operating income	$200,000
Add: Noncash deduction for depreciation	300,000
Net annual cash inflow	$500,000

2. The net present value is computed as follows:

Item	Year(s)	Amount of Cash Flows	12% Factor	Present Value of Cash Flows
Cost of new equipment	Now	$(2,400,000)	1.000	$(2,400,000)
Net annual cash inflow	1–8	$500,000	4.968	2,484,000
Net present value				$ 84,000

Yes, the project is acceptable because it has a positive net present value.

3. The formula for computing the factor of the internal rate of return is:

$$\text{Factor of the internal rate of return} = \frac{\text{Investment required}}{\text{Net annual cash inflow}}$$

$$= \frac{\$2{,}400{,}000}{\$500{,}000} = 4.800$$

Looking in Exhibit 13–23 in Appendix 13A at the end of the chapter and scanning along the eight-period line, we find that a factor of 4.800 represents a rate of return of about 13%.

4. The formula for the payback period is:

$$\text{Payback period} = \frac{\text{Investment required}}{\text{Net annual cash flow}}$$

$$= \frac{\$2{,}400{,}000}{\$500{,}000}$$

$$= 4.8 \text{ years}$$

5. The formula for the simple rate of return is:

$$\text{Simple rate of return} = \frac{\text{Annual incremental operating income}}{\text{Initial investment}}$$

$$= \frac{\$200{,}000}{\$2{,}400{,}000}$$

$$= 8.3\%$$

Review Problem 3: Capital Budgeting and Taxes

Ace Company is considering investing $70,000 in a passenger bus. The bus is expected to generate net annual cash inflows of $13,500 over an eight-year period. The bus will have a salvage value of $5,000 in eight years. The capital cost allowance is 30% and the income tax rate is 40%. Ace Company requires an after-tax return of 10% on all investments.

Required:

Compute the net present value of the investment. Should the investment be made?

Solution to Review Problem 3

1. The net present value analysis would be:

Items and Computations	Year(s)	(1) Amount	(2) Tax Effect	(1) × (2) After-Tax Cash-Flows	10% Factor	Present Value of Cash Flows
Investment in passenger bus	Now	$(70,000)		$(70,000)	1.000	$(70,000)
Net annual cash receipts	1–8	13,500	1–0.40	8,100	5.335	43,214
CCA tax shield	1–8					19,345
$\frac{Cdt}{d+k} \times \frac{1+.5k}{1+k} - \frac{Sdt \times (1+k)^{-n}}{d+k}$						
$\frac{70{,}000 \times .3 \times .4}{.3 + .10} \times \frac{1.05}{1.10} - \frac{5{,}000 \times .3 \times .4}{.3 + .10} \times .467$						
= ($21,000 × .9545) − ($1,500 × .467) = $19,345						
Salvage value of the bus	8	5,000		5,000	0.467	2,335
Net present value						$(5,106)

2. No, the investment project should not be undertaken. It has a negative net present value when the company's cost of capital is used as the discount rate.

Appendix 13A: The Concept of Present Value

LEARNING OBJECTIVE 8
Explain present value concepts and the use of present value tables.

The point was made in the main body of the chapter that a manager would rather receive a dollar today than a year from now. There are two reasons why this is true. First, a dollar received today is more valuable than a dollar received a year from now. The dollar received today can be invested immediately, and by the end of the year it will have earned some return, making the total amount in hand at the end of the year *greater* than the initial investment. The person receiving the dollar a year from now will simply have a dollar in hand at that time.

Second, the future involves uncertainty. The longer people have to wait to receive a dollar, the more uncertain it becomes that they will ever get the dollar. As time passes, conditions change. The changes may make future payments of the dollar impossible.

Since money has a time value, the manager needs a method of determining whether a cash outlay made now in an investment project can be justified in terms of expected receipts from the project in future years. That is, the manager must have a means of expressing future receipts in present dollar terms so that the future receipts can be compared *on an equivalent basis* with whatever investment is required in the project under consideration. The theory of interest provides managers with the means of making such a comparison.

The Theory of Interest

If a bank pays $105 one year from now in return for a deposit of $100 now, we would say that the bank is paying interest at an annual rate of 5%. The relationships involved in this notion can be expressed in mathematical terms by means of the following equation:

$$F_1 = P(1 + r) \quad (1)$$

where F_1 = the amount to be received in one year, P = the present outlay to be made, and r = the rate of interest involved.

If the present outlay is $100 deposited in a bank savings account that is to earn interest at 5%, then P = $100 and r = 0.05. Under these conditions, F_1 = $105, the amount to be received in one year.

The $100 present outlay is called the **present value** of the $105 amount to be received in one year. It is also known as the *discounted value* of the future $105 receipt. The $100 figure represents the value in present terms of a receipt of $105 to be received a year from now when the interest rate is 5%.

Present value
The value now of an amount that will be received in some future period.

Compound Interest What if the investor leaves her or his money in the bank for a second year? In that case, by the end of the second year, the original $100 deposit will have grown to $110.25:

Original deposit	$100.00
Interest for the first year:	
$100 × 0.05	5.00
Amount at the end of the first year	105.00
Interest for the second year:	
$105 × 0.05	5.25
Amount at the end of the second year	$110.25

Notice that the interest for the second year is $5.25, as compared to only $5 for the first year. The reason for the greater interest earned during the second year is that during the second year, interest is being paid *on interest.* That is, the $5 interest earned during the first year has been left in the account and has been added to the original $100 deposit in computing interest for the second year. This concept is known as **compound interest.** The compounding we have done is annual compounding. Interest can be compounded on a semi-annual, quarterly, or even more frequent basis. Many savings institutions are now compounding interest on a daily basis. The more frequently compounding is done, the more rapidly the invested balance will grow.

Compound interest
The process of paying interest on interest in an investment.

How is the concept of compound interest expressed in equation form? It is expressed by taking equation (1) and adjusting it to state the number of years, n, that a sum is going to be left deposited in the bank:

$$F_n = P(1 + r)^n \quad (2)$$

where n = years.

If n = 2 years, then our computation of the value of F in two years will be as follows:

$$F_2 = \$100(1 + 0.05)^2$$
$$F_2 = \$110.25$$

Present Value and Future Value Exhibit 13–17 shows the relationship between present value and future value as expressed in the theory of interest equations. As shown in the exhibit, if $100 is deposited in a bank at 5% interest, it will grow to $127.63 by the end of five years if interest is compounded annually.

Example N

A purchaser promises to pay $96,800 two years from now for a lot of land. This amount includes interest at an annual rate of 10%. What is the selling price of the land today?

As indicated in Exhibit 13–22 (10% column, down two rows) the present value of $1 is $0.826. The present value of $96,800 is $79,956.80 ($96,800 × .826). A more accurate answer is found as follows:

$$P = \$96{,}800(1 + .10)^{-2}$$
$$= \$80{,}000$$

Example O

A young woman in Vancouver plans to take a vacation trip four years from now. She estimates that she will need $18,000. At an annual interest rate of 16%, compounded quarterly, how much must be deposited into a bank account today to accumulate the required $18,000?

Because interest is compounded quarterly, the interest per period is 4% (the annual rate divided by four quarters). As shown in Exhibit 13–22, the present value of $1 to be received 16 periods in the future at 4% interest is $0.534. The present value of $18,000 is, therefore, $18,000 × .534, which is $9,612. The calculator solution is $18,000 × $(1 + .04)^{-16}$, which equals $9,610.35.

Present Value of a Series of Cash Flows (Annuity)

Annuity A series, or stream, of identical cash flows.

The present value of an **annuity** is the present value of a series of equal payments or receipts discounted at compound interest and made at regular intervals. Stated differently, it is the sum that allows the withdrawal of a series of equal amounts at regular intervals if left at compound interest.

The present value of $1 to be received at the end of each of four periods at 8% interest per period is shown graphically in Exhibit 13–18.

Two points are important in connection with Exhibit 13–18. First, notice that the farther we go forward in time, the smaller is the present value of the $1 interest receipt. The present value of $1 received a year from now is $0.926, as compared to only $0.735 for the $1 interest payment to be received four periods from now. This point simply underscores the fact that money has a time value.

The second point is that even though the computations involved in Exhibit 13–18 are accurate, they have involved unnecessary work. The same present value of $3.312 could have been obtained more easily by referring to Exhibit 13–23 (8% column, down four rows). Exhibit 13–23 contains the present value of $1 to be received each year over a *series* of years at various interest rates. Exhibit 13–23 has been derived by simply adding together the factors from Exhibit 13–22.

The mathematical formula for the present value (P_n) of an annuity of $1 per period compounded at the rate of r for n periods is:

EXHIBIT 13–17 The Relationship between Present Value and Future Value

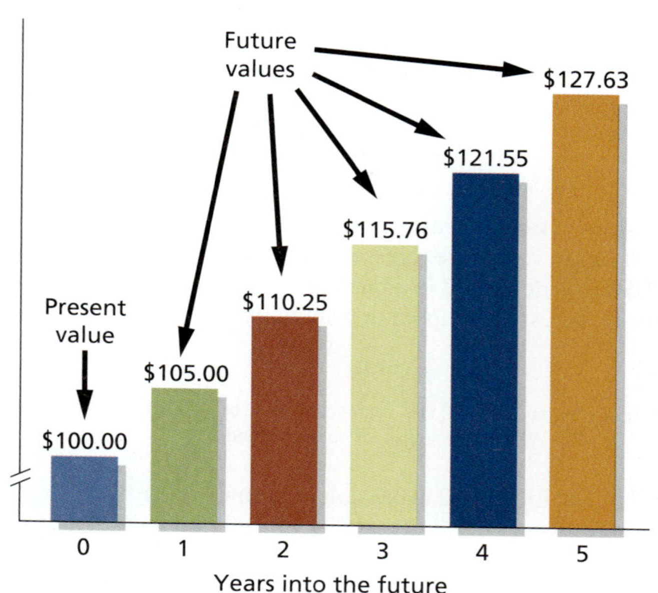

EXHIBIT 13–18 Illustration of Present Value of Ordinary Annuity

	Periods	0	1	2	3	4
			$1	$1	$1	$1
$ .926	$(1 + .08)^{-1}$		←			
.857	$(1 + .08)^{-2}$			←		
.794	$(1 + .08)^{-3}$				←	
.735	$(1 + .08)^{-4}$					←
$ 3.312						

$$P_n = \frac{1 - (1 + r)^{-n}}{r} \text{ or } \frac{1 - (1 + .08)^{-4}}{.08} = \$3.312 \quad (3)$$

Example P

What is the present value of a series of six semi-annual payments of $2,000 at 8% interest compounded annually? Assume that it is now January 1, 2000, and the first payment is made on June 30, 2000.

The purpose of solving this problem could be to determine (1) the sum that will provide for six semi-annual withdrawals of $2,000 if invested at 4% per period (8% divided by two interest periods per year), and (2) the sum that is payable in settlement of a series of obligations of $2,000 that are due at six semi-annual intervals and discounted at 4% per period. Using Exhibit 13–23 (4% column, down six periods) the value 5.242 is found. This present value of an annuity of $1 factor is then multiplied by $2,000 to give $10,484. Alternatively, using the present value of an ordinary annuity (annuity in arrears) formula:

$$P_n = \frac{1 - (1 + .04)^{-6}}{.04} \times \$2,000 = \$10,484.27$$

Example Q

How much money would a company be willing to invest in a project that would return $3,000 every three months for three years, and in addition, a lump sum of $20,000 at the end of the third year? The receipts begin three months from now. Interest is 16% per annum.

The $3,000 to be received at the end of each three-month period is an ordinary annuity. The number of interest periods is 12 (4 per year for three years) and the quarterly interest rate is 4% (16%/4 periods). Using Exhibit 13–23 (4% column, down 12 rows) the value of 9.385 is found. The present value of this annuity is $28,155 (9.385 × $3,000). The present value of the single sum of $20,000 is .625 (Exhibit 13–22, 4% column, down 12 rows) × $20,000, or $12,500. The present value of the series of receipts and the single lump sum is, therefore, $28,155 + $12,500, which totals $40,655. Note, the single amount is usually compounded at the same rate as the series of regulated payments.

Present Value of an Annuity Due

An annuity due is one in which the payments or receipts occur at the *beginning* of each period. Exhibit 13–19 compares the present value of an ordinary annuity of $1 for four periods with the present value of an annuity due for $1 for four periods. The interest rate is assumed to be 8%.

EXHIBIT 13–19 Present Value of an Ordinary Annuity and an Annuity Due

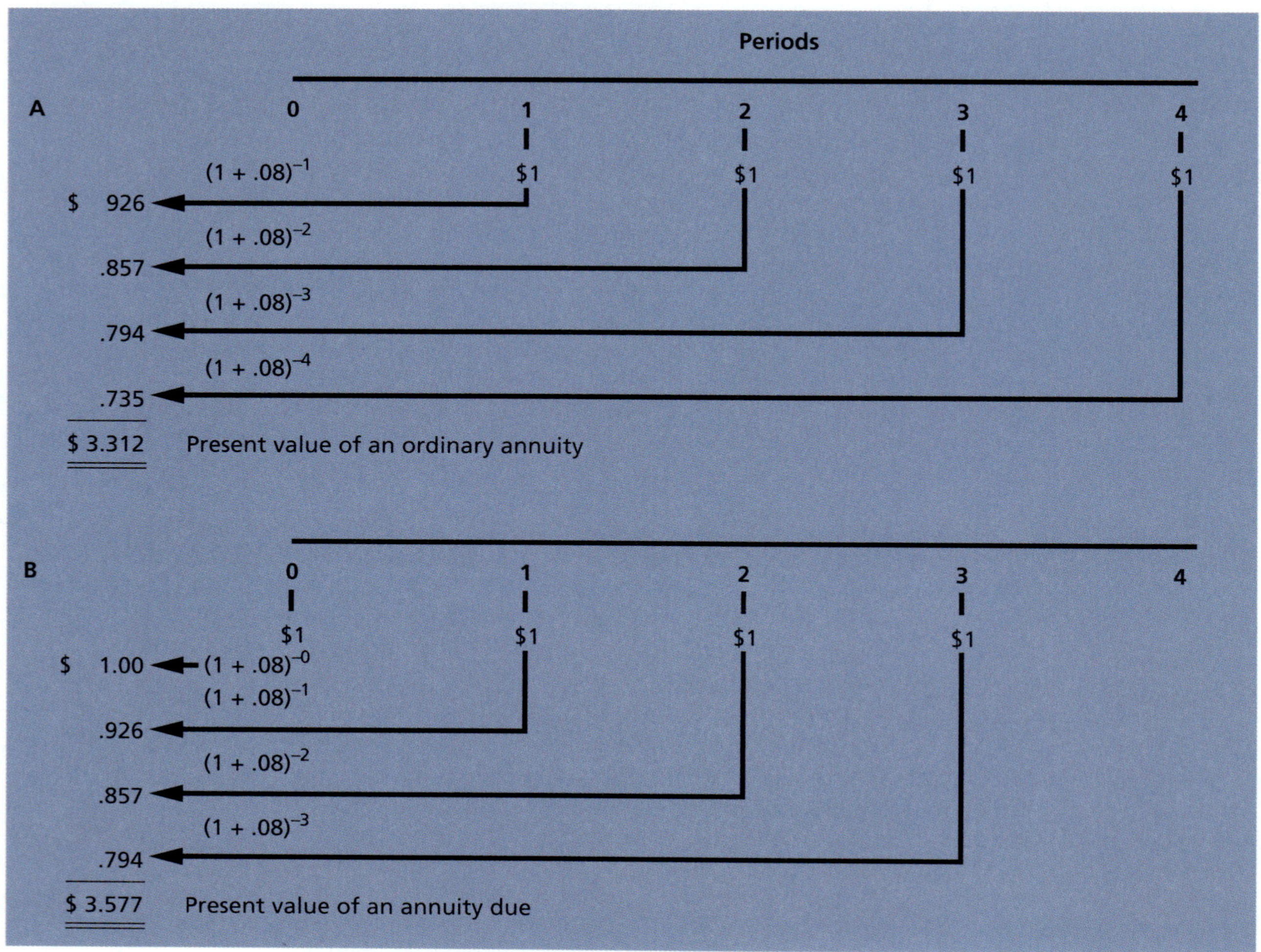

Computation of Present Value

An investment can be viewed in two ways: either in terms of its future value or in terms of its present value. We have seen from our computations above that if we know the present value of a sum (such as our $100 deposit), it is a relatively simple task to compute the sum's future value in n years by using equation (2). But what if the tables are reversed, and we know the *future* value of some amount but we do not know its present value?

For example, assume that you are to receive $200 two years from now. You know that the future value of this sum is $200, since this is the amount that you will be receiving in two years. But what is the sum's present value—what is it worth *right now?* The present value of any sum to be received in the future can be computed by turning equation (2) around and solving for P:

$$P = \frac{F_n}{(1 + r)^n} \tag{4}$$

In our example, $F = \$200$ (the amount to be received in the future), $r = 0.05$ (the rate of interest), and $n = 2$ (the number of years in the future that the amount is to be received):

$$P = \frac{\$200}{(1 + 0.05)^2}$$

$$P = \frac{\$200}{1.1025}$$

$$P = \$181.40$$

As shown by the computation above, the present value of a \$200 amount to be received two years from now is \$181.40 if the interest rate is 5%. In effect, we are saying that \$181.40 received *right now* is equivalent to \$200 received two years from now if the rate of return is 5%. The \$181.40 and the \$200 are just two ways of looking at the same item.

The process of finding the present value of a future cash flow, which we have just completed, is called **discounting.** We have *discounted* the \$200 to its present value of \$181.40. The 5% interest figure that we have used to find this present value is called the **discount rate.** Discounting of future sums to their present value is a common practice in business. A knowledge of the present value of a sum to be received in the future can be very useful to the manager, particularly in making capital budgeting decisions.

Discounting The process of finding the present value of a future cash flow.

Discount rate The rate of return that is used to find the present value of a future cash flow.

If you have a power key (y^x) on your calculator, the above calculations are fairly easy. However, some of the present value formulas we will be using are more complex and difficult to use. Fortunately, tables are available in which the calculations have already been done for you. For example, Exhibit 13–22 shows the discounted present value of \$1 to be received at various periods in the future at various interest rates. The table indicates that the present value of \$1 to be received two periods from now at 5% is 0.907. Since in our example we want to know the present value of \$200 rather than just \$1, we need to multiply the factor in the table by \$200:

$$\$200 \times 0.907 = \$181.40$$

The answer we obtain is the same answer as we obtained earlier using the formula in equation (4).

Note that part B of Exhibit 13–19 can be interpreted as an ordinary annuity for \$1 for three periods (\$0.926 + \$0.857 + \$0.794) to which we add \$1. We can calculate the present value of an annuity due by subtracting one period from n and calculating the present value of an ordinary annuity for $n - 1$ period. We then add \$1 to this annuity factor, which now gives the present value factor of an annuity due of \$1.

Example R

On February 1, 2008, Vacon Company signed an 18-month lease with Aucoin Leasing Company. The lease payments begin immediately. Calculate the present value of the lease, assuming that \$2,000 is paid each quarter and that the annual interest rate is 16%.

We can solve this problem by first determining the present value of an ordinary annuity for $n - 1$ periods, where n is equal to six periods (18 months = six quarters:)

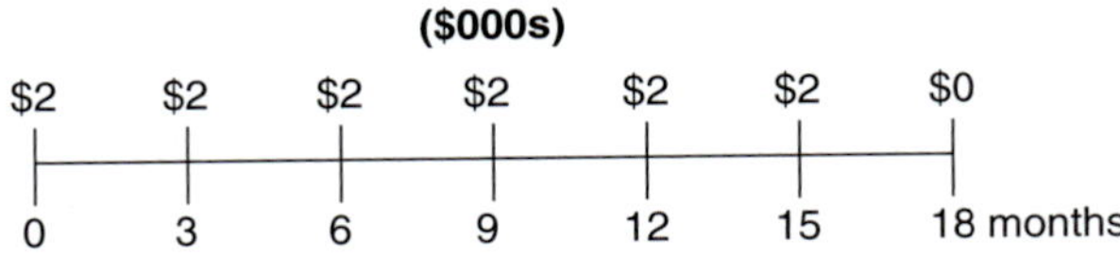

Using Exhibit 13–23, the present value of an annuity factor for five periods ($n - 1$) is 4.452 (4% column, five rows down). To this factor we add 1, resulting in an interest factor of 5.452. Next, we multiply the \$2,000 payments by 5.452 to arrive at \$10,904, the present value of the lease payments. Using the formula approach, the present value of an annuity due is as follows (calculator solution):

$$\text{PV(due)} = \$2{,}000 \times \left[1 + \frac{(1-(1+.04)^{-5}}{.04}\right]$$
$$= \$2{,}000 \times (1 + 4.4518223)$$
$$= \$2{,}000 \times 5.4518223$$
$$= \$10{,}903.65$$

Deferred Annuities

A deferred annuity is one in which the first payment or receipt does not begin until more than one interest period has expired. This is common for capital expenditure decisions that may take several periods to become operational.

Example S

What is the present value on January 1, 2008, of a series of five receipts of $1,000, the first of which is expected to be received on January 1, 2011? The interest rate is 10% per annum.

A graphical representation of the problem is as follows:

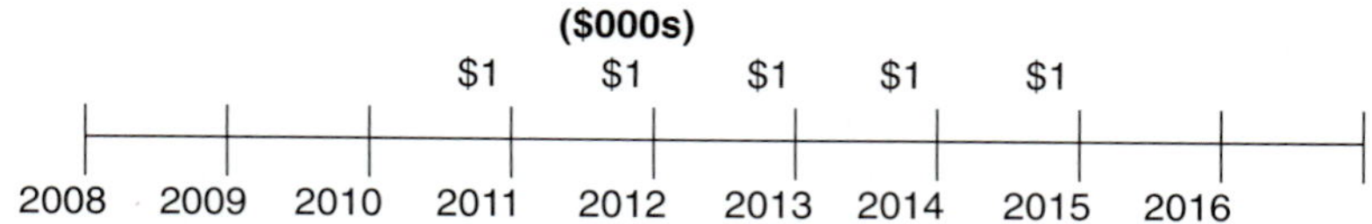

One way of solving this problem is by the following two-step procedure:

Step 1. Calculate the present value on January 1, 2010, of an ordinary annuity of a series of five receipts of $1,000. This is $1,000 times 3.791, or $3,791.

Step 2. The problem is now translated into a simple present value problem, depicted as follows:

$3,791

2008 2009 2010

The present value on January 1, 2008, can now be computed by discounting the $3,791 back two interest periods:

$$\text{PV (January 1, 2008)} = \$3{,}791(1+.10)^{-2}$$
$$= \$3{,}133$$

This problem could have also been solved by adding fictitious receipts on January 1, 2010, and on January 1, 2009, and calculating the present value of an ordinary annuity on January 1, 2008, for seven periods and then subtracting the present value of the receipts that did not occur:

Step 1:

$$\$1{,}000 \times \frac{(1-(1+.10)^{-7})}{.10}$$
$$= \$4{,}868$$

Step 2:

$$\$4{,}868 - \left(\$1{,}000 \times \frac{(1-(1+.10)^{-2})}{.10}\right)$$
$$= \$4{,}868 - \$1{,}735$$
$$= \$3{,}133$$

Future Value of an Annuity

Business transactions often involve a series of equal payments spaced evenly apart. As discussed earlier in the chapter, a series of equal payments at regular intervals is known as an *annuity*. The total that becomes due immediately after the last payment is the amount of an ordinary annuity or an annuity in arrears. If the payments are made or received at the beginning of the first interest period, the annuity is termed an *annuity due* or an *annuity in advance*.

The distinction between an ordinary annuity and an annuity due is presented graphically as follows:

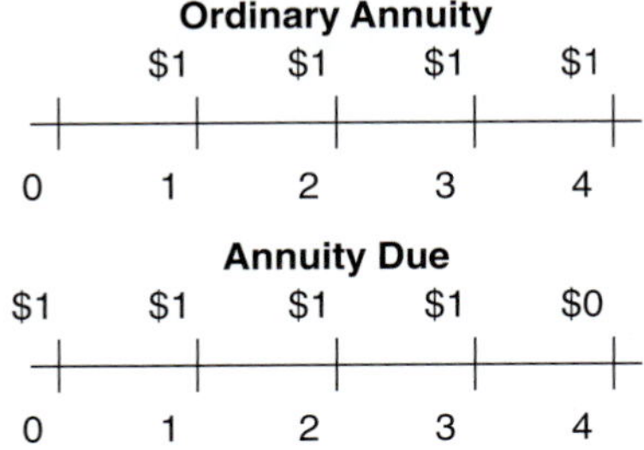

To illustrate how the future value of an ordinary annuity is determined, assume that $1 is deposited in a savings account at the end of each of four periods at 8% per period:

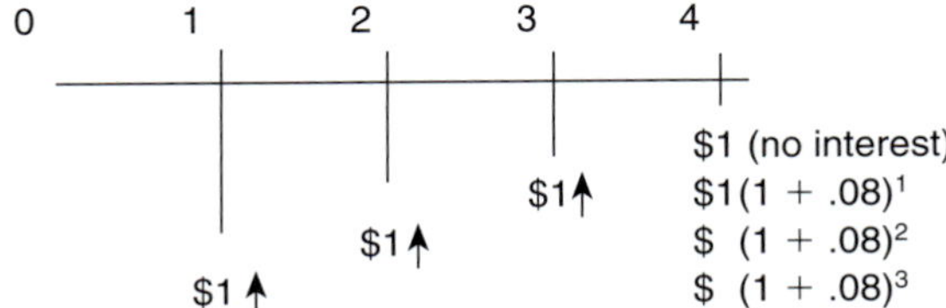

Thus, the value of an ordinary annuity of $1 due at the end of each period for four periods is:

$$\$1 + \$1\,(1 + .08)^1 + \$1(1 + .08)^2 + \$1(1 + .08)^3 =$$
$$\$1 + \quad \$1.08 \quad + \$1.1664 \quad + \quad \$1.2597 = \$4.5061$$

From the preceding illustration it can be seen that the $1 deposited at the end of the first year accumulates interest for a total of three periods, increasing to a value of $1.2597. The deposit at the end of the second year grows to $1.1664, and the $1 deposited at the end of the third period accumulates to $1.08. The $1 deposited at the end of the fourth period has not yet earned any interest. The series of four payments of $1 each period grows to $4.5061 at the end of the fourth period.

This problem can be solved quickly by using a mathematical expression based on a geometric progression. The future value of an annuity in arrears (F_n) compounded at an interest rate (r) for a given number of periods (n) is:

$$F_n = \frac{(1 + r)^n - 1}{r} \qquad (5)$$

The value of a series of $1 deposits made at the end of each of four years compounded at 8% annually is:

$$F_n = \$1 \times \frac{(1 + .08)^4 - 1}{.08} = \$4.5061$$

The same calculation, rounded at three decimal places, can be determined by referring to Exhibit 13–21 (8% column, down four rows) and multiplying this factor by the amount of each receipt ($1).

It should be apparent that Exhibit 13–20 and 13–21 are related. We can treat each cash flow of the annuity separately and find the future value of each cash flow (Exhibit 13–20) and sum them. Alternatively, it is much faster to find the sum of the annuity using Exhibit 13–21.

To find the future value of an annuity of $1 per period for four periods if each payment is made at the *beginning* of each period (an annuity due), we can modify the formula as follows:

$$F_n\,(\text{due}) = \frac{(1 + r)^n - 1}{r} \times (1 + r)$$

$$= \frac{(1 + .08)^4 - 1}{.08} \times (1 + .08)$$

$$= \$4{,}867$$

The same result can be reached by looking up the interest factor in Exhibit 13–21 for one additional interest period and then subtracting 1 from this factor (8% column, five rows down, deduct 1 from the factor 5.867 to give 4.867). This problem is illustrated by the following diagram:

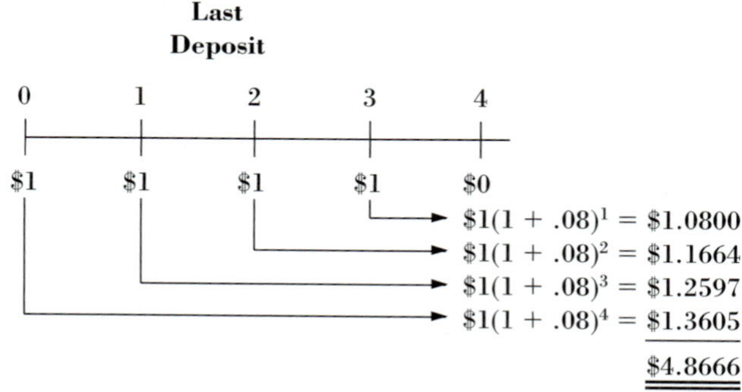

To summarize, the present value tables in Appendix 13A should be used as follows:

Exhibit 13–22: This table should be used to find the present value of a single cash flow (such as a single payment or receipt) occurring in the future.

Exhibit 13–23: This table should be used to find the present value of a series (or stream) of cash flows occurring in the future.

The use of these tables is illustrated in various exhibits in the main body of the chapter. *When a present value factor appears in an exhibit, the reader should take the time to trace it back in either Exhibit 13–22 or Exhibit 13–23 in order to get acquainted with the tables and how they work.*

Using Microsoft Excel

You can also perform compound interest calculations using the following Microsoft Excel functions:

RATE(nper,pmt,pv,fv,type,guess)
NPER(rate,pmt,pv,fv,type)
PV(rate,nper,pmt,fv,type)
FV(rate,nper,pmt,pv,type)

where

- *rate* is the interest rate per period.
- *nper* is the total number of payment periods in an annuity.
- *pv* is the present value, the total amount that a series of future payments is worth now.
- *fv* is the future value, or a cash balance you want to attain after the last payment is made. If *fv* is omitted, it is assumed to be 0 (the future value of a loan, for example, is 0).
- *pmt* is the payment made each period and cannot change over the life of the annuity.
- *type* is the number 0 or 1 and indicates when payments are due. (0 or omitted, payment is at the end of the period; 1, it is at the beginning of the period).

Excel functions are particularly useful when you want to calculate compound interest when making regular payments, as for a mortgage or an annuity. They are powerful but are a little complex to use.

EXHIBIT 13–20 Future Value of $1; $(1 + r)^n$

Periods	4%	5%	6%	7%	8%	9%	10%	11%	12%	13%	14%	15%	16%	17%	18%	19%	20%
1	1.040	1.050	1.060	1.070	1.080	1.090	1.100	1.110	1.120	1.130	1.140	1.150	1.160	1.170	1.180	1.190	1.200
2	1.082	1.103	1.124	1.145	1.166	1.188	1.210	1.232	1.254	1.277	1.300	1.323	1.346	1.369	1.392	1.416	1.440
3	1.125	1.158	1.191	1.225	1.260	1.295	1.331	1.368	1.405	1.443	1.482	1.521	1.561	1.602	1.643	1.685	1.728
4	1.170	1.216	1.262	1.311	1.360	1.412	1.464	1.518	1.574	1.630	1.689	1.749	1.811	1.874	1.939	2.005	2.074
5	1.217	1.276	1.338	1.403	1.469	1.539	1.611	1.685	1.762	1.842	1.925	2.011	2.100	2.192	2.288	2.386	2.488
6	1.265	1.340	1.419	1.501	1.587	1.677	1.772	1.870	1.974	2.082	2.195	2.313	2.436	2.565	2.700	2.840	2.986
7	1.316	1.407	1.504	1.606	1.714	1.828	1.949	2.076	2.211	2.353	2.502	2.660	2.826	3.001	3.185	3.379	3.583
8	1.369	1.477	1.594	1.718	1.851	1.993	2.144	2.305	2.476	2.658	2.853	3.059	3.278	3.511	3.759	4.021	4.300
9	1.423	1.551	1.689	1.838	1.999	2.172	2.358	2.558	2.773	3.004	3.252	3.518	3.803	4.108	4.435	4.785	5.160
10	1.480	1.629	1.791	1.967	2.159	2.367	2.594	2.839	3.106	3.395	3.707	4.046	4.411	4.807	5.234	5.695	6.192
11	1.539	1.710	1.898	2.105	2.332	2.580	2.853	3.152	3.479	3.836	4.226	4.652	5.117	5.624	6.176	6.777	7.430
12	1.601	1.796	2.012	2.252	2.518	2.813	3.138	3.498	3.896	4.335	4.818	5.350	5.936	6.580	7.288	8.064	8.916
13	1.665	1.886	2.133	2.410	2.720	3.066	3.452	3.883	4.363	4.898	5.492	6.153	6.886	7.699	8.599	9.596	10.699
14	1.732	1.980	2.261	2.579	2.937	3.342	3.797	4.310	4.887	5.535	6.261	7.076	7.988	9.007	10.147	11.420	12.839
15	1.801	2.079	2.397	2.759	3.172	3.642	4.177	4.785	5.474	6.254	7.138	8.137	9.266	10.539	11.974	13.590	15.407
16	1.873	2.183	2.540	2.952	3.426	3.970	4.595	5.311	6.130	7.067	8.137	9.358	10.748	12.330	14.129	16.172	18.488
17	1.948	2.292	2.693	3.159	3.700	4.328	5.054	5.895	6.866	7.986	9.276	10.761	12.468	14.426	16.672	19.244	22.186
18	2.026	2.407	2.854	3.380	3.996	4.717	5.560	6.544	7.690	9.024	10.575	12.375	14.463	16.879	19.673	22.901	26.623
19	2.107	2.527	3.026	3.617	4.316	5.142	6.116	7.263	8.613	10.197	12.056	14.232	16.777	19.748	23.214	27.252	31.948
20	2.191	2.653	3.207	3.870	4.661	5.604	6.727	8.062	9.646	11.523	13.743	16.367	19.461	23.106	27.393	32.429	38.338
30	3.243	4.322	5.743	7.612	10.063	13.268	17.449	22.892	29.960	39.116	50.950	66.212	85.850	111.065	143.371	184.675	237.376

EXHIBIT 13–21 Future Value of an Annuity of $1 in Arrears; $\frac{(1 + r)^n - 1}{r}$

Periods	4%	5%	6%	7%	8%	9%	10%	11%	12%	13%	14%	15%	16%	17%	18%	19%	20%
1	1.000	1.000	1.000	1.000	1.000	1.000	1.000	1.000	1.000	1.000	1.000	1.000	1.000	1.000	1.000	1.000	1.000
2	2.040	2.050	2.060	2.070	2.080	2.090	2.100	2.110	2.120	2.130	2.140	2.150	2.160	2.170	2.180	2.190	2.200
3	3.122	3.153	3.184	3.215	3.246	3.278	3.310	3.342	3.374	3.407	3.440	3.473	3.506	3.539	3.572	3.606	3.640
4	4.246	4.310	4.375	4.440	4.506	4.573	4.641	4.710	4.779	4.850	4.921	4.993	5.066	5.141	5.215	5.291	5.368
5	5.416	5.526	5.637	5.751	5.867	5.985	6.105	6.228	6.353	6.480	6.610	6.742	6.877	7.014	7.154	7.297	7.442
6	6.633	6.802	6.975	7.153	7.336	7.523	7.716	7.913	8.115	8.323	8.536	8.754	8.977	9.207	9.442	9.683	9.930
7	7.898	8.142	8.394	8.654	8.923	9.200	9.487	9.783	10.089	10.405	10.730	11.067	11.414	11.772	12.142	12.523	12.916
8	9.214	9.549	9.897	10.260	10.637	11.028	11.436	11.859	12.300	12.757	13.233	13.727	14.240	14.773	15.327	15.902	16.499
9	10.583	11.027	11.491	11.978	12.488	13.021	13.579	14.164	14.776	15.416	16.085	16.786	17.519	18.285	19.086	19.923	20.799
10	12.006	12.578	13.181	13.816	14.487	15.193	15.937	16.722	17.549	18.420	19.337	20.304	21.321	22.393	23.521	24.709	25.959
11	13.486	14.207	14.972	15.784	16.645	17.560	18.531	19.561	20.655	21.814	23.045	24.349	25.733	27.200	28.755	30.404	32.150
12	15.026	15.917	16.870	17.888	18.977	20.141	21.384	22.713	24.133	25.650	27.271	29.002	30.850	32.824	34.931	37.180	39.581
13	16.627	17.713	18.882	20.141	21.495	22.953	24.523	26.212	28.029	29.985	32.089	34.352	36.786	39.404	42.219	45.244	48.497
14	18.292	19.599	21.015	22.550	24.215	26.019	27.975	30.095	32.393	34.883	37.581	40.505	43.672	47.103	50.818	54.841	59.196
15	20.024	21.579	23.276	25.129	27.152	29.361	31.772	34.405	37.280	40.417	43.842	47.580	51.660	56.110	60.965	66.261	72.035
16	21.825	23.657	25.673	27.888	30.324	33.003	35.950	39.190	42.753	46.672	50.980	55.717	60.925	66.649	72.939	79.850	87.442
17	23.698	25.840	28.213	30.840	33.750	36.974	40.545	44.501	48.884	53.739	59.118	65.075	71.673	78.979	87.068	96.022	105.931
18	25.645	28.132	30.906	33.999	37.450	41.301	45.599	50.396	55.750	61.725	68.394	75.836	84.141	93.406	103.740	115.266	128.117
19	27.671	30.539	33.760	37.379	41.446	46.018	51.159	56.939	63.440	70.749	78.969	88.212	98.603	110.285	123.414	138.166	154.740
20	29.778	33.066	36.786	40.995	45.762	51.160	57.275	64.203	72.052	80.947	91.025	102.444	115.380	130.033	146.628	165.418	186.688
30	56.085	66.439	79.058	94.461	113.283	136.308	164.494	199.021	241.333	293.199	356.787	434.745	530.312	647.439	790.948	966.712	1181.882

EXHIBIT 13–22 Present Value of $1; $\frac{1}{(1 + r)^n}$ or $(1 + r)^{-n}$

Periods	4%	5%	6%	7%	8%	9%	10%	11%	12%	13%	14%	15%	16%	17%	18%	19%	20%	21%	22%	23%	24%	25%
1	0.962	0.952	0.943	0.935	0.926	0.917	0.909	0.901	0.893	0.885	0.877	0.870	0.862	0.855	0.847	0.840	0.833	0.826	0.820	0.813	0.806	0.800
2	0.925	0.907	0.890	0.873	0.857	0.842	0.826	0.812	0.797	0.783	0.769	0.756	0.743	0.731	0.718	0.706	0.694	0.683	0.672	0.661	0.650	0.640
3	0.889	0.864	0.840	0.816	0.794	0.772	0.751	0.731	0.712	0.693	0.675	0.658	0.641	0.624	0.609	0.593	0.579	0.564	0.551	0.537	0.524	0.512
4	0.855	0.823	0.792	0.763	0.735	0.708	0.683	0.659	0.636	0.613	0.592	0.572	0.552	0.534	0.516	0.499	0.482	0.467	0.451	0.437	0.423	0.410
5	0.822	0.784	0.747	0.713	0.681	0.650	0.621	0.593	0.567	0.543	0.519	0.497	0.476	0.456	0.437	0.419	0.402	0.386	0.370	0.355	0.341	0.328
6	0.790	0.746	0.705	0.666	0.630	0.596	0.564	0.535	0.507	0.480	0.456	0.432	0.410	0.390	0.370	0.352	0.335	0.319	0.303	0.289	0.275	0.262
7	0.760	0.711	0.665	0.623	0.583	0.547	0.513	0.482	0.452	0.425	0.400	0.376	0.354	0.333	0.314	0.296	0.279	0.263	0.249	0.235	0.222	0.210
8	0.731	0.677	0.627	0.582	0.540	0.502	0.467	0.434	0.404	0.376	0.351	0.327	0.305	0.285	0.266	0.249	0.233	0.218	0.204	0.191	0.179	0.168
9	0.703	0.645	0.592	0.544	0.500	0.460	0.424	0.391	0.361	0.333	0.308	0.284	0.263	0.243	0.225	0.209	0.194	0.180	0.167	0.155	0.144	0.134
10	0.676	0.614	0.558	0.508	0.463	0.422	0.386	0.352	0.322	0.295	0.270	0.247	0.227	0.208	0.191	0.176	0.162	0.149	0.137	0.126	0.116	0.107
11	0.650	0.585	0.527	0.475	0.429	0.388	0.350	0.317	0.287	0.261	0.237	0.215	0.195	0.178	0.162	0.148	0.135	0.123	0.112	0.103	0.094	0.086
12	0.625	0.557	0.497	0.444	0.397	0.356	0.319	0.286	0.257	0.231	0.208	0.187	0.168	0.152	0.137	0.124	0.112	0.102	0.092	0.083	0.076	0.069
13	0.601	0.530	0.469	0.415	0.368	0.326	0.290	0.258	0.229	0.204	0.182	0.163	0.145	0.130	0.116	0.104	0.093	0.084	0.075	0.068	0.061	0.055
14	0.577	0.505	0.442	0.388	0.340	0.299	0.263	0.232	0.205	0.181	0.160	0.141	0.125	0.111	0.099	0.088	0.078	0.069	0.062	0.055	0.049	0.044
15	0.555	0.481	0.417	0.362	0.315	0.275	0.239	0.209	0.183	0.160	0.140	0.123	0.108	0.095	0.084	0.074	0.065	0.057	0.051	0.045	0.040	0.035
16	0.534	0.458	0.394	0.339	0.292	0.252	0.218	0.188	0.163	0.141	0.123	0.107	0.093	0.081	0.071	0.062	0.054	0.047	0.042	0.036	0.032	0.028
17	0.513	0.436	0.371	0.317	0.270	0.231	0.198	0.170	0.146	0.125	0.108	0.093	0.080	0.069	0.060	0.052	0.045	0.039	0.034	0.030	0.026	0.023
18	0.494	0.416	0.350	0.296	0.250	0.212	0.180	0.153	0.130	0.111	0.095	0.081	0.069	0.059	0.051	0.044	0.038	0.032	0.028	0.024	0.021	0.018
19	0.475	0.396	0.331	0.277	0.232	0.194	0.164	0.138	0.116	0.098	0.083	0.070	0.060	0.051	0.043	0.037	0.031	0.027	0.023	0.020	0.017	0.014
20	0.456	0.377	0.312	0.258	0.215	0.178	0.149	0.124	0.104	0.087	0.073	0.061	0.051	0.043	0.037	0.031	0.026	0.022	0.019	0.016	0.014	0.012
21	0.439	0.359	0.294	0.242	0.199	0.164	0.135	0.112	0.093	0.077	0.064	0.053	0.044	0.037	0.031	0.026	0.022	0.018	0.015	0.013	0.011	0.009
22	0.422	0.342	0.278	0.226	0.184	0.150	0.123	0.101	0.083	0.068	0.056	0.046	0.038	0.032	0.026	0.022	0.018	0.015	0.013	0.011	0.009	0.007
23	0.406	0.326	0.262	0.211	0.170	0.138	0.112	0.091	0.074	0.060	0.049	0.040	0.033	0.027	0.022	0.018	0.015	0.012	0.010	0.009	0.007	0.006
24	0.390	0.310	0.247	0.197	0.158	0.126	0.102	0.082	0.066	0.053	0.043	0.035	0.028	0.023	0.019	0.015	0.013	0.010	0.008	0.007	0.006	0.005
25	0.375	0.295	0.233	0.184	0.146	0.116	0.092	0.074	0.059	0.047	0.038	0.030	0.024	0.020	0.016	0.013	0.010	0.009	0.007	0.006	0.005	0.004
26	0.361	0.281	0.220	0.172	0.135	0.106	0.084	0.066	0.053	0.042	0.033	0.026	0.021	0.017	0.014	0.011	0.009	0.007	0.006	0.005	0.004	0.003
27	0.347	0.268	0.207	0.161	0.125	0.098	0.076	0.060	0.047	0.037	0.029	0.023	0.018	0.014	0.011	0.009	0.007	0.006	0.005	0.004	0.003	0.002
28	0.333	0.255	0.196	0.150	0.116	0.090	0.069	0.054	0.042	0.033	0.026	0.020	0.016	0.012	0.010	0.008	0.006	0.005	0.004	0.003	0.002	0.002
29	0.321	0.243	0.185	0.141	0.107	0.082	0.063	0.048	0.037	0.029	0.022	0.017	0.014	0.011	0.008	0.006	0.005	0.004	0.003	0.002	0.002	0.002
30	0.308	0.231	0.174	0.131	0.099	0.075	0.057	0.044	0.033	0.026	0.020	0.015	0.012	0.009	0.007	0.005	0.004	0.003	0.003	0.002	0.002	0.001
40	0.208	0.142	0.097	0.067	0.046	0.032	0.022	0.015	0.011	0.008	0.005	0.004	0.003	0.002	0.001	0.001	0.001	0.000	0.000	0.000	0.000	0.000

EXHIBIT 13–23 Present Value of an Annuity of $1 in Arrears; $\frac{1}{r}\left[1 - \frac{1}{(1+r)^n}\right]$ or $\frac{1-(1+r)^{-n}}{r}$

Periods	4%	5%	6%	7%	8%	9%	10%	11%	12%	13%	14%	15%	16%	17%	18%	19%	20%	21%	22%	23%	24%	25%
1	0.962	0.952	0.943	0.935	0.926	0.917	0.909	0.901	0.893	0.885	0.877	0.870	0.862	0.855	0.847	0.840	0.833	0.826	0.820	0.813	0.806	0.800
2	1.886	1.859	1.833	1.808	1.783	1.759	1.736	1.713	1.690	1.668	1.647	1.626	1.605	1.585	1.566	1.547	1.528	1.509	1.492	1.474	1.457	1.440
3	2.775	2.723	2.673	2.624	2.577	2.531	2.487	2.444	2.402	2.361	2.322	2.283	2.246	2.210	2.174	2.140	2.106	2.074	2.042	2.011	1.981	1.952
4	3.630	3.546	3.465	3.387	3.312	3.240	3.170	3.102	3.037	2.974	2.914	2.855	2.798	2.743	2.690	2.639	2.589	2.540	2.494	2.448	2.404	2.362
5	4.452	4.329	4.212	4.100	3.993	3.890	3.791	3.696	3.605	3.517	3.433	3.352	3.274	3.199	3.127	3.058	2.991	2.926	2.864	2.803	2.745	2.689
6	5.242	5.076	4.917	4.767	4.623	4.486	4.355	4.231	4.111	3.998	3.889	3.784	3.685	3.589	3.498	3.410	3.326	3.245	3.167	3.092	3.020	2.951
7	6.002	5.786	5.582	5.389	5.206	5.033	4.868	4.712	4.564	4.423	4.288	4.160	4.039	3.922	3.812	3.706	3.605	3.508	3.416	3.327	3.242	3.161
8	6.733	6.463	6.210	5.971	5.747	5.535	5.335	5.146	4.968	4.799	4.639	4.487	4.344	4.207	4.078	3.954	3.837	3.726	3.619	3.518	3.421	3.329
9	7.435	7.108	6.802	6.515	6.247	5.995	5.759	5.537	5.328	5.132	4.946	4.772	4.607	4.451	4.303	4.163	4.031	3.905	3.786	3.673	3.566	3.463
10	8.111	7.722	7.360	7.024	6.710	6.418	6.145	5.889	5.650	5.426	5.216	5.019	4.833	4.659	4.494	4.339	4.192	4.054	3.923	3.799	3.682	3.571
11	8.760	8.306	7.887	7.499	7.139	6.805	6.495	6.207	5.938	5.687	5.453	5.234	5.029	4.836	4.656	4.486	4.327	4.177	4.035	3.902	3.776	3.656
12	9.385	8.863	8.384	7.943	7.536	7.161	6.814	6.492	6.194	5.918	5.660	5.421	5.197	4.988	4.793	4.611	4.439	4.278	4.127	3.985	3.851	3.725
13	9.986	9.394	8.853	8.358	7.904	7.487	7.103	6.750	6.424	6.122	5.842	5.583	5.342	5.118	4.910	4.715	4.533	4.362	4.203	4.053	3.912	3.780
14	10.563	9.899	9.295	8.745	8.244	7.786	7.367	6.982	6.628	6.302	6.002	5.724	5.468	5.229	5.008	4.802	4.611	4.432	4.265	4.108	3.962	3.824
15	11.118	10.380	9.712	9.108	8.559	8.061	7.606	7.191	6.811	6.462	6.142	5.847	5.575	5.324	5.092	4.876	4.675	4.489	4.315	4.153	4.001	3.859
16	11.652	10.838	10.106	9.447	8.851	8.313	7.824	7.379	6.974	6.604	6.265	5.954	5.668	5.405	5.162	4.938	4.730	4.536	4.357	4.189	4.033	3.887
17	12.166	11.274	10.477	9.763	9.122	8.544	8.022	7.549	7.120	6.729	6.373	6.047	5.749	5.475	5.222	4.990	4.775	4.576	4.391	4.219	4.059	3.910
18	12.659	11.690	10.828	10.059	9.372	8.756	8.201	7.702	7.250	6.840	6.467	6.128	5.818	5.534	5.273	5.033	4.812	4.608	4.419	4.243	4.080	3.928
19	13.134	12.085	11.158	10.336	9.604	8.950	8.365	7.839	7.366	6.938	6.550	6.198	5.877	5.584	5.316	5.070	4.843	4.635	4.442	4.263	4.097	3.942
20	13.590	12.462	11.470	10.594	9.818	9.129	8.514	7.963	7.469	7.025	6.623	6.259	5.929	5.628	5.353	5.101	4.870	4.657	4.460	4.279	4.110	3.954
21	14.029	12.821	11.764	10.836	10.017	9.292	8.649	8.075	7.562	7.102	6.687	6.312	5.973	5.665	5.384	5.127	4.891	4.675	4.476	4.292	4.121	3.963
22	14.451	13.163	12.042	11.061	10.201	9.442	8.772	8.176	7.645	7.170	6.743	6.359	6.011	5.696	5.410	5.149	4.909	4.690	4.488	4.302	4.130	3.970
23	14.857	13.489	12.303	11.272	10.371	9.580	8.883	8.266	7.718	7.230	6.792	6.399	6.044	5.723	5.432	5.167	4.925	4.703	4.499	4.311	4.137	3.976
24	15.247	13.799	12.550	11.469	10.529	9.707	8.985	8.348	7.784	7.283	6.835	6.434	6.073	5.746	5.451	5.182	4.937	4.713	4.507	4.318	4.143	3.981
25	15.622	14.094	12.783	11.654	10.675	9.823	9.077	8.422	7.843	7.330	6.873	6.464	6.097	5.766	5.467	5.195	4.948	4.721	4.514	4.323	4.147	3.985
26	15.983	14.375	13.003	11.826	10.810	9.929	9.161	8.488	7.896	7.372	6.906	6.491	6.118	5.783	5.480	5.206	4.956	4.728	4.520	4.328	4.151	3.988
27	16.330	14.643	13.211	11.987	10.935	10.027	9.237	8.548	7.943	7.409	6.935	6.514	6.136	5.798	5.492	5.215	4.964	4.734	4.524	4.332	4.154	3.990
28	16.663	14.898	13.406	12.137	11.051	10.116	9.307	8.602	7.984	7.441	6.961	6.534	6.152	5.810	5.502	5.223	4.970	4.739	4.528	4.335	4.157	3.992
29	16.984	15.141	13.591	12.278	11.158	10.198	9.370	8.650	8.022	7.470	6.983	6.551	6.166	5.820	5.510	5.229	4.975	4.743	4.531	4.337	4.159	3.994
30	17.292	15.372	13.765	12.409	11.258	10.274	9.427	8.694	8.055	7.496	7.003	6.566	6.177	5.829	5.517	5.235	4.979	4.746	4.534	4.339	4.160	3.995
40	19.793	17.159	15.046	13.332	11.925	10.757	9.779	8.951	8.244	7.634	7.105	6.642	6.233	5.871	5.548	5.258	4.997	4.760	4.544	4.347	4.166	3.999

Glossary

Visit the Online Learning Centre at **http://www.mcgrawhill.ca/olc/garrison/** for a review of key terms and definitions.

Questions

13–1 What is meant by the term *payback period?* How is the payback period determined? How can the payback method be useful?

13–2 What is the major criticism of the payback and simple rate of return methods of making capital budgeting decisions.?

13–3 What is the difference between capital budgeting screening decisions and capital budgeting preference decisions?

13–4 What is meant by the term *time value of money?*

13–5 What is meant by the term *discounting?*

13–6 Why isn't accounting net income used in the net present value and internal rate of return methods of making capital budgeting decisions?

13–7 Why are discounted cash flow methods of making capital budgeting decisions superior to other methods?

13–8 What is net present value? Can it ever be negative? Explain.

13–9 Identify two simplifying assumptions associated with discounted cash flow methods of making capital budgeting decisions.

13–10 If a company has to pay interest of 14% on long-term debt, then its cost of capital is 14%. Do you agree? Explain.

13–11 What is meant by an investment project's internal rate of return? How is the internal rate of return computed?

13–12 Explain how the cost of capital serves as a screening tool when dealing with (*a*) the net present value method and (*b*) the internal rate of return method.

13–13 As the discount rate increases, the present value of a given future cash flow also increases. Do you agree? Explain.

13–14 Refer to Exhibit 13–6. Is the return on this investment proposal exactly 14%, more than 14%, or less than 14%? Explain.

13–15 How is the project profitability index computed, and what does it measure?

13–16 What is meant by after-tax cost and how is the concept used in capital budgeting decisions?

13–17 What is a CCA tax shield and how does it affect capital budgeting decisions?

13–18 Ludlow Company is considering the introduction of a new product line. Would an increase in the income tax rate tend to make the new investment more or less attractive? Explain.

13–19 Assume that an old piece of equipment is sold at a loss. From a capital budgeting point of view, what two cash inflows will be associated with the sale?

13–20 Assume that a new piece of equipment costs $40,000 and that the tax rate is 30%. Should the new piece of equipment be included in the capital budgeting analysis as a cash outflow of $40,000, or as a cash outflow of $28,000 [$40,000 × (1 − 0.30)]? Explain.

Exercises

EXERCISE 13–1 Payback Method [LO1]

The management of Weimar Inc., a civil engineering design company, is considering an investment in a high-quality blueprint printer with the cash flows presented on the next page.

Required:

1. Determine the payback period of the investment.
2. Would the payback period be affected if the cash inflow in the last year were several times larger?

Year	Investment	Cash Inflow
1.........	$38,000	$2,000
2.........	$6,000	$4,000
3.........		$8,000
4.........		$9,000
5.........		$12,000
6.........		$10,000
7.........		$8,000
8.........		$6,000
9.........		$5,000
10.........		$5,000

EXERCISE 13–2 Simple Rate of Return Method [LO2]
The management of Wallingford MicroBrew is considering the purchase of an automated bottling machine for $80,000. The machine would replace an old piece of equipment that costs $33,000 per year to operate. The new machine would cost $10,000 per year to operate. The old machine currently in use could be sold now for a scrap value of $5,000. The new machine would have a useful life of 10 years with no salvage value.

Required:
Compute the simple rate of return on the new automated bottling machine.

EXERCISE 13–3 Net Present Value Method [LO3]
The management of Opry Company, a wholesale distributor of suntan products, is considering the purchase of a $25,000 machine that would reduce operating costs in its warehouse by $4,000 per year. At the end of the machine's 10-year useful life, it will have no scrap value. The company's required rate of return is 12%.

Required:
(Ignore income taxes.)
1. Determine the net present value of the investment in the machine.
2. What is the difference between the total, undiscounted cash inflows and cash outflows over the entire life of the machine?

EXERCISE 13–4 Internal Rate of Return [LO4]
Pisa Pizza Parlor is investigating the purchase of a new $45,000 delivery truck that would contain specially designed warming racks. The new truck would have a six-year useful life. It would save $5,400 per year over the present method of delivering pizzas. In addition, it would result in the sale of 1,800 more pizzas each year. The company realizes a contribution margin of $2 per pizza.

Required:
(Ignore income taxes.)
1. What would be the total annual cash inflows associated with the new truck for capital budgeting purposes?
2. Find the internal rate of return promised by the new truck to the nearest whole percent.
3. In addition to the data above, assume that due to the unique warming racks, the truck will have a $13,000 salvage value at the end of six years. Under these conditions, compute the internal rate of return to the nearest whole percent. (Hint: You may find it helpful to use the net present value approach; find the discount rate that will cause the net present value to be closest to zero. Use the format shown in Exhibit 13–6.)

EXERCISE 13–5 Uncertain Future Cash Flows [LO5]
Union Bay Plastics is investigating the purchase of automated equipment that would save $100,000 each year in direct labour and inventory carrying costs. This equipment costs $750,000 and is expected to have a 10-year useful life with no salvage value. The company requires a minimum 15% rate of return on all equipment purchases. This equipment would provide intangible benefits such as greater flexibility and higher-quality output that are difficult to estimate and yet are quite significant.

Required:
(Ignore income taxes.)
What dollar value per year would the intangible benefits have to be worth in order to make the equipment an acceptable investment?

EXERCISE 13–6 Preference Ranking [LO6]
Information on four investment proposals is given below:

	Investment Proposal			
	A	B	C	D
Investment required	$(85,000)	$(200,000)	$(90,000)	$(170,000)
Present value of cash inflows	119,000	250,000	135,000	221,000
Net present value	$ 34,000	$ 50,000	$ 45,000	$ 51,000
Life of the project	5 years	7 years	6 years	6 years

Required:
1. Compute the project profitability index for each investment proposal.
2. Rank the proposals in terms of preference.

EXERCISE 13–7 (Appendix 13A) Basic Present Value Concepts [LO8]

Each of the following parts is independent. (Ignore income taxes.)
1. Largo Freightlines plans to build a new garage in three years to have more space for repairing its trucks. The garage will cost $400,000. What lump-sum amount should the company invest now to have the $400,000 available at the end of the three-year period? Assume that the company can invest money at:
   a. Eight percent.
   b. Twelve percent.
2. Martell Products, Inc., can purchase a new copier that will save $5,000 per year in copying costs. The copier will last for six years and have no salvage value. What is the maximum purchase price that Martell Products would be willing to pay for the copier if the company's required rate of return is:
   a. Ten percent?
   b. Sixteen percent?
3. Sally has just won the million-dollar Big Slam jackpot at a gambling casino. The casino will pay her $50,000 per year for 20 years as the payoff. If Sally can invest money at a 10% rate of return, what is the present value of her winnings? Did she really win a million dollars? Explain.

EXERCISE 13–8 After-Tax Costs [LO7]

Solve each of the following parts independently:
a. Stoffer Company has hired a management consulting firm to review and make recommendations concerning Stoffer's organizational structure. The consulting firm's fee will be $100,000. What will be the after-tax cost of the consulting firm's fee if Stoffer's tax rate is 30%?
b. The Green Hills Riding Club has redirected its advertising toward a different sector of the market. As a result of this change in advertising, the club's annual revenues have increased by $40,000. If the club's tax rate is 30%, what is the after-tax benefit from the increased revenues?
c. The Golden Eagles Basketball Team has just installed an electronic scoreboard in its playing arena at a cost of $210,000. Determine the yearly tax savings from the CCA tax shield for the past three years. Assume that the income tax rate is 30%, the CCA rate is 30%, and the cost of capital is 10%.

EXERCISE 13–9 Comparison of Projects Using Net Present Value [LO6]

Sharp Company has $15,000 to invest. The company is trying to decide between two alternative uses of the funds as shown on the following page. Sharp Company uses a 16% discount rate.

Required:
(Ignore income taxes.) Which investment would you recommend that the company accept? Show all computations using net present value. Prepare separate computations for each investment.

	Invest in Project A	Invest in Project B
Investment required	$15,000	$15,000
Annual cash inflows	$4,000	$0
Single cash inflow at the end of 10 years		$60,000
Life of the project	10 years	10 years

EXERCISE 13–10 Basic Net Present Value Analysis [LO3]
On January 2, Fred Critchfield paid $18,000 for 900 common shares of Acme Company. Mr. Critchfield received an $0.80 per share dividend on the shares at the end of each year for four years. At the end of four years, he sold the shares for $22,500. Mr. Critchfield has a goal of earning a minimum return of 12% on all of his investments.

Required:
(Ignore income taxes.) Did Mr. Critchfield earn a 12% return on the shares? Use the net present value method and the general format shown in Exhibit 13–6. Round all computations to the nearest whole dollar.

EXERCISE 13–11 Internal Rate of Return and Net Present Value [LO3, LO4]
Scalia's Cleaning Service is investigating the purchase of an ultrasound machine for cleaning window blinds. The machine would cost $136,700, including invoice cost, freight, and training of employees to operate it. Scalia's has estimated that the new machine would increase the company's cash flows, net of expenses, by $25,000 per year. The machine would have a 14-year useful life with no expected salvage value.

Required:
(Ignore income taxes.)
1. Compute the machine's internal rate of return to the nearest whole percent.
2. Compute the machine's net present value. Use a discount rate of 16% and the format shown in Exhibit 13–7. Why do you have a zero net present value?
3. Suppose that the new machine would increase the company's annual cash flows, net of expenses, by only $20,000 per year. Under these conditions, compute the internal rate of return to the nearest whole percent.

EXERCISE 13–12 Uncertain Future Life [LO5]
Worldwide Travel Service has made an investment in certain equipment that cost the company $307,100. The equipment is expected to generate cash inflows of $50,000 each year.

Required:
How many years will the equipment have to be used in order to provide the company with a 14% return on its investment?

EXERCISE 13–13 Basic Payback Period and Simple Rate of Return Computations [LO1, LO2]
Martin Company is considering the purchase of a new piece of equipment. Relevant information concerning the equipment follows:

Purchase cost	$180,000
Annual cost savings that will be provided by the equipment	$37,500
Life of the equipment	12 years

Required:
(Ignore income taxes.)
1. Compute the payback period for the equipment. If the company rejects all proposals with a payback period of more than four years, would the equipment be purchased?
2. Compute the simple rate of return on the equipment. Use straight-line depreciation based on the equipment's useful life. Would the equipment be purchased if the company's required rate of return is 14%?

EXERCISE 13–14 (Appendix 13A) Basic Present Value Concepts [LO8]
Consider each of the following situations independently. (Ignore income taxes.)

1. Annual cash inflows from two competing investment opportunities are given below. Each investment opportunity will require the same initial investment. Compute the present value of the cash inflows for each investment using a 20% discount rate.

	Investment	
Year	**X**	**Y**
1	$ 1,000	$ 4,000
2	2,000	3,000
3	3,000	2,000
4	4,000	1,000
	$10,000	$10,000

2. At the end of three years, when you graduate from college, your father has promised to give you a used car that will cost $12,000. What lump sum must he invest now to have the $12,000 at the end of three years if he can invest money at:
   a. Six percent?
   b. Ten percent?
3. Mark has just won the grand prize on the "Hoot 'n' Holler " quiz show. He has a choice between (*a*) receiving $500,000 immediately and (*b*) receiving $60,000 per year for eight years plus a lump sum of $200,000 at the end of the eight-year period. If Mark can get a return of 10% on his investments, which option would you recommend that he accept? (Use present value analysis, and show all computations.)
4. You have just learned that you are a beneficiary in the will of your late Aunt Susan. The executrix of her estate has given you three options as to how you may receive your inheritance:
   a. You may receive $50,000 immediately.
   b. You may receive $75,000 at the end of six years.
   c. You may receive $12,000 at the end of each year for six years (a total of $72,000).
   If you can invest money at a 12% return, which option would you prefer?

EXERCISE 13–15 After-Tax Cash Flows in Net Present Value Analysis [LO7]
Kramer Corporation is considering two investment projects, each of which would require $50,000. Cost and cash flow data concerning the two projects are given below:

	Project A	Project B
Investment in high-speed photocopier	$50,000	
Investment in working capital		$50,000
Net annual cash inflows.	$9,000	$9,000
Life of the project.	8 years	8 years
CCA	20%	

The high-speed photocopier would have a salvage value of $5,000 in eight years. The photocopier would be depreciated over eight years. At the end of eight years, the investment in working capital would be released for use elsewhere. The company requires an after-tax return of 10% on all investments. The tax rate is 30%.

Required:
Compute the net present value of each investment project. (Round to the nearest whole dollar.)

EXERCISE 13–16 Working With Net Present Value [LO3]
Mountain View Hospital has purchased new lab equipment for $134,650. The equipment is expected to last for three years and to provide cash inflows as follows:

Year 1.	$45,000
Year 2.	$60,000
Year 3.	?

Required:
Assuming that the equipment will yield exactly a 16% rate of return, what is the expected cash inflow for Year 3?

EXERCISE 13–17 Basic Net Present Value and Internal Rate of Return Analysis [LO3, LO4]
(Ignore income taxes.) Consider each case below independently.

1. Minden Company's required rate of return is 15%. The company can purchase a new machine at a cost of $40,350. The new machine would generate cash inflows of $15,000 per year and have a four-year life with no salvage value. Compute the machine's net present value. (Use the format shown in Exhibit 13–3.) Is the machine an acceptable investment? Explain.
2. Leven Products, Inc., is investigating the purchase of a new grinding machine that has a projected life of 15 years. It is estimated that the machine will save $20,000 per year in cash operating costs. What is the machine's internal rate of return if it costs $111,500 new?
3. Sunset Press has just purchased a new trimming machine that cost $14,125. The machine is expected to save $2,500 per year in cash operating costs and to have a 10-year life. Compute the machine's internal rate of return. If the company's required rate of return is 16%, did it make a wise investment? Explain.

EXERCISE 13–18 Net Present Value Analysis of Two Alternatives [LO6]
Wriston Company has $300,000 to invest. The company is trying to decide between two alternative uses of the funds. The alternatives are as follows:

	A	B
Cost of equipment required	$300,000	$0
Working capital investment required	$0	$300,000
Annual cash inflows	$80,000	$60,000
Salvage value of equipment in seven years	$20,000	$0
Life of the project	7 years	7 years

The working capital needed for project B will be released for investment elsewhere at the end of seven years. Wriston Company uses a 20% discount rate.

Required:
(Ignore income taxes.) Which investment alternative (if either) would you recommend that the company accept? Show all computations using the net present value format. Prepare separate computations for each project.

EXERCISE 13–19 Payback Period and Simple Rate of Return [LO1, LO2]
The Heritage Amusement Park would like to construct a new ride called the Sonic Boom, which the park management feels would be very popular. The ride would cost $450,000 to construct, and it would have a 10% salvage value at the end of its 15-year useful life. The company estimates that the following annual costs and revenues would be associated with the ride:

Ticket revenues		$250,000
Less operating expenses:		
Maintenance.	$40,000	
Salaries.	90,000	
Depreciation	27,000	
Insurance	30,000	
Total operating expenses.		187,000
Operating income		$ 63,000

Required:
(Ignore income taxes.)

1. Assume that the Heritage Amusement Park will not construct a new ride unless the ride provides a payback period of six years or less. Does the Sonic Boom ride satisfy this requirement?

2. Compute the simple rate of return promised by the new ride. If Heritage Amusement Park requires a simple rate of return of at least 12%, does the Sonic Boom ride meet this criterion?

EXERCISE 13–20 Net Present Value Analysis Including Income Taxes [LO7]
Press Publishing Company hires students from the local university to collate pages on various printing jobs. This collating is all done by hand, at a cost of $60,000 per year. A collating machine has just come onto the market that could be used in place of the student help. The machine would cost $140,000 and have a 10-year useful life. It would require an operator at an annual cost of $18,000 and have annual maintenance costs of $7,000. New roller pads would be needed on the machine in five years at a total cost of $20,000. The salvage value of the machine in 10 years would be $40,000.

The CCA rate is 30 percent. Management requires a 14% after-tax return on all equipment purchases. The company's tax rate is 30%.

Required:
1. Determine the before-tax net annual cost savings that the new collating machine will provide.
2. Using the data from (1) above and other data from the exercise, compute the collating machine's net present value. (Round all dollar amounts to the nearest whole dollar.) Would you recommend that the machine be purchased?

Problems

PROBLEM 13–21 Simple Rate of Return; Payback [LO1, LO2]
Lugano's Pizza Parlor is considering the purchase of a large oven and related equipment for mixing and baking "crazy bread." The oven and equipment would cost $120,000 delivered and installed. It would be usable for about 15 years, after which it would have a 10% scrap value. The following additional information is available:

a. Mr. Lugano estimates that purchase of the oven and equipment would allow the pizza parlor to bake and sell 72,000 loaves of crazy bread each year. The bread sells for $1.25 per loaf.
b. The cost of the ingredients in a loaf of bread is 40% of the selling price. Mr. Lugano estimates that other costs each year associated with the bread would be the following: salaries, $18,000; utilities, $9,000; and insurance, $3,000.
c. The pizza parlor uses straight-line depreciation on all assets, deducting salvage value from original cost.

Required:
(Ignore income taxes.)
1. Prepare a contribution format income statement showing the operating income each year from production and sale of the crazy bread.
2. Compute the simple rate of return for the new oven and equipment. If a simple rate of return above 12% is acceptable to Mr. Lugano, will he purchase the oven and equipment?
3. Compute the payback period on the oven and equipment. If Mr. Lugano purchases any equipment with less than a six-year payback, will he purchase this equipment?

PROBLEM 13–22 Net Present Value Analysis; Uncertain Cash Flows [LO3, LO5]
Tiger Computers, Inc., of Singapore is considering the purchase of an automated etching machine for use in the production of its circuit boards. The machine would cost $900,000. (All currency amounts are in Singapore dollars.) An additional $650,000 would be required for installation costs and for software. Management believes that the automated machine would provide substantial annual reductions in costs, as shown below:

	Annual Reduction in Costs
Labour costs	$240,000
Material costs.......	$96,000

The new machine would require considerable maintenance work to keep it in proper adjustment. The company's engineers estimate that maintenance costs would increase by $4,250 per month if the machine were purchased. In addition, the machine would require a $90,000 overhaul at the end of the sixth year.

The new etching machine would be usable for 10 years, after which it would be sold for its scrap value of $210,000. It would replace an old etching machine that can be sold now for its scrap value of $70,000. Tiger Computers, Inc., requires a return of at least 18% on investments of this type.

Required:
(Ignore income taxes.)

1. Compute the net annual cost savings promised by the new etching machine.
2. Using the data from (1) above and other data from the problem, compute the new machine's net present value. (Use the incremental-cost approach.) Would you recommend that the machine be purchased? Explain.
3. Assume that management can identify several intangible benefits associated with the new machine, including greater flexibility in shifting from one type of circuit board to another, improved quality of output, and faster delivery as a result of reduced throughput time. What dollar value per year would management have to attach to these intangible benefits in order to make the new etching machine an acceptable investment?

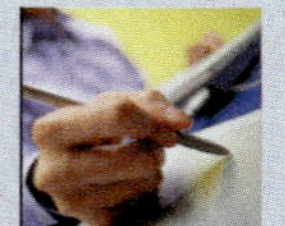

PROBLEM 13–23 Basic Net Present Value Analysis [LO3]
Renfree Mines, Inc., owns the mining rights to a large tract of land in a mountainous area. The tract contains a mineral deposit that the company believes might be commercially attractive to mine and sell. An engineering and cost analysis has been made, and it is expected that the following cash flows would be associated with opening and operating a mine in the area:

Cost of equipment required	$850,000
Net annual cash receipts	$230,000*
Working capital required	$100,000
Cost of road repairs in three years	$60,000
Salvage value of equipment in five years.	$200,000

*Receipts from sales of ore, less out-of-pocket costs for salaries, utilities, insurance, and so forth.

It is estimated that the mineral deposit would be exhausted after five years of mining. At that point, the working capital would be released for reinvestment elsewhere. The company's required rate of return is 14%.

Required:
(Ignore income taxes.) Determine the net present value of the proposed mining project. Should the project be accepted? Explain.

PROBLEM 13–24 Basic Net Present Value Analysis Including Income Taxes [LO7]
Rapid Parcel Service has been offered an eight-year contract to deliver mail and small parcels between army installations. To accept the contract, the company would have to purchase several new delivery trucks at a total cost of $450,000. Other data relating to the contract follow:

Net annual cash receipts (before taxes) from the contract	$108,000
Cost of overhauling the motors in the trucks in five years	$45,000
Salvage value of the trucks at termination of the contract	$20,000

If the contract were accepted, several old, fully depreciated trucks would be sold at a total price of $30,000. These funds would be used to help purchase the new trucks. For tax purposes, the company computes CCA deductions using the maximum rate of 30%. The company requires a 12% after-tax return on all equipment purchases. The tax rate is 30%.

Required:
Compute the net present value of this investment opportunity. Round all dollar amounts to the nearest whole dollar. Would you recommend that the contract be accepted?

PROBLEM 13–25 Basic Net Present Value Analysis [LO3]
Doughboy Bakery would like to buy a new machine for putting icing and other toppings on pastries. These are now put on by hand. The machine that the bakery is considering costs $90,000 new. It would last the bakery for eight years but would require a $7,500 overhaul at the end of the fifth year. After eight years, the machine could be sold for $6,000.

The bakery estimates that it will cost $14,000 per year to operate the new machine. The present manual method of putting toppings on the pastries costs $35,000 per year. In addition to reducing operating costs, the new machine will allow the bakery to increase its production of pastries by 5,000 packages per year. The bakery realizes a contribution margin of $0.60 per package. The bakery requires a 16% return on all investments in equipment.

Required:
(Ignore income taxes.)
1. What are the net annual cash inflows that will be provided by the new machine?
2. Compute the new machine's net present value. Use the incremental cost approach, and round all dollar amounts to the nearest whole dollar.

PROBLEM 13–26 Preference Ranking of Investment Projects [LO6]

Austin Company is investigating five different investment opportunities. Information on the four projects under study is given below:

	Project Number			
	1	2	3	4
Investment required	$(480,000)	$(360,000)	$(270,000)	$(450,000)
Present value of cash inflows at a 10% discount rate	567,270	433,400	336,140	522,970
Net present value	$ 87,270	$ 73,400	$ 66,140	$ 72,970
Life of the project	6 years	12 years	6 years	3 years
Internal rate of return	16%	14%	18%	19%

Since the company's required rate of return is 10%, a 10% discount rate has been used in the present value computations above. Limited funds are available for investment, so the company can't accept all of the available projects.

Required:
1. Compute the project profitability index for each investment project.
2. Rank the four projects according to preference, in terms of:
   a. Net present value
   b. Project profitability index
   c. Internal rate of return
3. Which ranking do you prefer? Why?

PROBLEM 13–27 Net Present Value Analysis [LO3]

Frank White will retire in six years. He wants to open some type of small business operation that can be managed in the free time he has available from his regular occupation, but that can be closed easily when he retires. He is considering several investment alternatives, one of which is to open a laundromat. After careful study, Mr. White has determined the following:

a. Washers, dryers, and other equipment needed to open the laundromat would cost $194,000. In addition, $6,000 in working capital would be required to purchase an inventory of soap, bleaches, and related items and to provide change for change machines. (The soap, bleaches, and related items would be sold to customers at cost.) After six years, the working capital would be released for investment elsewhere.
b. The laundromat would charge $1.50 per use for the washers and $0.75 per use for the dryers. Mr. White expects the laundromat to gross $1,800 each week from the washers and $1,125 each week from the dryers.
c. The only variable costs in the laundromat would be 7½ cents per use for water and electricity for the washers and 9 cents per use for gas and electricity for the dryers.
d. Fixed costs would be $3,000 per month for rent, $1,500 per month for cleaning, and $1,875 per month for maintenance, insurance, and other items.

e. The equipment would have a 10% disposal value in six years.

Mr. White will not open the laundromat unless it provides at least a 12% return.

Required:

(Ignore income taxes.)

1. Assuming that the laundromat would be open 52 weeks a year, compute the expected net annual cash receipts from its operation (gross cash receipts less cash disbursements). (Do not include the cost of the equipment, the working capital, or the salvage values in these computations.)
2. Would you advise Mr. White to open the laundromat? Show computations using the net present value method of investment analysis. Round all dollar amounts to the nearest whole dollar.

PROBLEM 13–28 Simple Rate of Return; Payback; Internal Rate of Return [LO1, LO2, LO4]

Chateau Beaune is a family-owned winery located in the Burgundy region of France, which is headed by Gerard Despinoy. The harvesting season in early fall is the busiest part of the year for the winery, and many part-time workers are hired to help pick and process grapes. Mr. Despinoy is investigating the purchase of a harvesting machine that would significantly reduce the amount of labour required in the picking process. The harvesting machine is built to straddle grapevines, which are laid out in low-lying rows. Two workers are carried on the machine just above ground level, one on each side of the vine. As the machine slowly crawls through the vineyard, the workers cut bunches of grapes from the vines, which then fall into a hopper. The machine separates the grapes from the stems and other woody debris. The debris are then pulverized and spread behind the machine as a rich ground mulch. Mr. Despinoy has gathered the following information relating to the decision of whether to purchase the machine:

a. The winery would save €190,000 per year in labour costs with the new harvesting machine. In addition, the company would no longer have to purchase and spread ground mulch—at an annual savings of €10,000. (The French currency is the euro, which is denoted by the symbol €.)

b. The harvesting machine would cost €480,000. It would have an estimated 12-year useful life and zero salvage value. The winery uses straight-line depreciation.

c. Annual out-of-pocket costs associated with the harvesting machine would be insurance, €1,000; fuel, €9,000; and a maintenance contract, €12,000. In addition, two operators would be hired and trained for the machine, and they would be paid a total of €70,000 per year, including all benefits.

d. Mr. Despinoy feels that the investment in the harvesting machine should earn at least a 16% rate of return.

Required:

(Ignore income taxes.)

1. Determine the annual net savings in cash operating costs that would be realized if the harvesting machine were purchased.
2. Compute the simple rate of return expected from the harvesting machine.
3. Compute the payback period on the harvesting machine. Mr. Despinoy will not purchase equipment unless it has a payback period of five years or less. Under this criterion, should the harvesting machine be purchased?
4. Compute (to the nearest whole percent) the internal rate of return promised by the harvesting machine. Based on this computation, does it appear that the simple rate of return is an accurate guide in investment decisions?

PROBLEM 13–29 Net Present Value; Uncertain Future Cash Flows; Postaudit [LO3, LO5]

"If we can get that new robot to combine with our other automated equipment, we'll have a complete flexible manufacturing system (FMS) in place in our Northridge plant," said Hal Swain, production manager for Diller Products.

"Let's just hope that reduced labour and inventory costs can justify its acquisition," replied Linda Wycoff, the controller. "Otherwise, we'll never get it. You know how the president feels about equipment paying for itself out of reduced costs."

Selected data relating to the robot are provided below:

Engineering studies suggest that use of the robot will result in a savings of 20,000 direct labour-hours each year. The labour rate is $16 per hour. Also, the smoother work flow made possible by the FMS will allow the company to reduce the amount of inventory on hand by $300,000. The released funds will be available for use elsewhere in the company. This inventory reduction will take place in the first year of operation. The company's required rate of return is 20%.

Cost of the robot.	$1,600,000
Software and installation.	$700,000
Annual savings in labour costs	?
Annual savings in inventory carrying costs	$190,000
Monthly increase in power and maintenance costs	$2,500
Salvage value in 12 years	$90,000
Useful life	12 years

Required:

(Ignore income taxes.)

1. Determine the net *annual* cost savings if the robot is purchased. (Do not include the $300,000 inventory reduction or the salvage value in this computation.)
2. Compute the net present value of the proposed investment in the robot. Based on these data, would you recommend that the robot be purchased? Explain.
3. Assume that the robot is purchased. At the end of the first year, Linda Wycoff has found that some items didn't work out as planned. Due to unforeseen problems, software and installation costs were $125,000 more than estimated, and direct labour has been reduced by only 17,500 hours per year, rather than by 20,000 hours. Assuming that all other cost data were accurate, does it appear that the company made a wise investment? Show computations, using the net present value format as in (2) above. (Hint: It might be helpful to place yourself back at the beginning of the first year, with the new data.)
4. Upon seeing your analysis in (3) above, the president stated, "That robot is the worst investment we've ever made. And here we'll be stuck with it for years."
   a. Explain to the president what benefits other than cost savings might accrue from using the new robot and FMS.
   b. Compute for the president the dollar amount of cash inflow that would be needed each year from the benefits in (*a*) above in order for the equipment to yield a 20% rate of return.

PROBLEM 13–30 Internal Rate of Return; Sensitivity Analysis [LO4]

Dr. Heidi Black is the managing partner of the Crestwood Dental Clinic. Dr. Black is trying to determine whether or not the clinic should move patient files and other items out of a spare room in the clinic and use the room for dental work. She has determined that it would require an investment of $142,950 for equipment and related costs of getting the room ready for use. Based on receipts being generated from other rooms in the clinic, Dr. Black estimates that the new room would generate a net cash inflow of $37,500 per year. The equipment purchased for the room would have a seven-year estimated useful life.

Required:

(Ignore income taxes.)

1. Compute the internal rate of return on the equipment for the new room to the nearest whole percent. Verify your answer by computing the net present value of the equipment using the internal rate of return you have computed as the discount rate.
2. Assume that Dr. Black will not purchase the new equipment unless it promises a return of at least 14%. Compute the amount of annual cash inflow that would provide this return on the $142,950 investment.
3. Although seven years is the average life for dental equipment, Dr. Black knows that due to changing technology this life can vary substantially. Compute the internal rate of return to the nearest whole percent if the life of the equipment were (*a*) five years and (*b*) nine years, rather than seven years. Is there any information provided by these computations that you would be particularly anxious to show Dr. Black?
4. Dr. Black is unsure about the estimated $37,500 annual cash inflow from the room. She thinks that the actual cash inflow could be as much as 20% greater or less than this figure.
   a. Assume that the actual cash inflow each year is 20% greater than estimated. Recompute the internal rate of return to the nearest whole percent using the seven-year life.
   b. Assume that the actual cash inflow each year is 20% less than estimated. Recompute the internal rate of return to the nearest whole percent using the seven-year life.
5. Refer to the original data. Assume that the equipment is purchased and that the room is opened for dental use. However, due to an increasing number of dentists in the area, the clinic is able

to generate only $30,000 per year in net cash receipts from the new room. At the end of five years, the clinic closes the room and sells the equipment to a newly licensed dentist for a cash price of $61,375. Compute the internal rate of return to the nearest whole percent that the clinic earned on its investment over the five-year period. Round all dollar amounts to the nearest whole dollar. (Hint: A useful way to proceed is to find the discount rate that will cause the net present value of the investment to be equal to, or near, zero).

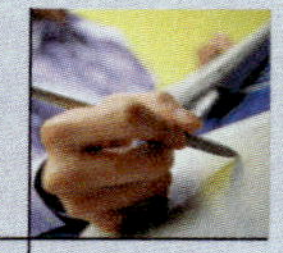

PROBLEM 13–31 Net Present Value Analysis of a Lease or Buy Decision [LO3]

Blinko Products wants an airplane for use by its corporate staff. The airplane that the company wishes to acquire, a Zephyr II, can be either purchased or leased from the manufacturer. The company has made the following evaluation of the two alternatives:

Purchase alternative. If the Zephyr II is purchased, then the costs incurred by the company would be as follows:

Purchase cost of the plane	$850,000
Annual cost of servicing, licenses, and taxes	$9,000
Repairs:	
First three years, per year..................	$3,000
Fourth year............................	$5,000
Fifth year..............................	$10,000

The plane would be sold after five years. Based on current resale values, the company would be able to sell it for about one-half of its original cost at the end of the five-year period.

Lease alternative. If the Zephyr II is leased, then the company would have to make an immediate deposit of $50,000 to cover any damage during use. The lease would run for five years, at the end of which time the deposit would be refunded. The lease would require an annual rental payment of $200,000 (the first payment is due at the end of Year 1). As part of this lease cost, the manufacturer would provide all servicing and repairs, license the plane, and pay all taxes. At the end of the five-year period, the plane would revert to the manufacturer, as owner.

Blinko Products' required rate of return is 18%.

Required:

(Ignore income taxes.)

1. Use the total-cost approach to determine the present value of the cash flows associated with each alternative.
2. Which alternative would you recommend that the company accept? Why?

PROBLEM 13–32 Simple Rate of Return; Payback [LO1, LO2]

Nagoya Amusements Corporation places electronic games and other amusement devices in supermarkets and similar outlets throughout Japan. Nagoya Amusements is investigating the purchase of a new electronic game called Mystic Invaders. The manufacturer will sell 20 games to Nagoya Amusements for a total price of ¥180,000. (The Japanese currency is yen, which is denoted by the symbol ¥.) Nagoya Amusements has determined the following additional information about the game:

a. The game would have a five-year useful life and a negligible salvage value. The company uses straight-line depreciation.
b. The game would replace other games that are unpopular and generating little revenue. These other games would be sold for a total of ¥30,000.
c. Nagoya Amusements estimates that Mystic Invaders would generate annual incremental revenues of ¥200,000 (total for all 20 games). Annual incremental out-of-pocket costs would be (in total): maintenance, ¥50,000; and insurance, ¥10,000. In addition, Nagoya Amusements would have to pay a commission of 40% of total revenues to the supermarkets and other outlets in which the games were placed.

Required:

(Ignore income taxes.)

1. Prepare a contribution format income statement showing the operating income each year from Mystic Invaders.
2. Compute the simple rate of return on Mystic Invaders. Will the game be purchased if Nagoya Amusements accepts any project with a simple rate of return greater than 14%?

3. Compute the payback period on Mystic Invaders. If the company accepts any investment with a payback period of less than three years, will the game be purchased?

PROBLEM 13–33 Preference Ranking of Investment Projects [LO6]

Yancey Company has limited funds available for investment and must ration the funds among four competing projects. Selected information on the four projects follows:

Project	Investment Required	Net Present Value	Life of the Project (years)	Internal Rate of Return
A	$800,000	$221,615	7	18%
B	$675,000	$210,000	12	16%
C	$500,000	$175,175	7	20%
D	$700,000	$152,544	3	22%

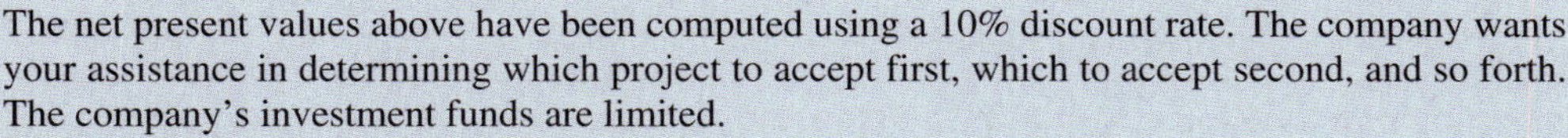

The net present values above have been computed using a 10% discount rate. The company wants your assistance in determining which project to accept first, which to accept second, and so forth. The company's investment funds are limited.

Required:

1. Compute the project profitability index for each project.
2. In order of preference, rank the four projects in terms of:
   a. Net present value.
   b. Project profitability index.
   c. Internal rate of return.
3. Which ranking do you prefer? Why?

PROBLEM 13–34 Net Present Value Analysis of a New Product [LO3]

Atwood Company has an opportunity to produce and sell a revolutionary new smoke detector for homes. To determine whether this would be a profitable venture, the company has gathered the following data on probable costs and market potential:

a. New equipment would have to be acquired to produce the smoke detector. The equipment would cost $100,000 and be usable for 12 years. After 12 years, it would have a salvage value equal to 10% of the original cost.
b. Production and sales of the smoke detector would require a working capital investment of $40,000 to finance accounts receivable, inventories, and day-to-day cash needs. This working capital would be released for use elsewhere after 12 years.
c. An extensive marketing study projects sales in units over the next 12 years as follows:

Year	Sales in Units
1	4,000
2	7,000
3	10,000
4–12	12,000

d. The smoke detectors would sell for $45 each; variable costs for production, administration, and sales would be $25 per unit.
e. To gain entry into the market, the company would have to advertise heavily in the early years of sales. The advertising program follows:

Year	Amount of Advertising
1–2	$70,000
3	$50,000
4–12	$40,000

f. Other fixed costs for salaries, insurance, maintenance, and straight-line depreciation on equipment would total $127,500 per year. (Depreciation is based on cost less salvage value.)

g. The company's required rate of return is 20%.

Required:
(Ignore income taxes.)

1. Compute the net cash inflow (cash receipts less yearly cash operating expenses) anticipated from sale of the smoke detectors for each year over the next 12 years.
2. Using the data computed in (1) above and other data provided in the problem, determine the net present value of the proposed investment. Would you recommend that Atwood Company accept the smoke detector as a new product?

PROBLEM: 13–35 A Comparison of Investment Alternatives Including Income Taxes [LO7]

Ms. Keri Lee, an expert in retrofitting buildings to meet seismic safety standards, has just received a $200,000 after-tax bonus for the successful completion of a project on time and under budget. Business has been so good that she is planning to retire in 12 years, spending her time relaxing in the sun, skiing, and doing charitable work. Ms. Lee is considering two alternatives for investing her bonus.

Alternative 1. Municipal bonds can be purchased that mature in 12 years and that bear interest at 8%. This interest would be paid semi-annually. (In discounting a cash flow that occurs semi-annually, the procedure is to halve the discount rate and double the number of periods. Use the same procedure for discounting the principal returned when the bonds reach maturity.) Do the calculations before income tax and convert to an after-tax return using a 40% income tax rate.

Alternative 2. A small discount perfume shop is available for sale at a nearby factory outlet centre. The business can be purchased from its current owner for $200,000. The following information relates to this alternative:

a. Of the purchase price, $80,000 would be for fixtures and other depreciable items. The remainder would be for the company's working capital (inventory, accounts receivable, and cash). The fixtures and other depreciable items would have a remaining useful life of at least 12 years but would be depreciated for tax reporting purposes using a CCA of 20%. Salvage value is expected to be negligible at the end of 12 years. At any rate, at the end of 12 years, these depreciable items would have a negligible salvage value; however, the working capital would be released for reinvestment elsewhere.
b. Store records indicate that sales have averaged $400,000 per year, and out-of-pocket costs have averaged $370,000 per year (*not* including income taxes). These out-of-pocket costs include rent on the building, cost of goods sold, utilities, and wages and salaries for the sales staff and the store manager. Ms. Lee plans to entrust the day-to-day operations of the store to the manager.
c. Ms. Lee's tax rate is 40% and she wishes to use an after tax discount rate of 8% given the risk involved.

Required:
Advise Ms. Lee as to which alternative should be selected. Use the total-cost approach to discounted cash flow in your analysis and a discount rate of 8%. (Round all dollar amounts to the nearest whole dollar.)

PROBLEM: 13–36 Net Present Value; Total and Incremental Approaches [LO3]

Eastbay Hospital has an auxiliary generator that is used when power failures occur. The generator is worn out and must be either overhauled or replaced with a new generator. The hospital has assembled the information presented on the following page.

If the company keeps and overhauls its present generator, then the generator will be usable for eight more years. If a new generator is purchased, it will be used for eight years, after which it will be replaced. The new generator would be diesel-powered, resulting in a substantial reduction in annual operating costs, as shown above.

The hospital computes depreciation on a straight-line basis. All equipment purchases are evaluated using a 16% discount rate.

Required:
(Ignore income taxes.)

1. Should Eastbay Hospital keep the old generator or purchase the new one? Use the total-cost approach to net present value in making your decision.
2. Redo (1) above, this time using the incremental-cost approach.

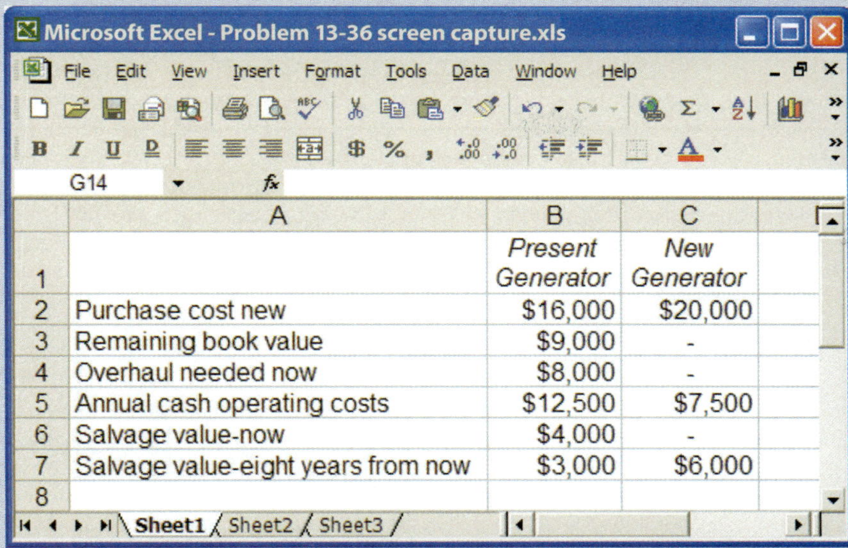
Microsoft Excel - Problem 13-36 screen capture.xls

	A	B	C
1		*Present Generator*	*New Generator*
2	Purchase cost new	$16,000	$20,000
3	Remaining book value	$9,000	-
4	Overhaul needed now	$8,000	-
5	Annual cash operating costs	$12,500	$7,500
6	Salvage value-now	$4,000	-
7	Salvage value-eight years from now	$3,000	$6,000
8			

PROBLEM: 13–37 Net Present Value Analysis Including Income Taxes [LO7]
The Crescent Drilling Company owns the drilling rights to several tracts of land on which natural gas has been found. The amount of gas on some of the tracts is somewhat marginal, and the company is unsure whether it would be profitable to extract and sell the gas that these tracts contain. One such tract is tract 410, on which the following information has been gathered:

Investment in equipment needed for extraction work	$600,000
Working capital investment needed	$85,000
Annual cash receipts from sale of gas, net of related cash operating expenses (before taxes)	$110,000
Cost of restoring land at completion of extraction work	$70,000

The natural gas in tract 410 would be exhausted after 10 years of extraction work. The equipment would have a useful life of 15 years, but it could be sold for only 15% of its original cost when extraction was completed. For tax purposes, the company would depreciate the equipment using a CCA of 20% and assuming zero salvage value. The tax rate is 30%, and the company's after-tax discount rate is 10%. The working capital would be released for use elsewhere at the completion of the project.

Required:
1. Compute the net present value of tract 410. Round all dollar amounts to the nearest whole dollar.
2. Would you recommend that the investment project be undertaken?

Cases

CASE 13–38 Ethics and the Manager; Postaudit [LO5]

After five years with a national accounting firm with mostly large manufacturing clients, Amy Kimbell joined Hi-Quality Productions Inc. (Hi-Q) as manager of Manufacturing Accounting.

Hi-Q is a publicly held company producing automotive components. One operation in the Alpha Division requires a highly automated process. Hi-Q's top management and board of directors had outsourced this particular high-tech operation to another company to avoid making a large investment in technology they viewed as constantly changing.

Each operating division of Hi-Q has a budget committee. Two years ago, the Alpha Division budget committee presented to the board its proposal to bring the high-tech operation in house. This would require a capital investment of approximately $4 million but would lead to more than enough cost savings to justify this expenditure. The board approved the proposal, and the investment was made. Later the same year, Amy Kimbell was promoted to assistant corporate controller. In this position, she sits on the budget committee of all divisions.

A little more than a year after the high-tech process was put into operation, the board requested a postaudit review of the actual cost savings. When the board requests such a review, the data are supplied by the management of the affected division and are reviewed by the division's budget committee. When the data were sent to the budget committee for review, Amy Kimbell noted that several of the projections in the original proposal were very aggressive. These included a very high salvage value for the equipment as well as a very long useful life over which cost savings were projected to occur. If more realistic projections had been used, Amy doubted that the board would have agreed to make the investment.

Also in the postaudit review, Amy noted that substantial amounts of incremental service department operating costs directly caused by the new investment were not being attributed to the high-tech operation. Instead, these costs were being allocated as general overhead to all departments. In addition, she noted that the estimated rate for spoiled and defective work contained in the proposal was being used in the review rather than the actual rate, which was considerably higher.

When Amy Kimbell brought these points to the attention of the division's budget committee, she was told that as a new member of the committee she would not be held responsible for decisions, such as the investment in the high-tech operation, that were made prior to her arrival. Accordingly, she should let the seasoned members of the committee handle this particular review. When Amy continued to express her concerns, she was firmly informed that it had been the unanimous decision of the committee to approve the original proposal because it was thought to be in the best long-run interest of the company. Given this consensus, it was felt that certain "adjustments and exceptions" to the postaudit review were justified to ensure the overall long-run well-being of the company.

Required:

1. What should Amy do?
2. Do you have any suggestions for revising the way in which postaudits are conducted at Hi-Q?

(Adapted from Roland L. Madison and Curtis C. Verschoor, "New Position Brings Ethical Dilemma," *Strategic Finance,* December 2000, pp. 22, 24. Used with permission from the IMA, Montvale, NJ, USA, www.imanet.org.)

CASE 13–39 Net Present Value Analysis of a Lease or Buy Decision [LO3]

Wyndham Stores operates a regional chain of upscale department stores. The company is going to open another store soon in a prosperous and growing suburban area. In discussing how the company can acquire the desired building and other facilities needed to open the new store, Harry Wilson, the company's marketing vice-president, stated, "I know most of our competitors are starting to lease facilities, rather than buy, but I just can't see the economics of it. Our development people tell me that we can buy the building site, put a building on it, and get all the store fixtures we need for $14 million. They also say that property taxes, insurance, maintenance, and repairs would run $200,000 a year. When you figure that we plan to keep a site for 20 years, that's a total cost of $18 million. But then when you realize that the building and property will be worth at least $5 million in 20 years, that's a net cost to us of only $13 million. Leasing costs a lot more than that."

"I'm not so sure," replied Erin Reilley, the company's executive vice-president. "Guardian Insurance Company is willing to purchase the building site, construct a building and install fixtures to our specifications, and then lease the facility to us for 20 years for an annual lease payment of only $1 million."

"That's just my point," said Harry. "At $1 million a year, it would cost us $20 million over the 20 years instead of just $13 million. What would we have left at the end? Nothing! The building would belong to the insurance company! I'll bet they would even want the first lease payment in advance."

"That's right," replied Erin. "We would have to make the first payment immediately and then one payment at the beginning of each of the following 19 years. However, you're overlooking a few things. For one thing, we would have to tie up a lot of our funds for 20 years under the purchase alternative. We would have to put $6 million down immediately if we buy the property, and then we would have to pay the other $8 million off over four years at $2 million a year."

"But that cost is nothing compared to $20 million for leasing," said Harry. "Also, if we lease, I understand we would have to put up a $400,000 security deposit that we wouldn't get back until the end. Besides that, we would still have to pay all the repair and maintenance costs just like we owned the property. No wonder those insurance companies are so rich if they can swing deals like this."

"Well, I'll admit that I don't have all the figures sorted out yet," replied Erin. "But I do have the operating cost breakdown for the building, which includes $90,000 annually for property taxes, $60,000 for insurance, and $50,000 for repairs and maintenance. If we lease, Guardian will handle its own insurance costs and will pay the property taxes, but we'll have to pay for the repairs and maintenance. I need to put all this together and see if leasing makes any sense with our 12% before-tax required rate of return. The president wants a presentation and recommendation in the executive committee meeting tomorrow."

Required:

(Ignore income taxes.)

1. Using the net present value approach, determine whether Wyndham Stores should lease or buy the new store. Assume that you will be making your presentation before the company's executive committee.
2. How will you reply in the meeting if Harry Wilson brings up the issue of the building's future sales value?

CASE 13–40 Comparison of Alternatives Using Net Present Value Analysis [LO3]

Woolrich Company's market research division has projected a substantial increase in demand over the next several years for one of the company's products. To meet this demand, the company will need to produce units as follows:

Year	Production in Units
1	20,000
2	30,000
3	40,000
4–10.......	45,000

At present, the company is using a single model 2600 machine to manufacture this product. To increase its productive capacity, the company is considering two alternatives:

Alternative 1. The company could purchase another model 2600 machine that would operate along with the one it now owns. The following information is available on this alternative:

a. The model 2600 machine now in use was purchased for $165,000 four years ago. Its present book value is $99,000, and its present market value is $90,000.
b. A new model 2600 machine costs $180,000 now. The old model 2600 machine will have to be replaced in six years at a cost of $200,000. The replacement machine will have a market value of about $100,000 when it is four years old.
c. The variable cost required to produce one unit of product using the model 2600 machine is given under the "general information" below.
d. Repairs and maintenance costs each year on a single model 2600 machine total $3,000.

Alternative 2. The company could purchase a model 5200 machine and use the old model 2600 machine as standby equipment. The model 5200 machine is a high-speed unit with double the capacity of the model 2600 machine. The following information is available on this alternative:

a. The cost of a new model 5200 machine is $250,000.
b. The variable cost required to produce one unit of product using the model 5200 machine is given under the "general information" below.
c. The model 5200 machine is more costly to maintain than the model 2600 machine. Repairs and maintenance on a model 5200 machine and on a model 2600 machine used as standby would total $4,600 per year.

The following general information is available on the two alternatives:

a. Both the model 2600 machine and the model 5200 machine have a 10-year life from the time they are first used in production. Straight-line depreciation is used by the company.
b. The two machine models are not equally efficient. Comparative variable costs per unit of product are as follows:

	Model 2600	Model 5200
Direct materials per unit	$0.36	$0.40
Direct labour per unit	0.50	0.22
Supplies and lubricants per unit	0.04	0.08
Total variable cost per unit.	$0.90	$0.70

c. No other factory costs would change as a result of the decision between the two machines.
d. Woolrich Company uses an 18% discount rate.

Required:
(Ignore income taxes.)

1. Which alternative should the company choose? Use the net present value approach. (Round to the nearest whole dollar.)
2. Suppose that the cost of direct materials increases by 50%. Would this make the model 5200 machine more or less desirable? Explain. No computations are needed.
3. Suppose that the cost of direct labour increases by 25%. Would this make the model 5200 machine more or less desirable? Explain. No computations are needed.

Research

R 13–41 Capital Budgeting Practices [LO1, LO2, LO3, LO4]
In recent years your college or university has probably undertaken a capital budgeting project such as building or renovating a facility. Investigate one of these capital budgeting projects. You will probably need the help of your school's accounting or finance office.

Required:

1. Determine the total cost of the project and the source of the funds for the project. Did the money come from provincial funds, gifts, grants, endowments, or the school's general fund?
2. Did the cost of the project stay within budget?
3. What financial criteria were used to evaluate the project?
4. If the net present value method or internal rate of return method was used, review the calculations. Do you agree with the calculations and methods used?
5. If the net present value method was not used to evaluate the project, estimate the project's new present value. If all of the required data are not available, make reasonable estimates for the missing data. What discount rate did you use? Why?
6. Evaluate the capital budgeting procedures that were actually used by your school.

R 13–42 Capital Cost Allowance Regulations [LO7]
Canadian income tax regulations have become mind-numbingly complex. As a result, the Canada Revenue Agency issues interpretation bulletins to assist corporations and others to comply. Refer to IT-128R—Capital Cost Allowance—Depreciable Property by going to the CRA web site.

After accessing the site, find six guidelines listed in the bulletin for determining whether an expenditure is capital in nature because depreciable property was acquired or improved, or whether it is currently deductible because it is in respect of the maintenance or repair of a property.

R 13–43 Capital Budgeting Practices [LO1, LO2, LO3, LO4, LO5]
In the business focus at the beginning of Chaptger 13, the proposed capital expenditures of Petro-Canada were presented as described in the 2006 Annual Report as part of their Management Discussion and Analysis.

Required:

1. Describe how Petro-Canada would structure its analysis of the $2,020 million proposed for advancing new growth projects. Given the uncertainty of finding new oil and gas, what analytical approaches might be employed by Petro-Canada to assess the benefit of such a large investment?
2. Comment on how appropriate the capital budgeting analysis presented in Chapter 13 would be to assess the viability of the $100 million proposed for complying with regulations such as environmental ones.

EXTERNAL REPORTING AND ANALYSIS

Online Chapter 14

Chapter 14 demonstrates how managers are observed by parties outside the organization. Managers are ultimately responsible to shareholders, creditors and other stakeholders who look at the results through financial accounting reports. Also many contracts for both remuneration and credit operate using financial accounting results.

In addition to how managers and business contracts are viewed, managers often wish to look at other organizations so they can compare themselves or invest. Chapter 14 provides a means of conducting such investigations.

Find Chapter 14 on the Managerial Accounting, eighth Canadian edition web site at www.mcgrawhill.ca/olc/garrison

Photo Credits

Chapter 1, Ryan McVay/Getty Images; Chapter 2, Skip Nall/Getty Images; Chapter 3, Steve Cole/Getty Images; Chapter 4, © Richard Hutchings; Chapter 5, Andrew Simpson; Chapter 6, Digital Vision/Getty Images; Chapter 7, Courtesy of Joie de Vivre Hospitality; Chapter 8, Steve Cole/Getty Images; Chapter 9, Rim Light/PhotoLink/Getty Images; Chapter 10, Steve Cole/Getty Images; Chapter 11, © CORBIS Images; Chapter 12, Ryan McVay/Getty Images; Chapter 13, Royalty-Free/CORBIS.

Company/Name Index

Subject Index

D

E

F

T